GATEWAYS TO
WORLD LITERATURE

VOLUME 1

The Ancient World through
the Early Modern Period

GATEWAYS TO
WORLD LITERATURE

VOLUME 1

The Ancient World through
the Early Modern Period

David Damrosch
General Editor

Boston Columbus Indianapolis New York San Francisco Upper Saddle River
Amsterdam Cape Town Dubai London Madrid Milan Munich Paris Montreal Toronto
Delhi Mexico City São Paulo Sydney Hong Kong Seoul Singapore Taipei Tokyo

Editor-in-Chief: *Joseph Terry*
Development Editor: *Erin Reilly*
Editorial Assistant: *Kelly Carroll*
Executive Marketing Manager: *Joyce Nilsen*
Senior Supplements Editor: *Donna Campion*
Production Manager: *Ellen MacElree*
Project Coordination, Text Design, and Page Makeup: *PreMediaGlobal, Inc.*
Senior Design Manager/Cover Designer: *John Callahan*
Cover Image: *Copyright © Robert Harding Picture Library Ltd/Alamy*
Senior Manufacturing Buyer: *Dennis J. Para*
Printer and Binder: *RR Donnelley/Crawfordsville*
Cover Printer: *Lehigh-Phoenix Color/Hagerstown*

For permission to use copyrighted material, grateful acknowledgment is made to the copyright
holders on page 1197–1200, which are hereby made part of this copyright page.

Library of Congress Cataloging-in-Publication Data

Gateways to world literature / David Damrosch, general editor.
    p. cm.
  Includes bibliographical references and index.
  ISBN 978-0-205-78710-4 (v. 1)
    1. Literature—Collections.   2. Literature—History and criticism.   I. Damrosch, David.
PN6014.G28 2012
808.8—dc23

2011032685

3 4 5 6 7 8 9 10—DOC—15 14

www.pearsonhighered.com   ISBN–13: 978-0-205-78710-4
ISBN–10:   0-205-78710-X

contents

List of Illustrations   xiv
Preface   xvii
Acknowledgments   xix

The Ancient World   1

Timeline   25

THE EPIC OF GILGAMESH (C. 1200 B.C.E.)
 (*trans. Stephanie Dalley*)   29

GENESIS (1st millennium B.C.E.)
 (*trans. Robert Alter*)   74
 Chapters 1—11   75

THE SONG OF SONGS (1st millennium B.C.E.)
 (*Jerusalem Bible translation*)   84

HOMER (8th century B.C.E.)   95
 The Iliad (*trans. Richmond Lattimore*)
  Book 1. The Wrath of Achilles   98
  Book 18. Achilles' Shield   111
  Book 22. The Death of Hektor   124
  Book 24. Achilles and Priam   135
 The Odyssey (*trans. Robert Fagles*)
  Book 1. Athena Inspires the Prince   152
  Book 6. The Princess and the Stranger   163
  Book 9. In the One-Eyed Giant's Cave   171
  Book 11. The Kingdom of the Dead   185
  Book 22. Slaughter in the Hall   201
  Book 23. The Great Rooted Bed   213
  Book 24. Peace   223

SAPPHO (early 7th century B.C.E.)   236
 Rich-throned immortal Aphrodite (*trans. M. L. West*)   236
 Come, goddess   237
 Some think a fleet   238
 He looks to me to be in heaven   238
 Love shakes my heart   239
 Honestly, I wish I were dead   239

. . . she worshipped you   239
Like the sweet-apple   240
The doorman's feet   240

SOPHOCLES (c. 496–406 B.C.E.)   240
Oedipus the King (*trans. David Grene*)   243

EURIPIDES (c. 480–405 B.C.E.)   281
The Medea (*trans. Rex Warner*)   284

PLATO (c. 429–347 B.C.E.)   315
Apology (*trans. Benjamin Jowett*)   315

THE RAMAYANA OF VALMIKI (last centuries B.C.E.)   331
from Book 2
[The Exile of Rama] (*trans. Sheldon Pollock*)   334
from Book 3
[The Abduction of Sita] (*trans. Sheldon Pollock*)   349
from Book 6
[The Death of Ravana] (*trans. Robert Goldman et al.*)   362
[The Fire Ordeal of Sita]   365

THE BOOK OF SONGS (1000–600 B.C.E.)   370
(*trans. Arthur Waley*)   371
1 The Ospreys Cry   371
5 Locusts   371
20 Plop Fall the Plums   372
23 In the Wilds Is a Dead Doe   372
26 Cypress Boat   372
45 Cypress Boat   373
76 I Beg of You, Zhong Zi   373
166 May Heaven Guard   374
189 The Beck   375
234 What Plant Is Not Faded?   376
238 Oak Clumps   376
245 Birth to the People   377
283 So They Appeared   379

CONFUCIUS (551–479 B.C.E.)   379
from The Analects (*trans. Simon Leys*)   380

VIRGIL (70–19 B.C.E.)   393
Aeneid (*trans. Robert Fitzgerald*)   397
from Book 1 [A Fateful Haven]   397
Book 4 [The Passion of the Queen]   414
from Book 12 [The Death of Turnus]   436

OVID (43 B.C.E.–18 C.E.)   442

  Metamorphoses (*trans. A. D. Melville*)   444

    from Book 1

      [Prologue]   444

    from Book 3

      [Tiresias]   444

      [Narcissus and Echo]   445

    from Book 6

      [Arachne]   449

    from Book 8

      [The Minotaur: Daedalus and Icarus]   454

    from Book 10

      [Orpheus and Eurydice]   456

      [Orpheus's Song: Ganymede, Hyacinth]   459

    from Book 11

      [The Death of Orpheus]   462

    from Book 15

      [Pythagoras]   463

CATULLUS (84–54 B.C.E.)   467

    3 ("Cry out lamenting, Venuses & Cupids") (*trans. Charles Martin*)   468

    5 ("Lesbia, let us live only for loving")   468

    13 ("You will dine well with me, my dear Fabullus")   469

    51 ("To me that man seems like a god in heaven")   469

    76 ("If any pleasure can come to a man through recalling")   470

    85 ("I hate & love")   470

    107 ("If ever something which someone with no expectation")   470

HORACE (65–8 B.C.E.)   471

  Satires (*trans. Niall Rudd*)   471

    1.5 ("Leaving the big city behind")   471

  Odes (*trans. David West*)   474

    1.9 ("You see Soracte standing white and deep")   474

    2.14 ("Ah how quickly, Postumus, Postumus")   475

The Medieval Era   477

Timeline   495

POETRY OF THE TANG DYNASTY   500

WANG WEI (701–761)   500

  from The Wang River Collection (*trans. Pauline Yu*)   501

    Preface   501

    1. Meng Wall Cove   501

    5. Deer Enclosure   501

    8. Sophora Path   502
    11. Lake Yi   502
    17. Bamboo Lodge   502
Bird Call Valley   502
Farewell   502
Farewell to Yuan the Second on His Mission to Anxi   502
Visiting the Temple of Gathered Fragrance   503
Zhongnan Retreat   503
In Response to Vice-Magistrate Zhang   503

LI BO (701–762)   **503**
    Drinking Alone with the Moon (*trans. Vikram Seth*)   504
    Fighting South of the Ramparts (*trans. Arthur Waley*)   506
    The Road to Shu Is Hard (*trans. Vikram Seth*)   506
    Bring in the Wine (*trans. Vikram Seth*)   507
    The Jewel Stairs' Grievance (*trans. Ezra Pound*)   508
    The River Merchant's Wife: A Letter (*trans. Ezra Pound*)   508
    Listening to a Monk from Shu Playing the Lute (*trans. Vikram Seth*)   509
    Farewell to a Friend (*trans. Pauline Yu*)   509
    In the Quiet Night (*trans. Vikram Seth*)   509
    Sitting Alone by Jingting Mountain (*trans. Stephen Owen*)   509
    Question and Answer in the Mountains (*trans. Vikram Seth*)   510

DU FU (712–770)   **510**
    Ballad of the Army Carts (*trans. Vikram Seth*)   511
    Moonlit Night (*trans. Vikram Seth*)   511
    Spring Prospect (*trans. Pauline Yu*)   512
    Traveling at Night (*trans. Pauline Yu*)   512
    Autumn Meditations (*trans. A. C. Graham*)   512
    Yangtse and Han (*trans. A. C. Graham*)   514

BO JUYI (772–846)   **514**
    A Song of Unending Sorrow (*trans. Witter Bynner*)   515

MURASAKI SHIKIBU (c. 978–c. 1014)   **517**
The Tale of Genji (*trans. Edward Seidensticker*)   520
   from Chapter 1. The Paulownia Court   520
   from Chapter 2. The Broom Tree   528
   from Chapter 5. Lavender   530
   from Chapter 7. An Autumn Excursion   538
   from Chapter 9. Heartvine   542
   from Chapter 10. The Sacred Tree   552
   from Chapter 12. Suma   555
   from Chapter 13. Akashi   557
   from Chapter 25. Fireflies   561

from Chapter 34. New Herbs (Part 1) 563
from Chapter 35. New Herbs (Part 2) 569
from Chapter 36. The Oak Tree 584
from Chapter 40. The Rites 587
from Chapter 41. The Wizard 590

THE QUR'AN (610 C.E.–632 C.E.) 592
   from Sura 41. Revelations Well Expounded (*trans. N. J. Dawood*) 594
   from Sura 79. The Soul-Snatchers 595
   from Sura 15. The Rocky Tract 595
   from Sura 2. The Cow 596
   from Sura 7. The Heights 597
   Sura 1. The Opening 598
   from Sura 4. Women 598
   from Sura 5. The Table 601
   from Sura 24. Light 602
   from Sura 36. Ya Sin 603
   from Sura 48. Victory 603
   Sura 71. Noah 604
   Sura 87. The Most High 605
   Sura 93. Daylight 605
   Sura 96. Clots of Blood 605
   Sura 110. Help 606

THE THOUSAND AND ONE NIGHTS (9th–14th centuries) 606
   Prologue: (*trans. Husain Haddawy*) 608
      [The Story of King Shahrayar and Shahrazad, His Vizier's Daughter] 608
      [The Tale of the Ox and the Donkey] 615
      [The Tale of the Merchant and His Wife] 616
   from The Tale of the Porter and the Young Girls
      (*trans. Powys Mathers after J. C. Mardrus*) 618
      [The Tale of Zubaidah, the First of the Girls] 629
   from The Tale of Sympathy the Learned 634
   Conclusion 644

BEOWULF (c. 750–950) 648
   (*trans. Alan Sullivan and Timothy Murphy*) 651

IBERIA, THE MEETING OF THREE WORLDS 712

CASTILIAN BALLADS AND TRADITIONAL SONGS
   (c. 11th–14th centuries) 715
      Ballad of Juliana (*trans. Edwin Honig*) 715
      Abenámar (*trans. William M. Davis*) 716
      Those mountains, mother (*trans. James Duffy*) 717

I will not pick verbena (*trans. James Duffy*)   717
Three Moorish Girls (*trans. Angela Buxton*)   717

MOZARABIC *KHARJAS* (10th–early 11th century)   718
As if you were a stranger (*trans. Peter Dronke*)   718
Ah tell me, little sisters (*trans. Peter Dronke*)   718
My lord Ibrahim (*trans. Peter Dronke*)   718
I'll give you such love! (*trans. Peter Dronke*)   719
Take me out of this plight (*trans. Peter Dronke*)   719
Mother, I shall not sleep (*trans. William M. Davis*)   719

IBN AL-'ARABI (1165–1240)   719
Gentle now, doves (*trans. Michael Sells*)   719

SOLOMON IBN GABIROL (c. 1021–c. 1057)   721
She looked at me and her eyelids burned (*trans. William M. Davis*)   721
Behold the sun at evening (*trans. Raymond P. Scheindlin*)   722
The mind is flawed, the way to wisdom blocked
   (*trans. Raymond P. Scheindlin*)   722
Winter wrote with the ink of its rains and showers
   (*trans. Raymond P. Scheindlin*)   722

YEHUDA HA-LEVI (before 1075–1141)   723
Cups without wine are lowly (*trans. William M. Davis*)   723
Ofra does her laundry with my tears (*trans. Raymond P. Scheindlin*)   723
Once when I fondled him upon my thighs (*trans. Raymond P. Scheindlin*)   723
From time's beginning, You were love's abode
   (*trans. Raymond P. Scheindlin*)   724
Your breeze, Western shore, is perfumed (*trans. David Goldstein*)   724
My heart is in the East (*trans. David Goldstein*)   724

RAMÓN LLULL (1232–1315)   725
from Blanquerna: The Book of the Lover and the Beloved
   (*trans. E. Allison Peers*)   725

DOM DINIS, KING OF PORTUGAL (1261–1325)   727
Provençals right well may versify (*trans. William M. Davis*)   727
Of what are you dying, daughter (*trans. Barbara Hughes Fowler*)   728
O blossoms of the verdant pine (*trans. Barbara Hughes Fowler*)   728
The lovely girl arose at earliest dawn (*trans. Barbara Hughes Fowler*)   729

MARTIN CODAX (fl. mid-13th century)   729
Ah God, if only my love could know (*trans. Peter Dronke*)   730
My beautiful sister, come hurry with me (*trans. Barbara Hughes Fowler*)   730
O waves that I've come to see (*trans. Barbara Hughes Fowler*)   731

MARIE DE FRANCE (mid-12th–early 13th century)   731
 Lais (*trans. Joan M. Ferrante and Robert W. Hanning*)   732
  Prologue   732
  Bisclavret (The Werewolf)   734
  Chevrefoil (The Honeysuckle)   740

DANTE ALIGHIERI (1265–1321)   743
 The Divine Comedy (*trans. Allen Mandelbaum*)   746
  Inferno   746

GEOFFREY CHAUCER (c. 1340–1400)   868
 The Canterbury Tales (*trans. J. U. Nicolson*)   870
  The General Prologue   870
  The Wife of Bath's Prologue   890
  The Wife of Bath's Tale   910

The Early Modern Period   919

Timeline   933

GIOVANNI BOCCACCIO (1313–1375)   936
 Decameron (*trans. G. H. McWilliam*)   938
  First Day [Introduction]   938
  First Day, Third Story [The Three Rings]   945
  Third Day, Tenth Story [Locking the Devil Up in Hell]   946
  Seventh Day, Fourth Story [The Woman Who Locked Her Husband Out]   950
  Tenth Day, Tenth Story [The Patient Griselda]   953

FRANCIS PETRARCH (1304–1374)   962
 Canzoniere (*trans. Mark Musa*)   964
  During the Life of My Lady Laura   964
   1 ("O you who hear within these scattered verses")   964
   3 ("It was the day the sun's ray had turned pale")   964
   16 ("The old man takes his leave, white-haired and pale")   965
   35 ("Alone and deep in thought I measure out")   965
   52 ("Diana never pleased her lover more")   966
   90 ("She'd let her gold hair flow free in the breeze")   966
   126 ("Clear, cool, sweet running waters")   966
   195 ("From day to day my face and hair are changing")   968
  After the Death of My Lady Laura   968
   267 ("O God! that lovely face, that gentle look")   968
   277 ("If Love does not give me some new advice")   969
   291 ("When I see coming down the sky Aurora")   969
   311 ("That nightingale so tenderly lamenting")   969
   353 ("O lovely little bird singing away")   970
   365 ("I go my way lamenting those past times")   970

MICHEL DE MONTAIGNE (1533–1592)   971

Essays (*trans. Donald Frame*)   973
  Of Idleness   973
  Of the Power of the Imagination   974
  Of Cannibals   981
  Of Repentance   989

MIGUEL DE CERVANTES SAAVEDRA (1547–1616)   999

Don Quixote (*trans. John Rutherford*)   1002
  Part 1   1002
    Chapter 1. [The character of the knight]   1002
    Chapter 2. [His first expedition]   1005
    Chapter 3. [He attains knighthood]   1009
    Chapter 4. [An adventure on leaving the inn]   1013
    Chapter 5. [The knight's misfortunes continue]   1017
    from Chapter 6. [The inquisition in the library]   1020
    Chapter 7. [His second expedition]   1022
    Chapter 8. [The adventure of the windmills]   1025
    Chapter 9. [The battle with the gallant Basque]   1030
    Chapter 10. [A conversation with Sancho]   1033
    from Chapter 18. [A second conversation with Sancho]   1037
    Chapter 22. [The liberation of the galley slaves]   1042
    from Chapter 25. [The knight's penitence]   1049
    from Chapter 52. [The last adventure]   1054
  Part 2   1060
    Chapter 3. [The knight, the squire and the bachelor]   1060
    Chapter 4. [Sancho provides answers]   1065
    Chapter 10. [Dulcinea enchanted]   1067
    Chapter 72. [Knight and squire return to their village]   1073
    Chapter 73. [A discussion about omens]   1076
    Chapter 74. [The death of Don Quixote]   1079

WILLIAM SHAKESPEARE (1564–1616)   1083

Sonnets   1085
    1 ("From fairest creatures we desire increase")   1085
    3 ("Look in thy glass, and tell the face thou viewest")   1085
    17 ("Who will believe my verse in time to come")   1086
    55 ("Not marble nor the gilded monuments")   1086
    73 ("That time of year thou mayst in me behold")   1086
    87 ("Farewell: thou art too dear for my possessing")   1087
    116 ("Let me not to the marriage of true minds")   1087
    126 ("O thou, my lovely boy, who in thy power")   1087
    127 ("In the old age black was not counted fair")   1088
    130 ("My mistress' eyes are nothing like the sun")   1088
The Tempest   1090

THE CONQUEST AND ITS AFTERMATH   1145

BERNAL DIAZ DEL CASTILLO (1492–1584)   1147
from The True History of the Conquest of New Spain
(*trans. Alfred Percival Maudslay*)   1148

from THE AZTEC-SPANISH DIALOGUES OF 1524   1159
(*trans. Jorge Klor de Alva*)   1159

SONGS OF THE AZTEC NOBILITY (15th–16th centuries)   1167
Make your beginning, you who sing (*trans. David Damrosch*)   1169
from Water-Pouring Song (*trans. John Bierhorst*)   1170
Moctezuma, you creature of heaven, you sing in Mexico (*trans.*
John Bierhorst)   1174

SOR JUANA INÉS DE LA CRUZ (c. 1651–1695)   1175
from The Loa for the Auto Sacramental of the Divine Narcissus
(*trans. Patricia A. Peters and Renée Domeier*)   1175

Bibliography   *1185*
Credits   *1197*
Index   *1201*

list of illustrations

The World According to Herodotus, C. 450 B.C.E.	Inside Front Cover
The Law Code of Hammurabi	1
Statue of Zeus or Poseidon	10
Marble statue of Augustus Caesar	20
Gilgamesh and Enkidu slaying the Bull of Heaven	30
Sappho and Alkaios	237
Maenad cup	282
Contemporary Indian comic book *Ramayana: The Death of Ravana*	332
King Arthur and His Knights	477
Calligraphy of the name of the Prophet Muhammad	486
Scenes from the Bayeux Tapestry	489
Liang Kai, *Li Bo Chanting a Poem*	505
Christian and Muslim playing chess, from the *Book of Games*	714
Dante's Earth, Hell, Purgatory, and Paradise	748—749
Don Cristobal Colon, Admiral of Ships Bound for the Indies	919
The Peking Mission	924
Aztec screenfold book	930
Gustave Doré, engraving for cervantes's *Don Quixote*	1001
Cortes accepting the Aztecs' surrender	1146
Henricus Hondius, *New Geographic and Hydrographic Map of the Entire Earth,* 1630.	Inside Back Cover

Maps

Asia, Europe, and North Africa in 1 C.E.	4
The Near East in 1250 B.C.E.	7
The Greek City-States in 450 B.C.E.	13
The Roman Empire in 150 C.E.	21
Africa, Asia, and Europe in 1000 C.E.	480
Medieval Europe, c. 1100 C.E.	491
The Iberian Peninsula, c. 1180	713
The World in 1500	921
Europe in 1590	926

Our world today is both expanding and growing smaller at the same time. Expanding, through a tremendous increase in the range of cultures that actively engage with each other; and yet growing smaller as well, as people and products surge across borders in the process known as globalization. This double movement creates remarkable opportunities for cross-cultural understanding, as well as new kinds of tensions, miscommunications, and uncertainties. Both the opportunities and the uncertainties are amply illustrated in the changing shape of world literature. A generation ago, when the term "world literature" was used in North America, it largely meant masterworks by European writers from Homer onward, together with a few favored North American writers, heirs to the Europeans. Today, however, it is generally recognized that Europe is only part of the story of the world's literatures, and only part of the story of North America's cultural heritage. An extraordinary range of exciting material is now in view, from the earliest Sumerian lyrics inscribed on clay tablets to the latest Kashmiri poetry circulated on the Internet. Many new worlds—and newly visible *older* worlds of classical traditions around the globe—await us today.

How can we best approach such varied materials from so many cultures? Can we deal with this embarrassment of riches without being overwhelmed by it, and without merely giving a glancing regard to less familiar traditions? This anthology has been designed to help readers successfully navigate "the sea of stories"—as Salman Rushdie has described the world's literary heritage. This preface will outline the ways we've gone about this challenging, fascinating task.

Connecting Distinctive Traditions

Works of world literature engage in a double conversation: with their culture of origin and with the varied contexts into which they travel away from home. To look broadly at world literature is therefore to see patterns of difference as well as points of contact and commonality. The world's disparate traditions have developed very distinct kinds of literature, even very different ideas as to what should be called "literature" at all. Beyond our immediate groupings, our overall selections have been made with an eye to fostering connections across time and space. We have worked to create an exceptionally coherent and well-integrated presentation of an extraordinary variety of works from around the globe, from the dawn of writing to the present. Recognizing that different sorts of works have counted as literature in differing times and places, we have taken an inclusive approach, centering on poems, plays, and fictional narratives but also including selections from rich historical, religious, and philosophical texts like the Bible and the Qur'an that have been important for much later literary work, even though they weren't conceived as literature themselves. We present many complete masterworks, including *The Epic of Gilgamesh* (in a beautiful verse translation) and Dante's *Inferno*, and we have extensive, teachable selections from such long works as *The Odyssey, The Tale of Genji,* and *Don Quixote*.

Along with these major selections we continue to present a great array of shorter works, some of which have been known only to specialists and only now are entering into world literature. It is our experience as readers and as teachers that the established classics themselves can best be understood when they're set in a varied literary landscape. Nothing is included here, though, simply to make a point: whether world-renowned or recently rediscovered, these are compelling works to read. Throughout our work on this book, we've tried to be highly inclusive in principle and yet carefully selective in practice, avoiding tokenism and also its inverse, the piling up of an unmanageable array of heterogeneous material. If we've succeeded as we hope, the result will be coherent as well as capacious, substantive as well as stimulating.

Aids to Understanding

A major emphasis of our work has been to introduce each culture and each work to best effect. Each major period and section of the anthology, each grouping of works, and each individual author has an introduction by a member of our editorial team. Our goal has been to write introductions informed by deep knowledge worn lightly. Neither talking down to our readers nor overwhelming them with masses of unassimilable information, our introductions don't seek to "cover" the material but instead try to uncover it, to provide ways in and connections outward. Similarly, our footnotes and glosses are concise and informative, rather than massive or interpretive. Timelines, maps, and pronunciation guides throughout the anthology all aim to foster an informed and pleasurable reading of the works.

Going Further

Gateways to World Literature makes connections beyond its covers as well as within them. Bibliographies at the end of the volume point the way to historical and critical readings for students wishing to go into greater depth for term papers. The website for the text offers practice quizzes, an interactive timeline, a searchable glossary of literary terms, audio pronunciation guides, and many more resources. Finally, an extensive instructor's manual is available to adopters at www.pearsonhighered.com.

We hope that the results of our work on this project will be as enjoyable to use as the book has been to create. We welcome you now inside our pages.

David Damrosch

acknowledgments

In the extended process of planning and preparing this anthology, the editors have been fortunate to have the support, advice, and assistance of many people. Our editor, Joe Terry, and our publisher, Roth Wilkofsky, have supported our project in every possible way and some seemingly impossible ones as well, helping us produce the best possible book despite all challenges to budgets and well-laid plans in a rapidly evolving field. Their associates, Erin Reilly and Kelly Carroll, have shown unwavering enthusiasm in developing the book and its related supplements.

We are grateful for the guidance of the many reviewers who advised us on the creation of this first edition of *Gateways* and our other World literature volumes, in their many incarnations: Adetutu Abatan (Floyd College); Roberta Adams (Fitchburg State College); Magda al-Nowaihi (Columbia University); Kyoka Amano (University of Indianapolis); Nancy Applegate (Floyd College); Susan Atefat-Peckham (Georgia College and State University); Evan Balkan (CCBC-Catonsville); Charles Bane (University of Central Arkansas); Michelle Barnett (University of Alabama, Birmingham); Colonel Bedell (Virginia Military Institute); Thomas Beebee (Pennsylvania State University); Paula Berggren (Baruch College); Mark Bernier (Blinn College); Ronald Bogue (University of Georgia); Laurel Bollinger (University of Alabama in Huntsville); Ashley S. Bonds (Copiah-Lincoln Community College); Theodore Bouabre (Jackson State University); Debra Taylor Bourdeau (Kennesaw State University); Terre Burton (Dixie State College); Patricia Cearley (South Plains College); Raj Chekuri (Laredo Community College); Sandra Clark (University of Wyoming); Maren Clegg-Hyer (Valdosta State University); Thomas F. Connolly (Suffolk University); Vilashini Cooppan (Yale University); Bradford Crain (College of the Ozarks); Robert W. Croft (Gainesville College); Patsy J. Daniels (Jackson State University); Frank Day (Clemson University); Michael Delahoyde (Washington State University); Elizabeth Otten Delmonico (Truman State University); Jo Devine (University of Alaska Southeast); Brian Doherty (University of Texas–Austin); Gene Doty (University of Missouri–Rolla); Jennifer Duncan (Chattagnooga State Technical Community College); James Earle (University of Oregon); Ed Eberhart (Troy University); R. Steve Eberly (Western Carolina University); Khalil Elayan (Kennesaw State University); Walter Evans (Augusta State University); Fidel Fajardo-Acosta (Creighton University); Gene C. Fant (Union University); Mike Felker (South Plains College); Kathy Flann (Eastern Kentucky University); Janice Gable (Valley Forge Christian College); Stanley Galloway (Bridgewater College); Doris Gardenshire (Trinity Valley Community College); Diana C. Gingo (Uniersity of Texas–Dallas); Jonathan Glenn (University of Central Arkansas); Kyle Glover (Lindenwood University); Lauri Goodling (Georgia Perimeter College); Michael Grimwood (North Carolina State University); Dean Hall (Kansas State University); Dorothy Hardman (Fort Valley State University); Katona D. Hargrave (Troy University); Joel Henderson (Chattanooga State Technical College); Nainsi J. Houston (Creighton University); Elissa Heil (University of the Ozarks); David Hesla (Emory University); Susan Hillabold (Purdue University North Central); Karen Hodges (Texas Wesleyan); David Hoegberg (Indiana University-Purdue University–Indianapolis); Sheri Hoem (Xavier University); Michael Hutcheson (Landmark College); Mary Anne Hutchinson (Utica College); Raymond Ide (Lancaster Bible College); James Ivory (Appalachian State University); Craig Kallendorf (Texas A & M University); Ernest N. Kaulbach (University of Texas–Austin); Bridget Keegan (Creighton University); Steven Kellman (University of Texas–San Antonio); Hans Kellner (North Carolina State University); Roxanne Kent-Drury (Northern Kentucky University); Robert M. Kirschen (University of Nevada–Las Vegas); Barry Kitterman (Austin Peay State University); Susan Kroeg (Eastern Kentucky University); Tamara Kuzmenkov (Tacoma Community College); Marta

Kvande (Valdosta State University); Jennifer Lawrence (Georgia State University); Heather Levy (University of Texas–Arlington); Patricia Lonchair (University of the Incarnate Word); Robert Lorenzi (Camden County College–Blackwood); David Lowery (Jones County Junior College); Mark Mazzone (Tennessee State University); David McCracken (Coker College); Judith Broome Mesa-Pelly (Austin Peay State University); George Mitrenski (Auburn University); J. Hunter Morgan (Glenville State College); Wayne Narey (Arkansas State University); James Nicholl (Western Carolina University); Roger Osterholm (Embry-Riddle University); James W. Parins (University of Arkansas–Little Rock); Joe Pellegrino (Eastern Kentucky University); Linda Lang-Peralta (Metropolitan State College of Denver); Sandra Petree (University of Arkansas); David E. Phillips (Charleston Southern University);Kevin R. Rahimzadeh (Eastern Kentucky University); Elizabeth L. Rambo (Campbell University); Melissa Rankin (University of Texas–Arlington); Terry Reilly (University of Alaska); Constance Relihan (Auburn University); Nelljean Rice (Coastal Carolina University); Gavin Richardson (Union University); Colleen Richmond (George Fox University); Elizabeth M. Richmond-Garza (University of Texas–Austin); Gretchen Ronnow (Wayne State University); Joseph Rosenblum (University of North Carolina at Greensboro); John Rothfork (West Texas A & M University); Elise Salem-Manganaro (Fairleigh Dickinson University); David P. Schenck (University of South Florida); Daniel Schierenbeck (Central Missouri State University); Asha Sen (University of Wisconsin Eau Claire); Richard Sha (American University); Edward Shaw (University of Central Florida); Jack Shreve (Allegany College of Maryland); Stephen Slimp (University of West Alabama); Jimmy Dean Smith (Union College); Gabriele Ulrike Stauf (Georgia Southwestern State University); Floyd C. Stuart (Norwich University); Barbara Szubinska (Eastern Kentucky University); Eleanor Sumpter-Latham (Central Oregon Community College); Ron Swigger (Albuquerque Technical Vocational Institute); Barry Tharaud (Mesa State College); Theresa Thompson (Valdosta State College); Douglass H. Thomson (Georgia Southern University); Teresa Thonney (Columbia Basin College); Charles Tita (Shaw University); Tomasz Warchol (Georgia Southern University); Scott D. Vander Ploeg (Madisonville Community College); Marian Wernicke (Pensacola Junior College); Sally Wheeler (Georgia Perimeter College); Nancy Wilson (Texas State University); Sallie Wolf (Arapahoe Community College); R. Paul Yoder (University of Arkansas–Little Rock); Racheal Yeatts (University of North Texas); Dede Yow (Kennesaw State University); and Jianqing Zheng (Mississippi Valley State University).

It has been a great pleasure to work with all these colleagues both at Longman and at schools around the country. This book exists for its readers, whose reactions and suggestions we warmly welcome, as *Gateways to World Literature* moves out into the world.

GATEWAYS TO
WORLD LITERATURE

VOLUME 1

The Ancient World through
the Early Modern Period

The Ancient World

Detail of stele inscribed with the Law Code of Hammurabi, c. 1750 B.C.E. The Babylonian King Hammurabi (reigned c. 1792–1750 B.C.E.) commissioned the major law code that bears his name, an ambitious effort to organize society under the rule of law. The seven-foot-tall stone column on which his laws are inscribed in cuneiform script is crowned with the scene showing Hammurabi conversing with the seated sun god, Shamash.

THE ANCIENT WORLD WAS SHAPED BY GREAT INNOVATIONS. The first nations and the first empires were founded, several great world religions—including Hinduism, Buddhism, and Christianity—were established, the first organized law codes were drawn up, and in many respects the outlines of civilization as we know it today began to emerge. A common term in all of these developments was the invention of systems of writing. With writing came effective long-distance communication and the ability to build nations and empires. While great religious leaders like Gautama Buddha, Jesus, and later the prophet Muhammad didn't write their teachings down, the scriptures compiled by their disciples and adherents played a major role in the worldwide spread of the religions they founded. Writing also gave cultures the ability to record their history and to create the textual records of their societies, preserving their imaginative works as well as more practical documents for later generations to read: literature was born.

The Beginnings of World Literature

The world's first great bodies of literary texts were created between four thousand and a little less than two thousand years ago, in Mesopotamia, in the Mediterranean world, in India, and in China. These works often have a double focus: preserving ancient traditions with roots in the distant past, they also respond to their own present situations. Ancient writers looked to the past to understand their present. Stories of creation would lead to the present world order, epic accounts of ancient battles would celebrate the founding of a people or nation, and even very recent laws would be portrayed as the wisdom of the ancients. Traditions could be invented as well as preserved, and as written texts became numerous, competing traditions could be compared, analyzed, and creatively reworked. The pleasures of imagination and of verbal beauty abound in these works as well, as ancient writers created the world's first written poems, dramas, and prose narratives. Their works became foundational for later writing in their own cultures and beyond, and have done much to shape our understanding and practice of literature to the present day. To read these texts now is to encounter a fascinating mixture of strangeness and familiarity, as the writers used radically new technology of writing to convey ancient wisdom and to adapt it to their own changing times.

Cities, Nations, and Empires

Ancient writing is largely urban in origins, for writing was employed mostly in courts and temples in the cities that grew rapidly in the second and first millennia B.C.E. The Greeks and Romans loved pastoral poems about shepherds and shepherdesses in the countryside, but the shepherds themselves couldn't write; the pastoral poetry we have was written by sophisticated urban poets dreaming of rural peace. Even so, the cities remained deeply dependent on the countryside; the great majority of all people in antiquity were engaged in growing crops and raising livestock. Primitive peoples had subsisted through hunting, fishing, and foraging for whatever edible plants they might happen to encounter, but between around 8000 and 6000 B.C.E. the settled cultivation of crops began. Farming produced substantial new surpluses of food and allowed for specialized roles to emerge in the growing cities: rulers and administrators, soldiers, priests, craftsmen, painters, musicians, and poets. As early as 5000 B.C.E., the Sumerians in southern Mesopotamia were building large cities complete with public water supplies and drainage, and by around 3100 B.C.E. the Sumerians had pioneered the use of written notations to record their dealings.

The rulers of major cities extended their reach to create the first nations, often relying on rivers as conduits of trade and communication. "Mesopotamia" takes its name from the Greek phrase "between the rivers," referring to the Tigris and Euphrates rivers on whose banks were built the great early cities of Ur, Akkad, Nippur, and Babylon. The Nile formed the backbone of Egypt, united into a single country around 3100 B.C.E., and the hieroglyphic writing developed in Egypt around that time greatly aided the new administrators in knitting their new country together. In China, cities grew up along rivers like the Yangzi, while in India a major early civilization grew up in the fertile valley of the Indus River. Sea routes could serve as well as rivers: the early Greek cities of Knossos in Crete and Mycenae on the mainland became centers of trade and of cultural production.

Over time, the most powerful city-states vied for control of larger regions, and the first empires were born in the third and second millennia B.C.E. The Babylonian and Assyrian empires waxed and waned across Mesopotamia and regions north and west; the Egyptians had long periods of control over Nubia and the Sudan to the south, and much of Palestine to the north and east. India and China, unified countries today, were (and still are) made up of many different ethnic groups speaking unrelated languages, and the governments that came to extend across their territories were creating empires rather than homogeneous nations. In late antiquity, vast empires extended from centers in Persia, in Northern Greece, and then in Rome, and great writers like Virgil both celebrated and probed the empires ruled by their patrons.

Travel, Migration, and Trade

Armies of conquest weren't the only groups on the move in the ancient world. Populations expanded rapidly in periods of prosperity but could come under severe stress in times of drought, or simply through outgrowing their resources. Entire peoples journeyed in search of new grazing lands and new fields to farm, in waves of migration that periodically transformed the social landscape, creating mixed populations in formerly unified regions. On a smaller scale, caravans of traders crossed long distances along the "silk road" that grew up from China to India and into Central Asia and Asia Minor, while Phoenician and Greek sailing ships established contacts around the Mediterranean. Like the tales that the great traveler Odysseus recounts to entertain his hosts, much ancient literature plays to people's fascination with hearing about distant peoples and their unusual customs, and many works explored what could happen when disparate cultures came into contact or conflict, either to comic effect or with tragic consequences.

Lyric and Epic

The invention of writing allowed ancient singers to record their poems, both short lyrics and the sweeping poetic narratives we call epics, and over time poetry came to be composed in writing, independent of oral tradition. Even written literature, though, remained closely tied to public performance: "lyric" poetry gets its name from the Greek poets' custom of singing their poems to the accompaniment of a lyre or small

Asia, Europe, and North Africa in 1 C.E.

ROMAN EMPIRE
PARTHIAN EMPIRE
PAHLAVAS
HAN EMPIRE

harp. The great early Chinese poetry collection, *The Book of Songs,* is equally a collection of works made to be sung. The poetic impulse seems to be universal, and indeed in all of the ancient cultures presented here, lyric poetry was recorded long before prose fiction emerged. At the same time, the very fact that poetry is found everywhere means that it was composed in many different settings and with different cultural assumptions, sometimes in close connection to religious ceremonies, other times purely as entertainment at banquets. Poets could be seen as powerful figures, verbal magicians whose words could have dangerous effects, or much more modestly as servants and entertainers. In China, poetry came to be regarded as an integral part of daily life: any educated person, male or female, was expected to be able to compose an apt poem for any occasion—the giving of a present, a friend's departure on a journey, or the downfall of a dynasty.

By contrast with the universality of lyric poetry, epic poetry is found in some ancient cultures (Babylonia, India, Greece, and Rome) and not others (Egypt, China). Works labeled "epic" are long narrative poems, usually several thousand lines or more, concerning a series of great struggles or adventures of a hero or group of heroes, aided and opposed by different gods, often leading to the forming of a people or nation. Often an epic centers on a great battle, as with Valmiki's *Ramayana* and Homer's *Iliad,* based on legendary struggles in India and Troy, respectively. Other epics, like the Bablyonian *Epic of Gilgamesh* and Homer's *Odyssey,* center more on an individual's voyage and the return home. The oldest epics are collective compositions, long developed in oral tradition, but as time went on they became increasingly shaped through rewriting. Eventually, they came to be composed by historically known individuals, like Virgil, whose *Aeneid* combines the two great themes of voyage and of battle. The epics present a range of forms and styles, through which their authors probe the fundamental limits and meaning of their culture.

Myth, Legend, and History

A distinct feature of ancient literature is the freedom with which it can mix kinds of material we usually think of as distinct, such as myths, legends, and verifiable historical facts. Most ancient cultures reckoned years by one monarch's reign and then the next, with spotty record-keeping if any, and no systematic marking of chronology. The dating of all the ancient texts in this anthology on the common scale of years B.C.E. ("before the common era") and C.E. ("common era") is based on efforts first made in the medieval era to date the year of Jesus's birth and organize history accordingly. (As is now common in world history texts, this anthology uses "B.C.E." and "C.E." in place of the traditional "B.C." and "A.D." with their direct theological emphasis.) With written records incomplete and inconsistent, the boundaries remained fluid in antiquity between what we would now separate as history versus legend or outright myth. "Myth" itself is a term with many meanings. Today we often call something a myth simply to say it isn't true, but in ancient Greek, the term *mythos* originally meant any speech or story. Gradually the term came to refer especially to poetic legends about the early doings of the gods, or the gods and mortals together, in a distant, shadowy past. Far from signifying falsehood, then, "myth" in the ancient world meant a story about ultimate truths. Myths were sometimes told to explain the origins of the world as a whole or of a particular custom or feature of the landscape; at other times, they were used as background or charter for a ritual, as when the Babylonian creation myth was recited as part of an annual New Year's ceremony. Anonymous in origin,

5

handed down over the years from one teller to another, a myth would vary in form and content as it circulated within a culture and beyond, and over time myths could be taken up and elaborated more for the sake of enjoyment than for any practical purpose. Throughout ancient literature, mythic elements continually reappear even in sober historical writing, and human history—like the earthly landscape itself—continued to bear the marks of the gods' deeds and intentions. In between myth and history proper are legends, traditional tales of relatively recent people and events. Often a single work will blend mythic, legendary, and historical materials, challenging us to see the world in a new way, interfusing what we often think of as separate realms of fact and fiction.

Most ancient texts existed in only one manuscript or a few copies at most, and over time the majority were lost. The ancient works we have today are the rare exceptions, works so treasured that they circulated widely and were preserved through centuries of warfare and disruption, or else works that simply happened to be preserved in a tomb or a ruined royal library, where they could be rediscovered long after their world had vanished. In many ways these foundational works set the course for much later writing around the globe, and they convey the first writers' excitement as they captured their world on paper, on clay tablets, on animal hides, and on stone.

The Ancient Near East

The story of world literature begins with the ancient cultures of Egypt and "the Fertile Crescent," a broad band of settled lands stretching from the Tigris and Euphrates rivers in what is now Iraq, up into Asia Minor and down through Palestine. Across this region a combination of favorable environmental conditions and human ingenuity led to the establishment of the world's first great cities, such as Thebes and Memphis in Egypt, and Ur and Babylon in Mesopotamia. As rulers sought to build empires and merchants created extensive trading networks, they began to develop means to communicate over large distances, settle their accounts, and extend their influence: writing was born.

Sometime around 3400 B.C.E. the Sumerian people of southern Mesopotamia began to inscribe clay tablets with symbolic representations of objects and then of sounds; by 3000 B.C.E. the world's first fully developed writing system had emerged, capable of conveying detailed information and increasingly complex thoughts through an intricate system of cuneiform ("wedge-shaped") signs. Hundreds of complex combinations of marks were used, each for a different syllable. Once baked, the clay tablets could easily be carried long distances, and to our good fortune they could last for thousands of years when buried in the region's dry, sandy soil.

By about 3000 B.C.E. the Egyptians had developed their own, openly pictorial form of writing, carved on stone or written with a brush on scrolls made from the fiber of the papyrus plant (our word "paper" comes from "papyrus"). Egyptian scribes created hundreds of hieroglyphic images of actual objects, and they found that they could employ these images to form many more words as well by using an image to signify just the initial sound of its object. Eventually, during the second millennium B.C.E., some traders in Egypt and Palestine began to use a simplified version of the alphabetic symbols and dropped the visual signs altogether: the first phonetic alphabet was created, and soon after 1000 B.C.E. several area languages, including Hebrew, were being written in purely alphabetic scripts. Through traders in Phoenicia an early alphabet spread to Greece and beyond, eventually becoming the alphabet we use today.

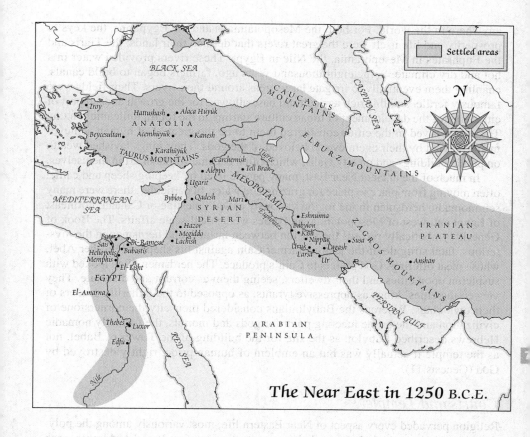

The Near East in 1250 B.C.E.

Empires, Cities, and Nomads

The first writers faced the challenge of recording a complex reality. Mesopotamia, where writing began, was made up of differing groups of widely different cultures. During the second and early first millennia, major empires extended out from Babylon, then from Nineveh—capital of the Babylonians' perennial rivals the Assyrians—and then from Babylon once again. The Hittite Empire in Anatolia (modern Turkey) also reached down into the area, and the Hittites adapted Babylonian cuneiform for their own use, as did early scribes in Persia, whose ruler Cyrus the Great eventually conquered Babylonia in 539 B.C.E.; Hellenistic Greek culture came into the area after Alexander the Great conquered Babylon in 331. Over the centuries Mesopotamia's ethnic composition steadily evolved through the immigration of new groups such as the Aramaeans, whose language of Aramaic is a close cousin of Hebrew and is used at times in the Bible itself; the legendary father of the Hebrew people, Abraham, is identified in Genesis and Deuteronomy as an Aramaean whom God commanded to leave Mesopotamia in order to found a new nation.

South of the other end of the Fertile Crescent, Egypt achieved early unity as a country in around 3100 B.C.E. Buffered by deserts on three sides and the Mediterranean to the north, Egypt remained a single country with an unbroken culture for a remarkable period of more than three thousand years, a record matched only by China anywhere in the world. For both the Mesopotamians and the Egyptians, the keys to prosperity and life itself were the great rivers that defined their lands: the Tigris and the Euphrates in Mesopotamia, the Nile in Egypt. These rivers provided water in a hot and dry climate. Some eight thousand years ago, farmers began to build canals, enabling them eventually to irrigate large areas around their rivers. Their fields were famously fertile, and this rich agricultural base allowed for the growth and support of cities and for the development of urban culture starting in the fourth millennium B.C.E. Those who lived in the cities considered them to be the greatest of human achievements, envied by their enemies and beloved of the gods. Their kings lavished wealth on public buildings and on city walls, which often became works of art in themselves.

In much of the ancient Near East, many people lived by keeping sheep and cattle, often moving from place to place for grazing and water. In particular, there were many seminomadic herdsmen in the region variously called Palestine or Canaan, northeast of Egypt and west of Mesopotamia, and cities were small-scale affairs. The Book of Genesis symbolically records the tension between farmers and herdsmen in the mysterious, fatal struggle of the jealous farmer Cain against his shepherd brother Abel, whose meat offerings God prefers to Cain's produce. The herdsmen often looked with suspicion upon cities and their dwellers, seeing them as corrupt and dissolute. They viewed the cities' kings as oppressive tyrants, as opposed to the fatherlike leaders of their own clans. Whereas the Babylonians considered their city the cornerstone of civilization and the prime meeting point for gods and mortals, the formerly nomadic Hebrews described Babylon as the site for the building of the Tower of Babel, not as the temple it actually was but an emblem of human pride, rightly destroyed by God (Genesis 11).

Courts and Temples

Religion pervaded every aspect of Near Eastern life, most variously among the polytheistic societies, which developed elaborate pantheons of gods and goddesses, each often associated with a particular city, natural force, or animal, and each of whom expected appropriate sacrifices and could be appealed to for different purposes. Typically a primordial generation of universal gods and goddesses was thought to have created the world and to have begotten further generations of divinities now in control of the world, usually with a large number of minor gods and goddesses ruled by a few preeminent divinities: a god associated with the sun (called Utu in Sumerian, Shamash in Akkadian, Amon Re or Aten in Egypt, Apollo in Greece), a moon goddess associated with fertility and love (Inanna or Ishtar in Mesopotamia, Isis in Egypt, Aphrodite in Greece, Venus in Rome), and other major divinities associated with such elemental forces as thunderstorms (Adad in Mesopotamia, Zeus in Greece) and water (Ea or Enki in Mesopotamia, Poseidon in Greece). The underworld was doubly ruled, in Mesopotamia by Nergal and his consort Ereshkigal, precursors of Hades and Persephone in Greek myth. In surviving poems, it is Ereshkigal who is the dominant figure, notably in chilling accounts of the underworld descent of her sister, the goddess of love (Inanna in Sumerian and Ishtar in Akkadian), who comes to visit her realm with nearly fatal results.

In the Near East as in medieval and early modern Europe, noble and especially royal women could wield substantial power, though only very rarely ruling outright as Cleopatra did in Egypt in the first century B.C.E. In Israel, women were powerful and sometimes dominant figures in clan-based life, and the Hebrew patriarchs are paired with imposing, and often cunning, matriarchs like Sarah, Rebekah, and Rachel. Women of modest circumstance are also periodically represented, as in the moving relationship of Ruth and Naomi in the Book of Ruth, or in the Song of Songs and the lyric poetry that has survived from Egypt. In Hebrew wisdom tradition, wisdom itself—a female noun in Hebrew, *hokmah*—came to be personified as a prime agent of God's guiding power. According to the Book of Proverbs, "I, Wisdom, dwell in prudence....By me kings reign, and nobles govern the earth." She prepares a banquet in her house of seven pillars and invites all to join her: "She has sent out her maidens to proclaim from the highest part of the town: 'Come in, you simpletons!' She says also to the fool, 'Come, dine with me and taste the wine that I have spiced. Cease to be foolish, and you will live, you will grow in understanding.'"

The Rebirth of the Past

During the last centuries of the first millennium B.C.E. the old Mesopotamian cultures went into steep decline, followed in the Roman period by Egypt as well; their texts were forgotten and their very scripts ceased to be known. For nearly two thousand years, the Bible contained the only ancient Near Eastern literature that anyone could read. The texts that follow in this section are the result of a long-distance collaboration between their ancient creators and their modern discoverers. The very name we commonly use for these works' place of origin, "the Near East," reflects the European perspective of the nineteenth-century archaeologists and scholars who sought out and deciphered these materials. The original authors, of course, didn't think of themselves as living in the East at all, whether near or middle: the residents of cities like Babylon and Thebes typically thought of themselves as living in the center of the world. The recovery of their large and varied world is one of the great intellectual achievements of the modern era, and it has given us new understandings of the biblical texts and a wealth of remarkable literature from the great ancient cultures at both ends of the Fertile Crescent.

Classical Greece

The ancient Greeks lived in pockets in what is now mainland Greece, throughout the islands of the eastern Mediterranean, and along the shores of the Mediterranean Sea. Like the writing of the ancient Near East, the earliest writing in the Greek world was often written on clay tablets, and it was used, so far as scholars know, to record the business of administering large bureaucracies and gathering tribute for the palace culture of the ancient Minoans (the indigenous people of Crete) and of the ancient Mycenaeans, the Greek-speakers who conquered them and adopted their writing system to record the sounds of Greek. The earliest surviving poems, the Homeric epics the *Iliad* and the *Odyssey,* record events of this age of heroes and warriors, of men and women close to the many gods and goddesses of the Greek pantheon. It was the time of Oedipus, the king who killed his father and married his mother, and of the expedition to Troy to retrieve the stolen Helen. These tales, passed on by word of mouth during a period when the skill of writing appears to have been lost, were first recorded in the eighth century B.C.E., when the many scattered communities of the Greeks began to grow and trade again after a period of devastation. They began to use an alphabet borrowed from the Phoenicians, adding vowels and making a supple and concise writing system that serves as the basis of our modern Roman alphabet.

Statue of Zeus or Poseidon from Cape Artemision, Greece, c. 450 B.C.E.

Immortals

Much of the early writing of the Greeks celebrates the many gods of this society. Hesiod in his *Theogony* tells the story of the succession of gods. The original goddess, Gaia, or "Earth," equal to her mate Ouranos, or "Sky," is replaced by many lesser female deities. The sky god is ambushed by his son Kronos, who castrates Ouranos with a sickle. The detached member mingles with the sea to produce Aphrodite, goddess of the foam and sexual desire. The time of Kronos is described as a golden age of mortals, which gives way to an age of silver, which is followed by a third race of bronze. After the time of heroes come the mortals of the present day, men of iron: "All toiling humanity will be blighted by envy, / grim and strident envy that takes its joy in the ruin of others." Hesiod's myth of the declining generations of mortals, perhaps derived from ancient Iranian sources, records the Greeks' sense of time and of distance from a heroic past. The gods too suffer through change but finally achieve stability when Zeus establishes himself as the preeminent divinity of the Olympians by conquering his father Kronos, who had been swallowing his children to prevent them from displacing him.

Although Zeus exercises a sort of monarchic sovereignty over the host of quarreling, rivalrous, and amorous lesser gods, the Greeks worshiped all of them. Aphrodite stood for the domain of sexual desire, pleasure, and yearning, Demeter for the reproductive powers of the citizen woman. Apollo, god of prophecy and of the foundation of new cities, watched over philosophers and murderers. Travelers consulted his oracle at Delphi, and the Pythian priestess there gave often enigmatic answers to their questions. Poseidon was the god of earthquakes, horses, and the sea, upon which many Greeks traveled great distances to lands known and unknown. Dionysos, god of wet things—wine, semen, milk, and honey—traveled from India with a band of ecstatic women, satyrs, and panthers, and was celebrated with new wine and with tragic performances. Hermes was the god of heralds, of traveling across boundaries—between cities, between properties, between life and death, the underworld and the mortal world, between Mount Olympus and earth. He was represented by herms, stone pillars with heads and erect phalluses. Worshipers at the mystery cult of Eleusis celebrated Demeter and her daughter Kore, or Persephone, who had been abducted by Hades, god of the underworld. Because she ate from a pomegranate while in the land of the dead, Persephone, though allowed to join her mother again on earth, returned to spend part of each year with her husband in the underworld, dramatizing the passage of the seasons. Participants in the mystery cult honored mother and daughter, and experienced the acting-out of some sacred ritual that brought comfort in the face of human mortality.

Greek polytheism encompasses many gods and goddesses, and many forms of worship, including animal sacrifice, ecstatic dancing, and ritualized sexual intercourse. Some of the most beautiful poems, before there were "poems" in a purely literary sense, are hymns sung in praise or celebration of the gods. Aphrodite appears to Anchises, father of Aeneas, founder of Rome:

> She was clothed in a robe more brilliant than gleaming fire
> and wore spiral bracelets and shining earrings,
> while round her tender neck there were beautiful necklaces,
> lovely, golden and of intricate design. Like the moon's
> was the radiance round her soft breasts, a wonder to the eye.

Cities

The *polis,* or "city-state" defined social experience in the classical age. The polis incorporated an urban complex and its surrounding territory, including towns, villages, sanctuaries dedicated to the gods, agricultural land, and wilderness. Relationships with the gods differed from city to city in the Greek world, as did political and social institutions. Sparta, a city of the Dorian tribe, organized its ruling elite as an army, bent on controlling subordinate inhabitants who lived like serfs, or communities of slaves. Although some early poets wrote poems of contest and battle, the later Spartans were respected more for their martial prowess than for their contributions to world literature. Corinth, a wealthy city known for its port, its ceramics, and its sacred prostitutes, sent out colonies to the rest of the Mediterranean, but left behind few literary remains. Thebes, city of Oedipus, achieved political glory in the fourth century B.C.E.; its greatest poet, Pindar, wrote earlier and sang the praises of athletes and their patrons, victorious in games like those held in Olympus in honor of Zeus and at Delphi, as a form of worship and celebration of the god Apollo. Although other cities have been excavated and explored in the modern period, we know most about ancient Athens, because of the rich record of writing left behind by the Athenians. It is in the city of Athens, in Attica, that the most important literary contributions of the Greek classical age were written. The citizens of this city worshiped with particular devotion Athena, goddess of wisdom, who was born from Zeus's head.

As the city-states grew they were governed by aristocracies, groups of nobles who often rivaled each other and engaged in repeated struggles for domination. The poet Sappho was supposedly exiled from Lesbos because of her implication in these struggles. Some aristocrats eventually set themselves up as what the Greeks called "tyrants"—that is, usurpers of monarchic power. The tyrants, who only gradually became associated with cruelty and despotism, sometimes allied themselves with popular elements in the cities to rise over their fellow aristocrats; they frequently tried to establish dynasties, in which their descendants would, like them, control their cities. The new form of government known as democracy evolved especially (though not only) in Athens after the late sixth century B.C.E. In the democracy, the free male citizen class, understanding themselves to be equal in principle, ruled themselves by means of assemblies in which each citizen had a vote, and they usually chose their magistrates through lot. The development of the Greek institution of democracy, although it excluded women, slaves, and noncitizens from participation in government, appears especially remarkable given the theocracies, empires, and monarchies that governed the states surrounding the Greeks in the ancient world.

Athenian democracy encouraged and supported the writing and performance of drama, in festivals celebrated for the god Dionysos. And the questioning of received truths, first explored in the works of the pre-Socratics like Parmenides, came to fruition in the circle of Socrates and his friends, including Plato, who took the drama of the fifth-century city and transformed it into philosophical dialogues. The Platonic dialogues presented fictional conversations in dramatic form, with directly quoted speech, often framed by a narrator; the author creates vividly realized characters who argue about knowledge, truth, and the proper conduct of life.

Drama

Greek drama grew up in the classical city, beginning probably in the sixth century. Athens organized the dramatic festivals, and committees of citizens chose the plays to be performed and then awarded victory to the best. The theaters of various

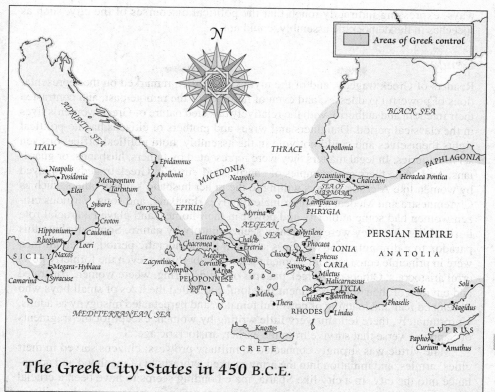

cities were situated in the open air, sometimes with a magnificent view. Stone benches for the spectators rose in ranks above thrones set in front for the priests of Dionysos; before them was the circular dancing floor, with a building facade, called a *skene*, a word originally meaning "tent," from which the actors emerged (the origin of our word "scene"). Some dramatists used a crane, ending plays with the appearance of a god or goddess on high, the *deus ex machina* or "god from the machine."

Tragedy was a crucial institution of the democratic city, dramatizing the engagement of the city with its own cultural and political history. The word "tragedy" means "goat song," and may have referred originally to a song sung at a goat sacrifice, connecting it perhaps with the part-animal satyrs who were Dionysos's companions. Tragedy as drama may have begun as the leaders of the "dithyramb," a choral hymn sung in honor of Dionysos, improvised and performed solos. The tragic performance shared the focus on *agon,* or "contest," with many other institutions of the Greek city, including the games, Olympian and others. In Athens, the tragedians presented their plays to a magistrate, who chose three plays to be performed, and a wealthy man for each, to pay for the training of the actors and the choruses, in a form of philanthropy or taxation that benefited the city as a whole. In general their stories were drawn from the epic cycle and concerned the gods and goddesses, heroes and heroines of the distant past. Nonetheless, the tragedies touched on contemporary concerns in many ways, expressing indirectly much that the political discourses of the city, such as speeches in the democratic assembly, could not.

Gender

Readers of Greek tragedy, and of the myths, have often remarked on the representations of powerful goddesses, and even of heroines of the remote past, and contrasted their freedom and authority with the relatively closeted nature of Greek women's lives in the classical period. Daughters and wives and mothers of citizens had no political rights themselves and could not vote in the assembly, hold political office, or even serve on juries. In legal matters they were represented by fathers, husbands, or guardians. And while there are examples of chastity and virtue in Greek tragedy displayed by women like Alcestis, who is willing to die in her husband's place, others, such as Clytemnestra and Medea, kill their male relatives, husband, and sons. Virtuous citizen women had some authority and power in their homes, and played a crucial role in ritual life. Yet they were frequently seen as unruly by nature. Some attribute this paradox to a diminution of women's status in the democratic period, when all men were in principle equal, and all women therefore subordinate, even the formerly powerful aristocrats. Others cite Greek patterns of child-rearing, where women, frustrated and envious of their sons' imminent freedom, controlled the lives of small boys who developed fear and loathing of powerful females, and perpetuated misogyny as adults. Unfortunately, there remains very little writing by women, except for the fragments of Sappho's verse that survive from the earlier, aristocratic age.

Male virtue was strongly connected to military prowess; citizens served in their cities' armies, and initiation into the army marked a threshold of manhood and acceptance into the city. In a city like Sparta, male bonding seems to have been a crucial element of military and citizen life; men dined together in messes, and the military unit seems to have been central to men's identities. Masculine existence focused on public life, in the military, in politics. Male homosexuality, a locus for intimacy among men, was an important institution in civic life; young men, and some older men, courted boys before their beards had grown, and much of the erotic, or sexual energy of the culture was focused on these relationships. The god Eros, son of Aphrodite, goddess of sexual desire, personified the attraction of males to females, males to males, females to females.

Barbarians

The Greeks lived in Greece itself but also came into contact with others around the Black Sea and the Mediterranean, whom they called "barbarians," because their language sounded to Greek ears like "bar-bar-bar": meaningless clumps of sound. Many of the barbarians familiar to the Greeks arrived as slaves and belonged to the free persons of the Greek city-states, working as domestic servants, agricultural laborers, and artisans, sometimes alongside the free. Other barbarians were free, passing through Greece or settling there. Still others were enemies in war. The Greeks were fascinated with them all: their skills, their customs, their luxury goods, their ways of organizing families and cities and empires.

The interest in the "barbarians" extends throughout the historical period of ancient Greece. Homer records contacts with non–Greek-speaking peoples, and Hesiod's work reflects the influence of Mesopotamian myth, religion, and poetry. The lyric poets of the Archaic period register trade with those surrounding the Greeks; Sappho sings: "A decorated slipper hid / her foot, a lovely piece of Lydian work." Herodotus wrote his history about the war between the Greeks and the Persians, interspersing it with elaborate accounts of the societies that made up the Persian empire, and beyond. Curious about what he saw, diligent in interviewing people about what they had seen, he describes the Egyptian phoenix, Arabia's flying snakes, the Arabians' harvesting of frankincense and cinnamon: "Let me only add that the whole country exhales a more than earthly fragrance." He reports that the Indians live farthest to the east of Greece, and that beyond them is uninhabitable desert. His interest in the Greeks' near and distant neighbors persists throughout Greek literature and makes the Greeks both proud of their innovations like democracy and conscious of the alternatives that surround them.

Alexander and After

After the Persian Wars, during which the Greek mainland was invaded by armies led by the Persian emperors, and after the Peloponnesian War, fought between the Spartans and the Athenians, struggles continued over which of the city-states would control Greece as a whole. This fighting came to an end with the victory of Philip of Macedon, who came from the north and defeated the alliance of Greek cities in 338 B.C.E. After his death, his kingdom was inherited by his son Alexander, said by some to be a son of Dionysos. During his short lifetime, Alexander not only conquered the Greeks but went deeply into the lands of the barbarians and overpowered army after army. Alexander swept through the Persian empire, conquering and dominating Egypt, where he was acclaimed as a god, and moving east, past the Persian capitals into what is now Afghanistan and beyond, to the Indus River. As he moved he founded cities, many named Alexandria in his honor.

When he died in Babylon in 323 B.C.E., Alexander left behind a contentious group of heirs, his generals, who fought over and divided the fragile empire he had established. The rulers of these "Hellenistic" kingdoms tried to impose the Greek language, Greek administrative policies, city-planning, and architecture on the indigenous cultures. One of the cities that flourished was the Egyptian Alexandria, which became the intellectual capital of the Hellenistic world, a multiethnic city inhabited by Egyptians, Jews, Lebanese, Sudanese, Greeks, and Macedonians and welcoming an immense variety of religious practices.

Alexandria was also the site of a monumental library that housed the greatest works of classical Greek antiquity. The poetry, literary criticism, science, and religious practices that were centered around the library had a great impact on the next conquering power, the Romans, who eventually brought Greece and the Hellenized East into their empire. After the fall of the Roman Empire, and the tenuous preservation of the legacy of Greek literature in the monasteries and libraries of medieval Europe, some of Greek learning was preserved by great Arab scholars fascinated with such thinkers as Plato and Aristotle, and was passed to the early humanists by Byzantine scholars and through Iberia, or medieval Spain. In the European Renaissance, artists, scholars, and writers looked back to Greece for inspiration. Enlightenment thinkers including the founders of the American republic looked back to Greek democracy and the Roman republic as they debated the shape of the American polity. Greece itself eventually become part of the Ottoman Empire, and some of its greatest treasures were destroyed or carted off by Europeans newly interested in Greek civilization. In the nineteenth century Lord Elgin sawed off large portions of the frieze of the Parthenon and took what wasn't destroyed or sunk in shipwreck back to London, where the fragments formed a key part of the collection that became the British Museum. The Romantics were stirred by the Greek struggle for independence from the Ottomans; Byron died at Missolonghi, in central Greece, having volunteered for the Greek war of liberation. Heinrich Schliemann, a wealthy German brewer, dug up the remains of preclassical civilization at Mycenae and at Troy, and the gold mask of Agamemnon dazzled a world accustomed to the white marble of the Parthenon and Michelangelo's classicizing sculpture. With all their contradictions and in all their variety, the Greeks remain the still-potent ancestors of the Western tradition.

Early South Asia

The history of early South Asia until around 500 B.C.E. is obscure and contested. Although not committed to writing until the second millennium C.E., the *Rig Veda Samhita* was composed beginning around 1500 B.C.E. by pastoralist settlers using a language related to many others now spoken in Iran and across Eastern, Central, and Western Europe, languages today classified as members of the "Indo-European" language family. Much of the Veda is in verse, often the same eleven-syllable meter found in ancient Greek poetry such as Sappho's (recreated in the English translation "He looks to me to be in heaven, that man" page 238); the composer was called a *kavi*, "seer," which in turn became the term for "poet." And although *kavya*, a word best translated as "literature," derives from this name, people before the modern period in South Asia were very careful to distinguish this "literature" from the sacred Veda.

The story of the invention of literature recounted in the first book of the Sanskrit epic the *Ramayana* of Valmiki, long known as the first poem, is provided on page 331. In the form we know it from manuscripts still available, the *Ramayana* was almost certainly composed around 200 B.C.E., not long after the first written documents of South Asia were produced at the court of Ashoka, the third king of the Maurya dynasty. The poem shares much of the political perspective of Ashoka, and it reflects on its oral origins in a way unlikely in a world truly ignorant of writing, which was almost certainly invented at Ashoka's court.

The second great epic of South Asia, the *Mahabharata*, ascribed to the sage Vyasa, is usually assigned to the genre of history rather than poetry. It is probable that the *Mahabharata* came into being a century or two before Ashoka though it continued to grow through addition of materials for some centuries even after Valmiki's work was completed. Like the *Ramayana*, it has as its principal theme the meaning of power as well as the extent of power—the nature of kingly rule and the limits of the world within which this rule makes sense. Like the ancient Greek epics the *Iliad* and the *Odyssey*, the *Ramayana* and *Mahabharata* may deal with particular people in particular places, but they contemplate problems that no one anywhere has escaped: war and the perceived need to kill in order to live; duty; family; love. Yet, the responses to these problems offered by the two South Asian epics are entirely dissimilar. The more steely-eyed, if more agonized, vision of the *Mahabharata* leaves us with the taste of ashes in our mouth, whereas in the more utopian vision of the *Ramayana* victory brings unending peace and prosperity.

The Maurya Empire vanished in the second century B.C.E., and we have only a shadowy idea of the period that followed until the Guptas established their polity around 320 C.E. and extended it far outward from the core area around today's Patna (in southern Bihar). In this new courtly world and elsewhere, Sanskrit literary culture dominated the cultural scene in South Asia up to and even beyond the vernacular revolutions in the early centuries of the second millennium, when regional languages began to replace Sanskrit for literary and political purposes.

The world of Vedic culture was one of punctilious observance of calendrical sacrifices. In time, perhaps around the middle of the first millennium B.C.E., many thinkers began to sense that sacrifice by itself might not encompass the ultimate meaning of human existence, and a true crisis of belief ensued. One response to this crisis was ascetic renunciation and physical self-mortification. Another response was a new and profound reflection on life and death; for the first time, we encounter the ideas of redeath and rebirth, or transmigration (*samsara*), in accordance with deeds committed in the previous life (*karma*). The texts in Sanskrit that these thinkers composed, including the Upanishads, played an important role in a more general critique of religious life that emerged among a wide range of spiritual masters on the margins of or outside the Vedic world. Chief among these was Siddhartha Gautama Shakyamuni, the Buddha or "Awakened One," whose new doctrine, distinctive forms of meditation, and new social practices—including the establishment of the monastic community—produced an alternative religious vision that, within a few centuries, was to spread across Asia like wildfire.

China: The Classical Tradition

Though not the earliest civilization in human history, China's has certainly been the longest continuing one, a record supported by material evidence and historical documents extending back in time at least five thousand years. Well-preserved pottery and other artifacts attest to the existence of several developed Neolithic cultures at multiple sites along the Yellow River in northern China, with at least one on the Yangzi River to the south as well. Although one of these cultures is dated to the fifth millennium B.C.E., the majority appear to have flourished during the third. This is also the beginning of a prehistoric mythological record constructed by later generations, who credited a series of sage emperors with innovations and principles that were instrumental in the development of Chinese civilization and that established abiding norms of ethical and political practice.

The historical record begins with the Shang dynasty (c. 1550–1040 B.C.E.), which developed in the central Yellow River basin, when Sumer had long since disappeared and Egypt was already an old civilization. The last ruler of the Shang was overthrown by the Zhou people to the west around 1040 B.C.E.. Like the Shang, the Zhou were an agrarian people and maintained a strong commitment to ancestor worship. Within three centuries, a non-Chinese tribe succeeded in sacking the Zhou capital near modern-day Xi'an in 770 B.C.E. A revived Eastern Zhou was established near Luoyang farther down the Yellow River, but the empire existed henceforth in name only, as its increasingly powerful feudal states engaged in a long struggle to take its place.

The duchy of Lu was most closely identified with ancient Zhou traditions, and for its native son Confucius (551–479 B.C.E.) the remedy for contemporary troubles lay in a return to those values, which centered on the primacy of a family-based morality and the extension of its ideal behaviors to all other relationships. There were numerous competing schools of thought contending for the attention of rulers. The king of

Qin, who succeeded in establishing his rule as the first emperor of China, adopted the advice of Han Fei (d. 233 B.C.E.) that only the power of power—of laws, rewards, and punishments—could order the state.

The Qin dynasty was remarkably and mercifully short-lived, lasting only from 221 to 206 B.C.E. Civil war then erupted, ending when a victorious general from the state of Han established a new dynasty that not only lasted for four hundred years but also remained for later generations the paragon of imperial power. Rejecting the excesses of the Qin, the Han dynasty (206 B.C.E.–220 C.E.) promoted Confucianism as state orthodoxy and implemented a rudimentary civil service competition in an attempt to match merit with responsibility. Five classical texts were also identified as the canon of the culture. Each of the "Five Classics" was associated in some way with Confucius, although later scholars have agreed that the links are tenuous at best. The *Book of Changes* (*Yijing* or *I Ching*) is a text used to interpret sixty-four hexagrams (patterns of six lines) connected to a divination process employing milfoil stalks that probably dates to the late Shang; Confucius was the supposed author of one of its most important affiliated commentaries. The *Book of Documents* (*Shujing* or *Shangshu*) was purported to contain pronouncements and other utterances of rulers and ministers dating back to the sage king Yao; though it was traditionally said to have been edited by Confucius, many sections are now agreed to be forgeries of much later date. The *Book of Songs* (*Shijing*) is an anthology of some three hundred poems that were composed across much of the Zhou dynasty and which were thought to have been compiled and edited by Confucius. The fourth classic contains ritual texts of which the *Record of Rites* (*Liji*) is the most important; it addresses issues of decorum both large and small and was supposedly collected and edited by Confucius as well. And the *Spring and Autumn Annals* chronicled events in Confucius's home state of Lu from 722 to 481 B.C.E. As Confucius looked back to the early Zhou; so all later dynasties would look back to the Han as the embodiment of imperial and cultural unity.

Rome and the Roman Empire

According to tradition, Romulus, a son of the god Mars suckled by a she-wolf with his twin brother Remus, founded Rome in 753 B.C.E. A legend popularized in the first century B.C.E. by the historian Livy and the poet Virgil attributed the genesis of the Roman people to the twelfth-century arrival on Italian shores of Aeneas, the Trojan hero who was said to have escaped the destruction by the Greeks of his ancestral city in Asia Minor. Aeneas's son Ascanius and their descendants ruled the region of Latium until Romulus took over the succession from his grandfather's usurper. The dual myth of origin expressed the double identity of the imperial city. On the one hand, it saw itself as grounded in the *mores maiorum,* the strict morality and customs of its rustic Latin ancestors. On the other hand, it saw itself as the cosmopolitan center of the world, steeped in the ancient and cultured traditions of the Hellenistic east.

The Roman republic, which lasted nearly five centuries until the ascension of emperor Augustus Caesar in 27 B.C.E., put a premium on gravity, dignity, austerity, integrity, fortitude, and disciplined obedience to the *mores maiorum*. For women, "old-fashioned mores" meant modesty, chastity, and subordination to the family of her father or her husband; for men, this meant fighting in the army and serving in government. As the famous lawyer and orator Cicero, staunch defender of the republican tradition, put it, "The Roman people hate private luxury but love public magnificence." Money was poured into great public works; victorious generals were feted with grand "triumphs"; martyrs and heroes of the republic were memorialized in statuary throughout the city. To be sure, the very insistence of so many writers on the austere virtue of the legendary past suggests that many wealthy and powerful Romans were in frequent need of admonition. Nevertheless, seldom has an ideology of self-restraint and self-sacrifice been more successfully employed. Nor is it difficult in this context to understand how the later empire and its citizenry would adapt so readily to the ascetic demands of early Christianity.

The World City

Rome was the center of religion, government, and cultural life from the early days of the republic until the division of the empire between east and west in the fourth century C.E. By the first century B.C.E., the tiny republic had become the dominant power in the Mediterranean; the capital city had some 250,000 inhabitants. By 100 C.E., over a million people lived there, far more than in any city for the next seven centuries. Notwithstanding severe overcrowding and the immense problems in feeding its population and disposing of their waste, the city's allure was irresistible. As the poet Ovid attested from unhappy exile on the Black Sea, the city (*urbs*) of Rome and the world (*orbis*) were one and the same: *Romanae spatium est urbis et orbis idem*.

Drainage and water supply were a priority from early on. By the late republic, the great central sewer known as the *cloaca maxima* had been enclosed; its tunnel ran nearly a kilometer and was large enough for the imperial administrator Agrippa to cruise through on a tour of inspection. Later sources list 144 public latrines within the city, in addition to those in the many public baths. These baths were central to the social life of Rome and its provincial towns, and they grew progressively larger and more spectacular as the empire expanded. The Caracalla baths, whose ruins can still be visited, could hold up to 1,500 persons, and included art galleries, libraries, and exercise halls. Display of wealth was an important aspect of the baths, but they also served the practical purpose of keeping a notoriously fastidious people clean. Given that the streets of Rome were extremely narrow, unlit at night, made of dirt, and strewn with filth and refuse, personal hygiene was a constant battle.

Nearly everyone in late republican and imperial Rome came from somewhere else. Although the poet Catullus was born in Verona and served on the staff of a governor in Asia Minor, he had no qualms in mocking his rival Egnatius as a provincial, with "untrimmed beard, and teeth polished in the Spanish / manner—with urine." Cicero, Livy, Virgil, Horace, and Ovid all came to Rome from other parts of Italy. Later writers arrived from farther afield: Tacitus from Gaul, the epic poet Lucan and the moralist Seneca from Córdoba in Spain, Apuleius and Augustine from North Africa. Spanish-born Trajan was the first emperor from beyond Italy (98–117 C.E.); later emperors came from all over the Mediterranean, often bringing their local customs and beliefs with them, as in the extreme case of the Syrian Elagabalus (218–22 C.E.), hereditary High Priest to the sun god of Emesa, whose exotic rituals and bizarre sexual practices contributed to his being assassinated in short order.

The Literature of Rome

The satirist Juvenal complained that there was no money in writing poetry. Several emperors were known as patrons of the arts, but writing was generally either integral to political activity—oratory and letter-writing—or conducted in one's leisure or by

Marble statue of Augustus Caesar, c. 20 B.C.E.

ARAL SEA

CASPIAN SEA

PARTHIAN EMPIRE
Ctesiphon

ARABIAN PENINSULA

CAUCASUS

ARMENIA

ASSYRIA
MESOPOTAMIA
Tigris
Euphrates

Trapezus

BLACK SEA

Sinope
Heraclea Pontica
BITHYNIA ET PONTUS
Nicomedia
Byzantium
Ancyra
GALATIA
CAPPADOCIA
Zeugma
SYRIA
Antioch
Seleucia
CILICIA
Tarsus
CYPRUS

SYRIAN DESERT

Heliopolis
Damascus
Tripolis
Bostra
Tyrus
Caesarea Maritima
JUDAEA
Jerusalem (Aelia Capitolina)
Petra
ARABIA

RED SEA

AEGYPTUS
Alexandria
Memphis
Nile

Pergamum
ASIA
Ephesus
Miletus
Cnidus
Thessalonica
MOESIA INFERIOR
MOESIA SUPERIOR
THRACIA
MACEDONIA
Delphi
Corinth
ACHAIA
Athens
EPIRUS
Sparta
Nicopolis
CRETA
CYRENE ET CRETA
Cyrene
Ptolemais
Apollonia

Sarmatians
BOSPORAN KINGDOM

Roxolani

DACIA
Danube

PANNONIA INFERIOR
PANNONIA SUPERIOR
Quadi
Marcomanni
DALMATIA
NORICUM

Burgundians
Elbe
GERMANIA
Colonia Agrippina
GERMANIA SUPERIOR
GERMANIA INFERIOR
RAETIA
ALPES GRAIAE ET POENINAE
ALPS

NORTH SEA

Hadrian's Wall
CALEDONIA
Londinium
Lutetia
BRITANNIA
HIBERNIA

BELGICA
GALLIA
Lugdunum
LUGDUNENSIS
Tolosa
AQUITANIA
Narbo
NARBONENSIS
Massilia
ALPES COTTIAE
ALPES MARITIMAE

Burdigala
Ebro
HISPANIA
TARRACONENSIS
Asturica
Valentia
Toletum
LUSITANIA
BAETICA
Corduba
Gades
Tingis

MAURETANIA TINGITANA
MAURETANIA CAESARIENSIS

ITALIA
Rome
Ostia
Ravenna
Bononia
Pisae
Florentia
Arretium
Capua
Naples (Napoli)
Puteoli
Brundisium
Tarentum
Rhegium
Messana
SICILIA
Syracuse

CORSICA
SARDINIA
SARDINIA ET CORSICA
BALEARES
Carthago Nova

Carthage
NUMIDIA
AFRICA

MEDITERRANEAN SEA

ATLANTIC OCEAN

N

The Roman Empire in 150 C.E.

those with independent incomes. All educated Romans were bilingual in Latin and Greek, and most higher education (rhetoric and philosophy) was conducted in Greek by teachers of Hellenistic origin. Latin literature grew out of imitation and translation from the Greek. Scrolls were status objects, and there was a vigorous publishing trade in classical Rome. Writing took place in one of three forms. Papyrus, made from the pith of an Egyptian marsh plant pounded into layers, was widely used in the east. More common in Italy and less expensive were parchment or vellum, made from the skins of cattle, sheep, or goats. All of these materials would be written upon with ink made from soot and water, and stored in rolls up to 16 feet in length. Wooden leaf tablets, thin enough to fold, could also be written on in ink. Alternatively, wooden stylus tablets with a recessed surface covered in colored wax could be inscribed with a bronze or iron stylus, and were reusable. By the fourth century, the parchment book or codex, bound down one edge, had replaced the scroll.

Perhaps the most Roman of all literary genres were the erotic elegy and the satire. The elegy was transformed from its Greek model by the addition of an apparently autobiographical first-person narrator. The erotic poet was single-minded in his pursuit of love, and generally turned his back on the traditionally public duties of the Roman citizen. A major influence on this poetry was Catullus (84–54 B.C.E.), whose school of "neoteric" poets was self-consciously modern, stressing emotionality, confessional detail, linguistic polish, and negligible subject matter over the rustic virtues of dignity, gravity and civic duty. Like the elegy, the satire focused primarily on individuals in nonofficial settings. Despite its capacity for character assassination, it seldom ventured into political territory or *ad hominem* attacks. Ovid, exiled by Augustus for "a poem and an indiscretion," Juvenal, banished by Domitian, and Petronius, forced to suicide by Nero, were all well aware that many subjects were off-limits to the poets of imperial Rome.

The primary genres of Roman expansion were history and epic. Rome was a record-keeping society, setting down numerous laws and treaties, and copious oratory and correspondence. The concern of historiographers such as Livy, Tacitus, and Suetonius with memorializing the past and their consciousness of the ideological power of historical narrative were especially influential on postmedieval writers, not least of whom was the celebrated chronicler Edward Gibbon, whose magnum opus, *The Decline and Fall of the Roman Empire* (1776–1788), molded the reception of Rome and its legacy for many generations. While historiography developed a distinctly Roman form, epic remained self-consciously indebted to its Greek antecedents, most notably the Homeric poems, the *Iliad* and the *Odyssey*. The paradigm was Virgil's *Aeneid,* which transferred the archaic, orally composed and mythic Homeric poems into a world simultaneously mythic and historical, archaic and contemporary. There had been some precedent for the *Aeneid,* but what followed it was a veritable explosion of epics concerning other episodes of Roman history and Greek myth. Two of the most enduring works of Latin literature, Lucretius's Epicurean account of the way the natural world, *On the Nature of Things* (c. 54 B.C.E.), and Ovid's protean retelling of the entire corpus of Greek and Roman mythology, the *Metamorphoses* (2–8 C.E.), brought the monumental scope and elevated style of epic to bear on subject matter and narrative forms that creatively stretched its boundaries. Latin epic and historiography reflected the new preeminence of Rome in their scope and ambition. Still, the accomplishments of empire were never recounted without at least a hint of ambivalence as to the sacrifice and suffering entailed by them.

Imperium Sine Fine

In the first book of the *Aeneid,* Jupiter prophesies that the land to be granted to the descendants of Aeneas will be an *imperium sine fine,* an empire with neither temporal nor geographical end. Virgil wrote these lines under the patronage of the first Roman emperor, Caesar Augustus (formerly Octavian), who reigned from 27 B.C.E. to 14 C.E. As Tacitus later wrote, Augustus "seduced everyone with the sweetness of peace." The restrictions of Augustus's rule seemed to many a small price to pay for putting an end to a hundred years of civil strife under the late republic and stabilizing a world now dominated by Rome. A series of both reforms and grabs for power that began somewhere in the late second century climaxed in 49 B.C.E. with the dictatorship of Julius Caesar. Caesar's power was based in the army he controlled and the reputation his victories had given him, most notably his subjugation of Gaul (present-day France). When Caesar was assassinated in 44 C.E. by a group of republican senators, war broke out among his heirs and rivals. His adopted son Octavian defeated Mark Antony and Antony's ally and lover Cleopatra at the decisive battle of Actium in 31 B.C.E., and the way was paved for him to become sole ruler of Rome.

The Roman empire was a complex combination of military prowess and political savvy. The Roman legions were highly trained and well-equipped, and they fought with disciplined efficiency. Repeated opposition, especially from rival powers, was savagely repressed. For the most part, however, defeated peoples retained a fair measure of autonomy as long as they paid the often severe taxes levied upon them by the central authority in Rome. The legionaries constructed carefully planned and laid-out provincial capitals throughout Roman territory, the origins of modern cities such as London, Paris, and Córdoba. They also built an extensive network of paved roads to allow rapid movement of persons and goods between Rome and the provinces, and aqueducts to transport water. Local peoples were usually allowed to preserve their own languages, customs, and religions. At the same time, they were gradually incorporated into Roman culture through citizenship and the privileges that went with it.

Expansion continued through the fourth century. The borders of Rome extended into Scotland in the British Isles, and as far north as the Rhine and the Danube rivers in Europe, circling the Mediterranean from Gaul, Spain, North Africa, and Egypt through Palestine, Syria, Asia Minor, Greece, and the Balkans. The military played an increasingly prominent role in choosing emperors, and succession often meant no more than a series of military coups. The need for military support would contribute to the eventual fall of Rome, as later emperors depended more and more on mercenaries from Germanic tribes to augment their forces.

The Eternal City in Ruins

The empire endured by name until the fall of Constantinople to the Ottoman Turks in 1453, but from a Roman point of view it was all over by 410 when Alaric led his Goths into Rome. The conversion of emperor Constantine in 324 had inaugurated the spread of Christianity through western Europe; it was also responsible for the shift of imperial power eastward to the city he established on the straits of the Bosphorus, free of the pagan temples and traditions that saturated Rome. The invading Goths were themselves converts to Christianity, partially acculturated into a western empire rapidly being eclipsed by the east. Evidently not everyone was sorry for the change. According to the Christian priest Salvanius, many in Gaul considered that "the enemy is more lenient to them than the tax collectors." Nevertheless, the symbolism of Rome in the hands of northern barbarians sent shockwaves through the empire. The church father Jerome, who while in Rome had begun the Vulgate, his enduring Latin translation of the Bible, lamented from Palestine that, "The head of the Roman empire was cut off, and, to speak more truly, the entire world perished with that single city." Rome continued to decline, and by the middle of the ninth century it had only seventeen thousand inhabitants. As the power of the medieval papacy grew from that point, so did the city revive, but ever since Alaric the ruins and the past of Rome have overshadowed its present. From Dante and Petrarch through Shakespeare and Montaigne to Thomas Mann and Sigmund Freud, few Western writers have been able to resist the allure of those ruins.

YEAR	THE WORLD	LITERATURE
3500 B.C.E.		
	3200–3100 Development of cuneiform writing in Mesopotamia	
	c. 3100 Unification of Egypt; development of hieroglyphics	
3000		
	3000–2501 Neolithic settlements on Crete	
	c. 2700 Gilgamesh, king of Uruk in southern Mesopotamia	
2500		
	2500–2001 Early Minoan culture on Crete	2500–2180 Pyramid Texts in Egypt
		2200–2000 Early Sumerian poems about Gilgamesh
2000		
	2000–1500 Greek-speakers begin to move from the East toward the eastern Mediterranean; Cecrops, legendary first king of Athens; Middle Minoan period of Crete; Decimal system on Crete; Late Minoan period of Crete (to 1400)	c. 1925 *The Story of Sinuhe*
	c. 1900 Hebrews begin to migrate from Babylonia to Palestine	
		c. 1600 Old Babylonian *Epic of Gilgamesh*
	c. 1550–1040 Shang dynasty in China	
1500		
	1500–1000 Wandering of pastoral nomadic groups across Eurasia	c. 1500–1000 Sanskrit Vedas
	1500–1200 Beginnings of Cretan-Mycenaean culture	
	c. 1372–1354 Reign of Akhnaten and "Amarna Revolution" in Egypt	c. 1360 Great Hymn to the Aten
		c. 1300–1200 Egyptian love poetry written down
	c. 1200 Traditional time of the Exodus of Israelites from captivity in Egypt	c. 1200 *Enuma Elish;* Sîn-liqe-unninni creates Standard Version of *The Epic of Gilgamesh*
	1193 Destruction of Troy, 6th level	
	c. 1100 According to legend, Aeneas arrives at Latium from Troy	
	c. 1040–256 Zhou dynasty in China	
	c. 1020 United Israel founded by King Saul	

continued

YEAR	THE WORLD	LITERATURE
1000		
	1000–900 Ionians, displaced from mainland Greece, found cities in Asia Minor, including Ephesus and Miletus. Political unification of Athens. Greek alphabet based on Semitic-Phoenician characters adds vowels	
	c. 1000–960 Reign of King David in Israel	c. 950 Yahwists compose first version of the Torah, including Genesis
	c. 960–931 Reign of King Solomon; after his death, Israel divided by civil war into Israel and Judah	
	900–700 Greek colonization throughout Mediterranean basin	c. 900 The Book of Job
		c. 900–700 Composition of *Iliad, Odyssey, Theogony, Works and Days*
	800–600 Rise of urbanism in northern India	c. 800–600 Upanishads
		c. 800–400 *Book of Songs*, China
	776 Legendary foundation of the Olympian games	
	753 Traditional date on which Romulus founds Rome	c. 750 Kabti-ilani-Marduk, *Erra and Ishum*
	722 Israel conquered by Assyrians; Judah remains independent	
	722–481 Spring and Autumn Period in China	
		700–600 Arkhilokhos, Sappho, and other Greek lyric poets flourish
	594–593 Solon reforms Athenian government	
	586 Babylonians conquer Judah, deport many Hebrews to Babylon	c. 550 Priestly writers among Hebrews in exile in Babylon revise Torah into canonical form
	c. 551–479 Life of Confucius	
	539 Cyrus the Great of Persia conquers Babylon and permits Hebrews to return to Israel. Founds Persian Empire	c. 500–450 *The Analects* of Confucius
	527 Death of Peisistratos, tyrant of Athens	500–429 *Dao De Jing*
	510 Cleisthenes's democratic reforms	
	509 Rome becomes a republic	
500		
	500–429 Life of Athenian leader Pericles	
	500 Ionians revolt from Persia	
	490–449 Persian Wars	
	490 Battle of Marathon	
	480 Battles of Thermopylae and Salamis	c. 475–450 Pindar, *Odes*
	470–399 Life of Socrates	458 Aeschylus, *Oresteia*
	469–399 Hippocrates	c. 450 *Discourses of the Buddha*
	448–433 Rebuilding of the Athenian Acropolis after Persian destruction	431 Pericles's Funeral Oration
		431 Euripides, *Medea*
	431–404 Peloponnesian War between Athens and Sparta	c. 430 Herodotus, *History*
	427–347 Life of Plato	c. 426 Sophocles, *Oedipus the King*
	411 Oligarchic coup in Athens	411 Aristophanes, *Lysistrata*
	405 Defeat of Athenians by Sparta	
	403–221 Warring States period in China	

YEAR	THE WORLD	LITERATURE
		c. 400 Thucydides, *History*
		c. 400 B.C.E.–400 C.E. *Mahabharata*
	399 Execution of Socrates	390 Plato, *Apology of Socrates*
	384–322 Life of Aristotle	
	369–286 Life of Zhuangzi	
	356–323 Alexander the Great conquers central Asia; founds Alexandria in Egypt in 332; dies in Babylon in 323	
	352–336 Philip II of Macedon	
	338 Philip defeats Greeks at Chaeronea	
	c. 300 Rise of the Mauryan Empire in India (to 100 C.E.)	c. 300 B.C.E.–100 C.E. Kautilya, *Treatise on Power*
	250 Buddhism begins to spread beyond India	250 Asoka, *Inscriptions*
	221–206 Qin dynasty in China	
	206 B.C.E.–220 C.E. Han dynasty in China	
		c. 200 Valmiki, *Ramayana*
	190 Palestine comes under Roman control	
	149–146 Third Punic War; Carthage is destroyed by Romans	
100	147 Romans take control of Greece	
	64–63 Conspiracy of Catiline in Rome against Cicero's consulship	
	58–50 Julius Caesar campaigns in Gaul	
		c. 55–54 Lucretius, *On the Nature of Things*
		c. 54 Catullus, *Poems*
	48 Caesar defeats Pompey at the battle of Pharsalus	
	44 Caesar murdered by Brutus and Cassius	
		39–29 Virgil, *Eclogues*
		35–30 Horace, *Satires*
	31 Octavian (Augustus) defeats Antony and Cleopatra at the battle of Actium, end of civil war; Egypt becomes a Roman province	
		29 B.C.E.–17 C.E. Livy, *History of Rome*
		19 Virgil, *Aeneid*
	c. 6 Birth of Jesus (traditionally estimated at 1 C.E.)	
		c. 1 B.C.E.–1 C.E. Ovid, *Art of Love, Remedy of Love*
1 C.E.		2–8 Ovid, *Metamorphoses*
	29 Augustus dies; succeeded after a month by Tiberius	
	c. 30 Jesus is crucified outside the walls of Jersualem	
		c. 45–64 Paul, *Epistles*

continued

YEAR	THE WORLD	LITERATURE
		c. 60–90 Gospels according to Matthew, Mark, and Luke; Acts of the Apostles
	64 The great fire in Rome; Nero persecutes Christians	
	65 Failure of the Pisonian conspiracy against Nero; Lucan and Seneca compelled to suicide	
		c. 66 Petronius, *Satyricon*
	70 Jewish revolt against Rome; Temple in Jerusalem destroyed	
		c. 75 *Priapea*
	98–117 Reign of Trajan	
100		c. 101–127 Juvenal, *Satires*
		c. 117 Tacitus, *Annals*
		c. 120 Suetonius, *Lives of the Caesars*
	150 Rule of the Kushanas and Indo-Scythians	150 Ashvaghosha, *Life of the Buddha*
	161–180 Reign of Marcus Aurelius	
	c. 200 Pandyas patronize Tamil culture in the south	c. 200 *Tamil Anthologies*
	c. 200 End of the Satavahana Empire in south-central India	c. 200 Hala, *The Seven Hundred Songs*
	200–500 End of Kushan rule and rise of the Gupta in northern India	c. 200–500 Early Buddhist *puranas*, including *Lore of the Dwarf Incarnation*
	313 Edict of Milan, Constantine proclaims toleration of the Christian religion	
	355–363 Reign of Julian "the Apostate"	
		384 Jerome, Vulgate Bible (New Testament)
		c. 400–425 Poetry of Tao Qian
		c. 400 Augustine, *Confessions*
		c. 400 Vatsyayana, *Kamasutra*
		406 Jerome, Vulgate Bible (Old Testament)
		413–427 Augustine, *City of God*
	420 Alaric sacks Rome	c. 450 Kalidasa, *Shakuntala*
	c. 450 Height of the Gupta Empire in India	

The greatest literary composition of ancient Mesopotamia, *The Epic of Gilgamesh* can rightly be called the first true work of world literature. It began to circulate widely around the ancient Near East as early as 1000 B.C.E., and it was translated into several of the region's languages. Tablets bearing portions of the epic have been found not only around Mesopotamia but also in Turkey and in Palestine. We know of no other work that crossed so many borders so early, as people in many areas began to respond to the epic's searching exploration of the meaning of culture in the face of death.

The story of Gilgamesh developed over many centuries from a kernel of historical fact. Gilgamesh was an early king of the city-state of Uruk in southern Mesopotamia; he lived sometime around 2750 B.C.E. Early records credit him with building a great wall around his city, "spread out across the countryside like a net for birds." In the years following his death a cult grew up around his memory, and he was honored as a judge of the underworld. By around 2000 B.C.E. a loosely connected cycle of songs had been written in Sumerian about his life and legendary adventures. These old songs portray Bilgames (as they call him) as a great warrior, describe his journey to a distant mountain where he kills a monster and brings home cedar trees for his palace, and tell of a descent by his servant Enkidu into the grim regions of the underworld. These early poems already signal what would become the organizing theme of the full epic: its hero's fear of death and his quest for immortality. As he decides to journey to slay the monster guarding the Cedar Mountain, Bilgames voices his anguish to Enkidu:

> O Enkidu, since no man can escape life's end,
> I will enter the mountain and set up my name.
> ....
> In my city, a man dies, and the heart is stricken,
> a man perishes, and the heart feels pain.
> I raised my head on the rampart,
> my gaze fell on a corpse drifting down the river, afloat on the water:
> I too shall become like that, just so shall I be!

Over the course of the Old Babylonian period (2000–1600 B.C.E.) a poet or poets in Babylon took up this theme and adapted the Sumerian poems into a connected epic, written in Akkadian, the increasingly dominant language of the region. Finally, around 1200 B.C.E., the epic was revised into its definitive form by a Babylonian priest named Sîn-liqe-unninni, whose additions include the poem's preface, which summarizes Gilgamesh's accomplishments and reflects directly on the recovery of ancient tradition—as the Gilgamesh story itself was by then.

The term "epic" is sometimes used loosely to describe ancient narrative poems in general, but full-scale epics do more than tell a story in poetic language. Epics like Homer's *Iliad* often center on the founding or defense of a city and its society, with extensive battle scenes in which a great hero attempts to overcome heavy odds presented both by human opponents and divine antagonism. Other epics, like Homer's *Odyssey,* have to do chiefly with a voyage of travel, exploration, or escape. Like Virgil's *Aeneid, The Epic of Gilgamesh* combines both kinds of epic subject matter. Ancient though it is, *Gilgamesh* is also like the *Aeneid* in being a developed reworking of earlier epic texts. Where Virgil used Homer and other sources, Sîn-liqe-unninni drew on older poems of the Flood and of the underworld, as well as of Gilgamesh and his adventures, to create a broad exploration of the uses and limits of human culture, poised between the realms of nature and of the gods.

The poem presents Gilgamesh as a mixed figure himself; like Homer's hero Achilles, he has a human father and a divine mother, and like Achilles he is a great but flawed hero. As the epic begins, he has been oppressing his own people, who appeal to the gods for

Impression from a stone cylinder seal, Babylonia, c. second millennium B.C.E. Scene showing Gilgamesh and Enkidu slaying the Bull of Heaven, as Ishtar angrily protests.

relief. The gods create Enkidu, no longer simply Gilgamesh's servant but now shown as a force of nature, a wild man who comes to Uruk and restrains Gilgamesh from his misbehavior. Becoming fast friends, Gilgamesh and Enkidu journey to a distant mountain and slay its guardian monster, and then enter into a fatal dispute with Ishtar, goddess of love. She tries to seduce Gilgamesh, who rejects her advances; she sends a great bull down from heaven to kill him, but Enkidu and Gilgamesh slaughter the bull. Then Enkidu goes too far: he rashly insults Ishtar, who decrees his death.

In despair at his friend's death, Gilgamesh sets off to find the distant, hidden home of his ancestor Utanapishtim, who with his wife was the sole survivor of a worldwide flood. Utanapishtim tells him the story of the Flood, in terms strikingly similar to the biblical account found in Genesis 6–9 (page 80). By weaving this formerly independent story into his epic, Sîn-liqe-unninni extends Gilgamesh's story to a wider context of the life and death of civilization itself. After telling his story, Utanapishtim gives Gilgamesh a plant that will give him immortality, but on his way home a serpent steals the plant, and Gilgamesh returns to Uruk distraught; his only comfort, in the poem's closing lines, is to survey his city's magnificent walls, in which he buries his story for later generations to read.

Gilgamesh is classically epic in its language as well as its story. The poem is written in an elevated style that moves with a grand, inexorable sweep, punctuated by haunting lyrical passages in which Gilgamesh and Enkidu voice their fears of the dangers they face and their grief at the prospect of death. Like later literary epics, *Gilgamesh* also makes thematic use of old patterns developed for earlier oral poetry. Sumerian poems relied heavily on repetition for verbal effect and to aid listeners in understanding when they were recited in ritual settings. *Gilgamesh* is clearly a written composition rather than an oral one, intended for private reading and reflection rather than for any public use, but Sîn-liqe-unninni availed himself fully of the resources of repetition. Series of mysterious dreams foreshadow future events and build a sense of brooding uncertainty. Variations within lines allow the reader to see more fully into events and images, as when Utanapishtim tells Gilgamesh, "I will reveal to you a thing that is hidden, a secret of the gods I will tell you!"

In a fitting reflection of the poem's own themes of loss and recovery, *The Epic of Gilgamesh* itself vanished from human knowledge for over two thousand years, following the defeat and destruction of the major Mesopotamian cities by Persian invaders in the seventh and sixth centuries B.C.E. It was not until the 1850s that an Iraqi archaeologist, Hormuzd Rassam, discovered the ruins of the great royal library of Ashurbanipal, King of the World and King of Assyria in the mid-seventh century. Rassam shipped thousands of tablets back to the British Museum, where scholars began to piece fragments together and puzzle out their contents. A full twenty years later a young curator named George Smith began to study the eleven tablets that would turn out to contain *Gilgamesh*. Smith was electrified when he came upon the Noah-like Utanapishtim's account of the Flood. "I am the first man to read that after two thousand years of oblivion," he exclaimed, and, according to his associate E. A. W. Budge, "he jumped up and rushed about the room in a state of great excitement, and, to the astonishment of those present, began to undress himself!"

Ever since then, modern readers have been gripped by this epic poem, though they have differed widely about how it should be understood. Nineteenth-century readers debated whether it was a work of fiction or a genuine historical account. The parallels between Utanapishtim and Noah were taken by some to demonstrate the factual basis of the biblical version, while others drew an opposite conclusion, that Noah must be as fictional a figure as his Akkadian counterpart. Readers today focus on the epic as a poetic masterpiece rather than a historical document, yet the poem remains open to many interpretations. In part, it is open-ended simply because it is fragmentary: extensive gaps remain in the set of tablets that Rassam found in Nineveh and in other copies that have been recovered elsewhere. Some of these gaps can be filled in with parallel passages in earlier and later versions, and in this way a reasonably complete translation can be pieced together, as is presented here. The poem's great theme of the fragility of human life and culture is well illustrated by gaps and ellipses that continue to dot the text.

Even in the poem's many well-preserved episodes, mysteries remain. We first meet Enkidu living happily in the open countryside, naked, among the animals; when a temple prostitute seduces him and brings him to Uruk, does this episode celebrate city culture's riches or satirize them? Is Gilgamesh displaying heroic boldness in going off to slay the demon Humbaba, or is he being foolhardy, as his own counselors tell him? When he rejects the goddess Ishtar's advances, is Gilgamesh standing up for humanity or making the mistake of his—and Enkidu's—life? What are we to make of the mysterious dreams that periodically visit both Gilgamesh and Enkidu? Does Utanapishtim sympathize with Gilgamesh's quest for immortality or mock him for believing he can transcend the human condition? Does the poem end in an affirmation of human culture or in despair?

First recorded a thousand years before either the Greeks or the Hebrews learned how to write, Gilgamesh's story circulated through the Near East and Asia Minor during the centuries in which both the legends of Genesis and the Homeric epics were developed and eventually written down. Both the Eden story and the Flood story have clear parallels in *Gilgamesh*, whose restless hero can also be well compared to Odysseus, even as his fated friendship with Enkidu can be related to the relationship of Achilles and his beloved friend Patroklos. Gilgamesh's story continued to live on in his own region in oral form, and his adventures have echoes in *The Thousand and One Nights* in such figures as Sindbad. Now that the epic itself has at last been recovered, its haunting images, its moving dialogues, and its engrossing drama make it once again, after two thousand years of oblivion, compelling reading today.

PRONUNCIATIONS:

Enkidu: AIN-key-dou
Gilgamesh: GILL-gah-mesh
Shamash: SHAY-mash
Shamhat: SHAHM-haht
Sîn-liqe-unninni: SEEN-LEE-kay-ooh-NEE-nee

Urshanabi: OOHR-sha-NAH-bee
Ut-napishtim: UT-nah-PEASH-team

The Epic of Gilgamesh[1]

Tablet 1

1   [Of him who] found out all things, I shall tell the land,
[Of him who] experienced everything, I shall teach the whole.
He searched lands everywhere.
He who experienced the whole gained complete wisdom.
5   He found out what was secret and uncovered what was hidden,
He brought back a tale of times before the Flood.
He had journeyed far and wide, weary and at last resigned.
He engraved all toils on a memorial monument of stone.
He had the wall of Uruk built, the sheepfold
10   Of holiest Eanna,[2] the pure treasury.
See its wall, which is like a copper band,
Survey its battlements, which nobody else can match,
Take the threshold, which is from time immemorial,
Approach Eanna, the home of Ishtar,
15   Which no future king nor any man will ever match!
Go up on to the wall of Uruk and walk around!
Inspect the foundation platform and scrutinize the brickwork!
Testify that its bricks are baked bricks,
And that the Seven Counsellors[3] must have laid its foundations!
20   One square mile is city, one square mile is orchards, one square mile is clay-
        pits, as well as the open ground of Ishtar's temple.
Three square miles and the open ground comprise Uruk.
Look for the copper tablet-box,
Undo its bronze lock,
Open the door to its secret,
25   Lift out the lapis lazuli tablet and read it,
The story of that man, Gilgamesh, who went through all kinds of sufferings.
He was superior to other kings, a warrior lord of great stature,
A hero born of Uruk, a goring wild bull.
He marches at the front as leader,
30   He goes behind, the support of his brothers,
A strong net, the protection of his men,
The raging flood-wave, which can destroy even a stone wall.
Son of Lugalbanda, Gilgamesh, perfect in strength,
Son of the lofty cow, the wild cow Ninsun.[4]
35   He is Gilgamesh, perfect in splendour,
Who opened up passes in the mountains,
Who could dig pits even in the mountainside,

1. Translated by Stephanie Dalley. Throughout the poem, brackets indicate missing lines or parts of lines. Some missing phrases have been restored on the basis of parallel passages elsewhere. In her Oxford edition, Dalley also marks uncertain terms with question marks; we have retained some of these question marks, but have accepted most of her readings, or in some cases have adopted translations for phrases from the translations by Andrew George and by John Gardner and John Maier.

2. Temple of Ishtar, patron goddess of Uruk.

3. Sent by Ea, god of wisdom, to teach humanity the arts of civilization.

	Who crossed the ocean, the broad seas, as far as the sunrise.

Who crossed the ocean, the broad seas, as far as the sunrise.
Who inspected the edges of the world, kept searching for eternal life,
40   Who reached Ut-napishtim the far-distant, by force.
Who restored to their rightful place cult centers which the Flood had ruined.
There is nobody among the kings of teeming humanity
Who can compare with him,
Who can say "I am king" beside Gilgamesh.
45   Gilgamesh was named from birth for fame.
Two-thirds of him was divine, and one-third mortal.
Belet-ili designed the shape of his body,[5]
Made his form perfect, [   ]
[   ] was proud [   ]
50   [   ]
[   ]
In Uruk the Sheepfold he would walk about,
Show himself superior, his head held high like a wild bull.
He had no rival, and at his drum
55   His weapons would rise up, his comrades have to rise up.
The young men of Uruk became dejected in their private [quarters].
Gilgamesh would not leave any son alone for his father.
Day and night his [behaviour] was overbearing.
He was the shepherd [   ]
60   He was their shepherd yet [   ]
Powerful, superb, [knowledgeable and expert],
Gilgamesh would not leave [young girls alone],
The daughters of warriors, the brides of young men.
The gods often heard their complaints.
65   The gods of heaven [   ] the lord of Uruk.
    "Did [Aruru] create such a rampant wild bull?
    Is there no rival? At the-drum
    His weapons rise up, his comrades have to rise up.
    Gilgamesh will not leave any son alone for his father.
70   Day and night his [behaviour] is overbearing.
    He is the shepherd of Uruk the Sheepfold,
    He is their shepherd, yet [   ]
    Powerful, superb, knowledgeable [and expert],
    Gilgamesh will not leave young girls [alone],
75   The daughters of warriors, the brides of young men.
    Anu often hears their complaints."
They called upon great Aruru:
    "You, Aruru, you created [mankind]!
    Now create someone for him, to match the ardour of his energies!
80   Let them be regular rivals, and let Uruk be allowed peace!"
When Aruru heard this, she created inside herself an image of Anu.
Aruru washed her hands, pinched off a piece of clay, cast it out into open country.
She created a [primitive man], Enkidu the warrior: offspring of silence, shooting
    star of Ninurta.[6]
85   His whole body was shaggy with hair, he was furnished with tresses like a woman,

5. Mother goddess, later called Aruru.
6. God of war.

His locks of hair grew luxuriant like grain.
He knew neither people nor country; he was dressed as cattle are.
With gazelles he eats vegetation,
With cattle he quenches his thirst at the watering place.
90   With wild beasts he presses forward for water.
A hunter, a brigand,
Came face to face with him beside the watering place.
He saw him on three successive days beside the watering place.
The hunter looked at him, and was dumbstruck to see him.
95   In perplexity he went back into his house
And was afraid, stayed mute, was silent,
And was ill at ease, his face worried.
[   ] the grief in his innermost being.
His face was like that of a long-distance traveller.
100 The hunter made his voice heard and spoke, he said to his father,
    "Father, there was a young man who came [from the mountain],
    [On the land] he was strong, he was powerful.
    His strength was very hard, like a sky-bolt of Anu.[7]
    He walks about on the mountain all the time,
105   All the time he eats vegetation with cattle,
    All the time he bathes his feet in the watering place.
    I am too frightened to approach him.
    He kept filling in the pits that I dug [   ],
    He kept pulling out the traps that I laid.
110   He kept helping cattle, wild beasts of open country, to escape my grasp.
    He will not allow me to work [in open country]."
His father spoke to him, to the hunter,
    "[A man lives in] Uruk, Gilgamesh.
    [   ] his open country.
115   [His strength is very hard, like a shooting star of Anu]
    [Go, set] your face [towards Uruk].
    [Tell him of   ] the strength of the man,
    [He will send a harlot], lead (her) forth, and
    [   ] the strong man.
120   When he approaches the cattle at the watering place,
    She must take off her clothes and reveal her attractions.
    He will see her and go close to her.
    Then his cattle, who have grown up in open country with him, will
        become alien to him."
[He listened] to the advice of his father [   ].
125 The hunter went off [to see Gilgamesh].
He took the road, set [his face] towards Uruk,
Entered the presence of Gilgamesh [   ]:
    "There was a young man who [came from the mountain],
    On the land he was strong, he was powerful.
130   His strength is very hard, like a shooting star of Anu.
    He walks about on the mountain all the time,
    All the time he eats vegetation with cattle,
    All the time he puts his feet in (the water) at the watering place."

I am too frightened to approach him.

135 He kept filling in the pits that I dug,
He kept pulling out the traps that I laid.
He kept helping cattle, wild beasts of open country, to escape my grasp.
He did not allow me to work in the open country."
Gilgamesh spoke to him, to the hunter,

140 "Go, hunter, lead forth the harlot Shamhat,
And when he approaches the cattle at the watering place,
She must take off her clothes and reveal her attractions.
He will see her and go close to her.
Then his cattle, who have grown up in open country with him, will
   become alien to him."

145 The hunter went; he led forth the harlot Shamhat with him,
And they took the road, they made the journey.
In three days they reached the appointed place.
Hunter and harlot sat down in their hiding place.
For one day, then a second, they sat at the watering place.

150 Then cattle arrived at the watering place; they drank.
Then wild beasts arrived at the water; they satisfied their need.
And he, Enkidu, whose origin is the mountain,
(Who) eats vegetation with gazelles,
Drinks (at) the watering place with cattle,

155 Satisfied his need for water with wild beasts.
Shamhat looked at the primitive man,
The murderous youth from the depths of open country.
   "Here he is, Shamhat, bare your bosom,
   Open your legs and let him take in your attractions!

160 Do not pull away, take wind of him!
   He will see you and come close to you.
   Spread open your garments, and let him lie upon you,
   Do for him, the primitive man, as women do.
   Then his cattle, who have grown up in open country with him, will
      become alien to him.

165 His love-making he will lavish upon you!"
Shamhat loosened her undergarments, opened her legs and he took
   in her attractions.
She did not pull away. She took wind of him,
Spread open her garments, and he lay upon her.
She did for him, the primitive man, as women do.

170 His love-making he lavished upon her.
For six days and seven nights Enkidu was aroused and poured himself
   into Shamhat.
When he was sated with her charms,
He set his face towards the open country of his cattle.
The gazelles saw Enkidu and scattered,

175 The cattle of open country kept away from his body.
For Enkidu had stripped; his body was too clean.
His legs, which used to keep pace with his cattle, were at a standstill.
Enkidu had been diminished, he could not run as before.
Yet he had acquired judgement, had become wiser.

180 He turned back, he sat at the harlot's feet.
The harlot was looking at his expression,
And he listened attentively to what the harlot said.
The harlot spoke to him, to Enkidu,
  "You have become [wise], Enkidu, you have become like a god.
185 Why should you roam open country with wild beasts?
Come, let me take you into Uruk the Sheepfold,
To the pure house, the dwelling of Anu and Ishtar,
Where Gilgamesh is perfect in strength,
And is like a wild bull, more powerful than (any of) the people."
190 She spoke to him, and her speech was acceptable.
Knowing his own mind now, he would seek for a friend.
Enkidu spoke to her, to the harlot,
  "Come, Shamhat; invite me
To the pure house, the holy dwelling of Anu and Ishtar,
195 Where Gilgamesh is perfect in strength,
And is like a wild bull, more powerful than any of the people.
Let me challenge him, and [   ]
(By saying:) 'In Uruk I shall be the strongest!'
I shall go in and alter destiny:
200 One who was born in open country has [superior] strength!"
Shamhat answered,
  "Come on, let us go forth, and let me please you!
  [   ] there are, I know.
Go, Enkidu, into Uruk the Sheepfold
205 Where young men are girded with sashes
And every day is a feast day,
Where the drums are beaten
And girls [show off] their figures,
Adorned with joy and full of happiness.
210 In bed at night great men [   ]
O Enkidu! You who [know nothing] of life!
Let me show you Gilgamesh, a man of joy and woe!
Look at him, observe his face,
He is beautiful in manhood, dignified,
215 His whole body is charged with seductive charm.
He is more powerful in strength of arms than you!
He does not sleep by day or night.
O Enkidu, change your plan for punishing him!
Shamash loves Gilgamesh,
220 And Anu, Ellil, and Ea made him wise![8]
Before you came from the mountains,
Gilgamesh was dreaming about you in Uruk.
Gilgamesh arose and described a dream, he told it to his mother,
  'Mother, I saw a dream in the night.
225 There were stars in the sky for me.
And something like a shooting star of Anu kept falling upon me!
I tried to lift it up, but it was too heavy for me.
I tried to turn it over, but I couldn't budge it.

8 Shamash is the sun god; Anu is the sky god, Ellil the storm god, and Ea the god of wisdom.

The countrymen of Uruk were standing over [it].
230   [The countrymen had gathered] over it,
The men crowded over it,
The young men massed over it,
They kissed its feet like very young children.
I loved it as a wife, doted on it,
235   [I carried it], laid it at your feet,
You treated it as equal to me.'
[The wise mother of Gilgamesh], all-knowing, understood,
She spoke to her lord.
[The wise wild cow Ninsun] all-knowing, understood,
240   She spoke to Gilgamesh,
'[When there were] stars in the sky for you,
And something like a shooting star of Anu kept falling upon you,
You tried to lift it up, but it was too heavy for you,
You tried to turn it over, but you couldn't budge it,
245   [You carried it], laid it at my feet,
I treated it as equal to you,
And you loved it as a wife, and doted on it:
It means a strong partner shall come to you,
      one who can save the life of a friend,
He will be the most powerful in strength of arms in the land.
250   His strength will be as great as that of a shooting star of Anu.
You will love him as a wife, you will dote upon him.
[And he will always] keep you safe.
[That is the meaning] of your dream.'
Gilgamesh spoke to her, to his mother.
255   'Mother, I have had a second dream.
An axe was thrown down in the street of Uruk the Sheepfold and
    they gathered over it,
The countrymen of Uruk stood over it.
The land gathered together over it,
The men massed over it.
260   [I carried it], laid it at your feet.
I loved it as a wife, doted upon it.
And you treated it as equal to me.'
The wise mother of Gilgamesh, all-knowing, understood, she spoke to her son.
The wise wild cow Ninsun, all-knowing, understood, she spoke to Gilgamesh,
265   'The copper axe which you saw is a man.
You will love it as a wife, you will dote upon it,
And I shall treat it as equal to you.
A strong partner will come to you, one who can save the life of a comrade.
He will be the most powerful in strength of arms in the land.
270   His strength will be as great as that of a shooting star of Anu.'
Gilgamesh spoke to his mother,
'Let it fall, then, according to the word of Ellil the great counsellor.
I shall gain a friend to advise me.'
Ninsun retold his dreams."
275   Thus Shamhat heard the dreams of Gilgamesh and told them to Enkidu.
"[The dreams mean that you will lo]ve one another."

Tablet II

[*Some sixty lines are missing here or very fragmentary. In them, Enkidu has his encounter with Shamhat, which can be restored from parallels in the briefer Old Babylonian version, given in the next twenty lines*]:

Enkidu sat before the woman.
The two of them made love together,
Enkidu forgot the hills where he was born.
Six days and seven nights Enkidu was erect,
5   mating with the temple harlot.
Shamhat opened her mouth, saying to Enkidu,
"When I look at you, Enkidu, you are like a god.
Why do you roam the wilderness with wild animals?
Come, let me lead you into Uruk of the broad places,
10   to the holy house, home of Anu,
the place where Gilgamesh is all-powerful,
and you [will embrace] him [like a wife],
you will love him like yourself.
Go, rise from the ground, bed of shepherds."
15   He heard her words and listened to what she said,
the advice of a woman came into his heart.
She took off part of her clothing and covered him;
another part she kept on herself.
She took his hand and led him like a child
20   to the shepherd-house, the place of the sheepfold.

(*The Standard Version resumes*):

The shepherds were gathered around him
Of their own accord, and by themselves—
    "The young man—how like Gilgamesh in build,
    Mature in build, as sturdy as battlements.
25   Why was he born in the mountains?
    He is just as powerful in strength of arms as a shooting star of Anu!"
They put food in front of him; [   ]
They put drink in front of him; [   ]
Enkidu would not eat the food; he narrowed his eyes and stared.

    (*gap of a few lines*)

30   [   ]   [   ]
He slew wolves and [   ]
[   ] the herdsmen [   ]
Enkidu [   ] a herdsman [   ]
[   ] you stayed at home [   ]
35   [   ] Uruk the Sheepfold [   ]

    (*gap*)

[He stood] in the street of Uruk [the Sheepfold]
[   ] the strong [   ]
He barred the way [of Gilgamesh]
The country of Uruk was standing around him

40 The country gathered together over him,
   The men massed over him,
   The young men crowded over him,
   Kissed his feet as if he were a toddler.
   When the young man [   ]
45 The bed was laid at night for Ishhara
   And for godlike Gilgamesh an equal match was found.
   Enkidu blocked his access at the door of the father-in-law's house,
   He would not allow Gilgamesh to enter.
   They grappled at the door of the father-in-law's house,
50 Wrestled in the street, in the public square.
   Doorframes shook, walls quaked.

           (about 37 lines missing)

       "He was the most powerful in strength of arms in the land,
        His strength was as great as that of a shooting star of Anu,
        A build as sturdy as battlements [   ]."
55 The [wise] mother of Gilgamesh, [all-knowing],
   Spoke [to her son].
   The wild cow Ninsun [spoke to Gilgamesh],
       "My son, [   ]
        Bitterly [   ]
60 [   ]
   Seized [   ].
   He brought up to his door [   ]
   Bitterly he was weeping [   ]"
       "Enkidu had no [   ]
65   His hair is allowed to hang loose [   ]
       He was born in open country, and who can prevail over him?"
   Enkidu stood, listened to him speaking,
   Pondered, and then sat down, began to cry.
   His eyes grew dim with tears.
70 His arms slackened, his strength [   ]
   (Then) they grasped one another,
   And embraced and held hands.
   [Gilgamesh made his voice heard and spoke],
   He said [to] Enkidu,
75   "[Why are your eyes] filled [with tears]?"

           (about 29 lines missing)

   "Ellil has destined him to keep the Cedar Forest safe,
    To be the terror of people.
    Humbaba, whose shout is the flood-weapon, whose utterance is Fire, and
        whose breath is Death,
    Can hear for a distance of sixty leagues through the . . . of the forest, so
        who can penetrate his forest?
80 Ellil has destined him to keep the Cedar Forest safe, to be the terror of
        people:
    Debility would seize anyone who penetrated his forest."
   Gilgamesh spoke to him, to Enkidu,

"Are you saying that [   ]?

(*gap of about 34 lines*)

[   ]

85 Gilgamesh [made his] voice heard [and spoke to Enkidu],
      "My friend, are there not [   ]
      Are there no children [   ]?"
    Enkidu made his voice heard and [spoke to Gilgamesh],
      "My friend, were we to go to him, [   ]
90   Humbaba [   ]"
    Gilgamesh made his voice heard [and spoke to Enkidu],
      "My friend, we really should [   ]

(*gap of a few lines*)

    They sat and pondered on [   ]
      "We made a *ḫaṣṣinnu*-axe [   ]
95   A *pāšu*-axe with a whole talent of [bronze for each half]
      Their swords weighed a whole talent each; [   ]
      Their belts weighed a whole talent each; their belts [   ]
      [   ]
      'Listen to me, young men
100   Young men of Uruk who know [   ]
      I am adamant: I shall take the road [to Humbaba].
      I shall face unknown opposition, [I shall ride along an unknown] road.
      Give me your blessing, since I [have decided] on the course,
      That I may enter the city-gate of Uruk [again in future]
105   And [celebrate] the New Year Festival once again in [future] years,
      And take part in the New Year Festival in years [to come].
      Let the New Year Festival be performed, let joy [resound],
      Let cries ring out in [   ]."'
    Enkidu gave advice to the elders,
110 The young men of Uruk [   ]
      "Tell him not to go to the Cedar Forest,
      That journey is not to be undertaken! A man [   ]
      The guardian of the Cedar [Forest   ]"

(*gap of a few lines*)

    The great counsellors of Uruk rose up
115 And gave an opinion to [Gilgamesh]:
      "You are [still young], Gilgamesh, you are impetuous to [   ],
      But you do not know what you will find [   ]
      Humbaba, whose shout is the flood-weapon,
      Whose utterance is Fire and whose breath is Death,
120   Can hear for up to sixty leagues the sounds of his forest.
      Whoever goes down to his forest
      [   ] or two.
      Who, even among the Igigi, can face him?
      Ellil destined him to keep the Cedar Forest safe, to be the terror of people."
125 Gilgamesh listened to the speech of the great counsellors.

(*gap of a few lines*)

Tablet III

"[   ]

Do not trust entirely, Gilgamesh, in your own strength.

When you have looked long enough, trust to your first blow.

He who leads the way will save his comrade.

5   He who knows the paths, he will guard his friend.

Let Enkidu go in front of you,

He knows the way of the Cedar Forest.

He can look at the fight and instruct in the battle.

Let Enkidu guard the friend, keep the comrade safe,

10   Bring him back safe in person for brides,

So that we in our assembly may rely on you as king,

And that you in turn as king may rely on us again."

Gilgamesh made his voice heard and spoke,

He said to Enkidu,

15   "Come, my friend, let us go to the great palace,

To Ninsun, the great queen.

Ninsun is wise, all-knowing, she understands,

She will set the steps of good advice at our feet."

They grasped each other by the hand,

20   And Gilgamesh and Enkidu went to the great palace,

To Ninsun the great queen.

Gilgamesh rose up and entered into [   ].

"Ninsun, I am adamant. [I shall take]

The distant path to where [Humbaba lives].

25   [I shall face] unknown [opposition],

[I shall ride along] an unknown [road]

Until the day when, having travelled far and wide,

I finally reach the Cedar Forest,

Until I slay ferocious Humbaba,

30   And exterminate from the land Something Evil, which Shamash hates.

(about 5 lines missing)

[   ] into your presence."

[Ninsun] paid attention [to all the words]

Of Gilgamesh, her son.

Ninsun entered her chamber.

35   [   ] soap-plant.

[She put on a garment], adornment of her body,

[Put on pins,] adornment of her breast,

[   ], wore her crown on her head.

[   ]...

40   [   ] she went up on to the roof.

She came before Shamash, made a smoke-offering,

Made a libation before Shamash and raised her arms:

"Why did you single out my son Gilgamesh and impose a restless spirit on him?

Now you have affected him and he will take

45   The distant path to where Humbaba lives,

He faces an unknown struggle,
He will ride along an unknown road
Until the day when, having travelled far and wide,
He finally reaches the Cedar Forest,
50 Until he slays ferocious Humbaba,
And exterminates from the land Something Evil which you hate.
On the day when you [   ] at the side of [   ],
May Aya,[9] the daughter-in-law, not be too fearful of you to commend
     him to you.
Entrust him (?) to the night watchmen,
55 [   ] whip [   ]"

    (gap of about 26 lines)

[   ] Gilgamesh [   ]
She extinguished the smoke-offering and [   ].
She called Enkidu to her and gave her decision.
    "Enkidu, you are a strong man, though not from my womb.
60   Now, your offspring [shall be dedicated to] Shamash with the oblates
     of Gilgamesh:
    Priestesses, devotees, and votaresses."
She placed symbols around Enkidu's neck, (saying)
    "Priestesses have accepted the orphan,
    The daughters of gods have adopted a foundling.
65   I hereby take Enkidu to be my son.
Gilgamesh shall accept Enkidu [as his brother]."

    (10 lines fragmentary)

    (gap of about 4 lines)

[A damaged fragment indicates that Gilgamesh and Enkidu make
offerings of juniper and incense at a shrine. A door of cedar is mentioned,
perhaps promised to Ellil in return for success against Humbaba.]

    (this gap and the next gap represent about 27 lines)

    "[Let Enkidu] guard the friend, [keep the comrade safe.]
    [Let him bring him back safe in person] for brides,
    So that we in our assembly may rely on you as king,
70   And that you in turn as king may rely on us again."
Enkidu made his voice heard and spoke,
He said to [Gilgamesh],
    "My friend, turn back [   ]
    A journey that is not [   ]"

    (gap)

Tablet IV

    (gap of about 5 lines?)

    At twenty leagues they ate their ration.
    At thirty leagues they stopped for the night.

Fifty leagues they travelled during the day.

The distance (took from) the new moon to the full moon, then three days
    more: they came to Lebanon.

5   (There) they dug a well in front of Shamash.

They [refilled their waterskins].

Gilgamesh went up on to the mountain,

And made his flour-offering to [   ]:

    "O mountain, bring me a dream, a favourable one!"

Enkidu arranged it for him, for Gilgamesh.

10   A dust-devil passed by, and he/it fixed (?) [   ]

He made him lie down inside the circle and [   ]

[   ] like wild barley [   ] blood [   ].

Gilgamesh sat with his chin on his knees.

Sleep, which spills out over people, overcame him.

15   In the middle watch he finished his sleep.

He rose up and said to his friend,

    "My friend, didn't you call me? Then why am I awake?

Didn't you touch me? Why am I so upset?

Didn't a god pass by? Then why is my flesh so feeble?

20   My friend, [I had a dream]

And the dream that I had was extremely upsetting.

At the foot of the mountain [   ]

[   ] fell/hit [   ].

We were like flies [   ]."

25   [He who] was born in open country, and [   ]

Enkidu explained the dream to his friend.

    "My friend, your dream is favourable.

The dream is very significant [   ]

My friend, the mountain which you saw [   ] (means:)

30   We shall seize Humbaba, sl[ay him],

And cast his corpse on to waste ground.

At the light of dawn we shall hear the favourable word of Shamash."

At twenty leagues they ate their ration.

At thirty leagues they stopped for the night.

35   (There) they dug a well in front of Shamash.

Gilgamesh went up on to [the mountain]

And made his flour-offering to [   ]:

    "O mountain, bring me a dream, a favourable one!"

Enkidu arranged it for him, for Gilgamesh.

    (gap into which the following may be restored:)

(A dust devil passed by, and he/it fixed [   ]

40   He made him lie down inside the circle and [   ]

[   ] like wild barley [   ]

Gilgamesh sat with his chin on his knees.

Sleep, which spills out over people, overcame him.

In the middle watch he finished his sleep,

45   He rose up and said to his friend,

    "My friend, didn't you call me? Then why am I awake?

Didn't you touch me? Why am I so upset?

My friend, I had a second dream,
50 And the dream that I had was extremely upsetting.)"

(The contents of the second dream are not preserved)

(about 20 lines missing)

"My friend, this [is the explanation of your dream]
Humbaba like [   ]
Until light flared up [   ]
We shall place on top of him [   ]
55 We were furious [at] Humbaba [   ]
[   ] we stood over him.
And in the morning the word of Shamash was favourable."
At twenty leagues they ate their ration.
At thirty leagues they stopped for the night.
60 Fifty leagues they travelled during the day.
(There) they dug a well in front of Shamash.
They refilled [their waterskins],
Gilgamesh went up on to [the mountain],
And made his flour-offering to [   ]:
"O mountain, bring me a dream, a favourable one!"
65 Enkidu arranged it for him, for Gilgamesh.
A dust-devil passed by, and he/it fixed [   ]
He made him lie down inside the circle and [   ]
[   ] like wild barley [   ]
Gilgamesh sat with his chin on his knees.
70 Sleep, which spills out over people, overcame him.
In the middle watch he finished his sleep.
He rose up and said to his friend,
"My friend, didn't you call me? Then why am I awake?
Didn't you touch me? Why am I so upset?
75 Didn't a god pass by? Then why is my flesh so feeble?
My friend, I had a third dream,
And the dream that I had was extremely upsetting.
Heaven cried out, earth groaned.
Day grew silent, darkness emerged,
80 Lightning flashed, fire broke out.
[Flames] crackled, death rained down.
(Then) sparks were dimmed, and the fire was extinguished.
[The coals which] kept falling turned to embers.
[Let us go back] down to open country where we can get advice."
85 Enkidu listened, and made him accept his dream; he spoke to Gilgamesh,

(interpretation of third dream missing)

(gap of about 23 lines)

(About 6 lines of 45 partly preserved)

"[One alone cannot (?)   ]
[They are strangers (?)   ]
It is a slippery path, and [one] does not [   ] But two [   ]
Two...[   ]
A three-stranded cord [is hardest to break]

A strong lion [cannot prevail over two of its own cubs.]
　　(*Column v not extant; gap of about 60 lines*)

Enkidu made his voice heard and spoke; he said to Gilgamesh,
　　"[How] can I go down into [the Cedar Forest?]
　　Or open up the path, when my arms are paralysed?"

95　Gilgamesh made his voice heard and spoke; he said to Enkidu,
　　"Why, my friend, do we [talk] like cowards?
　　We can cross all the mountains [　　　　　]
　　[　　　　　] to our face, before we have cut down [Cedars]
　　My friend, experienced in conflict, who has [　　] battle,
100　You have rubbed yourself with plants so you need not fear death.
　　Your shall have a double mantle of radiance like...
　　Your shout shall be as loud as a kettledrum.
　　Paralysis shall leave your arms, and impotence shall leave your loins.
　　Hold my hand, my friend, let us set off!
105　Your heart shall soon burn for conflict; forget death and [think only of] life.
　　Man is strong, prepared to fight, responsible.
　　He who goes in front (and) guards his (friend's) body, shall keep the comrade safe.
　　They shall have established fame for their [future]."
110　[　　　　　] they arrived together.
　　[　　　　　] of their words, they stood.

Tablet V

　　They stood at the edge of the forest,
　　Gazed and gazed at the height of the cedars,
　　Gazed and gazed at the entrance to the cedars,
　　Where Humbaba made tracks as he went to and fro.
5　The paths were well trodden and the road was excellent.
　　They beheld the Cedar Mountain, dwelling-place of gods, shrine of Irnini.
　　The cedar held up their luxuriance even on the face of the mountain.
　　Their shade was good, filling one with happiness.
　　Undergrowth burgeoned, entangling the forest.

　　　　(*8 fragmentary lines, then gap*)

　　　　(*They entered the forest and found Humbaba*)

10　Humbaba made his voice heard and spoke; he said to Gilgamesh,
　　"The fool Gilgamesh and the brutish man ought to ask themselves, why
　　　have you come to see me?
　　Your [friend] Enkidu is small fry who does not know his own father!
　　You are so very small that I regard you as I do a turtle or a tortoise
　　Which does not suck its mother's milk, so I do not approach you.
15　[Even if I] were to kill you, would I satisfy my stomach?
　　[Why,　　　　　], Gilgamesh, have you let (him) reach me,
　　[　　　　　　　　　]...
　　So I shall bite [through your/his] windpipe and neck, Gilgamesh,
　　And leave [your/his body] for birds of the forest, roaring (lions), birds of

20   Gilgamesh made his voice heard and spoke; he said to Enkidu,
       "My friend, Humbaba has changed his mood
       And...has come upon him [   ]
       And my heart [trembles lest he   ] suddenly!"
    Enkidu made his voice heard and spoke; he said to Gilgamesh,
25   "My friend, why do you talk like a coward?
       And your speech was feeble, and you tried to hide.
       Now, my friend, he has drawn you out
       With the (blow)pipe of the coppersmith for heating
       To count back each league swollen with the heat, each league of cold,
30   To dispatch the flood-weapon, to lash with the whip!
       Don't retrace your footsteps! Don't turn back!
       [   ] Make your blows harder!"

         (gap of a few lines)

    His (Gilgamesh's) tears flowed before Shamash [   ]
       "Remember what you said in Uruk!
35   Stand there and listen to me!"
    [Shamash] heard the words
    Of Gilgamesh, scion of Uruk, [and said],
       "As soon as a loud voice from the sky calls down to him,
       Rush, stand up to him, let him not [enter the forest],
40   Let him not go down to the wood, nor [   ].
       [Humbaba] will [not] be clothed in seven cloaks,
       He will be wearing [only one]; six are taken off.
       Like a charging wild bull which pierces [   ]
       He shouts only once, but fills one with terror.
45   The guardian of the forests will shout [   ]
       [   ]
       Humbaba like [   ] will shout."

        (gap of uncertain length)

    As soon as the swords [   ]
    [   ] from the sheaths [   ]
50   Streaked with verdigris (?) [   ]
    Dagger, sword [   ]
    One [   ]
    They wore [   ]
    Humbaba [made his voice heard and spoke]
55   "He will not go [   ]
       He will not go [   ]

        (7 lines illegible)

     May Ellil [   ]."
    Enkidu [made] his voice heard [and spoke],
    [He addressed his speech] to Humbaba,
60   "One alone [cannot   ]
       They are strangers [   ]
       It is a slippery path, and [one] does not
       [   ] but two [   ]

65   A three-stranded cord [is hardest to break]
    A strong lion [cannot prevail over] two of its own cubs."

(3 broken lines, then gap of uncertain length, then 2 broken lines)

    He struck (his) head, and matched him [   ]
    They stirred up the ground with the heels of their feet,
    Sirara and Lebanon were split apart at their gyrations,
70   White clouds grew black,
    Death dropped down over them like a fog.
    Shamash summoned up great tempests against Humbaba,
    South Wind, North Wind, East Wind, West Wind, Moaning Wind,
    Gale, *šaparziqqu*-Wind, *imhullu*-Wind, . . . -Wind
75   Asakku, Wintry Wind, Tempest, Whirlwind,
    Thirteen winds rose up at him and Humbaba's face grew dark.
    He could not charge forwards, he could not run backwards.
    Thus the weapons of Gilgamesh succeeded against Humbaba.
    Humbaba gasped for breath, he addressed Gilgamesh,
80   "You are young, Gilgamesh; your mother gave birth to you,
    And you are the offspring of [   ]
    You rose at the command of Shamash, Lord of the Mountain
    And you are the scion of Uruk, king Gilgamesh.
    [   ] Gilgamesh [   ]
85   [   ]
    Gilgamesh [   ]
    I shall make (them) grow luxuriantly for you in [   ]
    As many trees as you [   ]
    I shall keep for you myrtle wood, [   ]
90   Timbers to be the pride [of your palace]."
    Enkidu made his voice heard and spoke; he said to Gilgamesh,
    "[My friend], don't listen to [the words] of Humbaba.

(3 broken lines, gap of about 15 lines)

    "You have found out the nature of my forest, the nature [of my dwelling]
    And (now) you know all their . . . -s.
95   I should have taken you (and) slain you at the entrance to my forest's growth,
    I should have given your flesh to be eaten by the birds of the forest, roaring
        (lions), birds of prey, and scavengers.
    But now, Enkidu, it is in your power to . . . ,
    So tell Gilgamesh to spare my life!"
    Enkidu made his voice heard and spoke; he said to Gilgamesh,
100   "My friend, finish him off, slay him, grind him up, that [I may survive]
    Humbaba the guardian of the [Cedar] Forest!
    Finish him off, slay him, grind him up that [I may survive]
    Humbaba, the guardian of the forest.
    (Do it) before the leader Ellil hears, [   ]
105   [Lest] the gods be filled with fury at us [ ]
    Ellil in Nippur, Shamash in [Sippar].
    Set up an eternal [memorial]
    To [tell] how Gilgamesh [slew] Humbaba!"
    Humbaba listened, and [   ]

110 　　"You sit like a shepherd [　　　　　　　]
　　　　And just like...[　　　　　　　　]
　　　　Now, Enkidu, thus settle your own release
　　　　And tell Gilgamesh that he may save his life."
　　Enkidu made his voice heard and spoke; he said [to Gilgamesh],
115 　　　　"My friend, [finish off] Humbaba, the guardian of the Cedar Forest,
　　　　　　[finish him off], slay him [and grind him up, that I may survive].
　　　　(Do it) before the leader Ellil hears, [　　　　　　　]
　　　　Lest the gods be filled with fury at us [　　　　　　].
　　　　Ellil in Nippur, Shamash in Sippar. [Set up an eternal memorial]
120 　　　　To tell how Gilgamesh [slew] Humbaba."
　　Humbaba listened and [　　　　　　　　　]

　　　　　(gap of about 13 lines, in which Humbaba curses them)

　　　　"Neither one of them shall outlive
　　　　His friend! Gilgamesh and Enkidu shall never become old men."
　　Enkidu made his voice heard and spoke; he said to Gilgamesh,
125 　　　　"My friend, I talk to you but you don't listen to me!"

　　　　　(40 broken or missing lines)

　　　　　(gap of about 22 lines)

　　[　　　　] their dark patch (?) of verdigris.
　　Gilgamesh was cutting down the trees; Enkidu kept tugging at the stumps.
　　Enkidu made his voice heard and spoke; he said to Gilgamesh,
　　　　"My friend, I have had a fully mature cedar cut down,
130 　　　　The crown of which butted against the sky.
　　　　I made a door six poles high and two poles wide,
　　　　Its doorpost is a cubit..., its lower and upper hinges are (made) from
　　　　　a single [　　　].
　　　　Let the Euphrates carry [it] to Nippur; Nippur [　　　　　].
　　　　[　　　　　　　　　]."
135 　　They tied together a raft, they put down [　　　　　]
　　Enkidu embarked [　　　　　　　　]
　　And Gilgamesh [　　　　　] the head of Humbaba.
　　(Colophon)
　　Fifth tablet, series [of Gilgamesh]

Tablet VI

　　He washed his filthy hair, he cleaned his gear,
　　Shook out his locks over his back,
　　Threw away his dirty clothes and put on fresh ones.
　　He clothed himself in robes and tied on a sash.
5 　　Gilgamesh put his crown on his head
　　And Ishtar the princess raised her eyes to the beauty of Gilgamesh.
　　　　"Come to me, Gilgamesh, and be my lover!
　　　　Bestow on me the gift of your fruit!
　　　　You can be my husband, and I can be your wife.
10 　　　　I shall have a chariot of lapis lazuli and gold harnessed for you,
　　　　With wheels of gold, and horns of amber.

You shall harness storm demons as great mules!
Enter into our house through the fragrance of cedar!
When you enter our house
15 The wonderfully-wrought threshold shall kiss your feet!
Kings, nobles, princes shall bow down beneath you.
The verdure of mountain and country shall bring you produce,
Your goats shall bear triplets, your ewes twins,
Your loaded donkey shall outpace the mule.
20 Your horses shall run proud at the chariot,
[Your ox] shall be unrivalled at the yoke."
Gilgamesh made his voice heard and spoke,
He said to Ishtar the princess,
"What could I give you if I possessed you?
25 I would give you body oil and garments,
I would give you food and sustenance.
Could I provide you with bread fit for gods?
Could I provide you with ale fit for kings?
[   ]
30 Could I heap up [   ]
[   ] a robe?
[if] I possess you?
[You would be an oven that melts] ice,
A drafty door that can't keep out winds and gusts,
35 A palace wall that crushes its own warriors,
A well whose lid collapses,
Bitumen which [stains] its carrier,
A waterskin which [soaks] its carrier,
A limestone which crumbles in a stone wall,
40 A battering ram which shatters [in a land] of war,
A shoe which bites into the foot of its wearer.
Which of your lovers [lasted] forever?
Which of your masterful paramours went to heaven?
Come, let me [describe] your lovers to you!
45 He of the sheep [...   ...   .]
      knew him:
For Dumuzi the lover of your youth[1]
You decreed that he should keep weeping year after year.
You loved the colourful *allallu*-bird,
But you hit him and broke his wing.
50 He stays in the woods crying 'My wing!'
You loved the lion, whose strength is complete,
But you dug seven and seven pits for him.
You loved the horse, so trustworthy in battle,
But you decreed the whip, goad, and lash for him,
55 You decreed that he should gallop seven leagues non-stop,
You decreed that he should be overwrought and thirsty,
You decreed endless weeping for his mother Sililu.
You loved the shepherd, herdsman, and chief shepherd

1. Dumuzi was famous in Sumerian myths as the lover of the goddess Inanna/Ishtar, who rashly descends to the underworld to confront her sister, queen of the underworld: Dumuzi has to be offered as

Who was always heaping up the glowing ashes for you,
60 And cooked ewe-lambs for you every day.
But you hit him and turned him into a wolf,
His own herd-boys hunt him down
And his dogs tear at his haunches.
You loved Ishullanu, your father's gardener,
65 Who was always bringing you baskets of dates.
They brightened your table every day;
You lifted your eyes to him and went to him
'My own Ishullanu, let us enjoy your strength,
So put out your hand and touch our vulva!'
70 But Ishullanu said to you,
'Me? What do you want of me?
Did my mother not bake for me, and did I not eat?
What I eat with you would be loaves of dishonour and disgrace,
Rushes would be my only covering against the cold.'
75 You listened as he said this,
And you hit him, turned him into a frog,
Left him to stay amid the fruits of his labours,
Not able to move upward or down.
And how about me? You will love me and then [treat me] just like them!"
80 When Ishtar heard this,
Ishtar was furious, and [went up] to heaven.
Ishtar went up and wept before her father Anu,
Her tears flowed before her mother Antu.
"Father, Gilgamesh has shamed me again and again!
85 Gilgamesh spelt out to me my dishonour,
My dishonour and my disgrace."
Anu made his voice heard and spoke,
He said to the princess Ishtar,
"Why didn't you accuse Gilgamesh the king for yourself,
90 Since Gilgamesh spelt out your dishonour,
Your dishonour and your disgrace?"
Ishtar made her voice heard and spoke,
She said to her father Anu,
"Father, please give me the Bull of Heaven, and let me strike Gilgamesh
down !
95 Let me . . . Gilgamesh in his dwelling!
If you don't give me the Bull of Heaven,
I shall strike [   ]
I shall set my face towards the infernal regions,
I shall raise up the dead, and they will eat the living,
100 I shall make the dead outnumber the living!"
Anu made his voice heard and spoke,
He said to the princess Ishtar,
"On no account should you request the Bull of Heaven from me!
There would be seven years of chaff in the land of Uruk,
105 Have you stored up grain for the people?
Have you grown grass for the cattle?"

She said to her father Anu,
"I have heaped up a store [of grain in Uruk (?)],
110 I have ensured the production of [   ],
[   ] years of chaff.
[   ] has been gathered.
[   ] grass.
[   ] for him.

(gap of one or more lines)

115 [   ] of the Bull of Heaven [   ]."
Anu listened to Ishtar speaking,
And he put the Bull of Heaven's reins in her hands.
Ishtar [took hold] and directed it.
When it arrived in the land of Uruk
120 It [   ]
It went down to the river, and seven [   ] river [   ].
At the snorting of the Bull of Heaven a chasm opened up, and one hundred
    young men of Uruk fell into it,
Two hundred young men, three hundred young men.
At its second snorting another chasm opened up, and another hundred young
    men of Uruk fell into it,
125 Two hundred young men, three hundred young men fell into it.
At its third snorting a chasm opened up,
And Enkidu fell into it.
But Enkidu leapt out. He seized the Bull of Heaven by the horns.
The Bull of Heaven blew spittle into his face,
130 With its thick tail it whipped up its dung.
Enkidu made his voice heard and spoke,
He said to Gilgamesh,
    "My friend, we were too arrogant [when we killed Humbaba].
    How can we give recompense [for our action]?
135   My friend, I have seen [   ]
    And my strength [   ]
    Let me pull out [   ]
    [   ]
    Let me seize [   ]
140   Let me [   ]
    In [   ]
    And plunge your sword [   ]
    In between the base of the horns and the neck tendons."
Enkidu spun round [to] the Bull of Heaven,
145 And seized it by its thick tail,
And [   ]
Then Gilgamesh, like a but[cher] heroic and [   ]
Plunged his sword in between the base of the horns and the neck tendons.
When they had struck down the Bull of Heaven they pulled out its innards,
150 Set them before Shamash,
Backed away and prostrated themselves before Shamash.
Then the two brothers sat down.
Ishtar went up on to the wall of Uruk the Sheepfold

She was contorted with rage, she hurled down curses,
155   "That man Gilgamesh who reviled me has killed the Bull of Heaven!"
Enkidu listened to Ishtar saying this,
And he pulled out the Bull of Heaven's shoulder and slapped it into her face:
   "If I could only get at you as that does,
   I would do the same to you myself,
160   I would hang its intestines on your arms!"
Ishtar gathered the crimped courtesans,
Prostitutes and harlots.
She arranged for weeping over the Bull of Heaven's shoulder.
Gilgamesh called craftsmen, all the armourers,
165 And the craftsmen admired the thickness of its horns.
Thirty minas of lapis lazuli was (needed for) each of their pouring ends,
Two minas of gold (was needed for) each of their sheathings.
Six measures of oil was the capacity of both.
He dedicated (them) for anointing his god Lugalbanda,
170 Took them in and hung them on his bed (where he slept) as head of the family.
In the Euphrates they washed their hands
And held hands and came
Riding through the main street of Uruk.
The people of Uruk gathered and gazed at them.
175 Gilgamesh addressed a word to [his] retainers,
   "Who is finest among the young men?
   Who is proudest among the males?"
   "Gilgamesh is finest among the young men!
   Gilgamesh is proudest among the males!
180   [   ] we knew in our anger
   There is nobody like him who can please her [   ].
   [   ]"
Gilgamesh made merry in his palace.
Then they lay down, the young men were lying in bed for the night,
185 And Enkidu lay down and had a dream.
Enkidu got up and described the dream,
He said to his friend,

Tablet VII

   "My friend, why are the great gods consulting together?"

   (gap of about 20 lines, which may partly be filled in essence from a Hittite version, which is given here)

Then daylight came. [And] Enkidu said to Gilgamesh,
   "O my brother, what a dream [I saw] last night!
   Anu, Ellil, Ea, and heavenly Shamash [were in the assembly].
5   And Anu said to Ellil, 'As they have slain the Bull of Heaven,
   So too they have slain Huwawa, who [guarded] the mountains pla[nted]
      with cedars.'
   And Anu said, 'One of them [must die].'
   Ellil replied: 'Let Enkidu die, but let Gilgamesh not die.'
   Then heavenly Shamash said to valiant Ellil,

'Was it not according to your word that they slew the Bull of Heaven and
  Huwawa? Should now innocent Enkidu die?'
But Ellil turned in anger to heavenly Shamash, saying,
'(The fact is), you accompanied them daily, like one of their comrades.'"
Enkidu lay down before Gilgamesh, his tears flowing like streams.
  "O my brother, my brother is so dear to me.

  But they are taking me from my brother."
And: "I shall sit among the dead, I shall [   ] the threshold of the dead;
  Never again [shall I see] my dear brother with my own eyes."

  (end of Hittite insertion)

  (9 broken lines)

Enkidu lifted up [   ]
He discussed [   ] with the door.

  "Door, don't [you] remember the words?
  Are not... ...[   ]?
  I selected the timber for you over twenty leagues,
  Until I had found a fully mature cedar.
  There is no other wood like yours!

  Your height is six poles,[2] your width two poles,
  Your doorpost, your lower and upper hinge are made [from a single tree.]
  I made you, I carried you to Nippur [   ]
  Be aware, door, that this was a favour to you,
  And this was a good deed done for you [   ]

  I myself raised the axe, I cut you down,
  Loaded you myself on to the raft, [   ]
  I myself [   ] temple of Shamash
  [   ]
  I myself set (you) up in his gate [   ]

  [   ]
  I myself [   ]
  And in Uruk [   ]

  (2 broken lines)

Now, door, it was I who made you,
  I who carried you to Nippur.

  But the king who shall arise after me shall go through you,
  Gilgamesh shall [go through] your portals
  And change my name, and put on his own name!"
He tore out [the door and] hurled [   ].
He kept listening to his words, [   ] straight away

Gilgamesh kept listening to the words of his friend Enkidu, and his tears flowed.
Gilgamesh made his voice heard and spoke; he said to Enkidu [   ],
  "You, who used to be reasonable, [now speak] otherwise!
  Why, my friend, did your heart speak otherwise.
  The dream was very precious, and the warning awful; your lips buzzed like flies!

  The warning was awful, the dream was precious.

2. 48 feet.

They have left a legacy of grieving for next year.
The dream has left a legacy of grief for next year.
[I shall go] and offer prayers to the great gods,
I shall search out [your goddess], look for your god,
55 [   ] the father of the gods.
To Ellil the counsellor, father of the gods [   ].
I shall make a statue of you with countless gold [   ]"
[The words] he spoke were not like [   ],
[What] he said did not go back, did not [alter (?)]
60 [The] that he cast (?) did not go back, he did not erase. [   ]
[   ] to the people [   ]. At the first light of morning
Enkidu [raised] his head, wept before Shamash,
His tears flowed before the rays of the Sun.
  "I hereby beseech you, Shamash, because my fate is different (?),
65   [Because] the hunter, the brigand,
  Did not let me attain as much as my friend,
  Let the hunter never attain as much as his friend!
  Make his advantage vanish, make his strength less!
  [   ] his share from your presence,
70 Let [   ] not enter, let it go out through the window!"
When he had cursed the hunter as much as he wanted,
He decided to curse the harlot too.
  "Come, Shamhat, I shall fix a fate for you!
  [Curses] shall not cease for ever and ever.
75 I shall curse you with a great curse!
  Straight away my curses shall rise up against you!
  You shall never make your house voluptuous again,
  You shall not release [   ] of your young bulls,
  You shall not let them into the girls' rooms.
80 Filth shall impregnate your lovely lap,
  The drunkard shall soak your party dress with vomit,
  [   ] fingers,
  [Your cosmetic paint shall be] the potter's lump of clay,
  You shall never obtain the best cosmetic [oil,]
85 Bright silver, people's affluence, shall not accumulate in your house,
  The [   ] of your [   ] shall be your porch,
  The crossroads shall be your only sitting place,[3]
  Waste ground your only lying place,
  the shade of a city wall your only sitting place.
90 Thorns and spikes shall skin your feet,
  The drunkard and the thirsty shall slap your cheek,
  [   ] shall shout out against you.
  The builder shall never plaster the [walls of your house,]
  Owls will nest [in your roof beams (?),]
95 Feasting shall never take place in your house,

   (about 4 broken lines)

  Because you defiled me when I was pure,
  Because you seduced me in the open country when I was pure."

Shamash heard the utterance of his mouth.
Immediately a loud voice called down to him from the sky:
100   "Enkidu, why are you cursing my harlot Shamhat,
        Who fed you on food fit for gods,
        Gave you ale to drink, fit for kings,
        Clothed you with a great robe,
        Then provided you with Gilgamesh for a fine partner?
105   And now Gilgamesh, the friend who is a brother to you
        Will lay you to rest on a great bed
        And lay you to rest on a bed of loving care,
        And let you stay in a restful dwelling, the dwelling on the left.
        Princes of the earth will kiss your feet.
110   He will make the people of Uruk weep for you, mourn for you,
        Will fill the proud people with woe,
        And he himself will neglect his appearance after you(r death).
        Clothed only in a lionskin, he will roam the open country."
Enkidu listened to the speech of Shamash the warrior.
115   [His anger abated]; his heart became quiet.

            (*about 2 lines missing*)

        "Come, Shamhat, I shall change your fate!
        My utterance, which cursed you, shall bless you instead.
        Governors and princes shall love you,
        The single-league man shall smite his thigh (for you),
120   The double-league man shall shake out his locks (for you).
        The herdsman shall not hold back for you, he shall undo his belt for you.
        He shall give you ivory, lapis lazuli, and gold,
        Rings and brooches shall be presents for you.
        Rain shall pour down for him, his storage jars shall be heaped full.
125   The diviner shall lead you into the palace of the gods.
        Because of you, the mother of seven, the honoured wife, shall be deserted."
Then Enkidu [wept], for he was sick at heart.
[   ] he lay down alone.
He spoke what was in his mind to his friend.
130   "Listen again, my friend! I had a dream in the night.
        The sky called out, the earth replied,
        I was standing in between them.
        There was a young man, whose face was obscured.
        His face was like that of an Anzu-bird.[4]
135   He had the paws of a lion, he had the claws of an eagle.
        He seized me by my locks, using great force against me.
        I hit him, and he jumped like a *keppū*-toy,
        He hit me and forced me down like an [onager],
        Like a wild bull he trampled on me,
140   He squeezed my whole body.
        (I cried out:) 'Save me, my friend, don't desert me!'
        But you were afraid, and did not [help me (?)],
        You [   ].

            (*3 broken lines*)

[He hit me and] turned me into a dove.
145   [   ] my arms, like a bird.
He seized me, drove me down to the dark house, dwelling of Erkalla's god,
To the house which those who enter cannot leave,
On the road where travelling is one way only,
To the house where those who stay are deprived of light,
150   Where dust is their food, and clay their bread.
They are clothed, like birds, with feathers,
And they see no light, and they dwell in darkness.
Over the door [and the bolt, dust has settled.]
I looked at the house that I had entered,
155   And crowns were heaped up.
I [saw] those with crowns who had ruled the land from time
     immemorial,
[Priests of] Anu and Ellil regularly set out cooked meats,
Set out baked bread, set out cold water from waterskins.
In the house of dust that I had entered
160   Dwelt the *enu* and *lagaru*-priests,
Dwelt the *isippu* and *lumahhu*-priests,
Dwelt the *gudapsû*-priests of the great gods,
Dwelt Etana,[5] dwelt Shakkan
Dwelt Ereshkigal, the Queen of Earth.
165   Belet-seri, the scribe of Earth, was kneeling before her.
She was holding [a tablet] and kept reading aloud to her.
She raised her head and looked at me:
'[Who is it who] brought this man?'

          (*gap of about 50 lines*)

    [   ] experienced all kinds of troubles,
170   Remember me, my friend, and do not forget what I went through.
My friend saw an in[describable] dream."
From the day he saw the dream, his [strength] was finished.
Enkidu lay there the first day, then [a second day.]
[The illness] of Enkidu, as he lay in bed, [grew worse, his flesh weaker.]
175   A third day and a fourth day, the [illness] of [Enkidu grew worse, his flesh
     weaker,]
A fifth, sixth and seventh day, eighth, ninth [and tenth.]
The illness of Enkidu [grew worse, his flesh weaker].
An eleventh and twelfth day [his illness grew worse, his flesh weaker.]
Enkidu, as he lay in bed, [   ]
180   Gilgamesh cried out and [   ]
    "My friend is cursing me, [   ]
    Because in the midst of [   ]
    I was afraid of the fight [   ]
    My friend, who [was so strong] in the fight, [cursed me]
185   I, in [   ]

          (*gap of up to 30 lines*)

---

5. A famous ancient hero, subject of his own epic poem.

Tablet VIII

When the first light of dawn appeared
Gilgamesh said to his friend,
    "Enkidu, my friend, your mother a gazelle,
    And your father a wild donkey sired you,

5   Their milk was from onagers; they reared you,
    And cattle made you familiar with all the pastures.
    Enkidu's paths [led to] the Cedar Forest.
    They shall weep for you night and day, never fall silent,
    Weep for you, the elders of the broad city, of Uruk the Sheepfold.

10   The summit will bless (us) after our death,
    They shall weep for you, the [   ]s of the mountains,
    They shall mourn [   ]
    [The open country as if it were your father], the field as if it were your mother.
    They shall weep for you, [myrtle], cypress, and, cedar

15   In the midst of which we armed ourselves in our fury.
    They shall weep for you, the bear, hyena, leopard, tiger, stag, cheetah,
    Lion, wild bulls, deer, mountain goat, cattle, and other wild beasts of open
         country.
    It shall weep for you, the holy river Ulaya, along whose bank
    We used to walk so proudly.

20   It shall weep for you, the pure Euphrates,
    With whose water in waterskins we used to refresh ourselves.
    They shall weep for you, the young men of the broad city, of Uruk the
         Sheepfold,
    Who watched the fighting when we struck down the Bull of Heaven.
    He shall weep for you, the ploughman at [his plough]

25   Who extols your name with sweet Alala.
    He shall weep for you, [   ] of the broad city, of Uruk the Sheepfold,
    Who will extol your name in the first…
    He shall weep for you, the shepherd, the herdsman,
    Who used to make the beer mixture for your mouth.

30   She shall weep for you, [the wet-nurse]
    Who used to put butter on your lower parts.
    He shall weep for you, the elder
    Who used to put ale to your mouth.
    She shall weep for you, the harlot [   ]

35   By whom you were anointed with perfumed oil.
    They shall weep for you, [parents]-in-law
    Who [comfort] the wife…of your loins
    They shall weep for you, the young men, [like brothers]
    They shall weep for you and tear out their hair over you.

40   For you, Enkidu, I, like your mother, your father,
    Will weep on your plains [   ]
    Listen to me, young men, listen to me!
    Listen to me, elders of Uruk, listen to me!
    I myself must weep for Enkidu my friend,

45   Mourn bitterly, like a wailing woman.
    As for the axe at my side, spur to my arm,

The sword in my belt, the shield for my front,
My festival clothes, my manly sash:
Evil [Fate] rose up and robbed me of them.
50 My friend was the hunted mule, wild ass of the mountains, leopard of
     open country.
Enkidu the strong man was the hunted wild ass of [the mountains, leopard
     of open country].
We who met, and scaled the mountain,
Seized the Bull of Heaven and slew it,
Demolished Humbaba the mighty one of the Cedar Forest,
55 Now, what is the sleep that has taken hold of you?
Turn to me, you! You aren't listening to me!
But he cannot lift his head.
I touch his heart, but it does not beat at all."
He covered his friend's face like a daughter-in-law.
60 He circled over him like an eagle,
Like a lioness whose cubs are [trapped] in a pit,
He paced back and forth.
He tore out and spoilt well-curled hair,
He stripped off and threw away finery as if it were taboo.
65 When the first light of dawn appeared, Gilgamesh sent out a shout through
     the land.
The smith, the [   ], the coppersmith, the silversmith, the jeweller
     (were summoned).
He made [a likeness] of his friend, he fashioned a statue of his friend.
The four limbs of the friend were [made of   ], his chest was of lapis
     lazuli,
His skin was of gold [   ]

              (*gap of about 12 lines*)

70 "[I will lay you to rest] on a bed [of loving care]
And will let you stay [in a restful dwelling, a dwelling of the left].
Princes of the earth [will kiss your feet].
I will make the people [of Uruk] weep for you, [mourn for you].
[I will fill] the proud people with sorrow for you.
75 And I myself will neglect my appearance after you(r death)
Clad only in a lionskin, I will roam the open country."
When the first light of dawn appeared
Gilgamesh arose and [went to his treasury],
He undid its fastenings
80 And looked at the treasure.
He brought out carnelian, flint, alabaster,
[*Several fragmentary or missing lines describe Gilgamesh's elaborate offer-
     ings for Enkidu.*]
When the first light of dawn appeared, Gilgamesh opened [   ],
Set out a great table of *elammakku*-wood,
And filled a carnelian bowl with honey,
85 Filled a lapis lazuli bowl with butter.
[   ] he decorated and displayed it to Shamash.

              (*gap of up to 45 lines*)

Tablet IX

Gilgamesh mourned bitterly for Enkidu his friend,
And roamed open country.
    "Shall I die too? Am I not like Enkidu?
    Grief has entered my innermost being,
5   I am afraid of Death, and so I roam open country.
    I shall take the road and go quickly
    To see Ut-napishtim, son of Ubara-Tutu.
    (When) I reached the mountain passes at night,
    I saw lions and was afraid.
10   I raised my head, I prayed to Sin.[6]
    My prayers went to Sin, the [light] of the gods.
      '[   ], keep me safe!'"
[He   ] went to sleep, awoke at a dream
[And   ] was glad to be alive.
15 He took up an axe to his side
Drew the sword [from] his belt.
Like an arrow he fell among them,
Struck [   ], shattered the [   ].
Then [   ] of midday
20 He threw down/gave [   ]
He carved out [   ]
The name of the first [   ]
The name of the second [   ]

(6 lines fragmentary, then about 7 lines missing)

The name of the mountain [is] Mashu.
25 When he reached the mountain Mashu
Which daily guards the coming out [of Shamash]—
Their upper parts [touch] the sky's foundation,
Below, their breasts reach the underworld.
They guard its gate, Scorpion-men
30 Whose aura is frightful, and whose glance is death.
Their terrifying mantles of radiance drape the mountains.
They guard the sun at dawn and dusk—
Gilgamesh looked at them, and fear and terror clouded his face.
He took the initiative and gestured to them in greeting.
35 A Scorpion-man shouted to his woman,
    "Someone has come to us. His body is the flesh of gods."
The Scorpion-man's woman answered him,
    "Two-thirds of him is divine, and one-third of him mortal."
The Scorpion-man, the male, shouted,
40 Addressed his words to [Gilgamesh, the flesh of] gods.
    "[Who are you, that comes to us on] a distant journey?"

(gap of about 20 lines)

"Concerning Ut-napishtim, my father [   ]

---

6. The moon god.

Who stood in the gods' assembly and sought out eternal life.
    Death and Life [   ]."
45 The Scorpion-man made his voice heard and spoke,
    He said to Gilgamesh,
        "It is impossible, Gilgamesh, [   ]
        Nobody has passed through the mountain's inaccessible tract.
        For even after twelve leagues [   ]7
50   The darkness is too dense, there is no [light.]

           (gap of about 27 lines)

    In grief [   ]
    By cold and heat [my face is weathered]
    In exhaustion [   ]
    Now, you [   ]."
55 The Scorpion-man [made his voice heard and spoke],
    [He said to] Gilgamesh the [   ],
        "Go, Gilgamesh, [   ]
        Mashu [   ]
        Mountains [   ]
60   Safely [   ]
        The main gate of the land of [   ]."
    Gilgamesh [listened to the Scorpion-man],
    To the words of [the guardian of the gate].
    The path of Shamash [   ]
65 When he had achieved one league
    The darkness was dense, there was no light,
    It was impossible [for him to see] ahead or behind.
    When he had achieved two leagues

           (gap of about 8 lines)

    [When he had achieved] four leagues, [he hurried on];
70 [The darkness was] still dense, [there was no light],
    It was impossible [for him to see ahead or behind].
    [When he had achieved] five leagues, [he hurried on];
    [The darkness was] still dense, [there was no light],
    It was impossible [for him to see ahead or behind].
75 When [he had achieved six] leagues, [he hurried on];
    The darkness was still dense, [there was no light],
    It was impossible [for him to see ahead or behind].
    When he had achieved seven leagues, [he hurried on];
    The darkness was still dense, [there was] no [light],
80   It was impossible for him [to see] ahead or behind.
    When he had achieved eight leagues, he hurried on;
    The darkness was still dense, there was no light,
    It was [impossible for him to see] ahead or behind.
    [When he had achieved] nine leagues, the north wind [   ]
85   [   ] his face
    [But the darkness was still dense, there was no] light,
    [It was impossible for him to see] ahead or behind.

7 In 70 missing lines Gilgamesh persuades the scorpion-man to let him through.

[When he had] achieved [ten leagues]

[   ] came close.

90 [   ] leagues.

[he] came out in front of the sun.

[   ] brightness was everywhere.

All kinds of [thorny, prickly], spiky bushes were visible, blossoming with
   gemstones.

Carnelian° bore fruit   *a red gemstone*

95 Hanging in clusters, lovely to look at,

Lapis lazuli bore foliage,

Bore fruit, and was delightful to view.

           (gap of about 24 lines)

[   ] pine

Its fronds of banded agate [   ]

100 Sea-*laruššu* [   ] of *sāsu*-stone

Like brambles and thorn bushes [of]...-stone,

Carob trees [of] (green) *abašmû*-stone,

Šubû-stone, haematite [   ]

Riches and wealth [   ]

105 Like [   ] turquoise

Which [   ] the sea.

[   ]

As Gilgamesh walked around [at   ]

He raised [his eyes   ]

Tablet X

Siduri the alewife, who lives down by the sea,

Lives and [   ].

Vat-stands are made for her, [fermentation-vats] are made for her,

Covered by a covering and [   ].

5 Gilgamesh was pacing around and [   ]

Clad only in a (lion)skin [   ]

He had the flesh of gods upon [his body],

But grief was in [his innermost being].

His face was like that of a long-distance traveller.

10 The alewife looked at him from a distance.

She pondered in her heart, and [spoke] a word

To herself, and she [advised herself]:

   "Perhaps this man is an assassin.

   Is he going somewhere in [   ]?"

15 The alewife looked at him and locked [her door],

She locked her door, locked it [with a bolt].

Then he, Gilgamesh, noticed [   ]

Raised his chin and [   ]

Gilgamesh spoke to her, to the alewife;

20   "Alewife, why did you look at me [and lock] your door,

   Lock your door, [lock it] with a bolt?

   I will smash the door, I will shatter [the bolt]!

[We destroyed Humbaba, who lived in the] Cedar Forest.
[We killed] lions at the mountain passes."
25 [The alewife] spoke to him, to Gilgamesh,
"[If you are truly Gilgamesh], that struck down the Guardian,
[Destroyed] Humbaba, who lived in the Cedar Forest,
Killed lions at the mountain [passes],
[Seized the Bull of Heaven who came down from the sky, struck him down],
30 [Why are your cheeks wasted], your face dejected,
[Your heart so wretched, your appearance worn] out,
[And grief] in your innermost being?
Your face is like that of a long-distance traveller,
Your face is weathered by [cold and heat...],
35 [Clad only in a lionskin] you roam open country."
[Gilgamesh spoke to her, to Siduri the alewife],
"[How could my cheeks not be wasted, nor my face dejected],
[Nor my heart wretched, nor my appearance worn out],
[Nor grief in my innermost being],
40 [Nor my face like that of a long-distance traveller],
[Nor my face weathered by cold and heat...],
[Nor roaming open country, clad only in a lionskin?]
[My friend whom I love so much, who experienced every hardship with me],
[Enkidu, whom I love so much, who experienced every hardship with me—]
45 [The fate of mortals conquered him!] Six days [and seven nights I wept over him],
[I did not allow him to] be buried, [until a worm fell out of his nose].
[I was frightened and   ].
I am afraid of Death, [and so I roam open country].
The words of my friend [weigh upon me].
50 [I roam open country] for long distances; the words of my friend Enkidu weigh upon me.
I roam open country on long journeys.
[How, O how] could I stay silent, how, O how could I keep quiet [   ]?
My friend whom I love has turned to clay: Enkidu my friend whom I love [has turned to clay].
Am I not like him? Must I lie down too,
55 Never to rise, ever again?"[8]
Gilgamesh spoke to her, to the alewife,
"Now, alewife, which is the way to Ut-napishtim?
Give me directions, [whatever they are]; give me directions.
If it is possible, I shall cross the sea;
60 If it is impossible I shall roam open country again."
The alewife spoke to him, to Gilgamesh,
"There has never been a ferry of any kind, Gilgamesh,
And nobody from time immemorial has crossed the sea.
Shamash the warrior is the only one who has crossed the sea:
apart from Shamash, nobody has crossed the sea.
65 The crossing is difficult, the way of it very difficult,

---

8. The text omits a reply by the alewife. In the Old Babylonian version, she had urged Gilgamesh not to worry about death but to be content with the pleasures of life.

And in between are lethal waters which bar the way ahead.
Wherever, then, could you cross the sea, Gilgamesh?
And once you reached the lethal waters, what would you do?
(Yet) there is, Gilgamesh, a boatman of Ut-napishtim, Ur-shanabi,
70 He—the 'things of stone'° identify him—   *punting poles (?)*
  will be trimming a young pine in the forest.
 Go, and let him see your face.
 If it is possible, cross with him. If it is impossible, retreat back."
When Gilgamesh heard this
75 He took up an axe to his side,
Drew the sword from his belt,
Stole up and drove them off,
Like an arrow he fell among them.
In the midst of the forest the noise resounded.
80 Ur-shanabi looked and drew his sword,
Took up an axe and [crept up on (?)] him.
Then he, Gilgamesh, hit him on the head,
Seized his arms and [   ] of his chest.
And the "things of stone" [   ] the boat,
85 Which do not [   ] lethal [waters]
[   ] broad [sea]
In the waters [   ] held back.
He smashed [them and   ] to the river.
[   ] the boat
90 And [   ] on the bank.
[Gilgamesh spoke to him, to Ur-shanabi] the boatman,
  "[   ] I shall enter
  [   ] to you."
Ur-shanabi spoke to him, to Gilgamesh,
95 "Why are your cheeks wasted, your face dejected,
  Your heart so wretched, your appearance worn out,
  And grief in your innermost being?
  Your face is like that of a long-distance traveller.
  Your face is weathered by cold and heat [ ]
100 Clad only in a lionskin, you roam open country."
Gilgamesh spoke to him, to Ur-shanabi the boatman,
  "How could my cheeks not be wasted, nor my face dejected,
  Nor my heart wretched, nor my appearance worn out,
  Nor grief in my innermost being,
105 Nor my face like that of a long-distance traveller,
  Nor my face weathered by wind and heat [ ]
  Nor roaming open country clad only in a lionskin?
  My friend was the hunted mule, wild ass of the mountain, leopard of open
   country,
  Enkidu my friend was the hunted mule, wild ass of the mountain, leopard
   of open country.
110 We who met, and scaled the mountain,
  Seized the Bull of Heaven and slew it,
  Demolished Humbaba who dwelt in the Cedar Forest,
  Killed lions in the passes of the mountains,

My friend whom I love so much, who experienced every hardship with me,
115 Enkidu my friend whom I love so much, who experienced every hardship
with me—
The fate of mortals conquered him!
For six days and seven nights I wept over him: I did not allow him to be buried
Until a worm fell out of his nose.
I was frightened and [   ].
120 I am afraid of Death, and so I roam open country.
The words of my friend weigh upon me.
I roam open country for long distances; the words of Enkidu my friend
weigh upon me.
I roam open country on long journeys.
How, O how could I stay silent, how, O how could I keep quiet?
125 My friend whom I love has turned to clay: Enkidu my friend whom I love
has turned to clay.
Am I not like him? Must I lie down too,
Never to rise, ever again?"
Gilgamesh spoke to him, to Ur-shanabi the boatman,
"Now, Ur-shanabi, which is the way to Ut-napishtim?
130 Give me directions, whatever they are; give me directions.
If it is possible, I shall cross the sea;
If it is impossible, I shall roam open country again."
Ur-shanabi spoke to him, to Gilgamesh,
"Your own hands, Gilgamesh, have hindered [   ],
135 You have smashed the 'things of stone,' you have [   ].
The 'things of stone' are smashed, and their strings are pulled out.
Take up an axe, Gilgamesh, to your side,
Go down to the forest, [cut] three hundred poles each thirty metres (long).
Trim (them) and put 'knobs' (on them); then bring them to me [at the
boat]."
140 When Gilgamesh heard this,
He took up an axe to his side, drew a sword from his belt,
Went down to the forest and [cut] three hundred poles each thirty metres (long).
He trimmed (them) and put "knobs" (on them): he brought them [to
Ur-shanabi at the boat]
And Gilgamesh and Ur-shanabi embarked [in the boat(s)].
145 They cast off the *magillu*-boat and sailed away.
(After) a journey of a new moon and a full moon, on the third day [   ]
Ur-shanabi reached the lethal waters,
Ur-shanabi spoke to him, to Gilgamesh,
"Stay clear, Gilgamesh, take one pole at a time,
150 Don't let the lethal water wet your hand! [Hold] the knob!
Take a second, a third, then a fourth pole, Gilgamesh.
Take a fifth, a sixth, then a seventh pole, Gilgamesh.
Take an eighth, a ninth, then a tenth pole, Gilgamesh.
Take an eleventh, a twelfth pole, Gilgamesh."
155 Within seven hundred and twenty metres Gilgamesh had used up the poles.
Then he undid his belt, [   ]
Gilgamesh stripped himself; [   ]
With his arms he lifted up the cloth.

Ut-napishtim was looking on from a distance,
160   Pondered and spoke to himself,
Took counsel with himself:
    "Why are the [things of stone] broken,
    And the wrong gear aboard [   ]?
    Surely it can't be my man coming on? And on the right [   ].
165   I am looking, but I can't make [it out],
    I am looking, but [   ]
    I am looking, [   ]

(gap of about 20 lines, in which Gilgamesh comes ashore)

[Ut-napishtim spoke to him, to Gilgamesh],
    ["Why are your cheeks wasted, your face dejected],
170   [Your heart so wretched, your appearance worn out],
    [And grief in your innermost being]?
    [Your face is like that of a long-distance traveller].
    [Your face is weathered by cold and heat...]
    [Clad only in a lionskin you roam open country]."
175 [Gilgamesh spoke to him, to Ut-napishtim],
    ["How would my cheeks not be wasted, nor my face dejected],
    [Nor my heart wretched, nor] my appearance [worn out],
    [Nor grief in] my innermost being,
    [Nor] my face like [that of a long-distance traveller],
180   [Nor] my face [weathered by cold and heat...]
    [Nor] roaming open country [clad only in a lionskin]?
    My friend was the hunted mule, wild ass of the mountain, leopard of open
        country,
    Enkidu my friend was the hunted mule, wild ass of the mountain, leopard
        of open country.
    We who met and scaled the mountain,
185   Seized the Bull of Heaven and slew it,
    Demolished Humbaba who dwelt in the Cedar Forest,
    Killed lions in the passes of the mountains,
    My friend whom I love so much, who experienced every hardship with me,
    Enkidu my friend whom I love so much, who experienced every hardship
        with me—
190   The fate of mortals conquered him! For six days and seven nights I wept
        over him,
    I did not allow him to be buried
    Until a worm fell out of his nose.
    I was frightened [   ]. I am afraid of Death, [and so I roam open country].
    I roam open country for long distances;
195   The words of my friend weigh upon me.
    The words of Enkidu my friend weigh upon me.
    I roam the open country on long journeys.
    How, O how could I stay silent, how, O how could I keep quiet?
    My friend whom I love has turned to clay: Enkidu my friend whom I love
        has turned to clay.
200   Am I not like him? Must I lie down too,
    Never to rise, ever again?"

Gilgamesh spoke to him, to Ut-napishtim,
 "So I thought I would go to see Ut-napishtim the far-distant, of whom
  people speak.
 I searched, went through all countries,
205 Passed through and through difficult lands,
 And crossed to and fro all seas.
 My face never had enough of sweet sleep,
 My fibre was filled with grief.
 I made myself over-anxious by lack of sleep.
210 What did I gain from my toils?
 I did not make a good impression on the alewife, for my clothes were
  finished.
 I killed a bear, hyena, lion, leopard, tiger, deer, mountain goat, cattle, and
  other wild beasts of open country.
 I ate meat from them, I spread out their skins.
 Let her door be bolted against grief with pitch and bitumen!
215 Because of me, games are spoiled [   ],
 My own misfortunes have reduced me to misery."
Ut-napishtim spoke to him, to Gilgamesh,
 "Why do you prolong grief, Gilgamesh?
 Since [the gods made you] from the flesh of gods and mankind,
220 Since [the gods] made you like your father and mother,
 [Death is inevitable] at some time, both for Gilgamesh and for a fool,
 But a throne is set down [for you] in the assembly [ ].
 To a fool is given dregs instead of butter,
 Rubbish and sweepings which like [ ]
225 Clothed in a loincloth like [ ]
 Like a belt [   ]
 Because he has no [sense]
 Has no word of advice [ ]."
Gilgamesh raised his head,

     (17 broken lines)

230 "[Why] have you exerted yourself? What have you achieved?
 You have made yourself weary for lack of sleep,
 You only fill your flesh with grief,
 You only bring the distant days (of reckoning) closer.
 Mankind's fame is cut down like reeds in a reed-bed.
235 A fine young man, a fine girl,
 [   ] of Death.
 Nobody sees Death,
 Nobody sees the face of Death,
 Nobody hears the voice of Death.
240 Savage Death just cuts mankind down.
 Sometimes we build a house, sometimes we make a nest,
 But then brothers divide it upon inheritance.
 Sometimes there is hostility in [the land],
 But then the river rises and brings flood-water.
245 Dragonflies drift on the river,
 Their faces look upon the face of the Sun,

(But then) suddenly there is nothing.
The sleeping (?) and the dead are just like each other,
Death's picture cannot be drawn.
250 The primitive man (is as any) young man. When they blessed me,
The Anunnaki, the great gods, assembled;
Mammitum who creates fate decreed destinies with them.
They appointed death and life.
They did not mark out days for death,
255 But they did so for life."

Tablet XI

Gilgamesh spoke to him, to Ut-napishtim the far-distant,
"I look at you, Ut-napishtim
And your limbs are no different—you are just like me.
Indeed, you are not at all different—you are just like me.
5 I feel the urge to prove myself against you, to pick a fight.
[   ] you lie on your back.
[   ] how you came to stand in the gods' assembly and sought eternal life?"
Ut-napishtim spoke to him, to Gilgamesh,
"Let me reveal to you a closely guarded matter, Gilgamesh,
10 And let me tell you the secret of the gods.
Shuruppak is a city that you yourself know,
Situated [on the bank of] the Euphrates.
That city was already old when the gods within it
Decided that the great gods should make a flood.
15 There was Anu their father,
Warrior Ellil their counsellor,
Ninurta was their chamberlain,
Ennugi their canal-controller.
Far-sighted Ea swore the oath (of secrecy) with them,
20 So he repeated their speech to a reed hut,
'Reed hut, reed hut, brick wall, brick wall,
Listen, reed hut, and pay attention, brick wall:
(This is the message:)
Man of Shuruppak, son of Ubara-Tutu,
25 Dismantle your house, build a boat.
Leave possessions, search out living things.
Reject chattels and save lives!
Put aboard the seed of all living things, into the boat.
The boat that you are to build
30 Shall have her dimensions in proportion,
Her width and length shall be in harmony,
Roof her like the Apsu.'
I realized and spoke to my master Ea,
'I have paid attention to the words that you spoke in this way,
35 My master, and I shall act upon them.
But how can I explain myself to the city, the men and the elders?'
Ea made his voice heard and spoke,
He said to me, his servant,

'You shall speak to them thus:

40 "I think that Ellil has rejected me,
And so I cannot stay in your city,
And I cannot set foot on Ellil's land again.
I must go down to the Apsu° and stay with my master Ea.   *underworld sea*
Then he will shower abundance upon you,

45 A wealth of fowl, a treasure of fish.
[   ] prosperity, a harvest,
In the morning cakes he will shower down upon you,
And in the evening, a rain of wheat!"
When the first light of dawn appeared

50 The country gathered about me.
The carpenter brought his axe,
The reed-worker brought his stone,
The young men [   ]
[   ] oakum

55 Children carried the bitumen,
The poor fetched what was needed [   ].
On the fifth day I laid down her form.
One acre was her circumference, ten poles each the height of her walls,
Her top edge was likewise ten poles[9] all round.

60 I laid down her structure, drew it out,
Gave her six decks,
Divided her into seven.
Her middle I divided into nine,
Drove the water pegs into her middle.

65 I saw to the paddles and put down what was needed:
Three *sar* of bitumen I poured into the kiln,
Three *sar* of pitch I poured into the inside.
Three *sar* of oil they fetched, the workmen who carried the baskets.
Not counting the *sar* of oil which the dust soaked up,

70 The boatman stowed away two more *sar* of oil.
At the [   ] I slaughtered oxen.
I sacrificed sheep every day.
I gave the workmen ale and beer to drink,
Oil and wine as if they were river water

75 They made a feast, like the New Year's Day festival.
When the sun [rose] I provided hand oil.
[When] the sun went down the boat was complete.
[The launching was] very difficult;
Launching rollers had to be fetched (from) above (to) below.

80 Two-thirds of it [stood clear of the water line].
I loaded her with everything there was,
Loaded her with all the silver,
Loaded her with all the gold

---

9. The boat is described as a cube 80 feet on a side, making it a cross between a boat and a ziggurat, a pyramidal temple tower often with seven levels.

Loaded her with all the seed of living things, all of them.
85 I put on board the boat all my kith and kin.
Put on board cattle from open country, wild beasts from open country, all
    kinds of craftsmen.
Shamash had fixed the hour:
'In the morning cakes,
In the evening a rain of wheat
90 (I) shall shower down:
Enter into the boat and shut your door!'
That hour arrived;
In the morning cakes, in the evening a rain of wheat
    showered down.
I saw the shape of the storm,
95 The storm was terrifying to see.
I went aboard the boat and closed the door.
To seal the boat I handed over the (floating) palace with her cargo to
    Puzur-Amurru the boatman.
When the first light of dawn appeared,
A black cloud came up from the base of the sky.
100 Adad° kept rumbling inside it.   *storm god*
Shullat and Hanish were marching ahead,
Marched as chamberlains over mountain and country.
Erakal° pulled out the mooring poles,   *god of death*
Ninurta° marched on and made the weirs overflow.   *god of war*
105 The Anunnaki had to carry torches,
They lit up the land with their brightness.
The calm before the Storm-god came over the sky,
Everything light turned to darkness.
[   ]
110 On the first day the tempest [rose up],
Blew swiftly and [brought the flood-weapon],
Like a battle force [the destructive *kašūšu*-weapon] passed over
    [the people]
No man could see his fellow,
Nor could people be distinguished from the sky.
115 Even the gods were afraid of the flood-weapon.
They withdrew; they went up to the heaven of Anu.
The gods cowered, like dogs crouched by an outside wall.
Ishtar screamed like a woman giving birth;
The Mistress of the Gods, sweet of voice, was wailing,
120 'Has that time really returned to clay,
Because I spoke evil in the gods' assembly?
How could I have spoken such evil in the gods' assembly?
I should have ordered a battle to destroy my people;
I myself gave birth (to them), they are my own people,
125 Yet they fill the sea like fish spawn!'
The gods of the Anunnaki° were weeping with her.   *underworld gods*
The gods, humbled, sat there weeping.

Their lips were closed and covered with scab.
For six days and [seven] nights
130 The wind blew, flood and tempest overwhelmed the land;
When the seventh day arrived the tempest, flood and onslaught
Which had struggled like a woman in labour, blew themselves out.
The sea became calm, the *imhullu*-wind grew quiet, the flood held back.
I looked at the weather; silence reigned,
135 For all mankind had returned to clay.
The flood-plain was flat as a roof.
I opened a porthole and light fell on my cheeks.
I bent down, then sat. I wept.
My tears ran down my cheeks.
140 I looked for banks, for limits to the sea.
Areas of land were emerging everywhere.
The boat had come to rest on Mount Nimush.[1]
The mountain Nimush held the boat fast and did not let it budge.
The first and second day the mountain Nimush held the boat fast and did
not let it budge.
145 The third and fourth day the mountain Nimush held the boat fast and did
not let it budge.
The fifth and sixth day the mountain Nimush held the boat fast and did
not let it budge.
When the seventh day arrived,
I put out and released a dove.
The dove went; it came back,
150 For no perching place was visible to it, and it turned round.
I put out and released a swallow.
The swallow went; it came back,
For no perching place was visible to it, and it turned round.
I put out and released a raven.
155 The raven went, and saw the waters receding.
And it ate, preened, lifted its tail and did not turn round.
Then I put everything out to the four winds, and I made a sacrifice,
Set out a *surqinnu*-offering upon the mountain peak,
Arranged the jars seven and seven;
160 Into the bottom of them I poured essences of reeds, pine, and myrtle.
The gods smelt the fragrance,
The gods smelt the pleasant fragrance,
The gods like flies gathered over the sacrifice.
As soon as the Mistress of the Gods arrived
165 She raised the great flies which Anu had made to please her:
'Behold, O gods, I shall never forget (the significance of) my lapis lazuli
necklace,
I shall remember these times, and I shall never forget.
Let other gods come to the *surqinnu*-offering
But let Ellil not come to the *surqinnu*-offering,
170 Because he did not consult before imposing the flood,
And consigned my people to destruction!'

1. Likely a 9,000-foot mountain on the Persian border of northeastern Iraq.

As soon as Ellil arrived

He saw the boat. Ellil was furious,

Filled with anger at the Igigi gods.°   *sky gods*

175   'What sort of life survived? No man should have lived through the
           destruction!'

Ninurta made his voice heard and spoke,

He said to the warrior Ellil,

'Who other than Ea would have done such a thing?

For Ea can do everything!'

180   Ea made his voice heard and spoke,

He said to the warrior Ellil,

'You are the sage of the gods, warrior,

So how, O how, could you fail to consult, and impose the flood?

Punish the sinner for his sin, punish the criminal for his crime,

185   But ease off, let work not cease; be patient, let not [   ]

Instead of your imposing a flood, let a lion come up and diminish the
           people.

Instead of your imposing a flood, let a wolf come up and diminish the
           people.

Instead of your imposing a flood, let famine be imposed and [lessen] the land.

Instead of your imposing a flood, let Erra rise up and savage the people.

190   I did not disclose the secret of the great gods,

I just showed Atrahasis[2] a dream, and thus he heard the secret of the gods.'

Now the advice (that prevailed) was his advice.

Ellil came up into the boat,

And seized my hand and led me up.

195   He led up my woman and made her kneel down at my side.

He touched our foreheads, stood between us, blessed us:

'Until now Ut-napishtim was mortal,

But henceforth Ut-napishtim and his woman shall be as we gods are.

Ut-napishtim shall dwell far off at the mouth of the rivers.'

200   They took me and made me dwell far off, at the mouth of the rivers.

So now, who can gather the gods on your behalf, (Gilgamesh),

That you too may find eternal life which you seek?

For a start, you must not sleep for six days and seven nights."

As soon as he was sitting, (his head?) between his knees,

205   Sleep breathed over him like a fog.

Ut-napishtim spoke to her, to his wife,

"Look at the young man who wants eternal life!

Sleep breathes over him like a fog!"

His wife spoke to him, to Ut-napishtim the far-distant,

210   "Touch him, and let the man wake up.

Let him go back in peace the way he came,

Go back to his country through the great gate, through which he once left."

Ut-napishtim spoke to her, to his wife,

"Man behaves badly: he will behave badly towards you.

215   For a start, bake a daily portion for him, put it each time by his head,

And mark on the wall the days that he sleeps."

2. "Exceedingly Wise," the hero of an earlier poem on the flood story, a source for this tablet; here written by mistake for
"Ut-napishtim" or else deliberately used as an alternate name.

She baked a daily portion for him, put it each time by his head,
And marked on the wall for him the days that he slept.
His first day's portion was dried out,
220 The second was going bad, the third was soggy,
The fourth had white mould on
The fifth had discoloured,
The sixth was stinking,
The seventh—at that moment he touched him and the man woke up.
225 Gilgamesh spoke to him, to Ut-napishtim the far-distant,
 "No sooner had sleep come upon me
 Than you touched me, straight away, and roused me!"
Ut-napishtim spoke to him, to Gilgamesh,
 "[Look, Gil]gamesh, count your daily portions,
230 [That the number of days you slept] may be proved to you.
 Your [first] day's ration [is dried out],
 The second is going bad, the third is soggy,
 The fourth has white mould on,
 The fifth has discoloured, the sixth is stinking,
235 [The seventh—] at that moment you woke up."
Gilgamesh spoke to him, to Ut-napishtim the far-distant,
 "How, O how could I have done it, Ut-napishtim? Wherever can I go?
 The Snatchers have blocked my [routes]:
 Death is waiting in my bedroom,
240 And wherever I set my foot, Death is there too."
Ut-napishtim spoke to him, to Ur-shanabi the boatman,
 "Ur-shanabi, the quay will cast you out, the ferry will reject you.
 Be deprived of her side, at whose side you once went.
 The man whom you led: filthy hair fetters his body,
245 Skins have ruined the beauty of his flesh.
 Take him, Ur-shanabi, bring him to a wash-bowl,
 And let him wash in water his filthy hair, as clean as possible.
 Let him throw away his skins, and let the sea carry them off.
 Let his body be soaked (until it is) fresh.
250 Put a new headband on his head.
 Have him wear a robe as a proud garment
 Until he comes to his city,
 Until he reaches his journey's end.
 The garment shall not discolour, but stay absolutely new."
255 Ur-shanabi took him and brought him to a wash-bowl,
And he washed in water his filthy hair, as clean as possible.
He threw away his skins, and the sea carried them off.
His body was soaked (until it was) fresh.
He put a new headband on his head.
260 He wore a robe as a proud garment
Until he came to his city,
Until he reached his journey's end.
The garment would not discolour, and stayed absolutely new.
Gilgamesh and Ur-shanabi embarked on the boat.
265 They cast off the *magillu*-boat and sailed away.
His wife spoke to him, to Ut-napishtim the far-distant,

"Gilgamesh came, weary, striving,
What will you give him to take back to his country?"
And Gilgamesh out there raised the pole,
270　He brought the boat near the shore.
Ut-napishtim spoke to him, to Gilgamesh,
"Gilgamesh, you came, weary, striving,
What can I give you to take back to your country?
Let me reveal a closely guarded matter, Gilgamesh,
275　And let me tell you the secret of the gods.
There is a plant whose root is like camel-thorn,
Whose thorn, like a rose's, will spike [your hands].
If you yourself can win that plant, you will find [rejuvenation]."
When Gilgamesh heard this, he opened the pipe,
280　He tied heavy stones to his feet.
They dragged him down into the Apsu, and [he saw the plant].
He took the plant himself: it spiked [his hands].
He cut the heavy stones from his feet.
The sea threw him up on to its shore.
285　Gilgamesh spoke to him, to Ur-shanabi the boatman,
"Ur-shanabi, this plant is a plant to cure a crisis!
With it a man may win the breath of life.
I shall take it back to Uruk the Sheepfold; I shall give it to an elder to eat,
and so try out the plant.
Its name shall be: 'An old man grows into a young man.'[3]
290　I too shall eat it and turn into the young man that I once was,"
At twenty leagues they ate their ration.
At thirty leagues they stopped for the night.
Gilgamesh saw a pool whose water was cool,
And went down into the water and washed.
295　A snake smelt the fragrance of the plant.
It came up silently and carried off the plant.
As it took it away, it shed its scaly skin.
Thereupon Gilgamesh sat down and wept.
His tears flowed over his cheeks.
300　[He spoke to] Ur-shanabi the boatman,
"For what purpose, Ur-shanabi, have my arms grown weary?
For what purpose was the blood inside me so red?
I did not gain an advantage for myself,
I have given the advantage to the 'lion of the ground.'
305　Now the current will carry twenty leagues away.
While I was opening the pipe, [arranging] the gear,
I found a door-thong which must have been set there as an omen for me.
I shall give up.
And I have left the boat on the shore."
At twenty leagues they ate their ration.
310　At thirty leagues they stopped for the night.
They reached Uruk the Sheepfold.
Gilgamesh spoke to him, to Ur-shanabi the boatman,
"Go up on to the wall of Uruk, Ur-shanabi, and walk around,

3. This is probably the meaning of "Gilgamesh" in Sumerian.

Inspect the foundation platform and scrutinize the brickwork! Testify that
    its bricks are baked bricks,
315   And that the Seven Counsellors must have laid its foundations!
    One square mile is city, one square mile is orchards, one square mile is
    claypits, as well as the open ground of Ishtar's temple.
    Three square miles and the open ground comprise Uruk."

GENESIS 1–11 ■ (1st millennium B.C.E.)

The first eleven chapters of the Book of Genesis form a prologue for the entire Torah, the five books of Moses that begin the Hebrew Bible. In setting the stage for the national history that begins with Abraham in Genesis 12, the authors of Genesis reached back to old traditions of creation and of a primeval flood that was believed to have extinguished the ancient earthly order, after which modern societies began to be established. The biblical authors knew older versions of such stories, such as those found in the Babylonian *Enuma Elish* and *Epic of Gilgamesh,* yet they wished to tell the stories differently. First and most importantly, the older accounts had assumed a polytheistic universe, in which humanity was created to serve an entire pantheon of gods, whose disputes could be seen as causing earthly disruptions. Second, the older stories typically stemmed from long-settled civilizations based around great cities—a social order foreign to the nomadic Hebrews, who remained deeply suspicious of city culture and of elaborate social hierarchies even after they had begun to form a united kingdom of Israel, centered on their capital city of Jerusalem.

In comparison to works like *Enuma Elish,* Genesis 1–11 is notable for the absence of war in heaven, or even any multiplicity of divine beings: Genesis 1 goes so far as to give no name at all to the sun and moon—major divinities in earlier systems—simply calling them "the great light" and "the small light." Similarly, the ocean goddess Tiamat is demoted to an impersonal watery abyss, her name made into a common noun, *tehom* in Hebrew. At the same time, the absence of rival divinities like Tiamat posed a challenge for the biblical writers: with the entire universe firmly ruled by a single and just God, how could evil ever have come into the world? The story of the Garden of Eden—one of the most resonant stories in the history of Judeo-Christian culture—explores this problem in an enigmatic tale of prohibition, confusion, and disobedience, with the human actors manipulated by a serpent who is "cunning" rather than evil. Going on to the Flood story, the biblical writers saw human wickedness as the cause of this natural disaster, in contrast to the older Babylonian account, in which the gods had simply gotten tired of the noise made by the growing earthly population. Noah himself, like the patriarchs and matriarchs of later Hebrew history, becomes a complex figure who fails to fully maintain his covenant with God. The primeval history concludes with the building of the Tower of Babel—not as the triumphal inauguration of human culture, as with the construction of Babylon in *Enuma Elish,* but as an impious act of defiance to God.

Most biblical scholars consider that this sequence of stories is the product of several stages of development, reflecting successive reworkings of the old stories. The initial account, known as the Yahwistic version (from God's name *Yahweh*), was probably written down around the time of King Solomon in the early tenth century B.C.E. This version was evidently revised by later writers, most notably a writer or group of writers whom modern scholars have named the Priestly source; Genesis 1 is a product of this source, which emphasizes God's serene ordering power. Genesis 2 then picks up the older Yahwistic creation account, portraying a more mysterious and tentative relationship between God and his creation.

The stories of Genesis are distinctive in form as well as in content. The older Babylonian epics are all written in verse, reflecting long histories of literacy and poetic development; Genesis is in prose, reflecting years of oral storytelling in tents and around campfires. Robert Alter's lively translation beautifully captures the oral immediacy of the biblical creation story.

from Genesis

Chapter 1

When God began to create heaven and earth, and the earth then was welter and waste and darkness over the deep and God's breath hovering over the waters, God said, "Let there be light." And there was light. And God saw the light, that it was good, and God divided the light from the darkness. And God called the light Day, and the darkness He called Night. And it was evening and it was morning, first day. And God said, "Let there be a vault in the midst of the waters, and let it divide water from water." And God made the vault and it divided the water beneath the vault from the water above the vault, and so it was. And God called the vault Heavens, and it was evening and it was morning, second day. And God said, "Let the waters under the heavens be gathered in one place so that the dry land will appear," and so it was. And God called the dry land Earth and the gathering of waters He called Seas, and God saw that it was good. And God said, "Let the earth grow grass, plants yielding seed of each kind and trees bearing fruit of each kind, that has its seed within it." And so it was. And the earth put forth grass, plants yielding seed of each kind, and trees bearing fruit that has its seed within it of each kind, and God saw that it was good. And it was evening and it was morning, third day. And God said, "Let there be lights in the vault of the heavens to divide the day from the night, and they shall be signs for the fixed times and for days and years, and they shall be lights in the vault of the heavens to light up the earth." And so it was. And God made the two great lights, the great light for dominion of day and the small light for dominion of night, and the stars. And God placed them in the vault of the heavens to light up the earth and to have dominion over day and night and to divide the light from the darkness. And God saw that it was good. And it was evening and it was morning, fourth day. And God said, "Let the waters swarm with the swarm of living creatures and let fowl fly over the earth across the vault of the heavens." And God created the great sea monsters and every living creature that crawls, which the water had swarmed forth of each kind, and the winged fowl of each kind, and God saw that it was good. And God blessed them, saying, "Be fruitful and multiply and fill the water in the seas and let the fowl multiply in the earth." And it was evening and it was morning, fifth day. And God said, "Let the earth bring forth living creatures of each kind, cattle and crawling things and wild beasts of each kind." And so it was. And God made wild beasts of each kind and cattle of every kind and crawling things on the ground of each kind, and God saw that it was good.

And God said, "Let us make a human in our image, by our likeness, to hold sway over the fish of the sea and the fowl of the heavens and the cattle and the wild beasts and all the crawling things that crawl upon the earth.

> And God created the human in his image,
> in the image of God He created him,
> male and female He created them.

And God blessed them, and God said to them, "Be fruitful and multiply and fill the earth and conquer it, and hold sway over the fish of the sea and the fowl of the heavens and every beast that crawls upon the earth." And God said, "Look, I have given you every seed-bearing plant on the face of all the earth and every tree that has fruit bearing seed, yours they will be for food. And to all the beasts of the earth and to all the fowl of the heavens and to all that crawls on the earth, which has the breath of life within it, the green plants for food." And so it was. And God saw all that He had done, and, look, it was very good. And it was evening and it was morning, the sixth day.

Chapter 2

Then the heavens and the earth were completed, and all their array. And God completed on the seventh day the work He had done, and He ceased on the seventh day from all the work He had done. And God blessed the seventh day and hallowed it, for on it He had ceased from all His work that He had done. This is the tale of the heavens and the earth when they were created.

On the day the LORD God made earth and heavens, no shrub of the field being yet on the earth and no plant of the field yet sprouted, for the LORD God had not caused rain to fall on the earth and there was no human to till the soil, and wetness would well from the earth to water all the surface of the soil, then the LORD God fashioned the human, humus from the soil,[1] and blew into his nostrils the breath of life, and the human became a living creature. And the LORD God planted a garden in Eden, to the east, and He placed there the human He had fashioned. And the LORD God caused to sprout from the soil every tree lovely to look at and good for food, and the tree of life was in the midst of the garden, and the tree of knowledge, good and evil. Now a river runs out of Eden to water the garden and from there splits off into four streams. The name of the first is Pishon, the one that winds through the whole land of Havilah, where there is gold. And the gold of that land is goodly, bdellium is there, and lapis lazuli. And the name of the second river is Gihon, the one that winds through all the land of Cush. And the name of the third river is Tigris, the one that goes to the east of Ashur. And the fourth river is Euphrates.[2] And the LORD God took the human and set him down in the garden of Eden to till it and watch it. And the LORD God commanded the human, saying, "From every fruit of the garden you may surely eat. But from the tree of knowledge, good and evil, you shall not eat, for on the day you eat from it, you are doomed to die."

And the LORD God said, "It is not good for the human to be alone, I shall make him a sustainer beside him." And the LORD God fashioned from the soil each beast of the field and each fowl of the heavens and brought each to the human to see what he would call it, and whatever the human called a living creature, that was its name. And the human called names to all the cattle and to the fowl of the heavens and to all the beasts of the field, but for the human no sustainer beside him was found. And the LORD God cast a deep slumber on the human, and he slept, and He took one of his ribs and closed over the flesh where it had been, and the LORD God built the rib He had taken from the human into a woman and He brought her to the human. And the human said:

> This one at last, bone of my bones
> and flesh of my flesh,
> This one shall be called Woman,
> for from man was this one taken.[3]

1. The punning "human/humus" reflects the play in Hebrew between *adam*, "person," and *adamah*, "earth."
2. These rivers place Eden in southern Mesopotamia.
3. In Hebrew, "man" is *ish*, "woman" is *ishshah*.

Therefore does a man leave his father and his mother and cling to his wife and they become one flesh. And the two of them were naked, the human and his woman, and they were not ashamed.

Chapter 3

Now the serpent was most cunning of all the beasts of the field that the Lord God had made. And he said to the woman, "Though God said, you shall not eat from any tree of the garden—" And the woman said to the serpent, "From the fruit of the garden's trees we may eat, but from the fruit of the tree in the midst of the garden God has said, 'You shall not eat from it and you shall not touch it, lest you die.'" And the serpent said to the woman, "You shall not be doomed to die. For God knows that on the day you eat of it your eyes will be opened and you will become as gods knowing good and evil." And the woman saw that the tree was good for eating and that it was lust to the eyes and the tree was lovely to look at, and she took of its fruit and ate, and she also gave to her man, and he ate. And the eyes of the two were opened, and they knew they were naked, and they sewed fig leaves and made themselves loincloths.

And they heard the sound of the Lord God walking about in the garden in the evening breeze, and the human and his woman hid from the Lord God in the midst of the trees of the garden. And the Lord God called to the human and said to him, "Where are you?" And he said, "I heard your sound in the garden and I was afraid, for I was naked, and I hid." And He said, "Who told you that you were naked? From the tree I commanded you not to eat have you eaten?" And the human said, "The woman whom you gave by me, she gave me from the tree, and I ate." And the Lord God said to the woman, "What is this you have done?" And the woman said, "The serpent beguiled me and I ate." And the Lord God said to the serpent, "Because you have done this,

> Cursed be you
> of all cattle and all beasts of the field.
> On your belly shall you go
> and dust shall you eat all the days of your life.
> Enmity will I set between you and the woman,
> between your seed and hers.
> He will boot your head
> and you will bite his heel."

To the woman He said,

> "I will terribly sharpen your birth pangs,
> in pain shall you bear children.
> And for your man shall be your longing,
> and he shall rule over you."

And to the human he said, "Because you listened to the voice of your wife and ate from the tree that I commanded you, 'You shall not eat from it,'

> Cursed be the soil for your sake,
> with pangs shall you eat from it all the days of your life.
> Thorn and thistle shall it sprout for you
> and you shall eat the plants of the field.
> By the sweat of your brow shall you eat bread

>   till you return to the soil,
>   for from there were you taken,
>   for dust you are
>   and to dust shall you return."

And the human called his woman's name Eve, for she was the mother of all that lives.[4] And the LORD God made skin coats for the human and his woman, and He clothed them. And the LORD God said, "Now that the human has become like one of us, knowing good and evil, he may reach out and take as well from the tree of life and live forever." And the LORD God sent him from the garden of Eden to till the soil from which he had been taken. And he drove out the human and set up east of the garden of Eden the cherubim and the flame of the whirling sword to guard the way to the tree of life.

Chapter 4

And the human knew Eve his woman and she conceived and bore Cain, and she said, "I have got me a man with the LORD." And she bore as well his brother, Abel, and Abel became a herder of sheep while Cain was a tiller of the soil. And it happened in the course of time that Cain brought from the fruit of the soil an offering to the LORD. And Abel too had brought from the choice firstlings of his flock, and the LORD regarded Abel and his offering but He did not regard Cain and his offering, and Cain was very incensed, and his face fell. And the LORD said to Cain.

>   "Why are you incensed,
>   and why is your face fallen?
>   For whether you offer well,
>   or whether you do not,
>   at the tent flap sin crouches
>   and for you is its longing
>   but you will rule over it."

And Cain said to Abel his brother, "Let us go out to the field." And when they were in the field, Cain rose against Abel his brother and killed him. And the LORD said to Cain, "Where is Abel your brother?" And he said, "I do not know. Am I my brother's keeper?" And He said, "What have you done? Listen! your brother's blood cries out to me from the soil. And so, cursed shall you be by the soil that gaped with its mouth to take your brother's blood from your hand. If you till the soil, it will no longer give you its strength. A restless wanderer shall you be on the earth." And Cain said to the LORD, "My punishment is too great to bear. Now that You have driven me this day from the soil and I must hide from Your presence, I shall be a restless wanderer on the earth and whoever finds me will kill me." And the LORD said to him, "Therefore whoever kills Cain shall suffer sevenfold vengeance." And the LORD set a mark upon Cain so that whoever found him would not slay him.

And Cain went out from the LORD's presence and dwelled in the land of Nod[5] east of Eden. And Cain knew his wife and she conceived and bore Enoch. Then he became the builder of a city and called the name of the city, like his son's name, Enoch. And Irad was born to Enoch, and Irad begot Mehujael and Muhujael begot Methusael and

4. "Eve" means "living."
5. "Wandering."

Methusael begot Lamech. And Lamech took him two wives, the name of the one was Adah and the name of the other was Zillah. And Adah bore Jabal: he was the first of tent dwellers with livestock. And his brother's name was Jubal: he was the first of all who play on the lyre and pipe. As for Zillah, she bore Tubal-cain, who forged every tool of copper and iron. And the sister of Tubal-cain was Naamah. And Lamech said to his wives,

> "Adah and Zillah, O hearken my voice,
> You wives of Lamech, give ear to my speech.
> For a man have I slain for my wound,
> a boy for my bruising.
> For sevenfold Cain is avenged,
> and Lamech seventy and seven."

And Adam again knew his wife and she bore a son and called his name Seth,[6] as to say, "God has granted me other seed in place of Abel, for Cain has killed him." As for Seth, to him, too, a son was born, and he called his name Enosh. It was then that the name of the LORD was first invoked.

Chapter 5[7]

This is the book of the lineage of Adam: On the day God created the human, in the image of God He created him. Male and female He created them, and He blessed them and called their name humankind on the day they were created. And Adam lived a hundred and thirty years and he begot in his likeness by his image and called his name Seth. And the days of Adam after he begot Seth were eight hundred years, and he begot sons and daughters. And all the days Adam lived were nine hundred and thirty years. Then he died. And Seth lived a hundred and five years and he begot Enosh. And Seth lived after he begot Enosh eight hundred and seven years. Then he died. And all the days of Seth were nine hundred and twelve years. Then he died. And Enosh lived ninety years and he begot Kenan. And Enosh lived after he begot Kenan eight hundred and fifteen years, and he begot sons and daughters. And all the days of Enosh were nine hundred and five years. Then he died. And Kenan lived seventy years and he begot Mahalalel. And Kenan lived after he begot Mahalalel eight hundred and forty years, and he begot sons and daughters. And all the days of Kenan were nine hundred and ten years. Then he died. And Mahalalel lived sixty-five years and he begot Jared. And Mahalalel lived after he begot Jared eight hundred and thirty years, and he begot sons and daughters. And all the days of Mahalalel were eight hundred and ninety-five years. Then he died. And Jared lived a hundred and sixty-two years and he begot Enoch. And Jared lived after he begot Enoch eight hundred years, and he begot sons and daughters. And all the days of Jared were nine hundred and sixty-two years. Then he died. And Enoch lived sixty-five years and he begot Methuselah. And Enoch walked with God after he begot Methuselah three hundred years, and he begot sons and daughters. And all the days of Enoch were three hundred and sixty-five years. And Enoch walked with God and he was no more, for God took him. And Methuselah lived a hundred and eighty-seven years and he begot Lamech. And Methuselah lived after he begot Lamech seven hundred and eighty-two years, and he begot sons and daughters. And all the days of

---

6. "Granted."
7. This chapter gives a lineage of ten generations, linking Adam to Noah at the close of the primeval period.

Methuselah were nine hundred and sixty-nine years. Then he died. And Lamech lived a hundred and eighty-two years and he begot a son. And he called his name Noah,[8] as to say, "This one will console us for the pain of our hands' work from the soil which the LORD cursed." And Lamech lived after he begot Noah five hundred and ninety-five years, and he begot sons and daughters. And all the days of Lamech were seven hundred and seventy-seven years. Then he died. And Noah was five hundred years old and he begot Shem, Ham, and Japheth.

Chapter 6

And it happened as humankind began to multiply over the earth and daughters were born to them, that the sons of God saw that the daughters of man were comely, and they took themselves wives howsoever they chose. And the LORD said, "My breath shall not abide in the human forever, for he is but flesh. Let his days be a hundred and twenty years."

The Nephilim[9] were then on the earth, and afterward as well, the sons of God having come to bed with the daughters of man who bore them children: they are the heroes of yore, the men of renown.

And the LORD saw that the evil of the human creature was great on the earth and that every scheme of his heart's devising was only perpetually evil. And the LORD regretted having made the human on earth and was grieved to the heart. And the LORD said, "I will wipe out the human race I created from the face of the earth, from human to cattle to crawling thing to the fowl of the heavens, for I regret that I have made them." But Noah found favor in the eyes of the LORD. This is the lineage of Noah—Noah was a righteous man, he was blameless in his time, Noah walked with God—and Noah begot three sons, Shem and Ham and Japheth. And the earth was corrupt before God and the earth was filled with outrage. And God saw the earth and, look, it was corrupt, for all flesh had corrupted its ways on the earth. And God said to Noah, "The end of all flesh is come before me, for the earth is filled with outrage by them, and I am now about to destroy them, with the earth. Make yourself an ark of cypress wood, with cells you shall make the ark, and caulk it inside and out with pitch. This is how you shall make it: three hundred cubits, the ark's length; fifty cubits, its width; thirty cubits, its height.[1] Make a skylight in the ark, within a cubit of the top you shall finish it, and put an entrance in the ark on one side. With lower and middle and upper decks you shall make it. As for me, I am about to bring the Flood, water upon the earth, to destroy all flesh that has within it the breath of life from under the heavens, everything on the earth shall perish. And I will set up my covenant with you, and you shall enter the ark, you and your sons and your wife and the wives of your sons, with you. And from all that lives, from all flesh, two of each thing you shall bring to the ark to keep alive with you, male and female they shall be. From the fowl of each kind and from the cattle of each kind and from all that crawls on the earth of each kind, two of each thing shall come to you to be kept alive. As for you, take you from every food that is eaten and store it by you, to serve for you and for them as food." And this Noah did; as all that God commanded him, so he did.

8. "Comfort, rest."
9. Giants.
1. A cubit was about 18 inches.

Chapter 7

And the Lord said to Noah, "Come into the ark, you and all your household, for it is you I have seen righteous before me in this generation. Of every clean animal take you seven pairs, each with its mate, and of every animal that is not clean, one pair, each with its mate. Of the fowl of the heavens as well seven pairs, male and female, to keep seed alive over all the earth. For in seven days' time I will make it rain on the earth forty days and forty nights and I will wipe out from the face of the earth all existing things that I have made." And Noah did all that the Lord commanded him.

Noah was six hundred years old when the Flood came, water over the earth. And Noah and his sons and his wife and his sons' wives came into the ark because of the waters of the Flood. Of the clean animals and of the animals that were not clean and of the fowl and of all that crawls upon the ground two each came to Noah into the ark, male and female, as God had commanded Noah. And it happened after seven days, that the waters of the Flood were over the earth. In the six hundredth year of Noah's life, in the second month, on the seventeenth day of the month, on that day,

> All the wellsprings of the great deep burst
> and the casements of the heavens were opened.

And the rain was over the earth forty days and forty nights. That very day, Noah and Shem and Ham and Japheth, the sons of Noah, and Noah's wife, and the three wives of his sons together with them, came into the ark, they as well as beasts of each kind and cattle of each kind and each kind of crawling thing that crawls on the earth and each kind of bird, each winged thing. They came to Noah into the ark, two by two of all flesh that has the breath of life within it. And those that came in, male and female of all flesh they came, as God had commanded him, and the Lord shut him in. And the Flood was forty days over the earth, and the waters multiplied and bore the ark upward and it rose above the earth. And the waters surged and multiplied mightily over the earth, and the ark went on the surface of the water. And the waters surged most mightily over the earth, and all the high mountains under the heavens were covered. Fifteen cubits above them the waters surged as the mountains were covered. And all flesh that stirs on the earth perished, the fowl and the cattle and the beasts and all swarming things that swarm upon the earth, and all humankind. All that had the quickening breath of life in its nostrils, of all that was on dry land, died. And He wiped out all existing things from the face of the earth, from humans to cattle to crawling things to the fowl of the heavens, they were wiped out from the earth. And Noah alone remained, and those with him in the ark. And the waters surged over the earth one hundred and fifty days.

Chapter 8

And God remembered Noah and all the beasts and all the cattle that were with him in the ark. And God sent a wind over the earth and the waters subsided. And the wellsprings of the deep were dammed up, and the casements of the heavens, the rain from the heavens held back. And the waters receded from the earth little by little, and the waters ebbed. At the end of a hundred and fifty days the ark came to rest, on the seventeenth day of the seventh month, on the mountains of Ararat.[2] The waters continued to ebb, until the tenth month, on the first day of the tenth month, the mountaintops appeared. And it happened, at the end of forty days, that Noah opened the window of the ark he had made. And he let

2. A region in Armenia.

out the raven and it went forth to and fro until the waters should dry up from the earth. And he let out the dove to see whether the waters had abated from the surface of the ground. But the dove found no resting place for its foot and it returned to him to the ark, for the waters were over all the earth. And he reached out and took it and brought it back to him into the ark. Then he waited another seven days and again let the dove out of the ark. And the dove came back to him at eventide and, look, a plucked olive leaf was in its bill, and Noah knew that the waters had abated from the earth. Then he waited still another seven days and let out the dove, and it did not return to him again. And it happened in the six hundred and first year, in the first month, on the first day of the month, the waters dried up from the earth, and Noah took off the covering of the ark and he saw and, look, the surface of the ground was dry. And in the second month, on the twenty-seventh day of the month, the earth was completely dry. And God spoke to Noah, saying, "Go out of the ark, you and your wife and your sons and your sons' wives, with you. All the animals that are with you of all flesh, fowl and cattle and every crawling thing that crawls on the earth, take out with you, and let them swarm through the earth and be fruitful and multiply on the earth." And Noah went out, his sons and his wife and his sons' wives with him. Every beast, every crawling thing, and every fowl, everything that stirs on the earth, by families, came out of the ark. And Noah built an altar to the LORD and he took from every clean cattle and every clean fowl and offered burnt offerings on the altar. And the LORD smelled the fragrant odor and the LORD said in His heart, "I will not again damn the soil on humankind's score. For the devisings of the human heart are evil from youth. And I will not again strike down all living things as I did. As long as all the days of the earth—

    seedtime and harvest
    and cold and heat
    and summer and winter
    and day and night
    shall not cease."

Chapter 9

And God blessed Noah and his sons and He said to them, "Be fruitful and multiply and fill the earth. And the dread and fear of you shall be upon all the beasts of the field and all the fowl of the heavens, in all that crawls on the ground and in all the fish of the sea. In your hand they are given. All stirring things that are alive, yours shall be for food, like the green plants, I have given all to you. But flesh with its lifeblood still in it you shall not eat. And just so, your lifeblood I will requite, from every beast I will requite it, and from humankind, from every man's brother, I will requite human life.

    He who sheds human blood
    by humans his blood shall be shed,
    for in the image of God
    He made humankind.
    As for you, be fruitful and multiply,
    swarm through the earth, and hold sway over it."

And God said to Noah and to his sons with him, "And I, I am about to establish My covenant with you and with your seed after you, and with every living creature that is with you, the fowl and the cattle and every beast of the earth with you, all that have come out of the ark, every beast of the earth. And I will establish My covenant with you, that never again shall all flesh be cut off by the waters of the Flood, and never again shall there be a Flood to destroy the earth." And God said, "This is the sign of the covenant that I set between Me and you and every living creature that is with you, for everlasting generations: My bow I have set in the clouds to be a sign of the covenant between Me and the earth, and so, when I send clouds over the earth, the bow will appear in the cloud. Then I will remember My covenant, between Me and you and every living creature of all flesh, and the waters will no more become a Flood to destroy all flesh. And the bow shall be in the cloud and I will see it, to remember the everlasting covenant between God and all living creatures, all flesh that is on the earth." And God said to Noah, "This is the sign of the covenant I have established between Me and all flesh that is on the earth."

And the sons of Noah who came out from the ark were Shem and Ham and Japheth, and Ham was the father of Canaan. These three were the sons of Noah, and from these the whole earth spread out. And Noah, a man of the soil, was the first to plant a vineyard. And he drank of the wine and became drunk, and exposed himself within his tent. And Ham the father of Canaan saw his father's nakedness and told his two brothers outside.[3] And Shem and Japheth took a cloak and put it over both their shoulders and walked backward and covered their father's nakedness, their faces turned backward so they did not see their father's nakedness. And Noah woke from his wine and he knew what his youngest son had done to him. And he said,

> "Cursed be Canaan,
> the lowliest slave shall he be
> to his brothers."

And he said,

> "Blessed be the LORD
> the God of Shem,
> unto them shall Canaan be slave.
> May God enlarge Japheth,
> may he dwell in the tents of Shem,
> unto them shall Canaan be slave."

And Noah lived after the Flood three hundred and fifty years. And all the days of Noah were nine hundred and fifty years. Then he died.[4]

Chapter 11

And all the earth was one language, one set of words. And it happened as they journeyed from the east that they found a valley in the land of Shinar[5] and settled there. And they said to each other, "Come, let us bake bricks and burn them hard." And the brick served them as stone, and bitumen served them as mortar. And they said, "Come, let us build us a city and a tower with its top in the heavens, that we may make us a name, lest we be scattered over all the earth." And the LORD came down to see the city and the tower that the human creatures had built. And the LORD said, "As one people with one language for all, if this is what they have begun to do, nothing they plot will elude them. Come, let us go down and baffle their language there so that they will not understand each other's language." And the LORD scattered them from there over all the earth and they left off building the city. Therefore it is called Babel, for there the LORD made the language of all the earth babble. And from there the LORD scattered them over all the earth.

3. The story implies that Ham/Canaan had a sexual interest in Noah; later in the Bible (Leviticus 18), Canaanite sexual perversions are given as a reason God is displacing them in favor of the Hebrews.
4. Chapter 10, omitted here, gives a genealogy of Noah's descendants.
5. The lowlands of the Tigris-Euphrates basin in Mesopotamia.

This is the lineage of Shem: Shem was a hundred years old when he begot Arpachshad two years after the Flood. And Shem lived after begetting Arpachshad five hundred years and he begot sons and daughters. And Arpachshad lived thirty-five years and he begot Shelah. And Arpachshad lived after begetting Shelah four hundred and three years and he begot sons and daughters. And Shelah lived thirty years and he begot Eber. And Shelah lived after begetting Eber four hundred and three years and he begot sons and daughters. And Eber lived thirty-four years and he begot Peleg. And Eber lived after begetting Peleg four hundred and thirty years and he begot sons and daughters. And Peleg lived thirty years and he begot Reu. And Peleg lived after begetting Reu two hundred and nine years and he begot sons and daughters. And Reu lived thirty-two years and he begot Serug. And Reu lived after begetting Serug two hundred and seven years and he begot sons and daughters. And Serug lived thirty years and he begot Nahor. And Serug lived after begetting Nahor two hundred years and he begot sons and daughters. And Nahor lived twenty-nine years and he begot Terah. And Nahor lived after begetting Terah one hundred and nineteen years and he begot sons and daughters. And Terah lived seventy years and he begot Abram, Nahor, and Haran. And this is the lineage of Terah: Terah begot Abram, Nahor, and Haran, and Haran begot Lot. And Haran died in the lifetime of Terah his father in the land of his birth, Ur of the Chaldees. And Abram and Nahor took themselves wives. The name of Abram's wife was Sarai and the name of Nahor's wife was Milcah daughter of Haran, the father of Milcah and the father of Iscah. And Sarai was barren, she had no child. And Terah took Abram his son and Lot son of Haran, his grandson, and Sarai his daughter-in-law, the wife of his son Abram, and he set out with them from Ur of the Chaldees toward the land of Canaan, and they came to Haran and settled there. And the days of Terah were two hundred and five years, and Terah died in Haran.[6]

THE SONG OF SONGS ■ (1st millennium B.C.E.)

The phrase "song of songs," *shir ha-shirim* in Hebrew, means "best of all songs," a testimony to the power and beauty of the greatest love poem we have from the ancient Mediterranean world. Centuries of readers—and lovers—have relished the speakers' ecstatic praise of each other's bodies, the lyrical evocations of the beauties of nature and the landscape of Israel, and the mysterious episodes of abandonment and loss in the middle of the book. The title and opening line refer to it as a single song, and some editors over the centuries have inserted captions and dialogue markers to connect its parts into an extended dialogue between a woman, her beloved, and a chorus of her attendants or friends. The book can also be thought of, though, as a collection of older love poems. Many of these verses must have been sung individually, like the Egyptian poems they often resemble, long before they were collected together in around the third century B.C.E.

The Song of Songs was included in the Bible (after some ancient debate) thanks to the book's attribution to King Solomon. The rabbis who admitted it to the Bible interpreted the text allegorically as depicting the love of God for Israel. Later, Christian commentators adapted this line of interpretation, reading the collection as an allegory of the love of Christ for his Church. Modern scholarship tends instead to stress the poems' links to wedding songs and the older fertility myths that often underlay them. There was a developed tradition of "sacred marriage poetry" in the Near East. A list of hymn titles from the Mesopotamian city of Assur shows many that resemble verses in the Song of Songs:

6. In northwest Mesopotamia; a substantial number of people migrated from this region into Canaan in the early 2nd millennium B.C.E.—a migration that begins the story of Israel's patriarchs and matriarchs in the next section of Genesis, which concludes with the story of Joseph in Egypt.

"How do I long for the beautiful one!"
"The fragrance of cedar is thy love, O lord."
"To the door of the lord she did come."
"By night I thought of thee."
"Thou hast caressed me; be thou my lord!"

In Mesopotamia, these hymns would have been performed in festivals associated with planting and harvest, with the king and the queen, or the king and a temple prostitute, enacting the roles of the goddess of love (Inanna or Ishtar) and her consort (Dumuzi or Tammuz), who takes her place in the underworld for six months of the year; their union was the mythic underpinning for the seasonal fertility of crops. Tammuz and Ishtar (known in Palestine as Astarte) were worshiped in Jerusalem before the establishment of Hebrew monotheism—and probably long afterward as well, to the dismay of the prophets who continually condemned persisting pagan practices.

No direct use of such old traditions is found in the Song of Songs, though some of the verses use the older imagery, either in the context of a wedding between Solomon and a bride, or in other stanzas that seem to tell of a quite different, private love affair. We can think of these verses as infusing theology back into daily life, for these lyrics endow the lovers with qualities of divine power and mystery, and the lovers' encounters are set against a panoramic backdrop of Israel's sacred landscape and history.

The Song of Songs[1]

Chapter 1

The Song of Songs, which is Solomon's.

Let him kiss me with the kisses of his mouth.
Your love is more delightful than wine;
delicate is the fragrance of your perfume,
5   your name is an oil poured out,
and that is why the maidens love you.
Draw me in your footsteps, let us run.
The King has brought me into his rooms;
you will be our joy and our gladness.
10 We shall praise your love above wine;
how right it is to love you.
I am black but lovely, daughters of Jerusalem,
like the tents of Kedar,
like the pavilions of Salmah.
15 Take no notice of my swarthiness,
it is the sun that has burnt me.
My mother's sons turned their anger on me,
they made me look after the vineyards.
Had I only looked after my own!

20 Tell me then, you whom my heart loves:
Where will you lead your flock to graze,

1. Jerusalem Bible translation.

where will you rest it at noon?
That I may no more wander like a vagabond
beside the flocks of your companions.

25 If you do not know this, O loveliest of women,
follow the tracks of the flock,
and take your kids to graze
close by the shepherds' tents.

To my mare harnessed to Pharaoh's chariot
30 I compare you, my love.
Your cheeks show fair between their pendants
and your neck within its necklaces.
We shall make you golden earrings
and beads of silver.

35 —While the King rests in his own room
my nard yields its perfume.
My Beloved is a sachet of myrrh
lying between my breasts.
My Beloved is a cluster of henna flowers
40 among the vines of Engedi.

—How beautiful you are, my love,
how beautiful you are!
Your eyes are doves.

—How beautiful you are, my Beloved,
45 and how delightful!
All green is our bed.

—The beams of our house are of cedar,
the paneling of cypress.

Chapter 2

—I am the rose of Sharon,[2]
50 the lily of the valleys.
—As a lily among the thistles,
so is my love among the maidens.
—As an apple tree among the trees of the orchard,
so is my Beloved among the young men.
55 In his longed-for shade I am seated
and his fruit is sweet to my taste.
He has taken me to his banquet hall,
and the banner he raises over me is love.

2. A rich plain along the Mediterranean coast.

Feed me with raisin cakes,
60   restore me with apples,
for I am sick with love.
His left arm is under my head,
his right embraces me.

—I charge you, daughters of Jerusalem,
65   by the gazelles, by the hinds of the field,
not to stir my love, nor rouse it,
until it please to awake.

I hear my Beloved.
See how he comes
70   leaping on the mountains,
bounding over the hills.
My Beloved is like a gazelle,
like a young stag.
See where he stands
75   behind our wall.
He looks in at the window,
he peers through the lattice.

My Beloved lifts up his voice,
he says to me,
80   "Come then, my love,
my lovely one, come.
For see, winter is past,
the rains are over and gone.
The flowers appear on the earth.
85   The season of glad songs has come,
the cooing of the turtledove is heard in our land.
The fig tree is forming its first figs
and the blossoming vines give out their fragrance.
Come then, my love,
90   my lovely one, come.
My dove, hiding in the clefts of the rock,
in the coverts of the cliff,
show me your face,
let me hear your voice;
95   for your voice is sweet
and your face is beautiful."

Catch the foxes for us,
the little foxes that make havoc of the vineyards,
for our vineyards are in flower.
100   My Beloved is mine and I am his.
He pastures his flock among the lilies.

Before the dawn-wind rises,
before the shadows flee,

return! Be, my Beloved,
105 like a gazelle,
a young stag,
on the rugged mountains.

Chapter 3

On my bed, at night, I sought him
whom my heart loves.
110 I sought but did not find him.
So I will rise and go through the City;
in the streets and the squares
I will seek him whom my heart loves.

I sought but did not find him.
115 The watchmen came upon me
on their rounds in the City:
"Have you seen him whom my heart loves?"

Scarcely had I passed them
than I found him whom my heart loves.
120 I held him fast, nor would I let him go
till I had brought him into my mother's house,
into the room of her who conceived me.

I charge you, daughters of Jerusalem,
by the gazelles, by the hinds of the field,
125 not to stir my love, nor rouse it,
until it please to awake.

What is this coming up from the desert
like a column of smoke,
breathing of myrrh and frankincense
130 and every perfume the merchant knows?

See, it is the litter of Solomon.
Around it are sixty champions,
the flower of the warriors of Israel;
all of them skilled swordsmen,
135 veterans of battle.
Each man has his sword at his side,
against alarms by night.

King Solomon has made himself a throne
of wood from Lebanon.
140 The posts he has made of silver,
the canopy of gold,
the seat of purple;
the back is inlaid with ebony.

Daughters of Zion,
145 come and see King Solomon,

wearing the diadem with which his mother crowned him
on his wedding day,
on the day of his heart's joy.

Chapter 4

150
How beautiful you are, my love,
how beautiful you are!
Your eyes, behind your veil, are doves;
your hair is like a flock of goats
frisking down the slopes of Gilead.
Your teeth are like a flock of shorn ewes

155
as they come up from the washing.
Each one has its twin,
not one unpaired with another.
Your lips are a scarlet thread
and your words enchanting.

160
Your cheeks, behind your veil,
are halves of pomegranate.
Your neck is the tower of David
built as a fortress,
hung round with a thousand bucklers,

165
and each the shield of a hero.
Your two breasts are two fawns,
twins of a gazelle,
that feed among the lilies.

Before the dawn-wind rises,

170
before the shadows flee,
I will go to the mountain of myrrh,
to the hill of frankincense.

You are wholly beautiful, my love,
and without a blemish.

175
Come from Lebanon, my promised bride,
come from Lebanon, come on your way.
Lower your gaze, from the heights of Amana,
from the crests of Senir and Hermon,
the haunt of lions,

180
the mountains of leopards.

You ravish my heart,
my sister, my bride,[3]
you ravish my heart
with a single one of your glances,

3. As in Egyptian poetry, the lovers sometimes refer to each other as "sister" and "brother."

185   with one single pearl of your necklace.
What spells lie in your love,
my sister, my bride!
How delicious is your love, more delicious than wine!
How fragrant your perfumes,
190   more fragrant than all other spices!
Your lips, my promised one, distill wild honey.
Honey and milk are under your tongue;
and the scent of your garments
is like the scent of Lebanon.

195   She is a garden enclosed, my sister, my bride;
a garden enclosed, a sealed fountain.
Your shoots form an orchard of pomegranate trees,
the rarest essences are yours:
nard and saffron,
200   calamus and cinnamon,
with all the incense-bearing trees;
myrrh and aloes, with the subtlest odors.
Fountain that makes the gardens fertile,
well of living water,
205   streams flowing down from Lebanon.
Awake, north wind,
come, wind of the south!
Breathe over my garden,
to spread its sweet smell around.
210   Let my Beloved come into his garden,
let him taste its rarest fruits.

Chapter 5

I come into my garden,
my sister, my bride,
I gather my myrrh and balsam,
215   I eat my honey and my honeycomb,
I drink my wine and my milk.
Eat, friends, and drink,
drink deep, my dearest friends.

I sleep, but my heart is awake.
220   I hear my Beloved knocking.
"Open to me, my sister, my love,
my dove, my perfect one,
for my head is covered with dew,
my locks with the drops of night."
225   —"I have taken off my tunic,
am I to put it on again?
I have washed my feet,
am I to dirty them again?"

My Beloved thrust his hand
230　through the hole in the door;
I trembled to the core of my being.
Then I rose to open to my Beloved,
myrrh ran off my hands,
pure myrrh off my fingers,
235　on to the handle of the bolt.

I opened to my Beloved,
but he had turned his back and gone!
My soul failed at his flight.
I sought him but I did not find him,
240　I called to him but he did not answer.
The watchmen came upon me
as they made their rounds in the City.
They beat me, they wounded me,
they took away my cloak,
245　they who guard the ramparts.
I charge you, daughters of Jerusalem,
if you should find my Beloved,
what must you tell him . . . ?
That I am sick with love.

250　What makes your Beloved better than other lovers,
O loveliest of women?
What makes your Beloved better than other lovers,
to give us a charge like this?

My Beloved is fresh and ruddy,
255　to be known among ten thousand.
His head is golden, purest gold,
his locks are palm fronds and black as the raven.
His eyes are doves at a pool of water,
bathed in milk, at rest on a pool.
260　His cheeks are beds of spices,
banks sweetly scented.
His lips are lilies, distilling pure myrrh.
His hands are golden, rounded,
set with jewels of Tarshish.
265　His belly a block of ivory
covered with sapphires.
His legs are alabaster columns
set in sockets of pure gold.
His appearance is that of Lebanon,
270　unrivaled as the cedars.
His conversation is sweetness itself,
he is altogether lovable.
Such is my Beloved, such is my friend,
O daughters of Jerusalem.

Chapter 6

275   Where did your Beloved go,
           O loveliest of women?
           Which way did your Beloved turn
           so that we can help you to look for him?

           My Beloved went down to his garden,
280   to the beds of spices,
           to pasture his flock in the gardens
           and gather lilies.
           I am my Beloved's, and my Beloved is mine.
           He pastures his flock among the lilies.

285   You are beautiful as Tirzah,[4] my love,
           fair as Jerusalem.
           Turn your eyes away,
           for they hold me captive.
           Your hair is like a flock of goats
290   frisking down the slopes of Gilead.
           Your teeth are like a flock of sheep
           as they come up from the washing.
           Each one has its twin,
           not one unpaired with another.
295   Your cheeks, behind your veil,
           are halves of pomegranate.

           There are sixty queens
           and eighty concubines
           (and countless maidens).
300   But my dove is unique,
           mine, unique and perfect.
           She is the darling of her mother,
           the favorite of the one who bore her.
           The maidens saw her, and called her happy,
305   queens and concubines sang her praises:
           "Who is this arising like the dawn,
           fair as the moon,
           resplendent as the sun,
           terrible as an army with banners?"

310   I went down to the nut orchard
           to see what was sprouting in the valley,
           to see if the vines were budding
           and the pomegranate trees in flower.
           Before I knew ... my desire had hurled me
315   on the chariots of my people, as their prince.

---

4. A former capital of Israel.

Chapter 7

Return, return, O maid of Shulam,[5]
return, return, that we may gaze on you!

Why do you gaze on the maid of Shulam
dancing as though between two rows of dancers?

320 How beautiful are your feet in their sandals,
O prince's daughter!
The curve of your thighs is like the curve of a necklace,
work of a master hand.
Your navel is a bowl well rounded
325 with no lack of wine,
your belly a heap of wheat
surrounded with lilies.
Your two breasts are two fawns,
twins of a gazelle.
330 Your neck is an ivory tower.
Your eyes, the pools of Heshbon,
by the gate of Bath-rabbim.
Your nose, the Tower of Lebanon,
sentinel facing Damascus.
335 Your head is held high like Carmel,
and its plaits are as dark as purple;
a king is held captive in your tresses.
How beautiful you are, how charming,
my love, my delight!
340 In stature like the palm tree,
its fruit-clusters your breasts.
"I will climb the palm tree," I resolved,
"I will seize its clusters of dates."
May your breasts be clusters of grapes,
345 your breath sweet-scented as apples,
your speaking, superlative wine.

Wine flowing straight to my Beloved,
as it runs on the lips of those who sleep.
I am my Beloved's,
350 and his desire is for me.
Come, my Beloved,
let us go to the fields.
We will spend the night in the villages,
and in the morning we will go to the vineyards.
355 We will see if the vines are budding,

---

5. Perhaps a place name, or this may mean "Solomon's bride."

if their blossoms are opening,
if the pomegranate trees are in flower.
Then I shall give you the gift of my love.
The mandrakes yield their fragrance,
360   the rarest fruits are at our doors;
the new as well as the old,
I have stored them for you, my Beloved.

Chapter 8

Ah, why are you not my brother,
nursed at my mother's breast!
365   Then if I met you out of doors, I could kiss you
without people thinking ill of me.
I should lead you, I should take you
into my mother's house, and you would teach me!
I should give you spiced wine to drink,
370   juice of my pomegranates.

His left arm is under my head
and his right embraces me.
I charge you, daughters of Jerusalem,
not to stir my love, nor rouse it,
375   until it please to awake.

Who is this coming up from the desert
leaning on her Beloved?
I awakened you under the apple tree,
there where your mother conceived you,
380   there where she who gave birth to you conceived you.

Set me like a seal on your heart,
like a seal on your arm.
For love is strong as Death,
jealousy relentless as Sheol.
385   The flash of it is a flash of fire,
a flame of Yahweh himself.
Love no flood can quench,
no torrents drown.[6]

6. The translators of the Jerusalem Bible consider that the poem proper ends here. Several miscellaneous paragraphs follow in a kind of appendix, beginning with an aphorism: "Were a man to offer all the wealth of his house to buy love, contempt is all he would purchase." Then follows an obscure passage that may be a veiled criticism of the worldly policies of a late Jewish ruler in the 2nd century B.C.E.:

    Our sister is little: her breasts are not yet formed. What shall we do for our sister on the day she is spoken for? If she is a rampart, on the crest we will build a battlement of silver; if she is a door, we will board her up with planks of cedar.—I am a wall, and my breasts represent its towers. And under his eyes I have found true peace.

    Solomon had a vineyard at Baal-hamon. He entrusted it to overseers, and each one was to pay him the value of its produce, a thousand shekels of silver. But I look after my own vineyard myself. You, Solomon, may have your thousand shekels, and those who oversee its produce their two hundred.

    You who dwell in the gardens, my companions listen for your voice: deign to let me hear it. Haste away, my Beloved. Be like a gazelle, a young stag, on the spicy mountains.

The Greek word *homeros* means "hostage." Authorship of the great epic poems the *Iliad* and the *Odyssey* is attributed to someone bearing this name, but we don't know who or what he was. Several of the islands and cities of the eastern Mediterranean Sea claimed "Homer" as a native. What remains are the poems, amid passionate debates about when and where they were written down. Following research on the oral performance and composition of poetry in Serbia and Africa, scholars now believe that the poems represent the culmination of a long tradition of singers who assembled memories of a lost heroic age, vestiges of the story of the earliest Greeks' war against Troy in Asia Minor. The singers supplemented their oral tradition with more recent material and created two magnificent, long poems about the supposed ancestors, gods and men, of the aristocrats of the eighth century B.C.E.

Book 8 of the *Odyssey* shows us a scene of performance, where the singer Demodocus, blind as Homer was said to be, recounts part of the legend of Troy for feasting nobles:

> All reached out for the good things that lay at hand
> and when they'd put aside desire for food and drink,
> the Muse inspired the bard
> to sing the famous deeds of fighting heroes—
> the song whose fame had reached the skies those days:
> The Strife Between Odysseus and Achilles, Peleus' son...
> how once at the gods' flowing feast the captains clashed
> in a savage war of words, while Agamemnon, lord of armies,
> rejoiced at heart that Achaea's bravest men were battling so.

The Muse, a goddess, inspires the singer, who is seen as the channel through which memory and the divine pass to deliver these ancient stories, known to all the audience, drinking in the excellence of their retelling. Here the hero Odysseus, sitting disguised in the audience, is moved to tears.

The poems themselves preserve traces of the Mycenaean age (1500–1000 B.C.E.), hundreds of years before the date of their composition. Archaeologists have found, for example, an ivory figurine with a representation of a boar's tusk helmet like Odysseus's described in the *Iliad*. Both poems were composed in dactylic hexameter, that is, six feet based on a rhythm of a long syllable followed by two short syllables. The meter allowed the singers to retell and embellish the traditional stories of their people, while maintaining a steady flow of musical lines. Oral composition determined, with some flexibility, the "epithets," or qualifying terms used for the central figures of the poems; if Achilles, for example, is named in a certain position in a line, the words used to describe him, such as "swift-footed," must fit into the meter. If they don't, the song refers to him as the son of Peleus, or uses another qualifier that works rhythmically. Sometimes these epithets seem incongruous, or, some argue, ironic, where they fall:

> Aphrodite the sweetly laughing spoke...
> "Tydeus' son Diomedes, the too high-hearted, stabbed me
> as I was carrying my own beloved son out of the fighting...."

Even in pain, the goddess of eros can be "sweetly laughing" if the meter requires it. Other features of oral composition include repetitions, for example, in the highly conventional, formulaic scenes of warriors putting on armor, and what is sometimes called "ring" form, a pattern of *abccba*, for example, in set scenes in the poems. The dactylic hexameter preserved, like flies in amber, ancient allusions to features of warfare and of everyday life no longer familiar to the audience. The poems provide a rich, complex, and stratified record of all the centuries between the early Mycenaean period and the people of the eighth century B.C.E., who were engaged in trade and colonization with a wide Mediterranean world, stretching from the Aegean and its many islands east to Asia Minor, to the lands north and east of the Black Sea, to the northern coast of Africa, and to the far western edges of the Mediterranean Sea, to what is now Italy and southern France.

Early in the twentieth century, the anthropologist Milman Parry, exploring storytelling in preliterate societies, discovered features of composition that explained mysteries found in Homer. Some readers had preferred such ancient poets as Virgil to Homer because, as Alexander Pope put it, Homer sometimes nods. That is, Homer forgets and repeats and skips. Parry and his followers found that Yugoslavian oral poetry sung in the twentieth century showed similar patterns; its singers sang thousands of lines of heroic poetry that they forged in the moment, without memorization or writing, using "formulae," set phrases to define particular characters and to fill out lines as required by meter. They had typical scenes, such as arming scenes, that they used as templates for various characters, and other techniques for keeping their stories pouring forth, as they benefited from the experience and innovations of generations of singers who had preceded them.

The two Homeric poems share a language and a poetic tradition but tell very different stories. Both depend on the legend of a war with Troy, which the Greeks traced mythically to the abduction of the beautiful Helen of Sparta. The great god Zeus had raped her mother, Leda, appearing to her as a swan; Helen and her sister Clytemnestra were born from one egg, and their twin brothers, Castor and Pollux, later the Gemini in astrological lore, came from another. When Paris, son of King Priam of Troy, was promised the most beautiful woman in the world by the goddess of sexual love, Aphrodite, he came to the house of Menelaos in Sparta and stole away Menelaos's wife, Helen. Poets later differed on her willingness to be stolen. The Greeks' leaders, who had all courted Helen, had also pledged to get her back if she were ever taken from her husband; they set sail for Asia under the leadership of Menelaos's brother, Agamemnon, and fought for ten long years at Troy, finally winning the war through deception. The Greek army pretended to sail away from the battlefield, leaving an immense wooden horse as an offering. The Trojans pulled it inside the walls of their city, celebrated their victory, and in the night following, the Greeks, hidden inside the horse's belly, crept out and slaughtered and burned. The Greeks killed Priam, desecrated the altar of Athena, and killed children and enslaved the women of the city. The Trojan Aineias, whom the Romans called Aeneas, son of Venus, left burning Troy at the beginning of a long journey that culminated in the foundation of Rome. Because of sacrileges committed during the looting of Troy, the return of the Greek heroes to their homelands was often long and painful.

The singers of the Homeric tradition composed many poems recounting the events of this war and its aftermath. Most have been lost: poems that told of the giving of the prize, Helen, to Paris; of the arrival of the Amazons, women warriors, to help the Trojans on the battlefield; of the hero Achilles's falling in love with the queen of the Amazons, Penthesilea, even as he killed her with his spear; of the suicide of the hero Ajax; of the Trojan Horse and the sacking of Troy; and of the *nostoi,* or "returns," of the Greek heroes. The two Homeric poems that have come down to us focus vividly on two of the crucial stories contained within the greater epic tradition. The *Iliad* recounts the story of Achilles: his wrath at being slighted by Agamemnon, his withdrawal from battle, and the Trojan hero Hektor's killing of Achilles's beloved companion, Patroklos, dressed in Achilles's armor. Achilles's mother, the goddess Thetis, has warned him that he would either live a long life without fame or die young and glorious in battle. He chooses finally to enter the battle, to fight and die, and she asks Hephaistos, the artisan god, to make him new armor. The poem describes the divine making of Achilles's shield in a scene that connects it to ancient Near Eastern and Egyptian myths in which the artisan god, a metalworker or potter, creates the world and peoples it. Achilles returns to battle in a great rage of mourning and slaughters many Trojans, including Hektor. In Book 20 the poem compares him to fire:

As inhuman fire sweeps on in fury through the deep angles
Of a drywood mountain and sets ablaze the depth of the timber
And the blustering wind lashes the flame along, so Achilleus
Swept everywhere with his spear like something more than a mortal
Harrying them as they died, and the black earth ran blood.

The poem, which begins with a plague and the wrath of Achilles, ends with a scene of consolation between Priam, king of Troy, and his deadly enemy, Achilles, the warrior who killed his son.

Many of Homer's themes, characters, and even verbal patterns connect the epics with poems composed in the ancient Near East. The relationship between Achilles and the lost Patroklos echoes Gilgamesh's love for Enkidu in *The Epic of Gilgamesh* (see page 29), just as Homer's representation of Aphrodite recalls the ancient Near Eastern goddess Ishtar. The voyage of Odysseus to the land of the dead bears remarkable resemblances to the journey of Gilgamesh to visit his mentor, Utanapishtim, and scholars have linked such scenes as the Greek gods' assemblies with Sumerian, Akkadian, Ugaritic, Hittite, and Hebrew literature. While connecting with these earlier Eastern traditions, the Homeric poems began to elaborate crucial elements of the Greek civilization that followed them and were long used as the basis for classical education, as manuals for the proper conduct of a free citizen's life. Scholars have emphasized the ways in which classical Greek society posed all conflict in terms of the *agon,* the contest. The games, such as those held at Olympia every four years; the competition of the drama, in which the writers of tragedies and comedies were set against each other in a contest for a prize; even the law courts of the ancient Greek city-state repeated this shape of two or more antagonists, or combatants, who fought over a single prize, only one of whom left the contest as victor. The Trojan War and its battles defined the shape of conflict for Greek men in the centuries that followed.

The *Odyssey* differs radically from the *Iliad.* The *Iliad* in general confines its action to the battlefield around the walls of Troy, leaving the battlefield only to visit the world of the gods or to look outward through its similes, which compare the events of battle to natural phenomena and to the worlds of farmers, animals, and sailors on the "wine-dark sea." Although the goddesses play essential roles, as when Hera seduces her husband, Zeus, to distract him from the battlefield, the mortal women of the *Iliad* are taken like booty, or war prizes: traded, enslaved, and exchanged among the heroes. The women of the *Odyssey,* on the other hand, act: the poem begins with Odysseus's being held captive by the nymph Calypso, and it traces his long journey back to his waiting wife, Penelope, who both tantalizes and defends herself against a horde of suitors besieging her in their home on the island of Ithaca.

The *Odyssey* portrays a very different world from that of the battlefield around Troy; it presents a vast landscape of the Mediterranean that contains monsters, entrances to the underworld, and societies that test the Greeks' ideas of their own culture. This poem shows the noble household, with its dependent lordlings, slaves, farms, and palace, with all the tensions that grow out of such a hierarchical social arrangement. For a society that is about to form itself into many city-states and colonies overseas, the poem maps the imaginary geography of the Mediterranean and beyond, including societies of cannibals and one-eyed monsters, and explores the social hierarchies of class and gender and the border between the living and the dead. It bequeathes to the tradition a wily hero who lies when he needs to; who survives through endless ordeals to return home, kill his rivals, and then move on; and who visits the dead and manages to evade death through a cunning intelligence that the later Greeks both admired and despised. Both the *Iliad* and the *Odyssey* helped to define storytelling and the ideas of heroism, gender, and society for millennia. Virgil knew both poems intimately, and Dante, who didn't read Greek, knew of them. The *Odyssey* had its impact on tales of Sindbad in Arabic, on romance, and on all prose fiction following Homer.

PRONUNCIATIONS:[1]

Achaians: ah-KAI-uns
Achilleus: ah-KILL-yuss
Agamemnon: agg-ah-MEM-nohn
Aias: EYE-ahs
Athene: ah-THEE-nay
Atreides: ah-TRAY-deez
Atreus: AY-tree-us
Briseis: bre-SEE-iss
Chryseis: cry-SEE-iss
Circe: SEER-say
Danaans: DAY-nay-uns
Hektor: HEK-tor
Hephaistos: heh-FYS-tohs
Hermes: HER-meez
Menelaus: men-eh-LAY-us
Nausicaa: now-SEE-kay-ah
Odysseus: oh-DISS-yuss
Patroklos: pah-TRO-klos
Peleus: PEAL-yuss
Penelope: pen-EL-oh-pee
Phaiacia: fie-AY-sha
Phoibus: fo-EE-bus
Polyphemos: poll-ee-FEE-mos
Priam: PRY-am
Telemakhos: tel-EH-ma-khos
Thetis: THEH-tis
Xanthus: ZAN-thus

from The Iliad[1]

Book 1

[The Wrath of Achilles]

Sing, goddess,[2] the anger of Peleus' son Achilleus
and its devastation, which put pains thousandfold upon the Achaians,[3]
hurled in their multitudes to the house of Hades strong souls
of heroes, but gave their bodies to be the delicate feasting
5   of dogs, of all birds, and the will of Zeus[4] was accomplished
since that time when first there stood in division of conflict

---

1. The transliteration of Greek names varies widely. Some scholars prefer to follow very closely, in our Roman alphabet, the Greek spelling in the Greek alphabet. For example, they call the great hero of the Greek army in the Trojan War "Akhilleus." Others call him by the name the Romans later gave him, "Achilles." Still others prefer the compromise: "Achilleus." Most translations combine these solutions, using the Latin versions of names for the most familiar and transliterating more closely the less familiar names. Remember, Achilleus is Akhilleus is Achilles. Greek Odysseus becomes "Ulysses" in Rome and in James Joyce's novel of the same name. Agamemnon's queen is "Klytaimestra," "Clytaemestra," and even "Clytemnestra." Translated by Richmond Lattimore.

2. The Muse, goddess of epic poetry.

3. The Greeks.

4. Greatest of the gods, son of Kronos.

Atreus' son the lord of men[5] and brilliant Achilleus.

What god was it then set them together in bitter collision?
Zeus' son and Leto's, Apollo,[6] who in anger at the king drove
10 the foul pestilence along the host, and the people perished,
since Atreus' son had dishonoured Chryses, priest of Apollo,
when he came beside the fast ships of the Achaians to ransom
back his daughter, carrying gifts beyond count and holding
in his hands wound on a staff of gold the ribbons of Apollo
15 who strikes from afar, and supplicated all the Achaians,
but above all Atreus' two sons, the marshals of the people:
"Sons of Atreus and you other strong-greaved Achaians,
to you may the gods grant who have their homes on Olympos[7]
Priam's city[8] to be plundered and a fair homecoming thereafter,
20 but may you give me back my own daughter and take the ransom,
giving honour to Zeus' son who strikes from afar, Apollo."

Then all the rest of the Achaians cried out in favour
that the priest be respected and the shining ransom be taken;
yet this pleased not the heart of Atreus' son Agamemnon,
25 but harshly he drove him away with a strong order upon him:
"Never let me find you again, old sir, near our hollow
ships, neither lingering now nor coming again hereafter,
for fear your staff and the god's ribbons help you no longer.
The girl I will not give back; sooner will old age come upon her
30 in my own house, in Argos, far from her own land, going
up and down by the loom and being in my bed as my companion.
So go now, do not make me angry; so you will be safer."

So he spoke, and the old man in terror obeyed him
and went silently away beside the murmuring sea beach.
35 Over and over the old man prayed as he walked in solitude
to King Apollo, whom Leto of the lovely hair bore: "Hear me,
lord of the silver bow who set your power about Chryse
and Killa the sacrosanct, who are lord in strength over Tenedos,
Smintheus, if ever it pleased your heart that I built your temple,
40 if ever it pleased you that I burned all the rich thigh pieces
of bulls, of goats, then bring to pass this wish I pray for:
let your arrows make the Danaans[9] pay for my tears shed."
So he spoke in prayer, and Phoibos Apollo heard him,
and strode down along the pinnacles of Olympos, angered
45 in his heart, carrying across his shoulders the bow and the hooded
quiver; and the shafts clashed on the shoulders of the god walking
angrily. He came as night comes down and knelt then
apart and opposite the ships and let go an arrow.
Terrible was the clash that rose from the bow of silver.
50 First he went after the mules and the circling hounds, then let go
a tearing arrow against the men themselves and struck them.

5. Agamemnon.
6. God of disease, healing, prophecy, music, and poetry.
7. Sacred mountain home of the gods.
8. Troy, also called Ilion, city of Priam and his 50 sons and daughters, including Hektor, Paris, and Kassandra.
9. Like "Argives," another name for the Greeks.

The corpse fires burned everywhere and did not stop burning.
       Nine days up and down the host ranged the god's arrows,
but on the tenth Achilleus called the people to assembly;
55   a thing put into his mind by the goddess of the white arms, Hera,[1]
who had pity upon the Danaans when she saw them dying.
Now when they were all assembled in one place together,
Achilleus of the swift feet stood up among them and spoke forth:
"Son of Atreus, I believe now that straggling backwards
60   we must make our way home if we can even escape death,
if fighting now must crush the Achaians and the plague likewise.
No, come, let us ask some holy man, some prophet,
even an interpreter of dreams, since a dream also
comes from Zeus, who can tell why Phoibos Apollo is so angry,
65   if for the sake of some vow, some hecatomb he blames us,
if given the fragrant smoke of lambs, of he goats, somehow
he can be made willing to beat the bane aside from us."
       He spoke thus and sat down again, and among them stood up
Kalchas, Thestor's son, far the best of the bird interpreters,
70   who knew all things that were, the things to come and the things past,
who guided into the land of Ilion[2] the ships of the Achaians
through that seercraft of his own that Phoibos Apollo gave him.
He in kind intention toward all stood forth and addressed them:
"You have bidden me, Achilleus beloved of Zeus, to explain to
75   you this anger of Apollo the lord who strikes from afar. Then
I will speak; yet make me a promise and swear before me
readily by word and work of your hands to defend me,
since I believe I shall make a man angry who holds great kingship
over the men of Argos, and all the Achaians obey him.
80   For a king when he is angry with a man beneath him is too strong,
and suppose even for the day itself he swallow down his anger,
he still keeps bitterness that remains until its fulfilment
deep in his chest. Speak forth then, tell me if you will protect me."
       Then in answer again spoke Achilleus of the swift feet:
85   "Speak, interpreting whatever you know, and fear nothing.
In the name of Apollo beloved of Zeus to whom you, Kalchas,
make your prayers when you interpret the gods' will to the Danaans,
no man so long as I am alive above earth and see daylight
shall lay the weight of his hands on you beside the hollow ships,
90   not one of all the Danaans, even if you mean Agamemnon,
who now claims to be far the greatest of all the Achaians."
       At this the blameless seer took courage again and spoke forth:
"No, it is not for the sake of some vow or hecatomb[3] he blames us,
but for the sake of his priest whom Agamemnon dishonoured
95   and would not give him back his daughter nor accept the ransom.
Therefore the archer sent griefs against us and will send them
still, nor sooner thrust back the shameful plague from the Danaans
until we give the glancing-eyed girl back to her father

1. Goddess of marriage and the wife and sister of Zeus.
2. Troy.
3. Animal sacrifice.

100 without price, without ransom, and lead also a blessed hecatomb
to Chryse; thus we might propitiate and persuade him."
 He spoke thus and sat down again, and among them stood up
Atreus' son the hero wide-ruling Agamemnon
raging, the heart within filled black to the brim with anger
105 from beneath, but his two eyes showed like fire in their blazing.
First of all he eyed Kalchas bitterly and spoke to him:
"Seer of evil: never yet have you told me a good thing.
Always the evil things are dear to your heart to prophesy,
but nothing excellent have you said nor ever accomplished.
Now once more you make divination to the Danaans, argue
110 forth your reason why he who strikes from afar afflicts them,
because I for the sake of the girl Chryseis would not take
the shining ransom; and indeed I wish greatly to have her
in my own house; since I like her better than Klytaimestra
my own wife, for in truth she is no way inferior,
115 neither in build nor stature nor wit, nor in accomplishment.
Still I am willing to give her back, if such is the best way.
I myself desire that my people be safe, not perish.
Find me then some prize that shall be my own, lest I only
among the Argives go without, since that were unfitting;
120 you are all witnesses to this thing, that my prize goes elsewhere."
 Then in answer again spoke brilliant swift-footed Achilleus:
"Son of Atreus, most lordly, greediest for gain of all men,
how shall the great-hearted Achaians give you a prize now?
There is no great store of things lying about I know of.
125 But what we took from the cities by storm has been distributed;
it is unbecoming for the people to call back things once given.
No, for the present give the girl back to the god; we Achaians
thrice and four times over will repay you, if ever Zeus gives
into our hands the strong-walled citadel of Troy to be plundered."
130 Then in answer again spoke powerful Agamemnon:
"Not that way, good fighter though you be, godlike Achilleus,
strive to cheat, for you will not deceive, you will not persuade me.
What do you want? To keep your own prize and have me sit here
lacking one? Are you ordering me to give this girl back?
135 Either the great-hearted Achaians shall give me a new prize
chosen according to my desire to atone for the girl lost,
or else if they will not give me one I myself shall take her,
your own prize, or that of Aias, or that of Odysseus,
going myself in person; and he whom I visit will be bitter.
140 Still, these are things we shall deliberate again hereafter.
Come, now, we must haul a black ship down to the bright sea,
and assemble rowers enough for it, and put on board it
the hecatomb, and the girl herself, Chryseis of the fair cheeks,
and let there be one responsible man in charge of her,
145 either Aias or Idomeneus or brilliant Odysseus,
or you yourself, son of Peleus, most terrifying of all men,
to reconcile by accomplishing sacrifice the archer."
 Then looking darkly at him Achilleus of the swift feet spoke:

"O wrapped in shamelessness, with your mind forever on profit,
150 how shall any one of the Achaians readily obey you
either to go on a journey or to fight men strongly in battle?
I for my part did not come here for the sake of the Trojan
spearmen to fight against them, since to me they have done nothing.
Never yet have they driven away my cattle or my horses,
155 never in Phthia where the soil is rich and men grow great did they
spoil my harvest, since indeed there is much that lies between us,
the shadowy mountains and the echoing sea; but for your sake,
o great shamelessness, we followed, to do you favour,
you with the dog's eyes, to win your honour and Menelaos'[4]
160 from the Trojans. You forget all this or else you care nothing.
And now my prize you threaten in person to strip from me,
for whom I laboured much, the gift of the sons of the Achaians.
Never, when the Achaians sack some well-founded citadel
of the Trojans, do I have a prize that is equal to your prize.
165 Always the greater part of the painful fighting is the work of
my hands; but when the time comes to distribute the booty
yours is far the greater reward, and I with some small thing
yet dear to me go back to my ships when I am weary with fighting.
Now I am returning to Phthia, since it is much better
170 to go home again with my curved ships, and I am minded no longer
to stay here dishonoured and pile up your wealth and your luxury."
    Then answered him in turn the lord of men Agamemnon:
"Run away by all means if your heart drives you. I will not
entreat you to stay here for my sake. There are others with me
175 who will do me honour, and above all Zeus of the counsels.
To me you are the most hateful of all the kings whom the gods love.
Forever quarrelling is dear to your heart, and wars and battles;
and if you are very strong indeed, that is a god's gift.
Go home then with your own ships and your own companions,
180 be king over the Myrmidons. I care nothing about you.
I take no account of your anger. But here is my threat to you.
Even as Phoibos Apollo is taking away my Chryseis,
I shall convey her back in my own ship, with my own
followers; but I shall take the fair-cheeked Briseis,
185 your prize, I myself going to your shelter, that you may learn well
how much greater I am than you, and another man may shrink back
from likening himself to me and contending against me."
    So he spoke. And the anger came on Peleus' son, and within
his shaggy breast the heart was divided two ways, pondering
190 whether to draw from beside his thigh the sharp sword, driving
away all those who stood between and kill the son of Atreus,
or else to check the spleen within and keep down his anger.
Now as he weighed in mind and spirit these two courses
and was drawing from its scabbard the great sword, Athene descended
195 from the sky. For Hera the goddess of the white arms sent her,

02

4. Agamemnon's brother and the husband of Helen.

who loved both men equally in her heart and cared for them.
The goddess standing behind Peleus' son caught him by the fair hair,
appearing to him only, for no man of the others saw her.
Achilleus in amazement turned about, and straightway
200   knew Pallas Athene and the terrible eyes shining.
He uttered winged words and addressed her: "Why have you come now,
o child of Zeus of the aegis, once more? Is it that you may see
the outrageousness of the son of Atreus Agamemnon?
Yet will I tell you this thing, and I think it shall be accomplished.
205   By such acts of arrogance he may even lose his own life."
       Then in answer the goddess grey-eyed Athene spoke to him:
"I have come down to stay your anger—but will you obey me?—
from the sky; and the goddess of the white arms Hera sent me,
who loves both of you equally in her heart and cares for you.
210   Come then, do not take your sword in your hand, keep clear of fighting,
though indeed with words you may abuse him, and it will be that way.
And this also will I tell you and it will be a thing accomplished.
Some day three times over such shining gifts shall be given you
by reason of this outrage. Hold your hand then, and obey us."
215   Then in answer again spoke Achilleus of the swift feet:
"Goddess, it is necessary that I obey the word of you two,
angry though I am in my heart. So it will be better.
If any man obeys the gods, they listen to him also."
       He spoke, and laid his heavy hand on the silver sword hilt
220   and thrust the great blade back into the scabbard nor disobeyed
the word of Athene. And she went back again to Olympos
to the house of Zeus of the aegis with the other divinities.
       But Peleus' son once again in words of derision
spoke to Atreides, and did not yet let go of his anger:
225   "You wine sack, with a dog's eyes, with a deer's heart. Never
once have you taken courage in your heart to arm with your people
for battle, or go into ambuscade with the best of the Achaians.
No, for in such things you see death. Far better to your mind
is it, all along the widespread host of the Achaians
230   to take away the gifts of any man who speaks up against you.
King who feed on your people, since you rule nonentities;
otherwise, son of Atreus, this were your last outrage.
But I will tell you this and swear a great oath upon it:
in the name of this sceptre, which never again will bear leaf nor
235   branch, now that it has left behind the cut stump in the mountains,
nor shall it ever blossom again, since the bronze blade stripped
bark and leafage, and now at last the sons of the Achaians
carry it in their hands in state when they administer
the justice of Zeus. And this shall be a great oath before you:
240   some day longing for Achilleus will come to the sons of the Achaians,
all of them. Then stricken at heart though you be, you will be able
to do nothing, when in their numbers before man-slaughtering Hektor
they drop and die. And then you will eat out the heart within you
in sorrow, that you did no honour to the best of the Achaians."

245   Thus spoke Peleus' son and dashed to the ground the sceptre
studded with golden nails, and sat down again. But Atreides
raged still on the other side, and between them Nestor
the fair-spoken rose up, the lucid speaker of Pylos,
from whose lips the streams of words ran sweeter than honey.
250 In his time two generations of mortal men had perished,
those who had grown up with him and they who had been born to
these in sacred Pylos, and he was king in the third age.
He in kind intention toward both stood forth and addressed them:
"Oh, for shame. Great sorrow comes on the land of Achaia.
255 Now might Priam and the sons of Priam in truth be happy,
and all the rest of the Trojans be visited in their hearts with gladness,
were they to hear all this wherein you two are quarrelling,
you, who surpass all Danaans in council, in fighting.
Yet be persuaded. Both of you are younger than I am.
260 Yes, and in my time I have dealt with better men than
you are, and never once did they disregard me. Never
yet have I seen nor shall see again such men as these were,
men like Peirithoös, and Dryas, shepherd of the people,
Kaineus and Exadios, godlike Polyphemos,
265 or Theseus, Aigeus' son, in the likeness of the immortals.
These were the strongest generation of earth-born mortals,
the strongest, and they fought against the strongest, the beast men
living within the mountains, and terribly they destroyed them.
I was of the company of these men, coming from Pylos,
270 a long way from a distant land, since they had summoned me.
And I fought single-handed, yet against such men no one
of the mortals now alive upon earth could do battle. And also
these listened to the counsels I gave and heeded my bidding.
Do you also obey, since to be persuaded is better.
275 You, great man that you are, yet do not take the girl away
but let her be, a prize as the sons of the Achaians gave her
first. Nor, son of Peleus, think to match your strength with
the king, since never equal with the rest is the portion of honour
of the sceptred king to whom Zeus gives magnificence. Even
280 though you are the stronger man, and the mother who bore you was immortal,
yet is this man greater who is lord over more than you rule.
Son of Atreus, give up your anger; even I entreat you
to give over your bitterness against Achilleus, he who
stands as a great bulwark of battle over all the Achaians."
285   Then in answer again spoke powerful Agamemnon:
"Yes, old sir, all this you have said is fair and orderly.
Yet here is a man who wishes to be above all others,
who wishes to hold power over all, and to be lord of
all, and give them their orders, yet I think one will not obey him.
290 And if the everlasting gods have made him a spearman,
yet they have not given him the right to speak abusively."
      Then looking at him darkly brilliant Achilleus answered him:
"So must I be called of no account and a coward

	if I must carry out every order you may happen to give me.
295	Tell other men to do these things, but give me no more
	commands, since I for my part have no intention to obey you.
	And put away in your thoughts this other thing I tell you.
	With my hands I will not fight for the girl's sake, neither
	with you nor any other man, since you take her away who gave her.
300	But of all the other things that are mine beside my fast black
	ship, you shall take nothing away against my pleasure.
	Come, then, only try it, that these others may see also;
	instantly your own black blood will stain my spearpoint."
	So these two after battling in words of contention
305	stood up, and broke the assembly beside the ships of the Achaians.
	Peleus' son went back to his balanced ships and his shelter
	with Patroklos, Menoitios' son, and his own companions.
	But the son of Atreus drew a fast ship down to the water
	and allotted into it twenty rowers and put on board it
310	the hecatomb for the god and Chryseis of the fair cheeks
	leading her by the hand. And in charge went crafty Odysseus.
	These then putting out went over the ways of the water
	while Atreus' son told his people to wash off their defilement.
	And they washed it away and threw the washings into the salt sea.
315	Then they accomplished perfect hecatombs to Apollo,
	of bulls and goats along the beach of the barren salt sea.
	The savour of the burning swept in circles up to the bright sky.
	Thus these were busy about the army. But Agamemnon
	did not give up his anger and the first threat he made to Achilleus,
320	but to Talthybios he gave his orders and Eurybates
	who were heralds and hard-working henchmen to him: "Go now
	to the shelter of Peleus' son Achilleus, to bring back
	Briseis of the fair cheeks leading her by the hand. And if he
	will not give her, I must come in person to take her
325	with many men behind me, and it will be the worse for him."
	He spoke and sent them forth with this strong order upon them.
	They went against their will beside the beach of the barren
	salt sea, and came to the shelters and the ships of the Myrmidons.[5]
	The man himself they found beside his shelter and his black ship
330	sitting. And Achilleus took no joy at all when he saw them.
	These two terrified and in awe of the king stood waiting
	quietly, and did not speak a word at all nor question him.
	But he knew the whole matter in his own heart, and spoke first:
	"Welcome, heralds, messengers of Zeus and of mortals.
335	Draw near. You are not to blame in my sight, but Agamemnon
	who sent the two of you here for the sake of the girl Briseis.
	Go then, illustrious Patroklos, and bring the girl forth
	and give her to these to be taken away. Yet let them be witnesses
	in the sight of the blessed gods, in the sight of mortal
340	men, and of this cruel king, if ever hereafter

5. Achilleus' men.

there shall be need of me to beat back the shameful destruction
from the rest. For surely in ruinous heart he makes sacrifice
and has not wit enough to look behind and before him
that the Achaians fighting beside their ships shall not perish."

345 So he spoke, and Patroklos obeyed his beloved companion.
He led forth from the hut Briseis of the fair cheeks and gave her
to be taken away; and they walked back beside the ships of the Achaians,
and the woman all unwilling went with them still. But Achilleus
weeping went and sat in sorrow apart from his companions
350 beside the beach of the grey sea looking out on the infinite water.
Many times stretching forth his hands he called on his mother:[6]
"Since, my mother, you bore me to be a man with a short life,
therefore Zeus of the loud thunder on Olympos should grant me
honour at least. But now he has given me not even a little.
355 Now the son of Atreus, powerful Agamemnon,
has dishonoured me, since he has taken away my prize and keeps it."

So he spoke in tears and the lady his mother heard him
as she sat in the depths of the sea at the side of her aged father,
and lightly she emerged like a mist from the grey water.
360 She came and sat beside him as he wept, and stroked him
with her hand and called him by name and spoke to him: "Why then,
child, do you lament? What sorrow has come to your heart now?
Tell me, do not hide it in your mind, and thus we shall both know."

Sighing heavily Achilleus of the swift feet answered her:
365 "You know; since you know why must I tell you all this?
We went against Thebe, the sacred city of Eëtion,
and the city we sacked, and carried everything back to this place,
and the sons of the Achaians made a fair distribution
and for Atreus' son they chose out Chryseis of the fair cheeks.
370 Then Chryses, priest of him who strikes from afar, Apollo,
came beside the fast ships of the bronze-armoured Achaians to ransom
back his daughter, carrying gifts beyond count and holding
in his hands wound on a staff of gold the ribbons of Apollo
who strikes from afar, and supplicated all the Achaians,
375 but above all Atreus' two sons, the marshals of the people.
Then all the rest of the Achaians cried out in favour
that the priest be respected and the shining ransom be taken;
yet this pleased not the heart of Atreus' son Agamemnon,
but harshly he sent him away with a strong order upon him.
380 The old man went back again in anger, but Apollo
listened to his prayer, since he was very dear to him, and let go
the wicked arrow against the Argives. And now the people
were dying one after another while the god's shafts ranged
everywhere along the wide host of the Achaians, till the seer
385 knowing well the truth interpreted the designs of the archer.
It was I first of all urged then the god's appeasement;
and the anger took hold of Atreus' son, and in speed standing

6. The sea-nymph Thetis.

he uttered his threat against me, and now it is a thing accomplished.
For the girl the glancing-eyed Achaians are taking to Chryse
390 in a fast ship, also carrying to the king presents. But even
now the heralds went away from my shelter leading
Briseus' daughter, whom the sons of the Achaians gave me.
You then, if you have power to, protect your own son, going
to Olympos and supplicating Zeus, if ever before now
395 either by word you comforted Zeus' heart or by action.
Since it is many times in my father's halls I have heard you
making claims, when you said you only among the immortals
beat aside shameful destruction from Kronos' son the dark-misted,[7]
that time when all the other Olympians sought to bind him,
400 Hera and Poseidon and Pallas Athene. Then you,
goddess, went and set him free from his shackles, summoning
in speed the creature of the hundred hands to tall Olympos,
that creature the gods name Briareus, but all men
Aigaios' son, but he is far greater in strength than his father.
405 He rejoicing in the glory of it sat down by Kronion,
and the rest of the blessed gods were frightened and gave up binding him.
Sit beside him and take his knees and remind him of these things
now, if perhaps he might be willing to help the Trojans,
and pin the Achaians back against the ships and the water,
410 dying, so that thus they may all have profit of their own king,
that Atreus' son wide-ruling Agamemnon may recognize
his madness, that he did no honour to the best of the Achaians."
　　Thetis answered him then letting the tears fall: "Ah me,
my child. Your birth was bitterness. Why did I raise you?
415 If only you could sit by your ships untroubled, not weeping,
since indeed your lifetime is to be short, of no length.
Now it has befallen that your life must be brief and bitter
beyond all men's. To a bad destiny I bore you in my chambers.
But I will go to cloud-dark Olympos and ask this
420 thing of Zeus who delights in the thunder. Perhaps he will do it.
Do you therefore continuing to sit by your swift ships
be angry at the Achaians and stay away from all fighting.
For Zeus went to the blameless Aithiopians at the Ocean
yesterday to feast, and the rest of the gods went with him.
425 On the twelfth day he will be coming back to Olympos,
and then I will go for your sake to the house of Zeus, bronze-founded,
and take him by the knees and I think I can persuade him."
　　So speaking she went away from that place and left him
sorrowing in his heart for the sake of the fair-girdled woman
430 whom they were taking by force against his will. But Odysseus
meanwhile drew near to Chryse conveying the sacred hecatomb.
These when they were inside the many-hollowed harbour
took down and gathered together the sails and stowed them in the black
ship;

7. Zeus.

let down mast by the forestays, and settled it into the mast crutch
435   easily, and rowed her in with oars to the mooring.
They threw over the anchor stones and made fast the stern cables
and themselves stepped out on to the break of the sea beach,
and led forth the hecatomb to the archer Apollo,
and Chryseis herself stepped forth from the sea-going vessel.
440   Odysseus of the many designs guided her to the altar
and left her in her father's arms and spoke a word to him:
"Chryses, I was sent here by the lord of men Agamemnon
to lead back your daughter and accomplish a sacred hecatomb
to Apollo on behalf of the Danaans, that we may propitiate
445   the lord who has heaped unhappiness and tears on the Argives."
    He spoke, and left her in his arms. And he received gladly
his beloved child. And the men arranged the sacred hecatomb
for the god in orderly fashion around the strong-founded altar.
Next they washed their hands and took up the scattering barley.
450   Standing among them with lifted arms Chryses prayed in a great voice:
"Hear me, lord of the silver bow, who set your power about
Chryse and Killa the sacrosanct, who are lord in strength over
Tenedos; if once before you listened to my prayers
and did me honour and smote strongly the host of the Achaians,
455   so one more time bring to pass the wish that I pray for.
Beat aside at last the shameful plague from the Danaans."
    So he spoke in prayer, and Phoibos Apollo heard him.
And when all had made prayer and flung down the scattering barley
first they drew back the victims' heads and slaughtered them and skinned
    them,
460   and cut away the meat from the thighs and wrapped them in fat,
making a double fold, and laid shreds of flesh upon them.
The old man burned these on a cleft stick and poured the gleaming
wine over, while the young men with forks in their hands stood about him.
But when they had burned the thigh pieces and tasted the vitals,
465   they cut all the remainder into pieces and spitted them
and roasted all carefully and took off the pieces.
Then after they had finished the work and got the feast ready
they feasted, nor was any man's hunger denied a fair portion.
But when they had put away their desire for eating and drinking,
470   the young men filled the mixing bowls with pure wine, passing
a portion to all, when they had offered drink in the goblets.
All day long they propitiated the god with singing,
chanting a splendid hymn to Apollo, these young Achaians,
singing to the one who works from afar, who listened in gladness.
475   Afterwards when the sun went down and darkness came onward
they lay down and slept beside the ship's stern cables.
But when the young Dawn showed again with her rosy fingers,
they put forth to sea toward the wide camp of the Achaians.
And Apollo who works from afar sent them a favouring stern wind.
480   They set up the mast again and spread on it the white sails,
and the wind blew into the middle of the sail, and at the cutwater

a blue wave rose and sang strongly as the ship went onward.
She ran swiftly cutting across the swell her pathway.
But when they had come back to the wide camp of the Achaians
485 they hauled the black ship up on the mainland, high up
on the sand, and underneath her they fixed the long props.
Afterwards they scattered to their own ships and their shelters.

But that other still sat in anger beside his swift ships,
Peleus' son divinely born, Achilleus of the swift feet.
490 Never now would he go to assemblies where men win glory,
never more into battle, but continued to waste his heart out
sitting there, though he longed always for the clamour and fighting.

But when the twelfth dawn after this day appeared, the gods who
live forever came back to Olympos all in a body
495 and Zeus led them; nor did Thetis forget the entreaties
of her son, but she emerged from the sea's waves early
in the morning and went up to the tall sky and Olympos.
She found Kronos' broad-browed son apart from the others
sitting upon the highest peak of rugged Olympos.
500 She came and sat beside him with her left hand embracing
his knees, but took him underneath the chin with her right hand
and spoke in supplication to lord Zeus son of Kronos:
"Father Zeus, if ever before in word or action
I did you favour among the immortals, now grant what I ask for.
505 Now give honour to my son short-lived beyond all other
mortals. Since even now the lord of men Agamemnon
dishonours him, who has taken away his prize and keeps it.
Zeus of the counsels, lord of Olympos, now do him honour.
So long put strength into the Trojans, until the Achaians
510 give my son his rights, and his honour is increased among them."

She spoke thus. But Zeus who gathers the clouds made no answer
but sat in silence a long time. And Thetis, as she had taken
his knees, clung fast to them and urged once more her question:
"Bend your head and promise me to accomplish this thing,
515 or else refuse it, you have nothing to fear, that I may know
by how much I am the most dishonoured of all gods."

Deeply disturbed Zeus who gathers the clouds answered her:
"This is a disastrous matter when you set me in conflict
with Hera, and she troubles me with recriminations.
520 Since even as things are, forever among the immortals
she is at me and speaks of how I help the Trojans in battle.
Even so, go back again now, go away, for fear she
see us. I will look to these things that they be accomplished.
See then, I will bend my head that you may believe me.
525 For this among the immortal gods is the mightiest witness
I can give, and nothing I do shall be vain nor revocable
nor a thing unfulfilled when I bend my head in assent to it."

He spoke, the son of Kronos, and nodded his head with the dark brows,
and the immortally anointed hair of the great god
530 swept from his divine head, and all Olympos was shaken.

So these two who had made their plans separated, and Thetis
leapt down again from shining Olympos into the sea's depth,
but Zeus went back to his own house, and all the gods rose up
from their chairs to greet the coming of their father, not one had courage
535   to keep his place as the father advanced, but stood up to greet him.
Thus he took his place on the throne; yet Hera was not
ignorant, having seen how he had been plotting counsels
with Thetis the silver-footed, the daughter of the sea's ancient,
and at once she spoke revilingly to Zeus son of Kronos:
540   "Treacherous one, what god has been plotting counsels with you?
Always it is dear to your heart in my absence to think of
secret things and decide upon them. Never have you patience
frankly to speak forth to me the thing that you purpose."
Then to her the father of gods and men made answer:
545   "Hera, do not go on hoping that you will hear all my
thoughts, since these will be too hard for you, though you are my wife.
Any thought that it is right for you to listen to, no one
neither man nor any immortal shall hear it before you.
But anything that apart from the rest of the gods I wish to
550   plan, do not always question each detail nor probe me."
Then the goddess the ox-eyed lady Hera answered:
"Majesty, son of Kronos, what sort of thing have you spoken?
Truly too much in time past I have not questioned nor probed you,
but you are entirely free to think out whatever pleases you.
555   Now, though, I am terribly afraid you were won over
by Thetis the silver-footed, the daughter of the sea's ancient.
For early in the morning she sat beside you and took your
knees, and I think you bowed your head in assent to do honour
to Achilleus, and to destroy many beside the ships of the Achaians."
560   Then in return Zeus who gathers the clouds made answer:
"Dear lady, I never escape you, you are always full of suspicion.
Yet thus you can accomplish nothing surely, but be more
distant from my heart than ever, and it will be the worse for you.
If what you say is true, then that is the way I wish it.
565   But go then, sit down in silence, and do as I tell you,
for fear all the gods, as many as are on Olympos, can do nothing
if I come close and lay my unconquerable hands upon you."
He spoke, and the goddess the ox-eyed lady Hera was frightened
and went and sat down in silence wrenching her heart to obedience,
570   and all the Uranian gods in the house of Zeus were troubled.
Hephaistos the renowned smith rose up to speak among them,
to bring comfort to his beloved mother, Hera of the white arms:
"This will be a disastrous matter and not endurable
if you two are to quarrel thus for the sake of mortals
575   and bring brawling among the gods. There will be no pleasure
in the stately feast at all, since vile things will be uppermost.
And I entreat my mother, though she herself understands it,
to be ingratiating toward our father Zeus, that no longer
our father may scold her and break up the quiet of our feasting.

580 For if the Olympian who handles the lightning should be minded
to hurl us out of our places, he is far too strong for any.
Do you therefore approach him again with words made gentle,
and at once the Olympian will be gracious again to us."
He spoke, and springing to his feet put a two-handled goblet
585 into his mother's hands and spoke again to her once more:
"Have patience, my mother, and endure it, though you be saddened,
for fear that, dear as you are, I see you before my own eyes
struck down, and then sorry though I be I shall not be able
to do anything. It is too hard to fight against the Olympian.
590 There was a time once before now I was minded to help you,
and he caught me by the foot and threw me from the magic threshold,
and all day long I dropped helpless, and about sunset
I landed in Lemnos, and there was not much life left in me.
After that fall it was the Sintian men who took care of me."
595 He spoke, and the goddess of the white arms Hera smiled at him,
and smiling she accepted the goblet out of her son's hand.
Thereafter beginning from the left he poured drinks for the other
gods, dipping up from the mixing bowl the sweet nectar.
But among the blessed immortals uncontrollable laughter
600 went up as they saw Hephaistos bustling about the palace.
Thus thereafter the whole day long until the sun went under
they feasted, nor was anyone's hunger denied a fair portion,
nor denied the beautifully wrought lyre in the hands of Apollo
nor the antiphonal sweet sound of the Muses singing.
605 Afterwards when the light of the flaming sun went under
they went away each one to sleep in his home where
for each one the far-renowned strong-handed Hephaistos
had built a house by means of his craftsmanship and cunning.
Zeus the Olympian and lord of the lightning went to
610 his own bed, where always he lay when sweet sleep came on him.
Going up to the bed he slept and Hera of the gold throne beside him.

Book 18

[Achilles' Shield]

So these fought on in the likeness of blazing fire. Meanwhile,
Antilochos came, a swift-footed messenger, to Achilleus,
and found him sitting in front of the steep-horned ships, thinking
over in his heart of things which had now been accomplished.
5 Disturbed, Achilleus spoke to the spirit in his own great heart:
"Ah me, how is it that once again the flowing-haired Achaians
are driven out of the plain on their ships in fear and confusion?
May the gods not accomplish vile sorrows upon the heart in me
in the way my mother once made it clear to me, when she told me
10 how while I yet lived the bravest of all the Myrmidons
must leave the light of the sun beneath the hands of the Trojans.
Surely, then, the strong son of Menoitios has perished.

Unhappy! and yet I told him, once he had beaten the fierce fire
off, to come back to the ships, not fight in strength against Hektor."
15   Now as he was pondering this in his heart and his spirit,
meanwhile the son of stately Nestor was drawing near him
and wept warm tears, and gave Achilleus his sorrowful message:
"Ah me, son of valiant Peleus; you must hear from me
the ghastly message of a thing I wish never had happened.
20   Patroklos has fallen, and now they are fighting over his body
which is naked. Hektor of the shining helm has taken his armour."
He spoke, and the black cloud of sorrow closed on Achilleus.
In both hands he caught up the grimy dust, and poured it
over his head and face, and fouled his handsome countenance,
25   and the black ashes were scattered over his immortal tunic.
And he himself, mightily in his might, in the dust lay
at length, and took and tore at his hair with his hands, and defiled it.
And the handmaidens Achilleus and Patroklos had taken
captive, stricken at heart cried out aloud, and came running
30   out of doors about valiant Achilleus, and all of them
beat their breasts with their hands, and the limbs went slack in each of them.
On the other side Antilochos mourned with him, letting the tears fall,
and held the hands of Achilleus as he grieved in his proud heart,
fearing Achilleus might cut his throat with the iron. He cried out
35   terribly, aloud, and the lady his mother heard him
as she sat in the depths of the sea at the side of her aged father,
and she cried shrill in turn, and the goddesses gathered about her,
all who along the depth of the sea were daughters of Nereus.
For Glauke was there, Kymodoke and Thaleia,
40   Nesaie and Speio and Thoë, and ox-eyed Halia;
Kymothoë was there, Aktaia and Limnoreia,
Melite and Iaira, Amphithoë and Agauë,
Doto and Proto, Dynamene and Pherousa,
Dexamene and Amphinome and Kallianeira;
45   Doris and Panope and glorious Galateia,
Nemertes and Apseudes and Kallianassa;
Klymene was there, Ianeira and Ianassa,
Maira and Oreithyia and lovely-haired Amatheia,
and the rest who along the depth of the sea were daughters of Nereus.
50   The silvery cave was filled with these, and together all of them
beat their breasts, and among them Thetis led out the threnody:
"Hear me, Nereids, my sisters; so you may all know
well all the sorrows that are in my heart, when you hear of them from me.
Ah me, my sorrow, the bitterness in this best of child-bearing,
55   since I gave birth to a son who was without fault and powerful,
conspicuous among heroes; and he shot up like a young tree,
and I nurtured him, like a tree grown in the pride of the orchard.
I sent him away with the curved ships into the land of Ilion
to fight with the Trojans; but I shall never again receive him
60   won home again to his country and into the house of Peleus.
Yet while I see him live and he looks on the sunlight, he has

sorrows, and though I go to him I can do nothing to help him.
Yet I shall go, to look on my dear son, and to listen
to the sorrow that has come to him as he stays back from the fighting."

65   So she spoke, and left the cave, and the others together
went with her in tears, and about them the wave of the water
was broken. Now these, when they came to the generous Troad,
followed each other out on the sea-shore, where close together
the ships of the Myrmidons were hauled up about swift Achilleus.
70   There as he sighed heavily the lady his mother stood by him
and cried out shrill and aloud, and took her son's head in her arms, then
sorrowing for him she spoke to him in winged words: "Why then,
child, do you lament? What sorrow has come to your heart now?
Speak out, do not hide it. These things are brought to accomplishment
75   through Zeus: in the way that you lifted your hands and prayed for,
that all the sons of the Achaians be pinned on their grounded vessels
by reason of your loss, and suffer things that are shameful."
      Then sighing heavily Achilleus of the swift feet answered her:
"My mother, all these things the Olympian brought to accomplishment.
80   But what pleasure is this to me, since my dear companion has perished,
Patroklos, whom I loved beyond all other companions,
as well as my own life. I have lost him, and Hektor, who killed him,
has stripped away that gigantic armour, a wonder to look on
and splendid, which the gods gave Peleus, a glorious present,
85   on that day they drove you to the marriage bed of a mortal.
I wish you had gone on living then with the other goddesses
of the sea, and that Peleus had married some mortal woman.
As it is, there must be on your heart a numberless sorrow
for your son's death, since you can never again receive him
90   won home again to his country; since the spirit within does not drive me
to go on living and be among men, except on condition
that Hektor first be beaten down under my spear, lose his life
and pay the price for stripping Patroklos, the son of Menoitios."
      Then in turn Thetis spoke to him, letting the tears fall:
95   "Then I must lose you soon, my child, by what you are saying,
since it is decreed your death must come soon after Hektor's."
      Then deeply disturbed Achilleus of the swift feet answered her:
"I must die soon, then; since I was not to stand by my companion
when he was killed. And now, far away from the land of his fathers,
100   he has perished, and lacked my fighting strength to defend him.
Now, since I am not going back to the beloved land of my fathers,
since I was no light of safety to Patroklos, nor to my other
companions, who in their numbers went down before glorious Hektor,
but sit here beside my ships, a useless weight on the good land,
105   I, who am such as no other of the bronze-armoured Achaians
in battle, though there are others also better in council—
why, I wish that strife would vanish away from among gods and mortals,
and gall, which makes a man grow angry for all his great mind,
that gall of anger that swarms like smoke inside of a man's heart
110   and becomes a thing sweeter to him by far than the dripping of honey.

So it was here that the lord of men Agamemnon angered me.
Still, we will let all this be a thing of the past, and for all our
sorrow beat down by force the anger deeply within us.
Now I shall go, to overtake that killer of a dear life,
115 Hektor; then I will accept my own death, at whatever
time Zeus wishes to bring it about, and the other immortals.
For not even the strength of Herakles fled away from destruction,
although he was dearest of all to lord Zeus, son of Kronos,
but his fate beat him under, and the wearisome anger of Hera.
120 So I likewise, if such is the fate which has been wrought for me,
shall lie still, when I am dead. Now I must win excellent glory,
and drive some one of the women of Troy, or some deep-girdled
Dardanian woman, lifting up to her soft cheeks both hands
to wipe away the close bursts of tears in her lamentation,
125 and learn that I stayed too long out of the fighting. Do not
hold me back from the fight, though you love me. You will not persuade me."
    In turn the goddess Thetis of the silver feet answered him:
"Yes, it is true, my child, this is no cowardly action,
to beat aside sudden death from your afflicted companions.
130 Yet, see now, your splendid armour, glaring and brazen,
is held among the Trojans, and Hektor of the shining helmet
wears it on his own shoulders, and glories in it. Yet I think
he will not glory for long, since his death stands very close to him.
Therefore do not yet go into the grind of the war god,
135 not before with your own eyes you see me come back to you.
For I am coming to you at dawn and as the sun rises
bringing splendid armour to you from the lord Hephaistos."
    So she spoke, and turned, and went away from her son,
and turning now to her sisters of the sea she spoke to them:
140 "Do you now go back into the wide fold of the water
to visit the ancient of the sea and the house of our father,
and tell him everything. I am going to tall Olympos
and to Hephaistos, the glorious smith, if he might be willing
to give me for my son renowned and radiant armour."
145 She spoke, and they plunged back beneath the wave of the water,
while she the goddess Thetis of the silver feet went onward
to Olympos, to bring back to her son the glorious armour.
    So her feet carried her to Olympos; meanwhile the Achaians
with inhuman clamour before the attack of manslaughtering Hektor
150 fled until they were making for their own ships and the Hellespont;
nor could the strong-greaved Achaians have dragged the body
of Patroklos, henchman of Achilleus, from under the missiles,
for once again the men and the horses came over upon him,
and Hektor, Priam's son, who fought like a flame in his fury.
155 Three times from behind glorious Hektor caught him
by the feet, trying to drag him, and called aloud on the Trojans.
Three times the two Aiantes with their battle-fury upon them
beat him from the corpse, but he, steady in the confidence of his great strength,
kept making, now a rush into the crowd, or again at another time

160 stood fast, with his great cry, but gave not a bit of ground backward.
And as herdsmen who dwell in the fields are not able to frighten
a tawny lion in his great hunger away from a carcass,
so the two Aiantes, marshals of men, were not able
to scare Hektor, Priam's son, away from the body.

165 And now he would have dragged it away and won glory forever
had not swift wind-footed Iris come running from Olympos
with a message for Peleus' son to arm. She came secretly
from Zeus and the other gods, since it was Hera who sent her.
She came and stood close to him and addressed him in winged words:

170 "Rise up, son of Peleus, most terrifying of all men.
Defend Patroklos, for whose sake the terrible fighting
stands now in front of the ships. They are destroying each other;
the Achaians fight in defence over the fallen body
while the others, the Trojans, are rushing to drag the corpse off

175 to windy Ilion, and beyond all glorious Hektor
rages to haul it away, since the anger within him is urgent
to cut the head from the soft neck and set it on sharp stakes.
Up, then, lie here no longer; let shame come into your heart, lest
Patroklos become sport for the dogs of Troy to worry,

180 your shame, if the body goes from here with defilement upon it."
Then in turn Achilleus of the swift feet answered her:
"Divine Iris, what god sent you to me with a message?"
Then in turn swift wind-footed Iris spoke to him:
"Hera sent me, the honoured wife of Zeus; but the son of

185 Kronos, who sits on high, does not know this, nor any other
immortal, of all those who dwell by the snows of Olympos."
Then in answer to her spoke Achilleus of the swift feet:
"How shall I go into the fighting? They have my armour.
And my beloved mother told me I must not be armoured,

190 not before with my own eyes I see her come back to me.
She promised she would bring magnificent arms from Hephaistos.
Nor do I know of another whose glorious armour I could wear
unless it were the great shield of Telamonian Aias.
But he himself wears it, I think, and goes in the foremost

195 of the spear-fight over the body of fallen Patroklos."
Then in turn swift wind-footed Iris spoke to him:
"Yes, we also know well how they hold your glorious armour.
But go to the ditch, and show yourself as you are to the Trojans,
if perhaps the Trojans might be frightened, and give way

200 from their attack, and the fighting sons of the Achaians get wind
again after hard work. There is little breathing space in the fighting."
So speaking Iris of the swift feet went away from him;
but Achilleus, the beloved of Zeus, rose up, and Athene
swept about his powerful shoulders the fluttering aegis;

205 and she, the divine among goddesses, about his head circled
a golden cloud, and kindled from it a flame far-shining.
As when a flare goes up into the high air from a city
from an island far away, with enemies fighting about it

who all day long are in the hateful division of Ares
210 fighting from their own city, but as the sun goes down signal
fires blaze out one after another, so that the glare goes
pulsing high for men of the neighbouring islands to see it,
in case they might come over in ships to beat off the enemy;
so from the head of Achilleus the blaze shot into the bright air.
215 He went from the wall and stood by the ditch, nor mixed with the other
Achaians, since he followed the close command of his mother.
There he stood, and shouted, and from her place Pallas Athene
gave cry, and drove an endless terror upon the Trojans.
As loud as comes the voice that is screamed out by a trumpet
220 by murderous attackers who beleaguer a city,
so then high and clear went up the voice of Aiakides.[1]
But the Trojans, when they heard the brazen voice of Aiakides,
the heart was shaken in all, and the very floating-maned horses
turned their chariots about, since their hearts saw the coming afflictions.
225 The charioteers were dumbfounded as they saw the unwearied dangerous
fire that played above the head of great-hearted Peleion
blazing, and kindled by the goddess grey-eyed Athene.
Three times across the ditch brilliant Achilleus gave his great cry,
and three times the Trojans and their renowned companions were routed.
230 There at that time twelve of the best men among them perished
upon their own chariots and spears. Meanwhile the Achaians
gladly pulled Patroklos out from under the missiles
and set him upon a litter, and his own companions about him
stood mourning, and along with them swift-footed Achilleus
235 went, letting fall warm tears as he saw his steadfast companion
lying there on a carried litter and torn with the sharp bronze,
the man he had sent off before with horses and chariot
into the fighting; who never again came home to be welcomed.
    Now the lady Hera of the ox eyes drove the unwilling
240 weariless sun god to sink in the depth of the Ocean,
and the sun went down, and the brilliant Achaians gave over
their strong fighting, and the doubtful collision of battle.
    The Trojans on the other side moved from the strong encounter
in their turn, and unyoked their running horses from under the chariots,
245 and gathered into assembly before taking thought for their supper.
They stood on their feet in assembly, nor did any man have the patience
to sit down, but the terror was on them all, seeing that Achilleus
had appeared, after he had stayed so long from the difficult fighting.
First to speak among them was the careful Poulydamas,
250 Panthoös' son, who alone of them looked before and behind him.
He was companion to Hektor, and born on the same night with him,
but he was better in words, the other with the spear far better.
He in kind intention toward all stood forth and addressed them:
"Now take careful thought, dear friends; for I myself urge you
255 to go back into the city and not wait for the divine dawn

---

1. Achilleus, grandson of Aiakos, himself a son of Zeus.

in the plain beside the ships. We are too far from the wall now.
While this man was still angry with great Agamemnon,
for all that time the Achaians were easier men to fight with.
For I also used then to be one who was glad to sleep out
260 near their ships, and I hoped to capture the oarswept vessels.
But now I terribly dread the swift-footed son of Peleus.
So violent is the valour in him, he will not be willing
to stay here in the plain, where now Achaians and Trojans
from either side sunder between them the wrath of the war god.
265 With him, the fight will be for the sake of our city and women.
Let us go into the town; believe me; thus it will happen.
For this present, immortal night has stopped the swift-footed
son of Peleus, but if he catches us still in this place
tomorrow, and drives upon us in arms, a man will be well
270 aware of him, be glad to get back into sacred Ilion,
the man who escapes; there will be many Trojans the vultures
and dogs will feed on. But let such a word be out of my hearing!
If all of us will do as I say, though it hurts us to do it,
this night we will hold our strength in the market place, and the great walls
275 and the gateways, and the long, smooth-planed, close-joined gate timbers
that close to fit them shall defend our city. Then, early
in the morning, under dawn, we shall arm ourselves in our war gear
and take stations along the walls. The worse for him, if he endeavours
to come away from the ships and fight us here for our city.
280 Back he must go to his ships again, when he wears out the strong necks
of his horses, driving them at a gallop everywhere by the city.
His valour will not give him leave to burst in upon us
nor sack our town. Sooner the circling dogs will feed on him."
Then looking darkly at him Hektor of the shining helm spoke:
285 "Poulydamas, these things that you argue please me no longer
when you tell us to go back again and be cooped in our city.
Have you not all had your glut of being fenced in our outworks?
There was a time when mortal men would speak of the city
of Priam as a place with much gold and much bronze. But now
290 the lovely treasures that lay away in our houses have vanished,
and many possessions have been sold and gone into Phrygia
and into Maionia the lovely, when great Zeus was angry.
But now, when the son of devious-devising Kronos has given
me the winning of glory by the ships, to pin the Achaians
295 on the sea, why, fool, no longer show these thoughts to our people.
Not one of the Trojans will obey you. I shall not allow it.
Come, then, do as I say and let us all be persuaded.
Now, take your supper by positions along the encampment,
and do not forget your watch, and let every man be wakeful.
300 And if any Trojan is strongly concerned about his possessions,
let him gather them and give them to the people, to use them in common.
It is better for one of us to enjoy them than for the Achaians.
In the morning, under dawn, we shall arm ourselves in our war gear
and waken the bitter god of war by the hollow vessels.

305   If it is true that brilliant Achilleus is risen beside their
ships, then the worse for him if he tries it, since I for my part
will not run from him out of the sorrowful battle, but rather
stand fast, to see if he wins the great glory, or if I can win it.
The war god is impartial. Before now he has killed the killer."
310   So spoke Hektor, and the Trojans thundered to hear him;
fools, since Pallas Athene had taken away the wits from them.
They gave their applause to Hektor in his counsel of evil,
but none to Poulydamas, who had spoken good sense before them.
They took their supper along the encampment. Meanwhile the Achaians
315 mourned all night in lamentation over Patroklos.
Peleus' son led the thronging chant of their lamentation,
and laid his manslaughtering hands over the chest of his dear friend
with outbursts of incessant grief. As some great bearded lion
when some man, a deer hunter, has stolen his cubs away from him
320 out of the close wood; the lion comes back too late, and is anguished,
and turns into many valleys quartering after the man's trail
on the chance of finding him, and taken with bitter anger;
so he, groaning heavily, spoke out to the Myrmidons:
"Ah me. It was an empty word I cast forth on that day
325 when in his halls I tried to comfort the hero Menoitios.
I told him I would bring back his son in glory to Opous
with Ilion sacked, and bringing his share of war spoils allotted.
But Zeus does not bring to accomplishment all thoughts in men's minds.
Thus it is destiny for us both to stain the same soil
330 here in Troy; since I shall never come home, and my father,
Peleus the aged rider, will not welcome me in his great house,
nor Thetis my mother, but in this place the earth will receive me.
But seeing that it is I, Patroklos, who follow you underground,
I will not bury you till I bring to this place the armour
335 and the head of Hektor, since he was your great-hearted murderer.
Before your burning pyre I shall behead twelve glorious
children of the Trojans, for my anger over your slaying.
Until then, you shall lie where you are in front of my curved ships
and beside you women of Troy and deep-girdled Dardanian women
340 shall sorrow for you night and day and shed tears for you, those whom
you and I worked hard to capture by force and the long spear
in days when we were storming the rich cities of mortals."
     So speaking brilliant Achilleus gave orders to his companions
to set a great cauldron across the fire, so that with all speed
345 they could wash away the clotted blood from Patroklos.
They set up over the blaze of the fire a bath-water cauldron
and poured water into it and put logs underneath and kindled them.
The fire worked on the swell of the cauldron, and the water heated.
But when the water had come to a boil in the shining bronze, then
350 they washed the body and anointed it softly with olive oil
and stopped the gashes in his body with stored-up unguents
and laid him on a bed, and shrouded him in a thin sheet
from head to foot, and covered that over with a white mantle.

Then all night long, gathered about Achilleus of the swift feet,
355   the Myrmidons mourned for Patroklos and lamented over him.
But Zeus spoke to Hera, who was his wife and his sister:
"So you have acted, then, lady Hera of the ox eyes.
You have roused up Achilleus of the swift feet. It must be then
that the flowing-haired Achaians are born of your own generation."
360   Then the goddess the ox-eyed lady Hera answered him:
"Majesty, son of Kronos, what sort of thing have you spoken?
Even one who is mortal will try to accomplish his purpose
for another, though he be a man and knows not such wisdom as we do.
As for me then, who claim I am highest of all the goddesses,
365   both ways, since I am eldest born and am called your consort,
yours, and you in turn are lord over all the immortals,
how could I not weave sorrows for the men of Troy, when I hate them?"
Now as these two were saying things like this to each other,
Thetis of the silver feet came to the house of Hephaistos,
370   imperishable, starry, and shining among the immortals,
built in bronze for himself by the god of the dragging footsteps.
She found him sweating as he turned here and there to his bellows
busily, since he was working on twenty tripods
which were to stand against the wall of his strong-founded dwelling.
375   And he had set golden wheels underneath the base of each one
so that of their own motion they could wheel into the immortal
gathering, and return to his house: a wonder to look at.
These were so far finished, but the elaborate ear handles
were not yet on. He was forging these, and beating the chains out.
380   As he was at work on this in his craftsmanship and his cunning
meanwhile the goddess Thetis the silver-footed drew near him.
Charis of the shining veil saw her as she came forward,
she, the lovely goddess the renowned strong-armed one had married.
She came, and caught her hand and called her by name and spoke to her:
385   "Why is it, Thetis of the light robes, you have come to our house now?
We honour you and love you; but you have not come much before this.
But come in with me, so I may put entertainment before you."
She spoke, and, shining among divinities, led the way forward
and made Thetis sit down in a chair that was wrought elaborately
390   and splendid with silver nails, and under it was a footstool.
She called to Hephaistos the renowned smith and spoke a word to him:
"Hephaistos, come this way; here is Thetis, who has need of you."
Hearing her the renowned smith of the strong arms answered her:
"Then there is a goddess we honour and respect in our house.
395   She saved me when I suffered much at the time of my great fall
through the will of my own brazen-faced mother, who wanted
to hide me, for being lame. Then my soul would have taken much suffering
had not Eurynome and Thetis caught me and held me,
Eurynome, daughter of Ocean, whose stream bends back in a circle.
400   With them I worked nine years as a smith, and wrought many intricate
things; pins that bend back, curved clasps, cups, necklaces, working
there in the hollow of the cave, and the stream of Ocean around us

went on forever with its foam and its murmur. No other
among the gods or among mortal men knew about us
405 except Eurynome and Thetis. They knew, since they saved me.
Now she has come into our house; so I must by all means
do everything to give recompense to lovely-haired Thetis
for my life. Therefore set out before her fair entertainment
while I am putting away my bellows and all my instruments."

410   He spoke, and took the huge blower off from the block of the anvil
limping; and yet his shrunken legs moved lightly beneath him.
He set the bellows away from the fire, and gathered and put away
all the tools with which he worked in a silver strongbox.
Then with a sponge he wiped clean his forehead, and both hands,
415 and his massive neck and hairy chest, and put on a tunic,
and took up a heavy stick in his hand, and went to the doorway
limping. And in support of their master moved his attendants.
These are golden, and in appearance like living young women.
There is intelligence in their hearts, and there is speech in them
420 and strength, and from the immortal gods they have learned how to do
       things.
These stirred nimbly in support of their master, and moving
near to where Thetis sat in her shining chair, Hephaistos
caught her by the hand and called her by name and spoke a word to her:
"Why is it, Thetis of the light robes, you have come to our house now?
425 We honour you and love you; but you have not come much before this.
Speak forth what is in your mind. My heart is urgent to do it
if I can, and if it is a thing that can be accomplished."
       Then in turn Thetis answered him, letting the tears fall:
"Hephaistos, is there among all the goddesses on Olympos
430 one who in her heart has endured so many grim sorrows
as the griefs Zeus, son of Kronos, has given me beyond others?
Of all the other sisters of the sea he gave me to a mortal,
to Peleus, Aiakos' son, and I had to endure mortal marriage
though much against my will. And now he, broken by mournful
435 old age, lies away in his halls. Yet I have other troubles.
For since he has given me a son to bear and to raise up
conspicuous among heroes, and he shot up like a young tree,
I nurtured him, like a tree grown in the pride of the orchard.
I sent him away in the curved ships to the land of Ilion
440 to fight with the Trojans; but I shall never again receive him
won home again to his country and into the house of Peleus.
Yet while I see him live and he looks on the sunlight, he has
sorrows, and though I go to him I can do nothing to help him.
And the girl the sons of the Achaians chose out for his honour
445 powerful Agamemnon took her away again out of his hands.
For her his heart has been wasting in sorrow; but meanwhile the Trojans
pinned the Achaians against their grounded ships, and would not
let them win outside, and the elders of the Argives entreated
my son, and named the many glorious gifts they would give him.
450 But at that time he refused himself to fight the death from them;

nevertheless he put his own armour upon Patroklos
and sent him into the fighting, and gave many men to go with him.
All day they fought about the Skaian Gates, and on that day
they would have stormed the city, if only Phoibos Apollo
455 had not killed the fighting son of Menoitios there in the first ranks
after he had wrought much damage, and given the glory to Hektor.
Therefore now I come to your knees; so might you be willing
to give me for my short-lived son a shield and a helmet
and two beautiful greaves[2] fitted with clasps for the ankles
460 and a corselet. What he had was lost with his steadfast companion
when the Trojans killed him. Now my son lies on the ground, heart
  sorrowing."
  Hearing her the renowned smith of the strong arms answered her:
"Do not fear. Let not these things be a thought in your mind.
And I wish that I could hide him away from death and its sorrow
465 at that time when his hard fate comes upon him, as surely
as there shall be fine armour for him, such as another
man out of many men shall wonder at, when he looks on it."
  So he spoke, and left her there, and went to his bellows.
He turned these toward the fire and gave them their orders for working.
470 And the bellows, all twenty of them, blew on the crucibles,
from all directions blasting forth wind to blow the flames high
now as he hurried to be at this place and now at another,
wherever Hephaistos might wish them to blow, and the work went forward.
He cast on the fire bronze which is weariless, and tin with it
475 and valuable gold, and silver, and thereafter set forth
upon its standard the great anvil, and gripped in one hand
the ponderous hammer, while in the other he grasped the pincers.
  First of all he forged a shield that was huge and heavy,
elaborating it about, and threw around it a shining
480 triple rim that glittered, and the shield strap was cast of silver.
There were five folds composing the shield itself, and upon it
he elaborated many things in his skill and craftsmanship.
  He made the earth upon it, and the sky, and the sea's water,
and the tireless sun, and the moon waxing into her fullness,
485 and on it all the constellations that festoon the heavens,
the Pleiades and the Hyades and the strength of Orion
and the Bear, whom men give also the name of the Wagon,
who turns about in a fixed place and looks at Orion
and she alone is never plunged in the wash of the Ocean.
490 On it he wrought in all their beauty two cities of mortal
men. And there were marriages in one, and festivals.
They were leading the brides along the city from their maiden chambers
under the flaring of torches, and the loud bride song was arising.
The young men followed the circles of the dance, and among them
495 the flutes and lyres kept up their clamour as in the meantime
the women standing each at the door of her court admired them.

---

2. Shin-guards.

12

The people were assembled in the market place, where a quarrel
had arisen, and two men were disputing over the blood price
for a man who had been killed. One man promised full restitution
500   in a public statement, but the other refused and would accept nothing.
Both then made for an arbitrator, to have a decision;
and people were speaking up on either side, to help both men.
But the heralds kept the people in hand, as meanwhile the elders
were in session on benches of polished stone in the sacred circle
505   and held in their hands the staves of the heralds who lift their voices.
The two men rushed before these, and took turns speaking their cases,
and between them lay on the ground two talents of gold, to be given
to that judge who in this case spoke the straightest opinion.
      But around the other city were lying two forces of armed men
510   shining in their war gear. For one side counsel was divided
whether to storm and sack, or share between both sides the property
and all the possessions the lovely citadel held hard within it.
But the city's people were not giving way, and armed for an ambush.
Their beloved wives and their little children stood on the rampart
515   to hold it, and with them the men with age upon them, but meanwhile
the others went out. And Ares led them, and Pallas Athene.
These were gold, both, and golden raiment upon them, and they were
beautiful and huge in their armour, being divinities,
and conspicuous from afar, but the people around them were smaller.
520   These, when they were come to the place that was set for their ambush,
in a river, where there was a watering place for all animals,
there they sat down in place shrouding themselves in the bright bronze.
But apart from these were sitting two men to watch for the rest of them
and waiting until they could see the sheep and the shambling cattle,
525   who appeared presently, and two herdsmen went along with them
playing happily on pipes, and took no thought of the treachery.
Those others saw them, and made a rush, and quickly thereafter
cut off on both sides the herds of cattle and the beautiful
flocks of shining sheep, and killed the shepherds upon them.
530   But the other army, as soon as they heard the uproar arising
from the cattle, as they sat in their councils, suddenly mounted
behind their light-foot horses, and went after, and soon overtook them.
These stood their ground and fought a battle by the banks of the river,
and they were making casts at each other with their spears bronze-headed;
535   and Hate was there with Confusion among them, and Death the destructive;
she was holding a live man with a new wound, and another
one unhurt, and dragged a dead man by the feet through the carnage.
The clothing upon her shoulders showed strong red with the men's blood.
All closed together like living men and fought with each other
540   and dragged away from each other the corpses of those who had fallen.
      He made upon it a soft field, the pride of the tilled land,
wide and triple-ploughed, with many ploughmen upon it
who wheeled their teams at the turn and drove them in either direction.
And as these making their turn would reach the end-strip of the field,
545   a man would come up to them at this point and hand them a flagon

of honey-sweet wine, and they would turn again to the furrows
in their haste to come again to the end-strip of the deep field.
The earth darkened behind them and looked like earth that has been ploughed
though it was gold. Such was the wonder of the shield's forging.
550 He made on it the precinct of a king, where the labourers
were reaping, with the sharp reaping hooks in their hands. Of the cut swathes
some fell along the lines of reaping, one after another,
while the sheaf-binders caught up others and tied them with bind-ropes.
There were three sheaf-binders who stood by, and behind them
555 were children picking up the cut swathes, and filled their arms with them
and carried and gave them always; and by them the king in silence
and holding his staff stood near the line of the reapers, happily.
And apart and under a tree the heralds made a feast ready
and trimmed a great ox they had slaughtered. Meanwhile the women
560 scattered, for the workmen to eat, abundant white barley.
He made on it a great vineyard heavy with clusters,
lovely and in gold, but the grapes upon it were darkened
and the vines themselves stood out through poles of silver. About them
he made a field-ditch of dark metal, and drove all around this
565 a fence of tin; and there was only one path to the vineyard,
and along it ran the grape-bearers for the vineyard's stripping.
Young girls and young men, in all their light-hearted innocence,
carried the kind, sweet fruit away in their woven baskets,
and in their midst a youth with a singing lyre played charmingly
570 upon it for them, and sang the beautiful song for Linos
in a light voice, and they followed him, and with singing and whistling
and light dance-steps of their feet kept time to the music.
He made upon it a herd of horn-straight oxen. The cattle
were wrought of gold and of tin, and thronged in speed and with lowing
575 out of the dung of the farmyard to a pasturing place by a sounding
river, and beside the moving field of a reed bed.
The herdsmen were of gold who went along with the cattle,
four of them, and nine dogs shifting their feet followed them.
But among the foremost of the cattle two formidable lions
580 had caught hold of a bellowing bull, and he with loud lowings
was dragged away, as the dogs and the young men went in pursuit of him.
But the two lions, breaking open the hide of the great ox,
gulped the black blood and the inward guts, as meanwhile the herdsmen
were in the act of setting and urging the quick dogs on them.
585 But they, before they could get their teeth in, turned back from the lions,
but would come and take their stand very close, and bayed, and kept clear.
And the renowned smith of the strong arms made on it a meadow
large and in a lovely valley for the glimmering sheepflocks,
with dwelling places upon it, and covered shelters, and sheepfolds.
590 And the renowned smith of the strong arms made elaborate on it
a dancing floor, like that which once in the wide spaces of Knosos[3]
Daidalos[4] built for Ariadne of the lovely tresses.

3. Cretan city of King Minos, the father of Ariadne.
4. Mythic architect, artist, and inventor.

And there were young men on it and young girls, sought for their beauty
with gifts of oxen, dancing, and holding hands at the wrist. These
595   wore, the maidens long light robes, but the men wore tunics
of finespun work and shining softly, touched with olive oil.
And the girls wore fair garlands on their heads, while the young men
carried golden knives that hung from sword-belts of silver.
At whiles on their understanding feet they would run very lightly,
600   as when a potter crouching makes trial of his wheel, holding
it close in his hands, to see if it will run smooth. At another
time they would form rows, and run, rows crossing each other.
And around the lovely chorus of dancers stood a great multitude
happily watching, while among the dancers two acrobats
605   led the measures of song and dance revolving among them.

     He made on it the great strength of the Ocean River
which ran around the uttermost rim of the shield's strong structure.

     Then after he had wrought this shield, which was huge and heavy,
he wrought for him a corselet brighter than fire in its shining,
610   and wrought him a helmet, massive and fitting close to his temples,
lovely and intricate work, and laid a gold top-ridge along it,
and out of pliable tin wrought him leg-armour. Thereafter
when the renowned smith of the strong arms had finished the armour
he lifted it and laid it before the mother of Achilleus.
615   And she like a hawk came sweeping down from the snows of Olympos
and carried with her the shining armour, the gift of Hephaistos.

Book 22

[The Death of Hektor]

     So along the city the Trojans, who had run like fawns, dried
the sweat off from their bodies and drank and slaked their thirst, leaning
along the magnificent battlements. Meanwhile the Achaians
sloping their shields across their shoulders came close to the rampart.
5   But his deadly fate held Hektor shackled, so that he stood fast
in front of Ilion and the Skaian gates. Now Phoibos
Apollo spoke aloud to Peleion: "Why, son of Peleus,
do you keep after me in the speed of your feet, being mortal
while I am an immortal god? Even yet you have not
10   seen that I am a god, but strain after me in your fury.
Now hard fighting with the Trojans whom you stampeded means nothing
to you. They are crowded in the city, but you bent away here.
You will never kill me. I am not one who is fated."
     Deeply vexed Achilleus of the swift feet spoke to him:
15   "You have balked me, striker from afar, most malignant of all gods,
when you turned me here away from the rampart, else many Trojans
would have caught the soil in their teeth before they got back into Ilion.
Now you have robbed me of great glory, and rescued these people
lightly, since you have no retribution to fear hereafter.

20 Else I would punish you, if only the strength were in me."

  He spoke, and stalked away against the city, with high thoughts
in mind, and in tearing speed, like a racehorse with his chariot
who runs lightly as he pulls the chariot over the flat land.
Such was the action of Achilleus in feet and quick knees.

25 The aged Priam was the first of all whose eyes saw him
as he swept across the flat land in full shining, like that star
which comes on in the autumn and whose conspicuous brightness
far outshines the stars that are numbered in the night's darkening,
the star they give the name of Orion's Dog, which is brightest

30 among the stars, and yet is wrought as a sign of evil
and brings on the great fever for unfortunate mortals.
Such was the flare of the bronze that girt his chest in his running.
The old man groaned aloud and with both hands high uplifted
beat his head, and groaned amain, and spoke supplicating

35 his beloved son, who there still in front of the gateway
stood fast in determined fury to fight with Achilleus.
The old man stretching his hands out called pitifully to him:
"Hektor, beloved child, do not wait the attack of this man
alone, away from the others. You might encounter your destiny

40 beaten down by Peleion, since he is far stronger than you are.
A hard man: I wish he were as beloved of the immortal
as loved by me. Soon he would lie dead, and the dogs and the vultures
would eat him, and bitter sorrow so be taken from my heart.
He has made me desolate of my sons, who were brave and many.

45 He killed them, or sold them away among the far-lying islands.
Even now there are two sons, Lykaon and Polydoros,
whom I cannot see among the Trojans pent up in the city,
sons Laothoë a princess among women bore to me.
But if these are alive somewhere in the army, then I can

50 set them free for bronze and gold; it is there inside, since
Altes the aged and renowned gave much with his daughter.
But if they are dead already and gone down to the house of Hades,
it is sorrow to our hearts, who bore them, myself and their mother,
but to the rest of the people a sorrow that will be fleeting

55 beside their sorrow for you, if you go down before Achilleus.
Come then inside the wall, my child, so that you can rescue
the Trojans and the women of Troy, neither win the high glory
for Peleus' son, and yourself be robbed of your very life. Oh, take
pity on me, the unfortunate still alive, still sentient

60 but ill-starred, whom the father, Kronos' son, on the threshold of old age
will blast with hard fate, after I have looked upon evils
and seen my sons destroyed and my daughters dragged away captive
and the chambers of marriage wrecked and the innocent children taken
and dashed to the ground in the hatefulness of war, and the wives

65 of my sons dragged off by the accursed hands of the Achaians.
And myself last of all, my dogs in front of my doorway
will rip me raw, after some man with stroke of the sharp bronze
spear, or with spearcast, has torn the life out of my body;

those dogs I raised in my halls to be at my table, to guard my
70 gates, who will lap my blood in the savagery of their anger
and then lie down in my courts. For a young man all is decorous
when he is cut down in battle and torn with the sharp bronze, and lies there
dead, and though dead still all that shows about him is beautiful;
but when an old man is dead and down, and the dogs mutilate
75 the grey head and the grey beard and the parts that are secret,
this, for all sad mortality, is the sight most pitiful."

    So the old man spoke, and in his hands seizing the grey hairs
tore them from his head, but could not move the spirit in Hektor.
And side by side with him his mother in tears was mourning
80 and laid the fold of her bosom bare and with one hand held out
a breast, and wept her tears for him and called to him in winged words:
"Hektor, my child, look upon these and obey, and take pity
on me, if ever I gave you the breast to quiet your sorrow.
Remember all these things, dear child, and from inside the wall
85 beat off this grim man. Do not go out as champion against him,
o hard one; for if he kills you I can no longer
mourn you on the death-bed, sweet branch, o child of my bearing,
nor can your generous wife mourn you, but a big way from us
beside the ships of the Argives the running dogs will feed on you."

90   So these two in tears and with much supplication called out
to their dear son, but could not move the spirit in Hektor,
but he awaited Achilleus as he came on, gigantic.
But as a snake waits for a man by his hole, in the mountains,
glutted with evil poisons, and the fell venom has got inside him,
95 and coiled about the hole he stares malignant, so Hektor
would not give ground but kept unquenched the fury within him
and sloped his shining shield against the jut of the bastion.
Deeply troubled he spoke to his own great-hearted spirit:
"Ah me! If I go now inside the wall and the gateway,
100 Poulydamas will be first to put a reproach upon me,
since he tried to make me lead the Trojans inside the city
on that accursed night when brilliant Achilleus rose up,
and I would not obey him, but that would have been far better.
Now, since by my own recklessness I have ruined my people,
105 I feel shame before the Trojans and the Trojan women with trailing
robes, that someone who is less of a man than I will say of me:
'Hektor believed in his own strength and ruined his people.'
Thus they will speak; and as for me, it would be much better
at that time, to go against Achilleus, and slay him, and come back,
110 or else be killed by him in glory in front of the city.
Or if again I set down my shield massive in the middle
and my ponderous helm, and lean my spear up against the rampart
and go out as I am to meet Achilleus the blameless
and promise to give back Helen, and with her all her possessions,
115 all those things that once in the hollow ships Alexandros[1]

1. Paris.

brought back to Troy, and these were the beginning of the quarrel;
to give these to Atreus' sons to take away, and for the Achaians
also to divide up all that is hidden within the city,
and take an oath thereafter for the Trojans in conclave
120 not to hide anything away, but distribute all of it,
as much as the lovely citadel keeps guarded within it;
yet still, why does the heart within me debate on these things?
I might go up to him, and he take no pity upon me
nor respect my position, but kill me naked so, as if I were
125 a woman, once I stripped my armour from me. There is no
way any more from a tree or a rock to talk to him gently
whispering like a young man and a young girl, in the way
a young man and a young maiden whisper together.
Better to bring on the fight with him as soon as it may be.
130 We shall see to which one the Olympian grants the glory."
       So he pondered, waiting, but Achilleus was closing upon him
in the likeness of the lord of battles, the helm-shining warrior,
and shaking from above his shoulder the dangerous Pelian
ash spear, while the bronze that closed about him was shining
135 like the flare of blazing fire or the sun in its rising.
And the shivers took hold of Hektor when he saw him, and he could no
      longer
stand his ground there, but left the gates behind, and fled, frightened,
and Peleus' son went after him in the confidence of his quick feet.
As when a hawk in the mountains who moves lightest of things flying
140 makes his effortless swoop for a trembling dove, but she slips away
from beneath and flies and he shrill screaming close after her
plunges for her again and again, heart furious to take her;
so Achilleus went straight for him in fury, but Hektor
fled away under the Trojan wall and moved his knees rapidly.
145 They raced along by the watching point and the windy fig tree
always away from under the wall and along the wagon-way
and came to the two sweet-running well springs. There there are double
springs of water that jet up, the springs of whirling Skamandros.
One of these runs hot water and the steam on all sides
150 of it rises as if from a fire that was burning inside it.
But the other in the summer-time runs water that is like hail
or chill snow or ice that forms from water. Beside these
in this place, and close to them, are the washing-hollows
of stone, and magnificent, where the wives of the Trojans and their lovely
155 daughters washed the clothes to shining, in the old days
when there was peace, before the coming of the sons of the Achaians.
They ran beside these, one escaping, the other after him.
It was a great man who fled, but far better he who pursued him
rapidly, since here was no festal beast, no ox-hide
160 they strove for, for these are prizes that are given men for their running.
No, they ran for the life of Hektor, breaker of horses.
As when about the turnposts racing single-foot horses
run at full speed, when a great prize is laid up for their winning,

a tripod or a woman, in games for a man's funeral,
165 so these two swept whirling about the city of Priam
in the speed of their feet, while all the gods were looking upon them.
First to speak among them was the father of gods and mortals:
"Ah me, this is a man beloved whom now my eyes watch
being chased around the wall; my heart is mourning for Hektor
170 who has burned in my honour many thigh pieces of oxen
on the peaks of Ida with all her folds, or again on the uttermost
part of the citadel, but now the brilliant Achilleus
drives him in speed of his feet around the city of Priam.
Come then, you immortals, take thought and take counsel, whether
175 to rescue this man or whether to make him, for all his valour,
go down under the hands of Achilleus, the son of Peleus."

Then in answer the goddess grey-eyed Athene spoke to him:
"Father of the shining bolt, dark misted, what is this you said?
Do you wish to bring back a man who is mortal, one long since
180 doomed by his destiny, from ill-sounding death and release him?
Do it, then; but not all the rest of us gods shall approve you."

Then Zeus the gatherer of the clouds spoke to her in answer:
"Tritogeneia, dear daughter, do not lose heart; for I say this
not in outright anger, and my meaning toward you is kindly.
185 Act as your purpose would have you do, and hold back no longer."

So he spoke, and stirred on Athene, who was eager before this,
and she went in a flash of speed down the pinnacles of Olympos.

But swift Achilleus kept unremittingly after Hektor,
chasing him, as a dog in the mountains who has flushed from his covert
190 a deer's fawn follows him through the folding ways and the valleys,
and though the fawn crouched down under a bush and be hidden
he keeps running and noses him out until he comes on him;
so Hektor could not lose himself from swift-footed Peleion.
If ever he made a dash right on for the gates of Dardanos
195 to get quickly under the strong-built bastions, endeavouring
that they from above with missiles thrown might somehow defend him,
each time Achilleus would get in front and force him to turn back
into the plain, and himself kept his flying course next the city.
As in a dream a man is not able to follow one who runs
200 from him, nor can the runner escape, nor the other pursue him,
so he could not run him down in his speed, nor the other get clear.
How then could Hektor have escaped the death spirits, had not
Apollo, for this last and uttermost time, stood by him
close, and driven strength into him, and made his knees light?
205 But brilliant Achilleus kept shaking his head at his own people
and would not let them throw their bitter projectiles at Hektor
for fear the thrower might win the glory, and himself come second.
But when for the fourth time they had come around to the well springs
then the Father balanced his golden scales, and in them
210 he set two fateful portions of death, which lays men prostrate,
one for Achilleus, and one for Hektor, breaker of horses,
and balanced it by the middle; and Hektor's death-day was heavier

and dragged downward toward death, and Phoibos Apollo forsook him.
But the goddess grey-eyed Athene came now to Peleion

215 and stood close beside him and addressed him in winged words: "Beloved
of Zeus, shining Achilleus, I am hopeful now that you and I
will take back great glory to the ships of the Achaians, after
we have killed Hektor, for all his slakeless fury for battle.
Now there is no way for him to get clear away from us,

220 not though Apollo who strikes from afar should be willing to undergo
much, and wallow before our father Zeus of the aegis.
Stand you here then and get your wind again, while I go
to this man and persuade him to stand up to you in combat."

So spoke Athene, and he was glad at heart, and obeyed her,
225 and stopped, and stood leaning on his bronze-barbed ash spear. Meanwhile
Athene left him there, and caught up with brilliant Hektor,
and likened herself in form and weariless voice to Deïphobos.
She came now and stood close to him and addressed him in winged words:
"Dear brother, indeed swift-footed Achilleus is using you roughly

230 and chasing you on swift feet around the city of Priam.
Come on, then; let us stand fast against him and beat him back from us."

Then tall Hektor of the shining helm answered her: "Deïphobos,
before now you were dearest to me by far of my brothers,
of all those who were sons of Priam and Hekabe, and now

235 I am minded all the more within my heart to honour you,
you who dared for my sake, when your eyes saw me, to come forth
from the fortifications, while the others stand fast inside them."

Then in turn the goddess grey-eyed Athene answered him:
"My brother, it is true our father and the lady our mother, taking

240 my knees in turn, and my companions about me, entreated
that I stay within, such was the terror upon all of them.
But the heart within me was worn away by hard sorrow for you.
But now let us go straight on and fight hard, let there be no sparing
of our spears, so that we can find out whether Achilleus

245 will kill us both and carry our bloody war spoils back
to the hollow ships, or will himself go down under your spear."

So Athene spoke and led him on by beguilement.
Now as the two in their advance were come close together,
first of the two to speak was tall helm-glittering Hektor:

250 "Son of Peleus, I will no longer run from you, as before this
I fled three times around the great city of Priam, and dared not
stand to your onfall. But now my spirit in turn has driven me
to stand and face you. I must take you now, or I must be taken.
Come then, shall we swear before the gods? For these are the highest

255 who shall be witnesses and watch over our agreements.
Brutal as you are I will not defile you, if Zeus grants
to me that I can wear you out, and take the life from you.
But after I have stripped your glorious armour, Achilleus,
I will give your corpse back to the Achaians. Do you do likewise."

260 Then looking darkly at him swift-footed Achilleus answered:
"Hektor, argue me no agreements. I cannot forgive you.

As there are no trustworthy oaths between men and lions,
nor wolves and lambs have spirit that can be brought to agreement
but forever these hold feelings of hate for each other,
265 so there can be no love between you and me, nor shall there be
oaths between us, but one or the other must fall before then
to glut with his blood Ares the god who fights under the shield's guard.
Remember every valour of yours, for now the need comes
hardest upon you to be a spearman and a bold warrior.
270 There shall be no more escape for you, but Pallas Athene
will kill you soon by my spear. You will pay in a lump for all those
sorrows of my companions you killed in your spear's fury."

So he spoke, and balanced the spear far shadowed, and threw it;
but glorious Hektor kept his eyes on him, and avoided it,
275 for he dropped, watchful, to his knee, and the bronze spear flew over his
        shoulder
and stuck in the ground, but Pallas Athene snatched it, and gave it
back to Achilleus, unseen by Hektor shepherd of the people.
But now Hektor spoke out to the blameless son of Peleus:
"You missed; and it was not, o Achilleus like the immortals,
280 from Zeus that you knew my destiny; but you thought so; or rather
you are someone clever in speech and spoke to swindle me,
to make me afraid of you and forget my valour and war strength.
You will not stick your spear in my back as I run away from you
but drive it into my chest as I storm straight in against you;
285 if the god gives you that; and now look out for my brazen
spear. I wish it might be taken full length in your body.
And indeed the war would be a lighter thing for the Trojans
if you were dead, seeing that you are their greatest affliction."

So he spoke, and balanced the spear far shadowed, and threw it,
290 and struck the middle of Peleïdes' shield, nor missed it,
but the spear was driven far back from the shield, and Hektor was angered
because his swift weapon had been loosed from his hand in a vain cast.
He stood discouraged, and had no other ash spear; but lifting
his voice he called aloud on Deïphobos of the pale shield,
295 and asked him for a long spear, but Deïphobos was not near him.
And Hektor knew the truth inside his heart, and spoke aloud:
"No use. Here at last the gods have summoned me deathward.
I thought Deïphobos the hero was here close beside me,
but he is behind the wall and it was Athene cheating me,
300 and now evil death is close to me, and no longer far away,
and there is no way out. So it must long since have been pleasing
to Zeus, and Zeus' son who strikes from afar, this way; though before this
they defended me gladly. But now my death is upon me.
Let me at least not die without a struggle, inglorious,
305 but do some big thing first, that men to come shall know of it."

So he spoke, and pulling out the sharp sword that was slung
at the hollow of his side, huge and heavy, and gathering
himself together, he made his swoop, like a high-flown eagle
who launches himself out of the murk of the clouds on the flat land

310   to catch away a tender lamb or a shivering hare; so
Hektor made his swoop, swinging his sharp sword, and Achilleus
charged, the heart within him loaded with savage fury.
In front of his chest the beautiful elaborate great shield
covered him, and with the glittering helm with four horns
315   he nodded; the lovely golden fringes were shaken about it
which Hephaistos had driven close along the horn of the helmet.
And as a star moves among stars in the night's darkening,
Hesper, who is the fairest star who stands in the sky, such
was the shining from the pointed spear Achilleus was shaking
320   in his right hand with evil intention toward brilliant Hektor.
He was eyeing Hektor's splendid body, to see where it might best
give way, but all the rest of the skin was held in the armour,
brazen and splendid, he stripped when he cut down the strength of
        Patroklos;
yet showed where the collar-bones hold the neck from the shoulders,
325   the throat, where death of the soul comes most swiftly; in this place
brilliant Achilleus drove the spear as he came on in fury,
and clean through the soft part of the neck the spearpoint was driven.
Yet the ash spear heavy with bronze did not sever the windpipe,
so that Hektor could still make exchange of words spoken.
330   But he dropped in the dust, and brilliant Achilleus vaunted above him:
"Hektor, surely you thought as you killed Patroklos you would be
safe, and since I was far away you thought nothing of me,
o fool, for an avenger was left, far greater than he was,
behind him and away by the hollow ships. And it was I;
335   and I have broken your strength; on you the dogs and the vultures
shall feed and foully rip you; the Achaians will bury Patroklos."
      In his weakness Hektor of the shining helm spoke to him:
"I entreat you, by your life, by your knees, by your parents,
do not let the dogs feed on me by the ships of the Achaians,
340   but take yourself the bronze and gold that are there in abundance,
those gifts that my father and the lady my mother will give you,
and give my body to be taken home again, so that the Trojans
and the wives of the Trojans may give me in death my rite of burning."
      But looking darkly at him swift-footed Achilleus answered:
345   "No more entreating of me, you dog, by knees or parents.
I wish only that my spirit and fury would drive me
to hack your meat away and eat it raw for the things that
you have done to me. So there is no one who can hold the dogs off
from your head, not if they bring here and set before me ten times
350   and twenty times the ransom, and promise more in addition,
not if Priam son of Dardanos should offer to weigh out
your bulk in gold; not even so shall the lady your mother
who herself bore you lay you on the death-bed and mourn you:
no, but the dogs and the birds will have you all for their feasting."
355   Then, dying, Hektor of the shining helmet spoke to him:
"I know you well as I look upon you, I know that I could not
persuade you, since indeed in your breast is a heart of iron.

13

Be careful now; for I might be made into the gods' curse
upon you, on that day when Paris and Phoibos Apollo
360 destroy you in the Skaian gates, for all your valour."
     He spoke, and as he spoke the end of death closed in upon him,
and the soul fluttering free of the limbs went down into Death's house
mourning her destiny, leaving youth and manhood behind her.
Now though he was a dead man brilliant Achilleus spoke to him:
365 "Die: and I will take my own death at whatever time
Zeus and the rest of the immortals choose to accomplish it."
     He spoke, and pulled the brazen spear from the body, and laid it
on one side, and stripped away from the shoulders the bloody
armour. And the other sons of the Achaians came running about him,
370 and gazed upon the stature and on the imposing beauty
of Hektor; and none stood beside him who did not stab him;
and thus they would speak one to another, each looking at his neighbour:
"See now, Hektor is much softer to handle than he was
when he set the ships ablaze with the burning firebrand."
375 So as they stood beside him they would speak, and stab him.
But now, when he had despoiled the body, swift-footed brilliant
Achilleus stood among the Achaians and addressed them in winged words:
"Friends, who are leaders of the Argives and keep their counsel:
since the gods have granted me the killing of this man
380 who has done us much damage, such as not all the others together
have done, come, let us go in armour about the city
to see if we can find out what purpose is in the Trojans,
whether they will abandon their high city, now that this man
has fallen, or are minded to stay, though Hektor lives no longer.
385 Yet still, why does the heart within me debate on these things?
There is a dead man who lies by the ships, unwept, unburied:
Patroklos: and I will not forget him, never so long as
I remain among the living and my knees have their spring beneath me.
And though the dead forget the dead in the house of Hades,
390 even there I shall still remember my beloved companion.
But now, you young men of the Achaians, let us go back, singing
a victory song, to our hollow ships; and take this with us.
We have won ourselves enormous fame; we have killed the great Hektor
whom the Trojans glorified as if he were a god in their city."
395 He spoke, and now thought of shameful treatment for glorious Hektor.
In both of his feet at the back he made holes by the tendons
in the space between ankle and heel, and drew thongs of ox-hide through
     them,
and fastened them to the chariot so as to let the head drag,
and mounted the chariot, and lifted the glorious armour inside it,
400 then whipped the horses to a run, and they winged their way unreluctant.
A cloud of dust rose where Hektor was dragged, his dark hair was falling
about him, and all that head that was once so handsome was tumbled
in the dust; since by this time Zeus had given him over
to his enemies, to be defiled in the land of his fathers.
405 So all his head was dragged in the dust; and now his mother

tore out her hair, and threw the shining veil far from her
and raised a great wail as she looked upon her son; and his father
beloved groaned pitifully, and all his people about him
were taken with wailing and lamentation all through the city.
410   It was most like what would have happened, if all lowering
Ilion had been burning top to bottom in fire.
His people could scarcely keep the old man in his impatience
from storming out of the Dardanian gates; he implored them
all, and wallowed in the muck before them calling on each man
415   and naming him by his name: "Give way, dear friends,
and let me alone though you care for me, leave me to go out
from the city and make my way to the ships of the Achaians.
I must be suppliant to this man, who is harsh and violent,
and he might have respect for my age and take pity upon it
420   since I am old, and his father also is old, as I am,
Peleus, who begot and reared him to be an affliction
on the Trojans. He has given us most sorrow, beyond all others,
such is the number of my flowering sons he has cut down.
But for all of these I mourn not so much, in spite of my sorrow,
425   as for one, Hektor, and the sharp grief for him will carry me downward
into Death's house. I wish he had died in my arms, for that way
we two, I myself and his mother who bore him unhappy,
might so have glutted ourselves with weeping for him and mourning."
So he spoke, in tears, and beside him mourned the citizens.
430   But for the women of Troy Hekabe[2] led out the thronging
chant of sorrow: "Child, I am wretched. What shall my life be
in my sorrows, now you are dead, who by day and in the night
were my glory in the town, and to all of the Trojans
and the women of Troy a blessing throughout their city. They adored you
435   as if you were a god, since in truth you were their high honour
while you lived. Now death and fate have closed in upon you."
So she spoke in tears but the wife of Hektor had not yet
heard: for no sure messenger had come to her and told her
how her husband had held his ground there outside the gates;
440   but she was weaving a web in the inner room of the high house,
a red folding robe, and inworking elaborate figures.
She called out through the house to her lovely-haired handmaidens
to set a great cauldron over the fire, so that there would be
hot water for Hektor's bath as he came back out of the fighting;
445   poor innocent, nor knew how, far from waters for bathing,
Pallas Athene had cut him down at the hands of Achilleus.
She heard from the great bastion the noise of mourning and sorrow.
Her limbs spun, and the shuttle dropped from her hand to the ground. Then
she called aloud to her lovely-haired handmaidens: "Come here.
450   Two of you come with me, so I can see what has happened.
I heard the voice of Hektor's honoured mother; within me
my own heart rising beats in my mouth, my limbs under me

2. Hektor's mother.

are frozen. Surely some evil is near for the children of Priam.
May what I say come never close to my ear; yet dreadfully
455 I fear that great Achilleus might have cut off bold Hektor
alone, away from the city, and be driving him into the flat land,
might put an end to that bitter pride of courage, that always
was on him, since he would never stay back where the men were in
    numbers
but break far out in front, and give way in his fury to no man."
460   So she spoke, and ran out of the house like a raving woman
with pulsing heart, and her two handmaidens went along with her.
But when she came to the bastion and where the men were gathered
she stopped, staring, on the wall; and she saw him
being dragged in front of the city, and the running horses
465 dragged him at random toward the hollow ships of the Achaians.
The darkness of night misted over the eyes of Andromache.
She fell backward, and gasped the life breath from her, and far off
threw from her head the shining gear that ordered her headdress,
the diadem and the cap, and the holding-band woven together,
470 and the circlet, which Aphrodite the golden once had given her
on that day when Hektor of the shining helmet led her forth
from the house of Eëtion, and gave numberless gifts to win her.
And about her stood thronging her husband's sisters and the wives of his
    brothers
and these, in her despair for death, held her up among them.
475 But she, when she breathed again and the life was gathered back into her,
lifted her voice among the women of Troy in mourning:
"Hektor, I grieve for you. You and I were born to a single
destiny, you in Troy in the house of Priam, and I
in Thebe, underneath the timbered mountain of Plakos
480 in the house of Eëtion, who cared for me when I was little,
ill-fated he, I ill-starred. I wish he had never begotten me.
Now you go down to the house of Death in the secret places
of the earth, and left me here behind in the sorrow of mourning,
a widow in your house, and the boy is only a baby
485 who was born to you and me, the unfortunate. You cannot help him,
Hektor, any more, since you are dead. Nor can he help you.
Though he escape the attack of the Achaians with all its sorrows,
yet all his days for your sake there will be hard work for him
and sorrows, for others will take his lands away from him. The day
490 of bereavement leaves a child with no agemates to befriend him.
He bows his head before every man, his cheeks are bewept, he
goes, needy, a boy among his father's companions,
and tugs at this man by the mantle, that man by the tunic,
and they pity him, and one gives him a tiny drink from a goblet,
495 enough to moisten his lips, not enough to moisten his palate.
But one whose parents are living beats him out of the banquet
hitting him with his fists and in words also abuses him:
'Get out, you! Your father is not dining among us.'
And the boy goes away in tears to his widowed mother,

Astyanax, who in days before on the knees of his father
would eat only the marrow or the flesh of sheep that was fattest.
And when sleep would come upon him and he was done with his playing,
he would go to sleep in a bed, in the arms of his nurse, in a soft
bed, with his heart given all its fill of luxury.

505 Now, with his dear father gone, he has much to suffer:
he, whom the Trojans have called Astyanax, lord of the city,
since it was you alone who defended the gates and the long walls.
But now, beside the curving ships, far away from your parents,
the writhing worms will feed, when the dogs have had enough of you,

510 on your naked corpse, though in your house there is clothing laid up
that is fine-textured and pleasant, wrought by the hands of women.
But all of these I will burn up in the fire's blazing,
no use to you, since you will never be laid away in them;
but in your honour, from the men of Troy and the Trojan women."

515 So she spoke, in tears; and the women joined in her mourning.

Book 24

[Achilles and Priam]

And the games broke up, and the people scattered to go away, each man
to his fast-running ship, and the rest of them took thought of their dinner
and of sweet sleep and its enjoyment; only Achilleus
wept still as he remembered his beloved companion, nor did sleep

5 who subdues all come over him, but he tossed from one side to the other
in longing for Patroklos, for his manhood and his great strength
and all the actions he had seen to the end with him, and the hardships
he had suffered; the wars of men; hard crossing of the big waters.
Remembering all these things he let fall the swelling tears, lying

10 sometimes along his side, sometimes on his back, and now again
prone on his face; then he would stand upright, and pace turning
in distraction along the beach of the sea, nor did dawn rising
escape him as she brightened across the sea and the beaches.
Then, when he had yoked running horses under the chariot

15 he would fasten Hektor behind the chariot, so as to drag him,
and draw him three times around the tomb of Menoitios' fallen
son, then rest again in his shelter, and throw down the dead man
and leave him to lie sprawled on his face in the dust. But Apollo
had pity on him, though he was only a dead man, and guarded

20 the body from all ugliness, and hid all of it under the golden
aegis, so that it might not be torn when Achilleus dragged it.
So Achilleus in his standing fury outraged great Hektor.
The blessed gods as they looked upon him were filled with compassion
and kept urging clear-sighted Argeïphontes[1] to steal the body.

25 There this was pleasing to all the others, but never to Hera
nor Poseidon, nor the girl of the grey eyes,[2] who kept still

1. Hermes.
2. Athene.

their hatred for sacred Ilion as in the beginning,
and for Priam and his people, because of the delusion of Paris
who insulted the goddesses when they came to him in his courtyard
30   and favoured her who supplied the lust that led to disaster.
But now, as it was the twelfth dawn after the death of Hektor,
Phoibos Apollo spoke his word out among the immortals:
"You are hard, you gods, and destructive. Now did not Hektor
burn thigh pieces of oxen and unblemished goats in your honour?
35   Now you cannot bring yourselves to save him, though he is only
a corpse, for his wife to look upon, his child and his mother
and Priam his father, and his people, who presently thereafter
would burn his body in the fire and give him his rites of burial.
No, you gods; your desire is to help this cursed Achilleus
40   within whose breast there are no feelings of justice, nor can
his mind be bent, but his purposes are fierce, like a lion
who when he has given way to his own great strength and his haughty
spirit, goes among the flocks of men, to devour them.
So Achilleus has destroyed pity, and there is not in him
45   any shame; which does much harm to men but profits them also.
For a man must some day lose one who was even closer
than this; a brother from the same womb, or a son. And yet
he weeps for him, and sorrows for him, and then it is over,
for the Destinies put in mortal men the heart of endurance.
50   But this man, now he has torn the heart of life from great Hektor,
ties him to his horses and drags him around his beloved companion's
tomb; and nothing is gained thereby for his good, or his honour.
Great as he is, let him take care not to make us angry;
for see, he does dishonour to the dumb earth in his fury."
55   Then bitterly Hera of the white arms answered him, saying:
"What you have said could be true, lord of the silver bow, only
if you give Hektor such pride of place as you give to Achilleus.
But Hektor was mortal, and suckled at the breast of a woman,
while Achilleus is the child of a goddess, one whom I myself
60   nourished and brought up and gave her as bride to her husband
Peleus, one dear to the hearts of the immortals, for you all
went, you gods, to the wedding; and you too feasted among them
and held your lyre, o friend of the evil, faithless forever."
In turn Zeus who gathers the clouds spoke to her in answer:
65   "Hera, be not utterly angry with the gods, for there shall not
be the same pride of place given both. Yet Hektor also
was loved by the gods, best of all the mortals in Ilion.
I loved him too. He never failed of gifts to my liking.
Never yet has my altar gone without fair sacrifice,
70   the smoke and the savour of it, since that is our portion of honour.
The stealing of him we will dismiss, for it is not possible
to take bold Hektor secretly from Achilleus, since always
his mother is near him night and day; but it would be better
if one of the gods would summon Thetis here to my presence
75   so that I can say a close word to her, and see that Achilleus

is given gifts by Priam and gives back the body of Hektor."
      He spoke, and Iris storm-footed sprang away with the message,
and at a point between Samos and Imbros of the high cliffs
plunged in the dark water, and the sea crashed moaning about her.
80 She plummeted to the sea floor like a lead weight which, mounted
along the horn of an ox who ranges the fields, goes downward
and takes death with it to the raw-ravening fish. She found Thetis
inside the hollow of her cave, and gathered about her
sat the rest of the sea goddesses, and she in their midst
85 was mourning the death of her blameless son, who so soon was destined
to die in Troy of the rich soil, far from the land of his fathers.
Iris the swift-foot came close beside her and spoke to her:
"Rise, Thetis. Zeus whose purposes are infinite calls you."
      In turn Thetis the goddess, the silver-footed, answered her:
90 "What does he, the great god, want with me? I feel shamefast
to mingle with the immortals, and my heart is confused with sorrows.
But I will go. No word shall be in vain, if he says it."
      So she spoke, and shining among the divinities took up
her black veil, and there is no darker garment. She went
95 on her way, and in front of her rapid wind-footed Iris
guided her, and the wave of the water opened about them.
They stepped out on the dry land and swept to the sky. There they found
the son of Kronos of the wide brows, and gathered about him
sat all the rest of the gods, the blessed, who live forever.
100 She sat down beside Zeus father, and Athene made a place for her.
Hera put into her hand a beautiful golden goblet
and spoke to her to comfort her, and Thetis accepting drank from it.
The father of gods and men began the discourse among them:
"You have come to Olympos, divine Thetis, for all your sorrow,
105 with an unforgotten grief in your heart. I myself know this.
But even so I will tell you why I summoned you hither.
For nine days there has risen a quarrel among the immortals
over the body of Hektor, and Achilleus, stormer of cities.
They keep urging clear-sighted Argeïphontes to steal the body,
110 but I still put upon Achilleus the honour that he has, guarding
your reverence and your love for me into time afterwards. Go then
in all speed to the encampment and give to your son this message:
tell him that the gods frown upon him, that beyond all other
immortals I myself am angered that in his heart's madness
115 he holds Hektor beside the curved ships and did not give him
back. Perhaps in fear of me he will give back Hektor.
Then I will send Iris to Priam of the great heart, with an order
to ransom his dear son, going down to the ships of the Achaians
and bringing gifts to Achilleus which might soften his anger."
120   He spoke and the goddess silver-foot Thetis did not disobey him
but descended in a flash of speed from the peaks of Olympos
and made her way to the shelter of her son, and there found him
in close lamentation, and his beloved companions about him
were busy at their work and made ready the morning meal, and there

125 stood a great fleecy sheep being sacrificed in the shelter.
His honoured mother came close to him and sat down beside him,
and stroked him with her hand and called him by name and spoke to him:
"My child, how long will you go on eating your heart out in sorrow
and lamentation, and remember neither your food nor going
130 to bed? It is a good thing even to lie with a woman
in love. For you will not be with me long, but already
death and powerful destiny stand closely above you.
But listen hard to me, for I come from Zeus with a message.
He says that the gods frown upon you, that beyond all other
135 immortals he himself is angered that in your heart's madness
you hold Hektor beside the curved ships and did not redeem him.
Come, then, give him up and accept ransom for the body."
  Then in turn Achilleus of the swift feet answered her:
"So be it. He can bring the ransom and take off the body,
140 if the Olympian himself so urgently bids it."
  So, where the ships were drawn together, the son and his mother
conversed at long length in winged words. But the son of Kronos
stirred Iris to go down to sacred Ilion, saying:
"Go forth, Iris the swift, leaving your place on Olympos,
145 and go to Priam of the great heart within Ilion, tell him
to ransom his dear son, going down to the ships of the Achaians
and bringing gifts to Achilleus which might soften his anger:
alone, let no other man of the Trojans go with him, but only
let one elder herald attend him, one who can manage
150 the mules and the easily running wagon, so he can carry
the dead man, whom great Achilleus slew, back to the city.
Let death not be a thought in his heart, let him have no fear;
such an escort shall I send to guide him, Argeïphontes
who shall lead him until he brings him to Achilleus. And after
155 he has brought him inside the shelter of Achilleus, neither
will the man himself kill him, but will hold back all the others,
for he is no witless man nor unwatchful, nor is he wicked,
but will in all kindness spare one who comes to him as a suppliant."
  He spoke, and storm-footed Iris swept away with the message
160 and came to the house of Priam. There she found outcry and mourning.
The sons sitting around their father inside the courtyard
made their clothes sodden with their tears, and among them the old man
sat veiled, beaten into his mantle. Dung lay thick
on the head and neck of the aged man, for he had been rolling
165 in it, he had gathered and smeared it on with his hands. And his daughters
all up and down the house and the wives of his sons were mourning
as they remembered all those men in their numbers and valour
who lay dead, their lives perished at the hands of the Argives.
The messenger of Zeus stood beside Priam and spoke to him
170 in a small voice, and yet the shivers took hold of his body:
"Take heart, Priam, son of Dardanos, do not be frightened.
I come to you not eyeing you with evil intention
but with the purpose of good toward you. I am a messenger

of Zeus, who far away cares much for you and is pitiful.
175 The Olympian orders you to ransom Hektor the brilliant,
to bring gifts to Achilleus which may soften his anger:
alone, let no other man of the Trojans go with you, but only
let one elder herald attend you, one who can manage
the mules and the easily running wagon, so he can carry
180 the dead man, whom great Achilleus slew, back to the city.
Let death not be a thought in your heart, you need have no fear,
such an escort shall go with you to guide you, Argeïphontes
who will lead you till he brings you to Achilleus. And after
he has brought you inside the shelter of Achilleus, neither
185 will the man himself kill you but will hold back all the others;
for he is no witless man nor unwatchful, nor is he wicked
but will in all kindness spare one who comes to him as a suppliant."
So Iris the swift-footed spoke and went away from him.
Thereupon he ordered his sons to make ready the easily rolling
190 mule wagon, and to fasten upon it the carrying basket.
He himself went into the storeroom, which was fragrant
and of cedar, and high-ceilinged, with many bright treasures inside it.
He called out to Hekabe his wife, and said to her:
"Dear wife, a messenger came to me from Zeus on Olympos,
195 that I must go to the ships of the Achaians and ransom my dear son,
bringing gifts to Achilleus which may soften his anger.
Come then, tell me. What does it seem best to your own mind
for me to do? My heart, my strength are terribly urgent
that I go there to the ships within the wide army of the Achaians."
200 So he spoke, and his wife cried out aloud, and answered him:
"Ah me, where has that wisdom gone for which you were famous
in time before, among outlanders and those you rule over?
How can you wish to go alone to the ships of the Achaians
before the eyes of a man who has slaughtered in such numbers
205 such brave sons of yours? The heart in you is iron. For if
he has you within his grasp and lays eyes upon you, that man
who is savage and not to be trusted will not take pity upon you
nor have respect for your rights. Let us sit apart in our palace
now, and weep for Hektor, and the way at the first strong Destiny
210 spun with his life line when he was born, when I gave birth to him,
that the dogs with their shifting feet should feed on him, far from his
parents,
gone down before a stronger man; I wish I could set teeth
in the middle of his liver and eat it. That would be vengeance
for what he did to my son; for he slew him when he was no coward
215 but standing before the men of Troy and the deep-girdled women
of Troy, with no thought in his mind of flight or withdrawal."
In turn the aged Priam, the godlike, answered her saying:
"Do not hold me back when I would be going, neither yourself be
a bird of bad omen in my palace. You will not persuade me.
220 If it had been some other who ordered me, one of the mortals,
one of those who are soothsayers, or priests, or diviners,

I might have called it a lie and we might rather have rejected it.
But now, for I myself heard the god and looked straight upon her,
I am going, and this word shall not be in vain. If it is my destiny
225 to die there by the ships of the bronze-armoured Achaians,
then I wish that. Achilleus can slay me at once, with my own son
caught in my arms, once I have my fill of mourning above him."

He spoke, and lifted back the fair covering of his clothes-chest
and from inside took out twelve robes surpassingly lovely
230 and twelve mantles to be worn single, as many blankets,
as many great white cloaks, also the same number of tunics.
He weighed and carried out ten full talents of gold, and brought forth
two shining tripods, and four cauldrons, and brought out a goblet
of surpassing loveliness that the men of Thrace had given him
235 when he went to them with a message, but now the old man spared not
even this in his halls, so much was it his heart's desire
to ransom back his beloved son. But he drove off the Trojans
all from his cloister walks, scolding them with words of revilement:
"Get out, you failures, you disgraces. Have you not also
240 mourning of your own at home that you come to me with your sorrows?
Is it not enough that Zeus, son of Kronos, has given me sorrow
in losing the best of my sons? You also shall be aware of this
since you will be all the easier for the Achaians to slaughter
now he is dead. But, for myself, before my eyes look
245 upon this city as it is destroyed and its people are slaughtered,
my wish is to go sooner down to the house of the death god."

He spoke, and went after the men with a stick, and they fled outside
before the fury of the old man. He was scolding his children
and cursing Helenos, and Paris, Agathon the brilliant,
250 Pammon and Antiphonos, Polites of the great war cry,
Deïphobos and Hippothoös and proud Dios. There were nine
sons to whom now the old man gave orders and spoke to them roughly:
"Make haste, wicked children, my disgraces. I wish all of you
had been killed beside the running ships in the place of Hektor.
255 Ah me, for my evil destiny. I have had the noblest
of sons in Troy, but I say not one of them is left to me,
Mestor like a god and Troilos whose delight was in horses,
and Hektor, who was a god among men, for he did not seem like
one who was child of a mortal man, but of a god. All these
260 Ares has killed, and all that are left me are the disgraces,
the liars and the dancers, champions of the chorus, the plunderers
of their own people in their land of lambs and kids. Well then,
will you not get my wagon ready and be quick about it,
and put all these things on it, so we can get on with our journey?"

265 So he spoke, and they in terror at the old man's scolding
hauled out the easily running wagon for mules, a fine thing
new-fabricated, and fastened the carrying basket upon it.
They took away from its peg the mule yoke made of boxwood
with its massive knob, well fitted with guiding rings, and brought forth
270 the yoke lashing (together with the yoke itself) of nine cubits

and snugged it well into place upon the smooth-polished wagon-pole
at the foot of the beam, then slipped the ring over the peg, and lashed it
with three turns on either side to the knob, and afterwards
fastened it all in order and secured it under a hooked guard.
275   Then they carried out and piled into the smooth-polished mule wagon
all the unnumbered spoils to be given for the head of Hektor,
then yoked the powerful-footed mules who pulled in the harness
and whom the Mysians gave once as glorious presents to Priam;
but for Priam they led under the yoke those horses the old man
280   himself had kept, and cared for them at his polished manger.
    Now in the high house the yoking was done for the herald
and Priam, men both with close counsels in their minds. And now came
Hekabe with sorrowful heart and stood close beside them
carrying in her right hand the kind, sweet wine in a golden
285   goblet, so that before they went they might pour a drink-offering.
She stood in front of the horses, called Priam by name and spoke to him:
"Here, pour a libation to Zeus father, and pray you may come back
home again from those who hate you, since it seems the spirit
within you drives you upon the ships, though I would not have it.
290   Make your prayer then to the dark-misted, the son of Kronos
on Ida, who looks out on all the Troad, and ask him
for a bird of omen, a rapid messenger, which to his own mind
is dearest of all birds and his strength is the biggest, one seen
on the right, so that once your eyes have rested upon him
295   you can trust in him and go to the ships of the fast-mounted Danaans.
But if Zeus of the wide brows will not grant you his own messenger,
then I, for one, would never urge you on nor advise you
to go to the Argive ships, for all your passion to do it."
    Then in answer to her again spoke Priam the godlike:
300   "My lady, I will not disregard this wherein you urge me.
It is well to lift hands to Zeus and ask if he will have mercy."
    The old man spoke, and told the housekeeper who attended them
to pour unstained water over his hands. She standing beside them
and serving them held the washing-bowl in her hands, and a pitcher.
305   He washed his hands and took the cup from his wife. He stood up
in the middle of the enclosure, and prayed, and poured the wine out
looking up into the sky, and gave utterance and spoke, saying:
"Father Zeus, watching over us from Ida, most high, most honoured:
grant that I come to Achilleus for love and pity; but send me
310   a bird of omen, a rapid messenger which to your own mind
is dearest of all birds and his strength is biggest, one seen
on the right, so that once my eyes have rested upon him
I may trust in him and go to the ships of the fast-mounted Danaans."
    So he spoke in prayer, and Zeus of the counsels heard him.
315   Straightway he sent down the most lordly of birds, an eagle,
the dark one, the marauder, called as well the black eagle.
And as big as is the build of the door to a towering chamber
in the house of a rich man, strongly fitted with bars, of such size
was the spread of his wings on either side. He swept through the city

320 appearing on the right hand, and the people looking upon him
were uplifted and the hearts made glad in the breasts of all of them.
    Now in urgent haste the old man mounted into his chariot
and drove out through the forecourt and the thundering close. Before him
the mules hauled the wagon on its four wheels, Idaios
325 the sober-minded driving them, and behind him the horses
came on as the old man laid the lash upon them and urged them
rapidly through the town, and all his kinsmen were following
much lamenting, as if he went to his death. When the two men
had gone down through the city, and out, and come to the flat land,
330 the rest of them turned back to go to Ilion, the sons
and the sons-in-law. And Zeus of the wide brows failed not to notice
the two as they showed in the plain. He saw the old man and took pity
upon him, and spoke directly to his beloved son, Hermes:
"Hermes, for to you beyond all other gods it is dearest
335 to be man's companion, and you listen to whom you will, go now
on your way, and so guide Priam inside the hollow ships
of the Achaians, that no man shall see him, none be aware of him,
of the other Danaans, till he has come to the son of Peleus."
    He spoke, nor disobeyed him the courier, Argeïphontes.
340 Immediately he bound upon his feet the fair sandals
golden and immortal, that carried him over the water
as over the dry land of the main abreast of the wind's blast.
He caught up the staff, with which he mazes the eyes of those mortals
whose eyes he would maze, or wakes again the sleepers. Holding
345 this in his hands, strong Argeïphontes winged his way onward
until he came suddenly to Troy and the Hellespont, and there
walked on, and there took the likeness of a young man, a noble,
with beard new grown, which is the most graceful time of young manhood.
    Now when the two had driven past the great tomb of Ilos
350 they stayed their mules and horses to water them in the river,
for by this time darkness had descended on the land; and the herald
made out Hermes, who was coming toward them at a short distance.
He lifted his voice and spoke aloud to Priam: "Take thought,
son of Dardanos. Here is work for a mind that is careful.
355 I see a man; I think he will presently tear us to pieces.
Come then, let us run away with our horses, or if not, then
clasp his knees and entreat him to have mercy upon us."
    So he spoke, and the old man's mind was confused, he was badly
frightened, and the hairs stood up all over his gnarled body
360 and he stood staring, but the kindly god himself coming closer
took the old man's hand, and spoke to him and asked him a question:
"Where, my father, are you thus guiding your mules and horses
through the immortal night while other mortals are sleeping?
Have you no fear of the Achaians whose wind is fury,
365 who hate you, who are your enemies, and are near? For if one
of these were to see you, how you are conveying so many
treasures through the swift black night, what then could you think of?
You are not young yourself, and he who attends you is aged

for beating off any man who might pick a quarrel with you.
370 But I will do you no harm myself, I will even keep off
another who would. You seem to me like a beloved father."
In answer to him again spoke aged Priam the godlike:
"Yes, in truth, dear child, all this is much as you tell me;
yet still there is some god who has held his hand above me,
375 who sent such a wayfarer as you to meet me, an omen
of good, for such you are by your form, your admired beauty
and the wisdom in your mind. Your parents are fortunate in you."
Then in turn answered him the courier Argeïphontes:
"Yes, old sir, all this that you said is fair and orderly.
380 But come, tell me this thing and recite it to me accurately.
Can it be you convey these treasures in all their numbers and beauty
to outland men, so that they can be still kept safe for you?
Or are all of you by now abandoning sacred Ilion
in fear, such a one was he who died, the best man among you,
385 your son; who was never wanting when you fought against the Achaians."
In answer to him again spoke aged Priam the godlike:
"But who are you, o best of men, and who are your parents?
Since you spoke of my ill-starred son's death, and with honour."
Then in turn answered him the courier Argeïphontes:
390 "You try me out, aged sir. You ask me of glorious Hektor
whom many a time my eyes have seen in the fighting where men win
glory, as also on that time when he drove back the Argives
on their ships and kept killing them with the stroke of the sharp bronze,
and we stood by and wondered at him; for then Achilleus
395 would not let us fight by reason of his anger at Agamemnon.
For I am Achilleus' henchman, and the same strong-wrought vessel
brought us here; and I am a Myrmidon, and my father
is Polyktor; a man of substance, but aged, as you are.
He has six sons beside, and I am the seventh, and I shook
400 lots with the others, and it was my lot to come on this venture.
But now I have come to the plain away from the ships, for at daybreak
the glancing-eyed Achaians will do battle around the city.
They chafe from sitting here too long, nor have the Achaians'
kings the strength to hold them back as they break for the fighting."
405 In answer to him again spoke aged Priam the godlike:
"If then you are henchman to Peleïd Achilleus,
come, tell me the entire truth, and whether my son lies
still beside the ships, or whether by now he has been hewn
limb from limb and thrown before the dogs by Achilleus."
410 Then in turn answered him the courier Argeïphontes:
"Aged sir, neither have any dogs eaten him, nor have
the birds, but he lies yet beside the ship of Achilleus
at the shelters, and as he was; now here is the twelfth dawn
he has lain there, nor does his flesh decay, nor do worms feed
415 on him, they who devour men who have fallen in battle.
It is true, Achilleus drags him at random around his beloved
companion's tomb, as dawn on dawn appears, yet he cannot

mutilate him; you yourself can see when you go there
how fresh with dew he lies, and the blood is all washed from him,
420 nor is there any corruption, and all the wounds have been closed up
where he was struck, since many drove the bronze in his body.
So it is that the blessed immortals care for your son, though
he is nothing but a dead man; because in their hearts they loved him."

He spoke, and the old man was made joyful and answered him, saying:
425 "My child, surely it is good to give the immortals
their due gifts; because my own son, if ever I had one,
never forgot in his halls the gods who live on Olympos.
Therefore they remembered him even in death's stage. Come, then,
accept at my hands this beautiful drinking-cup, and give me
430 protection for my body, and with the gods' grace be my escort
until I make my way to the shelter of the son of Peleus."

In turn answered him the courier Argeïphontes:
"You try me out, aged sir, for I am young, but you will not
persuade me, telling me to accept your gifts when Achilleus
435 does not know. I fear him at heart and have too much reverence
to rob him. Such a thing might be to my sorrow hereafter.
But I would be your escort and take good care of you, even
till I came to glorious Argos in a fast ship or following
on foot, and none would fight you because he despised your escort."

440 The kind god spoke, and sprang up behind the horses and into
the chariot, and rapidly caught in his hands the lash and the guide reins,
and breathed great strength into the mules and horses. Now after
they had got to the fortifications about the ships, and the ditch, there
were sentries, who had just begun to make ready their dinner,
445 but about these the courier Argeïphontes drifted
sleep, on all, and quickly opened the gate, and shoved back
the door-bars, and brought in Priam and the glorious gifts on the wagon.
But when they had got to the shelter of Peleus' son: a towering
shelter the Myrmidons had built for their king, hewing
450 the timbers of pine, and they made a roof of thatch above it
shaggy with grass that they had gathered out of the meadows;
and around it made a great courtyard for their king, with hedgepoles
set close together; the gate was secured by a single door-piece
of pine, and three Achaians could ram it home in its socket
455 and three could pull back and open the huge door-bar; three other
Achaians, that is, but Achilleus all by himself could close it.
At this time Hermes, the kind god, opened the gate for the old man
and brought in the glorious gifts for Peleus' son, the swift-footed,
and dismounted to the ground from behind the horses, and spoke forth:
460 "Aged sir, I who came to you am a god immortal,
Hermes. My father sent me down to guide and go with you.
But now I am going back again, and I will not go in
before the eyes of Achilleus, for it would make others angry
for an immortal god so to face mortal men with favour.
465 But go you in yourself and clasp the knees of Peleion
and entreat him in the name of his father, the name of his mother

of the lovely hair, and his child, and so move the spirit within him."
　　So Hermes spoke, and went away to the height of Olympos,
but Priam vaulted down to the ground from behind the horses
470　and left Idaios where he was, for he stayed behind, holding
in hand the horses and mules. The old man made straight for the dwelling
where Achilleus the beloved of Zeus was sitting. He found him
inside, and his companions were sitting apart, as two only,
Automedon the hero and Alkimos, scion of Ares,
475　were busy beside him. He had just now got through with his dinner,
with eating and drinking, and the table still stood by. Tall Priam
came in unseen by the other men and stood close beside him
and caught the knees of Achilleus in his arms, and kissed the hands
that were dangerous and manslaughtering and had killed so many
480　of his sons. As when dense disaster closes on one who has murdered
a man in his own land, and he comes to the country of others,
to a man of substance, and wonder seizes on those who behold him,
so Achilleus wondered as he looked on Priam, a godlike
man, and the rest of them wondered also, and looked at each other.
485　But now Priam spoke to him in the words of a suppliant:
"Achilleus like the gods, remember your father, one who
is of years like mine, and on the door-sill of sorrowful old age.
And they who dwell nearby encompass him and afflict him,
nor is there any to defend him against the wrath, the destruction.
490　Yet surely he, when he hears of you and that you are still living,
is gladdened within his heart and all his days he is hopeful
that he will see his beloved son come home from the Troad.
But for me, my destiny was evil. I have had the noblest
of sons in Troy, but I say not one of them is left to me.
495　Fifty were my sons, when the sons of the Achaians came here.
Nineteen were born to me from the womb of a single mother,
and other women bore the rest in my palace; and of these
violent Ares broke the strength in the knees of most of them,
but one was left me who guarded my city and people, that one
500　you killed a few days since as he fought in defence of his country,
Hektor; for whose sake I come now to the ships of the Achaians
to win him back from you, and I bring you gifts beyond number.
Honour then the gods, Achilleus, and take pity upon me
remembering your father, yet I am still more pitiful;
505　I have gone through what no other mortal on earth has gone through;
I put my lips to the hands of the man who has killed my children."
　　So he spoke, and stirred in the other a passion of grieving
for his own father. He took the old man's hand and pushed him
gently away, and the two remembered, as Priam sat huddled
510　at the feet of Achilleus and wept close for manslaughtering Hektor
and Achilleus wept now for his own father, now again
for Patroklos. The sound of their mourning moved in the house. Then
when great Achilleus had taken full satisfaction in sorrow
and the passion for it had gone from his mind and body, thereafter
515　he rose from his chair, and took the old man by the hand, and set him

on his feet again, in pity for the grey head and the grey beard,
and spoke to him and addressed him in winged words: "Ah, unlucky,
surely you have had much evil to endure in your spirit.
How could you dare to come alone to the ships of the Achaians
520 and before my eyes, when I am one who have killed in such numbers
such brave sons of yours? The heart in you is iron. Come, then,
and sit down upon this chair, and you and I will even let
our sorrows lie still in the heart for all our grieving. There is not
any advantage to be won from grim lamentation.
525 Such is the way the gods spun life for unfortunate mortals,
that we live in unhappiness, but the gods themselves have no sorrows.
There are two urns that stand on the door-sill of Zeus. They are unlike
for the gifts they bestow: an urn of evils, an urn of blessings.
If Zeus who delights in thunder mingles these and bestows them
530 on man, he shifts, and moves now in evil, again in good fortune.
But when Zeus bestows from the urn of sorrows, he makes a failure
of man, and the evil hunger drives him over the shining
earth, and he wanders respected neither of gods nor mortals.
Such were the shining gifts given by the gods to Peleus
535 from his birth, who outshone all men beside for his riches
and pride of possession, and was lord over the Myrmidons. Thereto
the gods bestowed an immortal wife on him, who was mortal.
But even on him the god piled evil also. There was not
any generation of strong sons born to him in his great house
540 but a single all-untimely child he had, and I give him
no care as he grows old, since far from the land of my fathers
I sit here in Troy, and bring nothing but sorrow to you and your children.
And you, old sir, we are told you prospered once; for as much
as Lesbos, Makar's hold, confines to the north above it
545 and Phrygia from the north confines, and enormous Hellespont,
of these, old sir, you were lord once in your wealth and your children.
But now the Uranian gods brought us, an affliction upon you,
forever there is fighting about your city, and men killed.
But bear up, nor mourn endlessly in your heart, for there is not
550 anything to be gained from grief for your son; you will never
bring him back; sooner you must go through yet another sorrow."

    In answer to him again spoke aged Priam the godlike:
"Do not, beloved of Zeus, make me sit on a chair while Hektor
lies yet forlorn among the shelters; rather with all speed
555 give him back, so my eyes may behold him, and accept the ransom
we bring you, which is great. You may have joy of it, and go back
to the land of your own fathers, since once you have permitted me
to go on living myself and continue to look on the sunlight."

    Then looking darkly at him spoke swift-footed Achilleus:
560 "No longer stir me up, old sir. I myself am minded
to give Hektor back to you. A messenger came to me from Zeus,
my mother, she who bore me, the daughter of the sea's ancient.
I know you, Priam, in my heart, and it does not escape me
that some god led you to the running ships of the Achaians.

565 For no mortal would dare come to our encampment, not even
one strong in youth. He could not get by the pickets, he could not
lightly unbar the bolt that secures our gateway. Therefore
you must not further make my spirit move in my sorrows,
for fear, old sir, I might not let you alone in my shelter,
570 suppliant as you are; and be guilty before the god's orders."
        He spoke, and the old man was frightened and did as he told him.
The son of Peleus bounded to the door of the house like a lion,
nor went alone, but the two henchmen followed attending,
the hero Automedon and Alkimos, those whom Achilleus
575 honoured beyond all companions after Patroklos dead. These two
now set free from under the yoke the mules and the horses,
and led inside the herald, the old king's crier, and gave him
a chair to sit in, then from the smooth-polished mule wagon
lifted out the innumerable spoils for the head of Hektor,
580 but left inside it two great cloaks and a finespun tunic
to shroud the corpse in when they carried him home. Then Achilleus
called out to his serving-maids to wash the body and anoint it
all over; but take it first aside, since otherwise Priam
might see his son and in the heart's sorrow not hold in his anger
585 at the sight, and the deep heart in Achilleus be shaken to anger;
that he might not kill Priam and be guilty before the god's orders.
Then when the serving-maids had washed the corpse and anointed it
with olive oil, they threw a fair great cloak and a tunic
about him, and Achilleus himself lifted him and laid him
590 on a litter, and his friends helped him lift it to the smooth-polished
mule wagon. He groaned then, and called by name on his beloved
        companion:
"Be not angry with me, Patroklos, if you discover,
though you be in the house of Hades, that I gave back great Hektor
to his loved father, for the ransom he gave me was not unworthy.
595 I will give you your share of the spoils, as much as is fitting."
        So spoke great Achilleus and went back into the shelter
and sat down on the elaborate couch from which he had risen,
against the inward wall, and now spoke his word to Priam:
"Your son is given back to you, aged sir, as you asked it.
600 He lies on a bier. When dawn shows you yourself shall see him
as you take him away. Now you and I must remember our supper.
For even Niobe, she of the lovely tresses, remembered
to eat, whose twelve children were destroyed in her palace,
six daughters, and six sons in the pride of their youth, whom Apollo
605 killed with arrows from his silver bow, being angered
with Niobe, and shaft-showering Artemis killed the daughters;
because Niobe likened herself to Leto of the fair colouring
and said Leto had borne only two, she herself had borne many;
but the two, though they were only two, destroyed all those others.
610 Nine days long they lay in their blood, nor was there anyone
to bury them, for the son of Kronos made stones out of
the people; but on the tenth day the Uranian gods buried them.

But she remembered to eat when she was worn out with weeping.
And now somewhere among the rocks, in the lonely mountains,
615 in Sipylos, where they say is the resting place of the goddesses
who are nymphs, and dance beside the waters of Acheloios,
there, stone still, she broods on the sorrows that the gods gave her.
Come then, we also, aged magnificent sir, must remember
to eat, and afterwards you may take your beloved son back
620 to Ilion, and mourn for him; and he will be much lamented."

So spoke fleet Achilleus and sprang to his feet and slaughtered
a gleaming sheep, and his friends skinned it and butchered it fairly,
and cut up the meat expertly into small pieces, and spitted them,
and roasted all carefully and took off the pieces.
625 Automedon took the bread and set it out on the table
in fair baskets, while Achilleus served the meats. And thereon
they put their hands to the good things that lay ready before them.
But when they had put aside their desire for eating and drinking,
Priam, son of Dardanos, gazed upon Achilleus, wondering
630 at his size and beauty, for he seemed like an outright vision
of gods. Achilleus in turn gazed on Dardanian Priam
and wondered, as he saw his brave looks and listened to him talking.
But when they had taken their fill of gazing one on the other,
first of the two to speak was the aged man, Priam the godlike:
635 "Give me, beloved of Zeus, a place to sleep presently, so that
we may even go to bed and take the pleasure of sweet sleep.
For my eyes have not closed underneath my lids since that time
when my son lost his life beneath your hands, but always
I have been grieving and brooding over my numberless sorrows
640 and wallowed in the muck about my courtyard's enclosure.
Now I have tasted food again and have let the gleaming
wine go down my throat. Before, I had tasted nothing."

He spoke, and Achilleus ordered his serving-maids and companions
to make a bed in the porch's shelter and to lay upon it
645 fine underbedding of purple, and spread blankets above it
and fleecy robes to be an over-all covering. The maid-servants
went forth from the main house, and in their hands held torches,
and set to work, and presently had two beds made. Achilleus
of the swift feet now looked at Priam and said, sarcastic:
650 "Sleep outside, aged sir and good friend, for fear some Achaian
might come in here on a matter of counsel, since they keep coming
and sitting by me and making plans; as they are supposed to.
But if one of these come through the fleeting black night should notice you,
he would go straight and tell Agamemnon, shepherd of the people,
655 and there would be delay in the ransoming of the body.
But come, tell me this and count off for me exactly
how many days you intend for the burial of great Hektor.
Tell me, so I myself shall stay still and hold back the people."

In answer to him again spoke aged Priam the godlike:
660 "If you are willing that we accomplish a complete funeral
for great Hektor, this, Achilleus, is what you could do and give

me pleasure. For you know surely how we are penned in our city,
and wood is far to bring in from the hills, and the Trojans are frightened
badly. Nine days we would keep him in our palace and mourn him,
665   and bury him on the tenth day, and the people feast by him,
and on the eleventh day we would make the grave-barrow for him,
and on the twelfth day fight again; if so we must do."
    Then in turn swift-footed brilliant Achilleus answered him:
"Then all this, aged Priam, shall be done as you ask it.
670   I will hold off our attack for as much time as you bid me."
    So he spoke, and took the aged king by the right hand
at the wrist, so that his heart might have no fear. Then these two,
Priam and the herald who were both men of close counsel,
slept in the place outside the house, in the porch's shelter;
675   but Achilleus slept in the inward corner of the strong-built shelter,
and at his side lay Briseis of the fair colouring.
    Now the rest of the gods and men who were lords of chariots
slept nightlong, with the easy bondage of slumber upon them,
only sleep had not caught Hermes the kind god, who pondered
680   now in his heart the problem of how to escort King Priam
from the ships and not be seen by the devoted gate-wardens.
He stood above his head and spoke a word to him, saying:
"Aged sir, you can have no thought of evil from the way
you sleep still among your enemies now Achilleus has left you
685   unharmed. You have ransomed now your dear son and given much for him.
But the sons you left behind would give three times as much ransom
for you, who are alive, were Atreus' son Agamemnon
to recognize you, and all the other Achaians learn of you."
    He spoke, and the old man was afraid, and wakened his herald,
690   and lightly Hermes harnessed for them the mules and the horses
and himself drove them through the encampment. And no man knew of
        them.
    But when they came to the crossing-place of the fair-running river,
of whirling Xanthos, a stream whose father was Zeus the immortal,
there Hermes left them and went away to the height of Olympos,
695   and dawn, she of the yellow robe, scattered over all earth,
and they drove their horses on to the city with lamentation
and clamour, while the mules drew the body. Nor was any other
aware of them at the first, no man, no fair-girdled woman,
only Kassandra, a girl like Aphrodite the golden,
700   who had gone up to the height of the Pergamos. She saw
her dear father standing in the chariot, his herald and crier
with him. She saw Hektor drawn by the mules on a litter.
She cried out then in sorrow and spoke to the entire city:
"Come, men of Troy and Trojan women; look upon Hektor
705   if ever before you were joyful when you saw him come back living
from battle; for he was a great joy to his city, and all his people."
    She spoke, and there was no man left there in all the city
nor woman, but all were held in sorrow passing endurance.
They met Priam beside the gates as he brought the dead in.

710	First among them were Hektor's wife and his honoured mother
	who tore their hair, and ran up beside the smooth-rolling wagon,
	and touched his head. And the multitude, wailing, stood there about them.
	And now and there in front of the gates they would have lamented
	all day till the sun went down and let fall their tears for Hektor,
715	except that the old man spoke from the chariot to his people:
	"Give me way to get through with my mules; then afterwards
	you may sate yourselves with mourning, when I have him inside the palace."
	So he spoke, and they stood apart and made way for the wagon.
	And when they had brought him inside the renowned house, they laid him
720	then on a carved bed, and seated beside him the singers
	who were to lead the melody in the dirge, and the singers
	chanted the song of sorrow, and the women were mourning beside them.
	Andromache of the white arms led the lamentation
	of the women, and held in her arms the head of manslaughtering Hektor:
725	"My husband, you were lost young from life, and have left me
	a widow in your house, and the boy is only a baby
	who was born to you and me, the unhappy. I think he will never
	come of age, for before then head to heel this city
	will be sacked, for you, its defender, are gone, you who guarded
730	the city, and the grave wives, and the innocent children,
	wives who before long must go away in the hollow ships,
	and among them I shall also go, and you, my child, follow
	where I go, and there do much hard work that is unworthy
	of you, drudgery for a hard master; or else some Achaian
735	will take you by hand and hurl you from the tower into horrible
	death, in anger because Hektor once killed his brother,
	or his father, or his son; there were so many Achaians
	whose teeth bit the vast earth, beaten down by the hands of Hektor.
	Your father was no merciful man in the horror of battle.
740	Therefore your people are grieving for you all through their city,
	Hektor, and you left for your parents mourning and sorrow
	beyond words, but for me passing all others is left the bitterness
	and the pain, for you did not die in bed, and stretch your arms to me,
	nor tell me some last intimate word that I could remember
745	always, all the nights and days of my weeping for you."
	So she spoke in tears, and the women were mourning about her.
	Now Hekabe led out the thronging chant of their sorrow:
	"Hektor, of all my sons the dearest by far to my spirit;
	while you still lived for me you were dear to the gods, and even
750	in the stage of death they cared about you still. There were others
	of my sons whom at times swift-footed Achilleus captured,
	and he would sell them as slaves far across the unresting salt water
	into Samos, and Imbros, and Lemnos in the gloom of the mists. You,
	when he had taken your life with the thin edge of the bronze sword,
755	he dragged again and again around his beloved companion's
	tomb, Patroklos', whom you killed, but even so did not
	bring him back to life. Now you lie in the palace, handsome

and fresh with dew, in the likeness of one whom he of the silver
bow, Apollo, has attacked and killed with his gentle arrows."
760   So she spoke, in tears, and wakened the endless mourning.
Third and last Helen led the song of sorrow among them:
"Hektor, of all my lord's brothers dearest by far to my spirit:
my husband is Alexandros, like an immortal, who brought me
here to Troy; and I should have died before I came with him;
765   and here now is the twentieth year upon me since I came
from the place where I was, forsaking the land of my fathers. In this time
I have never heard a harsh saying from you, nor an insult.
No, but when another, one of my lord's brothers or sisters, a fair-robed
wife of some brother, would say a harsh word to me in the palace,
770   or my lord's mother—but his father was gentle always, a father
indeed—then you would speak and put them off and restrain them
by your own gentleness of heart and your gentle words. Therefore
I mourn for you in sorrow of heart and mourn myself also
and my ill luck. There was no other in all the wide Troad
775   who was kind to me, and my friend; all others shrank when they saw me."
So she spoke in tears, and the vast populace grieved with her.
Now Priam the aged king spoke forth his word to his people:
"Now, men of Troy, bring timber into the city, and let not
your hearts fear a close ambush of the Argives. Achilleus
780   promised me, as he sent me on my way from the black ships,
that none should do us injury until the twelfth dawn comes."
He spoke, and they harnessed to the wagons their mules
and their oxen
and presently were gathered in front of the city. Nine days
they spent bringing in an endless supply of timber. But when
785   the tenth dawn had shone forth with her light upon mortals,
they carried out bold Hektor, weeping, and set the body
aloft a towering pyre for burning. And set fire to it.
But when the young dawn showed again with her rosy fingers,
the people gathered around the pyre of illustrious Hektor.
790   But when all were gathered to one place and assembled together,
first with gleaming wine they put out the pyre that was burning,
all where the fury of the fire still was in force, and thereafter
the brothers and companions of Hektor gathered the white bones
up, mourning, as the tears swelled and ran down their cheeks. Then
795   they laid what they had gathered up in a golden casket
and wrapped this about with soft robes of purple, and presently
put it away in the hollow of the grave, and over it
piled huge stones laid close together. Lightly and quickly
they piled up the grave-barrow, and on all sides were set watchmen
800   for fear the strong-greaved Achaians might too soon set upon them.
They piled up the grave-barrow and went away, and thereafter
assembled in a fair gathering and held a glorious
feast within the house of Priam, king under God's hand.
Such was their burial of Hektor, breaker of horses.

from The Odyssey[1]

Book 1

Athena Inspires the Prince

Sing to me of the man, Muse,[2] the man of twists and turns
driven time and again off course, once he had plundered
the hallowed heights of Troy.
Many cities of men he saw and learned their minds,
5   many pains he suffered, heartsick on the open sea,
fighting to save his life and bring his comrades home.
But he could not save them from disaster, hard as he strove—
the recklessness of their own ways destroyed them all,
the blind fools, they devoured the cattle of the Sun
10   and the Sungod wiped from sight the day of their return.
Launch out on his story, Muse, daughter of Zeus,
start from where you will—sing for our time too.
                                              By now,
all the survivors, all who avoided headlong death
were safe at home, escaped the wars and waves.
15   But one man alone . . .
his heart set on his wife and his return—Calypso,
the bewitching nymph, the lustrous goddess, held him back,
deep in her arching caverns, craving him for a husband.
But then, when the wheeling seasons brought the year around,
20   that year spun out by the gods when he should reach his home,
Ithaca—though not even there would he be free of trials,
even among his loved ones—then every god took pity,
all except Poseidon.[3] He raged on, seething against
the great Odysseus till he reached his native land.
                                              But now
25   Poseidon had gone to visit the Ethiopians worlds away,
Ethiopians off at the farthest limits of mankind,
a people split in two, one part where the Sungod sets
and part where the Sungod rises. There Poseidon went
to receive an offering, bulls and rams by the hundred—
30   far away at the feast the Sea-lord sat and took his pleasure.
But the other gods, at home in Olympian Zeus's halls,
met for full assembly there, and among them now
the father of men and gods was first to speak,
sorely troubled, remembering handsome Aegisthus,
35   the man Agamemnon's son, renowned Orestes, killed.
Recalling Aegisthus, Zeus harangued the immortal powers:
"Ah how shameless—the way these mortals blame the gods.
From us alone, they say, come all their miseries, yes,

1. Translated by Robert Fagles.
2. Goddess of epic poetry, one of several Muses.
3. God of the sea, of earthquakes, and of horses.

but they themselves, with their own reckless ways,
40   compound their pains beyond their proper share.
Look at Aegisthus now...
above and beyond *his* share he stole Atrides'[4] wife,
he murdered the warlord coming home from Troy
though he knew it meant his own total ruin.
45   Far in advance we told him so ourselves,
dispatching the guide, the giant-killer Hermes.[5]
'Don't murder the man,' he said, 'don't court his wife.
Beware, revenge will come from Orestes, Agamemnon's son,
that day he comes of age and longs for his native land.'
50   So Hermes warned, with all the good will in the world,
but would Aegisthus' hardened heart give way?
Now he pays the price—all at a single stroke."

    And sparkling-eyed Athena drove the matter home:
"Father, son of Cronus, our high and mighty king,
55   surely he goes down to a death he earned in full!
Let them all die so, all who do such things.
But my heart breaks for Odysseus,
that seasoned veteran cursed by fate so long—
far from his loved ones still, he suffers torments
60   off on a wave-washed island rising at the center of the seas.
A dark wooded island, and there a goddess makes her home,
a daughter of Atlas, wicked Titan who sounds the deep
in all its depths, whose shoulders lift on high
the colossal pillars thrusting earth and sky apart.
65   Atlas' daughter it is who holds Odysseus captive,
luckless man—despite his tears, forever trying
to spellbind his heart with suave, seductive words
and wipe all thought of Ithaca from his mind.
But he, straining for no more than a glimpse
70   of hearth-smoke drifting up from his own land,
Odysseus longs to die...
                 Olympian Zeus,
have you no care for *him* in your lofty heart?
Did he never win your favor with sacrifices
burned beside the ships on the broad plain of Troy?
75   Why, Zeus, why so dead set against Odysseus?"

    "My child," Zeus who marshals the thunderheads replied,
"what nonsense you let slip through your teeth. Now,
how on earth could I forget Odysseus? Great Odysseus
who excels all men in wisdom, excels in offerings too
80   he gives the immortal gods who rule the vaulting skies?
No, it's the Earth-Shaker, Poseidon, unappeased,

4. "Son of Atreus," Agamemnon.
5. Messenger god.

forever fuming against him for the Cyclops
whose giant eye he blinded: godlike Polyphemus,
towering over all the Cyclops' clans in power.
85 The nymph Thoosa bore him, daughter of Phorcys,
lord of the barren salt sea—she met Poseidon
once in his vaulted caves and they made love.
And now for his blinded son the earthquake god—
though he won't quite kill Odysseus—
90 drives him far off course from native land.
But come, all of us here put heads together now,
work out his journey home so Odysseus can return.
Lord Poseidon, I trust, will let his anger go.
How can he stand his ground against the will
95 of all the gods at once—one god alone?"

Athena, her eyes flashing bright, exulted,
"Father, son of Cronus, our high and mighty king!
If now it really pleases the blissful gods
that wise Odysseus shall return—home at last—
100 let us dispatch the guide and giant-killer Hermes
down to Ogygia Island, down to announce at once
to the nymph with lovely braids our fixed decree:
Odysseus journeys home—the exile must return!
While I myself go down to Ithaca, rouse his son
105 to a braver pitch, inspire his heart with courage
to summon the flowing-haired Achaeans to full assembly,
speak his mind to all those suitors, slaughtering on and on
his droves of sheep and shambling longhorn cattle.
Next I will send him off to Sparta and sandy Pylos,
110 there to learn of his dear father's journey home.
Perhaps he will hear some news and make his name
throughout the mortal world."
                                So Athena vowed
and under her feet she fastened the supple sandals,
ever-glowing gold, that wing her over the waves
115 and boundless earth with the rush of gusting winds.
She seized the rugged spear tipped with a bronze point—
weighted, heavy, the massive shaft she wields to break the lines
of heroes the mighty Father's daughter storms against.
And down she swept from Olympus' craggy peaks
120 and lit on Ithaca, standing tall at Odysseus' gates,
the threshold of his court. Gripping her bronze spear,
she looked for all the world like a stranger now,
like Mentes, lord of the Taphians.
There she found the swaggering suitors, just then
125 amusing themselves with rolling dice before the doors,
lounging on hides of oxen they had killed themselves.
While heralds and brisk attendants bustled round them,
some at the mixing-bowls, mulling wine and water,

others wiping the tables down with sopping sponges,
130 setting them out in place, still other servants
jointed and carved the great sides of meat.

First by far to see her was Prince Telemachus,
sitting among the suitors, heart obsessed with grief.
He could almost see his magnificent father, here...
135 in the mind's eye—if only *he* might drop from the clouds
and drive these suitors all in a rout throughout the halls
and regain his pride of place and rule his own domains!
Daydreaming so as he sat among the suitors,
he glimpsed Athena now
140 and straight to the porch he went, mortified
that a guest might still be standing at the doors.
Pausing beside her there, he clasped her right hand
and relieving her at once of her long bronze spear,
met her with winged words: "Greetings, stranger!
145 Here in our house you'll find a royal welcome.
Have supper first, then tell us what you need."

He led the way and Pallas Athena followed.
Once in the high-roofed hall, he took her lance
and fixed it firm in a burnished rack against
150 a sturdy pillar, there where row on row of spears,
embattled Odysseus' spears, stood stacked and waiting.
Then he escorted her to a high, elaborate chair of honor,
over it draped a cloth, and here he placed his guest
with a stool to rest her feet. But for himself
155 he drew up a low reclining chair beside her,
richly painted, clear of the press of suitors,
concerned his guest, offended by their uproar,
might shrink from food in the midst of such a mob.
He hoped, what's more, to ask her about his long-lost father.
160 A maid brought water soon in a graceful golden pitcher
and over a silver basin tipped it out
so they might rinse their hands,
then pulled a gleaming table to their side.
A staid housekeeper brought on bread to serve them,
165 appetizers aplenty too, lavish with her bounty.
A carver lifted platters of meat toward them,
meats of every sort, and set beside them golden cups
and time and again a page came round and poured them wine.

But now the suitors trooped in with all their swagger
170 and took their seats on low and high-backed chairs.
Heralds poured water over their hands for rinsing,
serving maids brought bread heaped high in trays
and the young men brimmed the mixing-bowls with wine.
They reached out for the good things that lay at hand,

175 and when they'd put aside desire for food and drink
the suitors set their minds on other pleasures,
song and dancing, all that crowns a feast.
A herald placed an ornate lyre in Phemius' hands,
the bard who always performed among them there;
180 they forced the man to sing.
                                        A rippling prelude—
and no sooner had he struck up his rousing song
than Telemachus, head close to Athena's sparkling eyes,
spoke low to his guest so no one else could hear:
"Dear stranger, would you be shocked by what I say?
185 Look at them over there. Not a care in the world,
just lyres and tunes! It's easy for them, all right,
they feed on another's goods and go scot-free—
a man whose white bones lie strewn in the rain somewhere,
rotting away on land or rolling down the ocean's salty swells.
190 But that man—if they caught sight of him home in Ithaca,
by god, they'd all pray to be faster on their feet
than richer in bars of gold and heavy robes.
But now, no use, he's died a wretched death.
No comfort's left for us...not even if
195 someone, somewhere, says he's coming home.
The day of his return will never dawn.
                                        Enough.
Tell me about yourself now, clearly, point by point.
Who are you? where are you from? your city? your parents?
What sort of vessel brought you? Why did the sailors
200 land you here in Ithaca? Who did they say they are?
I hardly think you came this way on foot!
And tell me this for a fact—I need to know—
is this your first time here? Or are you a friend of father's,
a guest from the old days? Once, crowds of other men
205 would come to our house on visits—visitor that he was,
when he walked among the living."
                                        Her eyes glinting,
goddess Athena answered, "My whole story, of course,
I'll tell it point by point. Wise old Anchialus
was my father. My own name is Mentes,
210 lord of the Taphian men who love their oars.
And here I've come, just now, with ship and crew,
sailing the wine-dark sea to foreign ports of call,
to Temese, out for bronze—our cargo gleaming iron.
Our ship lies moored off farmlands far from town,
215 riding in Rithron Cove, beneath Mount Nion's woods.
As for the ties between your father and myself,
we've been friends forever, I'm proud to say,
and he would bear me out
if you went and questioned old lord Laertes.[6]

---

6. Odysseus's father.

220 He, I gather, no longer ventures into town
but lives a life of hardship, all to himself,
off on his farmstead with an aged serving-woman
who tends him well, who gives him food and drink
when weariness has taken hold of his withered limbs
225 from hauling himself along his vineyard's steep slopes.
And now I've come—and why? I heard that he was back...
your father, that is. But no, the gods thwart his passage.
Yet I tell you great Odysseus is not dead. He's still alive,
somewhere in this wide world, held captive, out at sea
230 on a wave-washed island, and hard men, savages,
somehow hold him back against his will.
                                        Wait,
I'll make you a prophecy, one the immortal gods
have planted in my mind—it will come true, I think,
though I am hardly a seer or know the flights of birds.
235 He won't be gone long from the native land he loves,
not even if iron shackles bind your father down.
He's plotting a way to journey home at last;
he's never at a loss.
                       But come, please,
tell me about yourself now, point by point.
240 You're truly Odysseus' son? You've sprung up so!
Uncanny resemblance...the head, and the fine eyes—
I see him now. How often we used to meet in the old days
before he embarked for Troy, where other Argive captains,
all the best men, sailed in the long curved ships.
245 From then to this very day
I've not set eyes on Odysseus or he on me."

     And young Telemachus cautiously replied,
"I'll try, my friend, to give you a frank answer.
Mother has always told me I'm his son, it's true,
250 but I am not so certain. Who, on his own,
has ever really known who gave him life?
Would to god I'd been the son of a happy man
whom old age overtook in the midst of his possessions!
Now, think of the most unlucky mortal ever born—
255 since you ask me, yes, they say I am his son."

     "Still," the clear-eyed goddess reassured him,
"trust me, the gods have not marked out your house
for such an unsung future,
not if Penelope has borne a son like you.
260 But tell me about all this and spare me nothing.
What's this banqueting, this crowd carousing here?
And what part do you play yourself? Some wedding-feast,
some festival? Hardly a potluck supper, I would say.
How obscenely they lounge and swagger here, look,
265 gorging in your house. Why, any man of sense

who chanced among them would be outraged,
seeing such behavior."
                              Ready Telemachus
took her up at once: "Well, my friend,
seeing you want to probe and press the question,
270   once this house was rich, no doubt, beyond reproach
when the man you mentioned still lived here, at home.
Now the gods have reversed our fortunes with a vengeance—
wiped that man from the earth like no one else before.
I would never have grieved so much about his death
275   if he'd gone down with comrades off in Troy
or died in the arms of loved ones,
once he had wound down the long coil of war.
Then all united Achaea would have raised his tomb
and he'd have won his son great fame for years to come.
280   But now the whirlwinds have ripped him away, no fame for him!
He's lost and gone now—out of sight, out of mind—and I...
he's left me tears and grief. Nor do I rack my heart
and grieve for him alone. No longer. Now the gods
have invented other miseries to plague me.
                                        Listen.
285   All the nobles who rule the islands round about,
Dulichion, and Same, and wooded Zacynthus too,
and all who lord it in rocky Ithaca as well—
down to the last man they court my mother,
they lay waste my house! And mother...
290   she neither rejects a marriage she despises
nor can she bear to bring the courting to an end—
while they continue to bleed my household white.
Soon—you wait—they'll grind *me* down as well."
                                    "Shameful!"—
brimming with indignation, Pallas Athena broke out.
295   "Oh how much you need Odysseus, gone so long—
how *he*'d lay hands on all these brazen suitors!
If only he would appear, now,
at his house's outer gates and take his stand,
armed with his helmet, shield and pair of spears,
300   as strong as the man I glimpsed that first time
in our own house, drinking wine and reveling there...
just come in from Ephyra, visiting Ilus, Mermerus' son.
Odysseus sailed that way, you see, in his swift trim ship,
hunting deadly poison to smear on his arrows' bronze heads.
305   Ilus refused—he feared the wrath of the everlasting gods—
but father, so fond of him, gave him all he wanted.
If only *that* Odysseus sported with these suitors,
a blood wedding, a quick death would take the lot!
True, but all lies in the lap of the great gods,
310   whether or not he'll come and pay them back,
here, in his own house.

But you, I urge you,
think how to drive these suitors from your halls.
Come now, listen closely. Take my words to heart.
At daybreak summon the island's lords to full assembly,
315   give your orders to all and call the gods to witness:
tell the suitors to scatter, each to his own place.
As for your mother, if the spirit moves her to marry,
let her go back to her father's house, a man of power.
Her kin will arrange the wedding, provide the gifts,
320   the array that goes with a daughter dearly loved.
                                            For you,
I have some good advice, if only you will accept it.
Fit out a ship with twenty oars, the best in sight,
sail in quest of news of your long-lost father.
Someone may tell you something
325   or you may catch a rumor straight from Zeus,
rumor that carries news to men like nothing else.
First go down to Pylos, question old King Nestor,
then cross over to Sparta, to red-haired Menelaus,
of all the bronze-armored Achaeans the last man back.
330   Now, if you hear your father's alive and heading home,
hard-pressed as you are, brave out one more year.
If you hear he's dead, no longer among the living,
then back you come to the native land you love,
raise his grave-mound, build his honors high
335   with the full funeral rites that he deserves—
and give your mother to another husband.
                                          Then,
once you've sealed those matters, seen them through,
think hard, reach down deep in your heart and soul
for a way to kill these suitors in your house,
340   by stealth or in open combat.
You must not cling to your boyhood any longer—
it's time you were a man. Haven't you heard
what glory Prince Orestes won throughout the world
when he killed that cunning, murderous Aegisthus,
345   who'd killed his famous father?
                                  And you, my friend—
how tall and handsome I see you now—be brave, you too,
so men to come will sing your praises down the years.
But now I must go back to my swift trim ship
and all my shipmates, chafing there, I'm sure,
350   waiting for my return. It all rests with you.
Take my words to heart."
                          "Oh stranger,"
heedful Telemachus replied, "indeed I will.
You've counseled me with so much kindness now,
like a father to a son. I won't forget a word.
355   But come, stay longer, keen as you are to sail,

so you can bathe and rest and lift your spirits,
then go back to your ship, delighted with a gift,
a prize of honor, something rare and fine
as a keepsake from myself. The kind of gift
360 a host will give a stranger, friend to friend."

          Her eyes glinting, Pallas declined in haste:
"Not now. Don't hold me here. I long to be on my way.
As for the gift—whatever you'd give in kindness—
save it for my return so I can take it home.
365 Choose something rare and fine, and a good reward
that gift is going to bring you."
                                With that promise,
off and away Athena the bright-eyed goddess flew
like a bird in soaring flight
but left his spirit filled with nerve and courage,
370 charged with his father's memory more than ever now.
He felt his senses quicken, overwhelmed with wonder—
this was a god, he knew it well and made at once
for the suitors, a man like a god himself.
                                    Amidst them still
the famous bard sang on, and they sat in silence, listening
375 as he performed The Achaeans' Journey Home from Troy:
all the blows Athena doomed them to endure.
                                    And now,
from high above in her room and deep in thought,
she caught his inspired strains...
Icarius' daughter Penelope, wary and reserved,
380 and down the steep stair from her chamber she descended,
not alone: two of her women followed close behind.
That radiant woman, once she reached her suitors,
drawing her glistening veil across her cheeks,
paused now where a column propped the sturdy roof,
385 with one of her loyal handmaids stationed either side.
Suddenly, dissolving in tears and bursting through
the bard's inspired voice, she cried out, "Phemius!
So many other songs you know to hold us spellbound,
works of the gods and men that singers celebrate.
390 Sing one of those as you sit beside them here
and they drink their wine in silence.
                                    But break off this song—
the unendurable song that always rends the heart inside me...
the unforgettable grief, it wounds me most of all!
How I long for my husband—alive in memory, always,
395 that great man whose fame resounds through Hellas
right to the depths of Argos!"
                                    "Why, mother,"
poised Telemachus put in sharply, "why deny
our devoted bard the chance to entertain us

any way the spirit stirs him on?
400 Bards are not to blame—
Zeus is to blame. He deals to each and every
laborer on this earth whatever doom he pleases.
Why fault the bard if he sings the Argives' harsh fate?
It's always the latest song, the one that echoes last
405 in the listeners' ears, that people praise the most.
Courage, mother. Harden your heart, and listen.
Odysseus was scarcely the only one, you know,
whose journey home was blotted out at Troy.
Others, so many others, died there too.

        So, mother,
410 go back to your quarters. Tend to your own tasks,
the distaff and the loom, and keep the women
working hard as well. As for giving orders,
men will see to that, but I most of all:
I hold the reins of power in this house."

           Astonished,
415 she withdrew to her own room. She took to heart
the clear good sense in what her son had said.
Climbing up to the lofty chamber with her women,
she fell to weeping for Odysseus, her beloved husband,
till watchful Athena sealed her eyes with welcome sleep.

420 But the suitors broke into uproar through the shadowed halls,
all of them lifting prayers to lie beside her, share her bed,
until discreet Telemachus took command: "You suitors
who plague my mother, you, you insolent, overweening...
for this evening let us dine and take our pleasure,
425 no more shouting now. What a fine thing it is
to listen to such a bard as we have here—
the man sings like a god.

        But at first light
we all march forth to assembly, take our seats
so I can give my orders and say to you straight out:
430 You must leave my palace! See to your feasting elsewhere,
devour your own possessions, house to house by turns.
But if you decide the fare is better, richer here,
destroying one man's goods and going scot-free,
all right then, carve away!
435 But I'll cry out to the everlasting gods in hopes
that Zeus will pay you back with a vengeance—all of you
destroyed in my house while I go scot-free myself!"

  So Telemachus declared. And they all bit their lips,
amazed the prince could speak with so much daring.

440 Eupithes' son Antinous broke their silence:
"Well, Telemachus, only the gods could teach you

to sound so high and mighty! Such brave talk.
I pray that Zeus will never make *you* king of Ithaca,
though your father's crown is no doubt yours by birth."

445   But cool-headed Telemachus countered firmly:
"Antinous, even though my words may offend you,
I'd be happy to take the crown if Zeus presents it.
You think that nothing worse could befall a man?
It's really not so bad to be a king. All at once
450   your palace grows in wealth, your honors grow as well.
But there are hosts of other Achaean princes, look—
young and old, crowds of them on our island here—
and any one of the lot might hold the throne,
now great Odysseus is dead...
455   But I'll be lord of my own house and servants,
all that King Odysseus won for me by force."

          And now Eurymachus, Polybus' son, stepped in:
"Surely this must lie in the gods' lap, Telemachus—
which Achaean will lord it over seagirt Ithaca.
460   Do hold on to your own possessions, rule your house.
God forbid that anyone tear your holdings from your hands
while men still live in Ithaca.
                    But about your guest,
dear boy, I have some questions. Where does he come from?
Where's his country, his birth, his father's old estates?
465   Did he bring some news of your father, his return?
Or did he come on business of his own?
How he leapt to his feet and off he went!
No waiting around for proper introductions.
And no mean man, not by the looks of him, I'd say."

470   "Eurymachus," Telemachus answered shrewdly,
"clearly my father's journey home is lost forever.
I no longer trust in rumors—rumors from the blue—
nor bother with any prophecy, when mother calls
some wizard into the house to ask him questions.
475   As for the stranger, though,
the man's an old family friend, from Taphos,
wise Anchialus' son. He says his name is Mentes,
lord of the Taphian men who love their oars."
                              So he said
but deep in his mind he knew the immortal goddess.
480   Now the suitors turned to dance and song,
to the lovely beat and sway,
waiting for dusk to come upon them there...
and the dark night came upon them, lost in pleasure.
Finally, to bed. Each to his own house.

485 off to his bedroom built in the fine courtyard—
 a commanding, lofty room set well apart—
 retired too, his spirit swarming with misgivings.
 His devoted nurse attended him, bearing a glowing torch,
 Eurycleia the daughter of Ops, Pisenor's son.
490 Laertes had paid a price for the woman years ago,
 still in the bloom of youth. He traded twenty oxen,
 honored her on a par with his own loyal wife at home
 but fearing the queen's anger, never shared her bed.
 She was his grandson's escort now and bore a torch,
495 for she was the one of all the maids who loved
 the prince the most—she'd nursed him as a baby.
 He spread the doors of his snug, well-made room,
 sat down on the bed and pulled his soft shirt off,
 tossed it into the old woman's conscientious hands,
500 and after folding it neatly, patting it smooth,
 she hung it up on a peg beside his corded bed,
 then padded from the bedroom,
 drawing the door shut with the silver hook,
 sliding the doorbolt home with its rawhide strap.
505 There all night long, wrapped in a sheep's warm fleece,
 he weighed in his mind the course Athena charted.

Book 6

The Princess and the Stranger

 So there he lay at rest, the storm-tossed great Odysseus,
 borne down by his hard labors first and now deep sleep
 as Athena traveled through the countryside
 and reached the Phaeacians' city. Years ago
5 they lived in a land of spacious dancing-circles,
 Hyperia, all too close to the overbearing Cyclops,
 stronger, violent brutes who harried them without end.
 So their godlike king, Nausithous, led the people off
 in a vast migration, settled them in Scheria,
10 far from the men who toil on this earth—
 he flung up walls around the city, built the houses,
 raised the gods' temples and shared the land for plowing.
 But his fate had long since forced him down to Death
 and now Alcinous ruled, and the gods made him wise.
15 Straight to his house the clear-eyed Pallas went,
 full of plans for great Odysseus' journey home.
 She made her way to the gaily painted room
 where a young girl lay asleep...
 a match for the deathless gods in build and beauty,
20 Nausicaa, the daughter of generous King Alcinous.

Two handmaids fair as the Graces slept beside her,
flanking the two posts, with the gleaming doors closed.
But the goddess drifted through like a breath of fresh air,
rushed to the girl's bed and hovering close she spoke,
in face and form like the shipman Dymas' daughter,
a girl the princess' age, and dearest to her heart.
Disguised, the bright-eyed goddess chided, "Nausicaa,
how could your mother bear a careless girl like you?
Look at your fine clothes, lying here neglected—
with your marriage not far off,
the day you should be decked in all your glory
and offer elegant dress to those who form your escort.
That's how a bride's good name goes out across the world
and it brings her father and queenly mother joy. Come,
let's go wash these clothes at the break of day—
I'll help you, lend a hand, and the work will fly!
You won't stay unwed long. The noblest men
in the country court you now, all Phaeacians
just like you, Phaeacia-born and raised. So come,
the first thing in the morning press your kingly father
to harness the mules and wagon for you, all to carry
your sashes, dresses, glossy spreads for your bed.
It's so much nicer for you to ride than go on foot.
The washing-pools are just too far from town."

                                    With that
the bright-eyed goddess sped away to Olympus, where,
they say, the gods' eternal mansion stands unmoved,
never rocked by galewinds, never drenched by rains,
nor do the drifting snows assail it, no, the clear air
stretches away without a cloud, and a great radiance
plays across that world where the blithe gods
live all their days in bliss. There Athena went,
once the bright-eyed one had urged the princess on.

      Dawn soon rose on her splendid throne and woke
Nausicaa finely gowned. Still beguiled by her dream,
down she went through the house to tell her parents now,
her beloved father and mother. She found them both inside.
Her mother sat at the hearth with several waiting-women,
spinning yarn on a spindle, lustrous sea-blue wool.
Her father she met as he left to join the lords
at a council island nobles asked him to attend.
She stepped up close to him, confiding, "Daddy dear,
I wonder, won't you have them harness a wagon for me,
the tall one with the good smooth wheels . . . so I
can take our clothes to the river for a washing?
Lovely things, but lying before me all soiled.
And you yourself, sitting among the princes,
debating points at your council,

you really should be wearing spotless linen.
Then you have five sons, full-grown in the palace,
70 two of them married, but three are lusty bachelors
always demanding crisp shirts fresh from the wash
when they go out to dance. Look at my duties—
that all rests on me."
                            So she coaxed, too shy
to touch on her hopes for marriage, young warm hopes,
75 in her father's presence. But he saw through it all
and answered quickly, "I won't deny you the mules,
my darling girl . . . I won't deny you anything.
Off you go, and the men will harness a wagon,
the tall one with the good smooth wheels,
80 fitted out with a cradle on the top."
                                With that
he called to the stablemen and they complied.
They trundled the wagon out now, rolling smoothly,
backed the mule-team into the traces, hitched them up,
while the princess brought her finery from the room
85 and piled it into the wagon's polished cradle.
Her mother packed a hamper—treats of all kinds,
favorite things to refresh her daughter's spirits—
poured wine in a skin, and as Nausicaa climbed aboard,
the queen gave her a golden flask of suppling olive oil
90 for her and her maids to smooth on after bathing.
Then, taking the whip in hand and glistening reins,
she touched the mules to a start and out they clattered,
trotting on at a clip, bearing the princess and her clothes
and not alone: her maids went with her, stepping briskly too.

95   Once they reached the banks of the river flowing strong
where the pools would never fail, with plenty of water
cool and clear, bubbling up and rushing through
to scour the darkest stains—they loosed the mules,
out from under the wagon yoke, and chased them down
100 the river's rippling banks to graze on luscious clover.
Down from the cradle they lifted clothes by the armload,
plunged them into the dark pools and stamped them down
in the hollows, one girl racing the next to finish first
until they'd scoured and rinsed off all the grime,
105 then they spread them out in a line along the beach
where the surf had washed a pebbly scree ashore.
And once they'd bathed and smoothed their skin with oil,
they took their picnic, sitting along the river's banks
and waiting for all the clothes to dry in the hot noon sun.
110 Now fed to their hearts' content, the princess and her retinue
threw their veils to the wind, struck up a game of ball.
White-armed Nausicaa led their singing, dancing beat . . .
as lithe as Artemis with her arrows striding down

from a high peak—Taygetus' towering ridge or Erymanthus—
115 thrilled to race with the wild boar or bounding deer,
and nymphs of the hills race with her,
daughters of Zeus whose shield is storm and thunder,
ranging the hills in sport, and Leto's heart exults
as head and shoulders over the rest her daughter rises,
120 unmistakable—she outshines them all, though all are lovely.
So Nausicaa shone among her maids, a virgin, still unwed.

But now, as she was about to fold her clothes
and yoke the mules and turn for home again,
now clear-eyed Pallas thought of what came next,
125 to make Odysseus wake and see this young beauty
and she would lead him to the Phaeacians' town.
The ball—
         the princess suddenly tossed it to a maid
but it missed the girl, it splashed in a deep swirling pool
and they all shouted out—
                    and that woke great Odysseus.
130 He sat up with a start, puzzling, his heart pounding:
"Man of misery, whose land have I lit on now?
What *are* they here—violent, savage, lawless?
or friendly to strangers, god-fearing men?
Listen: shouting, echoing round me—women, girls—
135 or the nymphs who haunt the rugged mountaintops
and the river springs and meadows lush with grass!
Or am I really close to people who speak my language?
Up with you, see how the land lies, see for yourself now..."

Muttering so, great Odysseus crept out of the bushes,
140 stripping off with his massive hand a leafy branch
from the tangled olive growth to shield his body,
hide his private parts. And out he stalked
as a mountain lion exultant in his power
strides through wind and rain and his eyes blaze
145 and he charges sheep or oxen or chases wild deer
but his hunger drives him on to go for flocks,
even to raid the best-defended homestead.
So Odysseus moved out . . .
about to mingle with all those lovely girls,
150 naked now as he was, for the need drove him on,
a terrible sight, all crusted, caked with brine—
they scattered in panic down the jutting beaches.
Only Alcinous' daughter held fast, for Athena planted
courage within her heart, dissolved the trembling in her limbs,
155 and she firmly stood her ground and faced Odysseus, torn now—
Should he fling his arms around her knees, the young beauty,
plead for help, or stand back, plead with a winning word,
beg her to lead him to the town and lend him clothing?
This was the better way, he thought. Plead now

with a subtle, winning word and stand well back,
don't clasp her knees, the girl might bridle, yes.
He launched in at once, endearing, sly and suave:
"Here I am at your mercy, princess—
are you a goddess or a mortal? If one of the gods

who rule the skies up there, you're Artemis to the life,
the daughter of mighty Zeus—I see her now—just look
at your build, your bearing, your lithe flowing grace . . .
But if you're one of the mortals living here on earth,
three times blest are your father, your queenly mother,

three times over your brothers too. How often their hearts
must warm with joy to see you striding into the dances—
such a bloom of beauty. True, but he is the one
more blest than all other men alive, that man
who sways you with gifts and leads you home, his bride!

I have never laid eyes on anyone like you,
neither man nor woman . . .
I look at you and a sense of wonder takes me.
                                                 Wait,
once I saw the like—in Delos,[1] beside Apollo's altar—
the young slip of a palm-tree springing into the light.

There I'd sailed, you see, with a great army in my wake,
out on the long campaign that doomed my life to hardship.
That vision! Just as I stood there gazing, rapt, for hours . . .
no shaft like that had ever risen up from the earth—
so now I marvel at *you*, my lady: rapt, enthralled,

too struck with awe to grasp you by the knees
though pain has ground me down.
                                          Only yesterday,
the twentieth day, did I escape the wine-dark sea.
Till then the waves and the rushing gales had swept me on
from the island of Ogygia. Now some power has tossed me here,

doubtless to suffer still more torments on your shores.
I can't believe they'll stop. Long before that
the gods will give me more, still more.
                                                 Compassion—
princess, please! You, after all that I have suffered,
you are the first I've come to. I know no one else,

none in your city, no one in your land.
Show me the way to town, give me a rag for cover,
just some cloth, some wrapper you carried with you here.
And may the good gods give you all your heart desires:
husband, and house, and lasting harmony too.

No finer, greater gift in the world than that . . .
when man and woman possess their home, two minds,
two hearts that work as one. Despair to their enemies,
a joy to all their friends. Their own best claim to glory."

1. Island between Greece and Asia Minor that was sacred to Apollo.

"Stranger," the white-armed princess answered staunchly,
205   "friend, you're hardly a wicked man, and no fool, I'd say—
it's Olympian Zeus himself who hands our fortunes out,
to each of us in turn, to the good and bad,
however Zeus prefers...
He gave you pain, it seems. You simply have to bear it.
210   But now, seeing you've reached our city and our land,
you'll never lack for clothing or any other gift,
the right of worn-out suppliants come our way.
I'll show you our town, tell you our people's name.
Phaeacians we are, who hold this city and this land,
215   and I am the daughter of generous King Alcinous.
All our people's power stems from him."

She called out to her girls with lovely braids:
"Stop, my friends! Why run when you see a man?
Surely you don't think *him* an enemy, do you?
220   There's no one alive, there never will be one,
who'd reach Phaeacian soil and lay it waste.
The immortals love us far too much for that.
We live too far apart, out in the surging sea,
off at the world's end—
225   no other mortals come to mingle with us.
But here's an unlucky wanderer strayed our way
and we must tend him well. Every stranger and beggar
comes from Zeus, and whatever scrap we give him
he'll be glad to get. So, quick, my girls,
230   give our newfound friend some food and drink
and bathe the man in the river,
wherever you find some shelter from the wind."
                             At that
they came to a halt and teased each other on
and led Odysseus down to a sheltered spot
235   where he could find a seat,
just as great Alcinous' daughter told them.
They laid out cloak and shirt for him to wear,
they gave him the golden flask of suppling olive oil
and pressed him to bathe himself in the river's stream.
240   Then thoughtful Odysseus reassured the handmaids,
"Stand where you are, dear girls, a good way off,
so I can rinse the brine from my shoulders now
and rub myself with oil...
how long it's been since oil touched my skin!
245   But I won't bathe in front of you. I would be embarrassed—
stark naked before young girls with lovely braids."

The handmaids scurried off to tell their mistress.
Great Odysseus bathed in the river, scrubbed his body
clean of brine that clung to his back and broad shoulders,

250   scoured away the brackish scurf that caked his head.
    And then, once he had bathed all over, rubbed in oil
    and donned the clothes the virgin princess gave him,
    Zeus's daughter Athena made him taller to all eyes,
    his build more massive now, and down from his brow
255   she ran his curls like thick hyacinth clusters
    full of blooms. As a master craftsman washes
    gold over beaten silver—a man the god of fire
    and Queen Athena trained in every fine technique—
    and finishes off his latest effort, handsome work,
260   so she lavished splendor over his head and shoulders now.
    And down to the beach he walked and sat apart,
    glistening in his glory, breathtaking, yes,
    and the princess gazed in wonder...
    then turned to her maids with lovely braided hair:
265   "Listen, my white-armed girls, to what I tell you.
    The gods of Olympus can't be all against this man
    who's come to mingle among our noble people.
    At first he seemed appalling, I must say—
    now he seems like a god who rules the skies up there!
270   Ah, if only a man like *that* were called my husband,
    lived right here, pleased to stay forever...
                            Enough.
    Give the stranger food and drink, my girls."
    They hung on her words and did her will at once,
    set before Odysseus food and drink, and he ate and drank,
275   the great Odysseus, long deprived, so ravenous now—
    it seemed like years since he had tasted food.

    The white-armed princess thought of one last thing.
    Folding the clothes, she packed them into her painted wagon,
    hitched the sharp-hoofed mules, and climbing up herself,
280   Nausicaa urged Odysseus, warmly urged her guest,
    "Up with you now, my friend, and off to town we go.
    I'll see you into my wise father's palace where,
    I promise you, you'll meet all the best Phaeacians.
    Wait, let's do it this way. You seem no fool to me.
285   While we're passing along the fields and plowlands,
    you follow the mules and wagon, stepping briskly
    with all my maids. I'll lead the way myself.
    But once we reach our city, ringed by walls
    and strong high towers too, with a fine harbor either side...
290   and the causeway in is narrow; along the road the rolling ships
    are all hauled up, with a slipway cleared for every vessel.
    There's our assembly, round Poseidon's royal precinct,
    built of quarried slabs planted deep in the earth.
    Here the sailors tend their black ships' tackle,
295   cables and sails, and plane their oarblades down.
    Phaeacians, you see, care nothing for bow or quiver,

only for masts and oars and good trim ships themselves—
we glory in our ships, crossing the foaming seas!
But I shrink from all our sea-dogs' nasty gossip.
Some old salt might mock us behind our backs—
we have our share of insolent types in town
and one of the coarser sort, spying us, might say,
'Now who's that tall, handsome stranger Nausicaa has in tow?
Where'd she light on *him?* Her husband-to-be, just wait!
But who—some shipwrecked stray she's taken up with,
some alien from abroad? Since nobody lives nearby.
Unless it's really a god come down from the blue
to answer all her prayers, and to have her all his days.
Good riddance! Let the girl go roving to find herself
a man from foreign parts. She only spurns her own—
countless Phaeacians round about who court her,
nothing but our best.'
                            So they'll scoff...
just think of the scandal that would face me then.
I'd find fault with a girl who carried on that way,
flouting her parents' wishes—father, mother, still alive—
consorting with men before she'd tied the knot in public.
No, stranger, listen closely to what I say, the sooner
to win your swift voyage home at my father's hands.
Now, you'll find a splendid grove along the road—
poplars, sacred to Pallas—
a bubbling spring's inside and meadows run around it.
There lies my father's estate, his blossoming orchard too,
as far from town as a man's strong shout can carry.
Take a seat there, wait a while, and give us time
to make it into town and reach my father's house.
Then, when you think we're home, walk on yourself
to the city, ask the way to my father's palace,
generous King Alcinous. You cannot miss it,
even an innocent child could guide you there.
No other Phaeacian's house is built like that:
so grand, the palace of Alcinous, our great hero.
Once the mansion and courtyard have enclosed you, go,
quickly, across the hall until you reach my mother.
Beside the hearth she sits in the fire's glare,
spinning yarn on a spindle, sea-blue wool—
a stirring sight, you'll see...
she leans against a pillar, her ladies sit behind.
And my father's throne is drawn up close beside her;
there he sits and takes his wine, a mortal like a god.
Go past him, grasp my mother's knees—if you want
to see the day of your return, rejoicing, soon,
even if your home's a world away.
If only the queen will take you to her heart,
then there's hope that you will see your loved ones,
reach your own grand house, your native land at last."

At that she touched the mules with her shining whip
and they quickly left the running stream behind.
The team trotted on, their hoofs wove in and out.
She drove them back with care so all the rest,
350   maids and Odysseus, could keep the pace on foot,
and she used the whip discreetly.
The sun sank as they reached the hallowed grove,
sacred to Athena, where Odysseus stopped and sat
and said a prayer at once to mighty Zeus's daughter:
355   "Hear me, daughter of Zeus whose shield is thunder—
tireless one, Athena! Now hear my prayer at last,
for you never heard me then, when I was shattered,
when the famous god of earthquakes wrecked my craft.
Grant that here among the Phaeacian people
360   I may find some mercy and some love!"

So he prayed and Athena heard his prayer
but would not yet appear to him undisguised.
She stood in awe of her Father's brother, lord of the sea
who still seethed on, still churning with rage against
365   the great Odysseus till he reached his native land.

Book 9

In the One-Eyed Giant's Cave

Odysseus, the great teller of tales, launched out on his story:
"Alcinous, majesty, shining among your island people,
what a fine thing it is to listen to such a bard
as we have here—the man sings like a god.
5   The crown of life, I'd say. There's nothing better
than when deep joy holds sway throughout the realm
and banqueters up and down the palace sit in ranks,
enthralled to hear the bard, and before them all, the tables
heaped with bread and meats, and drawing wine from a mixing-bowl
10   the steward makes his rounds and keeps the winecups flowing.
This, to my mind, is the best that life can offer.
                                                  But now
you're set on probing the bitter pains I've borne,
so I'm to weep and grieve, it seems, still more.
Well then, what shall I go through first,
15   what shall I save for last?
What pains—the gods have given me my share.
Now let me begin by telling you my name...
so you may know it well and I in times to come,
if I can escape the fatal day, will be your host,
20   your sworn friend, though my home is far from here.
I am Odysseus, son of Laertes, known to the world
for every kind of craft—my fame has reached the skies.
Sunny Ithaca is my home. Atop her stands

Mount Neriton's leafy ridges shimmering in the wind.
25 Around her a ring of islands circle side-by-side,
Dulichion, Same, wooded Zacynthus too, but mine
lies low and away, the farthest out to sea,
rearing into the western dusk
while the others face the east and breaking day.
30 Mine is a rugged land but good for raising sons—
and I myself, I know no sweeter sight on earth
than a man's own native country.
                                              True enough,
Calypso the lustrous goddess tried to hold me back,
deep in her arching caverns, craving me for a husband.
35 So did Circe, holding me just as warmly in her halls,
the bewitching queen of Aeaea keen to have me too.
But they never won the heart inside me, never.
So nothing is as sweet as a man's own country,
his own parents, even though he's settled down
40 in some luxurious house, off in a foreign land
and far from those who bore him.
                                              No more. Come,
let me tell you about the voyage fraught with hardship
Zeus inflicted on me, homeward bound from Troy . . .

      The wind drove me out of Ilium on to Ismarus,
45 the Cicones'[1] stronghold. There I sacked the city,
killed the men, but as for the wives and plunder,
that rich haul we dragged away from the place—
we shared it round so no one, not on my account,
would go deprived of his fair share of spoils.
50 Then I urged them to cut and run, set sail,
but would they listen? Not those mutinous fools;
there was too much wine to swill, too many sheep to slaughter
down along the beach, and shambling longhorn cattle.
And all the while the Cicones sought out other Cicones,
55 called for help from their neighbors living inland:
a larger force, and stronger soldiers too,
skilled hands at fighting men from chariots,
skilled, when a crisis broke, to fight on foot.
Out of the morning mist they came against us—
60 packed as the leaves and spears that flower forth in spring—
and Zeus presented us with disaster, me and my comrades
doomed to suffer blow on mortal blow. Lining up,
both armies battled it out against our swift ships,
both raked each other with hurtling bronze lances.
65 Long as morning rose and the blessed day grew stronger

1. In Thrace, across the opening of the Black Sea from Troy.

we stood and fought them off, massed as they were, but then,
when the sun wheeled past the hour for unyoking oxen,
the Cicones broke our lines and beat us down at last.
Out of each ship, six men-at-arms were killed;
70 the rest of us rowed away from certain doom.

   From there we sailed on, glad to escape our death
yet sick at heart for the dear companions we had lost.
But I would not let our rolling ships set sail until the crews
had raised the triple cry, saluting each poor comrade
75 cut down by the fierce Cicones on that plain.
Now Zeus who masses the stormclouds hit the fleet
with the North Wind—
       a howling, demonic gale, shrouding over
in thunderheads the earth and sea at once—
           and night swept down
from the sky and the ships went plunging headlong on,
80 our sails slashed to rags by the hurricane's blast!
We struck them—cringing at death we rowed our ships
to the nearest shoreline, pulled with all our power.
There, for two nights, two days, we lay by, no letup,
eating our hearts out, bent with pain and bone-tired.
85 When Dawn with her lovely locks brought on the third day,
then stepping the masts and hoisting white sails high,
we lounged at the oarlocks, letting wind and helmsmen
keep us true on course...
        And now, at long last,
I might have reached my native land unscathed,
90 but just as I doubled Malea's cape, a tide-rip
and the North Wind drove me way off course
careering past Cythera.
        Nine whole days
I was borne along by rough, deadly winds
on the fish-infested sea. Then on the tenth
95 our squadron reached the land of the Lotus-eaters,
people who eat the lotus, mellow fruit and flower.
We disembarked on the coast, drew water there
and crewmen snatched a meal by the swift ships.
Once we'd had our fill of food and drink I sent
100 a detail ahead, two picked men and a third, a runner,
to scout out who might live there—men like us perhaps,
who live on bread? So off they went and soon enough
they mingled among the natives, Lotus-eaters, Lotus-eaters
who had no notion of killing my companions, not at all,
105 they simply gave them the lotus to taste instead...
Any crewmen who ate the lotus, the honey-sweet fruit,
lost all desire to send a message back, much less return,
their only wish to linger there with the Lotus-eaters,

grazing on lotus, all memory of the journey home
110   dissolved forever. But *I* brought them back, back
to the hollow ships, and streaming tears—I forced them,
hauled them under the rowing benches, lashed them fast
and shouted out commands to my other, steady comrades:
'Quick, no time to lose, embark in the racing ships!'—
115   so none could eat the lotus, forget the voyage home.
They swung aboard at once, they sat to the oars in ranks
and in rhythm churned the water white with stroke on stroke.

      From there we sailed on, our spirits now at a low ebb,
and reached the land of the high and mighty Cyclops,
120   lawless brutes, who trust so to the everlasting gods
they never plant with their own hands or plow the soil.
Unsown, unplowed, the earth teems with all they need,
wheat, barley and vines, swelled by the rains of Zeus
to yield a big full-bodied wine from clustered grapes.
125   They have no meeting place for council, no laws either,
no, up on the mountain peaks they live in arching caverns—
each a law to himself, ruling his wives and children,
not a care in the world for any neighbor.
                                Now,
a level island stretches flat across the harbor,
130   not close inshore to the Cyclops' coast, not too far out,
thick with woods where the wild goats breed by hundreds.
No trampling of men to start them from their lairs,
no hunters roughing it out on the woody ridges,
stalking quarry, ever raid their haven.
135   No flocks browse, no plowlands roll with wheat;
unplowed, unsown forever—empty of humankind—
the island just feeds droves of bleating goats.
For the Cyclops have no ships with crimson prows,
no shipwrights there to build them good trim craft
140   that could sail them out to foreign ports of call
as most men risk the seas to trade with other men.
Such artisans would have made this island too
a decent place to live in...No mean spot,
it could bear you any crop you like in season.
145   The water-meadows along the low foaming shore
run soft and moist, and your vines would never flag.
The land's clear for plowing. Harvest on harvest,
a man could reap a healthy stand of grain—
the subsoil's dark and rich.
150   There's a snug deep-water harbor there, what's more,
no need for mooring-gear, no anchor-stones to heave,
no cables to make fast. Just beach your keels, ride out
the days till your shipmates' spirit stirs for open sea
and a fair wind blows. And last, at the harbor's head
155   there's a spring that rushes fresh from beneath a cave

and black poplars flourish round its mouth.   Well,
here we landed, and surely a god steered us in
through the pitch-black night.
Not that he ever showed himself, with thick fog
160   swirling around the ships, the moon wrapped in clouds
and not a glimmer stealing through that gloom.
Not one of us glimpsed the island—scanning hard—
or the long combers rolling us slowly toward the coast,
not till our ships had run their keels ashore.
165   Beaching our vessels smoothly, striking sail,
the crews swung out on the low shelving sand
and there we fell asleep, awaiting Dawn's first light.

When young Dawn with her rose-red fingers shone once more
we all turned out, intrigued to tour the island.
170   The local nymphs, the daughters of Zeus himself,
flushed mountain-goats so the crews could make their meal.
Quickly we fetched our curved bows and hunting spears
from the ships and, splitting up into three bands,
we started shooting, and soon enough some god
175   had sent us bags of game to warm our hearts.
A dozen vessels sailed in my command
and to each crew nine goats were shared out
and mine alone took ten. Then all day long
till the sun went down we sat and feasted well
180   on sides of meat and rounds of heady wine.
The good red stock in our vessels' holds
had not run out, there was still plenty left;
the men had carried off a generous store in jars
when we stormed and sacked the Cicones' holy city.
185   Now we stared across at the Cyclops' shore, so near
we could even see their smoke, hear their voices,
their bleating sheep and goats...
And then when the sun had set and night came on
we lay down and slept at the water's shelving edge.
190   When young Dawn with her rose-red fingers shone once more
I called a muster briskly, commanding all the hands,
'The rest of you stay here, my friends-in-arms.
I'll go across with my own ship and crew
and probe the natives living over there.
195   What *are* they—violent, savage, lawless?
or friendly to strangers, god-fearing men?'

With that I boarded ship and told the crew
to embark at once and cast off cables quickly.
They swung aboard, they sat to the oars in ranks
200   and in rhythm churned the water white with stroke on stroke.
But as soon as we reached the coast I mentioned—no long trip—

we spied a cavern just at the shore, gaping above the surf,
towering, overgrown with laurel. And here big flocks,
sheep and goats, were stalled to spend the nights,
205 and around its mouth a yard was walled up
with quarried boulders sunk deep in the earth
and enormous pines and oak-trees looming darkly...
Here was a giant's lair, in fact, who always pastured
his sheepflocks far afield and never mixed with others.
210 A grim loner, dead set in his own lawless ways.
Here was a piece of work, by god, a monster
built like no mortal who ever supped on bread,
no, like a shaggy peak, I'd say—a man-mountain
rearing head and shoulders over the world.
                                    Now then,
215 I told most of my good trusty crew to wait,
to sit tight by the ship and guard her well
while I picked out my dozen finest fighters
and off I went. But I took a skin of wine along,
the ruddy, irresistible wine that Maron gave me once,
220 Euanthes' son, a priest of Apollo, lord of Ismarus,
because we'd rescued him, his wife and children,
reverent as we were;
he lived, you see, in Apollo's holy grove.
And so in return he gave me splendid gifts,
225 he handed me seven bars of well-wrought gold,
a mixing-bowl of solid silver, then this wine...
He drew it off in generous wine-jars, twelve in all,
all unmixed—and such a bouquet, a drink fit for the gods!
No maid or man of his household knew that secret store,
230 only himself, his loving wife and a single servant.
Whenever they'd drink the deep-red mellow vintage,
twenty cups of water he'd stir in one of wine
and what an aroma wafted from the bowl—
what magic, what a godsend—
235 no joy in holding back when *that* was poured!
Filling a great goatskin now, I took this wine,
provisions too in a leather sack. A sudden foreboding
told my fighting spirit I'd soon come up against
some giant clad in power like armor-plate—
240 a savage deaf to justice, blind to law.

     Our party quickly made its way to his cave
but we failed to find our host himself inside;
he was off in his pasture, ranging his sleek flocks.
So we explored his den, gazing wide-eyed at it all,
245 the large flat racks loaded with drying cheeses,
the folds crowded with young lambs and kids,
split into three groups—here the spring-born,
here mid-yearlings, here the fresh sucklings

off to the side—each sort was penned apart.
250 And all his vessels, pails and hammered buckets
he used for milking, were brimming full with whey.
From the start my comrades pressed me, pleading hard,
'Let's make away with the cheeses, then come back—
hurry, drive the lambs and kids from the pens
255 to our swift ship, put out to sea at once!'
But I would not give way—
and how much better it would have been—
not till I saw him, saw what gifts he'd give.
But he proved no lovely sight to my companions.
260 There we built a fire, set our hands on the cheeses,
offered some to the gods and ate the bulk ourselves
and settled down inside, awaiting his return . . .
And back he came from pasture, late in the day,
herding his flocks home, and lugging a huge load
265 of good dry logs to fuel his fire at supper.
He flung them down in the cave—a jolting crash—
we scuttled in panic into the deepest dark recess.
And next he drove his sleek flocks into the open vault,
all he'd milk at least, but he left the males outside,
270 rams and billy goats out in the high-walled yard.
Then to close his door he hoisted overhead
a tremendous, massive slab—
no twenty-two wagons, rugged and four-wheeled,
could budge that boulder off the ground, I tell you,
275 such an immense stone the monster wedged to block
his cave!
Then down he squatted to milk his sheep and bleating goats,
each in order, and put a suckling underneath each dam.
And half of the fresh white milk he curdled quickly,
set it aside in wicker racks to press for cheese,
280 the other half let stand in pails and buckets,
ready at hand to wash his supper down.
As soon as he'd briskly finished all his chores
he lit his fire and spied us in the blaze and
'Strangers!' he thundered out, 'now who are you?
285 Where did you sail from, over the running sea-lanes?
Out on a trading spree or roving the waves like pirates,
sea-wolves raiding at will, who risk their lives
to plunder other men?'
The hearts inside us shook,
terrified by his rumbling voice and monstrous hulk.
290 Nevertheless I found the nerve to answer, firmly,
'Men of Achaea we are and bound now from Troy!
Driven far off course by the warring winds,
over the vast gulf of the sea—battling home
on a strange tack, a route that's off the map,
295 and so we've come to you . . .

so it must please King Zeus's plotting heart.
We're glad to say we're men of Atrides Agamemnon,
whose fame is the proudest thing on earth these days,
so great a city he sacked, such multitudes he killed!
But since we've chanced on you, we're at your knees
in hopes of a warm welcome, even a guest-gift,
the sort that hosts give strangers. That's the custom.
Respect the gods, my friend. We're suppliants—at
    your mercy!
Zeus of the Strangers guards all guests and suppliants:
strangers are sacred—Zeus will avenge their rights!'
    'Stranger,' he grumbled back from his brutal heart,
'you must be a fool, stranger, or come from nowhere,
telling *me* to fear the gods or avoid their wrath!
We Cyclops never blink at Zeus and Zeus's shield
of storm and thunder, or any other blessed god—
we've got more force by far.
I'd never spare you in fear of Zeus's hatred,
you or your comrades here, unless I had the urge.
But tell me, where did you moor your sturdy ship
when you arrived? Up the coast or close in?
I'd just like to know.'
                So he laid his trap
but he never caught me, no, wise to the world
I shot back in my crafty way, 'My ship?
Poseidon god of the earthquake smashed my ship,
he drove it against the rocks at your island's far cape,
he dashed it against a cliff as the winds rode us in.
I and the men you see escaped a sudden death.'

    Not a word in reply to that, the ruthless brute.
Lurching up, he lunged out with his hands toward my men
and snatching two at once, rapping them on the ground
he knocked them dead like pups—
their brains gushed out all over, soaked the floor—
and ripping them limb from limb to fix his meal
he bolted them down like a mountain-lion, left no scrap,
devoured entrails, flesh and bones, marrow and all!
We flung our arms to Zeus, we wept and cried aloud,
looking on at his grisly work—paralyzed, appalled.
But once the Cyclops had stuffed his enormous gut
with human flesh, washing it down with raw milk,
he slept in his cave, stretched out along his flocks.
And I with my fighting heart, I thought at first
to steal up to him, draw the sharp sword at my hip
and stab his chest where the midriff packs the liver—
I groped for the fatal spot but a fresh thought held me back.
There at a stroke we'd finish off ourselves as well—
how could *we* with our bare hands heave back

that slab he set to block his cavern's gaping maw?
So we lay there groaning, waiting Dawn's first light.

When young Dawn with her rose-red fingers shone once more
345   the monster relit his fire and milked his handsome ewes,
each in order, putting a suckling underneath each dam,
and as soon as he'd briskly finished all his chores
he snatched up two more men and fixed his meal.
Well-fed, he drove his fat sheep from the cave,
350   lightly lifting the huge doorslab up and away,
then slipped it back in place
as a hunter flips the lid of his quiver shut.
Piercing whistles—turning his flocks to the hills
he left me there, the heart inside me brooding on revenge:
355   how could I pay him back? would Athena give me glory?
Here was the plan that struck my mind as best . . .
the Cyclops' great club: there it lay by the pens,
olivewood, full of sap. He'd lopped it off to brandish
once it dried. Looking it over, we judged it big enough
360   to be the mast of a pitch-black ship with her twenty oars,
a freighter broad in the beam that plows through miles of sea—
so long, so thick it bulked before our eyes. Well,
flanking it now, I chopped off a fathom's length,
rolled it to comrades, told them to plane it down,
365   and they made the club smooth as I bent and shaved
the tip to a stabbing point. I turned it over
the blazing fire to char it good and hard,
then hid it well, buried deep under the dung
that littered the cavern's floor in thick wet clumps.
370   And now I ordered my shipmates all to cast lots—
who'd brave it out with me
to hoist our stake and grind it into his eye
when sleep had overcome him? Luck of the draw:
I got the very ones I would have picked myself,
375   four good men, and I in the lead made five . . .

Nightfall brought him back, herding his woolly sheep
and he quickly drove the sleek flock into the vaulted cavern,
rams and all—none left outside in the walled yard—
his own idea, perhaps, or a god led him on.
380   Then he hoisted the huge slab to block the door
and squatted to milk his sheep and bleating goats,
each in order, putting a suckling underneath each dam,
and as soon as he'd briskly finished all his chores
he snatched up two more men and fixed his meal.
385   But this time I lifted a carved wooden bowl,
brimful of my ruddy wine,
and went right up to the Cyclops, enticing,
'Here, Cyclops, try this wine—to top off

the banquet of human flesh you've bolted down!
390 Judge for yourself what stock our ship had stored.
I brought it here to make you a fine libation,
hoping you would pity me, Cyclops, send me home,
but your rages are insufferable. You barbarian—
how can any man on earth come visit you after *this?*
395 What you've done outrages all that's right!'

At that he seized the bowl and tossed it off
and the heady wine pleased him immensely—'More'—
he demanded a second bowl—'a hearty helping!
And tell me your name now, quickly,
400 so I can hand my guest a gift to warm *his* heart.
Our soil yields the Cyclops powerful, full-bodied wine
and the rains from Zeus build its strength. But this,
this is nectar, ambrosia—this flows from heaven!'

So he declared. I poured him another fiery bowl—
405 three bowls I brimmed and three he drank to the last drop,
the fool, and then, when the wine was swirling round his brain,
I approached my host with a cordial, winning word:
'So, you ask me the name I'm known by, Cyclops?
I will tell you. But you must give me a guest-gift
410 as you've promised. Nobody—that's my name. Nobody—
so my mother and father call me, all my friends.'

But he boomed back at me from his ruthless heart,
'*Nobody?* I'll eat Nobody last of all his friends—
I'll eat the others first! That's my gift to *you!*'

    With that
415 he toppled over, sprawled full-length, flat on his back
and lay there, his massive neck slumping to one side,
and sleep that conquers all overwhelmed him now
as wine came spurting, flooding up from his gullet
with chunks of human flesh—he vomited, blind drunk.
420 Now, at last, I thrust our stake in a bed of embers
to get it red-hot and rallied all my comrades:
'Courage—no panic, no one hang back now!'
And green as it was, just as the olive stake
was about to catch fire—the glow terrific, yes—
425 I dragged it from the flames, my men clustering round
as some god breathed enormous courage through us all.
Hoisting high that olive stake with its stabbing point,
straight into the monster's eye they rammed it hard—
I drove my weight on it from above and bored it home
430 as a shipwright bores his beam with a shipwright's drill
that men below, whipping the strap back and forth, whirl
and the drill keeps twisting faster, never stopping—
So we seized our stake with its fiery tip

and bored it round and round in the giant's eye
435 till blood came boiling up around that smoking shaft
and the hot blast singed his brow and eyelids round the core
and the broiling eyeball burst—
                                    its crackling roots blazed
and hissed—
                        as a blacksmith plunges a glowing ax or adze
in an ice-cold bath and the metal screeches steam
440 and its temper hardens—that's the iron's strength—
so the eye of the Cyclops sizzled round that stake!
He loosed a hideous roar, the rock walls echoed round
and we scuttled back in terror. The monster wrenched the spike
from his eye and out it came with a red geyser of blood—
445 he flung it aside with frantic hands, and mad with pain
he bellowed out for help from his neighbor Cyclops
living round about in caves on windswept crags.
Hearing his cries, they lumbered up from every side
and hulking round his cavern, asked what ailed him:
450 'What, Polyphemus, what in the world's the trouble?
Roaring out in the godsent night to rob us of our sleep.
Surely no one's rustling your flocks against your will—
surely no one's trying to kill you now by fraud or force!'

'Nobody, friends'—Polyphemus bellowed back from his cave—
455 'Nobody's killing me now by fraud and not by force!'
'If you're alone,' his friends boomed back at once,
'and nobody's trying to overpower you now—look,
it must be a plague sent here by mighty Zeus
and there's no escape from *that*.
460 You'd better pray to your father, Lord Poseidon.'

They lumbered off, but laughter filled my heart
to think how nobody's name—my great cunning stroke—
had duped them one and all. But the Cyclops there,
still groaning, racked with agony, groped around
465 for the huge slab, and heaving it from the doorway,
down he sat in the cave's mouth, his arms spread wide,
hoping to catch a comrade stealing out with sheep—
such a blithering fool he took me for!
But I was already plotting . . .
470 what was the best way out? how could I find
escape from death for my crew, myself as well?
My wits kept weaving, weaving cunning schemes—
life at stake, monstrous death staring us in the face—
till this plan struck my mind as best. That flock,
475 those well-fed rams with their splendid thick fleece,
sturdy, handsome beasts sporting their dark weight of wool:
I lashed them abreast, quietly, twisting the willow-twigs
the Cyclops slept on—giant, lawless brute—I took them

three by three; each ram in the middle bore a man
480   while the two rams either side would shield him well.
      So three beasts to bear each man, but as for myself?
      There was one bellwether ram, the prize of all the flock,
      and clutching him by his back, tucked up under
      his shaggy belly, there I hung, face upward,
485   both hands locked in his marvelous deep fleece,
      clinging for dear life, my spirit steeled, enduring...
      So we held on, desperate, waiting Dawn's first light.

                                                    As soon
      as young Dawn with her rose-red fingers shone once more
      the rams went rumbling out of the cave toward pasture,
490   the ewes kept bleating round the pens, unmilked,
      their udders about to burst. Their master now,
      heaving in torment, felt the back of each animal
      halting before him here, but the idiot never sensed
      my men were trussed up under their thick fleecy ribs.
495   And last of them all came my great ram now, striding out,
      weighed down with his dense wool and my deep plots.
      Stroking him gently, powerful Polyphemus murmured,
      'Dear old ram, why last of the flock to quit the cave?
      In the good old days you'd never lag behind the rest—
500   you with your long marching strides, first by far
      of the flock to graze the fresh young grasses,
      first by far to reach the rippling streams,
      first to turn back home, keen for your fold
      when night comes on—but now you're last of all.
505   And why? Sick at heart for your master's eye
      that coward gouged out with his wicked crew?—
      only after he'd stunned my wits with wine—
      that, that Nobody...
      who's not escaped his death, I swear, not yet.
510   Oh if only you thought like *me,* had words like *me*
      to tell me where that scoundrel is cringing from my rage!
      I'd smash him against the ground, I'd spill his brains—
      flooding across my cave—and that would ease my heart
      of the pains that good-for-nothing Nobody made me suffer!'

515   And with that threat he let my ram go free outside.
      But soon as we'd got one foot past cave and courtyard,
      first I loosed myself from the ram, then loosed my men,
      then quickly, glancing back again and again we drove
      our flock, good plump beasts with their long shanks,
520   straight to the ship, and a welcome sight we were
      to loyal comrades—we who'd escaped our deaths—
      but for all the rest they broke down and wailed.
      I cut it short, I stopped each shipmate's cries,
      my head tossing, brows frowning, silent signals
525   to hurry, tumble our fleecy herd on board,

launch out on the open sea!
They swung aboard, they sat to the oars in ranks
and in rhythm churned the water white with stroke on stroke.
But once offshore as far as a man's shout can carry,
530   I called back to the Cyclops, stinging taunts:
'So, Cyclops, no weak coward it was whose crew
you bent to devour there in your vaulted cave—
you with your brute force! Your filthy crimes
came down on your own head, you shameless cannibal,
535   daring to eat your guests in your own house—
so Zeus and the other gods have paid you back!'

       That made the rage of the monster boil over.
Ripping off the peak of a towering crag, he heaved it
so hard the boulder landed just in front of our dark prow
540   and a huge swell reared up as the rock went plunging under—
a tidal wave from the open sea. The sudden backwash
drove us landward again, forcing us close inshore
but grabbing a long pole, I thrust us off and away,
tossing my head for dear life, signaling crews
545   to put their backs in the oars, escape grim death.
They threw themselves in the labor, rowed on fast
but once we'd plowed the breakers twice as far,
again I began to taunt the Cyclops—men around me
trying to check me, calm me, left and right:
550   'So headstrong—why? Why rile the beast again?'

       'That rock he flung in the sea just now, hurling our ship
to shore once more—we thought we'd die on the spot!'

       'If he'd caught a sound from one of us, just a moan,
he would have crushed our heads and ship timbers
555   with one heave of another flashing, jagged rock!'

       'Good god, the brute can throw!'
                                       So they begged
but they could not bring my fighting spirit round.
I called back with another burst of anger, 'Cyclops—
if any man on the face of the earth should ask you
560   who blinded you, shamed you so—say Odysseus,
raider of cities, *he* gouged out your eye,
Laertes' son who makes his home in Ithaca!'

       So I vaunted and he groaned back in answer,
'Oh no, no—that prophecy years ago . . .
565   it all comes home to me with a vengeance now!
We once had a prophet here, a great tall man,
Telemus, Eurymus' son, a master at reading signs,
who grew old in his trade among his fellow-Cyclops.

All this, he warned me, would come to pass someday—
570 that I'd be blinded here at the hands of one Odysseus.
But I always looked for a handsome giant man to cross my path,
some fighter clad in power like armor-plate, but now,
look what a dwarf, a spineless good-for-nothing,
stuns me with wine, then gouges out my eye!
575 Come here, Odysseus, let me give you a guest-gift
and urge Poseidon the earthquake god to speed you home.
I am his son and he claims to be my father, true,
and he himself will heal me if he pleases—
no other blessed god, no man can do the work!'

                                        'Heal you!'—
580 here was my parting shot—'Would to god I could strip you
of life and breath and ship you down to the House of Death
as surely as no one will ever heal your eye,
not even your earthquake god himself!'

      But at that he bellowed out to lord Poseidon,
585 thrusting his arms to the starry skies, and prayed, 'Hear me—
Poseidon, god of the sea-blue mane who rocks the earth!
If I really am your son and you claim to be my father—
come, grant that Odysseus, raider of cities,
Laertes' son who makes his home in Ithaca,
590 never reaches home. Or if he's fated to see
his people once again and reach his well-built house
and his own native country, let him come home late
and come a broken man—all shipmates lost,
alone in a stranger's ship—
595 and let him find a world of pain at home!'

                                  So he prayed
and the god of the sea-blue mane, Poseidon, heard his prayer.
The monster suddenly hoisted a boulder—far larger—
wheeled and heaved it, putting his weight behind it,
massive strength, and the boulder crashed close,
600 landing just in the wake of our dark stern,
just failing to graze the rudder's bladed edge.
A huge swell reared up as the rock went plunging under,
yes, and the tidal breaker drove us out to our island's
far shore where all my well-decked ships lay moored,
605 clustered, waiting, and huddled round them, crewmen
sat in anguish, waiting, chafing for our return.
We beached our vessel hard ashore on the sand,
we swung out in the frothing surf ourselves,
and herding Cyclops' sheep from our deep holds
610 we shared them round so no one, not on my account,
would go deprived of his fair share of spoils.
But the splendid ram—as we meted out the flocks
my friends-in-arms made him my prize of honor,
mine alone, and I slaughtered him on the beach

Zeus of the thundercloud who rules the world.
But my sacrifices failed to move the god:
Zeus was still obsessed with plans to destroy
my entire oarswept fleet and loyal crew of comrades.
620 Now all day long till the sun went down we sat
and feasted on sides of meat and heady wine.
Then when the sun had set and night came on
we lay down and slept at the water's shelving edge.
When young Dawn with her rose-red fingers shone
        once more
625 I roused the men straightway, ordering all crews
to man the ships and cast off cables quickly.
They swung aboard at once, they sat to the oars in ranks
and in rhythm churned the water white with stroke on stroke.
And from there we sailed on, glad to escape our death
630 yet sick at heart for the comrades we had lost."

Book 11

The Kingdom of the Dead

"Now down we came to the ship at the water's edge,
we hauled and launched her into the sunlit breakers first,
stepped the mast in the black craft and set our sail
and loaded the sheep aboard, the ram and ewe,
5 then we ourselves embarked, streaming tears,
our hearts weighed down with anguish...
But Circe, the awesome nymph with lovely braids
who speaks with human voice, sent us a hardy shipmate,
yes, a fresh following wind ruffling up in our wake,
10 bellying out our sail to drive our blue prow on as we,
securing the running gear from stem to stern, sat back
while the wind and helmsman kept her true on course.
The sail stretched taut as she cut the sea all day
and the sun sank and the roads of the world grew dark.

15 And she made the outer limits, the Ocean River's bounds
where Cimmerian people have their homes—their realm and city
shrouded in mist and cloud. The eye of the Sun can never
flash his rays through the dark and bring them light,
not when he climbs the starry skies or when he wheels
20 back down from the heights to touch the earth once more—
an endless, deadly night overhangs those wretched men.
There, gaining that point, we beached our craft
and herding out the sheep, we picked our way
by the Ocean's banks until we gained the place
25 that Circe made our goal.
                            Here at the spot
Perimedes and Eurylochus held the victims fast,

dug a trench of about a forearm's depth and length
and around it poured libations out to all the dead,
30 first with milk and honey, and then with mellow wine,
then water third and last, and sprinkled glistening barley
over it all, and time and again I vowed to all the dead,
to the drifting, listless spirits of their ghosts,
that once I returned to Ithaca I would slaughter
35 a barren heifer in my halls, the best I had,
and load a pyre with treasures—and to Tiresias,
alone, apart, I would offer a sleek black ram,
the pride of all my herds. And once my vows
and prayers had invoked the nations of the dead,
40 I took the victims, over the trench I cut their throats
and the dark blood flowed in—and up out of Erebus they came,
flocking toward me now, the ghosts of the dead and gone...
Brides and unwed youths and old men who had suffered much
and girls with their tender hearts freshly scarred by sorrow
45 and great armies of battle dead, stabbed by bronze spears,
men of war still wrapped in bloody armor—thousands
swarming around the trench from every side—
unearthly cries—blanching terror gripped me!
I ordered the men at once to flay the sheep
50 that lay before us, killed by my ruthless blade,
and burn them both, and then say prayers to the gods,
to the almighty god of death and dread Persephone.
But I, the sharp sword drawn from beside my hip,
sat down on alert there and never let the ghosts
55 of the shambling, shiftless dead come near that blood
till I had questioned Tiresias myself.
                              But first
the ghost of Elpenor, my companion, came toward me.
He'd not been buried under the wide ways of earth,
not yet, we'd left his body in Circe's house,
60 unwept, unburied—this other labor pressed us.
But I wept to see him now, pity touched my heart
and I called out a winged word to him there: 'Elpenor,
how did you travel down to the world of darkness?
Faster on foot, I see, than I in my black ship.'

65   My comrade groaned as he offered me an answer:
'Royal son of Laertes, Odysseus, old campaigner,
the doom of an angry god, and god knows how much wine—
they were my ruin, captain...I'd bedded down
on the roof of Circe's house but never thought
70 to climb back down again by the long ladder—
headfirst from the roof I plunged, my neck snapped
from the backbone, my soul flew down to Death. Now,
I beg you by those you left behind, so far from here,
your wife, your father who bred and reared you as a boy,

75 and Telemachus, left at home in your halls, your only son.
Well I know when you leave this lodging of the dead
that you and your ship will put ashore again
at the island of Aeaea—then and there,
my lord, remember me, I beg you! Don't sail off
80 and desert me, left behind unwept, unburied, don't,
or my curse may draw god's fury on your head.
No, burn me in full armor, all my harness,
heap my mound by the churning gray surf—
a man whose luck ran out—
85 so even men to come will learn my story.
Perform my rites, and plant on my tomb that oar
I swung with mates when I rowed among the living.'

'All this, my unlucky friend,' I reassured him,
'I will do for you. I won't forget a thing.'
So we sat
90 and faced each other, trading our bleak parting words,
I on my side, holding my sword above the blood,
he across from me there, my comrade's phantom
dragging out his story.
But look, the ghost
of my mother came! My mother, dead and gone now...
95 Anticleia—daughter of that great heart Autolycus—
whom I had left alive when I sailed for sacred Troy.
I broke into tears to see her here, but filled with pity,
even throbbing with grief, I would not let her ghost
approach the blood till I had questioned Tiresias myself.

100 At last he came. The shade of the famous Theban prophet,
holding a golden scepter, knew me at once and hailed me:
'Royal son of Laertes, Odysseus, master of exploits,
man of pain, what now, what brings you here,
forsaking the light of day
105 to see this joyless kingdom of the dead?
Stand back from the trench—put up your sharp sword
so I can drink the blood and tell you all the truth.'

Moving back, I thrust my silver-studded sword
deep in its sheath, and once he had drunk the dark blood
110 the words came ringing from the prophet in his power:
'A sweet smooth journey home, renowned Odysseus,
that is what you seek
but a god will make it hard for you—I know—
you will never escape the one who shakes the earth,
115 quaking with anger at you still, still enraged
because you blinded the Cyclops, his dear son.
Even so, you and your crew may still reach home,
suffering all the way, if you only have the power

to curb their wild desire and curb your own, what's more,

120 from the day your good trim vessel first puts in
at Thrinacia Island, flees the cruel blue sea.
There you will find them grazing,
herds and fat flocks, the cattle of Helios,
god of the sun who sees all, hears all things.

125 Leave the beasts unharmed, your mind set on home,
and you all may still reach Ithaca—bent with hardship,
true—but harm them in any way, and I can see it now:
your ship destroyed, your men destroyed as well.
And even if *you* escape, you'll come home late

130 and come a broken man—all shipmates lost,
alone in a stranger's ship—
and you will find a world of pain at home,
crude, arrogant men devouring all your goods,
courting your noble wife, offering gifts to win her.

135 No doubt you will pay them back in blood when you come home!
But once you have killed those suitors in your halls—
by stealth or in open fight with slashing bronze—
go forth once more, you must...
carry your well-planed oar until you come

140 to a race of people who know nothing of the sea,
whose food is never seasoned with salt, strangers all
to ships with their crimson prows and long slim oars,
wings that make ships fly. And here is your sign—
unmistakable, clear, so clear you cannot miss it:

145 When another traveler falls in with you and calls
that weight across your shoulder a fan to winnow grain,
then plant your bladed, balanced oar in the earth
and sacrifice fine beasts to the lord god of the sea,
Poseidon—a ram, a bull and a ramping wild boar—

150 then journey home and render noble offerings up
to the deathless gods who rule the vaulting skies,
to all the gods in order.
And at last your own death will steal upon you...
a gentle, painless death, far from the sea it comes

155 to take you down, borne down with the years in ripe old age
with all your people there in blessed peace around you.
All that I have told you will come true.'
                                                  'Oh Tiresias,'
I replied as the prophet finished, 'surely the gods
have spun this out as fate, the gods themselves.

160 But tell me one thing more, and tell me clearly.
I see the ghost of my long-lost mother here before me.
Dead, crouching close to the blood in silence,
she cannot bear to look me in the eyes—
her own son—or speak a word to me. How,

165 lord, can I make her know me for the man I am?'

'One rule there is,' the famous seer explained,
'and simple for me to say and you to learn.
Any one of the ghosts you let approach the blood
will speak the truth to you. Anyone you refuse
170   will turn and fade away.'
                                  And with those words,
now that his prophecies had closed, the awesome shade
of lord Tiresias strode back to the House of Death.
But I kept watch there, steadfast till my mother
approached and drank the dark, clouding blood.
175   She knew me at once and wailed out in grief
and her words came winging toward me, flying home:
'Oh my son—what brings you down to the world
of death and darkness? You are still alive!
It's hard for the living to catch a glimpse of this....
180   Great rivers flow between us, terrible waters,
the Ocean first of all—no one could ever ford
that stream on foot, only aboard some sturdy craft.
Have you just come from Troy, wandering long years
with your men and ship? Not yet returned to Ithaca?
185   You've still not seen your wife inside your halls?'
                                       'Mother,'
I replied, 'I had to venture down to the House of Death,
to consult the shade of Tiresias, seer of Thebes.
Never yet have I neared Achaea, never once
set foot on native ground,
190   always wandering—endless hardship from that day
I first set sail with King Agamemnon bound for Troy,
the stallion-land, to fight the Trojans there.
But tell me about yourself and spare me nothing.
What form of death overcame you, what laid you low,
195   some long slow illness? Or did Artemis showering arrows
come with her painless shafts and bring you down?
Tell me of father, tell of the son I left behind:
do my royal rights still lie in their safekeeping?
Or does some stranger hold the throne by now
200   because men think that I'll come home no more?
Please, tell me about my wife, her turn of mind,
her thoughts...still standing fast beside our son,
still guarding our great estates, secure as ever now?
Or has she wed some other countryman at last,
205   the finest prince among them?'
                                'Surely, surely,'
my noble mother answered quickly, 'she's still waiting
there in your halls, poor woman, suffering so,
her life an endless hardship like your own...
wasting away the nights, weeping away the days.
210   No one has taken over your royal rights, not yet.

Telemachus still holds your great estates in peace,
he attends the public banquets shared with all,
the feasts a man of justice should enjoy,
for every lord invites him. As for your father,
215 he keeps to his own farm—he never goes to town—
with no bed for him there, no blankets, glossy throws;
all winter long he sleeps in the lodge with servants,
in the ashes by the fire, his body wrapped in rags.
But when summer comes and the bumper crops of harvest,
220 any spot on the rising ground of his vineyard rows
he makes his bed, heaped high with fallen leaves,
and there he lies in anguish...
with his old age bearing hard upon him, too,
and his grief grows as he longs for your return.
225 And I with the same grief, I died and met my fate.
No sharp-eyed Huntress showering arrows through the halls
approached and brought me down with painless shafts,
nor did some hateful illness strike me, that so often
devastates the body, drains our limbs of power.
230 No, it was my longing for *you,* my shining Odysseus—
you and your quickness, you and your gentle ways—
that tore away my life that had been sweet.'

　　　And I, my mind in turmoil, how I longed
to embrace my mother's spirit, dead as she was!
235 Three times I rushed toward her, desperate to hold her,
three times she fluttered through my fingers, sifting away
like a shadow, dissolving like a dream, and each time
the grief cut to the heart, sharper, yes, and I,
I cried out to her, words winging into the darkness:
240 'Mother—why not wait for me? How I long to hold you!—
so even here, in the House of Death, we can fling
our loving arms around each other, take some joy
in the tears that numb the heart. Or is this just
some wraith that great Persephone sends my way
245 to make me ache with sorrow all the more?'

　　　My noble mother answered me at once:
'My son, my son, the unluckiest man alive!
This is no deception sent by Queen Persephone,
this is just the way of mortals when we die.
250 Sinews no longer bind the flesh and bones together—
the fire in all its fury burns the body down to ashes
once life slips from the white bones, and the spirit,
rustling, flitters away...flown like a dream.
But you must long for the daylight. Go, quickly.
255 Remember all these things
so one day you can tell them to your wife.'

And so we both confided, trading parting words,
and there slowly came a grand array of women,
all sent before me now by august Persephone,
260   and all were wives and daughters once of princes.
They swarmed in a flock around the dark blood
while I searched for a way to question each alone,
and the more I thought, the more this seemed the best:
Drawing forth the long sharp sword from beside my hip,
265   I would not let them drink the dark blood, all in a rush,
and so they waited, coming forward one after another.
Each declared her lineage, and I explored them all.

And the first I saw there? Tyro, born of kings,
who said her father was that great lord Salmoneus,
270   said that she was the wife of Cretheus, Aeolus' son.
And once she fell in love with the river god, Enipeus,
far the clearest river flowing across the earth,
and so she'd haunt Enipeus' glinting streams,
till taking his shape one day
275   the god who girds the earth and makes it tremble
bedded her where the swirling river rushes out to sea,
and a surging wave reared up, high as a mountain, dark,
arching over to hide the god and mortal girl together.
Loosing her virgin belt, he lapped her round in sleep
280   and when the god had consummated his work of love
he took her by the hand and hailed her warmly:
'Rejoice in our love, my lady! And when this year
has run its course you will give birth to glorious children—
bedding down with the gods is never barren, futile—
285   and you must tend them, breed and rear them well.
Now home you go, and restrain yourself, I say,
never breathe your lover's name but know—
I am Poseidon, god who rocks the earth!'

With that he dove back in the heaving waves
290   and she conceived for the god and bore him Pelias, Neleus,
and both grew up to be stalwart aides of Zeus almighty,
both men alike. Pelias lived on the plains of Iolcos,
rich in sheepflocks, Neleus lived in sandy Pylos.
And the noble queen bore sons to Cretheus too:
295   Aeson, Pheres and Amythaon, exultant charioteer.

And after Tyro I saw Asopus' daughter Antiope,
proud she'd spent a night in the arms of Zeus himself
and borne the god twin sons, Amphion and Zethus,
the first to build the footings of seven-gated Thebes,
300   her bastions too, for lacking ramparts none could live
in a place so vast, so open—strong as both men were.

And I saw Alcmena next, Amphitryon's wife,
who slept in the clasp of Zeus and merged in love
and brought forth Heracles, rugged will and lion heart.
305 And I saw Megara too, magnanimous Creon's daughter
wed to the stalwart Heracles, the hero never daunted.

And I saw the mother of Oedipus, beautiful Epicaste.
What a monstrous thing she did, in all innocence—
she married her own son...
310 who'd killed his father, then he married *her!*
But the gods soon made it known to all mankind.
So he in growing pain ruled on in beloved Thebes,
lording Cadmus' people—thanks to the gods' brutal plan—
while she went down to Death who guards the massive gates.
315 Lashing a noose to a steep rafter, there she hanged aloft,
strangling in all her anguish, leaving her son to bear
the world of horror a mother's Furies bring to life.

And I saw magnificent Chloris, the one whom Neleus
wooed and won with a hoard of splendid gifts,
320 so dazzled by her beauty years ago...
the youngest daughter of Iasus' son Amphion,
the great Minyan king who ruled Orchomenos once.
She was his queen in Pylos, she bore him shining sons,
Nestor and Chromius, Periclymenus too, good prince.
325 And after her sons she bore a daughter, majestic Pero,
the marvel of her time, courted by all the young lords
round about. But Neleus would not give her to any suitor,
none but the man who might drive home the herds
that powerful Iphiclus had stolen. Lurching,
330 broad in the brow, those longhorned beasts,
and no small task to round them up from Phylace.
Only the valiant seer Melampus volunteered—
he would drive them home—
but a god's iron sentence bound him fast:
335 barbarous herdsmen dragged him off in chains.
Yet when the months and days had run their course
and the year wheeled round and the seasons came again,
then mighty Iphiclus loosed the prophet's shackles,
once he had told him all the gods' decrees.
340 And so the will of Zeus was done at last.

And I saw Leda next, Tyndareus' wife,
who'd borne the king two sons, intrepid twins,
Castor, breaker of horses, and the hardy boxer Polydeuces,
both buried now in the life-giving earth though still alive.
345 Even under the earth Zeus grants them that distinction:
one day alive, the next day dead, each twin by turns,
they both hold honors equal to the gods'.

And I saw Iphimedeia next, Aloeus' wife,
who claimed she lay in the Sea-lord's loving waves
350 and gave the god two sons, but they did not live long,
Otus staunch as a god and far-famed Ephialtes.
They were the tallest men the fertile earth has borne,
the handsomest too, by far, aside from renowned Orion.
Nine yards across they measured, even at nine years old,
355 nine fathoms tall they towered. They even threatened
the deathless gods they'd storm Olympus' heights
with the pounding rush and grinding shock of battle.
They were wild to pile Ossa upon Olympus, then on Ossa
Pelion dense with timber—their toeholds up the heavens.
360 And they'd have won the day if they had reached peak strength
but Apollo the son of Zeus, whom sleek-haired Leto bore,
laid both giants low before their beards had sprouted,
covering cheek and chin with a fresh crop of down.

Phaedra and Procris too I saw, and lovely Ariadne,
365 daughter of Minos, that harsh king. One day Theseus tried
to spirit her off from Crete to Athens' sacred heights
but he got no joy from her. Artemis killed her first
on wave-washed Dia's shores, accused by Dionysus.

And I saw Clymene, Maera and loathsome Eriphyle—
370 bribed with a golden necklace
to lure her lawful husband to his death . . .
But the whole cortege I could never tally, never name,
not all the daughters and wives of great men I saw there.
Long before that, the godsent night would ebb away.
375 But the time has come for sleep, either with friends
aboard your swift ship or here in your own house.
My passage home will rest with the gods and you."

Odysseus paused . . . They all fell silent, hushed,
his story holding them spellbound down the shadowed halls
380 till the white-armed queen Arete suddenly burst out,
"Phaeacians! How does this man impress you now,
his looks, his build, the balanced mind inside him?
The stranger is my guest
but each of you princes shares the honor here.
385 So let's not be too hasty to send him on his way,
and don't scrimp on his gifts. His need is great,
great as the riches piled up in your houses,
thanks to the gods' good will."
                              Following her,
the old revered Echeneus added his support,
390 the eldest lord on the island of Phaeacia:
"Friends, the words of our considerate queen—
they never miss the mark or fail our expectations.

So do as Arete says, though on Alcinous here
depend all words and action."
                              "And so it will be"—
395 Alcinous stepped in grandly—"sure as I am alive
and rule our island men who love their oars!
Our guest, much as he longs for passage home,
must stay and wait it out here till tomorrow,
till I can collect his whole array of parting gifts.
400 His send-off rests with every noble here
but with me most of all:
I hold the reins of power in the realm."

      Odysseus, deft and tactful, echoed back,
"Alcinous, majesty, shining among your island people,
405 if you would urge me now to stay here one whole year
then speed me home weighed down with lordly gifts,
I'd gladly have it so. Better by far, that way.
The fuller my arms on landing there at home,
the more respected, well received I'd be
410 by all who saw me sailing back to Ithaca."

      "Ah Odysseus," Alcinous replied, "one look at you
and we know that you are no one who would cheat us—
no fraud, such as the dark soil breeds and spreads
across the face of the earth these days. Crowds of vagabonds
415 frame their lies so tightly none can test them. But you,
what grace you give your words, and what good sense within!
You have told your story with all a singer's skill,
the miseries you endured, your great Achaeans too.
But come now, tell me truly: your godlike comrades—
420 did you see any heroes down in the House of Death,
any who sailed with you and met their doom at Troy?
The night's still young, I'd say the night is endless.
For us in the palace now, it's hardly time for sleep.
Keep telling us your adventures—they are wonderful.
425 I could hold out here till Dawn's first light
if only you could bear, here in our halls,
to tell the tale of all the pains you suffered."

      So the man of countless exploits carried on:
"Alcinous, majesty, shining among your island people,
430 there is a time for many words, a time for sleep as well.
But if you insist on hearing more, I'd never stint
on telling my own tale and those more painful still,
the griefs of my comrades, dead in the war's wake,
who escaped the battle-cries of Trojan armies
435 only to die in blood at journey's end—
thanks to a vicious woman's will.
                              Now then,
no sooner had Queen Persephone driven off

the ghosts of lovely women, scattering left and right,
than forward marched the shade of Atreus' son Agamemnon,
440 fraught with grief and flanked by all his comrades,
troops of his men-at-arms who died beside him,
who met their fate in lord Aegisthus' halls.
He knew me at once, as soon as he drank the blood,
and wailed out, shrilly; tears sprang to his eyes,
445 he thrust his arms toward me, keen to embrace me there—
no use—the great force was gone, the strength lost forever,
now, that filled his rippling limbs in the old days.
I wept at the sight, my heart went out to the man,
my words too, in a winging flight of pity:
450 'Famous Atrides, lord of men Agamemnon!
What fatal stroke of destiny brought you down?
Wrecked in the ships when lord Poseidon roused
some punishing blast of stormwinds, gust on gust?
Or did ranks of enemies mow you down on land
455 as you tried to raid and cut off herds and flocks
or fought to win their city, take their women?'

The field marshal's ghost replied at once:
'Royal son of Laertes, Odysseus, mastermind of war,
I was not wrecked in the ships when lord Poseidon
460 roused some punishing blast of stormwinds, gust on gust,
nor did ranks of enemies mow me down on land—
Aegisthus hatched my doom and my destruction,
he killed me, he with my own accursed wife...
he invited me to his palace, sat me down to feast
465 then cut me down as a man cuts down some ox at the trough!
So I died—a wretched, ignominious death—and round me
all my comrades killed, no mercy, one after another,
just like white-tusked boars
butchered in some rich lord of power's halls
470 for a wedding, banquet or groaning public feast.
You in your day have witnessed hundreds slaughtered,
killed in single combat or killed in pitched battle, true,
but if you'd laid eyes on this it would have wrenched your heart—
how we sprawled by the mixing-bowl and loaded tables there,
475 throughout the palace, the whole floor awash with blood.
But the death-cry of Cassandra,[1] Priam's daughter—
the most pitiful thing I heard! My treacherous queen,
Clytemnestra, killed her over my body, yes, and I,
lifting my fists, beat them down on the ground,
480 dying, dying, writhing around the sword.
But she, that whore, she turned her back on me,
well on my way to Death—she even lacked the heart
to seal my eyes with her hand or close my jaws.

1. Trojan princess and Agamemnon's war prize.

                                              So,
there's nothing more deadly, bestial than a woman
485   set on works like these—what a monstrous thing
she plotted, slaughtered her own lawful husband!
Why, I expected, at least, some welcome home
from all my children, all my household slaves
when I came sailing back again ... But she—
490   the queen hell-bent on outrage—bathes in shame
not only herself but the whole breed of womankind,
even the honest ones to come, forever down the years!'

        So he declared and I cried out, 'How terrible!
Zeus from the very start, the thunder king
495   has hated the race of Atreus with a vengeance—
his trustiest weapon women's twisted wiles.
What armies of us died for the sake of Helen ...
Clytemnestra schemed your death while you were worlds away!'

        'True, true,' Agamemnon's ghost kept pressing on,
500   'so even your own wife—never indulge her too far.
Never reveal the whole truth, whatever you may know;
just tell her a part of it, be sure to hide the rest.
Not that you, Odysseus, will be murdered by your wife.
She's much too steady, her feelings run too deep,
505   Icarius' daughter Penelope, that wise woman.
She was a young bride, I well remember ...
we left her behind when we went off to war,
with an infant boy she nestled at her breast.
That boy must sit and be counted with the men now—
510   happy man! His beloved father will come sailing home
and see his son, and he will embrace his father,
that is only right. But *my* wife—she never
even let me feast my eyes on my own son;
she killed me first, his father!
515   I tell you this—bear it in mind, you must—
when you reach your homeland steer your ship
into port in secret, never out in the open ...
the time for trusting women's gone forever!

        Enough. Come, tell me this, and be precise.
520   Have you heard news of my son? Where's he living now?
Perhaps in Orchomenos, perhaps in sandy Pylos
or off in the Spartan plains with Menelaus?
He's not dead yet, my Prince Orestes, no,
he's somewhere on the earth.'
                                    So he probed
525   but I cut it short: 'Atrides, why ask me that?
I know nothing, whether he's dead or alive.
It's wrong to lead you on with idle words.'

So we stood there, trading heartsick stories,
deep in grief, as the tears streamed down our faces.
530 But now there came the ghosts of Peleus' son Achilles,
Patroclus,[2] fearless Antilochus—and Great Ajax too,
the first in stature, first in build and bearing
of all the Argives after Peleus' matchless son.
The ghost of the splendid runner knew me at once
535 and hailed me with a flight of mournful questions:
'Royal son of Laertes, Odysseus, man of tactics,
reckless friend, what next?
What greater feat can that cunning head contrive?
What daring brought you down to the House of Death?—
540 where the senseless, burnt-out wraiths of mortals make their home.'

    The voice of his spirit paused, and I was quick to answer:
'Achilles, son of Peleus, greatest of the Achaeans,
I had to consult Tiresias, driven here by hopes
he would help me journey home to rocky Ithaca.
545 Never yet have I neared Achaea, never once
set foot on native ground...
my life is endless trouble.
                    But you, Achilles,
there's not a man in the world more blest than you—
there never has been, never will be one.
550 Time was, when you were alive, we Argives
honored you as a god, and now down here, I see,
you lord it over the dead in all your power.
So grieve no more at dying, great Achilles.'

    I reassured the ghost, but he broke out, protesting,
555 'No winning words about death to *me*, shining Odysseus!
By god, I'd rather slave on earth for another man—
some dirt-poor tenant farmer who scrapes to keep alive—
than rule down here over all the breathless dead.
But come, tell me the news about my gallant son.
560 Did he make his way to the wars,
did the boy become a champion—yes or no?
Tell me of noble Peleus, any word you've heard—
still holding pride of place among his Myrmidon hordes,
or do they despise the man in Hellas and in Phthia
565 because old age has lamed his arms and legs?
For I no longer stand in the light of day—
the man I was—comrade-in-arms to help my father
as once I helped our armies, killing the best fighters
Troy could field in the wide world up there...

2. Achilles's companion.

570 Oh to arrive at father's house—the man I was,
 for one brief day—I'd make my fury and my hands,
 invincible hands, a thing of terror to all those men
 who abuse the king with force and wrest away his honor!'

  So he grieved but I tried to lend him heart:
575 'About noble Peleus I can tell you nothing,
 but about your own dear son, Neoptolemus,
 I can report the whole story, as you wish.
 I myself, in my trim ship, I brought him
 out of Scyros to join the Argives under arms.
580 And dug in around Troy, debating battle-tactics,
 he always spoke up first, and always on the mark—
 godlike Nestor and I alone excelled the boy. Yes,
 and when our armies fought on the plain of Troy
 he'd never hang back with the main force of men—
585 he'd always charge ahead,
 giving ground to no one in his fury,
 and scores of men he killed in bloody combat.
 How could I list them all, name them all, now,
 the fighting ranks he leveled, battling for the Argives?
590 But what a soldier he laid low with a bronze sword:
 the hero Eurypylus, Telephus' son, and round him
 troops of his own Cetean comrades slaughtered,
 lured to war by the bribe his mother took.
 The only man I saw to put Eurypylus
595 in the shade was Memnon, son of the Morning.
 Again, when our champions climbed inside the horse
 that Epeus built with labor, and I held full command
 to spring our packed ambush open or keep it sealed,
 all our lords and captains were wiping off their tears,
600 knees shaking beneath each man—but not your son.
 Never once did I see his glowing skin go pale;
 he never flicked a tear from his cheeks, no,
 he kept on begging me there to let him burst
 from the horse, kept gripping his hilted sword,
605 his heavy bronze-tipped javelin, keen to loose
 his fighting fury against the Trojans. Then,
 once we'd sacked King Priam's craggy city,
 laden with his fair share and princely prize
 he boarded his own ship, his body all unscarred.
610 Not a wound from a flying spear or a sharp sword,
 cut-and-thrust close up—the common marks of war.
 Random, raging Ares plays no favorites.'
        So I said and
 off he went, the ghost of the great runner, Aeacus' grandson
 loping with long strides across the fields of asphodel,
615 triumphant in all I had told him of his son,
 his gallant, glorious son.

Now the rest of the ghosts, the dead and gone
came swarming up around me—deep in sorrow there,
each asking about the grief that touched him most.
620 Only the ghost of Great Ajax, son of Telamon,
kept his distance, blazing with anger at me still
for the victory I had won by the ships that time
I pressed my claim for the arms of Prince Achilles.
His queenly mother had set them up as prizes,
625 Pallas and captive Trojans served as judges.
Would to god I'd never won such trophies!
All for them the earth closed over Ajax,
that proud hero Ajax . . .
greatest in build, greatest in works of war
630 of all the Argives after Peleus' matchless son.
I cried out to him now, I tried to win him over:
'Ajax, son of noble Telamon, still determined,
even in death, not once to forget that rage
you train on me for those accursed arms?
635 The gods set up that prize to plague the Achaeans—
so great a tower of strength we lost when you went down!
For *your* death we grieved as we did for Achilles' death—
we grieved incessantly, true, and none's to blame
but Zeus, who hated Achaea's fighting spearmen
640 so intensely, Zeus sealed your doom.
Come closer, king, and listen to my story.
Conquer your rage, your blazing, headstrong pride!'

So I cried out but Ajax answered not a word.
He stalked off toward Erebus, into the dark
645 to join the other lost, departed dead.
Yet now, despite his anger,
he might have spoken to me, or I to him,
but the heart inside me stirred with some desire
to see the ghosts of others dead and gone.

650 And I saw Minos there, illustrious son of Zeus,
firmly enthroned, holding his golden scepter,
judging all the dead . . .
Some on their feet, some seated, all clustering
round the king of justice, pleading for his verdicts
655 reached in the House of Death with its all-embracing gates.

I next caught sight of Orion, that huge hunter,
rounding up on the fields of asphodel those wild beasts
the man in life cut down on the lonely mountain-slopes,
brandishing in his hands the bronze-studded club
660 that time can never shatter.
                              I saw Tityus too,
son of the mighty goddess Earth—sprawling there

on the ground, spread over nine acres—two vultures
hunched on either side of him, digging into his liver,
beaking deep in the blood-sac, and he with his frantic hands
665 could never beat them off, for he had once dragged off
the famous consort of Zeus in all her glory,
Leto, threading her way toward Pytho's ridge,
over the lovely dancing-rings of Panopeus.

    And I saw Tantalus too, bearing endless torture.
670 He stood erect in a pool as the water lapped his chin—
parched, he tried to drink, but he could not reach the surface,
no, time and again the old man stooped, craving a sip,
time and again the water vanished, swallowed down,
laying bare the caked black earth at his feet—
675 some spirit drank it dry. And over his head
leafy trees dangled their fruit from high aloft,
pomegranates and pears, and apples glowing red,
succulent figs and olives swelling sleek and dark,
but as soon as the old man would strain to clutch them fast
680 a gust would toss them up to the lowering dark clouds.

    And I saw Sisyphus too, bound to his own torture,
grappling his monstrous boulder with both arms working,
heaving, hands struggling, legs driving, he kept on
thrusting the rock uphill toward the brink, but just
685 as it teetered, set to topple over—
                                    time and again
the immense weight of the thing would wheel it back and
the ruthless boulder would bound and tumble down to the plain again—
so once again he would heave, would struggle to thrust it up,
sweat drenching his body, dust swirling above his head.

690   And next I caught a glimpse of powerful Heracles—
his ghost, I mean: the man himself delights
in the grand feasts of the deathless gods on high,
wed to Hebe, famed for her lithe, alluring ankles,
the daughter of mighty Zeus and Hera shod in gold.
695 Around him cries of the dead rang out like cries of birds,
scattering left and right in horror as on he came like night,
naked bow in his grip, an arrow grooved on the bowstring,
glaring round him fiercely, forever poised to shoot.
A terror too, that sword-belt sweeping across his chest,
700 a baldric of solid gold emblazoned with awesome work...
bears and ramping boars and lions with wild, fiery eyes,
and wars, routs and battles, massacres, butchered men.
May the craftsman who forged that masterpiece—
whose skills could conjure up a belt like that—
705 never forge another!
Heracles knew me at once, at first glance,

and hailed me with a winging burst of pity:
'Royal son of Laertes, Odysseus famed for exploits,
luckless man, you too? Braving out a fate as harsh
710   as the fate I bore, alive in the light of day?
Son of Zeus that I was, my torments never ended,
forced to slave for a man not half the man I was:
he saddled me with the worst heartbreaking labors.
Why, he sent me down here once, to retrieve the hound
715   that guards the dead—no harder task for me, he thought—
but I dragged the great beast up from the underworld to earth
and Hermes and gleaming-eyed Athena blazed the way!'

        With that he turned and back he went to the House of Death
but I held fast in place, hoping that others might still come,
720   shades of famous heroes, men who died in the old days
and ghosts of an even older age I longed to see,
Theseus and Pirithous, the gods' own radiant sons.
But before I could, the dead came surging round me,
hordes of them, thousands raising unearthly cries,
725   and blanching terror gripped me—panicked now
that Queen Persephone might send up from Death
some monstrous head, some Gorgon's staring face!
I rushed back to my ship, commanded all hands
to take to the decks and cast off cables quickly.
730   They swung aboard at once, they sat to the oars in ranks
and a strong tide of the Ocean River swept her on downstream,
sped by our rowing first, then by a fresh fair wind."

Book 22

Slaughter in the Hall

        Now stripping back his rags Odysseus master of craft and battle
vaulted onto the great threshold, gripping his bow and quiver
bristling arrows, and poured his flashing shafts before him,
loose at his feet, and thundered out to all the suitors:
5   "Look—your crucial test is finished, now, at last!
But another target's left that no one's hit before—
we'll see if *I* can hit it—Apollo give me glory!"

        With that he trained a stabbing arrow on Antinous...
just lifting a gorgeous golden loving-cup in his hands,
10   just tilting the two-handled goblet back to his lips,
about to drain the wine—and slaughter the last thing
on the suitor's mind: who could dream that one foe
in that crowd of feasters, however great his power,
would bring down death on himself, and black doom?
15   But Odysseus aimed and shot Antinous square in the throat
and the point went stabbing clean through the soft neck and out—

and off to the side he pitched, the cup dropped from his grasp
as the shaft sank home, and the man's life-blood came spurting
from his nostrils—

        thick red jets—

                a sudden thrust of his foot—

20   he kicked away the table—

                    food showered across the floor,
the bread and meats soaked in a swirl of bloody filth.
The suitors burst into uproar all throughout the house
when they saw their leader down. They leapt from their seats,
milling about, desperate, scanning the stone walls—
25   not a shield in sight, no rugged spear to seize.
They wheeled on Odysseus, lashing out in fury:
"Stranger, shooting at men will cost your life!"

      "Your game is over—you, you've shot your last!"

      "You'll never escape your own headlong death!"

30   "You killed the best in Ithaca—our fine prince!"

      "Vultures will eat your corpse!"

                    Groping, frantic—
each one persuading himself the guest had killed
the man by chance. Poor fools, blind to the fact
that all their necks were in the noose, their doom sealed.
35   With a dark look, the wily fighter Odysseus shouted back,
"You dogs! you never imagined I'd return from Troy—
so cocksure that you bled my house to death,
ravished my serving-women—wooed my wife
behind my back while I was still alive!
40   No fear of the gods who rule the skies up there,
no fear that men's revenge might arrive someday—
now all your necks are in the noose—your doom is sealed!"

      Terror gripped them all, blanched their faces white,
each man glancing wildly—how to escape his instant death?
45   Only Eurymachus had the breath to venture, "If you,
you're truly Odysseus of Ithaca, home at last,
you're right to accuse these men of what they've done—
so much reckless outrage here in your palace,
so much on your lands. But here he lies,
50   quite dead, and he incited it all—Antinous—
look, the man who drove us all to crime!
Not that he needed marriage, craved it so;
he'd bigger game in mind—though Zeus barred his way—
he'd lord it over Ithaca's handsome country, king himself,
55   once he'd lain in wait for your son and cut him down!
But now he's received the death that he deserved.

So spare your own people! Later we'll recoup
your costs with a tax laid down upon the land,
covering all we ate and drank inside your halls,
60 and each of us here will pay full measure too—
twenty oxen in value, bronze and gold we'll give
until we melt your heart. Before we've settled,
who on earth could blame you for your rage?"

But the battle-master kept on glaring, seething.
65 "No, Eurymachus! Not if you paid me all your father's wealth—
all you possess now, and all that could pour in from the world's end—
no, not even then would I stay my hands from slaughter
till all you suitors had paid for all your crimes!
Now life or death—your choice—fight me or flee
70 if you hope to escape your sudden bloody doom!
I doubt one man in the lot will save his skin!"

His menace shook their knees, their hearts too
but Eurymachus spoke again, now to the suitors: "Friends!
This man will never restrain his hands, invincible hands—
75 now that he's seized that polished bow and quiver, look,
he'll shoot from the sill until he's killed us all!
So fight—call up the joy of battle! Swords out!
Tables lifted—block his arrows winging death!
Charge him, charge in a pack—
80 try to rout the man from the sill, the doors,
race through town and sound an alarm at once—
our friend would soon see he's shot his bolt!"
                                        Brave talk—
he drew his two-edged sword, bronze, honed for the kill
and hurled himself at the king with a raw savage cry
85 in the same breath that Odysseus loosed an arrow
ripping his breast beside the nipple so hard
it lodged in the man's liver—
out of his grasp the sword dropped to the ground—
over his table, head over heels he tumbled, doubled up,
90 flinging his food and his two-handled cup across the floor—
he smashed the ground with his forehead, writhing in pain,
both feet flailing out, and his high seat tottered—
the mist of death came swirling down his eyes.

Amphinomus rushed the king in all his glory,
95 charging him face-to-face, a slashing sword drawn—
if only he could force him clear of the doorway, now,
but Telemachus—too quick—stabbed the man from behind,
plunging his bronze spear between the suitor's shoulders
and straight on through his chest the point came jutting out—
100 down he went with a thud, his forehead slammed the ground.
Telemachus swerved aside, leaving his long spearshaft

lodged in Amphinomus—fearing some suitor just might
lunge in from behind as he tugged the shaft,
impale him with a sword or hack him down,
105   crouching over the corpse.
He went on the run, reached his father at once
and halting right beside him, let fly, "Father—
now I'll get you a shield and a pair of spears,
a helmet of solid bronze to fit your temples!
110   I'll arm myself on the way back and hand out
arms to the swineherd, arm the cowherd too—
we'd better fight equipped!"
            "Run, fetch them,"
the wily captain urged, "while I've got arrows left
to defend me—or they'll force me from the doors
115   while I fight on alone!"

    Telemachus moved to his father's orders smartly.
Off he ran to the room where the famous arms lay stored,
took up four shields, eight spears, four bronze helmets
ridged with horsehair crests and, loaded with these,
120   ran back to reach his father's side in no time.
The prince was first to case himself in bronze
and his servants followed suit—both harnessed up
and all three flanked Odysseus, mastermind of war,
and he, as long as he'd arrows left to defend himself,
125   kept picking suitors off in the palace, one by one
and down they went, corpse on corpse in droves.
Then, when the royal archer's shafts ran out,
he leaned his bow on a post of the massive doors—
where walls of the hallway catch the light—and armed:
130   across his shoulder he slung a buckler four plies thick,
over his powerful head he set a well-forged helmet,
the horsehair crest atop it tossing, bristling terror,
and grasped two rugged lances tipped with fiery bronze.

    Now a side-door was fitted into the main wall—
135   right at the edge of the great hall's stone sill—
and led to a passage always shut by good tight boards.
But Odysseus gave the swineherd strict commands
to stand hard by the side-door, guard it well—
the only way the suitors might break out.
140   Agelaus called to his comrades with a plan:
"Friends, can't someone climb through the hatch?—
tell men outside to sound the alarm, be quick—
our guest would soon see he'd shot his last!"

    The goatherd Melanthius answered, "Not a chance,
145   my lord—the door to the courtyard's much too near,
dangerous too, the mouth of the passage cramped.

One strong man could block us, one and all!
No, I'll fetch you some armor to harness on,
out of the storeroom—there, nowhere else, I'm sure,
150   the king and his gallant son have stowed their arms!"

      With that the goatherd clambered up through smoke-ducts
high on the wall and scurried into Odysseus' storeroom,
bundled a dozen shields, as many spears and helmets
ridged with horsehair crests and, loaded with these,
155   rushed back down to the suitors, quickly issued arms.
Odysseus' knees shook, his heart too, when he saw them
buckling on their armor, brandishing long spears—
here was a battle looming, well he knew.
He turned at once to Telemachus, warnings flying:
160   "A bad break in the fight, my boy! One of the women's
tipped the odds against us—or could it be the goatherd?"

      "My fault, father," the cool clear prince replied,
"the blame's all mine. That snug door to the vault,
I left it ajar—they've kept a better watch than I.
165   Go, Eumaeus, shut the door to the storeroom,
check and see if it's one of the women's tricks
or Dolius' son Melanthius. He's our man, I'd say."

      And even as they conspired, back the goatherd
climbed to the room to fetch more burnished arms,
170   but Eumaeus spotted him, quickly told his king
who stood close by: "Odysseus, wily captain,
there he goes again, the infernal nuisance—
just as we suspected—back to the storeroom.
Give me a clear command!
175   Do I kill the man—if I can take him down—
or drag him back to you, here, to pay in full
for the vicious work he's plotted in your house?"

      Odysseus, master of tactics, answered briskly,
"I and the prince will keep these brazen suitors
180   crammed in the hall, for all their battle-fury.
You two wrench Melanthius' arms and legs behind him,
fling him down in the storeroom—lash his back to a plank
and strap a twisted cable fast to the scoundrel's body,
hoist him up a column until he hits the rafters—
185   let him dangle in agony, still alive,
for a good long time!"

      They hung on his orders, keen to do his will.
Off they ran to the storeroom, unseen by him inside—
Melanthius, rummaging after arms, deep in a dark recess
190   as the two men took their stand, either side of the doorposts,

poised till the goatherd tried to cross the doorsill...
one hand clutching a crested helmet, the other
an ample old buckler blotched with mildew,
the shield Laertes bore as a young soldier once
195 but there it lay for ages, seams on the handstraps split—
Quick, they rushed him, seized him, haled him back by the hair,
flung him down on the floor, writhing with terror, bound him
hand and foot with a chafing cord, wrenched his limbs
back, back till the joints locked tight—
200 just as Laertes' cunning son commanded—
they strapped a twisted cable round his body,
hoisted him up a column until he hit the rafters,
then you mocked him, Eumaeus, my good swineherd:
"Now stand guard through the whole night, Melanthius—
205 stretched out on a soft bed fit for *you,* your highness!
You're bound to see the Morning rising up from the Ocean,
mounting her golden throne—at just the hour you always
drive in goats to feast the suitors in the hall!"

So they left him, trussed in his agonizing sling;
210 they clapped on armor again, shut the gleaming doors
and ran to rejoin Odysseus, mastermind of war.
And now as the ranks squared off, breathing fury—
four at the sill confronting a larger, stronger force
arrayed inside the hall—now Zeus's daughter Athena,
215 taking the build and voice of Mentor, swept in
and Odysseus, thrilled to see her, cried out,
"Rescue us, Mentor, now it's life or death!
Remember your old comrade—all the service
I offered you! We were boys together!"
So he cried
220 yet knew in his bones it was Athena, Driver of Armies.
But across the hall the suitors brayed against her,
Agelaus first, his outburst full of threats:
"Mentor, never let Odysseus trick you into
siding with *him* to fight against the suitors.
225 Here's our plan of action, and we will see it through!
Once we've killed them both, the father and the son,
we'll kill you too, for all you're bent on doing
here in the halls—you'll pay with your own head!
And once our swords have stopped your violence cold—
230 all your property, all in your house, your fields,
we'll lump it all with Odysseus' rich estate
and never let your sons live on in your halls
or free your wife and daughters to walk through town!"

Naked threats—and Athena hit new heights of rage,
235 she lashed out at Odysseus now with blazing accusations:
"Where's it gone, Odysseus—your power, your fighting heart?

The great soldier who fought for famous white-armed Helen,
battling Trojans nine long years—nonstop, no mercy,
mowing their armies down in grueling battle—
240 you who seized the broad streets of Troy
with your fine strategic stroke! How can you—
now you've returned to your own house, your own wealth—
bewail the loss of your combat strength in a war with *suitors?*
Come, old friend, stand by me! You'll see action now,
245 see how Mentor the son of Alcimus, that brave fighter,
kills your enemies, pays you back for service!"
                                    Rousing words—
but she gave no all-out turning of the tide, not yet,
she kept on testing Odysseus and his gallant son,
putting their force and fighting heart to proof.
250 For all the world like a swallow in their sight
she flew on high to perch
on the great hall's central roofbeam black with smoke.

        But the suitors closed ranks, commanded now by Damastor's son
Agelaus, flanked by Eurynomus, Demoptolemus and Amphimedon,
255 Pisander, Polyctor's son, and Polybus ready, waiting—
head and shoulders the best and bravest of the lot
still left to fight for their lives,
now that the pelting shafts had killed the rest.
Agelaus spurred his comrades on with battle-plans:
260 "Friends, at last the man's invincible hands are useless!
Mentor has mouthed some empty boasts and flitted off—
just four are left to fight at the front doors. So now,
no wasting your long spears—all at a single hurl,
just six of us launch out in the first wave!
265 If Zeus is willing, we may hit Odysseus,
carry off the glory! The rest are nothing
once the captain's down!"
                              At his command,
concentrating their shots, all six hurled as one
but Athena sent the whole salvo wide of the mark—
270 one of them hit the jamb of the great hall's doors,
another the massive door itself, and the heavy bronze point
of a third ashen javelin crashed against the wall.
Seeing his men untouched by the suitors' flurry,
steady Odysseus leapt to take command:
275 "Friends! now it's for *us* to hurl at them, I say,
into this ruck of suitors! Topping all their crimes
they're mad to strip the armor off our bodies!"

        Taking aim at the ranks, all four let fly as one
and the lances struck home—Odysseus killed Demoptolemus,
280 Telemachus killed Euryades—the swineherd, Elatus—
and the cowherd cut Pisander down in blood.

They bit the dust of the broad floor, all as one.
Back to the great hall's far recess the others shrank
as the four rushed in and plucked up spears from corpses.

285   And again the suitors hurled their whetted shafts
but Athena sent the better part of the salvo wide—
one of them hit the jamb of the great hall's doors,
another the massive door itself, and the heavy bronze point
of a third ashen javelin crashed against the wall.
290   True, Amphimedon nicked Telemachus on the wrist—
the glancing blade just barely broke his skin.
Ctesippus sent a long spear sailing over
Eumaeus' buckler, grazing his shoulder blade
but the weapon skittered off and hit the ground.
295   And again those led by the brilliant battle-master
hurled their razor spears at the suitors' ranks—
and now Odysseus raider of cities hit Eurydamas,
Telemachus hit Amphimedon—Eumaeus, Polybus—
and the cowherd stabbed Ctesippus
300   right in the man's chest and triumphed over his body:
"Love your mockery, do you? Son of that blowhard
      Polytherses!
No more shooting off your mouth, you idiot, such big talk—
leave the last word to the gods—they're much stronger!
Take this spear, this guest-gift, for the cow's hoof
305   you once gave King Odysseus begging in his house!"

      So the master of longhorn cattle had his say—
as Odysseus, fighting at close quarters, ran Agelaus
through with a long lance—Telemachus speared Leocritus
so deep in the groin the bronze came punching out his back
310   and the man crashed headfirst, slamming the ground full-face.
And now Athena, looming out of the rafters high above them,
brandished her man-destroying shield of thunder, terrifying
the suitors out of their minds, and down the hall they panicked—
wild, like herds stampeding, driven mad as the darting gadfly
315   strikes in the late spring when the long days come round.
The attackers struck like eagles, crook-clawed, hook-beaked,
swooping down from a mountain ridge to harry smaller birds
that skim across the flatland, cringing under the clouds
but the eagles plunge in fury, rip their lives out—hopeless,
320   never a chance of flight or rescue—and people love the sport—
so the attackers routed suitors headlong down the hall,
wheeling into the slaughter, slashing left and right
and grisly screams broke from skulls cracked open—
the whole floor awash with blood.
                                    Leodes now—
325   he flung himself at Odysseus, clutched his knees,
crying out to the king with a sudden, winging prayer:
"I hug your knees, Odysseus—mercy! spare my life!

Never, I swear, did I harass any woman in your house—
never a word, a gesture—nothing, no, I tried
330   to restrain the suitors, whoever did such things.
They wouldn't listen, keep their hands to themselves—
so reckless, so they earn their shameful fate.
But I was just their prophet—
my hands are clean—and I'm to die their death!
335   Look at the thanks I get for years of service!"

    A killing look, and the wry soldier answered,
"Only a priest, a prophet for this mob, you say?
How hard you must have prayed in my own house
that the heady day of my return would never dawn—
340   my dear wife would be yours, would bear your children!
For that there's no escape from grueling death—you die!"

    And snatching up in one powerful hand a sword
left on the ground—Agelaus dropped it when he fell—
Odysseus hacked the prophet square across the neck
345   and the praying head went tumbling in the dust.
                           Now one was left,
trying still to escape black death. Phemius, Terpis' son,
the bard who always performed among the suitors—
they forced the man to sing . . .
There he stood, backing into the side-door,
350   still clutching his ringing lyre in his hands,
his mind in turmoil, torn—what should he do?
Steal from the hall and crouch at the altar-stone
of Zeus who Guards the Court, where time and again
Odysseus and Laertes burned the long thighs of oxen?
355   Or throw himself on the master's mercy, clasp his knees?
That was the better way—or so it struck him, yes,
grasp the knees of Laertes' royal son. And so,
cradling his hollow lyre, he laid it on the ground
between the mixing-bowl and the silver-studded throne,
360   then rushed up to Odysseus, yes, and clutched his knees,
singing out to his king with a stirring, winged prayer:
"I hug your knees, Odysseus—mercy! spare my life!
What a grief it will be to you for all the years to come
if you kill the singer now, who sings for gods and men.
365   I taught myself the craft, but a god has planted
deep in my spirit all the paths of song—
songs I'm fit to sing for you as for a god.
Calm your bloodlust now—don't take my head!
He'd bear me out, your own dear son Telemachus—
370   never of *my* own will, never for any gain did I
perform in your house, singing after the suitors
had their feasts. They were too strong, too many—
they forced me to come and sing—I had no choice!"

The inspired Prince Telemachus heard his pleas
375   and quickly said to his father close beside him,
       "Stop, don't cut him down! This one's innocent.
       So is the herald Medon—the one who always
       tended me in the house when I was little—
       spare him too. Unless he's dead by now,
380   killed by Philoetius or Eumaeus here—
       or ran into *you* rampaging through the halls."

       The herald pricked up his anxious ears at that...
       cautious soul, he cowered, trembling, under a chair—
       wrapped in an oxhide freshly stripped—to dodge black death.
385   He jumped in a flash from there, threw off the smelly hide
       and scuttling up to Telemachus, clutching his knees,
       the herald begged for life in words that fluttered:
       "Here I am, dear boy—spare me! Tell your father,
       flushed with victory, not to kill me with his sword—
390   enraged as he is with these young lords who bled
       his palace white and showed you no respect,
       the reckless fools!"
                            Breaking into a smile
       the canny Odysseus reassured him, "Courage!
       The prince has pulled you through, he's saved you now
395   so you can take it to heart and tell the next man too:
       clearly doing good puts doing bad to shame.
       Now leave the palace, go and sit outside—
       out in the courtyard, clear of the slaughter—
       you and the bard with all his many songs.
400   Wait till I've done some household chores
       that call for my attention."

       The two men scurried out of the house at once
       and crouched at the altar-stone of mighty Zeus—
       glancing left and right,
405   fearing death would strike at any moment.

       Odysseus scanned his house to see if any man
       still skulked alive, still hoped to avoid black death.
       But he found them one and all in blood and dust...
       great hauls of them down and out like fish that fishermen
410   drag from the churning gray surf in looped and coiling nets
       and fling ashore on a sweeping hook of beach—some noble catch
       heaped on the sand, twitching, lusting for fresh salt sea
       but the Sungod hammers down and burns their lives out...
       so the suitors lay in heaps, corpse covering corpse.
415   At last the seasoned fighter turned to his son:
       "Telemachus, go, call the old nurse here—
       I must tell her all that's on my mind."

Telemachus ran to do his father's bidding,
shook the women's doors, calling Eurycleia:
420 "Come out now! Up with you, good old woman!
You who watch over all the household hands—
quick, my father wants you, needs to have a word!"

Crisp command that left the old nurse hushed—
she spread the doors to the well-constructed hall,
425 slipped out in haste, and the prince led her on . . .
She found Odysseus in the thick of slaughtered corpses,
splattered with bloody filth like a lion that's devoured
some ox of the field and lopes home, covered with blood,
his chest streaked, both jaws glistening, dripping red—
430 a sight to strike terror. So Odysseus looked now,
splattered with gore, his thighs, his fighting hands,
and she, when she saw the corpses, all the pooling blood,
was about to lift a cry of triumph—here was a great exploit,
look—but the soldier held her back and checked her zeal
435 with warnings winging home: "Rejoice in your heart,
old woman—peace! No cries of triumph now.
It's unholy to glory over the bodies of the dead.
These men the doom of the gods has brought low,
and their own indecent acts. They'd no regard
440 for any man on earth—good or bad—
who chanced to come their way. And so, thanks
to their reckless work, they met this shameful fate.
Quick, report in full on the women in my halls—
who are disloyal to me, who are guiltless?"

                                    "Surely, child,"
445 his fond old nurse replied, "now here's the truth.
Fifty women you have inside your house,
women we've trained to do their duties well,
to card the wool and bear the yoke of service.
Some dozen in all went tramping to their shame,
450 thumbing their noses at me, at the queen herself!
And Telemachus, just now come of age—his mother
would never let the boy take charge of the maids.
But let me climb to her well-lit room upstairs
and tell your wife the news—
455 some god has put the woman fast asleep."

"Don't wake her yet," the crafty man returned,
"you tell those women to hurry here at once—
just the ones who've shamed us all along."

Away the old nurse bustled through the house
460 to give the women orders, rush them to the king.
Odysseus called Telemachus over, both herdsmen too,

with strict commands: "Start clearing away the bodies.
Make the women pitch in too. Chairs and tables—
scrub them down with sponges, rinse them clean.
And once you've put the entire house in order,
march the women out of the great hall—between
the roundhouse and the courtyard's strong stockade—
and hack them with your swords, slash out all their lives—
blot out of their minds the joys of love they relished
under the suitors' bodies, rutting on the sly!"

The women crowded in, huddling all together...
wailing convulsively, streaming live warm tears.
First they carried out the bodies of the dead
and propped them under the courtyard colonnade,
standing them one against another. Odysseus
shouted commands himself, moving things along
and they kept bearing out the bodies—they were forced.
Next they scrubbed down the elegant chairs and tables,
washed them with sopping sponges, rinsed them clean.
Then Telemachus and the herdsmen scraped smooth
the packed earth floor of the royal house with spades
as the women gathered up the filth and piled it outside.
And then, at last, once the entire house was put in order,
they marched the women out of the great hall—between
the roundhouse and the courtyard's strong stockade—
crammed them into a dead end, no way out from there,
and stern Telemachus gave the men their orders:
"No clean death for the likes of them, by god!
Not from me—they showered abuse on my head,
my mother's too!
                              You sluts—the suitors' whores!"

With that, taking a cable used on a dark-prowed ship
he coiled it over the roundhouse, lashed it fast to a tall column,
hoisting it up so high no toes could touch the ground.
Then, as doves or thrushes beating their spread wings
against some snare rigged up in thickets—flying in
for a cozy nest but a grisly bed receives them—
so the women's heads were trapped in a line,
nooses yanking their necks up, one by one
so all might die a pitiful, ghastly death...
they kicked up heels for a little—not for long.
                              Melanthius?
They hauled him out through the doorway, into the court,
lopped his nose and ears with a ruthless knife,
tore his genitals out for the dogs to eat raw
and in manic fury hacked off hands and feet.
                              Then,
once they'd washed their own hands and feet,

they went inside again to join Odysseus.
Their work was done with now.
But the king turned to devoted Eurycleia, saying,
"Bring sulfur, nurse, to scour all this pollution—
510   bring me fire too, so I can fumigate the house.
And call Penelope here with all her women—
tell all the maids to come back in at once."

          "Well said, my boy," his old nurse replied,
"right to the point. But wait,
515   let me fetch you a shirt and cloak to wrap you.
No more dawdling round the palace, nothing but rags
to cover those broad shoulders—it's a scandal!"

          "Fire first," the good soldier answered.
"Light me a fire to purify this house."

520   The devoted nurse snapped to his command,
brought her master fire and brimstone. Odysseus
purged his palace, halls and court, with cleansing fumes.

          Then back through the royal house the old nurse went
to tell the women the news and bring them in at once.
525   They came crowding out of their quarters, torch in hand,
flung their arms around Odysseus, hugged him, home at last,
and kissed his head and shoulders, seized his hands, and he,
overcome by a lovely longing, broke down and wept...
deep in his heart he knew them one and all.

Book 23

The Great Rooted Bed

          Up to the rooms the old nurse clambered, chuckling all
              the way,
to tell the queen her husband was here now, home at last.
Her knees bustling, feet shuffling over each other,
till hovering at her mistress' head she spoke:
5   "Penelope—child—wake up and see for yourself,
with your own eyes, all you dreamed of, all your days!
He's here—Odysseus—he's come home, at long last!
He's killed the suitors, swaggering young brutes
who plagued his house, wolfed his cattle down,
10   rode roughshod over his son!"

          "Dear old nurse," wary Penelope replied,
"the gods have made you mad. They have that power,
putting lunacy into the clearest head around
or setting a half-wit on the path to sense.

15 They've unhinged you, and you were once so sane.
Why do you mock me?—haven't I wept enough?—
telling such wild stories, interrupting my sleep,
sweet sleep that held me, sealed my eyes just now.
Not once have I slept so soundly since the day
20 Odysseus sailed away to see that cursed city...
Destroy, I call it—I hate to say its name!
Now down you go. Back to your own quarters.
If any other woman of mine had come to me,
rousing me out of sleep with such a tale,
25 I'd have her bundled back to her room in pain.
It's only your old gray head that spares you that!"

"Never"—the fond old nurse kept pressing on—
"dear child, I'd never mock you! No, it's all true,
he's here—Odysseus—he's come home, just as I tell you!
30 He's the stranger they all manhandled in the hall.
Telemachus knew he was here, for days and days,
but he knew enough to hide his father's plans
so *he* could pay those vipers back in kind!"

Penelope's heart burst in joy, she leapt from bed,
35 her eyes streaming tears, she hugged the old nurse
and cried out with an eager, winging word,
"Please, dear one, give me the whole story.
If he's really home again, just as you tell me,
how did he get those shameless suitors in his clutches?—
40 single-handed, braving an army always camped inside."

"I have no idea," the devoted nurse replied.
"I didn't see it, I didn't ask—all I heard
was the choking groans of men cut down in blood.
We crouched in terror—a dark nook of our quarters—
45 all of us locked tight behind those snug doors
till your boy Telemachus came and called me out—
his father rushed him there to do just that. And then
I found Odysseus in the thick of slaughtered corpses;
there he stood and all around him, over the beaten floor,
50 the bodies sprawled in heaps, lying one on another...
How it would have thrilled your heart to see him—
splattered with bloody filth, a lion with his kill!
And now they're all stacked at the courtyard gates—
he's lit a roaring fire,
55 he's purifying the house with cleansing fumes
and he's sent me here to bring you back to him.
Follow me down! So now, after all the years of grief,
you two can embark, loving hearts, along the road to joy.
Look, your dreams, put off so long, come true at last—

60   he's back alive, home at his hearth, and found you,
     found his son still here. And all those suitors
     who did him wrong, he's paid them back, he has,
     right in his own house!"
                              "Hush, dear woman,"
     guarded Penelope cautioned her at once.
65   "Don't laugh, don't cry in triumph—not yet.
     You know how welcome the sight of him would be
     to all in the house, and to me most of all
     and the son we bore together.
     But the story can't be true, not as you tell it,
70   no, it must be a god who's killed our brazen friends—
     up in arms at their outrage, heartbreaking crimes.
     They'd no regard for any man on earth—
     good or bad—who chanced to come their way. So,
     thanks to their reckless work they die their deaths.
75   Odysseus? Far from Achaea now, he's lost all hope
     of coming home ... he's lost and gone himself."

         "Child," the devoted old nurse protested,
     "what nonsense you let slip through your teeth.
     Here's your husband, warming his hands at his own hearth,
80   here—and you, you say he'll never come home again,
     always the soul of trust! All right, this too—
     I'll give you a sign, a proof that's plain as day.
     That scar, made years ago by a boar's white tusk—
     I spotted the scar myself, when I washed his feet,
85   and I tried to tell you, ah, but he, the crafty rascal,
     clamped his hand on my mouth—I couldn't say a word.
     Follow me down now. I'll stake my life on it:
     if I am lying to *you*—
     kill me with a thousand knives of pain!"

90   "Dear old nurse," composed Penelope responded,
     "deep as you are, my friend, you'll find it hard
     to plumb the plans of the everlasting gods.
     All the same, let's go and join my son
     so I can see the suitors lying dead
95   and see ... the one who killed them."
                                     With that thought
     Penelope started down from her lofty room, her heart
     in turmoil, torn ... should she keep her distance,
     probe her husband? Or rush up to the man at once
     and kiss his head and cling to both his hands?
100 As soon as she stepped across the stone threshold,
     slipping in, she took a seat at the closest wall
     and radiant in the firelight, faced Odysseus now.
     There he sat, leaning against the great central column,
     eyes fixed on the ground, waiting, poised for whatever words

105 his hardy wife might say when she caught sight of him.
A long while she sat in silence...numbing wonder
filled her heart as her eyes explored his face.
One moment he seemed...Odysseus, to the life—
the next, no, he was not the man she knew,
110 a huddled mass of rags was all she saw.

    "Oh mother," Telemachus reproached her,
"cruel mother, you with your hard heart!
Why do you spurn my father so—why don't you
sit beside him, engage him, ask him questions?
115 What other wife could have a spirit so unbending?
Holding back from her husband, home at last for *her*
after bearing twenty years of brutal struggle—
your heart was always harder than a rock!"
                                    "My child,"
Penelope, well-aware, explained, "I'm stunned with wonder,
120 powerless. Cannot speak to him, ask him questions,
look him in the eyes...But if he is truly
Odysseus, home at last, make no mistake:
we two will know each other, even better—
we two have secret signs,
125 known to us both but hidden from the world."

    Odysseus, long-enduring, broke into a smile
and turned to his son with pointed, winging words:
"Leave your mother here in the hall to test me
as she will. She soon will know me better.
130 Now because I am filthy, wear such grimy rags,
she spurns me—your mother still can't bring herself
to believe I am her husband.
                        But you and I,
put heads together. What's our best defense?
When someone kills a lone man in the realm
135 who leaves behind him no great band of avengers,
still the killer flees, goodbye to kin and country.
But *we* brought down the best of the island's princes,
the pillars of Ithaca. Weigh it well, I urge you."

    "Look to it all yourself now, father," his son
140 deferred at once. "You are the best on earth,
they say, when it comes to mapping tactics.
No one, no mortal man, can touch you there.
But we're behind you, hearts intent on battle,
nor do I think you'll find us short on courage,
145 long as our strength will last."
                            "Then here's our plan,"
the master of tactics said. "I think it's best.
First go and wash, and pull fresh tunics on

and tell the maids in the hall to dress well too.
And let the inspired bard take up his ringing lyre
150 and lead off for us all a dance so full of heart
that whoever hears the strains outside the gates—
a passerby on the road, a neighbor round about—
will think it's a wedding-feast that's under way.
No news of the suitors' death must spread through town
155 till we have slipped away to our own estates,
our orchard green with trees. There we'll see
what winning strategy Zeus will hand us then."

They hung on his words and moved to orders smartly.
First they washed and pulled fresh tunics on,
160 the women arrayed themselves—the inspired bard
struck up his resounding lyre and stirred in all
a desire for dance and song, the lovely lilting beat,
till the great house echoed round to the measured tread
of dancing men in motion, women sashed and lithe.
165 And whoever heard the strains outside would say,
"A miracle—someone's married the queen at last!"

"One of her hundred suitors."
                                                    "That callous woman,
too faithless to keep her lord and master's house
to the bitter end—"
                                    "Till he came sailing home."

170 So they'd say, blind to what had happened:
the great-hearted Odysseus was home again at last.
The maid Eurynome bathed him, rubbed him down with oil
and drew around him a royal cape and choice tunic too.
And Athena crowned the man with beauty, head to foot,
175 made him taller to all eyes, his build more massive,
yes, and down from his brow the great goddess
ran his curls like thick hyacinth clusters
full of blooms. As a master craftsman washes
gold over beaten silver—a man the god of fire
180 and Queen Athena trained in every fine technique—
and finishes off his latest effort, handsome work . . .
so she lavished splendor over his head and shoulders now.
He stepped from his bath, glistening like a god,
and back he went to the seat that he had left
185 and facing his wife, declared,
"Strange woman! So hard—the gods of Olympus
made you harder than any other woman in the world!
What other wife could have a spirit so unbending?
Holding back from her husband, home at last for *her*
190 after bearing twenty years of brutal struggle.
Come, nurse, make me a bed, I'll sleep alone.

She has a heart of iron in her breast."
                              "Strange *man,*"
wary Penelope said. "I'm not so proud, so scornful,
nor am I overwhelmed by your quick change...
You look—how well I know—the way he looked,
setting sail from Ithaca years ago
aboard the long-oared ship.

                    Come, Eurycleia,
move the sturdy bedstead out of our bridal chamber—
that room the master built with his own hands.
Take it out now, sturdy bed that it is,
and spread it deep with fleece,
blankets and lustrous throws to keep him warm."

        Putting her husband to the proof—but Odysseus
blazed up in fury, lashing out at his loyal wife:
"Woman—your words, they cut me to the core!
Who could move my bed? Impossible task,
even for some skilled craftsman—unless a god
came down in person, quick to lend a hand,
lifted it out with ease and moved it elsewhere.
Not a man on earth, not even at peak strength,
would find it easy to prise it up and shift it, no,
a great sign, a hallmark lies in its construction.
I know, I built it myself—no one else...
There was a branching olive-tree inside our court,
grown to its full prime, the bole like a column, thickset.
Around it I built my bedroom, finished off the walls
with good tight stonework, roofed it over soundly
and added doors, hung well and snugly wedged.
Then I lopped the leafy crown of the olive,
clean-cutting the stump bare from roots up,
planing it round with a bronze smoothing-adze—
I had the skill—I shaped it plumb to the line to make
my bedpost, bored the holes it needed with an auger.
Working from there I built my bed, start to finish,
I gave it ivory inlays, gold and silver fittings,
wove the straps across it, oxhide gleaming red.
There's our secret sign, I tell you, our life story!
Does the bed, my lady, still stand planted firm?—
I don't know—or has someone chopped away
that olive-trunk and hauled our bedstead off?"
                                    Living proof—
Penelope felt her knees go slack, her heart surrender,
recognizing the strong clear signs Odysseus offered.
She dissolved in tears, rushed to Odysseus, flung her arms
around his neck and kissed his head and cried out,
"Odysseus—don't flare up at me now, not you,
always the most understanding man alive!

The gods, it was the gods who sent us sorrow—
they grudged us both a life in each other's arms
from the heady zest of youth to the stoop of old age.
240 But don't fault me, angry with me now because I failed,
at the first glimpse, to greet you, hold you, so...
In my heart of hearts I always cringed with fear
some fraud might come, beguile me with his talk;
the world is full of the sort,
245 cunning ones who plot their own dark ends.
Remember Helen of Argos, Zeus's daughter—
would *she* have sported so in a stranger's bed
if she had dreamed that Achaea's sons were doomed
to fight and die to bring her home again?
250 Some god spurred her to do her shameless work.
Not till then did her mind conceive that madness,
blinding madness that caused her anguish, ours as well.
But now, since you have revealed such overwhelming proof—
the secret sign of our bed, which no one's ever seen
255 but you and I and a single handmaid, Actoris,
the servant my father gave me when I came,
who kept the doors of our room you built so well...
you've conquered my heart, my hard heart, at last!"

    The more she spoke, the more a deep desire for tears
260 welled up inside his breast—he wept as he held the wife
he loved, the soul of loyalty, in his arms at last.
Joy, warm as the joy that shipwrecked sailors feel
when they catch sight of land—Poseidon has struck
their well-rigged ship on the open sea with gale winds
265 and crushing walls of waves, and only a few escape,
        swimming,
struggling out of the frothing surf to reach the shore,
their bodies crusted with salt but buoyed up with joy
as they plant their feet on solid ground again,
spared a deadly fate. So joyous now to her
270 the sight of her husband, vivid in her gaze,
that her white arms, embracing his neck
would never for a moment let him go...
Dawn with her rose-red fingers might have shone
upon their tears, if with her glinting eyes
275 Athena had not thought of one more thing.
She held back the night, and night lingered long
at the western edge of the earth, while in the east
she reined in Dawn of the golden throne at Ocean's banks,
commanding her not to yoke the windswift team that brings men light,
280 Blaze and Aurora, the young colts that race the Morning on.
Yet now Odysseus, seasoned veteran, said to his wife,
"Dear woman...we have still not reached the end
of all our trials. One more labor lies in store—

285 boundless, laden with danger, great and long,
     and I must brave it out from start to finish.
     So the ghost of Tiresias prophesied to me,
     the day that I went down to the House of Death
     to learn our best route home, my comrades' and my own.
290 But come, let's go to bed, dear woman—at long last
     delight in sleep, delight in each other, come!"

     "If it's bed you want," reserved Penelope replied,
     "it's bed you'll have, whenever the spirit moves you,
     now that the gods have brought you home again
     to native land, your grand and gracious house.
295 But since you've alluded to it,
     since a god has put it in your mind,
     please, tell me about this trial still to come.
     I'm bound to learn of it later, I am sure—
     what's the harm if I hear of it tonight?"

                                         "Still so strange,"
300 Odysseus, the old master of stories, answered.
     "Why again, why force me to tell you all?
     Well, tell I shall. I'll hide nothing now.
     But little joy it will bring you, I'm afraid,
     as little joy for me.
                            The prophet said
305 that I must rove through towns on towns of men,
     that I must carry a well-planed oar until
     I come to a people who know nothing of the sea,
     whose food is never seasoned with salt, strangers all
     to ships with their crimson prows and long slim oars,
310 wings that make ships fly. And here is my sign,
     he told me, clear, so clear I cannot miss it,
     and I will share it with you now . . .
     When another traveler falls in with me and calls
     that weight across my shoulder a fan to winnow grain,
315 then, he told me, I must plant my oar in the earth
     and sacrifice fine beasts to the lord god of the sea,
     Poseidon—a ram, a bull and a ramping wild boar—
     then journey home and render noble offerings up
     to the deathless gods who rule the vaulting skies,
320 to all the gods in order.
     And at last my own death will steal upon me . . .
     a gentle, painless death, far from the sea it comes
     to take me down, borne down with the years in ripe old age
     with all my people here in blessed peace around me.
325 All this, the prophet said, will come to pass."

     "And so," Penelope said, in her great wisdom,
     "if the gods will really grant a happier old age,
     there's hope that we'll escape our trials at last."

So husband and wife confided in each other,
while nurse and Eurynome, under the flaring brands,
were making up the bed with coverings deep and soft.
And working briskly, soon as they'd made it snug,
back to her room the old nurse went to sleep
as Eurynome, their attendant, torch in hand,
lighted the royal couple's way to bed and,
leading them to their chamber, slipped away.
Rejoicing in each other, they returned to their bed,
the old familiar place they loved so well.

Now Telemachus, the cowherd and the swineherd
rested their dancing feet and had the women do the same,
and across the shadowed hall the men lay down to sleep.

But the royal couple, once they'd reveled in all
the longed-for joys of love, reveled in each other's stories,
the radiant woman telling of all she'd borne at home,
watching them there, the infernal crowd of suitors
slaughtering herds of cattle and good fat sheep—
while keen to win her hand—
draining the broached vats dry of vintage wine.
And great Odysseus told his wife of all the pains
he had dealt out to other men and all the hardships
he'd endured himself—his story first to last—
and she listened on, enchanted...
Sleep never sealed her eyes till all was told.

He launched in with how he fought the Cicones down,
then how he came to the Lotus-eaters' lush green land.
Then all the crimes of the Cyclops and how he paid him back
for the gallant men the monster ate without a qualm—
then how he visited Aeolus, who gave him a hero's welcome
then he sent him off, but the homeward run was not his fate,
not yet—some sudden squalls snatched him away once more
and drove him over the swarming sea, groaning in despair.
Then how he moored at Telepylus, where Laestrygonians
wrecked his fleet and killed his men-at-arms.
He told her of Circe's cunning magic wiles
and how he voyaged down in his long benched ship
to the moldering House of Death, to consult Tiresias,
ghostly seer of Thebes, and he saw old comrades there
and he saw his mother, who bore and reared him as a child.
He told how he caught the Sirens' voices throbbing in the wind
and how he had scudded past the Clashing Rocks, past grim Charybdis,
past Scylla—whom no rover had ever coasted by, home free—
and how his shipmates slaughtered the cattle of the Sun
and Zeus the king of thunder split his racing ship
with a reeking bolt and killed his hardy comrades,

375	all his fighting men at a stroke, but he alone
	escaped their death at sea. He told how he reached
	Ogygia's shores and the nymph Calypso held him back,
	deep in her arching caverns, craving him for a husband—
	cherished him, vowed to make him immortal, ageless, all his days,
380	yes, but she never won the heart inside him, never . . .
	then how he reached the Phaeacians—heavy sailing there—
	who with all their hearts had prized him like a god
	and sent him off in a ship to his own beloved land,
	giving him bronze and hoards of gold and robes . . .
385	and that was the last he told her, just as sleep
	overcame him . . . sleep loosing his limbs,
	slipping the toils of anguish from his mind.
	Athena, her eyes afire, had fresh plans.
	Once she thought he'd had his heart's content
390	of love and sleep at his wife's side, straightaway
	she roused young Dawn from Ocean's banks to her golden throne
	to bring men light and roused Odysseus too, who rose
	from his soft bed and advised his wife in parting,
	"Dear woman, we both have had our fill of trials.
395	You in our house, weeping over my journey home,
	fraught with storms and torment, true, and I,
	pinned down in pain by Zeus and other gods,
	for all my desire, blocked from reaching home.
	But now that we've arrived at our bed together—
400	the reunion that we yearned for all those years—
	look after the things still left me in our house.
	But as for the flocks those brazen suitors plundered,
	much I'll recoup myself, making many raids;
	the rest our fellow-Ithacans will supply
405	till all my folds are full of sheep again.
	But now I must be off to the upland farm,
	our orchard green with trees, to see my father,
	good old man weighed down with so much grief for me.
	And you, dear woman, sensible as you are,
410	I would advise you, still . . .
	quick as the rising sun the news will spread
	of the suitors that I killed inside the house.
	So climb to your lofty chamber with your women.
	Sit tight there. See no one. Question no one."
415	He strapped his burnished armor round his shoulders,
	roused Telemachus, the cowherd and the swineherd,
	and told them to take up weapons honed for battle.
	They snapped to commands, harnessed up in bronze,
	opened the doors and strode out, Odysseus in the lead.
420	By now the daylight covered the land, but Pallas,
	shrouding them all in darkness,
	quickly led the four men out of town.

Book 24

Peace

Now Cyllenian Hermes called away the suitors' ghosts,
holding firm in his hand the wand of fine pure gold
that enchants the eyes of men whenever Hermes wants
or wakes us up from sleep.
5   With a wave of this he stirred and led them on
and the ghosts trailed after with high thin cries
as bats cry in the depths of a dark haunted cavern,
shrilling, flittering, wild when one drops from the chain—
slipped from the rock face, while the rest cling tight...
10   So with their high thin cries the ghosts flocked now
and Hermes the Healer led them on, and down the dank
moldering paths and past the Ocean's streams they went
and past the White Rock and the Sun's Western Gates and past
the Land of Dreams, and they soon reached the fields of asphodel
15   where the dead, the burnt-out wraiths of mortals, make their home.

    There they found the ghosts of Peleus' son Achilles,
Patroclus, fearless Antilochus—and Great Ajax too,
the first in stature, first in build and bearing
of all the Argives after Peleus' matchless son.
20   They had grouped around Achilles' ghost, and now
the shade of Atreus' son Agamemnon marched toward them—
fraught with grief and flanked by all his comrades,
troops of his men-at-arms who died beside him,
who met their fate in lord Aegisthus' halls.
25   Achilles' ghost was first to greet him: "Agamemnon,
you were the one, we thought, of all our fighting princes
Zeus who loves the lightning favored most, all your days,
because you commanded such a powerful host of men
on the fields of Troy where we Achaeans suffered.
30   But you were doomed to encounter fate so early,
you too, yet no one born escapes its deadly force.
If only you had died your death in the full flush
of the glory you had mastered—died on Trojan soil!
Then all united Achaea would have raised your tomb
35   and you'd have won your son great fame for years to come.
Not so. You were fated to die a wretched death."

    And the ghost of Atrides Agamemnon answered,
"Son of Peleus, great godlike Achilles! Happy man,
you died on the fields of Troy, a world away from home,
40   and the best of Trojan and Argive champions died around you,
fighting for your corpse. And you... there you lay
in the whirling dust, overpowered in all your power
and wiped from memory all your horseman's skills.
That whole day we fought, we'd never have stopped

45   if Zeus had not stopped *us* with sudden gales.
        Then we bore you out of the fighting, onto the ships,
        we laid you down on a litter, cleansed your handsome flesh
        with warm water and soothing oils, and round your body
        troops of Danaans wept hot tears and cut their locks.
50   Hearing the news, your mother, Thetis, rose from the sea,
        immortal sea-nymphs in her wake, and a strange unearthly cry
        came throbbing over the ocean. Terror gripped Achaea's armies,
        they would have leapt in panic, boarded the long hollow ships
        if one man, deep in his age-old wisdom, had not checked them:
55   Nestor—from the first his counsel always seemed the best,
        and now, concerned for the ranks, he rose and shouted,
        'Hold fast, Argives! Sons of Achaea, don't run now!
        This is Achilles' mother rising from the sea
        with all her immortal sea-nymphs—
60   she longs to join her son who died in battle!'
        That stopped our panicked forces in their tracks
        as the Old Man of the Sea's daughters gathered round you—
        wailing, heartsick—dressed you in ambrosial, deathless robes
        and the Muses, nine in all, voice-to-voice in choirs,
65   their vibrant music rising, raised your dirge.
        Not one soldier would you have seen dry-eyed,
        the Muses' song so pierced us to the heart.
        For seventeen days unbroken, days and nights
        we mourned you—immortal gods and mortal men.
70   At the eighteenth dawn we gave you to the flames
        and slaughtered around your body droves of fat sheep
        and shambling longhorn cattle, and you were burned
        in the garments of the gods and laved with soothing oils
        and honey running sweet, and a long cortege of Argive heroes
75   paraded in review, in battle armor round your blazing pyre,
        men in chariots, men on foot—a resounding roar went up.
        And once the god of fire had burned your corpse to ash,
        at first light we gathered your white bones, Achilles,
        cured them in strong neat wine and seasoned oils.
80   Your mother gave us a gold two-handled urn,
        a gift from Dionysus, she said,
        a masterwork of the famous Smith, the god of fire.
        Your white bones rest in that, my brilliant Achilles,
        mixed with the bones of dead Patroclus, Menoetius' son,
85   apart from those of Antilochus, whom you treasured
        more than all other comrades once Patroclus died.
        Over your bones we reared a grand, noble tomb—
        devoted veterans all, Achaea's combat forces—
        high on its jutting headland over the Hellespont's[1]
90   broad reach, a landmark glimpsed from far out at sea
        by men of our own day and men of days to come.
                                 And then
        your mother, begging the gods for priceless trophies,

---

1. Strait between Europe and Asia, the modern Dardanelles.

set them out in the ring for all our champions.
You in your day have witnessed funeral games

95   for many heroes, games to honor the death of kings,
when young men cinch their belts, tense to win some prize—
but if you'd laid eyes on these it would have thrilled your heart,
magnificent trophies the goddess, glistening-footed Thetis,
held out in your honor. You were dear to the gods,

100   so even in death your name will never die . . .
Great glory is yours, Achilles,
for all time, in the eyes of all mankind!
                        But I?
What joy for *me* when the coil of war had wound down?
For my return Zeus hatched a pitiful death

105   at the hands of Aegisthus—and my accursed wife."

    As they exchanged the stories of their fates,
Hermes the guide and giant-killer drew up close to both,
leading down the ghosts of the suitors King Odysseus killed.
Struck by the sight, the two went up to them right away

110   and the ghost of Atreus' son Agamemnon recognized
the noted prince Amphimedon, Melaneus' dear son
who received him once in Ithaca, at his home,
and Atrides' ghost called out to his old friend now,
"Amphimedon, what disaster brings you down to the dark world?

115   All of you, good picked men, and all in your prime—
no captain out to recruit the best in any city
could have chosen better. What laid you low?
Wrecked in the ships when lord Poseidon roused
some punishing blast of gales and heavy breakers?

120   Or did ranks of enemies mow you down on land
as you tried to raid and cut off herds and flocks
or fought to win their city, take their women?
Answer me, tell me. I was once your guest.
Don't you recall the day I came to visit

125   your house in Ithaca—King Menelaus came too—
to urge Odysseus to sail with us in the ships
on our campaign to Troy? And the long slow voyage,
crossing wastes of ocean, cost us one whole month.
That's how hard it was to bring him round,

130   Odysseus, raider of cities."
                    "Famous Atrides!"
Amphimedon's ghost called back. "Lord of men, Agamemnon,
I remember it all, your majesty, as you say,
and I will tell you, start to finish now,
the story of our death,

135   the brutal end contrived to take us off.
We were courting the wife of Odysseus, gone so long.
She neither spurned nor embraced a marriage she despised,
no, she simply planned our death, our black doom!
This was her latest masterpiece of guile:

140 she set up a great loom in the royal halls
     and she began to weave, and the weaving finespun,
     the yarns endless, and she would lead us on: 'Young men,
     my suitors, now that King Odysseus is no more,
     go slowly, keen as you are to marry me, until
145 I can finish off this web...
     so my weaving won't all fray and come to nothing.
     This is a shroud for old lord Laertes, for that day
     when the deadly fate that lays us out at last will take him down.
     I dread the shame my countrywomen would heap upon me,
150 yes, if a man of such wealth should lie in state
     without a shroud for cover.'
                                   Her very words,
     and despite our pride and passion we believed her.
     So by day she'd weave at her great and growing web—
     by night, by the light of torches set beside her,
155 she would unravel all she'd done. Three whole years
     she deceived us blind, seduced us with this scheme...
     Then, when the wheeling seasons brought the fourth year on
     and the months waned and the long days came round once more,
     one of her women, in on the queen's secret, told the truth
160 and we caught her in the act—unweaving her gorgeous web.
     So she finished it off. Against her will. We forced her.
     But just as she bound off that great shroud and washed it,
     spread it out—glistening like the sunlight or the moon—
     just then some wicked spirit brought Odysseus back,
165 from god knows where, to the edge of his estate
     where the swineherd kept his pigs. And back too,
     to the same place, came Odysseus' own dear son,
     scudding home in his black ship from sandy Pylos.
     The pair of them schemed our doom, our deathtrap,
170 then lit out for town—
     Telemachus first in fact, Odysseus followed,
     later, led by the swineherd, and clad in tatters,
     looking for all the world like an old and broken beggar
     hunched on a stick, his body wrapped in shameful rags.
175 Disguised so none of us, not even the older ones,
     could spot that tramp for the man he really was,
     bursting in on us there, out of the blue. No,
     we attacked him, blows and insults flying fast,
     and he took it all for a time, in his own house,
180 all the taunts and blows—he had a heart of iron.
     But once the will of thundering Zeus had roused his blood,
     he and Telemachus bore the burnished weapons off
     and stowed them deep in a storeroom, shot the bolts
     and he—the soul of cunning—told his wife to set
185 the great bow and the gleaming iron axes out
     before the suitors—all of us doomed now—
     to test our skill and bring our slaughter on...

Not one of us had the strength to string that powerful weapon,
all of us fell far short of what it took. But then,
190 when the bow was coming round to Odysseus' hands,
we raised a hue and cry—he must not have it,
no matter how he begged! Only Telemachus
urged him to take it up, and once he got it
in his clutches, long-suffering great Odysseus
195 strung his bow with ease and shot through all the axes,
then, vaulting onto the threshold, stood there poised, and pouring
his flashing arrows out before him, glaring for the kill,
he cut Antinous down, then shot his painful arrows
into the rest of us, aiming straight and true,
200 and down we went, corpse on corpse in droves.
Clearly a god was driving him and all his henchmen,
routing us headlong in their fury down the hall,
wheeling into the slaughter, slashing left and right
and grisly screams broke from skulls cracked open—
205 the whole floor awash with blood.
                                                      So we died,
Agamemnon...our bodies lie untended even now,
strewn in Odysseus' palace. They know nothing yet,
the kin in our houses who might wash our wounds
of clotted gore and lay us out and mourn us.
210 These are the solemn honors owed the dead."
                                                      "Happy Odysseus!"
Agamemnon's ghost cried out. "Son of old Laertes—
mastermind—what a fine, faithful wife you won!
What good sense resided in your Penelope—
how well Icarius' daughter remembered you,
215 Odysseus, the man she married once!
The fame of her great virtue will never die.
The immortal gods will lift a song for all mankind,
a glorious song in praise of self-possessed Penelope.
A far cry from the daughter of Tyndareus, Clytemnestra—
220 what outrage she committed, killing the man *she* married once!—
yes, and the song men sing of her will ring with loathing.
She brands with a foul name the breed of womankind,
even the honest ones to come!"
                                                      So they traded stories,
the two ghosts standing there in the House of Death,
225 far in the hidden depths below the earth.

Odysseus and his men had stridden down from town
and quickly reached Laertes' large, well-tended farm
that the old king himself had wrested from the wilds,
years ago, laboring long and hard. His lodge was here
230 and around it stretched a row of sheds where fieldhands,
bondsmen who did his bidding, sat and ate and slept.
And an old Sicilian woman was in charge,

22

who faithfully looked after her aged master
out on his good estate remote from town.
235   Odysseus told his servants and his son,
"Into the timbered lodge now, go, quickly,
kill us the fattest porker, fix our meal.
And I will put my father to the test,
see if the old man knows me now, on sight,
240   or fails to, after twenty years apart."

       With that he passed his armor to his men
and in they went at once, his son as well. Odysseus
wandered off, approaching the thriving vineyard, searching,
picking his way down to the great orchard, searching,
245   but found neither Dolius nor his sons nor any hand.
They'd just gone off, old Dolius in the lead,
to gather stones for a dry retaining wall
to shore the vineyard up. But he did find
his father, alone, on that well-worked plot,
250   spading round a sapling—clad in filthy rags,
in a patched, unseemly shirt, and round his shins
he had some oxhide leggings strapped, patched too,
to keep from getting scraped, and gloves on his hands
to fight against the thorns, and on his head
255   he wore a goatskin skullcap
to cultivate his misery that much more...
Long-enduring Odysseus, catching sight of him now—
a man worn down with years, his heart racked with sorrow—
halted under a branching pear-tree, paused and wept.
260   Debating, head and heart, what should he do now?
Kiss and embrace his father, pour out the long tale—
how he had made the journey home to native land—
or probe him first and test him every way?
Torn, mulling it over, this seemed better:
265   test the old man first,
reproach him with words that cut him to the core.
Convinced, Odysseus went right up to his father.
Laertes was digging round the sapling, head bent low
as his famous offspring hovered over him and began,
270   "You want no skill, old man, at tending a garden.
All's well-kept here; not one thing in the plot,
no plant, no fig, no pear, no olive, no vine,
not a vegetable, lacks your tender, loving care.
But I must say—and don't be offended now—
275   your plants are doing better than yourself.
Enough to be stooped with age
but look how squalid you are, those shabby rags.
Surely it's not for sloth your master lets you go to seed.
There's nothing of slave about your build or bearing.
280   I have eyes: you look like a king to me. The sort

entitled to bathe, sup well, then sleep in a soft bed.
That's the right and pride of you old-timers.
Come now, tell me—in no uncertain terms—
whose slave are you? whose orchard are you tending?
285 And tell me this—I must be absolutely sure—
this place I've reached, is it truly Ithaca?
Just as that fellow told me, just now . . .
I fell in with him on the road here. Clumsy,
none too friendly, couldn't trouble himself
290 to hear me out or give me a decent answer
when I asked about a long-lost friend of mine,
whether he's still alive, somewhere in Ithaca,
or dead and gone already, lost in the House of Death.
Do you want to hear his story? Listen. Catch my drift.
295 I once played host to a man in my own country;
he'd come to my door, the most welcome guest
from foreign parts I ever entertained.
He claimed he came of good Ithacan stock,
said his father was Arcesius' son, Laertes.
300 So I took the new arrival under my own roof,
I gave him a hero's welcome, treated him in style—
stores in our palace made for princely entertainment.
And I gave my friend some gifts to fit his station,
handed him seven bars of well-wrought gold,
305 a mixing-bowl of solid silver, etched with flowers,
a dozen cloaks, unlined and light, a dozen rugs
and as many full-cut capes and shirts as well,
and to top it off, four women, perfect beauties
skilled in crafts—he could pick them out himself."

310 "Stranger," his father answered, weeping softly,
"the land you've reached is the very one you're after,
true, but it's in the grip of reckless, lawless men.
And as for the gifts you showered on your guest,
you gave them all for nothing.
315 But if you'd found him alive, here in Ithaca,
he would have replied in kind, with gift for gift,
and entertained you warmly before he sent you off.
That's the old custom, when one has led the way.
But tell me, please—in no uncertain terms—
320 how many years ago did you host the man,
that unfortunate guest of yours, my son . . .
there was a son, or was he all a dream?
That most unlucky man, whom now, I fear,
far from his own soil and those he loves,
325 the fish have swallowed down on the high seas
or birds and beasts on land have made their meal.
Nor could the ones who bore him—mother, father—
wrap his corpse in a shroud and mourn him deeply.

Nor could his warm, generous wife, so self-possessed,
330 Penelope, ever keen for her husband on his deathbed,
the fit and proper way, or close his eyes at last.
These are the solemn honors owed the dead.
But tell me your own story—that I'd like to know:
Who are you? where are you from? your city? your parents?
335 Where does the ship lie moored that brought you here,
your hardy shipmates too? Or did you arrive
as a passenger aboard some stranger's craft
and men who put you ashore have pulled away?"
                                             "The whole tale,"
his crafty son replied, "I'll tell you start to finish.
340 I come from Roamer-Town, my home's a famous place,
my father's Unsparing, son of old King Pain,
and my name's Man of Strife...
I sailed from Sicily, aye, but some ill wind
blew me here, off course—much against my will—
345 and my ship lies moored off farmlands far from town.
As for Odysseus, well, five years have passed
since he left my house and put my land behind him,
luckless man! But the birds were good as he launched out,
all on the right, and I rejoiced as I sent him off
350 and he rejoiced in sailing. We had high hopes
we'd meet again as guests, as old friends,
and trade some shining gifts."
                                      At those words
a black cloud of grief came shrouding over Laertes.
Both hands clawing the ground for dirt and grime,
355 he poured it over his grizzled head, sobbing, in spasms.
Odysseus' heart shuddered, a sudden twinge went shooting up
through his nostrils, watching his dear father struggle...
He sprang toward him, kissed him, hugged him, crying,
"Father—I am your son—myself, the man you're seeking,
360 home after twenty years, on native ground at last!
Hold back your tears, your grief.
Let me tell you the news, but we must hurry—
I've cut the suitors down in our own house,
I've paid them back their outrage, vicious crimes!"
                                             "Odysseus..."
365 Laertes, catching his breath, found words to answer.
"You—you're truly my son, Odysseus, home at last?
Give me a sign, some proof—I must be sure."
                                             "This scar first,"
quick to the mark, his son said, "look at this—
the wound I took from the boar's white tusk
370 on Mount Parnassus. There you'd sent me, you
and mother, to see her fond old father, Autolycus,
and collect the gifts he vowed to give me, once,
when he came to see us here.

23

Or these, these trees—
let me tell you the trees you gave me years ago,
375 here on this well-worked plot...
I begged you for everything I saw, a little boy
trailing you through the orchard, picking our way
among these trees, and you named them one by one.
You gave me thirteen pear, ten apple trees
380 and forty figs—and promised to give me, look,
fifty vinerows, bearing hard on each other's heels,
clusters of grapes year-round at every grade of ripeness,
mellowed as Zeus's seasons weigh them down."
Living proof—
and Laertes' knees went slack, his heart surrendered,
385 recognizing the strong clear signs Odysseus offered.
He threw his arms around his own dear son, fainting
as hardy great Odysseus hugged him to his heart
until he regained his breath, came back to life
and cried out, "Father Zeus—
390 you gods of Olympus, you still rule on high
if those suitors have truly paid in blood
for all their reckless outrage! Oh, but now
my heart quakes with fear that all the Ithacans
will come down on us in a pack, at any time,
395 and rush the alarm through every island town!"

"There's nothing to fear," his canny son replied,
"put it from your mind. Let's make for your lodge
beside the orchard here. I sent Telemachus on ahead,
the cowherd, swineherd too, to fix a hasty meal."

400 So the two went home, confiding all the way
and arriving at the ample, timbered lodge,
they found Telemachus with the two herdsmen
carving sides of meat and mixing ruddy wine.
Before they ate, the Sicilian serving-woman
405 bathed her master, Laertes—his spirits high
in his own room—and rubbed him down with oil
and round his shoulders drew a fresh new cloak.
And Athena stood beside him, fleshing out the limbs
of the old commander, made him taller to all eyes,
410 his build more massive, stepping from his bath,
so his own son gazed at him, wonderstruck—
face-to-face he seemed a deathless god...
"Father"—Odysseus' words had wings—"surely
one of the everlasting gods has made you
415 taller, stronger, shining in my eyes!"

Facing his son, the wise old man returned,
"If only—Father Zeus, Athena and lord Apollo—

I were the man I was, king of the Cephallenians
when I sacked the city of Nericus, sturdy fortress
out on its jutting cape! If I'd been young in arms
last night in our house with harness on my back,
standing beside you, fighting off the suitors,
how many I would have cut the knees from under—
the heart inside you would have leapt for joy!"

So father and son confirmed each other's spirits.
And then, with the roasting done, the meal set out,
the others took their seats on chairs and stools,
were just putting their hands to bread and meat
when old Dolius trudged in with his sons,
worn out from the fieldwork.
The old Sicilian had gone and fetched them home,
the mother who reared the boys and tended Dolius well,
now that the years had ground the old man down . . .
When they saw Odysseus—knew him in their bones—
they stopped in their tracks, staring, struck dumb,
but the king waved them on with a warm and easy air:
"Sit down to your food, old friend. Snap out of your wonder.
We've been cooling our heels here long enough,
eager to get our hands on all this pork,
hoping you'd all troop in at any moment."

Spreading his arms, Dolius rushed up to him,
clutched Odysseus by the wrist and kissed his hand,
greeting his king now with a burst of winging words:
"Dear master, you're back—the answer to our prayers!
We'd lost all hope but the gods have brought you home!
Welcome—health! The skies rain blessings on you!
But tell me the truth now—this I'd like to know—
shrewd Penelope, has she heard you're home?
Or should we send a messenger?"
                                    "She knows by now,
old man," his wily master answered brusquely.
"Why busy yourself with that?"

So Dolius went back to his sanded stool.
His sons too, pressing around the famous king,
greeted Odysseus warmly, grasped him by the hand
then took their seats in order by their father.

But now, as they fell to supper in the lodge,
Rumor the herald sped like wildfire through the city,
crying out the news of the suitors' bloody death and doom,
and massing from every quarter as they listened, kinsmen
    milled
with wails and moans of grief before Odysseus' palace.
And then they carried out the bodies, every family
buried their own, and the dead from other towns
they loaded onto the rapid ships for crews

to ferry back again, each to his own home . . .

465 Then in a long, mourning file they moved to assembly
where, once they'd grouped, crowding the meeting grounds,
old lord Eupithes rose in their midst to speak out.
Unforgettable sorrow wrung his heart for his son,
Antinous, the first that great Odysseus killed.

470 In tears for the one he lost, he stood and cried,
"My friends, what a mortal blow this man has dealt
to all our island people! Those fighters, many and brave,
he led away in his curved ships—he lost the ships
and he lost the men and back he comes again

475 to kill the best of our Cephallenian princes.
Quick, after him! Before he flees to Pylos
or holy Elis, where Epeans rule in power—
up, attack! Or we'll hang our heads forever,
all disgraced, even by generations down the years,

480 if we don't punish the murderers of our brothers and our sons!
Why, life would lose its relish—for me, at least—
I'd rather die at once and go among the dead.
Attack!—before the assassins cross the sea
and leave us in their wake."

He closed in tears
485 and compassion ran through every Achaean there.
Suddenly Medon and the inspired bard approached them,
fresh from Odysseus' house, where they had just awakened.
They strode into the crowds; amazement took each man
but the herald Medon spoke in all his wisdom:

490 "Hear me, men of Ithaca. Not without the hand
of the deathless gods did Odysseus do these things!
Myself, I saw an immortal fighting at his side—
like Mentor to the life. I saw the same god,
now in front of Odysseus, spurring him on,

495 now stampeding the suitors through the hall,
crazed with fear, and down they went in droves!"

Terror gripped them all, their faces ashen white.
At last the old warrior Halitherses, Mastor's son—
who alone could see the days behind and days ahead—

500 rose up and spoke, distraught for each man there:
"Hear me, men of Ithaca. Hear what I have to say.
Thanks to your own craven hearts these things were done!
You never listened to me or the good commander Mentor,
you never put a stop to your sons' senseless folly.

505 What fine work they did, so blind, so reckless,
carving away the wealth, affronting the wife
of a great and famous man, telling themselves
that he'd return no more! So let things rest now.
Listen to me for once—I say don't attack!

510 Else some will draw the lightning on their necks."

So he urged

sprang up with warcries now. They had no taste
for the prophet's sane plan—winning Eupithes
quickly won them over. They ran for armor
515   and once they'd harnessed up in burnished bronze
they grouped in ranks before the terraced city.
Eupithes led them on in their foolish, mad campaign,
certain he would avenge the slaughter of his son
but the father was not destined to return—
520   he'd meet his death in battle then and there.

        Athena at this point made appeals to Zeus:
"Father, son of Cronus, our high and mighty king,
now let me ask you a question...
tell me the secrets hidden in your mind.
525   Will you prolong the pain, the cruel fighting here
or hand down pacts of peace between both sides?"

        "My child," Zeus who marshals the thunderheads replied,
"why do you pry and probe me so intently? Come now,
wasn't the plan your own? You conceived it yourself:
530   Odysseus should return and pay the traitors back.
Do as your heart desires—
but let me tell you how it should be done.
Now that royal Odysseus has taken his revenge,
let both sides seal their pacts that he shall reign for life,
535   and let us purge their memories of the bloody slaughter
of their brothers and their sons. Let them be friends,
devoted as in the old days. Let peace and wealth
come cresting through the land."
                                        So Zeus decreed
and launched Athena already poised for action—
540   down she swept from Olympus' craggy peaks.

        By then Odysseus' men had had their fill
of hearty fare, and the seasoned captain said,
"One of you go outside—see if they're closing in."
A son of Dolius snapped to his command,
545   ran to the door and saw them all too close
and shouted back to Odysseus,
"They're on top of us! To arms—and fast!"
Up they sprang and strapped themselves in armor,
the three men with Odysseus, Dolius' six sons
550   and Dolius and Laertes clapped on armor too,
gray as they were, but they would fight if forced.
Once they had all harnessed up in burnished bronze
they opened the doors and strode out, Odysseus in the lead.

        And now, taking the build and voice of Mentor,
555   Zeus's daughter Athena marched right in.
The good soldier Odysseus thrilled to see her,
turned to his son and said in haste, "Telemachus,

you'll learn soon enough—as you move up to fight
where champions strive to prove themselves the best—
560   not to disgrace your father's line a moment.
In battle prowess we've excelled for ages
all across the world."

                            Telemachus reassured him,
"Now you'll see, if you care to watch, father,
now I'm fired up. Disgrace, you say?
565   I won't disgrace your line!"

      Laertes called out in deep delight,
"What a day for me, dear gods! What joy—
my son and my grandson vying over courage!"

                                  "Laertes!"
Goddess Athena rushed beside him, eyes ablaze:
570   "Son of Arcesius, dearest of all my comrades,
say a prayer to the bright-eyed girl and Father Zeus,
then brandish your long spear and wing it fast!"

      Athena breathed enormous strength in the old man.
He lifted a prayer to mighty Zeus's daughter,
575   brandished his spear a moment, winged it fast
and hit Eupithes, pierced his bronze-sided helmet
that failed to block the bronze point tearing through—
down Eupithes crashed, his armor clanging against his chest.
Odysseus and his gallant son charged straight at the front lines,
580   slashing away with swords, with two-edged spears and now
they would have killed them all, cut them off from home
if Athena, daughter of storming Zeus, had not cried out
in a piercing voice that stopped all fighters cold,
"Hold back, you men of Ithaca, back from brutal war!
585   Break off—shed no more blood—make peace at once!"

      So Athena commanded. Terror blanched their faces,
they went limp with fear, weapons slipped from their hands
and strewed the ground at the goddess' ringing voice.
They spun in flight to the city, wild to save their lives,
590   but loosing a savage cry, the long-enduring great Odysseus,
gathering all his force, swooped like a soaring eagle—
just as the son of Cronus hurled a reeking bolt
that fell at her feet, the mighty Father's daughter,
and blazing-eyed Athena wheeled on Odysseus, crying,
595   "Royal son of Laertes, Odysseus, master of exploits,
hold back now! Call a halt to the great leveler, War—
don't court the rage of Zeus who rules the world!"

      So she commanded. He obeyed her, glad at heart.
And Athena handed down her pacts of peace
600   between both sides for all the years to come—
the daughter of Zeus whose shield is storm and thunder,
yes, but the goddess still kept Mentor's build and voice.

The Greeks so valued Sappho's poetry that they called her the tenth Muse. Born to an aristocratic family on the island of Lesbos, she wrote poems reflecting a world of luxury, strongly marked by her island's proximity to the Asian coast and its wealthy cities. The fragmentary remains of her poetry reveal an aristocratic taste for adornments, flowers, perfumed oils, and erotic pleasures. Her poems include songs of sexual pursuit and remembrances of beloved women, sometimes framed as hymns to the goddess of *eros,* Aphrodite. Sappho was known for her verse celebrating same-sex desire, giving rise to the modern term "lesbian," which at root means simply "a native of Lesbos." Sappho also wrote wedding poems, poems of insult, and poems that refer to the heroic legends of the Trojan War. Her aesthetic oftens evokes what the Greeks called *pothos,* "yearning," a recollecting of scenes of pleasure or festival or the arrival among women of the immortal goddess. She belongs to the aristocratic world of the Archaic period, secure in its privileges and possibly even committed to preserving its way of life against tyrannical ambitions, since she was said to have been exiled in the turmoil of Lesbian politics during her lifetime. Although her poetry is fragmentary, it is the most substantial body of work by a woman that remains from classical antiquity.

PRONUNCIATION:
Sappho: SAF-fo

Rich-throned immortal Aphrodite[1]

> Rich-throned immortal Aphrodite,
> scheming daughter of Zeus, I pray you,
> with pain and sickness, Queen, crush not my heart,
>
> but come, if ever in the past you
> 5   heard my voice from afar and hearkened,
> and left your father's halls and came, with gold
>
> chariot yoked; and pretty sparrows
> brought you swiftly across the dark earth
> fluttering wings from heaven through the air.
>
> 10   Soon they were here, and you, Blest Goddess,
> smiling with your immortal features,
> asked why I'd called, what was the matter now,
>
> what was my heart insanely craving:
> "Who is it this time I must cozen
> 15   to love you, Sappho? Who's unfair to you?
>
> "For though she flee, soon she'll be chasing;
> though she refuse gifts, she'll be giving;
> though she love not, she'll love despite herself."

1. Translated by M. L. West.

The lyric poets Sappho and
Alkaios, red-figure vase,
c. 500 B.C.E.

20   Yes, come once more, from sore obsession
        free me; all that my heart desires
    fulfilled, fulfil—help me to victory!

Come, goddess

    Come, goddess, to your holy shrine,
        where your delightful apple grove
    awaits, and altars smoke with frankincense.

    A cool brook sounds through apple boughs,
5   and all's with roses overhung;
    from shimmering leaves a trancelike sleep takes hold.

    Here is a flowery meadow, too,
        where horses graze, and gentle blow

the breezes...

10　　　Here, then, Love-goddess much in mind,
　　　　　infuse our feast in gracious style
　　　with nectar poured in cups that turn to gold.

Some think a fleet

　　　　　Some think a fleet, a troop of horse
　　　　　or soldiery the finest sight
　　　in all the world; but I say, what one loves.

　　　　　Easy it is to make this plain
5　　　　　to anyone. She the most fair
　　　of mortals, Helen, having a man of the best,

　　　　　deserted him, and sailed to Troy,
　　　　　without a thought for her dear child
　　　or parents, led astray by [love's power.]

10　　　　[For though the heart be pr]oud [and strong,]
　　　　　[Love] quickly [bends it to his will.—]
　　　That makes me think of Anactoria.

　　　　　I'd sooner see her lovely walk
　　　　　and the bright sparkling of her face
15　　　than all the horse and arms of Lydia.[1]

He looks to me to be in heaven

　　　　　He looks to me to be in heaven,
　　　　　that man who sits across from you
　　　and listens near you to your soft speaking,

　　　　　your laughing lovely: that, I vow,
5　　　　　makes the heart leap in my breast;
　　　for watching you a moment, speech fails me,

　　　　　my tongue is paralysed, at once
　　　　　a light fire runs beneath my skin,
　　　my eyes are blinded, and my ears drumming,

10　　　　the sweat pours down me, and I shake
　　　　　all over, sallower than grass:
　　　I feel as if I'm not far off dying.

　　　　　But no thing is too hard to bear;
　　　　　for [God can make] the poor man [rich,
15　　　or bring to nothing heaven-high fortune.]

1. Wealthy kingdom near Lesbos in Asia Minor.

Love shakes my heart

                                                   Love
shakes my heart like the wind rushing down on
    the mountain oaks.

Honestly, I wish I were dead

    Honestly, I wish I were dead.
She was covered in tears as she went away,

      left me, saying "Oh, it's too bad!
      How unlucky we are! I swear,
5   Sappho, I don't want to be leaving you."

      This is what I replied to her:
      "Go, be happy, and think of me.
You remember how we looked after you;

      or if not, then let me remind
           . . . . .
10   all the lovely and beautiful times we had,

      all the garlands of violets
      and of roses and . . .
and . . . that you've put on in my company,

      all the delicate chains of flowers
15   that encircled your tender neck
           . . . . .
           . . . . .

      and the costly unguent with which
you anointed yourself, and the royal myrrh.

      On soft couches . . .
      Tender . . .
20   you assuaged your longing . . .

      There was never a . . .
      or a shrine or a . . .
    . . . that we were not present at,

      no grove . . . no festive dance . . .

. . . she worshipped you

    . . . she worshipped you
    and always in your singing she most delighted.

But now among the women of Lydia
she shines, as after the sun has set
5   the rosy-fingered moon will appear, surpassing

all the stars, bestowing her light alike
upon the waves of the briny sea
and on the fields that sparkle with countless flowers.

Everything is bathed in the lovely dew:
10   roses take their nourishment, and
soft chervil, and the blossoming honey-lotus.

Often, as she moves on her daily round,
she'll be eating her tender heart
when she thinks of her love for gentle Atthis.

15   And for us to go there...
...it's not possible...
with the wedding-song (?) ringing loud between us.

Like the sweet-apple

Like the sweet-apple that's gleaming red on the topmost bough,
right at the very end, that the apple-pickers forgot,
or rather didn't forget, but were just unable to reach.

Like the hyacinth on the hills that the passing shepherds
5   trample under their feet, and the purple bloom on the ground...

The doorman's feet

The doorman's feet are size 90:
five cowhides went into his sandals,
and it took ten cobblers to make them!

High must be the chamber—
5   Hymenaeum!
Make it high, you builders!

A bridegroom's coming—
        Hymenaeum!
like the War-god himself, the tallest of the tall!

SOPHOCLES ■ (C. 496–406 B.C.E.)

A citizen of Athens and its radical, innovative democracy, Sophocles won many victories
in the drama festivals of his native city. His great predecessor in the writing of tragedy,
Aeschylus, wrote the *Oresteia,* a trilogy consisting of three linked plays that celebrate the
founding of one of the city's important legal institutions and express a tenuous optimism

about the democratic experiment. Sophocles was a more conservative thinker, and he feared for his fellow citizens and for their city.

An ancient story records the piety of Sophocles. When the worship of Asclepius the healing god was introduced into the city of Athens in 420 B.C.E., Sophocles invited the god's representative, a snake, to live in his house until a suitable sanctuary was erected. Sophocles's piety was not at all otherworldly; he shared his fellow citizens' susceptibility to eros and the beauty of boys, and said at the end of his long life that he was glad no longer to be tormented by the goddess of sexuality, Aphrodite. Throughout his tragedies, one of the themes that concerns him is reverence for the gods, and he feared that democratic Athens, having turned away from the elite aristocratic form of government of earlier centuries, now risked abandoning the gods in a proud burst of wealth, confidence, and sometimes arrogant domination of its former allies in an Athenian empire. Among the Athenians of his day were intellectuals proud of their accomplishments in the development of logic, rhetoric, political theory, and philosophy. Radical thinkers such as the sophists insisted that human beings were the "measure of all things," rather than urging the traditional practices of worshiping the gods. Sophocles' tragedies intervene in the intense social, political, and religious debates of the fifth century B.C.E., when Athens participated in the victory over the huge Persian Empire's invasion at the beginning of the century, flourished in an atmosphere of risk and daring at midcentury, and went down to devastating defeat by the Spartans in the Peloponnesian War at the century's end.

In his long career, Sophocles wrote more than 120 tragedies, of which only a handful remain. His career began in 468 and ended with his death, just after the death of Euripides, the third of the great fifth-century tragedians. Sophocles lived in Athens at the time of Pericles, the brilliant aristocratic statesman of the classical age, which was also the time of Socrates, a founder of Greek philosophy, and of Aristophanes, the obscene, wild comic dramatist. This was also the period of Athens's great building program, when the treasures from the Athenians' empire were spent on embellishing the city with such magnificent buildings as the Parthenon, the temple of Athena, the patron goddess of Athens. Sophocles's plays take on some of the powerful myths the Greeks told themselves, seeking to reconcile the ideology of the democratic city, in which all men were said to be equal, with the myths of the preeminent heroes and gods they inherited from the Archaic age. Sophocles's *Electra* focuses on the unhappy family of Atreus, representing the daughter of the house as a wretched victim of her parents' enmity. His *Philoktetes* goes back to the myths of Homer and the Trojan War and shows the now-ruthless and rhetorically skilled Odysseus in conflict with the values of the past. *The Women of Trachis* portrays the great hero Herakles as he returns home from battle with a captive slave bride; his wife, having waited at home, tries to win him back to her with what she believes to be a love potion, but that is in fact a deadly poison that destroys him. In the *Ajax*, Sophocles portrays the great Homeric warrior driven mad by Athena, slaughtering his wife and children in a world he can no longer understand. In all of these plays, Sophocles engages questions of time and eternity and the conflict between the human values of the democratic city and the old Homeric virtues and devotion to the gods. In interrogating received stories and myths, he engages in a prolonged meditation on the relationship between civilization and its limits—nature, the gods, madness, death—all that cannot be known through the civilized discourses of human beings.

The myth of the Greek city of Thebes engaged Sophocles throughout his life as a tragedian, and in plays such as *Oedipus the King,* he gave a searching development to stark old stories that his audience would have known well. Thebes was said to have been founded by Kadmos, a prince from Tyre in Asia Minor; his sister Europa was one day playing on the beach with her friends when a lovely white bull took her off. This was Zeus in one of the many forms he assumed to seduce mortal women and boys. He took Europa to Crete, and she gave the continent of Europe her name. Kadmos journeyed to the mainland and after consulting with the oracle, came to the land of Thebes, where he had been instructed to kill the dragon guarding a spring. He took the dragon's teeth, sowed them in the ground, and warriors sprang up who fought to the death until only five survived. These were the Spartoi, the founding aristocratic families of Thebes. Kadmos founded the ruling dynasty, which suffered many troubles. One of the kings refused to worship Dionysos, even though the god was the son of Zeus and a Theban princess; he was dismembered and perhaps eaten alive by his own mother in a Dionysiac ecstasy. Another offspring of the house of Thebes was Aktaion, who while hunting one day came upon the virgin goddess Artemis bathing naked; enraged, she turned him into a stag to be eaten by his own dogs. The family also included Laios (or Laius), who in exile as a young man carried off his host's son, which, according to some legends, began the Greek practice of pederasty, the amorous, erotic relationship between men and young or adolescent boys. Laius returned to Thebes but was warned never to have children with his wife, Jocasta. When a son was born, they pierced the boy's ankles and gave him to a slave to expose on Mount Parnassos above the city of Thebes. He instead gave the child to a shepherd, who delivered him to the childless ruling family of Corinth.

This deliverance only plunged the child into new troubles. The boy, in Greek *Oidipous*, "Swollen-foot," was taunted as he grew up, and he went to visit the oracle of Apollo at Delphi, where he was told that he would kill his father and marry his mother. Seeking to avoid this fate, he traveled to Thebes, not Corinth, which he believed to be his home, and on the way killed a man on the road. When he arrived in Thebes, it was besieged by an uncanny monster called the Sphinx, who killed those who could not answer her riddle: What goes on four feet in the morning, two feet at noon, three at dusk? Only Oedipus knew the answer: the human being, who crawls as an infant, walks upright as an adult, and uses a stick in old age. He won both the city and its queen, Jocasta, and had children with her. Set after these events, Sophocles's play *Oedipus the King* portrays his anguished discovery of who he is.

The myth goes beyond the episodes portrayed in the tragedy: Oedipus cursed his sons just before the end of his life in Colonus, near Athens, where he blessed a shrine to protect the city of the Athenians from harm. Oedipus, who had known his mother's body twice (once as her child, once as her husband) with all his sufferings bestowed the benefit only a monster could give. His sons killed one another over the right to rule the city of Thebes; their sister, Antigone, went to her death defending her right to bury her despised brother, cast outside the city to be eaten by birds and dogs. Each of the great tragedians of classical Athens represented episodes from the Theban story of incest and horror for their audiences.

As presented in Athenian tragedy, archaic, mythic Thebes stands as a sort of anti-Athens, a place where repetition, terrible contact with the gods, sterility, dismemberment, incest, and filial hatred present a negative mirror for Athens, of all that Athens wishes not to bring forth as a *polis,* all that it fears as a dark side of its optimism. Sophocles returned to the myth of Thebes again and again, telling the story over many years. He probably first wrote *Antigone,* producing *Oedipus the King* some time after, and late in life gave the city *Oedipus at Colonus* at the end of the horrors of the Peloponnesian War, the great war among the Greeks. The tragedy *Oedipus the King* was probably first performed in a period of great trouble for the Athenians. Some have argued that in the tragedy, Oedipus stands as a figure for the city of Athens itself, as a model of intellectual confidence and seeking, exemplifying all the skills of rhetoric, science, mathematics, philosophy, and medicine on which the democratic city prided itself and on which it based its claims to the right to govern other cities in an empire. Others see Oedipus as a figure for the human being as such, existing between the gods and the animals, aspiring to godhood, brought down to the level of the beasts for that very aspiration, in an exemplary spectacle. The Athenians practiced both ostracism—the expulsion of dangerously powerful men from their midst—and a *pharmakos* ritual, like the scapegoating of the Hebrew Bible, expelling the lowest of their members. The Theban king, once compared to a god, becomes a blinded, wandering beast. Oedipus, whether an allegory for Athens itself or an exemplary human being, citizen of the city, has haunted the imagination of the West from Sophocles to Freud and beyond.

PRONUNCIATIONS:

> *Creon:* KREE-on
> *Jocasta:* jo-KAS-ta
> *Oedipus:* EE-di-pus
> *Teiresias:* ty-REE-see-as

Oedipus the King[1]

Characters

OEDIPUS, *King of Thebes*
JOCASTA, *his wife*
CREON, *his brother-in-law*
TEIRESIAS, *an old blind prophet*
A PRIEST

FIRST MESSENGER
SECOND MESSENGER
A HERDSMAN
A CHORUS OF OLD MEN OF THEBES

Scene: In front of the palace of Oedipus at Thebes. To the right of the stage near the altar stands the Priest with a crowd of children. Oedipus emerges from the central door.

OEDIPUS: Children, young sons and daughters of old Cadmus,[2]
       why do you sit here with your suppliant crowns?
       The town is heavy with a mingled burden
       of sounds and smells, of groans and hymns and incense;
5   I did not think it fit that I should hear
       of this from messengers but came myself,—
       I Oedipus whom all men call the Great.

   [*He turns to the Priest.*]

       You're old and they are young; come, speak for them.
       What do you fear or want, that you sit here
10   suppliant? Indeed I'm willing to give all
       that you may need; I would be very hard
       should I not pity suppliants like these.
PRIEST: O ruler of my country, Oedipus,
       you see our company around the altar;
15   you see our ages; some of us, like these,
       who cannot yet fly far, and some of us
       heavy with age; these children are the chosen
       among the young, and I the priest of Zeus.

1. Translated by David Grene.
2. Founder of Thebes.

24

Within the market place sit others crowned
20 with suppliant garlands, at the double shrine
of Pallas and the temple where Ismenus
gives oracles by fire. King, you yourself
have seen our city reeling like a wreck
already; it can scarcely lift its prow
25 out of the depths, out of the bloody surf.
A blight is on the fruitful plants of the earth,
a blight is on the cattle in the fields,
a blight is on our women that no children
are born to them; a God that carries fire,
30 a deadly pestilence, is on our town,
strikes us and spares not, and the house of Cadmus
is emptied of its people while black Death
grows rich in groaning and in lamentation.
We have not come as suppliants to this altar
35 because we thought of you as of a God,
but rather judging you the first of men
in all the chances of this life and when
we mortals have to do with more than man.
You came and by your coming saved our city,
40 freed us from tribute which we paid of old
to the Sphinx, cruel singer. This you did
in virtue of no knowledge we could give you,
in virtue of no teaching; it was God
that aided you, men say, and you are held
45 with God's assistance to have saved our lives.
Now Oedipus, Greatest in all men's eyes,
here falling at your feet we all entreat you,
find us some strength for rescue.
Perhaps you'll hear a wise word from some God,
50 perhaps you will learn something from a man
(for I have seen that for the skilled of practice
the outcome of their counsels live the most).
Noblest of men, go, and raise up our city,
go,—and give heed. For now this land of ours
55 calls you its savior since you saved it once.
So, let us never speak about your reign
as of a time when first our feet were set
secure on high, but later fell to ruin.
Raise up our city, save it and raise it up.
60 Once you have brought us luck with happy omen;
be no less now in fortune.
If you will rule this land, as now you rule it,
better to rule it full of men than empty.
For neither tower nor ship is anything
65 when empty, and none live in it together.
OEDIPUS: I pity you, children. You have come full of longing,
but I have known the story before you told it

only too well. I know you are all sick,
yet there is not one of you, sick though you are,
70   that is as sick as I myself.
Your several sorrows each have single scope
and touch but one of you. My spirit groans
for city and myself and you at once.
You have not roused me like a man from sleep;
75   know that I have given many tears to this,
gone many ways wandering in thought,
but as I thought I found only one remedy
and that I took. I sent Menoeceus' son
Creon, Jocasta's brother, to Apollo,
80   to his Pythian temple,
that he might learn there by what act or word
I could save this city. As I count the days,
it vexes me what ails him; he is gone
far longer than he needed for the journey.
85   But when he comes, then, may I prove a villain,
if I shall not do all the God commands.
PRIEST: Thanks for your gracious words. Your servants here
signal that Creon is this moment coming.
OEDIPUS: His face is bright. O holy Lord Apollo,
90   grant that his news too may be bright for us
and bring us safety.
PRIEST: It is happy news,
I think, for else his head would not be crowned
with sprigs of fruitful laurel.
OEDIPUS: We will know soon,
95   he's within hail. Lord Creon, my good brother,
what is the word you bring us from the God?

[*Creon enters.*]

CREON: A good word,—for things hard to bear themselves
if in the final issue all is well
I count complete good fortune.
OEDIPUS: What do you mean?
100   What you have said so far
leaves me uncertain whether to trust or fear.
CREON: If you will hear my news before these others
I am ready to speak, or else to go within.
OEDIPUS: Speak it to all;
105   the grief I bear, I bear it more for these
than for my own heart.
CREON: I will tell you, then,
what I heard, from the God.
King Phoebus[3] in plain words commanded us
to drive out a pollution from our land,

---

3. Apollo, god of the Pythian oracle at Delphi.

110   pollution grown ingrained within the land;
           drive it out, said the God, not cherish it,
           till it's past cure.
OEDIPUS: What is the rite
           of purification? How shall it be done?
CREON: By banishing a man, or expiation
115   of blood by blood, since it is murder guilt
           which holds our city in this destroying storm.
OEDIPUS: Who is this man whose fate the God pronounces?
CREON: My Lord, before you piloted the state
           we had a king called Laius.
OEDIPUS: I know of him by hearsay. I have not seen him.
CREON: The God commanded clearly: let some one
           punish with force this dead man's murderers.
OEDIPUS: Where are they in the world? Where would a trace
           of this old crime be found? It would be hard
           to guess where.
CREON: The clue is in this land;
           that which is sought is found;
           the unheeded thing escapes:
           so said the God.
OEDIPUS: Was it at home,
           or in the country that death came upon him,
130   or in another country travelling?
CREON: He went, he said himself, upon an embassy,
           but never returned when he set out from home.
OEDIPUS: Was there no messenger, no fellow traveller
           who knew what happened? Such a one might tell
135   something of use.
CREON: They were all killed save one. He fled in terror
           and he could tell us nothing in clear terms
           of what he knew, nothing, but one thing only.
OEDIPUS: What was it?
140   If we could even find a slim beginning
           in which to hope, we might discover much.
CREON: This man said that the robbers they encountered
           were many and the hands that did the murder
           were many; it was no man's single power.
OEDIPUS: How could a robber dare a deed like this
           were he not helped with money from the city,
           money and treachery?
CREON: That indeed was thought.
           But Laius was dead and in our trouble
           there was none to help.
OEDIPUS: What trouble was so great to hinder you
           inquiring out the murder of your king?
CREON: The riddling Sphinx induced us to neglect
           mysterious crimes and rather seek solution
           of troubles at our feet.

OEDIPUS: I will bring this to light again. King Phoebus
           fittingly took this care about the dead,
           and you too fittingly.
           And justly you will see in me an ally,
           a champion of my country and the God.
160   For when I drive pollution from the land
           I will not serve a distant friend's advantage,
           but act in my own interest. Whoever
           he was that killed the king may readily
           wish to dispatch me with his murderous hand;
165   so helping the dead king I help myself.

           Come, children, take your suppliant boughs and go;
           up from the altars now. Call the assembly
           and let it meet upon the understanding
           that I'll do everything. God will decide
170   whether we prosper or remain in sorrow.
PRIEST: Rise, children—it was this we came to seek,
           which of himself the king now offers us.
           May Phoebus who gave us the oracle
           come to our rescue and stay the plague.

           [*Exeunt all but the Chorus.*]

24

Strophe[4]

CHORUS: What is the sweet spoken word of God from the shrine of Pytho rich in gold
           that has come to glorious Thebes?
           I am stretched on the rack of doubt, and terror and trembling hold
           my heart, O Delian Healer, and I worship full of fears
           for what doom you will bring to pass, new or renewed in the revolving years.
180   Speak to me, immortal voice,
           child of golden Hope.

Antistrophe

           First I call on you, Athene, deathless daughter of Zeus,
           and Artemis, Earth Upholder,
           who sits in the midst of the market place in the throne which men call Fame,
185   and Phoebus, the Far Shooter, three averters of Fate,
           come to us now, if ever before, when ruin rushed upon the state,
           you drove destruction's flame away
           out of our land.

Strophe

           Our sorrows defy number;
190   all the ship's timbers are rotten;
           taking of thought is no spear for the driving away of the plague.

---

4. Strophe ("turn") and Antistrophe ("counterturn") refer to the moves the chorus would make, dancing as it sang.

There are no growing children in this famous land;
there are no women bearing the pangs of childbirth.
You may see them one with another, like birds swift on the wing,
195   quicker than fire unmastered,
speeding away to the coast of the Western God.[5]

Antistrophe

In the unnumbered deaths
of its people the city dies;
those children that are born lie dead on the naked earth
200   unpitied, spreading contagion of death; and grey haired mothers and wives
everywhere stand at the altar's edge, suppliant, moaning;
the hymn to the healing God rings out but with it the wailing voices are
    blended.
From these our sufferings grant us, O golden Daughter of Zeus,
glad-faced deliverance.

Strophe

205   There is no clash of brazen shields but our fight is with the War God,
a War God ringed with the cries of men, a savage God who burns us;
grant that he turn in racing course backwards out of our country's bounds
to the great palace of Amphitrite or where the waves of the Thracian sea
deny the stranger safe anchorage.
210   Whatsoever escapes the night
at last the light of day revisits;
so smite the War God, Father Zeus,
beneath your thunderbolt,
for you are the Lord of the lightning, the lightning that carries fire.

Antistrophe

215   And your unconquered arrow shafts, winged by the golden corded bow,
Lycean King, I beg to be at our side for help;
and the gleaming torches of Artemis with which she scours the Lycean hills,
and I call on the God with the turban of gold, who gave his name to this
    country of ours,
the Bacchic God with the wind flushed face,[6]
220   Evian One, who travel
with the Maenad company,
combat the God that burns us
with your torch of pine;
for the God that is our enemy is a God unhonoured among the Gods.

[*Oedipus returns.*]

OEDIPUS: For what you ask me—if you will hear my words,
and hearing welcome them and fight the plague,
you will find strength and lightening of your load.

---

5. Hades or death.
6. Dionysos, who traveled with frenzied female devotees, the Maenads.

Hark to me; what I say to you, I say
as one that is a stranger to the story
230 as stranger to the deed. For I would not
be far upon the track if I alone
were tracing it without a clue. But now,
since after all was finished, I became
a citizen among you, citizens—
235 now I proclaim to all the men of Thebes:
who so among you knows the murderer
by whose hand Laius, son of Labdacus,
died—I command him to tell everything
to me,—yes, though he fears himself to take the blame
240 on his own head; for bitter punishment
he shall have none, but leave this land unharmed.
Or if he knows the murderer, another,
a foreigner, still let him speak the truth.
For I will pay him and be grateful, too.
245 But if you shall keep silence, if perhaps
some one of you, to shield a guilty friend,
or for his own sake shall reject my words—
hear what I shall do then:
I forbid that man, whoever he be, my land,
250 my land where I hold sovereignty and throne;
and I forbid any to welcome him
or cry him greeting or make him a sharer
in sacrifice or offering to the Gods,
or give him water for his hands to wash.
255 I command all to drive him from their homes,
since he is our pollution, as the oracle
of Pytho's God proclaimed him now to me.
So I stand forth a champion of the God
and of the man who died.
260 Upon the murderer I invoke this curse—
whether he is one man and all unknown,
or one of many—may he wear out his life
in misery to miserable doom!
If with my knowledge he lives at my hearth
265 I pray that I myself may feel my curse.
On you I lay my charge to fulfill all this
for me, for the God, and for this land of ours
destroyed and blighted, by the God forsaken.

Even were this no matter of God's ordinance
270 it would not fit you so to leave it lie,
unpurified, since a good man is dead
and one that was a king. Search it out.
Since I am now the holder of his office,
and have his bed and wife that once was his,
275 and had his line not been unfortunate

we would have common children—[fortune leaped
upon his head]—because of all these things,
I fight in his defence as for my father,
and I shall try all means to take the murderer
280   of Laius the son of Labdacus
the son of Polydorus and before him
of Cadmus and before him of Agenor.
Those who do not obey me, may the Gods
grant no crops springing from the ground they plough
285   nor children to their women! May a fate
like this, or one still worse than this consume them!
For you whom these words please, the other Thebans,
may Justice as your ally and all the Gods
live with you, blessing you now and for ever!

CHORUS: As you have held me to my oath, I speak:
I neither killed the king nor can declare
the killer; but since Phoebus set the quest
it is his part to tell who the man is.

OEDIPUS: Right; but to put compulsion on the Gods
295   against their will—no man can do that.

CHORUS: May I then say what I think second best?

OEDIPUS: If there's a third best, too, spare not to tell it.

CHORUS: I know that what the Lord Teiresias
sees, is most often what the Lord Apollo
300   sees. If you should inquire of this from him
you might find out most clearly.

OEDIPUS: Even in this my actions have not been sluggard.
On Creon's word I have sent two messengers
and why the prophet is not here already
305   I have been wondering.

CHORUS: His skill apart
there is besides only an old faint story.

OEDIPUS: What is it?
I look at every story.

CHORUS: It was said
that he was killed by certain wayfarers.

OEDIPUS: I heard that, too, but no one saw the killer.

CHORUS: Yet if he has a share of fear at all,
his courage will not stand firm, hearing your curse.

OEDIPUS: The man who in the doing did not shrink
will fear no word.

CHORUS: Here comes his prosecutor:
315   led by your men the godly prophet comes
in whom alone of mankind truth is native.

[*Enter Teiresias, led by a little boy.*]

OEDIPUS: Teiresias, you are versed in everything,
things teachable and things not to be spoken,
things of the heaven and earth-creeping things.

320 You have no eyes but in your mind you know
with what a plague our city is afflicted.
My lord, in you alone we find a champion,
in you alone one that can rescue us.
Perhaps you have not heard the messengers,
325 but Phoebus sent in answer to our sending
an oracle declaring that our freedom
from this disease would only come when we
should learn the names of those who killed King Laius,
and kill them or expel from our country.
330 Do not begrudge us oracles from birds,
or any other way of prophecy
within your skill; save yourself and the city,
save me; redeem the debt of our pollution
that lies on us because of this dead man.
335 We are in your hands; pains are most nobly taken
to help another when you have means and power.
TEIRESIAS: Alas, how terrible is wisdom when
it brings no profit to the man that's wise!
This I knew well, but had forgotten it,
340 else I would not have come here.
OEDIPUS: What is this?
How sad you are now you have come!
TEIRESIAS: Let me
go home. It will be easiest for us both
to bear our several destinies to the end
if you will follow my advice.
OEDIPUS: You'd rob us
345 of this your gift of prophecy? You talk
as one who had no care for law nor love
for Thebes who reared you.
TEIRESIAS: Yes, but I see that even your own words
miss the mark; therefore I must fear for mine.
OEDIPUS: For God's sake if you know of anything,
do not turn from us; all of us kneel to you,
all of us here, your suppliants.
TEIRESIAS: All of you here know nothing. I will not
bring to the light of day my troubles, mine—
355 rather than call them yours.
OEDIPUS: What do you mean?
You know of something but refuse to speak.
Would you betray us and destroy the city?
TEIRESIAS: I will not bring this pain upon us both,
neither on you nor on myself. Why is it
360 you question me and waste your labour? I
will tell you nothing.
OEDIPUS: You would provoke a stone! Tell us, you villain,
tell us, and do not stand there quietly
unmoved and balking at the issue.

TEIRESIAS: You blame my temper but you do not see
           your own that lives within you; it is me
           you chide.
OEDIPUS: Who would not feel his temper rise
           at words like these with which you shame our city?
TEIRESIAS: Of themselves things will come, although I hide them
           and breathe no word of them.
OEDIPUS: Since they will come
           tell them to me.
TEIRESIAS: I will say nothing further.
           Against this answer let your temper rage
           as wildly as you will.
OEDIPUS: Indeed I am
375   so angry I shall not hold back a jot
           of what I think. For I would have you know
           I think you were complotter of the deed
           and doer of the deed save in so far
           as for the actual killing. Had you had eyes
380   I would have said alone you murdered him.
TEIRESIAS: Yes? Then I warn you faithfully to keep
           the letter of your proclamation and
           from this day forth to speak no word of greeting
           to these nor me; you are the land's pollution.
OEDIPUS: How shamelessly you started up this taunt!
           How do you think you will escape?
TEIRESIAS: I have.
           I have escaped; the truth is what I cherish
           and that's my strength.
OEDIPUS: And who has taught you truth?
           Not your profession surely!
TEIRESIAS: You have taught me,
390   for you have made me speak against my will.
OEDIPUS: Speak what? Tell me again that I may learn it better.
TEIRESIAS: Did you not understand before or would you
           provoke me into speaking?
OEDIPUS: I did not grasp it,
           not so to call it known. Say it again.
TEIRESIAS: I say you are the murderer of the king
           whose murderer you seek.
OEDIPUS: Not twice you shall
           say calumnies like this and stay unpunished.
TEIRESIAS: Shall I say more to tempt your anger more?
OEDIPUS: As much as you desire; it will be said
400   in vain.
TEIRESIAS: I say that with those you love best
           you live in foulest shame unconsciously
           and do not see where you are in calamity.
OEDIPUS: Do you imagine you can always talk
           like this, and live to laugh at it hereafter?

TEIRESIAS: Yes, if the truth has anything of strength.

OEDIPUS: It has, but not for you; it has no strength
for you because you are blind in mind and ears
as well as in your eyes.

TEIRESIAS: You are a poor wretch
to taunt me with the very insults which
410 every one soon will heap upon yourself.

OEDIPUS: Your life is one long night so that you cannot
hurt me or any other who sees the light.

TEIRESIAS: It is not fate that I should be your ruin,
Apollo is enough; it is his care
415 to work this out.

OEDIPUS: Was this your own design
or Creon's?

TEIRESIAS: Creon is no hurt to you,
but you are to yourself.

OEDIPUS: Wealth, sovereignty and skill outmatching skill
for the contrivance of an envied life!
420 Great store of jealousy fill your treasury chests,
if my friend Creon, friend from the first and loyal,
thus secretly attacks me, secretly
desires to drive me out and secretly
suborns this juggling, trick devising quack,
425 this wily beggar who has only eyes
for his own gains, but blindness in his skill.
For, tell me, where have you seen clear, Teiresias,
with your prophetic eyes? When the dark singer,
the sphinx, was in your country, did you speak
430 word of deliverance to its citizens?
And yet the riddle's answer was not the province
of a chance comer. It was a prophet's task
and plainly you had no such gift of prophecy
from birds nor otherwise from any God
435 to glean a word of knowledge. But I came,
Oedipus, who knew nothing, and I stopped her.
I solved the riddle by my wit alone.
Mine was no knowledge got from birds. And now
you would expel me,
440 because you think that you will find a place
by Creon's throne. I think you will be sorry,
both you and your accomplice, for your plot
to drive me out. And did I not regard you
as an old man, some suffering would have taught you
445 that what was in your heart was treason.

CHORUS: We look at this man's words and yours, my king,
and we find both have spoken them in anger.
We need no angry words but only thought
how we may best hit the God's meaning for us.

TEIRESIAS: If you are king, at least I have the right

no less to speak in my defence against you.
Of that much I am master. I am no slave
of yours, but Loxias',[7] and so I shall not
enroll myself with Creon for my patron.

455 Since you have taunted me with being blind,
here is my word for you.
You have your eyes but see not where you are
in sin, nor where you live, nor whom you live with.
Do you know who your parents are? Unknowing

460 you are an enemy to kith and kin
in death, beneath the earth, and in this life.
A deadly footed, double striking curse,
from father and mother both, shall drive you forth
out of this land, with darkness on your eyes,

465 that now have such straight vision. Shall there be
a place will not be harbour to your cries,
a corner of Cithaeron will not ring
in echo to your cries, soon, soon,—
when you shall learn the secret of your marriage,

470 which steered you to a haven in this house,—
haven no haven, after lucky voyage?
And of the multitude of other evils
establishing a grim equality
between you and your children, you know nothing.

475 So, muddy with contempt my words and Creon's!
Misery shall grind no man as it will you.

OEDIPUS: Is it endurable that I should hear
such words from him? Go and a curse go with you!
Quick, home with you! Out of my house at once!

TEIRESIAS: I would not have come either had you not called me.

OEDIPUS: I did not know then you would talk like a fool—
or it would have been long before I called you.

TEIRESIAS: I am a fool then, as it seems to you—
but to the parents who have bred you, wise.

OEDIPUS: What parents? Stop! Who are they of all the world?

TEIRESIAS: This day will show your birth and will destroy you.

OEDIPUS: How needlessly your riddles darken everything.

TEIRESIAS: But it's in riddle answering you are strongest.

OEDIPUS: Yes. Taunt me where you will find me great.

TEIRESIAS: It is this very luck that has destroyed you.

OEDIPUS: I do not care, if it has saved this city.

TEIRESIAS: Well, I will go. Come, boy, lead me away.

OEDIPUS: Yes, lead him off. So long as you are here,
you'll be a stumbling block and a vexation;

495 once gone, you will not trouble me again.

TEIRESIAS: I have said
what I came here to say not fearing your

7. Apollo's.

countenance: there is no way you can hurt me.
I tell you, king, this man, this murderer
(whom you have long declared you are in
    search of,
500   indicting him in threatening proclamation
as murderer of Laius)—he is here.
In name he is a stranger among citizens
but soon he will be shown to be a citizen
true native Theban, and he'll have no joy
505   of the discovery: blindness for sight
and beggary for riches his exchange,
he shall go journeying to a foreign country
tapping his way before him with a stick.
He shall be proved father and brother both
510   to his own children in his house; to her
that gave him birth, a son and husband both;
a fellow sower in his father's bed
with that same father that he murdered.
Go within, reckon that out, and if you find me
515   mistaken, say I have no skill in prophecy.

[*Exeunt separately Teiresias and Oedipus.*]

Strophe

CHORUS: Who is the man proclaimed
      by Delphi's prophetic rock
      as the bloody handed murderer,
      the doer of deeds that none dare name?
520   Now is the time for him to run
      with a stronger foot
      than Pegasus
      for the child of Zeus leaps in arms upon him
      with fire and the lightning bolt,
525   and terribly close on his heels
      are the Fates that never miss.

Antistrophe

Lately from snowy Parnassus
clearly the voice flashed forth,
bidding each Theban track him down,
530   the unknown murderer.
In the savage forests he lurks and in
the caverns like
the mountain bull.
He is sad and lonely, and lonely his feet
535   that carry him far from the navel of earth;
but its prophecies, ever living,
flutter around his head.

Strophe

The augur has spread confusion,
terrible confusion;
540   I do not approve what was said
nor can I deny it.
I do not know what to say;
I am in a flutter of foreboding;
I never heard in the present
545   nor past of a quarrel between
the sons of Labdacus and Polybus,
that I might bring as proof
in attacking the popular fame
of Oedipus, seeking
550   to take vengeance for undiscovered
death in the line of Labdacus.

Antistrophe

Truly Zeus and Apollo are wise
and in human things all knowing;
but amongst men there is no
555   distinct judgment, between the prophet
and me—which of us is right.
One man may pass another in wisdom
but I would never agree
with those that find fault with the king
560   till I should see the word
proved right beyond doubt. For once
in visible form the Sphinx
came on him and all of us
saw his wisdom and in that test
565   he saved the city. So he will not be condemned by my mind.

[*Enter Creon.*]

CREON: Citizens, I have come because I heard
deadly words spread about me, that the king
accuses me. I cannot take that from him.
If he believes that in these present troubles
570   he has been wronged by me in word or deed
I do not want to live on with the burden
of such a scandal on me. The report
injures me doubly and most vitally—
for I'll be called a traitor to my city
575   and traitor also to my friends and you.

CHORUS: Perhaps it was a sudden gust of anger
that forced that insult from him, and no judgment.

CREON: But did he say that it was in compliance
with schemes of mine that the seer told him lies?

CHORUS: Yes, he said that, but why, I do not know.

CREON: Were his eyes straight in his head? Was his mind right
          when he accused me in this fashion?

CHORUS: I do not know; I have no eyes to see
          what princes do. Here comes the king himself.

[*Enter Oedipus.*]

OEDIPUS: You, sir, how is it you come here? Have you so much
           brazen-faced daring that you venture in
           my house although you are proved manifestly
           the murderer of that man, and though you tried,
           openly, highway robbery of my crown?
590   For God's sake, tell me what you saw in me,
           what cowardice or what stupidity,
           that made you lay a plot like this against me?
           Did you imagine I should not observe
           the crafty scheme that stole upon me or
595   seeing it, take no means to counter it?
           Was it not stupid of you to make the attempt,
           to try to hunt down royal power without
           the people at your back or friends? For only
           with the people at your back or money can
600   the hunt end in the capture of a crown.

CREON: Do you know what you're doing? Will you listen
          to words to answer yours, and then pass judgment?

OEDIPUS: You're quick to speak, but I am slow to grasp you,
           for I have found you dangerous,—and my foe.

CREON: First of all hear what I shall say to that.

OEDIPUS: At least don't tell me that you are not guilty.

CREON: If you think obstinacy without wisdom
          a valuable possession, you are wrong.

OEDIPUS: And you are wrong if you believe that one,
610   a criminal, will not be punished only
           because he is my kinsman.

CREON: This is but just—
          but tell me, then, of what offense I'm guilty?

OEDIPUS: Did you or did you not urge me to send
           to this prophetic mumbler?

CREON: I did indeed,
615   and I shall stand by what I told you.

OEDIPUS: How long ago is it since Laius....

CREON: What about Laius? I don't understand.

OEDIPUS: Vanished—died—was murdered?

CREON: It is long,
          a long, long time to reckon.

OEDIPUS: Was this prophet
620   in the profession then?

CREON: He was, and honoured
          as highly as he is today.

OEDIPUS: At that time did he say a word about me?

CREON: Never, at least when I was near him.
OEDIPUS: You never made a search for the dead man?
CREON: We searched, indeed, but never learned of anything.
OEDIPUS: Why did our wise old friend not say this then?
CREON: I don't know; and when I know nothing, I
           usually hold my tongue.
OEDIPUS: You know this much,
           and can declare this much if you are loyal.
CREON: What is it? If I know, I'll not deny it.
OEDIPUS: That he would not have said that I killed Laius
           had he not met you first.
CREON: You know yourself
           whether he said this, but I demand that I
           should hear as much from you as you from me.
OEDIPUS: Then hear,—I'll not be proved a murderer.
CREON: Well, then. You're married to my sister.
OEDIPUS: Yes,
           that I am not disposed to deny.
CREON: You rule
           this country giving her an equal share
           in the government?
OEDIPUS: Yes, everything she wants
640   she has from me.
CREON: And I, as thirdsman to you,
           am rated as the equal of you two?
OEDIPUS: Yes, and it's there you've proved yourself false friend.
CREON: Not if you will reflect on it as I do.
           Consider, first, if you think anyone
645   would choose to rule and fear rather than rule
           and sleep untroubled by a fear if power
           were equal in both cases. I, at least,
           I was not born with such a frantic yearning
           to be a king—but to do what kings do.
650   And so it is with every one who has learned
           wisdom and self-control. As it stands now,
           the prizes are all mine—and without fear.
           But if I were the king myself, I must
           do much that went against the grain.
655   How should despotic rule seem sweeter to me
           than painless power and an assured authority?
           I am not so besotted yet that I
           want other honours than those that come with profit.
           Now every man's my pleasure; every man greets me;
660   now those who are your suitors fawn on me,—
           success for them depends upon my favour.
           Why should I let all this go to win that?
           My mind would not be traitor if it's wise;
           I am no treason lover, of my nature,
665   nor would I ever dare to join a plot.

Prove what I say. Go to the oracle
at Pytho and inquire about the answers,
if they are as I told you. For the rest,
if you discover I laid any plot
670 together with the seer, kill me, I say,
not only by your vote but by my own.
But do not charge me on obscure opinion
without some proof to back it. It's not just
lightly to count your knaves as honest men,
675 nor honest men as knaves. To throw away
an honest friend is, as it were, to throw
your life away, which a man loves the best.
In time you will know all with certainty;
time is the only test of honest men,
680 one day is space enough to know a rogue.
CHORUS: His words are wise, king, if one fears to fall.
Those who are quick of temper are not safe.
OEDIPUS: When he that plots against me secretly
moves quickly, I must quickly counterplot.
685 If I wait taking no decisive measure
his business will be done, and mine be spoiled.
CREON: What do you want to do then? Banish me?
OEDIPUS: No, certainly; kill you, not banish you.
CREON: I do not think that you've your wits about you.
OEDIPUS: For my own interests, yes.
CREON: But for mine, too,
you should think equally.
OEDIPUS: You are a rogue.
CREON: Suppose you do not understand?
OEDIPUS: But yet
I must be ruler.
CREON: Not if you rule badly.
OEDIPUS: O, city, city!
CREON: I too have some share
695 in the city; it is not yours alone.
CHORUS: Stop, my lords! Here—and in the nick of time
I see Jocasta coming from the house;
with her help lay the quarrel that now stirs you.

[*Enter Jocasta.*]

JOCASTA: For shame! Why have you raised this foolish squabbling
700 brawl? Are you not ashamed to air your private
griefs when the country's sick? Go in, you, Oedipus,
and you, too, Creon, into the house. Don't magnify
your nothing troubles.
CREON: Sister, Oedipus,
your husband, thinks he has the right to do
705 terrible wrongs—he has but to choose between
two terrors: banishing or killing me.

OEDIPUS: He's right, Jocasta; for I find him plotting
            with knavish tricks against my person.
CREON: That God may never bless me! May I die
710   accursed, if I have been guilty of
            one tittle of the charge you bring against me!
JOCASTA: I beg you, Oedipus, trust him in this,
            spare him for the sake of this his oath to God,
            for my sake, and the sake of those who stand here.
CHORUS: Be gracious, be merciful,
            we beg of you.
OEDIPUS: In what would you have me yield?
CHORUS: He has been no silly child in the past.
            He is strong in his oath now.
720   Spare him.
OEDIPUS: Do you know what you ask?
CHORUS: Yes.
OEDIPUS: Tell me then.
CHORUS: He has been your friend before all men's eyes; do not cast him
725   away dishonoured on an obscure conjecture.
OEDIPUS: I would have you know that this request of yours
            really requests my death or banishment.
CHORUS: May the Sun God, king of Gods, forbid! May I die without God's
            blessing, without friends' help, if I had any such thought. But my
730   spirit is broken by my unhappiness for my wasting country; and
            this would but add troubles amongst ourselves to the other troubles.
OEDIPUS: Well, let him go then—if I must die ten times for it,
            or be sent out dishonoured into exile.
            It is your lips that prayed for him I pitied,
735   not his; wherever he is, I shall hate him.
CREON: I see you sulk in yielding and you're dangerous
            when you are out of temper; natures like yours
            are justly heaviest for themselves to bear.
OEDIPUS: Leave me alone! Take yourself off, I tell you.
CREON: I'll go, you have not known me, but they have,
            and they have known my innocence.

            [Exit.]

CHORUS: Won't you take him inside, lady?
JOCASTA: Yes, when I've found out what was the matter.
CHORUS: There was some misconceived suspicion of a story, and on the other
            side the sting of injustice.
JOCASTA: So, on both sides?
CHORUS: Yes.
JOCASTA: What was the story?
CHORUS: I think it best, in the interests of the country, to leave it where
            it ended.

OEDIPUS: You see where you have ended, straight of judgment
        although you are, by softening my anger.
CHORUS: Sir, I have said before and I say again—be sure that I would have
        been proved a madman, bankrupt in sane council, if I should put
        you away, you who steered the country I love safely when she
        was crazed with troubles. God grant that now, too, you may
        prove a fortunate guide for us.
JOCASTA: Tell me, my lord, I beg of you, what was it
        that roused your anger so?
OEDIPUS: Yes, I will tell you.
760   I honour you more than I honour them.
        It was Creon and the plots he laid against me.
JOCASTA: Tell me—if you can clearly tell the quarrel—
OEDIPUS: Creon says
        that I'm the murderer of Laius.
JOCASTA: Of his own knowledge or on information?
OEDIPUS: He sent this rascal prophet to me, since
        he keeps his own mouth clean of any guilt.
JOCASTA: Do not concern yourself about this matter;
        listen to me and learn that human beings
        have no part in the craft of prophecy.
770   Of that I'll show you a short proof.
        There was an oracle once that came to Laius,—
        I will not say that it was Phoebus' own,
        but it was from his servants—and it told him
        that it was fate that he should die a victim
775   at the hands of his own son, a son to be born
        of Laius and me. But, see now, he,
        the king, was killed by foreign highway robbers
        at a place where three roads meet—so goes the story;
        and for the son—before three days were out
780   after his birth King Laius pierced his ankles
        and by the hands of others cast him forth
        upon a pathless hillside. So Apollo
        failed to fulfill his oracle to the son,
        that he should kill his father, and to Laius
785   also proved false in that the thing he feared,
        death at his son's hands, never came to pass.
        So clear in this case were the oracles,
        so clear and false. Give them no heed, I say;
        what God discovers need of, easily
790   he shows to us himself.
OEDIPUS: O dear Jocasta,
        as I hear this from you, there comes upon me
        a wandering of the soul—I could run mad.

JOCASTA:	What trouble is it, that you turn again
	and speak like this?
OEDIPUS:	I thought I heard you say
795	that Laius was killed at a crossroads.
JOCASTA:	Yes, that was how the story went and still
	that word goes round.
OEDIPUS:	Where is this place, Jocasta,
	where he was murdered?
JOCASTA:	Phocis is the country
	and the road splits there, one of two roads from Delphi,
800	another comes from Daulia.
OEDIPUS:	How long ago is this?
JOCASTA:	The news came to the city just before
	you became king and all men's eyes looked to you.
	What is it, Oedipus, that's in your mind?
OEDIPUS:	What have you designed, O Zeus, to do with me?
JOCASTA:	What is the thought that troubles your heart?
OEDIPUS:	Don't ask me yet—tell me of Laius—
	How did he look? How old or young was he?
JOCASTA:	He was a tall man and his hair was grizzled
	already—nearly white—and in his form
810	not unlike you.
OEDIPUS:	O God, I think I have
	called curses on myself in ignorance.
JOCASTA:	What do you mean? I am terrified
	when I look at you.
OEDIPUS:	I have a deadly fear
	that the old seer had eyes. You'll show me more
815	if you can tell me one more thing.
JOCASTA:	I will.
	I'm frightened,—but if I can understand,
	I'll tell you all you ask.
OEDIPUS:	How was his company?
	Had he few with him when he went this journey,
	or many servants, as would suit a prince?
JOCASTA:	In all there were but five, and among them
	a herald; and one carriage for the king.
OEDIPUS:	It's plain—it's plain—who was it told you this?
JOCASTA:	The only servant that escaped safe home.
OEDIPUS:	Is he at home now?
JOCASTA:	No, when he came home again
825	and saw you king and Laius was dead,
	he came to me and touched my hand and begged
	that I should send him to the fields to be
	my shepherd and so he might see the city
	as far off as he might. So I
830	sent him away. He was an honest man,
	as slaves go, and was worthy of far more
	than what he asked of me.

OEDIPUS: O, how I wish that he could come back quickly!

JOCASTA: He can. Why is your heart so set on this?

OEDIPUS: O dear Jocasta, I am full of fears
that I have spoken far too much; and therefore
I wish to see this shepherd.

JOCASTA: He will come;
but, Oedipus, I think I'm worthy too
to know what it is that disquiets you.

OEDIPUS: It shall not be kept from you, since my mind
has gone so far with its forebodings. Whom
should I confide in rather than you, who is there
of more importance to me who have passed
through such a fortune?

845   Polybus was my father, king of Corinth,
and Merope, the Dorian, my mother.
I was held greatest of the citizens
in Corinth till a curious chance befell me
as I shall tell you—curious, indeed,

850   but hardly worth the store I set upon it.
There was a dinner and at it a man,
a drunken man, accused me in his drink
of being bastard. I was furious
but held my temper under for that day.

855   Next day I went and taxed my parents with it;
they took the insult very ill from him,
the drunken fellow who had uttered it.
So I was comforted for their part, but
still this thing rankled always, for the story

860   crept about widely. And I went at last
to Pytho, though my parents did not know.
But Phoebus sent me home again unhonoured
in what I came to learn, but he foretold
other and desperate horrors to befall me,

865   that I was fated to lie with my mother,
and show to daylight an accursed breed
which men would not endure, and I was doomed
to be murderer of the father that begot me.
When I heard this I fled, and in the days

870   that followed I would measure from the stars
the whereabouts of Corinth—yes, I fled
to somewhere where I should not see fulfilled
the infamies told in that dreadful oracle.
And as I journeyed I came to the place

875   where, as you say, this king met with his death.
Jocasta, I will tell you the whole truth.
When I was near the branching of the crossroads,
going on foot, I was encountered by
a herald and a carriage with a man in it,

880   just as you tell me. He that led the way

and the old man himself wanted to thrust me
out of the road by force. I became angry
and struck the coachman who was pushing me.
When the old man saw this he watched his moment,
885 and as I passed he struck me from his carriage,
full on the head with his two pointed goad.
But he was paid in full and presently
my stick had struck him backwards from the car
and he rolled out of it. And then I killed them
890 all. If it happened there was any tie
of kinship twixt this man and Laius,
who is then now more miserable than I,
what man on earth so hated by the Gods,
since neither citizen nor foreigner
895 may welcome me at home or even greet me,
but drive me out of doors? And it is I,
I and no other have so cursed myself.
And I pollute the bed of him I killed
by the hands that killed him. Was I not born evil?
900 Am I not utterly unclean? I had to fly
and in my banishment not even see
my kindred nor set foot in my own country,
or otherwise my fate was to be yoked
in marriage with my mother and kill my father,
905 Polybus who begot me and had reared me.
Would not one rightly judge and say that on me
these things were sent by some malignant God?
O no, no, no—O holy majesty
of God on high, may I not see that day!
910 May I be gone out of men's sight before
I see the deadly taint of this disaster
come upon me.

CHORUS: Sir, we too fear these things. But until you see this man face to
     face and hear his story, hope.

OEDIPUS: Yes, I have just this much of hope—to wait until the herdsman comes.

JOCASTA: And when he comes, what do you want with him?

OEDIPUS: I'll tell you; if I find that his story is the same as yours, I at least
     will be clear of this guilt.

JOCASTA: Why, what so particularly did you learn from my story?

OEDIPUS: You said that he spoke of highway *robbers* who killed Laius. Now
     if he uses the same number, it was not I who killed him. One man
     cannot be the same as many. But if he speaks of a man travelling
     alone, then clearly the burden of the guilt inclines towards me.

JOCASTA: Be sure, at least, that this was how he told the story. He cannot
     unsay it now, for every one in the city heard it—not I alone. But,
     Oedipus, even if he diverges from what he said then, he shall
     never prove that the murder of Laius squares rightly with the
     prophecy—for Loxias declared that the king should be killed by

his own son. And that poor creature did not kill him surely,—
for he died himself first. So as far as prophecy goes, henceforward
I shall not look to the right hand or the left.

OEDIPUS: Right. But yet, send some one for the peasant to bring him here;
do not neglect it.

JOCASTA: I will send quickly. Now let me go indoors. I will do nothing
except what pleases you.

[*Exeunt.*]

Strophe

CHORUS: May destiny ever find me
pious in word and deed
prescribed by the laws that live on high:
940   laws begotten in the clear air of heaven,
whose only father is Olympus;[8]
no mortal nature brought them to birth,
no forgetfulness shall lull them to sleep;
for God is great in them and grows not old.

Antistrophe

945   Insolence breeds the tyrant, insolence
if it is glutted with a surfeit, unseasonable, unprofitable,
climbs to the roof-top and plunges
sheer down to the ruin that must be,
and there its feet are no service.
950   But I pray that the God may never
abolish the eager ambition that profits the state.
For I shall never cease to hold the God as our protector.

Strophe

If a man walks with haughtiness
of hand or word and gives no heed
955   to Justice and the shrines of Gods
despises—may an evil doom
smite him for his ill-starred pride of heart!—
if he reaps gains without justice
and will not hold from impiety
960   and his fingers itch for untouchable things.
When such things are done, what man shall contrive
to shield his soul from the shafts of the God?
When such deeds are held in honour,
why should I honour the Gods in the dance?

Antistrophe

965   No longer to the holy place,
to the navel of earth I'll go

8. Mountain throne of Zeus and home of the gods.

to worship, nor to Abae
nor to Olympia,
unless the oracles are proved to fit,
970   for all men's hands to point at.
O Zeus, if you are rightly called
the sovereign lord, all-mastering,
let this not escape you nor your ever-living power!
The oracles concerning Laius
975   are old and dim and men regard them not.
Apollo is nowhere clear in honour; God's service perishes.

[Enter Jocasta, carrying garlands.]

JOCASTA: Princes of the land, I have had the thought to go
to the Gods' temples, bringing in my hand
garlands and gifts of incense, as you see.
980   For Oedipus excites himself too much
at every sort of trouble, not conjecturing,
like a man of sense, what will be from what was,
but he is always at the speaker's mercy,
when he speaks terrors. I can do no good
985   by my advice, and so I came as suppliant
to you, Lycaean Apollo, who are nearest.
These are the symbols of my prayer and this
my prayer: grant us escape free of the curse.
Now when we look to him we are all afraid;
990   he's pilot of our ship and he is frightened.

[Enter Messenger.]

MESSENGER: Might I learn from you, sirs, where is the house of Oedipus?
Or best of all, if you know, where is the king himself?

CHORUS: This is his house and he is within doors. This lady is his wife and
mother of his children.

MESSENGER: God bless you, lady, and God bless your household! God bless
Oedipus' noble wife!

JOCASTA: God bless you, sir, for your kind greeting! What do you want
of us that you have come here? What have you to tell us?

MESSENGER: Good news, lady. Good for your house and for your husband.

JOCASTA: What is your news? Who sent you to us?

MESSENGER: I come from Corinth and the news I bring will give you pleasure.
Perhaps a little pain too.

JOCASTA: What is this news of double meaning?

MESSENGER: The people of the Isthmus will choose Oedipus to be their king.
1005   That is the rumour there.

JOCASTA: But isn't their king still old Polybus?

MESSENGER: No. He is in his grave. Death has got him.

JOCASTA: Is that the truth? Is Oedipus' father dead?

MESSENGER: May I die myself if it be otherwise!

JOCASTA *[to a servant]*:   Be quick and run to the King with the news! O oracles of the

Gods, where are you now? It was from this man Oedipus fled, lest
he should be his murderer! And now he is dead, in the course of
nature, and not killed by Oedipus.

[Enter Oedipus.]

OEDIPUS: Dearest Jocasta, why have you sent for me?

JOCASTA: Listen to this man and when you hear reflect what is the outcome
of the holy oracles of the Gods.

OEDIPUS: Who is he? What is his message for me?

JOCASTA: He is from Corinth and he tells us that your father Polybus is
dead and gone.

OEDIPUS: What's this you say, sir? Tell me yourself.

MESSENGER: Since this is the first matter you want clearly told: Polybus has
gone down to death. You may be sure of it.

OEDIPUS: By treachery or sickness?

MESSENGER: A small thing will put old bodies asleep.

OEDIPUS: So he died of sickness, it seems,—poor old man!

MESSENGER: Yes, and of age—the long years he had measured.

OEDIPUS: Ha! Ha! O dear Jocasta, why should one
look to the Pythian hearth? Why should one look
to the birds screaming overhead? They prophesied
1030   that I should kill my father! But he's dead,
and hidden deep in earth, and I stand here
who never laid a hand on spear against him,—
unless perhaps he died of longing for me,
and thus I am his murderer. But they,
1035   the oracles, as they stand—he's taken them
away with him, they're dead as he himself is,
and worthless.

JOCASTA: That I told you before now.

OEDIPUS: You did, but I was misled by my fear.

JOCASTA: Then lay no more of them to heart, not one.

OEDIPUS: But surely I must fear my mother's bed?

JOCASTA: Why should man fear since chance is all in all
for him, and he can clearly foreknow nothing?
Best to live lightly, as one can, unthinkingly.
As to your mother's marriage bed,—don't fear it.
1045   Before this, in dreams too, as well as oracles,
many a man has lain with his own mother.
But he to whom such things are nothing bears
his life most easily.

OEDIPUS: All that you say would be said perfectly
1050   if she were dead; but since she lives I must
still fear, although you talk so well, Jocasta.

JOCASTA: Still in your father's death there's light of comfort?

OEDIPUS: Great light of comfort; but I fear the living.

MESSENGER: Who is the woman that makes you afraid?

OEDIPUS: Merope, old man, Polybus' wife.

MESSENGER: What about her frightens the queen and you?

OEDIPUS: A terrible oracle, stranger, from the Gods.

MESSENGER: Can it be told? Or does the sacred law
        forbid another to have knowledge of it?

OEDIPUS: O no! Once on a time Loxias said
        that I should lie with my own mother and
        take on my hands the blood of my own father.
        And so for these long years I've lived away
        from Corinth; it has been to my great happiness;
1065   but yet it's sweet to see the face of parents.

MESSENGER: This was the fear which drove you out of Corinth?

OEDIPUS: Old man, I did not wish to kill my father.

MESSENGER: Why should I not free you from this fear, sir,
        since I have come to you in all goodwill?

OEDIPUS: You would not find me thankless if you did.

MESSENGER: Why, it was just for this I brought the news,—
        to earn your thanks when you had come safe home.

OEDIPUS: No, I will never come near my parents.

MESSENGER: Son,
        it's very plain you don't know what you're doing.

OEDIPUS: What do you mean, old man? For God's sake, tell me.

MESSENGER: If your homecoming is checked by fears like these.

OEDIPUS: Yes, I'm afraid that Phoebus may prove right.

MESSENGER: The murder and the incest?

OEDIPUS: Yes, old man;
        that is my constant terror.

MESSENGER: Do you know
1080   that all your fears are empty?

OEDIPUS: How is that,
        if they are father and mother and I their son?

MESSENGER: Because Polybus was no kin to you in blood.

OEDIPUS: What, was not Polybus my father?

MESSENGER: No more than I but just so much.

OEDIPUS: How can
1085   my father be my father as much as one
        that's nothing to me?

MESSENGER: Neither he nor I
        begat you.

OEDIPUS: Why then did he call me son?

MESSENGER: A gift he took you from these hands of mine.

OEDIPUS: Did he love so much what he took from another's hand?

MESSENGER: His childlessness before persuaded him.

OEDIPUS: Was I a child you bought or found when I
        was given to him?

MESSENGER: On Cithaeron's slopes
        in the twisting thickets you were found.

OEDIPUS: And why
        were you a traveller in those parts?

MESSENGER: I was

1095   in charge of mountain flocks.

OEDIPUS: You were a shepherd?
      A hireling vagrant?

MESSENGER: Yes, but at least at that time
      the man that saved your life, son.

OEDIPUS: What ailed me when you took me in your arms?

MESSENGER: In that your ankles should be witnesses.

OEDIPUS: Why do you speak of that old pain?

MESSENGER: I loosed you;
      the tendons of your feet were pierced and fettered,—

OEDIPUS: My swaddling clothes brought me a rare disgrace.

MESSENGER: So that from this you're called your present name.

OEDIPUS: Was this my father's doing or my mother's?
1105   For God's sake, tell me.

MESSENGER: I don't know, but he
      who gave you to me has more knowledge than I.

OEDIPUS: You yourself did not find me then? You took me
      from someone else?

MESSENGER: Yes, from another shepherd.

OEDIPUS: Who was he? Do you know him well enough
1110   to tell?

MESSENGER: He was called Laius' man.

OEDIPUS: You mean the king who reigned here in the old days?

MESSENGER: Yes, he was that man's shepherd.

OEDIPUS: Is he alive
      still, so that I could see him?

MESSENGER: You who live here
      would know that best.

OEDIPUS: Do any of you here
1115   know of this shepherd whom he speaks about
      in town or in the fields? Tell me. It's time
      that this was found out once for all.

CHORUS: I think he is none other than the peasant
      whom you have sought to see already; but
1120   Jocasta here can tell us best of that.

OEDIPUS: Jocasta, do you know about this man
      whom we have sent for? Is he the man he mentions?

JOCASTA: Why ask of whom he spoke? Don't give it heed;
      nor try to keep in mind what has been said.
1125   It will be wasted labour.

OEDIPUS: With such clues
      I could not fail to bring my birth to light.

JOCASTA: I beg you—do not hunt this out—I beg you,
      if you have any care for your own life.
      What I am suffering is enough.

OEDIPUS: Keep up
1130   your heart, Jocasta. Though I'm proved a slave,
      thrice slave, and though my mother is thrice slave,
      you'll not be shown to be of lowly lineage.

JOCASTA: O be persuaded by me, I entreat you;
      do not do this.
OEDIPUS: I will not be persuaded to let be
      the chance of finding out the whole thing clearly.
JOCASTA: It is because I wish you well that I
      give you this counsel—and it's the best counsel.
OEDIPUS: Then the best counsel vexes me, and has
1140   for some while since.
JOCASTA: O Oedipus, God help you!
      God keep you from the knowledge of who you are!
OEDIPUS: Here, some one, go and fetch the shepherd for me;
      and let her find her joy in her rich family!
JOCASTA: O Oedipus, unhappy Oedipus!
1145   that is all I can call you, and the last thing
      that I shall ever call you.

   [*Exit.*]

CHORUS: Why has the queen gone, Oedipus, in wild
      grief rushing from us? I am afraid that trouble
      will break out of this silence.
OEDIPUS: Break out what will! I at least shall be
      willing to see my ancestry, though humble.
      Perhaps she is ashamed of my low birth,
      for she has all a woman's high-flown pride.
      But I account myself a child of Fortune,
1155   beneficent Fortune, and I shall not be
      dishonoured. She's the mother from whom I spring;
      the months, my brothers, marked me, now as small,
      and now again as mighty. Such is my breeding,
      and I shall never prove so false to it,
1160   as not to find the secret of my birth.
CHORUS:

Strophe

      If I am a prophet and wise of heart
      you shall not fail, Cithaeron,
      by the limitless sky, you shall not!—
      to know at tomorrow's full moon
1165   that Oedipus honours you,
      as native to him and mother and nurse at once;
      and that you are honoured in dancing by us, as finding favour in
      sight of our king.
      Apollo, to whom we cry, find these things pleasing!

Antistrophe

1170   Who was it bore you, child? One of
      the long-lived nymphs who lay with Pan—
      the father who treads the hills?
      Or was she a bride of Loxias, your mother? The grassy slopes
      are all of them dear to him. Or perhaps Cyllene's king

1175   or the Bacchants' God that lives on the tops
         of the hills received you a gift from some
         one of the Helicon Nymphs, with whom he mostly plays?

[*Enter an old man, led by Oedipus' servants.*]

OEDIPUS: If some one like myself who never met him
         may make a guess,—I think this is the herdsman,
1180   whom we were seeking. His old age is consonant
         with the other. And besides, the men who bring him
         I recognize as my own servants. You
         perhaps may better me in knowledge since
         you've seen the man before.

CHORUS: You can be sure
1185   I recognize him. For if Laius
         had ever an honest shepherd, this was he.

OEDIPUS: You, sir, from Corinth, I must ask you first,
         is this the man you spoke of?

MESSENGER: This is he
         before your eyes.

OEDIPUS: Old man, look here at me
1190   and tell me what I ask you. Were you ever
         a servant of King Laius?

HERDSMAN: I was,—
         no slave he bought but reared in his own house.

OEDIPUS: What did you do as work? How did you live?

HERDSMAN: Most of my life was spent among the flocks.

OEDIPUS: In what part of the country did you live?

HERDSMAN: Cithaeron and the places near to it.

OEDIPUS: And somewhere there perhaps you knew this man?

HERDSMAN: What was his occupation? Who?

OEDIPUS: This man here,
         have you had any dealings with him?

HERDSMAN: No—
1200   not such that I can quickly call to mind.

MESSENGER: That is no wonder, master. But I'll make him remember what he
         does not know. For I know, that he well knows the country of
         Cithaeron, how he with two flocks, I with one kept company for
         three years—each year half a year—from spring till autumn time
1205   and then when winter came I drove my flocks to our fold home
         again and he to Laius' steadings. Well—am I right or not in what
         I said we did?

HERDSMAN: You're right—although it's a long time ago.

MESSENGER: Do you remember giving me a child
1210   to bring up as my foster child?

HERDSMAN: What's this?
         Why do you ask this question?

MESSENGER: Look old man,
         here he is—here's the man who was that child!

HERDSMAN: Death take you! Won't you hold your tongue?
OEDIPUS: No, no,
        do not find fault with him, old man. Your words
1215   are more at fault than his.
HERDSMAN: O best of masters,
        how do I give offense?
OEDIPUS: When you refuse
        to speak about the child of whom he asks you.
HERDSMAN: He speaks out of his ignorance, without meaning.
OEDIPUS: If you'll not talk to gratify me, you
1220   will talk with pain to urge you.
HERDSMAN: O please, sir,
        don't hurt an old man, sir.
OEDIPUS [*to the servants*]:   Here, one of you,
        twist his hands behind him.
HERDSMAN: Why, God help me, why?
        What do you want to know?
OEDIPUS: You gave a child
        to him,—the child he asked you of?
HERDSMAN: I did.
1225   I wish I'd died the day I did.
OEDIPUS: You will
        unless you tell me truly.
HERDSMAN: And I'll die
        far worse if I should tell you.
OEDIPUS: This fellow
        is bent on more delays, as it would seem.
HERDSMAN: O no, no! I have told you that I gave it.
OEDIPUS: Where did you get this child from? Was it your own or did you
        get it from another?
HERDSMAN: Not
        my own at all; I had it from some one.
OEDIPUS: One of these citizens? or from what house?
HERDSMAN: O master, please—I beg you, master, please
1235   don't ask me more.
OEDIPUS: You're a dead man if I
        ask you again.
HERDSMAN: It was one of the children
        of Laius.
OEDIPUS: A slave? Or born in wedlock?
HERDSMAN: O God, I am on the brink of frightful speech.
OEDIPUS: And I of frightful hearing. But I must hear.
HERDSMAN: The child was called his child; but she within,
        your wife would tell you best how all this was.
OEDIPUS: *She* gave it to you?
HERDSMAN: Yes, she did, my lord.
OEDIPUS: To do what with it?
HERDSMAN: Make away with it.

OEDIPUS: She was so hard—its mother?

HERDSMAN: Aye, through fear
1245   of evil oracles.

OEDIPUS: Which?

HERDSMAN: They said that he
          should kill his parents.

OEDIPUS: How was it that you
          gave it away to this old man?

HERDSMAN: O master,
          I pitied it, and thought that I could send it
          off to another country and this man
1250   was from another country. But he saved it
          for the most terrible troubles. If you are
          the man he says you are, you're bred
              to misery.

OEDIPUS: O, O, O, they will all come,
          all come out clearly! Light of the sun, let me
1255   look upon you no more after today!
          I who first saw the light bred of a match
          accursed, and accursed in my living
          with them I lived with, cursed in my killing.

[*Exeunt all but the Chorus.*]

CHORUS:

Strophe

          O generations of men, how I
1260   count you as equal with those who live
          not at all!
          What man, what man on earth wins more
          of happiness than a seeming
          and after that turning away?
1265   Oedipus, you are my pattern of this,
          Oedipus, you and your fate!
          Luckless Oedipus, whom of all men
          I envy not at all.

Antistrophe

          In as much as he shot his bolt
1270   beyond the others and won the prize
          of happiness complete—
          O Zeus—and killed and reduced to nought
          the hooked taloned maid of the riddling speech,
          standing a tower against death for my land:
1275   hence he was called my king and hence
          was honoured the highest of all
          honours; and hence he ruled
          in the great city of Thebes.

But now whose tale is more miserable?
1280 Who is there lives with a savager fate?
Whose troubles so reverse his life as his?

O Oedipus, the famous prince
for whom a great haven
the same both as father and son
1285 sufficed for generation,
how, O how, have the furrows ploughed
by your father endured to bear you, poor wretch,
and hold their peace so long?

Antistrophe

Time who sees all has found you out
1290 against your will; judges your marriage accursed,
begetter and begot at one in it.

O child of Laius,
would I had never seen you.
I weep for you and cry
1295 a dirge of lamentation.

To speak directly, I drew my breath
from you at the first and so now I lull
my mouth to sleep with your name.

[*Enter a second messenger.*]

SECOND MESSENGER: O Princes always honoured by our country,
1300 what deeds you'll hear of and what horrors see,
what grief you'll feel, if you as true born Thebans
care for the house of Labdacus's sons.
Phasis nor Ister cannot purge this house,
I think, with all their streams, such things
1305 it hides, such evils shortly will bring forth
into the light, whether they will or not;
and troubles hurt the most
when they prove self-inflicted.

CHORUS: What we had known before did not fall short
1310 of bitter groaning's worth; what's more to tell?

SECOND MESSENGER: Shortest to hear and tell—our glorious queen
Jocasta's dead.

CHORUS: Unhappy woman! How?

SECOND MESSENGER: By her own hand. The worst of what was done
you cannot know. You did not see the sight.
1315 Yet in so far as I remember it
you'll hear the end of our unlucky queen.
When she came raging into the house she went
straight to her marriage bed, tearing her hair
with both her hands, and crying upon Laius

1320 long dead—Do you remember, Laius,
that night long past which bred a child for us
to send you to your death and leave
a mother making children with her son?
And then she groaned and cursed the bed in which
1325 she brought forth husband by her husband, children
by her own child, an infamous double bond.
How after that she died I do not know,—
for Oedipus distracted us from seeing.
He burst upon us shouting and we looked
1330 to him as he paced frantically around,
begging us always: Give me a sword, I say,
to find this wife no wife, this mother's womb,
this field of double sowing whence I sprang
and where I sowed my children! As he raved
1335 some god showed him the way—none of us there.
Bellowing terribly and led by some
invisible guide he rushed on the two doors,—
wrenching the hollow bolts out of their sockets,
he charged inside. There, there, we saw his wife
1340 hanging, the twisted rope around her neck.
When he saw her, he cried out fearfully
and cut the dangling noose. Then, as she lay,
poor woman, on the ground, what happened after,
was terrible to see. He tore the brooches—
1345 the gold chased brooches fastening her robe—
away from her and lifting them up high
dashed them on his own eyeballs, shrieking out
such things as: they will never see the crime
I have committed or had done upon me!
1350 Dark eyes, now in the days to come look on
forbidden faces, do not recognize
those whom you long for—with such imprecations
he struck his eyes again and yet again
with the brooches. And the bleeding eyeballs gushed
1355 and stained his beard—no sluggish oozing drops
but a black rain and bloody hail poured down.

So it has broken—and not on one head
but troubles mixed for husband and for wife.
The fortune of the days gone by was true
1360 good fortune—but today groans and destruction
and death and shame—of all ills can be named
not one is missing.
CHORUS: Is he now in any ease from pain?
SECOND MESSENGER: He shouts
for some one to unbar the doors and show him
1365 to all the men of Thebes, his father's killer,
his mother's—no I cannot say the word,

it is unholy—for he'll cast himself,
out of the land, he says, and not remain
to bring a curse upon his house, the curse
1370   he called upon it in his proclamation. But
he wants for strength, aye, and some one to guide him;
his sickness is too great to bear. You, too,
will be shown that. The bolts are opening.
Soon you will see a sight to waken pity
1375   even in the horror of it.

[*Enter the blinded Oedipus.*]

CHORUS: This is a terrible sight for men to see!
        I never found a worse!
        Poor wretch, what madness came upon you!
        What evil spirit leaped upon your life
1380   to your ill-luck—a leap beyond man's strength!
        Indeed I pity you, but I cannot
        look at you, though there's much I want to ask
        and much to learn and much to see.
        I shudder at the sight of you.
OEDIPUS: O, O,
        where am I going? Where is my voice
        borne on the wind to and fro?
        Spirit, how far have you sprung?
CHORUS: To a terrible place whereof men's ears
1390   may not hear, nor their eyes behold it.
OEDIPUS: Darkness!
        Horror of darkness enfolding, resistless, unspeakable visitant
          sped by an ill wind in haste!
        madness and stabbing pain and memory
        of evil deeds I have done!
CHORUS: In such misfortunes it's no wonder
        if double weighs the burden of your grief.
OEDIPUS: My friend,
        you are the only one steadfast, the only one that attends on me;
        you still stay nursing the blind man.
1400   Your care is not unnoticed. I can know
        your voice, although this darkness is my world.
CHORUS: Doer of dreadful deeds, how did you dare
        so far to do despite to your own eyes?
        what spirit urged you to it?
OEDIPUS: It was Apollo, friends, Apollo,
        that brought this bitter bitterness, my sorrows to completion.
        But the hand that struck me
        was none but my own.
        Why should I see
1410   whose vision showed me nothing sweet to see?
CHORUS: These things are as you say.

OEDIPUS: What can I see to love?
            What greeting can touch my ears with joy?
            Take me away, and haste—to a place out of the way!
1415   Take me away, my friends, the greatly miserable,
            the most accursed, whom God too hates
            above all men on earth!
CHORUS: Unhappy in your mind and your misfortune,
            would I had never known you!
OEDIPUS: Curse on the man who took
            the cruel bonds from off my legs, as I lay in the field.
            He stole me from death and saved me,
            no kindly service.
            Had I died then
1425   I would not be so burdensome to friends.
CHORUS: I, too, could have wished it had been so.
OEDIPUS: Then I would not have come
            to kill my father and marry my mother infamously.
            Now I am godless and child of impurity,
1430   begetter in the same seed that created my wretched self.
            If there is any ill worse than ill,
            that is the lot of Oedipus.
CHORUS: I cannot say your remedy was good;
            you would be better dead than blind and living.
OEDIPUS: What I have done here was best done—don't tell me
            otherwise, do not give me further counsel.
            I do not know with what eyes I could look
            upon my father when I die and go
            under the earth, nor yet my wretched mother—
1440   those two to whom I have done things deserving
            worse punishment than hanging. Would the sight
            of children, bred as mine are, gladden me?
            No, not these eyes, never. And my city,
            its towers and sacred places of the Gods,
1445   of these I robbed my miserable self
            when I commanded all to drive *him* out,
            the criminal since proved by God impure
            and of the race of Laius.
            To this guilt I bore witness against myself—
1450   with what eyes shall I look upon my people?
            No. If there were a means to choke the fountain
            of hearing I would not have stayed my hand
            from locking up my miserable carcase,
            seeing and hearing nothing; it is sweet
1455   to keep our thoughts out of the range of hurt.

            Cithaeron, why did you receive me? Why
            having received me did you not kill me straight?
            And so I had not shown to men my birth.

            O Polybus and Corinth and the house,

1460 the old house that I used to call my father's—
what fairness you were nurse to, and what foulness
festered beneath! Now I am found to be
a sinner and a son of sinners. Crossroads,
and hidden glade, oak and the narrow way
1465 at the crossroads, that drank my father's blood
offered you by my hands, do you remember
still what I did as you looked on, and what
I did when I came here? O marriage, marriage!
you bred me and again when you had bred
1470 bred children of your child and showed to men
brides, wives and mothers and the foulest deeds
that can be in this world of ours.

Come—it's unfit to say what is unfit
to do.—I beg of you in God's name hide me
1475 somewhere outside your country, yes, or kill me,
or throw me into the sea, to be forever
out of your sight. Approach and deign to touch me
for all my wretchedness, and do not fear.
No man but I can bear my evil doom.

CHORUS: Here Creon comes in fit time to perform
or give advice in what you ask of us.
Creon is left sole ruler in your stead.

OEDIPUS: Creon! Creon! What shall I say to him?
How can I justly hope that he will trust me?
1485 In what is past I have been proved towards him
an utter liar.

[*Enter Creon.*]

CREON: Oedipus, I've come
not so that I might laugh at you nor taunt you
with evil of the past. But if you still
are without shame before the face of men
1490 reverence at least the flame that gives all life,
our Lord the Sun, and do not show unveiled
to him pollution such that neither land
nor holy rain nor light of day can welcome.

[*To a servant.*]

Be quick and take him in. It is most decent
1495 that only kin should see and hear the troubles
of kin.

OEDIPUS: I beg you, since you've torn me from
my dreadful expectations and have come
in a most noble spirit to a man
that has used you vilely—do a thing for me.
1500 I shall speak for your own good, not for my own.

CREON: What do you need that you would ask of me?

OEDIPUS: Drive me from here with all the speed you can

to where I may not hear a human voice.

CREON: Be sure, I would have done this had not I
1505   wished first of all to learn from the God the course
     of action I should follow.

OEDIPUS: But his word
     has been quite clear to let the parricide,
     the sinner, die.

CREON: Yes, that indeed was said.
     But in the present need we had best discover
1510   what we should do.

OEDIPUS: And will you ask about
     a man so wretched?

CREON: Now even you will trust
     the God.

OEDIPUS: So. I command you—and will beseech you—
     to her that lies inside that house give burial
     as you would have it; she is yours and rightly
1515   you will perform the rites for her. For me—
     never let this my father's city have me
     living a dweller in it. Leave me live
     in the mountains where Cithaeron is, that's called
     my mountain, which my mother and my father
1520   while they were living would have made my tomb.
     So I may die by their decree who sought
     indeed to kill me. Yet I know this much:
     no sickness and no other thing will kill me.
     I would not have been saved from death if not
1525   for some strange evil fate. Well, let my fate
     go where it will.
                  Creon, you need not care
     about my sons; they're men and so wherever
     they are, they will not lack a livelihood.
     But my two girls—so sad and pitiful—
1530   whose table never stood apart from mine,
     and everything I touched they always shared—
     O Creon, have a thought for them! And most
     I wish that you might suffer me to touch them
     and sorrow with them.

    [*Enter Antigone and Ismene, Oedipus' two daughters.*]

1535   O my lord! O true noble Creon! Can I
     really be touching them, as when I saw?
     What shall I say?
     Yes, I can hear them sobbing—my two darlings!
     and Creon has had pity and has sent me
1540   what I loved most?
     Am I right?

CREON: You're right: it was I gave you this
     because I knew from old days how you loved them
     as I see now.

OEDIPUS: God bless you for it, Creon,
1545   and may God guard you better on your road
        than he did me!
                        O children,
        where are you? Come here, come to my hands,
        a brother's hands which turned your father's eyes,
        those bright eyes you knew once, to what you see,
1550   a father seeing nothing, knowing nothing,
        begetting you from his own source of life.
        I weep for you—I cannot see your faces—
        I weep when I think of the bitterness
        there will be in your lives, how you must live
1555   before the world. At what assemblages
        of citizens will you make one? to what
        gay company will you go and not come home
        in tears instead of sharing in the holiday?
        And when you're ripe for marriage, who will he be,
1560   the man who'll risk to take such infamy
        as shall cling to my children, to bring hurt
        on them and those that marry with them? What
        curse is not there? "Your father killed his father
        and sowed the seed where he had sprung himself
1565   and begot you out of the womb that held him."
        These insults you will hear. Then who will marry you?
        No one, my children; clearly you are doomed
        to waste away in barrenness unmarried.
        Son of Menoeceus, since you are all the father
1570   left these two girls, and we, their parents, both
        are dead to them—do not allow them wander
        like beggars, poor and husbandless.
        They are of your own blood.
        And do not make them equal with myself
1575   in wretchedness; for you can see them now
        so young, so utterly alone, save for you only.
        Touch my hand, noble Creon, and say yes.
        If you were older, children, and were wiser,
        there's much advice I'd give you. But as it is,
1580   let this be what you pray: give me a life
        wherever there is opportunity
        to live, and better life than was my father's.
CREON: Your tears have had enough of scope; now go within the house.
OEDIPUS: I must obey, though bitter of heart.
CREON: In season, all is good.
OEDIPUS: Do you know on what conditions I obey?
CREON: You tell me them,
        and I shall know them when I hear.
OEDIPUS: That you shall send me out
        to live away from Thebes.
CREON: That gift you must ask of the God.

OEDIPUS:	But I'm now hated by the Gods.
CREON:	So quickly you'll obtain your prayer.
OEDIPUS:	You consent then?
CREON:	What I do not mean, I do not use to say.
OEDIPUS:	Now lead me away from here.
CREON:	Let go the children, then, and come.
OEDIPUS:	Do not take them from me.
CREON:	Do not seek to be master in everything,

for the things you mastered did not follow you throughout your life.

[*As Creon and Oedipus go out.*]

CHORUS: You that live in my ancestral Thebes, behold this Oedipus,—
1595   him who knew the famous riddles and was a man most masterful;
       not a citizen who did not look with envy on his lot—
       see him now and see the breakers of misfortune swallow him!
       Look upon that last day always. Count no mortal happy till
       he has passed the final limit of his life secure from pain.

EURIPIDES ■ (C. 480–405 B.C.E.)

The Greeks found Euripides peculiar. His tragedies featured talking slaves, extravagantly demonstrative women, and rhetorical excesses previously unheard in the works of his predecessors. He was said to be the son of a lettuce monger, to compose his tragedies in isolation in a cave, and even to own a library full of books, a great oddity in a world of limited literacy. In the drama contests organized by the city to honor the god Dionysos, in which Euripides's plays were performed, he often lost. Yet we have more of his tragedies than of any other Greek playwright, nineteen of the ninety he wrote.

In his tragedies, Euripides represents a complex mixture of the ordinary, the everyday, and the radically deviant, calling attention to the deep strangeness of tragedy, a genre that crosses the world of heroic legend with the daily life of the citizen audience. Maidservants scheme calmly about adultery. The deposed queen of Troy, Hecuba, who after the city's fall is a slave, murders her enemy's children; it is predicted in the tragedy named for her that she will end her life changed to a dog, "a bitch with blazing eyes."

Euripides's gods exhibit cruelty and petty selfishness and torment human beings for their own amusement. The goddesses Artemis and Aphrodite fight over the sexual fate of the chaste misogynist Hippolytus, entangled in the desire of his stepmother, Phaedra; accused of seduction, he dies a battered wreck in the arms of his father. The god Dionysos, in the *Bacchae,* seduces Thebes's king, Pentheus, into dressing as a woman so that he can spy on the maenads, the maddened women worshipers of the god. Dionysos provokes his devotees, including Pentheus's own mother, into a frenzy in which the king is torn to pieces, his head brought home as a trophy by his mother; in a devastating recognition scene, she slowly realizes what she carries.

Euripides takes seriously the human status of women, children, slaves, barbarians, foreigners, and prisoners of war and gives them voices in his tragedies, decentering the focus on the free Greek male citizen typical of the ancient city. He demonstrates a special fascination for women, their psychology, their motivations, and their fates. Several of his tragedies focus on idealistic young women who choose to sacrifice themselves for their idealism and are exploited by older characters of great cynicism; Iphigeneia, for example,

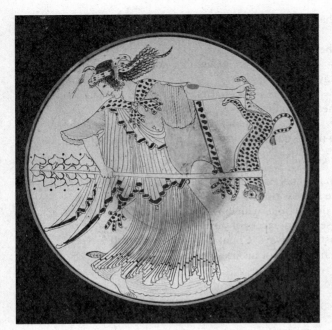

The Maenad cup by the Brygos Painter, mid-first millennium B.C.E. The maenad carries her thyrsus (a staff crowned with pine cones, symbol of Dionysos) and a small leopard she has just slain, probably to make another fur stole like the one she wears around her neck, identifying with the leopard's wild, foreign power.

dies at the hands of her father, Agamemnon, who sacrifices her so that the Greek fleet can sail to Troy from Aulis, where the fleet has been stalled for an offense committed against the goddess Artemis. In *Alcestis,* a husband allows his wife to die in his place and then, immediately after promising never to replace her, receives into his household what he believes to be another woman. In other plays, the choruses are made up of enslaved women who lament their losses of loved ones and of freedom, as in *The Trojan Women:*

> Beside their altars the Trojans
> died in their blood. Desolate now,
> men murdered, our sleeping rooms gave up
> their brides' beauty
> to breed sons for Greek men,
> sorrow for our own country.

Such lines speak to the audience of slaveholders and touch on both their status as the possessors of other human beings and their vulnerability to enslavement themselves, in a world of war where the killing of men and the enslaving of women in conquered cities was often a matter of course. It may be that radical thinkers of this period were questioning whether slaves were slaves "by nature." In one dramatic scene in the *Ion,* a slave pronounces what may have seemed to some like a heretical idea: "A slave bears only this/ Disgrace: the name. In every other way/An honest slave is equal to the free." Euripides returns several times to the aftermath of the fall of Troy, the paradigmatic city whose conquest stood for the loss of civilization itself. Rather than showing the scenes of warriors in the long battle that preceded the Greeks' victory, he concentrates on the Trojan victims, the humiliation and sexual slavery of the former free inhabitants, royal princesses taken to the lands of their conquerors and forced into new masters' beds.

In his own time Euripides was the object of mockery for his questioning of the status quo and for his peculiarities. The comic playwright Aristophanes ridicules him frequently, presenting in *The Women at the Thesmophoria* the case that the women of the city are furious at Euripides for his misogyny and want to destroy him. In his play *The Frogs,* first performed in 405 B.C.E., Aristophanes sends the god Dionysos, portrayed as a coward and a fool, and his slave Xanthias into the underworld to bring the recently deceased Euripides back from the dead. The comedy engages in a merciless and hilarious attack on Euripides, who is seen ultimately, after a drama contest between him and Aeschylus, as precisely not what the world above needs.

Euripides's plays call into question the heroism of traditional heroes such as Jason, husband of Medea, or Admetus, Alcestis' mate. They expose the all-too-human motives of the gods. They deploy the highly wrought argumentation of the contemporary rhetoricians and the sophists. They put into play new forms of music and almost operatic lyricism. The plays partake of the critical, questioning spirit of the later fifth century B.C.E., a world of exhausting war, with the Athenian democracy rocked by power struggles between manipulative orators, soon to be overwhelmed in defeat by the Spartans and their allies. The intellectual climate favored questioning everything—received ideas about the gods, forms of government and political hierarchies, the divine or noble origin of the Athenians, differences among Greeks and between Greeks and barbarians, the ambiguous power of rhetorical speech, the nature of slavery, and gender roles and relations. And Euripides, without committing himself definitively, presents the contradictory difficulties for his audiences.

One of the plays that most dramatically embodies these contradictions, *The Medea,* was produced in 431 B.C.E., at the time when the Peloponnesian War between the Athenians and the Spartans began and when the Athenians suffered a devastating plague that eventually carried off the great statesman Perikles. The play shares many of the concerns of other Euripidean dramas: a focus on women, with a servant taking an important role; rhetoric influenced by philosophical developments of the latter half of the fifth century; a questioning of traditional morality; and a central role for an outsider, in this case a barbarian woman, Medea, brought into the heart of Greece by her husband, Jason. The play fastens on her difference—her exotic origins and her history as a sorceress, her murder of her own brother and the fatal boiling of an old man in a fake effort of rejuvenation. It places this barbarian witch in the heart of the household and gives her a speech in which she laments the fate of the Greek woman. She stands apart by virtue of her foreign birth, yet expresses the common dismay of a wife whose man can seek comfort elsewhere while she is confined to the house. Medea says she would prefer military combat to childbirth.

Greek brides, often half the age of husbands they had barely met by their wedding day, were taken from their fathers' houses and moved into the houses of their husbands' fathers as strangers in the midst of an unfamiliar domestic life. Like the mythical women warriors called the Amazons, or the women of the island of Lemnos, who killed their husbands and administered their island themselves, Medea represents the danger at the center of the Greek household, the female brought inside, a potential source of discontent and even violence. Euripides shows Medea first as dangerously jealous, then scheming, and then violent, vengeful, and destructive, escaping from the city of Corinth only to flee to Athens, to the site of the play's first performance. Euripides cunningly twists his portrait of Medea in the course of the play. She may begin as an object of sympathy, suffering like any wife at the prospect of her husband's new alliance. As the play continues, her bestial, barbaric nature comes into the foreground, and she becomes an exemplar of the ruthless, violent, and strange. Her extreme violence may exceed the incipient sympathy of the audience and send it away from the theater in horror and revulsion. Some scholars see Euripides representing Medea throughout as the object of sympathy and identification; others argue, however, that Euripides seems to understand her, along with other women, as vulnerable,

as the canary in the mine, liable to break down in situations of extremity and, victims
themselves, to turn toward acts of passionate despair and hatred that bring down the world.

PRONUNCIATIONS:

    Aegeus: ay-GEE-us
    Euripides: you-RIP-pid-eez
    Medea: meh-DEE-ah

The Medea[1]

Characters

MEDEA, *princess of Colchis and wife of Jason*
JASON, *son of Aeson, king of Iolcus*
TWO CHILDREN OF MEDEA AND JASON
CREON, *king of Corinth*
AEGEUS, *king of Athens*
NURSE TO MEDEA
TUTOR TO MEDEA'S CHILDREN
MESSENGER
CHORUS OF CORINTHIAN WOMEN

In front of Medea's house in Corinth. Enter from the house Medea's nurse.

NURSE:	How I wish the Argo[2] never had reached the land
	Of Colchis,[3] skimming through the blue Symplegades,[4]
	Nor ever had fallen in the glades of Pelion
	The smitten fir-tree to furnish oars for the hands
5	Of heroes who in Pelias' name attempted
	The Golden Fleece! For then my mistress Medea
	Would not have sailed for the towers of the land of Iolcus,[5]
	Her heart on fire with passionate love for Jason;
	Nor would she have persuaded the daughters of Pelias
10	To kill their father, and now be living here
	In Corinth with her husband and children. She gave
	Pleasure to the people of her land of exile,
	And she herself helped Jason in every way.
	This is indeed the greatest salvation of all—
15	For the wife not to stand apart from the husband.
	But now there's hatred everywhere, Love is diseased.
	For, deserting his own children and my mistress,
	Jason has taken a royal wife to his bed,
	The daughter of the ruler of this land, Creon.
20	And poor Medea is slighted, and cries aloud on the
	Vows they made to each other, the right hands clasped
	In eternal promise. She calls upon the gods to witness

1. Translated by Rex Warner.
2. Ship of Jason and the Argonauts.
3. On the east coast of the Black Sea.
4. The "Clashing Rocks" at the entrance to the Black Sea.
5. In northern Greece.

What sort of return Jason has made to her love.
She lies without food and gives herself up to suffering,
25 Wasting away every moment of the day in tears.
So it has gone since she knew herself slighted by him.
Not stirring an eye, not moving her face from the ground,
No more than either a rock or surging sea water
She listens when she is given friendly advice.
30 Except that sometimes she twists back her white neck and
Moans to herself, calling out on her father's name,
And her land, and her home betrayed when she came away with
A man who now is determined to dishonor her.
Poor creature, she has discovered by her sufferings
35 What it means to one not to have lost one's own country.
She has turned from the children and does not like to see them.
I am afraid she may think of some dreadful thing,
For her heart is violent. She will never put up with
The treatment she is getting. I know and fear her
40 Lest she may sharpen a sword and thrust to the heart,
Stealing into the palace where the bed is made,
Or even kill the king and the new-wedded groom,
And thus bring a greater misfortune on herself.
She's a strange woman. I know it won't be easy
45 To make an enemy of her and come off best.
But here the children come. They have finished playing.
They have no thought at all of their mother's trouble.
Indeed it is not usual for the young to grieve.

[*Enter from the right the slave who is the tutor to Medea's two small children.
The children follow him.*]

TUTOR: You old retainer of my mistress' household,
50 Why are you standing here all alone in front of the
Gates and moaning to yourself over your misfortune?
Medea could not wish you to leave her alone.

NURSE: Old man, and guardian of the children of Jason,
If one is a good servant, it's a terrible thing
55 When one's master's luck is out; it goes to one's heart.
So I myself have got into such a state of grief
That a longing stole over me to come outside here
And tell the earth and air of my mistress' sorrows.

TUTOR: Has the poor lady not yet given up her crying?

NURSE: Given up? She's at the start, not halfway through her tears.

TUTOR: Poor fool—if I may call my mistress such a name—
How ignorant she is of trouble more to come.

NURSE: What do you mean, old man? You needn't fear to speak.

TUTOR: Nothing. I take back the words which I used just now.

NURSE: Don't, by your beard, hide this from me, your fellow-servant.
If need be, I'll keep quiet about what you tell me.

TUTOR: I heard a person saying, while I myself seemed
Not to be paying attention, when I was at the place

Where the old draught-players sit, by the holy fountain,
70 That Creon, ruler of the land, intends to drive
These children and their mother in exile from Corinth.
But whether what he said is really true or not
I do not know. I pray that it may not be true.

NURSE: And will Jason put up with it that his children
75 Should suffer so, though he's no friend to their mother?

TUTOR: Old ties give place to new ones. As for Jason, he
No longer has a feeling for this house of ours.

NURSE: It's black indeed for us, when we add new to old
Sorrows before even the present sky has cleared.

TUTOR: But you be silent, and keep all this to yourself.
It is not the right time to tell our mistress of it.

NURSE: Do you hear, children, what a father he is to you?
I wish he were dead—but no, he is still my master.
Yet certainly he has proved unkind to his dear ones.

TUTOR: What's strange in that? Have you only just discovered
That everyone loves himself more than his neighbor?
Some have good reason, others get something out of it.
So Jason neglects his children for the new bride.

NURSE: Go indoors, children. That will be the best thing.
90 And you, keep them to themselves as much as possible.
Don't bring them near their mother in her angry mood.
For I've seen her already blazing her eyes at them
As though she meant some mischief and I am sure that
She'll not stop raging until she has struck at someone.
95 May it be an enemy and not a friend she hurts!

[*Medea is heard inside the house.*]

MEDEA: Ah, wretch! Ah, lost in my sufferings,
I wish, I wish I might die.

NURSE: What did I say, dear children? Your mother
Frets her heart and frets it to anger.
100 Run away quickly into the house,
And keep well out of her sight.
Don't go anywhere near, but be careful
Of the wildness and bitter nature
Of that proud mind.
105 Go now! Run quickly indoors.
It is clear that she soon will put lightning
In that cloud of her cries that is rising
With a passion increasing. O, what will she do,
Proud-hearted and not to be checked on her course,
110 A soul bitten into with wrong?

[*The Tutor takes the children into the house.*]

MEDEA: Ah, I have suffered
What should be wept for bitterly. I hate you,

Children of a hateful mother. I curse you
And your father. Let the whole house crash.
NURSE: Ah, I pity you, you poor creature.
How can your children share in their father's
Wickedness? Why do you hate them? Oh children,
How much I fear that something may happen!
Great people's tempers are terrible, always
120   Having their own way, seldom checked,
Dangerous they shift from mood to mood.
How much better to have been accustomed
To live on equal terms with one's neighbors.
I would like to be safe and grow old in a
125   Humble way. What is moderate sounds best,
Also in practice *is* best for everyone.
Greatness brings no profit to people.
God indeed, when in anger, brings
Greater ruin to great men's houses.

[*Enter, on the right, a Chorus of Corinthian Women. They have come to inquire about Medea and to attempt to console her.*]

CHORUS: I heard the voice, I heard the cry
Of Colchis' wretched daughter.
Tell me, mother, is she not yet
At rest? Within the double gates
Of the court I heard her cry. I am sorry
135   For the sorrow of this home. O, say, what has happened?
NURSE: There is no home. It's over and done with.
Her husband holds fast to his royal wedding,
While she, my mistress, cries out her eyes
There in her room, and takes no warmth from
140   Any word of any friend.
MEDEA: Oh, I wish
That lightning from heaven would split my head open.
Oh, what use have I now for life?
I would find my release in death
145   And leave hateful existence behind me.
CHORUS: O God and Earth and Heaven!
Did you hear what a cry was that
Which the sad wife sings?
Poor foolish one, why should you long
150   For that appalling rest?
The final end of death comes fast.
No need to pray for that.
Suppose your man gives honor
To another woman's bed.
155   It often happens. Don't be hurt.
God will be your friend in this.
You must not waste away
Grieving too much for him who shared your bed.

MEDEA:	Great Themis, lady Artemis,[6] behold
160	The things I suffer, though I made him promise,
	My hateful husband. I pray that I may see him,
	Him and his bride and all their palace shattered
	For the wrong they dare to do me without cause.
	Oh, my father! Oh, my country! In what dishonor
165	I left you, killing my own brother for it.
NURSE:	Do you hear what she says, and how she cries
	On Themis, the goddess of Promises, and on Zeus,
	Whom we believe to be the Keeper of Oaths?
	Of this I am sure, that no small thing
170	Will appease my mistress' anger.
CHORUS:	Will she come into our presence?
	Will she listen when we are speaking
	To the words we say?
	I wish she might relax her rage
175	And temper of her heart.
	My willingness to help will never
	Be wanting to my friends.
	But go inside and bring her
	Out of the house to us,
180	And speak kindly to her: hurry,
	Before she wrongs her own.
	This passion of hers moves to something great.
NURSE:	I will, but I doubt if I'll manage
	To win my mistress over.
185	But still I'll attempt it to please you.
	Such a look she will flash on her servants
	If any comes near with a message,
	Like a lioness guarding her cubs.
	It is right, I think, to consider
190	Both stupid and lacking in foresight
	Those poets of old who wrote songs
	For revels and dinners and banquets,
	Pleasant sounds for men living at ease;
	But none of them all has discovered
195	How to put to an end with their singing
	Or musical instruments grief,
	Bitter grief, from which death and disaster
	Cheat the hopes of a house. Yet how good
	If music could cure men of this! But why raise
200	To no purpose the voice at a banquet? For *there* is
	Already abundance of pleasure for men
	With a joy of its own.

[*The Nurse goes into the house.*]

CHORUS:	I heard a shriek that is laden with sorrow.

6. Goddess of justice, virgins, and the hunt.

205 Shrilling out her hard grief she cries out
Upon him who betrayed both her bed and her marriage.
Wronged, she calls on the gods,
On the justice of Zeus, the oath sworn,
Which brought her away
210 To the opposite shore of the Greeks
Through the gloomy salt straits to the gateway
Of the salty unlimited sea.

[*Medea, attended by servants, comes out of the house.*]

MEDEA: Women of Corinth, I have come outside to you
Lest you should be indignant with me; for I know
That many people are overproud, some when alone,
215 And others when in company. And those who live
Quietly, as I do, get a bad reputation.
For a just judgment is not evident in the eyes
When a man at first sight hates another, before
Learning his character, being in no way injured;
220 And a foreigner especially must adapt himself.
I'd not approve of even a fellow-countryman
Who by pride and want of manners offends his neighbors.
But on me this thing has fallen so unexpectedly,
It has broken my heart. I am finished. I let go
225 All my life's joy. My friends, I only want to die.
It was everything to me to think well of one man,
And he, my own husband, has turned out wholly vile.
Of all things which are living and can form a judgment
We women are the most unfortunate creatures.
230 Firstly, with an excess of wealth it is required
For us to buy a husband and take for our bodies
A master; for not to take one is even worse.
And now the question is serious whether we take
A good or bad one; for there is no easy escape
235 For a woman, nor can she say no to her marriage.
She arrives among new modes of behavior and manners,
And needs prophetic power, unless she has learned at home,
How best to manage him who shares the bed with her.
And if we work out all this well and carefully,
240 And the husband lives with us and lightly bears his yoke,
Then life is enviable. If not, I'd rather die.
A man, when he's tired of the company in his home,
Goes out of the house and puts an end to his boredom
And turns to a friend or companion of his own age.
245 But we are forced to keep our eyes on one alone.
What they say of us is that we have a peaceful time
Living at home, while they do the fighting in war.
How wrong they are! I would very much rather stand
Three times in the front of battle than bear one child.
250 Yet what applies to me does not apply to you.

You have a country. Your family home is here.
You enjoy life and the company of your friends.
But I am deserted, a refugee, thought nothing of
By my husband—something he won in a foreign land.
255   I have no mother or brother, nor any relation
With whom I can take refuge in this sea of woe.
This much then is the service I would beg from you:
If I can find the means or devise any scheme
To pay my husband back for what he has done to me—
260   Him and his father-in-law and the girl who married him—
Just to keep silent. For in other ways a woman
Is full of fear, defenseless, dreads the sight of cold
Steel; but, when once she is wronged in the matter of love,
No other soul can hold so many thoughts of blood.

CHORUS: This I will promise. You are in the right, Medea,
In paying your husband back. I am not surprised at you
For being sad.
               But look! I see our King Creon
Approaching. He will tell us of some new plan.

[*Enter, from the right, Creon, with attendants.*]

CREON: You, with that angry look, so set against your husband,
270   Medea, I order you to leave my territories
An exile, and take along with you your two children,
And not to waste time doing it. It is my decree,
And I will see it done. I will not return home
Until you are cast from the boundaries of my land.

MEDEA: Oh, this is the end for me. I am utterly lost.
Now I am in the full force of the storm of hate
And have no harbor from ruin to reach easily.
Yet still, in spite of it all, I'll ask the question:
What is your reason, Creon, for banishing me?

CREON: I am afraid of you—why should I dissemble it?—
Afraid that you may injure my daughter mortally.
Many things accumulate to support my feeling.
You are a clever woman, versed in evil arts,
And are angry at having lost your husband's love.
285   I hear that you are threatening, so they tell me,
To do something against my daughter and Jason
And me, too. I shall take my precautions first.
I tell you, I prefer to earn your hatred now
Than to be soft-hearted and afterward regret it.

MEDEA: This is not the first time, Creon. Often previously
Through being considered clever I have suffered much
A person of sense ought never to have his children
Brought up to be more clever than the average.
For, apart from cleverness bringing them no profit,
295   It will make them objects of envy and ill-will.
If you put new ideas before the eyes of fools

They'll think you foolish and worthless into the bargain;
And if you are thought superior to those who have
Some reputation for learning, you will become hated.

300 I have some knowledge myself of how this happens;
For being clever, I find that some will envy me,
Others object to me. Yet all my cleverness
Is not so much.

               Well, then, are you frightened, Creon,
That I should harm you? There is no need. It is not

305 My way to transgress the authority of a king.
How have you injured me? You gave your daughter away
To the man you wanted. Oh, certainly I hate
My husband, but you, I think, have acted wisely;
Nor do I grudge it you that your affairs go well.

310 May the marriage be a lucky one! Only let me
Live in this land. For even though I have been wronged,
I will not raise my voice, but submit to my betters.

CREON: What you say sounds gentle enough. Still in my heart
I greatly dread that you are plotting some evil,

315 And therefore I trust you even less than before.
A sharp-tempered woman, or, for that matter, a man,
Is easier to deal with than the clever type
Who holds her tongue. No. You must go. No need for more
Speeches. The thing is fixed. By no manner of means

320 Shall you, an enemy of mine, stay in my country.

MEDEA: I beg you. By your knees, by your new-wedded girl.

CREON: Your words are wasted. You will never persuade me.

MEDEA: Will you drive me out, and give no heed to my prayers?

CREON: I will, for I love my family more than you.

MEDEA: O my country! How bitterly now I remember you!

CREON: I love my country too—next after my children.

MEDEA: Oh what an evil to men is passionate love!

CREON: That would depend on the luck that goes along with it.

MEDEA: O God, do not forget who is the cause of this!

CREON: Go. It is no use. Spare me the pain of forcing you.

MEDEA: I'm spared no pain. I lack no pain to be spared me.

CREON: Then you'll be removed by force by one of my men.

MEDEA: No, Creon, not that! But do listen, I beg you.

CREON: Woman, you seem to want to create a disturbance.

MEDEA: I *will* go into exile. *This* is not what I beg for.

CREON: Why then this violence and clinging to my hand?

MEDEA: Allow me to remain here just for this one day,
So I may consider where to live in my exile,
And look for support for my children, since their father

340 Chooses to make no kind of provision for them.
Have pity on them! You have children of your own.
It is natural for you to look kindly on them.
For myself I do not mind if I go into exile.
It is the children being in trouble that I mind.

CREON: There is nothing tyrannical about my nature,
    And by showing mercy I have often been the loser.
    Even now I know that I am making a mistake.
    All the same you shall have your will. But this I tell you,
    That if the light of heaven tomorrow shall see you,
350 You and your children in the confines of my land,
    You die. This word I have spoken is firmly fixed.
    But now, if you must stay, stay for this day alone.
    For in it you can do none of the things I fear.

[*Exit Creon with his attendants.*]

CHORUS: Oh, unfortunate one! Oh, cruel!
355 Where will you turn? Who will help you?
    What house or what land to preserve you
    From ill can you find?
    Medea, a god has thrown suffering
    Upon you in waves of despair.
MEDEA: Things have gone badly every way. No doubt of that
    But not these things this far, and don't imagine so.
    There are still trials to come for the new-wedded pair,
    And for their relations pain that will mean something.
    Do you think that I would ever have fawned on that man
365 Unless I had some end to gain or profit in it?
    I would not even have spoken or touched him with my hands.
    But he has got to such a pitch of foolishness
    That, though he could have made nothing of all my plans
    By exiling me, he has given me this one day
370 To stay here, and in this I will make dead bodies
    Of three of my enemies—father, the girl, and my husband.
    I have many ways of death which I might suit to them,
    And do not know, friends, which one to take in hand;
    Whether to set fire underneath their bridal mansion,
375 Or sharpen a sword and thrust it to the heart,
    Stealing into the palace where the bed is made.
    There is just one obstacle to this. If I am caught
    Breaking into the house and scheming against it,
    I shall die, and give my enemies cause for laughter.
380 It is best to go by the straight road, the one in which
    I am most skilled, and make away with them by poison.
    So be it then.
    And now suppose them dead. What town will receive me?
    What friend will offer me a refuge in his land,
385 Or the guaranty of his house and save my own life?
    There is none. So I must wait a little time yet,
    And if some sure defense should then appear for me,
    In craft and silence I will set about this murder.
    But if my fate should drive me on without help,
390 Even though death is certain, I will take the sword

Myself and kill, and steadfastly advance to crime.
It shall not be—I swear it by her, my mistress,
Whom most I honor and have chosen as partner,
Hecate,[7] who dwells in the recesses of my hearth—
395 That any man shall be glad to have injured me.
Bitter I will make their marriage for them and mournful,
Bitter the alliance and the driving me out of the land.
Ah, come, Medea, in your plotting and scheming
Leave nothing untried of all those things which you know.
400 Go forward to the dreadful act. The test has come
For resolution. You see how you are treated. Never
Shall you be mocked by Jason's Corinthian wedding,
Whose father was noble, whose grandfather Helius.[8]
You have the skill. What is more, you were born a woman,
405 And women, though most helpless in doing good deeds,
Are of every evil the cleverest of contrivers.

CHORUS: Flow backward to your sources, sacred rivers,
And let the world's great order be reversed.
It is the thoughts of *men* that are deceitful,
410 *Their* pledges that are loose.
Story shall now turn my condition to a fair one,
Women are paid their due.
No more shall evil-sounding fame be theirs.

Cease now, you muses of the ancient singers,
415 To tell the tale of my unfaithfulness;
For not on us did Phoebus, lord of music,[9]
Bestow the lyre's divine
Power, for otherwise I should have sung an answer
To the other sex. Long time
420 Has much to tell of us, and much of them.

You sailed away from your father's home,
With a heart on fire you passed
The double rocks of the sea.
And now in a foreign country
425 You have lost your rest in a widowed bed,
And are driven forth, a refugee
In dishonor from the land.

Good faith has gone, and no more remains
In great Greece a sense of shame.
430 It has flown away to the sky.
No father's house for a haven
Is at hand for you now, and another queen

7. Goddess associated with witchcraft.
8. God of the sun.
9. The god Apollo.

Of your bed has dispossessed you and
Is mistress of your home.

[*Enter Jason, with attendants.*]

JASON: This is not the first occasion that I have noticed
How hopeless it is to deal with a stubborn temper.
For, with reasonable submission to our ruler's will,
You might have lived in this land and kept your home.
As it is you are going to be exiled for your loose speaking.

440   Not that I mind myself. You are free to continue
Telling everyone that Jason is a worthless man.
But as to your talk about the king, consider
Yourself most lucky that exile is your punishment.
I, for my part, have always tried to calm down

445   The anger of the king, and wished you to remain.
But you will not give up your folly, continually
Speaking ill of him, and so you are going to be banished.
All the same, and in spite of your conduct, I'll not desert
My friends, but have come to make some provision for you,

450   So that you and the children may not be penniless
Or in need of anything in exile. Certainly
Exile brings many troubles with it. And even
If you hate me, I cannot think badly of you.

MEDEA: O coward in every way—that is what I call you,

455   With bitterest reproach for your lack of manliness,
You have come, you, my worst enemy, have come to me!
It is not an example of overconfidence
Or of boldness thus to look your friends in the face,
Friends you have injured—no, it is the worst of all

460   Human diseases, shamelessness. But you did well
To come, for I can speak ill of you and lighten
My heart, and you will suffer while you are listening.
And first I will begin from what happened first.
I saved your life, and every Greek knows I saved it,

465   Who was a shipmate of yours aboard the Argo,
When you were sent to control the bulls that breathed fire
And yoke them, and when you would sow that deadly field.
Also that snake, who encircled with his many folds
The Golden Fleece and guarded it and never slept,

470   I killed, and so gave you the safety of the light.
And I myself betrayed my father and my home,
And came with you to Pelias' land of Iolcus.
And then, showing more willingness to help than wisdom,
I killed him, Pelias, with a most dreadful death

475   At his own daughters' hands,[1] and took away your fear.
This is how I behaved to you, you wretched man,

---

1. Convinced by Medea that they would rejuvenate him, his daughters boiled Pelias.

And you forsook me, took another bride to bed,
Though you had children; for, if that had not been,
You would have had an excuse for another wedding.
480 Faith in your word has gone. Indeed, I cannot tell
Whether you think the gods whose names you swore by then
Have ceased to rule and that new standards are set up,
Since you must know you have broken your word to me.
O my right hand, and the knees which you often clasped
485 In supplication, how senselessly I am treated
By this bad man, and how my hopes have missed their mark!
Come, I will share my thoughts as though you were a friend—
You! Can I think that you would ever treat me well?
But I will do it, and these questions will make you
490 Appear the baser. Where am I to go? To my father's?
Him I betrayed and his land when I came with you.
To Pelias' wretched daughters? What a fine welcome
They would prepare for me who murdered their father!
For this is my position—hated by my friends
495 At home, I have, in kindness to you, made enemies
Of others whom there was no need to have injured.
And how happy among Greek women you have made me
On your side for all this! A distinguished husband
I have—for breaking promises. When in misery
500 I am cast out of the land and go into exile,
Quite without friends and all alone with my children,
That will be a fine shame for the new-wedded groom,
For his children to wander as beggars and she who saved him.
O God, you have given to mortals a sure method
505 Of telling the gold that is pure from the counterfeit;
Why is there no mark engraved upon men's bodies,
By which we could know the true ones from the false ones?

CHORUS: It is a strange form of anger, difficult to cure,
When two friends turn upon each other in hatred.

JASON: As for me, it seems I must be no bad speaker.
But, like a man who has a good grip of the tiller,
Reef up his sail, and so run away from under
This mouthing tempest, woman, of your bitter tongue.
Since you insist on building up your kindness to me,
515 My view is that Cypris[2] was alone responsible
Of men and gods for the preserving of my life.
You are clever enough—but really I need not enter
Into the story of how it was love's inescapable
Power that compelled you to keep my person safe.
520 On this I will not go into too much detail.
In so far as you helped me, you did well enough.

---

2. Aphrodite, goddess of sexual desire.

But on this question of saving me, I can prove
You have certainly got from me more than you gave.
Firstly, instead of living among barbarians,
525 You inhabit a Greek land and understand our ways,
How to live by law instead of the sweet will of force.
And all the Greeks considered you a clever woman.
You were honored for it; while, if you were living at
The ends of the earth, nobody would have heard of you.
530 For my part, rather than stores of gold in my house
Or power to sing even sweeter songs than Orpheus,
I'd choose the fate that made me a distinguished man.
There is my reply to your story of my labors.
Remember it was you who started the argument.
535 Next for your attack on my wedding with the princess:
Here I will prove that, first, it was a clever move,
Secondly, a wise one, and, finally, that I made it
In your best interests and the children's. Please keep calm.
When I arrived here from the land of Iolcus,
540 Involved, as I was, in every kind of difficulty,
What luckier chance could I have come across than this,
An exile to marry the daughter of the king?
It was not—the point that seems to upset you—that I
Grew tired of your bed and felt the need of a new bride;
545 Nor with any wish to outdo your number of children.
We have enough already. I am quite content.
But—this was the main reason—that we might live well,
And not be short of anything. I know that all
A man's friends leave him stone-cold if he becomes poor.
550 Also that I might bring my children up worthily
Of my position, and, by producing more of them
To be brothers of yours, we would draw the families
Together and all be happy. You need no children.
And it pays me to do good to those I have now
555 By having others. Do you think this a bad plan?
You wouldn't if the love question hadn't upset you.
But you women have got into such a state of mind
That, if your life at night is good, you think you have
Everything; but, if in that quarter things go wrong,
560 You will consider your best and truest interests
Most hateful. It would have been better far for men
To have got their children in some other way, and women
Not to have existed. Then life would have been good.

CHORUS: Jason, though you have made this speech of yours look well,
565 Still I think, even though others do not agree,
You have betrayed your wife and are acting badly.

MEDEA: Surely in many ways I hold different views
From others, for I think that the plausible speaker
Who is a villain deserves the greatest punishment.
570 Confident in his tongue's power to adorn evil,

He stops at nothing. Yet he is not really wise.
As in your case. There is no need to put on the airs
Of a clever speaker, for one word will lay you flat.
If you were not a coward, you would not have married
575 Behind my back, but discussed it with me first.
JASON: And you, no doubt, would have furthered the proposal,
If I had told you of it, you who even now
Are incapable of controlling your bitter temper.
MEDEA: It was not that. No, you thought it was not respectable
580 As you got on in years to have a foreign wife.
JASON: Make sure of this: it was not because of a woman
I made the royal alliance in which I now live,
But, as I said before, I wished to preserve you
And breed a royal progeny to be brothers
585 To the children I have now, a sure defense to us.
MEDEA: Let me have no happy fortune that brings pain with it,
Or prosperity which is upsetting to the mind!
JASON: Change your ideas of what you want, and show more sense.
Do not consider painful what is good for you,
590 Nor, when you are lucky, think yourself unfortunate.
MEDEA: You can insult me. You have somewhere to turn to.
But I shall go from this land into exile, friendless.
JASON: It was what you chose yourself. Don't blame others for it.
MEDEA: And how did I choose it? Did I betray my husband?
JASON: You called down wicked curses on the king's family.
MEDEA: A curse, that is what I am become to your house too.
JASON: I do not propose to go into all the rest of it;
But, if you wish for the children or for yourself
In exile to have some of my money to help you,
600 Say so, for I am prepared to give with open hand,
Or to provide you with introductions to my friends
Who will treat you well. You are a fool if you do not
Accept this. Cease your anger and you will profit.
MEDEA: I shall never accept the favors of friends of yours,
605 Nor take a thing from you, so you need not offer it.
There is no benefit in the gifts of a bad man.
JASON: Then, in any case, I call the gods to witness that
I wish to help you and the children in every way,
But you refuse what is good for you. Obstinately
610 You push away your friends. You are sure to suffer for it.
MEDEA: Go! No doubt you hanker for your virginal bride,
And are guilty of lingering too long out of her house.
Enjoy your wedding. But perhaps—with the help of God—
You will make the kind of marriage that you will regret.

[*Jason goes out with his attendants.*]

CHORUS: When love is in excess
It brings a man no honor
Nor any worthiness.

But if in moderation Cypris comes,
There is no other power at all so gracious.
620   O goddess, never on me let loose the unerring
Shaft of your bow in the poison of desire.

Let my heart be wise.
It is the gods' best gift.
On me let mighty Cypris
625   Inflict no wordy wars or restless anger
To urge my passion to a different love.
But with discernment may she guide women's weddings,
Honoring most what is peaceful in the bed.

O country and home,
630   Never, never may I be without you,
Living the hopeless life,
Hard to pass through and painful,
Most pitiable of all.
Let death first lay me low and death
635   Free me from this daylight.
There is no sorrow above
The loss of a native land.

I have seen it myself,
Do not tell of a secondhand story.
640   Neither city nor friend
Pitied you when you suffered
The worst of sufferings.
O let him die ungraced whose heart
Will not reward his friends,
645   Who cannot open an honest mind
No friend will he be of mine.

[*Enter Aegeus, king of Athens, an old friend of Medea.*]

AEGEUS: Medea, greeting! This is the best introduction
        Of which men know for conversation between friends.
MEDEA: Greeting to you too, Aegeus, son of King Pandion.
650   Where have you come from to visit this country's soil?
AEGEUS: I have just left the ancient oracle of Phoebus.
MEDEA: And why did you go to earth's prophetic center?
AEGEUS: I went to inquire how children might be born to me.
MEDEA: Is it so? Your life still up to this point is childless?
AEGEUS: Yes. By the fate of some power we have no children.
MEDEA: Have you a wife, or is there none to share your bed?
AEGEUS: There is. Yes, I am joined to my wife in marriage.
MEDEA: And what did Phoebus say to you about children?
AEGEUS: Words too wise for a mere man to guess their meaning.
MEDEA: It is proper for me to be told the god's reply?
AEGEUS: It is. For sure what is needed is cleverness.
MEDEA: Then what was his message? Tell me, if I may hear.

AEGEUS: I am not to loosen the hanging foot of the wine-skin ...

MEDEA: Until you have done something, or reached some country?

AEGEUS: Until I return again to my hearth and house.

MEDEA: And for what purpose have you journeyed to this land?

AEGEUS: There is a man called Pittheus, king of Troezen.

MEDEA: A son of Pelops, they say, a most righteous man.

AEGEUS: With him I wish to discuss the reply of the god.

MEDEA: Yes. He is wise and experienced in such matters.

AEGEUS: And to me also the dearest of all my spear-friends.

MEDEA: Well, I hope you have good luck, and achieve your will.

AEGEUS: But why this downcast eye of yours, and this pale cheek?

MEDEA: O Aegeus, my husband has been the worst of all to me.

AEGEUS: What do you mean? Say clearly what has caused this grief.

MEDEA: Jason wrongs me, though I have never injured him.

AEGEUS: What has he done? Tell me about it in clearer words.

MEDEA: He has taken a wife to his house, supplanting me.

AEGEUS: Surely he would not dare to do a thing like that.

MEDEA: Be sure he has. Once dear, I now am slighted by him.

AEGEUS: Did he fall in love? Or is he tired of your love?

MEDEA: He was greatly in love, this traitor to his friends.

AEGEUS: Then let him go, if, as you say, he is so bad.

MEDEA: A passionate love—for an alliance with the king.

AEGEUS: And who gave him his wife? Tell me the rest of it.

MEDEA: It was Creon, he who rules this land of Corinth.

AEGEUS: Indeed, Medea, your grief was understandable.

MEDEA: I am ruined. And there is more to come: I am banished.

AEGEUS: Banished? By whom? Here you tell me of a new wrong.

MEDEA: Creon drives me an exile from the land of Corinth.

AEGEUS: Does Jason consent? I cannot approve of this.

MEDEA: He pretends not to, but he will put up with it.
        Ah, Aegeus, I beg and beseech you, by your beard
        And by your knees I am making myself your suppliant,

695   Have pity on me, have pity on your poor friend,
        And do not let me go into exile desolate,
        But receive me in your land and at your very hearth.
        So may your love, with God's help, lead to the bearing
        Of children, and so may you yourself die happy.

700   You do not know what a chance you have come on here.
        I will end your childlessness, and I will make you able
        To beget children. The drugs I know can do this.

AEGEUS: For many reasons, woman, I am anxious to do
        This favor for you. First, for the sake of the gods,

705   And then for the birth of children which you promise,
        For in that respect I am entirely at my wits' end.
        But this is my position: if you reach my land,
        I, being in my rights, will try to befriend you.
        But this much I must warn you of beforehand:

710   I shall not agree to take you out of this country;
        But if you by yourself can reach my house, then you

MEDEA: Shall stay there safely. To none will I give you up
           But from this land you must make your escape yourself,
           For I do not wish to incur blame from my friends.

MEDEA: It shall be so. But, if I might have a pledge from you
           For this, then I would have from you all I desire.

AEGEUS: Do you not trust me? What is it rankles with you?

MEDEA: I trust you, yes. But the house of Pelias hates me,
           And so does Creon. If you are bound by this oath,
720   When they try to drag me from your land, you will not
           Abandon me; but if our pact is only words,
           With no oath to the gods, you will be lightly armed,
           Unable to resist their summons. I am weak,
           While they have wealth to help them and a royal house.

AEGEUS: You show much foresight for such negotiations.
           Well, if you will have it so, I will not refuse.
           For, both on my side this will be the safest way
           To have some excuse to put forward to your enemies,
           And for you it is more certain. You may name the gods.

MEDEA: Swear by the plain of Earth, and Helius, father
           Of my father, and name together all the gods...

AEGEUS: That I will act or not act in what way? Speak.

MEDEA: That you yourself will never cast me from your land,
           Nor, if any of my enemies should demand me,
735   Will you, in your life, willingly hand me over.

AEGEUS: I swear by the Earth, by the holy light of Helius,
           By all the gods, I will abide by this you say.

MEDEA: Enough. And, if you fail, what shall happen to you?

AEGEUS: What comes to those who have no regard for heaven.

MEDEA: Go on your way. Farewell. For I am satisfied.
           And I will reach your city as soon as I can,
           Having done the deed I have to do and gained my end.

[Aegeus goes out.]

CHORUS: May Hermes, god of travelers,
           Escort you, Aegeus, to your home!
745   And may you have the things you wish
           So eagerly; for you
           Appear to me to be a generous man.

MEDEA: God, and God's daughter, justice, and light of Helius!
           Now, friends, has come the time of my triumph over
750   My enemies, and now my foot is on the road.
           Now I am confident they will pay the penalty.
           For this man, Aegeus, has been like a harbor to me
           In all my plans just where I was most distressed.
           To him I can fasten the cable of my safety
755   When I have reached the town and fortress of Pallas.[3]

---

3. Athena, goddess of Athens.

And now I shall tell to you the whole of my plan.
Listen to these words that are not spoken idly.
I shall send one of my servants to find Jason
And request him to come once more into my sight.
760 And when he comes, the words I'll say will be soft ones.
I'll say that I agree with him, that I approve
The royal wedding he has made, betraying me.
I'll say it was profitable, an excellent idea.
But I shall beg that my children may remain here:
765 Not that I would leave in a country that hates me
Children of mine to feel their enemies' insults,
But that by a trick I may kill the king's daughter.
For I will send the children with gifts in their hands
To carry to the bride, so as not to be banished—
770 A finely woven dress and a golden diadem.
And if she takes them and wears them upon her skin
She and all who touch the girl will die in agony;
Such poison will I lay upon the gifts I send.
But there, however, I must leave that account paid.
775 I weep to think of what a deed I have to do
Next after that; for I shall kill my own children.
My children, there is none who can give them safety.
And when I have ruined the whole of Jason's house,
I shall leave the land and flee from the murder of my
780 Dear children, and I shall have done a dreadful deed.
For it is not bearable to be mocked by enemies.
So it must happen. What profit have I in life?
I have no land, no home, no refuge from my pain.
My mistake was made the time I left behind me
785 My father's house, and trusted the words of a Greek,
Who, with heaven's help, will pay me the price for that.
For those children he had from me he will never
See alive again, nor will he on his new bride
Beget another child, for she is to be forced
790 To die a most terrible death by these my poisons.
Let no one think me a weak one, feeble-spirited,
A stay-at-home, but rather just the opposite,
One who can hurt my enemies and help my friends;
For the lives of such persons are most remembered.

CHORUS: Since you have shared the knowledge of your plan with us,
I both wish to help you and support the normal
Ways of mankind, and tell you not to do this thing.
MEDEA: I can do no other thing. It is understandable
For you to speak thus. You have not suffered as I have.
CHORUS: But can you have the heart to kill your flesh and blood?
MEDEA: Yes, for this is the best way to wound my husband.
CHORUS: And you, too. Of women you will be most unhappy.
MEDEA: So it must be. No compromise is possible.

[*She turns to the Nurse.*]

Go, you, at once, and tell Jason to come to me.
805 You I employ on all affairs of greatest trust.
Say nothing of these decisions which I have made,
If you love your mistress, if you were born a woman.

CHORUS: From of old the children of Erechtheus are
Splendid, the sons of blessed gods. They dwell
810 In Athens' holy and unconquered land,
Where famous Wisdom feeds them and they pass gaily
Always through that most brilliant air where once, they say,
That golden Harmony gave birth to the nine
Pure Muses of Pieria.

815 And beside the sweet flow of Cephisus' stream,
Where Cypris sailed, they say, to draw the water,
And mild soft breezes breathed along her path,
And on her hair were flung the sweet-smelling garlands
Of flowers of roses by the Lovers, the companions
820 Of Wisdom, her escort, the helpers of men
In every kind of excellence.

How then can these holy rivers
Or this holy land love you,
Or the city find you a home,
825 You, who will kill your children,
You, not pure with the rest?
O think of the blow at your children
And think of the blood that you shed.
O, over and over I beg you,
830 By your knees I beg you do not
Be the murderess of your babes!

O where will you find the courage
Or the skill of hand and heart,
When you set yourself to attempt
835 A deed so dreadful to do?
How, when you look upon them,
Can you tearlessly hold the decision
For murder? You will not be able,
When your children fall down and implore you,
840 You will not be able to dip
Steadfast your hand in their blood.

[*Enter Jason with attendants.*]

JASON: I have come at your request. Indeed, although you are
Bitter against me, this you shall have: I will listen
To what new thing you want, woman, to get from me.

MEDEA: Jason, I beg you to be forgiving toward me
For what I said. It is natural for you to bear with
My temper, since we have had much love together.
I have talked with myself about this and I have

	Reproached myself. "Fool" I said, "why am I so mad?
850	Why am I set against those who have planned wisely?
	Why make myself an enemy of the authorities
	And of my husband, who does the best thing for me
	By marrying royalty and having children who
	Will be as brothers to my own? What is wrong with me?
855	Let me give up anger, for the gods are kind to me.
	Have I not children, and do I not know that we
	In exile from our country must be short of friends?"
	When I considered this I saw that I had shown
	Great lack of sense, and that my anger was foolish.
860	Now I agree with you. I think that you are wise
	In having this other wife as well as me, and I
	Was mad. I should have helped you in these plans of yours,
	Have joined in the wedding, stood by the marriage bed,
	Have taken pleasure in attendance on your bride.
865	But we women are what we are—perhaps a little
	Worthless; and you men must not be like us in this,
	Nor be foolish in return when we are foolish.
	Now, I give in, and admit that then I was wrong.
	I have come to a better understanding now.

[*She turns toward the house.*]

870	Children, come here, my children, come outdoors to us!
	Welcome your father with me, and say goodbye to him,
	And with your mother, who just now was his enemy,
	Join again in making friends with him who loves us.

[*Enter the children, attended by the Tutor.*]

	We have made peace, and all our anger is over.
875	Take hold of his right hand—O God, I am thinking
	Of something which may happen in the secret future.
	O children, will you just so, after a long life,
	Hold out your loving arms at the grave? O children,
	How ready to cry I am, how full of foreboding!
880	I am ending at last this quarrel with your father,
	And, look my soft eyes have suddenly filled with tears.
CHORUS:	And the pale tears have started also in my eyes.
	O may the trouble not grow worse than now it is!
JASON:	I approve of what you say. And I cannot blame you
885	Even for what you said before. It is natural
	For a woman to be wild with her husband when he
	Goes in for secret love. But now your mind has turned
	To better reasoning. In the end you have come to
	The right decision, like the clever woman you are.
890	And of you, children, your father is taking care.
	He has made, with God's help, ample provision for you.
	For I think that a time will come when you will be
	The leading people in Corinth with your brothers.
	You must grow up. As to the future, your father

895 And those of the gods who love him will deal with that.
I want to see you, when you have become young men,
Healthy and strong, better men than my enemies.
Medea, why are your eyes all wet with pale tears?
Why is your cheek so white and turned away from me?
900 Are not these words of mine pleasing for you to hear?
MEDEA: It is nothing. I was thinking about these children.
JASON: You must be cheerful. I shall look after them well.
MEDEA: I will be. It is not that I distrust your words,
But a woman is a frail thing, prone to crying.
JASON: But why then should you grieve so much for these children?
MEDEA: I am their mother. When you prayed that they might live
I felt unhappy to think that these things will be.
But come, I have said something of the things I meant
To say to you, and now I will tell you the rest.
910 Since it is the king's will to banish me from here—
And for me, too, I know that this is the best thing,
Not to be in your way by living here or in
The king's way, since they think me ill-disposed to them—
I then am going into exile from this land;
915 But do you, so that you may have the care of them,
Beg Creon that the children may not be banished.
JASON: I doubt if I'll succeed, but still I'll attempt it.
MEDEA: Then you must tell your wife to beg from her father
That the children may be reprieved from banishment.
JASON: I will, and with her I shall certainly succeed.
MEDEA: If she is like the rest of us women, you will.
And I, too, will take a hand with you in this business,
For I will send her some gifts which are far fairer,
I am sure of it, than those which now are in fashion,
925 A finely woven dress and a golden diadem,
And the children shall present them. Quick, let one of you
Servants bring here to me that beautiful dress.

[*One of her attendants goes into the house.*]

She will be happy not in one way, but in a hundred,
Having so fine a man as you to share her bed,
930 And with this beautiful dress which Helius of old,
My father's father, bestowed on his descendants.

[*Enter attendant carrying the poisoned dress and diadem.*]

There, children, take these wedding presents in your hands.
Take them to the royal princess, the happy bride,
And give them to her. She will not think little of them.
JASON: No, don't be foolish, and empty your hands of these.
Do you think the palace is short of dresses to wear?
Do you think there is no gold there? Keep them, don't give them
Away. If my wife considers me of any value,
She will think more of me than money, I am sure of it.

MEDEA: No, let me have my way. They say the gods themselves
          Are moved by gifts, and gold does more with men than words.
          Hers is the luck, her fortune that which god blesses;
          She is young and a princess; but for my children's reprieve
          I would give my very life, and not gold only.
945   Go children, go together to that rich palace,
          Be suppliants to the new wife of your father,
          My lady, beg her not to let you be banished.
          And give her the dress—for this is of great importance,
          That she should take the gift into her hand from yours.
950   Go, quick as you can. And bring your mother good news
          By your success of those things which she longs to gain.

     [*Jason goes out with his attendants, followed by the Tutor and the children carrying the poisoned gifts.*]

CHORUS: Now there is no hope left for the children's lives.
          Now there is none. They are walking already to murder.
          The bride, poor bride, will accept the curse of the gold,
955   Will accept the bright diadem.
          Around her yellow hair she will set that dress
          Of death with her own hands.

          The grace and the perfume and glow of the golden robe
          Will charm her to put them upon her and wear the wreath,
960   And now her wedding will be with the dead below,
          Into such a trap she will fall,
          Poor thing, into such a fate of death and never
          Escape from under that curse.
          You, too, O wretched bridegroom, making your match with kings,
965   You do not see that you bring
          Destruction on your children and on her,
          Your wife, a fearful death.
          Poor soul, what a fall is yours!

          In your grief, too, I weep, mother of little children,
970   You who will murder your own,
          In vengeance for the loss of married love
          Which Jason has betrayed
          As he lives with another wife.

     [*Enter the Tutor with the children.*]

TUTOR: Mistress, I tell you that these children are reprieved,
975   And the royal bride has been pleased to take in her hands
          Your gifts. In that quarter the children are secure.
          But come,
          Why do you stand confused when you are fortunate?
          Why have you turned round with your cheek away from me?
980   Are not these words of mine pleasing for you to hear?
MEDEA: Oh! I am lost!
TUTOR: That word is not in harmony with my tidings.

MEDEA:	I am lost, I am lost!
TUTOR:	Am I in ignorance telling you
	Of some disaster, and not the good news I thought?
MEDEA:	You have told what you have told. I do not blame you.
TUTOR:	Why then this downcast eye, and this weeping of tears?
MEDEA:	Oh, I am forced to weep, old man. The gods and I,
	I in a kind of madness, have contrived all this.
TUTOR:	Courage! You, too, will be brought home by your children.
MEDEA:	Ah, before that happens I shall bring others home.
TUTOR:	Others before you have been parted from their children.
	Mortals must bear in resignation their ill luck.
MEDEA:	That is what I shall do. But go inside the house,
	And do for the children your usual daily work.

[*The Tutor goes into the house. Medea turns to her children.*]

995 O children, O my children, you have a city,
You have a home, and you can leave me behind you,
And without your mother you may live there forever.
But I am going in exile to another land
Before I have seen you happy and taken pleasure in you,
1000 Before I have dressed your brides and made your marriage beds
And held up the torch at the ceremony of wedding.
Oh, what a wretch I am in this my self-willed thought!
What was the purpose, children, for which I reared you?
For all my travail and wearing myself away?
1005 They were sterile, those pains I had in the bearing of you.
Oh surely once the hopes in you I had, poor me,
Were high ones: you would look after me in old age,
And when I died would deck me well with your own hands;
A thing which all would have done. Oh but now it is gone,
1010 That lovely thought. For, once I am left without you,
Sad will be the life I'll lead and sorrowful for me.
And you will never see your mother again with
Your dear eyes, gone to another mode of living.
Why, children, do you look upon me with your eyes?
1015 Why do you smile so sweetly that last smile of all?
Oh, Oh, what can I do? My spirit has gone from me,
Friends, when I saw that bright look in the children's eyes.
I cannot bear to do it. I renounce my plans
I had before. I'll take my children away from
1020 This land. Why should I hurt their father with the pain
They feel, and suffer twice as much of pain myself?
No, no, I will not do it. I renounce my plans.
Ah, what is wrong with me? Do I want to let go
My enemies unhurt and be laughed at for it?
1025 I must face this thing. Oh, but what a weak woman
Even to admit to my mind these soft arguments.
Children, go into the house. And he whom law forbids
To stand in attendance at my sacrifices,

Let him see to it. I shall not mar my handiwork.
1030 Oh! Oh!
Do not, O my heart, you must not do these things!
Poor heart, let them go, have pity upon the children.
If they live with you in Athens they will cheer you.
No! By Hell's avenging furies it shall not be—
1035 This shall never be, that I should suffer my children
To be the prey of my enemies' insolence.
Every way is it fixed. The bride will not escape.
No, the diadem is now upon her head, and she,
The royal princess, is dying in the dress, I know it.
1040 But—for it is the most dreadful of roads for me
To tread, and them I shall send on a more dreadful still—
I wish to speak to the children.

[*She calls the children to her.*]

Come, children, give
Me your hands, give your mother your hands to kiss them.
Oh the dear hands, and O how dear are these lips to me,
1045 And the generous eyes and the bearing of my children!
I wish you happiness, but not here in this world.
What is here your father took. Oh how good to hold you!
How delicate the skin, how sweet the breath of children!
Go, go! I am no longer able, no longer
1050 To look upon you. I am overcome by sorrow.

[*The children go into the house.*]

I know indeed what evil I intend to do,
But stronger than all my afterthoughts is my fury,
Fury that brings upon mortals the greatest evils.

[*She goes out to the right, toward the royal palace.*]

CHORUS: Often before
1055 I have gone through more subtle reasons,
And have come upon questionings greater
Than a woman should strive to search out.
But we too have a goddess to help us
And accompany us into wisdom.
1060 Not all of us. Still you will find
Among many women a few,
And our sex is not without learning.
This I say, that those who have never
Had children, who know nothing of it,
1065 In happiness have the advantage
Over those who are parents.
The childless, who never discover
Whether children turn out as a good thing
Or as something to cause pain, are spared
1070 Many troubles in lacking this knowledge.

And those who have in their homes
The sweet presence of children, I see that their lives
Are all wasted away by their worries.
First they must think how to bring them up well and
1075 How to leave them something to live on.
And then after this whether all their toil
Is for those who will turn out good or bad,
Is still an unanswered question.
And of one more trouble, the last of all,
1080 That is common to mortals I tell.
For suppose you have found them enough for their living,
Suppose that the children have grown into youth
And have turned out good, still, if God so wills it,
Death will away with your children's bodies,
1085 And carry them off into Hades.
What is our profit, then, that for the sake of
Children the gods should pile upon mortals
After all else
This most terrible grief of all?

[*Enter Medea, from the spectators' right.*]

MEDEA: Friends, I can tell you that for long I have waited
For the event. I stare toward the place from where
The news will come. And now, see one of Jason's servants
Is on his way here, and that labored breath of his
Shows he has tidings for us, and evil tidings.

[*Enter, also from the right, the Messenger.*]

MESSENGER: Medea, you who have done such a dreadful thing,
So outrageous, run for your life, take what you can,
A ship to bear you hence or chariot on land.
MEDEA: And what is the reason deserves such flight as this?
MESSENGER: She is dead, only just now, the royal princess,
1100 And Creon dead, too, her father, by your poisons.
MEDEA: The finest words you have spoken. Now and hereafter
I shall count you among my benefactors and friends.
MESSENGER: What! Are you right in the mind? Are you not mad,
Woman? The house of the king is outraged by you.
1105 Do you enjoy it? Not afraid of such doings?
MEDEA: To what you say I on my side have something too
To say in answer. Do not be in a hurry, friend,
But speak. How did they die? You will delight me twice
As much again if you say they died in agony.
MESSENGER: When those two children, born of you, had entered in,
Their father with them, and passed into the bride's house,
We were pleased, we slaves who were distressed by your wrongs.
All through the house we were talking of but one thing,
How you and your husband had made up your quarrel.
1115 Some kissed the children's hands and some their yellow hair,

And I myself was so full of my joy that I
Followed the children into the women's quarters.
Our mistress, whom we honor now instead of you,
Before she noticed that your two children were there,
1120 Was keeping her eye fixed eagerly on Jason.
Afterwards, however, she covered up her eyes,
Her cheek paled, and she turned herself away from him,
So disgusted was she at the children's coming there.
But your husband tried to end the girl's bad temper,
1125 And said "You must not look unkindly on your friends.
Cease to be angry. Turn your head to me again.
Have as your friends the same ones as your husband has.
And take these gifts, and beg your father to reprieve
These children from their exile. Do it for my sake."
1130 She, when she saw the dress, could not restrain herself.
She agreed with all her husband said, and before
He and the children had gone far from the palace,
She took the gorgeous robe and dressed herself in it,
And put the golden crown around her curly locks,
1135 And arranged the set of the hair in a shining mirror,
And smiled at the lifeless image of herself in it.
Then she rose from her chair and walked about the room,
With her gleaming feet stepping most soft and delicate,
All overjoyed with the present. Often and often
1140 She would stretch her foot out straight and look along it.
But after that it was a fearful thing to see.
The color of her face changed, and she staggered back,
She ran, and her legs trembled, and she only just
Managed to reach a chair without falling flat down.
1145 An aged woman servant who, I take it, thought
This was some seizure of Pan or another god,
Cried out "God bless us," but that was before she saw
The white foam breaking through her lips and her rolling
The pupils of her eyes and her face all bloodless.
1150 Then she raised a different cry from that "God bless us,"
A huge shriek, and the women ran, one to the king,
One to the newly wedded husband to tell him
What had happened to his bride; and with frequent sound
The whole of the palace rang as they went running.
1155 One walking quickly round the course of a race-track
Would now have turned the bend and be close to the goal,
When she, poor girl, opened her shut and speechless eye,
And with a terrible groan she came to herself.
For a twofold pain was moving up against her.
1160 The wreath of gold that was resting around her head
Let forth a fearful stream of all-devouring fire,
And the finely woven dress your children gave to her,
Was fastening on the unhappy girl's fine flesh.
She leapt up from the chair, and all on fire she ran,

1165	Shaking her hair now this way and now that, trying
	To hurl the diadem away; but fixedly
	The gold preserved its grip, and, when she shook her hair,
	Then more and twice as fiercely the fire blazed out.
	Till, beaten by her fate, she fell down to the ground,
1170	Hard to be recognized except by a parent.
	Neither the setting of her eyes was plain to see,
	Nor the shapeliness of her face. From the top of
	Her head there oozed out blood and fire mixed together.
	Like the drops on pine-bark, so the flesh from her bones
1175	Dropped away, torn by the hidden fang of the poison.
	It was a fearful sight; and terror held us all
	From touching the corpse. We had learned from what had happened.
	But her wretched father, knowing nothing of the event,
	Came suddenly to the house, and fell upon the corpse,
1180	And at once cried out and folded his arms about her,
	And kissed her and spoke to her, saying, "O my poor child,
	What heavenly power has so shamefully destroyed you?
	And who has set me here like an ancient sepulcher,
	Deprived of you? O let me die with you, my child!"
1185	And when he had made an end of his wailing and crying,
	Then the old man wished to raise himself to his feet;
	But, as the ivy clings to the twigs of the laurel,
	So he stuck to the fine dress, and he struggled fearfully.
	For he was trying to lift himself to his knee,
1190	And she was pulling him down, and when he tugged hard
	He would be ripping his aged flesh from his bones.
	At last his life was quenched, and the unhappy man
	Gave up the ghost, no longer could hold up his head.
	There they lie close, the daughter and the old father,
1195	Dead bodies, an event he prayed for in his tears.
	As for your interests, I will say nothing of them,
	For you will find your own escape from punishment.
	Our human life I think and have thought a shadow,
	And I do not fear to say that those who are held
1200	Wise among men and who search the reasons of things
	Are those who bring the most sorrow on themselves.
	For of mortals there is no one who is happy.
	If wealth flows in upon one, one may be perhaps
	Luckier than one's neighbor, but still not happy.

[*Exit.*]

CHORUS: Heaven, it seems, on this day has fastened many
Evils on Jason, and Jason has deserved them.
Poor girl, the daughter of Creon, how I pity you
And your misfortunes, you who have gone quite away
To the house of Hades because of marrying Jason.

MEDEA: Women, my task is fixed: as quickly as I may
To kill my children, and start away from this land,

And not, by wasting time, to suffer my children
To be slain by another hand less kindly to them.
Force every way will have it they must die, and since
1215   This must be so, then I, their mother, shall kill them.
Oh, arm yourself in steel, my heart! Do not hang back
From doing this fearful and necessary wrong.
Oh, come, my hand, poor wretched hand, and take the sword,
Take it, step forward to this bitter starting point,
1220   And do not be a coward, do not think of them,
How sweet they are, and how you are their mother. Just for
This one short day be forgetful of your children,
Afterward weep; for even though you will kill them,
They were very dear—Oh, I am an unhappy woman!

[*With a cry she rushes into the house.*]

CHORUS: O Earth, and the far shining
                 Ray of the Sun, look down, look down upon
                 This poor lost woman, look, before she raises
                 The hand of murder against her flesh and blood.
                 Yours was the golden birth from which
1230   She sprang, and now I fear divine
                 Blood may be shed by men.
                 O heavenly light, hold back her hand,
                 Check her, and drive from out the house
                 The bloody Fury raised by fiends of Hell.

1235   Vain waste, your care of children;
                 Was it in vain you bore the babes you loved,
                 After you passed the inhospitable strait
                 Between the dark blue rocks, Symplegades?
                 O wretched one, how has it come,
1240   This heavy anger on your heart,
                 This cruel bloody mind?
                 For God from mortals asks a stern
                 Price for the stain of kindred blood
                 In like disaster falling on their homes.

[*A cry from one of the children is heard.*]

CHORUS: Do you hear the cry, do you hear the children's cry?
                 O you hard heart, O woman fated for evil!
ONE OF THE CHILDREN [*from within*]:   What can I do and how escape my mother's
       hands?
ANOTHER CHILD [*from within*]:   O my dear brother, I cannot tell. We are lost.
CHORUS: Shall I enter the house? Oh, surely I should
1250   Defend the children from murder.
A CHILD [*from within*]:   O help us, in God's name, for now we need your help.
                 Now, now we are close to it. We are trapped by the sword.
CHORUS: O your heart must have been made of rock or steel,
                 You who can kill

1255	With your own hand the fruit of your own womb.
	Of one alone I have heard, one woman alone
	Of those of old who laid her hands on her children,
	Ino, sent mad by heaven when the wife of Zeus
	Drove her out from her home and made her wander;
1260	And because of the wicked shedding of blood
	Of her own children she threw
	Herself, poor wretch, into the sea and stepped away
	Over the sea-cliff to die with her two children.
	What horror more can be? O women's love,
1265	So full of trouble,
	How many evils have you caused already!

[*Enter Jason, with attendants.*]

JASON: You women, standing close in front of this dwelling,
Is she, Medea, she who did this dreadful deed,
Still in the house, or has she run away in flight?
1270 For she will have to hide herself beneath the earth,
Or raise herself on wings into the height of air,
If she wishes to escape the royal vengeance.
Does she imagine that, having killed our rulers,
She will herself escape uninjured from this house?
1275 But I am thinking not so much of her as for
The children—her the king's friends will make to suffer
For what she did. So I have come to save the lives
Of my boys, in case the royal house should harm them
While taking vengeance for their mother's wicked deed.

CHORUS: O Jason, if you but knew how deeply you are
Involved in sorrow, you would not have spoken so.

JASON: What is it? That she is planning to kill me also?

CHORUS: Your children are dead, and by their own mother's hand.

JASON: What! That is it? O woman, you have destroyed me!

CHORUS: You must make up your mind your children are no more.

JASON: Where did she kill them? Was it here or in the house?

CHORUS: Open the gates and there you will see them murdered.

JASON: Quick as you can unlock the doors, men, and undo
The fastenings and let me see this double evil,
1290 My children dead and her—Oh her I will repay.

[*His attendants rush to the door. Medea appears above the house in a chariot drawn by dragons. She has the dead bodies of the children with her.*]

MEDEA: Why do you batter these gates and try to unbar them,
Seeking the corpses and for me who did the deed?
You may cease your trouble, and, if you have need of me,
Speak, if you wish. You will never touch me with your hand,
1295 Such a chariot has Helius, my father's father,
Given me to defend me from my enemies.

JASON: You hateful thing, you woman most utterly loathed
By the gods and me and by all the race of mankind,

You who have had the heart to raise a sword against
1300   Your children, you, their mother, and left me childless—
You have done this, and do you still look at the sun
And at the earth, after these most fearful doings?
I wish you dead. Now I see it plain, though at that time
I did not, when I took you from your foreign home
1305   And brought you to a Greek house, you, an evil thing,
A traitress to your father and your native land.
The gods hurled the avenging curse of yours on me.
For your own brother you slew at your own hearthside,
And then came aboard that beautiful ship, the Argo.
1310   And that was your beginning. When you were married
To me, your husband, and had borne children to me,
For the sake of pleasure in the bed you killed them.
There is no Greek woman who would have dared such deeds,
Out of all those whom I passed over and chose you
1315   To marry instead, a bitter destructive match,
A monster, not a woman, having a nature
Wilder than that of Scylla in the Tuscan sea.
Ah! no, not if I had ten thousand words of shame
Could I sting you. You are naturally so brazen.
1320   Go, worker in evil, stained with your children's blood.
For me remains to cry aloud upon my fate,
Who will get no pleasure from my newly wedded love,
And the boys whom I begot and brought up, never
Shall I speak to them alive. Oh, my life is over!

MEDEA: Long would be the answer which I might have made to
These words of yours, if Zeus the father did not know
How I have treated you and what you did to me.
No, it was not to be that you should scorn my love,
And pleasantly live your life through, laughing at me;
1330   Nor would the princess, nor he who offered the match,
Creon, drive me away without paying for it.
So now you may call me a monster, if you wish,
A Scylla housed in the caves of the Tuscan sea.
I too, as I had to, have taken hold of your heart.

JASON: You feel the pain yourself. You share in my sorrow.
MEDEA: Yes, and my grief is gain when you cannot mock it.
JASON: O children, what a wicked mother she was to you!
MEDEA: They died from a disease they caught from their father.
JASON: I tell you it was not my hand that destroyed them.
MEDEA: But it was your insolence, and your virgin wedding.
JASON: And just for the sake of that you chose to kill them.
MEDEA: Is love so small a pain, do you think, for a woman?
JASON: For a wise one, certainly. But you are wholly evil.
MEDEA: The children are dead. I say this to make you suffer.
JASON: The children, I think, will bring down curses on you.
MEDEA: The gods know who was the author of this sorrow.
JASON: Yes, the gods know indeed, they know your loathsome heart.

MEDEA: Hate me. But I tire of your barking bitterness.

JASON: And I of yours. It is easier to leave you.

MEDEA: How then? What shall I do? I long to leave you too.

JASON: Give me the bodies to bury and to mourn them.

MEDEA: No, that I will not. I will bury them myself,
Bearing them to Hera's temple on the promontory;
So that no enemy may evilly treat them
1355 By tearing up their grave. In this land of Corinth
I shall establish a holy feast and sacrifice
Each year for ever to atone for the blood guilt.
And I myself go to the land of Erechtheus
To dwell in Aegeus' house, the son of Pandion.
1360 While you, as is right, will die without distinction,
Struck on the head by a piece of the Argo's timber,
And you will have seen the bitter end of my love.

JASON: May a Fury for the children's sake destroy you,
And justice, Requitor of blood.

MEDEA: What heavenly power lends an ear
To a breaker of oaths, a deceiver?

JASON: Oh, I hate you, murderess of children.

MEDEA: Go to your palace. Bury your bride.

JASON: I go, with two children to mourn for.

MEDEA: Not yet do you feel it. Wait for the future.

JASON: Oh, children I loved!

MEDEA: I loved them, you did not.

JASON: You loved them, and killed them.

MEDEA: To make you feel pain.

JASON: Oh, wretch that I am, how I long
To kiss the dear lips of my children!

MEDEA: Now you would speak to them, now you would kiss them.
Then you rejected them.

JASON: Let me, I beg you,
Touch my boys' delicate flesh.

MEDEA: I will not. Your words are all wasted.

JASON: O God, do you hear it, this persecution,
1380 These my sufferings from this hateful
Woman, this monster, murderess of children?
Still what I can do that I will do:
I will lament and cry upon heaven,
Calling the gods to bear me witness
1385 How you have killed my boys and prevent me from
Touching their bodies or giving them burial.
I wish I had never begot them to see them
Afterward slaughtered by you.

CHORUS: Zeus in Olympus is the overseer
1390 Of many doings. Many things the gods
Achieve beyond our judgment. What we thought
Is not confirmed and what we thought not god
Contrives. And so it happens in this story.

[Curtain.]

PLATO ■ (c. 429–347 B.C.E.)

The Athenians executed Socrates, Plato's beloved teacher, in 399 B.C.E., in the aftermath of their defeat in the Peloponnesian War, condemning him on charges of impiety and for the corruption of young men. Socrates, who wrote nothing, left behind Plato, who wrote the founding texts of Western philosophy. His dialogues recorded or invented conversations among Socrates, his circle, and other men. Though Plato himself isn't a character in these dialogues, he used them as his vehicle for setting out defining issues for the Western traditions of ethics, political theory, logic, linguistics, theory of knowledge, rhetoric, and metaphysics. Plato was brought to remarkably sophisticated considerations of definition and knowledge by his dissatisfactions with the teachings of earlier thinkers including the pre-Socratics, the first physicists; the sophists, traveling teachers of rhetoric; and the politics of the city of his day. He portrays Socrates and his friends seeking to clarify such questions as the difference between opinion and true knowledge, the relationship between rhetoric and philosophy, the nature of language, the place of the gods in ethical life, and the role of poetry in society. What are often seen as earlier dialogues conclude with the participants' mutual recognition of ignorance. Later conversations explore such matters as the ideal society and its laws. In the course of Plato's writings, philosophy itself, "the love of wisdom," emerges for the first time as a distinct enterprise. Plato's dialogues combine highly rhetorical prose with dramatic techniques in order to explore the limits of knowledge and human existence, sometimes offering vivid portraits of men in flirtatious or passionate debate. Plato demonstrates an enduring suspicion of democracy, which allowed all citizen men to engage in politics, a task he believed should be conducted by experts—the guardian class he proposed to govern his ideal city, described in the *Republic*. The *Apology* is presented as the speech Socrates offers in his defense when put on trial by his enemies in Athens, written by Plato after Socrates was executed by being forced to drink hemlock, dying a martyr's death. In Plato's moving presentation, Socrates's trial becomes nothing less than a struggle for the soul of the Athenian polity.

Apology[1]

How you, O Athenians, have been affected by my accusers, I cannot tell; but I know that they almost made me forget who I was—so persuasively did they speak; and yet they have hardly uttered a word of truth. But of the many falsehoods told by them, there was one which quite amazed me;—I mean when they said that you should be upon your guard and not allow yourselves to be deceived by the force of my eloquence. To say this, when they were certain to be detected as soon as I opened my lips and proved myself to be anything but a great speaker, did indeed appear to me most shameless—unless by the force of eloquence they mean the force of truth; for if such is their meaning, I admit that I am eloquent. But in how different a way from theirs!

Well, as I was saying, they have scarcely spoken the truth at all; but from me you shall hear the whole truth; not, however, delivered after their manner in a set oration duly ornamented with words and phrases. No, by heaven! but I shall use the words and arguments which occur to me at the moment; for I am confident in the justice of my cause: at my time of life I ought not to be appearing before you, O men of Athens, in the character of a juvenile orator—let no one expect it of me. And I must beg of you to grant me a favour:—If I defend myself in my accustomed manner, and you hear me using the words which I have been in the habit of using in the agora,[2] at the

---

1. Translated by Benjamin Jowett.
2. Place of assembly, a marketplace.

tables of the money-changers, or anywhere else, I would ask you not to be surprised, and not to interrupt me on this account. For I am more than seventy years of age, and appearing now for the first time in a court of law, I am quite a stranger to the language of the place; and therefore I would have you regard me as if I were really a stranger, whom you would excuse if he spoke in his native tongue, and after the fashion of his country:—Am I making an unfair request of you? Never mind the manner, which may or may not be good; but think only of the truth of my words, and give heed to that: let the speaker speak truly and the judge decide justly.

And first, I have to reply to the older charges and to my first accusers, and then I will go on to the later ones. For of old I have had many accusers, who have accused me falsely to you during many years; and I am more afraid of them than of Anytus and his associates, who are dangerous, too, in their own way. But far more dangerous are the others, who began when you were children, and took possession of your minds with their falsehoods, telling of one Socrates, a wise man, who speculated about the heaven above, and searched into the earth beneath, and made the worse appear the better cause. The disseminators of this tale are the accusers whom I dread; for their hearers are apt to fancy that such enquirers do not believe in the existence of the gods. And they are many, and their charges against me are of ancient date, and they were made by them in the days when you were more impressible than you are now—in childhood, or it may have been in youth—and the cause when heard went by default, for there was none to answer. And hardest of all, I do not know and cannot tell the names of my accusers; unless in the chance case of a Comic poet. All who from envy and malice have persuaded you—some of them having first convinced themselves— all this class of men are most difficult to deal with; for I cannot have them up here, and cross-examine them, and therefore I must simply fight with shadows in my own defence, and argue when there is no one who answers. I will ask you then to assume with me, as I was saying, that my opponents are of two kinds; one recent, the other ancient: and I hope that you will see the propriety of my answering the latter first, for these accusations you heard long before the others, and much oftener.

Well, then, I must make my defence, and endeavor to clear away in a short time, a slander which has lasted a long time. May I succeed, if to succeed be for my good and yours, or likely to avail me in my cause! The task is not an easy one; I quite understand the nature of it. And so leaving the event with God, in obedience to the law I will now make my defence.

I will begin at the beginning, and ask what is the accusation which has given rise to the slander of me, and in fact has encouraged Meletus to prefer this charge against me. Well, what do the slanderers say? They shall be my prosecutors, and I will sum up their words in an affidavit: "Socrates is an evil-doer, and a curious person, who searches into things under the earth and in heaven, and he makes the worse appear the better cause; and he teaches the aforesaid doctrines to others." Such is the nature of the accusation: it is just what you have yourselves seen in the comedy of Aristophanes, who has introduced a man whom he calls Socrates, going about and saying that he walks in air, and talking a deal of nonsense concerning matters of which I do not pretend to know either much or little[3]—not that I mean to speak disparagingly of any one who is a student of natural philosophy. I should be very sorry if Meletus could bring so grave a charge against me. But the simple truth is, O Athenians, that I have nothing to do with physical speculations. Very many of those here present are witnesses to the truth of this, and to them I appeal. Speak then, you who have heard me, and tell your neighbours whether any of you have ever known me hold forth in

3. In Aristophanes's *Clouds*, which attacks Socrates as a ridiculous master of false reasoning.

few words or in many upon such matters.... You hear their answer. And from what they say of this part of the charge you will be able to judge of the truth of the rest.

As little foundation is there for the report that I am a teacher, and take money; this accusation has no more truth in it than the other.[4] Although, if a man were really able to instruct mankind, to receive money for giving instruction would, in my opinion, be an honour to him. There is Gorgias of Leontium, and Prodicus of Ceos, and Hippias of Elis, who go the round of the cities, and are able to persuade the young men to leave their own citizens by whom they might be taught for nothing, and come to them whom they not only pay, but are thankful if they may be allowed to pay them. There is at this time a Parian philosopher residing in Athens, of whom I have heard; and I came to hear of him in this way:—I came across a man who has spent a world of money on the Sophists, Callias, the son of Hipponicus, and knowing that he had sons, I asked him: "Callias," I said "if your two sons were foals or calves, there would be no difficulty in finding some one to put over them; we should hire a trainer of horses, or a farmer probably, who would improve and perfect them in their own proper virtue and excellence; but as they are human beings, whom are you thinking of placing over them? Is there any one who understands human and political virtue? You must have thought about the matter, for you have sons; is there any one?" "There is," he said. "Who is he?" said I; "and of what country? and what does he charge?" "Evenus the Parian," he replied; "he is the man, and his charge is five minae." Happy is Evenus, I said to myself, if he really has this wisdom, and teaches at such a moderate charge. Had I the same, I should have been very proud and conceited; but the truth is that I have no knowledge of the kind.

I dare say, Athenians, that some one among you will reply, "Yes, Socrates, but what is the origin of these accusations which are brought against you; there must have been something strange which you have been doing? All these rumours and this talk about you would never have arisen if you had been like other men: tell us, then, what is the cause of them, for we should be sorry to judge hastily of you." Now I regard this as a fair challenge, and I will endeavour to explain to you the reason why I am called wise and have such an evil fame. Please to attend then. And although some of you may think that I am joking, I declare that I will tell you the entire truth. Men of Athens, this reputation of mine has come of a certain sort of wisdom which I possess. If you ask me what kind of wisdom, I reply, wisdom such as may perhaps be attained by man, for to that extent I am inclined to believe that I am wise; whereas the persons of whom I was speaking have a superhuman wisdom, which I may fail to describe, because I have it not myself; and he who says that I have, speaks falsely, and is taking away my character. And here, O men of Athens, I must beg you not to interrupt me, even if I seem to say something extravagant. For the word which I will speak is not mine. I will refer you to a witness who is worthy of credit; that witness shall be the God of Delphi[5]—he will tell you about my wisdom, if I have any, and of what sort it is. You must have known Chaerephon; he was early a friend of mine, and also a friend of yours, for he shared in the recent exile of the people, and returned with you. Well, Chaerephon, as you know, was very impetuous in all his doings, and he went to Delphi and boldly asked the oracle to tell him whether—as I was saying, I must beg you not to interrupt—he asked the oracle to tell him whether any one was wiser than I was, and the Pythian prophetess answered, that there was no man wiser. Chaerephon is dead himself; but his brother, who is in court, will confirm the truth of what I am saying.

Why do I mention this? Because I am going to explain to you why I have such an evil name. When I heard the answer, I said to myself, What can the god mean? and what

---

4. Protagoras and other popular teachers of rhetoric made fortunes by their teaching.

5. Apollo

is the interpretation of his riddle? for I know that I have no wisdom, small or great. What then can he mean when he says that I am the wisest of men? And yet he is a god, and cannot lie; that would be against his nature. After long consideration, I thought of a method of trying the question. I reflected that if I could only find a man wiser than myself, then I might go to the god with a refutation in my hand. I should say to him, "Here is a man who is wiser than I am; but you said that I was the wisest." Accordingly I went to one who had the reputation of wisdom, and observed him—his name I need not mention; he was a politician whom I selected for examination—and the result was as follows: When I began to talk with him, I could not help thinking that he was not really wise, although he was thought wise by many, and still wiser by himself; and thereupon I tried to explain to him that he thought himself wise, but was not really wise; and the consequence was that he hated me, and his enmity was shared by several who were present and heard me. So I left him, saying to myself, as I went away: Well, although I do not suppose that either of us knows anything really beautiful and good, I am better off than he is,—for he knows nothing, and thinks that he knows; I neither know nor think that I know. In this latter particular, then, I seem to have slightly the advantage of him. Then I went to another who had still higher pretensions to wisdom, and my conclusion was exactly the same. Whereupon I made another enemy of him, and of many others besides him.

Then I went to one man after another, being not unconscious of the enmity which I provoked, and I lamented and feared this: But necessity was laid upon me,—the word of God, I thought, ought to be considered first. And I said to myself, Go I must to all who appear to know, and find out the meaning of the oracle. And I swear to you, Athenians, by the dog I swear!—for I must tell you the truth—the result of my mission was just this: I found that the men most in repute were all but the most foolish; and that others less esteemed were really wiser and better. I will tell you the tale of my wanderings and of the "Herculean" labours, as I may call them, which I endured only to find at last the oracle irrefutable.

After the politicians, I went to the poets; tragic, dithyrambic, and all sorts. And there, I said to myself, you will be instantly detected; now you will find out that you are more ignorant than they are. Accordingly, I took them some of the most elaborate passages in their own writings, and asked what was the meaning of them—thinking that they would teach me something. Will you believe me? I am almost ashamed to confess the truth, but I must say that there is hardly a person present who would not have talked better about their poetry than they did themselves. Then I knew that not by wisdom do poets write poetry, but by a sort of genius and inspiration; they are like diviners or soothsayers who also say many fine things, but do not understand the meaning of them. The poets appeared to me to be much in the same case; and I further observed that upon the strength of their poetry they believed themselves to be the wisest of men in other things in which they were not wise. So I departed, conceiving myself to be superior to them for the same reason that I was superior to the politicians.

At last I went to the artisans, for I was conscious that I knew nothing at all, as I may say; and I was sure that they knew many fine things; and here I was not mistaken, for they did know many things of which I was ignorant, and in this they certainly were wiser than I was. But I observed that even the good artisans fell into the same error as the poets;—because they were good workmen they thought that they also knew all sorts of high matters, and this defect in them overshadowed their wisdom; and therefore I asked myself on behalf of the oracle, whether I would like to be as I was, neither having their knowledge nor their ignorance, or like them in both; and I made answer to myself and to the oracle that I was better off as I was.

This inquisition has led to my having many enemies of the worst and most dangerous kind, and has given occasion also to many calumnies. And I am called wise, for my hearers always imagine that I myself possess the wisdom which I find wanting in others: but the truth is, O men of Athens, that God only is wise; and by his answer he intends to show that the wisdom of men is worth little or nothing; he is not speaking of Socrates, he is only using my name by way of illustration, as if he said, He, O men, is the wisest, who, like Socrates, knows that his wisdom is in truth worth nothing. And so I go about the world, obedient to the god, and search and make enquiry into the wisdom of any one, whether citizen or stranger, who appears to be wise; and if he is not wise, then in vindication of the oracle I show him that he is not wise; and my occupation quite absorbs me, and I have no time to give either to any public matter of interest or to any concern of my own, but I am in utter poverty by reason of my devotion to the god.

There is another thing:—young men of the richer classes, who have not much to do, come about me of their own accord; they like to hear the pretenders examined, and they often imitate me, and proceed to examine others; there are plenty of persons, as they quickly discover, who think that they know something, but really know little or nothing; and then those who are examined by them instead of being angry with themselves are angry with me: This confounded Socrates, they say; this villainous misleader of youth!— and then if somebody asks them, Why, what evil does he practise or teach? they do not know, and cannot tell; but in order that they may not appear to be at a loss, they repeat the ready-made charges which are used against all philosophers about teaching things up in the clouds and under the earth, and having no gods, and making the worse appear the better cause; for they do not like to confess that their pretence of knowledge has been detected—which is the truth; and as they are numerous and ambitious and energetic, and are drawn up in battle array and have persuasive tongues, they have filled your ears with their loud and inveterate calumnies. And this is the reason why my three accusers, Meletus and Anytus and Lycon, have set upon me; Meletus, who has a quarrel with me on behalf of the poets; Anytus, on behalf of the craftsmen and politicians; Lycon, on behalf of the rhetoricians: and as I said at the beginning, I cannot expect to get rid of such a mass of calumny all in a moment. And this, O men of Athens, is the truth and the whole truth; I have concealed nothing, I have dissembled nothing. And yet, I know that my plainness of speech makes them hate me, and what is their hatred but a proof that I am speaking the truth?—Hence has arisen the prejudice against me; and this is the reason of it, as you will find out either in this or in any future enquiry.

I have said enough in my defence against the first class of my accusers; I turn to the second class. They are headed by Meletus, that good man and true lover of his country, as he calls himself. Against these, too, I must try to make a defence:—Let their affidavit be read: it contains something of this kind: It says that Socrates is a doer of evil, who corrupts the youth; and who does not believe in the gods of the state, but has other new divinities of his own. Such is the charge; and now let us examine the particular counts. He says that I am a doer of evil, and corrupt the youth; but I say, O men of Athens, that Meletus is a doer of evil, in that he pretends to be in earnest when he is only in jest, and is so eager to bring men to trial from a pretended zeal and interest about matters in which he really never had the smallest interest. And the truth of this I will endeavour to prove to you.

Come hither, Meletus, and let me ask a question of you. You think a great deal about the improvement of youth?

Yes, I do.

Tell the judges, then, who is their improver; for you must know, as you have taken the pains to discover their corrupter, and are citing and accusing me before them. Speak, then, and tell the judges who their improver is.—Observe, Meletus, that you are silent, and have nothing to say. But is not this rather disgraceful, and a very considerable proof of what I was saying, that you have no interest in the matter? Speak up, friend, and tell us who their improver is.

The laws.

But that, my good sir, is not my meaning. I want to know who the person is, who, in the first place, knows the laws.

The judges,[6] Socrates, who are present in court.

What, do you mean to say, Meletus, that they are able to instruct and improve youth?

Certainly they are.

What, all of them, or some only and not others?

All of them.

By the goddess Hera, that is good news! There are plenty of improvers, then. And what do you say of the audience,—do they improve them?

Yes, they do.

And the senators?

Yes, the senators improve them.

But perhaps the members of the assembly corrupt them?—or do they too improve them?

They improve them.

Then every Athenian improves and elevates them; all with the exception of myself; and I alone am their corrupter? Is that what you affirm?

That is what I stoutly affirm.

I am very unfortunate if you are right. But suppose I ask you a question: How about horses? Does one man do them harm and all the world good? Is not the exact opposite the truth? One man is able to do them good, or at least not many;—the trainer of horses, that is to say, does them good, and others who have to do with them rather injure them? Is not that true, Meletus, of horses, or of any other animals? Most assuredly it is; whether you and Anytus say yes or no. Happy indeed would be the condition of youth if they had one corrupter only, and all the rest of the world were their improvers. But you, Meletus, have sufficiently shown that you never had a thought about the young: your carelessness is seen in your not caring about the very things which you bring against me.

And now, Meletus, I will ask you another question—by Zeus I will: Which is better, to live among bad citizens, or among good ones? Answer, friend, I say; the question is one which may be easily answered. Do not the good do their neighbours good, and the bad do them evil?

Certainly.

And is there any one who would rather be injured than benefited by those who live with him? Answer, my good friend, the law requires you to answer—does any one like to be injured?

Certainly not.

And when you accuse me of corrupting and deteriorating the youth, do you allege that I corrupt them intentionally or unintentionally?

6. Or jury; cases were judged by panels of as many as 500 fellow citizens.

Intentionally, I say.

But you have just admitted that the good do their neighbours good, and evil do them evil. Now, is that a truth which your superior wisdom has recognized thus early in life, and am I, at my age, in such darkness and ignorance as not to know that if a man with whom I have to live is corrupted by me, I am very likely to be harmed by him; and yet I corrupt him, and intentionally, too—so you say, although neither I nor any other human being is ever likely to be convinced by you. But either I do not corrupt them, or I corrupt them unintentionally; and on either view of the case you lie. If my offense is unintentional, the law has no cognizance of unintentional offences: you ought to have taken me privately, and warned and admonished me; for if I had been better advised, I should have left off doing what I only did unintentionally—no doubt I should; but you would have nothing to say to me and refused to teach me. And now you bring me up in this court, which is a place not of instruction, but of punishment.

It will be very clear to you, Athenians, as I was saying, that Meletus has no care at all, great or small, about the matter. But still I should like to know, Meletus, in what I am affirmed to corrupt the young. I suppose you mean, as I infer from your indictment, that I teach them not to acknowledge the gods which the state acknowledges, but some other new divinities or spiritual agencies in their stead. These are the lessons by which I corrupt the youth, as you say.

Yes, that I say emphatically.

Then, by the gods, Meletus, of whom we are speaking, tell me and the court, in somewhat plainer terms, what you mean! for I do not as yet understand whether you affirm that I teach other men to acknowledge some gods, and therefore that I do believe in gods, and am not an entire atheist—this you do not lay to my charge,—but only you say that they are not the same gods which the city recognizes—the charge is that they are different gods. Or, do you mean that I am an atheist simply, and a teacher of atheism?

I mean the latter—that you are a complete atheist.

What an extraordinary statement! Why do you think so, Meletus? Do you mean that I do not believe in the godhead of the sun or moon, like other men?

I assure you, judges, that he does not: for he says that the sun is stone, and the moon earth.

Friend Meletus, you think that you are accusing Anaxagoras:[7] and you have but a bad opinion of the judges, if you fancy them illiterate to such a degree as not to know that these doctrines are found in the books of Anaxagoras the Clazomenian, which are full of them. And so, forsooth, the youth are said to be taught them by Socrates, when there are not unfrequently exhibitions of them at the theatre (price of admission one drachma at the most); and they might pay their money, and laugh at Socrates if he pretends to father these extraordinary views. And so, Meletus, you really think that I do not believe in any god?

I swear by Zeus that you believe absolutely in none at all.

Nobody will believe you, Meletus, and I am pretty sure that you do not believe yourself. I cannot help thinking, men of Athens, that Meletus is reckless and impudent, and that he has written this indictment in a spirit of mere wantonness and youthful bravado. Has he not compounded a riddle, thinking to try me? He said to himself:—I shall see whether the wise Socrates will discover my facetious contradiction, or whether I shall be able to deceive him and the rest of them. For he certainly

___
7. A philosopher tried for impiety.

does appear to me to contradict himself in the indictment as much as if he said that Socrates is guilty of not believing in the gods, and yet of believing in them—but this is not like a person who is in earnest.

I should like you, O men of Athens, to join me in examining what I conceive to be his inconsistency; and do you, Meletus, answer. And I must remind the audience of my request that they would not make a disturbance if I speak in my accustomed manner:

Did ever man, Meletus, believe in the existence of human things, and not of human beings?...I wish, men of Athens, that he would answer, and not be always trying to get up, an interruption. Did ever any man believe in horsemanship, and not in horses? or in flute-playing, and not in flute-players? No, my friend; I will answer to you and to the court, as you refuse to answer for yourself. There is no man who ever did. But now please to answer the next question: Can a man believe in spiritual and divine agencies, and not in spirits or demigods?

He cannot.

How lucky I am to have extracted that answer, by the assistance of the court! But then you swear in the indictment that I teach and believe in divine or spiritual agencies (new or old, no matter for that); at any rate, I believe in spiritual agencies,—so you say and swear in the affidavit; and yet if I believe in divine beings, how can I help believing in spirits or demigods;—must I not? To be sure I must; and therefore I may assume that your silence gives consent. Now what are spirits or demigods? are they not either gods or the sons of gods?

Certainly they are.

But this is what I call the facetious riddle invented by you: the demigods or spirits are gods, and you say first that I do not believe in gods, and then again that I do believe in gods; that is, if I believe in demigods. For if the demigods are the illegitimate sons of gods, whether by the nymphs or by any other mothers, of whom they are said to be the sons—what human being will ever believe that there are no gods if they are the sons of gods? You might as well affirm the existence of mules, and deny that of horses and asses. Such nonsense, Meletus, could only have been intended by you to make trial of me. You have put this into the indictment because you had nothing real of which to accuse me. But no one who has a particle of understanding will ever be convinced by you that the same men can believe in divine and superhuman things, and yet not believe that there are gods and demigods and heroes.

I have said enough in answer to the charge of Meletus: any elaborate defence is unnecessary; but I know only too well how many are the enmities which I have incurred, and this is what will be my destruction if I am destroyed;—not Meletus, nor yet Anytus, but the envy and detraction of the world, which has been the death of many good men, and will probably be the death of many more; there is no danger of my being the last of them.

Someone will say: And are you not ashamed, Socrates, of a course of life which is likely to bring you to an untimely end? To him I may fairly answer: There you are mistaken: a man who is good for anything ought not to calculate the chance of living or dying; he ought only to consider whether in doing anything he is doing right or wrong—acting the part of a good man or of a bad. Whereas, upon your view, the heroes who fell at Troy were not good for much, and the son of Thetis[8] above all, who altogether despised danger in comparison with disgrace; and when he was so eager

---

8. Achilles.

to slay Hector, his goddess mother said to him, that if he avenged his companion Patroclus, and slew Hector, he would die himself—"Fate," she said, in these or the like words, "waits for you next after Hector"; he, receiving this warning, utterly despised danger and death, and instead of fearing them, feared rather to live in dishonour, and not to avenge his friend. "Let me die forthwith," he replies, "and be avenged of my enemy, rather than abide here by the beaked ships, a laughing-stock and a burden of the earth." Had Achilles any thought of death and danger? For wherever a man's place is, whether the place which he has chosen or that in which he has been placed by a commander, there he ought to remain in the hour of danger; he should not think of death or of anything but of disgrace. And this, O men of Athens, is a true saying.

Strange, indeed, would be my conduct, O men of Athens, if I who, when I was ordered by the generals whom you chose to command me at Potidaea and Amphipolis and Delium,[9] remained where they placed me, like any other man, facing death—if now, when, as I conceive and imagine, God orders me to fulfil the philosopher's mission of searching into myself and other men, I were to desert my post through fear of death, or any other fear; that would indeed be strange, and I might justly be arraigned in court for denying the existence of the gods, if I disobeyed the oracle because I was afraid of death, fancying that I was wise when I was not wise. For the fear of death is indeed the pretence of wisdom, and not real wisdom, being a pretence of knowing the unknown; and no one knows whether death, which men in their fear apprehend to be the greatest evil, may not be the greatest good. Is not this ignorance of a disgraceful sort, the ignorance which is the conceit that man knows what he does not know? And in this respect only I believe myself to differ from men in general, and may perhaps claim to be wiser than they are:—that whereas I know but little of the world below, I do not suppose that I know: but I do know that injustice and disobedience to a better, whether God or man, is evil and dishonourable, and I will never fear or avoid a possible good rather than a certain evil.

And therefore if you let me go now, and are not convinced by Anytus, who said that since I had been prosecuted I must be put to death (or if not that I ought never to have been prosecuted at all); and that if I escape now, your sons will all be utterly ruined by listening to my words—if you say to me, Socrates, this time we will not mind Anytus, and you shall be let off, but upon one condition, that you are not to enquire and speculate in this way any more, and that if you are caught doing so again you shall die;—if this was the condition on which you let me go, I should reply: Men of Athens, I honour and love you; but I shall obey God rather than you, and while I have life and strength I shall never cease from the practice and teaching of philosophy, exhorting any one whom I meet and saying to him after my manner: You, my friend,—a citizen of the great and mighty and wise city of Athens,—are you not ashamed of heaping up the greatest amount of money and honour and reputation, and caring so little about wisdom and truth and the greatest improvement of the soul, which you never regard or heed at all? And if the person with whom I am arguing, says: Yes, but I do care; then I do not leave him or let him go at once; but I proceed to interrogate and examine and cross-examine him, and if I think that he has no virtue in him, but only says that he has, I reproach him with undervaluing the greater, and over-valuing the less. And I shall repeat the same words to every one whom I meet, young and old, citizen and alien, but especially to the citizens, inasmuch as they are my brethren.

9. As a younger man, Socrates had been a foot soldier in these battles during the Peloponnesian War.

For know that this is the command of God; and I believe that no greater good has ever happened in the state than my service to the God. For I do nothing but go about persuading you all, old and young alike, not to take thought for your persons or your properties, but first and chiefly to care about the greatest improvement of the soul. I tell you that virtue is not given by money, but that from virtue comes money and every other good of man, public as well as private. This is my teaching, and if this is the doctrine which corrupts the youth, I am a mischievous person. But if any one says that this is not my teaching, he is speaking an untruth. Wherefore, O men of Athens, I say to you, do as Anytus bids or not as Anytus bids, and either acquit me or not; but whichever you do, understand that I shall never alter my ways, not even if I have to die many times.

Men of Athens, do not interrupt, but hear me; there was an understanding between us that you should hear me to the end: I have something more to say, at which you may be inclined to cry out; but I believe that to hear me will be good for you, and therefore I beg that you will not cry out. I would have you know, that if you kill such a one as I am, you will injure yourselves more than you will injure me. Nothing will injure me, not Meletus nor yet Anytus—they cannot, for a bad man is not permitted to injure a better than himself. I do not deny that Anytus may, perhaps, kill him, or drive him into exile, or deprive him of civil rights; and he may imagine, and others may imagine, that he is inflicting a great injury upon him: but there I do not agree. For the evil of doing as he is doing—the evil of unjustly taking away the life of another—is greater far.

And now, Athenians, I am not going to argue for my own sake, as you may think, but for yours, that you may not sin against the God by condemning me, who am his gift to you. For if you kill me you will not easily find a successor to me, who, if I may use such a ludicrous figure of speech, am a sort of gadfly,[1] given to the state by God; and the state is a great and noble steed who is tardy in his motions owing to his very size, and requires to be stirred into life. I am that gadfly which God has attached to the state, and all day long and in all places am always fastening upon you, arousing and persuading and reproaching you. You will not easily find another like me, and therefore I would advise you to spare me. I dare say that you may feel out of temper (like a person who is suddenly awakened from sleep), and you think that you might easily strike me dead as Anytus advises, and then you would sleep on for the remainder of your lives, unless God in his care of you sent you another gadfly. When I say that I am given to you by God, the proof of my mission is this:—if I had been like other men, I should not have neglected all my own concerns or patiently seen the neglect of them during all these years, and have been doing yours, coming to you individually like a father or elder brother, exhorting you to regard virtue; such conduct, I say, would be unlike human nature. If I had gained anything, or if my exhortations had been paid, there would have been some sense in my doing so; but now, as you will perceive, not even the impudence of my accusers dares to say that I have ever exacted or sought pay of any one; of that they have no witness. And I have a sufficient witness to the truth of what I say—my poverty.

Some one may wonder why I go about in private giving advice and busying myself with the concerns of others, but do not venture to come forward in public and advise the state. I will tell you why. You have heard me speak at sundry times and in divers places of an oracle or sign which comes to me, and is the divinity which Meletus

1. Horsefly.

ridicules in the indictment. This sign, which is a kind of voice, first began to come to me when I was a child; it always forbids but never commands me to do anything which I am going to do. This is what deters me from being a politician. And rightly, as I think. For I am certain, O men of Athens, that if I had engaged in politics, I should have perished long ago, and done no good either to you or to myself. And do not be offended at my telling you the truth: for the truth is, that no man who goes to war with you or any other multitude, honestly striving against the many lawless and unrighteous deeds which are done in a state, will save his life; he who will fight for the right, if he would live even for a brief space, must have a private station and not a public one.

I can give you convincing evidence of what I say, not words only, but what you value far more—actions. Let me relate to you a passage of my own life which will prove to you that I should never have yielded to injustice from any fear of death, and that "as I should have refused to yield" I must have died at once. I will tell you a tale of the courts, not very interesting perhaps, but nevertheless true. The only office of state which I ever held, O men of Athens, was that of senator: the tribe Antiochis, which is my tribe, had the presidency at the trial of the generals who had not taken up the bodies of the slain after the battle of Arginusae;[2] and you proposed to try them in a body, contrary to law, as you all thought afterwards; but at the time I was the only one of the Prytanes who was opposed to the illegality, and I gave my vote against you; and when the orators threatened to impeach and arrest me, and you called and shouted, I made up my mind that I would run the risk, having law and justice with me, rather than take part in your injustice because I feared imprisonment and death. This happened in the days of the democracy. But when the oligarchy of the Thirty[3] was in power, they sent for me and four others into the rotunda, and bade us bring Leon the Salaminian from Salamis, as they wanted to put him to death. This was a specimen of the sort of commands which they were always giving with the view of implicating as many as possible in their crimes; and then I showed, not in word only but in deed, that, if I may be allowed to use such an expression, I cared not a straw for death, and that my great and only care was lest I should do an unrighteous or unholy thing. For the strong arm of that oppressive power did not frighten me into doing wrong; and when we came out of the rotunda the other four went to Salamis and fetched Leon, but I went quietly home. For which I might have lost my life, had not the power of the Thirty shortly afterwards come to an end. And many will witness to my words.

Now do you really imagine that I could have survived all these years, if I had led a public life, supposing that like a good man I had always maintained the right and had made justice, as I ought, the first thing? No indeed, men of Athens, neither I nor any other man. But I have been always the same in all my actions, public as well as private, and never have I yielded any base compliance to those who are slanderously termed my disciples, or to any other. Not that I have any regular disciples. But if anyone likes to come and hear me while I am pursuing my mission, whether he be young or old, he is not excluded. Nor do I converse only with those who pay; but anyone, whether he be rich or poor, may ask and answer me and listen to my words; and whether he turns out to be a bad man or a good one, neither result can be justly imputed to me; for I never taught or professed to teach him anything. And if anyone says that he has ever learned or heard anything from me in private which all the world has not heard, let me tell you that he is lying.

2. Athenian victory in the Peloponnesian War in 406 B.C.E.
3. Members of the antidemocratic coup of 404 B.C.E.

But I shall be asked, Why do people delight in continually conversing with you? I have told you already, Athenians, the whole truth about this matter: they like to hear the cross-examination of the pretenders to wisdom; there is amusement in it. Now this duty of cross-examining other men has been imposed upon me by God; and has been signified to me by oracles, visions, and in every way in which the will of divine power was ever intimated to any one. This is true, O Athenians; or, if not true, would be soon refuted. If I am or have been corrupting the youth, those of them who are now grown up and become sensible that I gave them bad advice in the days of their youth should come forward as accusers, and take their revenge; or if they do not like to come themselves, some of their relatives, fathers, brothers, or other kinsmen, should say what evil their families have suffered at my hands.

Now is their time. Many of them I see in the court. There is Crito, who is of the same age and of the same deme with myself, and there is Critobulus his son, whom I also see. Then again there is Lysanias of Sphettus, who is the father of Aeschines—he is present; and also there is Antiphon of Cephisus, who is the father of Epigenes; and there are the brothers of several who have associated with me. There is Nicostratus the son of Theosdotides, and the brother of Theodotus (now Theodotus himself is dead, and therefore he, at any rate, will not seek to stop him); and there is Paralus the son of Demodocus, who had a brother Theages; and Adeimantus the son of Ariston, whose brother Plato is present; and Aeantodorus, who is the brother of Apollodorus, whom I also see. I might mention a great many others, some of whom Meletus should have produced as witnesses in the course of his speech; and let him still produce them, if he has forgotten—I will make way for him. And let him say, if he has any testimony of the sort which he can produce. Nay, Athenians, the very opposite is the truth. For all these are ready to witness on behalf of the corrupter, of the injurer of their kindred, as Meletus and Anytus call me; not the corrupted youth only—there might have been a motive for that—but their uncorrupted elder relatives. Why should they too support me with their testimony? Why, indeed, except for the sake of truth and justice, and because they know that I am speaking the truth, and that Meletus is a liar.

Well, Athenians, this and the like of this is all the defence which I have to offer. Yet a word more. Perhaps there may be some one who is offended at me, when he calls to mind how he himself on a similar, or even a less serious occasion, prayed and entreated the judges with many tears, and how he produced his children in court, which was a moving spectacle, together with a host of relations and friends; whereas I, who am probably in danger of my life, will do none of these things. The contrast may occur to his mind, and he may be set against me, and vote in anger because he is displeased at me on this account. Now if there be such a person among you,—mind, I do not say that there is,—to him I may fairly reply: My friend, I am a man, and like other men, a creature of flesh and blood, and not "of wood or stone," as Homer says;[4] and I have a family, yes, and sons, O Athenians, three in number, one almost a man, and two others who are still young; and yet I will not bring any of them hither in order to petition you for an acquittal. And why not? Not from any self-assertion or want of respect for you. Whether I am or am not afraid of death is another question, of which I will not now speak. But, having regard to public opinion, I feel that such conduct would be discreditable to myself, and to you, and to the whole state. One who has reached my years, and who has a name for wisdom, ought not to demean himself.

Whether this opinion of me be deserved or not, at any rate the world has decided that Socrates is in some way superior to other men. And if those among you who are

4. In the *Odyssey*, Book 19, line 184.

said to be superior in wisdom and courage, and any other virtue, demean themselves in this way, how shameful is their conduct! I have seen men of reputation, when they have been condemned, behaving in the strangest manner: they seemed to fancy that they were going to suffer something dreadful if they died, and that they could be immortal if you only allowed them to live; and I think that such are a dishonour to the state, and that any stranger coming in would have said of them that the most eminent men of Athens, to whom the Athenians themselves give honour and command, are no better than women. And I say that these things ought not to be done by those of us who have a reputation; and if they are done, you ought not to permit them; you ought rather to show that you are far more disposed to condemn the man who gets up a doleful scene and makes the city ridiculous, than him who holds his peace.

But, setting aside the question of public opinion, there seems to be something wrong in asking a favour of a judge, and thus procuring an acquittal, instead of informing and convincing him. For his duty is, not to make a present of justice, but to give judgment; and he has sworn that he will judge according to the laws, and not according to his own good pleasure; and we ought not to encourage you, nor should you allow yourself to be encouraged, in this habit of perjury—there can be no piety in that. Do not then require me to do what I consider dishonourable and impious and wrong, especially now, when I am being tried for impiety on the indictment of Meletus. For if, O men of Athens, by force of persuasion and entreaty I could overpower your oaths, then I should be teaching you to believe that there are no gods, and in defending should simply convict myself of the charge of not believing in them. But that is not so—far otherwise. For I do believe that there are gods, and in a sense higher than that in which any of my accusers believe in them. And to you and to God I commit my cause, to be determined by you as is best for you and me.

There are many reasons why I am not grieved, O men of Athens, at the vote of condemnation. I expected it, and am only surprised that the votes are so nearly equal; for I had thought that the majority against me would have been far larger; but now, had thirty votes gone over to the other side, I should have been acquitted. And I may say, I think, that I have escaped Meletus. I may say more; for without the assistance of Anytus and Lycon, anyone may see that he would not have had a fifth part of the votes, as the law requires, in which case he would have incurred a fine of a thousand drachmae.

And so he proposes death as the penalty. And what shall I propose on my part, O men of Athens? Clearly that which is my due. And what is my due? What return shall be made to the man who has never had the wit to be idle during his whole life; but has been careless of what the many care for—wealth, and family interests, and military offices, and speaking in the assembly, and magistracies, and plots, and parties. Reflecting that I was really too honest a man to be a politician and live, I did not go where I could do no good to you or to myself; but where I could do the greatest good privately to every one of you, thither I went, and sought to persuade every man among you that he must look to himself, and seek virtue and wisdom before he looks to his private interests, and look to the state before he looks to the interests of the state; and that this should be the order which he observes in all his actions. What shall be done to such a one? Doubtless some good thing, O men of Athens, if he has his reward; and the good should be of a kind suitable to him. What would be a reward suitable to a poor man who is your benefactor, and who desires leisure that he may instruct you? There can be no reward so fitting as maintenance in the Prytaneum,[5] O men of Athens, a reward which he deserves far more than the citizen who has won the

5. Building where officials dined at the democratic city's expense.

prize at Olympia in the horse or chariot race, whether the chariots were drawn by two horses or by many. For I am in want, and he has enough; and he only gives you the appearance of happiness, and I give you the reality. And if I am to estimate the penalty fairly, I should say that maintenance in the Prytaneum is the just return.

Perhaps you think that I am defying you in what I am saying now, as in what I said before about the tears and prayers. But this is not so. I speak rather because I am convinced that I never intentionally wronged any one, although I cannot convince you—the time has been too short; if there were a law at Athens, as there is in other cities, that a capital cause should not be decided in one day, then I believe that I should have convinced you. But I cannot in a moment refute great slanders; and, as I am convinced that I never wronged another, I will assuredly not wrong myself. I will not say of myself that I deserve any evil, or propose any penalty. Why should I? Because I am afraid of the penalty of death which Meletus proposes? When I do not know whether death is a good or an evil, why should I propose a penalty which would certainly be an evil? Shall I say imprisonment? And why should I live in prison, and be the slave of the magistrates of the year—of the Eleven? Or shall the penalty be a fine, and imprisonment until the fine is paid? There is the same objection. I should have to lie in prison, for money I have none, and cannot pay. And if I say exile (and this may possibly be the penalty which you will affix), I must indeed be blinded by the love of life, if I am so irrational as to expect that when you, who are my own citizens, cannot endure my discourses and words, and have found them so grievous and odious that you will have no more of them, others are likely to endure me. No indeed, men of Athens, that is not very likely. And what a life should I lead, at my age, wandering from city to city, ever changing my place of exile, and always being driven out! For I am quite sure that wherever I go, there, as here, the young men will flock to me; and if I drive them away, their elders will drive me out at their request; and if I let them come, their fathers and friends will drive me out for their sakes.

Some one will say: Yes, Socrates, but cannot you hold your tongue, and then you may go into a foreign city, and no one will interfere with you? Now I have great difficulty in making you understand my answer to this. For if I tell you that to do as you say would be a disobedience to the God, and therefore that I cannot hold my tongue, you will not believe that I am serious; and if I say again that daily to discourse about virtue, and of those other things about which you hear me examining myself and others, is the greatest good of man, and that the unexamined life is not worth living, you are still less likely to believe me. Yet I say what is true, although a thing of which it is hard for me to persuade you. Also, I have never been accustomed to think that I deserve to suffer any harm. Had I money I might have estimated the offence at what I was able to pay, and not have been much the worse. But I have none, and therefore I must ask you to proportion the fine to my means. Well, perhaps I could afford a mina,[6] and therefore I propose that penalty: Plato, Crito, Critobulus, and Apollodorus, my friends here, bid me say thirty minae, and they will be the sureties. Let thirty minae be the penalty; for which sum they will be ample security to you.

Not much time will be gained, O Athenians, in return for the evil name which you will get from the detractors of the city, who will say that you killed Socrates, a wise man; for they will call me wise, even although I am not wise, when they want to reproach you. If you had waited a little while, your desire would have been fulfilled in the course of nature. For I am far advanced in years, as you may perceive, and not far from

28

---

6. According to Xenophon, this modest sum was a fifth of Socrates's possessions.

death. I am speaking now not to all of you, but only to those who have condemned me to death. And I have another thing to say to them: You think that I was convicted because I had no words of the sort which would have procured my acquittal—I mean, if I had thought fit to leave nothing undone or unsaid. Not so; the deficiency which led to my conviction was not of words—certainly not. But I had not the boldness or impudence or inclination to address you as you would have liked me to do, weeping and wailing and lamenting, and saying and doing many things which you have been accustomed to hear from others, and which, as I maintain, are unworthy of me.

I thought at the time that I ought not to do anything common or mean when in danger: nor do I now repent of the style of my defence; I would rather die having spoken after my manner, than speak in your manner and live. For neither in war nor yet at law ought I or any man to use every way of escaping death. Often in battle there can be no doubt that if a man will throw away his arms, and fall on his knees before his pursuers, he may escape death; and in other dangers there are other ways of escaping death, if a man is willing to say and do anything. The difficulty, my friends, is not to avoid death, but to avoid unrighteousness; for that runs faster than death. I am old and move slowly, and the slower runner has overtaken me, and my accusers are keen and quick, and the faster runner, who is unrighteousness, has overtaken them. And now I depart hence condemned by you to suffer the penalty of death,—they too go their ways condemned by the truth to suffer the penalty of villainy and wrong; and I must abide by my award—let them abide by theirs. I suppose that these things may be regarded as fated,—and I think that they are well.

And now, O men who have condemned me, I would like to prophesy to you; for I am about to die, and in the hour of death men are gifted with prophetic power. And I prophesy to you who are my murderers, that immediately after my departure punishment far heavier than you have inflicted on me will surely await you. Me you have killed because you wanted to escape the accuser, and not to give an account of your lives. But that will not be as you suppose: far otherwise. For I say that there will be more accusers of you than there are now; accusers whom hitherto I have restrained: and as they are younger they will be more inconsiderate with you, and you will be more offended at them. If you think that by killing men you can prevent some one from censuring your evil lives, you are mistaken; that is not a way of escape which is either possible or honourable; the easiest and the noblest way is not to be disabling others, but to be improving yourselves. This is the prophecy which I utter before my departure to the judges who have condemned me.

Friends, who would have acquitted me, I would like also to talk with you about the thing which has come to pass, while the magistrates are busy, and before I go to the place at which I must die. Stay then a little, for we may as well talk with one another while there is time. You are my friends, and I should like to show you the meaning of this event which has happened to me. O my judges—for you I may truly call judges— I should like to tell you of a wonderful circumstance. Hitherto the divine faculty of which the internal oracle is the source has constantly been in the habit of opposing me even about trifles, if I was going to make a slip or error in any matter; and now as you see there has come upon me that which may be thought, and is generally believed to be, the last and worst evil. But the oracle made no sign of opposition, either when I was leaving my house in the morning, or when I was on my way to the court, or while I was speaking, at anything which I was going to say; and yet I have often been stopped in the middle of a speech, but now in nothing I either said or did touching the matter in hand has the oracle opposed me. What do I take to be the explanation of this silence? I will tell you. It is an intimation that what has happened to me is a good, and that those of us who think that death is an evil are in error. For the customary sign would surely have opposed me had I been going to evil and not to good.

Let us reflect in another way, and we shall see that there is great reason to hope that death is a good; for one of two things—either death is a state of nothingness and utter unconsciousness, or, as men say, there is a change and migration of the soul from this world to another. Now if you suppose that there is no consciousness, but a sleep like the sleep of him who is undisturbed even by dreams, death will be an unspeakable gain. For if a person were to select the night in which his sleep was undisturbed even by dreams, and were to compare with this the other days and nights of his life, and then were to tell us how many days and nights he had passed in the course of his life better and more pleasantly than this one, I think that any man, I will not say a private man, but even the great king[7] will not find many such days or nights, when compared with the others. Now if death be of such a nature, I say that to die is gain; for eternity is then only a single night.

But if death is the journey to another place, and there, as men say, all the dead abide, what good, O my friends and judges, can be greater than this? If indeed when the pilgrim arrives in the world below, he is delivered from the professors of justice in this world, and finds the true judges who are said to give judgment there, Minos and Rhadamanthus and Aeacus and Triptolemus, and other sons of God who were righteous in their own life, that pilgrimage will be worth making. What would not a man give if he might converse with Orpheus and Musaeus and Hesiod and Homer?[8] Nay, if this be true, let me die again and again. I myself, too, shall have a wonderful interest in there meeting and conversing with Palamedes, and Ajax the son of Telamon, and any other ancient hero who has suffered death through an unjust judgment; and there will be no small pleasure, as I think, in comparing my own sufferings with theirs. Above all, I shall then be able to continue my search into true and false knowledge; as in this world, so also in the next; and I shall find out who is wise, and who pretends to be wise, and is not. What would not a man give, O judges, to be able to examine the leader of the great Trojan expedition; or Odysseus or Sisyphus, or numberless others, men and women too! What infinite delight would there be in conversing with them and asking them questions! In another world they do not put a man to death for asking questions: assuredly not. For besides being happier than we are, they will be immortal, if what is said is true.

Wherefore, O judges, be of good cheer about death, and know of a certainty, that no evil can happen to a good man, either in life or after death. He and his are not neglected by the gods; nor has my own approaching end happened by mere chance. But I see clearly that the time had arrived when it was better for me to die and be released from trouble; wherefore the oracle gave no sign. For which reason, also, I am not angry with my condemners, or with my accusers; they have done me no harm, although they did not mean to do me any good; and for this I may gently blame them.

Still I have a favour to ask of them. When my sons are grown up, I would ask you, O my friends, to punish them; and I would have you trouble them, as I have troubled you, if they seem to care about riches, or anything, more than about virtue; or if they pretend to be something when they are really nothing,—then reprove them, as I have reproved you, for not caring about that for which they ought to care, and thinking that they are something when they are really nothing. And if you do this, both I and my sons will have received justice at your hands.

The hour of departure has arrived, and we go our ways—I to die, and you to live. Which is better God only knows.

---

7. The Persian emperor.

8. The four legendary founders of poetry.

A teller of tales, so the story goes, was once reciting the *Ramayana*. He got to the part where Prince Rama explains to Sita, his wife, that she must stay in the city of Ayodhya and not accompany him into forest exile. After trying to dissuade him without success, Sita cries out, "Thousands of *Ramayanas* have been composed before this, and there isn't one in which Sita doesn't go with her husband!" The argument is persuasive, and Rama agrees to take her along.

Thousands of *Ramayanas?* Yes, quite likely, if we include all the versions from across Asia in all the different regional languages over the past two thousand years, to say nothing of the countless modern films, performance genres, and forms of popular culture ranging from peasant songs to comic books. And many of these versions are as self-aware as the little story recounted above, as far as their relationship to other tellings and their social, political, or historical location. The fact is indisputable: the story of Rama—his banishment to the forest on the eve of his coronation, the abduction of his wife, Sita, by the demon king Ravana, his defeat of the enemy and recovery of Sita—has had an impact on the literary imagination of India and wider Asia that is more intense and enduring than any other narrative, bar none. *Ramayanas* are found from Kashmir to Tibet to China and from Sri Lanka to Thailand, Laos, and Java. And it isn't just literary imagination that has been influenced by the story. The different *Ramayanas,* each of them making a particular argument appropriate for its own time and place, have contributed to shaping the spheres of religion, politics, and everyday morality to a degree unmatched by any other work in Indian history.

The version of the *Ramayana* to which many retellings explicitly or implicitly respond—retellings are always responses—is the Sanskrit work of Valmiki. As is so often the case in early Sanskrit literature, we have no reliable historical knowledge about the author, and dating his poem has proved to be difficult. The *Ramayana* contains an account of its own creation: it presents itself as the "first literary work" (*kavya*), a thing said to be previously unknown in Indian culture. But what its newness actually consists of is not entirely clear. The text itself links its novelty with the metrical form of the poem, but the verse structure used for most of the work is far older than the *Ramayana* of Valmiki could possibly be. Its self-identification as the first poem, along with everything else we know about it, suggests a relatively late date. Although tradition holds that the events of the *Mahabharata* took place in the Second Age from the present, whereas the *Ramayana* took place in the third, previous age, the *Ramayana* is later than the core text of the Bharata epic (c. 300 B.C.E.) since Valmiki knows the main story and has used it to deftly structure his own narrative. His thought world has features in common with that of King Ashoka, who issued his inscriptions in the middle of the third century B.C.E. And the history of Sanskrit literature, as "literature" comes to be defined in the Sanskrit tradition, begins only around the start of the Common Era. All these considerations point toward 200 B.C.E. or so as the likeliest period of the creation of the poem that came to bear Valmiki's name.

Some scholars dispute the proposition that any one person created the *Ramayana*. The manuscript history of the work clearly reveals substantial variation owing to a period of oral transmission. And like the *Mahabharata,* Valmiki's text was subject to continual expansion; an entire book, the seventh and last, was added at some point (perhaps along with the greater part of the first). Yet the oral variation of the *Ramayana* remains a variation of one and the same poem. The text was probably more or less memorized (the poem itself says as much) and was committed to writing at different times and places; it was assuredly not composed anew with each telling, as occurred in other oral epic traditions, such as the

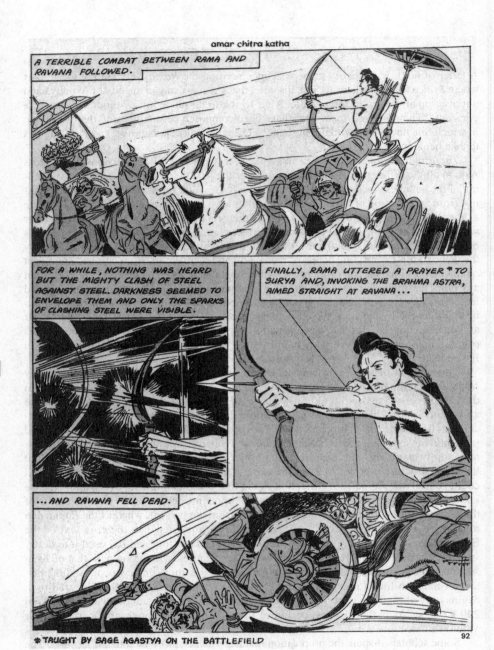

A TERRIBLE COMBAT BETWEEN RAMA AND RAVANA FOLLOWED.

FOR A WHILE, NOTHING WAS HEARD BUT THE MIGHTY CLASH OF STEEL AGAINST STEEL. DARKNESS SEEMED TO ENVELOPE THEM AND ONLY THE SPARKS OF CLASHING STEEL WERE VISIBLE.

FINALLY, RAMA UTTERED A PRAYER * TO SURYA AND, INVOKING THE BRAHMA ASTRA, AIMED STRAIGHT AT RAVANA...

...AND RAVANA FELL DEAD.

* TAUGHT BY SAGE AGASTYA ON THE BATTLEFIELD

92

A contemporary Indian comic book rendering depicts the death of Ravana in Valmiki's *Ramayana*.

Serbo-Croatian. A single voice can clearly be heard in Books 2 through 6, a voice of a sort that had never been heard before in Sanskrit.

There is a degree of literary artistry present in every level of the text—from the cohesiveness and sustained momentum of the grand narrative all the way down to the individual image—that is consistent across the poem and quite unlike anything else found in earlier Sanskrit works. One small example of this occurs in Book 3: Rama has gone off to hunt a magic deer, which in reality is a demon sent by Ravana, who had gotten word of Sita's beauty, to lure Rama away from the hermitage where he is living out his exile. Rama's younger brother, Lakshmana, told to guard Sita, has reluctantly left her alone after hearing what he thinks is Rama's cry for help (it is, of course, the demon's cry). This is Ravana's opening, and Valmiki describes his approach with the unobtrusive skill of a meticulous artist, using a half dozen different verbs of motion to bring our apprehension slowly to a climax:

> Assuming the guise of a wandering mendicant, he turned his steps toward Vaidehi...
> Clad in a soft saffron robe, with topknot, parasol, and sandals...he approached Vaidehi...
> Both brothers had left her, and in his pride of power he advanced upon her...
> Ten-necked Ravana had waited for an opening...In the guise of a beggar he drew near to Vaidehi...
> As Vaidehi sat grieving for her husband, the unholy Ravana in the guise of a holy man edged closer to her...
> The blackhearted stalker of the night stole ever closer to Vaidehi

This kind of expressive care is in evidence throughout the poem, and often achieves a level of artistry with which the aesthetic of the *Mahabharata* narrative—powerful, even overwhelming in its own right—has nothing in common.

There are many other differences between these two defining works of Indian culture, but the most telling are at the level of argument and ethic. In fact, Valmiki's poem can be read as a response to the apocalyptic vision of social and political disintegration encountered in the *Mahabharata*. The basic narrative problem is identical to that found in the other text: when their aged father, King Dasharatha, declares his intention to abdicate, the two brothers Rama and Bharata would be expected to contest the succession of power. But no struggle ensues, since Rama is ready to withdraw and Bharata is ready to submit to Rama (it is almost as if no one wants the kingship). Again, like Draupadi, wife of the five Pandava brothers in the *Mahabharata*, Sita is the target of a violent attack. In this case, however, it is not a brother who attacks her but a (literally) demonized outsider, Ravana, king of the *rakshasas*, imaginary beings who embody all that is most feared—and perhaps most desired—by traditional Indian readers. In these two episodes we glimpse a major transformation in the epic narrative tradition that is the ongoing concern of Valmiki's work: the conundrum of power is solved, and its dangerous energies are displaced from brothers to Others.

Key to this transformation is the character of Rama. Almost from their first acquaintance with the poem, Western scholars without exception believed that the hero's divinity was the result of later revision. The original *Ramayana*, they thought, must have been a tale of a simple human hero struggling against evil; the text was eventually appropriated by devotees of the god Vishnu, who turned the work into a theological tract. This long-held interpretation has been shown to be false. The divinity of Rama—not as the major god Vishnu, but as an undoubtedly transcendent being—is a constitutive part of the poem, not only textually but logically. Now that a reasonably complete picture of the manuscript history of the work is available, it has become clear that no textual criticism allows for the removal of all references to Rama's divinity; it is an inexpungable part of the text. The logic of the story shows what kind of divinity this is, one similar to the semidivine status of epic heroes such as Gilgamesh (see page 29) and Achilles (see page 95), but far transcending it. When the demon king Ravana accepts the wish he has been granted from the great god Shiva, he couches it in terms he believes will ensure his immortality: he asks to be invincible to gods, demigods, men, and animals. What he fails to include in his list is what proves to be his undoing: a life-form that is part man and part god. Just such a being is Rama, both man and god at once. And this, as the text powerfully suggests, is what all real kings are supposed to be.

This mode of being also points toward a mode of behaving that enables Rama to escape the paralyzing moral dilemma of the *Mahabharata*. Can any acceptable definition of *dharma*— right, law, duty—require the slaughter of one's kinsmen? The *Mahabharata* has no workable answer to this horrific predicament; not even the doctrine of the *Bhagavad Gita*, the disinterested execution of one's *dharma*, seems an adequate response. Instead, the *Mahabharata* only shows what happens when the logic especially of the duty of the warrior is allowed to follow its course. This is precisely what Rama rejects. He juxtaposes the warrior's duty (Kshatriya *dharma*) to a higher law, that of hierarchical obedience—of son to father, younger brother to elder brother. This ethic ensures peace among the contestants to power, and, in the end, a utopian reign in the kingdom. Equally important is that those who in any way oppose this vision are not truly human; they are demonic beings and can with justice be destroyed.

Because of its success in framing moral problems, Valmiki's *Ramayana* has long been held to provide models of conduct for the everyday lives of everyday people; even today, opinion polls show that Sita is the most influential figure in the lives of young Indian girls. As an old proverb advises, "Act like Rama, and never like Ravana." No one was ever told to "act like Krishna"; it is what Krishna and other such deities say, not what they do, that readers and listeners are told to follow. But the *Ramayana* offers positive paradigms for life, and no other work remotely approximates it for the didactic force it has exercised throughout India's history.

WHO'S WHO IN THE *RAMAYANA*

Dasharatha: DUH-shuh-RUH-thuh; king of Ayodhya (uh-YOH-dhyah)
His four sons:

Rama: RAH-muh
Bharata: BHUH-ruh-tuh
Lakshmana: LUHK-shmuh-nuh
Shatrughna: SHUH-troo-ghnuh

Kausalya: kow-SUHL-yah; mother of Rama
Kaikeyi: kai-KAY-yee; mother of Bharata
Sumitra: su-MEE-trah; mother of Lakshmana and Shatrughna
Sita: SEE-tah; wife of Rama

The Ramayana of Valmiki
from Book 2[1]

[The Exile of Rama]

Sarga 7

Now, Kaikeyī's family servant, who had lived with her from the time of her birth, had happened to ascend to the rooftop terrace that shone like the moon.

1. Translated by Sheldon Pollock.

From the terrace Mantharā could see all Ayodhyā[2]—the king's way newly sprinkled, the lotuses and waterlilies strewn about, the costly ornamental pennants and banners, the sprinkling of sandalwood water, and the crowds of freshly bathed people.

Seeing a nursemaid standing nearby, Mantharā asked, "Why is Rāma's mother so delighted and giving away money to people, when she has always been so miserly? Tell me, why are the people displaying such boundless delight? Has something happened to delight the lord of earth? What is he planning to do?"

Bursting with delight and out of sheer gladness the nursemaid told the hunchback Mantharā about the greater majesty in store for Rāghava:

"Tomorrow on Puṣya day[3] King Daśaratha is going to consecrate Rāma Rāghava[4] as prince regent, the blameless prince who has mastered his anger."

When she heard what the nursemaid said, the hunchback was furious and descended straightway from the terrace that was like the peak of Mount Kailāsa.[5]

Consumed with rage, the malevolent Mantharā approached Kaikeyī as she lay upon her couch, and she said:

"Get up, you foolish woman! How can you lie there when danger is threatening you? Don't you realize that a flood of misery is about to overwhelm you?

"Your beautiful face has lost its charm. You boast of the power of your beauty, but it has proved to be as fleeting as a river's current in the hot season."

So she spoke, and Kaikeyī was deeply distraught at the bitter words of the angry, malevolent hunchback.

"Mantharā," she replied, "is something wrong? I can tell by the distress in your face how sorely troubled you are."

Hearing Kaikeyī's gentle words the wrathful Mantharā spoke—and a very clever speaker she was.

The hunchback grew even more distraught, and with Kaikeyī's best interests at heart, spoke out, trying to sharpen her distress and turn her against Rāghava:

"Something is very seriously wrong, my lady, something that threatens to ruin you. For King Daśaratha is going to consecrate Rāma as prince regent.

"I felt myself sinking down into unfathomable danger, stricken with grief and sorrow, burning as if on fire. And so I have come here, with your best interests at heart.

2. The capital of the kingdom of Kosala, in what is today the Indian state of Uttar Pradesh.
3. A favorable alignment of the constellation Pushya (consisting of the three stars of Cancer) marks an auspicious day on which important ceremonies are held.
4. Rama (literally, "descendent of Raghu," Rama's paternal great-grandfather).
5. A mountain in the Himalayan range, said to be the dwelling place of the great god Shiva.

"When you are sorrowful, Kaikeyī, I am too, and even more, and, when you prosper, so do I. There is not the slightest doubt of this.

"You were born into a family of kings, you are a queen of the lord of earth. My lady, how can you fail to know that the ways of kings are ruthless?

"Your husband talks of righteousness, but he is deceiving you; his words are gentle but he is cruel. You are too innocent to understand, and so he has utterly defrauded you like this.

"When expedient, your husband reassures you, but it is all worthless. Now that there is something of real worth he is ready to bestow it upon Kausalyā.

"Having got Bharata[6] out of the way by sending him off to your family, the wicked man shall tomorrow establish Rāma in unchallenged kingship.

"He is an enemy pretending to be your husband. He is like a viper, child, whom you have taken to your bosom and lovingly mothered.

"For what an enemy or a snake would do if one ignored them, King Daśaratha is now doing to you and your son.

"The man is evil, his assurances false, and, by establishing Rāma in the kingship, dear child who has always known comfort, he will bring ruin upon you and your family.

"Kaikeyī, the time has come to act, and you must act swiftly, for your own good. You must save your son, yourself, and me, my enchanting beauty."

After listening to Mantharā's speech, the lovely woman rose from the couch and presented the hunchback with a lovely piece of jewelry.

And, when she had given the hunchback the jewelry, Kaikeyī, most beautiful of women, said in delight to Mantharā,

"What you have reported to me is the most wonderful news. How else may I reward you, Mantharā, for reporting such good news to me?

"I draw no distinction between Rāma and Bharata, and so I am perfectly content that the king should consecrate Rāma as king.

"You could not possibly tell me better news than this, or speak more welcome words, my well-deserving woman. For what you have told me I will give you yet another boon, something you might like more—just choose it!"

Sarga 8

But Mantharā was beside herself with rage and sorrow. She threw the jewelry away and said spitefully:

6. Bharata and his younger brother Shatrughna were sent off to their maternal uncle's home by Dasharatha himself.

"You foolish woman, how can you be delighted at such a moment? Are you not aware that you stand in the midst of a sea of grief?

"It is Kausalyā who is fortunate; it is her son the eminent brahmans will consecrate as the powerful prince regent tomorrow, on Puṣya day.

"Once Kausalyā secures this great object of joy, she will cheerfully eliminate her enemies. And you will have to wait on her with hands cupped in reverence, like a serving woman.

"Delight is truly in store for Rāma's exalted women, and all that is in store for your daughters-in-law is misery, at Bharata's down-fall."

Seeing how deeply distressed Mantharā was as she spoke, Queen Kaikeyī began to extol Rāma's virtues:

"Rāma knows what is right, his gurus have taught him self-restraint. He is grateful, truthful, and honest, and as the king's eldest son, he deserves to be prince regent.

"He will protect his brothers and his dependents like a father; and long may he live! How can you be upset, hunchback, at learning of Rāma's consecration?

"Surely Bharata as well, the bull among men, will obtain the kingship of his fathers and forefathers after Rāma's one hundred years.

"Why should you be upset, Mantharā, when we have prospered in the past, and prosper now, and shall have good fortune in the future? For he obeys me even more scrupulously than he does Kausalyā."

When she heard what Kaikeyī said, Mantharā was still more sorely troubled. She heaved a long and hot sigh and then replied:

"You are too simple-minded to see what is good for you and what is not. You are not aware that you are sinking in an ocean of sorrow fraught with disaster and grief.

"Rāghava will be king, Kaikeyī, and then the son of Rāghava, while Bharata will be debarred from the royal succession altogether.

"For not all the sons of a king stand in line for the kingship, my lovely. Were all of them to be so placed, grave misfortune would ensue.

"That is why kings place the powers of kingship in the hands of the eldest, faultless Kaikeyī, however worthy the others.

"Like a helpless boy that son of yours, the object of all your motherly love, will be totally excluded from the royal succession and from its pleasures as well.

"Here I am, come on your behalf, but you pay me no heed. Instead, you want to reward me in token of your rival's good luck!

"Surely once Rāma secures unchallenged kingship he will have Bharata sent off to some other country—if not to the other world!

"And you had to send Bharata, a mere boy, off to your brother's, though knowing full well that proximity breeds affection, even in insentient things.

"Now, Rāghava will protect Lakṣmaṇa, just as Saumitri will protect Rāma, for their brotherly love is as celebrated as that of the Aśvins.

"And so Rāma will do no harm to Lakṣmaṇa, but he will to Bharata without question.

"So let your son go straight from Rājagṛha[7] to the forest. That is the course I favor, and it is very much in your own best interests.

"For in this way good fortune may still befall your side of the family—if, that is, Bharata secures, as by rights he should, the kingship of his forefathers.

"Your child has known only comfort, and, at the same time, he is Rāma's natural enemy. How could the one, with his fortunes lost, live under the sway of the other, whose fortunes are thriving?

"Like the leader of an elephant herd attacked by a lion in the forest, your son is about to be set upon by Rāma, and you must save him.

"Then, too, because of your beauty's power you used to spurn your co-wife, Rāma's mother, so proudly. How could she fail to repay that enmity?

"When Rāma secures control of the land, Bharata will be lost for certain. You must therefore devise some way of making your son the king and banishing his enemy this very day."

Sarga 9

So Mantharā spoke, and Kaikeyī, her face glowing with rage, heaved a long and burning sigh and said to her:

"Today, at once, I will have Rāma banished to the forest, and at once have Bharata consecrated as prince regent.

"But now, Mantharā, think: In what way can Bharata, and not Rāma, secure the kingship?"

So Queen Kaikeyī spoke, and the malevolent Mantharā answered her, to the ruin of Rāma's fortunes:

"Well then, I shall tell you, Kaikeyī—and pay close attention—how your son Bharata may secure sovereign kingship."

7. The capital city of Kekaya in Kashmir, the kingdom from which Kaikeyī hails.

Hearing Mantharā's words, Kaikeyī half rose from her sumptuous couch and exclaimed:

"Tell me the way, Mantharā! How can Bharata, and not Rāma, secure the kingship?"

So the queen spoke, and the malevolent hunchback answered her, to the ruin of Rāma's fortunes:

"When the gods and *asuras* were at war, your husband went with the royal seers to lend assistance to the king of the gods, and he took you along. He set off toward the south, Kaikeyī, to the Daṇḍakas and the city called Vaijayanta. It was there that Timidhvaja ruled, the same who is called Śambara, a great *asura* of a hundred magic powers. He had given battle to Śakra, and the host of gods could not conquer him.[8]

"In the great battle that followed, King Daśaratha was struck unconscious, and you, my lady, conveyed him out of battle. But there, too, your husband was wounded by weapons, and once again you saved him, my lovely. And so in his gratitude he granted you two boons.

"Then, my lady, you said to your husband. 'I shall choose my two boons when I want them,' and the great king consented. I myself was unaware of this, my lady, until you yourself told me, long ago.

"You must now demand these two boons of your husband: the consecration of Bharata and the banishment of Rāma for fourteen years.

"Now go into your private chamber, daughter of Aśvapati, as if in a fit of rage. Put on a dirty garment, lie down on the bare ground, and don't speak to him, don't even look at him.

"Your husband has always adored you, I haven't any doubt of it. For your sake the great king would even go through fire.

"The king could not bring himself to anger you, nor even bear to look at you when you are angry. He would give up his own life to please you.

"The lord of the land is powerless to refuse your demand. Dull-witted girl, recognize the power of your beauty.

"King Daśaratha will offer gems, pearls, gold, a whole array of precious gifts—but pay no mind to them.

"Just keep reminding Daśaratha of those two boons he granted at the battle of the gods and *asuras*. Illustrious lady, you must not let this opportunity pass you by.

---

8. The battle between the gods and *asuras*, or antigods, forms part of many ancient legends. In earlier Sanskrit works, Shambara is the enemy of Indra, the king of the gods, who is also known as Shakra (literally, "the able one"). The city Vaijayanta and the name Timidhvaja are obscure.

"When the great king Rāghava helps you up himself and offers you a boon, then you must ask him for this one, first making sure he swears to it: 'Banish Rāma to the forest for nine years and five, and make Bharata king of the land, the bull among kings.'

"In this way Rāma will be banished and cease to be 'the pleasing prince,' and your Bharata, his rival eliminated, will be king.

"And by the time Rāma returns from the forest, your steadfast son and his supporters will have struck deep roots and won over the populace.

"I think it high time you overcame your timidity. You must forcibly prevent the king from carrying out Rāma's consecration."

And so Mantharā induced her to accept such evil by disguising it as good, and Kaikeyī, now cheered and delighted, replied:

"Hunchback, I never recognized your excellence, nor how excellent your advice. Of all the hunchbacks in the land there is none better at devising plans.

"You are the only one who has always sought my advantage and had my interests at heart. I might never have known, hunchback, what the king intended to do.

"There are hunchbacks who are misshapen, crooked and hideously ugly—but not you, you are lovely, you are bent no more than a lotus in the breeze.

"Your chest is arched, raised as high as your shoulders, and down below your waist, with its lovely navel, seems as if it had grown thin in envy of it.

"Your girdle-belt beautifies your hips and sets them jingling. Your legs are set strong under you, while your feet are long.

"With your wide buttocks, Mantharā, and your garment of white linen, you are as resplendent as a wild goose when you go before me.

"And this huge hump of yours, wide as the hub of a chariot wheel—your clever ideas must be stored in it, your political wisdom and magic powers.

"And there, hunchback, is where I will drape you with a garland made of gold, once Bharata is consecrated and Rāghava has gone to the forest.

"When I have accomplished my purpose, my lovely, when I am satisfied, I will anoint your hump with precious liquid gold.

"And for your face I will have them fashion an elaborate and beautiful forehead mark of gold and exquisite jewelry for you, hunchback.

"Dressed in a pair of lovely garments you shall go about like a goddess; with that face of yours that challenges the moon, peerless in visage; and you shall strut holding your head high before the people who hate me.

"You too shall have hunchbacks, adorned with every sort of ornament, to humbly serve you, hunchback, just as you always serve me."

Being flattered in this fashion, she replied to Kaikeyī, who still lay on her luxurious couch like a flame of fire on an altar:

"One does not build a dike, my precious, after the water is gone. Get up, apprise the king, and see to your own welfare!"

Thus incited, the large-eyed queen went with Mantharā to her private chamber, puffed up with the intoxicating power of her beauty.

There the lovely lady removed her pearl necklace, worth many hundred thousands, and her other costly and beautiful jewelry.

And then, under the spell of the hunchback Mantharā's words, the golden Kaikeyī got down upon the floor and said to her:

"Hunchback, go inform the king that I will surely die right here unless Bharata receives as his portion the land and Rāghava, as his, the forest."

And uttering these ruthless words, the lady put all her jewelry aside and lay down upon the ground bare of any spread, like a fallen *kinnara* woman.[9]

Her face enveloped in the darkness of her swollen rage, her fine garlands and ornaments stripped off, the wife of the lord of men grew distraught and took on the appearance of a darkened sky, when all the stars have set.

Sarga 10

Now, when the great king had given orders for Rāghava's consecration, he gladly entered the inner chamber to tell his beloved wife the good news.

But when the lord of the world saw her fallen on the ground and lying there in a posture so ill-befitting her, he was consumed with sorrow.

The guileless old man saw her on the floor, that guileful young wife of his, who meant more to him than life itself.

He began to caress her affectionately, as a great bull elephant in the wilderness might caress his cow wounded by the poisoned arrow of a hunter lurking in the forest.

And, as he caressed his lotus-eyed wife with his hands, sick with worry and desire, he said to her:

"I do not understand, my lady, why you should be angry. Has someone offended you, or shown you disrespect, that you should lie here in the dust, my precious, and

---

9. *Kinnaras* ("part-man") are obscure mythical creatures; female *kinnaras* are renowned for their beauty.

cause me such sorrow? What reason have you to lie upon the floor as if possessed by a spirit, driving me to distraction, when you are so precious to me?

"I have skilled physicians, who have been gratified in every way. They will make you well again. Tell me what hurts you, my lovely.

"Is there someone to whom you would have favor shown, or has someone aroused your disfavor? The one shall find favor at once, the other incur my lasting disfavor.

"Is there some guilty man who should be freed, or some innocent man I should execute? What poor man should I enrich, what rich man impoverish?

"I and my people, we all bow to your will. I could not bring myself to thwart any wish of yours, not if it cost me my life. Tell me what your heart desires, for all the earth belongs to me, as far as the wheel of my power reaches."

So he spoke, and now encouraged she resolved to tell her hateful plan. She then commenced to cause her husband still greater pain.

"No one has mistreated me, my lord, or shown me disrespect. But there is one wish I have that I should like you to fulfill.

"You must first give me your promise that you are willing to do it. Then I shall reveal what it is I desire."

So his beloved Kaikeyī spoke, and the mighty king, hopelessly under the woman's power, said to her with some surprise:

"Do you not yet know, proud lady, that except for Rāma, tiger among men, there is not a single person I love as much as you?

"Take hold of my heart, rip it out, and examine it closely, my lovely Kaikeyī; then tell me if you do not find it true.

"Seeing that I have the power, you ought not to doubt me. I will do what will make you happy, I swear to you by all my acquired merit."

His words filled her with delight, and she made ready to reveal her dreadful wish, which was like a visitation of death:

"Let the three and thirty gods, with Indra at their head, hear how you in due order swear an oath and grant me a boon.

"Let the sun and moon, the sky, the planets, night and day, the quarters of space, heaven and earth, let all the *gandharvas* and *rākṣasas,* the spirits that stalk the night, the household gods in every house, and all the other spirits take heed of what you have said.[1]

---

1. *Gandharvas* are heavenly beings renowned for their musical skills. *Rakshasas,* often called "stalkers of the night," are demonic creatures known to eat humans and disrupt the sacrifices of forest ascetics.

"This mighty king, who is true to his word and knows the ways of righteousness, in full awareness grants me a boon—let the deities give ear to this for me."

Thus the queen ensnared the great archer and called upon witnesses. She then addressed the king, who in his mad passion had granted her a boon.

"I will now claim the two boons you once granted me, my lord. Hear my words, your Majesty.

"Let my son Bharata be consecrated with the very rite of consecration you have prepared for Rāghava.

"Let Rāma withdraw to Daṇḍaka wilderness[2] and for nine years and five live the life of an ascetic, wearing hides and barkcloth garments and matted hair.[3]

"Let Bharata today become the uncontested prince regent, and let me see Rāghava depart this very day for the forest."

When the great king heard Kaikeyī's ruthless demands, he was shaken and unnerved, like a stag at the sight of a tigress.

The lord of men gasped as he sank down upon the bare floor. "Oh damn you!" he cried in uncontrollable fury before he fell into a stupor, his heart crushed by grief.

Gradually the king regained his senses and then, in bitter sorrow and anger, he spoke to Kaikeyī, with fire in his eyes:

"Malicious, wicked woman, bent on destroying this House! Evil woman, what evil did Rāma or I ever do to you?

"Rāghava has always treated you just like his own mother. What reason can you have for trying to wreck his fortunes, of all people?

"It was sheer suicide to bring you into my home. I did it unwittingly, thinking you a princess—and not a deadly poisonous viper.

"When praise for Rāma's virtues is on the lips of every living soul, what crime could I adduce as pretext for renouncing my favorite son?

"I would sooner renounce Kausalyā, or Sumitrā, or sovereignty, or life itself, than Rāma, who so cherishes his father.

"The greatest joy I know is seeing my first-born son. If I cannot see Rāma, I shall lose my mind.

2. The country of King Dandaka was laid waste by Indra's curse or, according to another source, the curse of a Brahman whose daughter was raped by the king.

3. As a mark of renunciation, forest-dwelling ascetics are said to wear "barkcloth" (perhaps cloth woven of bast fiber) and to leave their hair unkempt.

"The world might endure without the sun, or crops without water, but without Rāma life could not endure within my body.

"Enough then, give up this scheme, you evil-scheming woman. I beg you! Must I get down and bow my head to your feet?"

His heart in the grip of a woman who knew no bounds, the guardian of the earth began helplessly to cry, and as the queen extended her feet he tried in vain to touch them, and collapsed like a man on the point of death.

Sarga 11

The king lay there, in so unaccustomed a posture, so ill-befitting his dignity, like Yayāti himself, his merit exhausted, fallen from the world of the gods.[4] But the woman was unafraid, for all the fear she awoke. She was misfortune incarnate and had yet to secure her fortunes. Once more she tried to force him to fulfill the boon.

"You are vaunted, great king, as a man true to his word and firm in his vows. How then can you be prepared to withhold my boon?"

So Kaikeyī spoke, and King Daśaratha, faltering for a moment, angrily replied:

"Vile woman, mortal enemy! Will you not be happy, will you not be satisfied until you see me dead, and Rāma, the bull among men, gone to the forest?

"To satisfy Kaikeyī Rāma must be banished to the forest, but if I keep my word in this, then I must be guilty of another lie. My infamy will be unequaled in the eyes of the people and my disgrace inevitable."

While he was lamenting like this, his mind in a whirl, the sun set and evening came on.

To the anguished king lost in lamentation, the night, adorned with the circlet of the moon, no longer seemed to last a mere three watches.

Heaving burning sighs, aged King Daśaratha sorrowfully lamented in his anguish, his eyes fixed upon the sky.

"I do not want you to bring the dawn—here, I cup my hands in supplication. But no, pass as quickly as you can, so that I no longer have to see this heartless, malicious Kaikeyī, the cause of this great calamity."

But with this, the king cupped his hands before Kaikeyī and once more, begging her mercy, he spoke:

"Please, I am an old man, my life is nearly over. I am desolate, I place myself in your hands. Dear lady, have mercy on me for, after all, I am king.

4. A legendary emperor who through ascetic discipline reached heaven, only to be expelled by Indra because of his pride.

"Truly it was thoughtless of me, my fair-hipped lady, to have said those things just now. Have mercy on me, please, my child. I know you have a heart."

So the pure-hearted king lamented, frantically and piteously, his eyes reddened and dimmed by tears, but the malicious, black-hearted woman only listened and made no reply.

And as the king stared at the woman he loved but could not appease, whose demand was so perverse—for the exile of his own son—he once again was taken faint, overcome with grief, and dropped unconscious to the floor.

* * *

Sarga 16

Rāma saw his father, with a wretched look and his mouth all parched, slumped upon his lovely couch, Kaikeyī at his side.

First he made an obeisance with all deference at his father's feet and then did homage most scrupulously at the feet of Kaikeyī.

"Rāma!" cried the wretched king, his eyes brimming with tears, but he was unable to say anything more or to look at him.

As if his foot had grazed a snake, Rāma was seized with terror to see the expression on the king's face, one more terrifying than he had ever seen before.

For the great king lay heaving sighs, racked with grief and remorse, all his senses numb with anguish, his mind stunned and confused.

It was as if the imperturbable, wave-wreathed ocean had suddenly been shaken with perturbation, as if the sun had been eclipsed, or a seer had told a lie.

His father's grief was incomprehensible to him, and the more he pondered it, the more his agitation grew, like that of the ocean under a full moon.

With his father's welfare at heart, Rāma struggled to comprehend, "Why does the king not greet me, today of all days?

"On other occasions, when Father might be angry, the sight of me would calm him. Why then, when he looked at me just now, did he instead become so troubled?

"He seems desolate and grief-stricken, and his face has lost its glow." Doing obeisance to Kaikeyī, Rāma spoke these words:

"I have not unknowingly committed some offense, have I, to anger my father? Tell me, and make him forgive me.

"His face is drained of color, he is desolate and does not speak to me. It cannot be, can it, that some physical illness or mental distress afflicts him? But it is true, well-being is not something one can always keep.

"Some misfortune has not befallen the handsome prince Bharata, has it, or coura-geous Śatrughna, or one of my mothers?

"I should not wish to live an instant if his majesty, the great king, my father, were angered by my failure to satisfy him or do his bidding.

"How could a man not treat him as a deity incarnate, in whom he must recognize the very source of his existence in this world?

"Can it be that in anger you presumed to use harsh words with my father, and so threw his mind into such turmoil?

"Answer my questions truthfully, my lady: What has happened to cause this un-precedented change in the lord of men?

"At the bidding of the king, if enjoined by him, my guru, father, king, and bene-factor, I would hurl myself into fire, drink deadly poison, or drown myself in the sea.

"Tell me then, my lady, what the king would have me do. I will do it, I promise. Rāma need not say so twice."

The ignoble Kaikeyī then addressed these ruthless words to Rāma, the upright and truthful prince:

"Long ago, Rāghava, in the war of the gods and *asuras,* your father bestowed two boons on me, for protecting him when he was wounded in a great battle.

"By means of these I have demanded of the king that Bharata be consecrated and that you, Rāghava, be sent at once to Daṇḍaka wilderness.

"If you wish to ensure that your father be true to his word, and you to your own, best of men, then listen to what I have to say.

"Abide by your father's guarantee, exactly as he promised it, and enter the forest for nine years and five.

"Forgo the consecration and withdraw to Daṇḍaka wilderness, live there seven years and seven, wearing matted hair and barkcloth garments.

"Let Bharata rule this land from the city of the Kosalans, with all the treasures it contains, all its horses, chariots, elephants."

When Rāma, slayer of enemies, heard Kaikeyī's hateful words, like death itself, he was not the least disconcerted, but only replied,

"So be it. I shall go away to live in the forest, wearing matted hair and barkcloth garments, to safeguard the promise of the king.

"But I want to know why the lord of earth, the invincible tamer of foes, does not greet me as he used to?

"You need not worry, my lady. I say it to your face: I shall go to the forest—rest assured—wearing barkcloth and matted hair.

"Enjoined by my father, my benefactor, guru, and king, a man who knows what is right to do, what would I hesitate to do in order to please him?

"But there is still one thing troubling my mind and eating away at my heart: that the king does not tell me himself that Bharata is to be consecrated.

"For my wealth, the kingship, Sītā, and my own dear life I would gladly give up to my brother Bharata on my own, without any urging.

"How much more readily if urged by my father himself, the lord of men, in order to fulfill your fond desire and safeguard his promise?

"So you must reassure him. Why should the lord of earth keep his eyes fixed upon the ground and fitfully shed these tears?

"This very day let messengers depart on swift horses by order of the king to fetch Bharata from his uncle's house.

"As for me, I shall leave here in all haste for Daṇḍaka wilderness, without questioning my father's word, to live there fourteen years."

Kaikeyī was delighted to hear these words of Rāma's, and trusting them implicitly, she pressed Rāghava to set out at once.

"So be it. Men shall go as messengers on swift horses to bring home Bharata from his uncle's house.

"But since you are now so eager, Rāma, I do not think it wise to linger. You should therefore proceed directly from here to the forest.

"That the king is ashamed and does not address you himself, that is nothing, best of men, you needn't worry about that.

"But so long as you have not hastened from the city and gone to the forest, Rāma, your father shall neither bathe nor eat."

"Oh curse you!" the king gasped, overwhelmed with grief, and upon the gilt couch he fell back in a faint.

Rāma raised up the king, pressed though he was by Kaikeyī—like a horse whipped with a crop—to make haste and depart for the forest.

Listening to the ignoble Kaikeyī's hateful words, so dreadful in their consequences, Rāma remained unperturbed and only said to her,

"My lady, it is not in the hopes of gain that I suffer living in this world. You should know that, like the seers, I have but one concern and that is righteousness.

"Whatever I can do to please this honored man I will do at any cost, even if it means giving up my life.

"For there is no greater act of righteousness than this: obedience to one's father and doing as he bids.

"Even unbidden by this honored man, at your bidding alone I shall live for fourteen years in the desolate forest.

"Indeed, Kaikeyī, you must ascribe no virtue to me at all if you had to appeal to the king, when you yourself are so venerable in my eyes.

"Let me only take leave of my mother, and settle matters with Sītā. Then I shall go, this very day, to the vast forest of the Daṇḍakas.

"You must see to it that Bharata obeys Father and guards the kingdom, for that is the eternal way of righteousness."

When his father heard Rāma's words, he was stricken with such deep sorrow that he could not hold back his sobs in his grief and broke out in loud weeping.

Splendid Rāma did homage at the feet of his unconscious father and at the feet of that ignoble woman, Kaikeyī; then he turned to leave.

Reverently Rāma circled his father and Kaikeyī, and, withdrawing from the inner chamber, he saw his group of friends.

Lakṣmaṇa, the delight of Sumitrā, fell in behind him, his eyes brimming with tears, in a towering rage.

Reverently circling the equipment for the consecration, but careful not to gaze at it, Rāma slowly went away.

The loss of the kingship diminished his great majesty as little as night diminishes the loveliness of the cool-rayed moon, beloved of the world.

Though he was on the point of leaving his native land and going to the forest, he was no more discomposed than one who has passed beyond all things of this world.

Holding back his sorrow within his mind, keeping his every sense in check, and fully self-possessed he made his way to his mother's residence to tell her the sad news.

As Rāma entered her residence, where joy still reigned supreme, as he reflected on the sudden wreck of all his fortunes, even then he showed no sign of discomposure, for fear it might endanger the lives of those he loved.

from Book 3[1]

[The Abduction of Sita]

Sarga 42

After instructing his brother the mighty prince, delight of the Raghus,[2] strapped on his gold-hilted sword.

He then strapped on a pair of quivers and took up his proper ornament—the bow with triple curve—and set off at a rapid pace.

The deer spied the lord of kings rushing toward him and he led him on, now timorously hiding, now showing himself again.

With sword strapped on and taking up his bow, Rāma ran toward the deer, imagining he saw his form shimmering before him.

At one moment he would spot him running through the deep forest, temptingly near, and would take his bow in hand, only to look once more and find the deer beyond the range of his arrow. In one stretch of forest he came into sight leaping through the air in frightful panic, and then he passed into another stretch and out of sight.

Like the disk of the autumn moon veiled in tatters of cloud, he was seen one instant and gone the next.

Now appearing, now disappearing, he drew Rāghava far away, and helplessly deluded by him Kākutstha[3] flew into a rage.

Then the deer halted in exhaustion and withdrew to a shady spot in the meadow, not far away, where Rāma spotted him surrounded by other animals of the forest.

Seeing the deer mighty Rāma was determined to kill him. The powerful prince nocked his sturdy bow and drew it back with power.

Aiming at the deer he shot a gleaming, flaming arrow fashioned by Brahmā[4] that glared like a snake as it darted forth.

1. Translated by Sheldon Pollock.
2. Rama.
3. Rama (literally, "a descendant of Kakutstha," an ancestor in Rama's lineage).
4. Rama had earlier received the god Brahma's heavenly weapons from the sage Agastya.

The supreme arrow penetrated the illusory deer form and like a bolt of lightning pierced the heart, Mārīca's heart.[5]

The deer leaped high as a palm tree and with a ghastly shriek fell to the ground, tormented by the arrow, his life ebbing away. And as Mārīca lay there dying, the shape he had assumed began to disappear.

Knowing the time had come, in Rāghava's own voice he cried out, "Oh Sītā! Oh Lakṣmaṇa!"

Pierced to the quick by an arrow unlike any other, Mārīca once more took on the form of a massive *rākṣasa,* giving up the deer form and his life.

Struck by the arrow, he became a *rākṣasa* once more, with huge fangs, a necklace of gold, sparkling earrings, and every other ornament to adorn him.

Seeing that dreadful sight, the *rākṣasa* fallen on the ground, Rāma thought suddenly of Sītā and recalled what Lakṣmaṇa had said.[6]

"With his dying breath this *rākṣasa* cried out at the top of his voice, 'Oh Sītā! Oh Lakṣmaṇa!' How will Sītā react to hearing this?

"And great-armed Lakṣmaṇa, what will be his state of mind?" As these thoughts came to righteous Rāma, the hair on his body bristled with dread.

Then Rāma's consternation gave way to a feeling of fear that shot through him with sharp pangs: The deer he had slain was in fact a *rākṣasa,* the voice it had used was his own.

He killed another dappled deer and taking the meat hurriedly retraced his steps to Janasthāna.[7]

Sarga 43

Now, when Sītā heard that cry of distress, in her husband's own voice, coming from the forest, she said to Lakṣmaṇa, "Go and find out what has happened to Rāghava.

"My heart—my very life—is jarred from its place by the sound of his crying in deep distress that I heard so clearly.

"You must rescue your brother, who cries out in the forest. Run to your brother at once, for he needs help! The *rākṣasas* have him in their power, like a bull fallen among lions." So she spoke, but Lakṣmaṇa, heeding his brother's command, did not go.

---

5. The *rakshasa* compelled by Ravana to assume the form of a bejeweled deer in order to draw Rama away from the hermitage.
6. At the first sight of the magical deer, Lakshmana had a premonition that it must be a *rakshasa.*
7. The region of the Dandaka forest located near Rama's hermitage.

Then the daughter of Janaka[8] angrily said to him, "You wear the guise of a friend to your brother, Saumitri,[9] but act like his foe, refusing to aid him in his extremity. You hope Rāma perishes, Lakṣmaṇa, isn't that so? And it is all because of me.

"I think you would be happy should some disaster befall your brother. You have no real affection for him, so you stand there calmly with the splendid prince gone from sight.

"For with him in danger and me here, how could I prevent what you came here with the sole intention of doing?"

So Sītā, princess of Videha, spoke, overwhelmed with tears and grief, and Lakṣmaṇa replied to her as she stood there frightened as a doe.

"My lady, there is no one, god or man, *gandharva,* great bird, or *rākṣasa, piśāca, kinnara,* beast, or dreaded *dānava*—no one, fair lady, who could match Rāma, the peer of Vāsava, in battle.[1]

"Rāma cannot be killed in battle. You must not talk this way, for I dare not leave you in the forest with Rāghava gone.

"His power cannot be withstood, not by any powers however vast, not by all three worlds up in arms, or the deathless gods themselves, their lord included.

"Let your heart rest easy, do not be alarmed. Your husband will soon return, after killing that splendid deer.

"That was clearly not his voice, or any belonging to a god. It was the magic of that *rākṣasa,* unreal as a mirage.

"You were entrusted to my safekeeping, shapely Vaidehī,[2] by the great Rāma. I dare not leave you here alone.

"Then too, dear lady, because of the slaughter at Janasthāna, where Khara perished, we have earned the hostility of the night-stalkers.[3]

"*Rākṣasas* delight in causing trouble, Vaidehī, they make all kinds of noises in the deep forest. You need not worry."

Though what he said was true, Sītā was enraged by Lakṣmaṇa's words. Her eyes blazed bright red as she made this harsh reply:

8. Sita is the adopted daughter of King Janaka of Mithila in Videha country, where he discovered her as baby in a furrowed field.
9. Lakshmana (literally, "son of Sumitra").
1. *Pishacas* and *danavas* are two more categories of nonhuman beings. "Vasava" is an epithet of Indra, king of the gods.
2. Sita (literally, "woman of Videha").
3. The *rakshasa* Khara, a brother of Ravana, was killed when he and his 14,000 soldiers attacked Rama.

"Ignoble, cruel man, disgrace to your House! How pitiful this attempt of yours. I feel certain you are pleased with all this, and that is why you can talk the way you do.

"It is nothing new, Lakṣmaṇa, for rivals to be so evil, cruel rivals like you always plotting in secret.

"You treacherously followed Rāma to the forest, the two of you alone: You are either in the employ of Bharata or secretly plotting to get me.

"I am married to Rāma, a husband dark as a lotus, with eyes like lotus petals. How could I ever give my love to some ordinary man?

"I would not hesitate to take my life before your very eyes, Saumitri, for I could not live upon this earth one moment without Rāma."

Such were the words Sītā spoke to Lakṣmaṇa, so harsh they made his hair bristle with horror. But he controlled himself, and with hands cupped in reverence he addressed her:

"I dare not answer, Maithilī,[4] for you are a deity in my eyes. And yet inappropriate words from a woman come as nothing new.

"This is the nature of women the whole world over: Women care nothing for righteousness, they are flighty, sharp-tongued, and divisive.

"May all the inhabitants of the forest give ear and bear me witness how my words of reason met so harsh a reply from you.

"Curse you and be damned, that you could so suspect me, when I am only following the orders of my guru. How like a woman to be so perverse!

"I am going to Kākutstha. I wish you well, fair woman. May the spirits of the forest, each and every one, protect you, large-eyed lady.

"How ominous the portents that manifest themselves to me! I pray I find you here when I return with Rāma."

Now, when Lakṣmaṇa addressed her in this fashion, Janaka's daughter began to weep. Overwhelmed with tears she hotly replied:

"Parted from Rāma I will drown myself in the Godāvarī,[5] Lakṣmaṇa, I will hang myself or hurl my body upon some rocky place.

"Or I will drink deadly poison or throw myself into a blazing fire. I would never touch any man but Rāghava, not even with my foot!"

4. Sita (literally, "woman of Mithila").
5. A river in the southern region of India.

Such were the insults Sītā hurled at Lakṣmaṇa in her sorrow, and sorrowfully she wept and struck her belly with her fists.

At the sight of large-eyed Sītā so deeply anguished and weeping, Saumitri was beside himself and tried to comfort her, but she would say nothing more to her husband's brother.

Then, cupping his hands in reverence and bowing slightly, Lakṣmaṇa, the self-respecting prince, said goodbye to Sītā. And as he set forth to find Rāma, he turned around again and again and looked back at Maithilī.

Sarga 44

Rāghava's younger brother, angered by her harsh words and sorely longing for Rāma, set forth without further delay.

This was the opening ten-necked Rāvaṇa had been waiting for, and he took advantage of it at once. Assuming the guise of a wandering mendicant, he turned his steps toward Vaidehī.

Clad in a soft saffron robe, with topknot, parasol, and sandals, and goodly staff and water pitcher hanging at his left shoulder—disguised like this, as a mendicant—he approached Vaidehī.

Both brothers had left her, and in his pride of power he advanced upon her, like total darkness advancing upon the twilight, when both sun and moon have left.

He gazed at the glorious young princess as ominously as a planet might gaze upon the star Rohiṇī when the hare-marked moon is absent.[6]

At the appearance of the dreaded, evil creature, the trees that grew in Janasthāna stopped rustling and the wind died down.

At the sight of him peering around with his blood-red eyes, the swift current of the Godāvarī river began to slacken in fear.

Ten-necked Rāvaṇa had waited for an opening, and Rāma had given him one. In the guise of a beggar he drew near to Vaidehī.

As Vaidehī sat grieving for her husband, the unholy Rāvaṇa in the guise of a holy man edged closer to her, like the sluggish planet, Saturn, closing in on Citrā, the sparkling star.

Like a deep well concealed by grass, the evil one in the guise of a holy man stood watching Vaidehī, illustrious wife of Rāma—the beautiful woman with lovely teeth

---

6. The planet is Mercury and the star-cluster Rohini is the beloved of the moon. In Sanskrit literature, dramatic moments are often rendered through astronomical tropes because of the prominence given to astral phenomena in traditional Indian rituals and beliefs.

and lips, and a face like the full moon—as she sat in the leaf hut tormented with grief and tears.

The blackhearted stalker of the night stole ever closer to Vaidehī, the woman dressed in garments of yellow silk, and with eyes like lotus petals.

With arrows of Manmatha, god of love, lodged deep within his heart, and the sounds of the *vedas*[7] on his lips, the overlord of *rākṣasas* appeared before the deserted hut and courteously spoke.

Rāvaṇa began singing her praises, that loveliest of women in the three worlds, a radiant beauty, like the goddess Śrī herself without the lotus.

"Who are you, golden woman dressed in garments of yellow silk, wearing a lovely lotus garland, and like a lotus pond yourself?

"Are you the goddess Modesty or Fame? Are you Śrī or lovely Lakṣmī or perhaps an *apsaras,* lovely lady? Could you be Prosperity, shapely woman, or easygoing Pleasure?[8]

"Your teeth are bright white, tapered, and even; your eyes are large and clear, rosy at the corner, black in the center.

"Your hips are full and broad, your thighs smooth as an elephant's trunk. And these, your delightful breasts, how round they are, so firm and gently heaving; how full and lovely, smooth as two palm fruits, with their nipples standing stiff and the rarest gems to adorn them.

"Graceful lady with your lovely smile, lovely teeth, and lovely eyes, you have swept my heart away like a river in flood that sweeps away its banks.

"Your waist I could compass with my fingers; how fine is your hair, how firm your breasts. No goddess, no *gandharva* woman, no *yakṣa* or *kinnara* woman, no mortal woman so beautiful have I ever seen before on the face of this earth.[9]

"Your beauty, unrivaled in all the worlds, your delicacy and youth, and the fact of your living here in the woods stir the deepest feelings in me.

"I urge you to go home, this is no place for you to be living. For this is the lair of dreaded *rākṣasas,* who can change their form at will.

"In the most delightful palaces, in luxuriant, fragrant city gardens is where you should be strolling.

---

7. Ancient wisdom texts.

8. Shri and Lakshmi, goddesses of royalty and wealth, are normally taken to be one and the same, and the consort of Vishnu. *Apsaras* are celestial nymphs.

9. *Yakshas* are yet another category of divine beings whose women are famous for their beauty.

"To my mind you deserve the finest garlands and beverages and raiment, and the finest husband, lovely black-eyed lady.

"Could you be one of the Rudras or Maruts, sweet-smiling, shapely woman, or one of the Vasus, perhaps? You look like a goddess to me.

"But *gandharvas* do not pass this way, nor do gods or *kinnaras,* for this is the lair of *rākṣasas.* How is it you have come here?

"There are monkeys here, lions, panthers, and tigers, apes, hyenas, and flesh-eating birds. How is it you do not fear them?

"And the dreaded elephants that go running wild, maddened by rut—how is it you do not fear them, lovely lady, all alone in the deep wilderness?

"Who are you, to whom do you belong, where do you come from, my precious, and why are you wandering all alone through Daṇḍaka, the haunt of dreaded *rākṣasas?*"

Such was the praise evil Rāvaṇa lavished on Vaidehī. But seeing he had come in the garb of a brahman, Maithilī honored him with all the acts of hospitality due a guest.

First she brought forward a cushion and offered water for his feet, and then she called him when food was ready, for he looked kindly enough.

35

When Maithilī observed that he had come in the garb of a twice-born[1]—a brahman with a begging bowl and saffron robe; when she saw these accoutrements, it was impossible to refuse him, and so she extended him an invitation befitting a brahman.

"Here is a cushion, brahman, please be seated and accept this water for your feet. Here I have made ready for you the best fare the forest has to offer. You may partake of it freely."

So Maithilī extended him a cordial invitation, and as Rāvaṇa gazed at her, the wife of the lord of men, he confirmed his resolve to take her by force, and with that, consigned himself to death.

Her husband in his honest garb had gone to hunt the magic deer, and she waited for him and Lakṣmaṇa, scanning the horizon. But she saw neither Rāma nor Lakṣmaṇa—only the deep, green forest.

Sarga 45

When Rāvaṇa came in the guise of a mendicant to carry off Vaidehī, he had first put some questions to her. Of her own accord she now began to tell her story.

For Sītā had thought a moment: "He is a brahman and my guest. If I do not reply he will curse me." She then spoke these words:

1. A term used primarily of Brahmans. (They are said to be born a second time when initiated into studentship by their teacher.)

"I am the daughter of Janaka, the great king of Mithilā. My name is Sītā, may it please the best of twice-born, and I am the wife of Rāma.

"For twelve years I lived in the house of Rāghava, enjoying such pleasures as mortals enjoy. I had all I could desire.

"Then, in the thirteenth year, the king in concert with his kingly counselors approved the royal consecration of my husband.

"But just as the preparations for Rāghava's consecration were under way, a mother-in-law of mine named Kaikeyī asked her husband for a boon.

"You see, Kaikeyī had already married my father-in-law for a consideration. So she had two things she now could ask of her husband, the best of kings and a man who always kept his word: One was the consecration of Bharata, the other, my husband's banishment.

"'From this day forth I will not eat, or drink, or sleep, I will put an end to my life if Rāma is consecrated.'

"Such were Kaikeyī's words, and though my father-in-law, who had always shown her respect, begged her with offers of commensurate riches, she would not do what he begged of her.

"Rāma, my mighty husband, was then twenty-five years old, and I had just passed my eighteenth birthday.

"His name is renowned throughout the world, his eyes are large, his arms strong. He is virtuous, honest, truthful, and devoted to the welfare of all people.

"When Rāma came into his father's presence for the consecration to begin, it was Kaikeyī who addressed my husband, in a rush of words:

"'Listen to me, Rāghava, and hear what your father has decreed. The kingship is to be given to Bharata uncontested.

"'As for you, you are to live in the forest for nine years and five. Go into banishment, Kākutstha, and save your father from falsehood.'

"Without a trace of fear my husband Rāma answered Kaikeyī, 'So be it,' and in firm compliance with his vow did just as she had told him.

"For Rāma has taken a solemn vow, brahman, one never to be broken: always to give and not receive, to tell the truth and not lie.

"Rāma has a constant companion, his half brother Lakṣmaṇa, a tiger among men and mighty slayer of enemies in battle.

"This brother Lakṣmaṇa, who keeps to the ways of righteousness, firm in his vows, followed bow in hand when Rāma went into banishment with me.

"And so the three of us were driven from the kingdom for the sake of Kaikeyī. Thus it is under compulsion, best of twice-born, that we now wander the dense forest.

"Rest a moment; or you can even pass the night here if you like. My husband will soon return bringing an abundance of food from the forest.

"But can you just tell me your name, your clan, and family? How is it that you, a brahman, wander all alone in Daṇḍaka wilderness?"

So Sītā, wife of Rāma, spoke, and powerful Rāvaṇa, overlord of *rākṣasas,* made a reply that froze her blood:

"I am he who terrifies the worlds, with all their gods, *asuras,* and great serpents. I am Rāvaṇa, Sītā, supreme lord of the hosts of *rākṣasas.*

"Now that I have set eyes on you, flawless, golden lady dressed in silk, I shall no longer take any pleasure in my own wives.

"From one place and another I have carried off many splendid women. May it please you to become chief queen over every one of them.

"In the middle of the ocean lies my vast city Laṅkā, perched upon a mountain peak and ringed by the sea.

"There, my radiant Sītā, you shall stroll with me through the forests, never longing for this life you are leading in the wilderness.

"Five thousand slave women all adorned with ornaments shall wait upon you hand and foot, Sītā, if you become my wife."

So Rāvaṇa spoke, but Janaka's daughter, that faultless beauty, angrily and with utter contempt for the *rākṣasa* replied:

"I am faithful to Rāma, my husband, the equal of great Indra, unshakable as a great mountain, imperturbable as the great sea.

"I am faithful to Rāma, the great-armed, great-chested prince, who moves with the boldness of a lion, a lionlike man, a lion among men.

"I am faithful to Rāma, the king's most cherished son, a great-armed, mighty prince of wide renown and strict self-control, whose face is like the full moon.

"As for you, you are a jackal in the presence of a lioness, to come here seeking me, whom you can never have. You could no more touch me than touch the radiance of the sun.

"You must be seeing many a golden tree of death, ill-fated Rāvaṇa, if you seek to gain the beloved wife of Rāghava.

"You are seeking to pluck the fang from the mouth of a poisonous snake, the tooth from the mouth of a hungry lion in pursuit, the foe to all beasts.

"You are seeking to carry off Mandara, greatest of mountains, in your hand, to drink the *kālakūṭa* poison and take no harm of it.[2]

"You are rubbing your eye with a needle, licking a razor with your tongue, if you seek to violate the beloved wife of Rāghava.

"You are seeking to cross the ocean with a boulder tied around your neck, to take into your hands the very sun and moon, if you seek to assault the beloved wife of Rāghava.

"You have seen a blazing fire and seek to carry it away in a cloth, if you seek to carry off the virtuous wife of Rāma.

"You are seeking to walk atop a row of iron-headed spears, if you seek to violate the proper wife of Rāma.

"As different as a lion and a jackal in the forest, the ocean and a ditch, rare wine and gruel, so different are Dāśarathi[3] and you.

"As different as gold and lead, sandalwood paste and slime, a bull elephant and a cat in the forest, so different are Dāśarathi and you.

"As different as Garuda, the son of Vinatā,[4] and a crow, a peacock and a gull, a vulture and a crane in the forest, so different are Dāśarathi and you.

"As long as Rāma walks the earth, mighty as thousand-eyed Indra, armed with his bow and arrow, you may take me but could never enjoy me, no more than a fly the diamond chip it swallows."

Such were the words the good woman addressed to the evil nightstalker, but a shudder passed through her body, and she began to quiver like a slender plantain tree tossed by the wind.

And when Rāvaṇa, mighty as Death himself, observed how Sītā was trembling, he thought to frighten her still further by telling of his House, his power, the name he had won for himself, and the deeds he had done.

---

2. The legendary Mt. Mandara was made the churning stick when the gods and antigods churned the milk ocean for the drink of immortality. The cosmic serpent used as the twirling string spewed forth the terrible *kalakuta* poison, which Shiva swallowed to protect the world.
3. Rama (literally "descendent of Dasharatha").
4. King of birds and the mount of the god Vishnu.

Sarga 46

Even as Sītā was speaking in this manner, Rāvaṇa flew into a passion, and knitting his brow into a frown he harshly replied:

"I am half brother to Vaiśravaṇa,[5] lovely lady. My name is Rāvaṇa, if you please, the mighty ten-necked one.

"In fear of me the gods, *gandharvas, piśācas,* great birds, and serpents flee in terror, as all things born are put to flight by fear of Death.

"In connection with some issue between us Vaiśravaṇa, my half brother, and I came into conflict. In a rage I attacked and defeated him in battle.

"Tormented by fear of me he left his own prosperous realm and now dwells on Kailāsa, highest of mountains, with only men to convey him.

"For the aerial chariot that flies where one desires, the lovely Puṣpaka, once belonged to him. But I took it by force of arms, my beauty, and now ride upon it through the sky.

"At the mere sight of my face, Maithilī, once my anger has been provoked, the gods with Indra at their head flee in terror.

"In my presence the wind blows cautiously, and the sun's hot rays turn cold in fear.

"The leaves on the trees stop rustling, and the rivers slacken their current wherever I am, wherever I go.

"On the further shore of the ocean lies my lovely city, Laṅkā, grand as Indra's Amarāvatī, thronged with dreaded *rākṣasas.*

"It is a lovely, dazzling city ringed by a white rampart, with gateways made of gold and towers of cat's-eye beryl.

"It is crowded with elephants, horses, and chariots, the sound of pipes resounds there, and its gardens are beautiful, filled with trees bearing any fruit one wants.

"Living there with me, proud princess Sītā, you shall forget what it was like to have been a mortal woman.

"Enjoying not only the pleasures mortals enjoy, lovely lady, but divine pleasures, too, you shall soon forget that short-lived mortal, Rāma.

"So meager is his power that King Daśaratha, in order to enthrone a favored son, was able to drive him into the forest, first-born though he was.

---

5. Kubera, god of wealth. In his more common, wrathful form, Ravana has ten necks and twenty arms.

"What use is this witless Rāma to you, large-eyed woman, a miserable ascetic who lets himself be deposed from the kingship?

"The lord of all *rākṣasas* has come here in person, of his own accord. Do not reject him, whom the arrows of Manmatha, god of love, have so badly wounded.

"For if you do reject me, timid lady, you shall live to regret it, just like Urvaśī after she spurned Purūravas."[6]

So he spoke, but Vaidehī was overcome with rage—her eyes grew red, and though all alone in that deserted spot, she made this harsh reply to the lord of *rākṣasas:*

"How can you want to commit such an outrage, you who claim Vaiśravaṇa as brother, a god to whom all beings pay homage?

"The *rākṣasas* shall inevitably perish, Rāvaṇa, all who have you for their king, a cruel, imprudent, intemperate king.

"A man might abduct Indra's wife, Úacī herself, and still hope to save his life, but he who carries me off, the wife of Rāma, has no life left to save.

"One might steal the incomparable Úacī from the hand that wields the thunderbolt and long remain alive. But violate a woman like me, *rākṣasa,* and even drinking the nectar of immortality will be no escape for you."

Sarga 47

Hearing Sītā's words the awesome ten-necked Rāvaṇa struck his hands together and made ready to assume his massive form.

Again he addressed Maithilī, and far more severely than before: "It seems you did not hear, madwoman, when I spoke of my strength and valor.

"I can lift the earth in my arms while standing in the sky; I can drink up the ocean, I can slay Death in battle.

"I can shatter the earth with my sharp arrows, madwoman, or bring the sun to a halt. I can take on any form at will. You see before you a husband ready to grant your every wish."

And as Rāvaṇa spoke thus in his wild rage, his yellow-rimmed eyes turned fiery red.

Then suddenly Rāvaṇa, younger brother to Vaiśravaṇa, abandoned the kindly form of beggar and assumed his true shape, one such as Doom itself must have.

With eyes flaming bright red, with earrings of burnished gold, with bow and arrows, he became once more the majestic ten-faced stalker of the night.

6. The celestial nymph Urvashi fell in love with the mortal king Pururavas. The reference here to her misfortune when she left Pururavas is unclear.

He had thrown off the guise of mendicant and assumed his own form again, the colossal shape of Rāvaṇa, overlord of *rākṣasas*.

With eyes flaming bright red in his rage, lowering like a bank of storm clouds, clad in a red garment Rāvaṇa stood before Maithilī, staring at her, perfect jewel of a woman, with her jet-black hair, her sunlike radiance, and the fine clothes and ornaments that she wore. And he said:

"If you seek a husband whose fame has spread throughout the three worlds, shapely woman, be mine. I am a lord worthy of you.

"Love me forever. I shall be a lover to win your praise, and never, my beauty, will I do anything to displease you. Give up this love for a mortal being, and bestow your love on me.

"What possible virtues could make you love this short-lived Rāma, a failure, stripped of kingship? You think you are so smart, but what a fool you really are!

"He is a simpleton, who at the bidding of a woman abandoned his kingdom and loved ones to come and live in this forest, the haunt of wild beasts."

And so speaking to Sītā, princess of Mithilā, who deserved the same kindness she always showed others, Rāvaṇa seized her as the planet Budha might seize the star Rohiṇī in the sky.

With his left hand he seized lotus-eyed Sītā by her hair and with his right hand by her thighs.

With his long arms and sharp fangs he resembled a mountain peak; seeing him advancing like Death himself, the spirits of the forest fled overpowered by fear.

Then with a dreadful rumble Rāvaṇa's great chariot came into view, that unearthly chariot fashioned by magic, with wheels of gold, and harnessed with asses.

With loud, harsh threats he then clutched Vaidehī to his breast and boarded the chariot.

Caught in Rāvaṇa's grip and wild with despair, the glorious Sītā screamed at the top of her voice, crying, "Rāma!" But Rāma was far away in the forest.

Filled with desire for one who was filled with loathing for him, Rāvaṇa flew up holding her writhing like a serpent queen.

As the lord of *rākṣasas* carried her off through the sky, she screamed shrilly like a woman gone mad, in agony, or delirious:

"Oh great-armed Lakṣmaṇa, you have always sought favor with your guru. Don't you know that I am being carried off by a *rākṣasa*, who can change his form at will?

"And you, Rāghava, you renounced all life's pleasures, everything of value, for the sake of righteousness. Don't you see me being carried off in defiance of all that is right?

"And surely, slayer of enemies, you are the one to discipline wrongdoers. Why then don't you punish so evil a creature as Rāvaṇa?

"But no, the result of wrongdoing is not seen right away. Time is a factor in this, as in the ripening of grain.

"And as for you, Doom must have robbed you of your senses to do what you have done. Disaster shall befall you at the hands of Rāma, a terrible disaster that will end your life.

"Ah, now Kaikeyī and all her family must be satisfied. Rāma's lawful wife has been taken from him, that glorious prince whom nothing but righteousness could satisfy.

"Janasthāna, I call on you and you *karṇikāra* trees in full blossom: Tell Rāma at once that Rāvaṇa is carrying off Sītā.

"I greet you, Mount Prasravaṇa,[7] with your flower garlands and massive peaks: Quickly tell Rāma that Rāvaṇa is carrying off Sītā.

"I greet you, Godāvarī river, alive with the call of geese and cranes: Tell Rāma at once that Rāvaṇa is carrying off Sītā.

"And you spirits that inhabit the different trees of this forest, I salute you all: Tell my husband that I have been carried off.

"All creatures that live in this place, I appeal to you for help, all you flocks of birds and herds of beasts: Tell my husband that the woman he loves more than life itself is being carried off, that Sītā has been carried away, helpless, by Rāvaṇa.

"Once the powerful, great-armed prince discovers where I am—albeit in the other world—he shall come in all his valor and bring me home, were it Vaivasvata himself, god of death, who had carried me off.

* * *

from Book 6[1]

[The Death of Ravana]

from *Sarga 96*

The great battle raged all night long as the gods, *dānavas, yakṣas, piśācas,* great serpents, and *rākṣasas* stood watching.

---

7. A peak in the Vindhya range in central India, where Rama, Sita, and Lakshmana spent time during their exile.
1. Translated by Robert Goldman, Barend A. van Nooten, and Sally Sutherland Goldman.

Indeed the duel between Rāma and Rāvaṇa went on day and night not pausing for an hour or even a moment.

Sarga 97

But then Mātali[2] alerted Rāghava, saying, "Why, heroic prince, do you merely match him blow for blow, as if you knew no better?

"In order to kill him, my lord, you must shoot him with the missile of Grandfather Brahmā. For the moment ordained by the gods for his destruction is now at hand."

Alerted by Mātali's words, Rāma drew forth that blazing arrow which, as he did so, made a hissing sound like that of a snake.

It had been given to him earlier by the mighty and blessed seer Agastya. It was a mighty arrow, the gift of Brahmā and unfailing in battle.

Brahmā whose power is immeasurable had fashioned it long ago for the sake of Indra and had presented it to that lord of the gods, who was eager to conquer the three worlds.

Pavana, the god of the wind, resided in its feathers; Pāvaka, the god of fire, and Bhâskara, the sun god, were in its arrowhead. Its shaft was made of cosmic space; and the mountains Meru and Mandara lent it their weight.

Radiant in its appearance, beautifully feathered, and adorned with gold, it was fashioned with the radiant energy of all the elements, and it was as brilliant as the sun.

It looked like the smoking fire of doom and glistened like a venomous snake. It could shatter hosts of chariots, elephants, and horses; and its effects were instantaneous.

It could shatter gateways and their iron beams and even mountains. With its shaft drenched with the blood of various creatures and smeared with their marrow it was truly frightful.

Roaring deafeningly and charged with the power of the thunderbolt, it was the scourge of many hosts. Dreadful, hissing like a serpent, it inspired terror in all beings.

It was fearsome and looked like Yama, the god of death. It provided a constant supply of food to flocks of cranes and vultures, *rākṣasas*, and packs of jackals.

Fletched with the various, beautiful and variegated feathers of Garuḍa, it brought joy to the monkey chiefs and despair to the *rākṣasas*.

Then strong and mighty Rāma invoked that great, unequalled arrow—an arrow that robbed one's enemies of their glory but brought joy to oneself. It was destined

---

2. As Ravana fought from a chariot while Rama was on foot, Indra, king of the gods, dispatched his charioteer Matali to provide Rama with a comparable conveyance.

to destroy that menace to the Ikṣvākus[3] and all the worlds; and Rāma placed it on his bow in the manner prescribed in the *veda*.

Filled with fury and exerting himself to the utmost, he bent the bow fully and loosed the arrow towards Rāvaṇa, tearing at his vitals.

As unstoppable as the thunderbolt and released by those arms of adamant, it struck Rāvaṇa's breast, inevitable as death.

Loosed with tremendous speed the deadly arrow pierced evil-minded Rāvaṇa's heart.

Drenched with blood the fatal arrow swiftly entered the earth, carrying with it the life breaths of Rāvaṇa.

Once the arrow had accomplished its purpose in killing Rāvaṇa, it obediently returned to its quiver, glistening with its still-wet blood.

Meanwhile the bow and arrows of him who had been struck down so swiftly slipped from his grasp along with his life breaths as he lay dying.

The lord of the sons of chaos, once so swift and splendid, fell lifeless to the ground from his chariot like Vṛtra[4] smitten by the thunderbolt.

Seeing him fallen to the ground, the surviving rangers of the night, their lord slain, fled terrified in all directions.

But as for the monkeys, whose weapons were trees, when they saw that ten-necked Rāvaṇa had been slain and that Rāghava was victorious, they pursued the *rākṣasas,* roaring loudly.

Hard pressed by the jubilant monkeys, their protector slain, the *rākṣasas* fled in fear to Laṅkā, their piteous faces drenched with tears.

Then the rejoicing monkeys, acting the part of victors, roared triumphantly, proclaiming Rāghava's victory and the death of Rāvaṇa.

The auspicious kettledrums of the thirty gods then resounded in the heavens; and a pleasant breeze blew, wafting a divine fragrance.

Then an extraordinary and delightful shower of blossoms fell from the sky to the earth, covering Rāma's chariot.

The beautiful voice of the great gods filled with the praise of Rāghava could be heard in the heavens crying, "Well done! Well done!"

3. The family name of the royal dynasty of Ayodhya.
4. A demon slain by Indra, who as the god of rain wields a thunderbolt.

Now that fierce Rāvaṇa, the terror of all the worlds, had been slain, great joy filled the gods and celestial bards.

Then, having slain that bull among *rākṣasas,* Rāghava, in great delight, fulfilled the wishes of Sugrīva and mighty Aṅgada.[5]

The hosts of the Māruts[6] regained tranquility, the directions were limpid, and the sky grew clear. The earth ceased its trembling, and soft breezes blew, while the sun, the bringer of day, shone with a steady light.

Sugrīva, Vibhīṣaṇa,[7] and the rest of splendid Rāghava's close allies, together with Lakṣmaṇa, gathered around him on the battlefield in the joy of victory and paid him homage with all due ceremony.

And the mighty prince, the delight of the king of the Raghu dynasty, having slain his enemy, became true to his vow. Surrounded by his kinsmen and armies there on the field of battle, he looked as resplendent as Indra surrounded by the hosts of the thirty gods.

* * *

[*After the killing of Rāvaṇa, Sītā is recovered and brought before Rāma.*]

[The Fire Ordeal of Sita]

Sarga 103

Looking at Maithilī who stood so meekly beside him, Rāma began to speak as rage simmered in his heart.

"So here you are, my lady. I have won you back after conquering my enemy in battle. I did all this in accordance with the demands of manly valor.

"I have wiped clean the affront and so my wrath is appeased. For I have eliminated both the insult and my enemy at the same time.

"Today I have demonstrated my manly valor. Today my efforts have borne fruit. Today, having fulfilled my vow, I am once more master of myself.

"You were carried off by that wanton *rākṣasa* when you were left alone, but now through manly action I have expunged that affront caused by fate.

"Of what use to anyone is a weakling who cannot wipe clean an insult through his own power?

"The leaping of the ocean and the razing of Laṅkā—today those praiseworthy deeds of Hanumān have borne fruit.

5. Sugriva is the monkey king of Kishkindha who aided Rama in the recovery of Sita. Angada is his nephew and successor.
6. The wind gods.
7. The virtuous *rakshasa* brother of Ravana, who allies himself with Rama.

"And today the efforts of Sugrīva and his army through their valor in battle and their beneficial counsel to me have borne fruit as well.

"And the efforts of my devoted Vibhīṣaṇa, who abandoned his worthless brother and came to me of his own accord, have likewise borne fruit."

Now as Rāma was saying these words in this fashion, Sītā, who looked like a wide-eyed doe, was overcome with tears.

But as Rāma gazed upon her, his anger flared up once more, like a blazing fire drenched with melted butter.

Knitting his brows on his forehead and glancing at her from the corner of his eye, he spoke harshly to Sītā there in the midst of the monkeys and *rākṣasas*.

"In wiping away this affront, Sītā, I have accomplished all that a man could do. In my wrath, I have won you back from the hands of my enemy just as through his austerities, the contemplative sage Agastya won back the southern lands that had been inaccessible to all living beings.

"Please understand that I did not undertake this great war effort—now brought to completion through the valor of my allies—on your account. Instead I did all this in order to protect my reputation and in every way to wipe clean the insult and disgrace to my illustrious lineage.

"Since, however, your virtue is now in doubt, your presence has become as unbearable to me as a bright lamp to a man afflicted with a disease of the eye.

"Go, therefore, as you please with my permission, daughter of Janaka, in any of the ten directions. I have no further use for you, my lady.

"For what powerful man born in a respectable family—his heart tinged with affection—would take back a woman who had lived in the house of another man?

"How could I who boast of my noble lineage possibly take you back—just risen from Rāvaṇa's lap and gazed upon by his lustful eye?

"I have restored my reputation; and that is the purpose for which I won you back. I have no further interest in you. Go from here wherever you like.

"I have made up mind in saying this, my lady. Choose Lakṣmaṇa or Bharata as you please.

"Or, Sītā, turn your heart to Sugrīva, lord of the monkeys, or the *rākṣasa* lord Vibhīṣaṇa, whichever pleases you.

"For surely, Sītā, once he had seen you with your heavenly beauty so enchanting, Rāvaṇa would not long have left you unmolested while you were dwelling in his house."

When Maithilī, who deserved to hear only kind words, had heard those cruel words of her beloved after so long a time, she shed tears and trembled violently like a *vallarī* creeper struck down by the trunk of a mighty elephant.

Sarga 104

When Vaidehī was addressed in this cruel and horrifying manner by the furious Rāghava, she was deeply wounded.

Hearing those cutting words of her husband before that great multitude, words such as she had never heard before, Maithilī was overcome with shame.

Pierced, as it were, by those verbal barbs, the daughter of Janaka, seemed to shrink within herself and gave way to bitter tears.

Wiping her tear-stained face, she replied softly to her husband in a faltering voice:

"How can you, heroic prince, speak to me with such cutting and improper words, painful to the ears, as some vulgar man might speak to his vulgar wife?

"I am not as you think of me, great armed prince. You must believe in me, for I swear to you by my own virtue.

"You harbor suspicion against all women because of the conduct of the vulgar ones. If you really knew me, you would abandon your suspicion.

"If I touched another's body against my will, lord, it was not by my choice. It is fate that was to blame here.

"My heart, which I control, was always devoted to you. But I was helpless. What could I have done regarding my body, which was in the power of another?

"If, my love, you do not truly know me despite our long-nurtured love and intimacy, then surely I am lost forever.

"When you dispatched the heroic Hanumān to search for me, why, heroic prince, did you not repudiate me then, while I was still in Laṅkā?

"No sooner had I heard your message, heroic prince, then abandoned by you, I would have abandoned my own life right before the eyes of that monkey lord.

"Then you would not have had to risk your life in a useless effort nor would your allies have had to undergo hardships to no purpose.

"But now, tiger among men, you give way to anger like some lesser man, thinking of me only as a typical woman.

"Since I am named after Janaka, you fail to take into account that I was born from the Goddess Earth, nor, though you know my conduct well, do you give it proper consideration.

"You give no weight to the fact that you took my hand when we were both still children. My devotion, my virtuous conduct—all that you have set aside."

When she had spoken in this fashion, Sītā turned weeping to Lakṣmaṇa, who stood there despondent and brooding, and spoke, her voice choked with tears.

"Build me a pyre, Saumitri, the only cure for this calamity. I cannot bear to live under the cloud of this false allegation.

"Rejected in the assembly of the people by my husband, who is not satisfied with my virtues, I shall enter the fire, bearer of oblations, so that I may follow the only path proper for me."

When Lakṣmaṇa, slayer of heroic foes, had been addressed in this fashion by Vaidehī, he glared at Rāghava's face, gripped by indignation.

But, sensing Rāma's intentions, which were betrayed by his facial expression, mighty Saumitri, ever obedient to Rāma's wishes, built the pyre.

Then reverently circumambulating Rāma, who stood with his face downcast, Vaidehī approached the blazing fire, eater of oblations.

After making her obeisance to the gods and the brahmans, Maithilī cupped her hands in reverence and facing Agni, god of fire, said this:

"Since my heart has never once strayed from Rāghava, so may the purifying fire, witness of all the world, protect me in every way."

When she had spoken in this fashion, Vaidehī reverently circumambulated the fire, eater of oblations. Then she entered the blazing flames, with a fearless heart.

The vast crowd assembled there, filled with children and the aged, watched as Maithilī entered the fire, eater of oblations.

As Sītā entered the fire, a vast and prodigious cry of, "Alas! Alas!" arose from the *rākṣasas* and monkeys.

* * *

[*The gods appear to ask how Rāma, who is chief among the gods, could remain unmoved as Sītā throws herself into the fire. Led by Brahmā they then remind Rāma of his divinity and utter a hymn of praise to him.*]

Sarga 106

Upon hearing that auspicious speech uttered by Grandfather Brahmā, the shining god of fire took Vaidehī on his lap and rose.

She resembled the rising sun and was adorned with ornaments of burnished gold. She was young and wore red garments and her hair was dark and curling. Her garland and ornaments were undamaged. Her mind was calm and her appearance unchanged. Taking Vaidehī on his lap the shining god of fire presented her to Rāma.

Then the purifying god of fire, witness of all the world, spoke to Rāma, saying, "Here is your Vaidehī, Rāma. She has committed no sin.

"She is of pure conduct and high moral character and has never betrayed you in word, thought, imagination, or glance.

"When you had left her alone she was carried off, helpless and sorrowful, from the deserted forest by the *rākṣasa* Rāvaṇa, arrogant in his power.

"Hidden and imprisoned in the inner apartments, thinking only of you and having you for her only recourse, she was guarded by hordes of hideous *rākṣasa* women, dreadful to behold.

"Although she was enticed and threatened in various ways, Maithilī would not even think of the *rākṣasa,* since her heart was utterly devoted to you.

"You must take her back, Rāghava, for her heart is pure and she is free from sin. Say no more, I am giving you an order."

When mighty Rāma, steadfast and firm in his valor, had been addressed in this fashion, that best of those who maintain righteousness, replied to that foremost among the thirty gods.

"Unquestionably Sītā needed to be proven innocent before the three worlds, since the auspicious woman had long dwelt in Rāvaṇa's inner apartments.

"For had I not put Jānakī to the test, the virtuous would say of me, 'Daśaratha's son Rāma is a lustful fool.'

36

"I know full well that Janaka's daughter Maithilī could give her heart to no other, since she is devoted to me and obeys my every thought.

"But in order that the three worlds too should have faith in her, I, whose ultimate recourse is truth, took no notice as Vaidehī entered the fire, eater of oblations.

"Rāvaṇa could no more have violated that wide-eyed lady, protected by her own blazing energy, than could the mighty ocean violate its boundary.

"That evil-minded brute was incapable of assaulting Maithilī even in his thoughts. For she is as unapproachable as a blazing flame of fire.

"This auspicious woman was not destined to rule over Rāvaṇa's inner apartments. For she is as inseparable from me as is its radiance from the sun.

"Janaka's daughter Maithilī has been proven innocent before the three worlds, and I am no more able to give her up than is a self-controlled man his good reputation.

"Moreover, I must follow the good advice that all of you affectionate friends, respected throughout the world, have uttered for my own good."

When he had uttered these words, powerful Rāma, praised by his mighty companions for the feat he had accomplished, was reunited with his beloved. Then Rāghava, who well deserved it, experienced happiness.

The *Book of Songs* (*Shi jing,* or Classic of Poetry), compiled by the sixth century B.C.E, is the oldest anthology in China, whose literary tradition begins with the lyric. According to one historical tradition, the poems were collected by Zhou dynasty officials as evidence for contemporary mores to be presented to the ruler, but the prevailing account of the text's compilation appears in the *Grand Scribe's Records* of Sima Qian. There we are told that it was edited by none other than Confucius himself, who selected its 305 songs from a larger group of over three thousand stored in the archives of the Zhou feudal states, edited their musical accompaniments (now lost), and arranged them in their present order. However unlikely, this attribution remained unquestioned until modern times, and already by the fourth century B.C.E. the anthology had been canonized as one of the five Confucian classics. This ensured the text's preservation, and its inclusion in the educational curriculum of the elite (more specifically, on the civil service examination), and brought a scholarly attention that generated many volumes of commentary over the ages.

The poems were most likely composed between 1000 and 600 B.C.E. Many appear to be simple folk songs, whereas others reveal a more aristocratic and literary origin, and some are clearly temple hymns to the dynasty's ruling house. All but six are anonymous, and the majority treat themes familiar to folk and ballad traditions worldwide: friendship, courtship, marriage, and death; planting, harvesting, hunting, and fishing; and the glories and sorrows of war. The natural images with which many poems open (sometimes repeated elsewhere) offer a cue to what follows, but their often enigmatic quality has elicited centuries of scholarly speculation. Unlike most early poetry in other cultures, the *Book of Songs* features a great deal of rhyme, and the most common form employs three stanzas of four (or six) four-syllable lines each.

The numbers assigned to the poems refer to their sequence in the standard edition from the second century B.C.E. The poems are grouped into four sections of varying size, of which the first and largest contains 160 "Airs of the States" (*Guo feng*). *Feng* literally means "wind" but can also denote "customs" and is closely related to a word meaning "to criticize," and the States represent fifteen of the Zhou feudal domains. These are among the latest of the poems in the anthology and among the most accessible; all but the last six included here are from this group. The next seventy-four poems, "Lesser Elegances" (*xiao ya*), treat similar subjects drawn from daily life but sometimes placed within a more elite context; poems 166, 189, and 234 belong to this section. The thirty-one "Greater Elegances" (*da ya*) that follow (including poems 238 and 245) are sometimes difficult to distinguish from the preceding group but tend to include the longest poems in the anthology, narratives of historical and legendary events and figures. Finally, the forty "Hymns" (*song*), of which 283 is an example, may be among the oldest works in the collection. They were said to have been used in ritual performances by the Zhou rulers and two other feudal courts; many lack both rhyme and divisions into stanzas.

Traditions of reading the *Book of Songs* are important for understanding not only the collection itself but also later presumptions about all literature, and poetry in particular. The *Songs* are the most frequently cited work in Confucius's *Analects,* and other early texts demonstrate that the poems were often quoted in political and diplomatic discussions to convey opinions obliquely but effectively. Such trust in the poems' didactic utility, coupled with the fact that some clearly are accounts of actual events, led early scholars to assume that the entire anthology was commenting either directly or indirectly on history. The premises for this belief are articulated most clearly in what is known as the "Great Preface" to the collection: poetry (or song, the two being interchangeable) expresses naturally and spontaneously what is in one's heart or mind, and the impulse arises from the external world of nature, society, and the body politic, which are linked by correlative networks. Any poetic expression could therefore be assumed to implicate something larger than the individual, construed as a response to a particular set of circumstances in a particular context. Thus poem 5, "Locusts," was read as praise of the Zhou queen, whose freedom from jealousy and willingness to allow the king other consorts produced, happily, a multitude of progeny. Such interpretations may represent far-fetched distortions of the poems' original import, but they also provided valuable explanations for often perplexing vignettes. These practices also dignified texts that might otherwise have been devalued or lost (much as allegory served the Hebrew Bible's Song of Songs), and they continued to shape the later poetic and critical tradition in profound ways.

The linguistic difficulty of the *Book of Songs* has challenged both traditional Chinese commentators and translators into Western languages. Arthur Waley's translations offer the best compromise between philological accuracy and poetic fluency, but they may be usefully compared with two alternatives. Swedish sinologist Bernhard Karlgren (1889–1978) translated the poems into philologically accurate prose. The poet Ezra Pound (1885–1972), who knew no Chinese but considered himself a Confucian, sought to highlight the resemblance of the *Songs* to English ballads and was said by T. S. Eliot to have been "the inventor of Chinese poetry for our time."

from Book of Songs[1]

1: The Ospreys Cry

"Fair, fair," cry the ospreys
On the island in the river.
Lovely is this noble lady,
Fit bride for our lord.

5 In patches grows the water mallow;
To left and right one must seek it.
Shy was this noble lady;
Day and night he sought her.

Sought her and could not get her;
10 Day and night he grieved.
Long thoughts, oh, long unhappy thoughts,
Now on his back, now tossing on to his side.

In patches grows the water mallow;
To left and right one must gather it.
15 Shy is this noble lady;
With great zither and little we hearten her.

In patches grows the water mallow;
To left and right one must choose it.
Shy is this noble lady;
20 With bells and drums we will gladden her.

5: Locusts

The locusts' wings say "throng, throng";
Well may your sons and grandsons
Be a host innumerable.

1 Translated by Arthur Waley

The locusts' wings say "bind, bind";
5   Well may your sons and grandsons
Continue in an endless line.

The locusts' wings say "join, join";[1]
Well may your sons and grandsons
Be forever at one.

20: Plop Fall the Plums

Plop fall the plums; but there are still seven.
Let those gentlemen that would court me
Come while it is lucky!

Plop fall the plums; there are still three.
5   Let any gentleman that would court me
Come before it is too late!

Plop fall the plums, in shallow baskets we lay them
Any gentleman who would court me
Had better speak while there is time.

23: In the Wilds Is a Dead Doe

In the wilds there is a dead doe;
With white rushes we cover her.
There was a lady longing for the spring;
A fair knight seduced her.

5   In the wood there is a clump of oaks,
And in the wilds a dead deer
With white rushes well bound;
There was a lady fair as jade.

"Heigh, not so hasty, not so rough;
10 Heigh, do not touch my handkerchief.
Take care, or the dog will bark."

26: Cypress Boat[1]

Tossed is that cypress boat,
Wave-tossed it floats.
My heart is in turmoil, I cannot sleep.
But secret is my grief.
5   Wine I have, all things needful
For play, for sport.

My heart is not a mirror,
To reflect what others will.

1. The three noises that the locusts' wings make are being punned upon and interpreted as omens.
1. Traditional commentators believe that this is a song of a woman being married against her will.

Brothers too I have;
10 I cannot be snatched away.
But lo, when I told them of my plight
I found that they were angry with me.

My heart is not a stone;
It cannot be rolled.
15 My heart is not a mat;
It cannot be folded away.
I have borne myself correctly
In rites more than can be numbered.

My sad heart is consumed, I am harassed
20 By a host of small men.
I have borne vexations very many,
Received insults not few.
In the still of night I brood upon it;
In the waking hours I rend my breast.

25 O sun, ah, moon,
Why are you changed and dim?
Sorrow clings to me
Like an unwashed dress.
In the still of night I brood upon it,
30 Long to take wing and fly away.

45: Cypress Boat

Unsteady is that cypress boat
In the middle of the river.
His two locks looped over his brow[1]
He swore that truly he was my comrade,
5 And till death would love no other.
Oh, mother, ah, Heaven,
That a man could be so false!

Unsteady is that boat of cypress-wood
By that river's side.
10 His two locks looped over his brow
He swore that truly he was my mate,
And till death would not fail me.
Oh, mother, ah, Heaven,
That a man could be so false!

76: I Beg of You, Zhong Zi

I beg of you, Zhong Zi,
Do not climb into our homestead,
Do not break the willows we have planted.

1. A sign that he has not yet come of age.

Not that I mind about the willows,
5 But I am afraid of my father and mother.
Zhong Zi I dearly love;
But of what my father and mother say
Indeed I am afraid.

I beg of you, Zhong Zi,
10 Do not climb over our wall,
Do not break the mulberry-trees we have planted.
Not that I mind about the mulberry-trees,
But I am afraid of my brothers.
Zhong Zi I dearly love;
15 But of what my brothers say
Indeed I am afraid.

I beg of you, Zhong Zi,
Do not climb into our garden,
Do not break the hard-wood we have planted.
20 Not that I mind about the hard-wood,
But I am afraid of what people will say.
Zhong Zi I dearly love;
But of all that people will say
Indeed I am afraid.

166: May Heaven Guard

May Heaven guard and keep you
In great security,
Make you staunch and hale;
What blessing not vouchsafed?
5 Give you much increase,
Send nothing but abundance.

May Heaven guard and keep you,
Cause your grain to prosper,
Send you nothing that is not good.
10 May you receive from Heaven a hundred boons,
May Heaven send down to you blessings so many
That the day is not long enough for them all.

May Heaven guard and keep you,
Cause there to be nothing in which you do not rise higher,
15 Like the mountains, like the uplands,
Like the ridges, the great ranges,
Like a stream coming down in flood;
In nothing not increased.
Lucky and pure are your viands of sacrifice
20 That you use in filial offering,
Offerings of invocation, gift-offerings, offering in dishes and offering of first-
    fruits
To dukes and former kings.
Those sovereigns say: "We give you

Myriad years of life, days unending."

25 The Spirits are good,
They will give you many blessings.
The common people are contented,
For daily they have their drink and food.
The thronging herd, the many clans
30 All side with you in deeds of power.

To be like the moon advancing to its full,
Like the sun climbing the sky,
Like the everlastingness of the southern hills,
Without failing or falling,
35 Like the pine-tree, the cypress in their verdure—
All these blessings may you receive!

189: The Beck[1]

Ceaseless flows that beck,
Far stretch the southern hills.
May you be sturdy as the bamboo,
May you flourish like the pine,
5 May elder brother and younger brother
Always love one another,
Never do evil to one another.

To give continuance to foremothers and forefathers
We build a house, many hundred cubits of wall;
10 To south and west its doors.
Here shall we live, here rest,
Here laugh, here talk.

We bind the frames, creak, creak;
We hammer the mud, tap, tap,
15 That it may be a place where wind and rain cannot enter,
Nor birds and rats get in,
But where our lord may dwell.

As a halberd, even so plumed,
As an arrow, even so sharp,
20 As a bird, even so soaring,
As wings, even so flying
Are the halls to which our lord ascends.

Well leveled is the courtyard,
Firm are the pillars,
25 Cheerful are the rooms by day,
Softly gloaming by night,
A place where our lord can be at peace.

Below, the rush-mats; over them the bamboo-mats.
Comfortably he sleeps,
30 He sleeps and wakes

And interprets his dreams.
"Your lucky dreams, what were they?"
"They were of black bears and brown,
Of serpents and snakes."

35   The diviner thus interprets it:
"Black bears and brown
Mean men-children.
Snakes and serpents
Mean girl-children."

40   So he bears a son,
And puts him to sleep upon a bed,
Clothes him in robes,
Gives him a jade scepter to play with.
The child's howling is very lusty;
45   In red greaves shall he flare,
Be lord and king of house and home.
Then he bears a daughter,

And puts her upon the ground,
Clothes her in swaddling-clothes,
50   Gives her a loom-whorl to play with.
For her no decorations, no emblems;
Her only care, the wine and food,
And how to give no trouble to father and mother.

234: What Plant Is Not Faded?

What plant is not faded?
What day do we not march?
What man is not taken
To defend the four bounds?

5   What plant is not wilting?
What man is not taken from his wife?
Alas for us soldiers,
Treated as though we were not fellow-men!

Are we buffaloes, are we tigers
10   That our home should be these desolate wilds?
Alas for us soldiers,
Neither by day nor night can we rest!

The fox bumps and drags
Through the tall, thick grass.
15   Inch by inch move our barrows
As we push them along the track.

238: Oak Clumps

Thick grow the oak clumps;

Great is the magnificence of the lord king;
On either hand are those that speed for him.

5 Great is the magnificence of the lord king;
On either hand are those that hold up scepters before him,
Hold up scepters in solemn state,
As befits doughty knights.

Spurt goes that boat on the Jing;
10 A host of oarsmen rows it.
When the King of Zhou goes forth,
His six armies are with him.

How it stands out, the Milky Way,
Making a blazon in the sky!
15 Long life to the King of Zhou,
And a portion for his people!

Chiseled and carved are his emblems,
Of bronze and jade are they made.
Ceaseless are the labors of our king
20 Fashioning the network of all the lands.

245: Birth to the People

She who in the beginning gave birth to the people,
This was Jiang Yuan.
How did she give birth to the people?
Well she sacrificed and prayed
5 That she might no longer be childless.
She trod on the big toe of God's footprint,
Was accepted and got what she desired.
Then in reverence, then in awe
She gave birth, she nurtured;
10 And this was Hou Ji.°   *"Lord Millet"*

Indeed, she had fulfilled her months,
And her first-born came like a lamb
With no bursting or rending,
With no hurt or harm.
15 To make manifest His magic power
God on high gave her ease.
So blessed were her sacrifice and prayer
That easily she bore her child.

Indeed, they[1] put it in a narrow lane;
20 But oxen and sheep tenderly cherished it.
Indeed, they put it in a far-off wood;
But it chanced that woodcutters came to this wood.
Indeed, they put it on the cold ice;

1. The ballad does not tell us who exposed the child. According to one version it was the mother herself; according to

But the birds covered it with their wings.
25   The birds at last went away,
And Hou Ji began to wail.

Truly far and wide
His voice was very loud.
Then sure enough he began to crawl;
30   Well he straddled, well he reared,
To reach food for his mouth.
He planted large beans;
His beans grew fat and tall.
His paddy-lines were close set,
35   His hemp and wheat grew thick,
His young gourds teemed.

Truly Hou Ji's husbandry
Followed the way that had been shown.
He cleared away the thick grass,
40   He planted the yellow crop.
It failed nowhere, it grew thick,
It was heavy, it was tall,
It sprouted, it eared,
It was firm and good,
45   It nodded, it hung—
He made house and home in Tai.

Indeed, the lucky grains were sent down to us,
The black millet, the double-kerneled,
Millet pink-sprouted and white.
50   Far and wide the black and the double-kerneled
He reaped and acred;
Far and wide the millet pink and white
He carried in his arms, he bore on his back,
Brought them home, and created the sacrifice.

55   Indeed, what are they, our sacrifices?
We pound the grain, we bale it out,
We sift, we tread,
We wash it—soak, soak;
We boil it all steamy.
60   Then with due care, due thought
We gather southernwood, make offering of fat,
Take lambs for the rite of expiation,
We roast, we broil,
To give a start to the coming year.

65   High we load the stands,
The stands of wood and of earthenware.
As soon as the smell rises
God on high is very pleased:
"What smell is this, so strong and good?"
70   Hou Ji founded the sacrifices,

And without blemish or flaw
They have gone on till now.

283: So They Appeared

So they appeared before their lord the king
To get from him their emblems,
Dragon-banners blazing bright,
Tuneful bells tinkling,
5   Bronze-knobbed reins jangling—
The gifts shone with glorious light.
Then they showed them to their shining ancestors
Piously, making offering,
That they might be vouchsafed long life,
10   Everlastingly be guarded.
Oh, a mighty store of blessings!
Glorious and mighty, those former princes and lords
Who secure us with many blessings,
Through whose bright splendors
15   We greatly prosper.

CONFUCIUS ▦ (551–479 B.C.E.)

"Ever since man came into this world, there has never been one greater than Confucius." So declared the fourth-century B.C.E. thinker Mencius, who developed his predecessor's key ideas in ways that would prove instrumental in securing their influence throughout the course of Chinese history. About this great man himself, however, we know remarkably little. Confucius lived during the waning years of the Zhou dynasty in China, when the ruling house had lost virtually all of its power to a ravenous set of competing kingdoms headed by more or less distant relatives. Warfare, economic growth, and social change had destabilized social and political structures and the language that had come to justify them, putting into question the actual and the conceptual bases of received authority.

Confucius probably belonged to the lower ranks of a hereditary nobility whose status was in jeopardy; he was a native of the state of Lu, which supported the legitimacy and rituals of the Zhou rulers. He attributed the social chaos of his time to a falling away from these practices and devoted his life to the attempt to restore them. Failing to secure appointment as a political counselor despite extensive travels to one feudal state after another, he settled for a job as a professional teacher, probably China's first, back home in Lu. *The Analects* (*Lun yu*), best understood as "selected sayings," comprise quotations, conversations, and anecdotes often centering on his response to a specific question. Compiled by multiple generations of later students, it has come down to us in twenty sections or books, of which 3–8 and 11–15 are agreed by scholars to be the oldest and 16–20 the newest. Loosely organized at best, the text contains occasionally repeated passages and material that might even be considered anti-Confucian. By the first century B.C.E., however, *The Analects* were taken as the key to the thoughts of Confucius, who had become identified as the fundamental shaper and transmitter of the cultural heritage.

Obsessed with the prevailing chaos around him, Confucius sought a remedy in a renewal of values and behavior embodied for him in an idealized vision of the founders of the Zhou dynasty. Followers of Confucius were to become known as *ru,* a term evoking a respect for traditional scholarship and ritual. He explicitly disavowed any claims to being an innovator, but many implications of his teachings were in fact quite novel. He articulated his ideas within the context of human relationships, both large and small. Although clearly mindful of notions of heaven and destiny that in earlier eras were probably associated with divine or cosmic forces, Confucius focused not on "gods and spirits" but rather on the realm of the concrete and human. And rather than consider morality in the abstract, he sought to explicate the actions of a specific individual in a particular context. For him, principles of mutual respect and obligation rooted in the family were extended to the community and the body politic, creating a social order consisting of a specific set of appropriate roles, a hierarchical relationship among them, and a governing code of conduct. A key concept is that of the *junzi,* or "gentleman," a term that had denoted social nobility but that Confucius transformed into a state of moral excellence that is attainable, in principle, by almost anyone. Equally important is the term *ren,* translated here as "humanity" and "goodness," which is rooted etymologically in a notion of "human-heartedness," or what it means to be one human being associating with another. Ethical behavior is grounded in a refusal to do to another what one would not want done to oneself and is manifested in respect for one's elders and observance of ritual decorum. It can be learned, cultivated, performed, and, ultimately, perfected when precept and behavior become one.

Traditions (now largely discounted) linked Confucius with the compilation of the Five Classics that became identified as canonical: the *Book of Songs, Book of Documents, Book of Changes,* the *Records of Rites,* and the *Spring and Autumn Annals* (a chronicle of Confucius's home state of Lu). By the beginning of the second millennium, *The Analects* had joined them on the classical curriculum for the imperial civil service examination, the most important entry into the career of choice for the literate elite in the government bureaucracy. Rote, uncomprehending memorization of the text as a child would be followed by a lifetime of reflection and, even more important, action upon its meaning. That generations of scholars in China were to aspire to this goal, seeing the educated person as morally superior but obliged to serve others, is owing in no small measure to the lessons of the text itself.

from The Analects[1]

1.1. The Master[2] said: "To learn something and then to put it into practice at the right time: is this not a joy? To have friends coming from afar: is this not a delight? Not to be upset when one's merits are ignored: is this not the mark of a gentleman?"

1.2. Master You[3] said: "A man who respects his parents and his elders would hardly be inclined to defy his superiors. A man who is not inclined to defy his superiors will never foment a rebellion. A gentleman works at the root. Once the root is secured, the Way unfolds. To respect parents and elders is the root of humanity."

1.3. The Master said: "Clever talk and affected manners are seldom signs of goodness."

1.4. Master Zeng[4] said: "I examine myself three times a day. When dealing on behalf of others, have I been trustworthy? In intercourse with my friends, have I been faithful? Have I practiced what I was taught?"

1. Translated by Simon Leys.
2. "The Master" is Confucius himself.
3. Confucius's disciple Zhong You (d. 480 B.C.E.), also known as Zilu.
4. Another disciple, Zeng Can, who played a prominent role in early Confucianism.

1.5. The Master said: "To govern a state of middle size, one must dispatch business with dignity and good faith; be thrifty and love all men; mobilize the people only at the right times."

1.6. The Master said: "At home, a young man must respect his parents; abroad, he must respect his elders. He should talk little, but with good faith; love all people, but associate with the virtuous. Having done this, if he still has energy to spare, let him study literature."

1.16. The Master said: "Don't worry if people don't recognize your merits; worry that you may not recognize theirs."

2.1 The Master said: "He who rules by virtue is like the polestar, which remains unmoving in its mansion while all the other stars revolve respectfully around it."

2.3. The Master said: "Lead them by political maneuvers, restrain them with punishments: the people will become cunning and shameless. Lead them by virtue, restrain them with ritual: they will develop a sense of shame and a sense of participation."

2.4. The Master said: "At fifteen, I set my mind upon learning. At thirty, I took my stand. At forty, I had no doubts. At fifty, I knew the will of Heaven. At sixty, my ear was attuned. At seventy, I follow all the desires of my heart without breaking any rule."

2.5. Lord Meng Yi asked about filial piety. The Master said: "Never disobey."
As Fan Chi was driving him in his chariot, the Master told him: "Meng Yi asked me about filial piety and I replied: 'Never disobey.'" Fan Chi said: "What does that mean?" The Master said: "When your parents are alive, serve them according to the ritual. When they die, bury them according to the ritual, make sacrifices to them according to the ritual."

2.6. Lord Meng Wu asked about filial piety. The Master said: "The only time a dutiful son ever makes his parents worry is when he is sick."

2.7. Ziyou[5] asked about filial piety. The Master said: "Nowadays people think they are dutiful sons when they feed their parents. Yet they also feed their dogs and horses. Unless there is respect, where is the difference?"

2.8. Zixia[6] asked about filial piety. The Master said: "It is the attitude that matters. If young people merely offer their services when there is work to do, or let their elders drink and eat when there is wine and food, how could this ever pass as filial piety?"

2.9. The Master said: "I can talk all day to Yan Hui[7]—he never raises any objection, he looks stupid. Yet, observe him when he is on his own: his actions fully reflect what he learned. Oh no, Hui is not stupid!"

2.11. The Master said: "He who by revising the old knows the new, is fit to be a teacher."

2.12. The Master said: "A gentleman is not a pot."[8]

---

5. The disciple Yan Yan, about whom little is known except that he was one of Confucius's younger students.
6. Bu Shang, a disciple who played a major role in the transmission of the Confucian classics.
7. Also known as Yan Yuan, one of Confucius's most gifted and favorite disciples.
8. That is, he is not a specialist, in the way a vessel is designed for one specific purpose.

2.13. Zigong[9] asked about the true gentleman. The Master said: "He preaches only what he practices."

2.14. The Master said: "The gentleman considers the whole rather than the parts. The small man considers the parts rather than the whole."

2.15. The Master said: "To study without thinking is futile. To think without studying is dangerous."

2.16. The Master said: "To attack a question from the wrong end—this is harmful indeed."

2.17. The Master said: "Zilu, I am going to teach you what knowledge is. To take what you know for what you know, and what you do not know for what you do not know, that is knowledge indeed."

2.18. Zizhang[1] was studying in the hope of securing an official position. The Master said: "Collect much information, put aside what is doubtful, repeat cautiously the rest; then you will seldom say something wrong. Make many observations, leave aside what is suspect, apply cautiously the rest; then you will seldom have cause for regret. With few mistakes in what you say and few regrets for what you do, your career is made."

2.19. Duke Ai asked: "What should I do to win the hearts of the people?" Confucius replied: "Raise the straight and set them above the crooked, and you will win the hearts of the people. If you raise the crooked and set them above the straight, the people will deny you their support."

2.20. Lord Ji Kang asked: "What should I do in order to make the people respectful, loyal, and zealous?" The Master said: "Approach them with dignity and they will be respectful. Be yourself a good son and a kind father, and they will be loyal. Raise the good and train the incompetent, and they will be zealous."

4.1. The Master said: "It is beautiful to live amidst humanity. To choose a dwelling place destitute of humanity is hardly wise."

4.3. The Master said: "Only a good man can love people and can hate people."

4.4. The Master said: "Seeking to achieve humanity leaves no room for evil."

4.5. The Master said: "Riches and rank are what every man craves; yet if the only way to obtain them goes against his principles, he should desist from such a pursuit. Poverty and obscurity are what every man hates; yet if the only escape from them goes against his principles, he should accept his lot. If a gentleman forsakes humanity, how

9. Duanmu Si, the only one of the three best-known disciples to survive Confucius. He was a successful merchant and diplomat.
1. Zhuansun Shi, another disciple about whom little is known.

can he make a name for himself? Never for a moment does a gentleman part from humanity; he clings to it through trials, he clings to it through tribulations."

4.6. The Master said: "I have never seen a man who truly loved goodness and hated evil. Whoever truly loves goodness would put nothing above it; whoever truly hates evil would practice goodness in such a way that no evil could enter him. Has anyone ever devoted all his strength to goodness just for one day? No one ever has, and yet it is not for want of strength—there may be people who do not have even the small amount of strength it takes, but I have never seen any."

4.8. The Master said: "In the morning hear the Way; in the evening die content."

4.9. The Master said: "A scholar sets his heart on the Way; if he is ashamed of his shabby clothes and coarse food, he is not worth listening to."

4.10. The Master said: "In the affairs of the world, a gentleman has no *parti pris:* he takes the side of justice."

4.14. The Master said: "Do not worry if you are without a position; worry lest you do not deserve a position. Do not worry if you are not famous; worry lest you do not deserve to be famous."

4.15. The Master said: "Shen, my doctrine has one single thread running through it." Master Zeng Shen replied: "Indeed."
The Master left. The other disciples asked: "What did he mean?" Master Zeng said: "The doctrine of the Master is: Loyalty and reciprocity, and that is all."

4.16. The Master said: "A gentleman considers what is just; a small man considers what is expedient."

4.18. The Master said: "When you serve your parents, you may gently remonstrate with them. If you see that they do not take your advice, be all the more respectful and do not contradict them. Let not your efforts turn to bitterness."

4.19. The Master said: "While your parents are alive, do not travel afar. If you have to travel, you must leave an address."

4.20. The Master said: "If three years after his father's death, the son does not alter his father's ways, he is a good son indeed."

4.21. The Master said: "Always keep in mind the age of your parents. Let this thought be both your joy and your worry."

4.25. The Master said: "Virtue is not solitary; it always has neighbors."

5.7. The Master said: "The Way does not prevail. I shall take a raft and put out to sea. I am sure Zilu will accompany me." Hearing this, Zilu was overjoyed. The Master said: "Zilu is bolder than I. Still, where would we get the timber for our craft?"

5.10. Zai Yu[2] was sleeping during the day. The Master said: "Rotten wood cannot be carved; dung walls cannot be troweled. What is the use of scolding him?"

The Master said: "There was a time when I used to listen to what people said and trusted that they would act accordingly, but now I listen to what they say and watch what they do. It is Zai Yu who made me change."

5.11. The Master said: "I have never seen a man who was truly steadfast." Someone replied: "Shen Cheng?" The Master said: "Shen Cheng is driven by his desires. How could he be called steadfast?"

5.14. When Zilu had learned one thing, his only fear was that he might learn another one before he had the chance to practice the first.

5.20. Lord Ji Wen always thought thrice before acting. Hearing this, the Master said: "Twice is enough."

5.27. The Master said: "Alas, I have never seen a man capable of seeing his own faults and of exposing them in the tribunal of his heart."

5.28. The Master said: "In a hamlet of ten houses, you will certainly find people as loyal and faithful as I, but you will not find one man who loves learning as much as I do."

6.3. Duke Ai asked: "Which of the disciples has a love of learning?" Confucius replied: "There was Yan Hui who loved learning; he never vented his frustrations upon others; he never made the same mistake twice. Alas, his allotted span of life was short: he is dead. Now, for all I know, there is no one with such a love of learning."

6.11. The Master said: "How admirable was Yan Hui! A handful of rice to eat, a gourd of water for drink, a hovel for your shelter—no one would endure such misery, yet Yan Hui's joy remained unaltered. How admirable was Yan Hui!"

6.17. The Master said: "Who would leave a house without using the door? Why do people seek to walk outside the Way?"

6.18. The Master said: "When nature prevails over culture, you get a savage; when culture prevails over nature, you get a pedant. When nature and culture are in balance, you get a gentleman."

6.23. The Master said: "The wise find joy on the water, the good find joy in the mountains. The wise are active, the good are quiet. The wise are joyful, the good live long."

6.27. The Master said: "A gentleman enlarges his learning through literature and restrains himself with ritual; therefore, he is not likely to go wrong."

2. Also known as Zai Wo, a disciple who tended to disappoint Confucius.

6.29. The Master said: "The moral power of the Middle Way is supreme, and yet it is not commonly found among the people anymore."

7.1. The Master said: "I transmit, I invent nothing. I trust and love the past. In this, I dare to compare myself to our venerable Peng."

7.7. The Master said: "I never denied my teaching to anyone who sought it, even if he was too poor to offer more than a token present for his tuition."

7.8. The Master said: "I enlighten only the enthusiastic; I guide only the fervent. After I have lifted up one corner of a question, if the student cannot discover the other three, I do not repeat."

7.12. The Master said: "If seeking wealth were a decent pursuit, I too would seek it, even if I had to work as a janitor. As it is, I'd rather follow my inclinations."

7.13. Matters which the Master approached with circumspection: fasting; war; illness.

7.14. When the Master was in Qi, he heard the Coronation Hymn of Shun. For three months, he forgot the taste of meat. He said: "I never imagined that music could reach such a point."

7.15. Ran Qiu[3] said: "Does our Master support the Duke of Wei?" Zigong said: "Well, I am going to ask him."
Zigong went in and asked Confucius: "What sort of people were Boyi and Shuqi?"—"They were virtuous men of old."—"Did they complain?"—"They sought goodness, they got goodness. Why should they have complained?"
Zigong left and said to Ran Qiu: "Our Master does not support the Duke of Wei."[4]

7.18. Occasions when the Master did not use dialect: when reciting the *Poems* and the *Documents,* and when performing ceremonies. In all these occasions, he used the correct pronunciation.

7.19. The Governor of She asked Zilu about Confucius. Zilu did not reply. The Master said: "Why did you not say 'He is the sort of man who, in his enthusiasm, forgets to eat, in his joy forgets to worry, and who ignores the approach of old age'?"

7.20. The Master said: "For my part, I am not endowed with innate knowledge. I am simply a man who loves the past and who is diligent in investigating it."

7.21. The Master never talked of: miracles; violence; disorders; spirits.

7.22. The Master said: "Put me in the company of any two people at random—they will invariably have something to teach me. I can take their qualities as a model and their defects as a warning."

7.23. The Master said: "Heaven vested me with moral power. What do I have to fear from Huan Tui?"[5]

7.26. The Master said: "A saint, I cannot hope to meet. I would be content if only I could meet a gentleman."
The Master said: "A perfect man, I cannot hope to meet. I would be content if only I could meet a principled man. When Nothing pretends to be Something, Emptiness pretends to be Fullness, and Penury pretends to be Affluence, it is hard to have principles."

7.29. The people of Huxiang were deaf to all teaching; but a boy came to visit the Master. The disciples were perplexed. The Master said: "To approve his visit does not mean approving what he does besides. Why be so finicky? When a man makes himself clean before a visit, we appreciate his cleanliness, we do not endorse his past or his future."

7.30. The Master said: "Is goodness out of reach? As soon as I long for goodness, goodness is at hand."

7.34. The Master said: "I make no claims to wisdom or to human perfection—how would I dare? Still, my aim remains unflagging and I never tire of teaching people." Gongxi Chi[6] said: "This is precisely what we disciples fail to emulate."

7.35. The Master was severely ill. Zilu asked leave to pray. The Master said: "Is there such a practice?" Zilu said: "Oh yes, and the invocation goes like this: 'We pray you, Spirits from above and Spirits from below.'" The Master said: "In that case, I have been praying for a long time already."

8.4. Master Zeng was ill. Lord Mengjing came to visit him. Master Zeng said: "When a bird is about to die, his song is sad; when a man is about to die, his words are true. In following the Way, a gentleman pays special attention to three things: in his attitude, he eschews rashness and arrogance; in his expression, he clings to good faith; in his speech, he eschews vulgarity and nonsense. As to the details of liturgy, leave these to the sextons."

8.9. The Master said: "You can make the people follow the Way, you cannot make them understand it."

8.17. The Master said: "Learning is like a chase in which, as you fail to catch up, you fear to lose what you have already gained."

---

5. Tradition has it that this was said when Huan Tui, minister of war in the state of Song, attempted to kill Confucius.
6. Also known as Gongxi Hua, another disciple who was said to have been in charge of Confucius's funeral.

9.2. A man from Daxiang said: "Your Confucius is really great! With his vast learning, he has still not managed to excel in any particular field." The Master heard of this and said to his disciples: "Which skill should I cultivate? Shall I take up charioteering? Shall I take up archery? All right, I shall take up charioteering."

9.4. The Master absolutely eschewed four things: capriciousness, dogmatism, willfulness, self-importance.

9.5. The Master was trapped in Kuang. He said: "King Wen is dead; is civilization not resting now on me? If Heaven intends civilization to be destroyed, why was it vested in me? If Heaven does not intend civilization to be destroyed, what should I fear from the people of Kuang?"

9.11. Yan Hui said with a sigh: "The more I contemplate it, the higher it is; the deeper I dig into it, the more it resists; I saw it in front of me, and then suddenly it was behind me. Step by step, our Master really knows how to entrap people. He stimulates me with literature, he restrains me with ritual. Even if I wanted to stop, I could not. Just as all my resources are exhausted, the goal is towering right above me; I long to embrace it, but cannot find the way."

9.13. Zigong said: "If you had a precious piece of jade, would you hide it safely in a box, or would you try to sell it for a good price?" The Master said: "I would sell it! I would sell it! All I am waiting for is the right offer."

9.14. The Master wanted to settle among the nine barbarian tribes of the East. Someone said: "It is wild in those parts. How would you cope?" The Master said: "How could it be wild, once a gentleman has settled there?"

9.16. The Master said: "I have never found it difficult to serve my superiors abroad and my elders at home; or to bury the dead with due reverence; or to hold my wine."

9.17. The Master stood by a river and said: "Everything flows like this, without ceasing, day and night."

9.18. The Master said: "I have never seen anyone who loved virtue as much as sex."

9.20. The Master said: "What was unique in Yan Hui was his capacity for attention whenever one spoke to him."

9.21. The Master said of Yan Hui: "Alas, I watched his progress, but did not see him reach the goal."

9.22. The Master said: "There are shoots that bear no flower, and there are flowers that bear no fruit."

9.24. The Master said: "How could words of admonition fail to win our assent? Yet the main thing should be actually to amend our conduct. How could words of praise fail to delight us? Yet the main thing should be actually to understand their purpose. Some people show delight but no understanding, or they assent without changing their ways—I really don't know what to do with them."

9.29. The Master said: "The wise are without perplexity; the good are without sorrow; the brave are without fear."

9.30. The Master said: "There are people with whom you may share information, but not share the Way. There are people with whom you may share the Way, but not share a commitment. There are people with whom you may share a commitment, but not share counsel."

9.31.

> The cherry tree
> Waves its blossoms.
> It is not that I do not think of you
> But your house is so far away!

The Master said: "He does not really love her; if he did, would he mind the distance?"

11.10. Yan Hui died. The Master wailed wildly. His followers said: "Master, such grief is not proper." The Master said: "In mourning such a man, what sort of grief would be proper?"

11.11. Yan Hui died. The disciples wanted to give him a grand burial. The Master said: "This is not right."

The disciples gave him a grand burial. The Master said: "Yan Hui treated me as his father, and yet I was not given the chance to treat him as my son. This is not my fault, but yours, my friends."

11.12. Zilu asked how to serve the spirits and gods. The Master said: "You are not yet able to serve men, how could you serve the spirits?"

Zilu said: "May I ask you about death?" The Master said: "You do not yet know life, how could you know death?"

11.22. Zilu asked: "Should I practice at once what I have just learned?" The Master said: "Your father and your elder brother are still alive; how could you practice at once what you have just learned?"

Ran Qiu asked: "Should I practice at once what I have just learned? The Master said: "Practice it at once."

Gongxi Chi said: "When Zilu asked if he should practice at once what he had just learned, you told him to consult first with his father and elder brother. When Ran Qiu asked if he should practice at once what he had just learned, you told him to practice it at once. I am confused; may I ask you to explain?" The Master said: "Ran Qiu is slow, therefore I push him; Zilu has energy for two, therefore I hold him back."

12.1. Yan Hui asked about humanity. The Master said: "The practice of humanity comes down to this: tame the self and restore the rites. Tame the self and restore the rites for but one day, and the whole world will rally to your humanity. The practice of humanity comes from the self, not from anyone else."

Yan Hui said: "May I ask which steps to follow?" The Master said: "Observe the rites in this way: don't look at anything improper; don't listen to anything improper; don't say anything improper; don't do anything improper."

Yan Hui said: "I may not be clever, but with your permission, I shall endeavor to do as you have said."

12.2. Ran Yong asked about humanity. The Master said: "When abroad, behave as if in front of an important guest. Lead the people as if performing a great ceremony. What you do not wish for yourself, do not impose upon others. Let no resentment enter public affairs; let no resentment enter private affairs."

Ran Yong said: "I may not be clever, but with your permission I shall endeavor to do as you have said."

12.5. Sima Niu[7] was grieving: "All men have brothers; I alone have none." Zixia said: "I have heard this: life and death are decreed by fate, riches and honors are allotted by Heaven. Since a gentleman behaves with reverence and diligence, treating people with deference and courtesy, all within the Four Seas are his brothers. How could a gentleman ever complain that he has no brothers?"

12.7. Zigong asked about government. The Master said: "Sufficient food, sufficient weapons, and the trust of the people." Zigong said: "If you had to do without one of these three, which would you give up?"—"Weapons."—"If you had to do without one of the remaining two, which would you give up?"—"Food; after all, everyone has to die eventually. But without the trust of the people, no government can stand."

12.10. Zizhang asked how to accumulate moral power and how to recognize emotional incoherence. The Master said: "Put loyalty and faith above everything, and follow justice. That is how one accumulates moral power. When you love someone, you wish him to live; when you hate someone, you wish him to die. Now, if you simultaneously wish him to live and to die, this is an instance of incoherence."

> If not for the sake of wealth.
> Then for the sake of change...

12.11. Duke Jing of Qi asked Confucius about government. Confucius replied: "Let the lord be a lord; the subject a subject; the father a father; the son a son." The Duke said: "Excellent! If indeed the lord is not a lord, the subject not a subject, the father not a father, the son not a son, I could be sure of nothing anymore—not even of my daily food."

12.18. Lord Ji Kang was troubled by burglars. He consulted with Confucius. Confucius replied: "If you yourself were not covetous, they would not rob you, even if you paid them to."

---

7. A brother of Huan Tui, who made an attempt on Confucius's life.

12.19. Lord Ji Kang asked Confucius about government, saying: "Suppose I were to kill the bad to help the good: how about that?" Confucius replied: "You are here to govern; what need is there to kill? If you desire what is good, the people will be good. The moral power of the gentleman is wind, the moral power of the common man is grass. Under the wind, the grass must bend."

13.3. Zilu asked: "If the ruler of Wei were to entrust you with the government of the country, what would be your first initiative?" The Master said: "It would certainly be to rectify the names." Zilu said: "Really? Isn't this a little farfetched? What is this rectification for?" The Master said: "How boorish can you get! Whereupon a gentleman is incompetent, thereupon he should remain silent. If the names are not correct, language is without an object. When language is without an object, no affair can be effected. When no affair can be effected, rites and music wither. When rites and music wither, punishments and penalties miss their target. When punishments and penalties miss their target, the people do not know where they stand. Therefore, whatever a gentleman conceives of, he must be able to say; and whatever he says, he must be able to do. In the matter of language, a gentleman leaves nothing to chance."

13.9. The Master was on his way to Wei, and Ran Qiu was driving. The Master said: "So many people!" Ran Qiu said: "Once the people are many, what next should be done?"—"Enrich them."—"Once they are rich, what next should be done?"—"Educate them."

13.10. The Master said: "If a ruler could employ me, in one year I would make things work, and in three years the results would show."

13.11. The Master said: "'When good men have been running the country for a hundred years, cruelty can be overcome, and murder extirpated.' How true is this saying!"

13.15. Duke Ding asked: "Is there one single maxim that could ensure the prosperity of a country?" Confucius replied: "Mere words could not achieve this. There is this saying, however: 'It is difficult to be a prince, it is not easy to be a subject.' A maxim that could make the ruler understand the difficulty of his task would come close to ensuring the prosperity of the country."

"Is there one single maxim that could ruin a country?"

Confucius replied: "Mere words could not achieve this. There is this saying, however: 'The only pleasure of being a prince is never having to suffer contradiction.' If you are right and no one contradicts you, that's fine; but if you are wrong and no one contradicts you—is this not almost a case of 'one single maxim that could ruin a country'?"

13.20. Zigong asked: "How does one deserve to be called a gentleman?" The Master said: "He who behaves with honor, and, being sent on a mission to the four corners of the world, does not bring disgrace to his lord, deserves to be called a gentleman."

"And next to that, if I may ask?"

"His relatives praise his filial piety and the people of his village praise the way he respects the elders."

"And next to that, if I may ask?"

"His word can be trusted; whatever he undertakes, he brings to completion. In this, he may merely show the obstinacy of a vulgar man; still, he should probably qualify as a gentleman of lower category."

"In this respect, how would you rate our present politicians?"

"Alas! These puny creatures are not even worth mentioning!"

13.24. Zigong asked: "What would you think of a man, if all the people in his village liked him?" The Master said: "This is not enough."—"And what if all the people in the village disliked him?"—"This is not enough. It would be better if the good people in the village were to like him, and the bad people to dislike him."

13.25. The Master said: "It is easy to work for a gentleman, but not easy to please him. Try to please him by immoral means, and he will not be pleased; but he never demands anything that is beyond your capacity. It is not easy to work for a vulgar man, but easy to please him. Try to please him, even by immoral means, and he will be pleased; but his demands know no limits."

13.26. The Master said: "A gentleman shows authority, but no arrogance. A vulgar man shows arrogance, but no authority."

14.4. The Master said: "A virtuous man is always of good counsel; a man of good counsel is not always virtuous. A good man is always brave: a brave man is not always good."

14.6. The Master said: "Gentlemen may not always achieve the fullness of humanity. Small men never achieve the fullness of humanity."

14.23. The Master said: "A gentleman reaches up. A vulgar man reaches down."

14.24. The Master said: "In the old days, people studied to improve themselves. Now they study in order to impress others."

14.27. The Master said: "A gentleman would be ashamed should his deeds not match his words."

14.28. The Master said: "A gentleman abides by three principles which I am unable to follow: his humanity knows no anxiety; his wisdom knows no hesitation; his courage knows no fear." Zigong said: "Master, you have just drawn your own portrait."

14.29. Zigong was criticizing other people. The Master said: "Zigong must have already reached perfection, which affords him a leisure I do not possess."

14.30. The Master said: "It is not your obscurity that should distress you, but your incompetence."

14.35. The Master said: "No one understands me!" Zigong said: "Why is it that no one understands you?" The Master said: "I do not accuse Heaven, nor do I blame men; here below I am learning, and there above I am being heard. If I am understood, it must be by Heaven."

14.38. Zilu stayed for the night at the Stone Gate. The gatekeeper said: "Where are you from?" Zilu said: "I am from Confucius's household."—"Oh, is that the one who keeps pursuing what he knows is impossible?"

15.16. The Master said: "With those who cannot say 'What should I do? what should I do?,' I really do not know what I should do."

15.24. Zigong asked: "Is there any single word that could guide one's entire life?" The Master said: "Should it not be *reciprocity?* What you do not wish for yourself, do not do to others."

15.27. The Master said: "Clever talk ruins virtue. Small impatiences ruin great plans."

15.36. The Master said: "In the pursuit of virtue, do not be afraid to overtake your teacher."

17.2. The Master said: "What nature put together, habit separates."

17.19. The Master said: "I wish to speak no more." Zigong said: "Master, if you do not speak, how would little ones like us still be able to hand down any teachings?" The Master said: "Does Heaven speak? Yet the four seasons follow their course and the hundred creatures continue to be born. Does Heaven speak?"

17.20. Ru Bei wanted to see Confucius. Confucius declined on the grounds of illness. As Ru Bei's messenger was leaving, the Master took up his zithern and sang loudly enough for him to hear.

17.21. Zai Yu asked: "Three years mourning for one's parents—this is quite long. If a gentleman stops all ritual practices for three years, the practices will decay; if he stops all musical performances for three years, music will be lost. As the old crop is consumed, a new crop grows up, and for lighting the fire, a new lighter is used with each season. One year of mourning should be enough." The Master said: "If after only one year, you were again to eat white rice and to wear silk, would you feel at ease?"—"Absolutely."—"In that case, go ahead! The reason a gentleman prolongs his mourning is simply that, since fine food seems tasteless to him, and music offers him no enjoyment, and the comfort of his house makes him uneasy, he prefers to do without all these pleasures. But now, if you can enjoy them, go ahead!"

Zai Yu left. The Master said: "Zai Yu is devoid of humanity. After a child is born, for the first three years of his life, he does not leave his parents' bosom. Three years mourning is a custom that is observed everywhere in the world. Did Zai Yu never enjoy the love of his parents, even for three years?"

17.24. Zigong said: "Does a gentleman have hatreds?" The Master said: "Yes. He hates those who dwell on what is hateful in others. He hates those inferiors who slander their superiors. He hates those whose courage is not tempered by civilized manners. He hates the impulsive and the stubborn." He went on: "And you? Don't you have your own hatreds?"— "I hate the plagiarists who pretend to be learned. I hate the arrogant who pretend to be brave. I hate the malicious who pretend to be frank."

17.25. The Master said: "Women and underlings are especially difficult to handle: be friendly, and they become familiar; be distant, and they resent it."

17.26. The Master said: "Whoever, by the age of forty, is still disliked, will remain so till the end."

18.5. Jieyu, the Madman of Chu, went past Confucius, singing:

> Phoenix, oh Phoenix!
> The past cannot be retrieved,
> But the future still holds a chance.
> Give up, give up!
> The days of those in office are numbered!

Confucius stopped his chariot, for he wanted to speak with him, but the other hurried away and disappeared. Confucius did not succeed in speaking to him.

18.6. Changju and Jieni were ploughing together. Confucius, who was passing by, sent Zilu to ask where the ford was. Changju said: "Who is in the chariot?" Zilu said: "It is Confucius." "The Confucius from Lu?"—"Himself."—"Then he already knows where the ford is."

Zilu then asked Jieni, who replied: "Who are you?"—"I am Zilu."—"The disciple of Confucius, from Lu?"—"Yes."—"The whole universe is swept along by the same flood; who can reverse its flow? Instead of following a gentleman who keeps running from one patron to the next, would it not be better to follow a gentleman who has forsaken the world?" All the while he kept on tilling his field.

Zilu came back and reported to Confucius. Rapt in thought, the Master sighed: "One cannot associate with birds and beasts. With whom should I keep company, if not with my own kind? If the world were following the Way, I would not have to reform it."

VIRGIL ■ (70–19 B.C.E.)

From shortly after his death until just a few centuries ago, Publius Vergilius Maro was commonly regarded not only as the poet of Rome and the Roman Empire but also as a philosopher, prophet, sage, and even magician. One result of the legends surrounding Virgil was that the *Aeneid* was customarily used as a book of divination. Seeking guidance, readers would close their eyes, open the pages at random, and point a blind finger at a line of poetry by which they would direct their actions from that moment onward. In his medieval epic poem *The Divine Comedy,* Dante gave a similar authority to the *Aeneid,* invoking its words and its author as guide to the perilous task of journeying through the afterlife (see page 743). Virgil would perhaps not have been surprised by such responses to the *Aeneid,* for seldom has a work of literature been so self-consciously focused on the effect it would have on its readers, on its culture, and on posterity.

There are several ways in which the *Aeneid* signals these intentions. The first is the thoroughness with which it revisits and revises the two founding epics of ancient Greece, the *Iliad* and the *Odyssey.* Because it sets its action during the aftermath of the Trojan War and because the path of its hero, Aeneas, follows in the trail of Odysseus's journey, the *Aeneid* operates as a Roman sequel to Homer. Because it switches allegiance, glorifying Troy and denigrating the Greek forces, it significantly reinterprets the Homeric epics as well. And because it tells its tale of the legendary past with one eye always fixed on the meaning of that past for the Roman present under the rule of Emperor Augustus, the *Aeneid* displays a consciousness of its place in history quite alien to the oral tradition represented by the Homeric poems.

Born in 70 B.C.E. near the small Italian town of Mantua, Virgil came of age during a traumatic period of Roman history, nearly a century of recurring civil war. When Octavian defeated the forces of Marc Antony and Cleopatra in 31 B.C.E. and acceded soon after to the reins of empire as Augustus Caesar, he inaugurated a long-desired stretch of peace and stability as well as an end to the cherished tradition of the republic over which so much blood had been spilled. Both emotions are strongly registered in the ancient world depicted in the *Aeneid*, balanced as it is between repeated prophecies of the destined glories of Rome to come and the enormous suffering and hardship that will be required to get there. So the opening to Book 1 concludes majestically but also with a touch of exhaustion: "So hard and huge a task it was to found the Roman people."

Following the publication of his first collection of poetry, the *Bucolics*, or *Eclogues* (42–39 B.C.E.)—ten fairly short, loose adaptations of the Greek pastoral poems of Theocritus—Virgil found himself, like his younger friend Horace, a member of Octavian's inner circle by virtue of the patronage and friendship of Maecenas, an influential member of the aristocracy and one of Octavian's ministers. Over the next years, Virgil slowly polished his second collection, the *Georgics*, four books of verse concerning farming and beekeeping but equally immersed in mythology and contemporary events. Octavian reportedly ordered a preview reading of the barely completed *Georgics* by their author in 29 B.C.E.; Virgil's canonical status has never been in doubt since. He spent the last ten years of his life at work on the *Aeneid*. Apparently not yet satisfied with its form at the end of his life, he left orders for it to be burned. Augustus countermanded the order, consigning the manuscript to Virgil's colleague Varius to prepare it for publication (i.e., copying and circulation in manuscript form). It immediately became a school text, used for teaching grammar, verse, and philosophy; commented and glossed repeatedly; and frequently imitated, although for the most part timorously and from afar. Because the fourth of his *Eclogues* includes an enigmatic prophecy of a savior to come, Virgil was also rapidly assimilated as a forerunner of Christianity, and the *Aeneid* functioned throughout late antiquity and the Middle Ages as a linking text between Christian doctrine and the classical tradition, most famously in Dante's work.

The *Aeneid* is composed of twelve books containing a total of just under ten thousand lines in the traditional six-beat meter of epic. The first six books recount the difficult journey of Aeneas from the defeated city of Troy to the shores of Italy, where he is fated to found Rome. The poem plunges *in medias res*—into the middle of the story—with Aeneas's fleet nearly destroyed by a storm roused by the goddess Juno, who bears various grudges against the Trojans and is determined to prevent or at least delay their ambitions. They manage to land safely on the North African coast, where they are taken in by Queen Dido, herself an exile engaged in building Carthage, a city that would much later become the opponent of Rome in three brutal conflicts, the so-called Punic Wars of the third and second centuries B.C.E. In Books 2 and 3, Aeneas tells Dido and her court the story of the fall of Troy and the early stages of his journey. Then, following the machinations of his mother, Venus, the pair conduct a short-lived but passionate affair that ends in catastrophe when Aeneas is ordered by the gods to return to his fated duty. Following further difficulties, Aeneas decides after a dream vision to journey into the underworld to meet and consult with the shade of his father, Anchises. In the Elysian Fields, Anchises shows Aeneas the souls waiting to return to the world above and sketches out his descendants in a prophetic history of Rome dating all the way through the recent civil war and the time of Augustus.

The final six books of the poem describe the war that awaits Aeneas after he lands in Latium on the coast of Italy. A series of broken treaties and much maneuvering by Juno and Venus lead to a conflict between the Trojans and their allies and the local king, Turnus, and his allies. Although traditionally neglected in favor of the more varied material of the first six books, the "Iliadic" second half of the *Aeneid* offers a sustained meditation on the costs of civil war and the pros and cons of empire building. The poem ends abruptly, offering not the closure of Aeneas's impending marriage with the Latinian princess Lavinia or his promised deification but his summary execution of Turnus as the defeated leader pleads for mercy.

Like much else in the poem, the ending has prompted debate over the years as to how we are meant to interpret Aeneas's action. This would appear to be a consistent artistic strategy throughout the poem. The *Aeneid* possesses a typological structure, constantly sending the reader back and forth between the legendary period of the poem's setting and the contemporary period of its composition. The character and choices of Aeneas constantly reflect on those of the current ruler, Augustus, who had recently concluded a civil war himself. The Dido episode is not only a tragic rendition of the conflict between individual desire and public duty but also a complex foreshadowing of the three Punic Wars, which ended in the destruction of Carthage by Rome in 146 B.C.E. The sympathy that Virgil imparts to Dido in this episode casts a shadow on the later episode, just as the wrath to which Aeneas succumbs in killing Turnus implicates in some way the character of Augustus. Virgil never makes a direct equation between past and present, nor does he give straightforward, symbolic meaning to any specific episodes. Instead, he sets up a framework of correspondences between the past and the present that invites the reader to seek meaning through a chain of comparisons.

A similar relationship exists with the Homeric epics, with which Virgil assumed his readers would be intimately familiar. One of Virgil's goals in rewriting episodes from the *Iliad* and the *Odyssey* was to define what was specifically Roman about his own characters and epic. In Book 2, for example, the bloody encounter between Troy's ruler Priam and Achilles's son Pyrrhus can be compared to the concluding book of the *Iliad,* where Priam persuades Achilles to relent in his anger and return the body of Priam's son, Hektor, for proper burial (see page 135). In Virgil's account of the fall of Troy, Pyrrhus first slaughters another of Priam's sons before the father's eyes at the family altar and then butchers the aged man himself. The story is striking on its own terms, but the additional resonance of the Homeric comparison places the issues of heroism, piety, loss, exile, and fathers and sons in especially sharp relief.

On the level of language, the *Aeneid* also shuttles its readers back and forth between the ancient world of the Homeric epic and Virgil's contemporary world. He borrows techniques of oral composition to give his poem an archaic feel, heightening its effect of sublime distance from everyday life. Characters are referred to repeatedly by epithets such as "pious Aeneas" or "faithful Achates"; particular formulae such as "marvelous to tell" are repeated; different forces receive lengthy catalogues of names and lineage. The epic hexameter, a line composed of six equal parts, or "feet," is weighty and serious, although carefully varied to avoid monotony. Like the Greek, Latin meter was based on the length of vowels, determined by default (certain vowels are long by rule) and by placement (vowels are usually long when followed by two consonants, for example). The dactyl was the standard foot (long—short—short), but various of the six dactyls in a line could be changed to spondees (long—long) according to certain rules. In the previously cited line, "So hard and huge a task it was to found the Roman people" (Book 1, line 33), for example, an opening spondee and two more in the center lay a heavy stress on the solemn meaning of the line and on the key adjective, "Roman," in its middle:

tāntǣ mōlǐs ěrǎt / Rōmānām // cōndĕrě gēntěm.[1]

Word order in Latin is extremely flexible, allowing *Romanam* to come in the middle, and for the act of founding to be flanked by the adjective and noun being founded; a word-by-word rendering of the translator's language would read: "So hard and huge—task—was—Roman—to found—people."

At the same time that Virgil strove to echo Homer, he also grounded his poem in the language and experience of his own day. He coined a good number of new words, and especially in his use of simile he was frequently and self-consciously anachronistic. The very first simile of the poem, for example, compares Neptune calming the waves to a veteran quieting a rioting crowd in the Roman Forum, a space that wouldn't be created until hundreds of years after the time in which the poem is set. Later in Book 1, we find Aeneas looking down on the rising walls of Carthage, marveling at the laws being enacted and the "magistrates and sacred senate" being chosen, as if Carthage were already modern Rome. Virgil chooses here to use the traditional epic device of a natural simile to describe a human phenomenon, comparing the scene to "bees in early summer." Here he also alludes to the final book of his previous work, the *Georgics,* which uses a long treatise on beekeeping to comment on the proper functioning of Roman society. The *Aeneid* can be read as a self-contained epic tale of exile and war, but the more one follows its many threads backward to Greek literature and forward to contemporary Rome, the deeper and more satisfying that tale becomes.

Virgil equally encourages and rewards the reader who follows the imagery forward and backward within the body of the poem. There are myriad formal patterns in the *Aeneid;* one of the most striking and most disturbing is the set of attributes Virgil associates with many of the female characters in the poem, beginning with the goddess Juno, whose implacably "black rage" determines that every time it seems a resolution has finally been reached, all hell will break loose once again. A divine, overpowering, and contagious anger that descends thematically from the rage of Achilles in the *Iliad* and before that, the fury of the goddess Ishtar in *The Epic of Gilgamesh* (see page 29), Juno's rage (*ira*) has a terrifying effect on every character it infects. It transforms the steady and pious ruler Dido into a raving fury; it causes the Trojan women to torch their own fleet; through the fury Allecto it feeds Turnus's seething fire of injustice and the passions of the Latin queen Amata. It is particularly associated with imagery of fire and serpents, and although Virgil never quite identifies it with a feminine force per se, he certainly relates it to forces of uncontrollable emotion usually undergone by female characters in the mythological tradition before him.

The split between male and female is a primary opposition in a poem built around oppositions. Like all of the polarities we find in the poem, however, it becomes more complicated the more we study its details; after all, the last person in the poem to be overcome with *ira* is Aeneas himself in the final scene, even though Juno has agreed finally to give up her own wrath. Because of so many built-in cross-references and so much historical mirroring, the *Aeneid* is readily allegorized into symbolic meanings. This is particularly the case with the gods, who drive most of the poem's plot, causing events to occur by their conflicting machinations. The gods were also pretty much an archaism by the time Virgil was writing, at least in the sense of divine figures who interacted openly with mortals. Here, too, Virgil seems careful not to reduce them to a single meaning. There are moments when the gods behave like the distanced immortals of legend, moments when they react with petty human emotions, moments when they insist on the traditional virtues of Roman society, and moments when they appear irreligious and well-nigh immoral. Virgil's human characters, too, straddle a space between heroic, sometimes tragic paradigms of humanity and fully fleshed individuals with idiosyncratic, subjective takes on the world around them. Witness Aeneas's reaction when his father wants to show him his heroic future, the great tradition of Rome he is destined to sire. Rather than embrace his heroic role, Aeneas responds in the baffled tone of a long-suffering trooper who cannot imagine anyone being eager about anything related to the cruel world above:

> Must we imagine,
> Father, there are souls that go from here
> Aloft to upper heaven, and once more
> Return to bodies' dead weight? The poor souls,
> How can they crave our daylight so?

It is not just because of its philosophical and prophetic gravity that the *Aeneid* has laid such a claim on posterity; it is because Virgil was able to balance that gravity through a constant reminder of how it must have felt weighing on the hearts and minds of those required to sacrifice themselves to the goals they were responsible for achieving.

PRONUNCIATIONS:

Aeneas: eh-NEE-uhs
Aeneid: eh-NEE-id
Allecto: ah-LEC-toh
Amata: ah-MAH-tah
Anchises: an-KAI-seez
Ascanius: as-KAY-nee-uhs
Dido: DAI-doh
Eclogues: EH-klogs
Elysian: eh-LEE-zhuhn
Lavinia: lah-VI-nee-uh
Pyrrhus: PIR-ruhs
Turnus: TUR-nuhs

from Aeneid[1]

from Book 1

[A Fateful Haven]

I sing of warfare and a man at war.[2]
From the sea-coast of Troy in early days
He came to Italy by destiny,
To our Lavinian western shore,
5   A fugitive, this captain, buffeted
Cruelly on land as on the sea
By blows from powers of the air—behind them
Baleful Juno[3] in her sleepless rage.
And cruel losses were his lot in war,
10   Till he could found a city and bring home
His gods to Latium, land of the Latin race,
The Alban lords, and the high walls of Rome.
Tell me the causes now, O Muse, how galled
In her divine pride, and how sore at heart
15   From her old wound, the queen of gods compelled him—
A man apart, devoted to his mission—
To undergo so many perilous days
And enter on so many trials. Can anger
Black as this prey on the minds of heaven?
20   Tyrian settlers in that ancient time
Held Carthage, on the far shore of the sea,

---

1. Translated by Robert Fitzgerald.
2. Virgil echoes the opening lines of Homer's *Iliad* and *Odyssey*. As does Homer, he begins in the midst of events; we find out how this situation arose only in Books 2 and 3.

Set against Italy and Tiber's mouth,
A rich new town, warlike and trained for war.[4]
And Juno, we are told, cared more for Carthage
25   Than for any walled city of the earth,
More than for Samos,[5] even. There her armor
And chariot were kept, and, fate permitting,
Carthage would be the ruler of the world.
So she intended, and so nursed that power.
30   But she had heard long since
That generations born of Trojan blood
Would one day overthrow her Tyrian walls,
And from that blood a race would come in time
With ample kingdoms, arrogant in war,
35   For Libya's ruin: so the Parcae spun.[6]
In fear of this, and holding in memory
The old war she had carried on at Troy
For Argos'° sake (the origins of that anger,   *the Greeks*
That suffering, still rankled: deep within her,
40   Hidden away, the judgment Paris gave,[7]
Snubbing her loveliness; the race she hated;
The honors given ravished Ganymede),[8]
Saturnian Juno,[9] burning for it all,
Buffeted on the waste of sea those Trojans
45   Left by the Greeks and pitiless Achilles,[1]
Keeping them far from Latium. For years
They wandered as their destiny drove them on
From one sea to the next: so hard and huge
A task it was to found the Roman people.

50   They were all under sail in open water
With Sicily just out of sight astern,
Lighthearted as they plowed the whitecapped sea
With stems of cutting bronze. But never free
Of her eternal inward wound, the goddess
55   Said to herself:

                "Give up what I began?
Am I defeated? Am I impotent
To keep the king of Teucrians[2] from Italy?
The Fates forbid me, am I to suppose?
Could Pallas° then consume the Argive° fleet   *Athena / Greek*

4. The historical Carthage was founded by Phoenicians from the eastern Mediterranean island harbor of Tyre around the 9th or 8th century B.C.E. on the northeast coast of Tunisia. All of the North African coastal zone, and sometimes all of Africa, was known to the Greeks as "Libya."

5. Aegean island, legendary birthplace of Hera.

6. The Fates, who were represented as three old women spinning.

7. According to Greek myth, Hera and Athena (Roman: Minerva) supported the Greeks in the Trojan War because Paris had chosen Aphrodite as the most beautiful goddess in return for her promise to grant him Helen as a prize.

8. Son of Troy's founder, Tros. Because of his great beauty, he was carried off by Zeus to be his cupbearer on Mt. Olympus.

9. "Saturnian" because she was the daughter of Cronos, who was identified with the Roman god Saturnus.

1. Champion of the Greeks and the hero of the *Iliad*.

2. Teucer was a legendary king in the region of Troy whose daughter Zeus's son Dardanus married. Because of him the

60   With fire, and drown the crews,
      Because of one man's one mad act—the crime
      Of Ajax, son of Oïleus?[3] She—yes, she!—
      Hurled out of cloudland lancing fire of Jove,
      Scattered the ships, roughed up the sea with gales,
65   Then caught the man, bolt-struck, exhaling flames,
      In a whirlwind and impaled him on a rock.
      But I who walk as queen of all the gods,
      Sister and wife of Jove,[4] I must contend
      For years against one people! Who adores
70   The power of Juno after this, or lays
      An offering with prayer upon her altar?"

      Smouldering, putting these questions to herself,
      The goddess made her way to stormcloud country,
      Aeolia, the weather-breeding isle.
75   Here in a vast cavern King Aeolus[5]
      Rules the contending winds and moaning gales
      As warden of their prison. Round the walls
      They chafe and bluster underground. The din
      Makes a great mountain murmur overhead.
80   High on a citadel enthroned,
      Scepter in hand, he mollifies their fury,
      Else they might flay the sea and sweep away
      Land masses and deep sky through empty air.
      In fear of this, Jupiter hid them away
85   In caverns of black night. He set above them
      Granite of high mountains—and a king
      Empowered at command to rein them in
      Or let them go. To this king Juno now
      Made her petition:
                "Aeolus, the father
90   Of gods and men decreed and fixed your power
      To calm the waves or make them rise in wind.
      The race I hate is crossing the Tuscan° sea,   *Tyrrhenian*
      Transporting Ilium° with her household gods[6]—   *Troy*
      Beaten as they are—to Italy.
                   Put new fury
95   Into your winds, and make the long ships founder!
      Drive them off course! Throw bodies in the sea!
      I have fourteen exquisite nymphs, of whom
      The loveliest by far, Deïopëa,[7]
      Shall be your own. I'll join you two in marriage,

3. Minor hero of the *Iliad,* said by legend to be hated by Athena because he had disrupted Athena's statue when he dragged Cassandra from it before raping her.

4. Another name for Jupiter, chief of the gods in Roman religion, who is identified with the Greek Zeus, the brother and husband of Hera.

5. Ruler of the winds who aids Odysseus in Homer's *Odyssey,* Book 10. Later tradition made him a deity.

6. The Penates, or household gods, were Roman spirits connected with the inner part of the house—in essence, the souls of the ancestors of the race.

7. In Greek mythology, nymphs were divinities of trees, mountains, and rivers, who were personified as young and beau-

100   So she will spend all future years with you,
    As you so well deserve,
    And make you father of her lovely children."

    Said Aeolus:
              "To settle on what you wish
    Is all you need to do, your majesty.
105   I must perform it. You have given me
    What realm I have. By your good offices
    I rule with Jove's consent, and I recline
    Among the gods at feasts, for you appoint me
    Lord of wind and cloud."
                    Spearhaft reversed,
110   He gave the hollow mountainside a stroke,
    And, where a portal opened, winds in ranks,
    As though drawn up for battle, hurtled through,
    To blow across the earth in hurricane.
    Over the sea, tossed up from the sea-floor,
115   Eastwind and Southwind, then the wild Southwest
    With squall on squall came scudding down,
    Rolling high combers shoreward.
                    Now one heard
    The cries of men and screech of ropes in rigging
    Suddenly, as the stormcloud whipped away
120   Clear sky and daylight from the Teucrians'° eyes,   *Trojans'*
    And gloom of night leaned on the open sea.
    It thundered from all quarters, as it lightened
    Flash on flash through heaven. Every sign
    Portended a quick death for mariners.
125   Aeneas on the instant felt his knees
    Go numb and slack, and stretched both hands to heaven,
    Groaning out:
              "Triply lucky, all you men
    To whom death came before your fathers' eyes
    Below the wall at Troy! Bravest Danaan,°   *Greek*
130   Diomedes, why could I not go down
    When you had wounded me, and lose my life
    On Ilium's battlefield?[8] Our Hector lies there,
    Torn by Achilles' weapon; there Sarpedon,
    Our giant fighter, lies; and there the river
135   Simoïs washes down so many shields
    And helmets, with strong bodies taken under!"[9]

    As he flung out these words, a howling gust
    From due north took the sail aback and lifted
    Wavetops to heaven; oars were snapped in two;

---

8. Diomedes was one of the principal Achaean warriors in the *Iliad*; in Book 5 he fought Aeneas. He appears in Book 11 of the *Aeneid*, where he refuses to join the forces massed against Aeneas. "Danaans" is a word used by Homer and other poets to mean the Greeks.

9. Hector was the leader of the Trojans, killed by Achilles (*Iliad*, bk. 22); Sarpedon, a son of Zeus and an ally of the Trojans, was killed by Achilles's companion Patroclus (*Iliad*, bk. 16); Simoïs was a river of Troy.

140	The prow sheered round and left them broadside on
	To breaking seas; over her flank and deck
	A mountain of grey water crashed in tons.
	Men hung on crests; to some a yawning trough
	Uncovered bottom, boiling waves and sand.
145	The Southwind caught three ships and whirled them down
	On reefs, hidden midsea, called by Italians
	"The Altars"—razorbacks just under water.
	The Eastwind drove three others from deep water
	Into great shoals and banks, embedding them
150	And ringing them with sand, a desperate sight.
	Before Aeneas' eyes a toppling billow
	Struck the Lycians' ship, Orontës' ship,
	Across the stern, pitching the steersman down
	And overboard. Three times the eddying sea
155	Carried the ship around in the same place
	Until the rapid whirlpool gulped it down.
	A few men swimming surfaced in the welter.
	So did shields, planks, precious things of Troy.
	Ilioneus' good ship, brave Achatës' ship,
160	The ship that carried Abas, and the one
	Aletës sailed in, hale in his great age,
	Were all undone by the wild gale: their seams
	Parted and let the enemy pour in.
	During all this, Neptune[1] became aware
165	Of hurly-burly and tempest overhead,
	Bringing commotion to the still sea-depth
	And rousing him. He lifted his calm brow
	Above the surface, viewing the great sea,
	And saw Aeneas' squadron far and wide
170	Dispersed over the water, saw the Trojans
	Overwhelmed, the ruining clouds of heaven,
	And saw his angry sister's hand in all.
	He called to him Eastwind and South and said:
	"Are you so sure your line is privileged?
175	How could you dare to throw heaven and earth
	Into confusion, by no will of mine,
	And make such trouble? You will get from me—
	But first to calm the rough sea; after this,
	You'll pay a stricter penalty for your sins.
180	Off with you! Give this message to your king:
	Power over the sea and the cruel trident
	Were never his by destiny, but mine.
	He owns the monstrous rocks, your home, Eastwind.
	Let Aeolus ruffle in that hall alone
185	And lord it over winds shut in their prison."

1. Roman version of the Greek sea god, Poseidon, brother of Zeus and Hera.

Before the words were out, he quieted
The surging water, drove the clouds away,
And brought the sunlight back. Cymothoë
And Triton,[2] side by side, worked to dislodge
190   The grounded ships; then Neptune with his trident
Heaved them away, opened the miles of shoals,
Tempered the sea, and in his car departed
Gliding over the wave-tops on light wheels.

When rioting breaks out in a great city,
195   And the rampaging rabble goes so far
That stones fly, and incendiary brands—
For anger can supply that kind of weapon—
If it so happens they look round and see
Some dedicated public man, a veteran
200   Whose record gives him weight, they quiet down,
Willing to stop and listen.
Then he prevails in speech over their fury
By his authority, and placates them.
Just so, the whole uproar of the great sea
205   Fell silent, as the Father of it all,
Scanning horizons under the open sky,
Swung his team around and gave free rein
In flight to his eager chariot.[3]
                    Tired out,
Aeneas' people made for the nearest land,
210   Turning their prows toward Libya. There's a spot
Where at the mouth of a long bay an island
Makes a harbor, forming a breakwater
Where every swell divides as it comes in
And runs far into curving recesses.
215   There are high cliffs on this side and on that,
And twin peaks towering heavenward impend
On reaches of still water. Over these,
Against a forest backdrop shimmering,
A dark and shaggy grove casts a deep shade,
220   While in the cliffside opposite, below
The overhanging peaks, there is a cave
With fresh water and seats in the living rock,
The home of nymphs. Here never an anchor chain,
Never an anchor's biting fluke need hold
225   A tired ship.
                    Aeneas put in here,
With only seven ships from his full number,
And longing for the firm earth underfoot

2. Cymothoë was one of the Nereids, or sea maidens. Triton was a son of Poseidon.

3. The first of the poem's epic similes, intentionally anachronistic in its comparison of Neptune to a "public man" placating a rioting crowd, embodying the Roman ideal of the *vir pietate gravis*, the man solemn and weighty with piety.

The Trojans disembarked, to take possession
Of the desired sand-beach. Down they lay,
230 To rest their brinesoaked bodies on the shore.
Achatës promptly struck a spark from flint
And caught it in dry leaves; he added tinder
Round about and waved it for a flame-burst.
Then they brought out the grain of Ceres, tainted
235 By sea water, and Ceres' implements,[4]
And, weary of their troubles, made all ready
To dry and grind with millstones what they had.[4]

Meanwhile, Aeneas climbed one of the peaks
For a long seaward view, hoping to sight
240 Gale-worn Antheus and the Phrygian° biremes,[5]   *Trojan*
Capys, or high poops bearing Caïcus' arms.
He found no ship in sight, but on the shore
Three wandering stags.[6] Behind them whole herds followed,
Grazing in a long line down the valleys.
245 Planting his feet, he took in hand the bow
And arrows carried by his aide, Achatës,
Then, aiming for the leaders with heads high
And branching antlers, brought them first to earth.
Next he routed the whole herd,
250 Driving them with his shafts through leafy places,
Shooting and shooting till he won the hunt
By laying seven carcasses on the ground,
A number equal to his ships. Then back
To port he went, and parcelled out the game
255 To his ships' companies. There he divided
The wine courtly Acestës had poured out
And given them on the Sicilian shore—
Full jugs of it—when they were about to sail.[7]
By this and by a simple speech Aeneas
260 Comforted his people:
                              "Friends and companions,
Have we not known hard hours before this?
My men, who have endured still greater dangers,
God will grant us an end to these as well.
You sailed by Scylla's rage, her booming crags,
265 You saw the Cyclops' boulders.[8] Now call back
Your courage, and have done with fear and sorrow.
Some day, perhaps, remembering even this

---

4. The Italian goddess Ceres was identified with the Greek Demeter, goddess of agriculture and fertility—hence the word "cereal" for edible grains. Her implements are the millstones and other tools for grinding grain.

5. Rowing ships with two levels of oars.

6. Many classical commentators interpreted the three stags as a figure representing the three Punic Wars that Rome would fight with Carthage.

7. Acestës was a Sicilian king who had hosted the Trojans in Sicily on their way to Carthage; he welcomes them again at his shores in Book 5.

8. The monster Scylla was traditionally said to be located across from the whirlpool of Charybdis in the straits of Messina between the island of Sicily and the boot of Italy. The Cyclops were one-eyed giants whom tradition placed on Sicily. Both monsters are encountered by Odysseus; Aeneas recounts both adventures in Book 3 of the *Aeneid*.

Will be a pleasure. Through diversities
Of luck, and through so many challenges,
270 We hold our course for Latium, where the Fates
Hold out a settlement and rest for us.
Troy's kingdom there shall rise again. Be patient:
Save yourselves for more auspicious days."

So ran the speech. Burdened and sick at heart,
275 He feigned hope in his look, and inwardly
Contained his anguish. Now the Trojan crews
Made ready for their windfall and their feast.
They skinned the deer, bared ribs and viscera,
Then one lot sliced the flesh and skewered it
280 On spits, all quivering, while others filled
Bronze cooking pots and tended the beach fires.
All got their strength back from the meal, reclining
On the wild grass, gorging on venison
And mellowed wine. When hunger had been banished,
285 And tables put away, they talked at length
In hope and fear about their missing friends:
Could one believe they might be still alive,
Or had they suffered their last hour,
Never again to hear a voice that called them?
290 Aeneas, more than any, secretly
Mourned for them all—for that fierce man, Orontës,
Then for Amycus, then for the bitter fate
Of Lycus, for brave Gyas, brave Cloanthus.

It was the day's end when from highest air
295 Jupiter looked down on the broad sea
Flecked with wings of sails, and the land masses,
Coasts, and nations of the earth. He stood
On heaven's height and turned his gaze toward Libya,
And, as he took the troubles there to heart,
300 Venus[9] appealed to him, all pale and wan,
With tears in her shining eyes:
                                        "My lord who rule
The lives of men and gods now and forever,
And bring them all to heel with your bright bolt,
What in the world could my Aeneas do,
305 What could the Trojans do, so to offend you
That after suffering all those deaths they find
The whole world closed to them, because of Italy?
Surely from these the Romans are to come
In the course of years, renewing Teucer's line,
310 To rule the sea and all the lands about it,
According to your promise. What new thought

9. Goddess of love, Aphrodite to the Greeks, daughter of Zeus and Dione. She was the mother of Aeneas by Anchises, a member of the royal house of Troy. In the *Iliad*, she rescues Aeneas from duels with Diomedes and Achilles.

Has turned you from them, Father? I consoled myself
For Troy's fall, that grim ruin, weighing out
One fate against another in the scales.[1]
315 But now, when they have borne so many blows,
The same misfortune follows them. Great king,
What finish to their troubles will you give?
After Antenor slipped through the Achaeans
He could explore Illyrian coves and reach
320 In safety the Liburnians' inland kingdoms
And source of the Timavus.[2] Through nine openings
With a great rumble in the mountain wall
It bursts from the ground there and floods the fields
In a rushing sea. And yet he chose that place
325 For Padua and new homes for Teucrians,
Gave them a name, set up the arms of Troy,
And now rests in his peace. As for ourselves,
Your own children, whom you make heirs of heaven,
Our ships being lost (this is unspeakable!),
330 We are forsaken through one enemy's rage
And kept remote from Italy. Is this
The palm for loyalty? This our power restored?"

He smiled at her, the father of gods and men,
With that serenity that calms the weather,[3]
335 And lightly kissed his daughter. Then he said:

"No need to be afraid, Cytherëa.[4]
Your children's destiny has not been changed.
As promised, you shall see Lavinium's walls[5]
And take up, then, amid the stars of heaven
340 Great-souled Aeneas.[6] No new thought has turned me.
No, he, your son—now let me speak of him,
In view of your consuming care, at length,
Unfolding secret fated things to come[7]—
In Italy he will fight a massive war,
345 Beat down fierce armies, then for the people there
Establish city walls and a way of life.
When the Rutulians[8] are subdued he'll pass
Three summers of command in Latium,
Three years of winter quarters. But the boy,
350 Ascanius, to whom the name of Iulus

1. The image of Zeus weighing two fates on the golden scales appears twice in the *Iliad* (8.69 and 22.209).

2. A spring in northern Italy. In mythology, Antenor was an elderly and upright counselor in Troy during the siege. In Roman times, he was said to have settled at the head of the Adriatic, where he founded Padua. The Liburni were an Illyrian (Balkan) people on the northeast coast of the Adriatic, famous as seafarers and pirates in Roman times.

3. In Greek mythology, Zeus was the god of the sky and the weather.

4. Venus. Cythera is an island off the Peloponnese that in Greek myth was the birthplace of Aphrodite, who had a sanctuary there.

5. The large town founded where Aeneas will first land in Latium.

6. Jove predicts the eventual deification of Aeneas. A hero-cult of Aeneas existed by the 3rd century B.C.E.

7. The next 44 lines contain the first of the poem's prophecies linking Aeneas's legendary voyage with actual as well as mythical events in more recent Roman history.

8. The subjects of Turnus, Aeneas's rival in Italy.

Now is added—Ilus while Ilium stood[9]—
Will hold the power for all of thirty years,
Great rings of wheeling months. He will transfer
His capital from Lavinium and make
355 A fortress, Alba Longa.[1] Three full centuries
That kingdom will be ruled by Hector's race,
Until the queen and priestess, Ilia,[2]
Pregnant by Mars, will bear twin sons to him.
Afterward, happy in the tawny pelt
360 His nurse, the she-wolf, wears, young Romulus
Will take the leadership, build walls of Mars,
And call by his own name his people Romans.
For these I set no limits, world or time,
But make the gift of empire without end.
365 Juno, indeed, whose bitterness now fills
With fear and torment sea and earth and sky,
Will mend her ways, and favor them as I do,
Lords of the world, the toga-bearing Romans.
Such is our pleasure. As the years fall away,
370 An age comes when Assaracus' royal house
Will bring to servitude Thessalian Phthia,
Renowned Mycenae, too; and subjugate
Defeated Argos.[3] From that comely line
The Trojan Caesar comes, to circumscribe
375 Empire with Ocean, fame with heaven's stars.
Julius his name, from Iulus handed down:
All tranquil shall you take him heavenward
In time, laden with plunder of the East,
And he with you shall be invoked in prayer.[4]
380 Wars at an end, harsh centuries then will soften,
Ancient Fides and Vesta, Quirinus
With Brother Remus, will be lawgivers,[5]
And grim with iron frames, the Gates of War
Will then be shut: inside, unholy Furor,
385 Squatting on cruel weapons, hands enchained
Behind him by a hundred links of bronze,

---

9. Ascanius was Aeneas's son. The Julian clan (whose members included Julius Caesar and Augustus) called him "Iulus" and claimed descent from him. According to Virgil, they derived the name from "Ilus," the founder of Troy.

1. A city in the Alban hills about 13 miles southeast of Rome. Tradition placed the founding of Alba Longa c. 1152 B.C.E. It lost its primacy in Latium not long after the founding of Rome.

2. According to Roman legend, Ilia was a Vestal Virgin who bore two sons to the war god Mars (Greek: Ares). She was thrown into the river Tiber by her usurping uncle, and Romulus and Remus were raised by a she-wolf.

3. Jove predicts Trojan revenge in the form of the eventual Roman conquest of Greece. At the time of Homer, Phthia was the kingdom of Achilles, Mycenae of Agamemnon, and Argos of Diomedes. Greece and Macedonia became the Roman province of Achaea in 146 B.C.E.

4. Virgil presents the claim of the *gens Iulia* to descent from Ascanius and predicts the career of either Julius Caesar (100–44 B.C.E.) or his adopted son, Julius Caesar Octavianus (63 B.C.E.–14 C.E.), known also as "Augustus." Julius Caesar was officially deified as Divus Iulius in 42 B.C.E.; Virgil predicts the deification of Augustus, which occurred after the poet's death, at the time of the emperor's funeral.

5. Fides was the Roman personification of Faith, and Vesta was the goddess of the hearth. Quirinus was the local deity of the Sabine community who settled on the Quirinal hill, later identified with Romulus.

Will grind his teeth and howl with bloodied mouth."[6]

That said, he sent the son of Maia[7] down
From his high place to make the land of Carthage,
390   The new-built town, receptive to the Trojans,
Not to allow Queen Dido, all unknowing
As to the fated future, to exclude them.
Through the vast air with stroking wings he flew
And came down quickly on the Libyan coast,
395   Performing Jove's command, so that at once
Phoenicians put aside belligerence
As the god willed. Especially the queen
Took on a peaceful mood, an open mind
Toward Teucrians.

               But the dedicated man,
400   Aeneas, thoughtful through the restless night,
Made up his mind, as kindly daylight came,
To go out and explore the strange new places,
To learn what coast the wind had brought him to
And who were living there, men or wild creatures—
405   For wilderness was all he saw—and bring
Report back to his company. The ships
He hid beneath a hollowed rocky cliff
And groves that made a vault, trees all around
And deep shade quivering. He took his way
410   With only one man at his side, Achatës,
Hefting two hunting spears with broad steel points.
Then suddenly, in front of him,
His mother crossed his path in mid-forest,
Wearing a girl's shape and a girl's gear—
415   A Spartan girl, or like that one of Thrace,
Harpalycë,[8] who tires horses out,
Outrunning the swift Hebrus. She had hung
About her shoulders the light, handy bow
A huntress carries, and had given her hair
420   To the disheveling wind; her knees were bare,
Her flowing gown knotted and kirtled up.
She spoke first:

             "Ho, young fellows, have you seen—
Can you say where—one of my sisters here,
In a spotted lynx-hide, belted with a quiver,
425   Scouting the wood, or shouting on the track
Behind a foam-flecked boar?"

                To Venus then

---

40

6. In times of complete peace, the temple of Janus Geminus (the god of doors and gates) in the Forum in Rome would be closed, most famously in 29, following Augustus's victory in the civil war. *Furor,* the Latin word for fury or rage, personifies the irrationality of war, especially of the civil variety.

7. Hermes, the messenger of the gods, identified in Roman religion with Mercury, was originally a god of trade.

8. A mythical Thracian princess raised by her father to be a warrior.

The son of Venus answered:
                                    "No, I've heard
Or seen none of your sisters—only, how
Shall I address you, girl? Your look's not mortal,
430 Neither has your accent a mortal ring.
O Goddess, beyond doubt! Apollo's sister?[9]
One of the family of nymphs? Be kind,
Whoever you may be, relieve our trouble,
Tell us under what heaven we've come at last,
435 On what shore of the world are we cast up,
Wanderers that we are, strange to this country,
Driven here by wind and heavy sea.
By my right hand many an offering
Will be cut down for you before your altars."
440 Venus replied:
                        "Be sure I am not fit
For any such devotion. Tyrian girls
Are given to wearing quivers and hunting boots
Of crimson, laced on the leg up to the knee.
This is the Punic kingdom that you see,
445 The folk are Tyrian, the town Agenor's.[1]
But neighboring lands belong to Libya,
A nation hard to fight against in war.
The ruler here is Dido,[2] of Tyre city,
In flight here from her brother—a long tale
450 Of wrong endured, mysterious and long.
But let me tell the main events in order.
Her husband was Sychaeus, of all Phoenicians
Richest in land, and greatly loved by her,
Ill-fated woman. Her father had given her,
455 A virgin still, in marriage, her first rite.
Her brother, though, held power in Tyre—Pygmalion,
A monster of wickedness beyond all others.
Between the two men furious hate arose,
And sacrilegiously before the altars,
460 Driven by a blind lust for gold, Pygmalion
Took Sychaeus by surprise and killed him
With a dagger blow in secret, undeterred
By any thought of Dido's love. He hid
What he had done for a long time, cozening° her,   *deceiving*
465 Deluding the sick woman with false hope.
But the true form of her unburied husband
Came in a dream: lifting his pallid face
Before her strangely, he made visible

---

9. Artemis, the daughter of Zeus and Leto, was a virgin and huntress who was identified with the Italian moon goddess, Diana.

1. In Greek mythology, Agenor was the Phoenician king of Tyre and the father of Cadmus and Europa.

2. Dido was originally the name of a Phoenician goddess but was later given to Elissa, the legendary daughter of Belus of Tyre, whose story Venus tells here.

470	The cruel altars and his body pierced,
	Uncovering all the dark crime of the house.

He urged her then to make haste and take flight,
Leaving her fatherland, and to assist the journey
Revealed a buried treasure of old time,
Unknown to any, a weight of gold and silver.
475   Impelled by this, Dido laid her plans
To get away and to equip her company.
All who hated the tyrant, all in fear
As bitter as her own, now came together,
And ships in port, already fitted out,
480   They commandeered, to fill with gold: the riches
Pygmalion had itched for went to sea,
And captaining the venture was a woman.
They sailed to this place where today you'll see
Stone walls going higher and the citadel
485   Of Carthage, the new town. They bought the land,
Called Drumskin from the bargain made, a tract
They could enclose with one bull's hide.[3]
What of yourselves? From what coast do you come?
Where are you bound?"
                    Then to the questioner
490   He answered sighing, bringing out the words
From deep within him:
                    "Goddess, if I should tell
Our story from the start, if you had leisure
To hear our annals of adversity,
Before I finished, the fair evening star
495   Would come to close Olympus and the day.
From old Troy—if the name of Troy has fallen
Perhaps upon your ears—we sailed the seas,
And yesterday were driven by a storm,
Of its own whim, upon this Libyan coast.
500   I am Aeneas, duty-bound, and known
Above high air of heaven by my fame,
Carrying with me in my ships our gods
Of hearth and home, saved from the enemy.
I look for Italy to be my fatherland,
505   And my descent is from all-highest Jove.
With twenty ships I mounted the Phrygian° sea,   *Aegean*
As my immortal mother showed the way.
I followed the given fates. Now barely seven
Ships are left, battered by wind and sea,
510   And I myself, unknown and unprovisioned,
Cross the Libyan wilderness, an exile
Driven from Europe and from Asia—"

3. According to legend, a Libyan king granted Dido as much land as she could cover with a bull's hide. By cutting the hide into narrow strips, she obtained enough space to found Carthage.

But Venus chose to hear no more complaints
And broke in, midway through his bitterness:

515 "Whoever you are, I doubt Heaven is unfriendly
To you, as you still breathe life-giving air
On your approach to the Tyrian town. Go on:
Betake yourself this way to the queen's gate.
Your friends are back. This is my news for you:
520 Your ships were saved and brought to shore again
By winds shifting north, or else my parents
Taught me augury to no purpose. Look:
See the twelve swans in line rejoicing there!
Jove's eagle, like a bolt out of the blue,
525 Had flurried them in open heaven, but now
They seem to be alighting one by one
Or looking down on those already grounded.
As they disport themselves, with flapping wings,
After their chanting flight about the sky,
530 Just so your ships and your ships' companies
Are either in port or entering under sail.
Go on then, where the path leads, go ahead!"

On this she turned away. Rose-pink and fair
Her nape shone, her ambrosial hair exhaled
535 Divine perfume, her gown rippled full length,
And by her stride she showed herself a goddess.
Knowing her for his mother, he called out
To the figure fleeting away:
                              "You! cruel, too!
Why tease your son so often with disguises?
540 Why may we not join hands and speak and hear
The simple truth?"
                    So he called after her,
And went on toward the town. But Venus muffled
The two wayfarers in grey mist, a cloak
Of dense cloud poured around them, so that no one
545 Had the power to see or to accost them,
Make them halt, or ask them what they came for.
Away to Paphos[4] through high air she went
In joy to see her home again, her shrine
And hundred altars where Sabaean incense[5]
550 Fumed and garlands freshened the air.
                                        Meanwhile
The two men pressed on where the pathway led,
Soon climbing a long ridge that gave a view
Down over the city and facing towers.
Aeneas found, where lately huts had been,
555 Marvelous buildings, gateways, cobbled ways,

4. City-kingdom on the island of Cyprus and home of one of the most famous Aphrodite cults.
5. The Sabaeans were one of the chief peoples of Arabia, famous for precious spices and perfumes.

And din of wagons. There the Tyrians
Were hard at work: laying courses for walls,
Rolling up stones to build the citadel,
While others picked out building sites and plowed
560 A boundary furrow. Laws were being enacted,
Magistrates and a sacred senate chosen.
Here men were dredging harbors, there they laid
The deep foundation of a theatre,
And quarried massive pillars to enhance
565 The future stage—as bees in early summer
In sunlight in the flowering fields
Hum at their work, and bring along the young
Full-grown to beehood; as they cram their combs
With honey, brimming all the cells with nectar,
570 Or take newcomers' plunder, or like troops
Alerted, drive away the lazy drones,
And labor thrives and sweet thyme scents the honey.
Aeneas said: "How fortunate these are
Whose city walls are rising here and now!"[6]

575 He looked up at the roofs, for he had entered,
Swathed in cloud—strange to relate—among them,
Mingling with men, yet visible to none.
In mid-town stood a grove that cast sweet shade
Where the Phoenicians, shaken by wind and sea,
580 Had first dug up that symbol Juno showed them,
A proud warhorse's head:[7] this meant for Carthage
Prowess in war and ease of life through ages.
Here being built by the Sidonian[8] queen
Was a great temple planned in Juno's honor,
585 Rich in offerings and the godhead there.
Steps led up to a sill of bronze, with brazen
Lintel, and bronze doors on groaning pins.
Here in this grove new things that met his eyes
Calmed Aeneas' fear for the first time.
590 Here for the first time he took heart to hope
For safety, and to trust his destiny more
Even in affliction. It was while he walked
From one to another wall of the great temple
And waited for the queen, staring amazed
595 At Carthaginian promise, at the handiwork
Of artificers and the toil they spent upon it:
He found before his eyes the Trojan battles
In the old war, now known throughout the world—
The great Atridae, Priam, and Achilles,

41

---

6. The founding of Carthage was traditionally dated to 814 or 813 B.C.E., some four centuries after the destruction of Troy. This makes the meeting between Dido and Aeneas chronologically tricky but allows a profound symmetry between the two cities being founded by two exiles.

7. Tanit, the great goddess of Carthage, was identified early on with Juno. It was she who, according to legend, had led the Tyrians to the spot where they dug up a horse's head, a divine portent of the future site of their city.

8. Phoenician. Sidon was a Phoenician city on the coast of modern Lebanon.

600   Fierce in his rage at both sides. Here Aeneas
        Halted, and tears came.
                         "What spot on earth,"
        He said, "what region of the earth, Achatës,
        Is not full of the story of our sorrow?
        Look, here is Priam. Even so far away

605   Great valor has due honor; they weep here
        For how the world goes, and our life that passes
        Touches their hearts. Throw off your fear. This fame
        Insures some kind of refuge."[9]
                        He broke off
        To feast his eyes and mind on a mere image,

610   Sighing often, cheeks grown wet with tears,
        To see again how, fighting around Troy,
        The Greeks broke here, and ran before the Trojans,
        And there the Phrygians ran, as plumed Achilles
        Harried them in his warcar. Nearby, then,

615   He recognized the snowy canvas tents
        Of Rhesus,[1] and more tears came: these, betrayed
        In first sleep, Diomedes devastated,
        SY Swording many, till he reeked with blood,
        Then turned the mettlesome horses toward the beachhead

620   Before they tasted Trojan grass or drank
        At Xanthus[2] ford.
                  And on another panel
        Troilus,[3] without his armor, luckless boy,
        No match for his antagonist, Achilles,
        Appeared pulled onward by his team: he clung

625   To his warcar, though fallen backward, hanging
        On to the reins still, head dragged on the ground,
        His javelin scribbling S's in the dust.
        Meanwhile to hostile Pallas'° shrine   *Athena's*
        The Trojan women walked with hair unbound,

630   Bearing the robe of offering, in sorrow,
        Entreating her, beating their breasts. But she,
        Her face averted, would not raise her eyes.[4]

---

9. The scenes from the Trojan War on the temple walls that Virgil recounts here constitute the poem's first use of the classical rhetorical figure of *ekphrasis,* the verbal description of a work of visual art. The scenes also serve to preview Aeneas's own account of the fall of Troy in Book 2.

1. A Thracian ally of the Trojans who was victimized by Odysseus and Diomedes in the night raid of the *Iliad,* Book 10, described here.

2. A river of Troy; its god was a son of Zeus.

3. One of the sons of Hecuba and Priam, king of Troy. Non-Homeric sources told of his ambush by Achilles and slaughter at the altar of Apollo.

4. Like Hera, Athena sided with the Greeks; in this scene from the *Iliad,* Trojan women attempt unsuccessfully to appease her anger.

And there was Hector, dragged around Troy walls
Three times, and there for gold Achilles sold him,
635   Bloodless and lifeless.[5] Now indeed Aeneas
Heaved a mighty sigh from deep within him,
Seeing the spoils, the chariot, and the corpse
Of his great friend, and Priam, all unarmed,
Stretching his hands out.
              He himself he saw
640   In combat with the first of the Achaeans,[6]
And saw the ranks of Dawn, black Memnon's arms;[7]
Then, leading the battalion of Amazons
With half-moon shields, he saw Penthesilëa
Fiery amid her host, buckling a golden
645   Girdle beneath her bare and arrogant breast,
A girl who dared fight men, a warrior queen.[8]
Now, while these wonders were being surveyed
By Aeneas of Dardania, while he stood
Enthralled, devouring all in one long gaze,
650   The queen paced toward the temple in her beauty,
Dido, with a throng of men behind.

[*Under Venus's influence, Dido welcomes Aeneas and his people. At dinner, Venus sends down Cupid to take the shape of Ascanius and awaken love for Aeneas in Dido. Dido asks Aeneas to recount the story of the fall of Troy and of his travels thereafter. Aeneas's tale includes a description of the Trojan Horse, which the Trojans believed was left outside their city gates as a gift from the Greeks after their defeat. In actuality, the Horse was filled with Greek warriors who opened the city gates at night and invaded Troy. Aeneas relates how he watched as Pyrrhus killed Polites in front of his father, King Priam, and then killed the king in front of his wife, Queen Hecuba. Returning home, Aeneas convinces his stubborn father to abandon Troy with him. He carries his father and leads his son Ascanius and his wife Creusa. Aeneas loses Creusa in the commotion of war and briefly meets her ghost. After a winter's preparation, the remaining Trojan survivors set out in search of their promised new home. They attempt unsuccessfully to settle in Thrace and Crete. After several years, Aeneas receives a detailed prophecy from Helenus, a son of Priam and Hecuba who has married Hector's wife, Andromache, and settled in Epirus. They cross over to Italy and sail on to Sicily, where they pick up one of Ulysses's men near Mount Aetna, the haunt of the Cyclopes. They make their way around the south coast of Sicily to Drepanum, where Anchises dies.*]

---

5. Achilles dragged Hector's body around the city in the *Iliad,* Book 22 (the scene is described in further detail in bk. 2); he ransomed the body to Hector's father, Priam, in the *Iliad,* Book 24.

6. The duel with Achilles in the *Iliad,* Book 20, from which Aeneas's mother rescues him.

7. A mythical king of Ethiopia, son of Aurora, goddess of Dawn, and Priam's brother Tithonus; he arrived after Hector's death and was killed by Achilles.

8. A mythical Amazon queen who led an army to aid Priam after Hector's death; she was killed by Achilles.

Book 4

[The Passion of the Queen]

The queen, for her part, all that evening ached
With longing that her heart's blood fed, a wound
Or inward fire eating her away.
The manhood of the man, his pride of birth,
5   Came home to her time and again; his looks,
His words remained with her to haunt her mind,
And desire for him gave her no rest.

When Dawn
Swept earth with Phoebus' torch° and burned away   *the sun*
Night-gloom and damp, this queen, far gone and ill,
10   Confided to the sister of her heart:
"My sister Anna, quandaries and dreams
Have come to frighten me—such dreams!

Think what a stranger
Yesterday found lodging in our house:
How princely, how courageous, what a soldier.
15   I can believe him in the line of gods,
And this is no delusion. Tell-tale fear
Betrays inferior souls. What scenes of war
Fought to the bitter end he pictured for us!
What buffetings awaited him at sea!
20   Had I not set my face against remarriage
After my first love died and failed me, left me
Barren and bereaved—and sick to death
At the mere thought of torch and bridal bed—
I could perhaps give way in this one case
25   To frailty. I shall say it: since that time
Sychaeus, my poor husband, met his fate,
And blood my brother shed stained our hearth gods,
This man alone has wrought upon me so
And moved my soul to yield. I recognize
30   The signs of the old flame, of old desire.
But O chaste life, before I break your laws,
I pray that Earth may open, gape for me
Down to its depth, or the omnipotent
With one stroke blast me to the shades, pale shades
35   Of Erebus[1] and the deep world of night!
That man who took me to himself in youth
Has taken all my love; may that man keep it,
Hold it forever with him in the tomb."

At this she wept and wet her breast with tears.
40   But Anna answered:
"Dearer to your sister

---

1. Primeval darkness, sprung from Chaos, the father of Day by his sister, Night.

Than daylight is, will you wear out your life,
Young as you are, in solitary mourning,
Never to know sweet children, or the crown
Of joy that Venus brings? Do you believe
45 This matters to the dust, to ghosts in tombs?
Granted no suitors up to now have moved you,
Neither in Libya nor before, in Tyre—
Iarbas[2] you rejected, and the others,
Chieftains bred by the land of Africa
50 Their triumphs have enriched—will you contend
Even against a welcome love? Have you
Considered in whose lands you settled here?
On one frontier the Gaetulans, their cities,
People invincible in war—with wild
55 Numidian horsemen, and the offshore banks,
The Syrtës; on the other, desert sands,
Bone-dry, where fierce Barcaean nomads range.[3]
Or need I speak of future wars brought on
From Tyre, and the menace of your brother?
60 Surely by dispensation of the gods
And backed by Juno's will, the ships from Ilium
Held their course this way on the wind.
                                        Sister,
What a great city you'll see rising here,
And what a kingdom, from this royal match!
65 With Trojan soldiers as companions in arms
By what exploits will Punic glory grow!
Only ask the indulgence of the gods,
Win them with offerings, give your guests ease,
And contrive reasons for delay, while winter
70 Gales rage, drenched Orion[4] storms at sea,
And their ships, damaged still, face iron skies."

This counsel fanned the flame, already kindled,
Giving her hesitant sister hope, and set her
Free of scruple. Visiting the shrines
75 They begged for grace at every altar first,
Then put choice rams and ewes to ritual death
For Ceres Giver of Laws, Father Lyaeus,
Phoebus, and for Juno most of all
Who has the bonds of marriage in her keeping.[5]

2. The Libyan king with whom Dido made the bargain of the bull's hide.

3. The Berber inhabitants of Numidia, west and south of Carthaginian territory, were nomadic herdsmen who had become warlike by the Second Punic War. The Syrtës were dangerous shoals and shallows of the Libyan continental shelf.

4. A mighty hunter who was eventually transformed into the constellation known by his name.

5. "Lyaeus" was a frequent poetic cult title for Bacchus; "pater" ("father") was often used for gods and heroes as a mark of respect. One of the roles Juno took from Hera was the protector of marriage.

80   Dido herself, splendidly beautiful,
        Holding a shallow cup, tips out the wine
        On a white shining heifer, between the horns,
        Or gravely in the shadow of the gods
        Approaches opulent altars. Through the day
85   She brings new gifts, and when the breasts are opened
        Pores over organs, living still, for signs.
        Alas, what darkened minds have soothsayers!
        What good are shrines and vows to maddened lovers?
        The inward fire eats the soft marrow away,
90   And the internal wound bleeds on in silence.

        Unlucky Dido, burning, in her madness
        Roamed through all the city, like a doe
        Hit by an arrow shot from far away
        By a shepherd hunting in the Cretan woods—
95   Hit by surprise, nor could the hunter see
        His flying steel had fixed itself in her;
        But though she runs for life through copse and glade
        The fatal shaft clings to her side.
                                        Now Dido
        Took Aeneas with her among her buildings,
100   Showed her Sidonian wealth, her walls prepared,
        And tried to speak, but in mid-speech grew still.
        When the day waned she wanted to repeat
        The banquet as before, to hear once more
        In her wild need the throes of Ilium,
105   And once more hung on the narrator's words.
        Afterward, when all the guests were gone,
        And the dim moon in turn had quenched her light,
        And setting stars weighed weariness to sleep,
        Alone she mourned in the great empty hall
110   And pressed her body on the couch he left:
        She heard him still, though absent—heard and saw him.
        Or she would hold Ascanius in her lap,
        Enthralled by him, the image of his father,
        As though by this ruse to appease a love
115   Beyond all telling.
                                Towers, half-built, rose
        No farther; men no longer trained in arms
        Or toiled to make harbors and battlements
        Impregnable. Projects were broken off,
        Laid over, and the menacing huge walls
120   With cranes unmoving stood against the sky.

        As soon as Jove's dear consort saw the lady
        Prey to such illness, and her reputation
        Standing no longer in the way of passion,
        Saturn's daughter[6] said to Venus:
                                        "Wondrous!

125   Covered yourself with glory, have you not,
      You and your boy, and won such prizes, too.
      Divine power is something to remember
      If by collusion of two gods one mortal
      Woman is brought low.
                       I am not blind.
130   Your fear of our new walls has not escaped me,
      Fear and mistrust of Carthage at her height.
      But how far will it go? What do you hope for,
      Being so contentious? Why do we not
      Arrange eternal peace and formal marriage?
135   You have your heart's desire: Dido in love,
      Dido consumed with passion to her core.
      Why not, then, rule this people side by side
      With equal authority? And let the queen
      Wait on her Phrygian lord, let her consign
140   Into your hand her Tyrians as a dowry."

      Now Venus knew this talk was all pretence,
      All to divert the future power from Italy
      To Libya; and she answered:
                    "Who would be
      So mad, so foolish as to shun that prospect
145   Or prefer war with you? That is, provided
      Fortune is on the side of your proposal.
      The fates here are perplexing: would one city
      Satisfy Jupiter's will for Tyrians
      And Trojan exiles? Does he approve
150   A union and a mingling of these races?
      You are his consort: you have every right
      To sound him out. Go on, and I'll come, too."

      But regal Juno pointedly replied:
      "That task will rest with me. Just now, as to
155   The need of the moment and the way to meet it,
      Listen, and I'll explain in a few words.
      Aeneas and Dido in her misery
      Plan hunting in the forest, when the Titan
      Sun[7] comes up with rays to light the world,
160   While beaters in excitement ring the glens
      My gift will be a black raincloud, and hail,
      A downpour, and I'll shake heaven with thunder.
      The company will scatter, lost in gloom,
      As Dido and the Trojan captain come
165   To one same cavern. I shall be on hand,

7. The Greek sun god Helios was the son of the Titan Hyperion; Helios became identified by the Greeks with Apollo, the

And if I can be certain you are willing,
There I shall marry them and call her his.
A wedding, this will be."
                              Then Cytherëa,
Not disinclined, nodded to Juno's plea,
170   And smiled at the stratagem now given away.

Dawn came up meanwhile from the Ocean stream,
And in the early sunshine from the gates
Picked huntsmen issued: wide-meshed nets and snares,
Broad spearheads for big game, Massylian[8] horsemen
175   Trooping with hounds in packs keen on the scent.
But Dido lingered in her hall, as Punic
Nobles waited, and her mettlesome hunter
Stood nearby, cavorting in gold and scarlet,
Champing his foam-flecked bridle. At long last
180   The queen appeared with courtiers in a crowd,
A short Sidonian cloak edged in embroidery
Caught about her, at her back a quiver
Sheathed in gold, her hair tied up in gold,
And a brooch of gold pinning her scarlet dress.
185   Phrygians came in her company as well,
And Iulus, joyous at the scene. Resplendent
Above the rest, Aeneas walked to meet her,
To join his retinue with hers. He seemed—
Think of the lord Apollo in the spring
190   When he leaves wintering in Lycia
By Xanthus torrent, for his mother's isle
Of Delos, to renew the festival;
Around his altars Cretans, Dryopës,
And painted Agathyrsans raise a shout,
195   But the god walks the Cynthian ridge alone
And smooths his hair, binds it in fronded laurel,
Braids it in gold; and shafts ring on his shoulders.[9]
So elated and swift, Aeneas walked
With sunlit grace upon him.
                              Soon the hunters,
200   Riding in company to high pathless hills,
Saw mountain goats shoot down from a rocky peak
And scamper on the ridges; toward the plain
Deer left the slopes, herding in clouds of dust
In flight across the open lands. Alone,
205   The boy Ascanius, delightedly riding
His eager horse amid the lowland vales,

---

8. The Massyli were a people of northern Africa.

9. Xanthus was the major river of the region of Lycia in southwest Asia Minor, where there was an important sanctuary of Leto, the mother of Apollo. Delos is a small island in the Aegean, mythological birthplace of Apollo and Artemis, an important center of worship, and the seat of an oracle of Apollo. Cynthia is a mountain of Delos. Cretans, Dryopës, and Agathyrsans were peoples associated with the cult of Apollo.

Outran both goats and deer. Could he only meet
Amid the harmless game some foaming boar,
Or a tawny lion down from the mountainside!

210 Meanwhile in heaven began a rolling thunder,
And soon the storm broke, pouring rain and hail.
Then Tyrians and Trojans in alarm—
With Venus' Dardan grandson—ran for cover
Here and there in the wilderness, as freshets
215 Coursed from the high hills.
                              Now to the self-same cave
Came Dido and the captain of the Trojans.
Primal Earth herself and Nuptial Juno
Opened the ritual, torches of lightning blazed,
High Heaven became witness to the marriage,
220 And nymphs cried out wild hymns from a mountain top.

That day was the first cause of death, and first
Of sorrow. Dido had no further qualms
As to impressions given and set abroad;
She thought no longer of a secret love
225 But called it marriage. Thus, under that name,
She hid her fault.
                   Now in no time at all
Through all the African cities Rumor[1] goes—
Nimble as quicksilver among evils. Rumor
Thrives on motion, stronger for the running,
230 Lowly at first through fear, then rearing high,
She treads the land and hides her head in cloud.
As people fable it, the Earth, her mother,
Furious against the gods, bore a late sister
To the giants Coeus and Enceladus,[2]
235 Giving her speed on foot and on the wing:
Monstrous, deformed, titanic. Pinioned, with
An eye beneath for every body feather,
And, strange to say, as many tongues and buzzing
Mouths as eyes, as many pricked-up ears,
240 By night she flies between the earth and heaven
Shrieking through darkness, and she never turns
Her eye-lids down to sleep. By day she broods,
On the alert, on rooftops or on towers,
Bringing great cities fear, harping on lies
245 And slander evenhandedly with truth.
In those days Rumor took an evil joy
At filling countrysides with whispers, whispers,

---

41

1. Rumor appears in Hesiod as a Greek god whose work is "never quite in vain"; Virgil portrays her as midway between a god and an allegory of the social effects of rumor (*fama*).

2. According to Hesiod, the giants were sons of Ge (Earth). After the defeat of their rebellion against the gods, the giants were buried under volcanoes in Greece and Italy, Enceladus under Aetna in Sicily.

Gossip of what was done, and never done:
How this Aeneas landed, Trojan born,
250   How Dido in her beauty graced his company,
Then how they reveled all the winter long
Unmindful of the realm, prisoners of lust.

These tales the scabrous goddess put about
On men's lips everywhere. Her twisting course
255   Took her to King Iarbas, whom she set
Ablaze with anger piled on top of anger.
Son of Jupiter Hammon by a nymph,
A ravished Garamantean,³ this prince
Had built the god a hundred giant shrines,
260   A hundred altars, each with holy fires.
Alight by night and day, sentries on watch,
The ground enriched by victims' blood, the doors
Festooned with flowering wreaths. Before his altars
King Iarbas, crazed by the raw story,
265   Stood, they say, amid the Presences,°   *spirits*
With supplicating hands, pouring out prayer:
"All powerful Jove, to whom the feasting Moors
At ease on colored couches tip their wine,
Do you see this? Are we then fools to fear you
270   Throwing down your bolts? Those dazzling fires
Of lightning, are they aimless in the clouds
And rumbling thunder meaningless? This woman
Who turned up in our country and laid down
A tiny city at a price, to whom
275   I gave a beach to plow—and on my terms—
After refusing to marry me has taken
Aeneas to be master in her realm.
And now Sir Paris with his men, half-men,
His chin and perfumed hair tied up
280   In a Maeonian bonnet, takes possession.⁴
As for ourselves, here we are bringing gifts
Into these shrines—supposedly your shrines—
Hugging that empty fable."
                            Pleas like this
From the man clinging to his altars reached
285   The ears of the Almighty. Now he turned
His eyes upon the queen's town and the lovers
Careless of their good name; then spoke to Mercury,
Assigning him a mission:
                         "Son, bestir yourself,
Call up the Zephyrs,° take to your wings and glide.   *winds*
290   Approach the Dardan captain where he tarries

---

3. An African people; Hammon was a Libyan god identified with Jupiter.

4. Iarbas compares Aeneas to Paris, the abductor of Helen, who was regarded as unmanly, more interested in seduction than warfare. "Maeonia" was an old name for Lydia and denotes the Asiatic origin of the Trojans.

Rapt in Tyrian Carthage, losing sight
Of future towns the fates ordain. Correct him,
Carry my speech to him on the running winds:
No son like this did his enchanting mother
295   Promise to us, nor such did she deliver
Twice from peril at the hands of Greeks.
He was to be the ruler of Italy,
Potential empire, armorer of war;
To father men from Teucer's noble blood
300   And bring the whole world under law's dominion.
If glories to be won by deeds like these
Cannot arouse him, if he will not strive
For his own honor, does he begrudge his son,
Ascanius, the high strongholds of Rome?
305   What has he in mind? What hope, to make him stay
Amid a hostile race, and lose from view
Ausonian[5] progeny, Lavinian lands?
The man should sail: that is the whole point.
Let this be what you tell him, as from me."

310   He finished and fell silent. Mercury
Made ready to obey the great command
Of his great father, and he first tied on
The golden sandals, winged, that high in air
Transport him over seas or over land
315   Abreast of gale winds; then he took the wand
With which he summons pale souls out of Orcus
And ushers others to the undergloom,
Lulls men to slumber or awakens them,
And opens dead men's eyes.[6] This wand in hand,
320   He can drive winds before him, swimming down
Along the stormcloud. Now aloft, he saw
The craggy flanks and crown of patient Atlas,[7]
Giant Atlas, balancing the sky
Upon his peak—his pine-forested head
325   In vapor cowled, beaten by wind and rain.
Snow lay upon his shoulders, rills cascaded
Down his ancient chin and beard a-bristle,
Caked with ice. Here Mercury of Cyllenë[8]
Hovered first on even wings, then down
330   He plummeted to sea-level and flew on
Like a low-flying gull that skims the shallows
And rocky coasts where fish ply close inshore.

42

5. Italian. From an ancient name for central and southern Italy.

6. In addition to his role as messenger, Mercury was the conductor of souls of the dead to the underworld. Orcus was an infernal deity in Greek mythology, identified in Roman religion with Dis, god of the underworld.

7. The Atlas mountains run through northern Africa; Greek mythology made them a Titan's son who was punished by having to support the skies on his head and hands.

8. Hermes was born on Mt. Cyllenë in Arcadia.

So, like a gull between the earth and sky,
The progeny of Cyllenë, on the wing
From his maternal grandsire, split the winds
To the sand bars of Libya.
                              Alighting tiptoe
On the first hutments, there he found Aeneas
Laying foundations for new towers and homes.
He noted well the swordhilt the man wore,
Adorned with yellow jasper; and the cloak
Aglow with Tyrian dye upon his shoulders—
Gifts of the wealthy queen, who had inwoven
Gold thread in the fabric. Mercury
Took him to task at once:[9]
                              "Is it for you
To lay the stones for Carthage's high walls,
Tame husband that you are, and build their city?
Oblivious of your own world, your own kingdom!
From bright Olympus he that rules the gods
And turns the earth and heaven by his power—
He and no other sent me to you, told me
To bring this message on the running winds:
What have you in mind? What hope, wasting your days
In Libya? If future history's glories
Do not affect you, if you will not strive
For your own honor, think of Ascanius,
Think of the expectations of your heir,
Iulus, to whom the Italian realm, the land
Of Rome, are due."
                              And Mercury, as he spoke,
Departed from the visual field of mortals
To a great distance, ebbed in subtle air.
Amazed, and shocked to the bottom of his soul
By what his eyes had seen, Aeneas felt
His hackles rise, his voice choke in his throat.
As the sharp admonition and command
From heaven had shaken him awake, he now
Burned only to be gone, to leave that land
Of the sweet life behind. What can he do? How tell
The impassioned queen and hope to win her over?
What opening shall he choose? This way and that
He let his mind dart, testing alternatives,
Running through every one. And as he pondered
This seemed the better tactic: he called in
Mnestheus, Sergestus and stalwart Serestus,
Telling them:
                              "Get the fleet ready for sea,

335

340

345

350

355

360

365

370

9. Mercury repeats Jove's speech word for word. This is one of the many ways Virgil mimics Homeric oral conventions.

375 But quietly, and collect the men on shore.
Lay in ship stores and gear."
                                        As to the cause
For a change of plan, they were to keep it secret,
Seeing the excellent Dido had no notion,
No warning that such love could be cut short;
380 He would himself look for the right occasion,
The easiest time to speak, the way to do it.
The Trojans to a man gladly obeyed.

The queen, for her part, felt some plot afoot
Quite soon—for who deceives a woman in love?
385 She caught wind of a change, being in fear
Of what had seemed her safety. Evil Rumor,
Shameless as before, brought word to her
In her distracted state of ships being rigged
In trim for sailing. Furious, at her wits' end,
390 She traversed the whole city, all aflame
With rage, like a Bacchantë driven wild
By emblems shaken, when the mountain revels
Of the odd year possess her, when the cry
Of Bacchus rises and Cithaeron calls
395 All through the shouting night.[1] Thus it turned out
She was the first to speak and charge Aeneas:

"You even hoped to keep me in the dark
As to this outrage, did you, two-faced man,
And slip away in silence? Can our love
400 Not hold you, can the pledge we gave not hold you,
Can Dido not, now sure to die in pain?
Even in winter weather must you toil
With ships, and fret to launch against high winds
For the open sea? Oh, heartless!
                                        Tell me now,
405 If you were not in search of alien lands
And new strange homes, if ancient Troy remained,
Would ships put out for Troy on these big seas?
Do you go to get away from me? I beg you,
By these tears, by your own right hand, since I
410 Have left my wretched self nothing but that—
Yes, by the marriage that we entered on,
If ever I did well and you were grateful
Or found some sweetness in a gift from me,
Have pity now on a declining house!
415 Put this plan by, I beg you, if a prayer

---

1. Bacchantës, or maenads, were initiates in the cult of Bacchus (Greek: Dionysus), usually women, whose ritual behavior when possessed by their god was characterized by wild dancing and ecstatic behavior. The most famous and most extreme portrait of Dionysiac behavior was in Euripides's play *The Bacchae*, where King Pentheus is torn apart by his mother on Mt. Cithaeron when he refuses to recognize the new god.

Is not yet out of place.
Because of you, Libyans and nomad kings
Detest me, my own Tyrians are hostile;
Because of you, I lost my integrity
420 And that admired name by which alone
I made my way once toward the stars.
                                    To whom
Do you abandon me, a dying woman,
Guest that you are—the only name now left
From that of husband? Why do I live on?
425 Shall I, until my brother Pygmalion comes
To pull my walls down? Or the Gaetulan
Iarbas leads me captive? If at least
There were a child by you for me to care for,
A little one to play in my courtyard
430 And give me back Aeneas, in spite of all,
I should not feel so utterly defeated,
Utterly bereft."
                              She ended there.
The man by Jove's command held fast his eyes
And fought down the emotion in his heart.
435 At length he answered:
                              "As for myself, be sure
I never shall deny all you can say,
Your majesty, of what you meant to me.
Never will the memory of Elissa°   *Dido*
Stale for me, while I can still remember
440 My own life, and the spirit rules my body.
As to the event, a few words. Do not think
I meant to be deceitful and slip away.
I never held the torches of a bridegroom,
Never entered upon the pact of marriage.
445 If Fate permitted me to spend my days
By my own lights, and make the best of things
According to my wishes, first of all
I should look after Troy and the loved relics
Left me of my people. Priam's great hall
450 Should stand again; I should have restored the tower
Of Pergamum for Trojans in defeat.
But now it is the rich Italian land
Apollo tells me I must make for: Italy,
Named by his oracles.[2] There is my love;
455 There is my country. If, as a Phoenician,
You are so given to the charms of Carthage,
Libyan city that it is, then tell me,
Why begrudge the Teucrians new lands

---

2. Aeneas recounted this episode to Dido as part of his wanderings in Book 3.

	For homesteads in Ausonia? Are we not
460	Entitled, too, to look for realms abroad?
	Night never veils the earth in damp and darkness,
	Fiery stars never ascend the east,
	But in my dreams my father's troubled ghost
	Admonishes and frightens me. Then, too,
465	Each night thoughts come of young Ascanius,
	My dear boy wronged, defrauded of his kingdom,
	Hesperian lands of destiny. And now
	The gods' interpreter, sent by Jove himself—
	I swear it by your head and mine—has brought
470	Commands down through the racing winds! I say
	With my own eyes in full daylight I saw him
	Entering the building! With my very ears
	I drank his message in! So please, no more
	Of these appeals that set us both afire.
475	I sail for Italy not of my own free will."

	During all this she had been watching him
	With face averted, looking him up and down
	In silence, and she burst out raging now:

	"No goddess was your mother. Dardanus
480	Was not the founder of your family.
	Liar and cheat! Some rough Caucasian cliff
	Begot you on flint. Hyrcanian tigresses[3]
	Tendered their teats to you. Why should I palter?
	Why still hold back for more indignity?
485	Sigh, did he, while I wept? Or look at me?
	Or yield a tear, or pity her who loved him?
	What shall I say first, with so much to say?
	The time is past when either supreme Juno
	Or the Saturnian father viewed these things
490	With justice. Faith can never be secure.
	I took the man in, thrown up on this coast
	In dire need, and in my madness then
	Contrived a place for him in my domain,
	Rescued his lost fleet, saved his shipmates' lives.
495	Oh, I am swept away burning by furies!
	Now the prophet Apollo, now his oracles,
	Now the gods' interpreter, if you please,
	Sent down by Jove himself, brings through the air
	His formidable commands! What fit employment
500	For heaven's high powers! What anxieties
	To plague serene immortals! I shall not
	Detain you or dispute your story. Go,
	Go after Italy on the sailing winds,

3. Caucasian and Hyrcanian (referring to regions near the Caspian Sea) are used as epitomes of Asian barbarism and savagery in contrast to the Roman civility claimed by Aeneas.

Look for your kingdom, cross the deepsea swell!
505 If divine justice counts for anything,
I hope and pray that on some grinding reef
Midway at sea you'll drink your punishment
And call and call on Dido's name!
From far away I shall come after you
510 With my black fires, and when cold death has parted
Body from soul I shall be everywhere
A shade° to haunt you! You will pay for this,   *spirit*
Unconscionable! I shall hear! The news will reach me
Even among the lowest of the dead!"

515 At this abruptly she broke off and ran
In sickness from his sight and the light of day,
Leaving him at a loss, alarmed, and mute
With all he meant to say. The maids in waiting
Caught her as she swooned and carried her
520 To bed in her marble chamber.
                                                      Duty-bound,
Aeneas, though he struggled with desire
To calm and comfort her in all her pain,
To speak to her and turn her mind from grief,
And though he sighed his heart out, shaken still
525 With love of her, yet took the course heaven gave him
And went back to the fleet. Then with a will
The Teucrians fell to work and launched the ships
Along the whole shore: slick with tar each hull
Took to the water. Eager to get away,
530 The sailors brought oar-boughs out of the woods
With leaves still on, and oaken logs unhewn.
Now you could see them issuing from the town
To the water's edge in streams, as when, aware
Of winter, ants will pillage a mound of spelt
535 To store it in their granary; over fields
The black battalion moves, and through the grass
On a narrow trail they carry off the spoil;
Some put their shoulders to the enormous weight
Of a trundled grain, while some pull stragglers in
540 And castigate delay; their to-and-fro
Of labor makes the whole track come alive.
At that sight, what were your emotions, Dido?
Sighing how deeply, looking out and down
From your high tower on the seething shore
545 Where all the harbor filled before your eyes
With bustle and shouts! Unconscionable Love,
To what extremes will you not drive our hearts!
She now felt driven to weep again, again
To move° him, if she could, by supplication,
550 Humbling her pride before her love—to leave

Nothing untried, not to die needlessly.

"Anna, you see the arc of waterfront
All in commotion: they come crowding in
From everywhere. Spread canvas calls for wind,
555   The happy crews have garlanded the sterns.
If I could brace myself for this great sorrow,
Sister, I can endure it, too. One favor,
Even so, you may perform for me.
Since that deserter chose you for his friend
560   And trusted you, even with private thoughts,
Since you alone know when he may be reached,
Go, intercede with our proud enemy.
Remind him that I took no oath at Aulis[4]
With Danaans to destroy the Trojan race;
565   I sent no ship to Pergamum.° Never did I   *Troy*
Profane his father Anchises' dust and shade.
Why will he not allow my prayers to fall
On his unpitying ears? Where is he racing?
Let him bestow one last gift on his mistress:
570   This, to await fair winds and easier flight.
Now I no longer plead the bond he broke
Of our old marriage, nor do I ask that he
Should live without his dear love, Latium,
Or yield his kingdom. Time is all I beg,
575   Mere time, a respite and a breathing space
For madness to subside in, while my fortune
Teaches me how to take defeat and grieve.
Pity your sister. This is the end, this favor—
To be repaid with interest when I die."

580   She pleaded in such terms, and such, in tears,
Her sorrowing sister brought him, time and again.
But no tears moved him, no one's voice would he
Attend to tractably. The fates opposed it;
God's will blocked the man's once kindly ears.
585   And just as when the north winds from the Alps
This way and that contend among themselves
To tear away an oaktree hale with age,
The wind and tree cry, and the buffeted trunk
Showers high foliage to earth, but holds
590   On bedrock, for the roots go down as far
Into the underworld as cresting boughs
Go up in heaven's air: just so this captain,
Buffeted by a gale of pleas
This way and that way, dinned all the day long,
595   Felt their moving power in his great heart,

4. Aulis was the launching point of the Greek expedition to Troy.

And yet his will stood fast; tears fell in vain.

On Dido in her desolation now
Terror grew at her fate. She prayed for death,
Being heartsick at the mere sight of heaven.
600   That she more surely would perform the act
And leave the daylight, now she saw before her
A thing one shudders to recall: on altars
Fuming with incense where she placed her gifts,
The holy water blackened, the spilt wine
605   Turned into blood and mire. Of this she spoke
To no one, not to her sister even. Then, too,
Within the palace was a marble shrine
Devoted to her onetime lord, a place
She held in wondrous honor, all festooned
610   With snowy fleeces and green festive boughs.
From this she now thought voices could be heard
And words could be made out, her husband's words,
Calling her, when midnight hushed the earth;
And lonely on the rooftops the night owl
615   Seemed to lament, in melancholy notes,
Prolonged to a doleful cry. And then, besides,
The riddling words of seers in ancient days,
Foreboding sayings, made her thrill with fear.
In nightmare, fevered, she was hunted down
620   By pitiless Aeneas, and she seemed
Deserted always, uncompanioned always,
On a long journey, looking for her Tyrians
In desolate landscapes—

               as Pentheus gone mad
Sees the oncoming Eumenidës and sees
625   A double sun and double Thebes appear,[5]
Or as when, hounded on the stage, Orestës
Runs from a mother armed with burning brands,
With serpents hellish black,
And in the doorway squat the Avenging Ones.[6]

630   So broken in mind by suffering, Dido caught
Her fatal madness and resolved to die.
She pondered time and means, then visiting
Her mournful sister, covered up her plan
With a calm look, a clear and hopeful brow.

635   "Sister, be glad for me! I've found a way
To bring him back or free me of desire.

---

5. Here Virgil cites a scene from the *Bacchae* of Euripides in which Dionysus has driven mad Pentheus, King of Thebes, causing him to see the world double as the Bacchantes approach to tear him to pieces. Virgil equates them with the Furies (Eumenides), female powers of the underworld who punish blood guilt.

6. Son of Clytemnestra and Agamemnon, Orestes kills his mother and her lover to revenge her murder of his father. He is then pursued by the Furies (the Avenging Ones). Virgil's description comes from the *Oresteia* of Aeschylus.

Near to the Ocean boundary, near sundown,
The Aethiops' farthest territory lies,
Where giant Atlas turns the sphere of heaven
640   Studded with burning stars. From there
A priestess of Massylian stock has come;
She had been pointed out to me: custodian
Of that shrine named for daughters of the west,
Hesperidës; and it is she who fed
645   The dragon, guarding well the holy boughs
With honey dripping slow and drowsy poppy.[7]
Chanting her spells she undertakes to free
What hearts she wills, but to inflict on others
Duress of sad desires; to arrest
650   The flow of rivers, make the stars move backward,
Call up the spirits of deep Night.[8] You'll see
Earth shift and rumble underfoot and ash trees
Walk down mountainsides. Dearest, I swear
Before the gods and by your own sweet self,
655   It is against my will that I resort
For weaponry to magic powers. In secret
Build up a pyre in the inner court
Under the open sky, and place upon it
The arms that faithless man left in my chamber,
660   All his clothing, and the marriage bed
On which I came to grief—solace for me
To annihilate all vestige of the man,
Vile as he is: my priestess shows me this."

While she was speaking, cheek and brow grew pale.
665   But Anna could not think her sister cloaked
A suicide in these unheard-of rites;
She failed to see how great her madness was
And feared no consequence more grave
Than at Sychaeus' death. So, as commanded,
670   She made the preparations. For her part,
The queen, seeing the pyre in her inmost court
Erected huge with pitch-pine and sawn ilex,°   *holm oak*
Hung all the place under the sky with wreaths
And crowned it with funereal cypress boughs.
675   On the pyre's top she put a sword he left
With clothing, and an effigy on a couch,
Her mind fixed now ahead on what would come.
Around the pyre stood altars, and the priestess,
Hair unbound, called in a voice of thunder

---

7. The garden tended by the Hesperides, the daughters of Hesperus (West) and Atlas, was traditionally located beyond the Atlas mountains at the western border of the Ocean. The garden contained a tree of golden apples given by Earth to Hera following her marriage. The tree was guarded by a dragon, who was slain by Hercules.

8. Another tradition made the Hesperides the daughters of Night and Erebus. As is his custom, Virgil combines elements of different versions of the myth in Dido's description.

680   Upon three hundred gods, on Erebus,
        On Chaos, and on triple Hecatë,
        Three-faced Diana.[9] Then she sprinkled drops
        Purportedly from the fountain of Avernus.[1]
        Rare herbs were brought out, reaped at the new moon
685   By scythes of bronze, and juicy with a milk
        Of dusky venom; then the rare love-charm
        Or caul torn from the brow of a birthing foal
        And snatched away before the mother found it.
        Dido herself with consecrated grain
690   In her pure hands, as she went near the altars,
        Freed one foot from sandal straps, let fall
        Her dress ungirdled, and, now sworn to death,
        Called on the gods and stars that knew her fate.
        She prayed then to whatever power may care
695   In comprehending justice for the grief
        Of lovers bound unequally by love.

        The night had come, and weary in every land
        Men's bodies took the boon of peaceful sleep.
        The woods and the wild seas had quieted
700   At that hour when the stars are in mid-course
        And every field is still; cattle and birds
        With vivid wings that haunt the limpid lakes
        Or nest in thickets in the country places
        All were asleep under the silent night.
705   Not, though, the agonized Phoenician queen:
        She never slackened into sleep and never
        Allowed the tranquil night to rest
        Upon her eyelids or within her heart.
        Her pain redoubled; love came on again,
710   Devouring her, and on her bed she tossed
        In a great surge of anger.
                                    So awake,
        She pressed these questions, musing to herself:

        "Look now, what can I do? Turn once again
        To the old suitors, only to be laughed at—
715   Begging a marriage with Numidians
        Whom I disdained so often? Then what? Trail
        The Ilian ships and follow like a slave
        Commands of Trojans? Seeing them so agreeable,
        In view of past assistance and relief,
720   So thoughtful their unshaken gratitude?
        Suppose I wished it, who permits or takes

---

9. Hecatë was a sinister goddess associated with magic, witchcraft, the night, the underworld, and crossroads, which she haunted. She was frequently depicted with three faces representing her three aspects and sometimes identified with Artemis (Roman: Diana).

1. A lake near Cumae and Naples. Near it is a cave reputed to contain an entrance to the underworld (see bk. 6). Avernus was used by Virgil and others to refer to the underworld in general.

Aboard their proud ships one they so dislike?
Poor lost soul, do you not yet grasp or feel
The treachery of the line of Laömedon?
725   What then? Am I to go alone, companion
Of the exultant sailors in their flight?
Or shall I set out in their wake, with Tyrians,
With all my crew close at my side, and send
The men I barely tore away from Tyre
730   To sea again, making them hoist their sails
To more sea-winds? No: die as you deserve,
Give pain quietus° with a steel blade.   rest
                          Sister,
You are the one who gave way to my tears
In the beginning, burdened a mad queen
735   With sufferings, and thrust me on my enemy.
It was not given me to lead my life
Without new passion, innocently, the way
Wild creatures live, and not to touch these depths.
The vow I took to the ashes of Sychaeus
740   Was not kept."
                          So she broke out afresh
In bitter mourning. On his high stern deck
Aeneas, now quite certain of departure,
Everything ready, took the boon of sleep,
In dream the figure of the god returned
745   With looks reproachful as before: he seemed
Again to warn him, being like Mercury
In every way, in voice, in golden hair,
And in the bloom of youth.
                          "Son of the goddess,
Sleep away this crisis, can you still?
750   Do you not see the dangers growing round you,
Madman, from now on? Can you not hear
The offshore westwind blow? The woman hatches
Plots and drastic actions in her heart,
Resolved on death now, whipping herself on
755   To heights of anger. Will you not be gone
In flight, while flight is still within your power?
Soon you will see the offing boil with ships
And glare with torches; soon again
The waterfront will be alive with fires,
760   If Dawn comes while you linger in this country.
Ha! Come, break the spell! Woman's a thing
Forever fitful and forever changing."

At this he merged into the darkness. Then
As the abrupt phantom filled him with fear,
765   Aeneas broke from sleep and roused his crewmen:
"Up, turn out now! Oarsmen, take your thwarts!
Shake out sail! Look here, for the second time

A god from heaven's high air is goading me
To hasten our break away, to cut the cables.
770 Holy one, whatever god you are,
We go with you, we act on your command
Most happily! Be near, graciously help us,
Make the stars in heaven propitious ones!"

He pulled his sword aflash out of its sheath
775 And struck at the stern hawser.° All the men   mooring cable
Were gripped by his excitement to be gone,
And hauled and hustled. Ships cast off their moorings,
And an array of hulls hid inshore water
As oarsmen churned up foam and swept to sea.

780 Soon early Dawn, quitting the saffron bed
Of old Tithonus,[2] cast new light on earth,
And as air grew transparent, from her tower
The queen caught sight of ships on the seaward reach
With sails full and the wind astern. She knew
785 The waterfront now empty, bare of oarsmen.
Beating her lovely breast three times, four times,
And tearing her golden hair,

"O Jupiter,"
She said, "will this man go, will he have mocked
My kingdom, stranger that he was and is?
790 Will they not snatch up arms and follow him
From every quarter of the town? And dockhands
Tear our ships from moorings? On! Be quick
With torches! Give out arms! Unship the oars!
What am I saying? Where am I? What madness
795 Takes me out of myself? Dido, poor soul,
Your evil doing has come home to you.
Then was the right time, when you offered him
A royal scepter. See the good faith and honor
Of one they say bears with him everywhere
800 The hearthgods of his country! One who bore
His father, spent with age, upon his shoulders!
Could I not then have torn him limb from limb
And flung the pieces on the sea?[3] His company,
Even Ascanius could I not have minced
805 And served up to his father at a feast?[4]
The luck of battle might have been in doubt—
So let it have been! Whom had I to fear,

---

2. In Greek mythology, Tithonus, a son of Laomedon and the brother of Priam, was loved by Eos (Roman: Aurora), the goddess of Dawn. She begged Zeus to make Tithonus immortal but forgot to ask for eternal youth for him as well.

3. As Medea did to her brother, Apsyrtus, to aid her escape with her lover, Jason. In revenge for Jason's later betrayal of her, she killed their two children as well. See Euripides' *Medea* (page 281).

4. When Procne, daughter of a legendary king of Athens, discovered that her husband, Tereus, had raped and mutilated her sister, Philomela, she killed their son, Itys, and served him to his father as punishment.

Being sure to die? I could have carried torches
Into his camp, filled passage ways with flame,
810 Annihilated father and son and followers
And given my own life on top of all!
O Sun, scanning with flame all works of earth,
And thou, O Juno, witness and go-between
Of my long miseries; and Hecatë,
815 Screeched for at night at crossroads in the cities;
And thou, avenging Furies, and all gods
On whom Elissa dying may call: take notice,
Overshadow this hell with your high power,
As I deserve, and hear my prayer!
820 If by necessity that impious wretch
Must find his haven and come safe to land,
If so Jove's destinies require, and this,
His end in view, must stand, yet all the same
When hard beset in war by a brave people,
825 Forced to go outside his boundaries
And torn from Iulus, let him beg assistance,
Let him see the unmerited deaths of those
Around and with him, and accepting peace
On unjust terms, let him not, even so,
830 Enjoy his kingdom or the life he longs for,
But fall in battle before his time and lie
Unburied on the sand! This I implore,
This is my last cry, as my last blood flows.
Then, O my Tyrians, besiege with hate
835 His progeny and all his race to come:
Make this your offering to my dust. No love,
No pact must be between our peoples; No,
But rise up from my bones, avenging spirit!
Harry with fire and sword the Dardan countrymen
840 Now, or hereafter, at whatever time
The strength will be afforded. Coast with coast
In conflict, I implore, and sea with sea,
And arms with arms: may they contend in war,
Themselves and all the children of their children!"[5]

845 Now she took thought of one way or another,
At the first chance, to end her hated life,
And briefly spoke to Barcë, who had been
Sychaeus' nurse; her own an urn of ash
Long held in her ancient fatherland.
                                    "Dear nurse,
850 Tell Sister Anna to come here, and have her
Quickly bedew herself with running water

5. Virgil creates a myth of the origins of the conflict between Carthage and Rome. More immediately, he motivates the difficulty faced by the Trojans when they reach Latium in defeating an obviously inferior foe.

Before she brings our victims for atonement.
Let her come that way. And you, too, put on
Pure wool around your brows. I have a mind
855 To carry out that rite to Stygian Jove[6]
That I have readied here, and put an end
To my distress, committing to the flames
The pyre of that miserable Dardan."

At this with an old woman's eagerness
860 Barcë hurried away. And Dido's heart
Beat wildly at the enormous thing afoot.
She rolled her bloodshot eyes, her quivering cheeks
Were flecked with red as her sick pallor grew
Before her coming death. Into the court
865 She burst her way, then at her passion's height
She climbed the pyre and bared the Dardan sword—
A gift desired once, for no such need.
Her eyes now on the Trojan clothing there
And the familiar bed, she paused a little,
870 Weeping a little, mindful, then lay down
And spoke her last words:
                                        "Remnants dear to me
While god and fate allowed it, take this breath
And give me respite from these agonies.
I lived my life out to the very end
875 And passed the stages Fortune had appointed.
Now my tall shade goes to the underworld.
I built a famous town, saw my great walls,
Avenged my husband, made my hostile brother
Pay for his crime. Happy, alas, too happy,
880 If only the Dardanian keels had never
Beached on our coast." And here she kissed the bed.
"I die unavenged," she said, "but let me die.
This way, this way, a blessed relief to go
Into the undergloom. Let the cold Trojan,
885 Far at sea, drink in this conflagration
And take with him the omen of my death!"

Amid these words her household people saw her
Crumpled over the steel blade, and the blade
Aflush with red blood, drenched her hands. A scream
890 Pierced the high chambers. Now through the shocked city
Rumor went rioting, as wails and sobs
With women's outcry echoed in the palace
And heaven's high air gave back the beating din,

34

6. Dis, god of the underworld, "ruler of the Styx."

As though all Carthage or old Tyre fell
895   To storming enemies, and, out of hand,
        Flames billowed on the roofs of men and gods.
        Her sister heard the trembling, faint with terror,
        Lacerating her face, beating her breast,
        Ran through the crowd to call the dying queen:

900   "It came to this, then, sister? You deceived me?
        The pyre meant this, altars and fires meant this?
        What shall I mourn first, being abandoned? Did you
        Scorn your sister's company in death?
        You should have called me out to the same fate!
905   The same blade's edge and hurt, at the same hour,
        Should have taken us off. With my own hands
        Had I to build this pyre, and had I to call
        Upon our country's gods, that in the end
        With you placed on it there, O heartless one,
910   I should be absent? You have put to death
        Yourself and me, the people and the fathers
        Bred in Sidon, and your own new city.
        Give me fresh water, let me bathe her wound
        And catch upon my lips any last breath
915   Hovering over hers."
                              Now she had climbed
        The topmost steps and took her dying sister
        Into her arms to cherish, with a sob,
        Using her dress to stanch the dark blood flow.
        But Dido trying to lift her heavy eyes
920   Fainted again. Her chest-wound whistled air.
        Three times she struggled up on one elbow
        And each time fell back on the bed. Her gaze
        Went wavering as she looked for heaven's light
        And groaned at finding it. Almighty Juno,
925   Filled with pity for this long ordeal
        And difficult passage, now sent Iris[7] down
        Out of Olympus to set free
        The wrestling spirit from the body's hold.
        For since she died, not at her fated span
930   Nor as she merited, but before her time
        Enflamed and driven mad, Proserpina
        Had not yet plucked from her the golden hair,
        Delivering her to Orcus of the Styx.[8]
        So humid Iris through bright heaven flew

---

7. The goddess of the rainbow, and also messenger of the gods, especially Hera/Juno.

8. Proserpina (Greek: Persephone) was the goddess of the underworld and the wife of Dis (Greek: Hades). In sacrifices, the hair of the victim would be removed and offered as first fruits. When men and women died at their appointed time, Proserpina herself was said to cut their locks for a similar reason; however, she cannot do this for the untimely dead, so Iris is sent out of special compassion in her place.

935   On saffron-yellow wings, and in her train
        A thousand hues shimmered before the sun.
        At Dido's head she came to rest.

                          "This token
        Sacred to Dis I bear away as bidden
        And free you from your body."

                             Saying this,
940   She cut a lock of hair. Along with it
        Her body's warmth fell into dissolution,
        And out into the winds her life withdrew.

[*Leaving Carthage, the Trojans stop again at Drepinum in Sicily, where they conduct funeral games for the anniversary of Anchises' death. The games—naval and foot races, boxing, and archery—are interrupted when the women of Troy, goaded by Juno, set fire to the ships. Anchises visits Aeneas in a dream, telling him that he must descend to the underworld to meet him. To travel through the underworld, Aeneas finds the Sibyl of Cumaea to advise and guide him. She instructs him to find a golden bough to present to Persephone, Queen of the Dead. Aeneas begins his descent into the underworld, meeting the three-headed dog Cerberus, crossing the Styx, and passing through the abysses of Hell. Aeneas finally enters the fields of Elysium, where he meets his father who explains how most souls are purified and reincarnated, but those who have lived extraordinarily ethical lives are permitted to stay in Elysium. Aeneas disembarks at the mouth of the Tiber, and the fulfillment of certain signs leads him to recognize the land promised him. He makes a pact with King Latinus, which Juno disrupts by sending the Fury Allecto to assail Latinus's wife, Amata, and the Rutulian leader, Turnus. The pact is broken, and a powerful alliance of Italian peoples marches on the Trojan camp. Following divine advice, Aeneas sails up the Tiber in search of aid, where he finds Evander, king of a small nation of Arcadians on the site where Rome one day will be. The two leaders make an alliance, and Evander entrusts his son, Pallas, to Aeneas's care in the war. Aeneas collects further allies, and his mother presents him with a suit of armor made by Vulcan, including a shield adorned with scenes from the future history of Rome. Turnus seizes on Aeneas's absence to attack the Trojan camp, nearly succeeding in taking it. The return of Aeneas with his allies tips the balance in the other direction. Turnus kills Pallas in single combat, stripping him of his sword belt, which he dons as a token of his victory. Further battles ensue, including the death of the virgin warrior Camilla on the Latin side. Turnus accepts decisive single combat with Aeneas, but Juno persuades his sister, the nymph Juturna, to cause the truce to fail, and the seemingly endless battle recommences.*]

from Book 12

[The Death of Turnus]

        Omnipotent Olympus' king meanwhile
1070   Had words for Juno, as she watched the combat
        Out of a golden cloud. He said:

                        "My consort,
        What will the end be? What is left for you?

	You yourself know, and say you know, Aeneas
	Born for heaven, tutelary° of this land, *protector*
1075	By fate to be translated to the stars.
	What do you plan? What are you hoping for,
	Keeping your seat apart in the cold clouds?
	Fitting, was it, that a mortal archer
	Wound an immortal? That a blade let slip
1080	Should be restored to Turnus, and new force
	Accrue to a beaten man? Without your help
	What could Juturna do?[1] Come now, at last
	Have done, and heed our pleading, and give way.
	Let yourself no longer be consumed
1085	Without relief by all that inward burning;
	Let care and trouble not forever come to me
	From your sweet lips. The finish is at hand.
	You had the power to harry men of Troy
	By land and sea, to light the fires of war
1090	Beyond belief, to scar a family
	With mourning before marriage. I forbid
	Your going further."[2]

                       So spoke Jupiter,
And with a downcast look Juno replied:

	"Because I know that is your will indeed,
1095	Great Jupiter, I left the earth below,
	Though sore at heart, and left the side of Turnus.
	Were it not so, you would not see me here
	Suffering all that passes, here alone,
	Resting on air. I should be armed in flames
1100	At the very battle-line, dragging the Trojans
	Into a deadly action. I persuaded
	Juturna—I confess—to help her brother
	In his hard lot, and I approved her daring
	Greater difficulties to save his life,
1105	But not that she should fight with bow and arrow.
	This I swear by Styx' great fountainhead
	Inexorable, which high gods hold in awe.[3]
	I yield now and for all my hatred leave
	This battlefield. But one thing not retained
1110	By fate I beg for Latium, for the future
	Greatness of your kin: when presently
	They crown peace with a happy wedding day—
	So let it be—and merge their laws and treaties,
	Never command the land's own Latin folk

1. Jupiter is referring to earlier incidents in the war involving divine meddling. The water nymph Juturna was the sister and protectress of Turnus.

2. Jupiter outlines the limits of Juno's power against fate, which legislates the outcome of events but not necessarily the way in which they unroll.

3. It was customary for the Olympian gods to swear on the river Styx. Such oaths were held by the gods to be inviolable.

1115	To change their old name, to become new Trojans,
	Known as Teucrians; never make them alter
	Dialect or dress. Let Latium be.
	Let there be Alban kings for generations,
	And let Italian valor be the strength
1120	Of Rome in after times. Once and for all
	Troy fell, and with her name let her lie fallen."[4]

The author of men and of the world replied
With a half-smile:
                    "Sister of Jupiter
Indeed you are, and Saturn's other child,
1125 To feel such anger, stormy in your breast.
But come, no need; put down this fit of rage.
I grant your wish. I yield, I am won over
Willingly. Ausonian folk will keep
Their fathers' language and their way of life,
1130 And, that being so, their name. The Teucrians
Will mingle and be submerged, incorporated.
Rituals and observances of theirs
I'll add, but make them Latin, one in speech.
The race to come, mixed with Ausonian blood,
1135 Will outdo men and gods in its devotion,
You shall see—and no nation on earth
Will honor and worship you so faithfully."[5]

To all this Juno nodded in assent
And, gladdened by his promise, changed her mind.
1140 Then she withdrew from sky and cloud.
                                    That done,
The Father set about a second plan—
To take Juturna from her warring brother.
Stories are told of twin fiends, called the Dirae,[6]
Whom, with Hell's Megaera, deep Night bore
1145 In one birth. She entwined their heads with coils
Of snakes and gave them wings to race the wind.
Before Jove's throne, a step from the cruel king,
These twins attend him and give piercing fear
To ill mankind, when he who rules the gods
1150 Deals out appalling death and pestilence,
Or war to terrify our wicked cities.[7]
Jove now dispatched one of these, swift from heaven,
Bidding her be an omen to Juturna.
Down she flew, in a whirlwind borne to earth,

---

4. Virgil provides an explanation for the disappearance of any historical trace of the Trojan origins of Rome.

5. The temple of Jupiter Capitolinus was dedicated to Jupiter, Juno, and Minerva.

6. The Latin word for the Furies, whom the tragedian Aeschylus called the daughters of Night. Megaera was one of the three Furies named in antiquity.

7. Here, rather than summoned from the underworld, the Furies are depicted as acting in the service of Olympian justice.

1155 Just like an arrow driven through a cloud
   From a taut string, an arrow armed with gall
   Of deadly posion, shot by a Parthian[8]—
   A Parthian or a Cretan—for a wound
   Immedicable; whizzing unforeseen
1160 It goes through racing shadows: so the spawn
   Of Night went diving downward to the earth.

   On seeing Trojan troops drawn up in face
   Of Turnus' army, she took on at once
   The shape of that small bird that perches late
1165 At night on tombs or desolate roof-tops
   And troubles darkness with a gruesome song.[9]
   Shrunk to that form, the fiend in Turnus' face
   Went screeching, flitting, flitting to and fro
   And beating with her wings against his shield.
1170 Unstrung by numbness, faint and strange, he felt
   His hackles rise, his voice choke in his throat.
   As for Juturna, when she knew the wings,
   The shriek to be the fiend's, she tore her hair,
   Despairing, then she fell upon her cheeks
1175 With nails, upon her breast with clenched hands.

   "Turnus, how can your sister help you now?
   What action is still open to me, soldierly
   Though I have been? Can I by any skill
   Hold daylight for you? Can I meet and turn
1180 This deathliness away? Now I withdraw,
   Now leave this war. Indecent birds, I fear you;
   Spare me your terror. Whip-lash of your wings
   I recognize, that ghastly sound, and guess
   Great-hearted Jupiter's high cruel commands.
1185 Returns for my virginity, are they?
   He gave me life eternal—to what end?
   Why has mortality been taken from me?
   Now beyond question I could put a term
   To all my pain, and go with my poor brother
1190 Into the darkness, his companion there.
   Never to die? Will any brook of mine
   Without you, brother, still be sweet to me?
   If only earth's abyss were wide enough
   To take me downward, goddess though I am,
1195 To join the shades below!"
          So she lamented,
   Then with a long sigh, covering up her head
   In her grey mantle, sank to the river's depth.

43

---

8. The Parthians held an empire in what is now eastern Iran.
9. The Fury takes the form of an owl, a bird closely associated with death.

Aeneas moved against his enemy
And shook his heavy pine-tree spear. He called
1200   From his hot heart:
               "Rearmed now, why so slow?
Why, even now, fall back? The contest here
Is not a race, but fighting to the death
With spear and sword. Take on all shapes there are,
Summon up all your nerve and skill, choose any
1205   Footing, fly among the stars, or hide
In caverned earth—"
                   The other shook his head,
Saying:
         "I do not fear your taunting fury,
Arrogant prince. It is the gods I fear
And Jove my enemy."
                He said no more,
1210   But looked around him. Then he saw a stone,
Enormous, ancient, set up there to prevent
Landowners' quarrels. Even a dozen picked men
Such as the earth produces in our day
Could barely lift and shoulder it. He swooped
1215   And wrenched it free, in one hand, then rose up
To his heroic height, ran a few steps,
And tried to hurl the stone against his foe—
But as he bent and as he ran
And as he hefted and propelled the weight
1220   He did not know himself. His knees gave way,
His blood ran cold and froze. The stone itself,
Tumbling through space, fell short and had no impact.

Just as in dreams when the night-swoon of sleep
Weighs on our eyes, it seems we try in vain
1225   To keep on running, try with all our might,
But in the midst of effort faint and fail;
Our tongue is powerless, familiar strength
Will not hold up our body, not a sound
Or word will come: just so with Turnus now:
1230   However bravely he made shift to fight
The immortal fiend blocked and frustrated him.
Flurrying images passed through his mind.
He gazed at the Rutulians, and beyond them,
Gazed at the city, hesitant, in dread.
1235   He trembled now before the poised spear-shaft
And saw no way to escape; he had no force
With which to close, or reach his foe, no chariot
And no sign of the charioteer, his sister.[1]
At a dead loss he stood. Aeneas made
1240   His deadly spear flash in the sun and aimed it,

---

1. In an earlier scene in Book 12, where Juturna replaces Turnus's charioteer and spirits him away from the scene of battle.

Narrowing his eyes for a lucky hit.
Then, distant still, he put his body's might
Into the cast. Never a stone that soared
From a wall-battering catapult went humming

1245 Loud as this, nor with so great a crack
Burst ever a bolt of lightning. It flew on
Like a black whirlwind bringing devastation,
Pierced with a crash the rim of sevenfold shield,
Cleared the cuirass'° edge, and passed clean through   *breastplate's*

1250 The middle of Turnus' thigh. Force of the blow
Brought the huge man to earth, his knees buckling,
And a groan swept the Rutulians as they rose,
A groan heard echoing on all sides from all
The mountain range, and echoed by the forests.

1255 The man brought down, brought low, lifted his eyes
And held his right hand out to make his plea:

"Clearly I earned this, and I ask no quarter.
Make the most of your good fortune here.
If you can feel a father's grief—and you, too,

1260 Had such a father in Anchises—then
Let me bespeak your mercy for old age
In Daunus,° and return me, or my body,   *Turnus's father*
Stripped, if you will, of life, to my own kin.
You have defeated me. The Ausonians

1265 Have seen me in defeat, spreading my hands.
Lavinia is your bride. But go no further
Out of hatred."
                    Fierce under arms, Aeneas
Looked to and fro, and towered, and stayed his hand
Upon the sword-hilt. Moment by moment now

1270 What Turnus said began to bring him round
From indecision. Then to his glance appeared
The accurst swordbelt surmounting Turnus' shoulder,
Shining with its familiar studs—the strap
Young Pallas wore when Turnus wounded him

1275 And left him dead upon the field; now Turnus
Bore that enemy token on his shoulder—
Enemy still. For when the sight came home to him,
Aeneas raged at the relic of his anguish
Worn by this man as trophy. Blazing up

1280 And terrible in his anger, he called out:

"You in your plunder, torn from one of mine,
Shall I be robbed of you? This wound will come
From Pallas: Pallas makes this offering
And from your criminal blood exacts his due."

1285 He sank his blade in fury in Turnus' chest.
Then all the body slackened in death's chill,
And with a groan for that indignity
His spirit fled into the gloom below

The poet Publius Ovidius Naso had the misfortune to experience the extremes of life in imperial Rome: after some years at the height of fame in the center of the world, he was abruptly exiled to the far reaches of the empire, on the weather-beaten shore of the Black Sea, where, he complained bitterly, the barbarous inhabitants couldn't even understand Latin and he lived in fear for his life. While we will never know the precise reasons behind this precipitous change in fortunes, the usual explanation that he was accused of immorality does at least resonate with the irreverent and unpredictable tone of Ovid's poetry. For example, the erotic verses that first made his name—the *Loves* (sometime after 20 B.C.E.), *The Art of Love* (c. 1 B.C.E.), and *Remedy of Love* (1 B.C.E.– 1 C.E.)—sometimes celebrate and sometimes satirize the single-minded pursuit of sexual pleasure. The *Metamorphoses* (2–8 C.E.), Ovid's *magnum opus,* recounts the history of the world from the first creation through the reign of Augustus. It too is a double-edged work, a collection of wondrous transformations and beautiful myths but also a chronicle of the disaster and suffering of mortals and the misdeeds perpetrated by the ancient gods.

Much about the *Metamorphoses* can be viewed as a response to Virgil's epic of the founding of Rome, the *Aeneid* (19 B.C.E.), and to Virgil's status as the preeminent poet of his time. Ovid was seventeen years Virgil's junior and spent his formative years under the peace of Augustus rather than the tumultuous years of civil war that forged Virgil's poetry. Consequently, where Virgil's concern had been how best to represent the costs of war and the demands of peace, Ovid's was how to compose a great work when Virgil's had already been written. There are many underlying similarities in theme and structure. Both poems employ hexameter, the six-footed meter characteristic of classical epic; both are also epic in length, although Ovid divides his poem into fifteen books rather than the *Aeneid*'s twelve or the twenty-four of the Homeric poems. Both poems place the Roman Empire of Augustus at the end point of their narratives, and both refer to their lord and patron as a god. Moreover, the *Metamorphoses* includes within its historical trajectory the *Aeneid*'s material—the fall of Troy and the difficult journey of Aeneas from Troy to found Rome. Nevertheless, these similarities serve more to emphasize the differences than to efface them.

Ovid calls his poem a "book of changes" in the opening verses, and it is truly a dazzling compendium of transformations. Nothing is stable in the world of the *Metamorphoses*. There is no unifying protagonist, no single character who makes more than a few cameo appearances, and no continuity of setting or chronology. Ovid took as his raw material basically everything that had been written in Greek and Latin up to that point, with a particular focus on the many myths about the interaction, primarily erotic, between the Olympian gods and the mortals of the ancient world. Rather than link his many episodes in any consistently causal manner, Ovid chose a looser range of associations: sometimes there is a similarity in type of transformation; sometimes the tale of one family's child will lead to the story of another child of the same generation; and sometimes one story frames a series of further, unrelated tales. So when Orpheus loses Eurydice and sits down to sing of his sorrows, he sings about other transformations. Part of the artistry of the *Metamorphoses* lies in the way it encourages us to seek meanings and connections not just along the chain of its interlinked tales but between the different levels of its sets of tales inside tales, or between the different parts of a myth split up and scattered throughout the poem for the reader to reconstruct.

In the *Aeneid,* the reader is constantly being reminded of the role played by each event in the grand narrative of the founding of Rome. The *Metamorphoses,* by contrast, is resolutely focused on how a particular event looks and feels to its participants. We are given but a single glimpse of the weaver Arachne, but it is the defining moment of her life: her weaving duel with the goddess Minerva. Ovid paints the duel in great detail, especially the fabrics themselves, for they too tell cautionary tales of transformation. Minerva weaves scenes of contest, "the sorry fate" of mortals who challenged gods; Arachne responds with scenes of divine deception and abuse of mortals. The climax of nearly every episode is the transformation scene, where Ovid shows the full range of his powers of description and variation, always catching in words the moment of change, the moment when the person being transformed is neither one thing nor the other. Here is Arachne's metamorphosis into a spider:

> Touched by the bitter lotion, all her hair
> Falls off and with it go her nose and ears.
> Her head shrinks tiny; her whole body's small;
> Instead of legs slim fingers line her sides.
> The rest is belly; yet from that she sends
> A fine-spun thread and, as a spider, still
> Weaving her web, pursues her former skill.

Characteristically, the change is both beautiful and horrible, and Arachne is both utterly transformed and yet strangely still herself.

The closest thing to a guiding philosophy in the *Metamorphoses,* a program that would gather its disparate gems into a fixed setting, is the speech of the Greek mathematician Pythagoras in Book 15. This speech, the longest in the poem, asserts what looks like a general moral: "Nothing retains its form; new shapes from old / Nature, the great inventor, ceaselessly / Contrives." For Pythagoras, the principle of change implies the transmigration of souls from one body to the next; every thing and every creature on the earth is sentient, and the world's souls are constantly migrating from one being to another. Pythagoras, consequently, is a vegetarian. Many scholars have taken Pythagoras seriously as the voice of the author and argued that his speech gives shape and substance to the poem; many others have argued that it is just another Ovidian parody of a blowhard who takes himself too seriously. Strong arguments can be made both ways, and we need not exclude the possibility that Ovid has perversely placed the secrets of his poem's meaning in the mouth of a character he may also have thought was ridiculous. There is great pleasure to be found in the endless invention and playfulness of the *Metamorphoses* and great satisfaction in its profound glimpses of human emotions and tragedy. Perhaps its most enduring quality, however, and what has made it such an influential compendium of myth over the past two millennia, is the myriad combinations and recombinations of the extremes of experience that Ovid achieves at every turn in his exploration of the meanings of change in our lives.

PRONUNCIATIONS:
Arachne: ah-RAK-nee
Daedalus: DEH-dah-luhs
Echo: EH-koh
Eurydice: yur-RI-di-see
Ganymede: GA-ni-meed
Hyacinth: HAI-uh-sinth
Icarus: IH-kah-ruhs
Metamorphoses: me-tuh-MOR-foh-seez
Minotaur: MI-nah-tawr

Narcissus: nahr-SI-suhs
Orpheus: OR-fee-uhs
Phaethon: FAY-tuhn
Pygmalion: pig-MAY-lee-uhn
Pythagoras: pi-THA-gor-uhs
Tiresias: tai-REE-see-uhs

from Metamorphoses[1]

from Book 1

[PROLOGUE]

Of bodies changed to other forms I tell;
You Gods, who have yourselves wrought every change,
Inspire my enterprise and lead my lay
In one continuous song from nature's first
5 Remote beginnings to our modern times.

from Book 3

[TIRESIAS]

While down on earth as destiny ordained
These things took place, and Bacchus, babe twice born,
Was cradled safe and sound,[1] it chanced that Jove,
Well warmed with nectar, laid his weighty cares
5 Aside and, Juno too in idle mood,
The pair were gaily joking, and Jove said
"You women get more pleasure out of love
Than we men do, I'm sure." She disagreed.
So they resolved to get the views of wise
10 Tiresias.[2] He knew both sides of love.
For once in a green copse when two huge snakes
Were mating, he attacked them with his stick,
And was transformed (a miracle!) from man
To woman; and spent seven autumns so;
15 Till in the eighth he saw the snakes once more
And said "If striking you has magic power
To change the striker to the other sex,
I'll strike you now again." He struck the snakes
And so regained the shape he had at birth.

---

1. Translated by A. D. Melville.

1. Bacchus (Greek: Dionysus) was the son of Jove and Cadmus's daughter Semele. He is called "twice born" because after his mother was killed by a trick of the jealous Juno, Jove sewed him up in his thigh. The god of wine and intoxication, Bacchus was associated with the ecstatic rituals of his Bacchantes, or female followers.

2. The resident seer of Thebes, Tiresias is the most celebrated prophet of classical myth and literature. Odysseus consults his ghost in the *Odyssey*, and Tiresias plays a central role in *Oedipus the King*.

20	Asked then to give his judgement on the joke,
	He found for Jove; and Juno (so it's said)
	Took umbrage beyond reason, out of all
	Proportion, and condemned her judge to live
	In the black night of blindness evermore.
25	But the Almighty Father (since no god
	Has right to undo what any god has done)
	For his lost sight gave him the gift to see
	What things should come, the power of prophecy,
	An honour to relieve that penalty.

[NARCISSUS and ECHO]

30	So blind Tiresias gave to all who came
	Faultless and sure reply and far and wide
	Through all Boeotia's cities[3] spread his fame.
	To test his truth and trust the first who tried
	Was wave-blue water-nymph Liriope,
35	Whom once Cephisus in his sinuous flow
	Embracing held and ravished. In due time
	The lovely sprite bore a fine infant boy,
	From birth adorable, and named her son
	Narcissus; and of him she asked the seer,
40	Would he long years and ripe old age enjoy,
	Who answered "If he shall himself not know."
	For long his words seemed vain; what they concealed
	The lad's strange death and stranger love revealed.
	Narcissus now had reached his sixteenth year
45	And seemed both man and boy; and many a youth
	And many a girl desired him, but hard pride
	Ruled in that delicate frame, and never a youth
	And never a girl could touch his haughty heart.
	Once as he drove to nets the frightened deer
50	A strange-voiced nymph observed him, who must speak
	If any other speak and cannot speak
	Unless another speak, resounding Echo.
	Echo was still a body, not a voice,
	But talkative as now, and with the same
55	Power of speaking, only to repeat,
	As best she could, the last of many words.
	Juno had made her so; for many a time,
	When the great goddess might have caught the nymphs
	Lying with Jove upon the mountainside,
60	Echo discreetly kept her talking till
	The nymphs had fled away; and when at last
	The goddess saw the truth, "Your tongue," she said,

3. Boeotia was a region of central Greece. Thebes, in the south, was its dominant city.

"With which you tricked me, now its power shall lose,
Your voice avail but for the briefest use."
65   The event confirmed the threat: when speaking ends,
All she can do is double each last word,
And echo back again the voice she's heard.
      Now when she saw Narcissus wandering
In the green byways, Echo's heart was fired;
70   And stealthily she followed, and the more
She followed him, the nearer flamed her love,
As when a torch is lit and from the tip
The leaping sulphur grasps the offered flame.
She longed to come to him with winning words,
75   To urge soft pleas, but nature now opposed;
She might not speak the first but—what she might—
Waited for words her voice could say again.
      It chanced Narcissus, searching for his friends,
Called "Anyone here?" and Echo answered "Here!"
80   Amazed he looked all round and, raising his voice,
Called "Come this way!" and Echo called "This way!"
He looked behind and, no one coming, shouted
"Why run away?" and heard his words again.
He stopped and, cheated by the answering voice,
85   Called "Join me here!" and she, never more glad
To give her answer, answered "Join me here!"
And graced her words and ran out from the wood
To throw her longing arms around his neck.
He bolted, shouting "Keep your arms from me!
90   Be off! I'll die before I yield to you."
And all she answered was "I yield to you."
Shamed and rejected in the woods she hides
And has her dwelling in the lonely caves;
Yet still her love endures and grows on grief,
95   And weeping vigils waste her frame away;
Her body shrivels, all its moisture dries;
Only her voice and bones are left; at last
Only her voice, her bones are turned to stone.
So in the woods she hides and hills around,
100 For all to hear, alive, but just a sound.
      Thus had Narcissus mocked her; others too,
Hill-nymphs and water-nymphs and many a man
He mocked; till one scorned youth, with raised hands, prayed,
"So may *he* love—and never win his love!"
105 And Nemesis[4] approved the righteous prayer.
      There was a pool, limpid and silvery,
Whither no shepherd came nor any herd,
Nor mountain goat; and never bird nor beast
Nor falling branch disturbed its shining peace;

4. Nemesis personified the concept of divine retribution for human pride; she was also worshipped as a goddess.

110 Grass grew around it, by the water fed,
    And trees to shield it from the warming sun.
    Here—for the chase and heat had wearied him—
    The boy lay down, charmed by the quiet pool,
    And, while he slaked his thirst, another thirst
115 Grew; as he drank he saw before his eyes
    A form, a face, and loved with leaping heart
    A hope unreal and thought the shape was real.
    Spellbound he saw himself, and motionless
    Lay like a marble statue staring down.
120 He gazes at his eyes, twin constellation,
    His hair worthy of Bacchus or Apollo,
    His face so fine, his ivory neck, his cheeks
    Smooth, and the snowy pallor and the blush;
    All he admires that all admire in him,
125 Himself he longs for, longs unwittingly,
    Praising is praised, desiring is desired,
    And love he kindles while with love he burns.
    How often in vain he kissed the cheating pool
    And in the water sank his arms to clasp
130 The neck he saw, but could not clasp himself!
    Not knowing what he sees, he adores the sight;
    That false face fools and fuels his delight.
    You simple boy, why strive in vain to catch
    A fleeting image? What you see is nowhere;
135 And what you love—but turn away—you lose!
    You see a phantom of a mirrored shape;
    Nothing itself; with you it came and stays;
    With you it too will go, if you can go!
        No thought of food or rest draws him away;
140 Stretched on the grassy shade he gazes down
    On the false phantom, staring endlessly,
    His eyes his own undoing. Raising himself
    He holds his arms towards the encircling trees
    And cries "You woods, was ever love more cruel!
145 You know! For you are lovers' secret haunts.
    Can you in your long living centuries
    Recall a lad who pined so piteously?
    My joy! I see it; but the joy I see
    I cannot find" (so fondly love is foiled!)
150 "And—to my greater grief—between us lies
    No mighty sea, no long and dusty road,
    Nor mountain range nor bolted barbican.°   *fortification*
    A little water sunders us. He longs
    For my embrace. Why, every time I reach
155 My lips towards the gleaming pool, he strains
    His upturned face to mine. I surely could
    Touch him, so slight the thing that thwarts our love.
    Come forth, whoever you are! Why, peerless boy,

Elude me? Where retreat beyond my reach?
160 My looks, my age—indeed it cannot be
That you should shun—the nymphs have loved me too!
Some hope, some nameless hope, your friendly face
Pledges; and when I stretch my arms to you
You stretch your arms to me, and when I smile
165 You smile, and when I weep, I've often seen
Your tears, and to my nod your nod replies,
And your sweet lips appear to move in speech,
Though to my ears your answer cannot reach.
Oh, I am he! Oh, now I know for sure
170 The image is my own; it's for myself
I burn with love; I fan the flames I feel.
What now? Woo or be wooed? Why woo at all?
My love's myself—my riches beggar me.
Would I might leave my body! I could wish
175 (Strange lover's wish!) my love were not so near!
Now sorrow saps my strength; of my life's span
Not long is left; I die before my prime.
Nor is death sad for death will end my sorrow;
Would he I love might live a long tomorrow!
180 But now we two—one soul—one death will die."
  Distraught he turned towards the face again;
His tears rippled the pool, and darkly then
The troubled water veiled the fading form,
And, as it vanished, "Stay," he shouted, "stay!
185 Oh, cruelty to leave your lover so!
Let me but gaze on what I may not touch
And feed the aching fever in my heart."
Then in his grief he tore his robe and beat
His pale cold fists upon his naked breast,
190 And on his breast a blushing redness spread
Like apples, white in part and partly red,
Or summer grapes whose varying skins assume
Upon the ripening vine a blushing bloom.
And this he saw reflected in the pool,
195 Now still again, and could endure no more.
But as wax melts before a gentle fire,
Or morning frosts beneath the rising sun,
So, by love wasted, slowly he dissolves
By hidden fire consumed. No colour now,
200 Blending the white with red, nor strength remains
Nor will, nor aught that lately seemed so fair,
Nor longer lasts the body Echo loved.
But she, though angry still and unforgetting,
Grieved for the hapless boy, and when he moaned
205 "Alas," with answering sob she moaned "alas,"
And when he beat his hands upon his breast,
She gave again the same sad sounds of woe.

His latest words, gazing and gazing still,
He sighed "alas! the boy I loved in vain!"
210 And these the place repeats, and then "farewell,"
And Echo said "farewell." On the green grass
He drooped his weary head, and those bright eyes
That loved their master's beauty closed in death.
Then still, received into the Underworld,
215 He gazed upon himself in Styx's pool.

His Naiad sisters wailed and sheared their locks
In mourning for their brother; the Dryads too
Wailed[5] and sad Echo wailed in answering woe.
And then the brandished torches, bier and pyre
220 Were ready—but no body anywhere;
And in its stead they found a flower—behold,
White petals clustered round a cup of gold![6]

from Book 6

[ARACHNE]

Pallas[1] had listened to the tale she told
With warm approval of the Muses' song
And of their righteous rage.[2] Then to herself—
"To praise is not enough; I should have praise
5 Myself, not suffer my divinity
To be despised unscathed." She had in mind
Arachne's doom, the girl of Lydia,[3]
Who in the arts of wool-craft claimed renown
(So she had heard) to rival hers. The girl
10 Had no distinction in her place of birth
Or pedigree, only that special skill.
Her father was Idmon of Colophon,
Whose trade it was to dye the thirsty wool
With purple of Phocaea.[4] She had lost
15 Her mother, but she too had been low-born
And matched her husband. Yet in all the towns
Of Lydia Arachne's work had won
A memorable name, although her home
Was humble and Hypaepae where she lived
20 Was humble too. To watch her wondrous work

5. Naiads are freshwater nymphs, or minor female deities, often daughters of river gods; hence their kinship to the river's son, Narcissus. Dryads are tree nymphs.

6. Narcissus is a genus of fragrant, bulbous flowers including the daffodil, jonquil, and the poet's narcissus, which most closely matches Ovid's description.

1. Minerva (Greek: Pallas Athena) was born fully formed from the head of Jove. She was the goddess of crafts, wisdom, and war. She was also the patroness of the Greek city-state of Athens.

2. The nine Muses, goddesses of the arts, especially music and poetry, made their home on Helicon, a mountain in southwest Boeotia. They have just finished relating to Minerva their singing contest with the Pierides, nine daughters of Pierus of Pella in Macedonia. To punish their presumption, the Muses had transformed the sisters into magpies.

3. A region in Asia Minor, now western Turkey.

4. Colophon and Phocaea were Ionian cities in western Asia Minor.

The nymphs would often leave their vine-clad slopes
Of Tmolus, often leave Pactolus' stream,
Delighted both to see the cloth she wove
And watch her working too; such grace she had.
25 Forming the raw wool first into a ball,
Or fingering the flock and drawing out
Again and yet again the fleecy cloud
In long soft threads, or twirling with her thumb,
Her dainty thumb, the slender spindle, or
30 Embroidering the pattern—you would know
Pallas had trained her. Yet the girl denied it
(A teacher so distinguished hurt her pride)
And said, "Let her contend with me. Should I
Lose, there's no forfeit that I would not pay."
35   Pallas disguised herself as an old woman.
A fringe of false grey hair around her brow,
Her tottering steps supported by a stick,
And speaking to the girl, "Not everything
That old age brings," she said, "we'd wish to avoid.
40 With riper years we gain experience.
Heed my advice. Among the world of men
Seek for your wool-craft all the fame you will,
But yield the goddess place, and humbly ask
Pardon for those rash words of yours; she'll give
45 You pardon if you ask." With blazing eyes
Arachne stared at her and left her work.
She almost struck her; anger strong and clear
Glowed as she gave the goddess (in disguise)
Her answer: "You're too old, your brain has gone.
50 You've lived too long, your years have done for you.
Talk to your daughters, talk to your sons' wives!
My own advice is all I need. Don't think
Your words have any weight. My mind's unchanged.
Why doesn't Pallas come herself? Why should
55 She hesitate to match herself with me?"
Then Pallas said, "She's come!" and threw aside
The old crone's guise and stood revealed. The nymphs
And Lydian women knelt in reverence.
Only Arachne had no fear. Yet she
60 Blushed all the same; a sudden colour tinged
Her cheeks against her will, then disappeared;
So when Aurora rises in the dawn,
The eastern sky is red and, as the sun
Climbs, in a little while is pale again.
65   She stood by her resolve, setting her heart,
Her stupid heart, on victory, and rushed
To meet her fate. Nor did the child of Jove
Refuse or warn her further or postpone
The contest. Then, with no delay, they both,

70	Standing apart, set up their separate looms
	And stretched the slender warp. The warp is tied
	To the wide cross-beam; a cane divides the threads;
	The pointed shuttles carry the woof through,
	Sped by their fingers. When it's through the warp,
75	The comb's teeth, tapping, press it into place.
	Both work in haste, their dresses girdled tight
	Below their breasts; the movements of their arms
	Are skilled and sure; their zeal beguiles their toil.
	Here purple threads that Tyrian vats have dyed[5]
80	Are woven in, and subtle delicate tints
	That change insensibly from shade to shade.
	So when the sunshine strikes a shower of rain,
	The bow's huge arc will paint the whole wide sky,
	And countless different colours shine, yet each
85	Gradation dupes the gaze, the tints that touch
	So similar, the extremes so far distinct.
	Threads too of golden wire were woven in,
	And on the loom an ancient tale was traced.[6]
	The rock of Mars in Cecrops' citadel[7]
90	Is Pallas' picture and that old dispute
	About the name of Athens. Twelve great gods,
	Jove in their midst, sit there on lofty thrones,
	Grave and august, each pictured with his own
	Familiar features: Jove in regal grace,
95	The Sea-god standing, striking the rough rock
	With his tall trident, and the wounded rock
	Gushing sea-brine, his proof to clinch his claim.
	Herself she gives a shield, she gives a spear
	Sharp-tipped, she gives a helmet for her head;
100	The aegis guards her breast,[8] and from the earth,
	Struck by her spear, she shows an olive tree,
	Springing pale-green with berries on the boughs;
	The gods admire; and Victory ends the work.
	Yet to provide examples to instruct
105	Her rival what reward she should expect
	For her insensate daring, she designed
	In each of the four corners four small scenes
	Of contest, brightly coloured miniatures.
	There in one corner Thracian Rhodope
110	And Haemon, icy mountains now, but once

---

5. Tyre was a city of the Phoenicians in the ancient Middle East. An important trading center, it founded colonies in Cyprus and Carthage and was famed for its purple dye and its glass.

6. Athena weaves the tale of her dispute with the sea god Neptune (Greek: Poseidon) over who should be the patron deity of Athens.

7. The Areopagus, or "Hill of Mars," was the meeting place of the ancient council of Athens, which took its name from it. Cecrops was the legendary founder of the city.

8. The aegis was a goatskin cloak or breastplate with tassels. Worn by Minerva, it terrified her enemies and granted protection from attack.

Mortals, who claimed the names of gods most high.[9]
Another showed the Pygmy matron's doom,
Her pitiable doom, when Juno won
The contest and transformed her to a crane
115   And made her fight her folk, her kith and kin.[1]
Antigone she pictured too, who once
Challenged the royal consort of great Jove.
And Juno changed her to a bird, and Troy
Availed her nothing nor Laomedon,
120   Her father—no! with snowy feathers clothed,
In self-applause she claps her stork's loud bill.[2]
In the last corner Cinyras, bereaved,
Embraced the temple steps, his daughters' limbs,
And lying on the marble seemed to weep.[3]
125   All round the border ran an olive-branch,
The branch of peace. That was the end, and she
Finished her picture with her own fair tree.°   *the olive*
     Arachne shows Europa cheated by
The bull's disguise, a real bull you'd think,
130   And real sea.[4] The girl was gazing at
The shore she'd left and calling to her friends,
Seeming to dread the leaping billows' touch,
Shrinking and drawing up her feet in fear.
Asterie in the struggling eagle's clutch
135   She wove, and pictured Leda as she lay
Under the white swan's wings, and added too
How Jove once in a satyr's guise had got
Antiope with twins, and, as Amphitryon,
Bedded Alcmena; in a golden shower
140   Fooled Danae, Aegina in a flame,
And as a shepherd snared Mnemosyne,
And as a spotted serpent Proserpine.[5]
Neptune she drew, changed to a savage bull
For love of Canace; and Neptune too
145   Sired, as Enipeus, the Aloidae;

---

9. Rhodope and Haemon were an incestuous brother-and-sister pair who called themselves "Jove" and "Juno" (who were also brother and sister). They were transformed into mountains in Thrace, a region in the southeastern Balkans.

1. Oenoe was a pygmy, one of a race of dwarves located by Greek mythology variously in Thrace, India, the Nile, or elsewhere. The battle between the pygmies and the cranes was a common topic in ancient art and poetry.

2. Antigone (not to be confused with the Theban daughter of Oedipus and Jocasta) was the sister of Priam and daughter of Laomedon of Troy. This is the only known account of her dispute with Juno.

3. Cinyras was an Assyrian king; this is the only known account of his daughter's presumption toward Juno.

4. Arachne's weaving offers a lengthy list of the gods' seductions or rapes of mortals, a number of which Ovid recounts in more detail elsewhere in the poem. Europa was abducted by Jove, who was disguised as a white bull.

5. Asterie was a Titan's daughter; Leda was the mother of Helen, Castor, and Pollux; Antiope bore the Theban twins Amphion and Zethus; Jove fathered Hercules on Alcmena, disguised as her husband, the king of Thebes; Danae bore the hero Perseus; Aegina was a daughter of the river god Asopus, and Aeacus, the son of the union, was the grandfather of both Achilles and Ajax; Jove's seduction of Mnemosyne yielded the nine Muses; Proserpine (Greek: Persephone) was Jove's daughter by Ceres (Greek: Demeter), and their son was the second Dionysus, Dionysus-Zagreus.

Bisaltes' child he cheated as a ram;
The corn's most gracious mother, golden-haired,
Suffered him as a horse, and, as a bird,
The snake-tressed mother of the flying steed;
150 And poor Melantho knew him as a dolphin.[6]
To all of them Arachne gave their own
Features and proper features of the scene.
She wove too Phoebus in a herdsman's guise,
And how he sometimes wore a lion's skin,
155 Sometimes hawk's plumage; how he fooled Isse,
Macareus' daughter, as a shepherd;[7] how
Bacchus with bunches of false grapes deceived
Erigone, and Saturn, as a horse,
Begot the centaur Chiron.[8] Round the edge
160 A narrow band of flowers she designed,
Flowers and clinging ivy intertwined.
  In all that work of hers Pallas could find,
Envy could find, no fault. Incensed at such
Success the warrior goddess, golden-haired,
165 Tore up the tapestry, those crimes of heaven,
And with the boxwood shuttle in her hand
(Box of Cytorus)[9] three times, four times, struck
Arachne on her forehead. The poor wretch,
Unable to endure it, bravely placed
170 A noose around her neck; but, as she hung,
Pallas in pity raised her. "Live!" she said,
"Yes, live but hang, you wicked girl, and know
You'll rue the future too: that penalty
Your kin shall pay to all posterity!"
175 And as she turned to go, she sprinkled her
With drugs of Hecate,[1] and in a trice,
Touched by the bitter lotion, all her hair
Falls off and with it go her nose and ears.
Her head shrinks tiny; her whole body's small;
180 Instead of legs slim fingers line her sides.
The rest is belly; yet from that she sends
A fine-spun thread and, as a spider, still
Weaving her web, pursues her former skill.

---

6. Neptune's amours: Canace was a daughter of Aeolus of Thessaly and the sister of Macareus; the Thessalian river god Enipeus was Tyro's lover, a story Ovid combines with Neptune's siring the giants Otus and Ephialtes on Aloeus's wife, Iphimedia; Neptune turned himself into a ram and Bisaltes's daughter Theophane into a ewe, and their offspring was the Ram with the Golden Fleece; in Arcadia, Ceres was said to have mated as a mare with Neptune in horse shape; raped in Athena's temple by Neptune, the girl Medusa had her hair transformed into serpents, and the winged horse Pegasus emerged when Perseus cut off her head; Melantho was the daughter of Deucalion and Pyrrha.

7. As a shepherd, Apollo seduces Isse, or Amphisse, the daughter of Macareus and his sister, Canace.

8. Erigone was a daughter of Icarius, who was killed by shepherds unfamiliar with the novel effects of Bacchus's grape-vines; both became stars in the heavens. The sea nymph Philyra, loved by Saturn as horse and mare, gave birth to the wise centaur Chiron, the teacher of Asclepius, Jason, and Achilles, among others.

9. Cytorus is a mountain in northern Asia Minor that is proverbial for its box trees, which produced a hard and fine-grained wood.

1. A sinister goddess associated with magic, witchcraft, the night, the underworld, and crossroads.

from Book 8

Minos reached harbour in the isle of Crete[1]
155 And, disembarking, paid his vows to Jove,
A hundred bulls, and hung the spoils of war
To adorn his palace walls. His dynasty's
Disgrace had grown; the monstrous hybrid beast
Declared the queen's obscene adultery.[2]
160 To rid his precincts of this shame the king
Planned to confine him shut away within
Blind walls of intricate complexity.
The structure was designed by Daedalus,
That famous architect.[3] Appearances
165 Were all confused; he led the eye astray
By a mazy multitude of winding ways,
Just as Maeander plays among the meads
Of Phrygia and in its puzzling flow
Glides back and forth and meets itself and sees
170 Its waters on their way and winds along,
Facing sometimes its source, sometimes the sea.[4]
So Daedalus in countless corridors
Built his bafflement, and hardly could himself
Make his way out, so puzzling was the maze.
175 Within this labyrinth Minos shut fast
The beast, half bull, half man, and fed him twice
On Attic blood, lot-chosen each nine years,
Until the third choice mastered him.[5] The door,
So difficult, which none of those before
180 Could find again, by Ariadne's aid
Was found, the thread that traced the way rewound.
Then Theseus, seizing Minos' daughter,[6] spread
His sails for Naxos,[7] where, upon the shore,
That cruel prince abandoned her and she,
185 Abandoned, in her grief and anger found
Comfort in Bacchus' arms. He took her crown
And set it in the heavens to win her there

---

1. Minos, a son of Europa and Jove, was king of the island-kingdom of Crete.

2. Inspired with the love of a bull sent by the sea god Neptune, Minos's wife, Pasiphaë, had the inventor Daedalus create a wooden cow covered with a leather hide. The bull impregnated her inside this contraption, and she gave birth to the Minotaur, a man with the head of a bull.

3. A member of the royal family of Athens, Daedalus came to Crete after he had been banished for the murder of Perdix, out of fear that his sister's son would prove to be the greater inventor.

4. Maeander was in southern Asia Minor; its name was synonymous with the idea of a winding river.

5. Minos exacted an annual tribute of seven young men and seven young women from Athens to feed the Minotaur. In the third year, the Athenian hero (and later king) Theseus joined the tribute.

6. Ariadne, Minos's daughter, fell in love with Theseus and offered to help him in return for leaving with him and becoming his wife. Daedalus revealed to her the secret of the labyrinth.

7. Naxos is an island in the Cyclades between Crete and Athens.

A star's eternal glory; and the crown
Flew through the soft light air and, as it flew,
190 Its gems were turned to gleaming fires, and still
Shaped as a crown their place in heaven they take
Between the Kneeler and him who grasps the Snake.[8]

Hating the isle of Crete and the long years
Of exile, Daedalus was pining for
195 His native land, but seas on every side
Imprisoned him. "Though land and sea," he thought,
"The king may bar to me, at least the sky
Is open; through the sky I'll set my course.[9]
Minos may own all else; he does not own
200 The air." So then to unimagined arts
He set his mind and altered nature's laws.
Row upon row of feathers he arranged,
The smallest first, then larger ones, to form
A growing graded shape, as rustic pipes
205 Rise in a gradual slope of lengthening reeds;
Then bound the middle and the base with wax
And flaxen threads, and bent them, so arranged,
Into a gentle curve to imitate
Wings of a real bird. His boy stood by,
210 Young Icarus, who, blithely unaware
He plays with his own peril, tries to catch
Feathers that float upon the wandering breeze,
Or softens with his thumb the yellow wax,
And by his laughing mischief interrupts
215 His father's wondrous work. Then, when the last
Sure touch was given, the craftsman poised himself
On his twin wings and hovered in the air.
Next he prepared his son. "Take care," he said,
"To fly a middle course, lest if you sink
220 Too low the waves may weight your feathers; if
Too high, the heat may burn them. Fly half-way
Between the two. And do not watch the stars,
The Great Bear or the Wagoner or Orion,
With his drawn sword, to steer by. Set your course
225 Where I shall lead." He fixed the strange new wings
On his son's shoulders and instructed him
How he should fly; and, as he worked and warned,
The old man's cheeks were wet, the father's hands
Trembled. He kissed his son (the last kisses
230 He'd ever give) and rising on his wings

---

8. One version of the myth relates that Bacchus married her, and she was transformed into the constellation Corona Borealis, or the Crown, in the stars between the Kneeler, or Hercules, and the Snake, once the guardian dragon of the Hesperides.

9. Daedalus had been imprisoned with his son, Icarus, by Minos for telling Ariadne how to escape from the labyrinth.

He flew ahead, anxious for his son's sake,
Just like a bird that from its lofty nest
Launches a tender fledgeling in the air.
Calling his son to follow, schooling him
235 In that fatal apprenticeship, he flapped
His wings and watched the boy flapping behind.
  An angler fishing with his quivering rod,
A lonely shepherd propped upon his crook,
A ploughman leaning on his plough, looked up
240 And gazed in awe, and thought they must be gods
That they could fly. Delos and Paros lay
Behind them now; Samos, great Juno's isle,
Was on the left, Lebinthos on the right
And honey-rich Calymne,[1] when the boy
245 Began to enjoy his thrilling flight and left
His guide to roam the ranges of the heavens,
And soared too high. The scorching sun so close
Softened the fragrant wax that bound his wings;
The wax melted; his waving arms were bare;
250 Unfledged, they had no purchase on the air!
And calling to his father as he fell,
The boy was swallowed in the blue sea's swell,
The blue sea that for ever bears his name.[2]
His wretched father, now no father, cried
255 "Oh, Icarus, where are you? Icarus,
Where shall I look, where find you?" On the waves
He saw the feathers. Then he cursed his skill,
And buried his boy's body in a grave,
And still that island keeps the name he gave.

from Book 10

[ORPHEUS and EURYDICE]

Thence Hymen° came, in saffron mantle clad,   *god of marriage*
At Orpheus'[1] summons through the boundless sky
To Thessaly, but vain the summons proved.
True he was present, but no hallowed words
5 He brought nor happy smiles nor lucky sign;
Even the torch he held sputtered throughout
With smarting smoke, and caught no living flame
For all his brandishing. The ill-starred rite

---

1. Islands in the Aegean between Crete and Asia Minor.
2. The Icarian Sea surrounds the island of Icaria, near Samos in the Aegean Sea.

1. The son of Apollo and the Muse Calliope, the Thracian Orpheus was the preeminent singer of classical myth.
Voyaging with the Argonauts, he outsang the Sirens. His journey to the underworld to rescue Eurydice was at the root of
an important mystery cult, and many hymns, most of them related to Dionysus, were attributed to Orpheus.

Led to a grimmer end. The new-wed bride,° *Eurydice*
10   Roaming with her gay Naiads through the grass,
Fell dying when a serpent struck her heel.
And when at last the bard of Rhodope° *Thrace*
Had mourned his fill in the wide world above,
He dared descend through Taenarus' dark gate
15   To Hades[2] to make trial of the shades;
And through the thronging wraiths and grave-spent ghosts
He came to pale Persephone and him,
Lord of the shades, who rules the unlovely realm,
And as he struck his lyre's sad chords he said:
20   "Ye deities who rule the world below,
Whither we mortal creatures all return,
If simple truth, direct and genuine,
May by your leave be told, I have come down
Not with intent to see the glooms of Hell,
25   Nor to enchain the triple snake-haired necks
Of Cerberus,[3] but for my dear wife's sake,
In whom a trodden viper poured his venom
And stole her budding years. My heart has sought
Strength to endure; the attempt I'll not deny;
30   But love has won, a god whose fame is fair
In the world above; but here I doubt, though here
Too, I surmise; and if that ancient tale
Of ravishment is true, you too were joined
In love.[4] Now by these regions filled with fear,
35   By this huge chaos, these vast silent realms,
Reweave, I implore, the fate unwound too fast
Of my Eurydice. To you are owed
Ourselves and all creation; a brief while
We linger; then we hasten, late or soon,
40   To one abode; here one road leads us all;
Here in the end is home; over humankind
Your kingdom keeps the longest sovereignty.
She too, when ripening years reach their due term,
Shall own your rule. The favour that I ask
45   Is but to enjoy her love; and, if the Fates
Will not reprieve her, my resolve is clear
Not to return: may two deaths give you cheer."
     So to the music of his strings he sang,
And all the bloodless spirits wept to hear;
50   And Tantalus forgot the fleeing water,
Ixion's wheel was tranced; the Danaids
Laid down their urns; the vultures left their feast,

---

2. Taenarum, the central of the three southern fingers of the Peloponnesus, was known to contain a cave leading to the underworld, used by Hercules, among others.

3. The three-headed dog Cerberus was the legendary guardian of the underworld.

4. Pluto (Greek: Hades) had snatched his niece Proserpine, the daughter of Jove and Ceres, down to the underworld to be his queen.

And Sisyphus sat rapt upon his stone.[5]
Then first by that sad singing overwhelmed,
55 The Furies' cheeks, it's said, were wet with tears;[6]
And Hades' queen and he whose sceptre rules
The Underworld could not deny the prayer,
And called Eurydice. She was among
The recent ghosts and, limping from her wound,
60 Came slowly forth; and Orpheus took his bride
And with her this compact that, till he reach
The world above and leave Avernus' vale,[7]
He look not back or else the gift would fail.
         The track climbed upwards, steep and indistinct,
65 Through the hushed silence and the murky gloom;
And now they neared the edge of the bright world,
And, fearing lest she faint, longing to look,
He turned his eyes—and straight she slipped away.
He stretched his arms to hold her—to be held—
70 And clasped, poor soul, naught but the yielding air.
And she, dying again, made no complaint
(For what complaint had she save she was loved?)
And breathed a faint farewell, and turned again
Back to the land of spirits whence she came.
75   The double death of his Eurydice
Stole Orpheus' wits away; (like him who saw
In dread the three-necked hound of Hell with chains
Fast round his middle neck, and never lost
His terror till he lost his nature too
80 And turned to stone; or Olenos, who took
Upon himself the charge and claimed the guilt
When his ill-starred Lethaea trusted to
Her beauty, hearts once linked so close, and now
Two rocks on runnelled Ida's mountainside).
85 He longed, he begged, in vain to be allowed
To cross the stream of Styx a second time.
The ferryman repulsed him.[8] Even so
For seven days he sat upon the bank,
Unkempt and fasting, anguish, grief and tears
90 His nourishment, and cursed Hell's cruelty.
Then he withdrew to soaring Rhodope

5. Celebrated underworld punishments. Tantalus, a son of Jove, sat at the gods' table but for revealing their secrets was punished by the torment of food and drink always just out of his reach. Ixion, the king of the Lapithae and the father of Pirithous, was bound to a wheel for the attempted rape of Juno. The 50 daughters of Danaus, the king of Argos, killed their husbands on their collective wedding night, for which they were forced eternally to carry water in leaky urns. Prometheus was punished for his theft of fire by having his liver eternally eaten by a vulture. Sisyphus, a son of Aeolus and the founder of Corinth, was renowned for his cunning and trickery; he was punished for them as well, forced to roll a boulder up a hill that would always escape him just as he reached the summit.

6. Born like the Giants from Earth and the blood of Uranus's severed genitals, the Furies were female powers of the underworld who punished transgressions.

7. Avernus, near Naples, was another reputed entrance to the underworld.

8. It was the task of Charon to ferry newly arrived souls across the river Styx.

And Haemus battered by the northern gales.
    Three times the sun had reached the watery Fish
That close the year,[9] while Orpheus held himself
95   Aloof from love of women, hurt perhaps
By ill-success or bound by plighted troth.
Yet many a woman burned with passion for
The bard, and many grieved at their repulse.
It was his lead that taught the folk of Thrace
100   The love for tender boys, to pluck the buds,
The brief springtime, with manhood still to come.
    There was a hill, and on the hill a wide
Level of open ground, all green with grass.
The place lacked any shade. But when the bard,
105   The heaven-born bard, sat there and touched his strings,
Shade came in plenty. Every tree was there:[1]
Dodona's holy durmast, poplars once
The Sun's sad daughters, oaks with lofty leaves,
Soft limes, the virgin laurel and the beech;[2]
110   The ash, choice wood for spearshafts, brittle hazels,
The knotless fir, the ilex curving down
With weight of acorns, many-coloured maples,
The social plane, the river-loving willow,
The water-lotus, box for ever green,
115   Thin tamarisks and myrtles double-hued,
Viburnums bearing berries of rich blue.
Twist-footed ivy came and tendrilled vines,
And vine-clad elms, pitch-pines and mountain-ash,
Arbutus laden with its blushing fruit,
120   Lithe lofty palms, the prize of victory,
And pines, high-girdled, in a leafy crest,
The favourite of Cybele, the gods'
Great mother, since in this tree Attis doffed
His human shape and stiffened in its trunk.[3]

                   * * *

[ORPHEUS'S SONG: GANYMEDE, HYACINTH]

Such was the grove the bard assembled. There
He sat amid a company of beasts,
A flock of birds, and when he'd tried his strings
And, as he tuned, was satisfied the notes,
175   Though different, agreed in harmony,

9. Three years have passed. The twelfth and final sign of the zodiac, Pisces ("the Fish"), marks the end of winter (mid-February to mid-March).

1. The catalogue of trees includes several whose transformations Ovid has already described.

2. Dodona in Epirus was said to be the oldest Greek oracle; the durmast, or oak, was her sacred tree. The sun's three daughters were Phaethon's sisters, who wept so long at his tomb that they were transformed into poplars. The river Peneus's daughter, Daphne, was changed by her father into a laurel to escape the advances of Apollo; he chose the laurel as his tree and its wreath as the victor's crown.

3. Attis was a Phrygian, or Lydian, youth beloved of Cybele, the Anatolian fertility goddess, who castrated himself in a fit of madness.

He sang this song: "From Jove, great Mother Muse,[4]
Inspire my song: to Jove all creatures bow;
Jove's might I've often hymned in days gone by.
I sang the giants in a graver theme
180   And bolts victorious in Phlegra's plains.[5]
But now I need a lighter strain, to sing
Of boys beloved of gods and girls bewitched
By lawless fires who paid the price of lust.
        The King of Heaven once was fired with love
185   Of Ganymede,[6] and something was devised
That Jove would rather be than what he was.
Yet no bird would he deign to be but one
That had the power to bear his thunderbolts.[7]
At once his spurious pinions° beat the breeze   *wings*
190   And off he swept the Trojan lad; who now,
Mixing the nectar, waits in heaven above
(Though Juno frowns) and hands the cup to Jove.
        Hyacinth, too, Apollo would have placed
In heaven had the drear° Fates given time   *dreary*
195   To place him there. Yet in the form vouchsafed
He is immortal. Year by year, when spring
Drives winter flying and the Ram succeeds
The watery Fish, he rises from the earth
And in the greensward° brings his bloom to birth.[8]   *grassy ground*

200   Hyacinth was my father's favourite,
And Delphi, chosen centre of the world,
Lost its presiding god, who passed his days
Beside Eurotas° in the martial land   *Sparta's river*
Of unwalled Sparta, and no more esteemed
205   Zither or bow. Forgetting his true self,
He was content to bear the nets, to hold
The hounds in leash and join the daylong chase
Through the rough mountain ridges, nourishing
His heart's desire with long companionship.

210   One day, near noon, when the high sun midway
Between the night past and the night to come
At equal distance stood from dawn and dusk,
They both stripped off their clothes and oiled their limbs,
So sleek and splendid, and began the game,
215   Throwing the discus; and Apollo first
Poised, swung and hurled it skywards through the air,
Up, soaring up, to cleave the waiting clouds.

4. Orpheus was the son of Calliope, the Muse of epic poetry.
5. The battle with the Giants took place on the plain of Phlegra in Thrace.
6. Ganymede was a brother of Ilos, the founder of Troy. Both were sons of Tros, a grandson of Jove.
7. The eagle was closely associated with Jove and was said to fetch his thunderbolts after he threw them.
8. Pisces ("Fish") is the last month of the solar year (mid-February to mid-March); Aries ("the Ram") is the first of the
new year (mid-March to mid-April). Although not the same as the modern hyacinth, the name also refers here to a flower,
to be described below.

The heavy disk at longest last fell back
To the familiar earth, a proof of skill,
220   And strength with skill. Then straightway Hyacinth,
Unthinking, in the excitement of the sport,
Ran out to seize it, but it bounded back
From the hard surface full into his face.
The god turned pale, pale as the boy himself,
225   And catching up the huddled body, tried
To revive him, tried to staunch the tragic wound
And stay the fading soul with healing herbs.
His skill was vain; the wound was past all cure.
And as, when in a garden violets
230   Or lilies tawny-tongued or poppies proud
Are bruised and bent, at once they hang their heads
And, drooping, cannot stand erect and bow
Their gaze upon the ground; so dying lies
That face so fair and, all strength ebbed away,
235   His head, too heavy, on his shoulder sinks.

"My Hyacinth," Apollo cried, "laid low
And cheated of youth's prime! I see your wound,
My condemnation, you my grief and guilt!
I, I have caused your death; on my own hand,
240   My own, your doom is written. Yet what wrong
Is mine unless to join the game with you
Were wrong or I were wrong to love you well?
Oh, would for you—or with you—I might give
My life! But since the laws of fate forbid,
245   You shall be with me always; you shall stay
For ever in remembrance on my lips,
And you my lyre and you my song shall hymn.
A new flower you shall be with letters marked
To imitate my sobs, and time shall come
250   When to that flower the bravest hero born
Shall add his name on the same petals writ."
    So with prophetic words Apollo spoke,
And lo! the flowing blood that stained the grass
Was blood no longer; and a flower rose
255   Gorgeous as Tyrian dye, in form a lily,
Save that a lily wears a silver hue,
This richest purple. And, not yet content,
Apollo (who had wrought the work of grace)
Inscribed upon the flower his lament,
260   AI AI, AI AI, and still the petals show
The letters written there in words of woe.
And Sparta's pride in Hyacinth, her son,
Endures undimmed; with pomp and proud display
Each year his feast returns in the ancient way.[9]

* * *

9. The three-day festival honoring Apollo and Hyacinth was an important date in the Spartan year.

from Book 11

While Orpheus sang his minstrel's songs and charmed
The rocks and woods and creatures of the wild
To follow, suddenly, as he swept his strings
In concord with his song, a frenzied band
5　Of Thracian women, wearing skins of beasts,
From some high ridge of ground caught sight of him.[1]
"Look!" shouted one of them, tossing her hair
That floated in the breeze, "Look, there he is,
The man who scorns us!" and she threw her lance
10　Full in Apollo's minstrel's face, but, tipped
With leaves, it left a bruise but drew no blood.
Another hurled a stone; that, in mid air,
Was vanquished by the strains of voice and lyre
And grovelled at his feet, as if to ask
15　Pardon for frenzy's daring. Even so
The reckless onslaught swelled; their fury knew
No bounds; stark madness reigned. And still his singing
Would have charmed every weapon, but the huge
Clamour, the drums, the curving Phrygian fifes,°　　*small flutes*
20　Hand-clapping, Bacchic screaming drowned the lyre.
And then at last, his song unheard, his blood
Reddened the stones. The Maenads first pounced on
The countless birds still spellbound by his song,
The snakes, the host of creatures of the wild,
25　His glory and his triumph. Next they turned
Their bloody hands on Orpheus, flocking like
Birds that have seen a midnight owl abroad
By day, or in the amphitheatre
Upon the morning sand a pack of hounds
30　Round a doomed stag. They rushed upon the bard,
Hurling their leaf-dressed lances, never meant
For work like that; and some slung clods, some flints,
Some branches torn from trees. And, lest they lack
Good weapons for their fury, as it chanced,
35　Oxen were toiling there to plough the land
And brawny farmhands digging their hard fields
Not far away, and sweating for their crop.
Seeing the horde of women, they fled and left
Their labour's armoury, and all across
40　The empty acres lay their heavy rakes,
Hoes and long-handled mattocks. Seizing these,
Those frantic women tore apart the oxen
That threatened with their horns, and streamed to slay

---

1. Maenads, or Bacchantes, were followers of Bacchus (Greek: Dionysos), intoxicated by the god's power. They dressed in panther skins and carried a *thyrsos,* or ivy-covered staff.

The bard. He pleaded then with hands outstretched
45   And in that hour for the first time his words
Were useless and his voice of no avail.
In sacrilege they slew him. Through those lips
(Great Lord of Heaven!) that held the rocks entranced,
That wild beasts understood, he breathed his last,
50   And forth into the winds his spirit passed.
      The sorrowing birds, the creatures of the wild,
The woods that often followed as he sang,
The flinty rocks and stones, all wept and mourned
For Orpheus; forest trees cast down their leaves,
55   Tonsured in grief, and rivers too, men say,
Were swollen with their tears, and Naiads wore,
And Dryads too, their mourning robes of black
And hair dishevelled. All around his limbs
Lay scattered. Hebrus'² stream received his head
60   And lyre, and floating by (so wonderful!)
His lyre sent sounds of sorrow and his tongue,
Lifeless, still murmured sorrow, and the banks
Gave sorrowing reply. And then they left
Their native river, carried out to sea,
65   And gained Methymna's shore on Lesbos' isle.³
There, as his head lay on that foreign sand,
Its tumbled tresses dripping, a fierce snake
Threatened, until at last Apollo came
To thwart it as it struck and froze to stone
70   That serpent's open mouth and petrified,
Just as they were, its jaws that gaped so wide.
      The ghost of Orpheus passed to the Underworld,
And all the places that he'd seen before
He recognized again and, searching through
75   The Elysian fields, he found Eurydice
And took her in his arms with leaping heart.
There hand in hand they stroll, the two together;
Sometimes he follows as she walks in front,
Sometimes he goes ahead and gazes back—
80   No danger now—at his Eurydice.

from Book 15

[PYTHAGORAS]

A man lived here, a Samian by birth,
60   But he had fled from Samos and its masters
And, hating tyranny, by his own choice

---

2. A Thracian river that flowed into the Aegean Sea.
3. Methymna was a city on Lesbos, a large island off the coast of Asia Minor.

Became an exile.[1] Though the gods in heaven
Live far removed, he approached them in his mind,
And things that nature kept from mortal sight
65 His inward eye explored. When meditation
And vigils of long study had surveyed
All things that are, he made his wisdom free
For all to share; and he would teach his class,
Hanging in silent wonder on his words,
70 The great world's origin, the cause of things,
What nature is, what god, and whence the snow,
What makes the lightning, whether thunder comes
From Jove or from the winds when clouds burst wide,
Why the earth quakes, what ordinance controls
75 The courses of the stars, and the whole sum
Of nature's secrets. He was first to ban
As food for men the flesh of living things:
These are the doctrines he was first to teach,
Wise words, though wisdom powerless to persuade.[2]

* * *

"Now since the sea's great surges sweep me on,
All canvas spread, hear me! In all creation
Nothing endures, all is in endless flux,
Each wandering shape a pilgrim passing by.
180 And time itself glides on in ceaseless flow,
A rolling stream—and streams can never stay,
Nor lightfoot hours. As wave is driven by wave
And each, pursued, pursues the wave ahead,
So time flies on and follows, flies and follows,
185 Always, for ever new. What was before
Is left behind; what never was is now;
And every passing moment is renewed.
"You see how day extends as night is spent,
And this bright radiance succeeds the dark;
190 Nor, when the tired world lies in midnight peace,
Is the sky's sheen the same as in the hour
When on his milk-white steed the Morning Star
Rides forth, or when, bright harbinger of day,
Aurora gilds the globe to greet the sun.
195 The sun's round shield at morning when he climbs
From earth's abyss glows red, and when he sinks
To earth's abyss at evening red again,
And at his zenith gleaming bright, for there

---

1. Pythagoras was born on the island of Samos in the mid-6th century B.C.E. He left for Croton, a Greek colony in southern Italy, around 530. He was held to have brought to Greece the doctrine of the transmigration of souls on which Ovid has him speak here. He was also credited with important discoveries in music, astronomy, and mathematics, including the Pythagorean theorem.

2. Vegetarianism was one of the tenets of the ancient cult of Pythagoreanism. After arguing that vegetarianism hearkens back to the Golden Age, Pythagoras goes on to dismiss the fear of death: because of the transmigration of souls, nothing dies.

The air is pure and earth's dross far away.
200   Nor can the queenly moon ever retain
Her shape unchanged, but always, as her orb
Waxes or wanes, tomorrow, she must shine
Larger or smaller than she is today.
    "Again, you notice how the year in four
205   Seasons revolves, completing one by one
Fit illustration of our human life.
The young springtime, the tender suckling spring,
Is like a child; the swelling shoots so fresh,
So soft and fragile, fill the farmers' hearts
210   With hope and gladness. Flowers are everywhere;
Their colours dance across the fostering fields,
While the green leaves still lack their strength and pride.
Spring passes, and the year, grown sturdier,
Rolls on to summer like a strong young man;
215   No age so sturdy, none so rich, so warm.
Then autumn follows, youth's fine fervour spent,
Mellow and ripe, a temperate time between
Youth and old age, his temples flecked with grey.
And last, with faltering footsteps, rough and wild,
220   His hair, if any, white, old winter comes.
    "Our bodies too are always, endlessly
Changing; what we have been, or are today,
We shall not be tomorrow. Years ago
We hid, mere seeds and promise, in the womb;
225   Nature applied her artist's hands to free
Us from our swollen mother's narrow home,
And sent us forth into the open air.
Born to the shining day, the infant lies
Strengthless, but soon on all fours like the beasts
230   Begins to crawl, and then by slow degrees,
Weak-kneed and wobbling, clutching for support
Some helping upright, learns at last to stand.
Then swift and strong he traverses the span
Of youth, and when the years of middle life
235   Have given their service too, he glides away
Down the last sunset slope of sad old age—
Old age that saps and mines and overthrows
The strength of earlier years. Milo, grown old,
Sheds tears to see how shrunk and flabby hang
240   Those arms on which the muscles used to swell,
Massive like Hercules; and, when her glass
Shows every time-worn wrinkle, Helen weeps
And wonders why she twice was stolen for love.[3]

---

3. Milo was a wrestler from Croton who won many victories at the Olympic and the Pythian Games and a disciple of Pythagoras. Helen was first carried off by Theseus and then later, after she had married Menelaus, by Paris of Troy.

Time, the devourer, and the jealous years
245   With long corruption ruin all the world
       And waste all things in slow mortality.
          "The elements themselves do not endure;
       Examine how they change and learn from me.
       The everlasting universe contains
250   Four generative substances; of these
       Two, earth and water, sink of their own weight;
       Two, air and fire (fire purer still than air),
       Weightless, unburdened, seek the heights above.
       Though spaced apart, all issue from each other
255   And to each other fall. So earth, reduced,
       Is rarefied to water; moisture, thinned,
       Dissolves to air and wind; air, losing weight,
       So light, so insubstantial, flashes up
       To empyrean fire. Then they return
260   In reverse order as the skein° unwinds.   *bundle of yarn*
       Thus fire, condensed, passes to heavier air,
       Air into water, water in its turn
       Compressed, conglobed, solidifies to earth.
          "Nothing retains its form; new shapes from old
265   Nature, the great inventor, ceaselessly
       Contrives. In all creation, be assured,
       There is no death—no death, but only change
       And innovation; what we men call birth
       Is but a different new beginning; death
270   Is but to cease to be the same. Perhaps
       This may have moved to that and that to this,
       Yet still the sum of things remains the same.

                              * * *

          "So—lest I range too far and my steeds lose
       Their course—the earth and all therein, the sky
455   And all thereunder change and change again.
       We too ourselves, who of this world are part,
       Not only flesh and blood but pilgrim souls,
       Can make our homes in creatures of the wild
       Or of the farm. These creatures might have housed
460   Souls of our parents, brothers, other kin,
       Or men at least, and we must keep them safe,
       Respected, honoured, lest we gorge ourselves
       On such a banquet as Thyestes ate.[4]
       How vilely he's inured, how wickedly
465   He fits himself to kill his human kin,
       He who can slit his calf's throat, hear its cries
       Unmoved, who has the heart to kill his kid
       That screams like a small child, or eat the bird

---

4. The sons of Thyestes were killed and served to their father in a meal by his brother, Atreus.

His hand has reared and fed! How far does this
470 Fall short of murder? Where else does it lead?
No! Let the oxen plough and owe their death
To length of days; let the sheep give their shield
Against the north wind's fury; let the goats
Bring their full udders for your hand to milk.
475 Away with traps and snares and lures and wiles!
Never again lime twigs to cheat the birds,
Nor feather ropes to drive the frightened deer,
Nor hide the hook with dainties that deceive!
Destroy what harms; destroy, but never eat;
480 Choose wholesome fare and never feast on meat!"

CATULLUS ■ (84–54 B.C.E.)

In the small corpus of verse he completed before his untimely death at age 30, Gaius Valerius Catullus celebrated novelty, obscenity, youth, brevity, charm, wit, passion, and urban-
ity. His 113 poems, most of them quite short, reproduce everyday life and take us inside
the mind of a young man-about-town in first-century B.C.E Rome. Meals and journeys are
described; friends are praised and heckled, enemies mocked and reviled; loves and disap-
pointments are chronicled in graphic detail; and everywhere there is the writing, reciting,
and criticism of poetry.

Born into a well-to-do family in Verona, Catullus soon made his way to the capital,
where he moved among the preeminent political and literary figures of his day. He had
a brother, whose sudden death in Asia Minor around 57 B.C.E. was the occasion of a sea
voyage to the distant grave near Troy and a moving poem that strove "to speak in vain
to your unspeaking ashes." He conducted a love affair with the powerful (and, according
to Cicero, notorious) Clodia, half-sister of the tribune Publius Clodius Pulcher and wife
of Quintus Caecilius Metellus, consul in the year 60. This was the "Lesbia" to whom
many of the poems refer and with whom the poet explores the extremes of passion; her
name itself pays homage to the erotic lyrics of Sappho, the archaic Greek poet of the
island of Lesbos (page 236; an imitation of one of her poems is included in the selection below, page 469). Catullus's depiction of love is central to his portrayal of life as a
paradoxical mix of emotions, a heady brew both sweet and sour in which despair and joy
are inseparable.

Catullus's poetic intensity is well illustrated by this deservedly famous epigram:

> Odi et amo. quare id faciam fortasse requiris?
> nescio sed fieri sentio et excrucior.

> I hate & love. And if you should ask how I can do both,
> I couldn't say; but I feel it, and it shivers me.

The compression and power of these two lines derive in large part from the elimination
of adjectives and of images. The poet gives us only verbs of condensed sensation: *hate,
love, do, feel, shiver.* Rather than explaining the paradox of the opening antithesis, *odi et
amo*, this string of verbs heightens its effect. Half the verbs are active; half are passive: the
poet hates and loves; he rules and is ruled by his lover and his love. With its capacity to
concentrate opposites of emotion and sense perceptions into concrete feelings through a

masterful control of language and meter, the lyric form allowed Catullus to render vividly
the chaotic experience of an individual in the late Republic.

PRONUNCIATION:
Catullus: kah-TUHL-luhs

from Poems[1]

3[2]

Cry out lamenting, Venuses & Cupids,
and mortal men endowed with Love's refinement:
the sparrow of my lady lives no longer!
Sparrow, the darling pet of my beloved,
5   that was more precious to her than her eyes were;
it was her little honey, and it knew her
as well as any girl knows her own mother;
it would not ever leave my lady's bosom
but leapt up, fluttering from yon to hither,
10   chirruping always only to its mistress.
It now flits off on its way, goes, gloom-laden
down to where—word is—there is no returning.
Damn you, damned shades of Orcus[3] that devour
all mortal loveliness, for such a lovely
15   sparrow it was you've stolen from my keeping!
O hideous deed! O poor little sparrow!
It's your great fault that my lady goes weeping,
reddening, ruining her eyes from sorrow.

5

Lesbia, let us live only for loving,
and let us value at a single penny
all the loose flap of senile busybodies!
Suns when they set are capable of rising,
5   but at the setting of our own brief light
night is one sleep from which we never waken.
Give me a thousand kisses, then a hundred,
another thousand next, another hundred,
a thousand without pause & then a hundred,
10   until when we have run up our thousands
we will cry bankrupt, hiding our assets

1. Translated by Charles Martin.
2. This poem is in the form of a mock threnody, or funeral dirge.
3. An infernal deity in Greek mythology. Identified in Roman religion with Dis, the god of the underworld.

from ourselves & any who would harm us,
knowing the volume of our trade in kisses.

13

You will dine well with me, my dear Fabullus,[1]
in a few days or so, the gods permitting.
—Provided you provide the many-splendored
feast, and invite your fair-complected° lady,   complexioned
5 your wine, your salt & all the entertainment!
Which is to say, my dear, if you bring dinner
you will dine well, for these days your Catullus
finds that his purse is only full of cobwebs.
But in return, you'll have from me Love's Essence,
10 —or what (if anything) is more delicious:
I'll let you sniff a certain charming fragrance
which Venuses & Cupids gave my lady;
one whiff of it, Fabullus, and you'll beg the
gods to transform you into nose, completely!

51[1]

To me that man seems like a god in heaven,
seems—may I say it?—greater than all gods are,
who sits by you & without interruption
  watches you, listens

5 to your light laughter, which casts such confusion
onto my senses, Lesbia, that when I
gaze at you merely, all of my well-chosen
  words are forgotten

as my tongue thickens & a subtle fire
10 runs through my body while my ears are deafened
by their own ringing & at once my eyes are
  covered in darkness!

Leisure, Catullus. More than just a nuisance,
leisure: you riot, overmuch enthusing.
15 Fabulous cities & their sometime kings have
  died of such leisure.

---

1. Fabullus was a colleague in the Roman province of Spain with Veranius, a friend of Catullus who, we are told, sent the poet a set of fine napkins of Spanish linen as a souvenir. The poem's number comes from its place in the manuscript. It is not known if this order reflects the author's intention.

1. A free translation of Sappho's poem "He looks to me to be in heaven" (see page 238), in Sapphic strophes, with a final stanza of his own.

76[1]

If any pleasure can come to a man through recalling
    decent behavior in his relations with others,
not breaking his word, and never, in any agreement,
    deceiving men by abusing vows sworn to heaven,
5 then countless joys will await you in old age, Catullus,
    as a reward for this unrequited passion!
For all of those things which a man could possibly say or
    do have all been said & done by you already,
and none of them counted for anything, thanks to her vileness!
10   Then why endure your self-torment any longer?
Why not abandon this wretched affair altogether,
    spare yourself pain the gods don't intend you to suffer!
It's hard to break off with someone you've loved such a long time:
    it's hard, but you have to do it, somehow or other.
15 Your only chance is to get out from under this sickness,
    no matter whether or not you think you're able.
O gods, if pity is yours, or if ever to any
    who lay near death you offered the gift of your mercy,
look on my suffering: if my life seems to you decent,
20   then tear from within me this devouring cancer,
this heavy dullness wasting the joints of my body,
    completely driving every joy from my spirit!
Now I no longer ask that she love me as I love her,
    or—even less likely—that she give up the others:
25 all that I ask for is health, an end to this foul sickness!
    O gods, grant me this in exchange for my worship.

85

I hate & love. And if you should ask how I can do both,
    I couldn't say; but I feel it, and it shivers me.

107

If ever something which someone with no expectation
    desired should happen, we are rightly delighted!
And so this news is delightful—it's dearer than gold is:
    you have returned to me, Lesbia, my desired!
5 Desired, yet never expected—but you *have* come back
    to me! A holiday, a day of celebration!
What living man is luckier than I am? Or able
    to say that anything could possibly be better?

---

1. The mood, subject, and meter of this poem anticipate the classical Roman love elegies of Propertius, Tibullus, and Ovid.

HORACE ▪ (65–8 B.C.E.)

Son of a freedman farmer of modest means, Quintus Horatius Flaccus was by the end of his life a close acquaintance of Emperor Augustus. Through his often topical poetry and through his actions, Horace was intimately involved in the events of his day. In 42 B.C.E., he fought on the losing side of Caesar's murderers, Brutus and Cassius, at Philippi against Mark Antony and Octavian. His family farm was confiscated, but Horace eventually landed on his feet, gaining the patronage of the influential Etruscan noble and minister of Octavian, Maecenas, with the aid of his friend Virgil. In 33, Maecenas presented Horace with a farm in the rich Sabine country northeast of Rome. Horace published his *Satires* (*Sermones*) between 34 and 30 B.C.E, the *Epodes* in 30, three books of *Odes* in 23, the *Epistles* in 20, and a fourth book of *Odes* around 13.

The *Satires* are more conversational in tone and subject matter, while the *Odes* are more formal and morally instructive; but both the *Satires* and the *Odes* are built around a series of oppositions: country versus city, a simple versus a complicated life, poverty versus wealth, past versus present, private versus public. Central to these oppositions is the Epicurean conception of the *aurea mediocritas,* or golden mean, the desire to avoid extremes in life and to focus on the simple pleasures of the present. Horace prides himself on puncturing pretensions and unreasonable behavior, including his own. The strategy of comic deflation allows Horace to introduce philosophical concerns with the lightest of touches.

from SATIRES

1.5 Leaving the big city behind I found lodgings at Aricia[1]

	Leaving the big city° behind I found lodgings at Aricia	*Rome*
	in a smallish pub. With me was Heliodorus, the professor	
	of rhetoric, the greatest scholar in the land of Greece. From there	
	to Forum Appi crammed with bargees° and stingy landlords.	*bargemen*
5	Being lazy types we split this stretch into two, though speed-merchants	

Leaving the big city° behind I found lodgings at Aricia   *Rome*
in a smallish pub. With me was Heliodorus, the professor
of rhetoric, the greatest scholar in the land of Greece. From there
to Forum Appi crammed with bargees° and stingy landlords.   *bargemen*
5   Being lazy types we split this stretch into two, though speed-merchants
do it in one. The Appian[2] is easier when you take it slowly.
Here I declared war on my stomach because of the water
which was quite appalling, and waited impatiently as the other travellers
enjoyed their dinner.
          Now night was preparing to draw her shadows
10   over the earth and to sprinkle the heavens with glimmering lights
when the lads started to shout at the boatmen, who replied in kind.[3]
"Bring her over here!" "How many hundred are you going to pack in?"
"Whoah, that's enough!"
          While the fares are collected and the mule harnessed,
a whole hour goes by. The blasted mosquitoes and the marsh
15   frogs make sleep impossible. The boatman, who has had a skinful

1. Translated by Niall Rudd.
2. Their route follows the Appian Way, most ancient of the roads for which the Romans were celebrated. It ran south from Rome to Brindisi in the heel of Italy, a major port for travel to Greece and other eastern destinations.
3. This leg of the Appian Way was a canal that ran through the Pomptine Marshes.

of sour wine, sings of his distant loved one, and a traveller
takes up the refrain. Weariness finally gets the better of the traveller
and he nods off. The lazy boatman lets the mule graze;
he ties the rope to a stone and lies on his back snoring.
When day dawns we realize the barge is making no progress.
This is remedied when a furious passenger jumps ashore,
seizes a branch of willow, and wallops the mule and the boatman
on the head and back.
         It was almost ten before we landed.
We washed our hands and face in Feronia's holy spring.[4]
Then after breakfast we crawled three miles up to Anxur
perched on its white rocks which can be seen from far and wide.
This was where the admirable Maecenas was due to come,
along with Cocceius; both were envoys on a mission of immense
importance; both had experience in reconciling friends who had quarrelled.[5]
I went indoors to smear some black ointment on my eyes,
which were rather bloodshot. Meanwhile Maecenas and Cocceius arrived,
and also Fonteius Capito, a man of consummate charm
and tact, who held a unique place in Antony's affections.

We left Fundi with relief in the Praetorship° of Aufidius Luscus,   *control*
laughing at the regalia of that fatuous official—the toga complete
with border, the broad-striped tunic, and the pan of glowing charcoal.
Then, after a weary journey, we stopped at the Mamurras' city.
Murena lent us his house, Capito provided the food.

Dawn the next day found us in a state of high
excitement, for on reaching Sinuessa we were joined by Plotius, Varius,
and Virgil.[6] No finer men have ever walked the face
of the earth; and no one is more dearly attached to them all than I am.
You can imagine how delighted we were and how warmly we greeted one
    another.
For me there's nothing in life to compare with the joy of friendship.
Near the Campanian Bridge accommodation was provided
by a small house, fuel and salt by official caterers.[7]
Then, at Capua, the mules laid down their packs early.
Maecenas went off to take exercise; Virgil and I had a sleep,
for ball-games are bad for inflamed eyes and dyspeptic stomachs.

Next we put up at a well-stocked villa belonging to Cocceius,
which overlooks the inns of Caudium. Now, O Muse,
recount in brief, I pray thee, the clash of Sarmentus the clown
with Messius Cicirrus, and from what lineage each entered
the fray. Messius comes of glorious stock—Oscans!

---

4. The local goddess, Feronia, had a temple and holy spring near Anxur (modern Terracina).

5. Horace was on the trip as companion to Maecenas at an important diplomatic meeting that took place in 38 or 37 between representatives of Octavian and Antony ("friends who had quarrelled"). Lucius Cocceius Nerva was a politician who had helped negotiate an earlier treaty.

6. Plotius Tucca and Lucius Varius would later edit the *Aeneid* after Virgil's death in 19 B.C.E.

7. Roman law required that traveling officials be provided with accommodations and supplies along major roads.

55   Sarmentus' lady owner is still alive.[8] With such
      pedigrees they joined battle. Sarmentus was the first to strike:
      "I declare you're the image of a wild horse!"
                                          "Right!" says Messius,
      amid general laughter, and tosses his head.
                                          "Hey," says the other,
      "If you can threaten us like that when your horn's cut off, what would you do
60   if it was still on your head?" (The point being that the left side
      of his hairy brow was in fact disfigured by an ugly scar.)
      After making a string of jokes about Messius' face and his Campanian
      disease he begged him to do the dance of the shepherd Cyclops,
      swearing he would have no need of a mask or tragic buskins.[9]

65   Cicirrus wasn't lost for an answer. Had Sarmentus got around to offering
      his chain, as promised, to the household gods? His status of clerk
      in no way diminished his mistress's claim on him. Finally, why
      had he ever bothered to run away when a single pound of meal
      would have been quite enough for a tiny miserable scrap like him?

70   We had great fun as the party continued into the night.

      From there we went straight to Beneventum, where the fussy host very
           nearly
      burnt his house down while turning some skinny thrushes on the fire.
      For Vulcan fell out sideways through the old stove, and his darting
      flame instantly shot up to lick the roof overhead.
75   Then, what a sight! greedy guests and frightened servants
      snatching up the dinner and all struggling to put out the blaze.

      From that point on Apulia began to bring into view
      her old familiar hills.[1] They were scorched as usual by the Scirocco
      and we'd never have crawled across them had it not been for a house
80   near Trivicum which provided shelter—plus a lot of weepy smoke.
      (Damp branches were burning in the stove, leaves and all.)

      Here, like an utter fool, I stayed awake till midnight
      waiting for a girl who broke her promise. Sleep eventually
      overtook me, still keyed up for sex. Then scenes from a dirty
85   dream spattered my nightshirt and stomach as I lay on my back.

      From there we bowled along in waggons for twenty-four miles
      putting up at a little town which can't be identified in verse,
      though it can very easily by its features: there they sell the most common
      of all commodities—water, but their bread is quite unbeatable,
90   and a traveller, if he's wise, usually carries some with him on his journey;
      for the sort you get at Canusium (founded of yore by Diomede

473

---

8. Sarmentus was a freed slave of Maecenas's household, and Messius descended from the ancient Oscan people of
Campania, the butts of many Roman jokes. Like many comic duos, one is tiny, and the other huge. Horace parodies the
form of the epic combat.
9. The thick-soled boots and mask worn by tragic actors.
1. Apulia occupies the heel of southern Italy; Horace was born there in the town of Venusia. The hot sirocco wind blows
there from northern Africa.

the bold)[2] is gritty, and your jug is no better off for water.
Here Varius said a sad good-bye to his tearful friends.

95   The following night we arrived at Rubi, worn out
after covering a long stretch of road damaged by heavy rain.
On the next day the weather was better but the road worse
all the way to the walls of Bari, famous for fish.

Then Gnatia, on whose construction the water-nymphs scowled, provided
fun and amusement by trying to persuade us that incense melts
100   without fire on the temple steps; Apella the Jew may believe it—
not me, for I have learned that the gods live a life of calm,
and that if nature presents some strange occurrence it is not
sent down by the gods in anger from their high home in the sky.

Brindisi marks the end of this long tale and journey.

from ODES[1]

1.9 You see Soracte standing white and deep

You see Soracte[2] standing white and deep
with snow, the woods in trouble, hardly able
    to carry their burden, and the rivers
        halted by sharp ice.

5   Thaw out the cold. Pile up the logs
on the hearth and be more generous, Thaliarchus,[3]
    as you draw the four-year-old Sabine[4]
        from its two-eared cask.

Leave everything else to the gods. As soon as
10   they still the winds battling it out
    on the boiling sea, the cypresses stop waving
        and the old ash trees.

Don't ask what will happen tomorrow.
Whatever day Fortune[5] gives you, enter it
15   as profit, and don't look down on love
        and dancing while you're still a lad,

---

2. After the end of the Trojan War, the Greek hero Diomedes was said to have gone to Apulia and was credited with the founding of several towns there.

1. Translated by David West.

2. An isolated mountain to the north of Rome that was home of the Hirpi, priests of the cult of Soranus, an underworld deity identified with Apollo, who also happened to be the special patron of Emperor Augustus.

3. Most of Horace's poems address real-life acquaintances; however, "Thaliarchus" is simply Greek for "master of the revels," an apt name for this poem, one of several by Horace on the theme of *carpe diem,* or "seize the day."

4. A proverbially excellent wine from the region northeast of Rome where Horace's estate was located.

5. The goddess of chance or luck, of great importance in Roman religion.

while the gloomy grey keeps away from the green.
Now is the time for the Campus[6] and the squares
    and soft sighs at the time arranged
        as darkness falls.

20

Now is the time for the lovely laugh from the secret corner
giving away the girl in her hiding-place,
    and for the token snatched from her arm
        or finger feebly resisting.

2.14 Ah how quickly, Postumus, Postumus

Ah how quickly, Postumus, Postumus,[1]
the years glide by, and piety will not delay
    the wrinkles, and old age, and death, the unsubdued,
        pressing at their heels,

5   no, my friend, not if every day that passes you sacrificed
three hundred bulls to appease Pluto, the god
    who cannot weep, who confines Tityos
        and the three-bodied giant Geryon

in the prison of those gloomy waters
10   that we know all of us must cross[2]
    who feed upon the bounty of the earth,
        whether we be kings or poor tenant farmers.

In vain shall we avoid the bloody god of war
and the roaring breakers of the Adriatic.[3]
15   In vain autumn after long autumn shall we tremble
        for our health when the south wind blows.

We must go and see black Cocytus meandering
in its sluggish flow,[4] the infamous daughters of Danaus,
    and Sisyphus, son of Aeolus,
20   at his long sentence of hard labour.[5]

We must leave the earth, our home,
and the wife we love, and none of these trees you tend

---

6. The Campus Martius was a center of public life and leisure in 1st-century Rome, full of baths, theaters, and temples.

1. Perhaps Propertius Postumus, a relation of the poet Propertius.

2. Pluto was the god of the underworld, the Roman equivalent of the Greek Hades. The Giant Tityos was punished in the underworld for his attempted rape of Leto, the mother of Apollo and Diana; composed of three men joined together, Geryon was killed by the hero Hercules. The Styx was the principal river of the underworld.

3. The sea located between Italy and the Balkans.

4. The Cocytus was another underworld river.

5. Mythical figures punished for their misdeeds on earth. Danaus's 50 daughters had killed their husbands on their wedding night. Sisyphus was a legendary trickster who was condemned to push up hill a boulder that always rolled down again just as he reached the top.

                    except the hated cypresses[6]
                        will go with their short-lived master.

25   Your heir, worthier than yourself, will drink off
                    the Caecuban[7] you laid down behind a hundred locks,
                        and stain your paving with proud wine undiluted
                            and too good for the banquets of priests.

---

6. The cypress tree was traditionally associated by the Romans with mortality, especially in the case of rich and important men. Its branches were placed at the door of the mourning house, on the funeral altar, and on the pyre itself; the cypress was also planted around graves.

7. A prized wine from a region of Latium.

The Medieval Era

King Arthur and His Knights, from a manuscript of the *Prose Lancelot,* France, 13th century. In this illustration from a collection of Arthurian romances, King Arthur is majestically enthroned, and in keeping with his royal stature he towers over his knights. He is shown requesting a central commodity in the Arthurian stories—more stories. "Now tell the tales," he commands, "that have befallen you since the day of Pentecost before all the companions of the Quest returned."

THE TERM "MEDIEVAL" WAS COINED LONG AFTER THE CLOSE OF the period to which it refers, as people looking back from early modern times sought a name for the thousand years or so between their day and classical antiquity, roughly the fourth through the fourteenth centuries C.E.; "medieval" comes from the Latin for "middle era." Originally applied specifically to Europe, the term has come to be used for a "middle" period in a range of cultures around the world. The beginnings of this middle era vary from place to place, but each of the ancient literary cultures presented in this anthology went through a major time of transition in late antiquity, roughly between the first and fourth centuries C.E. By that point, a body of ancient works had been established as foundational for the later culture: the Confucian classics in China and Indochina; the Vedas and early epics of India; the Bible and the Greek and Roman classics in the Mediterranean world. These and other classic works continued to have a lasting influence, yet many more texts were lost in the upheavals of late antiquity; only a small fraction of Sappho's lyrics and Sophocles's plays survived, for example, and some entire civilizations vanished, such as those of Mesopotamia and ancient Egypt.

Even as one era was passing away, another was coming into being. Distinctly new literatures were created in many areas, sometimes in languages that had never been written before, such as Japanese, Arabic, and German, sometimes through creative transformation of classical languages such as Chinese, Sanskrit, and Latin.

Lords and Ladies, Knights and Samurai

The vast majority of the medieval world's population consisted of peasantry: farmers tilling small plots of land (or fishing, in coastal areas), often as virtual or outright slaves of powerful lords who controlled the land. In Europe and sometimes elsewhere, authority and land ownership were organized feudally, a system in which an overlord held title to all land in his domain and granted it to noble vassals in exchange for their loyalty and support; the vassals in turn controlled the lives of the serfs who worked their lands. Monarchs often tried to gather their nobility round them, to enhance the glory of their courts and to keep a watchful eye on their powerful underlings. Royal courts in China, Japan, India, Persia, Iraq, and Europe were sites of feasting and of seduction, where court poets celebrated noble deeds in heroic epics and romances, and sang the sorrows of love in enticing lyrics.

Women weren't only the idealized objects of poetic devotion; increasingly, they were poets themselves as well. Court life, and the convents to which women might withdraw from court life, provided new opportunities for women to become writers. With a few important exceptions such as Sappho, women in antiquity had had little access to literacy and no opportunity to record their stories and songs. In the medieval era, women began to play important roles in patronizing and also creating literature and other works of art. The pre-Islamic woman poet al-Khansa' became a founding figure for Arabic poetry, and in several regions aristocratic women in particular gained a new stature as writers. In Japan, a remarkable series of courtly women wrote poetry and became pioneers in prose writing. *The Tale of Genji*, by the noblewoman known as Murasaki Shikibu, has long been recognized as one of the greatest narratives ever written. In Europe, Marie de France and Béatrice, the countess of Dia, were two among a number of celebrated women poets.

Medieval knights in Europe, and their Japanese counterparts the samurai, sought fame as much as wealth, and became the subjects of great poems and prose tales concerning their exploits battling one another or dragons and other monsters. Writers including Marie de France and the anonymous author of *Gawain and the Green Knight* celebrated the adventures of the legendary King Arthur's knights, while the great Japanese samurai clans had their deeds commemorated in medieval epics and many later works, even starring in very recent times in such movies as Kurosawa's *The Seven Samurai*. The common folk sang songs and told stories, but they were rarely literate and their oral traditions generally went unmarked. Yet folk songs and tales survived when they were recorded for upper-class consumption, as notably happened with the stories included in *The Thousand and One Nights*. That text actually dramatizes this process of transmission, in tales in which the Caliph Haroun al-Rashid goes out into Baghdad dressed as a common merchant, accompanied by his vizier and executioner, to seek adventure and hear marvelous stories; back home in his palace, he regularly has the best of these stories recorded in letters of gold.

Medieval writers typically portray their royal patrons as vastly wise, powerful, and generous, yet the reality was often a good deal less glorious. In many regions, transportation was poor and long-distance communication was awkward, rendering central control difficult, and subsistence-level farming didn't produce very great surpluses that could support both a local aristocracy and the royal household in the style to which both aspired. There were frequent struggles for position and ascendancy, both between the lords of neighboring regions and between vassals and their overlords. Feuding and open warfare are constant themes in medieval literature. A partial exception to this pattern was China. Unified in ancient times under the feudal Han dynasty (202 B.C.E.–220 C.E.), early medieval China experienced a long phase of conflict and division, but was then reunified under the Sui dynasty in the late sixth century. A period of great prosperity ensued, with much of central China linked by canals as well as rivers, and older feudal patterns were replaced by a national bureaucracy controlled by the emperor and his administration. The Tang dynasty (618–907) became the golden age of Chinese poetry as of several other arts, and in this sense China's "middle" period became its *central* period in the eyes of later historians, writers, and artists.

47

Travel, Trade, and Conquest

The medieval period saw steadily increasing contacts across regions, promoted especially by two kinds of travelers: merchants and missionaries or pilgrims. A "Silk Road" was established from East Asia to the shores of the Mediterranean, and Constantinople and Venice became major connecting links between Europe and points east. Armies were on the move as well, often fueled by religious fervor as well as political ambition. Following the establishment of Islam in Arabia in the early seventh century, a wave of conversion and consolidation spread westward across North Africa, and north and east into Mesopotamia and Turkey. Baghdad became a major cultural as well as political center, and by the eighth century much of Spain had come under Muslim control. Regional empires waxed and waned elsewhere as well, particularly in Europe, in South Asia, and among the Maya in what is now Mexico and Guatemala; in East Asia, Japan and Korea became consolidated as unified and strong countries, and China influenced many regions around its borders directly or indirectly.

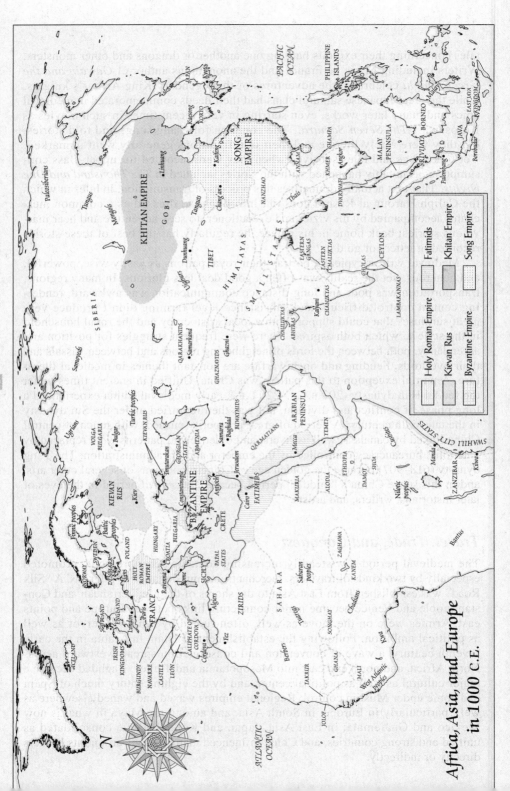

Africa, Asia, and Europe
in 1000 C.E.

The Growth of World Religions

Every aspect of medieval life was profoundly marked by religion, and several faiths gained an increasingly global scope during the period: Buddhism spread from India to China, Tibet, Korea, Japan, and beyond; Islam spread far beyond the boundaries of any one empire, reaching as far east as Indonesia, west to Spain, and south into central Africa. Christianity pressed back against the advance of Islam, and Christian missionaries began to fan out across the known world (a process that accelerated at the start of the early modern period with the European discovery of the "New World"). The intermingling of old and new forms of belief produced conflict but also gave people new options in orienting themselves toward the universe and the social world. Medieval literature often registers these intermixtures: in the Anglo-Saxon *Beowulf,* written in Christian times but set in pagan times; in the mixing of pre-Islamic and post-Islamic motifs in *The Thousand and One Nights;* in the interplay of Buddhist and Confucian elements in Chinese poetry.

The need to define one's religion against alternatives also stimulated the growth of organized theological reflection: theologians in Paris and Rome, in Baghdad, Mecca, and Andalusian Spain, and in the courts of India and elsewhere debated proper modes of understanding, forms of worship, and ethical behavior. Building on these philosophical discussions, many medieval works of literature join theological and aesthetic themes, from the deceptively simple poetry of the Buddhist Wang Wei to the Islamic mysticism of Ibn al-'Arabi to Dante's transcendent vision blending earthly life and afterlife in his *Divine Comedy*. The medieval world was both resolutely worldly and thoroughly otherworldly. "The medieval world" was many worlds, in fact, including the many richly imaginative worlds here.

Medieval China

As was the case in Western Europe, what is often referred to as the medieval period in China followed on the collapse of the first great empire, the Han, between the late second and early fourth centuries C.E. and the rule of much of the land by "barbarians," non-Chinese tribes from the north. Unlike its Western counterpart, China's middle ages also included the eventual reunification of the empire under the Sui rulers from the north in 589, almost immediately followed by the Tang dynasty, which lasted from 618 to 907. The political instability that marked the centuries from the downfall of the Han to the reunification of the Sui hindered the engagement in public life that Confucius had sought to foster and that had gradually become institutionalized during the Han.

Arguments for attention to individual, as opposed to collective, needs were provided by Daoist and Buddhist doctrines that attracted increasing numbers of adherents at this time. The Buddhist focus on the individual's renunciation of the duties and rewards of this world marked a radical departure from Confucianism's emphasis on social and ethical responsibility. Buddhism made significant inroads in both northern and southern China during the period of division. Its monasteries became repositories of some of the most important works of art produced during the middle ages, and for centuries thereafter Buddhist rituals would mark milestones such as birth, marriage, and death in the lives of both commoners and the imperial household.

Reunification of China returned the center of government to the northern capital of Chang'an, within whose city walls approximately a million people resided during the Tang dynasty's most prosperous period, the reign of Emperor Xuanzong (712–756). Diplomats, students, and Buddhist monks from Japan and Korea stayed for extended periods in the capital, as well as artists, musicians, nomads, and merchants from India, Persia, and the Middle East. Governing an empire that extended a thousand miles from the Great Wall to the north to Hainan Island in the south, with a registered population of nearly fifty million, required a complex system of taxation, state monopolies, and forced labor, as well as an elaborate structure of provincial and county administration staffed by educated bureaucrats. As had always been the case, aristocratic birth offered the easiest entry into government office, but the civil service examination now began to vie for importance as a means of qualification.

Five major examinations, which conferred five different degrees, were offered throughout the Tang, but the one requiring the most sophisticated literary talent quickly became the most prestigious one; it led to the degree of "presented scholar" (*jinshi*), someone suitable for presentation to the emperor. The range of knowledge tested on the *jinshi* examination was relatively broad; its basic curriculum included literature, the classics, current affairs, and administrative issues, thereby approaching fairly closely the Confucian ideal of a liberal education. During the Tang, a test of poetic composition was included at various times on the examination, providing testimony not only to the stature of poetry as a literary form during the dynasty but also an index of its deep embeddedness in official life. Court appointees had to be prepared to write at the command of a member of the ruling family. If the emperor composed a poem inspired by some outing or memorable event, courtiers would be expected to "respond respectfully," using the same form and rhyme scheme. (Tang forms regulated line length and number of words per line, required a single rhyme for all even-numbered lines, and called for strict parallelism of syntax and meaning between lines as well as patterns of alternation between tones of words.) Or a member of the ruling family might simply set the topic, with officials in attendance composing poems at his command or using a rhyme assigned by him. Anecdotes surviving from such events typically record who finished his poem first and whose was judged of the highest quality.

The practices of court poetry were honed to perfection by poets of the Tang in nonofficial contexts as well. Older forms permitted greater metrical freedom and maintained their popularity, and all forms of Chinese poetry, whether old or new, could take advantage of features of the classical language itself, which seems spare and sometimes ambiguous when compared with Western European languages, owing to its lack of inflection and characteristic omission of indications of person, tense, and other grammatical relationships. To an experienced reader familiar with the conventions, a typical poem would not—as has been argued by some—be read as "telegraphic," but it would leave much unspecified in the text. A good example is the following quatrain by Li Bo (701–770) that is still memorized by Chinese schoolchildren today. A word-for-word rendering is shown beneath the Chinese characters:

靜 夜 思

Quiet Night Thought

牀 前 明 月 光

Bed front bright moon radiance

疑 是 地 上 霜

Suspect is ground upon frost

舉 頭 望 明 月

Raise head gaze bright moon

低 頭 思 故 鄉

Lower head think old province

Thoughts on a Quiet Night

Before my bed the bright moon's gleam
I take to be frost on the ground.
Lifting my head I gaze at the bright moon;
Lowering my head I think of home.

Readers have long appreciated the way in which these twenty words convey a powerful sense of a traveler's longing without making any overt emotional reference. Skilled poets such as Wang Wei or Du Fu excelled in the ability to manipulate the many requirements of the regulated verse forms in the service of nuanced expression and evocative description.

Japan

Politics, Religion, and Culture

From the fourth century onward, a number of powerful clans dominated the Japanese archipelago. Gradually the Yamato clan conquered the other clans and formed an imperial court centered on a sovereign who claimed descent from the Sun Goddess (Amaterasu), incorporating the heads of the other clans into a state administrative system. This imperial clan was to rule Japan or stand as a figurehead for political authority for many centuries up until the present.

Buddhism was introduced to Japan from China in the middle of the sixth century, and it became a major carrier of Chinese civilization. The animistic folk beliefs later called Shintō saw the divine in nature and focused on fertility and life in this world. In contrast, Buddhism focused on suffering and death. The seventh and eighth centuries saw the introduction of a writing system based on Chinese graphs, Chinese literature, and Chinese philosophy, particularly Confucianism, which established a sociopolitical and moral code based on the family, with filial piety as the highest virtue. Chinese became the official language of government and religion in Japan, creating a double system of spoken Japanese and written Chinese.

In 794, the imperial capital moved to Heian, present-day Kyoto, marking the beginning of four centuries of cultural efflorescence centered on the imperial court and aristocratic life. The Fujiwara clan came to the fore in the Heian period, taking firm control of the throne in the latter half of the tenth century, using regents to rule in place of a child emperor. The Fujiwara married their daughters to the emperor, thereby becoming the uncles of future emperors, and placing a clan member in position to be ruling chancellor. They poured vast resources into the entourages and residences of these imperial consorts, enabling women's court literature to flourish at this time. The most powerful of these regents was Fujiwara Michinaga (966–1027), whose eldest daughter Shōshi became empress and consort of Emperor Ichijō (r. 986–1011). Murasaki Shikibu probably wrote much of *The Tale of Genji* while serving as a lady in waiting to Empress Shōshi.

The Tale of Genji reveals the high level of cultural accomplishment of the imperial court—in such diverse fields as calligraphy, painting, poetry, incense, dance, and music—even as it focuses on the vicissitudes of a wide range of very distinctive women. Much of vernacular literature from the Heian period through the medieval period exists in a larger Buddhist context that regards excessive attachment—especially deep emotions such as resentment, hatred, and love—as the cause for suffering and a serious deterrent to individual salvation. In *The Tale of Genji,* the Buddhist notion of impermanence is embodied in the fleeting cherry blossoms and many of the most moving, powerfully emotional scenes are those that are the result of the sorrowful and fleeting nature of things.

At the end of the twelfth century, two major warrior clans, the Heike (Taira) and the Genji (Minamoto), engaged in an extended war for control of the capital and the court, ushering in the age of the samurai. The result was two political centers, a Heike court government in Kyoto and a Genji military government in the East, with the latter asserting ever greater control. Out of this struggle developed a new warrior culture: the frugal lifestyle of the samurai, the strong fighting spirit, and samurai ethics of self-sacrifice, honor, and loyalty. During this period, the Buddhist temples became the institutional centers of learning and culture, much as the church did in medieval Europe. In the late medieval period, from 1336 to 1572, the political center shifted back to Kyoto. The Ashikaga shogunate, or military government, was to rule over Japan for almost two and a half centuries. It came of age with its third shogun, Ashikaga Yoshimitsu (r. 1368–1394), who unified the rival imperial courts, took control of the imperial court in Kyoto, and became a great patron of the arts.

General Characteristics of Japanese Literature

Japanese literature often stresses brevity, condensation, and overtones. The paring down of form and expression occurs in a wide variety of forms: poetry such as the haiku, the shortest poetic form in world literature, Noh drama, gardens, bonsai, tea ceremony, and ink painting, to mention only the most obvious. Japanese drama and prose fiction, while sometimes possessing elaborate and complex plot structures, are usually concerned with the elaboration of a particular mood or state of mind. *The Tale of Genji* is highlighted by a series of partings, including the deaths and departures of major characters throughout the book. The closeness of traditional social ties—between parent and child, lord and retainer, husband and wife, individual and group—makes the parting an emotionally explosive situation, which is often presented in highly poetical language.

The lyrical character of Japanese vernacular literature derives in significant part from the fusion of genres and media that in European literature are generally thought of as being separate. In Japan, prose fiction and prose writing are extensively interwoven with poetry and poetic diction. Since the Renaissance, European theater has generally been split into three basic forms—drama, opera, and ballet—whereas traditional Japanese theater has combined these elements (acting, music, and dance) in Noh drama, kabuki, and jōruri, or puppet theater (for an extraordinary example of the latter, see Chikamatsu Mon'zaemon's *The Love Suicides at Amijima,* Volume 2, page 70). This multimedia quality often means that instead of emphasizing the world being represented, the dramatic work calls attention to itself as a medium of performance.

Like the structure of the prose narratives, Japanese literary forms tend to add on to rather than replace one another. Every major historical era gave birth to new literary and artistic genres, but usually without destroying or abandoning the earlier forms. The thirty-one syllable classical poem emerged in the Nara and Heian periods, linked verse in the medieval period, the seventeen-syllable haiku in the Edo period, and free verse in the modern period (under the influence of Western poetry). With the exception of linked verse, all of these poetic genres continue to flourish today in Japan. The same is true of Japanese drama. Noh and its comic counterpart, kyōgen, emerged in the Muromachi period; jōruri and kabuki became dominant in the Edo theater, and modern theater came to the fore in the twentieth century. Instead of each new form displacing the previous one, these dramatic forms have continued to coexist even today. An early masterpiece such as *The Tale of Genji* thus remains an ongoing presence in Japanese literature in the twenty-first century.

48

The Islamic World

When it comes to the word, the language that played a substantial role in the shaping and development of Arabic culture, Islam shares the emphasis on language and writing that also governed Judaism and Christianity. The emergence of Islam and the codification of the Arabic language in the Qur'an ensured the continuous development of Arabic over two millennia. The oldest record of Arabic appeared in an Assyrian account of fighting from 853 to 626 B.C.E. Mecca, the commercial center of Arabia, acted as a linguistic melting pot that developed a standard language out of a myriad of different dialects. By the sixth century, there was a widely recognized literary language distinct from all forms of the spoken language in common currency in Arabia.

Arabic poetry is deeply rooted in oral tradition, and it was a voice long before it was expressed through an alphabet. Poets did not create poetry for themselves but for the tribe and on behalf of the whole community. This poetry was often connected to religious ritual, a dimension that was enhanced by the concept of divine inspiration. Both poets and their audiences believed that the poet was touched by a *jinn*

Calligraphy of the name of the Prophet Muhammad, Turkey, 1827. Based on centuries-old calligraphic traditions, this dynamic verbal "image" of the Prophet is surrounded by a description (*hilyah*) of the Prophet by his son-in-law 'Ali, which concludes: "When walking, he leaned forward, as if descending a slope. If he turned to see something, he would turn with his whole body. Between his shoulders he had the Seal of Prophethood. He was the last of the Prophets."

(a demon or Muse), who revealed the poem to him. Poetry played the role of the media in our present time: poets spread the news, elaborated the official line on issues, and attacked the enemies of the caliphs, Muhammad's successors. The Qur'an too developed poetic oral recitation and used it very effectively; it is no coincidence that the only miracle of Muhammad was a verbal miracle, the Qur'an itself. Poetry maintained its position in the culture for centuries, even though Muhammad had an early aversion to poetry and the Qur'an says of poets that "most of them are liars" who "wander distractedly in every valley" (26:223–25).

Muhammad was born around 570 C.E. into a distinguished Meccan family. Orphaned in early childhood, he was brought up by a succession of relatives and around 595 married a rich, older Meccan woman, Khadija. Little is known of the period between his marriage at the age of twenty-five and the revelation of the message of Islam to him at the age of forty around the year 610. One clear explanation is theological: the archangel Gabriel suddenly appeared to him and gave him a prophetic call. The early Meccan verses of the Qur'an enumerated the various manifestations of God in nature that should convince those who have time to reflect and logically deduce that there is sublime power greater than human power—*islam* means "surrender" to God. Muhammad's early preaching was tolerated because it didn't threaten the gods of Mecca or disturb its social hierarchy. Things changed when he openly attacked polytheism and the gods of Mecca, and declared that the Ka'bah, the traditional Meccan sanctuary, belonged only to the one true God, Allah. The powerful merchant class turned against Muhammad when he called for justice, attacked greed and the oppression of the poor, and asked people to free themselves from love of wealth and from all forms of deceit.

The acceleration and severity of the opposition of the notables of Mecca to his call, combined with the death of his wife, led to Muhammad's migration, or *hijra*, to Medina in 622. The *hijra* marked the beginning of the formative years of Islam itself as a major religion and the emergence of the community of believers as a force to reckon with. In 628 a treaty was negotiated with Mecca, allowing Muhammad and his followers to make their annual pilgrimage there. When the Meccans broke the treaty the following year, Muhammad decided to invade his birthplace, and achieved the conquest of Mecca in 630, becoming the strongest man in Arabia. Muhammad succeeded in uniting the complementary resources of the nomadic and the urban Arabs, and the Arab area within the peninsula was integrated in a manner never before attained. Soon the nation became a vast empire, and developed a civilization religious in spirit and manifestation.

The Muslim domain continued to expand after Mohammad's death in 632, conquering the whole of Persia, Syria, Palestine, Jerusalem, Egypt, and North Africa as far as present-day Tunis. A civil war ensued between the followers of the Prophet's cousin and son-in-law 'Ali and the 'Umayyad caliphate, resulting in the split between Sunni or orthodox Muslims and supporters of 'Ali, known as the Shi'ites ("followers"). The Umayyads expanded the Muslim Empire to India and sub-Saharan Africa, and to Andalusia in Spain. The Umayyads were supportive patrons of poetry and theology, but it was during the reign of the subsequent Abbasid Caliphate (750–1258) that Muslim civilization reached its peak culturally, economically, scientifically, and militarily, extending the boundaries of the empire to China and Southeast Asia and spreading Islam through a large part of Africa. "The Tale of Sympathy the Learned" in *The Thousand and One Nights* gives the reader a glimpse of the cultural atmosphere in the court the Abbasids had established in Baghdad.

Most of the major classical poets are from this period, including Abu Nuwas and Ibn al-Rumi. The study of language flourished and the intricate forms of Arabic poetry were skillfully codified. The first Arabic dictionary was compiled and literary history and criticism of Arabic literature were initiated. This was also the period that saw the advancement of Arabic mathematics and sciences: geometry, algebra, medicine, alchemy, physics, chemistry, and anatomy all flourished. Most of the knowledge developed during this period was later translated into Latin and formed a key basis for the late Middle Ages and the Renaissance in Europe. Without the translations made at the Baghdad center known as the School of Wisdom, we might not now be able to enjoy the critical insights of Aristotle, whose *Poetics* was preserved thanks to the Arabic translation.

Islamic culture also continued to develop in Persian and other languages of the Muslim world. Following the fall of the Abbasid dynasty in 1258, the principal center of power moved from Baghdad first to Egypt and then to Turkey with the rise of the

Ottomans (1500–1900). The most notable developments took place in Andalusia, in the field of intellectual inquiry and Islamic philosophy, and in Egypt in the field of narrative and popular epics. The work of the most distinguished Islamic philosopher, Ibn Rushd or Averroës of Córdoba, is a product of the Arabic culture in Andalusia. He had immense influence on the Jewish and Christian worlds of philosophy. In Egypt, a proliferation of popular literature gave rise to exquisite epics such as those of Bani-Hilal and 'Antara, and a large number of the stories of *The Thousand and One Nights* were elaborated.

With the Qur'an, Arabic became a world language, the language of medieval Islamic civilization, the Latin of the Muslim world. With the expansion of the Islamic *'umma* (community or nation) into a multiracial and multicultural civilization, many other cultural influences have been absorbed into Arabic culture and enriched its capacity for expression. Similarly, Arabic forms and Islamic traditions have penetrated many other languages and cultures, as can be seen in the section Iberia: The Meeting of Three Worlds.

Medieval Europe

There is no doubt that medieval Europe was a difficult place in which to live. Waves of raids, invasions, and tribal migrations rolled through and destabilized the former Roman Empire: Germanic tribes in the fifth and sixth centuries, followed by Vikings from the north, Muslims from the south, and Magyar and other Central Asian tribes from the east. War remained a way of life through the thirteenth century, with myriad territorial skirmishes and numerous Crusades into Iberia, the Middle East, and North Africa. Then, in the mid-fourteenth century, the Black Plague killed off a third of Europe's population. For all of its terrors the Middle Ages bequeathed to later European culture much of its identity and heritage: the geographic, social, and political conceptions of Europe and most of the European nations; the cathedrals, castles, and cities; the institutions of government and religion; the codes of honor and chivalry; the languages, the poetry of love, and the stories of adventure. A good argument can be made that the Renaissance was itself a medieval invention.

Imperial rule had spread the Latin language across the continent, and Latin continued to play a key role in ecclesiastical and monastic life as well as in government, administration, and law. As economic expansion brought relative social and political stability in the twelfth and thirteenth centuries, the vernacular languages as we know them today began to predominate—English, French, Spanish, German, and Italian among others—and many of the national borders (and border disputes) began to solidify. In this period, usually known as the High Middle Ages, internationalism came to mean not so much a shared culture and authority as a broad knowledge of many different cultures and authorities. The English poet Geoffrey Chaucer was a professional diplomat equally at ease in local dialects around Britain, in French in Paris and in Tuscan Italian in Florence; the Florentine poet Dante Alighieri wrote a treatise on the Romance languages and incorporated the vocabulary of Latin, Occitan (also known as Provençal), French, and many Italian dialects into his *Divine Comedy*. England was ruled for several centuries by Normans, descendants of the original "Northmen," ninth-century Danish invaders who had settled in Normandy in northwest France; the court language was Anglo-Norman, a version of Old

Scenes from the Bayeux Tapestry, France, late 11th century. Attributed to Queen Matilda (wife of William the Conqueror) and her attendants, this great scroll of embroidered linen (230 feet long by 20 inches high) depicts the Norman Conquest of England in exuberant detail.

French. A mix of Byzantine, Muslim, Jewish, Lombard, Norman and later peoples made long- established cities such as Palermo in Sicily new centers of cultural interchange and innovation. Muslim rulers long controlled southern Iberia, known then as al-Andalus: their administrations were full of Jewish courtiers, their cities crowded with Mozarabs, or arabized Christians, and their armies strengthened by complex alliances with neighboring Christian rulers.

Language and Culture

After they had sacked Rome in 410, Germanic tribes out of northern and southeastern Europe eventually took over and settled different regions of the now-dissolved empire. Monastic communities and ambitious churchmen and rulers invested much time, money and artistry into copying ancient manuscripts and attempting to preserve a Latin heritage in danger of vanishing forever. Most of the literature that has come down to us from before the eleventh century is in the medieval or low Latin that was the lingua franca of the time. It is handwritten in ink on sheets of parchment (made from the skin of cattle, sheep, or goats) bound together down one edge, in what is known as a codex. In addition to lyrics of nature and of love, hymns and other forms of religious poetry were dominant genres; both forms were often emotional and direct in their language and imagery. Alongside these written examples of Latin poetry, there were local oral traditions such as the Celtic tales or *lais,* the Anglo-Saxon epic of the great chieftain Beowulf, and popular songs all over the continent.

Most educated Romans had been fluent in both Latin and Greek, but once the empire had been divided between East and West in the fourth century, this gradually ceased to be the case. Greek was a lost language in western Europe. Homer was known only by reputation, and the philosophy of Plato and Aristotle only through Roman commentaries of a few minor works. Greek thought eventually made its way back into Christian Europe across the boundary between Islam and Christianity and by means of Arabic translations, accompanied by learned glosses by contemporary philosophers such as the Jewish scholar Moses Maimonides and Ibn Rushd, also known as Averroës the Commentator. In important frontier cities such as Toledo (recaptured from al-Andalus in 1058) and Palermo (known as the city of the three-fold tongue, taken by the Normans in 1072), Jewish, Muslim, and Christian scholars debated while they translated the wisdom of the ancients into Latin. Translators at work in the 13th-century Galician-Portuguese court of Alfonso X, for instance, included five Jews, four Spanish Christians, four Italians, a Muslim converted to Christianity, technical editors to deal with difficult terms, and secretaries to write everything down.

Religion and the Church

Catholic Christianity was simultaneously the strongest link between the Middle Ages and the classical world and the strongest impediment to that link. Until the twelfth century, scholarship was conducted almost entirely under the auspices of the church, first in the monasteries and later in cathedral towns and in the courts of rulers such as Charlemagne, founder of the Holy Roman Empire in 800. As opposed to the courtier's life that characterized the southern frontier cities and Islamic capitals, monastic scholarship prided itself on detachment from worldly concerns.

By contrast, the papacy, increasingly embroiled in the temporal demands of politics and governance and generally suspicious of new ideas, more closely resembled the southern courts than the monasteries. The papal states accumulated vast wealth and power through being a principal player or influence in nearly every one of the countless negotiations, treaties, wars, and betrayals that raged throughout the period. The worldly preeminence of the papacy was seen by many reformers to be at odds with the Gospel message of Jesus that salvation was to be found in discarding wealth and earthly ties. Great damage was done to papal prestige when in 1378 the Great Schism led to thirty-seven years of competing French and Italian popes in Avignon and Rome. The stage was set for the Protestant Reformation to challenge the papacy's thousand-year supremacy as the spiritual voice of the Christian church.

Reform took many shapes before Martin Luther's definitive rebellion in 1518, from powerful figures within the ecclesiastical inner circles to abbots, abbesses, monks and nuns to laymen and -women whom divine inspiration led to take up preaching or writing. One of the earliest was Saint Benedict (c. 480–c. 550), whose celebrated "Rule" guided the rituals of daily monastic life for centuries to come, covering even details of eating, drinking and sleeping. Benedictines and later orders were also invested in expanding the frontiers of Christianity through conversion.

Crusading was an important way of uniting the Christians of Europe and channeling outward their military energy and thirst for plunder. Quixotic enthusiasts such as the founder of the Franciscan order of mendicant (or begging) friars saw it as their duty to convert the heathens across the Mediterranean (Saint Francis of Assisi traveled to Egypt to preach to the Sultan after five of his brethren had been martyred there), but the customary ecclesiastical response was to kill them. The first Crusade was proclaimed by Pope Urban II in 1095 following the Byzantine emperor's request for aid against the Muslims. The inflamed piety of the Crusaders marching eastward took its toll on non-Christians along the way, especially the Jews, who were slaughtered indiscriminately. The Crusaders made it all the way to Jerusalem, which they captured on July 15, 1099, killing, plundering, and weeping for pious joy. Following

this initial triumph, there were seven named Crusades through to the end of the thirteenth century, nearly all ending in calamitous defeat, as well as many other related expeditions, and even a disastrous Children's Crusade in 1212.

Feudalism

Warfare was a viable way of life for an entire estate of the medieval population, the *chevalier,* or knight. After the death of Charlemagne in 814, the empire crumbled into pieces of various sizes and influence, each one occupied by a lord with a certain amount of land under his control, himself often beholden to other lords, dukes or kings with broader jurisdictions. It was customary for holdings to be divided among all descendants upon the death of a lord, so there was no stable pattern of inheritance from first-born to first-born (the practice known as primogeniture). Lands were constantly being brought together and split apart in an endless, many-sided tug-of-war. As families intermarried and allegiances overlapped and intertwined, the form of social and political organization known as feudalism emerged as a way of giving some sort of structure to this chaos.

Feudalism varied across Europe, but there were some fundamental features. The primary relation was between lord and vassal, formalized by an oath of fealty, swearing mutual aid, protection, and vengeance if one party were killed. Lord and vassal were bound by a set of laws and a broader set of customs and traditions of which many elements survive to this day in the abstract concepts of honor and chivalry, a phenomenon explored at uproarious length many centuries later in Cervantes's novel, *Don Quixote*. In practice, of course, things were not as simple as Don Quixote would regard them: vassals were often obligated to several lords simultaneously, allegiances were bartered and sold, and a bond could dissolve in an instant if something better (for one party) came along. The Occitan poet Bertran de Born, for example, spent much of his life fighting with his brother for sole possession of the family castle.

The other principal component of the feudal hierarchy was the worker. The traditional use of slaves for field labor was less customary by this time. There were some peasants of free status who owed only rent, but most were serfs, bound to both lord and land. In the commonest scenario, a serf would be allowed to cultivate a plot of land for himself in return for cultivating other plots belonging to the lord. The serf would also receive a place to live in the village appended to the local manor, with protection in the event of attack from outside. Hunger, however, was the immediate concern. The clergy was equally embroiled in the feudal web, for local parish appointments and bishoprics were often controlled by local lords. Unsurprisingly, in a milieu rife with alliances and intrigues, the culture of feudalism excelled in the portrayal of situational ethics, using tales of knight errantry and epic heroism to explore the costs and benefits of the different choices of action and different types of behavior possible (or impossible) within the constraints of its world.

Lyric and Song

The cultural milieu of the feudal world was the court. The love lyric was elaborated in the worldly Andalusian cities of Córdoba, Granada, and Seville, and it flourished in the isolated castles of Occitania, the Anglo-Norman courts of England, the northern French seats such as Troyes in Champagne, and the courts of the German monarchs.

When not off fighting in battle, the knights and their lords required entertainment. This was the role of the *jongleur,* who would perform the songs produced by the troubadours and other songwriters around Europe. The lyrics reflect the interests of the audience: there is some singing of battle, a little of God, and much of the courtly pastimes of hunting, falconing, and, above all, lovemaking. For several centuries during the High Middle Ages, there was not a court without its resident poets, and the love lyrics they perfected remain with us to this day.

Song was not restricted to the feudal courts. Hymns and chants were integral to the experience of mass, and to the everyday life of many monks and nuns. Many working songs survive as well, songs for spinning, songs of injustice and rebellion, songs mimicking the sounds of different occupations. The *jongleurs* and other performers who traveled from court to court were well versed in many genres besides the love lyric. At court, they might also perform traditional epics, such as the *Song of Roland,* the legendary tale of Charlemagne's worthy vassal, or folktales, such as those Marie de France translated in her *Lais,* or satirical and parodic songs. Perhaps not at court, but at inns and on the road, they might also perform from a broad repertory of popular songs for less cultivated audiences. Traveling performers and pilgrims, such as the Goliards, or vagabond scholars, carried both sacred and profane tunes and lyrics back and forth across the continent, adapting and transforming them to suit different audiences, different musical instruments, and different expectations.

The Rise of the Cities

49

The irreverent songs of the vagabond scholars had little in common with the isolated refinement of the courts. The Goliard phenomenon was directly linked to the rise of cities and the universities within them in the twelfth and thirteenth centuries. Through the first part of the Middle Ages, the only large Western cities were in the south of Europe, in Muslim Iberia and in Sicily. Better crop rotation, a healthier diet, and new technology—the heavy plow, pulled by teams of horse or oxen, the water mill and later the windmill—helped the population of Europe to double between the eleventh century and the fourteenth, to around seventy or eighty million. Increased political stability and long-distance trade contributed to growth, as did a marked warming trend in the weather. The new population migrated to the growing cities, first in Italy, center of trade with the East and with North Africa, and later in northern Europe. Plying the rivers of Europe, commercial networks developed to link north and south further.

During these same centuries, European society was transformed from an oral to a literate culture. By 1300 commerce and government were dependent on written records and financial recordkeeping, introduced by Jewish merchants familiar with the practice from the wealthier and more sophisticated cultures of Islam and Byzantium. One reason for the rise of the universities was the need to train a body of clerks in these newly required skills. Many of these universities, such as those in Bologna, Paris, Oxford, Cambridge, Heidelberg, and Salamanca, survive to this day. Students and teachers were frequently planning to be or already were members of the secular clergy, unattached to a monastery or particular church. This "clerkly" culture was instrumental in the philosophical and literary movement known as the twelfth-century renaissance: a renewed interest in classical philosophy and literature paired with an increased investment in rational argumentation and the study of the physical world. It also gave rise to a body of writings that used women as the target for an attack against marriage and sensuality steeped in the ascetic tradition of ancient Roman *virtus* while reveling in the worldliness it detailed. The ambivalence of clerkly misogyny was captured well in Chaucer's "Wife of Bath's Prologue."

The newly intellectual focus on rationality and experience was seen by many religious figures to come at the expense of the basic tenets of the Christian faith. In a similar way, the new manufacturers and traders, or burghers, of the towns were for the most part also pious, although their piety did not always manifest itself in ways pleasing to the ecclesiastical authorities. A common ground was found in the magnificent cathedrals erected during these centuries, and funded in large part by the new urban wealth. Cathedrals such as Chartres or Notre-Dame de Paris, by far the tallest buildings in the land and visible for many miles, were holy places, but they were also the skyscrapers of their day, a brand-new architectural form symbolizing the new wealth and power of secular cities. The stained-glass windows (a twelfth-century innovation) are wonders of biblical storytelling; they also epitomize the art and invention of the urban artisans and manufacturers and the resources of the benefactors able to fund their artistry. Cathedrals were not simply houses of worship: they were guardians of relics and places of pilgrimage, the center of the social calendar, and the site of baptisms, marriages, and funerals. Since they often had at their feet the largest open spaces in the densely packed medieval city, they were the focal point of nearly every aspect of urban life.

Allegory and Adventure

One of the reasons that so many different uses and contradictions could coexist in the same place and in a single person is that the medieval mind preferred analogy to symbolism. Symbolic thinking typically attaches a unique and unchanging meaning to a specific word or object (the cathedral as a sacred place of worship), and an individual to a single, fixed identity from cradle to grave. By contrast, medieval thought tended to conceptualize the world in terms of a complex network of parallel relations. A critical device in this analogical way of thinking about the world was allegory, a mode of writing that marks nearly every aspect of medieval culture, most memorably perhaps in the realm of literature. To approach the world allegorically is to regard it as simultaneously possessing a multitude of meanings. Just as the medieval person was accustomed to juggling several languages and several different cultures, so was she or he accustomed to keeping multiple meanings in mind simultaneously, or to singing sacrilegious songs in the tavern while piously praying in church, without feeling obligated to choose irrevocably between any of the several apparently contradictory possibilities. The mysterious behavior of the Green Knight in the fourteenth-century romance *Sir Gawain and the Green Knight,* for example, is neither psychologically consistent nor immediately comprehensible; nevertheless, it compels the reader's attention, demanding that his riddle be solved even as the complexities of the characters and events belie any simple answer.

The medieval world, like the literature that has survived from it, is a fascinating combination of familiarity and alienness. Much that seems to us traditional, even timeless, was in fact brand new in the Middle Ages, from chivalry and love poetry to the cathedrals and cities to the Catholic Christian church and the very idea of Europe. And much of what the Renaissance chose to exclude from the Middle Ages, especially the legacy of the classical world, was for the medieval person a fact of everyday life. To think medievally is to think several ways at once; that was their great accomplishment and the great challenge and joy their literature poses to a modern reader, accustomed to thinking in one language, one culture, and one identity at a time.

THE MEDIEVAL ERA

YEAR	THE WORLD	LITERATURE
200		
	220 End of Han dynasty in China	
	220–265 Three Kingdoms period in China	
	265–419 Chin dynasty in China	
300		
	335–470 Gupta dynasty in northern India	
		365–427 Life of Chinese poet Tao Qian
400		
	c. 400 Unification of Japan	c. 400 *Mahabharata* achieves established form
	410 Visigoths sack Rome	
	420 China divided between Southern and Northern dynasties (to 589)	
	450 Anglo-Saxons invade England	
500		524 Boethius, *The Consolation of Philosophy*
	530 Justinian Code	
	c. 550 Buddhism introduced to Japan	
	c. 570–632 Life of the Prophet Muhammad	
	588 Lombards invade Italy	
	589 Sui dynasty in China (to 618)	
600		
		c. 600–646 Life of pre-Islamic woman poet al-Khansa'
	618 Tang dynasty in China (to 907)	
	622 Hijra of Muhammad from Mecca; foundation of Islam	
	638 Arab conquest of Jerusalem	
		651–652 Text of Qur'an established
		c. 658–680 Caedmon's dream hymn
	698 Arabs take Carthage	
700		
	700 Benedictine missionaries complete the Christianization of England begun by Gregory the Great	
		701 Birth of Chinese poets Wang Wei (d. 761) and Li Bo (d. 762)
	710–784 Nara period in Japan	
	711–715 Arabs arrive in Spain and in western India	
		712–770 Life of poet Du Fu
		731 The Venerable Bede, *Ecclesiastical History of the English Nation*
	732 Charles Martel halts Arab invasion at Poitiers	
	750 Abbasid dynasty in Middle East and North Africa (to 1258)	c. 750 Irish monks produce the *Book of Kells;* Ibn Ishaq writes *The Biography of the Prophet*
		c. 750–950 *Beowulf*
		753 The Venerable Bede dies
		759 *Manyōshū,* collection of Japanese court poetry

YEAR	THE WORLD	LITERATURE
	763 Tibetans invade Tang China 772–804 Saxon Wars 786–809 Haroun al-Rashid is Caliph in Baghdad 794–1185 Heian period in Japan	
800		
	800 Fujiwara clan achieves dominance in Japan (to 12th century) 800 Charlemagne is crowned Holy Roman Emperor (dies in 814)	
	819 Samanid dynasty in Persia (to 1005) 870 Vikings discover Iceland 899 Alfred the Great of England dies	810–850 Writings by al-Jahiz, Arabic prose master 868 *The Diamond Sutra,* world's oldest surviving printed book
900		
	907 Five Dynasties period in China (to 959) 960 Song dynasty in China (to 1279) 979 Paper money introduced in China	
1000		
	1000 Sweden begins to be converted to Christianity; Iceland converted to Christianity c. 1000 Vikings reach North America	10th century First Mozarabic *kharjas* in Spain 1002 Sei Shōnagon, *The Pillow Book* c. 1000–1019 Murasaki Shikibu, *The Tale of Genji*
1010		1010 Firdawsi's Persian epic, the *Shahname*
	1018 Tamils conquer Sri Lanka	
1020		1027 Ibn Hazm, *The Dove's Neckring*
1030		
	1031 Christian reconquest of Spain begins	
1040		
	c. 1045 Chinese invent movable type printing	
1050	1054 Great Schism between the Eastern and Western Churches	
1060		
	1066 Battle of Hastings: William the Conqueror and Normans begin their rule over the British Isles	1063–1078 Anselm of Canterbury, *Proslogion*
1070		
	1071 Seljuk Turks defeat Byzantines at Manzikert	1071–1127 William of Aquitaine, the first known troubadour 1075–1141 Yehuda ha-Levi, author of poems and *The Book of the Khazars*
1080		
	1085 Yorimoto becomes first shogun of Japan; Christians recapture Toledo, Spain	

YEAR	THE WORLD	LITERATURE
1090	1095 Pope Urban II preaches the First Crusade 1099 Fall of Jerusalem to Christian crusaders	
1100	c. 1100 Anasazi build cliff dwellings at Mesa Verde and Chaco Canyon	
1110		
1120	c. 1122–1204 Eleanor of Aquitaine, queen consort of Louis VII of France (1137–1152) and of Henry II of England (1152–1204)	
1130	1130 Song move capital to Huangzhou	1130–1145 Bernard of Clairvaux, *Sermons on the Song of Songs* c. 1133–1140 Letters of Abelard and Heloise
1140	1147–1149 Second Crusade	1141–1152 Hildegard von Bingen, *Scivias* 1146–1174 *The Play of Adam*
1150	1152 Temple of Angkor Wat completed	c. 1150 Geoffrey of Monmouth, *History of the Kings of Britain*
1160	1163 Foundation stone laid for the cathedral of Notre-Dame de Paris 1167 Foundation of Oxford University	1160–1180 Marie de France, *Lais* 1165–1180 Chrétien de Troyes, Arthurian romances 1169–1196 Ibn Rushd (Averroës), summaries and commentaries on Aristotle
1170	1170 Death of Thomas Becket ordered by Henry II	1177 Farid ud-Din al'Attar, *The Conference of the Birds*
1180	1187 Saladin retakes Jerusalem from the Christians 1189–1192 Third Crusade led by Richard I the Lion-Heart and Frederick Barbarossa	1180–1194 Bertran de Born, *Songs* 1186–1196 Andreas Capellanus, *The Art of Courtly Love*
1190	1198 Innocent III founds the Papal State and organizes the Fourth Crusade to recapture Jerusalem from the Arabs	1190–1230 Walther von der Vogelweide, *Songs*
1200	1206 Genghis Khan unites Mongols 1208 Innocent III proclaims the Albigensian Crusade	late 12th–early 13th century *The Poem of the Cid* 1207–1283 Life of Persian mystical poet Jalaloddin Rumi
1210	1215 Magna Carta 1216 Dominican order founded by St. Dominic of Spain	c. 1210 Gottfried von Strassburg, *Tristan* 1212 Kamo no Chomei, *An Account of My Ten-Foot-Square Hut* 1218 First version of *Tales of Heike*

YEAR	THE WORLD	LITERATURE
1220	1222–1242 Mongols invade Europe, rule Russia for two centuries 1227 Death of Genghis Khan 1226 Francis of Assisi dies	c. 1225 Guillaume de Lorris, *The Romance of the Rose*
1230		
1240	1244 Muslims capture Jerusalem; West doesn't recapture Jerusalem until 1917 1248 Construction of the Alhambra begins in Granada	c. 1240 Snorri Sturluson, *The Prose Edda*
1250	1258 Mongols sack Baghdad and end Abbasid dynasty	c. 1250 Alfonso the Wise, *Cantigas of Santa Maria* c. 1250–1275 Mechthild von Magdeburg, *A Flowing Light of the Godhead*
1260	1260 Consecration of Chartres Cathedral 1267 Giotto begins his school of painting in Florence	c. 1265–1273 Thomas Aquinas, *Summa Theologica* 1267 Brunetto Latini, *Book of the Treasure*
1270	1270 Eighth Crusade 1279 The Mongols under Kublai Khan crush final Song resistance	
1280	1280 Yuan (Mongol) dynasty in China (to 1368) 1281 Beginning of Ottoman power in Turkey	c. 1280 *Njal's Saga* c. 1284 Ramon Llull, *Blanquerna*
1290	1292 Marco Polo returns from travels	1295 Dante Alighieri, *La Vita Nuova* 1298 Marco Polo, *The Book of Marvels*
1300	1309–1377 Papacy at Avignon	early 13th century Ibn al-Arabi, *Gentle Now, Doves* mid-13th century Martin Codax, *Songs* late 13th century Jean de Meun's continuation of *The Romance of the Rose* c. 1300–1325 *Songs* by Dom Dinis, King of Portugal 1307–1321 Dante, *The Divine Comedy*
1310		
1320	1324 Pilgrimage to Mecca of Mansa Musa of Mal	1321 Dante Alighieri dies
1330	1337 Hundred Years' War begins 1338 Beginning of Muromachi period in Japan (to 1573)	

YEAR	THE WORLD	LITERATURE
1340	1345–1346 Ibn Battuta travels in Southeast Asia and China 1347–1351 Black Death in Europe	1340–1374 Francis Petrarch, *Scattered Rhymes* 1343 Juan Ruiz, *The Book of Good Love* 1349 Giovanni Boccaccio, *The Decameron*
1350	1354 Ottomans begin conquest of the Balkan Peninsula	
1360	1365 First German university is opened at Heidelberg; the universities of Bologna and Oxford date from the 12th century 1368 Ming dynasty in China (to 1644)	
1370		1374 Francis Petrarch dies 1378 Death of Muslim world traveler Ibn Battuta
1380	c. 1380 Ottomans found Janissary corps	c. 1388–1400 Geoffrey Chaucer, *The Canterbury Tales*
1390	1398 Tamerlane sacks Delhi	
1400	1405 Zheng He's first voyage to the Indian Ocean	1400 Geoffrey Chaucer dies late 14th century *Sir Gawain and the Green Knight* 1404–1405 Christine de Pizan, *The Book of the City of Ladies*
1410		
1420		
1430	1431 Joan of Arc dies 1434 Medici family gains control over government of Florence	
1440	1441 Portuguese capture slaves in Africa; start of Atlantic Slave Trade	1444 Juan de Mena, *The Labyrinth of Fortune*
1450	1450 Gutenberg invents the printing press 1453 Fall of Constantinople; Ottoman Turks end the Eastern Empire 1455 Henry VI wages the Wars of the Roses (between Lancaster and York)	
1460	1469 Ferdinand of Aragon marries Isabella of Castile and unites the kingdom of Spain	1461 François Villon, *The Testament*
1470		
1480		
1490	1492 Ferdinand and Isabella annex Granada and expel Jews from Spain; discovery of America	

Poetry of the Tang Dynasty

Chinese literature began with the lyric, whose period of greatest flowering, by common agreement, was the Tang dynasty (618–907). Artistic achievement of all sorts benefited from the reunification of the country that had been accomplished during the preceding, short-lived Sui dynasty (581–618) and the political consolidation and expansion that followed for over a century until the brief but disruptive rebellion led by An Lushan between 755 and 757. The imperial capital of Chang'an thrived, thanks to elaborate transportation systems that brought goods in from the provinces, as well as equally sophisticated administrative structures that dispatched bureaucrats in all directions to manage them. Government policies fostered the institutional growth of both Buddhism and Daoism, while still maintaining a commitment to Confucian texts and values, encouraging an atmosphere of pluralism that was further enlivened by the many influences generated by rich contacts with foreign cultures, especially those of central Asia.

The earliest theories of poetry in China regarded it as a spontaneous, if crafted, response to an external stimulus, a form of writing of unquestioned value as a means of communication, instruction, and critique. Poetic composition was a skill that any scholar/bureaucrat would be expected to display, on occasions both serious and trivial. The standard collection of Tang poetry contains almost 49,000 works by 2,200 poets and testifies in its variety to its deep integration in the daily life of the educated class, for whom poetry was a widely accepted currency of personal, social, and political exchange. It is difficult to imagine how depleted the collections of the past would be had such circumstances not inspired, or compelled, the composition of a poem. In particular, the typically peripatetic career of government bureaucrats is responsible for the thick chapters of farewell and keepsake poems in almost all individual collections. The cultural importance of poetry was further institutionalized during the Tang by the introduction of a test of poetic composition on the most prestigious imperial civil service examination that, when passed, conferred on the successful candidate the most prestigious degree, that of the *jinshi,* or "presented scholar." This requirement was in fact removed at various points during the dynasty, and debates raged almost immediately regarding its reliability as an indicator of future administrative competence and its influence on the quality of poetic production in general. Its presence does certainly attest, nonetheless, to the stature and popularity of poetry during the Tang and confirms that it was a means of articulating the relationship between an individual and the body politic.

Chinese literary historians have long been fond of demarcating periods and categories, and the Tang was no exception to this practice. The history of Tang poetry has thus typically been divided into four periods—Early, High, Middle, and Late—with its peak, unsurprisingly, during the High Tang, or the first half of the eighth century. The three most esteemed poets of the period—Wang Wei, Li Bo, and Du Fu—were also conveniently associated with the three major belief systems of the epoch, Buddhism, Daoism, and Confucianism, respectively. Their works together epitomize the varied creativity of this central period of Chinese poetry.

WANG WEI ■ (701–761)

One of the most prominent poets of his time, Wang Wei was born into a distinguished family and earned youthful renown as poet, painter, and musician. After passing the most literary of the imperial civil service examinations in 721, he enjoyed a slow but steady rise through government ranks that took him through various offices at the capital, to several provincial posts, and finally in 759 back to court in a high-ranking position with few duties. A minor infraction and the death of his mother briefly interrupted his progress, but the most important setback occurred when he was captured by the rebel general An Lushan, who took over the Tang capital of Chang'an from 755 to 757 and forced Wang Wei to serve under his puppet government. Only the intercession of Wang Wei's powerful younger brother led to his pardon and rehabilitation upon the imperial family's return to the capital.

Wang Wei was an accomplished master of both old and new poetic forms and was especially admired for his quatrains in regulated verse. His poetry displays the hallmarks of the urbane courtly style—impersonal, witty, and decorous—whose mastery is best revealed, perhaps paradoxically, in his limpid evocations of life in retreat, and especially scenes from his country estate on the Wang River outside the capital. After his mother's death in 730, he converted part of this property to a monastery, and his poetry demonstrates his commitment to Buddhism, sometimes in its themes, but even more so in language and style. Wang Wei was also an influential painter, and in one poem in fact declares that he was "mistakenly a poet" and in an earlier life "must have been a painter." His depictions of landscape, however, are noteworthy not for elaborate descriptive detail but rather for their apparently artless language and tranquil mood. In accord with Chan (Zen) doctrine, he appears to accept both the simple and concrete reality of nature and its ultimate illusoriness, and his poetry conveys this dual awareness in a tone of contemplative, dispassionate detachment.

from The Wang River Collection[1]

Preface

My retreat is in the Wang River mountain valley. The places to walk to include: Meng Wall Cove, Huazi Hill, Grained Apricot Lodge, Clear Bamboo Range, Deer Enclosure, Magnolia Enclosure, Dogwood Bank, Sophora Path, Lakeside Pavilion, Southern Hillock, Lake Yi, Willow Waves, Luan Family Shallows, Gold Powder Spring, White Rock Rapids, Northern Hillock, Bamboo Lodge, Magnolia Bank, Lacquer Tree Garden, and Pepper Tree Garden. When Pei Di and I were at leisure, we each composed the following quatrains.

1. Meng Wall Cove

> A new home at the mouth of Meng Wall:
> Ancient trees, the last withered willows.
> The one who comes again—who will it be?
> Grieving in vain for former men's possessions.

5. Deer Enclosure

> Empty mountain, no man is seen.
> Only heard are echoes of men's talk.
> Reflected light enters the deep wood
> And shines again on blue-green moss.

1. Translated by Pauline Yu. Inspired by sites on his country estate in Lantian, outside the capital of Chang'an, Wang Wei composed a series of 20 quatrains that were matched by a set written by his close friend Pei Di (b. 716). Wang also painted a long handscroll depicting the same scenic spots; the scroll has been lost, though numerous imitations exist.

8. Sophora Path

> The bypath is shaded by sophoras;
> In secluded shadows, green moss is thick.
> But the gatekeeper sweeps it in welcome
> In case the mountain monk should come.

11. Lake Yi

> Blowing flutes cross to the distant shore.
> At day's dusk I bid farewell to you.
> On the lake with one turn of the head:
> Mountain green rolls into white clouds.

17. Bamboo Lodge

> Alone I sit amid the dark bamboo,
> Play the zither and whistle[2] loud again.
> In the deep wood men do not know
> The bright moon comes to shine on me.

Bird Call Valley[1]

> Man at leisure, cassia flowers fall.
> The night still, spring mountain empty.
> The moon emerges, startling mountain birds:
> At times they call within the spring valley.

Farewell

> Dismounting I give you wine to drink,
> And inquire where you are going.
> You say you did not achieve your wishes
> And return to rest at the foot of Southern Mountain.
> 5 But go—do not ask again:
> White clouds have no ending time.

Farewell to Yuan the Second on His Mission to Anxi[1]

> In Wei City morning rain dampens the light dust.
> By the travelers' lodge, green upon green—the willows' color is new.
> I urge you to drink up yet another glass of wine:
> Going west from Yang Pass, there are no old friends.

2. This was probably a combination of Daoist breathing techniques and whistling, and was said to express feelings while harmonizing with nature and facilitating the achievement of immortality.

1. The first of a series of five quatrains composed at a friend's estate, "Miscellaneous Poems Written at Huangfu Yue's Cloud Valley."

1. One of many poems to often unidentified fellow officials setting off to distant posts. The city of Wei was in Shaanxi Province, near the imperial capital, whereas Anxi was located far to the northwest in Xinjiang. This quatrain was set to music and became a popular farewell tune.

Visiting the Temple of Gathered Fragrance[1]

      I do not know the Temple of Gathered Fragrance,
      For several miles, entering cloudy peaks.
      Ancient trees, paths without people;
      Deep in the mountains, where is the bell?
5   Noise from the spring swallows up lofty rocks;
      The color of the sun chills green pines.
      Toward dusk by the curve of an empty pond,
      Peaceful meditation controls poison dragons.[2]

Zhongnan Retreat

      In middle years I am rather fond of the Dao;
      My late home is at the foot of Southern Mountain.
      When the feeling comes, each time I go there alone.
      That splendid things are empty, of course, I know.
5   I walk to the place where the water ends
      And sit and watch the time when clouds rise.
      Meeting by chance an old man of the forest,
      I chat and laugh without a date to return.

In Response to Vice-Magistrate Zhang

      In late years I care for tranquility alone—
      A myriad affairs do not concern my heart.
      A glance at myself: there are no long-range plans.
      I only know to return to the old forest.
5   Pine winds blow, loosening my belt;
      The mountain moon shines as I pluck my zither.
      You ask about reasons for success and failure:
      A fisherman's song enters the shore's deeps.[1]

LI BO ▪ (701–762)

About Li Bo's family little is known for certain, despite the richness of legends concerning his background—for which the poet himself was probably largely responsible. Possibly of Turkish origin, he was raised in what is now Sichuan province and appears to have treated his birth in the wild west of China as a license to flout accepted norms of behavior. Unlike most of his peers he never attempted the civil service examination, thus sparing himself the humiliation of failure. But his career aspirations were no less ambitious, perhaps

1. A Buddhist monastery located south of Chang'an.
2. Most likely referring to illusions or passions that serve as obstacles to enlightenment.
1. Among other things, Wang Wei is alluding to an anonymous fisherman's song included in an anthology of poetry from the southern kingdom of Chu. Responding to the lament of a political exile about having been banished for his high moral principles, the fisherman's gently mocking song speaks of the greater wisdom of being able to adapt to circumstances: "If the waters are clear, I'll wash my hat, / If they're muddy I'll wash my feet."

owing to his claim of kinship with the imperial family, also surnamed Li. Thanks to a friendship he cultivated with a powerful Daoist adept, in 742 he succeeded in securing a post in the court bureau responsible for producing official documents, where he initially attracted favorable attention from the emperor and his entourage, but then his drunken audacity led to his expulsion two years later. Lamenting the alleged failure of those in power to appreciate him, he wandered for over a decade and finally provided the emperor with a legitimate reason to mistrust him by becoming involved in a minor revolt. For this he was arrested for treason, and though he was eventually pardoned he died without having secured the patronage he had sought. A popular legend tells of his drowning while trying to embrace the reflection of the moon in the water, although overindulgence in alcohol and long-life elixirs (typically containing mercury) were more likely to blame.

Li Bo traveled extensively to Daoist retreats, and he became known as the "Poet-Immortal." Although he clearly didn't spurn political engagement, his outsider image entitled him to excesses and eccentricities that also characterize his poetry, and his poems often display a playful fantasy that can have the poet, for example, engaging in conversation with the moon. Of his nearly one thousand poems, the majority consist not of the newer regulated verse patterns but of older forms that allowed greater liberties of expression. Li Bo especially enjoyed imitating folk songs, and the colloquial diction and bold expression of longer examples like "The Road to Shu Is Hard" are especially distinctive. As was true for all Tang poets, much of his work consists of responses to occasions like visits and farewells. Li Bo made much of the spontaneity and facility with which he composed, and the disarming simplicity of his diction and imagery in these occasional pieces can suggest deep feeling with extraordinary effectiveness.

Reasonably well known during his lifetime, Li Bo was singled out by later generations as an inspired genius and complement to the more serious and sober Du Fu. Comparative evaluations of the two figures have occupied critics for centuries, but they are generally agreed to be the two most important poets of the Tang dynasty.

Drinking Alone with the Moon[1]

> A pot of wine among the flowers.
> I drink alone, no friend with me.
> I raise my cup to invite the moon.
> He and my shadow and I make three.
>
> 5 The moon does not know how to drink;
> My shadow mimes my capering;
> But I'll make merry with them both—
> And soon enough it will be Spring.
>
> I sing—the moon moves to and fro.
> 10 I dance—my shadow leaps and sways.
> Still sober, we exchange our joys.
> Drunk—and we'll go our separate ways.
>
> Let's pledge—beyond human ties—to be friends,
> And meet where the Silver River ends.

1. Translated by Vikram Seth.

Liang Kai, *Li Bo Chanting a Poem,* hanging scroll, 13th century. An honored member of the imperial painting academy, Liang Kai chose, for unknown reasons, to retreat to a Chan Buddhist monastery outside Hangzhou. The spare brushwork of this imaginary portrait captures the nonchalant abandon that Li Bo (701–761) sought to convey in his poetry.

Fighting South of the Ramparts[1]

Last year we were fighting at the source of the Sang-kan;
This year we are fighting on the Onion River road.
We have washed our swords in the surf of Parthian seas;
We have pastured our horses among the snows of the T'ien Shan.
5   The King's armies have grown grey and old
Fighting ten thousand leagues away from home.
The Huns have no trade but battle and carnage;
They have no fields or ploughlands,
But only wastes where white bones lie among yellow sands.
10   Where the house of Ch'in built the Great Wall that was to keep away the
       Tartars,
There, in its turn, the House of Han lit beacons of war.
The beacons are always alight, fighting and marching never stop.
Men die in the field, slashing sword to sword;
The horses of the conquered neigh piteously to Heaven.
15   Crows and hawks peck for human guts,
Carry them in their beaks and hang them on the branches of withered trees.
Captains and soldiers are smeared on the bushes and grass;
The general schemed in vain.
Know therefore that the sword is a cursed thing
20   Which the wise man uses only if he must.

The Road to Shu Is Hard[1]

Ah! it's fearsome—oh! it's high!
The road to Shu is hard, harder than climbing to the sky.
    The kings Can Cong and Yu Fu
    Founded long ago the land of Shu,
5   Then for forty-eight thousand years
    Nothing linked it to the Qin frontiers.
    White Star Peak blocked the western way.
A bird-track tried to cut across to Mount Emei—
And only when the earth shook, hills collapsed, and brave men died
10   Did cliff-roads and sky-ladders join it to the world outside.
Above—high peaks turn back the dragon-chariot of the sun.
Below—great whirlpools turn around the waves that rush and stun.
    Not even yellow cranes can fly across—
    Even the clambering apes are at a loss.
15   At Green Mud Ridge the path coils to and fro:
Nine twists for every hundred steps—up a sheer cliff we go.
The traveller, touching the stars, looks upwards, scared out of his wits.
He clutches his heart with a deep sigh—down on the ground he sits!
Sir, from this journey to the West, will you return some day?
20   How can you hope to climb the crags along this fearful way?

---

1. Translated by Arthur Waley.
1. Translated by Vikram Seth.

Mournful birds in ancient trees—you'll hear no other sound
Of life: the male bird follows his mate as they fly round and round.
    You'll hear the cuckoo call in the moonlight,
    Sad that the mountain's bare at night.
25   The road to Shu is hard, harder than climbing to the sky.
Just speak these words to someone's face—you'll see its colour fly.
A hand's breadth from the sky peaks join to crown a precipice
Where withered pines, bent upside down, lean over the abyss.
Swift rapids, wrestling cataracts descend in roaring spasms,
30   Pound cliffs, boil over rocks, and thunder through ten thousand chasms.
    To face such danger and such fear,
    Alas, from such a distance, Sir, what could have brought you here?
    Dagger Peak is high and steep—
    Even a single man can keep
35   The pass from thousands—though he may
    Become a wolf or jackal—and betray.
    By day we dread the savage tiger's claws,
    By night the serpent's jaws,
    Its sharp, blood-sucking fangs bared when
40   It mows down like hemp stalks the lives of men.
    Though Chengdu is a pleasure dome,
    Better to quickly turn back home.
The road to Shu is hard, harder than climbing to the sky.
Leaning, I stare into the west and utter a long sigh.

Bring in the Wine[1]

The waters of the Yellow River come down from the sky,
Never once returning as towards the sea they flow.
The mirrors of high palaces are sad with once-bright hair:
Though silken-black at morning it has changed by night to snow.
5   Fulfil your wishes in this life, exhaust your every whim
And never raise an empty golden goblet to the moon.
Fate's loaded me with talent and it must be put to use!
Scatter a thousand coins—they'll all come winging homeward soon.
Cook a sheep, slaughter an ox—and for our further pleasure
10   Let's drink three hundred cups of wine down in a single measure.
    So here's to you, Dan Qiu—
    And Master Cen, drink up.
    Bring in, bring in the wine—
    Pour on, cup after cup.
15   I'll sing a song for you—
    So lend your ears and hear me through.
Bells and drums and feasts and jade are all esteemed in vain:
Just let me be forever drunk and never be sober again.
The sages and the virtuous men are all forgotten now.

1. Translated by Vikram Seth.

20 It is the drinkers of the world whose names alone remain.
 Chen Wang, the prince and poet,[2] once at a great banquet paid
 Ten thousand for a cask of wine with laughter wild and free.
 How can you say, my host, that you have fallen short of cash?
 You've got to buy more wine and drink it face to face with me.
25 My furs so rare—
  My dappled mare—
 Summon the boy to go and get the choicest wine for these
 And we'll dissolve the sorrows of a hundred centuries.

The Jewel Stairs' Grievance[1]

 The jewelled steps are already quite white with dew,
 It is so late that the dew soaks my gauze stockings,
 And I let down the crystal curtain
 And watch the moon through the clear autumn.

The River Merchant's Wife: A Letter[1]

 While my hair was still cut straight across my forehead
 I played about the front gate, pulling flowers.
 You came by on bamboo stilts, playing horse,
 You walked about my seat, playing with blue plums.
5 And we went on living in the village of Chokan:
 Two small people, without dislike or suspicion.

 At fourteen I married My Lord you.
 I never laughed, being bashful.
 Lowering my head, I looked at the wall.
10 Called to, a thousand times, I never looked back.

 At fifteen I stopped scowling,
 I desired my dust to be mingled with yours
 Forever and forever and forever.
 Why should I climb the look out?

15 At sixteen you departed,
 You went into far Ku-to-yen, by the river of swirling eddies,
 And you have been gone five months.
 The monkeys make sorrowful noise overhead.

 You dragged your feet when you went out.
20 By the gate now, the moss is grown, the different mosses,
 Too deep to clear them away!
 The leaves fall early this autumn, in wind.

2. Chen Wang (Prince Chen) was Cao Zhi (192–232).

1. Translated by Ezra Pound. Pound didn't know classical Chinese, but he worked from the notes made by Ernest Fenellosa, a scholar of Japanese culture. With his first volume of these translations, *Cathay* (1915), Pound was said by T. S. Eliot to have become "the inventor of Chinese poetry for our time."

1. Translated by Ezra Pound.

The paired butterflies are already yellow with August
Over the grass in the West garden;
25   They hurt me. I grow older.
If you are coming down through the narrows of the river Kiang,
Please let me know beforehand,
And I will come out to meet you

As far as Cho-fu-Sa.

Listening to a Monk from Shu Playing the Lute[1]

The monk from Shu with his green lute-case walked
Westward down Emei Shan, and at the sound
Of the first notes he strummed for me I heard
A thousand valleys' rustling pines resound.
5   My heart was cleansed, as if in flowing water.
In bells of frost I heard the resonance die.
Dusk came unnoticed over the emerald hills
And autumn clouds layered the darkening sky.

Farewell to a Friend[1]

Verdant mountains behind the northern ramparts.
White waters wind around the east city wall.
From this place once parting has ended,
The lone tumbleweed flies a myriad miles.
5   Floating clouds: a traveler's thoughts.
Setting sun: an old friend's feelings.
Waving hands, you go from here—
Horses neigh gently as they leave.

In the Quiet Night[1]

The floor before my bed is bright:
Moonlight—like hoarfrost—in my room.
I lift my head and watch the moon.
I drop my head and think of home.

Sitting Alone by Jingting Mountain[1]

The flocks of birds have flown high and away,
A solitary cloud goes off calmly alone.
We look at each other and never get bored—
Just me and Ching-t'ing Mountain.

1. Translated by Vikram Seth.
1. Translated by Pauline Yu.
1. Translated by Vikram Seth.
1. Translated by Stephen Owen.

Question and Answer in the Mountains[1]

They ask me why I live in the green mountains.
I smile and don't reply; my heart's at ease.
Peach blossoms flow downstream, leaving no trace—
And there are other earths and skies than these.

DU FU ■ (712–770)

By common consensus Du Fu wears the heavy mantle of China's greatest poet, but during his lifetime he struggled unsuccessfully for recognition of another sort. The grandson of a prominent court poet, he took the most literary and difficult civil service examination twice to qualify for a position in the central government but failed both times. He attracted the emperor's attention by sending him examples of his literary work and passed a special examination set for him, but when he eventually secured a court position his forthrightness led to dismissal within days. Offered minor provincial posts, he soon opted to resign and embarked on what was to be a lifetime of travel in search of better employment. The separation and hardship he and his family endured were great; one young son died of starvation, and Du Fu himself suffered from chronic and often severe illness and died never having attained his goal.

A failure as a public man, Du Fu nonetheless produced a body of poetry whose concerns and compassion have been seen to embody the highest Confucian ideals. He was the first poet to write directly and often critically about contemporary political and social conditions in China, on a scale both large and small, and has been dubbed as a consequence both the "Poet-Sage" and the "Poet-Historian." He was deeply affected by the devastating effect of the rebellion of general An Lushan in 755, even after the recapture of the capital by imperial troops in 757. The government never regained its past stability or glory, and a sense of irrevocable loss is developed especially powerfully in Du Fu's eight-poem sequence "Autumn Meditations," written while he was in Kuizhou, Sichuan, frustratingly far from the center of activity. What has impressed later readers is his ability to situate his own personal fate within the grand course of events. No poet before him had written so extensively about himself and his own family and with such detail about his daily existence. Du Fu further intertwines this history with that of the nation with great poignancy, the frequent image of a solitary figure in the landscape conveying both his aspirations and his agony at not being able to translate his compassion into broader action.

Du Fu was also the first poet to speak extensively of his own writing, and his work expresses the hope that his poetry could play the role that eluded him in public service. Highly conscious of his craft, he preferred the newer regulated verse forms that allowed him to test the limits of poetic expression under technically demanding conditions. In a poem of eight five- or seven-word lines, a poet would be expected to introduce a topic in the first couplet, provide illustrative descriptive imagery in the next two couplets, and then finish with a witty or enigmatic closure, while conforming to established tonal patterns and observing syntactic and semantic parallelism. The poems written during the last decade of his life are especially noteworthy for their densely packed, ambiguous and allusive language, and his constant concern with the effort of his art made him the poet's poet for succeeding generations and, by the eleventh century, afforded him an undisputed place at the top of the literary hierarchy.

1. Translated by Vikram Seth.

Ballad of the Army Carts[1]

Carts rattle and squeak,
Horses snort and neigh—
Bows and arrows at their waists, the conscripts march away.
Fathers, mothers, children, wives run to say goodbye.
5   The Xianyang Bridge in clouds of dust is hidden from the eye.
They tug at them and stamp their feet, weep, and obstruct their way.
    The weeping rises to the sky.
    Along the road a passer-by
    Questions the conscripts. They reply:

10 They mobilize us constantly. Sent northwards at fifteen
To guard the River, we were forced once more to volunteer,
Though we are forty now, to man the western front this year.
The headman tied our headcloths for us when we first left here.
We came back white-haired—to be sent again to the frontier.
15 Those frontier posts could fill the sea with the blood of those who've died,
But still the Martial Emperor's aims remain unsatisfied.
In county after county to the east, Sir, don't you know,
In village after village only thorns and brambles grow.
Even if there's a sturdy wife to wield the plough and hoe,
20 The borders of the fields have merged, you can't tell east from west.
It's worse still for the men from Qin, as fighters they're the best—
And so, like chickens or like dogs, they're driven to and fro.

Though you are kind enough to ask,
Dare we complain about our task?
25 Take, Sir, this winter. In Guanxi
The troops have not yet been set free.
The district officers come to press
The land tax from us nonetheless.
But, Sir, how can we possibly pay?
30 Having a son's a curse today.
Far better to have daughters, get them married—
A son will lie lost in the grass, unburied.
Why, Sir, on distant Qinghai shore
The bleached ungathered bones lie year on year.
35 New ghosts complain, and those who died before
Weep in the wet gray sky and haunt the ear.

Moonlit Night[1]

In Fuzhou, far away, my wife is watching
The moon alone tonight, and my thoughts fill
With sadness for my children, who can't think
Of me here in Changan; they're too young still.
5 Her cloud-soft hair is moist with fragrant mist.
In the clear light her white arms sense the chill.

1. Translated by Vikram Seth.

When will we feel the moonlight dry our tears,
Leaning together on our window-sill?

Spring Prospect[1]

The country shattered, mountains and rivers remain.
Spring in the city—grasses and trees are dense.
Feeling the times, flowers draw forth tears.
Hating to part, birds alarm the heart.
5   Beacon fires for three months in a row:
A letter from home worth ten thousand in gold.
White hairs scratched grow even shorter—
Soon too few to hold a hatpin on.[2]

Traveling at Night[1]

Slender grass, a faint wind on the shore.
Tall mast, a lonely night on the boat.
Stars hang down on the flat plain's expanse.
The moon surges up in the great river, flowing.
5   A name—how can writing make it known?
An office—for age and sickness given up.
Fluttering, floating, what is there for likeness?
On heaven and earth, one sandy gull.

Autumn Meditations[1]

1

Gems of dew wilt and wound the maple trees in the wood:
From Wu mountains, from Wu gorges, the air blows desolate.
The waves between the river banks merge in the seething sky,
Clouds in the wind above the passes touch their shadows on the ground.
5   Clustered chrysanthemums have opened twice, in tears of other days:
The forlorn boat, once and for all, tethers my homeward thoughts.
    In the houses quilted clothes speed scissors and ruler.
The washing blocks pound, faster each evening, in Pai Ti[2] high on the hill.

2

On the solitary walls of K'uei-chou the sunset rays slant,
10   Each night guided by the Dipper I gaze towards the capital.
It is true then that tears start when we hear the gibbon cry thrice:[3]
Useless my mission adrift on the raft which came by this eighth month.[4]

1. Translated by Pauline Yu.
2. Used to anchor the cap of an official.
1. Translated by Pauline Yu.
1. Translated by A. C. Graham. Du Fu wrote this sequence in 766 while in exile in Kuizhou, on the middle Yangzi River far south of the capital of Chang'an.
2. White Emperor City, adjacent to Kuizhou.
3. According to a traditional fishermen's song, the gibbon's three cries in the Wu gorges sounded so mournful they could not but elicit tears.
4. In two separate legends, a fisherman and a Han dynasty official were carried on rafts to the Milky Way.

Fumes of the censers by the pictures in the ministry elude my sickbed pillow,
The whitewashed parapets of turrets against the hills dull the mournful bugles.
15   Look! On the wall, the moon in the ivy
Already, by the shores of the isle, lights the blossoms on the reeds.

3

A thousand houses rimmed by the mountains are quiet in the morning light,
Day after day in the house by the river I sit in the blue of the hills.
20 Two nights gone the fisher-boats once more come bobbing on the waves,
Belated swallows in cooling autumn still flit to and fro....
A disdained K'uang Heng, as a critic of policy:
As promoter of learning, a Liu Hsiang who failed.[5]
    Of the school-friends of my childhood, most did well.
By the Five Tombs[6] in light cloaks they ride their sleek horses.

4

25 Well said Ch'ang-an looks like a chess-board:[7]
A hundred years of the saddest news.
The mansions of princes and nobles all have new lords:
Another breed is capped and robed for office.
Due north on the mountain passes the gongs and drums shake,
30 To the chariots and horses campaigning in the west the winged dispatches hasten.
    While the fish and the dragons fall asleep and the autumn river turns cold
My native country, untroubled times, are always in my thoughts.

5

The gate of P'eng-lai Palace faces the South Mountain:
Dew collects on the bronze stems out of the Misty River.
35 See in the west on Jasper Lake the Queen Mother descend:
Approaching from the east the purple haze fills the Han-ku pass.[8]
The clouds roll back, the pheasant-tail screens open before the throne:
Scales ringed by the sun on dragon robes! I have seen the majestic face.
    I lay down once by the long river, wake left behind by the years,
40 Who so many times answered the roll of court by the blue chain-patterned door.

6

From the mouth of Ch'üt-t'ang gorges here, to the side of Crooked River there,
For ten thousand miles of mist in the wind the touch of pallid autumn.
Through the walled passage from Calyx Hall the royal splendour coursed,
To Hibiscus Park the griefs of the frontier came.
45 Pearl blinds and embellished pillars closed in the yellow cranes,
Embroidered cables and ivory masts startled the white seagulls.
    Look back and pity the singing, dancing land!
Ch'in from most ancient times was the seat of princes.

5. A famous statesman and a famous editor of the Han dynasty. Between 757 and 758, Du Fu held a position charged with "reminding" the emperor of oversights, but fell out of favor owing to critical memorials.

6. Imperial tombs outside the capital.

7. Recently invaded by rebel troops, Chang'an's streets were also laid out as a symmetrical grid.

8. Du Fu refers variously to the Penglai Palace in Chang'an, named after one of the fairy islands in the Eastern sea; the copper pans raised on pillars which the Emperor Wu (140–87 B.C.E) made to collect dew for the elixir; the Misty River is the empyrean; the Western Queen Mother (Xiwangmu) who banqueted King Mu (1001–947 B.C.E) at Jasper Lake in his country far to the west, an incident which the poet fuses with her later descent from the sky to teach the arts of immortality to the Emperor Wu; the philosopher Laozi coming through the passes preceded by a purple cloud on his final journey to the west [translator's note].

K'un-ming Pool was the Han time's monument,
50   The banners of the Emperor Wu are here before my eyes.[9]
Vega threads her loom in vain by night under the moon,
And the great stone fish's plated scales veer in the autumn wind.
The waves toss a zizania seed, over sunken clouds as black:
Dew on the calyx chills the lotus, red with dropped pollen.
55   Over the pass, all the way to the sky, a road for none but the birds.
On river and lakes, to the ends of the earth, one old fisherman.

8

The K'un-wu road by Yü-su river ran its meandering course,
The shadow of Purple Turret Peak fell into Lake Mei-p'i,
Grains from the fragrant rice-stalks, pecked and dropped by the parrots;
60   On the green *wu-t'ung* tree branches which the perching phoenix aged.
Beautiful girls gathered kingfisher feathers for spring gifts:
Together in the boat, a troop of immortals, we set forth again in the evening....
        This brush of many colours once forced the elements.
Chanting, peering into the distance, in anguish my white head droops.

Yangtse and Han[1]

By Yangtse and Han, a stranger who thinks of home,
One withered pedant between the Ch'ien and K'un.[2]
Under as far a sky as that streak of cloud,
The moon in the endless night no more alone.
5   In sunset hale of heart still:
In the autumn wind, risen from sickness.
There's always a place kept for an old horse
Though it can take no more to the long road.

BO JUYI (772–846)

Born into a scholar-official family of limited means, Bo Juyi passed the most rigorous civil service examination in 800 and held government posts fairly steadily thereafter, although only briefly in the capital. Appointed to relatively powerful positions in the provinces as prefect, he became attracted to Buddhism later in life and thus grew increasingly remote spiritually as well as geographically from the center of political activity. Reacting against tendencies toward increasingly difficult and obscure poetic styles, Bo wrote prolifically and cultivated a plain style that he hoped would be accessible even to a peasant woman. Much of his poetry deals with surprising frankness with details of his daily life, ranging from topics like eating bamboo shoots to the aggravations of child-rearing and the virtues of baldness.

    Bo Juyi also took seriously the Confucian mandate to employ poetry as a vehicle of social and political protest. With his lifelong friend Yuan Zhen, he promoted a revival of folk song traditions based on those collected by the Han dynasty Music Bureau, but whose subject

9. Kunming Pool near Chang'an was made by Wu of Han for naval exercises. Near it was a statue of the Weaving Girl (the star Vega) and in it a stone whale with movable fins and tail [translator's note].

1. Translated by A. C. Graham.

2. Ch'ien (qian) and K'un (kun) represent heaven and earth in the divination system of the *Book of Changes*.

matter, unlike that of those predecessors, would focus resolutely on contemporary bureaucratic abuses. But his best-loved work, somewhat to his chagrin, was the tragic story of the Tang emperor Minghuang (or Xuanzong, r. 713–755) and his prized consort, Yang Guifei. She was blamed for preparing the way for the disastrous rebellion of An Lushan, owing both to her infatuating beauty and to the seditious behavior of her relatives. When the emperor was forced to flee the capital with her, his soldiers reportedly refused to protect him unless she was first executed. This anguished tale of conflict between the affairs of the heart and the interests of the state was the subject of numerous other poems, stories, and dramas as well.

A Song of Unending Sorrow[1]

China's Emperor, craving beauty that might shake an empire,
Was on the throne, for many years, searching, never finding,
Till a little child of the Yang clan, hardly even grown,
Bred in an inner chamber, with no one knowing her,
5   But with graces granted by heaven and not to be concealed,
At last one day was chosen for the imperial household.
If she but turned her head and smiled, there were cast a hundred spells,
And the powder and paint of the Six Palaces faded into nothing....
It was early spring. They bathed her in the Flower-Pure Pool,
10   Which warmed and smoothed the creamy-tinted crystal of her skin,
And, because of her languor, a maid was lifting her
When first the Emperor noticed her and chose her for his bride.
The cloud of her hair, petal of her cheek, gold ripples of her crown when
        she moved,
Were sheltered on spring evenings by warm hibiscus-curtains;
15   But nights of spring were short and the sun arose too soon,
And the Emperor, from that time forth, forsook his early hearings
And lavished all his time on her with feasts and revelry,
His mistress of the spring, his despot of the night.
There were other ladies in his court, three thousand of rare beauty,
20   But his favors to three thousand were concentered in one body.
By the time she was dressed in her Golden Chamber, it would be almost
        evening;
And when tables were cleared in the Tower of Jade, she would loiter, slow
        with wine.
Her sisters and brothers all were given titles;
And, because she so illumined and glorified her clan,
25   She brought to every father, every mother through the empire,
Happiness when a girl was born rather than a boy....
High rose Li Palace, entering blue clouds,
And far and wide the breezes carried magical notes
Of soft song and slow dance, of string and bamboo music.
30   The Emperor's eyes could never gaze on her enough—
Till war-drums, booming from Yü-yang, shocked the whole earth
And broke the tunes of "The Rainbow Skirt and the Feathered Coat."
The Forbidden City, the nine-tiered palace, loomed in the dust
From thousands of horses and chariots headed southwest.

1. Translated by Witter Bynner.

35 The imperial flag opened the way, now moving and now pausing—
   But thirty miles from the capital, beyond the western gate,
   The men of the army stopped, not one of them would stir
   Till under their horses' hoofs they might trample those moth-eyebrows...
   Flowery hairpins fell to the ground, no one picked them up,
40 And a green and white jade hair-tassel and a yellow-gold hair-bird.
   The Emperor could not save her, he could only cover his face.
   And later when he turned to look, the place of blood and tears
   Was hidden in a yellow dust blown by a cold wind....
   At the cleft of the Dagger-Tower Trail they crisscrossed through a cloud-line
45 Under O-mei Mountain. The last few came.
   Flags and banners lost their color in the fading sunlight...
   But as waters of Shu are always green and its mountains always blue,
   So changeless was his majesty's love and deeper than the days.
   He stared at the desolate moon from his temporary palace,
50 He heard bell-notes in the evening rain, cutting at his breast.
   And when heaven and earth resumed their round and the dragon-car faced
      home,
   The Emperor clung to the spot and would not turn away
   From the soil along the Ma-wei slope, under which was buried
   That memory, that anguish. Where was her jade-white face?
55 Ruler and lords, when eyes would meet, wept upon their coats
   As they rode, with loose rein, slowly eastward, back to the capital....
   The pools, the gardens, the palace, all were just as before,
   The Lake T'ai-yi hibiscus, the Wei-yang Palace willows;
   But a petal was like her face and a willow-leaf her eyebrow—
60 And what could he do but cry whenever he looked at them?...
   Peach-trees and plum-trees blossomed, in the winds of spring;
   Lakka-foliage fell to the ground, after autumn rains;
   The Western and Southern Palaces were littered with late grasses,
   And the steps were mounded with red leaves that no one swept away.
65 Her Pear-Garden Players became white-haired
   And the eunuchs thin-eyebrowed in her Court of Pepper-Trees;
   Over the throne flew fireflies, while he brooded in the twilight.
   He would lengthen the lamp-wick to its end and still could never sleep.
   Bell and drum would slowly toll the dragging night-hours
70 And the River of Stars grow sharp in the sky, just before dawn,
   And the porcelain mandarin-ducks on the roof grow thick with morning frost
   And his covers of kingfisher-blue feel lonelier and colder
   With the distance between life and death year after year;
   And yet no beloved spirit ever visited his dreams....
75 At Ling-ch'ün lived a Taoist priest who was a guest of heaven,
   Able to summon spirits by his concentrated mind.
   And people were so moved by the Emperor's constant brooding
   That they besought the Taoist priest to see if he could find her.
   He opened his way in space and clove the ether like lightning
80 Up to heaven, under the earth, looking everywhere.
   Above, he searched the Green Void, below, the Yellow Spring;
   But he failed, in either place, to find the one he looked for.
   And then he heard accounts of an enchanted isle at sea,

A part of the intangible and incorporeal world,
With pavilions and fine towers in the five-colored air,
And of exquisite immortals moving to and fro,
And of one among them—whom they called The Ever True—
With a face of snow and flowers resembling hers he sought.
So he went to the West Hall's gate of gold and knocked at the jasper door
And asked a girl, called Morsel-of-Jade, to tell The Doubly-Perfect.
And the lady, at news of an envoy from the Emperor of China,
Was startled out of dreams in her nine-flowered canopy.
She pushed aside her pillow, dressed, shook away sleep,
And opened the pearly shade and then the silver screen.
Her cloudy hair-dress hung on one side because of her great haste,
And her flower-cap was loose when she came along the terrace,
While a light wind filled her cloak and fluttered with her motion
As though she danced "The Rainbow Skirt and the Feathered Coat."
And the tear-drops drifting down her sad white face
Were like a rain in spring on the blossom of the pear.
But love glowed deep within her eyes when she bade him thank her liege,
Whose form and voice had been strange to her ever since their parting—
Since happiness had ended at the Court of the Bright Sun,
And moons and dawns had become long in Fairy-Mountain Palace.
But when she turned her face and looked down toward the earth
And tried to see the capital, there were only fog and dust.
So she took out, with emotion, the pledges he had given
And, through his envoy, sent him back a shell box and gold hairpin,
But kept one branch of the hairpin, and one side of the box,
Breaking the gold of the hairpin, breaking the shell of the box;
"Our souls belong together," she said, "like this gold and this shell—
Somewhere, sometime, on earth or in heaven, we shall surely meet."
And she sent him, by his messenger, a sentence reminding him
Of vows which had been known only to their two hearts:
"On the seventh day of the Seventh-month, in the Palace of Long Life,
We told each other secretly in the quiet midnight world
That we wished to fly in heaven, two birds with the wings of one,
And to grow together on the earth, two branches of one tree."...
Earth endures, heaven endures; sometime both shall end,
While this unending sorrow goes on and on forever.

[END OF POETRY OF THE TANG DYNASTY]

MURASAKI SHIKIBU ■ (c. 978–c. 1014)

Murasaki Shikibu belonged to the Northern Branch of the Fujiwara clan, the same branch
that produced the Regent family. Both sides of her family can in fact be traced back to
Fujiwara no Fuyutsugu (775–826), whose son Yoshifusa became the first regent. Murasaki
Shikibu's family line, however, subsequently declined, and by her grandfather's generation had settled at the provincial governor level. Murasaki Shikibu's father, Fujiwara no
Tametoki (d. 1029), while eventually receiving the governorships of Echizen and Echigo
provinces, had an undistinguished and uncertain career as a bureaucrat. He was, however,
able to distinguish himself as a scholar of Chinese literature and as a poet

In 996 Murasaki Shikibu accompanied her father to his new post as provincial governor in Echizen, on the north side of Japan. A year or two later she returned to the capital to marry Fujiwara no Nobutaka, who was old enough to be her father and who came from the same middle tier of the aristocracy. Murasaki Shikibu bore a daughter named Kenshi, probably in 999, and Nobutaka died only a few years later, in 1001.

It is generally believed that Murasaki Shikibu started writing *The Tale of Genji* (*Genji monogatari*) after her husband's death, perhaps in response to the sorrow it caused her, and it was probably the reputation of the early chapters that resulted in her being summoned to the imperial court around 1005–1006. She became a lady-in-waiting to Empress Shōshi, the consort of Emperor Ichijō and the eldest daughter of Fujiwara no Michinaga (966–1027), who had become regent. At least half of the *Diary of Murasaki Shikibu* is devoted to a long-awaited event in Michinaga's career—the birth of a son to Empress Shōshi in 1008—which would make Michinaga the grandfather of a future emperor. Murasaki Shikibu was the sobriquet given to her as a lady-in-waiting at the imperial court and is not her actual name, which remains unknown. "Shikibu" probably comes from the position in the Shikibu-shō (Ministry of Ceremonial) occupied by her father, while "Murasaki" may refer to the lavender color of the flower of her clan (Fujiwara, Wisteria Fields) or it may be that her nickname came from the heroine of *The Tale of Genji*.

The Tale of Genji The title of *The Tale of Genji* comes from the surname of the hero, the son of the reigning emperor at the beginning of the narrative. *The Tale of Genji* is generally divided into three parts: the first thirty-three chapters follow Genji's career, from his birth to exile to triumphant return to his rise to the pinnacle of society, focusing equally, if not more, on the fate of the various women that he becomes involved with. The second part, Chapters 34 to 41, explores the darkness that gathers over Genji's private life and that of his great love Murasaki, who eventually succumbs and dies, and ends with Genji's own death. The third part consists of the thirteen chapters following Genji's death, which are primarily concerned with the affairs of Kaoru, Genji's supposed son, and with three sisters (particularly Oigimi and Ukifune) with whom Kaoru becomes involved. A significant shift of focus occurs in the third part: from the capital and court to the countryside, and from a society concerned with refinement, elegance, and the various arts, to an otherworldly, ascetic perspective—a shift that anticipates the movement of mid-Heian court culture toward the religious literature of the medieval period, focused on hermits who withdrew from the world.

The Tale of Genji both follows and works against a common plot convention of the Heian vernacular tale (*monogatari*) in which the heroine, whose family has declined or disappeared, is discovered and loved by an illustrious noble. This association of love and inferior social status appears from the opening line of the *Genji* and extends to the last relationship between Kaoru and Ukifune. In the opening chapter, the reigning emperor, like all Heian emperors, was expected to devote himself to his principal consort (the Kokiden lady), the lady of the highest rank, and yet he dotes on a woman of considerably lower status—a social and political violation that eventually results in the woman's death. Like his monogatari predecessor, Ariwara no Narihira, the hero of *The Tales of Ise,* and like his father, Genji pursues love where it is forbidden and most unlikely to be found or attained. In "Lavender," the fifth chapter, Genji discovers his future wife, the young Murasaki, who has lost her mother and is in danger of losing her only guardian when Genji takes her into his home.

In Murasaki Shikibu's day, it would have been unheard of for a man of Genji's high rank to take a girl of Murasaki's low position into his own residence and marry her. In the upper levels of Heian aristocratic society, the man usually lived in his wife's residence, either in the house of her parents or in a dwelling nearby (as Genji does with Aoi, his principal wife). The prospective groom had high stakes in marriage, for the bride's family provided not only a residence but other forms of support as well. When Genji takes a girl (such as the young Murasaki) with no backing or social support into his house, he openly flouts the conventions of marriage as they were known to Murasaki Shikibu's audience. In the monogatari tradition, however, this action becomes a sign of excessive, romantic love.

A number of other sequences in the story—those of Yūgao, the Akashi lady, Oigimi, and Ukifune—start on a similar note. All of these women come from upper- or middle-rank aristocratic families (much like that of the author herself) that have, for various reasons, fallen into social obscurity and must struggle to survive. The appearance of the highborn hero implies, at least for the attendants surrounding the woman, an opportunity for social redemption. However, Murasaki Shikibu focuses on the difficulties that the woman subsequently encounters, either in dealing with the man, or failing to make the social transition between her own social background and that of the highborn hero. The woman may, for example, be torn between pride and material need, or between emotional dependence and a desire to be more independent, or she may feel abandoned and betrayed—all conflicts explored in *The Tale of Genji*. In classical Japanese poetry, love has a similar fate: it is never about happiness or the blissful union of souls. Instead, it dwells on unfulfilled hopes, regretful partings, fears of abandonment, and lingering resentment.

The Tale of Genji is remarkable for the manner in which it absorbs the exploration of identity and social position found in earlier women's diaries, the social romance of the early monogatari, and the poetry and imagery of *The Tales of Ise,* blending these strands into a deeply psychological narrative that evolves around distinctive characters. But while bearing a striking resemblance to the modern psychological novel, *The Tale of Genji* wasn't conceived and written as a single work and then published and distributed to a mass audience as novels are today. Instead, it was issued in limited installments, chapter by chapter or sequence by sequence, to an circumscribed, aristocratic audience over an extended period of time. As a result *The Tale of Genji* can be appreciated as a closely interrelated series of texts that can be read either individually or as a whole and that is the product of an author whose attitudes, interests, and techniques evolved significantly with time and experience. For example, the reader of the Ukifune narrative can appreciate this sequence both independently and as an integral part of the previous narrative. The *Genji* can also be understood as a kind of multiple Bildungsroman or novel of the development of a character through time and experience. Yet in this work, the development occurs not only in the life of a single hero or heroine but over different generations, with two or more characters. Genji, for example, attains an awareness of death, mutability, and the illusory nature of the world through repeated suffering. By contrast, Kaoru, his supposed son, begins his life, or rather his narrative, with a profound grasp and acceptance of these darker aspects of life. In the second part, in the "New Herbs" chapters, the heroine Murasaki has long assumed that she can monopolize Genji's affections and act as his principal wife. Genji's unexpected marriage to the Third Princess, however, crushes these assumptions, causing Murasaki to fall mortally ill. In the third part, the Uji sequence, Oigimi never suffers the way Murasaki does, but she quickly comes to a similar awareness of the inconstancy of men, love, and marriage, even though Kaoru appears to be an ideal companion.

Murasaki Shikibu probably first wrote a short sequence of chapters, perhaps beginning with "Lavender," and then, in response to reader demand, wrote a sequel or another related series of chapters, and so forth. Certain sequences, which appear to have been inserted later, focus on women of the middle and lower aristocracy, as opposed to the main chapters of the first part which deal with Fujitsubo and other upper-rank women related to the throne. The only chapters in which authorship has been questioned are three chapters following the death of Genji at the end of the second part. The following selections condense this extended narrative by leaving out those chapters and sections that were later additions, of questionable authorship, or tangential to the lives of the central characters.

51

PRONUNCIATIONS:
Murasaki Shikibu: moo-ra-sa-ki shi-ki-boo
Genji: gen-jee
Aoi: ah-oh-ee
Rokujō: ro-koo-joh

The Tale of Genji[1]

from *Chapter 1. The Paulownia Court*

In a certain reign there was a lady not of the first rank whom the emperor loved more
than any of the others. The grand ladies with high ambitions thought her a presumptuous upstart, and lesser ladies were still more resentful. Everything she did offended
someone. Probably aware of what was happening, she fell seriously ill and came to
spend more time at home than at court. The emperor's pity and affection quite passed
bounds. No longer caring what his ladies and courtiers might say, he behaved as if
intent upon stirring gossip.

His court looked with very great misgiving upon what seemed a reckless infatuation. In China just such an unreasoning passion had been the undoing of an emperor
and had spread turmoil through the land. As the resentment grew, the example of
Yang Kuei-fei[2] was the one most frequently cited against the lady.

She survived despite her troubles, with the help of an unprecedented bounty
of love. Her father, a grand councilor, was no longer living. Her mother, an old-
fashioned lady of good lineage, was determined that matters be no different for her
than for ladies who with paternal support were making careers at court. The mother
was attentive to the smallest detail of etiquette and deportment. Yet there was a limit
to what she could do. The sad fact was that the girl was without strong backing, and
each time a new incident arose she was next to defenseless.

It may have been because of a bond in a former life that she bore the emperor a
beautiful son, a jewel beyond compare. The emperor was in a fever of impatience to see
the child, still with the mother's family; and when, on the earliest day possible, he was
brought to court, he did indeed prove to be a most marvelous babe. The emperor's eldest son was the grandson of the Minister of the Right. The world assumed that with this
powerful support he would one day be named crown prince; but the new child was far
more beautiful. On public occasions the emperor continued to favor his eldest son. The
new child was a private treasure, so to speak, on which to lavish uninhibited affection.

The mother was not of such a low rank as to attend upon the emperor's personal
needs. In the general view she belonged to the upper classes. He insisted on having her
always beside him, however, and on nights when there was music or other entertainment
he would require that she be present. Sometimes the two of them would sleep late, and
even after they had risen he would not let her go. Because of his unreasonable demands
she was widely held to have fallen into immoderate habits out of keeping with her rank.

With the birth of the son, it became yet clearer that she was the emperor's favorite. The mother of the eldest son began to feel uneasy. If she did not manage carefully,
she might see the new son designated crown prince. She had come to court before the

---

1. Translated by Edward Seidensticker, with notes adapted from Seidensticker.
2. The beautiful concubine of the Tang emperor Hsüan Tsung. The emperor's infatuation with her was viewed as the
cause of the An Lushan Rebellion, and led to her execution.

emperor's other ladies, she had once been favored over the others, and she had borne several of his children. However much her complaining might trouble and annoy him, she was one lady whom he could not ignore.

Though the mother of the new son had the emperor's love, her detractors were numerous and alert to the slightest inadvertency. She was in continuous torment, feeling that she had nowhere to turn. Her quarters were in the Kiritsubo.[3] The emperor had to pass the apartments of other ladies to reach hers, and it must be admitted that their resentment at his constant comings and goings was not unreasonable. Her visits to the royal chambers were equally frequent. The robes of her women were in a scandalous state from trash strewn along bridges and galleries. Once some women conspired to have both doors of a gallery she must pass bolted shut, and so she found herself unable to advance or retreat. Her anguish over the mounting list of insults was presently more than the emperor could bear. He moved a lady out of rooms adjacent to his own and assigned them to the Kiritsubo lady and so, of course, aroused new resentment.

When the young prince reached the age of three,[4] the resources of the treasury and the stewards' offices were exhausted to make the ceremonial bestowing of trousers as elaborate as that for the eldest son. Once more there was malicious talk; but the prince himself, as he grew up, was so superior of mien and disposition that few could find it in themselves to dislike him. Among the more discriminating, indeed, were some who marveled that such a paragon had been born into this world.

In the summer the boy's mother, feeling vaguely unwell, asked that she be allowed to go home. The emperor would not hear of it. Since they were by now used to these indispositions, he begged her to stay and see what course her health would take. It was steadily worse, and then, suddenly, everyone could see that she was failing. Her mother came pleading that he let her go home. At length he agreed.

Fearing that even now she might be the victim of a gratuitous insult, she chose to go off without ceremony, leaving the boy behind. Everything must have an end, and the emperor could no longer detain her. It saddened him inexpressibly that he was not even permitted to see her off. A lady of great charm and beauty, she was sadly emaciated. She was sunk in melancholy thoughts, but when she tried to put them into words her voice was almost inaudible. The emperor was quite beside himself, his mind a confusion of things that had been and things that were to come. He wept and vowed undying love, over and over again. The lady was unable to reply. She seemed listless and drained of strength, as if she scarcely knew what was happening. Wanting somehow to help, the emperor ordered that she be given the honor of a hand-drawn carriage. He returned to her apartments and still could not bring himself to the final parting.

"We vowed that we would go together down the road we all must go. You must not leave me behind."

She looked sadly up at him. "If I had suspected that it would be so—" She was gasping for breath.

> "I leave you, to go the road we all must go.
> The road I would choose, if only I could, is the other."

It was evident that she would have liked to say more; but she was so weak that it had been a struggle to say even this much.

---

3. The Paulownia Court, in the northeast corner of the residential compound of the palace. The distance of the Kiritsubo lady's quarters from the emperor's, near the middle of the compound, is a reflection of her relatively low rank.

4. All ages are by the Asian count, not of the full years but of the number of years in which one has lived, therefore one or two years above the full count: someone born near the end of a year would turn "two" at New Year's.

The emperor was wondering again if he might not keep her with him and have her with him to the end.

But a message came from her mother, asking that she hurry. "We have obtained the agreement of eminent ascetics to conduct the necessary services, and I fear that they are to begin this evening."

So, in desolation, he let her go. He passed a sleepless night.

He sent off a messenger and was beside himself with impatience and apprehension even before there had been time for the man to reach the lady's house and return. The man arrived to find the house echoing with laments. She had died at shortly past midnight. He returned sadly to the palace. The emperor closed himself up in his private apartments. He would have liked at least to keep the boy with him, but no precedent could be found for having him away from his mother's house through the mourning. The boy looked in bewilderment at the weeping courtiers, at his father too, the tears streaming over his face. The death of a parent is sad under any circumstances, and this one was indescribably sad.

But there must be an end to weeping, and orders were given for the funeral. If only she could rise to the heavens with the smoke from the pyre, said the mother between her sobs. She rode in the hearse with several attendants, and what must her feelings have been when they reached Mount Otaki?[5] It was there that the services were conducted with the utmost solemnity and dignity.

She looked down at the body. "With her before me, I cannot persuade myself that she is dead. At the sight of her ashes I can perhaps accept what has happened."

The words were rational enough, but she was so distraught that she seemed about to fall from the carriage. The women had known that it would be so and did what they could for her.

A messenger came from the palace with the news that the lady had been raised to the Third Rank, and presently a nunciary arrived to read the official order. For the emperor, the regret was scarcely bearable that he had not had the courage of his resolve to appoint her an imperial consort, and he wished to make amends by promoting her one rank. There were many who resented even this favor. Others, however, of a more sensitive nature, saw more than ever what a dear lady she had been, simple and gentle and difficult to find fault with. It was because she had been excessively favored by the emperor that she had been the victim of such malice. The grand ladies were now reminded of how sympathetic and unassuming she had been. It was for just such an occasion, they remarked to one another, that the phrase "how well one knows" had been invented.

The days went dully by. The emperor was careful to send offerings for the weekly memorial services. His grief was unabated and he spent his nights in tears, refusing to summon his other ladies. His serving women were plunged into dew-drenched autumn.

There was one lady, however, who refused to be placated. "How ridiculous," said the lady of the Kokiden Pavilion, mother of his eldest son, "that the infatuation should continue even now."

The emperor's thoughts were on his youngest son even when he was with his eldest. He sent off intelligent nurses and serving women to the house of the boy's grandmother, where he was still in residence, and made constant inquiry after him.

The autumn tempests blew and suddenly the evenings were chilly. Lost in his grief, the emperor sent off a note to the grandmother. His messenger was a woman of middle rank called Myōbu, whose father was a guards officer. It was on a beautiful moonlit night that he dispatched her, a night that brought memories. On such nights he and the dead lady had played the koto for each other. Her koto had somehow had overtones lacking in other instruments, and when she would interrupt the music to speak, the words too carried echoes of their own. Her face, her manner—they seemed to cling to him, but with "no more substance than the lucent dream."

[*Myōbu visits the Kiritsubo lady's grieving mother, and delivers a letter in which the emperor hints that he would like his young son to return to the palace.*]

Myōbu was much moved to find the emperor waiting up for her. Making it seem that his attention was on the small and beautifully planted garden before him, now in full autumn bloom, he was talking quietly with four or five women, among the most sensitive of his attendants. He had become addicted to illustrations by the emperor Uda for "The Song of Everlasting Sorrow"[6] and to poems by Ise and Tsurayuki on that subject, and to Chinese poems as well.

He listened attentively as Myōbu described the scene she had found so affecting. He took up the letter she had brought from the grandmother.

"I am so awed by this august message that I would run away and hide; and so violent are the emotions it gives rise to that I scarcely know what to say.

> The tree that gave them shelter has withered and died.
> One fears for the plight of the hagi[7] shoots beneath."

A strange way to put the matter, thought the emperor; but the lady must still be dazed with grief. He chose to overlook the suggestion that he himself could not help the child.

He sought to hide his sorrow, not wanting these women to see him in such poor control of himself. But it was no use. He reviewed his memories over and over again, from his very earliest days with the dead lady. He had scarcely been able to bear a moment away from her while she lived. How strange that he had been able to survive the days and months since on memories alone. He had hoped to reward the grandmother's sturdy devotion, and his hopes had come to nothing.

"Well," he sighed, "she may look forward to having her day, if she will only live to see the boy grow up."

Looking at the keepsakes Myōbu had brought back, he thought what a comfort it would be if some wizard were to bring him, like that Chinese emperor, a comb from the world where his lost love was dwelling. He whispered:

> "And will no wizard search her out for me,
> That even he may tell me where she is?"

There are limits to the powers of the most gifted artist. The Chinese lady in the paintings did not have the luster of life. Yang Kuei-fei was said to have resembled the lotus of the Sublime Pond, the willows of the Timeless Hall. No doubt she was very beautiful in her Chinese finery. When he tried to remember the quiet charm of his lost lady, he found that there was no color of flower, no song of bird, to summon her up. Morning and night, over and over again, they had repeated to each other the lines from "The Song of Everlasting Sorrow":

> In the sky, as birds that share a wing.
> On earth, as trees that share a branch.

It had been their vow, and the shortness of her life had made it an empty dream.

---

6. By Po Chü-i, describing the grief of the Tang emperor Hsüan Tsung upon the death of his concubine Yang Kuei-fei. Uda reigned in the late ninth century and died in 931. Tsurayuki and Ise (one of Uda's concubines) were active in the early 10th century.

7. A kind of clover.

Everything, the moaning of the wind, the humming of autumn insects, added to the sadness. But in the apartments of the Kokiden lady matters were different. It had been some time since she had last waited upon the emperor. The moonlight being so beautiful, she saw no reason not to have music deep into the night. The emperor muttered something about the bad taste of such a performance at such a time, and those who saw his distress agreed that it was an unnecessary injury. Kokiden was of an arrogant and intractable nature and her behavior suggested that to her the emperor's grief was of no importance.

The moon set. The wicks in the lamps had been trimmed more than once and presently the oil was gone. Still he showed no sign of retiring. His mind on the boy and the old lady, he jotted down a verse:

> Tears dim the moon, even here above the clouds.[8]
> Dim must it be in that lodging among the reeds.

Calls outside told him that the guard was being changed. It would be one or two in the morning. People would think his behavior strange indeed. He at length withdrew to his bedchamber. He was awake the whole night through, and in dark morning, his thoughts on the blinds that would not open,[9] he was unable to interest himself in business of state. He scarcely touched his breakfast, and lunch seemed so remote from his inclinations that his attendants exchanged looks and whispers of alarm.

Not all voices were sympathetic. Perhaps, some said, it had all been foreordained, but he had dismissed the talk and ignored the resentment and let the affair quite pass the bounds of reason; and now to neglect his duties so—it was altogether too much. Some even cited the example of the Chinese emperor who had brought ruin upon himself and his country.

The months passed and the young prince returned to the palace. He had grown into a lad of such beauty that he hardly seemed meant for this world—and indeed one almost feared that he might only briefly be a part of it. When, the following spring, it came time to name a crown prince, the emperor wanted very much to pass over his first son in favor of the younger, who, however, had no influential maternal relatives. It did not seem likely that the designation would pass unchallenged. The boy might, like his mother, be destroyed by immoderate favors. The emperor told no one of his wishes. There did after all seem to be a limit to his affections, people said; and Kokiden regained her confidence.

The boy's grandmother was inconsolable. Finally, because her prayer to be with her daughter had been answered, perhaps, she breathed her last. Once more the emperor was desolate. The boy, now six, was old enough to know grief himself. His grandmother, who had been so good to him over the years, had more than once told him what pain it would cause her, when the time came, to leave him behind.

He now lived at court. When he was seven he went through the ceremonial reading of the Chinese classics, and never before had there been so fine a performance. Again a tremor of apprehension passed over the emperor—might it be that such a prodigy was not to be long for this world?

"No one need be angry with him now that his mother is gone." He took the boy to visit the Kokiden Pavilion. "And now most especially I hope you will be kind to him."

Admitting the boy to her inner chambers, even Kokiden was pleased. Not the sternest of warriors or the most unbending of enemies could have held back a smile. Kokiden was reluctant to let him go. She had two daughters, but neither could compare

---

8. Even here in the palace.
9. Referring to a poem by Ise on "The Song of Everlasting Sorrow": "The jeweled blinds are drawn, the morning is dark. / I had not thought I would not even dream."

with him in beauty. The lesser ladies crowded about, not in the least ashamed to show their faces, all eager to amuse him, though aware that he set them off to disadvantage. I need not speak of his accomplishments in the compulsory subjects, the classics and the like. When it came to music his flute and koto made the heavens echo—but to recount all his virtues would, I fear, give rise to a suspicion that I distort the truth.

An embassy came from Korea. Hearing that among the emissaries was a skilled physiognomist, the emperor would have liked to summon him for consultation. He decided, however, that he must defer to the emperor Uda's injunction against receiving foreigners, and instead sent this favored son to the Kōro mansion,[1] where the party was lodged. The boy was disguised as the son of the grand moderator, his guardian at court. The wise Korean cocked his head in astonishment.

"It is the face of one who should ascend to the highest place and be father to the nation," he said quietly, as if to himself. "But to take it for such would no doubt be to predict trouble. Yet it is not the face of the minister, the deputy, who sets about ordering public affairs."

The moderator was a man of considerable learning. There was much of interest in his exchanges with the Korean. There were also exchanges of Chinese poetry, and in one of his poems the Korean succeeded most skillfully in conveying his joy at having been able to observe such a countenance on this the eve of his return to his own land, and sorrow that the parting must come so soon. The boy offered a verse that was received with high praise. The most splendid of gifts were bestowed upon him. The wise man was in return showered with gifts from the palace.

Somehow news of the sage's remarks leaked out, though the emperor himself was careful to say nothing. The Minister of the Right, grandfather of the crown prince and father of the Kokiden lady, was quick to hear, and again his suspicions were aroused. In the wisdom of his heart, the emperor had already analyzed the boy's physiognomy after the Japanese fashion and had formed tentative plans. He had thus far refrained from bestowing imperial rank on his son, and was delighted that the Korean view should so accord with his own. Lacking the support of maternal relatives, the boy would be most insecure as a prince without court rank, and the emperor could not be sure how long his own reign would last. As a commoner he could be of great service. The emperor therefore encouraged the boy in his studies, at which he was so proficient that it seemed a waste to reduce him to common rank. And yet—as a prince he would arouse the hostility of those who had cause to fear his becoming emperor. Summoning an astrologer of the Indian school, the emperor was pleased to learn that the Indian view coincided with the Japanese and the Korean; and so he concluded that the boy should become a commoner with the name Minamoto or Genji.

The months and the years passed and still the emperor could not forget his lost love. He summoned various women who might console him, but apparently it was too much to ask in this world for one who even resembled her. He remained sunk in memories, unable to interest himself in anything. Then he was told of the Fourth Princess, daughter of a former emperor, a lady famous for her beauty and reared with the greatest care by her mother, the empress. A woman now in attendance upon the emperor had in the days of his predecessor been most friendly with the princess, then but a child, and even now saw her from time to time.

"I have been at court through three reigns now," she said, "and never had I seen anyone who genuinely resembled my lady. But now the daughter of the empress dowager is growing up, and the resemblance is most astonishing. One would be hard put to find her equal."

52

1. In the southern part of the city.

Hoping that she might just possibly be right, the emperor asked most courteously to have the princess sent to court. Her mother was reluctant and even fearful, however. One must remember, she said, that the mother of the crown prince was a most willful lady who had subjected the Kiritsubo lady to open insults and presently sent her into a fatal decline. Before she had made up her mind she followed her husband in death, and the daughter was alone. The emperor renewed his petition. He said that he would treat the girl as one of his own daughters.

Her attendants and her maternal relatives and her older brother, Prince Hyōbu, consulted together and concluded that rather than languish at home she might seek consolation at court; and so she was sent off. She was called Fujitsubo. The resemblance to the dead lady was indeed astonishing. Because she was of such high birth (it may have been that people were imagining things) she seemed even more graceful and delicate than the other. No one could despise her for inferior rank, and the emperor need not feel shy about showing his love for her. The other lady had not particularly encouraged his attentions and had been the victim of a love too intense; and now, though it would be wrong to say that he had quite forgotten her, he found his affections shifting to the new lady, who was a source of boundless comfort. So it is with the affairs of this world.

Since Genji never left his father's side, it was not easy for this new lady, the recipient of so many visits, to hide herself from him. The other ladies were disinclined to think themselves her inferior, and indeed each of them had her own merits. They were all rather past their prime, however. Fujitsubo's beauty was of a younger and fresher sort. Though in her childlike shyness she made an especial effort not to be seen, Genji occasionally caught a glimpse of her face. He could not remember his own mother and it moved him deeply to learn, from the lady who had first told the emperor of Fujitsubo, that the resemblance was striking. He wanted to be near her always.

"Do not be unfriendly," said the emperor to Fujitsubo. "Sometimes it almost seems to me too that you are his mother. Do not think him forward, be kind to him. Your eyes, your expression: you are really so uncommonly like her that you could pass for his mother."

Genji's affection for the new lady grew, and the most ordinary flower or tinted leaf became the occasion for expressing it. Kokiden was not pleased. She was not on good terms with Fujitsubo, and all her old resentment of Genji came back. He was handsomer than the crown prince, her chief treasure in the world, well thought of by the whole court. People began calling Genji "the shining one." Fujitsubo, ranked beside him in the emperor's affections, became "the lady of the radiant sun."

It seemed a pity that the boy must one day leave behind his boyish attire; but when he reached the age of twelve he went through his initiation ceremonies and received the cap of an adult. Determined that the ceremony should be in no way inferior to the crown prince's, which had been held some years earlier in the Grand Hall, the emperor himself bustled about adding new details to the established forms. As for the banquet after the ceremony, he did not wish the custodians of the storehouses and granaries to treat it as an ordinary public occasion.

The throne faced east on the east porch, and before it were Genji's seat and that of the minister who was to bestow the official cap. At the appointed hour in mid-afternoon Genji appeared. The freshness of his face and his boyish coiffure were again such as to make the emperor regret that the change must take place. The ritual cutting of the boy's hair was performed by the secretary of the treasury. As the beautiful locks fell the emperor was seized with a hopeless longing for his dead lady. Repeatedly he found himself struggling to keep his composure. The ceremony over, the boy withdrew to change to adult trousers and descended into the courtyard for ceremonial thanksgiving. There was not a person in the assembly who did not feel his eyes misting over. The emperor was stirred by the deepest of emotions. He had on brief occasions been able to forget the past, and now it all came back again. Vaguely apprehensive lest the initiation of so young a boy bring a sudden aging, he was astonished to see that his son delighted him even more.

The Minister of the Left, who bestowed the official cap, had only one daughter, named Aoi, his chief joy in life. Her mother, the minister's first wife, was a princess of the blood. The crown prince had sought the girl's hand, but the minister thought rather of giving her to Genji. He had heard that the emperor had similar thoughts. When the emperor suggested that the boy was without adequate sponsors for his initiation and that the support of relatives by marriage might be called for, the minister quite agreed.

* * *

The nuptial observances were conducted with great solemnity. The groom seemed to the minister and his family quite charming in his boyishness. The bride was older, and somewhat ill at ease with such a young husband.

The minister had the emperor's complete confidence, and his principal wife, the girl's mother, was the emperor's sister. Both parents were therefore of the highest standing. And now they had Genji for a son-in-law. The Minister of the Right, who as grandfather of the crown prince should have been without rivals, was somehow eclipsed. The Minister of the Left had numerous children by several ladies. One of the sons, named Tō no Chūjō, a very handsome lad by his principal wife, was already a guards lieutenant. Relations between the two ministers were not good but the Minister of the Right found it difficult to ignore such a talented youth, to whom he offered the hand of his fourth and favorite daughter. His esteem for his new son-in-law rivaled the other minister's esteem for Genji. To both houses the new arrangements seemed ideal.

Constantly at his father's side, Genji spent little time at the Sanjō mansion of his bride. Fujitsubo was for him a vision of sublime beauty. If he could have someone like her—but in fact there was no one really like her. His bride too was beautiful, and she had had the advantage of every luxury; but he was not at all sure that they were meant for each other. The yearning in his young heart for the other lady was agony. Now that he had come of age, he no longer had his father's permission to go behind her curtains. On evenings when there was music, he would play the flute to her koto and so communicate something of his longing, and take some comfort from her voice, soft through the curtains. Life at court was for him much preferable to life at Sanjō. Two or three days at Sanjō would be followed by five or six days at court. For the minister, youth seemed sufficient excuse for this neglect. He continued to be delighted with his son-in-law.

The minister selected the handsomest and most accomplished of ladies to wait upon the young pair and planned the sort of diversions that were most likely to interest Genji. At the palace the emperor assigned him the apartments that had been his mother's and took care that her retinue was not dispersed. Orders were handed down to the offices of repairs and fittings to remodel the house that had belonged to the lady's family. The results were magnificent. The plantings and the artificial hills had always been remarkably tasteful, and the grounds now swarmed with workmen widening the lake. If only, thought Genji, he could have with him the lady he yearned for.

The sobriquet "the shining Genji," one hears, was bestowed upon him by the Korean.

from *Chapter 2. The Broom Tree*

"The shining Genji": it was almost too grand a name. Yet he did not escape criticism for numerous little adventures. It seemed indeed that his indiscretions might give him a name for frivolity, and he did what he could to hide them. But his most secret affairs (such is the malicious work of the gossips) became common talk. If, on the other hand, he were to go through life concerned only for his name and avoid all these interesting and amusing little affairs, then he would be laughed to shame by the likes of the lieutenant of Katano.[1]

Still a guards captain, Genji spent most of his time at the palace, going infrequently to the Sanjō mansion of his father-in-law. The people there feared that he might have been stained by the lavender of Kasugano.[2] Though in fact he had an instinctive dislike for the promiscuity he saw all around him, he had a way of sometimes turning against his own better inclinations and causing unhappiness.

The summer rains came, the court was in retreat, and an even longer interval than usual had passed since his last visit to Sanjō. Though the minister and his family were much put out, they spared no effort to make him feel welcome. The minister's sons were more attentive than to the emperor himself. Genji was on particularly good terms with Tō no Chūjō. They enjoyed music together and more frivolous diversions as well. Tō no Chūjō was of an amorous nature and not at all comfortable in the apartments which his father-in-law, the Minister of the Right, had at great expense provided for him. At Sanjō with his own family, on the other hand, he took very good care of his rooms, and when Genji came and went the two of them were always together. They were a good match for each other in study and at play. Reserve quite disappeared between them.

It had been raining all day. There were fewer courtiers than usual in the royal presence. Back in his own palace quarters, also unusually quiet, Genji pulled a lamp near and sought to while away the time with his books. He had Tō no Chūjō with him. Numerous pieces of colored paper, obviously letters, lay on a shelf. Tō no Chūjō made no attempt to hide his curiosity.

"Well," said Genji, "there are some I might let you see. But there are some I think it better not to."

"You miss the point. The ones I want to see are precisely the ones you want to hide. The ordinary ones—I'm not much of a hand at the game, you know, but even I am up to the ordinary give and take. But the ones from ladies who think you are not doing right by them, who sit alone through an evening and wait for you to come—those are the ones I want to see."

It was not likely that really delicate letters would be left scattered on a shelf, and it may be assumed that the papers treated so carelessly were the less important ones.

"You do have a variety of them," said Tō no Chūjō, reading the correspondence through piece by piece. This will be from her, and this will be from her, he would say. Sometimes he guessed correctly and sometimes he was far afield, to Genji's great amusement. Genji was brief with his replies and let out no secrets.

"It is I who should be asking to see your collection. No doubt it is huge. When I have seen it I shall be happy to throw my files open to you."

---

1. Evidently the hero of a romance that has been lost.

2. *Tales of Ise* 1: "Kasugano lavender stains my robe / in deep disorder, like my secret loves." Kasugano is on the outskirts of Nara. Here as elsewhere lavender (*murasaki*) suggests a romantic affinity.

"I fear there is nothing that would interest you." Tō no Chūjō was in a contemplative mood. "It is with women as it is with everything else: the flawless ones are very few indeed. This is a sad fact which I have learned over the years. All manner of women seem presentable enough at first. Little notes, replies to this and that, they all suggest sensibility and cultivation. But when you begin sorting out the really superior ones you find that there are not many who have to be on your list. Each has her little tricks and she makes the most of them, getting in her slights at rivals, so broad sometimes that you almost have to blush. Hidden away by loving parents who build brilliant futures for them, they let word get out of this little talent and that little accomplishment and you are all in a stir. They are young and pretty and amiable and carefree, and in their boredom they begin to pick up a little from their elders, and in the natural course of things they begin to concentrate on one particular hobby and make something of it. A woman tells you all about it and hides the weak points and brings out the strong ones as if they were everything, and you can't very well call her a liar. So you begin keeping company, and it is always the same. The fact is not up to the advance notices."

Tō no Chūjō sighed, a sigh clearly based on experience. Some of what he had said, though not all, accorded with Genji's own experience. "And have you come upon any," said Genji, smiling, "who would seem to have nothing at all to recommend them?"

"Who would be fool enough to notice such a woman? And in any case, I should imagine that women with no merits are as rare as women with no faults. If a woman is of good family and well taken care of, then the things she is less than proud of are hidden and she gets by well enough. When you come to the middle ranks, each woman has her own little inclinations and there are thousands of ways to separate one from another. And when you come to the lowest—well, who really pays much attention?"

He appeared to know everything. Genji was by now deeply interested.

"You speak of three ranks," he said, "but is it so easy to make the division? There are well-born ladies who fall in the world and there are people of no background who rise to the higher ranks and build themselves fine houses as if intended for them all along. How would you fit such people into your system?"

At this point two young courtiers, a guards officer and a functionary in the ministry of rites, appeared on the scene, to attend the emperor in his retreat. Both were devotees of the way of love and both were good talkers. Tō no Chūjō, as if he had been waiting for them, invited their views on the question that had just been asked. The discussion progressed, and included a number of rather unconvincing points.

"Those who have just arrived at high position," said one of the newcomers, "do not attract the same sort of notice as those who were born to it. And those who were born to the highest rank but somehow do not have the right backing—in spirit they may be as proud and noble as ever, but they cannot hide their deficiencies. And so I think that they should both be put in your middle rank.

"There are those whose families are not quite of the highest rank but who go off and work hard in the provinces. They have their place in the world, though there are all sorts of little differences among them. Some of them would belong on anyone's list. So it is these days. Myself, I would take a woman from a middling family over one who has rank and nothing else. Let us say someone whose father is almost but not quite a councilor. Someone who has a decent enough reputation and comes from a decent enough family and can live in some luxury. Such people can be very pleasant. There is nothing wrong with the household arrangements, and indeed a daughter can sometimes be set out in a way that dazzles you. I can think of several such women it would be hard to find fault with. When they go into court service, they are the ones the unexpected favors have a way of falling on. I have seen cases enough of it, I can tell you."

Genji smiled. "And so a person should limit himself to girls with money?"

"That does not sound like you," said Tō no Chūjō.

"When a woman has the highest rank and a spotless reputation," continued the other, "but something has gone wrong with her upbringing, something is wrong in the way she puts herself forward, you wonder how it can possibly have been allowed to happen. But when all the conditions are right and the girl herself is pretty enough, she is taken for granted. There is no cause for the least surprise. Such ladies are beyond the likes of me, and so I leave them where they are, the highest of the high. There are surprisingly pretty ladies wasting away behind tangles of weeds, and hardly anyone even knows of their existence. The first surprise is hard to forget. There she is, a girl with a fat, sloppy old father and boorish brothers and a house that seems common at best. Off in the women's rooms is a proud lady who has acquired bits and snatches of this and that. You get wind of them, however small the accomplishments may be, and they take hold of your imagination. She is not the equal of the one who has every-thing, of course, but she has her charm. She is not easy to pass by."

He looked at his companion, the young man from the ministry of rites. The latter was silent, wondering if the reference might be to his sisters, just then coming into their own as subjects for conversation. Genji, it would seem, was thinking that on the highest levels there were sadly few ladies to bestow much thought upon. He was wearing several soft white singlets with an informal court robe thrown loosely over them. As he sat in the lamplight leaning against an armrest, his companions almost wished that he were a woman. Even the "highest of the high" might seem an inad-equate match for him.

[*Although Genji remains aloof from the discussion, the other young men continue trading notes about desirable and undesirable qualities in women they have known. Tō no Chūjō describes an affair he had with a reticent, undemanding woman (Yūgao) by whom he had a child, but who was eventually driven off by his principal wife. Throughout, Genji's thoughts remain on Fujitsubo, who seems to him without flaw.*]

from *Chapter 5. Lavender*

[*Genji falls ill and goes to the Northern Hills, where he is treated by a Sage and remains to recover.*]

The evening was long. Genji took advantage of a dense haze to have a look at the house behind the wattle fence. Sending back everyone except Koremitsu, he took up a position at the fence. In the west room sat a nun who had a holy image before her. The blinds were slightly raised and she seemed to be offering flowers. She was leaning against a pillar and had a text spread out on an armrest. The effort to read seemed to take all her strength. Perhaps in her forties, she had a fair, delicate skin and a pleasantly full face, though the effects of illness were apparent. The features sug-gested breeding and cultivation. Cut cleanly at the shoulders, her hair seemed to him far more pleasing than if it had been permitted to trail the usual length. Beside her were two attractive women, and little girls scampered in and out. Much the prettiest was a girl of perhaps ten in a soft white singlet and a russet robe. She would one day be a real beauty. Rich hair spread over her shoulders like a fan. Her face was flushed from weeping.

"What is it?" The nun looked up. "Another fight?" He thought he saw a resemblance. Perhaps they were mother and daughter.

"Inuki let my baby sparrows loose." The child was very angry. "I had them in a basket."

"That stupid child," said a rather handsome woman with rich hair who seemed to be called Shōnagon and was apparently the girl's nurse. "She always manages to do the wrong thing, and we are forever scolding her. Where will they have flown off to? They were getting to be such sweet little things too! How awful if the crows find them." She went out.

"What a silly child you are, really too silly," said the nun. "I can't be sure I will last out the day, and here you are worrying about sparrows. I've told you so many times that it's a sin to put birds in a cage. Come here."

The child knelt down beside her. She was charming, with rich, unplucked eyebrows and hair pushed childishly back from the forehead. How he would like to see her in a few years! And a sudden realization brought him close to tears: the resemblance to Fujitsubo, for whom he so yearned, was astonishing.

The nun stroked the girl's hair. "You will not comb it and still it's so pretty. I worry about you, you do seem so very young. Others are much more grown up at your age. Your poor dead mother: she was only ten when her father died, and she understood everything. What will become of you when I am gone?"

She was weeping, and a vague sadness had come over Genji too. The girl gazed attentively at her and then looked down. The hair that fell over her forehead was thick and lustrous.

> "Are these tender grasses to grow without the dew
> which holds itself back from the heavens that would receive it?"

There were tears in the nun's voice, and the other woman seemed also to be speaking through tears:

> "It cannot be that the dew will vanish away
> ere summer comes to these early grasses of spring."

The bishop came in. "What is this? Your blinds up? And today of all days you are out on the veranda? I have just been told that General Genji is up at the hermitage being treated for malaria. He came in disguise and I was not told in time to pay a call."

"And what a sight we are. You don't suppose he saw us?" She lowered the blinds.

"The shining one of whom the whole world talks. Wouldn't you like to see him? Enough to make a saint throw off the last traces of the vulgar world, they say, and feel as if new years had been added to his life. I will get off a note."

He hurried away, and Genji too withdrew. What a discovery! It was for such unforeseen rewards that his amorous followers were so constantly on the prowl. Such a rare outing for him, and it had brought such a find! She was a perfectly beautiful child. Who might she be? He was beginning to make plans: the child must stand in the place of the one whom she so resembled.

[*After Genji has retired to his quarters, the bishop, the brother of Murasaki's grandmother, arrives and invites him to pay a visit.*]

The bishop talked of this ephemeral world and of the world to come. His own burden of sin was heavy, thought Genji, that he had been lured into an illicit and profitless affair. He would regret it all his life and suffer even more terribly in the life to come. What joy to withdraw to such a place as this! But with the thought came thoughts of the young face he had seen earlier in the evening.

"Do you have someone with you here? I had a dream that suddenly begins to make sense."

"How quick you are with your dreams, sir! I fear my answer will disappoint you. It has been a very long time since the Lord Inspector died. I don't suppose you will even have heard of him. He was my brother-in-law. His widow turned her back on the world and recently she has been ill, and since I do not go down to the city she has come to stay with me here. It was her thought that I might be able to help her."

"I have heard that your sister had a daughter. I ask from no more than idle curiosity, you must believe me."

"There was an only daughter. She too has been dead these ten years and more. He took very great pains with her education and hoped to send her to court; but he died before that ambition could be realized, and the nun, my sister, was left to look after her. I do not know through whose offices it was that Prince Hyōbu began visiting the daughter in secret. His wife is from a very proud family, you know, sir, and there were unpleasant incidents, which finally drove the poor thing into a fatal decline. I saw before my own eyes how worry can destroy a person."

So the child he had seen would be the daughter of Prince Hyōbu and the unfortunate lady; and it was Fujitsubo, the prince's sister, whom she so resembled. He wanted more than ever to meet her. She was an elegant child, and she did not seem at all spoiled. What a delight if he could take her into his house and make her his ideal!

"A very sad story." He wished to be completely sure. "Did she leave no one behind?"

"She had a child just before she died, a girl, a great source of worry for my poor sister in her declining years."

There could be no further doubt. "What I am about to say will, I fear, startle you—but might I have charge of the child? I have rather good reasons, for all the suddenness of my proposal. If you are telling yourself that she is too young—well, sir, you are doing me an injustice. Other men may have improper motives, but I do not."

"Your words quite fill me with delight. But she is indeed young, so very young that we could not possibly think even in jest of asking you to take responsibility for her. Only the man who is presently to be her husband can take that responsibility. In a matter of such import I am not competent to give an answer. I must discuss the matter with my sister." He was suddenly remote and chilly.

Genji had spoken with youthful impulsiveness and could not think what to do next.

[Genji spends the night at the bishop's and engages in an exchange of poetry with the nun, making his interest in the girl known, much to the consternation of the nun and the attendants. The bishop and the nun agree that Genji's proposal is rather precipitate, and suggest that he wait until the girl grows up. Genji returns to the city and grudgingly accedes to his father-in-law's request that he spend some time at Sanjō to continue his recuperation.]

At the minister's Sanjō mansion everything was in readiness. It had been polished and refitted until it was a jeweled pavilion, perfect to the last detail. As always,

Genji's wife Aoi secluded herself in her private apartments, and it was only at her father's urging that she came forth; and so Genji had her before him, immobile, like a princess in an illustration for a romance. It would have been a great pleasure, he was sure, to have her comment even tartly upon his account of the mountain journey. She seemed the stiffest, remotest person in the world. How odd that the aloofness seemed only to grow as time went by.

"It would be nice, I sometimes think, if you could be a little more wifely. I have been very ill, and I am hurt, but not really surprised, that you have not inquired after my health."

"Like the pain, perhaps, of awaiting a visitor who does not come?"

She cast a sidelong glance at him as she spoke, and her cold beauty was very intimidating indeed.

"You so rarely speak to me, and when you do you say such unpleasant things. 'A visitor who does not come'—that is hardly an appropriate way to describe a husband, and indeed it is hardly civil. I try this approach and I try that, hoping to break through, but you seem intent on defending all the approaches. Well, one of these years, perhaps, if I live long enough."

He withdrew to the bedchamber. She did not follow. Though there were things he would have liked to say, he lay down with a sigh. He closed his eyes, but there was too much on his mind to permit sleep.

He thought of the little girl and how he would like to see her grown into a woman. Her grandmother was of course right when she said that the girl was still too young for him. He must not seem insistent. And yet—was there not some way to bring her quietly to Nijō and have her beside him, a comfort and a companion? Prince Hyōbu was a dashing and stylish man, but no one could have called him remarkably handsome. Why did the girl so take after her aunt? Perhaps because aunt and father were children of the same empress. These thoughts seemed to bring the girl closer, and he longed to have her for his own.

* * *

Fujitsubo was ill and had gone home to her family. Genji managed a sympathetic thought or two for his lonely father, but his thoughts were chiefly on the possibility of seeing Fujitsubo. He quite halted his visits to other ladies. All through the day, at home and at court, he sat gazing off into space, and in the evening he would press Omyōbu to be his intermediary. How she did it I do not know; but she contrived a meeting. It is sad to have to say that his earlier attentions, so unwelcome, no longer seemed real, and the mere thought that they had been successful was for Fujitsubo a torment. Determined that there would not be another meeting, she was shocked to find him in her presence again. She did not seek to hide her distress, and her efforts to turn him away delighted him even as they put him to shame. There was no one else quite like her. In that fact was his undoing: he would be less a prey to longing if he could find in her even a trace of the ordinary. And the tumult of thoughts and feelings that now assailed him—he would have liked to consign it to the Mountain of Obscurity.[1] It might have been better, he sighed, so short was the night, if he had not come at all.

> "So few and scattered the nights, so few the dreams,
> Would that the dream tonight might take me with it."

1. Kurabunoyama, thought to have been in present-day Kyoto.

He was in tears, and she did, after all, have to feel sorry for him.

> "Were I to disappear in the last of dreams
> Would yet my name live on in infamy?"

She had every right to be unhappy, and he was sad for her. Omyōbu gathered his clothes and brought them out to him.

Back at Nijō he spent a tearful day in bed. He had word from Omyōbu that her lady had not read his letter. So it always was, and yet he was hurt. He remained in distraught seclusion for several days. The thought that his father might be wondering about his absence filled him with terror.

Lamenting the burden of sin that seemed to be hers, Fujitsubo was more and more unwell, and could not bestir herself, despite repeated messages summoning her back to court. She was not at all her usual self—and what was to become of her? She took to her bed as the weather turned warmer. Three months had now passed and her condition was clear; and the burden of sin now seemed to have made it necessary that she submit to curious and reproving stares. Her women thought her behavior very curious indeed. Why had she let so much time pass without informing the emperor? There was of course a crucial matter of which she spoke to no one. Ben, the daughter of her old nurse, and Omyōbu, both of whom were very close to her and attended her in the bath, had ample opportunity to observe her condition. Omyōbu was aghast. Her lady had been trapped by the harshest of fates. The emperor would seem to have been informed that a malign spirit had possession of her, and to have believed the story, as did the court in general. He sent a constant stream of messengers, which terrified her and allowed no pause in her sufferings.

Genji had a strange, rather awful dream. He consulted a soothsayer, who said that it portended events so extraordinary as to be almost unthinkable.

"It contains bad omens as well. You must be careful."

"It was not my own dream but a friend's. We will see whether it comes true, and in the meantime you must keep it to yourself."

What could it mean? He heard of Fujitsubo's condition, thought of their night together, and wondered whether the two might be related. He exhausted his stock of pleas for another meeting. Horrified that matters were so out of hand, Omyōbu could do nothing for him. He had on rare occasions had a brief note, no more than a line or two, but now even these messages ceased coming.

Fujitsubo returned to court in the Seventh Month. The emperor's affection for her had only grown in her absence. Her condition was now apparent to everyone. A slight emaciation made her beauty seem if anything nearer perfection, and the emperor kept her always at his side. The skies as autumn approached called more insistently for music. Keeping Genji too beside him, the emperor had him try his hand at this and that instrument. Genji struggled to control himself, but now and then a sign of his scarcely bearable feelings did show through, to remind the lady of what she wanted more than anything to forget.* * *

In the autumn evening, his thoughts on his unattainable love, he longed more than ever, unnatural though the wish may have seemed, for the company of the little girl who sprang from the same roots. The thought of the evening when the old nun had described herself as dew holding back from the heavens made him even more impatient—and at the same time he feared that if he were to bring the girl to Nijō he would be disappointed in her.

> I long to have it, to bring it in from the moor,
> The lavender[2] that shares its roots with another.

In the Tenth Month the emperor was to visit the Suzaku Palace. From all the great families and the middle and upper courtly ranks the most accomplished musicians and dancers were selected to go with him, and grandees and princes of the blood were busy at the practice that best suited their talents. Caught up in the excitement, Genji was somewhat remiss in inquiring after the nun.

When, finally, he sent off a messenger to the northern hills, a sad reply came from the bishop: "We lost her toward the end of last month. It is the way of the world, I know, and yet I am sad."

If the news shocked even him into a new awareness of evanescence, thought Genji, how must it be for the little girl who had so occupied the nun's thoughts? Young though she was, she must feel utterly lost. He remembered, though dimly, how it had been when his mother died, and he sent off an earnest letter of sympathy. Shōnagon's answer seemed rather warmer. He went calling on an evening when he had nothing else to occupy him, some days after he learned that the girl had come out of mourning and returned to the city. The house was badly kept and almost deserted. The poor child must be terrified, he thought. He was shown to the same room as before. Sobbing, Shōnagon told him of the old lady's last days. Genji too was in tears.

"My young lady's father would seem to have indicated a willingness to take her in, but she is at such an uncomfortable age, not quite a child and still without the discernment of an adult; and the thought of having her in the custody of the lady who was so cruel to her mother is too awful. Her sisters will persecute her dreadfully, I know. The fear of it never left my lady's mind, and we have had too much evidence that the fear was not groundless. We have been grateful for your expressions of interest, though we have hesitated to take them seriously. I must emphasize that my young lady is not at all what you must think her to be. I fear that we have done badly by her, and that our methods have left her childish even for her years."

"Must you continue to be so reticent and apologetic? I have made my own feelings clear, over and over again. It is precisely the childlike quality that delights me most and makes me think I must have her for my own. You may think me complacent and self-satisfied for saying so, but I feel sure that we were joined in a former life. Let me speak to her, please.

> "Rushes hide the sea grass at Wakanoura.
> Must the waves that seek it out turn back to sea?

That would be too much to ask of her."

> "The grass at Wakanoura were rash indeed
> To follow waves that go it knows not whither.

It would be far, far too much to ask."

---

2. *Murasaki,* a millet from the roots of which a lavender dye is extracted. Lavender, in general the color of affinity or intimacy, suggests more specifically the *fuji* of Fujitsubo, "Wisteria Court." It is because of this poem that the girl is presently to be called Murasaki. The name Murasaki Shikibu also derives from it.

The easy skill with which she turned her poem made it possible for him to forgive its less than encouraging significance. "After so many years," he whispered, "the gate still holds me back."[3]

The girl lay weeping for her grandmother. Her playmates came to tell her that a gentleman in court dress was with Shōnagon. Perhaps it would be her father?

She came running in. "Where is the gentleman, Shōnagon? Is Father here?"

What a sweet voice she had!

"I'm not your father, but I'm someone just as important. Come here."

She saw that it was the other gentleman, and child though she was, she flushed at having spoken out of turn. "Let's go." She tugged at Shōnagon's sleeve. "Let's go. I'm sleepy."

"Do you have to keep hiding yourself from me? Come here. You can sleep on my knee."

"She is really very young, sir." But Shōnagon urged the child forward, and she knelt obediently just inside the blinds.

He ran his hand over a soft, rumpled robe, and, a delight to the touch, hair full and rich to its farthest ends. He took her hand. She pulled away—for he was, after all, a stranger.

"I said I'm sleepy." She went back to Shōnagon.

He slipped in after her. "I am the one you must look to now. You must not be shy with me."

"Please, sir. You forget yourself. You forget yourself completely. She is simply not old enough to understand what you have in mind."

"It is you who do not understand. I see how young she is, and I have nothing of the sort in mind. I must again ask you to be witness to the depth and purity of my feelings."

It was a stormy night. Sleet was pounding against the roof.

"How can she bear to live in such a lonely place? It must be awful for her." Tears came to his eyes. He could not leave her. "I will be your watchman. You need one on a night like this. Come close to me, all of you."

Quite as if he belonged there, he slipped into the girl's bedroom. The women were astounded, Shōnagon more than the rest. He must be mad! But she was in no position to protest. Genji pulled a singlet over the girl, who was trembling like a leaf. Yes, he had to admit that his behavior must seem odd; but, trying very hard not to frighten her, he talked of things he thought would interest her.

"You must come to my house. I have all sorts of pictures, and there are dolls for you to play with."

She was less frightened than at first, but she still could not sleep. The storm blew all through the night, and Shōnagon quite refused to budge from their side. They would surely have perished of fright, whispered the women, if they had not had him with them. What a pity their lady was not a little older!

It was still dark when the wind began to subside and he made his departure, and all the appearances were as of an amorous expedition. "What I have seen makes me very sad and convinces me that she must not be out of my sight. She must come and live with me and share my lonely days. This place is quite impossible. You must be in constant terror."

3. Fujiwara Koretada, *Gosenshū* 732: "Alone, in secret, I hurry to Meeting Hill. / After so many years, the gate still holds me back."

"Her father has said that he will come for her. I believe it is to be after the memorial services."

"Yes, we must think of him. But they have lived apart, and he must be as much of a stranger as I am. I really do believe that in this very short time my feelings for her are stronger than his." He patted the girl on the head and looked back smiling as he left.

[Genji decides to retrieve the young Murasaki before her father, Prince Hyōbu, comes to pick her up.]

He went into her bedroom, where the women were too surprised to cry out. He took her in his arms and smoothed her hair. Her father had come for her, she thought, only half awake.

"Let's go. I have come from your father's." She was terrified when she saw that it was not after all her father. "You are not being nice. I have told you that you must think of me as your father." And he carried her out.

A chorus of protests now came from Shōnagon and the others.

"I have explained things quite well enough. I have told you how difficult it is for me to visit her and how I want to have her in a more comfortable and accessible spot; and your way of making things easier is to send her off to her father. One of you may come along, if you wish."

"Please, sir." Shōnagon was wringing her hands. "You could not have chosen a worse time. What are we to say when her father comes? If it is her fate to be your lady, then perhaps something can be done when the time comes. This is too sudden, and you put us in an extremely difficult position."

"You can come later if you wish."

His carriage had been brought up. The women were fluttering about helplessly and the child was sobbing. Seeing at last that there was nothing else to be done, Shōnagon took up several of the robes they had been at work on the night before, changed to presentable clothes of her own, and got into the carriage.

It was still dark when they reached Nijō, only a short distance away. Genji ordered the carriage brought up to the west wing and took the girl inside.

"It is like a nightmare," said Shōnagon. "What am I to do?"

"Whatever you like. I can have someone see you home if you wish."

Weeping helplessly, poor Shōnagon got out of the carriage. What would her lady's father think when he came for her? And what did they now have to look forward to? The saddest thing was to be left behind by one's protectors. But tears did not augur well for the new life. With an effort she pulled herself together.

Since no one was living in this west wing, there was no curtained bedchamber. Genji had Koremitsu put up screens and curtains, sent someone else to the east wing for bedding, and lay down. Though trembling violently, the girl managed to keep from sobbing aloud.

"I always sleep with Shōnagon," she said softly in childish accents.

"Imagine a big girl like you still sleeping with her nurse."

Weeping quietly, the girl lay down.

Shōnagon sat up beside them, looking out over the garden as dawn came on. The buildings and grounds were magnificent, and the sand in the garden was like jewels. Not used to such affluence, she was glad there were no other women in this west wing. It was here that Genji received occasional callers. A few guards beyond the blinds were the only attendants.

They were speculating on the identity of the lady he had brought with him. "Someone worth looking at, you can bet."

Water pitchers and breakfast were brought in. The sun was high when Genji arose. "You will need someone to take care of you. Suppose you send this evening for the ones you like best." He asked that children be sent from the east wing to play with her. "Pretty little girls, please." Four little girls came in, very pretty indeed.

The new girl, his Murasaki, still lay huddled under the singlet he had thrown over her.

"You are not to sulk, now, and make me unhappy. Would I have done all this for you if I were not a nice man? Young ladies should do as they are told." And so the lessons began.

She seemed even prettier here beside him than from afar. His manner warm and fatherly, he sought to amuse her with pictures and toys he had sent for from the east wing. Finally she came over to him. Her dark mourning robes were soft and unstarched, and when she smiled, innocently and unprotestingly, he had to smile back. She went out to look at the trees and pond after he had departed for the east wing. The flowers in the foreground, delicately touched by frost, were like a picture. Streams of courtiers, of the medium ranks and new to her experience, passed back and forth. Yes, it was an interesting place. She looked at the pictures on screens and elsewhere and (so it is with a child) soon forgot her troubles. ✳✳✳

Presently Murasaki had all her women with her. She was a bright, lively child, and the boys and girls who were to be her playmates felt quite at home with her. Sometimes on lonely nights when Genji was away she would weep for her grand-mother. She thought little of her father. They had lived apart and she scarcely knew him. She was by now extremely fond of her new father. She would be the first to run out and greet him when he came home, and she would climb on his lap, and they would talk happily together, without the least constraint or embarrassment. He was delighted with her. A clever and watchful woman can create all manner of difficulties. A man must be always on his guard, and jealousy can have the most unwelcome consequences. Murasaki was the perfect companion, a toy for him to play with. He could not have been so free and uninhibited with a daughter of his own. There are restraints upon paternal intimacy. Yes, he had come upon a remarkable little treasure.

from *Chapter 7. An Autumn Excursion*

Fujitsubo had gone home to her family. Looking restlessly, as always, for a chance to see her, Genji was much criticized by his father-in-law's people at Sanjō. And rumors of the young Murasaki were out. Certain of the women at Sanjō let it be known that a new lady had been taken in at Nijō. Genji's wife was intensely displeased. It was most natural that she should be, for she did not of course know that the "lady" was a mere child. If she had complained to him openly, as most women would have done, he might have told her everything, and no doubt eased her jealousy. It was her arbitrary judgments that sent him wandering. She had no specific faults, no vices or blemishes, which he could point to. She had been the first lady in his life, and in an abstract way he admired and treasured her. Her feelings would change, he felt sure, once she was more familiar with his own. She was a perceptive woman, and the change was certain to come. She still occupied first place among his ladies.

Murasaki was by now thoroughly comfortable with him. She was maturing in appearance and manner, and yet there was artlessness in her way of clinging to him.

Thinking it too early to let the people in the main hall know who she was, he kept her in one of the outer wings, which he had had fitted to perfection. He was constantly with her, tutoring her in the polite accomplishments and especially calligraphy. It was as if he had brought home a daughter who had spent her early years in another house. He had studied the qualifications of her stewards and assured himself that she would have everything she needed. Everyone in the house, save only Koremitsu, was consumed with curiosity. Her father still did not know of her whereabouts. Sometimes she would weep for her grandmother. Her mind was full of other things when Genji was with her, and often he stayed the night; but he had numerous other places to look in upon, and he was quite charmed by the wistfulness with which she would see him off in the evening. Sometimes he would spend two and three days at the palace and go from there to Sanjō. Finding a pensive Murasaki upon his return, he would feel as if he had taken in a little orphan. He no longer looked forward to his nocturnal wanderings with the same eagerness. Her granduncle the bishop kept himself informed of her affairs, and was pleased and puzzled. Genji sent most lavish offerings for memorial services.

Longing for news of Fujitsubo, still with her family, he paid a visit. Omyōbu, Chūnagon, Nakatsukasa, and others of her women received him, but the lady whom he really wanted to see kept him at a distance. He forced himself to make conversation. Prince Hyōbu, her brother and Murasaki's father, came in, having heard that Genji was on the premises. He was a man of great and gentle elegance, someone, thought Genji, who would interest him enormously were they of opposite sexes. Genji felt very near this prince so near the two ladies, and to the prince their conversation seemed friendly and somehow significant as earlier conversations had not. How very handsome Genji was! Not dreaming that it was a prospective son-in-law he was addressing, he too was thinking how susceptible (for he was a susceptible man) he would be to Genji's charms if they were not of the same sex.

When, at dusk, the prince withdrew behind the blinds, Genji felt pangs of jealousy. In the old years he had followed his father behind those same blinds, and there addressed the lady. Now she was far away—though of course no one had wronged him, and he had no right to complain.

"I have not been good about visiting you," he said stiffly as he got up to leave. "Having no business with you, I have not wished to seem forward. It would give me great pleasure if you would let me know of any services I might perform for you."

Omyōbu could do nothing for him. Fujitsubo seemed to find his presence even more of a trial than before, and showed no sign of relenting. Sadly and uselessly the days went by. What a frail, fleeting union theirs had been!

Shōnagon, Murasaki's nurse, continued to marvel at the strange course their lives had taken. Perhaps some benign power had arranged it, the old nun having mentioned Murasaki in all her prayers. Not that everything was perfect. Genji's wife at Sanjō was a lady of the highest station, and other affairs, indeed too many of them, occupied him as well. Might not the girl face difficult times as she grew into womanhood? Yet he did seem fond of her as of none of the others, and her future seemed secure. The period of mourning for a maternal grandmother being set at three months, it was on New Year's Eve that Murasaki took off her mourning weeds. The old lady had been for her both mother and grandmother, however, and so she chose to limit herself to pale, unfigured pinks and lavenders and yellows. Pale colors seemed to suit her even better than rich ones.

"And do you feel all grown up, now that a new year has come?" Smiling, radiating youthful charm, Genji looked in upon her. He was on his way to the morning festivities at court.

She had already taken out her dolls and was busy seeing to their needs. All manner of furnishings and accessories were laid out on a yard-high shelf. Dollhouses threatened to overflow the room.

"Inuki knocked everything over chasing out devils last night and broke this." It was a serious matter. "I'm gluing it."

"Yes, she really is very clumsy, that Inuki. We'll ask someone to repair it for you. But today you must not cry. Crying is the worst way to begin a new year."

And he went out, his retinue so grand that it overflowed the wide grounds. The women watched from the veranda, the girl with them. She set out a Genji among her dolls and saw him off to court.

"This year you must try to be just a little more grown up," said Shōnagon. "Ten years old, no, even more, and still you play with dolls. It will not do. You have a nice husband, and you must try to calm down and be a little more wifely. Why, you fly into a tantrum even when we try to brush your hair." A proper shaming was among Shōnagon's methods.

So she had herself a nice husband, thought Murasaki. The husbands of these women were none of them handsome men, and hers was so very young and handsome. The thought came to her now for the first time, evidence that, for all this play with dolls, she was growing up. It sometimes puzzled her women that she should still be such a child. It did not occur to them that she was in fact not yet a wife.

From the palace Genji went to Sanjō. His wife, as always, showed no suggestion of warmth or affection; and as always he was uncomfortable.

"How pleasant if this year you could manage to be a little friendlier."

But since she had heard of his new lady she had become more distant than ever. She was convinced that the other was now first among his ladies, and no doubt she was as uncomfortable as he. But when he jokingly sought to make it seem that nothing was amiss, she had to answer, if reluctantly. Everything she said was uniquely, indefinably elegant. She was four years his senior and made him feel like a stripling. Where, he asked, was he to find a flaw in this perfection? Yet he seemed determined to anger her with his other affairs. She was a proud lady, the single and treasured daughter, by a princess, of a minister who overshadowed the other grandees, and she was not prepared to tolerate the smallest discourtesy. And here he was behaving as if these proud ways were his to make over. They were completely at cross purposes, he and she.

* * *

Genji did not pay many New Year calls. He called upon his father, the crown prince, the old emperor,[1] and, finally, Fujitsubo, still with her family. Her women thought him handsomer than ever. Yes, each year, as he matured, his good looks produced a stronger shudder of delight and foreboding. Fujitsubo was assailed by innumerable conflicting thoughts.

The Twelfth Month, when she was to have been delivered of her child, had passed uneventfully. Surely it would be this month, said her women, and at court everything was in readiness; but the First Month too passed without event. She was greatly troubled by rumors that she had fallen under a malign influence. Her worries had made

---

1. Perhaps the father of the reigning emperor, he is mentioned nowhere else. The reign of the present emperor seems to have been preceded by that of Fujitsubo's father, now dead.

her physically ill and she began to wonder if the end was in sight. More and more certain as time passed that the child was his, Genji quietly commissioned services in various temples. More keenly aware than most of the evanescence of things, he now found added to his worries a fear that he would not see her again. Finally toward the end of the Second Month she bore a prince, and the jubilation was unbounded at court and at her family palace. She had not joined the emperor in praying that she be granted a long life, and yet she did not want to please Kokiden, an echo of whose curses had reached her. The will to live returned, and little by little she recovered.

The emperor wanted to see his little son the earliest day possible. Genji, filled with his own secret paternal solicitude, visited Fujitsubo at a time when he judged she would not have other visitors.

"Father is extremely anxious to see the child. Perhaps I might have a look at him first and present a report."

She refused his request, as of course she had every right to do. "He is still very shriveled and ugly."

There was no doubt that the child bore a marked, indeed a rather wonderful, resemblance to Genji. Fujitsubo was tormented by feelings of guilt and apprehension. Surely everyone who saw the child would guess the awful truth and damn her for it. People were always happy to seek out the smallest and most trivial of misdeeds. Hers had not been trivial, and dreadful rumors must surely be going the rounds. Had ever a woman been more sorely tried?

Genji occasionally saw Omyōbu and pleaded that she intercede for him; but there was nothing she could do.

"This insistence, my lord, is very trying," she said, at his constant and passionate pleas to see the child. "You will have chances enough later." Yet secretly she was as unhappy as he was.

"In what world, I wonder, will I again be allowed to see her?" The heart of the matter was too delicate to touch upon.

> "What legacy do we bring from former lives that
> Loneliness should be our lot in this one?"

"I do not understand. I do not understand at all."

His tears brought her to the point of tears herself. Knowing how unhappy her lady was, she could not bring herself to turn him brusquely away.

> "Sad at seeing the child, sad at not seeing.
> The heart of the father, the mother, lost in darkness."[2]

And she added softly: "There seems to be no lessening of the pain for either of you."

She saw him off, quite unable to help him. Her lady had said that because of the danger of gossip she could not receive him again, and she no longer behaved toward Omyōbu with the old affection. She behaved correctly, it was true, and did nothing that might attract attention, but Omyōbu had done things to displease her. Omyōbu was very sorry for them.

In the Fourth Month the little prince was brought to the palace. Advanced for his age both mentally and physically, he was already able to sit up and to right himself when he rolled over. He was strikingly like Genji. Unaware of the truth, the emperor

2. Fujiwara Kanesuke, *Gosenshū* 1103: "The heart of a parent is not darkness, / and yet he wanders lost in thoughts upon his child."

would say to himself that people of remarkable good looks did have a way of looking alike. He doted upon the child. He had similarly doted upon Genji, but, because of strong opposition—and how deeply he regretted the fact—had been unable to make him crown prince. The regret increased as Genji, now a commoner, improved in looks and in accomplishments. And now a lady of the highest birth had borne the emperor another radiant son. The infant was for him an unflawed jewel, for Fujitsubo a source of boundless guilt and foreboding.

One day, as he often did, Genji was enjoying music in Fujitsubo's apartments. The emperor came out with the little boy in his arms.

"I have had many sons, but you were the only one I paid a great deal of attention to when you were this small. Perhaps it is the memory of those days that makes me think he looks like you. Is it that all children look alike when they are very young?" He made no attempt to hide his pleasure in the child.

Genji felt himself flushing crimson. He was frightened and awed and pleased and touched, all at the same time, and there were tears in his eyes. Laughing and babbling, the child was so beautiful as to arouse fears that he would not be long in this world. If indeed he resembled the child, thought Genji, then he must be very handsome. He must take better care of himself. (He seemed a little self-satisfied at times.) Fujitsubo was in such acute discomfort that she felt herself breaking into a cold sweat. Eager though he had been to see the child, Genji left in great agitation.

[*In "The Festival of the Cherry Blossoms," the next chapter, Genji has his first encounter with Oborozukiyo, the daughter of the powerful Minister of the Right and sister of the Kokiden lady, who is slated to become the consort of the crown prince (the future Suzaku emperor). "Heartvine," the following chapter, opens with a change of guard: Genji's father, the Kiritsubo emperor, has abdicated, bringing to the throne the Suzaku emperor, son of the Kokiden lady and the Minister of the Right. Fujitsubo's son (and secretly that of Genji), the future Reizei emperor, is made the heir apparent.*]

from *Chapter 9. Heartvine*

With the new reign Genji's career languished, and since he must be the more discreet about his romantic adventures as he rose in rank, he had less to amuse him. Everywhere there were complaints about his aloofness.

As if to punish him, there was one lady who continued to cause him pain with her own aloofness. Fujitsubo saw more of the old emperor, now abdicated, than ever. She was always at his side, almost as if she were a common housewife. Annoyed at this state of affairs, Kokiden did not follow the old emperor when he left the main palace. Fujitsubo was happy and secure. The concerts in the old emperor's palace attracted the attention of the whole court, and altogether life was happier for the two of them than while he had reigned. Only one thing was lacking: he greatly missed the crown prince, Fujitsubo's son, and worried that he had no strong backers. Genji, he said, must be the boy's adviser and guardian. Genji was both pleased and embarrassed.

And there was the matter of the lady at Rokujō. With the change of reigns, her daughter, who was also the daughter of the late crown prince, had been appointed high priestess of the Ise Shrine. No longer trusting Genji's affections, the Rokujō lady had been thinking that, making the girl's youth her excuse, she too would go to Ise.

The old emperor heard of her plans. "The crown prince was so very fond of her," he said to Genji, in open displeasure. "It is sad that you should have made light of her, as if she were any ordinary woman. I think of the high priestess as one of my own children, and you should be good to her mother, for my sake and for the sake of the dead prince. It does you no good to abandon yourself to these affairs quite as the impulse takes you."

It was perfectly true, thought Genji. He waited in silence.

"You should treat any woman with tact and courtesy, and be sure that you cause her no embarrassment. You should never have a woman angry with you."

What would his father think if he were to learn of Genji's worst indiscretion? The thought made Genji shudder. He bowed and withdrew.

The matter his father had thus reproved him for did no good for either of them, the woman or Genji himself. It was a scandal, and very sad for her. She continued to be very much on his mind, and yet he had no thought of making her his wife. She had grown cool toward him, worried about the difference in their ages. He made it seem that it was because of her wishes that he stayed away. Now that the old emperor knew of the affair the whole court knew of it. In spite of everything, the lady went on grieving that he had not loved her better. ✳ ✳ ✳

At Sanjō, his wife and her family were even unhappier about his infidelities, but, perhaps because he did not lie to them, they for the most part kept their displeasure to themselves. His wife was with child and in considerable distress mentally and physically. For Genji it was a strange and moving time. Everyone was delighted and at the same time filled with apprehension, and all manner of retreats and abstinences were prescribed for the lady. Genji had little time to himself. While he had no particular wish to avoid the Rokujō lady and the others, he rarely visited them.

At about this time the high priestess of Kamo resigned. She was replaced by the old emperor's third daughter, whose mother was Kokiden. The new priestess was a favorite of both her brother, the new emperor, and her mother, and it seemed a great pity that she should be shut off from court life; but no other princess was qualified for the position. The installation ceremonies, in the austere Shinto tradition, were of great dignity and solemnity. Many novel details were added to the Kamo festival in the Fourth Month, so that it was certain to be the finest of the season. Though the number of high courtiers attending the princess at the lustration was limited by precedent, great care was taken to choose handsome men of good repute. Similar care was given to their uniforms and to the uniform trappings of their horses. Genji was among the attendants, by special command of the new emperor. Courtiers and ladies had readied their carriage far in advance, and Ichijō was a frightening crush, without space for another vehicle. The stands along the way had been appointed most elaborately. The sleeves that showed beneath the curtains fulfilled in their brightness and variety all the festive promise.

Genji's wife seldom went forth on sightseeing expeditions and her pregnancy was another reason for staying at home.

But her young women protested. "Really, my lady, it won't be much fun sneaking off by ourselves. Why, even complete strangers—why, all the country folk have come in to see our lord! They've brought their wives and families from the farthest provinces. It will be too much if you make us stay away."

Her mother, Princess Omiya, agreed. "You seem to be feeling well enough, my dear, and they will be very disappointed if you don't take them."

And so carriages were hastily and unostentatiously decked out, and the sun was already high when they set forth. The waysides were by now too crowded to admit the elegant Sanjō procession. Coming upon several fine carriages not attended by grooms and footmen, the Sanjō men commenced clearing a space. Two palm-frond carriages remained, not new ones, obviously belonging to someone who did not wish to attract attention. The curtains and the sleeves and aprons to be glimpsed beneath them, some in the gay colors little girls wear, were in very good taste.

The men in attendance sought to defend their places against the Sanjō invaders. "We aren't the sort of people you push around."

There had been too much drink in both parties, and the drunken ones were not responsive to the efforts of their more mature and collected seniors to restrain them.

The palm-frond carriages were from the Rokujō house of the high priestess of Ise. The Rokujō lady had come quietly to see the procession, hoping that it might make her briefly forget her unhappiness. The men from Sanjō had recognized her, but preferred to make it seem otherwise.

"They can't tell us who to push and not to push," said the more intemperate ones to their fellows. "They have General Genji to make them feel important."

Among the newcomers were some of Genji's men. They recognized and felt a little sorry for the Rokujō lady, but, not wishing to become involved, they looked the other way. Presently all the Sanjō carriages were in place. The Rokujō lady, behind the lesser ones, could see almost nothing. Quite aside from her natural distress at the insult, she was filled with the bitterest chagrin that, having refrained from display, she had been recognized. The stools for her carriage shafts had been broken and the shafts propped on the hubs of perfectly strange carriages, a most undignified sight. It was no good asking herself why she had come. She thought of going home without seeing the procession, but there was no room for her to pass; and then came word that the procession was approaching, and she must, after all, see the man who had caused her such unhappiness. How weak is the heart of a woman! Perhaps because this was not "the bamboo by the river Hinokuma,"[1] he passed without stopping his horse or looking her way; and the unhappiness was greater than if she had stayed at home.

Genji seemed indifferent to all the grandly decorated carriages and all the gay sleeves, such a flood of them that it was as if ladies were stacked in layers behind the carriage curtains. Now and again, however, he would have a smile and a glance for a carriage he recognized. His face was solemn and respectful as he passed his wife's carriage. His men bowed deeply, and the Rokujō lady was in misery. She had been utterly defeated.

She whispered to herself:

"A distant glimpse of the River of Lustration.
His coldness is the measure of my sorrow."

She was ashamed of her tears. Yet she thought how sorry she would have been if she had not seen that handsome figure set off to such advantage by the crowds.

The high courtiers were, after their several ranks, impeccably dressed and caparisoned and many of them were very handsome; but Genji's radiance dimmed the strongest lights. Among his special attendants was a guards officer of the Sixth Rank, though attendants of such standing were usually reserved for the most splendid royal processions. His retinue made such a fine procession itself that every tree and blade of grass along the way seemed to bend forward in admiration.

It is not on the whole considered good form for veiled ladies of no mean rank and even nuns who have withdrawn from the world to be jostling and shoving one

---

1. Anonymous, *Kokinshū* 1080: "In the bamboo by the river Hinokuma, / stop that your horse may drink, and I may see you."

another in the struggle to see, but today no one thought it out of place. Hollow-mouthed women of the lower classes, their hair tucked under their robes, their hands brought respectfully to their foreheads, were hopping about in hopes of catching a glimpse. Plebeian faces were wreathed in smiles which their owners might not have enjoyed seeing in mirrors, and daughters of petty provincial officers of whose existence Genji would scarcely have been aware had set forth in carriages decked out with the most exhaustive care and taken up posts which seemed to offer a chance of seeing him. There were almost as many things by the wayside as in the procession to attract one's attention.

And there were many ladies whom he had seen in secret and who now sighed more than ever that their station was so out of keeping with his. Prince Shikibu viewed the procession from a stand. Genji had matured and did indeed quite dazzle the eye, and the prince thought with foreboding that some god might have noticed, and was making plans to spirit the young man away. His daughter, Princess Asagao, having over the years found Genji a faithful correspondent, knew how remarkably steady his feelings were. She was aware that attentions moved ladies even when the donor was a most ordinary man; yet she had no wish for further intimacy. As for her women, their sighs of admiration were almost deafening.

No carriages set out from the Sanjō mansion on the day of the festival proper.

Genji presently heard the story of the competing carriages. He was sorry for the Rokujō lady and angry at his wife. It was a sad fact that, so deliberate and fastidious, she lacked ordinary compassion. There was indeed a tart, forbidding quality about her. She refused to see, though it was probably an unconscious refusal, that ladies who were to each other as she was to the Rokujō lady should behave with charity and forbearance. It was under her influence that the men in her service flung themselves so violently about. Genji sometimes felt uncomfortable before the proud dignity of the Rokujō lady, and he could imagine her rage and humiliation now.

He called upon her. The high priestess, her daughter, was still with her, however, and, making reverence for the sacred sakaki tree[2] her excuse, she declined to receive him.

She was right, of course. Yet he muttered to himself: "Why must it be so? Why cannot the two of them be a little less prickly?" * * *

For the Rokujō lady the pain was unrelieved. She knew that she could expect no lessening of his coldness, and yet to steel herself and go off to Ise with her daughter—she would be lonely, she knew, and people would laugh at her. They would laugh just as heartily if she stayed in the city. Her thoughts were as the fisherman's bob at Ise.[3] Her very soul seemed to jump wildly about, and at last she fell physically ill.

Genji discounted the possibility of her going to Ise. "It is natural that you should have little use for a reprobate like myself and think of discarding me. But to stay with me would be to show admirable depths of feeling."

These remarks did not seem very helpful. Her anger and sorrow increased. A hope of relief from this agony of indecision had sent her to the river of lustration, and there she had been subjected to violence.

At Sanjō, Genji's wife seemed to be in the grip of a malign spirit. It was no time for nocturnal wanderings. Genji paid only an occasional visit to his own Nijō mansion.

---

2. A glossy-leafed tree related to the camellia. Its branches are used in Shinto ritual.

3. Anonymous, *Kokinshū* 509: "Has my heart become the fisherman's bob at Ise? / It jumps and bobs and knows not calm or resolve."

His marriage had not been happy, but his wife was important to him and now she was carrying his child. He had prayers read in his Sanjō rooms. Several malign spirits were transferred to the medium and identified themselves, but there was one which quite refused to move. Though it did not cause great pain, it refused to leave her for so much as an instant. There was something very sinister about a spirit that eluded the powers of the most skilled exorcists. The Sanjō people went over the list of Genji's ladies one by one. Among them all, it came to be whispered, only the Rokujō lady and the lady at Nijō seemed to have been singled out for special attentions, and no doubt they were jealous. The exorcists were asked about the possibility, but they gave no very informative answers. Of the spirits that did announce themselves, none seemed to feel any deep enmity toward the lady. Their behavior seemed random and purposeless. There was the spirit of her dead nurse, for instance, and there were spirits that had been with the family for generations and had taken advantage of her weakness.

The confusion and worry continued. The lady would sometimes weep in loud wailing sobs, and sometimes be tormented by nausea and shortness of breath.

The old emperor sent repeated inquiries and ordered religious services. That the lady should be worthy of these august attentions made the possibility of her death seem even more lamentable. Reports that they quite monopolized the attention of court reached the Rokujō mansion, to further embitter its lady. No one can have guessed that the trivial incident of the carriages had so angered a lady whose sense of rivalry had not until then been strong.

Not at all herself, she left her house to her daughter and moved to one where Buddhist rites would not be out of place.[4] Sorry to hear of the move, Genji bestirred himself to call on her. The neighborhood was a strange one and he was in careful disguise. He explained his negligence in terms likely to make it seem involuntary and to bring her forgiveness, and he told her of Aoi's illness and the worry it was causing him.

"I have not been so very worried myself, but her parents are beside themselves. It has seemed best to stay with her. It would relieve me enormously if I thought you might take a generous view of it all." He knew why she was unwell, and pitied her.

They passed a tense night. As she saw him off in the dawn she found that her plans for quitting the city were not as firm as on the day before. Her rival was of the highest rank and there was this important new consideration; no doubt his affections would finally settle on her. She herself would be left in solitude, wondering when he might call. The visit had only made her unhappier. In upon her gloom, in the evening, came a letter.

"Though she had seemed to be improving, she has taken a sudden and drastic turn for the worse. I cannot leave her."

The usual excuses, she thought. Yet she answered:

> "I go down the way of love and dampen my sleeves,
>   and go yet further, into the muddy fields.

A pity the well is so shallow."[5]

The hand was the very best he knew. It was a difficult world, which refused to give satisfaction. Among his ladies there was none who could be dismissed as completely beneath consideration and none to whom he could give his whole love.

---

4. They were out of place in the house of a Shinto priestess.
5. Anonymous, *Kokin Rokujō, Zoku Kokka Taikan* 31863: "A pity the mountain well should be so shallow. / I seek to take water and only wet my sleeves."

Despite the lateness of the hour, he got off an answer: "You only wet your sleeves—what can this mean? That your feelings are not of the deepest, I should think.

> You only dip into the shallow waters,
> And I quite disappear into the slough?

"Do you think I would answer by letter and not in person if she were merely indisposed?"

The malign spirit was more insistent, and Aoi was in great distress. Unpleasant rumors reached the Rokujō lady, to the effect that it might be her spirit or that of her father, the late minister. Though she had felt sorry enough for herself, she had not wished ill to anyone; and might it be that the soul of one so lost in sad thoughts went wandering off by itself? She had, over the years, known the full range of sorrows, but never before had she felt so utterly miserable. There had been no release from the anger since the other lady had so insulted her, indeed behaved as if she did not exist. More than once she had the same dream: in the beautifully appointed apartments of a lady who seemed to be a rival she would push and shake the lady, and flail at her blindly and savagely. It was too terrible. Sometimes in a daze she would ask herself if her soul had indeed gone wandering off. The world was not given to speaking well of people whose transgressions had been far slighter. She would be notorious. It was common enough for the spirits of the angry dead to linger on in this world. She had thought them hateful, and it was her own lot to set a hateful example while she still lived. She must think no more about the man who had been so cruel to her. But so to think was, after all, to think.

The high priestess, her daughter, was to have been presented at court the year before, but complications had required postponement. It was finally decided that in the Ninth Month she would go from court to her temporary shrine. The Rokujō house was thus busy preparing for two lustrations, but its lady, lost in thought, seemed strangely indifferent. A most serious state of affairs—the priestess's attendants ordered prayers. There were no really alarming symptoms. She was vaguely unwell, no more. The days passed. Genji sent repeated inquiries, but there was no relief from his worries about another invalid, a more important one.

It was still too early for Aoi to be delivered of her child. Her women were less than fully alert; and then, suddenly, she was seized with labor pains. More priests were put to more strenuous prayers. The malign spirit refused to move. The most eminent of exorcists found this stubbornness extraordinary, and could not think what to do. Then, after renewed efforts at exorcism, more intense than before, it commenced sobbing as if in pain.

"Stop for a moment, please. I want to speak to General Genji."

It was as they had thought. The women showed Genji to a place at Aoi's curtains. Thinking—for she did seem on the point of death—that Aoi had last words for Genji, her parents withdrew. The effect was grandly solemn as priests read from the Lotus Sutra in hushed voices. Genji drew the curtains back and looked down at his wife. She was heavy with child, and very beautiful. Even a man who was nothing to her would have been saddened to look at her. Long, heavy hair, bound at one side, was set off by white robes, and he thought her lovelier than when she was most carefully dressed and groomed.

He took her hand. "How awful. How awful for you." He could say no more.

Usually so haughty and forbidding, she now gazed up at him with languid eyes that were presently filled with tears. How could he fail to be moved? This violent weeping, he thought, would be for her parents, soon to be left behind, and perhaps, at this last leave-taking, for him too.

"You mustn't fret so. It can't be as bad as you think. And even if the worst comes, we will meet again. And your good mother and father: the bond between parents and children lasts through many lives. You must tell yourself that you will see them again."

"No, no. I was hurting so, I asked them to stop for a while. I had not dreamed that I would come to you like this. It is true: a troubled soul will sometimes go wandering off." The voice was gentle and affectionate.

> "Bind the hem of my robe, to keep it within,
> the grieving soul that has wandered through the skies."[6]

It was not Aoi's voice, nor was the manner hers. Extraordinary—and then he knew that it was the voice of the Rokujō lady. He was aghast. He had dismissed the talk as vulgar and ignorant fabrication, and here before his eyes he had proof that such things did actually happen, he was horrified and repelled.

"You may say so. But I don't know who you are. Identify yourself."

It was indeed she. "Aghast"—is there no stronger word? He waved the women back.

Thinking that these calmer tones meant a respite from pain, her mother came with medicine; and even as she drank it down she gave birth to a baby boy. Everyone was delighted, save the spirits that had been transferred to mediums. Chagrined at their failure, they were raising a great stir, and all in all it was a noisy and untidy scene. There was still the afterbirth to worry about. Then, perhaps because of all the prayers, it too was delivered. The grand abbot of Hiei and all the other eminent clerics departed, looking rather pleased with themselves as they mopped their foreheads. Sure that the worst was past after all the anxious days, the women allowed themselves a rest.

The prayers went on as noisily as ever, but the house was now caught up in the happy business of ministering to a pretty baby. It hummed with excitement on each of the festive nights.[7] Fine and unusual gifts came from the old emperor and from all the princes and high courtiers. Ceremonies honoring a boy baby are always interesting.

The Rokujō lady received the news with mixed feelings. She had heard that her rival was critically ill, and now the crisis had passed. She was not herself. The strangest thing was that her robes were permeated with the scent of the poppy seeds burned at exorcisms. She changed clothes repeatedly and even washed her hair, but the odor persisted. She was overcome with self-loathing. And what would others be thinking? It was a matter she could discuss with no one. She could only suffer in distraught silence.

Somewhat calmer, Genji was still horrified at the unsolicited remarks he had had from the possessive spirit. He really must get off a note to the Rokujō lady. Or should he have a talk with her? He would find it hard to be civil, and he did not wish to hurt her. In the end he made do with a note.

Aoi's illness had been critical, and the strictest vigil must be continued. Genji had been persuaded to stop his nocturnal wanderings. He still had not really talked to his wife, for she was still far from normal. The child was so beautiful as to arouse forebodings, and preparations were already under way for a most careful and elaborate education. The minister was pleased with everything save the fact that his daughter had still not recovered. But he told himself that he need not worry. A slow convalescence was to be expected after so serious an illness.

---

6. Tying the skirt of a robe was a device for keeping an errant spirit at home.
7. There were celebrations on the third, fifth, seventh, and ninth nights.

Especially around the eyes, the baby bore a strong resemblance to the crown prince, whom Genji suddenly felt an intense longing to see. He could not sit still. He had to be off to court.

"I have been neglecting my duties," he said to the women, "and am feeling rather guilty. I think today I will venture out. It would be good if I might see her before I go. I am not a stranger, you know."

"Quite true, sir. You of all people should be allowed near. She is badly emaciated, I fear, but that is scarcely a reason for her to hide herself from you."

And so a place was set out for him at her bedside. She answered from time to time, but in a very weak voice. Even so little, from a lady who had been given up for dead, was like a dream. He told her of those terrible days. Then he remembered how, as if pulling back from a brink, she had begun talking to him so volubly and so eagerly. A shudder of revulsion passed over him.

"There are many things I would like to say to you, but you still seem very tired."

He even prepared medicine for her. The women were filled with admiration. When had he learned to be so useful?

She was sadly worn and lay as if on the border of death, pathetic and still lovely. There was not a tangle in her lustrous hair. The thick tresses that poured over her pillows seemed to him quite beyond compare. He gazed down at her, thinking it odd that he should have felt so dissatisfied with her over the years.

"I must see my father, but I am sure I will not be needed long. How nice if we could always be like this. But your mother is with you so much, I have not wanted to seem insistent. You must get back your strength and move back to your own rooms. Your mother pampers you too much. That may be one reason why you are so slow getting well."

As he withdrew in grand court dress she lay looking after him as she had not been in the habit of doing.

There was to be a conference on promotions and appointments. The minister too set off for court, in procession with all his sons, each of them with a case to plead and determined not to leave his side.

The Sanjō mansion was almost deserted. Aoi was again seized with a strangling shortness of breath; and very soon after a messenger had been sent to court she was dead. Genji and the others left court, scarcely aware of where their feet were taking them. Appointments and promotions no longer concerned them. Since the crisis had come at about midnight there was no possibility of summoning the grand abbot and his suffragans. Everyone had thought that the worst was over, and now of course everyone was stunned, dazed, wandering aimlessly from room to room, hardly knowing a door from a wall. Messengers crowded in with condolences, but the house was in such confusion that there was no one to receive them. The intensity of the grief was almost frightening. Since malign spirits had more than once attacked the lady, her father ordered the body left as it was for two or three days in hopes that she might revive. The signs of death were more and more pronounced, however, and, in great anguish, the family at length accepted the truth. Genji, who had private distress to add to the general grief, thought he knew as well as anyone ever would what unhappiness love can bring. Condolences even from the people most important to him brought no comfort. The old emperor, himself much grieved, sent a personal message; and so for the minister there was new honor, happiness to temper the sorrow. Yet there was no relief from tears.

Every reasonable suggestion was accepted toward reviving the lady, but, the ravages of death being ever more apparent, there was finally no recourse but to see her to Toribe Moor. There were many heartrending scenes along the way. The crowds of mourners and priests invoking the holy name quite overflowed the wide moor. Messages continued to pour in, from the old emperor, of course, and from the empress and crown prince and all the great houses as well.

The minister was desolate. "Now in my last years to be left behind by a daughter who should have had so many years before her." No one could see him without sharing his sorrow.

Grandly the services went on through the night, and as dawn came over the sky the mourners turned back to the city, taking with them only a handful of ashes. Funerals are common enough, but Genji, who had not been present at many, was shaken as never before. Since it was late in the Eighth Month a quarter moon still hung in a sky that would have brought melancholy thoughts in any case; and the figure of his father-in-law, as if groping in pitch darkness, seemed proper to the occasion and at the same time indescribably sad.

A poem came to his lips as he gazed up into the morning sky:

> "Might these clouds be the smoke that mounts from her pyre?
> They fill my heart with feelings too deep for words."

[*Genji remains in seclusion at Sanjō for seven weeks, grieving for Aoi. At last he takes leave of his in-laws, leaving his newborn son Yūgiri in their care, and returns to his own Nijō mansion.*]

The Nijō mansion had been cleaned and polished for his return. The whole household assembled to receive him. The higher-ranking ladies had sought to outdo one another in dress and grooming. The sight of them made him think of the sadly dejected ladies at Sanjō. Changing to less doleful clothes, he went to the west wing. The fittings, changed to welcome the autumn, were fresh and bright, and the young women and little girls were all very pretty in autumn dress. Shōnagon had taken care of everything.

Murasaki too was dressed to perfection. "You have grown," he said, lifting a low curtain back over its frame.

She looked shyly aside. Her hair and profile seemed in the lamplight even more like those of the lady he so longed for.

He had worried about her, he said, coming nearer. "I would like to tell you everything, but it is not a very lucky sort of story. Maybe I should rest awhile in the other wing. I won't be long. From now on you will never be rid of me. I am sure you will get very bored with me."

Shōnagon was pleased but not confident. He had so many wellborn ladies, another demanding one was certain to take the place of the one who was gone. She was a dry, unsentimental sort.

Genji returned to his room. Asking Chūjō to massage his legs, he lay down to rest. The next morning he sent off a note for his baby son. He gazed on and on at the answer, from one of the women, and all the old sadness came back.

It was a tedious time. He no longer had any enthusiasm for the careless night wanderings that had once kept him busy. Murasaki was much on his mind. She seemed peerless, the nearest he could imagine to his ideal. Thinking that she was no longer too young for marriage, he had occasionally made amorous overtures; but she had not seemed to understand. They had passed their time in games of Go and *hentsugi.*[8] She was clever and she had many delicate ways of pleasing him in the most trivial diversions. He had not seriously thought of her as a wife. Now he could not restrain himself. It would be a shock, of course.

What had happened? Her women had no way of knowing when the line had been crossed. One morning Genji was up early and Murasaki stayed on and on in bed. It was not at all like her to sleep so late. Might she be unwell? As he left for his own rooms, Genji pushed an inkstone inside her bed curtains.

At length, when no one else was near, she raised herself from her pillow and saw beside it a tightly folded bit of paper. Listlessly she opened it. There was only this verse, in a casual hand:

> Many have been the nights we have spent together
> Purposelessly, these coverlets between us.

She had not dreamed he had anything of the sort on his mind. What a fool she had been, to repose her whole confidence in so gross and unscrupulous a man.

It was almost noon when Genji returned. "They say you're not feeling well. What can be the trouble? I was hoping for a game of Go."

She pulled the covers over her head. Her women discreetly withdrew. He came up beside her.

"What a way to behave, what a very unpleasant way to behave. Try to imagine, please, what these women are thinking."

He drew back the covers. She was bathed in perspiration and the hair at her forehead was matted from weeping.

"Dear me. This does not augur well at all." He tried in every way he could think of to comfort her, but she seemed genuinely upset and did not offer so much as a word in reply.

"Very well. You will see no more of me. I do have my pride."

He opened her writing box but found no note inside. Very childish of her—and he had to smile at the childishness. He stayed with her the whole day, and he thought the stubbornness with which she refused to be comforted most charming.

Boar-day sweets[9] were served in the evening. Since he was still in mourning, no great ceremony attended upon the observance. Glancing over the varied and tastefully arranged foods that had been brought in cypress boxes to Murasaki's rooms only, Genji went out to the south veranda and called Koremitsu.

"We will have more of the same tomorrow night," he said, smiling, "though not in quite such mountains. This is not the most propitious day."

Koremitsu had a quick mind. "Yes, we must be careful to choose lucky days for our beginnings." And, solemnly and deliberately: "How many rat-day sweets am I asked to provide?"[1]

"Oh, I should think one for every three that we have here."

Koremitsu went off with an air of having informed himself adequately. A clever and practical young fellow, thought Genji.

Koremitsu had the nuptial sweets prepared at his own house. He told no one what they signified.

8. Guessing concealed parts of Chinese characters.

9. Eaten on the first Day of the Boar in the Tenth Month, to ensure good health, and perhaps too by way of prayer for a fruitful marriage, the wild boar being a symbol of fertility.

1. There were no "rat-day sweets." The words for "rat" and "sleep" sound the same, and the Day of the Rat follows the Day of the Boar; Koremitsu is referring obliquely to the nuptial bed.

Genji felt like a child thief. The role amused him and the affection he now felt for the girl seemed to reduce his earlier affection to the tiniest mote. A man's heart is a very strange amalgam indeed! He now thought that he could not bear to be away from her for a single night.

The sweets he had ordered were delivered stealthily, very late in the night. A man of tact, Koremitsu saw that Shōnagon, an older woman, might make Murasaki uncomfortable, and so he called her daughter.

"Slip this inside her curtains, if you will," he said, handing her an incense box. "You must see that it gets to her and to no one else. A solemn celebration. No carelessness permitted."

She thought it odd. "Carelessness? Of that quality I have had no experience."

"The very word demands care. Use it sparingly."

Young and somewhat puzzled, she did as she was told. It would seem that Genji had explained the significance of the incense box to Murasaki.

The women had no warning. When the box emerged from the curtains the next morning, the pieces of the puzzle began to fall into place. Such numbers of dishes—when might they have been assembled?—and stands with festooned legs, bearing sweets of a most especial sort. All in all, a splendid array. How very nice that he had gone to such pains, thought Shōnagon. He had overlooked nothing. She wept tears of pleasure and gratitude.

"But he really could have let us in on the secret," the women whispered to one another. "What can the gentleman who brought them have thought?"

When he paid the most fleeting call on his father or put in a brief appearance at court, he would be impossibly restless, overcome with longing for the girl. Even to Genji himself it seemed excessive. He had resentful letters from women with whom he had been friendly. He was sorry, but he did not wish to be separated from his bride for even a night. He had no wish to be with these others and let it seem that he was indisposed.

from *Chapter 10. The Sacred Tree*

The Rokujō lady was more and more despondent as the time neared for her daughter's departure. Since the death of Aoi, who had caused her such pain, Genji's visits, never frequent, had stopped altogether. They had aroused great excitement among her women and now the change seemed too sudden. Genji must have very specific reasons for having turned against her—there was no explaining his extreme coldness otherwise. She would think no more about him. She would go with her daughter. There were no precedents for a mother's accompanying a high priestess to Ise, but she had as her excuse that her daughter would be helpless without her. The real reason, of course, was that she wanted to flee these painful associations.

In spite of everything, Genji was sorry when he heard of her decision. He now wrote often and almost pleadingly, but she thought a meeting out of the question at this late date. She would risk disappointing him rather than have it all begin again.

She occasionally went from the priestess's temporary shrine[1] to her Rokujō house, but so briefly and in such secrecy that Genji did not hear of the visits. The temporary shrine did not, he thought, invite casual visits. Although she was much on his mind, he let the days and months go by. His father, the old emperor, had begun to

---

1. In the western part of the city.

suffer from recurrent aches and cramps, and Genji had little time for himself. Yet he did not want the lady to go off to Ise thinking him completely heartless, nor did he wish to have a name at court for insensitivity. He gathered his resolve and set off for the shrine.

It was on about the seventh of the Ninth Month. The lady was under great tension, for their departure was imminent, possibly only a day or two away. He had several times asked for a word with her. He need not go inside, he said, but could wait on the veranda. She was in a torment of uncertainty but at length reached a secret decision: she did not want to seem like a complete recluse and so she would receive him through curtains.

It was over a reed plain of melancholy beauty that he made his way to the shrine. The autumn flowers were gone and insects hummed in the wintry tangles. A wind whistling through the pines brought snatches of music to most wonderful effect, though so distant that he could not tell what was being played. Not wishing to attract attention, he had only ten outrunners, men who had long been in his service, and his guards were in subdued livery. He had dressed with great care. His more perceptive men saw how beautifully the melancholy scene set him off, and he was having regrets that he had not made the journey often. A low wattle fence, scarcely more than a suggestion of an enclosure, surrounded a complex of board-roofed buildings, as rough and insubstantial as temporary shelters.

The shrine gates, of unfinished logs, had a grand and awesome dignity for all their simplicity, and the somewhat forbidding austerity of the place was accentuated by clusters of priests talking among themselves and coughing and clearing their throats as if in warning. It was a scene quite unlike any Genji had seen before. The fire lodge[2] glowed faintly. It was all in all a lonely, quiet place, and here away from the world a lady already deep in sorrow had passed these weeks and months. Concealing himself outside the north wing, he sent in word of his arrival. The music abruptly stopped and the silence was broken only by a rustling of silken robes.

Though several messages were passed back and forth, the lady herself did not come out.

"You surely know that these expeditions are frowned upon. I find it very curious that I should be required to wait outside the sacred paling. I want to tell you everything, all my sorrows and worries."

He was right, said the women. It was more than a person could bear, seeing him out there without even a place to sit down. What was she to do? thought the lady. There were all these people about, and her daughter would expect more mature and sober conduct. No, to receive him at this late date would be altogether too undignified. Yet she could not bring herself to send him briskly on his way. She sighed and hesitated and hesitated again, and it was with great excitement that he finally heard her come forward.

"May I at least come up to the veranda?" he asked, starting up the stairs.

The evening moon burst forth and the figure she saw in its light was handsome beyond describing.

Not wishing to apologize for all the weeks of neglect, he pushed a branch of the sacred tree[3] in under the blinds.

---

2. There are several theories about the use of this building. The most likely are that it was for preparing offerings and that it was for lighting torches and flares.

3. *Sakaki,* related to the camellia.

> "With heart unchanging as this evergreen,
> this sacred tree, I enter the sacred gate."

She replied:

> "You err with your sacred tree and sacred gate.
> No beckoning cedars stand before my house."[4]

And he:

> "Thinking to find you here with the holy maidens,
> I followed the scent of the leaf of the sacred tree."

Though the scene did not encourage familiarity, he made bold to lean inside the blinds.

He had complacently wasted the days when he could have visited her and perhaps made her happy. He had begun to have misgivings about her, his ardor had cooled, and they had become the near strangers they were now. But she was here before him, and memories flooded back. He thought of what had been and what was to be, and he was weeping like a child.

She did not wish him to see her following his example. He felt even sadder for her as she fought to control herself, and it would seem that even now he urged her to change her plans. Gazing up into a sky even more beautiful now that the moon was setting, he poured forth all his pleas and complaints, and no doubt they were enough to erase the accumulated bitterness. She had resigned herself to what must be, and it was as she had feared. Now that she was with him again she found her resolve wavering.

Groups of young courtiers came up. It was a garden which aroused romantic urges and which a young man was reluctant to leave.

Their feelings for each other, Genji's and the lady's, had run the whole range of sorrows and irritations, and no words could suffice for all they wanted to say to each other. The dawn sky was as if made for the occasion. Not wanting to go quite yet, Genji took her hand, very gently.

> "A dawn farewell is always drenched in dew,
> But sad is the autumn sky as never before."

A cold wind was blowing, and a pine cricket seemed to recognize the occasion. It was a serenade to which a happy lover would not have been deaf. Perhaps because their feelings were in such tumult, they found that the poems they might have exchanged were eluding them.

At length the lady replied:

> "An autumn farewell needs nothing to make it sadder.
> Enough of your songs, O crickets on the moors!"

It would do no good to pour forth all the regrets again. He made his departure, not wanting to be seen in the broadening daylight. His sleeves were made wet along the way with dew and with tears.

The lady, not as strong as she would have wished, was sunk in a sad reverie. The shadowy figure in the moonlight and the perfume he left behind had the younger women in a state only just short of swooning.

---

4. Anonymous, *Kokinshū 982:* "Should you seek my house at the foot of Mount Miwa, / you need only look for the cedars by the gate."

"What kind of journey could be important enough, I ask you," said one of them, choking with tears, "to make her leave such a man?"

His letter the next day was so warm and tender that again she was tempted to reconsider. But it was too late: a return to the old indecision would accomplish nothing. Genji could be very persuasive even when he did not care a great deal for a woman, and this was no ordinary parting. He sent the finest travel robes and supplies, for the lady and for her women as well. They were no longer enough to move her. It was as if the thought had only now come to her of the ugly name she seemed fated to leave behind.

[*In the Tenth Month of the same year, Genji's father the old emperor dies. On his deathbed, he instructs his son, the Suzaku emperor, to look to Genji for advice in public affairs, and to be good to the crown prince (the future Reizei emperor). The following year Genji makes further overtures to Fujitsubo, driving her to become a nun after the anniversary of the old emperor's death. In the summer of the next year the Minister of the Right discovers Genji with Oborozukiyo, now a favored concubine of the Suzaku emperor. The Kokiden faction uses this episode as a pretext to destroy Genji politically.*]

from *Chapter 12. Suma*

[*In the Third Month of the year following his scandal with Oborozukiyo, Genji, now twenty-five, opts to go into voluntary exile in Suma, an isolated area to the southwest of the capital, near the sea, rather than face further adversity in the capital. He is accompanied by only a few close associates.*]

At Suma, melancholy autumn winds were blowing. Genji's house was some distance from the sea, but at night the wind that blew over the barriers, now as in Yukihira's day, seemed to bring the surf to his bedside. Autumn was hushed and lonely at a place of exile. He had few companions. One night when they were all asleep he raised his head from his pillow and listened to the roar of the wind and of the waves, as if at his ear. Though he was unaware that he wept, his tears were enough to set his pillow afloat.[1] He plucked a few notes on his koto, but the sound only made him sadder.

> The waves on the strand, like moans of helpless longing.
> The winds—like messengers from those who grieve?

He had awakened the others. They sat up, and one by one they were in tears.

This would not do. Because of him they had been swept into exile, leaving families from whom they had never before been parted. It must be very difficult for them, and his own gloom could scarcely be making things easier. So he set about cheering them. During the day he would invent games and make jokes, and set down this and that poem on multicolored patchwork, and paint pictures on fine specimens of figured Chinese silk. Some of his larger paintings were masterpieces. He had long ago been told of this Suma coast and these hills and had formed a picture of them in his mind, and he found now that his imagination had fallen short of the actuality. What a pity, said his men, that they could not summon Tsunenori and Chieda[2] and other famous painters of the day to add colors to Genji's monochromes. This resolute cheerfulness

---

1. This extravagant figure of speech is to be found in *Kokin Rokujō, Zoku Kokka Taikan* 34087.
2. Tsunenori seems to have been active some three quarters of a century before; so too, presumably, was Chieda.

had the proper effect. His men, four or five of whom were always with him, would not have dreamed of leaving him.

There was a profusion of flowers in the garden. Genji came out, when the evening colors were at their best, to a gallery from which he had a good view of the coast. His men felt chills of apprehension as they watched him, for the loneliness of the setting made him seem like a visitor from another world. In a dark robe tied loosely over singlets of figured white and aster-colored trousers, he announced himself as "a disciple of the Buddha" and slowly intoned a sutra, and his men thought that they had never heard a finer voice. From offshore came the voices of fishermen raised in song. The barely visible boats were like little seafowl on an utterly lonely sea, and as he brushed away a tear induced by the splashing of oars and the calls of wild geese overhead, the white of his hand against the jet black of his rosary was enough to bring comfort to men who had left their families behind.

* * *

It was the day of the serpent, the first such day in the Third Month.

"The day when a man who has worries goes down and washes them away," said one of his men, admirably informed, it would seem, in all of the annual observances.

Wishing to have a look at the seashore, Genji set forth. Plain, rough curtains were strung up among the trees, and a soothsayer who was doing the circuit of the province was summoned to perform the lustration.

Genji thought he could see something of himself in the rather large doll being cast off to sea, bearing away sins and tribulations.

> "Cast away to drift on an alien vastness,
> I grieve for more than a doll cast out to sea."

The bright, open seashore showed him to wonderful advantage. The sea stretched placid into measureless distances. He thought of all that had happened to him, and all that was still to come.

> "You eight hundred myriad gods must surely help me,
> For well you know that blameless I stand before you."

Suddenly a wind came up and even before the services were finished the sky was black. Genji's men rushed about in confusion. Rain came pouring down, completely without warning. Though the obvious course would have been to return straightway to the house, there had been no time to send for umbrellas. The wind was now a howling tempest, everything that had not been tied down was scuttling off across the beach. The surf was biting at their feet. The sea was white, as if spread over with white linen. Fearful every moment of being struck down, they finally made their way back to the house.

"I've never seen anything like it," said one of the men. "Winds do come up from time to time, but not without warning. It is all very strange and very terrible."

The lightning and thunder seemed to announce the end of the world, and the rain to beat its way into the ground; and Genji sat calmly reading a sutra. The thunder subsided in the evening, but the wind went on through the night.

"Our prayers seem to have been answered. A little more and we would have been carried off. I've heard that tidal waves do carry people off before they know what is happening to them, but I've not seen anything like this."

Towards dawn sleep was at length possible. A man whom he did not recognize came to Genji in a dream.

"The court summons you." He seemed to be reaching for Genji. "Why do you not go?"

It would be the king of the sea, who was known to have a partiality for handsome men. Genji decided that he could stay no longer at Suma.

from *Chapter 13. Akashi*

The days went by and the thunder and rain continued. What was Genji to do? People would laugh if, in this extremity, out of favor at court, he were to return to the city. Should he then seek a mountain retreat? But if it were to be noised about that a storm had driven him away, then he would cut a ridiculous figure in history.

His dreams were haunted by that same apparition. Messages from the city almost entirely ceased coming as the days went by without a break in the storms. Might he end his days at Suma? No one was likely to come calling in these tempests.

A messenger did come from Murasaki, a sad, sodden creature. Had they passed in the street, Genji would scarcely have known whether he was man or beast, and of course would not have thought of inviting him to come near. Now the man brought a surge of pleasure and affection—though Genji could not help asking himself whether the storm had weakened his moorings.

Murasaki's letter, long and melancholy, said in part: "The terrifying deluge goes on without a break, day after day. Even the skies are closed off, and I am denied the comfort of gazing in your direction.

> What do they work, the sea winds down at Suma?
> At home, my sleeves are assaulted by wave after wave."

Tears so darkened his eyes that it was as if they were inviting the waters to rise higher.

The man said that the storms had been fierce in the city too, and that a special reading of the Prajñāpāramitā Sutra had been ordered. "The streets are all closed and the great gentlemen can't get to court, and everything has closed down."

The man spoke clumsily and haltingly, but he did bring news. Genji summoned him near and had him questioned.

"It's not the way it usually is. You don't usually have rain going on for days without a break and the wind howling on and on. Everyone is terrified. But it's worse here. They haven't had this hail beating right through the ground and thunder going on and on and not letting a body think." The terror written so plainly on his face did nothing to improve the spirits of the people at Suma.

Might it be the end of the world? From dawn the next day the wind was so fierce and the tide so high and the surf so loud that it was as if the crags and the mountains must fall. The horror of the thunder and lightning was beyond description. Panic spread at each new flash. For what sins, Genji's men asked, were they being punished? Were they to perish without another glimpse of their mothers and fathers, their dear wives and children?

Genji tried to tell himself that he had been guilty of no misdeed for which he must perish here on the seashore. Such were the panic and confusion around him, however, that he bolstered his confidence with special offerings to the god of Sumiyoshi.

"O you of Sumiyoshi who protect the lands about: if indeed you are an avatar of the Blessed One, then you must save us."

His men were of course fearful for their lives; but the thought that so fine a gentleman (and in these deplorable circumstances) might be swept beneath the waters seemed altogether too tragic. The less distraught among them prayed in loud voices to this and that favored deity, Buddhist and Shinto, that their own lives be taken if it meant that his might be spared.

They faced Sumiyoshi and prayed and made vows: "Our lord was reared deep in the fastnesses of the palace, and all blessings were his. You who, in the abundance of your mercy, have brought strength through these lands to all who have sunk beneath the weight of their troubles: in punishment for what crimes do you call forth these howling waves? Judge his case if you will, you gods of heaven and earth. Guiltless, he is accused of a crime, stripped of his offices, driven from his house and city, left as you see him with no relief from the torture and the lamentation. And now these horrors, and even his life seems threatened. Why? we must ask. Because of sins in some other life, because of crimes in this one? If your vision is clear, O you gods, then take all this away."

Genji offered prayers to the king of the sea and countless other gods as well. The thunder was increasingly more terrible, and finally the gallery adjoining his rooms was struck by lightning. Flames sprang up and the gallery was destroyed. The confusion was immense; the whole world seemed to have gone mad. Genji was moved to a building out in back, a kitchen or something of the sort it seemed to be. It was crowded with people of every station and rank. The clamor was almost enough to drown out the lightning and thunder. Night descended over a sky already as black as ink.

Presently the wind and rain subsided and stars began to come out. The kitchen being altogether too mean a place, a move back to the main hall was suggested. The charred remains of the gallery were an ugly sight, however, and the hall had been badly muddied and all the blinds and curtains blown away. Perhaps, Genji's men suggested somewhat tentatively, it might be better to wait until dawn. Genji sought to concentrate upon the holy name, but his agitation continued to be very great.

He opened a wattled door and looked out. The moon had come up. The line left by the waves was white and dangerously near, and the surf was still high. There was no one here whom he could turn to, no student of the deeper truths who could discourse upon past and present and perhaps explain these wild events. All the fisherfolk had gathered at what they had heard was the house of a great gentleman from the city. They were as noisy and impossible to communicate with as a flock of birds, but no one thought of telling them to leave.

"If the wind had kept up just a little longer," someone said, "absolutely everything would have been swept under. The gods did well by us."

There are no words—"lonely" and "forlorn" seem much too weak—to describe his feelings.

> "Without the staying hand of the king of the sea
> the roar of the eight hundred waves would have taken us under."

Genji was as exhausted as if all the buffets and fires of the tempest had been aimed at him personally. He dozed off, his head against some nondescript piece of furniture.

The old emperor came to him, quite as when he had lived. "And why are you in this wretched place?" He took Genji's hand and pulled him to his feet. "You must do as the god of Sumiyoshi tells you. You must put out to sea immediately. You must leave this shore behind."

"Since I last saw you, sir," said Genji, overjoyed, "I have suffered an unbroken series of misfortunes. I had thought of throwing myself into the sea."

"That you must not do. You are undergoing brief punishment for certain sins. I myself did not commit any conscious crimes while I reigned, but a person is guilty of transgressions and oversights without his being aware of them. I am doing penance and have no time to look back towards this world. But an echo of your troubles came to me and I could not stand idle. I fought my way through the sea and up to this shore and I am very tired; but now that I am here I must see to a matter in the city." And he disappeared.

Genji called after him, begging to be taken along. He looked around him. There was only the bright face of the moon. His father's presence had been too real for a dream, so real that he must still be here. Clouds traced sad lines across the sky. It had been clear and palpable, the figure he had so longed to see even in a dream, so clear that he could almost catch an afterimage. His father had come through the skies to help him in what had seemed the last extremity of his sufferings. He was deeply grateful, even to the tempests; and in the aftermath of the dream he was happy.

Quite different emotions now ruffled his serenity. He forgot his immediate troubles and only regretted that his father had not stayed longer. Perhaps he would come again. Genji would have liked to go back to sleep, but he lay wakeful until daylight.

A little boat had pulled in at the shore and two or three men came up.

"The revered monk who was once governor of Harima has come from Akashi. If the former Minamoto councillor, Lord Yoshikiyo, is here, we wonder if we might trouble him to come down and hear the details of our mission."

Yoshikiyo pretended to be surprised and puzzled. "He was once among my closer acquaintances here in Harima, but we had a falling out and it has been some time since we last exchanged letters. What can have brought him through such seas in that little boat?"

Genji's dream had given intimations. He sent Yoshikiyo down to the boat immediately. Yoshikiyo marveled that it could even have been launched upon such a sea.

These were the details of the mission, from the mouth of the old governor: "Early this month a strange figure came to me in a dream. I listened, though somewhat incredulously, and was told that on the thirteenth there would be a clear and present sign. I was to ready a boat and make for this shore when the waves subsided. I did ready a boat, and then came this savage wind and lightning. I thought of numerous foreign sovereigns who have received instructions in dreams on how to save their lands, and I concluded that even at the risk of incurring his ridicule I must on the day appointed inform your lord of the import of the dream. And so I did indeed put out to sea. A strange jet blew all the way and brought us to this shore. I cannot think of it except as divine intervention. And might I ask whether there have been corresponding manifestations here? I do hate to trouble you, but might I ask you to communicate all of this to your lord?"

Yoshikiyo quietly relayed the message, which brought new considerations. There had been these various unsettling signs conveyed to Genji dreaming and waking. The possibility of being laughed at for having departed these shores under threat now seemed the lesser risk. To turn his back on what might be a real offer of help from the gods would be to ask for still worse misfortunes. It was not easy to reject ordinary advice, and personal reservations counted for little when the advice came from great eminences. "Defer to them; they will cause you no reproaches," a wise man of old once said.[1] He could scarcely face worse misfortunes by deferring than by not deferring, and he did not seem likely to gain great merit and profit by hesitating out of concern for his brave name. Had not his own father come to him? What room was there for doubts?

---

1. Lao-tze, say early commentaries; but the advice is not to be found in his extant writings.

He sent back his answer: "I have been through a great deal in this strange place, and I hear nothing at all from the city. I but gaze upon a sun and moon going I know not where as comrades from my old home; and now comes this angler's boat, happy tidings on an angry wind.[2] Might there be a place along your Akashi coast where I can hide myself?

The old man was delighted. Genji's men pressed him to set out even before sunrise. Taking along only four or five of his closest attendants, he boarded the boat. That strange wind came up again and they were at Akashi as if they had flown. It was very near, within crawling distance, so to speak; but still the workings of the wind were strange and marvelous.

The Akashi coast was every bit as beautiful as he had been told it was. He would have preferred fewer people, but on the whole he was pleased. Along the coast and in the hills the old monk had put up numerous buildings with which to take advantage of the four seasons: a reed-roofed beach cottage with fine seasonal vistas; beside a mountain stream a chapel of some grandeur and dignity, suitable for rites and meditation and invocation of the holy name; and rows of storehouses where the harvest was put away and a bountiful life assured for the years that remained. Fearful of the high tides, the old monk had sent his daughter and her women off to the hills. The house on the beach was at Genji's disposal.

The sun was rising as Genji left the boat and got into a carriage. This first look by daylight at his new guest brought a happy smile to the old man's lips. He felt as if the accumulated years were falling away and as if new years had been granted him. He gave silent thanks to the god of Sumiyoshi. He might have seemed ridiculous as he bustled around seeing to Genji's needs, as if the radiance of the sun and the moon had become his private property; but no one laughed at him.

I need not describe the beauty of the Akashi coast. The careful attention that had gone into the house and the rocks and plantings of the garden, the graceful line of the coast—it was infinitely pleasanter than Suma, and one would not have wished to ask a less than profoundly sensitive painter to paint it. The house was in quiet good taste. The old man's way of life was as Genji had heard it described, hardly more rustic than that of the grandees at court. In sheer luxury, indeed, he rather outdid them.

[Genji remains in Akashi for nearly a year and a half, during which the Akashi priest succeeds in bringing about a union between Genji and his daughter, the Akashi lady. The same violent storm that hit Suma also hit the capital, bringing other omens and disturbances with it: the Kiritsubo emperor appears to his son, the reigning Suzaku emperor, in a dream, reproving him for his treatment of Genji. The Suzaku emperor suffers subsequently a painful eye ailment, the Kokiden lady falls ill, and the Minister of the Right dies. Finally, a year later, Suzaku grants Genji a pardon, summoning him back to the capital in the Seventh Month. Early the following year, Suzaku yields the throne to Reizei, and Genji returns to power. His liaison with the Akashi lady results in a daughter, who is eventually brought to the capital to be raised by Murasaki. Shortly thereafter, Fujitsubo dies. Reizei is informed of his true parentage, and tries to abdicate in favor of his father Genji. Genji refuses but rises rapidly in political rank, eventually being appointed Chancellor. In his thirty-fourth year, Genji constructs a lavish residence, the Rokujō mansion, a virtual court where he gathers all of his women around him. Among these women is Tamakazura, a lost daughter of

---

2. Ki no Tsurayuki, *Gosenshū* 1225: "An angler's boat upon the waves that pound us, / happy tidings on an angry wind."

Tō no Chūjō whom Genji has discovered, adopted, and treats as though she were his own daughter. The following passage from the Tamakazura sequence is known as the "defense of fiction."]

from *Chapter 25. Fireflies*

The rains of early summer continued without a break, even gloomier than in most years. The ladies at Rokujō amused themselves with illustrated romances. The Akashi lady, a talented painter, sent pictures to her daughter.

Tamakazura was the most avid reader of all. She quite lost herself in pictures and stories and would spend whole days with them. Several of her young women were well informed in literary matters. She came upon all sorts of interesting and shocking incidents (she could not be sure whether they were true or not), but she found little that resembled her own unfortunate career. There was *The Tale of Sumiyoshi,* popular in its day, of course, and still well thought of. She compared the plight of the heroine, within a hairbreadth of being taken by the chief accountant,[1] with her own escape from the Higo person.[2]

Genji could not help noticing the clutter of pictures and manuscripts. "What a nuisance this all is," he said one day. "Women seem to have been born to be cheerfully deceived. They know perfectly well that in all these old stories there is scarcely a shred of truth, and yet they are captured and made sport of by the whole range of trivialities and go on scribbling them down, quite unaware that in these warm rains their hair is all dank and knotted."

He smiled. "What would we do if there were not these old romances to relieve our boredom? But amid all the fabrication I must admit that I do find real emotions and plausible chains of events. We can be quite aware of the frivolity and the idleness and still be moved. We have to feel a little sorry for a charming princess in the depths of gloom. Sometimes a series of absurd and grotesque incidents which we know to be quite improbable holds our interest, and afterwards we must blush that it was so. Yet even then we can see what it was that held us. Sometimes I stand and listen to the stories they read to my daughter, and I think to myself that there certainly are good talkers in the world. I think that these yarns must come from people much practiced in lying. But perhaps that is not the whole of the story?"

She pushed away her inkstone. "I can see that that would be the view of someone much given to lying himself. For my part, I am convinced of their truthfulness."

He laughed. "I have been rude and unfair to your romances, haven't I? They have set down and preserved happenings from the age of the gods to our own. *The Chronicles of Japan* and the rest are a mere fragment of the whole truth. It is your romances that fill in the details.

"We are not told of things that happened to specific people exactly as they happened; but the beginning is when there are good things and bad things, things that happen in this life which one never tires of seeing and hearing about, things which one cannot bear not to tell of and must pass on for all generations. If the storyteller wishes to speak well, then he chooses the good things; and if he wishes to hold the reader's attention he chooses bad things, extraordinarily bad things. Good things and bad things alike, they are things of this world and no other.

---

1. There is no such incident in the version which survives today.
2. A rustic man who had pursued her in Kyūshu, before her arrival in the capital and adoption by Genji.

"Writers in other countries approach the matter differently. Old stories in our own are different from new. There are differences in the degree of seriousness. But to dismiss them as lies is itself to depart from the truth. Even in the writ which the Buddha drew from his noble heart are parables, devices for pointing obliquely at the truth. To the ignorant they may seem to operate at cross purposes. The Greater Vehicle is full of them, but the general burden is always the same. The difference between enlightenment and confusion is of about the same order as the difference between the good and the bad in a romance. If one takes the generous view, then nothing is empty and useless."

He now seemed bent on establishing the uses of fiction.

"But tell me: is there in any of your old stories a proper, upright fool like myself?" He came closer. "I doubt that even among the most unworldly of your heroines there is one who manages to be as distant and unnoticing as you are. Suppose the two of us set down our story and give the world a really interesting one."

"I think it very likely that the world will take notice of our curious story even if we do not go to the trouble." She hid her face in her sleeves.

"Our curious story? Yes, incomparably curious, I should think." Smiling and playful, he pressed nearer.

> "Beside myself, I search through all the books,
> and come upon no daughter so unfilial."

"You are breaking one of the commandments."

He stroked her hair as he spoke, but she refused to look up. Presently, however, she managed a reply:

> "So too it is with me. I too have searched,
> and found no cases quite so unparental."

Somewhat chastened, he pursued the matter no further. Yet one worried. What was to become of her?

Murasaki too had become addicted to romances. Her excuse was that Genji's little daughter insisted on being read to.

"Just see what a fine one this is," she said, showing Genji an illustration for *The Tale of Kumano.*[3] The young girl in tranquil and confident slumber made her think of her own younger self. "How precocious even very little children seem to have been. I suppose I might have set myself up as a specimen of the slow, plodding variety. I would have won that competition easily."

Genji might have been the hero of some rather more eccentric stories.

"You must not read love stories to her. I doubt that clandestine affairs would arouse her unduly, but we would not want her to think them commonplace."

What would Tamakazura have made of the difference between his remarks to her and these remarks to Murasaki?

"I would not of course offer the wanton ones as a model," replied Murasaki, "but I would have doubts too about the other sort. Lady Atemiya in *The Tale of the Hollow Tree,* for instance. She is always very brisk and efficient and in control of things, and she never makes mistakes; but there is something unwomanly about her cool manner and clipped speech."

"I should imagine that it is in real life as in fiction. We are all human and we all have our ways. It is not easy to be unerringly right. Proper, well-educated parents go

---

3. Or *The Tale of Komano.* It does not survive.

to great trouble over a daughter's education and tell themselves that they have done well if something quiet and demure emerges. It seems a pity when defects come to light one after another and people start asking what her good parents can possibly have been up to. Yet the rewards are very great when a girl's manner and behavior seem just right for her station. Even then empty praise is not satisfying. One knows that the girl is not perfect and looks at her more critically than before. I would not wish my own daughter to be praised by people who have no standards."

He was genuinely concerned that she acquit herself well in the tests that lay before her.

Wicked stepmothers are of course standard fare for the romancers, and he did not want them poisoning relations between Murasaki and the child. He spent a great deal of time selecting romances he thought suitable, and ordered them copied and illustrated.

from Chapter 34. New Herbs (Part 1)

[*Genji is now forty years old. His daughter by the Akashi lady has gone to court as a consort to the crown prince. He has retired as Chancellor, and been accorded benefices equivalent to those of a retired emperor. Meanwhile, the Suzaku emperor falls ill, and is worried about the future of his favorite daughter, the Third Princess. Although he considers Genji's son Yūgiri, Tō no Chūjō's son Kashiwagi, and Genji's half brother Prince Hotaru as potential husbands for her, he asks Genji to take care of her. Despite his fear of hurting Murasaki, Genji agrees to marry the girl (spurred on, perhaps, by the fact that, like Murasaki, the Third Princess is a niece of Fujitsubo).*]

And so the contract was made.

In the evening there was a banquet for Genji's party and the Suzaku household. The priest's fare was unpretentious but beautifully prepared and served. The tableware and the trays of light aloeswood also suggested the priestly vocation and brought tears to the eyes of the guests. The melancholy and moving details were innumerable, but I fear that they would clutter my story.

It was late in the night when Genji and his men departed, the men bearing lavish gifts. The Fujiwara councilor was among those who saw them off. There had been a fall of snow and the Suzaku emperor had caught cold. But he was happy. The future of the Third Princess seemed secure.

Genji was worried. Murasaki had heard vague rumors, but she had told herself that it could not be. Genji had once been very serious about the high priestess of Ise, it seemed, but in the end he had held himself back. She had not worried a great deal, and asked no questions.

How would she take this news? Genji knew that his feelings towards her would not change, or if they did it would be in the direction of greater intensity. But only time could assure her of that fact, and there would be cruel uncertainty in the meantime. Nothing had been allowed to come between them in recent years, and the thought of having a secret from her for even a short time made him very unhappy.

He said nothing to her that night.

The next day was dark, with flurries of snow.

"I went yesterday to call on the Suzaku emperor. He is in very poor health indeed." It was in the course of a leisurely conversation that Genji brought the matter up. "He said many sad things, but what seems to trouble him most as he goes off to his retreat is the future of the Third Princess." And he described that part of the interview. "I was really so extremely sorry for him that I found it impossible to refuse. I suppose people will make a great thing of it. The thought of taking a bride at my age has seemed so utterly preposterous that I have tried through this and that intermediary to suggest a certain want of ardor. But to see him in person and have it directly from him—I simply could not bring myself to refuse. Do you think that when the time does finally come for him to go off into the mountains we might have her come here? Would that upset you terribly? Please do not let it. Trust me, and tell yourself what is the complete truth, that nothing is going to change. She has more right to feel insecure than you do. But I am sure that we can arrange things happily enough for her too."

She was always torturing herself over the smallest of his affairs, and he had dreaded telling her of this one.

But her reply was quiet and unassertive, "Yes, it is sad for her. The only thing that worries me is the possibility that she might feel less than completely at home. I shall be very happy if our being so closely related persuades her that I am no stranger."

"How silly that this very willingness to accept things should bother me. But it does. It makes me start looking for complications, and I am sure I will feel guiltier as the two of you get used to each other. You must pay no attention to what people say. Rumors are strange things. It is impossible to know where they come from, but there they are, like living creatures bent on poisoning relations between a man and a woman. You must listen only to yourself and let matters take their course. Do not start imagining things, and do not torture yourself with empty jealousies."

It was a tempest out of the blue which there was no escaping. Murasaki was determined that she would not complain or give any hint of resentment. She knew that neither her wishes nor her advice would have made any difference. She did not want the world to think that she had been crushed by what had to come. There was her sharp-tongued stepmother, so quick to blame and to gloat.... She was certain to gloat over this, and to say that Murasaki deserved exactly what had come to her. Though very much in control of herself, Murasaki was prey to these worries. The very durability of her relations with Genji was sure to make people laugh harder. But she gave no hint of her unhappiness.

The New Year came, and at the Suzaku Palace the Third Princess's wedding plans kept people busy. Her several suitors were deeply disappointed. The emperor, who had let it be known that he would welcome her at court, was among them.

[In due course, the Third Princess is installed in the Rokujō mansion.]

It was an unsettling time for Murasaki. No doubt Genji was giving an honest view of the matter when he said that she would not be overwhelmed by the Third Princess. Yet for the first time in years she felt genuinely threatened. The new lady was young and, it would seem, rather showy in her ways, and of such a rank that Murasaki could not ignore her. All very unsettling; but she gave no hint of her feelings, and indeed helped with all the arrangements. Genji saw more than ever that there was really no one like her.

The Third Princess was, as her father had said, a mere child. She was tiny and immature physically, and she gave a general impression of still greater, indeed quite extraordinary, immaturity. He thought of Murasaki when he had first taken her in. She had even then been interesting. She had had a character of her own. The Third Princess was like a baby. Well, thought Genji, the situation had something to recommend it: she was not likely to intrude and make Murasaki unhappy with fits of jealousy. Yet he did think he might have hoped for someone a *little* more interesting. For the first three nights he was faithfully in attendance upon her. Murasaki was unhappy but said nothing. She gave herself up to her thoughts and to such duties, now performed with unusual care, as scenting his robes. He thought her splendid. Why, he asked himself, whatever the pressures and the complications, had he taken another wife? He had been weak and he had given an impression of inconstancy, and brought it all upon himself. Yūgiri had escaped because the Suzaku emperor had seen what an unshakable pillar of fidelity he was.

Genji was near tears. "Please excuse me just this one more night. I have no alternative. If after this I neglect you, then you may be sure that I will be angrier with myself than you can ever be with me. We do have to consider her father's feelings."

"Do not ask us bystanders," she said, a faint smile on her lips, "to tell you how to behave."

He turned away, chin in hand, to hide his confusion.

> "I had grown so used to thinking it would not change,
> and now, before my very eyes, it changes."

He took up the paper on which she had jotted down old poems that fitted her mood as well as this poem of her own. It was not the most perfect of poems, perhaps, but it was honest and to the point.

> "Life must end. It is a transient world.
> The one thing lasting is the bond between us."

He did not want to leave, but she said that he was only making things more difficult for her. He was wearing the soft robes which she had so carefully scented. She had over the years seen new threats arise only to be turned away, and she had finally come to think that there would be no more. Now this had happened, and everyone was talking. She knew how susceptible he had been in his earlier years, and now the whole future seemed uncertain. It was remarkable that she showed no sign of her disquiet.

Her women were talking as of the direst happenings.

"Who would have expected it? He has always kept himself well supplied with women, but none of them has seemed the sort to raise a challenge. So things have been quiet. I doubt that our lady will let them defeat her—but we must be careful. The smallest mistake could make things very difficult."

Murasaki pretended that nothing at all was amiss. She talked pleasantly with them until late in the night. She feared that silence on the most important subject might make it seem more important than it was.

"I am so glad that she has come to us. We have had a full house, but I sometimes think he has been a little bored with us, poor man. None of us is grand enough to be really interesting. I somehow hope that we will be the best of friends. Perhaps it is because they say that she is still a mere child. And here you all are digging a great chasm between us. If we were of the same rank, or perhaps if I had some slight reason to think myself a little her superior, then I would feel that I had to be careful. But as it is—you may think it impertinent of me to say so—I only want to be friendly."

Nakatsukasa and Chūjō exchanged glances. "Such kindness," one of them, I do not know which, would seem to have muttered. They had once been recipients of Genji's attentions but they had been with Murasaki for some years now, and they were among her firmer allies.

Inquiries came from the ladies in the other quarters, some of them suggesting that they who had long ago given up their ambitions might be the more fortunate ones. Murasaki sighed. They meant to be kind, of course, but they were not making things easier. Well, there was no use in tormenting herself over things she could not change, and the inconstancy of the other sex was among them.

Her women would think it odd if she spent the whole night talking with them. She withdrew to her boudoir and they helped her into bed. She was lonely, and the presence of all these women did little to disguise the fact. She thought of the years of his exile. She had feared that they would not meet again, but the agony of waiting for word that he was still alive was in itself a sort of distraction from the sorrow and longing. She sought to comfort herself now with the thought that those confused days could so easily have meant the end of everything.

The wind was cold. Not wanting her women to know that she could not sleep, she lay motionless until she ached from the effort. Still deep in the cold night, the call of the first cock seemed to emphasize the loneliness and sorrow.

She may not have been in an agony of longing, but she was deeply troubled, and perhaps for that reason she came to Genji in his dreams. His heart was racing. Might something have happened to her? He lay waiting for the cock as if for permission to leave, and at its first call rushed out as if unaware that it would not yet be daylight for some time. Still a child, the princess kept her women close beside her. One of them saw him out through a corner door. The snow caught the first traces of dawn, though the garden was still dark. "In vain the spring's darkness,"[1] whispered her nurse, catching the scent he had left behind.

The patches of snow were almost indistinguishable from the white garden sands. "There is yet snow by the castle wall,"[2] he whispered to himself as he came to Murasaki's wing of the house and tapped on a shutter. No longer in the habit of accommodating themselves to nocturnal wanderings, the women let him wait for a time.

"How slow you are," he said, slipping in beside her. "I am quite congealed, as much from terror as from cold. And I have done nothing to deserve it."

He thought her rather wonderful. She did nothing at all, and yet, hiding her wet sleeves, she somehow managed to keep him at a distance. Not even among ladies of the highest birth was there anyone quite like her. He found himself comparing her with the little princess he had just left.

He spent the day beside her, going over their years together, and charging her with evasion and deviousness.

He sent a note saying that he would not be calling on the princess that day. "I seem to have caught a chill from the snow and think I would be more comfortable here."

Her nurse sent back tartly by word of mouth that the note had been passed on to her lady. Not a very amiable sort, thought Genji.

He did not want the Suzaku emperor to know of his want of ardor, but he did not seem capable even of maintaining appearances. Things could scarcely have been worse. For her part, Murasaki feared that the Suzaku emperor would hold her responsible.

---

1. Oshikōchi Mitsune, *Kokinshū* 40: "In vain the spring night's darkness accosts the plum, / destroying the color but not the scent of its blossoms."

2. Po Chü-i, Collected Works 16, "Dawn from *Yü Hsin's Tower*."

Waking this time in the familiar rooms, he got off another note to the princess. He took great trouble with it, though he was not sure that she would notice. He chose white paper and attached it to a sprig of plum blossom.

> "Not heavy enough to block the way between us,
> the flurries of snow this morning yet distress me."

He told the messenger that the note was to be delivered at the west gallery.[3] * * *

An answer did presently come. It was on red tissue paper and folded neatly in an envelope. He opened it with trepidation, hoping that it would not be too irredeemably childish. He did not want to have secrets from Murasaki, and yet he did not want her to see the princess's hand, at least for a time. To display the princess in all her immaturity seemed somehow insulting. But it would be worse to make Murasaki yet unhappier. She sat leaning against an armrest. He laid the note half open beside her.

> "You do not come. I fain would disappear,
> a veil of snow upon the rough spring winds."

It was every bit as bad as he had feared, scarcely even a child's hand—and of course in point of years she was not a child at all. Murasaki glanced at it and glanced away as if she had not seen it. He would have offered it up for what it was, evidence of almost complete uselessness, had it been from anyone else.

"So you see you have nothing to worry about," he said.

He paid his first daytime call upon the princess. He had dressed with unusual care and no doubt his good looks had an unusually powerful effect on women not used to them. For the older and more experienced of them, the nurse, for instance, the effect was of something like apprehension. He was so splendid that they feared complications. Their lady was such a pretty little child of a thing, reduced to almost nothing at all by the brilliance of her surroundings. It was as if there were no flesh holding up the great mounds of clothing. She did not seem shy before him, and if it could have been said that her openness and freedom from mannerism were for purposes of putting him at ease, then it could also have been said that they succeeded very well. Her father was not generally held to be a virile sort of man, but no one denied his superior taste and refinement, and the mystery was that he had done so little by way of training her. And of course Genji, like everyone else, knew that she was his favorite, and that he worried endlessly about her. It all seemed rather sad. The other side of the matter was that she did undeniably have a certain girlish charm. She listened quietly and answered with whatever came into her mind. He must be good to her. In his younger days his disappointment would have approached contempt, but he had become more tolerant. They all had their ways, and none was enormously superior to the others. There were as many sorts of women as there were women. A disinterested observer would probably have told him that he had made a good match for himself. Murasaki was the only remarkable one among them all, more remarkable now than ever, he thought, and he had known her very well for a very long time. He had no cause for dissatisfaction with his efforts as guardian and mentor. A single morning or evening away from her and the sense of deprivation was so intense as to bring a sort of foreboding.

* * *

A frequenter of the Suzaku Palace, Kashiwagi had known all about the Third Princess and the Suzaku emperor's worries. He had offered himself as a candidate for

5

---

3. His reasons are not clear. There is a theory that he doesn't want Murasaki to see, but it is not very tenable.

her hand. His candidacy had not been dismissed, and then, suddenly and to his very great disappointment, she had gone to Genji. He still could not reconcile himself to what had happened. He seems to have taken some comfort in exchanging reports with women whom he had known in her maiden days. He of course heard what everyone else heard, that she was no great competitor for Genji's affection.

He was forever complaining to Koji.

[*On a pleasant day in the Third Month, a number of young men, including Yūgiri (Genji's son by Aoi) and Kashiwagi (Tō no Chūjō's son), assemble at Rokujō and engage in a game of kickball* (kemari), *while Genji looks on.*]

Taking their places under a fine cherry in full bloom, Yūgiri and Kashiwagi were very handsome in the evening light. Genji's less than genteel sport—such things do happen—took on something of the elegance of the company and the place. Spring mists enfolded trees in various stages of bud and bloom and new leaf. The least subtle of games does have its skills and techniques, and each of the players was determined to show what he could do. Though Kashiwagi played only briefly, he was clearly the best of them all. He was handsome but retiring, intense and at the same time lively and expansive. Though the players were now under the cherry directly before the south stairs, they had no eye for the blossoms. Genji and Prince Hotaru were at a corner of the veranda.

Yes, there were many skills, and as one inning followed another a certain abandon was to be observed and caps of state were pushed rather far back on noble foreheads. Yūgiri could permit himself a special measure of abandon, and his youthful spirits and vigor were infectious. He had on a soft white robe lined with red. His trousers were gently taken in at the ankles, but by no means untidy. He seemed very much in control of himself despite the abandon, and cherry petals fell about him like a flurry of snow. He broke off a twig from a dipping branch and went to sit on the stairs.

"How quick they are to fall," said Kashiwagi, coming up behind him. "We must teach the wind to blow wide and clear."[4]

He glanced over toward the Third Princess's rooms. They seemed to be in the usual clutter. The multicolored sleeves pouring from under the blinds and through openings between them were like an assortment of swatches to be presented to the goddess of spring. Only a few paces from him a woman had pushed her curtains carelessly aside and looked as if she might be in a mood to receive a gentleman's addresses. A Chinese cat, very small and pretty, came running out with a larger cat in pursuit. There was a noisy rustling of silk as several women pushed forward to catch it. On a long cord which had become badly tangled, it would not yet seem to have been fully tamed. As it sought to free itself the cord caught in a curtain, which was pulled back to reveal the women behind. No one, not even those nearest the veranda, seemed to notice. They were much too worried about the cat.

A lady in informal dress stood[5] just inside the curtains beyond the second pillar to the west. Her robe seemed to be of red lined with lavender, and at the sleeves and throat the colors were as bright and varied as a book of paper samples. Her cloak was of white figured satin lined with red. Her hair fell as cleanly as sheaves of thread and fanned out towards the neatly trimmed edges some ten inches beyond her feet. In the

---

4. Fujiwara Yoshikaze, *Kokinshū* 85: "Blow wide and clear, spring wind, of the cherry blossoms. / Let us see if they will fall of their own accord."

5. The verb is important. Well-behaved ladies did not permit themselves to be seen standing.

rich billowing of her skirts the lady scarcely seemed present at all. The white profile framed by masses of black hair was pretty and elegant—though unfortunately the room was dark and he could not see her as well in the evening light as he would have wished. The women had been too delighted with the game, young gentlemen heedless of how they scattered the blossoms, to worry about blinds and concealment. The lady turned to look at the cat, which was mewing piteously, and in her face and figure was an abundance of quiet, unpretending young charm.

Yūgiri saw and strongly disapproved, but would only have made matters worse by stepping forward to lower the blind. He coughed warningly. The lady slipped out of sight. He too would have liked to see more, and he sighed when, the cat at length disengaged, the blind fell back into place. Kashiwagi's regrets were more intense. It could only have been the Third Princess, the lady who was separated from the rest of the company by her informal dress. He pretended that nothing had happened, but Yūgiri knew that he had seen the princess, and was embarrassed for her. Seeking to calm himself, Kashiwagi called the cat and took it up in his arms. It was delicately perfumed. Mewing prettily, it brought the image of the Third Princess back to him (for he had been ready to fall in love).

from *Chapter 35. New Herbs (Part 2)*

The royal cat had had a large litter of kittens, which had been put out here and there. One of them, a very pretty little creature, was scampering about the crown prince's rooms. Kashiwagi was of course reminded of the Rokujō cat.

"The Third Princess has a really fine cat. You would have to go a very long way to find its rival. I only had the briefest glimpse, but it made a deep impression on me."

Very fond of cats, the crown prince asked for all the details. Kashiwagi perhaps made the Rokujō cat seem more desirable than it was.

"It is a Chinese cat, and Chinese cats are different. All cats have very much the same disposition, I suppose, but it does seem a little more affectionate than most. A perfectly charming little thing."

The crown prince made overtures through the Akashi princess and presently the cat was delivered. Everyone was agreed that it was a very superior cat. Guessing that the crown prince meant to keep it, Kashiwagi waited a few days and paid a visit. He had been a favorite of the Suzaku emperor's and now he was close to the crown prince, to whom he gave lessons on the koto and other instruments.

"Such numbers of cats as you do seem to have. Where is my own special favorite?"
The Chinese cat was apprehended and brought in. He took it in his arms.

"Yes, it is a handsome beast," said the crown prince, "but it does not seem terribly friendly. Maybe it is not used to us. Do you really think it so superior to our own cats?"

"Cats do not on the whole distinguish among people, though perhaps the more intelligent ones do have the beginnings of a rational faculty. But just look at them all, such swarms of cats and all of them such fine ones. Might I have the loan of it for a few days?"

He was afraid that he was being rather silly. But he had his cat. He kept it with him at night, and in the morning would see to its toilet and pet it and feed it. Once the initial shyness had passed it proved to be a most affectionate animal. He loved its way of sporting with the hem of his robe or entwining itself around a leg. Sometimes when he was sitting at the veranda lost in thought it would come up and speak to him.

"What an insistent little beast you are." He smiled and stroked its back. "You are here to remind me of someone I long for, and what is it you long for yourself? We must have been together in an earlier life, you and I."

He looked into its eyes and it returned the gaze and mewed more emphatically. Taking it in his arms, he resumed his sad thoughts.

"Now why should a cat all of a sudden dominate his life?" said one of the women. "He never paid much attention to cats before."

The crown prince asked to have the cat back, but in vain. It had become Kashiwagi's constant and principal companion.

[*Several years pass. The Akashi princess has since given birth to several children, one of whom will be the next crown prince. Although Murasaki and Genji remain happily married, she has begun asking him to allow her to become a nun, but he refuses.*]

Murasaki was now busy being grandmother to the royal children. She did nothing that might have left her open to charges of bad judgment. Hers was a perfection, indeed, that was somehow ominous. It aroused forebodings. The evidence is that such people are not meant to have long lives. Genji had known many women and he knew what a rarity she was. She was thirty-seven this year.[1]

He was thinking over the years they had been together. "You must be especially careful this year. You must overlook none of the prayers and services. I am very busy and sometimes careless, and I must rely on you to keep track of things. If there is something that calls for special arrangements I can give the orders. It is a pity that your uncle, the bishop, is no longer living. He was the one who really knew about these things.

"I have always been rather spoiled and there can be few precedents for the honors I enjoy. The other side of the story is that I have had more than my share of sorrow. The people who have been fond of me have left me behind one after another, and there have been events in more recent years that I think almost anyone would call very sad. As for nagging little worries, it almost seems as if I were a collector of them. I sometimes wonder if it might be by way of compensation that I have lived a longer life than I would have expected to. You, on the other hand—I think that except for our years apart you have been spared real worries. There are the troubles that go with the glory of being an empress or one of His Majesty's other ladies. They are always being hurt by the proud people they must be with and they are engaged in a competition that makes a terrible demand on their nerves. You have lived the life of a cloistered maiden, and there is none more comfortable and secure. It is as if you had never left your parents. Have you been aware, my dear, that you have been luckier than most? I know that it has not been easy for you to have the princess move in on us all of a sudden. We sometimes do not notice the things that are nearest to us, and you may not have noticed that her presence has made me fonder of you. But you are quick to see these things, and perhaps I do you an injustice."

"You are right, of course. I do not much matter, and it must seem to most people that I have been more fortunate than I deserve. And that my unhappiness should sometimes have seemed almost too much for me—perhaps that is the prayer that has sustained me." She seemed to be debating whether to go on. He thought her splendid.

---

1. She should be 39 or 40. The thirty-seventh year by the Asian count was thought to be a dangerous one. It was then that Fujitsubo died.

"I doubt that I have much longer to live. Indeed, I have my doubts about getting through this year if I pretend that no changes are needed. It would make me very happy if you would let me do what I have so long wanted to do."

"Quite out of the question. Do you think I could go on without you? Not very much has happened these last years, I suppose, but knowing that you are here has been the most important thing. You must see to the end how very much I have loved you."

It was the usual thing, all over again.

A very little more and she would be in tears, he could see. He changed the subject.

"I have not known enormous numbers of women, but I have concluded that they all have their good points, and that the genuinely calm and equable ones are very rare indeed.

"There was Yūgiri's mother. I was a mere boy when we were married and she was one of the eminences in my life, someone I could not think of dismissing. But things never went well. To the end she seemed very remote. It was sad for her, but I cannot convince myself that the fault was entirely mine. She was an earnest lady with no faults that one would have wished to single out, but it might be said that she was the cold intellectual, the sort you might turn to for advice and find yourself uncomfortable with.

"There was the Rokujō lady, Akikonomu's mother. I remember her most of all for her extraordinary subtlety and cultivation, but she was a difficult lady too, indeed almost impossible to be with. Even when her anger seemed justified it lasted too long, and her jealousy was more than a man could be asked to endure. The tensions went on with no relief, and the reservations on both sides made easy companionship quite impossible. I stood too much on my dignity, I suppose. I thought that if I gave in she would gloat and exult. And so it ended. I could see how the gossip hurt her and how she condemned herself for conduct which she thought unworthy of her position, and I could see that difficult though she might be I was at fault myself. It is because I have so regretted what finally happened that I have gone to such trouble for her daughter. I do not claim all the credit, of course. It is obvious that she was meant all along for important things. But I made enemies for myself because of what I did for her, and I like to think that her mother, wherever she is, has forgiven me. I have on the impulse of the moment done many things I have come to regret. It was true long ago and it is true now." By fits and starts, he spoke of his several ladies.

"There is the Akashi lady. I looked down upon her and thought her no more than a plaything. But she has depths. She may seem docile and uncomplicated, but there is a firm core underneath it all. She is not easily slighted."

"I was not introduced to the other ladies and can say nothing about them," replied Murasaki. "I cannot pretend to know very much about the Akashi lady either, but I have had a glimpse of her from time to time, and would agree with you that she has very great pride and dignity. I often wonder if she does not think me a bit of a simpleton. As for your daughter, I should imagine that she forgives me my faults."

It was affection for the Akashi princess, thought Genji, that had made such good friends of Murasaki and a lady she had once so resented. Yes, she was splendid indeed.

"You may have your little blank spots," he said, "but on the whole you manage things as the people and the circumstances demand. I have as I have said known numbers of ladies and not one of them has been quite like you. Not"—he smiled—"that you always keep your feelings to yourself."

In the evening he went off to the main hall. "I must commend the princess for having carried out her instructions so faithfully."

Immersed in her music, she was as youthful as ever. It did not seem to occur to her that anyone might be less than happy with her presence.

"Let me have a few days off," said Genji, "and you take a few off too. You have quite satisfied your teacher. You worked hard and the results were worthy of the effort. I have no doubts now about your qualifications." He pushed the koto aside and lay down.

As always when he was away, Murasaki had her women read stories to her. In the old stories that were supposed to tell what went on in the world, there were men with amorous ways and women who had affairs with them, but it seemed to be the rule that in the end the man settled down with one woman. Why should Murasaki herself live in such uncertainty? No doubt, as Genji had said, she had been unusually fortunate. But were the ache and the scarcely endurable sense of deprivation to be with her to the end? She had much to think about and went to bed very late, and towards daylight she was seized with violent chest pains. Her women were immediately at her side. Should they call Genji? Quite out of the question, she replied. Presently it was daylight. She was running a high fever and still in very great pain. No one had gone for Genji. Then a message came from the Akashi princess and she was informed of Murasaki's illness, and in great trepidation sent word to Genji. He immediately returned to Murasaki's wing of the house, to find her still in great pain.

"And what would seem to be the matter?" He felt her forehead. It was flaming hot.

He was in terror, remembering that only the day before he had warned her of the dangerous year ahead. Breakfast was brought but he sent it back. He was at her side all that day, seeing to her needs. She was unable to sit up and refused even the smallest morsel of fruit.

The days went by. All manner of prayers and services were commissioned. Priests were summoned to perform esoteric rites. Though the pain was constant, it would at times be of a vague and generalized sort, and then, almost unbearable, the chest pains would return. An endless list of abstinences was drawn up by the soothsayers, but it did no good. Beside her all the while, Genji was in anguish, looking for the smallest hopeful sign, the barely perceptible change that can brighten the prospects in even the most serious illness. She occupied the whole of his attention. Preparations for the visit to the Suzaku emperor, who sent frequent and courteous inquiries, had been put aside.

The Second Month was over and there was no improvement. Thinking that a change of air might help, Genji moved her to his Nijō mansion. Anxious crowds gathered there and the confusion was enormous. The Reizei emperor was much troubled and Yūgiri even more so. There were others who were in very great disquiet. Were Murasaki to die, then Genji would almost certainly follow through with his wish to retire from the world. Yūgiri saw to the usual sort of prayers and rites, of course, and extraordinary ones as well.

"Do you remember what I asked for?" Murasaki would say when she was feeling a little more herself. "May I not have it even now?"

"I have longed for many years to do exactly that," Genji would reply, thinking that to see her even briefly in nun's habit would be as painful as to know that the final time had come. "I have been held back by the thought of what it would mean to you if I were to insist on having my way. Can you now think of deserting me?"

But it did indeed seem that the end might be near. There were repeated crises, each of which could have been the last. Genji no longer saw the Third Princess. Music had lost all interest and koto and flute were put away. Most of the Rokujō household moved to Nijō. At Rokujō, where only women remained, it was as if the fires had gone out. One saw how much of the old life had depended on a single lady.

The Akashi princess was at Genji's side.

"But whatever I have might take advantage of your condition," said Murasaki, weak though she was. "Please go back immediately."

The princess's little children were with them, the prettiest children imaginable. Murasaki looked at them and wept. "I doubt that I shall be here to see you grow up. I suppose you will forget all about me"

The princess too was weeping.

"You must not even think of it," said Genji. "Everything will be all right if only we manage to think so. When we take the broad, easy view we are happy. It may be the destiny of the meaner sort to rise to the top, but the fretful and demanding ones do not stay there very long. It is the calm ones who survive. I could give you any number of instances."

He described her virtues to all the native and foreign gods and told them how very little she had to atone for. The venerable sages entrusted with the grander services and the priests in immediate attendance as well, including the ones on night duty, were sorry that they seemed to be accomplishing so little. They turned to their endeavors with new vigor and intensity. For five and six days there would be some improvement and then she would be worse again, and so time passed. How would it all end? The malign force that had taken possession of her refused to come forth. She was wasting away from one could not have said precisely what ailment, and there was no relief from the worry and sorrow.

I have been neglecting Kashiwagi. Now a councilor of the middle rank, he enjoyed the special confidence of the emperor and was one of the more promising young officials of the day. But fame and honor had done nothing to satisfy the old longing. He took for his bride the Second Princess, daughter of the Suzaku emperor by a low-ranking concubine. It must be admitted that he thought her less than the very best he could have found. She was an agreeable lady whose endowments were far above the ordinary, but she was not capable of driving the Third Princess from his thoughts. He did not, to be sure, treat her like one of the old women who are cast out on mountain-sides to die, but he was not as attentive as he might have been.

The Kojijū[2] to whom he went with the secret passion he was unable to quell was a daughter of Jijū, the Third Princess's nurse. Jijū's elder sister was Kashiwagi's own nurse, and so he had long known a great deal about the princess. He had known when she was still a child that she was very pretty and that she was her father's favorite. It was from these early beginnings that his love had grown.

Guessing that the Rokujō mansion would be almost deserted, he called Kojijū and warmly pleaded his case. "My feelings could destroy me, I fear. You are my tie with her and so I have asked you about her and hoped that you might let her know something of my uncontrollable longing. You have been my hope and you have done nothing. Someone was saying to her royal father that Genji had many ladies to occupy his attention and that one of them seemed to have monopolized it, and the Third Princess was spending lonely nights and days of boredom. It would seem that her father might have been having second thoughts. If his daughters had to marry commoners, he said, it would be nice if they were commoners who had a little time for them. Someone told me that he might even think the Second Princess the more fortunate of the two. She is the one who has long years of comfort and security ahead of her. I cannot tell you how it all upsets me." He sighed. "They are daughters of the same royal father, but the one is the one and the other is the other."

"I think, sir, that you might be a little more aware of your place in the world. You have one princess and you want another? Your greed seems boundless."

He smiled. "Yes, I suppose so. But her father gave me some encouragement and so did her brother. Though it may be, as you say, that I am not as aware of my place in the world as I should be, I have let myself think of her. Both of them found occasion to say that they did not consider me so very objectionable. You are the one who is at fault—you should have worked just a little harder."

"It was impossible. I have been told that there is such a thing as fate. It may have been fate which made Genji ask for her so earnestly and ceremoniously. Do you really think His Majesty's affection for you such that, had you made similar overtures, they would have prevailed over His Lordship's? It is true that you have a little more dignity and prestige now than you had then."

He did not propose to answer this somewhat intemperate outburst. "Let us leave the past out of the matter. The present offers a rare opportunity. There are very few people around her and you can, if you will, contrive to admit me to her presence and let me tell her just a little of what has been on my mind. As for the possibility of my doing anything improper—look at me, if you will, please. Do I seem capable of anything of the sort?"

"This is preposterous, utterly preposterous. The very thought of it terrifies me. Why did I even come?"

"Not entirely preposterous, I think. Marriage is an uncertain arrangement. Are you saying that these things never under any circumstances happen to His Majesty's own ladies? I should think that the chances might be more considerable with someone like the princess. On the surface everything may seem to be going beautifully, but I should imagine that she has her share of private dissatisfactions. She was her father's favorite and now she is losing out to ladies of no very high standing. I know everything. It is an uncertain world we live in and no one can legislate to have things exactly as he wants them."

"You are not telling me, are you, that she is losing out to others and so she must make fine new arrangements for herself? The arrangements she has already made for herself are rather fine, I should think, and of a rather special nature. Her royal father would seem to have thought that with His Lordship to look after her as if she were his daughter she would have no worries. I should imagine that they have both of them accepted the relationship for what it is. Do you think it is quite your place to suggest changes?"

He must not let her go away angry. "You may be sure that I am aware of my own inadequacy and would not dream of exposing myself to the critical eye of a lady who is used to the incomparable Genji. But it would not be such a dreadful thing, I should think, to approach her curtains and speak with her very briefly? It is not considered such a great sin, I believe, for a person to speak the whole truth to the powers above."

He seemed prepared to swear by all the powers, and she was young and somewhat heedless, and when a man spoke as if he were prepared to throw his life away she could not resist forever.

"I will see what I can do if I find what seems the right moment. On nights when His Lordship does not come the princess has swarms of women in her room, and always several of her favorites right beside her, and I cannot imagine what sort of moment it will be."

Frowning, she left him.

He was after her constantly. The moment finally came, it seemed, and she got off a note to him. He set out in careful disguise, delighted but in great trepidation. It did not occur to him that a visit might only add to his torments. He wanted to see a little more of her whose sleeves he had glimpsed that spring evening. If he were to tell her what was in his heart, she might pity him, she might even answer him briefly.

It was about the middle of the Fourth Month, the eve of the lustration for the Kamo festival. Twelve women from the Third Princess's household were to be with the high priestess, and girls and young women of no very high rank who were going to watch the procession were busy at their needles and otherwise getting ready. No one had much time for the princess. Azechi, one of her most trusted intimates, had been summoned by the Minamoto captain with whom she was keeping company and had gone back to her room. Only Kojijū was with the princess. Sensing that the time was right, she led him to a seat in an east corner of the princess's boudoir. And was that not a little extreme?

The princess had gone serenely off to bed. She sensed that a man was in her room and thought that it would be Genji. But he seemed rather too polite—and then suddenly he put his arms around her and took her from her bed. She was terrified. Had some evil power seized her? She forced herself to look up and saw that it was a stranger. And here he was babbling complete nonsense. She called for her women, but no one came. She was trembling and bathed in perspiration. Though he could not help feeling sorry for her, he thought this agitation rather charming.

"I know that I am nothing, but I would not have expected quite such unfriendliness. I once had ambitions that were perhaps too grand for me. I could have kept them buried in my heart, I suppose, eventually to die there, but I spoke to someone of a small part of them and they came to your father's attention. I took courage from the fact that he did not seem to consider them entirely beneath his notice, and I told myself that the regret would be worse than anything if a love unique for its depth and intensity should come to nothing, and my low rank and only that must be held responsible. It was a very deep love indeed, and the sense of regret, the injury, the fear, the yearning, have only grown stronger as time has gone by. I know that I am being reckless and I am very much ashamed of myself that I cannot control my feelings and must reveal myself to you as someone who does not know his proper place. But I vow to you that I shall do nothing more. You will have no worse crimes to charge me with."

She finally guessed who he was, and was appalled. She was speechless.

"I know how you must feel; but it is not as if this sort of thing had never happened before. Your coldness is what has no precedent. It could drive me to extremes. Tell me that you pity me and that will be enough. I will leave you."

He had expected a proud lady whom it would not be easy to talk to. He would tell her a little of his unhappiness, he had thought, and say nothing he might later regret. But he found her very different. She was pretty and gentle and unresisting, and far more graceful and elegant, in a winsome way, than most ladies he had known. His passion was suddenly more than he could control. Was there no hiding place to which they might run off together?

He presently dozed off (it cannot be said that he fell asleep) and dreamed of the cat of which he had been so fond. It came up to him mewing prettily. He seemed to be dreaming that he had brought it back to the princess. As he awoke he was asking himself why he should have done that. And what might the dream have meant?

The princess was still in a state of shock. She could not believe that it had all happened.

"You must tell yourself that there were ties between us which we could not escape. I am in as much of a daze as you can possibly be."

He told her of the surprising event that spring evening, of the cat and the cord and the raised blind. So it had actually happened! Sinister forces seemed to preside over her affairs. And how could she face Genji? She wept like a little child and he looked on with respectful pity. Brushing away her tears, he let them mingle with his own.

There were traces of dawn in the sky. He felt that he had nowhere to go and that it might have been better had he not come at all. "What am I to do? You seem to dislike me most extravagantly, and I find it hard to think of anything more to say. And I have not even heard your voice."

He was only making things worse. Her thoughts in a turmoil, she was quite unable to speak.

"This muteness is almost frightening. Could anything be more awful? I can see no reason for going on. Let me die. Life has seemed to have some point and so I have lived, and even now it is not easy to think that I am at the end of it. Grant me some small favor, some gesture, anything at all, and I will not mind dying."

He took her in his arms and carried her out. She was terrified. What could he possibly mean to do with her? He spread a screen in a corner room and opened the door beyond. The south door of the gallery, through which he had come the evening before, was still open. It was very dark. Wanting to see her face, even dimly, he pushed open a shutter.

"This cruelty is driving me mad. If you wish to still the madness, then say that you pity me."

She did want to say something. She wanted to say that his conduct was outrageous. But she was trembling like a frightened child. It was growing lighter.

"I would like to tell you of a rather startling dream I had, but I suppose you would not listen. You seem to dislike me very much indeed. But I think it might perhaps mean something to you."

The dawn sky seemed sadder than the saddest autumn sky.

"I arise and go forth in the dark before the dawn.
I know not where, nor whence came the dew on my sleeve."

He showed her a moist sleeve.

He finally seemed to be leaving. So great was her relief that she managed an answer:

"Would I might fade away in the sky of dawn,
and all of it might vanish as a dream."

She spoke in a tiny, wavering voice and she was like a beautiful child. He hurried out as if he had only half heard, and felt as if he were leaving his soul behind.

He went quietly off to his father's house, preferring it to his own and the company of the Second Princess. He lay down but was unable to sleep. He did not know what if anything the dream had meant. He suddenly longed for the cat—and he was frightened. It was a terrible thing he had done. How could he face the world? He remained in seclusion and his secret wanderings seemed to be at an end. It was a terrible thing for the Third Princess, of course, and for himself as well. Supposing he had seduced the emperor's own lady and the deed had come to light—could the punishment be worse? Even if he were to avoid specific punishment he did not know how he could face a reproachful Genji.

There are wellborn ladies of strongly amorous tendencies whose dignity and formal bearing are a surface that falls away when the right man comes with the right overtures. With the Third Princess it was a matter of uncertainty and a want of firm principles. She was a timid girl and she felt as vulnerable as if one of her women had already broadcast her secret to the world. She could not face the sun. She wanted to brood in darkness.

She said that she was unwell. The report was passed on to Genji, who came hurrying over. He had thought that he already had worries enough. There was nothing emphatically wrong with her, it would seem, but she refused to look at him. Fearing that she was out of sorts because of his long absence, he told her about Murasaki's illness.

"It may be the end. At this time of all times I would not want her to think me unfeeling. She has been with me since she was a child and I cannot abandon her now. I am afraid I have not had time these last months for anyone else. It will not go on forever, and I know that you will presently understand."

She was ashamed and sorry. When she was alone she wept a great deal.

For Kashiwagi matters were worse. The conviction grew that it would have been better not to see her. Night and day he could only lament his impossible love. A group of young friends, in a hurry to be off to the Kamo festival, urged him to go with them, but he pleaded illness and spent the day by himself. Though correct in his behavior toward the Second Princess, he was not really fond of her. He passed the tedious hours in his own rooms. The little girl came in with a sprig of aoi, the heartvine of the Kamo festival.

> "In secret, without leave, she brings this heartvine.
> A most lamentable thing, a blasphemous thing."

He could think only of the Third Princess. He heard the festive roar in the distance as if it were no part of his life and passed a troubled day in a tedium of his own making.

The Second Princess was used to these low spirits. She did not know what might be responsible for them, but she felt unhappy and inadequate. She had almost no one with her, most of the women having gone off to the festival. In her gloom she played a sad, gentle strain on a koto. Yes, she was very beautiful, very delicate and refined; but had the choice been his he would have taken her sister. He had not, of course, been fated to make the choice.

> "Laurel branches twain, so near and like.
> Why was it that I took the fallen leaf?"[3]

It was a poem he jotted down to while away the time—and not very complimentary to the Second Princess.

Though Genji was in a fever of impatience to be back at Nijō, he so seldom visited Rokujō that it would be bad manners to leave immediately.

A messenger came. "Our lady has expired."

He rushed off. The road was dark before his eyes, and ever darker. At Nijō the crowds overflowed into the streets. There was weeping within. The worst did indeed seem to have happened. He pushed his way desperately through.

"She had seemed better these last few days," said one of the women, "and now this."

---

3. The Second Princess is often called Ochiba, "Fallen Leaf." The name comes from this poem.

The confusion was enormous. The women were wailing and asking her to take them with her. The altars had been dismantled and the priests were leaving, only the ones nearest the family remaining behind. For Genji it was like the end of the world.

He set about quieting the women. "Some evil power has made it seem that she is dead. Nothing more. Certainly this commotion does not seem called for."

He made vows more solemn and detailed than before and summoned ascetics known to have worked wonders.

"Even if her time has come and she must leave us," they said, "let her stay just a little longer. There was the vow of the blessed Fudō.[4] Let her stay even that much longer."

So intense and fevered were their efforts that clouds of black smoke seemed to coil over their heads.

Genji longed to look into her eyes once more. It had been too sudden, he had not even been allowed to say goodbye. There seemed a possibility—one can only imagine the dread which it inspired—that he too was on the verge of death.

Perhaps the powers above took note. The malign spirit suddenly yielded after so many tenacious weeks and passed from Murasaki to the little girl who was serving as medium, and who now commenced to thrash and writhe and moan. To Genji's joy and terror Murasaki was breathing once more.

The medium was now weeping and flinging her hair madly about. "Go away, all of you. I want a word with Lord Genji and it must be with him alone. All these prayers and chants all these months have been an unrelieved torment. I have wanted you to suffer as I have suffered. But then I saw that I had brought you to the point of death and I pitied you, and so I have come out into the open. I am no longer able to seem indifferent, though I am the wretch you see. It is precisely because the old feelings have not died that I have come to this. I had resolved to let myself be known to no one."

He had seen it before. The old terror and anguish came back. He took the little medium by the hand lest she do something violent.

"Is it really you? I have heard that foxes and other evil creatures sometimes go mad and seek to defame the dead. Tell me who you are, quite plainly. Or give me a sign, something that will be meaningless to others but unmistakable to me. Then I will try to believe you."

Weeping copiously and speaking in a loud wail, the medium seemed at the same time to cringe with embarrassment.

"I am horribly changed, and you pretend not to know me. You are the same. Oh dreadful, dreadful."

Even in these wild rantings there was a suggestion of the old aloofness. It added to the horror. He wanted to hear no more.

But there was more. "From up in the skies I saw what you did for my daughter and was pleased. But it seems to be a fact that the ways of the living are not the ways of the dead and that the feeling of mother for child is weakened. I have gone on thinking you the cruelest of men. I heard you tell your dear lady what a difficult and unpleasant person you once found me, and the resentment was worse than when you insulted me to my face and finally abandoned me. I am dead, and I hoped that you had forgiven me and would defend me against those who spoke ill of me and say that it was none of it true. The hope was what twisted a twisted creature more cruelly and brought this horror. I do not hate her; but the powers have shielded you and only let me hear your voice in the distance. Now this has happened. Pray for me. Pray that my

---

4. Early commentaries say that Fudō vowed to give six more months of life to those of the faithful who wished it.

sins be forgiven. These services, these holy texts, they are an unremitting torment, they are smoke and flames, and in the roar and crackle I cannot hear the holy word. Tell my child of my torments. Tell her that she is never to fall into rivalries with other ladies, never to be a victim of jealousy. Her whole attention must go to atoning for the sins of her time at Ise, far from the Good Law. I am sorry for everything."

It was not a dialogue which he wished to pursue. He had the little medium taken away and Murasaki quietly moved to another room.

The crowds swarming through the house seemed themselves to bode ill. All the high courtiers had been off watching the return procession from the Kamo Shrine and it was on their own way home that they heard the news.

"What a really awful thing," said someone, and there was no doubting the sincerity of the words. "A light that should for every reason have gone on shining has been put out, and we are left in a world of drizzling rain."

But someone else whispered: "It does not do to be too beautiful and virtuous. You do not live long. 'Nothing in this world would be their rival,' the poet said.[5] He was talking about cherry blossoms, of course, but it is so with her too. When such a lady lives to know all the pleasures and successes, her fellows must suffer. Maybe now the Third Princess will enjoy some of the attention that should have been hers all along. She has not had an easy time of it, poor thing."

Not wanting another such day, Kashiwagi had ridden off with several of his brothers to watch the return procession. The news of course came as a shock. They turned towards Nijō.

"Nothing is meant in this world to last forever,"[6] he whispered to himself. He went in as if inquiring after her health, for it had after all been only a rumor. The wailing and lamenting proclaimed that it must be true.

Prince Hyōbu had arrived and gone inside and was too stunned to receive him. A weeping Yūgiri came out.

"How is she? I heard these awful reports and was unable to believe them, though I had of course known of her illness."

"Yes, she has been very ill for a very long time. This morning at dawn she stopped breathing. But it seems to have been a possession. I am told that although she has revived and everyone is enormously relieved the crisis has not yet passed. We are still very worried."

His eyes were red and swollen. It was his own unhappy love, perhaps, that made Kashiwagi look curiously at his friend, wondering why he should grieve so for a stepmother of whom he had not seen a great deal.

"She was dangerously ill," Genji sent out to the crowds. "This morning quite suddenly it appeared that she had breathed her last. The shock, I fear, was such that we were all quite deranged and given over to loud and unbecoming grief. I have not myself been as calm and in control of things as I ought to have been. I will thank you properly at another time for having been so good as to call."

It would not have been possible for Kashiwagi to visit Rokujō except in such a crisis. He was in acute discomfort even so—evidence, no doubt, of a very bad conscience.

Genji was more worried than before. He commissioned numberless rites of very great dignity and grandeur. The Rokujō lady had done terrible things while she lived,

5. Anonymous, *Kokinshū* 70: "If cherry blossoms waited at our command / nothing in this world would be their rival."
6. *Tales of Ise* 82: "The cherry blossom is dearest when it falls. / Nothing is meant in this world to last forever."

and what she had now become was utterly horrible. He even felt uncomfortable about his relations with her daughter, the Reizei empress. The conclusion was inescapable: women were creatures of sin. He wanted to be done with them. He could not doubt that it was in fact the Rokujō lady who had addressed him. His remarks about her had been in an intimate conversation with Murasaki overheard by no one. Disaster still seemed imminent. He must do what he could to forestall it. Murasaki had so earnestly pleaded to become a nun. He thought that tentative vows might give her strength and so he permitted a token tonsure and ordered that the five injunctions be administered. There were noble and moving phrases in the sermon describing the admirable power of the injunctions. Weeping and hovering over Murasaki quite without regard for appearances, Genji too invoked the holy name. There are crises that can unsettle the most superior of men. He wanted only to save her, to have her still beside him, whatever the difficulties and sacrifices. The sleepless nights had left him dazed and emaciated.

Murasaki was better, but still in pain through the Fourth Month. It was now the rainy Fifth Month, when the skies are their most capricious. Genji commissioned a reading of the Lotus Sutra in daily installments and other solemn services as well towards freeing the Rokujō lady of her sins. At Murasaki's bedside there were continuous readings by priests of good voice. From time to time the Rokujō lady would make dolorous utterances through the medium, but she refused all requests that she go away.

Murasaki was troubled with a shortness of breath and seemed even weaker as the warm weather came on. Genji was in such a state of distraction that Murasaki, ill though she was, sought to comfort him. She would have no regrets if she were to die, but she did not want it to seem that she did not care. She forced herself to take broth and a little food and from the Sixth Month she was able to sit up. Genji was delighted but still very worried. He stayed with her at Nijō.

The Third Princess had been unwell since that shocking visitation. There were no specific complaints or striking symptoms. She felt vaguely indisposed and that was all. She had eaten very little for some weeks and was pale and thin. Unable to contain himself, Kashiwagi would sometimes come for visits as fleeting as dreams. She did not welcome them. She was so much in awe of Genji that to rank the younger man beside him seemed almost blasphemous. Kashiwagi was an amiable and personable young man, and people who were no more than friends were quite right to think him superior; but she had known the incomparable Genji since she was a child and Kashiwagi scarcely seemed worth a glance. She thought herself very badly treated indeed that he should be the one to make her unhappy. Her nurse and a few others knew the nature of her indisposition and grumbled that Genji's visits were so extremely infrequent. He did finally come to inquire after her.

It was very warm. Murasaki had had her hair washed and otherwise sought renewal. Since she was in bed with her hair spread about her, it was not quick to dry. It was smooth and without a suggestion of a tangle to the farthest ends. Her skin was lovely, so white that it almost seemed iridescent, as if a light were shining through. She was very beautiful and as fragile as the shell of a locust.

The Nijō mansion had been neglected and was somewhat run-down, and compared to the Rokujō mansion it seemed very cramped and narrow. Taking advantage of a few days when she was somewhat more herself, Genji sent gardeners to clear the brook and restore the flower beds, and the suddenly renewed expanse before her made Murasaki marvel that she should be witness to such things. The lake was very cool, a carpet of lotuses. The dew on the green of the pads was like a scattering of jewels.

"Just look, will you," said Genji. "As if it had a monopoly on coolness. I cannot tell you how pleased I am that you have improved so." She was sitting up and her pleasure in the scene was quite open. There were tears in his eyes. "I was almost afraid at times that I too might be dying."

She was near tears herself.

> "It is a life in which we cannot be sure of lasting
> as long as the dew upon the lotus."

And he replied:

> "To be as close as the drops of dew on the lotus
> must be our promise in this world and the next."

Though he felt no eagerness to visit Rokujō, it had been some time since he had learned of the Third Princess's indisposition. Her brother and father would probably have heard of it too. They would think his inability to leave Murasaki rather odd and his failure to take advantage of a break in the rains even odder.

The princess looked away and did not answer his questions. Interpreting her silence as resentment at his long absence, he set about reasoning with her.

He called some of her older women and made detailed inquiries about her health.

"She is in an interesting condition, as they say."

"Really, now! And at this late date! I couldn't be more surprised."

It was his general want of success in fathering children that made the news so surprising. Ladies he had been with for a very long while had remained childless. He thought her sweet and pathetic and did not pursue the matter. Since it had taken him so long to collect himself for the visit, he could not go back to Nijō immediately. He stayed with her for several days. Murasaki was always on his mind, however, and he wrote her letter after letter.

"He certainly has thought of a great deal to say in a very short time," grumbled a woman who did not know that the lady was the more culpable party. "It does not seem like a marriage with the firmest sort of foundations."

Kojijū was frantic with worry.

Hearing that Genji was at Rokujō, Kashiwagi was a victim of a jealousy that might have seemed out of place. He wrote a long letter to the Princess describing his sorrows. Kojijū took advantage of a moment when Genji was in another part of the house to show her the letter.

"Take it away. It makes me feel worse." She lay down and refused to look at it.

"But do just glance for a minute at the beginning here." Kojijū unfolded the letter. "It is very sad."

Someone was coming. She pulled the princess's curtains closed and went off.

It was Genji. In utter confusion, the princess had time only to push it under the edge of a quilt.

He would be going back to Rokujō that evening, said Genji. "You do not seem so very ill. The lady in the other house is very ill indeed and I would not want her to think I have deserted her. You are not to pay any attention to what they might be saying about me. You will presently see the truth."

So cheerful and even frolicsome at other times, she was subdued and refused to look at him. It must be that she thought he did not love her. He lay down beside her and as they talked it was evening. He was awakened from a nap by a clamor of evening cicadas.

"It will soon be dark," he said, getting up to change clothes.

"Can you not stay at least until you have the moon to guide you?"[7]

She seemed so very young. He thought her charming. At least until then—it was a very small request.

> "The voice of the evening cicada says you must leave.
> 'Be moist with evening dews,' you say to my sleeves?"

Something of the cheerful innocence of old seemed to come back. He sighed and knelt down beside her.

> "How do you think it sounds in yonder village,
> the cicada that summons me there and summons me here?"

He was indeed pulled in two directions. Finally deciding that it would be cruel to leave, he stayed the night. Murasaki continued to be very much on his mind. He went to bed after a light supper.

He was up early, thinking to be on his way while it was still cool.

"I left my fan somewhere. This one is not much good." He searched through her sitting room, where he had had his nap the day before.

He saw a corner of pale-green tissue paper at the edge of a slightly disarranged quilt. Casually he took it up. It was a note in a man's hand. Delicately perfumed, it somehow had the look of a rather significant document. There were two sheets of paper covered with very small writing. The hand was without question Kashiwagi's.

The woman who opened the mirror for him paid little attention. It would of course be a letter he had every right to see. But Kojijū noted with horror that it was the same color as Kashiwagi's of the day before. She quite forgot about breakfast. It could not be. Nothing so awful could have been permitted to happen. Her lady absolutely must have hidden it.

The princess was still sleeping soundly. What a child she was, thought Genji, not without a certain contempt. Supposing someone else had found the letter. That was the thing: the heedlessness that had troubled him all along.

He had left and the other women were some distance away. "And what did you do with the young gentleman's letter?" asked Kojijū. "His Lordship was reading a letter that was very much the same color."

The princess collapsed in helpless weeping.

Kojijū was sorry for her, of course, but shocked and angry too. "Really, my lady— where did you put it? There were others around and I went off because I did not want him to think we were conspiring. That was how I felt. And you had time before he came in. Surely you hid it?"

"He came in on me while I was reading it. I didn't have time. I slipped it under something and forgot about it."

Speechless, Kojijū went to look for the letter. It was of course nowhere to be found.

"How perfectly, impossibly awful. The young gentleman was terrified of His Lordship, terrified that the smallest word might reach him. And now this has happened, and in no time at all. You are such a child, my lady. You let him see you, and he could not forget you however many years went by, and came begging to me. But that we should lose control of things so completely—it just did not seem possible. Nothing could be worse for either of you."

---

7. Oyakeme of Buzen, *Manyōshū* 709, with variations in other anthologies: "Dark the way and dangerous. / Can you not stay at least until you have the moon to guide you?"

She did not mince words. The princess was too good-natured and still too much of a child to argue back. Her tears flowed on.

She quite lost her appetite. Her women thought Genji cruel and unfeeling. "She is so extremely unwell, and he ignores her. He gives all his attention to a lady who has quite recovered."

Genji was still puzzled. He read the letter over and over again. He tested the hypothesis that one of her women had deliberately set about imitating Kashiwagi's hand. But it would not do. The idiosyncrasies were all too clearly Kashiwagi's. He had to admire the style, the fluency and clear detail with which Kashiwagi had described the fortuitous consummation of all his hopes, and all his sufferings since. But Genji had felt contemptuous of the princess and he must feel contemptuous of her young friend too. A man simply did not set these matters down so clearly in writing. Kashiwagi was a man of discernment and some eminence, and he had written a letter that could easily embarrass a lady. Genji himself had in his younger years never forgotten that letters have a way of going astray. His own letters had always been laconic and evasive even when he had longed to make them otherwise. Caution had not always been easy.

And how was he to behave towards the princess? He understood rather better the reasons for her condition. He had come upon the truth himself, without the aid of informers. Was there to be no change in his manner? He would have preferred that there be none but feared that things could not be the same again. Even in affairs which he had not from the outset taken seriously, the smallest evidence that the lady might be interested in someone else had always been enough to kill his own interest; and here he had more, a good deal more. What an impertinent trifler the young man was! It was not unknown for a young man to seduce even one of His Majesty's own ladies, but this seemed different. A young man and lady might in the course of their duties in the royal service find themselves favorably disposed towards each other and do what they ought not to have done. Such things did happen. Royal ladies were, after all, human. Some of them were not perhaps as sober and careful as they might be and they made mistakes. The man would remain in the court service and unless there was a proper scandal the mistake might go undetected. But this—Genji snapped his fingers in irritation. He had paid more attention to the princess than the lady he really loved, the truly priceless treasure, and she had responded by choosing a man like Kashiwagi!

He thought that there could be no precedent for it. Life had its frustrations for His Majesty's ladies when they obediently did their duty. There might come words of endearment from an honest man and there might be times when silence seemed impossible, and in a lady's answers would be the start of a love affair. One did not condone her behavior but one could understand it. But Genji thought himself neither fatuous nor conceited in wondering how the Third Princess could possibly have divided her affections between him and a man like Kashiwagi.

Well, it was all very distasteful. But he would say nothing. He wondered if his own father had long ago known what was happening and said nothing. He could remember his own terror very well, and the memory told him that he was hardly the one to reprove others who strayed from the narrow path.

Despite his determined silence, Murasaki knew that something was wrong. She herself had quite recovered, and she feared that he was feeling guilty about the Third Princess.

"I really am very much better. They tell me that Her Highness is not well. You should have stayed with her a little longer."

58

"Her Highness—it is true that she is indisposed, but I cannot see that there is a great deal wrong with her. Messenger after messenger has come from court. I gather that there was one just today from her father. Her brother worries about her because her father worries about her, and I must worry about both of them."

"I would worry less about them than about the princess herself if I thought she was unhappy. She may not say very much, but I hate to think of all those women giving her ideas."

Genji smiled and shrugged his shoulders. "You are the important one and you have no troublesome relatives, and you think of all these things. I think about her important brother and you think about her women. I fear I am not a very sensitive man." But of her suggestion that he return to Rokujō he said only: "There will be time when you are well enough to go with me."

"I would like to stay here just a little while longer. Do please go ahead and make her happy. I won't be long."

And so the days went by. The princess was of course in no position to charge him with neglect. She lived in dread lest her father get some word of what had happened.

Letter after passionate letter came from Kashiwagi. Finally, pushed too far, Kojijū told him everything. He was horrified. When had it happened? It had been as if the skies were watching him, so fearful had he been that something in the air might arouse Genji's suspicions. And now Genji had irrefutable evidence. It was a time of still, warm weather even at night and in the morning, but he felt as if a cold wind were cutting through him. Genji had singled him out for special favors and made him a friend and adviser, and for all this Kashiwagi had been most grateful. How could he now face Genji—who must think him an intolerable upstart and interloper! Yet if he were to avoid Rokujō completely people would notice and think it odd, and Genji would of course have stronger evidence than before. Sick with worry, Kashiwagi stopped going to court. It was not likely that he would face specific punishment, but he feared that he had ruined his life. Things could not be worse. He hated himself for what he had let happen.

[*Tormented by guilt, and fearful of Genji's displeasure, Kashiwagi falls seriously ill.*]

from *Chapter 36. The Oak Tree*

The New Year came and Kashiwagi's condition had not improved. He knew how troubled his parents were and he knew that suicide was no solution, for he would be guilty of the grievous sin of having left them behind. He had no wish to live on. Since his very early years he had had high standards and ambitions and had striven in private matters and public to outdo his rivals by even a little. His wishes had once or twice been thwarted, however, and he had so lost confidence in himself that the world had come to seem unrelieved gloom. A longing to prepare for the next world had succeeded his ambitions, but the opposition of his parents had kept him from following the mendicant way through the mountains and over the moors. He had delayed, and time had gone by. Then had come events, and for them he had only himself to blame, which had made it impossible for him to show his face in public. He did not blame the gods. His own deeds were working themselves out. A man does not have the thousand years of the pine, and he wanted to go now, while there were still those who might mourn for him a little, and perhaps even a sigh from her would be the reward for his burning passion. To die now and perhaps win the forgiveness of the man who must feel so aggrieved would be far preferable to living on and bringing sorrow and dishonor upon the lady and upon himself. In his last moments everything must disappear.

Perhaps, because he had no other sins to atone for, a part of the affection with which Genji had once honored him might return.

The same thoughts, over and over, ran uselessly through his mind. And why, he asked himself in growing despair, had he so deprived himself of alternatives? His pillow threatened to float away on the river of his woes.

He took advantage of a slight turn for the better, when his parents and the others had withdrawn from his bedside, to get off a letter to the Third Princess.

"You may have heard that I am near death. It is natural that you should not care very much, and yet I am sad." His hand was so uncertain that he gave up any thought of saying all that he would have wished to say.

> "My thoughts of you: will they stay when I am gone
> like smoke that lingers over the funeral pyre?

One word of pity will quiet the turmoil and light the dark road I am taking by my own choice."

Unchastened, he wrote to Kojijū of his sufferings, at considerable length. He longed, he said, to see her lady one last time. She had from childhood been close to his house, in which she had near relatives. Although she had strongly disapproved of his designs upon a royal princess who should have been far beyond his reach, she was extremely sorry for him in what might be his last illness.

"Do answer him, please, my lady," she said, in tears. "You must, just this once. It may be your last chance."

"I am sorry for him, in a general sort of way. I am sorry for myself too. Any one of us could be dead tomorrow. But what happened was too awful. I cannot bear to think of it. I could not possibly write to him."

She was not by nature a very careful sort of lady, but the great man to whom she was married had terrorized her with hints, always guarded, that he was displeased with her.

Kojijū insisted and pushed an inkstone towards her, and finally, very hesitantly, she set down an answer which Kojijū delivered under cover of evening.

Tō no Chūjō had sent to Mount Katsuragi for an ascetic famous as a worker of cures, and the spells and incantations in which he immersed himself might almost have seemed overdone. Other holy men were recommended and Tō no Chūjō's sons would go off to seek in mountain recesses men scarcely known in the city. Mendicants quite devoid of grace came crowding into the house. The symptoms did not point to any specific illness, but Kashiwagi would sometimes weep in great, racking sobs. The soothsayers were agreed that a jealous woman had taken possession of him. They might possibly be right, thought Tō no Chūjō. But whoever she was she refused to withdraw, and so it was that the search for healers reached into these obscure corners. The ascetic from Katsuragi, an imposing man with cold, forbidding eyes, intoned mystic spells in a somewhat threatening voice.

"I cannot stand a moment more of it," said Kashiwagi. "I must have sinned grievously. These voices terrify me and seem to bring death even nearer."

Slipping from bed, he instructed the women to tell his father that he was asleep and went to talk with Kojijū. Tō no Chūjō and the ascetic were conferring in subdued tones. Tō no Chūjō was robust and youthful for his years and in ordinary times much given to laughter. He told the holy man how it had all begun and how a respite always seemed to be followed by a relapse.

"Do please make her go away, whoever she might be," he said entreatingly.

A hollow shell of his old self, Kashiwagi was meanwhile addressing Kojijū in a faltering voice sometimes interrupted by a suggestion of a laugh.

"Listen to them. They seem to have no notion that I might be ill because I misbehaved. If, as these wise men say, some angry lady has taken possession of me, then I would expect her presence to make me hate myself a little less. I can say that others have done much the same thing, made mistakes in their longing for ladies beyond their reach, and ruined their prospects. I can tell myself all this, but the torment goes on. I cannot face the world knowing that he knows. His radiance dazzles and blinds me. I would not have thought the misdeed so appalling, but since the evening when he set upon me I have so lost control of myself that it has been as if my soul were wandering loose. If it is still around the house somewhere, please lay a trap for it."[1]

She told him of the Third Princess, lost in sad thoughts and afraid of prying eyes. He could almost see the forlorn little figure. Did unhappy spirits indeed go wandering forth disembodied?

"I shall say no more of your lady. It has all passed as if it had never happened at all. Yet I would be very sorry indeed if it were to stand in the way of her salvation. I have only one wish left, to know that the consequences of the sad affair have been disposed of safely. I have my own interpretation of the dream I had that night and have had very great trouble keeping it to myself."

Kojijū was frightened at the inhuman tenacity which these thoughts suggested. Yet she had to feel sorry for him. She was weeping bitterly.

He sent for a lamp and read the princess's note. Though fragile and uncertain, the hand was interesting. "Your letter made me very sad, but I cannot see you. I can only think of you. You speak of the smoke that lingers on, and yet

> I wish to go with you, that we may see
> whose smoldering thoughts last longer, yours or mine."

That was all, but he was grateful for it.

"The smoke—it will follow me from this world. What a useless, insubstantial affair it was!"

Weeping uncontrollably, he set about a reply. There were many pauses and the words were fragmentary and disconnected and the hand like the tracks of a strange bird.

> "As smoke I shall rise uncertainly to the heavens,
> and yet remain where my thoughts will yet remain.

Look well, I pray you, into the evening sky. Be happy, let no one reprove you; and, though it will do no good, have an occasional thought for me."

Suddenly worse again, he made his way tearfully back to his room. "Enough. Go while it is still early, please, and tell her of my last moments. I would not want anyone who already thinks it odd to think it even odder. What have I brought from other lives, I wonder, to make me so unhappy?"

Usually he kept her long after their business was finished, but today he dismissed her briefly. She was very sorry for him and did not want to go.

His nurse, who was her aunt, told Kojijū of his illness, weeping all the while.

Tō no Chūjō was in great alarm. "He had seemed better these last few days. Why the sudden change?"

---

1. *Tales of Ise* 110: "In longing my soul has ventured forth alone. / If you see it late in the night, please seek to trap it."

"I cannot see why you are surprised," replied his son. "I am dying. That is all."

That evening the Third Princess was taken with severe pains.

Guessing that they were birth pangs, her women sent for Genji in great excitement. He came immediately. How vast and unconditional his joy would be, he thought, were it not for his doubts about the child. But no one must be allowed to suspect their existence. He summoned ascetics and put them to continuous spells and incantations, and he summoned all the monks who had made names for themselves as healers. The Rokujō mansion echoed with mystic rites. The princess was in great pain through the night and at sunrise was delivered of a child. It was a boy. Most unfortunate, thought Genji. It would not be easy to guard the secret if the resemblance to the father was strong. There were devices for keeping girls in disguise and of course girls did not have to appear in public as did boys. But there was the other side of the matter: given these nagging doubts from the outset, a boy did not require the attention which must go into rearing a girl.

But how very strange it all was! Retribution had no doubt come for the deed which had terrified him then and which he was sure would go on terrifying him to the end. Since it had come, all unexpectedly, in this world, perhaps the punishment would be lighter in the next.

Unaware of these thoughts, the women quite lost themselves in ministering to the child. Because it was born of such a mother in Genji's late years, it must surely have the whole of his affection.

[*Kashiwagi dies, and after the Third Princess gives birth to his son, Kaoru, she immediately takes Buddhist vows despite Genji's protests. Kaoru, a beautiful little boy, is thought by the world to be Genji's son, and is raised in the Rokujō mansion.*]

from *Chapter 40. The Rites*

[*Three years have passed. Murasaki has continued to be in uncertain health since her great illness, and again seeks permission from Genji to take Buddhist vows, but Genji stubbornly refuses. The Akashi daughter, who was raised by Murasaki and has since been named empress, visits her sickbed.*]

Murasaki had always found the heat very trying. This summer she was near prostration. Though there were no marked symptoms and though there was none of the unsightliness that usually goes with emaciation, she was progressively weaker. Her women saw the world grow dark before their eyes as they contemplated the future.

Distressed at reports that there was no improvement, the empress visited Nijō. She was given rooms in the east wing and Murasaki waited to receive her in the main hall. Though there was nothing unusual about the greetings, they reminded Murasaki, as indeed did everything, that the empress's little children would grow up without her. The attendants announced themselves one by one, some of them very high courtiers. A familiar voice, thought Murasaki, and another. She had not seen the empress in a very long while and hung on the conversation with fond and eager attention.

Genji looked in upon them briefly. "You find me disconsolate this evening," he said to the empress, "a bird turned away from its nest. But I shall not bore you with my complaints." He withdrew. He was delighted to see Murasaki out of bed, but feared that the pleasure must be a fleeting one.

"We are so far apart that I would not dream of troubling you to visit me, and I fear that it will not be easy for me to visit you."[1]

After a time the Akashi lady came in. The two ladies addressed each other affectionately, though Murasaki left a great deal unsaid. She did not want to be one of those who eloquently prepare the world to struggle along without them. She did remark briefly and quietly upon the evanescence of things, and her wistful manner said more than her words.

Genji's royal grandchildren were brought in.

"I spend so much time imagining futures for you, my dears. Do you suppose that I do after all hate to go?"

Still very beautiful, she was in tears. The empress would have liked to change the subject, but could not think how.

"May I ask a favor?" said Murasaki, very casually, as if she hesitated to bring the matter up at all. "There are numbers of people who have been with me for a very long while, and some of them have no home but this. Might I ask you to see that they are taken care of?" And she gave the names.

Having commissioned a reading from the holy writ, the empress returned to her rooms.

Little Niou, the prettiest of them all, seemed to be everywhere at once. Choosing a moment when she was feeling better and there was no one else with her, she seated him before her.

"I may have to go away. Will you remember me?"

"But I don't want you to go away." He gazed up at her, and presently he was rubbing at his eyes, so charming that she was smiling through her tears. "I like my granny,[2] better than Father and Mother. I don't want you to go away."

"This must be your own house when you grow up. I want the rose plum and the cherries over there to be yours. You must take care of them and say nice things about them, and sometimes when you think of it you might put flowers on the altar."

He nodded and gazed up at her, and then abruptly, about to burst into tears, he got up and ran out. It was Niou and the First Princess whom Murasaki most hated to leave. They had been her special charges, and she would not live to see them grow up.

The cool of autumn, so slow to come, was at last here. Though far from well, she felt somewhat better. The winds were still gentle, but it was a time of heavy dews all the same. She would have liked the empress to stay with her just a little while longer but did not want to say so. Messengers had come from the emperor, all of them summoning the empress back to court, and she did not want to put the empress in a difficult position. She was no longer able to leave her room, however much she might want to respect the amenities, and so the empress called on her. Apologetic and at the same time very grateful, for she knew that this might be their last meeting, she had made careful preparations for the visit.

Though very thin, she was more beautiful than ever—one would not have thought it possible. The fresh, vivacious beauty of other years had asked to be likened to the flowers of this earth, but now there was a delicate serenity that seemed to go beyond such present similes. For the empress the slight figure before her, the very serenity bespeaking evanescence, was utter sadness.

---

1. The speaker may be either Murasaki or the empress.
2. *Haha,* the most common word for "mother." Some commentators argue for *baba,* "old woman" or "grandmother."

Wishing to look at her flowers in the evening light, Murasaki pulled herself from bed with the aid of an armrest.

Genji came in. "Isn't this splendid? I imagine Her Majesty's visit has done wonders for you."

How pleased he was at what was in fact no improvement at all—and how desolate he must soon be!

"So briefly rests the dew upon the hagi.
Even now it scatters in the wind."

It would have been a sad evening in any event, and the plight of the dew even now being shaken from the tossing branches, thought Genji, must seem to the sick lady very much like her own.

"In the haste we make to leave this world of dew,
may there be no time between the first and last."

He did not try to hide his tears.

And this was the empress's poem:

"A world of dew before the autumn winds.
Not only theirs, these fragile leaves of grass."

Gazing at the two of them, each somehow more beautiful than the other, Genji wished that he might have them a thousand years just as they were; but of course time runs against these wishes. That is the great, sad truth.

"Would you please leave me?" said Murasaki. "I am feeling rather worse. I do not like to know that I am being rude and find myself unable to apologize." She spoke with very great difficulty.

The empress took her hand and gazed into her face. Yes, it was indeed like the dew about to vanish away. Scores of messengers were sent to commission new services. Once before it had seemed that she was dying, and Genji hoped that whatever evil spirit it was might be persuaded to loosen its grip once more. All through the night he did everything that could possibly be done, but in vain. Just as light was coming she faded away. Some kind power above, he thought, had kept the empress with her through the night. He might tell himself, as might all the others who had been with her, that these things have always happened and will continue to happen, but there are times when the natural order of things is unacceptable. The numbing grief made the world itself seem like a twilight dream. The women tried in vain to bring their wandering thoughts together. Fearing for his father, more distraught even than they, Yūgiri had come to him.

"It seems to be the end," said Genji, summoning him to Murasaki's curtains. "To be denied one's last wish is a cruel thing. I suppose that their reverences will have finished their prayers and left us, but someone qualified to administer vows must still be here. We did not do a great deal for her in this life, but perhaps the Great Buddha can be persuaded to turn a little light on the way she must take into the next. Tell them, please, that I want someone to give the tonsure. There is still someone with us who can do it, surely?"

He spoke with studied calm, but his face was drawn and he was weeping.

"But these evil spirits play very cruel tricks," replied Yūgiri, only slightly less benumbed than his father. "Don't you suppose the same thing has happened all over again? Your suggestion is of course quite proper. We are told that even a day and a night of the holy life brings untold blessings. But suppose this really is the end—can we hope that anything we do will throw so very much light on the way she must go? No, let us come to terms with the sorrow we have before us and try not to make it worse."

But he summoned several of the priests who had stayed on, wishing to be of service through the period of mourning, and asked them to do whatever could still be done.

He could congratulate himself on his filial conduct over the years, upon the fact that he had permitted himself no improper thoughts; but he had had one fleeting glimpse of her, and he had gone on hoping that he might one day be permitted another, even as brief, or that he might hear her voice, even faintly. The second hope had come to nothing, and the other—if he did not see her now he never would see her. He was in tears himself, and the room echoed with the laments of the women.

"Do please try to be a little quieter, just for a little while." He lifted the curtains as he spoke, making it seem that Genji had summoned him. In the dim morning twilight Genji had brought a lamp near Murasaki's dead face. He knew that Yūgiri was beside him, but somehow felt that to screen this beauty from his son's gaze would only add to the anguish.

"Exactly as she was," he whispered. "But as you see, it is all over."

He covered his face. Yūgiri too was weeping. He brushed the tears away and struggled to see through them as the sight of the dead face brought them flooding back again. Though her hair had been left untended through her illness, it was smooth and lustrous and not a strand was out of place. In the bright lamplight the skin was a purer, more radiant white than the living lady, seated at her mirror, could have made it. Her beauty, as if in untroubled sleep, emptied words like "peerless" of all content. He almost wished that the spirit which seemed about to desert him might be given custody of the unique loveliness before him.

Since Murasaki's women were none of them up to such practical matters, Genji forced himself to think about the funeral arrangements. He had known many sorrows, but none quite so near at hand, demanding that he and no one else do what must be done. He had known nothing like it, and he was sure that there would be nothing like it in what remained of his life.

from *Chapter 41. The Wizard*

Already at the beginning of the Eighth Month the autumn winds were lonely. Genji was busy with preparations for the memorial services. How swiftly the months had gone by! Everyone went through fasting and penance and the Paradise Mandala was dedicated. Chūjō[1] as usual brought holy water for Genji's vesper devotions. He took up her fan, on which she had written a poem:

> "This day, we are told, announces an end to mourning.
> How can it be, when there is no end to tears?"

He wrote beside it:

> "The days are numbered for him who yet must mourn.
> And are they numbered, the tears that yet remain?"

---

1. One of Murasaki's women.

Early in the Ninth Month came the chrysanthemum festival. As always, the festive bouquets were wrapped in cotton to catch the magic dew.

> "On other mornings we took the elixir together.
> This morning lonely sleeves are wet with dew."

The Tenth Month was as always a time of gloomy winter showers. Looking up into the evening sky, he whispered to himself: "The rains are as the rains of other years." He envied the wild geese overhead, for they were going home.

> "O wizard flying off through boundless heavens,
> find her whom I see not even in my dreams."[2]

The days and months went by, and he remained inconsolable.

Presently the world was buzzing with preparations for the harvest festival and the Gosechi dances. Yūgiri brought two of his little boys, already in court service, to see their grandfather. They were very nearly the same age, and very pretty indeed. With them were several of their uncles, spruce and elegant in blue Gosechi prints, a very grand escort indeed for two little boys. At the sight of them all, so caught up in the festive gaiety, Genji thought of memorable occurrences on ancient festival days.

> "Our lads go off to have their Day of Light.[3]
> For me it is as if there were no sun."

And so he had made his way through the year, and the time had come to leave the world behind. He gave his attendants, after their several ranks, gifts to remember him by. He tried to avoid grand farewells, but they knew what was happening, and the end of the year was a time of infinite sadness. Among his papers were letters which he had put aside over the years but which he would not wish others to see. Now, as he got his affairs in order, he would come upon them and burn them. There was a bundle of letters from Murasaki among those he had received at Suma from his various ladies. Though a great many years had passed, the ink was as fresh as if it had been set down yesterday. They seemed meant to last a thousand years. But they had been for him, and he was finished with them. He asked two or three women who were among his closest confidantes to see to destroying them. The handwriting of the dead always has the power to move us, and these were not ordinary letters. He was blinded by the tears that fell to mingle with the ink until presently he was unable to make out what was written.

> "I seek to follow the tracks of a lady now gone
> to another world. Alas, I lose my way."

Not wanting to display his weakness, he pushed them aside.

The women were permitted glimpses of this and that letter, and the little they saw was enough to bring the old grief back anew. Murasaki's sorrow at being those few miles from him now seemed to remove all bounds to their own sorrow. Seeking to control a flow of tears that must seem hopelessly exaggerated, Genji glanced at one of the more affectionate notes and wrote in the margin:

2. In "The Song of Everlasting Sorrow" the emperor sends a wizard in search of the dead Yang Kuei-fei. In Chapter 1, Genji's grieving father is put in mind of the same passage. The word *maboroshi*, "wizard," occurs in the tale only these two times.

3. Toyonoakari, the day following the harvest festival proper.

"I gather sea grasses no more, nor look upon them.
Now they are smoke, to join her in distant heavens."

And so he consigned them to flames.

In the Twelfth Month the clanging of croziers as the holy name was invoked was more moving than in other years, for Genji knew that he would not again be present at the ceremony. These prayers for longevity—he did not think that they would please the Blessed One. There had been a heavy fall of snow, which was now blowing into drifts. The repast in honor of the officiant was elaborate and Genji's gifts were even more lavish than usual. The holy man had often presided over services at court and at Rokujō. Genji was sorry to see that his hair was touched with gray. As always, there were numerous princes and high courtiers in the congregation. The plum trees, just coming into bloom, were lovely in the snow. There should have been music, but Genji feared that this year music would make him weep. Poems were read, in keeping with the time and place.

There was this poem as Genji offered a cup of wine to his guest of honor:

"Put blossoms in your caps today. Who knows
that there will still be life when spring comes round?"

This was the reply:

"I pray that these blossoms may last a thousand springs.
For me the years are as the deepening snowdrifts."

There were many others, but I neglected to set them down.

It was Genji's first appearance in public. He was handsomer than ever, indeed almost unbelievably handsome. For no very good reason, the holy man was in tears.

Genji was more and more despondent as the New Year approached.

Niou scampered about exorcising devils, that the New Year might begin auspiciously.

"It takes a lot of noise to get rid of them. Do you have any ideas?"

Everything about the scene, and especially the thought that he must say goodbye to the child, made Genji fear that he would soon be weeping again.

"I have not taken account of the days and months.
The end of the year—the end of a life as well?"

The festivities must be more joyous than ever, he said, and his gifts to all the princes and officials, high and low—or so one is told—quite shattered precedent.

THE QUR'AN (610 C.E.–632 C.E.)

The Qur'an, also known as *al-kitab* (the Book) or *Kitab Allah* (the Book of God) is the name of the Muslim scripture. It contains the divine text that was revealed in its fixed and finite form to the Prophet Muhammad through the archangel Gabriel, a celestial messenger serving as intermediary between God and Muhammad. It is the word of Allah revealed to his Prophet, Muhammad, over some twenty years (between 610 C.E.–632 C.E.), to transmit to the whole of humanity. Moses parted the Red Sea, Jesus had the ability to walk on water and resurrect the dead; the Qur'an was Muhammad's sole miracle. It has been approached as a linguistic miracle by Muslim scholars for centuries.

The earliest attested use of the word *qur'an* is in the Qur'an itself, where it occurs about seventy times; *al-kitab* ("the book") occurs 255 times, establishing self-reference as one of the book's textual strategies. The word *qur'an* comes from the Arabic root *qara'a*, "read," which is the first word of the first verse that was revealed to Muhammad. In the Qur'an itself, the most frequently used synonym for the Qur'an is *al-kitab*, which is also used to refer to the books revealed to Moses and to Jesus's disciples, thus establishing the genealogy of the Qur'an as the final version of previous divine revelations that were, according to the Qur'an, subjected to human interference. Thus the preservation of the accurate text of the Qur'an was of paramount importance if it was not to suffer the fate of previous revelations.

The Qur'an was preserved orally and in written form during the life of Muhammad. Upon revelation, each verse was committed to memory by several of his followers and written down by others known as the scribes of the revelation, the most famous of them being Zayd ibn Thabit, the Prophet's secretary. Before his death, Muhammad read the final version of the Qur'an in its entirety to his followers and secretaries. This was later preserved in written form during the time of his successor, Abu Bakr (r. 632–634) under the auspices of Thabit. Thus within two years of Muhammad's death a definitive text was written down, kept by Abu Bakr, then passed to his successor 'Umar (634–644). In the time of the third caliph, 'Uthman (644–656), several manuscripts were made on the basis of the first one ordered by Abu Bakr and distributed to conquered lands outside Arabia.

The verses of the Qur'an vary in length from a few letters to 128 words, and these are grouped in sections or chapters (suras), which vary in length from 3 to 286 verses. They are roughly arranged in decreasing order of length. The first sura, "The Opening," is liturgical in nature, as are the final short suras, a number of which have the form of incantations. The other suras are in many different forms and genres, which vary from the short oath to a lengthy narrative of several biblical and nonbiblical stories.

The Qur'an consists of 114 suras, eighty-five revealed in Mecca, and twenty-nine revealed in Medina. The early Meccan suras call for belief in one God and in social justice, transcendent truths, and the practice of personal and altruistic virtues. They are mainly short and their language is full of poetic imagery and eloquent appeals to the hearer to worship and embrace Islam as the final creed. The suras of the middle Meccan period are longer and more prosaic, though they still retain some poetic qualities, referring mainly to the manifestations of God in nature and his divine attributes, while the late Meccan suras are full of narrative stories and sermons. The Medinan suras tend to be more prescriptive and legislative, and they contain more narrative concerning the organization of the community and the lessons it should learn from the mistakes of the past. They were revealed after the creation of the first Islamic community in Medina and aimed to provide it with guidance and consolidate its identity and cohesion.

As will be seen in the selections included here, the Qur'an embraces many literary and linguistic forms, from the oath and prophetic utterance, to the imperative and didactic "say-passages," to dramatic and narrative forms. Many of the Qur'anic narratives retell traditional stories found in Near and Middle Eastern cultures, such as the story of creation. Others are derived from biblical or apocryphal Christian texts and oral tradition. The Qur'an relates the stories of the prophets or messengers of God from Noah to Jesus, including Abraham, Ishmael, David, Elijah, Jonah, Jacob, Joseph, Job, Moses, and Solomon. The stories of these biblical characters are retold with some variations and often major alterations. The story of Joseph (Sura 12) follows the biblical account rather closely, while that of Jesus differs in some essential details. It accepts the biblical story but denies an essential aspect of the Christian account, the resurrection of Jesus. In addition to all these biblical characters, the Qur'an has many nonbiblical ones, including several from Greek sources.

59

Narrative stories comprise a substantial part of the Qur'an, and many of them were augmented and elaborated in several commentaries and exegeses. As a text, the Qur'an relies on cross-referencing and it often relates a story in more than one chapter. It relates segments or kernels of a specific story in one sura, picks it up again in another to complement or enforce certain aspects of its narrative, then gives its final parts in a third sura. This serves many different functions—to sustain the reader's attention and interest in the story, or test our comprehension of its implications, or even enforce its significance in the text. The story of creation is a good example. In order to get the complete story and to understand its relations with other biblical variants, one has to gather its scattered segments from four or five suras, as in the opening selections given here. One finds a segment on the creation of earth in one sura, the nature of its oval shape in another, and the time of this creation and how to calculate it in our modern manner in a third sura.

This narrative strategy was elaborated and developed into a fine art centuries later in *The Thousand and One Nights,* in which one finds fascinating and artistic renderings of many Qur'anic stories, notably those of Solomon, of the Kings of ancient Persia, and of Alexander the Great, to mention but a few. The Qur'anic concern with mythic and fantastic narrative may have provided a further source of inspiration for *The Thousand and One Nights.* The most important link between the Qur'an and *The Thousand and One Nights* is the cultural one. The Qur'anic worldview and its whole system of values and beliefs inform the world of *The Thousand and One Nights* and structure its ethos. In addition the Qur'anic concept of destiny and preordained fate is essential to the understanding of narrative progression in Scheherazade's text. Without a clear understanding of the philosophical assumptions underlying this concept, one cannot fathom the constant interplay between the frame tale and the enframed stories of *The Thousand and One Nights.* What appears in this wonderful narrative text as mere chance should be understood as the vicissitudes of destiny that conceal a deeper wisdom. Such wisdom is often beyond the comprehension of mere mortals, and this is the source of its never-ending fascination.

The Qur'an has had an immense influence on later Arabic literature, and it is treasured for its own language as well. The beauty of its language is majestic, not seductively entrancing; it amazes rather than excites, and arouses pleasure through repose not movement. Its dialogic nature implies respect for the reader and emphasizes the text's rational dimension as well as its spiritual nature. It was and still remains the pinnacle of the Arabic word, the reservoir of its rhetorical, poetic, and stylistic devices.

PRONUNCIATIONS:

Iblīs: ee-BLEES
Qur'an: coo-RAHN
sura: SUE-rah

from The Qur'an[1]

from *Sura 41. Revelations Well Expounded*

IN THE NAME OF GOD, THE COMPASSIONATE, THE MERCIFUL

Revealed by the Compassionate, the Merciful: a Book of revelations well expounded, an Arabic Qur'an for men of knowledge.

---

1. Translated by N. J. Dawood. The first five selections (from Suras 41, 79, 15, 2, and 7) bring together some of the Qur'an's major passages on creation.

It proclaims good news and a warning: yet most men turn their backs and pay no heed. They say: "Our hearts are proof against the faith to which you call us. Our ears are stopped, and a thick veil stands between us. Do as you think fit, and so will we."

Say: "I am but a mortal like yourselves. It is revealed to me that your God is one God. Therefore take the straight path to Him and implore His forgiveness. Woe betide those who serve other gods besides Him; who give no alms and disbelieve in the life to come. As for those who have faith and do good works, an endless recompense awaits them."

Say: "Do you indeed disbelieve in Him who created the earth in two days? And do you make other gods His equals? The Lord of the Universe is He."

He set upon the earth mountains towering high above it. He pronounced His blessing upon it, and in four days provided it with sustenance for all alike. Then, turning to the sky, which was but a cloud of vapour, He said to it and to the earth: "Come forward both, willingly or perforce."

"We will come willingly," they answered. In two days He formed the sky into seven heavens, and to each heaven He assigned its task. We decked the lowest heaven with brilliant stars and guardian comets. Such is the design of the Mighty One, the All-knowing.

from *Sura 79. The Soul-Snatchers*

Are you harder to create than the heaven which He has built? He raised it high and fashioned it, giving darkness to its night and brightness to its day.

After that He spread the earth, and, drawing water from its depth, brought forth its pastures. He set down the mountains, for you and for your cattle to delight in.

from *Sura 15. The Rocky Tract*

It was We that revealed the Admonition, and shall Ourself preserve it. We have sent forth apostles before you to the older nations: but they scoffed at each apostle We sent them. Thus do We put doubt into the hearts of the guilty: they deny him, despite the example of the ancients.

If we opened for the unbelievers a gate in heaven and they ascended through it higher and higher, still they would say: "Our eyes were dazzled: truly, we must have been bewitched."

We have decked the heavens with constellations and made them lovely to behold. We have guarded them from every cursèd devil. Eavesdroppers are pursued by fiery comets.

We have spread out the earth and set upon it immovable mountains. We have planted it with every seasonable fruit, providing sustenance for yourselves and for those whom you do not provide for. We hold the store of every blessing and send it down in appropriate measure. We let loose the fertilizing winds and bring down water from the sky for you to drink; its stores are beyond your reach.

It is surely We who ordain life and death. We are the Heir of all things.

We know those who have gone before you, and know those who will come hereafter. It is your Lord who will gather them all before Him. He is wise and all-knowing.

We created man from dry clay, from black moulded loam, and before him Satan from smokeless fire. Your Lord said to the angels: "I am creating man from dry clay, from black moulded loam. When I have fashioned him and breathed of My spirit into him, kneel down and prostrate yourselves before him."

The angels, one and all, prostrated themselves, except Satan. He refused to prostrate himself as the others did.

"Satan," said God, "why do you not prostrate yourself?"

He replied: "I will not bow to a mortal whom You created of dry clay, of black moulded loam."

"Get you hence," said God, "you are accursed. The curse shall be on you till Judgement-day."

"Lord," said Satan, "reprieve me till the Day of Resurrection."

He answered: "You are reprieved till the Appointed Day."

"Lord," said Satan, "since You have thus seduced me, I will tempt mankind on earth: I will seduce them all, except those of them who are your faithful servants."

He replied: "This is My straight path. You shall have no power over My servants, only the sinners who follow you. They are all destined for Hell. It has seven gates, and through each gate they shall come in separate bands. But the righteous shall dwell among gardens and fountains; in peace and safety they shall enter them."

from *Sura 2. The Cow*

He created for you all that the earth contains; then, ascending to the sky, He fashioned it into seven heavens. He has knowledge of all things.

When your Lord said to the angels: "I am placing on the earth one that shall rule as My deputy," they replied: "Will You put there one that will do evil and shed blood, when we have for so long sung Your praises and sanctified Your name?"

He said: "I know what you know not."

He taught Adam the names of all things and then set them before the angels, saying: "Tell Me the names of these, if what you say be true."

"Glory be to You," they replied, "we have no knowledge except that which You have given us. You alone are all-knowing and wise."

Then said He: "Adam, tell them their names." And when Adam had named them, He said: "Did I not tell you that I know the secrets of the heavens and the earth, and know all that you reveal and all that you conceal?"

And when We said to the angels: "Prostrate yourselves before Adam," they all prostrated themselves except Satan, who in his pride refused and became an unbeliever.

We said: "Adam, dwell with your wife in Paradise and eat of its fruits to your hearts' content wherever you will. But never approach this tree or you shall both become transgressors."

But Satan lured them thence and brought about their banishment. "Get you down," We said, "and be enemies to each other. The earth will for a while provide your dwelling and your sustenance."

Then Adam received commandments from his Lord, and his Lord relented towards him. He is the Relenting One, the Merciful.

"Get you down hence, all," We said. "When My guidance is revealed to you, those that follow My guidance shall have nothing to fear or to regret; but those that deny and reject Our revelations shall be the inmates of the Fire, and there shall they abide for ever."

* * *

God: there is no god but Him, the Living, the Eternal One.[2] Neither slumber nor sleep overtakes Him. His is what the heavens and the earth contain. Who can intercede with Him except by His permission? He knows what is before and behind men. They can grasp only that part of His knowledge which He wills. His throne is as vast as the heavens and the earth, and the preservation of both does not weary Him. He is the Exalted, the Immense One.

from *Sura 7. The Heights*

IN THE NAME OF GOD, THE COMPASSIONATE, THE MERCIFUL

Alif lām mim sād.[3] This Book has been revealed to you—let not your heart be troubled about it—so that you may thereby give warning and admonish the faithful.

Observe that which is brought down to you from your Lord and follow no other masters besides Him. But you seldom take warning.

How many cities have We destroyed! In the night Our scourge fell upon them, or at midday, when they were drowsing.

And when Our scourge fell upon them, their only cry was: "We have indeed been wicked men."

We will surely question those to whom the messengers were sent, and We will question the messengers themselves. With knowledge We will recount to them what they have done, for We were never away from them.

On that day all shall be weighed with justice. Those whose good deeds weigh heavy in the scales shall triumph, but those whose deeds are light shall lose their souls, because they have denied Our revelations.

We have given you power in the land and provided you with a livelihood: yet you are seldom thankful.

We created you and gave you form. Then We said to the angels: "Prostrate yourselves before Adam." They all prostrated themselves except Satan, who refused to prostrate himself.

"Why did you not prostrate yourself when I commanded you?" He asked.

"I am nobler than he," he replied. "You created me from fire, but You created him from clay."

He said: "Get you down hence! This is no place for your contemptuous pride. Away with you! Humble shall you henceforth be."

He replied: "Reprieve me till the Day of Resurrection."

"You are reprieved," said He.

"Because You have led me into sin," he declared, "I will waylay Your servants as they walk on Your straight path, then spring upon them from the front and from the rear, from their right and from their left. Then You will find the greater part of them ungrateful."

"Begone!" He said. "A despicable outcast you shall henceforth be. As for those that follow you, I shall fill Hell with you all."

To Adam He said: "Dwell with your wife in Paradise, and eat of any fruit you please; but never approach this tree or you shall both become transgressors."

But Satan tempted them, so that he might reveal to them their shameful parts, which they had never seen before. He said: "Your Lord has forbidden you to approach

2. This paragraph is a prayer that is believed to have a magic, incantatory power.
3. Several suras begin with a set of Arabic letters, whose meaning is uncertain.

this tree only to prevent you from becoming angels or immortals." Then he swore to them that he would give them friendly counsel.

Thus did he cunningly seduce them. And when they had eaten of the tree, their shame became visible to them, and they both covered themselves with the leaves of the garden.

Their Lord called out to them, saying: "Did I not forbid you to approach that tree, and did I not say to you that Satan was your inveterate foe?"

They replied: "Lord, we have wronged our souls. Pardon us and have mercy on us, or we shall surely be among the lost."

He said: "Get you down hence, and may your descendants be enemies to each other. The earth will for a while provide your dwelling and your comforts. There you shall live and there shall you die, and thence shall you be raised to life."

Children of Adam! We have given you clothes to cover your shameful parts, and garments pleasing to the eye; but the finest of all these is the robe of piety.

That is one of God's revelations. Perchance they will take heed.

Children of Adam! Let not Satan tempt you, as he seduced your parents out of Paradise. He stripped them of their garments to reveal to them their shameful parts. He and his minions see you whence you cannot see them. We have made the devils guardians over the unbelievers.

Sura 1. The Opening[4]

IN THE NAME OF GOD THE COMPASSIONATE THE MERCIFUL

Praise be to God, Lord of the Universe,
The Compassionate, the Merciful,
Sovereign of the Day of Judgement!
You alone we worship, and to You alone we turn for help.
Guide us to the straight path,
The path of those whom You have favoured,
Not of those who have incurred Your wrath,
Nor of those who have gone astray.

from Sura 4. Women[5]

IN THE NAME OF GOD, THE COMPASSIONATE, THE MERCIFUL

You people! Have fear of your Lord, who created you from a single soul. From that soul He created its spouse, and through them He bestrewed the earth with countless men and women.

Fear God, in whose name you plead with one another, and honour the mothers who bore you. God is ever watching you.

Give orphans the property which belongs to them. Do not exchange their valuables for worthless things or cheat them of their possessions; for this would surely be a grievous sin. If you fear that you cannot treat orphans[6] with fairness, then you may

---

4. This sura is read in every prayer, and often several times during each of the five prayers of the day.

5. This sura pays detailed attention to women and to family issues. It is exceptional for its era in giving women a definite share in their family's inheritance.

6. Orphan girls.

marry other women who seem good to you: two, three, or four of them. But if you fear that you cannot maintain equality among them, marry one only or any slave-girls you may own. This will make it easier for you to avoid injustice.

Give women their dowry as a free gift; but if they choose to make over to you a part of it, you may regard it as lawfully yours.

Do not give the feeble-minded the property with which God has entrusted you for their support; but maintain and clothe them with its proceeds, and speak kind words to them.

Put orphans to the test until they reach a marriageable age. If you find them capable of sound judgement, hand over to them their property, and do not deprive them of it by squandering it before they come of age.

Let not the rich guardian touch the property of his orphan ward; and let him who is poor use no more than a fair portion of it for his own advantage.

When you hand over to them their property, call in some witnesses; sufficient is God's accounting of your actions.

Men shall have a share in what their parents and kinsmen leave; and women shall have a share in what their parents and kinsmen leave: whether it be little or much, they shall be legally entitled to a share.

If relatives, orphans, or needy men are present at the division of an inheritance, give them, too, a share of it, and speak kind words to them.

Let those who are solicitous about the welfare of their young children after their own death take care not to wrong orphans. Let them fear God and speak for justice.

Those that devour the property of orphans unjustly, swallow fire into their bellies; they shall burn in a mighty conflagration.

God has thus enjoined you concerning your children:

A male shall inherit twice as much as a female. If there be more than two girls, they shall have two-thirds of the inheritance; but if there be one only, she shall inherit the half. Parents shall inherit a sixth each, if the deceased have a child; but if he leave no child and his parents be his heirs, his mother shall have a third. If he have brothers, his mother shall have a sixth after payment of any legacy he may have bequeathed or any debt he may have owed.

You may wonder whether your parents or your children are more beneficial to you. But this is the law of God; surely God is all-knowing and wise.

You shall inherit the half of your wives' estate if they die childless. If they leave children, a quarter of their estate shall be yours after payment of any legacy they may have bequeathed or any debt they may have owed.

Your wives shall inherit one quarter of your estate if you die childless. If you leave children, they shall inherit one-eighth, after payment of any legacy you may have bequeathed or any debt you may have owed.

If a man or a woman leave neither children nor parents and have a brother or a sister, they shall each inherit one-sixth. If there be more, they shall equally share the third of the estate, after payment of any legacy he may have bequeathed or any debt he may have owed, without prejudice to the rights of the heirs. That is a commandment from God. God is all-knowing, and gracious.

Such are the bounds set by God. He that obeys God and His apostle shall dwell for ever in gardens watered by running streams. That is the supreme triumph. But he that defies God and His apostle and transgresses His bounds, shall be cast into a Fire wherein he will abide for ever. Shameful punishment awaits him.

If any of your women commit a lewd act, call in four witnesses from among yourselves against them; if they testify to their guilt confine them to their houses till death overtakes them or till God finds another way for them.

If two men among you commit a lewd act, punish them both. If they repent and mend their ways, let them be. God is forgiving and merciful.

God forgives those who commit evil in ignorance and then quickly turn to Him in penitence. God will pardon them. God is all-knowing and wise. But He will not forgive those who do evil and, when death comes to them, say: "Now we repent!" Nor those who die unbelievers: for them We have prepared a woeful scourge.

Believers, it is unlawful for you to inherit the women of your deceased kinsmen against their will, or to bar them from re-marrying, in order that you may force them to give up a part of what you have given them, unless they be guilty of a proven lewd act. Treat them with kindness; for even if you dislike them, it may well be that you dislike a thing which God has meant for your own abundant good.

If you wish to replace one wife with another, do not take from her the dowry you have given her even if it be a talent of gold. That would be improper and grossly unjust; for how can you take it back when you have lain with each other and entered into a firm contract?

You shall not marry the women whom your fathers married: all previous such marriages excepted. That was an evil practice, indecent and abominable.

Forbidden to you are your mothers, your daughters, your sisters, your paternal and maternal aunts, the daughters of your brothers and sisters, your foster-mothers, your foster-sisters, the mothers of your wives, your step-daughters who are in your charge, born of the wives with whom you have lain (it is no offence for you to marry your step-daughters if you have not consummated your marriage with their mothers), and the wives of your own begotten sons. You are also forbidden to take in marriage two sisters at one and the same time: all previous such marriages excepted. Surely God is forgiving and merciful. Also married women, except those whom you own as slaves. Such is the decree of God. All women other than these are lawful for you, provided you court them with your wealth in modest conduct, not in fornication. Give them their dowry for the enjoyment you have had of them as a duty; but it shall be no offence for you to make any other agreement among yourselves after you have fulfilled your duty. Surely God is all-knowing and wise.

If any one of you cannot afford to marry a free believing woman, let him marry a slave-girl who is a believer (God best knows your faith: you are born one of another). Marry them with the permission of their masters and give them their dowry in all justice, provided they are honourable and chaste and have not entertained other men. If after marriage they commit adultery, they shall suffer half the penalty inflicted upon free adulteresses. Such is the law for those of you who fear to commit sin: but if you abstain, it will be better for you. God is forgiving and merciful.

* * *

The People of the Book ask you to bring down for them a book from heaven. Of Moses they demanded a harder thing than that. They said to him: "Show us God distinctly." And for their wickedness the thunderbolt smote them. They worshipped the calf after clear signs had been revealed to them; yet We forgave them that, and bestowed on Moses clear authority.

When We made a covenant with them We raised the Mount above them and said: "Enter the gates in adoration. Do not break the Sabbath." We took from them a solemn covenant. But they broke their covenant, denied the revelations of God, and killed the prophets unjustly. They said: "Our hearts are sealed."

It is God who has sealed their hearts, on account of their unbelief. They have no faith, except a few of them.

They denied the truth and uttered a monstrous falsehood against Mary.[7] They declared: "We have put to death the Messiah, Jesus son of Mary, the apostle of God." They did not kill him, nor did they crucify him, but they thought they did.

Those that disagreed about him were in doubt concerning him; they knew nothing about him that was not sheer conjecture; they did not slay him for certain. God lifted him up to Him; God is mighty and wise. There is none among the People of the Book but will believe in him before his death; and on the Day of Resurrection he will bear witness against them.

Because of their iniquity, We forbade the Jews wholesome things which were formerly allowed them; because time after time they have debarred others from the path of God; because they practise usury—although they were forbidden it—and cheat others of their possessions. Woeful punishment have We prepared for those that disbelieve. But those of them that have deep learning, and those that truly believe in what has been revealed to you and what was revealed before you; who attend to their prayers and render the alms levy and have faith in God and the Last Day—these shall be richly recompensed.

We have revealed Our will to you as We revealed it to Noah and to the prophets who came after him; as We revealed it to Abraham, Ishmael, Isaac, Jacob, and the tribes; to Jesus, Job, Jonah, Aaron, Solomon and David, to whom We gave the Psalms. Of some apostles We have already told you, but there are others of whom We have not yet spoken (God spoke directly to Moses): apostles who brought good news to mankind and admonished them, so that they might have no plea against God after their coming. God is mighty and wise.

God bears witness, by that which He has revealed to you, that He revealed it with His knowledge; and so do the angels. There is no better witness than God.

Those that disbelieve and debar others from the path of God have strayed far into error. God will not forgive those who disbelieve and act unjustly; nor will He guide them to any path other than the path of Hell, wherein they shall abide for ever. Surely that is easy enough for God.

from *Sura 5. The Table*[8]

Believers, when death approaches you, let two just men from among you act as witnesses when you make your testament; or two men from another tribe if the calamity of death overtakes you while you are travelling the land. Detain them after prayers, and if you doubt their honesty, let them swear by God: "We will not sell our testimony for any price even to a kinsman. We will not hide the testimony of God; for we should then be evil-doers." If both prove dishonest, replace them by another pair from among those immediately concerned, and let them both swear by God, saying: "Our testimony is truer than theirs. We have told no lies, for we should then be wrongdoers." Thus will they be more likely to bear true witness or to fear that the oaths of others may contradict theirs. Have fear of God and be obedient. God does not guide the evil-doers.

---

7. Understanding Jesus as a human prophet rather than divine, the Qur'an criticizes the Christian treatment of Mary as the Mother of God.

8. A further discussion of Jesus and his mission.

One day God will gather all the apostles and ask them: "How were you received?" They will reply: "We have no knowledge. You alone know what is hidden." God will say: "Jesus son of Mary, remember the favour I bestowed on you and on your mother: how I strengthened you with the Holy Spirit, so that you preached to men in your cradle and in the prime of manhood; how I instructed you in the Book and in wisdom, in the Torah and in the Gospel; how by My leave you fashioned from clay the likeness of a bird and breathed into it so that, by My leave, it became a living bird; how, by My leave, you healed the blind man and the leper, and by My leave restored the dead to life; how I protected you from the Israelites when you had come to them with clear signs: when those of them who disbelieved declared: 'This is but plain sorcery'; how, when I enjoined the disciples to believe in Me and in My apostle, they replied: 'We believe; bear witness that we submit.'"

"Jesus son of Mary," said the disciples, "can your Lord send down to us from heaven a table spread with food?"

He replied: "Have fear of God, if you are true believers."

"We wish to eat of it," they said, "so that we may reassure our hearts and know that what you said to us is true, and that we may be witnesses of it."

"Lord," said Jesus son of Mary, "send down to us from heaven a table spread with food, that it may mark a feast for the first of us and the last of us: a sign from You. Give us our sustenance; You are the best provider."

God replied: "I am sending one to you. But whoever of you disbelieves hereafter shall be punished as no man will ever be punished."

Then God will say: "Jesus son of Mary, did you ever say to mankind: 'Worship me and my mother as gods besides God?'"

"Glory be to You," he will answer, "I could never have claimed what I have no right to. If I had ever said so, You would have surely known it. You know what is in my mind, but I know not what is in Yours. You alone know what is hidden. I told them only what You bade me. I said: 'Serve God, my Lord and your Lord.' I watched over them while living in their midst, and ever since You took me to Yourself, You have been watching them. You are the witness of all things. If You punish them, they surely are Your servants; and if You forgive them, surely You are mighty and wise."

God will say: "This is the day when their truthfulness will benefit the truthful. They shall forever dwell in gardens watered by running streams. God is pleased with them, and they are pleased with Him. That is the supreme triumph."

God has sovereignty over the heavens and the earth and all that they contain. He has power over all things.

from *Sura 24. Light*

God is the light of the heavens and the earth. His light may be compared to a niche that enshrines a lamp, the lamp within a crystal of star-like brilliance. It is lit from a blessed olive tree neither eastern nor western. Its very oil would almost shine forth, though no fire touched it. Light upon light; God guides to His light whom He will.

God speaks in parables to mankind. God has knowledge of all things.

His light is found in temples which God has sanctioned to be built for the remembrance of His name. In them, morning and evening, His praise is sung by men whom neither trade nor profit can divert from remembering God, from offering prayers, or from giving alms; who dread the day when men's hearts and eyes shall writhe with anguish; who hope that God will requite them for their noblest deeds and lavish His grace upon them. God gives without reckoning to whom He will.

from *Sura 36. Ya Sin*[9]

We have taught him no poetry, nor does it become him to be a poet. This is but an admonition: an eloquent Qur'an to exhort the living and to pass judgement on the unbelievers.

Do they not see how, among the things Our hands have made, We have created for them the beasts of which they are masters? We have subjected these to them, that they may ride on some and eat the flesh of others; they drink their milk and put them to other uses. Will they not give thanks?

They have set up other gods besides God, hoping that they may help them. They cannot help them: yet their worshippers stand like warriors ready to defend them.

Let not their words grieve you. We have knowledge of all that they conceal and all that they reveal.

Is man not aware that We created him from a little germ? Yet is he flagrantly contentious. He answers back with arguments, and forgets his own creation. He asks: "Who will give life to rotten bones?"

Say: "He who first brought them into being will give them life again: He has knowledge of every creature; He who gives you from the green tree a flame, and lo! you light a fire."

Has He who created the heavens and the earth no power to create others like them? That He surely has. He is the all-knowing Creator. When He decrees a thing He need only say: "Be," and it is.

Glory be to Him who has control of all things. To Him shall you all be recalled.

from *Sura 48. Victory*

IN THE NAME OF GOD, THE COMPASSIONATE, THE MERCIFUL

We have given you a glorious victory,[1] so that God may forgive you your past and future sins, and perfect His goodness to you; that He may guide you to a straight path and bestow on you His mighty help.

It was He who sent down tranquillity into the hearts of the faithful, so that their faith might grow stronger (God's are the legions of the heavens and the earth: God is all-knowing and wise); that He may bring the believers, both men and women, into gardens watered by running streams, there to abide for ever; that He may forgive them their sins (this, in God's sight, is a glorious triumph); and that He may punish the hypocrites and the idolaters, men and women, who think evil thoughts about God. A turn of evil shall befall them, for God is angry with them. He has laid on them His curse and prepared for them the fire of Hell: an evil fate.

God's are the legions of the heavens and the earth. God is mighty and wise.

We have sent you[2] forth as a witness and as a bearer of good news and warnings, so that you may have faith in God and His apostle and that you may assist Him, honour Him, and praise Him morning and evening.

Those that swear fealty to you, swear fealty to God Himself. The Hand of God is above their hands. He that breaks his oath breaks it at his own peril, but he that keeps his pledge to God shall be richly recompensed by Him.

---

60

9. On Muhammad's mission as prophet, not poet.
1. Probably the taking of Mecca in 630.
2. The Meccans

The desert Arabs who stayed behind[3] will say to you: "We were occupied with our goods and families. Implore God to pardon us." They will say with their tongues what they do not mean in their hearts.

Say: "Who can intervene on your behalf with God if it be His will to do you harm or good? Indeed, God is cognizant of all your actions."

No. You[4] thought the Apostle and the believers would never return to their people; and with this fancy your hearts were delighted. You harboured evil thoughts and thus incurred damnation.

As for those that disbelieve in God and His apostle, We have prepared a blazing Fire for the unbelievers. God has sovereignty over the heavens and the earth. He pardons whom He will and punishes whom He pleases. God is forgiving and merciful.

Sura 71. Noah

In the Name of God, the Compassionate, the Merciful

We sent forth Noah to his people, saying: "Give warning to your people before a woeful scourge overtakes them."

He said: "My people, I come to warn you plainly. Serve God and fear Him, and obey me. He will forgive you your sins and give you respite for an appointed term. When God's time arrives, none shall put it back. Would that you understood this!"

"Lord," said Noah, "night and day I have pleaded with my people, but my pleas have only aggravated their aversion. Each time I call on them to seek Your pardon, they thrust their fingers into their ears and draw their cloaks over their heads, persisting in sin and bearing themselves with insolent pride. I called out loud to them, and appealed to them in public and in private. 'Seek forgiveness of your Lord,' I said. 'He is ever ready to forgive. He sends down abundant water from the sky for you and bestows upon you wealth and children. He has provided you with gardens and with running brooks. Why do you deny the greatness of God when He created you in gradual stages? Can you not see how God created the seven heavens one above the other, placing in them the moon for a light and the sun for a lantern? God has brought you forth from the earth like a plant, and to the earth He will restore you. Then He will bring you back afresh. God has made the earth a vast expanse for you, so that you may roam its spacious paths.'"

And Noah said: "Lord, my people disobey me, and follow those whose wealth and offspring will only hasten their perdition. They have devised an outrageous plot, and said to each other: 'Do not renounce your gods. Do not forsake Wadd or Suwā' or Yaghūth or Ya'ūq or Naṣr.'[5] They have led numerous men astray. You surely drive the wrongdoers to further error."

And because of their sins they were overwhelmed by the Flood and cast into the Fire. They found none besides God to help them.

And Noah said: "Lord, do not leave a single unbeliever on the earth. If You spare them, they will mislead Your servants and beget none but sinners and unbelievers. Forgive me, Lord, and forgive my parents and every true believer who seeks refuge in my house. Forgive all the faithful, men and women, and hasten the destruction of the wrongdoers."

3. Away from battle.
4. The desert Arabs.
5. Different idols.

Sura 87. The Most High

IN THE NAME OF GOD, THE COMPASSIONATE, THE MERCIFUL

Praise the Name of your Lord, the Most High, who has created all things and gave them due proportions; who has ordained their destinies and guided them; who brings forth the green pasture, then turns it to withered grass.

We shall make you recite Our revelations, so that you shall forget none of them except as God pleases. He has knowledge of all that is manifest, and all that is hidden.

We shall guide you to the smoothest path. Therefore give warning, if warning will avail. He that fears God will heed it, but the wicked sinner will flout it. He shall burn in the gigantic Fire, where he shall neither die nor live. Happy shall be the man who keeps himself pure, who remembers the name of his Lord and prays.

Yet you[6] prefer this life, although the life to come is better and more lasting.

All this is written in earlier scriptures; the scriptures of Abraham and Moses.

Sura 93. Daylight

IN THE NAME OF GOD, THE COMPASSIONATE, THE MERCIFUL

By the light of day, and by the dark of night, your Lord has not forsaken you,[7] nor does He abhor you.

The life to come holds a richer prize for you than this present life. You shall be gratified with what your Lord will give you.

Did He not find you an orphan and give you shelter?

Did He not find you in error and guide you?

Did He not find you poor and enrich you?

Therefore do not wrong the orphan, nor chide away the beggar. But proclaim the goodness of your Lord.

Sura 96. Clots of Blood[8]

IN THE NAME OF GOD, THE COMPASSIONATE, THE MERCIFUL

Recite in the name of your Lord who created—created man from clots of blood.

Recite! Your Lord is the Most Bountiful One, who by the pen taught man what he did not know.

Indeed, man transgresses in thinking himself his own master: for to your Lord all things return.

Observe the man who rebukes Our servant when he prays. Think: does he follow the right guidance or enjoin true piety?

Think: if he denies the Truth and pays no heed, does he not realize that God observes all?

No. Let him desist, or We will drag him by the forelock, his lying, sinful forelock.

Then let him call his helpmates. We will call the guards of Hell.

No, never obey him! Prostrate yourself and come nearer.

---

6. Unbelievers.

7. Muhammad.

8. These are the first lines ever revealed to Muhammad.

Sura 110. Help

In the Name of God, the Compassionate, the Merciful

When God's help and victory come, and you see men embrace God's faith in multitudes, give glory to your Lord and seek His pardon. He is ever disposed to mercy.

THE THOUSAND AND ONE NIGHTS ■ (9th–14th centuries)

Apart from the Qur'an, *Alf Layla wa-Layla* (*The Thousand and One Nights* or *The Arabian Nights*) is perhaps the most influential, well-known and widely read work of Arabic and Islamic culture. The earliest evidence that a work or a compilation of this nature existed goes back to the ninth century, and certainly by the twelfth century there are many manuscripts of *The Thousand and One Nights* in Egypt, Syria, and Iraq. The present title of the work is a twelfth-century coinage, for earlier mentions of the work refer to it simply as *Alf Layla* ("The Thousand Nights"). Earlier manuscripts are incomplete and led to speculation that the title *The Thousand Nights* was only meant to denote a large number of stories rather than a formal organization of the work. Recent scholarship and application of modern critical approaches have challenged this assumption and established the structural cohesion of the work. Similarly there is much speculation concerning the origin of the work, its genealogy, and development. It has been suggested that a Persian collection of tales, *Hazar Afsana* ("Thousand Tales"), is the source of *The Thousand and One Nights*. Others claim that its source text is an Indian narrative of different stories similar to the frame story of *The Thousand and One Nights,* yet neither of these accounts for the richness of the work and its infinite variety of narratives.

The text's unity is grounded in a constant interplay between the frame story and the enframed stories. In the famous frame tale, the vizier's daughter Scheherazade or Shahrazad offers her stories as ransom for her life to avert the violence of a tyrant king, but the ransom only works through the suspension of time by using storytelling to stop its flow. Narrative manipulates time, and the suspension of time enhances the power of narrative, hence the circular nature of *The Thousand and One Nights*. Because of this circularity, the structural unity of the work develops through variations, echoes, and references forward and back, rather than through cause-and-effect progressions. This linking can be seen in the first set of stories, when the threat of violence is averted or postponed by the telling of stories. But in certain tales the link with the frame story is different. In "The Tale of Sympathy the Learned" one sees the whole work mirrored in one of its stories of how a learned woman is able to tame the powerful men around her. This tale may be studied as the first ever "feminist" literary text, which enhances the position of the woman, subverting the patriarchal order and exposing its weaknesses. In other stories on the other hand, the link to the frame tale seems weak, yet they often involve themes—the evanescence of worldly pleasures, ascetic piety, and the need for humble acceptance of God—that are basic Islamic tenets also implied in the main frame.

The tales are further connected by the fact that tales often generate other tales or kernels of tales within themselves. The narrative of *The Thousand and One Nights* is similar in form to nested Russian dolls, one hidden inside another. Unlike the Russian doll, the tales aren't identical or symmetrical and are varied in location, characters, and action. Yet there is a deep structure that makes them a whole within every tale, and at the same time part of the organic whole that is *The Thousand and One Nights*. The nested tales often replicate in their flow the very structure of the whole work—that is, a basic frame story and a number of enframed stories within its overreaching thematic unity. This confirms both the circularity and the self-reference of the work.

Another dimension of the work enhances its coherence. The set of philosophical and religious assumptions underpinning the deep structure of *The Thousand and One Nights* is essentially Islamic in its tenets and uniquely Arabic in its orientation. As a result, the book has often been known as *The Arabian Nights*. Early European translators noted its cultural difference. Richard Burton, for example, noted the parallels between the cultural ethos of *The Thousand and One Nights* and the Muslim customs in the Arab and Indian worlds, which he himself witnessed in his travels. These philosophical and religious aspects of the work are an essential part of the motivation of its narrative, whose ultimate aim is to re-educate the tyrant king, to acclimate him to a tolerant and humane civilization. The various strata or cycles of stories correspond to the different Arabic/Islamic virtues and concepts that are necessary for a comprehensive re-education of a tyrant. *The Thousand and One Nights* reflects the culmination of Arabic and Islamic civilization at the peak of its assimilation of many elements of the older cultures that embraced Islam, such as Persian, Egyptian, Iraqi, Indian, and even Chinese.

Yet the work is primarily the product of the Arabic imagination and the Islamic worldview embodied in the Qur'an, for it carries the distinct mark of Arabic culture in two of its major centers: Iraq and Egypt. Although the majority of characters in *The Thousand and One Nights* are of Arabic origin and carry Arabic names, there are characters with Indian, Persian, Turkish, Hebrew, and other foreign names. This makes *The Thousand and One Nights* a mirror of the Islamic world with people from a myriad of cultures and nations, and of the Islamic civilization's ability to assimilate various strands of other cultures. Another aspect of this is that one finds Christians, Zoroastrians, and pagans converting to Islam but not Muslims being converted to Christianity or any other religion in these tales, for *The Thousand and One Nights* is a reflection of the triumph of Islamic culture.

The Thousand and One Nights is generally considered as a work of collective imagination rather than of one author, but it is an imagination that puts the woman, Scheherazade, in the center of the creative assembly. It is usually divided into two parts. In the Baghdad part, characters, action, and space are dominated by this Islamic metropolis during the peak of the Abbasid period in the days of Haroun al-Rashid. In the Egyptian part, the location and characters reflect the specificity of Egyptian culture as demonstrated in the use of Egyptian names and places, the Coptic names of months, and the manipulation of *jinn* through a talisman or magic object, rather than directly as in the Baghdad section. The tales in which jinn or genies act independently are seen to be inspired by Persian or Indian stories. Another group of tales reflects influences of ancient Babylonian and Mesopotamian narratives and of some historic events and characters, particularly those related to Alexander the Great. *The Thousand and One Nights* is also brimming with characters, motifs, and stories that come to it from the Qur'an, or via the Qur'an, such as those of the Hebrew king Solomon.

Most of the stories in our selection are from the Baghdad part, with the partial exception of "The Tale of Sympathy the Learned," which originated in Baghdad and was reshaped in Egypt, demonstrating the convergence of the two parts. Since Baghdad was the metropolis of a large empire, its stories reflect the life of an affluent capital and the myriad of cultural influences on it. The tales of the Caliph and that of the poet Abu-Nuwas demonstrate this. The Egyptian stories provided *The Thousand and One Nights* with different narrative genres, such as tales of thieves, tricksters, and rogues, tales in which people use talismans to control genies and demons, and stories that might be called "bourgeois romances" of love and adultery. Between them, the two parts of *The Thousand and One Nights* embrace an impressive number of narrative genres, from travel narratives and romances to fairy tales, legends, humorous or fantasy tales, didactic stories, anecdotes, and short stories. One can identify every conceivable narrative configuration in *The Thousand and One Nights,* from early narrative kernels to the most developed fiction, from realistic rendering to the fantastic and the absurd. In addition there are 1,420 poems or fragments of poetry; this interweaving of poetry and prose can be compared to that found in *The Tale of Genji* (page 517).

    The Thousand and One Nights is often considered the archetypal narrative text, or the mother of all narrative, and this may explain its universal appeal and enduring influence through the ages. There is ample evidence to suggest that medieval Europeans knew it, and the comic tales of Boccaccio can well be compared to those of the *Nights*. Like any long collectively composed oral text, it went through many stages of development. The text in the form that we know now in the West owes its existence to the first European translation by a French orientalist, Jean Antoine Galland (1646–1715), who used a manuscript that dates from 1536. The first volume of his *Les Mille et Une Nuits: Contes Arabes Traduits en Français* appeared in 1704, with eleven more volumes thereafter. The work was a great success, thus inspiring its translation into other European languages, including into English in 1792 and German in 1823.

    Since its first appearance in Europe, *The Thousand and One Nights* fascinated writers and poets from Coleridge to Robert Louis Stevenson (who wrote a *New Thousand and One Nights* in 1882), to the father of modern magic realism, Jorge Luis Borges. In the Arab world the impact of this archetypal text is ubiquitous, and no study of modern Arabic narrative is possible without a clear knowledge of its rubrics. The Egyptian Nobel laureate, Naguib Mahfouz, has endeavored to rewrite certain tales in his *Arabian Nights and Days* (1982), selections from which are included in Volume 2.

PRONUNCIATIONS:

Dunyazad: DOON-yah-zadh
Shahrazad: SHAH-rah-zahd
Shahrayar: SHAH-ree-yar
Shahzaman: SHAH-zah-MANN

from The Thousand and One Nights

Prologue[1]

[The Story of King Shahrayar and Shahrazad, His Vizier's Daughter]

It is related—but God knows and sees best what lies hidden in the old accounts of bygone peoples and times—that long ago, during the time of the Sasanid dynasty,[2] in the peninsulas of India and Indochina, there lived two kings who were brothers. The older brother was named Shahrayar, the younger Shahzaman. The older,

---

1. The Prologue is translated by Husain Haddawy, in a lively oral-flavored style, using an Egyptian manuscript that gives the heroine's name as Shahrazad, her sister (usually called Dunyazad) as Dinarzad, and the king as Shahrayar rather than the more usual Shahryar.

2. A dynasty of Persian kings who ruled from c. 226–641 C.E.

Shahrayar, was a towering knight and a daring champion, invincible, energetic, and implacable. His power reached the remotest corners of the land and its people, so that the country was loyal to him, and his subjects obeyed him. Shahrayar himself lived and ruled in India and Indochina, while to his brother he gave the land of Samarkand to rule as king.[3]

Ten years went by, when one day Shahrayar felt a longing for his brother the king, summoned his vizier[4] (who had two daughters, one called Shahrazad, the other Dinarzad) and bade him go to his brother. Having made preparations, the vizier journeyed day and night until he reached Samarkand. When Shahzaman heard of the vizier's arrival, he went out with his retainers to meet him. He dismounted, embraced him, and asked him for news from his older brother, Shahrayar. The vizier replied that he was well, and that he had sent him to request his brother to visit him. Shahzaman complied with his brother's request and proceeded to make preparations for the journey. In the meantime, he had the vizier camp on the outskirts of the city, and took care of his needs. He sent him what he required of food and fodder, slaughtered many sheep in his honor, and provided him with money and supplies, as well as many horses and camels.

For ten full days he prepared himself for the journey; then he appointed a chamberlain in his place, and left the city to spend the night in his tent, near the vizier. At midnight he returned to his palace in the city, to bid his wife good-bye. But when he entered the palace, he found his wife lying in the arms of one of the kitchen boys. When he saw them, the world turned dark before his eyes and, shaking his head, he said to himself, "I am still here, and this is what she has done when I was barely outside the city. How will it be and what will happen behind my back when I go to visit my brother in India? No. Women are not to be trusted." He got exceedingly angry, adding, "By God, I am king and sovereign in Samarkand, yet my wife has betrayed me and has inflicted this on me." As his anger boiled, he drew his sword and struck both his wife and the cook. Then he dragged them by the heels and threw them from the top of the palace to the trench below. He then left the city and going to the vizier ordered that they depart that very hour. The drum was struck, and they set out on their journey, while Shahzaman's heart was on fire because of what his wife had done to him and how she had betrayed him with some cook, some kitchen boy. They journeyed hurriedly, day and night, through deserts and wilds, until they reached the land of King Shahrayar, who had gone out to receive them.

When Shahrayar met them, he embraced his brother, showed him favors, and treated him generously. He offered him quarters in a palace adjoining his own, for King Shahrayar had built two beautiful towering palaces in his garden, one for the guests, the other for the women and members of his household. He gave the guest house to his brother, Shahzaman, after the attendants had gone to scrub it, dry it, furnish it, and open its windows, which overlooked the garden. Thereafter, Shahzaman would spend the whole day at his brother's, return at night to sleep at the palace, then go back to his brother the next morning. But whenever he found himself alone and thought of his ordeal with his wife, he would sigh deeply, then stifle his grief, and say, "Alas, that this great misfortune should have happened to

3. Samarkand is in central Asia.
4. A caliph's or king's chief administrator.

one in my position!" Then he would fret with anxiety, his spirit would sag, and he would say, "None has seen what I have seen." In his depression, he ate less and less, grew pale, and his health deteriorated. He neglected everything, wasted away, and looked ill.

When King Shahrayar looked at his brother and saw how day after day he lost weight and grew thin, pale, ashen, and sickly, he thought that this was because of his expatriation and homesickness for his country and his family, and he said to himself, "My brother is not happy here. I should prepare a goodly gift for him and send him home." For a month he gathered gifts for his brother; then he invited him to see him and said, "Brother, I would like you to know that I intend to go hunting and pursue the roaming deer, for ten days. Then I shall return to prepare you for your journey home. Would you like to go hunting with me?" Shahzaman replied, "Brother, I feel distracted and depressed. Leave me here and go with God's blessing and help." When Shahrayar heard his brother, he thought that his dejection was because of his homesickness for his country. Not wishing to coerce him, he left him behind, and set out with his retainers and men. When they entered the wilderness, he deployed his men in a circle to begin trapping and hunting.

After his brother's departure, Shahzaman stayed in the palace and, from the window overlooking the garden, watched the birds and trees as he thought of his wife and what she had done to him, and sighed in sorrow. While he agonized over his misfortune, gazing at the heavens and turning a distracted eye on the garden, the private gate of his brother's palace opened, and there emerged, strutting like a dark-eyed deer, the lady, his brother's wife, with twenty slave-girls, ten white and ten black. While Shahzaman looked at them, without being seen, they continued to walk until they stopped below his window, without looking in his direction, thinking that he had gone to the hunt with his brother. Then they sat down, took off their clothes, and suddenly there were ten slave-girls and ten black slaves dressed in the same clothes as the girls. Then the ten black slaves mounted the ten girls, while the lady called, "Mas'ud, Mas'ud!" and a black slave jumped from the tree to the ground, rushed to her, and, raising her legs, went between her thighs and made love to her. Mas'ud topped the lady, while the ten slaves topped the ten girls, and they carried on till noon. When they were done with their business, they got up and washed themselves. Then the ten slaves put on the same clothes again, mingled with the girls, and once more there appeared to be twenty slave-girls. Mas'ud himself jumped over the garden wall and disappeared, while the slave-girls and the lady sauntered to the private gate, went in and, locking the gate behind them, went their way.

All of this happened under King Shahzaman's eyes. When he saw this spectacle of the wife and the women of his brother the great king—how ten slaves put on women's clothes and slept with his brother's paramours and concubines and what Mas'ud did with his brother's wife, in his very palace—and pondered over this calamity and great misfortune, his care and sorrow left him and he said to himself, "This is our common lot. Even though my brother is king and master of the whole world, he cannot protect what is his, his wife and his concubines, and suffers misfortune in his very home. What happened to me is little by comparison. I used to think that I was the only one who has suffered, but from what I have seen, everyone suffers. By God, my misfortune is lighter than that of my brother." He kept marveling and blaming life, whose trials none can escape, and he began to find consolation in his own affliction and forget his grief. When supper came, he ate and drank with relish and zest and, feeling better, kept eating and drinking, enjoying himself and feeling happy. He thought to himself, "I am no longer alone in my misery; I am well."

For ten days, he continued to enjoy his food and drink, and when his brother, King Shahrayar came back from the hunt, he met him happily, treated him attentively, and greeted him cheerfully. His brother, King Shahrayar, who had missed him, said, "By God, brother, I missed you on this trip and wished you were with me." Shahzaman thanked him and sat down to carouse with him, and when night fell, and food was brought before them, the two ate and drank, and again Shahzaman ate and drank with zest. As time went by, he continued to eat and drink with appetite, and became light-hearted and carefree. His face regained color and became ruddy, and his body gained weight, as his blood circulated and he regained his energy; he was himself again, or even better. King Shahrayar noticed his brother's condition, how he used to be and how he had improved, but kept it to himself until he took him aside one day and said, "My brother Shahzaman, I would like you to do something for me, to satisfy a wish, to answer a question truthfully." Shahzaman asked, "What is it, brother?" He replied, "When you first came to stay with me, I noticed that you kept losing weight, day after day, until your looks changed, your health deteriorated, and your energy sagged. As you continued like this, I thought that what ailed you was your homesickness for your family and your country, but even though I kept noticing that you were wasting away and looking ill, I refrained from questioning you and hid my feelings from you. Then I went hunting, and when I came back, I found that you had recovered and had regained your health. Now I want you to tell me everything and to explain the cause of your deterioration and the cause of your subsequent recovery, without hiding anything from me." When Shahzaman heard what King Shahrayar said, he bowed his head, then said, "As for the cause of my recovery, that I cannot tell you, and I wish that you would excuse me from telling you." The king was greatly astonished at his brother's reply and, burning with curiosity, said, "You must tell me. For now, at least, explain the first cause."

Then Shahzaman related to his brother what happened to him with his own wife, on the night of his departure, from beginning to end, and concluded, "Thus all the while I was with you, great King, whenever I thought of the event and the misfortune that had befallen me, I felt troubled, careworn, and unhappy, and my health deteriorated. This then is the cause." Then he grew silent. When King Shahrayar heard his brother's explanation, he shook his head, greatly amazed at the deceit of women, and prayed to God to protect him from their wickedness, saying, "Brother, you were fortunate in killing your wife and her lover, who gave you good reason to feel troubled, careworn, and ill. In my opinion, what happened to you has never happened to anyone else. By God, had I been in your place, I would have killed at least a hundred or even a thousand women. I would have been furious; I would have gone mad. Now praise be to God who has delivered you from sorrow and distress. But tell me what has caused you to forget your sorrow and regain your health?" Shahzaman replied, "King, I wish that for God's sake you would excuse me from telling you." Shahrayar said, "You must." Shahzaman replied, "I fear that you will feel even more troubled and careworn than I." Shahrayar asked, "How could that be, brother? I insist on hearing your explanation."

61

Shahzaman then told him about what he had seen from the palace window and the calamity in his very home—how ten slaves, dressed like women, were sleeping with his women and concubines, day and night. He told him everything from beginning to end (but there is no point in repeating that). Then he concluded, "When I saw your own misfortune, I felt better—and said to myself, 'My brother is king of the world, yet such a misfortune has happened to him, and in his very home.' As a result I forgot my care and sorrow, relaxed, and began to eat and drink. This is the cause of my cheer and good spirits."

When King Shahrayar heard what his brother said and found out what had happened to him, he was furious and his blood boiled. He said, "Brother, I can't believe what you say unless I see it with my own eyes." When Shahzaman saw that his brother was in a rage, he said to him, "If you do not believe me, unless you see your misfortune with your own eyes, announce that you plan to go hunting. Then you and I shall set out with your troops, and when we get outside the city, we shall leave our tents and camp with the men behind, enter the city secretly, and go together to your palace. Then the next morning you can see with your own eyes."

King Shahrayar realized that his brother had a good plan and ordered his army to prepare for the trip. He spent the night with his brother, and when God's morning broke, the two rode out of the city with their army, preceded by the camp attendants, who had gone to drive the poles and pitch the tents where the king and his army were to camp. At nightfall King Shahrayar summoned his chief chamberlain and bade him take his place. He entrusted him with the army and ordered that for three days no one was to enter the city. Then he and his brother disguised themselves and entered the city in the dark. They went directly to the palace where Shahzaman resided and slept there till the morning. When they awoke, they sat at the palace window, watching the garden and chatting, until the light broke, the day dawned, and the sun rose. As they watched, the private gate opened, and there emerged as usual the wife of King Shahrayar, walking among twenty slave-girls. They made their way under the trees until they stood below the palace window where the two kings sat. Then they took off their women's clothes, and suddenly there were ten slaves, who mounted the ten girls and made love to them. As for the lady, she called, "Mas'ud, Mas'ud," and a black slave jumped from the tree to the ground, came to her, and said, "What do you want, you slut? Here is Sa'ad al-Din Mas'ud." She laughed and fell on her back, while the slave mounted her and like the others did his business with her. Then the black slaves got up, washed themselves, and, putting on the same clothes, mingled with the girls. Then they walked away, entered the palace, and locked the gate behind them. As for Mas'ud, he jumped over the fence to the road and went on his way.

When King Shahrayar saw the spectacle of his wife and the slave-girls, he went out of his mind, and when he and his brother came down from upstairs, he said, "No one is safe in this world. Such doings are going on in my kingdom, and in my very palace. Perish the world and perish life! This is a great calamity, indeed." Then he turned to his brother and asked, "Would you like to follow me in what I shall do?" Shahzaman answered, "Yes. I will." Shahrayar said, "Let us leave our royal state and roam the world for the love of the Supreme Lord. If we should find one whose misfortune is greater than ours, we shall return. Otherwise, we shall continue to journey through the land, without need for the trappings of royalty." Shahzaman replied, "This is an excellent idea. I shall follow you."

Then they left by the private gate, took a side road, and departed, journeying till nightfall. They slept over their sorrows, and in the morning resumed their day journey until they came to a meadow by the seashore. While they sat in the meadow amid the thick plants and trees, discussing their misfortunes and the recent events, they suddenly heard a shout and a great cry coming from the middle of the sea. They trembled with fear, thinking that the sky had fallen on the earth. Then the sea parted, and there emerged a black pillar that, as it swayed forward, got taller and taller, until it touched the clouds. Shahrayar and Shahzaman were petrified; then they ran in terror and, climbing a very tall tree, sat hiding in its foliage. When they looked again, they saw that the black pillar was cleaving the sea, wading in the water toward the green meadow, until it touched the shore. When they looked again, they saw that it was a black demon, carrying on his head a large glass chest with four steel locks. He came out, walked into the meadow, and where should he stop but under the very tree where the two kings were hiding. The demon sat down and placed the glass chest on the ground. He took out four keys and, opening the locks of the chest, pulled out a full-grown woman. She had a beautiful figure, and a face like the full moon, and a lovely smile. He took her out, laid her under the tree, and looked at her, saying, "Mistress of all noble women, you whom I carried away on your wedding night, I would like to sleep a little." Then he placed his head on the young woman's lap, stretched his legs to the sea, sank into sleep, and began to snore.

Meanwhile, the woman looked up at the tree and, turning her head by chance, saw King Shahrayar and King Shahzaman. She lifted the demon's head from her lap and placed it on the ground. Then she came and stood under the tree and motioned to them with her hand, as if to say, "Come down slowly to me." When they realized that she had seen them, they were frightened, and they begged her and implored her, in the name of the Creator of the heavens, to excuse them from climbing down. She replied, "You must come down to me." They motioned to her, saying, "This sleeping demon is the enemy of mankind. For God's sake, leave us alone." She replied, "You must come down, and if you don't, I shall wake the demon and have him kill you." She kept gesturing and pressing, until they climbed down very slowly and stood before her. Then she lay on her back, raised her legs, and said, "Make love to me and satisfy my need, or else I shall wake the demon, and he will kill you." They replied, "For God's sake, mistress, don't do this to us, for at this moment we feel nothing but dismay and fear of this demon. Please, excuse us." She replied, "You must," and insisted, swearing, "By God who created the heavens, if you don't do it, I shall wake my husband the demon and ask him to kill you and throw you into the sea." As she persisted, they could no longer resist and they made love to her, first the older brother, then the younger. When they were done and withdrew from her, she said to them, "Give me your rings," and, pulling out from the folds of her dress a small purse, opened it, and shook out ninety-eight rings of different fashions and colors. Then she asked them, "Do you know what these rings are?" They answered, "No." She said, "All the owners of these rings slept with me, for whenever one of them made love to me, I took a ring from him. Since you two have slept with me, give me your rings, so that I may add them to the rest, and make a full hundred. A hundred men have known me under the very horns of this filthy, monstrous cuckold, who has imprisoned me in this chest, locked it with four locks, and kept me in the middle of this raging, roaring sea. He has guarded me and tried to keep me pure and chaste, not realizing that nothing can prevent or alter what is predestined and that when a woman desires something, no one can stop her." When Shahrayar and Shahzaman heard what the young woman said, they were greatly amazed, danced with joy, and said, "O God, O God! There is no power and no strength, save in God the Almighty, the Magnificent. Great is women's cunning." Then each of them took off his ring and handed it to her. She took them and put them with the rest in the purse. Then sitting again by the demon, she lifted his head, placed it back on her lap, and motioned to them, "Go on your way, or else I shall wake him."

They turned their backs and took to the road. Then Shahrayar turned to his brother and said, "My brother Shahzaman, look at this sorry plight. By God, it is worse than ours. This is no less than a demon who has carried a young woman away on her wedding night, imprisoned her in a glass chest, locked her up with four locks, and kept her in the middle of the sea, thinking that he could guard her from what God had foreordained, and you saw how she has managed to sleep with ninety-eight men, and added the two of us to make a hundred. Brother, let us go back to our kingdoms and our cities, never to marry a woman again. As for myself, I shall show you what I will do."

Then the two brothers headed home and journeyed till nightfall. On the morning of the third day, they reached their camp and men, entered their tent, and sat on their thrones. The chamberlains, deputies, princes, and viziers came to attend King Shahrayar, while he gave orders and bestowed robes of honor, as well as other gifts. Then at his command everyone returned to the city, and he went to his own palace and ordered his chief vizier, the father of the two girls Shahrazad and Dinarzad, who will be mentioned below, and said to him, "Take that wife of mine and put her to death." Then Shahrayar went to her himself, bound her, and handed her over to the vizier, who took her out and put her to death. Then King Shahrayar grabbed his sword, brandished it, and, entering the palace chambers, killed every one of his slave-girls and replaced them with others. He then swore to marry for one night only and kill the woman the next morning, in order to save himself from the wickedness and cunning of women, saying, "There is not a single chaste woman anywhere on the entire face of the earth." Shortly thereafter he provided his brother Shahzaman with supplies for his journey and sent him back to his own country with gifts, rarities, and money. The brother bade him good-bye and set out for home.

Shahrayar sat on his throne and ordered his vizier, the father of the two girls, to find him a wife from among the princes' daughters. The vizier found him one, and he slept with her and was done with her, and the next morning he ordered the vizier to put her to death. That very night he took one of his army officers' daughters, slept with her, and the next morning ordered the vizier to put her to death. The vizier, who could not disobey him, put her to death. The third night he took one of the merchants' daughters, slept with her till the morning, then ordered his vizier to put her to death, and the vizier did so. It became King Shahrayar's custom to take every night the daughter of a merchant or a commoner, spend the night with her, then have her put to death the next morning. He continued to do this until all the girls perished, their mothers mourned, and there arose a clamor among the fathers and mothers, who called the plague upon his head, complained to the Creator of the heavens, and called for help on Him who hears and answers prayers.

Now, as mentioned earlier, the vizier, who put the girls to death, had an older daughter called Shahrazad and a younger one called Dinarzad. The older daughter, Shahrazad, had read the books of literature, philosophy, and medicine. She knew poetry by heart, had studied historical reports, and was acquainted with the sayings of men and the maxims of sages and kings. She was intelligent, knowledgeable, wise, and refined. She had read and learned. One day she said to her father, "Father, I will tell you what is in my mind." He asked, "What is it?" She answered, "I would like you to marry me to King Shahrayar, so that I may either succeed in saving the people or perish and die like the rest." When the vizier heard what his daughter Shahrazad said, he got angry and said to her, "Foolish one, don't you know that King Shahrayar has sworn to spend but one night with a girl and have her put to death the next morning? If I give you to him, he will sleep with you for one night and will ask me to put you to death the next morning, and I shall have to do it, since I cannot disobey him." She said, "Father, you must give me to him, even if he kills me." He asked, "What has possessed you that you wish to imperil yourself?" She replied, "Father, you must give me to him. This is absolute and final." Her father the vizier became furious and said to her, "Daughter, 'He who misbehaves, ends up in trouble,' and 'He who considers not the end, the world is not his friend.' As the popular saying goes, 'I would be sitting pretty, but for my curiosity.' I am afraid that what happened to the donkey and the ox with the merchant will happen to you." She asked, "Father, what happened to the donkey, the ox, and the merchant?" He said:

[The Tale of the Ox and the Donkey]

There was a prosperous and wealthy merchant who lived in the countryside and labored on a farm. He owned many camels and herds of cattle and employed many men, and he had a wife and many grown-up as well as little children. This merchant was taught the language of the beasts,[5] on condition that if he revealed his secret to anyone, he would die; therefore, even though he knew the language of every kind of animal, he did not let anyone know, for fear of death. One day, as he sat, with his wife beside him and his children playing before him, he glanced at an ox and a donkey he kept at the farmhouse, tied to adjacent troughs, and heard the ox say to the donkey, "Watchful one, I hope that you are enjoying the comfort and the service you are getting. Your ground is swept and watered, and they serve you, feed you sifted barley, and offer you clear, cool water to drink. I, on the contrary, am taken out to plow in the middle of the night. They clamp on my neck something they call yoke and plow, push me all day under the whip to plow the field, and drive me beyond my endurance until my sides are lacerated, and my neck is flayed. They work me from nighttime to nighttime, take me back in the dark, offer me beans soiled with mud and hay mixed with chaff, and let me spend the night lying in urine and dung. Meanwhile you rest on well-swept, watered, and smoothed ground, with a clean trough full of hay. You stand in comfort, save for the rare occasion when our master the merchant rides you to do a brief errand and returns. You are comfortable, while I am weary; you sleep, while I keep awake."

When the ox finished, the donkey turned to him and said, "Green-horn, they were right in calling you ox, for you ox harbor no deceit, malice, or meanness. Being sincere, you exert and exhaust yourself to comfort others. Have you not heard the saying 'Out of bad luck, they hastened on the road'? You go into the field from early morning to endure your torture at the plow to the point of exhaustion. When the plowman takes you back and ties you to the trough, you go on butting and beating with your horns, kicking with your hoofs, and bellowing for the beans, until they toss them to you; then you begin to eat. Next time, when they bring them to you, don't eat or even touch them, but smell them, then draw back and lie down on the hay and straw. If you do this, life will be better and kinder to you, and you will find relief."

As the ox listened, he was sure that the donkey had given him good advice. He thanked him, commended him to God, and invoked His blessing on him, and said,

---

5. This ability has precedence in the Qur'an, which records that God taught Solomon the language of the beasts.

"May you stay safe from harm, watchful one." All of this conversation took place, daughter, while the merchant listened and understood. On the following day, the plowman came to the merchant's house and, taking the ox, placed the yoke upon his neck and worked him at the plow, but the ox lagged behind. The plowman hit him, but following the donkey's advice, the ox, dissembling, fell on his belly, and the plowman hit him again. Thus the ox kept getting up and falling until nightfall, when the plowman took him home and tied him to the trough. But this time the ox did not bellow or kick the ground with his hoofs. Instead, he withdrew, away from the trough. Astonished, the plowman brought him his beans and fodder, but the ox only smelled the fodder and pulled back and lay down at a distance with the hay and straw, complaining till the morning. When the plowman arrived, he found the trough as he had left it, full of beans and fodder, and saw the ox lying on his back, hardly breathing, his belly puffed, and his legs raised in the air. The plowman felt sorry for him and said to himself, "By God, he did seem weak and unable to work." Then he went to the merchant and said, "Master, last night, the ox refused to eat or touch his fodder."

The merchant, who knew what was going on, said to the plowman, "Go to the wily donkey, put him to the plow, and work him hard until he finishes the ox's task." The plowman left, took the donkey, and placed the yoke upon his neck. Then he took him out to the field and drove him with blows until he finished the ox's work, all the while driving him with blows and beating him until his sides were lacerated and his neck was flayed. At nightfall he took him home, barely able to drag his legs under his tired body and his drooping ears. Meanwhile the ox spent his day resting. He ate all his food, drank his water, and lay quietly, chewing his cud in comfort. All day long he kept praising the donkey's advice and invoking God's blessing on him. When the donkey came back at night, the ox stood up to greet him, saying, "Good evening, watchful one! You have done me a favor beyond description, for I have been sitting in comfort. God bless you for my sake." Seething with anger, the donkey did not reply, but said to himself, "All this happened to me because of my miscalculation. 'I would be sitting pretty, but for my curiosity.' If I don't find a way to return this ox to his former situation, I will perish." Then he went to his trough and lay down, while the ox continued to chew his cud and invoke God's blessing on him.

"You, my daughter, will likewise perish because of your miscalculation. Desist, sit quietly, and don't expose yourself to peril. I advise you out of compassion for you." She replied, "Father, I must go to the king, and you must give me to him." He said, "Don't do it." She insisted, "I must." He replied, "If you don't desist, I will do to you what the merchant did to his wife." She asked, "Father, what did the merchant do to his wife?" He said:

[The Tale of the Merchant and His Wife]

After what had happened to the donkey and the ox, the merchant and his wife went out in the moonlight to the stable, and he heard the donkey ask the ox in his own language, "Listen, ox, what are you going to do tomorrow morning, and what will you do when the plowman brings you your fodder?" The ox replied, "What shall I do but follow your advice and stick to it? If he brings me my fodder, I will pretend to be ill, lie down, and puff my belly." The donkey shook his head, and said, "Don't do it. Do you know what I heard our master the merchant say to the plowman?" The ox asked, "What?" The donkey replied, "He said that if the ox failed to get up and eat his fodder, he would call the butcher to slaughter him and skin him and would distribute the meat for alms and use the skin for a mat. I am afraid for you, but good advice is a matter of faith; therefore, if he brings you your fodder, eat it and look alert lest they cut your throat and skin you." The ox farted and bellowed.

The merchant got up and laughed loudly at the conversation between the donkey and the ox, and his wife asked him, "What are you laughing at? Are you making fun of me?" He said, "No." She said, "Tell me what made you laugh." He replied, "I cannot tell you. I am afraid to disclose the secret conversation of the animals." She asked, "And what prevents you from telling me?" He answered, "The fear of death." His wife said, "By God, you are lying. This is nothing but an excuse. I swear by God, the Lord of heaven, that if you don't tell me and explain the cause of your laughter, I will leave you. You must tell me." Then she went back to the house crying, and she continued to cry till the morning. The merchant said, "Damn it! Tell me why you are crying. Ask for God's forgiveness, and stop questioning and leave me in peace." She said, "I insist and will not desist." Amazed at her, he replied, "You insist! If I tell you what the donkey said to the ox, which made me laugh, I shall die." She said, "Yes, I insist, even if you have to die." He replied, "Then call your family," and she called their two daughters, her parents and relatives, and some neighbors. The merchant told them that he was about to die, and everyone, young and old, his children, the farmhands, and the servants began to cry until the house became a place of mourning. Then he summoned legal witnesses, wrote a will, leaving his wife and children their due portions, freed his slave-girls, and bid his family good-bye, while everybody, even the witnesses, wept. Then the wife's parents approached her and said, "Desist, for if your husband had not known for certain that he would die if he revealed his secret, he wouldn't have gone through all this." She replied, "I will not change my mind," and everybody cried and prepared to mourn his death.

Well, my daughter Shahrazad, it happened that the farmer kept fifty hens and a rooster at home, and while he felt sad to depart this world and leave his children and relatives behind, pondering and about to reveal and utter his secret, he overheard a dog of his say something in dog language to the rooster, who, beating and clapping his wings, had jumped on a hen and, finishing with her, jumped down and jumped on another. The merchant heard and understood what the dog said in his own language to the rooster, "Shameless, no-good rooster. Aren't you ashamed to do such a thing on a day like this?" The rooster asked, "What is special about this day?" The dog replied, "Don't you know that our master and friend is in mourning today? His wife is demanding that he disclose his secret, and when he discloses it, he will surely die. He is in this predicament, about to interpret to her the language of the animals, and all of us are mourning for him, while you clap your wings and get off one hen and jump on another. Aren't you ashamed?" The merchant heard the rooster reply, "You fool, you lunatic! Our master and friend claims to be wise, but he is foolish, for he has only one wife, yet he does not know how to manage her." The dog asked, "What should he do with her?"

The rooster replied, "He should take an oak branch, push her into a room, lock the door, and fall on her with the stick, beating her mercilessly until he breaks her arms and legs and she cries out, 'I no longer want you to tell me or explain anything.' He should go on beating her until he cures her for life, and she will never oppose him in anything. If he does this, he will live, and live in peace, and there will be no more grief, but he does not know how to manage." Well, my daughter Shahrazad, when the merchant heard the conversation between the dog and the rooster, he jumped up and, taking an oak branch, pushed his wife into a room, got in with her, and locked the door. Then he began to beat her mercilessly on her chest and shoulders and kept beating her until she cried for mercy, screaming, "No, no, I don't want to know anything. Leave me alone, leave me alone. I don't want to know anything," until he got tired of hitting her and opened the door. The wife emerged penitent, the husband learned good management, and everybody was happy, and the mourning turned into a celebration.

"If you don't relent, I shall do to you what the merchant did to his wife." She said, "Such tales don't deter me from my request. If you wish, I can tell you many such tales. In the end, if you don't take me to King Shahrayar, I shall go to him by myself behind your back and tell him that you have refused to give me to one like him and that you have begrudged your master one like me." The vizier asked, "Must you really do this?" She replied, "Yes, I must."

Tired and exhausted, the vizier went to King Shahrayar and, kissing the ground before him, told him about his daughter, adding that he would give her to him that very night. The king was astonished and said to him, "Vizier, how is it that you have found it possible to give me your daughter, knowing that I will, by God, the Creator of heaven, ask you to put her to death the next morning and that if you refuse, I will have you put to death too?" He replied, "My King and Lord, I have told her everything and explained all this to her, but she refuses and insists on being with you tonight." The king was delighted and said, "Go to her, prepare her, and bring her to me early in the evening."

The vizier went down, repeated the king's message to his daughter, and said, "May God not deprive me of you." She was very happy and, after preparing herself and packing what she needed, went to her younger sister, Dinarzad, and said, "Sister, listen well to what I am telling you. When I go to the king, I will send for you, and when you come and see that the king has finished with me, say, 'Sister, if you are not sleepy, tell us a story.' Then I will begin to tell a story, and it will cause the king to stop his practice, save myself, and deliver the people." Dinarzad replied, "Very well."

At nightfall the vizier took Shahrazad and went with her to the great King Shahrayar. But when Shahrayar took her to bed and began to fondle her, she wept, and when he asked her, "Why are you crying?" she replied, "I have a sister, and I wish to bid her goodbye before daybreak." Then the king sent for the sister, who came and went to sleep under the bed. When the night wore on, she woke up and waited until the king had satisfied himself with her sister Shahrazad and they were by now all fully awake. Then Dinarzad cleared her throat and said, "Sister, if you are not sleepy, tell us one of your lovely little tales to while away the night, before I bid you goodbye at daybreak, for I don't know what will happen to you tomorrow." Shahrazad turned to King Shahrayar and said, "May I have your permission to tell a story?" He replied, "Yes," and Shahrazad was very happy and said, "Listen."

from The Tale of the Porter and the Young Girls[1]

There was once a young man in the city of Baghdad, who was by faith a bachelor and by trade a porter.

One day, as he was leaning idly against his basket in the market-place, a woman, wearing a full veil of Mosul silk, tasselled with gold and turned with rare brocade,

---

1. This tale and the remaining selections are translated by Powys Mathers from the classic French translation by J. C. Mardrus. Whereas Haddawy's translation of the Prologue is based on a lean early manuscript, the Mardrus/Mathers version reflects the ongoing, expansive tradition, which added in poetry and many tales not found in the earlier manuscripts. From this point onward, Shahrazad's sister's name is found in its best-known form, Dunyazad. Shahrazad tells the story of the Porter beginning on the ninth night, after a series of shorter stories (always leading onward at daybreak) has fascinated the king and enticed him to postpone her murder night by night.

stopped before him and raised the veil a little from her face. Above it there showed dark eyes with long lashes of silk and lids to set a man dreaming. Her body was slight, her feet were very small, and clear perfection shone about her. She said, and oh, but her voice was sweet: "Take up your basket, porter, and follow me." Hardly believing that so exquisite words could have been said to him, the porter took up his basket and followed the girl, who stopped eventually before the door of a house. She knocked at the door and immediately a Christian opened to her, who gave her, in exchange for a dīnār, a great measure of olive-clear wine which she put into the basket,[2] saying to the porter: "Lift and follow me." "By Allah, this is a day of days!" exclaimed the porter, as he lifted his basket and followed the girl. Arrived at the stall of a fruiterer, she bought Syrian apples, Osmāni quinces, peaches from Uman, jasmine of Aleppo, Damascene nenuphars, cucumbers from the Nile, limes from Egypt, Sultāni citrons, myrtle berries, flowers of henna, blood-red anemones, violets, pomegranate bloom, and the narcissus. All these she put into the porter's basket, and said: "Lift!"; so he lifted and followed her until she came to a butcher's stall. Here she said: "Cut me ten pounds of mutton." So they cut her ten pounds which she wrapped in banana leaves and put into the basket, and said: "Lift!" He lifted and followed her to an almond seller, from whom she bought every kind of almond that there is. Then the porter followed her to a sweetmeat seller from whom she bought a great platter which she covered with things from the stall: open-work sugar tarts with butter, velvet pastries perfumed with musk and stuffed deliciously, sābūnīyah biscuits, small cakes, lime tarts, honey-tasting jam, those sweets called mushabbak, little souffléd patties called lukaimāt al-Kādī,[3] and those others named combs of Zainab which are made with butter and mingled with milk and honey. All these pleasant things she put upon the platter and then placed the platter in the basket. "If you had told me, I would have brought a mule," said the porter. Smiling at his jest, she stopped at the stall of a distiller of perfumes and bought ten sorts of waters, rose water, water of orange flowers, willow flower, violet and other kinds; she bought also a spray of rose-musk-scented water, grains of male incense, aloe wood, ambergris and musk; finally she selected candles of Alexandrian wax and put all in the basket, saying: "Lift and follow!" Obediently the porter took up his basket and followed the young lady until she came to a splendid palace, having a great court set in an inner garden; it was tall, magnificent and four-square, and the door had two leaves of ebony, plated with plates of red gold.

The young girl rapped gently upon the door and it flew wide open. Then the porter looked at her who had opened the door and saw that she was a child having a slim and gracious body, the very model of all a young girl should be, not only for her round and prominent breasts, not only for her beauty and her air of breeding, but also for the perfection of her waist and of her carriage. Her brow was as white as the first ray fallen from the new moon, her eyes were the eyes of a gazelle, and the brows above them were as the crescent moons of Ramadān.[4] Her cheeks were anemones, her mouth the scarlet seal of Sulaiman, her face pale as the full moon when she first rises above the grasses, her breasts twin passion-fruit. As for her young white pliant belly, it lay hid beneath her robe like some precious love letter in a silken case. Seeing her, the porter felt that he was losing his wits and nearly let the basket slip from his shoulders. "As Allah lives, this is the most blessed day of all my life!" he said. Standing

2. Since wine is fobidden in Islam, only Christians are licensed to trade in it.

3. Mushabbak and lukaimat al-Kadi are two types of doughnut-like sweets soaked in honey.

4. The new moons that mark the beginning and end of the holy month of Ramadan, a time of fasting and atonement.

within, the young portress said to her sister the cateress and also to the porter: "Enter, and be your welcome as great as it is good!"

They went in and came at last to an ample hall giving on the central court, hung over with silk brocade and gold brocade, and full of fair gold-crusted furniture. There were vases and carved seats, curtains and close-shut presses all about it, and in the middle a marble couch, inlaid with pearl and diamond, covered with a red satin quilt. On the bed lay a third girl who exceeded all the marvel that a girl can be. Her eyes were Babylonian, for all witchcraft has its seat in Babylon. Her body was slim as the letter alif,[5] her face so fair as to confuse the bright sun. She was as a star among the shining of the stars, a true Arabian woman, as the poet says:

> Who sings your slender body is a reed
> His simile a little misses,
> Reeds must be naked to be fair indeed
> While your sweet garments are but added blisses.
>
> Who sings your body is a slender bough
> Also commits a kindred folly,
> Boughs to be fair must have green leaves enow
> And you, my white one, must be naked wholly.

The young girl got up from the bed, moved a few paces into the middle of the hall until she was near her two sisters and then said to them: "Why are you standing still like this? Take the basket from the porter's head." Then the cateress came in front of the porter, the portress came behind him and, helped by their third sister, they relieved him of his burden. When they had taken everything out of the basket, they arranged all neatly and gave two dīnārs to the porter, saying: "Turn and be gone, O porter!" But he looked at the young girls, admiring the perfection of their beauty, and thought that he had never seen the like. He noticed that there was no man with them and, marvelling at all the drinks, fruits, perfumed flowers, and other good things, had no desire to go away.

The eldest of the girls said: "Why do you not go? Do you find your payment too little?" and then, turning to her sister the cateress: "Give him a third dīnār." But the porter said: "As Allah lives, fair ladies, my ordinary pay is but two half dīnārs; you have paid me well enough and yet all my heart and the inner parts of my soul are troubled about you. I cannot help asking myself what this life of yours is, that you live alone and have no man here to bear you human company. Do you not know that a minaret is of no value unless it be one of the four minarets of a mosque? You are but three, my ladies, you need a fourth. Women cannot be truly happy without men. The poet has said: 'There can be no harmony save with four joined instruments: the lute, the harp, the cithern and flagiolet.' Now you are only three, my ladies; you need a flagiolet, a fourth instrument, a man of discretion, full both of sentiment and intellect, a gifted artist with sealed lips!"

"But, porter," said the young girls, "do you not know that we are virgins and so are fearful of confiding ourselves to the indiscretion of a man? We also have read the poets, and they say: 'Confide in none; a secret told is a secret spoiled.'"

Hearing this, the porter cried: "I swear on your dear lives, my ladies, that I am a man sure, faithful and discreet, one who has studied the annals and read books.

---

5. The first letter of the Arabic alphabet, which looks like the English letter l.

I speak of only pleasing things and am carefully silent about all the rest. I act always according to the saying of the poet:

> I know the duties of high courtesy,
> Your dearest secrets shall be safe with me;
> I'll shut them in a little inner room
> And seal the lock and throw away the key.

Their hearts were much moved towards the porter when they heard his verses and all the rhymes and rhythms he recited, and in jest they said: "You must know that we have spent a great sum of money on this place. Have you the silver to pay us back? For we would not ask you to sit with us unless you paid the reckoning. We take it you desire to stay here, to become our companion in the wine and, above all, to keep us waking all the night until the shadow of the dawn fall on our faces." "Love without gold is a poor make-weight in the scales," added the eldest of the girls, the mistress of the house; and the portress said: "If you have nothing, get you gone with nothing!" But here the cateress interrupted, saying: "Let us leave this joke, my sisters. As Allah lives, this boy has not spoiled our day and another might not have been so patient. I myself will undertake to pay for him."

At this the porter rejoiced with all his heart and said to the cateress: "By Allah, I owe this wonderful bargain all to you!" "Stay with us, then, brave porter," she replied, "and rest assured that you shall be the darling of our eyes." So saying, she rose and, after clasping his waist, began to arrange the flasks, to clarify and pour the wine, and to set places for the feast near a pool of water in the center of the hall. She brought in everything of which they might have need, handed the wine, and saw that all were seated. The porter with these girls on every hand thought that he was dreaming in his sleep.

Soon the cateress took the wine flagon and filled a cup from which each drank three times. Then she filled it afresh and passed it to her sisters and then to the porter, who drank and said these lines:

> In this red wine is liveliness
> And strength and well-being,
> In this red wine is all caress
> And every wanton thing;
> Drink deep and you will find, I trust,
> In this red wine is very lust.

On this he kissed the hands of the three girls and drained the cup. Then he went up to the mistress of the house, saying: "Mistress, I am your slave, your thing, your chattel!" and he recited, in her honour, this stanza of a certain poet:

> I stand most like a slave
> Outside your door,
> Must I an entrance crave
> In vain for ever more?
> There is one gift I have—
> I stand most like a slave.

Then, "Drink, my friend," said she, "and may the wine be sweet and wholesome in its going down: may it give you strength to set out upon that road where lies all bodily well-being." The porter took the cup, kissed the girl's hand and, in a sweetly-modulated voice, sang very low these verses of the poet:

> I gave my love a wine
> Splendidly red as are her cheeks, I said.
> Then she: "I cannot drink these cheeks of mine."
> "Ah, let me speak," I said,
> "Thou can'st not drink those cheeks of thine;
> Then drink these tears and blood of mine!"

Again the young girl took the cup to the porter and, after holding it to his lips, sat down beside her sister. Soon they began to dance and sing and to play with the wonderful petals, the porter all the time taking them in his arms and kissing them, while one said saucy things to him, another drew him to her, and the third beat him with flowers. They went on drinking until the grape sat throned above their reason, and, when her reign was fully established, the portress rose and stripped off all her clothes until she was naked. Jumping into the water of the fountain, she began to play with it, taking it in her mouth and blowing it noisily at the porter, washing all her body, and letting it run between her childish thighs. At length she got out of the fountain, threw herself on the porter's lap, stretched out on her back and, pointing to the thing which was between her thighs, said:

"My darling, do you know the name of that?" "Aha," answered the porter, "usually that is called the house of compassion." Then she cried: "Yū, yū! Are you not ashamed?" and taking him by the neck she began to slap him. "No, no!" he cried. "It is called the thing." But she shook her head, and "Then it is your behind piece," said the porter. Again she shook her head, and "It is your hornet," said he. At these words she began to slap him so hard that she abraded his skin. "You tell me its name!" he shouted, and she told him: "Basil of the bridges." "At last," cried the porter. "Praise be to Allah for your safety, O my basil of the bridges!"

After that, they let the cup go round and round; and the second girl, taking off her clothes, jumped into the basin. There she did as her sister had done and then, getting out, threw herself on to the porter's lap. Pointing to her thighs and the thing between them, she said: "Light of my life, what is the name of that?" "Your crack," he answered. "O listen to his naughty word!" she cried, and slapped him so hard that the hall echoed with the sound. "Then it is basil of the bridges," he hazarded, but she again cried that it was not and went on slapping his neck. "Well, what is its name?" he yelled, and she answered: "The husked sesame."

Now the third girl, in her turn, got up, undressed, and went down into the basin, where she did as her sisters had done. Afterwards she put on some of her clothes and stretched herself over the thighs of the porter. "Guess the name of that," she said, pointing to her delicate parts. The porter tried this name and that and ended by asking her to tell him and cease her slapping. "The khān of Abu-Mansūr," she replied.

Then, in reprisal, the porter rose, undressed and went down into the water, and lo! his blade swam level with the surface. He washed as the girls had done, came out of the basin, and, throwing himself into the lap of the portress, rested his feet in that of the cateress. Pointing to his organ, he asked the mistress of the house: "What is his name, my queen?" At this all the girls laughed till they fell over on their backs, and cried together: "Your zabb!" "No," he said, and took a little bite at each by way of forfeit. Then they cried: "Your tool, then!" But he said: "No," and pinched their breasts.

"But it is your tool," they cried in astonishment, "for it is hot. It is your zabb, because it moves." Each time the porter shook his head and kissed and bit and pinched and hugged them until they laughed again. In the end they had to ask him to tell them; and the porter reflected a moment, looked between his thighs, and winking, said: "Ladies, this child, my zabb, says for himself:

'My name is the Mighty Ungelt Mule who feeds on the basil of bridges, feasts on husked sesame, and stays the night in father Mansūr's khān.'"

At these words, the girls laughed so much that they fell over on their bottoms; and afterwards all four went on drinking from the same cup until the approach of evening. When night fell, they said to the porter: "Be gone, now, turn your face and let us see the width of your shoulders." But the porter cried: "By Allah, it is easier for my soul to quit my body than for me to quit your house, my ladies! Let us make the night continue the sweet day, and tomorrow all can part and follow their destiny upon the road of Allah." The young cateress then spoke up saying: "By my life, sisters, let us ask him to pass the night with us; we will have many good laughs at the naughty fellow who is so shameless and yet so gentle." The others agreed, and said to the porter: "Very well, you can stay with us this night on condition that you obey implicitly and ask no reason or explanation of anything you see." "I agree to that, ladies," he said. "Get up, then, and read what is over the door," they commanded; so he rose, and found over the door these words lettered in gold:

"Speak not of that which concerns you not or you will hear that which shall please you not."

Reading this, the porter said: "Ladies, I call you to witness that I will never speak of that which concerns me not."

At this point Shahrazād saw the approach of morning and discreetly fell silent.

But when the tenth night had come

Dunyazād said: "Finish your tale, dear sister."

So Shahrazād answered: "Gladly and as in duty bound," and thus continued:

It is related, O auspicious King, that when the porter had made his promise to the girls, the cateress rose and set meat before them all, which they ate with good appetite. After the meal, candles were lighted, perfumed wood and incense burned, and all began to drink again and to eat the various delicacies from the market; especially the porter who also recited well-formed verses all the time, shutting his eyes and shaking his head. Suddenly they heard a knocking on the door, which, though it did not interrupt their pleasure, caused the portress to rise. She came back, saying: "Indeed, tonight's pleasure is to be perfect, for there are three strangers at the door with shaved beards and each blind of the left eye, which is a strange coincidence. It is easy to see that they come from the lands of Rūm, each has different features and yet their faces all match in their fittingness for being laughed at. If we let them in, we can have much fun at their expense." She persuaded her companions, who said: "Tell them that they may come in, but be sure they understand the condition: 'Speak not of that which concerns you not or you will hear that which shall please you not.'" So the young girl ran joyously to the door and came back leading the three one-eyed men, who indeed had shaved beards, moustaches twisted back, and all the signs of that brotherhood of beggars called kalandars. As soon as they came in, they wished peace to the company, backing one by one as they did so; on which the girls stood up and invited them to be seated. The three men, after they had sat down, looked at the porter, who was very drunk, and supposing him to belong to their brotherhood, said among themselves: "Here is another kalandar; he is sure to bear us friendly company." But the porter, who had heard what they said, jumped to his feet and, eyeing them sternly and a little squintingly, said: "All right, all right, my friends, make yourselves at home; and begin by digesting those words written above the door." The girls burst out laughing at his words and said to each other: "We are going to have fun with these kalandars and the porter." They set food before the kalandars—who ate like kalandars!—then wine— and the kalandars drank turn and turn about, reaching out again and again for the cup. When the drink was passing round at a rare pace, the porter said: "Come, brothers, have you not some good tale of marvellous adventure in your scrips to amuse us?" Cheered by this suggestion, the kalandars asked for musical instruments and, when the portress had fetched out a Mosul drum fitted with crotals, a lute of Irāq, and a Persian flagiolet, they stood up and began to play while the girls sang with them. The porter became frenzied with pleasure and kept on shouting: "Ha! yā Allah!", so struck was he by the harmonious voices of the singers.

In the middle of all this, knocking was again heard upon the door and the portress rose to see who was there.

Now this was the reason for the second knocking on the door:

That night the Khalīfah, Hārūn al-Rashīd, had gone down to wander about his city to see and hear for himself what might be going on there. He was accompanied by his wazīr, Jafar al-Barmaki,[6] and by Masrūr, his sword-bearer, the instrument of his justice. You must know that it was a habit of his to disguise himself as a merchant and make such expeditions.

While he was walking through the streets of the city, he passed that palace and heard the sounds of music and gaiety which issued from it. Then said the Khalīfah to Jafar: "I wish to enter that place to see those singers." Jafar answered: "They must be a crowd of drunkards. If we go in some hurt may come to you." But the Khalīfah said: "Certainly we must go in. I wish to find a way in which we can enter and take them by surprise." "I hear and I obey," said Jafar at this command and, going up to the door, he knocked.

When the young portress opened the door, the wazīr said to her: "My mistress, we are merchants from Tiberias. Ten days ago we came to Baghdad with our goods and took lodging in the khān of the merchants. One of the other traders at the khān asked us to his house tonight to eat with him. After the meal, which lasted an hour in which we ate and drank excellently, he gave us leave to depart. We came out but, the night being dark and we strangers, lost our way to the khān where we lodge. So now we beg you of your great goodness to let us come in and pass the night at your house. Allah will reward your kindness." The portress looked at them closely and, seeing that they had the appearance of most respectable merchants, went in to ask the advice of her two companions. The other two said: "Let them come in!" So she returned to the door, crying: "Enter!" On this invitation the Khalīfah and Jafar and Masrūr came in and the girls rose, putting themselves at their service and saying: "Be very welcome. Take your ease here, dear companions; but accept, we pray, this one condition: 'Speak not of that which concerns you not or you will hear that which shall please you not.'" The newcomers answered: "Be it so," and sat down with the others. While they were being invited to drink and to send round the cup, the Khalīfah looked at

---

6. The trusted vizier and companion of Harun (or Haroun) al-Rashid (r. 786–809), the most famous of all the Abbasid Caliphs.

the three kalandars and was astonished to see that each was blind of the left eye; then at the girls and was overcome with surprise at all their beauty and grace. When the girls, in their ministrations to the guests, offered the Khalīfah a cup of the rarest wine, he refused, saying: "I am vowed to pilgrimage." So the portress got up and placed a little table of finest inlay before him on which she set a cup of Chinese porcelain into which she poured spring water refreshed with snow, mingling sugar and rose-water within it. The Khalīfah accepted this, thanking her cordially and saying to himself: "Tomorrow I shall reward her for her kindness."

The girls continued to act the hostess and pass about the wine till the wits of the companions were dancing dizzily. Then she who was the mistress of the house rose up and, having asked if any wanted more, took the cateress by the hand saying: "Rise, my sister, that we may do that which we have to do." "Be it as you say," the other answered. On this the portress also rose and, telling the kalandars to get up from the center of the hall and seat themselves by the door, herself cleared and tidied the central space. The other two called to the porter: "By Allah, your friendship is of but little use! You are no stranger here but belong to the house." On this the porter stood up, lifted the skirts of his robe and tightened his belt, saying: "Tell me what to do and I shall do it." "Follow me," said the portress. So he followed her out of the hall and saw two black bitches with chains round their necks, which, as he was bid, he led back into the middle of the hall. Then the eldest pulled up her sleeves, took a whip, and told the porter to lead forward one of the bitches. When he had done so, dragging her by the chain, the animal began to weep, raising its head piteously towards the girl; but the latter, without seeming to notice, fell upon it, beating it over the head with her whip till the bitch yelled and wept and she herself could strike no more. Then she threw down the whip and, taking the bitch in her arms, clasped it to her breast, wiped away its tears, and kissed its head which she held between her hands. After a little, she said to the porter: "Bring me the other, and take this one back." So the porter brought the other bitch forward and the girl treated it as she had the first.

The Khalīfah felt his heart filled with pity at this sight; his breast shook with grief and he signed with his eye to Jafar to question the young woman. But Jafar signed to him that it were better to keep silent. Soon the mistress of the house turned to her sisters saying: "Come, let us do as is our custom." They answered: "Yes"; so she got up on to the marble bed which was plated with gold and silver and said to the other two: "Let it be done!" Then the portress also got up on to the bed; but the cateress went into her own room and brought back a satin bag fringed with green silk. Halting before the other two, she opened the bag and drew a lute from it. First tuning this and then playing upon it, she sang these lines of love and all the sadness of love:

> Love at my door
> Knocked and I gave him bed.
> When sleep saw this
> He took offence and fled.
> "Give me back sleep;
> Where has he gone?" I said.
>   * * *
> It's not that time
> Has passed, but that so has she,
> It's not that love

Won't last, but that nor will she,
Not that life's gone,
But that she's gone from me.

My soul is bound
By the scents of her body,
Jasmine and musk
And rose of her body,
Amber and nard,
The scents of her body.

"Allah comfort you, my sister," cried out the portress, when the song was finished; then, tearing all her clothes in an ecstasy of grief, she fell in a faint upon the floor.

Her body being in some sort bared, the Khalīfah was able to see upon it the prints of whips and rods, a circumstance which astonished and appalled him. But the cateress came and cast water in her sister's face until she recovered consciousness; then she brought her a new robe and helped her into it.

The Khalīfah whispered to Jafar: "You do not seem moved by this. Do you not see the marks of the scourge on the woman? I can hardly keep silent and I will know no rest until I have found out the truth of all this and of the matter of the two bitches." "Lord and Master," answered Jafar, "remember the condition: 'Speak not of that which concerns you not or you will hear that which shall please you not.'"

While they were talking thus, the cateress again took up the lute and, pressing it against her rounded breast, sounded the chords and sang:

If one came to us plaining of love,
What would we answer?
Seeing that we also are drowned in love,
What would we do?
If we charged a speaker to speak for us,
What would he know of it?

* * *

Again the portress fell fainting and again her naked body showed the marks of whips and rods.

The three kalandars began whispering together when they saw this: "It had been better for us if we had never come into this house, even though we had to sleep on the naked ground; for what we have just seen is enough to melt the marrow in our spines." The Khalīfah turned to them and said: "Why is that?" "We are afraid of what has happened," they answered. "Is that so?" said the Khalīfah, "then you are not of this house?" "We are not," they answered, "we imagined it belonged to that man beside you." "By Allah, it does not!" cried the porter. "This is the very first time that I have entered here. Also, God knows, it would have been better for me to have slept on the rubbish heaps among the ruins."

So they concerted with each other and said: "We are seven men to three women, let us demand an explanation of these things and, if they will not answer willingly, we can use force." They all agreed to this except Jafar, who said: "Do you think that right and equitable? Remember, we are their guests and that they laid down certain conditions which we swore to keep. The night is nearly over; it would be better for each of us to go forth and seek his destiny upon the road of Allah." Then, winking at the Khalīfah and drawing him aside, he continued: "We have but one more hour to stay here. Tomorrow I promise that I will bring them up before you, and then we can compel them to tell their story." But the Khalīfah said: "I have not the patience to wait till tomorrow." The others continued their planning, some saying this and some saying that, but it all came back to the question: "Who is to ask them?" At last it was decided that the porter should do so.

So, when the girls said: "Good folk, what are you talking about?", the porter rose to his feet and, standing up straight before the lady of the house, addressed her courteously: "My queen, I ask and pray you in the name of Allah, on behalf of all us jolly fellows, to tell us the tale of those two bitches and why you so beat them and then weep over them and kiss them. Tell us, too, for we wait to hear it, the cause of the marks of whips and rods on the body of your sister. This we ask of you; that is all, my queen." Then the lady of the house questioned them: "Is this that the porter has said asked in the name of all?" And each, with the exception of Jafar, answered: "Yes." Jafar said nothing.

The eldest girl, hearing this answer of theirs, exclaimed: "As Allah lives, you who are our guests have done us here the most grievous of wrongs. We bound you to this condition: 'Speak not of that which concerns you not or you will hear that which shall please you not.' Was it not enough for you to come into our house and eat our good food? Perhaps, though, it was less your fault than the fault of our sister who let you in."

So saying, she pulled the sleeves of her robe away from her wrist and beat the floor with her foot three times, calling: "Come quick, come quick!" The door of one of the great curtained presses opened and out glided seven strong negroes carrying sharpened swords. To these she said: "Bind the arms of these prattling guests and fasten them one to the other." This the negroes did, saying: "O mistress, O hidden flower beyond the sight of men, may we cut off their heads?" "Have patience for an hour," she answered. "I wish to know what sort of men they are before they die."

On this the porter cried: "By Allah, mistress queen, do not kill me for the crime of others. All these have sinned, committing a notable crime against you, but not I. As God lives, how happy, how paradisal would our night have been if we had never set eyes on these ill-omened kalandars.[7] I have always said that kalandars could lay waste the loveliest of cities just by coming into it." And he added these lines:

> The fairest gift of strength is clemency
> If the weak offend;
> So do not, for our love's sake, punish me
> For the fault of a friend.

The eldest girl burst out laughing when the porter had finished speaking.

At this point Shahrazād saw the approach of day and discreetly fell silent.

But when the eleventh night had come

She said:

It is related, O auspicious King, that when the eldest girl burst out laughing after having been angry, she came down to the company and said: "Tell me all that there is to tell, for you have but one hour to live. I give you this indulgence because you are

---

7. There was a superstitious belief that one-eyed people bring bad luck.

poor folk. If you were among the most noble, great ones of your tribes or even governors, it is true that I would hurry on your punishment."

"Jafar, we are in sorry case," said the Khalīfah, "tell her who we are or she may kill us." "Which is exactly what we deserve," said Jafar. Then said the Khalīfah: "There is a time for being witty and a time for being serious, there is a time for everything."

Now first of all the eldest girl approached the kalandars and asked them: "Are you brothers?" To this they answered: "No, by Allah, we are only poor men of the poorest who live by cupping and scarifying."[8] Then she turned to one of them and said: "Were you born without one eye?" "As God lives, I was not," he answered, "but the tale of the way I lost my eye is so extraordinary that, if it were written with a needle in the corner of another eye, yet would it be a lesson to the circumspect." The second and the third made the same kind of answer; then all three said: "Each of us was born in a different country; the stories of our lives are strange and our adventures pass the marvellous." "Well, then," said the girl, "each of you must tell his story and the reason of his coming to our house. Should the tale seem good to us, each then may make his bow and go his way."

The first who came forward was the porter; and he said: "My queen, I am a porter, nothing more. Your cateress here gave me things to carry and led me to you. You know well what happened to me after I got here and, if I refuse to be more particular, you know why. That is all my tale. I will not add another word to it, and Allah bless you." Then said the eldest girl: "Get you gone, make your bow and let us see the last of you." "But," said the porter, "no, by God, I will not stir until I have heard the tales of these friends of mine."

[*The three kalandars proceed to tell their tales of adventure and misfortune, and then the owner of the house asks Haroun al-Rashid for his story.*]

The young girl then turned to the Khalīfah, Jafar and Masrur, asking for their stories. So Jafar went up and told her the fable that he had already told the portress at the door. After she had heard him, the girl said: "I will pardon you all. Depart quickly and in peace."

When they were safely out in the road, the Khalīfah asked the kalandars whither they were going and, when they answered that they did not know, instructed Jafar to take them to his home and bring them before him in the morning, so that he might see what could be done for them.

After Jafar had done his bidding, the Khalīfah returned to his palace, where he tried in vain to sleep. Early in the morning he rose and, mounting his throne, held audience of all the chief men of his empire. When these had departed, he turned to Jafar, saying: "Bring to me the three young girls and the two bitches and the three kalandars." Jafar brought them all forthwith and, when they stood before the Khalīfah, the girls being heavily veiled, addressed these words to them: "We hold you free of any unkindness; you knew not who we were and yet you pardoned us and treated us well. Now learn that you have come into the hands of the fifth of the line of Abbās, Hārūn al-Rashīd, the Khalīfah. It is unwise to tell him aught but the truth."

When Jafar had thus spoken for the Prince of Believers, the eldest girl came forward, saying: "Prince of Believers, my story is so strange that if it were written with a needle on the corner of an eye yet would it serve as a lesson to the circumspect!"

At this point Shahrazād saw the approach of morning and discreetly fell silent.

8. Performing simple medical treatments.

But when the sixteenth night had come

She said:

It is related, O auspicious King, that the eldest of the young girls stood up before the Prince of Believers and told this story:

[The Tale of Zubaidah, the First of the Girls]

Prince of Believers; my name is Zubaidah, my sister who opened the door for you is Amīnah, and our youngest is called Fahīmah. We were all three born of the same father but not of the same mother; these two bitches, on the other hand, are full sisters to me, being born of the same father and the same mother. When our father died, leaving five thousand dīnars to be divided equally among us, Amīnah and Fahīmah left us to live with their mother, while I and my two sisters lived together. I was the youngest of the three, though I am older than Amīnah and Fahīmah.

Soon after our father's death, my two elder sisters married and, in a little while, their husbands fitted out commercial ventures with their wives' inheritances and set sail, each taking his wife with him and leaving me alone.

My sisters were away for four years, and during that time their husbands, becoming bankrupt, lost all their goods and made off, abandoning them among strangers in strange lands. After bitter sufferings they managed to make their ways back to me, but they looked so like beggars that at first I did not recognise them. Yet when they spoke to me I knew who they were and questioned them tenderly as to what had happened. "Sister, words cannot help us now," they answered. "Allah took the reed pen and wrote that it was to be." I pitied them from the bottom of my heart, sent them to the bath, and put fair new garments upon them, saying: "Sisters, you are the elder, while I am the younger; you stand to me in the place of both father and mother. My inheritance, by Allah's grace, has prospered and increased. Come, use the profit of it as your own and live with me in honour and in peace."

I loaded them with benefits and they stayed with me for a year, sharing my substance. But one day they said: "Marriage would be better for us, we cannot do without it any longer, we have no more patience with living alone." "I fear that you will get little good from marriage," I said, "for an honest man is hard to come by in these days. You tried marriage once; have you forgotten how you found it?"

But they would not listen to me, being set on marrying without my consent; so I married them to husbands, giving them money and the necessary clothes. And the new husbands took them away as before.

It was not long, however, before the new husbands deceived them and decamped with all the dowry which I had provided. Naked and full of excuses, they returned to me, saying: "Do not blame us, we are older than you but you are wiser than we. We promise never to say a word again on the subject of marriage." "Sweet welcome to you, my sisters," I answered, "there are none dearer to me in the world than you." So I kissed them and behaved bountifully towards them as before.

After they had lived with me for another year, it came into my head to fit out a ship with merchandise and to voyage in it to do business at Basrah. So I got ready a vessel, filling it with merchandise and goods of all kinds as well as necessaries for the voyage. I asked my sisters whether they would rather stay at home while I was away or come with me. They decided to accompany me, so I took them with me and we set sail. But first I divided my money into two halves, one of which I took with me and one of which I hid at home in case some misfortune befell the ship and we escaped with our lives.

We sailed on night and day, but by ill-luck the captain lost his course, so that we were driven to the outer ocean and into a sea quite other than the one we had designed to reach. Driving before the wind for ten days, we saw at last a city far off and asked the captain what its name might be. "As Allah lives, I do not know," he answered. "I have never seen it in my life, nor the sea in which we are. But the important thing is that we are now out of danger. It only remains for you to enter that city and offer your merchandise. I suggest that you should sell it there if you can."

An hour later he came to us again, saying: "Disembark now and go into the city to see the marvels of Allah there. Call on His name and you shall go in safety."

We entered the city and saw to our stupefaction that all the inhabitants had been turned into black rocks, but that, while they had been petrified, everything else in the markets and the streets was as it had been, goods of every kind and appointments of gold and silver all about the place. We were delighted with what we saw and, saying to each other: "Surely there must be some extraordinary reason for all this," separated, each going in different directions about the streets, to collect as much as might be conveniently carried of gold, silver and precious fabrics.

It was towards the citadel that I made my way. There I found the King's palace and, entering by a great door of solid gold and lifting a velvet curtain, I saw that all the furniture and everything else there was of fine gold or silver. In the courtyard and in all the rooms soldiers and chamberlains stood or sat, all turned to stone; and in the central hall, filled with chamberlains, lieutenants and wazīrs, I saw the King sitting on his throne, petrified also but arrayed in such noble and costly garments as took my breath away. Fifty silk-clad mamelūks[9] holding naked swords stood there in stone about the King. His throne was encrusted with great pearls lying among other jewels. And each pearl shone so like a star that I thought I should lose my wits in gazing on them.

Going on, I reached the harīm, which I found to be more wonderful than all the rest, built even to the window-bars of solid gold and with silken hangings on the walls and with velvet and satin curtains hanging before the doors and windows. In the midst of a group of women, all turned to stone, I saw the Queen herself dressed in a robe sewn with noble pearls, crowned with a mass of great jewels, with collars and necklaces about her throat of pleasantly carved gold; but herself changed to black stone.

Wandering further, I came to an open door made with two leaves of virgin silver, and beyond it I saw a porphyry staircase of seven steps. Mounting this, I came to a white marble hall, covered with a carpet of gold thread, in the middle of which there rose, between great golden torches, a dais also of solid gold picked out with emeralds and turquoises. An alabaster bed, studded with pearls and upholstered with precious embroidery, stood on the dais with a great light shining by it. I came near and found that the light proceeded from a diamond, as large as an ostrich's egg, lying on a stool by the bedside and shining from all its facets so that the whole hall was filled with radiance.

Although the diamond outshone them utterly, the torches were lighted; therefore I deduced that some human hand was near and went on searching among the other halls, marvelling at all I saw and hunting everywhere for a human being. I was so entranced that I forgot all about my voyage, my ship, and my sisters. Night fell suddenly while I was still in a dream at all that beauty, and when I tried to leave the palace I could not find my way. In my search I came again to the hall with the alabaster bed, the diamond, and the lighted torches. Lying down, I half covered myself with a blue

9. Warrior slaves.

satin quilt wrought with silver and pearl, and took up a copy of our Koran, that sacred book. It was written out in stately gold characters with red devices and illuminations in all colours. From it I read a few verses to the glory of Allah and to reprove myself that my sleep might be holy. I meditated on the words of the Prophet, whom may Allah bless, and tried to sleep.

When the middle of the night had come and I was still awake, I heard a sweet and learned voice reciting the Koran. I rose in haste and, going in the direction of the voice, came to a little room with an open door. I entered softly, leaving the torch which I had caught up outside, and saw that the place was a kind of sanctuary. It was lighted by little green glass lamps and on its floor, facing the East, lay a prayer-rug upon which a very beautiful young man was reading the Koran aloud with grave attention and perfect eloquence. In my astonishment I asked myself how this young man alone could have escaped the fate of all the city. I came towards him and wished him peace. When he turned his eyes upon me and wished me peace, I said: "I conjure you by the truth of the sacred words which you are reading from the book of Allah to answer my question truly."

Calmly and sweetly he smiled at me, saying: "First, O woman, tell me how it is that you have come into this place where I pray, and then I will answer any question you like to put to me." When he had listened in astonishment to my story, I questioned him concerning the extraordinary appearance of the city. He shut the sacred book and, placing it in a satin bag, bade me sit at his side. I did so and, gazing attentively at him, found in him that full perfection which is in the moon: sympathy, beauty of face, proportioned elegance of body. His cheeks were as clear as crystal, his face had the delicate tint of the fresh date, as if it had been he of whom the poet was thinking when he wrote these lines:

> A watcher of the stars at night
> Looked up and saw to rose and white
> A boy, with such delicious grace,
> Such brilliant tint of breast and face,
> So curved and delicate of limb,
> That he exclaimed on seeing him:
> "Sure it was Saturn gave that hair,
> A black star falling in the air;
> Those roses were a gift from Mars;
> The Archer of the seven stars
> Gave all his arrows to that eye;
> While great sagacious Mercury
> Did sweet intelligence impart;
> Queen Venus forged his golden heart
> And…and…" But here the sage's art
> Stopped short; and his old wits went wild
> When the new star drew near and smiled.

Red flames were lighted in my heart when I looked at him and, in the violent trouble of my senses, I regretted that I had not met him long before. "Master and sovereign," I said, "I pray you answer me." "I hear and I obey," he replied, and told me the following remarkable story:

Honourable lady, this was my father's city, filled with his subjects and the people of his kin. He it was whom you saw petrified upon his throne, the Queen you saw was my mother. Both were magicians, worshippers of terrible Nardūn, who swore by fire and light, by shade and heat, and all the turning stars.

For a long time my father had no children. I was the child of his age and he reared me carefully throughout my boyhood, that I might be bred up to the true happiness of kingship.

Now in the palace there was a very old woman who in secret was a Believer in Allah and his Messenger, though in public she pretended to fall in with the creed of my parents. My father had great confidence in her as a faithful and chaste woman, he heaped benefits upon her and firmly believed that she was of his own faith. When I began to grow up, he put me in her charge, commanding her to give me a good education and a grounding in the laws of Nardūn.

The old woman took me into her charge and at once declared to me the religion of Islām, from its rites of purification and ablution to the sacred forms of its prayers. She taught and expounded the Koran to me in the Prophet's own tongue[1] and, when she had taught me all that she knew, warned me to keep my knowledge sedulously from my father lest he should kill me. I did so and, when a short time afterwards that saintly old woman died breathing her last words into my ear, I continued a secret believer in Allah and His Prophet. Far different were the inhabitants of this city who hardened their hearts and dwelt in darkness. But one day, while they continued their idolatry, a voice like thunder spoke from an invisible muezzin to far and near, saying: "O people of the city, leave the worship of fire and Nardūn, and turn to the one Almighty King."

Terrified by this voice the inhabitants of the city sought the King, my father, and asked the meaning of these awful words. But my father told them not to be frightened or amazed, and bade them stand firm in their old beliefs.

So for another year they blindly worshipped fire, until the day came round again on which the voice had been heard. Then the voice boomed out once more, and this it did on the same day for the next three years. But the people continued to worship their false god until one morning, out of the clear sky of dawn, wrath and sorrow fell upon them and they were suddenly turned to black stone, they and their horses, their mules and their camels, and all their beasts. I alone, who was the sole Believer in the city, escaped the doom.

Since then I have remained here, praying, fasting, and reciting from the Book, but I have been very lonely, lovely lady, with no one to bear me human company.

On this I said to him: "Youth of every perfection, will you not come with me to the city of Baghdad, where are sages and venerable old men steeped in the teachings of our Religion? There your learning and your faith will be increased together, and I, though I am a woman of some account, will be your slave there. In Baghdad I am mistress among my people, with a following of men, servants and young boys; also I have a ship here full of all necessary goods. Fate threw me upon your coast and Destiny has seen fit to bring us together." I did not cease from fanning his desire to go with me until he consented to do so.

At this point Shahrazād saw the approach of morning and discreetly fell silent as was her custom.

But when the seventeenth night had come

---

1. Arabic.

She said:

It is related, O auspicious King, that the girl Zubaidah did not cease from fanning the desire of the young man to go with her until he consented to do so.

They talked long together until sleep overcame them, and Zubaidah slept that night at the feet of the young man. I leave you to imagine whether she was happy or no.

Zubaidah continued her story to the Khalīfah Hārūn al-Rashīd, in the hearing of Jafar and the three kalandars in these words:

When morning broke, we chose out from all the treasures of the palace the best we could carry, and went down towards the city, where we met my slaves and the captain who had been looking for me a long time. They were delighted to see me again and more than a little astonished when I gave them the outline of my story and of the young man's tale concerning the doom which had fallen upon the city. But hardly had my sisters seen the handsome young man than they were filled with violent jealousy and began in their hatred secretly to plot my hurt.

We all went aboard, I in great joy because I loved the youth, and, taking advantage of a favourable wind, sailed away. My sisters never left us alone, and one day they asked me directly what I intended to do with the youth. I told them that I meant to marry him and, turning towards him, I said: "Master, I desire to become your slave. Do not refuse me this." "Indeed, I do not refuse," he answered and, our troth being thus plighted, I said to my sisters: "This young man is enough property for me. All else I have I give to you." "Your wish is law," they answered, but at the same time they schemed against me in their hearts.

We came with favouring winds from the Dread Sea to the Sea of Safety, across which we sailed for several days till we saw the buildings of Basrah rising from the water. That night we cast anchor and all slept.

While we slept, my sisters rose and, lifting the youth and myself, cast us, mattresses and all, into the sea. The poor young man, who could not swim, was drowned. It was written by Allah that he should become one of the martyrs, just as it was written that I should be saved. For, when I fell into the water, Allah sent me a spar of wood to which I clung and supported by which I was carried by the waves to the shore of a nearby island. There I dried my clothes and slept, rising in the morning to look for some track which should lead me to safety. Soon I found a road worn by human feet which I followed into the interior of the island, until I had gone right across it and came out on the other side, opposite the city of Basrah. Suddenly I saw a little snake hurrying towards me, hotly pursued by a much larger snake who was trying to kill it. I felt pity for the little snake which was so weary that its tongue hung out. So I lifted a great stone and smashed in the head of the large snake, killing it on the spot. Immediately to my surprise the little snake spread two wings and, flying up into the air, disappeared from my sight.

Being broken by fatigue, I lay down where I was and slept for about an hour. When I woke, I found a beautiful young negress seated at my feet, rubbing and kissing them. I snatched them away in considerable shame, not knowing whether her intentions towards me were honourable or not, and asked her sharply who she was and what she wanted. "I hastened to come to you," she said, "because of the great service you have done me in killing my enemy. I am a Jinnīyah and was in the likeness of that little snake. The big snake was my enemy, a Jinnī who wished to rape me and to kill me. You saved me, so I flew at once to the ship from which your two sisters threw you. I changed them into black bitches and have brought them to you." Sure enough, there were two black bitches tied to the tree behind me. "Lastly," went on the Jinnīyah, "I transported all your riches to your house in Baghdad and then sank the ship. As for your young man, he is drowned. I can do nothing against death. Allah alone is Almighty."

With these words she took me in her arms together with my sisters, the bitches, and, flying with us through the air, set us down safely on the terrace of my house here in Baghdad.

Looking about me I found all the treasures and the goods that had been in my ship ranged in careful order round the rooms, not one having been lost or spoiled. Before she left, the Jinnīyah said to me: "I command you by the sacred symbol on the Seal of Sulaimān to give each of these bitches three hundred strokes of the whip every day. If you forget even once I shall be obliged to come back and change you also into the same shape."

What could I answer save: "I hear and I obey"?

Ever since then, O Prince of Believers, I have beaten them and then pitifully caressed them as you have seen. That is my story.

* * *

But when the eighteenth night had come

Shahrazād continued in this wise:

It is related, O auspicious King, that, on hearing the stories of the girls Zubaidah and Amīnah, who with their little sister Fahīmah, the two black bitches, and the three kalandars, had been brought before him, the Khalīfah Hārūn al-Rashīd rejoiced at the marvel of the two tales and ordered them to be written out in fair calligraphy by his scribes. * * *

Then al-Amīn was remarried to the young Amīnah, Zubaidah to the first kalandar who was a king's son, the other two sisters to the other two kalandars, princes both, and the Khalīfah himself wedded the youngest of the five sisters, the maiden Fahīmah, the witty and agreeable cateress.

Hārūn al-Rashīd had a palace built for each couple and endowed them with riches that they might live happily. Also, hardly had night fallen when he himself hastened to bed with the young Fahīmah, and they passed the sweetest of nights together.

from The Tale of Sympathy the Learned

But when the two-hundred-and-seventieth night had come

Little Dunyazād waited until Shahrazād had finished her act with the King, and then raised her head, crying: "O sister, why do you not start at once the anecdotes which you promised us concerning that delightful poet Abū Nuwās,[1] the Khalifah's friend, the sweetest singer of Irāq and Arabia?" Shahrazād smiled at her sister, saying: "I only wait the King's permission before telling you some of the adventures of Abū Nuwās, who was not only an exquisite poet but a notorious evil-liver."

Dunyazād ran to her sister and embraced her, saying: "What did he do? Tell us at once, if you please."

But King Shahryār turned to Shahrazād and said: "O Shahrazād, it would give me great pleasure to hear one or two of these adventures, for I am sure that they are most

---

1. One of the major poets of the Abbasid period.

entertaining; but tonight my mind is more inclined to higher things and would rather hear words of wisdom from you. If you know some tale which can fortify our souls with moral precepts and help us to profit by the experience of the wise, do not scruple to begin at once. Afterwards, if my patience be not exhausted, you may recount the adventures of Abū Nuwās."

Shahrazād hastened to reply: "By chance I have been thinking all day, O auspicious King, of a story which concerns a girl who was called Sympathy, a slave unequalled both in beauty and learning; I am ready to tell you all that I have heard of what she did and what she knew."

"As Allah lives," cried King Shahryār, "you may begin at once; for nothing pleases me more than to learn wisdom from the lips of beauty. I hope that the tale will satisfy and profit me with an example of that learning which becomes a faithful Muslim woman."

Shahrazād reflected for a short time and then raised her finger, saying:

It is related—but Allah is all-wise and all-knowing—that there was once a very rich merchant in Baghdad, who had honour and privilege of every kind, but whom Allah had deprived of one happiness. He had no child, not even a daughter. He grew old in sorrow, seeing his bones becoming more and more transparent, his back more and more arched, without being able to obtain any consoling result from his numerous wives. One day, however, after he had distributed a great alms, visited saints, fasted and prayed fervently, he lay with his youngest wife and, by Allah's grace, got her with child.

At the end of nine months to a day she bore him a man-child as fair as a fragment of the moon; therefore the merchant in gratitude to Allah entertained the poor, the widow, and the orphan for seven whole days, and then named his son Abū al-Husn.[2]

The child was carried in the arms of nurses and beautiful slaves, cared for like some jewel of price by all the women, until he reached the age when he might begin to learn. Then wise masters were given to him, who taught him the wonderful words of the Koran, beautiful writing, poetry, arithmetic, and especially the science of shooting with the bow.

Not only was his education finer than that of any other child then living, but his beauty was almost a magic thing. His boyish graces, the fresh colour of his cheeks, the flowers of his lips, and the young down of his face were thus celebrated by a poet:

> Though spring has passed already over the rose trees,
> Here are some buds not fully opened yet,
> In this sweet garden ignorant of weather:
> See, the down feather
> Of the violet
> Under those trees!

Young Abū al-Husn was his father's joy and the light of his eyes, during the old man's remaining term upon this earth. When he felt that his debt was to be paid to Allah, he called his son to him, saying: "My child, quittance nears and I have nothing left to do but prepare myself to stand before the Master. I leave you great riches, money and goods, rich fields and farms, which should last your lifetime and the lifetime of your children's children. Enjoy your property without excess, thanking the Giver and being mindful of Him all your days." With that the old merchant died, and his son shut himself in with grief, after superintending his father's funeral.

2. "The handsome one."

Soon, however, his friends led him away from his sorrow and persuaded him to go to the hammām and change his garments, saying: "He who is born again in a son like yourself does not die. Have done with tears; make the most of your riches and your youth."

So Abū al-Husn little by little forgot the counsels of his father and learnt to look upon happiness and gold as inexhaustible. He satisfied every caprice of his nature, frequenting singers and musicians, eating enormous quantities of chicken every day (for he was very fond of chicken), unsealing old jars of strong wine, and hearing ever about him the noise of chinking goblets. He exhausted all that he could exhaust and spent all that he could spend, until he woke one morning to find that there remained of all his possessions only a single slave girl.

But here you must pause to admire the workings of Fate, who had decreed that this one remaining slave should be the supreme marvel of Western and Eastern women. She was called Sympathy; and never had a name been better given. She was as up-right as the letter alif, and her figure was so slim that she might defy the sun to cast a shadow by her; the colouring of her young face was wonderful, and its expression was both fortunate and filled with blessing. Her mouth seemed to have been sealed with the seal of Sulaimān to guard the pearls within; the two pomegranates of her breasts were separated by a valley of shadows and delights; and her navel was carved so deep that it would have held an ounce of nutmeg butter. Her reed-like waist ended in so heavy a croup that she left deep prints of it in every sofa and mattress which she used. A certain poet had her in mind when he wrote:

> If you can call the sun and the moon and the rose tree
> Sad-coloured,
> Call her sad-coloured also.
>
> Hearts beat the advance as she advances,
> And the retreat when she retreats.
> The river of life flows through the meadows of Eden,
> And the meadows of Eden are below her garment,
> The moon is beneath her mantle.
>
> Her body is a song of colours:
> Carnation of roses answers to silver,
> Black ripe berries
> And new-cut sandal-wood
> Are one note.
>
> The man who takes her is more blessed
> Than the God who gives her;
> And He is continually called blessed.

Such was the slave Sympathy, the last possession of the prodigal Abū al-Husn of Baghdad.

At this point Shahrazād saw the approach of morning and discreetly fell silent.

But when the two-hundred-and-seventy-first night had come

She said:

Seeing that he was ruined for ever, Abū al-Husn fell into a desolation which robbed him of both hunger and sleep; for three days and three nights he refused food and drink and sleep, so that the slave Sympathy thought he was on the point of dying and determined to save him at any cost to herself.

She put on the rest of her jewels and those robes which remained most fit to be seen; then she went to her master and said with an encouraging smile: "Allah will put an end to your misfortunes by my help. You have only to take me with you to the Commander of the Faithful, Hārūn al-Rashīd, fifth of the line of Abbās, and offer me to him for ten thousand dīnārs. If he objects that the price is too high, you must say: 'Prince of Believers, this girl is worth more; as you will discover if you put her to the proof. You will find that she is without equal or near equal, and worthy to serve the Khalīfah.'" She finished by recommending that he should not bate his price on any consideration.

Abū al-Husn had neglected, in his careless way, to notice the supreme gifts of his beautiful slave; therefore he merely thought that the idea was not a bad one and held some chances of success. He led Sympathy into the presence of the Khalīfah without delay, and repeated the offer which she had recommended to him.

The Khalīfah turned towards her, asking: "What is your name?" "I am called Sympathy," she answered, and he continued: "O Sympathy, are you indeed learned, and can you tell me the various branches of knowledge in which you excel?" "My master," she answered, "I have studied syntax, poetry, civil and canon law, music, astronomy, geometry, arithmetic, the law concerning inheritance, the art of elucidating books of spells and reading ancient inscriptions. I know the Sublime Book by heart and can read it in seven different ways;[3] I know the exact number of its chapters, verses, divisions, parts, and combinations; how many lines, words, consonants, and vowels there are in it; I know which are the inspired chapters written at Mecca and those which were dictated at Madinah. I know both laws and dogmas, and can determine the degrees of authenticity among them from the point of tradition; I am acquainted with architecture, logic, and philosophy; with eloquence, language, rhetoric, and the rules of versification. I know every artifice by which words can be ordered into musical lines. I am equally at home in the construction of simply flowing verses and very complicated examples suited for subtle palates alone; if I introduce an occasional obscurity into my compositions, it is to hold the attention and to delight such minds as can disentangle a fragile thread. I have learnt many things and remembered all I have learnt. I can sing perfectly, dance like a bird, play the lute and the flute, and perform in fifty different ways on every stringed instrument. When I dance and sing, those who see and hear me are damned by my beauty; when I walk in my perfumed clothing, balanced upon my feet, I kill; when I move my bottom, I overthrow; when I wink, I pierce; when I shake my bracelets, I make blind; I give life with a touch, and death by going away; I am skilful in all the arts and have carried my education so far that only those who have worn out their life in study may see it, as it were, upon the far horizon."

Hārūn al-Rashīd was delighted and astonished to find so much eloquence and beauty in the child who stood before him with lowered eyes. He turned to Abū al-Husn, saying: "I shall send at once for all the masters of art and science in my kingdom, to put the knowledge of your slave to public proof. If she comes victorious from the trial, I will not give you ten thousand dīnārs but cover you with honours for having brought so great a marvel to me. If she fails in her examination, she shall remain your property."

3. The seven ways of reciting the Qur'an.

The Khalīfah straightway sent for the most learned man of that time, Ibrāhīm ibn Siyyār,[4] a sage who had gone to the depths of all human knowledge; and he also commanded the presence of the chief poets, grammarians, theologians, doctors, philosophers, astronomers and lawyers of his kingdom. They hastened to the palace and assembled in the great hall, without knowing why they had been summoned. They seated themselves in a circle upon carpets about the Khalīfah's golden chair, while Sympathy stood meekly in their presence, smiling upon them through her light veil.

At this point Shahrazād saw the approach of morning and discreetly fell silent.

But when the two-hundred-and-seventy-second night had come

She said:

When a silence had fallen upon this assembly so deep that the far-off fall of a needle upon the ground might have been heard, Sympathy made a graceful and dignified bow to those present and said to the Khalīfah in a melodious voice:

"Prince of Believers, it is for you to order and for me to obey; I stand ready to answer any question posed to me by these venerable sages, these readers of the Koran, lawyers, doctors, architects, astronomers, geometrists, grammarians, philosophers and poets."

Hārūn al-Rashīd turned to those who were about him, saying: "I have called you hither that you may examine the learning of this girl in all directions and to any depth; it is for you to spare no pains in exhibiting your own scholarship and erudition." All the sages bowed to the earth, carrying their hands to their eyes and foreheads, and answering: "Obedience and obeisance to Allah and to you, O Prince of Believers!"

The slave Sympathy stood for some moments in thought with lowered head; then she looked up, saying: "Tell me, my masters, which of you is the most learned in the Koran and the traditions of our Prophet (upon whom be prayer and peace!)." All fingers were pointed to one of the doctors, who rose, saying: "I am that man." Then said Sympathy: "Ask me what you will of your own subject." So the learned reader of the Koran said:

"O young girl, since you have studied the sacred Book of Allah, you must know the number of the chapters, words, and letters in it; and also the precepts of our faith. Tell me first who is your Lord, who is your Prophet, who is your Imām, what is your orientation, what is your rule of life, what is your guide, and who are your brothers?"

She answered: "Allah is my Lord, Muhammad (upon whom be prayer and peace!) is my Prophet; the Koran is my law and therefore my Imām; the Kaabah, the house of Allah builded by Abraham at Mecca, is my orientation; the example of our holy Prophet is my rule of life; the Sunnah,[5] the collection of traditions, is my guide; and all Believers are my brothers."

While the Khalīfah marvelled to hear such precise answers from such lovely lips, the sage said:

"Tell me, how do you know that there is a God?"

She answered: "By reason."

"What is reason?"

---

4. One of the most erudite intellectuals of the era of Harun Al-Rashid.

5. The set of rules derived from the conduct and sayings of the Prophet Muhammad. The Kaabah is the central shrine in Mecca; an imam is a prayer leader.

"Reason is a double gift: it is both innate and acquired. Innate wisdom is that which Allah has placed in the hearts of His chosen servants that they may walk in the way of truth. Acquired wisdom is the fruit of education and labour in an intelligent man."

"That is an excellent answer. But can you tell me, where is the seat of reason?"

"In the heart, whence inspirations rise to the brain."

"That is so. How have you learnt to know the Prophet (upon whom be prayer and peace!)?"

"By reading the Book of Allah, by the phrases contained therein, by the proofs and witnessings of His divine mission."

"What are the indispensable duties of our religion?"

"The indispensable duties of our religion are five: the profession of Faith: 'There is no God but Allah and Muhammad is the messenger of Allah!', prayer, alms, fasting during the month of Ramadān, and pilgrimage to Mecca when that is possible."

"What are the most praiseworthy acts of piety?"

"They are six in number: prayer, alms, fasting, pilgrimage, fighting bad instincts and forbidden things, to take part in a holy war."

"What is the aim of prayer?"

"To offer the homage of my virtue to the Lord, to celebrate His praises, and to lift my soul towards the calm places."

"Yā Allah! That is an excellent reply. Does not prayer necessitate certain indispensable preparations?"

"Certainly it does. It is necessary to purify the whole body by ritual ablutions, to put on garments which have no stain of dirt, to choose a clean place in which to pray, to protect that part of the body which lies between the navel and the knees, to have pure intent, and to turn towards the Kaabah, in the direction of holy Mecca."

"What is the value of prayer?"

"It sustains faith, of which it is the foundation."

"What is the fruit or utility of prayer?"

"True prayer has no terrestrial use; it should be regarded only as a spiritual tie between the creature and his Lord. It can produce ten immaterial results: it lights the heart, it brightens the face, it pleases the Compassionate, it infuriates the devil, it attracts pity, it repels evil, it preserves from ill, it protects against enemies, it fortifies the wavering spirit, and brings the slave nearer to his Master."

"What is the key of prayer? And what is the key of that key?"

"The key of prayer is ablution and the key of ablution is the preparatory formula: 'In the name of Allah, the Merciful, the Compassionate.'"***

When the learned commentator of the Book heard Sympathy's answers, he could not but admit to himself that she knew as much as he did; but, being unwilling to confess his inability to catch her out, he asked her the following subtle question: "What is the linguistic meaning of the word *ablution?*"

"To get rid of all internal or external impurity by washing."

"What is the meaning of the word to *fast?*"

"To abstain."

"What is the meaning of the word to *give?*"

"To enrich oneself."

"To go on a *pilgrimage?*"

"To attain the end."

"To make *war?*"

"To defend oneself."

The sage rose up, crying: "In truth I am short of questions and arguments. This slave astonishes me with her knowledge and the clearness of her exposition, O Commander of the Faithful!"

Sympathy smiled slightly, saying: "I would like, in my turn, to ask you one question: can you tell me what are the foundations of Islām?"

He reflected for a moment, and then replied: "They are four in number: faith illuminated by sane reason; righteousness; knowledge of duty and equity, together with discretion; and the fulfilment of all promises."

Sympathy said again: "Allow me to ask you a further question. If you cannot answer it, it will be my right to take away the distinctive garment which you wear as a learned reader of the Book."

"I accept," he answered, "put your question, O slave."

"What are the branches of Islām?" she asked.

After a long time spent in reflection, the wise man could not answer, so the Khalīfah said to Sympathy: "If you can give us the answer yourself, the gown belongs to you."

Sympathy bowed and answered: "The branches of Islām are twenty: strict observance of the Book's teaching, conformation with the traditions and oral instructions of the Prophet, the avoidance of injustice, eating permitted food, never to eat unpermitted food, to punish evil doers that vice may not increase owing to the exaggerated clemency of the virtuous, repentance, profound study of religion, to do good to enemies, to be modest, to succour the servants of Allah, to avoid all innovation and change, to show courage in adversity and strength in time of trial, to pardon when one is strong, to be patient in misfortune, to know Allah, to know His Prophet (upon whom be prayer and peace!), to resist the suggestions of the Evil One, to fight against the passions and wicked instincts of the soul, to be wholly vowed in confidence and submission to the service of Allah."

When the Khalīfah Hārūn al-Rashīd heard this answer, he ordered the sage's gown to be stripped from him and given to Sympathy; this was immediately done, and the learned man left the hall in confusion, with his head bowed.

Then a second theologian, famous for his subtlety, to whom all eyes voted the honour of next questioning the girl, rose and turned towards Sympathy, saying: "I will only ask you a few short questions, O slave. What duties are to be observed while eating?"

"In eating a man must first wash his hands and invoke the name of Allah. He must sit upon the left haunch, and use only the thumb and two first fingers in conveying the food to his mouth. He must take small mouthfuls, masticate each piece of food thoroughly, and not look at his neighbour for fear of embarrassing him and spoiling his appetite."

"Can you tell me what is something, what is half something, and what is less than something?"

"A Believer is something, a hypocrite is half something, and an infidel is less than something."

"That is correct. Now can you tell me where faith is found?"

"Faith abides in four places: in the heart, in the head, in the tongue, and in the members. The strength of the heart consists in joy, the strength of the head in knowledge of the truth, the strength of the tongue in sincerity, and the strength of the members in submission."

"How many hearts are there?"

"There are several: the heart of the Believer is a pure and healthy heart, the heart of an Infidel is exactly the opposite." ***

At this point Shahrazād saw the approach of morning and discreetly fell silent.

But when the two-hundred-and-seventy-sixth night had come

She said:

"There is a heart attached to the things of this world, and a heart attached to spiritual joys; there is a heart mastered by the passions, by hate or avarice; there is a slack heart, a heart burning with love, a heart puffed with pride; there is a lighted heart like that of the companions of our holy Prophet; and there is the heart of the Prophet himself, which is the heart of the Chosen."

When the learned theologian heard this answer, he cried: "You have won my approbation, O slave!"

Sympathy looked at the Khalīfah, saying: "O Commander of the Faithful, allow me to ask one question of my examiner and to take his gown if he cannot answer." Hārūn al-Rashīd gave his permission, and she asked:

"Can you tell me what duty must be fulfilled before all other duties, however important those may be?"

The wise man did not know what to say, so the girl took his gown from him and herself answered the question:

"The duty of ablution; for we are bidden to purify ourselves before fulfilling the least of religious duties or any of those acts prescribed by the Book or the Sunnah."

Sympathy cast a glance round the assembly, and this was answered by one of the most celebrated men of the century, supposed without equal in a knowledge of the Koran. He rose and said:

"Since you know the Book of Allah, O girl full of the sweet perfume of the spirit, can you give me a sample of your study?"

"The Koran is composed of a hundred and fourteen chapters, seventy of which were dictated at Mecca and forty-four at Madinah. It is divided into six hundred and twenty-one divisions, called decades, and into six thousand two hundred and thirty-six verses. It contains seventy-nine thousand, four hundred and thirty-nine words, and three hundred and twenty-three thousand, six hundred and seventy letters, to each of which attach ten special virtues. The names of twenty-five prophets are mentioned: Adam, Noah, Ishmael, Isaac, Jacob, Joseph, Elisha, Jonah, Lot, Sālih, Hūd, Shuaib, David, Solomon, Dhūl-kafl, Idrīs, Elias, Yahyā, Zacharias, Job, Moses, Aaron, Jesus, and Muhammad (upon all these be prayer and peace!). Nine birds or winged beasts are mentioned: the gnat, the bee, the fly, the hoopoe, the crow, the grasshopper, the ant, the bulbul, and the bird of Jesus (upon whom be prayer and peace!), which is none other than the bat."

"You are marvellously exact. Now can you tell me in what verse our holy Prophet judges the Unbelievers?"

"In this verse: 'The Jews say that the Christians are wrong and the Christians say that the Jews are wrong; to this extent both are right!'" ***

The learned questioner could contain himself no longer, but cried out: "I bear witness, O Prince of Believers, that this young girl is unequalled in knowledge!"

Sympathy demanded leave to ask a question in her turn, and said:

"Can you tell me which verse of the Koran contains the letter kāf twenty-three times, which contains the letter mīm sixteen times, and which contains the letter ain forty times?"

The sage stayed with his mouth open, unable to make the least attempt at an answer; so Sympathy first took away his gown and then herself indicated the required verses to the general stupefaction of all.

Next, a learned doctor of medicine rose in the assembly, one famous for the studies he had made and the books he had written, and said:

"You have spoken excellently of the things of the spirit; now it is time that we turn our attention to the body. I require you, O beautiful slave, to give us some information about the body of man, its composition, its nerves, its bones, its vertebrae, and why Adam was called Adam."

"The name of Adam comes from the Arabic word adīm, which signifies the surface of the earth; it was given to the first man because he was created from earth taken from different parts of the world. His head was made from the soil of the East, his breast from the soil of the Kaabah, and his feet from the soil of the West. Allah made seven entrances and two exits for the body: the two eyes, the two ears, the two nostrils, and the mouth for entrances, and for exits, one before and one behind. Then the Creator united in Adam four elements to give him a nature: water, earth, fire and air; so that a bilious temperament is of the nature of fire, which is hot and dry; a nervous temperament is of the nature of earth, which is dry; a lymphatic temperament is of the nature of water, which is cold and moist; and a sanguine temperament is of the nature of air, which is warm and dry. After this Allah assembled the human body. He placed within it three hundred and sixty ducts and two hundred and forty bones. He gave it three instincts: of life, reproduction, and appetite. He gave it a heart, a spleen, lungs, six intestines, a liver, two kidneys, a brain, two eggs, a member, and a skin. He dowered it with five senses, guided by seven vital spirits. As for the position of the organs, he placed the heart upon the left of the breast, and the stomach below it, the lungs to act as fans for the heart, the liver on the right to guard the heart, and, for the same purpose, he placed the interlacing intestines and the articulation of the ribs. The head is composed of forty-eight bones, the chest of twenty-four ribs and twenty-five in a woman; this extra rib is on the right, and is useful to fasten the child in the belly of its mother and to support it, as it were, by an arm."***

"So far there has been nothing lacking in your answers. Now I wish to ask you a question of capital importance, which will show if you have a true knowledge of the facts of life. Can you give us a clear account of copulation?"

On hearing this question the young girl blushed and lowered her head, so that the Khalīfah thought that she was unable to answer: but she turned towards him, saying: "As Allah lives, O Commander of the Faithful, my silence is not due to ignorance; for the answer is upon the tip of my tongue, but refuses to leave my lips because of my respect for the Khalīfah." Hārūn al-Rashīd answered: "It would give me very great pleasure to hear such an answer from your mouth. Speak freely, explicitly, and without fear." So the learned Sympathy spoke as follows:

"Copulation is that act which unites the sexes of man and woman. It is an excellent thing, having many virtues and conferring many benefits: it lightens the body and relieves the soul, it cures melancholy, tempers the heat of passion, attracts love, contents the heart, consoles in absence, and cures insomnia. These are its effects when a man couples with a young woman: it is far otherwise when he has to do with an old one. Connection with an old woman exposes a man to many maladies, among others disease of the eyes, disease of the kidneys, disease of the thighs, and disease of the back. In a word, it is a terrible thing, to be avoided as one would avoid a deadly poison. Best of all is to choose a woman expert in the art, one who understands a wink, who can speak with her feet and hands, and spare her owner the necessity of keeping a garden and flower beds.

All complete copulation is followed by moisture. In the woman this moisture is produced by the emotion felt in her honourable parts; in the man, by the running of that sap which is secreted by the two eggs. This sap follows a complicated road; man possesses one large vein which gives birth to all the other veins; the blood which fortifies these three hundred and sixty smaller veins runs at last into a tube which debouches in the left egg; in this egg the blood turns about, clarifies, and changes into a white liquid which thickens because of the heat of the egg, and smells like palm milk."

At this point Shahrazād saw the approach of morning and discreetly fell silent.

But when the two-hundred-and-eighty-second night had come

She said:

"You have answered wisely!" cried the sage. "I have only two more questions to ask. Can you tell me what thing lives always in prison and dies when it breathes the free air? Also, what are the best fruits?"

"The first is a fish; and the second, citrons and pomegranates."

When the doctor heard the wonderful replies of Sympathy, he confessed himself incapable of making her stumble and would have returned to his place, but Sympathy signed to him to remain, saying: "I will now ask you a question. Can you tell me what is round like the earth, and lives in an eye, sometimes going through that eye, and sometimes separated from it, copulating without an organ, leaving its companion for the night, and embracing her again during the day, choosing its habitation upon the edge of things?"

The learned man cudgelled his brains for an answer but could find none, so Sympathy took away his gown and gave the answer herself: "The button and the button-loop." ***

Hārūn al-Rashīd was edified in the extreme by so much knowledge and wisdom, and ordered the learned Ibrāhīm ibn Siyyār to give his own gown to the girl. The sage did so and then, lifting his right hand, witnessed publicly that the slave had surpassed him in scholarship and was the marvel of the age.

"Can you play upon instruments of music and accompany yourself while you sing?" asked the Khalīfah, and, when Sympathy replied that she could, had a lute brought to her, which was contained in a red satin case with a tassel of saffron coloured silk and a gold clasp. Sympathy drew the lute from its covering and found carved about it, in interlaced and flowering character, the following verses:

> I was the green branch of a tree
> Birds loved and taught their songs to.
> Haply the teaching lingers,
> For, when I lie on beauty's knee,
> Remember under beauty's fingers,
> The woodland song I sing belongs to
> The birds who sang to me.

She leaned over the lute as a mother over her nursling and, drawing twelve different harmonies from the strings, sang in a voice that echoed long after in all hearts and brought tears of emotion to every eye.

When she had finished, the Khalīfah rose up, crying: "May Allah increase your gifts within you, O Sympathy, and have in His benign keeping those who taught you and those who gave you birth!" So saying, he had ten thousand golden dīnārs, in a hundred sacks, given to Abū al-Husn and then turned to Sympathy, saying: "Tell me, O child of marvel, would you rather enter my harīm and have a palace and retinue for yourself, or return home with this young man?"

At this point Shahrazād saw the approach of morning and discreetly fell silent.

But when the two-hundred-and-eighty-seventh night had come

She said:

Sympathy kissed the earth between the Khalīfah's hands and answered: "May Allah continue to shower His blessings upon our master! Your slave would prefer to return to the house of him who brought her here."

Instead of being offended by this answer, the Khalīfah immediately gave Sympathy a further five thousand dīnārs, saying: "May you be found as expert in love as you are in answering questions!" After this he put the crown upon his generosity by raising Abū al-Husn to high employment and numbering him among his intimate favourites.

The two young people left the hall, one staggering under all the gowns of the sages, and the other under all the sacks of gold. As they went, they were followed by the whole marvelling assembly, who lifted their arms, crying: "Was ever in the world a liberality like that of the descendants of Abbās?"

Such, O auspicious King, continued Shahrazād, were the answers given by Sympathy before the assembly of sages and handed down in the royal annals to be an instruction to every woman of the Faith.

Then Shahrazād, seeing that King Shahryār was still frowning and racking his brains, began at once upon the Adventures of the Poet Abū Nuwās.

Little Dunyazād, who had been half asleep, woke up suddenly on hearing the name of Abū Nuwās and, large-eyed with attention, made ready to listen with all her ears.

Conclusion

Then she fell silent, and King Shahryār cried: "O Shahrazād, that was a noble and admirable story! O wise and subtle one, you have taught me many lessons, letting me see that every man is at the call of Fate; you have made me consider the words of kings and peoples passed away; you have told me some things which were strange, and many that were worthy of reflection. I have listened to you for a thousand nights and one night, and now my soul is changed and joyful, it beats with an appetite for life. I give thanks to Him Who has perfumed your mouth with so much eloquence and has set wisdom to be a seal upon your brow!"

Little Dunyazād rose quite up from her carpet, and ran to throw her arms about her sister, crying: "O Shahrazād, how soft and delicate are your words, how moving and delightful! With what a savour they have filled our hearts! Oh, how beautiful are your words, my sister!"

Shahrazād leaned over the child and, as she embraced her, whispered some words which caused her to glide from the room, as camphor melts before the sun.

Shahrazād stayed alone with Shahryār, but, as he was preparing to take this marvellous bride between his joyful arms, the curtains opened and Dunyazād reappeared, followed by a nurse with twin children hanging at her breasts. A third child hurried after them on all fours.

Shahrazād embraced the three little ones and then ranged them before Shahryār; her eyes filled with tears, as she said: "O King of time, behold these three whom Allah has granted to us in three years."

While Shahryār kissed the children and was moved with joy through all his body to touch them, Shahrazād said again: "Your eldest son is more than two years old, and these twins will soon be one. Allah protect them from the evil-eye! You remember, O King of time, that I was absent through sickness for twenty days between the six hundred and seventy-ninth night of my telling and the seven hundredth. It was during that absence that I gave birth to the twins. They pained and wearied me a great deal more than their elder brother in the previous year. With him I was so little disturbed that I had no need to interrupt the tale of Sympathy the Learned, even for one night."

She fell silent, and King Shahryār, looking from her to his sons and from his sons to her, could say no word.

Then little Dunyazād turned from kissing the infants a twentieth time, and said to Shahryār: "Will you cut off my sister's head, O King? Will you destroy the mother of your sons, and leave three little kings to miss her love?"

"Be quiet and have no fear, young girl," answered King Shahryār, between two fits of sobbing. It was not for a long time that he could master his emotion, and say: "O Shahrazād, I swear by the Lord of Pity that you were already in my heart before the coming of these children. He had given you gifts with which to win me; I loved you in my soul because I had found you pure, holy, chaste, tender, straightforward, unassailable, ingenious, subtle, eloquent, discreet, smiling, and wise. May Allah bless you, my dear, your father and mother, your root and race! O Shahrazād, this thousand and first night is whiter for us than the day!" When he had said these things, he rose and embraced the woman's head.

Shahrazād took her King's hand and carried it to her lips, her heart, and her brow, saying: "O lord of time, I beg you to call your old wazīr, that he may rejoice at my salvation and partake in the benediction of this night."

So the King sent for his wazīr, and the old man entered carrying Shahrazād's winding-sheet over his arm, for he was sure that her hour had come at last. Shahryār rose in his honour and kissed him between the eyes, saying: "O father of Shahrazād, O begetter of benediction, Allah has raised up your daughter to be the salvation of my people. Repentance has come to me through her!" Joy penetrated the old man's heart so suddenly that he fell into a swoon. When rose-water had brought him to himself, Shahrazād and Dunyazād kissed his hand, and he blessed them. The rest of that night passed for them all in a daze of happiness.

Shahryār sent for his brother Shahzamān, King of Samarkand al-Ajam, and went out to meet his coming with a glorious retinue. The city was gay with flags, and in the streets and markets the people burnt incense, sublimated camphor, aloes, Indian musk, nard and ambergris. They put fresh henna upon their fingers and saffron upon their faces. Drums, flutes, clarinets, fifes, cymbals and dulcimers filled every ear with a rejoicing sound.

While great feasts were being given at the royal expense, King Shahryār took his brother aside and spoke of the life which he had led with Shahrazād for the last three years. He recounted for Shahzamān's benefit some of the maxims, phrases, tales, proverbs, jests, anecdotes, characteristics, marvels, poems, and recitations which he had heard during that time. He praised the wazīr's daughter for her eloquence, wisdom, purity, piety, sweetness, honesty and discretion. "She is my wife," he said, "the mother of my children."

When King Shahzamān had a little recovered from his astonishment, he said: "Since you have been so fortunate, I too will marry. I will marry Shahrazād's sister, the little one, I do not know her name. We shall be two brothers married to two sure and honest sisters; we will forget our old misfortune. That calamity touched me first, and then through me it reached to you. If I had not discovered mine, you would never have known of yours. Alas, my brother, I have been mournful and loveless during these years. Each night I have followed your example by taking a virgin to my bed, and every morning I have avenged our ills upon her life. Now I will follow you in a better deed, and marry your wazīr's second daughter."

Shahryār went joyfully to Shahrazād and told her that his brother had, of his own accord, elected Dunyazād for his bride. "We consent, O King of time," she said, "on condition that your brother stays henceforth with us. I could not bear to be separated from my little sister, even for one hour. I brought her up and educated her; she could not part from me. If Shahzamān will give this undertaking, Dunyazād shall be his slave. If not, we will keep her."

When Shahzamān heard Shahrazād's answer, he said: "As Allah lives, my brother, I had intended no less than to remain with you always. I feel now that I can never abide to be parted from you again. As for the throne of Samarkand, Allah will send to fill it." "I have longed for this," answered King Shahryār. "Join with me in thanks to Allah, my brother, that He has brought our hearts together again after so many months!"

The kādī and witnesses were summoned, and a marriage contract was written out for King Shahzamān and Dunyazād. Rejoicing and illuminations with coloured fire followed upon the news of this; and all the city ate and drank at the King's expense for forty days and forty nights. The two brothers and two sisters entered the hammām and bathed there in rose-water, flower-water, scented willow-water, and perfumed water of musk, while eagle wood and aloes were burned about them.

Shahrazād combed and tressed her little sister's hair, and sprinkled it with pearls. Then she dressed her in a robe of antique Persian stuff, stitched with red gold and enhanced by drunken animals and swooning birds embroidered in the very colours of life. She put a fairy collar about her neck, and Dunyazād became below her fingers fairer than Alexander's wife.

When the two Kings had left the hammām and seated themselves upon their thrones, the bridal company, the wives of the amīrs and notables, stood in two motionless lines to right and left. Time came, and the sisters entered between these living walls, each sustaining the other, and having the appearance of two moons in one night sky.

Then the noblest ladies there took Dunyazād by the hand and, after removing her robes, dressed her in a garment of blue satin, a sea tint to make reason fail upon her throne. A poet said of her:

> Her veil is torn from the bright blue
> Which all the stars are hasting to,
> Her lips control a hive of bees,
> And roses are about her knees,
> The white flakes of the jasmine twine
> Round her twin sweetness carnaline,
> Her waist is a slight reed which stands
> Swayed on a hill of moving sands.

Shahzamān came down to be the first to look upon her. When he had admired her in this dress, he sat upon his throne again, and this was a signal for the second change. So Shahrazād and the women clad their bride in a robe of apricot silk. As she passed before her husband's throne, she justified the words of the poet:

> You are more fair than a summer moon
> On a winter night, you are more fair.
> I said when I saw your falling hair:
> "Night's black wing is hiding day."
> "A cloud, but lo! the moon is there,"
> You, rose child, found to say.

When Shahzamān had come down and admired her in this dress, Shahrazād put a tunic of grenade velvet upon her sister. *** Shahrazād slipped her hand to her sister's waist, and they walked before the Kings and between the guests toward the inner chambers. Then the Queen undressed little Dunyazād and laid her upon the bed with such recommendations as were suitable. They kissed and wept in each other's arms for a little, as it was the first night for which they had been separated.

That was a white and joyful night for the two brothers and the two sisters, it was a fair continuation of the thousand and one which had gone before, a love tale better than them all, the dawn of a new era for the subjects of King Shahryār.

When the brothers had come from the hammām in the morning and joined their wives, the wazīr sought permission to enter. They rose in his honour and the two women kissed his hand; but, when he asked for the day's orders, the four said with one voice: "O father, we wish that you should give commands in the future and not receive them. That is why we make you King of Samarkand al-Ajam." "I yield my throne to you," said Shahzamān; and Shahryār cried: "I will only give you leave to do so, my brother, if you will consent to share my royalty and reign with me day and day about." "I hear and I obey," said Shahzamān.

The wazīr kissed his daughters in farewell, embraced the three little sons, and departed for Samarkand al-Ajam at the head of a magnificent escort. Allah had written him security in his journey, and the inhabitants of his new kingdom hailed his coming with delight. He reigned over them in all justice and became a King among great Kings. So much for him.

After these things, King Shahryār called together the most renowned annalists and proficient scribes from all the quarters of Islām, and ordered them to write out the tales of Shahrazād from beginning to end, without the omission of a single detail. So they sat down and wrote thirty volumes in gold letters, and called this sequence of marvels and astonishments: THE BOOK OF THE THOUSAND NIGHTS AND ONE NIGHT. Many faithful copies were made, and King Shahryār sent them to the four corners of his empire, to be an instruction to the people and their children's children. But he shut the original manuscript in the gold cupboard of his reign and made his wazīr of treasure responsible for its safe keeping.

King Shahryār and Queen Shahrazād, King Shahzamān and Queen Dunyazād, and Shahrazād's three small sons, lived year after year in all delight, knowing days each more admirable than the last and nights whiter than days, until they were visited by the Separator of friends, the Destroyer, the Builder of tombs, the Inexorable, the Inevitable.

Such are the excellent tales called THE THOUSAND NIGHTS AND ONE NIGHT, together with all that is in them of wonder and instruction, prodigy and marvel, astonishment and beauty.

But Allah knows all! He alone can distinguish between the true and the false. He knows all!

64

"I had always thought of English literature as the richest in the world," wrote the Argentine poet Jorge Luis Borges of his experience of first reading Old English poetry; "the discovery now of a secret chamber at the very threshold of that literature came to me as an additional gift." It is easy to fall under the spell of *Beowulf*'s strangeness and antiquity, of a poetry that makes its characters feel both alien and intensely present, as if freshly arisen from centuries of oblivion beneath the earthen mounds where the Geats and other Germanic tribes would bury their fallen leaders. *Beowulf* is replete with the pagan customs of the *comitati*, the warrior-bands that in the fifth century had swept across Europe from their strongholds in the north: Angles, Saxons, and Jutes across the North Sea to England, Ostrogoths and other tribes southward to topple the Roman Empire. Their heroic code, steeped in values such as revenge, honor, and the gift-giving recalled by Borges above, imbues the poem with the sense of an epoch already lost to time, just as the narrative mirrors its account of the youthful exploits of the hero Beowulf with the story of the end of his long life, battling against a marauding dragon. Composed several centuries later, in a world since converted to Christianity, and set in a land across the North Sea, *Beowulf* is intensely engaged with the ways in which change occurs—from old customs to new, kings to heirs, heathen to Christian, oral culture to the written word—and the deeply conflicted feelings such changes never fail to elicit.

Much of the history of the poem's reception resembles the "secret chamber" of which Borges wrote. We don't know when or where it was composed—hypotheses range from seventh-century East Anglia or Northumbria to tenth-century England—nor do we know who wrote it, layperson or cleric, or whether it was originally written at all—some scholars believe it was dictated by a *scop,* a bard or singer of tales at an Anglo-Saxon court. It survives, by chance, in a single manuscript known as the Nowell Codex, which was copied by two scribes around the year 1000. Nothing is known of its history before the sixteenth century; it was scorched in a fire and nearly destroyed in 1731, and no one realized its value until the early nineteenth century, when it was transcribed and edited by a Danish scholar. Although the author assumed his audience had prior knowledge of the underlying history, there are few known sources for the events described, nor did the poem leave a discernible trace on the literature that came after it—until, that is, the nineteenth century. Like its hero, it seems to stand alone.

Also like its hero, however, *Beowulf* is immersed in a highly developed and sophisticated social world. Its first two parts are set in the land of the Danes, the Scyldings, or descendants of Scyld, a people blessed by fate, prosperous and secure. When they construct a glorious mead-hall, a gathering place for drinking and feasting, their harp-songs disturb a neighbor, the man-monster Grendel, who plagues their land for a dozen years. The young retainer Beowulf hears of their plight, journeys across the sea from his home in Geatland (in what is now southwestern Sweden), and purges the land of its monsters. In the second part, some thousand lines, more than fifty years have passed, and Beowulf himself now rules the Geats, who find themselves threatened by a monster of their own, a treasure-hoarding dragon awakened from its slumber by a clumsy thief. Beowulf slays the dragon but loses his life, and the poem concludes as the Geats bury their leader and lament their fate, exposed to the might of the neighboring peoples—the Swedes, the Frisians, the Franks—who will lose no time in seizing their land and goods, and probably their lives. *Lif is læne,* the poem tells us, "life is transitory."

The main action revolves around three fights with three superbly imagined monsters: Beowulf pitted against Grendel in the mead-hall, against Grendel's vengeful mother in her underwater lair, and against the dragon in its buried barrow-mound. And while the poem gives ample space to the battle descriptions that were essential to any heroic narrative, the poet was equally engrossed by the intricate web of events and associations touched upon during these duels or arising out of them. Rather than using the linear narration familiar from classical Greek and Latin literature, the *Beowulf* poet structured his story in what scholars of oral poetry call "ring composition"—interlinked rings radiating out from the central events. Viewed this way, the fight with Grendel's mother would occupy the poem's center, while the prior battle with her son and the subsequent combat with the dragon would "ring" the center, developing related themes in parallel and in contrast. Similarly, paired episodes with queens both introduce (Hildeburh and Wealhtheow) and follow (Hygd and Modthryth) the encounter with Grendel's mother, raising other questions of succession and conflict between generations, and probing the place of women in the warrior-code of the Germanic tribes.

The poet—and we can assume his audience as well—delighted in interpolating episodes from other times and places, sometimes flashbacks to prior conflicts—such as the tale of Sigemund the dragon-slayer—sometimes glimpses of events to come in the future, and sometimes barely connected tales of past blood-feuds. He (or perhaps she, as a few critics have conjectured) expected the audience or readers not only to fill in the context behind the often brief hints of famous or infamous deeds, but also to read laterally, moving sideways through the text from connection to connection, comparing and contrasting different characters, different situations, different outcomes. As in the *Lais* of Marie de France, the *Poem of the Cid,* and many other medieval narratives, an entire social milieu and a complex ethic emerge not so much from individual psychology or particular events, as from a broader mirroring. The narrative's multiple detours and asides take a call-and-response form, filled with repetitions of situations and events, even ones we have already seen, as when Beowulf, returned to his lord Hygelac, recounts the fights we have already heard about, but gives them a new meaning for a new context.

In addition to this horizontal structure of parallels and contrasts, there is also a vertical structure to the poem that derives from the gap in time between the date of the events and the date of composition. Although most of the characters (with the exception of Beowulf, who seems to have been a fictional creation) appear elsewhere in Scandinavian legend and genealogies, only Hygelac's death in battle with the Frisians (in what is now the northern Netherlands) can actually be documented (somewhere between 515 and 530 C.E.). Between this period and the composition of the poem, Christianity had spread through the region, and the poet depicted the lives of the heathen Germans from the point of view of a pious Christian. Like the Norse writer Snorri Sturluson, however, rather than simply dismiss their pre-Christian practices or transform these ancestors into practicing Christians, the poet struck a fragile balance, leaving much unsaid. The pagan characters voice pious sentiments—"put aside pride," counsels the wise old Danish king Hrothgar—somewhere between the harsh realities of the heroic code and the metaphysical dictates of the Christian virtues. When depicting certain practices incompatible with the rituals of the newer religion—burial rites, for example, or the Danes' panicked prayer to "war-idols" (lines 155–61)—the narrator will sometimes note the distinction. For the most part, however, the peoples of the poem exist in a threshold world neither wholly pagan nor wholly Christian, where God is known but the mysteries of Christ and the sacraments are not, and where a heathen delight in booty and pride in fighting prowess do not preclude a deep-seated religiosity—a situation perhaps not so different from that of the recently converted Angles and Saxons of early-medieval England. The poem's audience could read the poem in either direction, finding the descendants of Cain in Grendel and Satan in the serpentine Dragon, and an allegory of the ideal Christian ruler in Beowulf, or recalling the blood-feuds, gift-giving, and pleasures of the mead-hall in the old customs, or merging them together in their imagination.

Names were a key component of the ability to view the world doubly, for Christianity entered the language through already existing words. It is impossible to know to what degree the poem's original audience would have heard a Norse god or the Christian God in words such as *metod* (which originally meant "fate") or *dryhten* ("ruler," "king"), that could now refer to either figure. Similarly, a phrase such as "the Lord lent them aid in their anguish, weaving their war-luck" (page 665, lines 623–624) combines a Christian sentiment of a grace-bestowing God with a pagan image of a God weaving a web of fate. A term like *wyrd,* another word for fate, which appears throughout the poem to describe the destined moment of a warrior's death, could be accepted either as a natural force ruling the world or as a synonym for divine Providence, inscrutable to mortals but part of God's plan. Word-weaving was fundamental to the composition of Old English poetry, and just as new concepts could be grafted onto preexistent names and terms, so the *scop*'s skill was demonstrated by the ability to make new and unforeseen combinations out of the "word-hoard" of the oral tradition.

Characters' names are themselves compounds. Scyld Scefing ("shield of the sheaf") is the founder of the Danish royal house; the name Beowulf means "bear," literally a "bee-wolf," a plunderer of bees for their honey. The fundamental facts of the warriors' world are likewise not granted simple names, but "kennings," combinations evoking their attributes, their uses, their greater meaning—the poem contains more than 1,500 compounds. The sea can be a "whale-road" or a "swan's road"; a king a "ring-giver" or a "treasure-giver"; weapons, ships, and sails receive similar treatment. Words have power in this world—to define and to enhance a character, to provoke, as when the *scop*'s song arouses Grendel to carnage, or to send to defeat, as when Beowulf humbles the envious Unferth in a *flyting,* or verbal duel. Part of this variation is due to the requirements of oral composition: different epithets, names of different metrical lengths can be used as needed to fill out the lines of the heroic song, but this variety equally bespeaks a way of thinking about the world as an interconnected web of relationships, just as genealogies defined people in terms of their heritage, and alliances and blood-feuds alternated in a give-and-take of gifts and blows.

Repetition and variation are at the heart of Old English poetry, for its unrhymed meter is based in alliteration, a repeated consonant in different words. The lines of *Beowulf* consist of two half-verses separated by a caesura, or pause, with two beats or stressed syllables in each half. The first beat of the first half always alliterates with the first beat of the second half; the second beat of the first half may also alliterate, but not the final beat of the line. Thus the dragon's revenge on the Geats for the theft of its treasure:

> ...Hord-weard onbād
> earfoðlīce, oððæt æfen cwōm;
> wæs ðā gebolgen beorges hyrde
> wolde [s]e lāða līge forgyldan
> drinc-fæt dȳre. þā wæs dæg sceacen
> wyrme on willan; nō on wealle læ[n]g
> bīdan wolde, ac mid bæle fōr,
> fȳre gefȳsed.

A literal translation by Howard J. Chickering gives a good sense of the word-choice and rhythm of the passage:

> ...The hoard-keeper waited,
> miserable, impatient, till evening came.
> By then the barrow-snake was swollen with rage,
> wanted revenge for that precious cup,
> a payment by fire. The day was over
> and the dragon rejoiced, could no longer lie
> coiled within walls but flew out in fire,
> with shooting flames.[1]

Standard formulae—*oððæt æfen cwōm, þā wæs dæg sceacen*—punctuate the passage of time as the dragon waits for its nighttime revenge. The repetition of its names stresses its waiting and its power, while the variation in kennings—*Hord-weard, beorges hyrde*—and the earthy metaphor of its proper name, *wyrme,* allies the dragon's character both with man—hoard-keeper,

1. This rendering makes a useful comparison to the fluidity and compactness of Sullivan and Murphy's version used in this anthology (page 695, lines 2030–35).

miserable, vengeful, enraged, rejoicing—and beast—coiled, fire-breathing, monstrous. Through it all, the lines keep the forward beat as the alliteration also looks back to the beginning of the line, undulating like the dragon as it awaits its burst into freedom, *fȳre gefȳsed.*

As the scholar of Old English, J. R. R. Tolkien, wrote in an influential essay on a poem he would incorporate in significant ways into his novels of epic fantasy, the poet "esteemed dragons, as rare as they are dire.... He liked them—as a poet, not as a sober zoologist; and he had good reason." The poet's gift was to make a dragon that was simultaneously real and marvelous, symbolic and deadly, human and bestial. In just the same way he blended Christian borrowings with Scandinavian legend, the incompatible opposites of which the medieval world would be wrought, refusing to yield either to one or to the other, holding past and future counterbalanced together.

PRONUNCIATIONS:

Beowulf: BAY-oh-woolf
Jorge Luis Borges: HOR-hay loo-WEES BOR-hayz
Geats: KHAY-ahts
Hrothgar: HRAWTH-gahr
Hygd: heegd
Hygelac: HEE-ah-lack
Wealhtheow: WAYL-thay-oh
Weohstan: WAY-oh-stan

Beowulf[1]

1. Grendel

So! The Spear-Danes   in days of old
were led by lords   famed for their forays.
We learned of those princes'   power and prowess.
Often Scyld Scefing[2]   ambushed enemies,
5   took their mead-benches,   mastered their troops,
though first he was found   forlorn and alone.[3]
His early sorrows   were swiftly consoled:
he grew under heaven,   grew to a greatness
renowned among men   of neighboring lands,
10   his rule recognized   over the whale-road,
tribute granted him.   That was a good king!

Afterward God   gave him an heir,
a lad in the hall   to lighten all hearts.
The Lord had seen   how long and sorely
15   the people had languished   for lack of a leader.
Beow[4] was blessed   with boldness and honor;
throughout the North   his name became known.

1. The modern English translation is by Alan Sullivan and Timothy Murphy (2002, revised 2003).

2. The traditional founder of the Danish royal house. His name means "shield" or protection of the "sheaf," suggesting an earlier association in Norse mythology with the god of vegetation. The Danes are known afterward as "Scyldings," descendants of Scyld.

3. Scyld Scefing arrives among the Danes as a foundling, a dangerous position in both Norse and Anglo-Saxon cultures. Solitaries and outcasts were generally regarded with suspicion; it is a tribute to Scyld Scefing that he surmounted these obstacles to become the leader and organizer of the Danish people.

4. The manuscript reads "Beowulf" here, the copyist's mind having skipped ahead to the story's protagonist.

A soldierly son   should strive in his youth
to do great deeds,   give generous gifts
20 and defend his father.   Then in old age,
when strife besets him,   his comrades will stand
and his folk follow.   Through fair dealing
a prince shall prosper   in any kingdom.

Still hale on the day   ordained for his journey,
25 Scyld went to dwell   with the World's Warder.
His liegemen bore   his bier to the beach:
so he had willed   while wielding his words
as lord of the land,   beloved by all.
With frost on its fittings,   a lordly longboat
30 rode in the harbor,   ring-bowed and ready.
They placed their prince,   the gold-giver,
the famous man   at the foot of the mast,
in the hollow hull   heaped with treasures
from far-off lands.   I have not heard another
35 ship ever sailed   more splendidly stocked
with war-weapons,   arms and armor.
About his breast   the booty was strewn,
keepsakes soon to be   claimed by the sea.
So he'd been sent   as a child chosen
40 to drift on the deep.   The Danes now returned
treasures no less   than those they had taken,
and last they hoisted   high overhead
a golden banner   as they gave the great one
back to the Baltic   with heavy hearts
45 and mournful minds.   Though clever in council
or strong under sky,   men cannot say
or know for certain   who landed that shipload.

But the son of Scyld   was hailed in the strongholds
after the father   had fared far away,
50 and he long ruled   the lordly Scyldings.
A son was born   unto Beow also:
proud Healfdene,   who held his high seat,
battle-hardened   and bold in old age.
Four offspring   descended from Healfdene,
55 awake in the world: Heorogar, Hrothgar,
kindly Halga;   I have heard that the fourth
was Onela's queen[5]   and slept with the sovereign
of warlike Swedes.
                        Hrothgar was granted
swiftness for battle   and staunchness in strife,[6]
60 so friends and kinfolk   followed him freely.
His band of young soldiers   swelled to a swarm.

---

5. The daughters of Germanic royal families were married to the heads of opposing tribes in an attempt to cement military alliances. Often, as here, they are not named in the poem.

6. Significantly, Hrothgar is not the first-born of his generation. Leadership of the tribe was customarily conferred by acclamation upon the royal candidate who showed the greatest promise and ability.

In his mind he mulled   commanding a meadhall
higher than humankind   ever had heard of,
and offering everyone,   young and old,
65   all he could give   that God had granted,
save common land   and commoners' lives.
Then, I am told,   he tackled that task,
raising the rafters   with craftsmen summoned
from many kingdoms   across Middle-Earth.
70   They covered it quickly   as men count the time,
and he whose word   held the land whole
named it Heorot,[7]   highest of houses.
The prince did not fail   to fulfill his pledge:
feasts were given,   favor and fortune.
75   The roof reared up;   the gables were great,
awaiting the flames   which would flare fiercely
when oaths were broken,   anger awakened;
but Heorot's ruin   was not yet at hand.[8]

Each day, one evil   dweller in darkness
80   spitefully suffered   the din from that hall
where Hrothgar's men   made merry with mead.
Harp-strings would sound,   and the song of the scop
would recount the tales   told of time past:
whence mankind had come,   and how the Almighty
85   had fashioned flat land,   fair to behold,
surrounded with water.   The worker of wonders
lifted and lit   the sun and moon
for Earth's dwellers;   He filled the forests
with branches and blooms;   He breathed life
90   into all kinds of creatures.
                              So the king's thanes
gathered in gladness;   then crime came calling,
a horror from hell,   hideous Grendel,
wrathful rover   of borders and moors,
holder of hollows,   haunter of fens.
95   He had lived long   in the homeland of horrors,
born to the band   whom God had banished
as kindred of Cain,   thereby requiting
the slayer of Abel.[9]   Many such sprang
from the first murderer: monsters and misfits,
100   elves and ill-spirits,   also those giants
whose wars with the Lord   earned them exile.

After nightfall   he nosed around Heorot,
saw how swordsmen   slept in the hall,
unwary and weary   with wine and feasting,

7. The name of Hrothgar's hall in Anglo-Saxon literally means "hart" or "stag," a male deer. The epithet "adorned with horns," which is applied to Heorot later, may further suggest its function as a hunting lodge.
8. The peace concluded between the Danes and the Heathobards through intermarriage is already doomed before it has taken place. The events foreshadowed here will occur long after the time of the poem.
9. See Genesis 4:3–16.

105	numb to the sorrows suffered by men.
	The cursed creature, cruel and remorseless,
	swiftly slipped in. He seized thirty thanes
	asleep after supper, shouldered away
	what trophies he would, and took to his lair
110	pleased with the plunder, proud of his murders.

When daylight dawned   on the spoils of slaughter,
the strength of the fiend   was readily seen.
The feast was followed   by fits of weeping,
and cries of outrage   rose in the morning.
Hrothgar the strong   sank on his throne,
helpless and hopeless   beholding the carnage,
the trail of the terror,   a trouble too wrathful,
a foe too ferocious,   too steadfast in rage,
ancient and evil.   The evening after
he murdered again   with no more remorse,
so fixed was his will   on that wicked feud.
Henceforth the fearful   were easily found
elsewhere, anywhere   far from the fiend,
bedding in barns,   for the brutal hall-thane
was truly betokened   by terrible signs,
and those who escaped   stayed safer afar.

So wrath fought alone   against rule and right;
one routed many;   the mead-hall stood empty.
Strongest of Spear-Danes,   Hrothgar suffered
this fell affliction   for twelve winters' time.
As his woes became known   widely and well,
sad songs were sung   by the sons of men:
how season on season,   with ceaseless strife,
Grendel assailed   the Scylding's sovereign.
The monster craved   no kinship with any,
no end to the evil   with wergeld[1] owed;
nor might a king's   council have reckoned
on quittance come   from the killer's hand.
The dark death-shadow   daunted them all,
lying in ambush   for old and young,
secretly slinking   and stalking by night.
No man knows where   on the misty moor
the heathen keepers   of hell-runes[2] wander.

So over and over   the loathsome ogre
mortally menaced   mankind with his crimes.
Raiding by night,   he reigned in the hall,
and Heorot's high   adornments were his,

---

1. A cash payment for someone's death. *Wergeld* was regarded as an improvement over violent revenge, and Grendel is marked as uncivilized because he refuses to acknowledge this practice.

2. By rendering the Old English *helrunan*, which means "those adept in the mysteries of hell," as "heathen keepers of hell-runes," the translators are taking the liberty of suggesting that "demons" such as Grendel are familiar with runes—the letters of the early Germanic alphabet.

but God would not grant   throne-gifts to gladden
a scourge who spurned   the Sovereign of Heaven.

150   Stricken in spirit,   Hrothgar would often
closet his council   to ponder what plan
might be deemed best   by strong-minded men.
Sometimes the elders   swore before altars
of old war-idols,   offering prayers
155   for the soul-slayer   to succor their people.[3]
Such was their habit,   the hope of heathens:
with hell in their hearts,   they were lost to the Lord.
Their inmost minds   knew not the Almighty;
they never would worship   the world's true protector.
160   Sorry is he   who sears his soul,
afflicted by flames   he freely embraced.
No cheer for the chastened!   No change in his fate!
But happy is he   whom heaven welcomes,
and after his death-day   he dwells with the Father.

165   So in his sorrow   the son of Healfdene[4]
endlessly weighed   how a wise warrior
might fend off harm.   The hardship this foe
of his folk inflicted   was fierce and long-lasting,
most ruinous wrath   and wracking night-evil.

170   A thane[5] of Hygelac   heard in his homeland
of Grendel's deeds.   Great among Geats,[6]
this man was more mighty   than any then living.
He summoned and stocked   a swift wave-courser,
and swore to sail   over the swan-road
175   as one warrior should   for another in need.
His elders could find   no fault with his offer,
and awed by the omens,   they urged him on.
He gathered the bravest   of Geatish guardsmen.
One of fifteen,   the skilled sailor
180   strode to his ship   at the ocean's edge.

He was keen to embark: his keel was beached
under the cliff   where sea-currents curled
surf against sand;   his soldiers were ready.
Over the bow   they boarded in armor,
185   bearing their burnished   weapons below,
their gilded war-gear   to the boat's bosom.
Other men shoved   the ship from the shore,
and off went the band,   their wood-braced vessel
bound for the venture   with wind on the waves

---

3. In their fear, the Danes resume heathen practices. In Christian belief, the pagan gods were transformed into devils.
4. Hrothgar. He is referred to by his patronymic, his father's name, as is frequent with male characters in the poem.
5. One of the king's principal retainers, chief among these being the earls.
6. A Germanic tribe who lived along the southwestern coast of what is now Sweden.

190   and foam under bow,   like a fulmar in flight.[7]

       On the second day   their upswept prow
       slid into sight   of steep hillsides,
       bright cliffs, wide capes   at the close of their crossing,
       the goal of their voyage   gained in good time.
195   Swiftly the sailors   steered for the shore,
       moored their boat   and debarked on the berm.
       Clad in corselets   of clattering mail,
       they saluted the Lord   for their smooth sailing.

       From the post he held   high on the headland,
200   a Scylding had spied   the strangers bearing
       bright bucklers   and battle-armor
       over their gangplank.   Avid for answers
       and minded to know   what men had come hence,
       Hrothgar's thane   hastened on horseback
205   down to the beach   where he brusquely brandished
       spear-haft in hand   while speaking stern words:

       "What warriors are you,   wearers of armor,
       bearers of weapons,   daring to bring
       your lofty longboat   over the sea-lane?
210   Long have I looked   out on the ocean
       so foreign foes   might never float hither
       and harry our homeland   with hostile fleets.
       No men have ever   more brazenly borne
       shields to our shores,   nor have you sought
215   leave from our lords   to land in this place,
       nor could you have known   my kin would consent.
       I have never beheld   an earl on this earth
       more mighty in arms   than one among you.
       This is no hall-warmer,   handsome in harness,
220   showy with shield,   but the noblest of knights
       unless looks belie him.   Now let me know
       who are your fathers   before you fare further
       or spy on the Danes.   I say to you, sailors
       far from your homes: hear me and hasten
225   to answer me well.   Whence have you wandered?
       Why have you come?"
                            Wisest with words,
       the eldest offered   an answer for all:
       "From Geat-land we come;   we are Geatish men,
       sharers of Hygelac's   hearth and hall.
230   My father was famous   among our folk
       as a lordly leader   who lived many winters
       before, full of years,   he departed our fastness.
       His name was Ecgtheow.   All over Earth
       every wise man   remembers him well.

7. Gull-like sea bird of the far north Atlantic.

235 We have landed in friendship   to look for your lord,
the son of Healfdene,   sovereign of Scyldings.
Give us good guidance: a great errand
has driven us hence   to the holder of Danes.
Our purpose is open;   this I promise;
240 but you could attest   if tales tell the truth.
They speak of some scourge,   none can say what,
secretly stalking   by night among Scyldings,
a shadowy shape   whose malice to men
is shown by a shameful   shower of corpses.
245 I offer Hrothgar,   with honest heart,
the means to make   an end to this menace.
Wise and good,   he will win his reward,
the scalding surges   of care will be cooled
if ever such awful   evil is vanquished.
250 So his sorrows   shall swiftly be soothed
or else his anguish   haunt him, unaltered,
as long as his house   holds on the hilltop."

Astride his steed,   the guard spoke again:
"A sharp-witted warrior   often must weigh
255 words against works   when judging their worth.
This I have learned: you honor our lord.
Thus you may come,   though clad in corselets
and weaponed for war.   I shall show you the way.
Meanwhile those thanes   who are mine to command
260 shall stand by the ship   you steered to our shore.
No thief will trouble   your newly-tarred craft
before you return   and take to the tide.
A swan-necked bow   will bear you back
to your windward coast.   Most welcome of men,
265 may you be granted   good fortune in battle,
enduring unharmed   the deed you would do."

So they set out   while the ship sat at rest,
the broad-beamed vessel   bound to the beach,
lashed by its lines.   Lustrous boar-icons
270 glinted on cheek-guards.   Adorned with gold,
the flame-hardened helms   defended their lives.
Glad of their mettle   while marching together,
the troop hastened   until they beheld
the highest of halls   raised under heaven,
275 most famed among folk   in foreign lands.
Sheathed with gold   and grandly gabled,
the roof of the ruler   lit up his realm.
The foremost warrior   waved them forward
and bade the band go   straight to that building,
280 court of the king   and his brave kinsmen.
Reining his steed,   he spoke a last word:
"It is time I returned.   May All-Ruling Father
favor your errand.   I fare to the ocean,

to watch and ward off   wrathful marauders."

285   The street was stone-paved;   a straight path
       guided the band.   Byrnies glittered,
       jackets of chain-mail   whose jingling rings,
       hard and hand-linked,   sang on harnesses.
       Marshaled for battle,   they marched to the building.
290   Still sea-weary,   they set their broad-shields
       of well-hardened wood   against Heorot's wall.
       Their corselets clinked   as they bent to a bench
       and stood their sturdy   spears in a row,
       gray from the ash grove,   ground to sharp points.
295   This was a war party   worthy of weapons.

       Then a proud prince   questioned their purpose:
       "Where are you bringing   these burnished bosses,
       these gray mail-shirts,   grimly-masked helms
       and serried spears?   I am Hrothgar's
300   herald and door-ward.   I have never beheld
       a band of wanderers   with bearings so brave.
       I believe that boldness   has brought you to Hrothgar,
       not banishment's shame."
                              The eldest answered,
       hard and hardy   under his helmet,
305   a warlike prince   of the Weder[8] people:
       "We are Hygelac's   hearth-companions.
       My name is Beowulf;   my purpose, to bear
       unto Healfdene's son,   your lordly leader,
       a message meant   for that noblest of men,
310   if he will allow us   leave to approach."

       Wise Wulfgar,   man of the Wendels,
       known to many   for boldness in battle,
       stoutly spoke out: "I shall ask our sovereign,
       well-wisher of Danes   and awarder of wealth,
315   about this boon   you have come to request
       and bear you back,   as soon as may be,
       whatever answer   the great man offers."

       He went straightaway   where Hrothgar waited,
       old and gray-haired,   with thanes gathered round.
320   Squarely he stood   for his king to assess him.
       Such was the Scylding   custom at court,
       and so Wulfgar spoke   to his sovereign and friend:
       "Far-sailing Geats   have come to our kingdom
       across the wide water.   These warriors call
325   their leader *Beowulf*   and bid me bring
       their plea to our prince,   if it pleases him
       to allow them entrance   and offer them audience.

58

8. An alternate name for Geat.

I implore you to hear them,   princely Hrothgar,
for I deem them worthy   of wearing their armor
330 and treating with earls.   Truly the elder
who led them hither   is a lord of some stature."

Helm of the Scyldings,   Hrothgar held forth:
"I knew him once.   He was only a lad.
His honored father,   old Ecgtheow,
335 received the sole   daughter of Hrethel.
The son now seeks us   solely from friendship.
Seamen have said,   after sailing hence
with gifts for the Geats,   that his hand-grip would match
the might and main   of thirty strong men.
340 The West-Danes[9] have long   awaited God's grace.
Here is our hope   against Grendel's dread,
if I reckon rightly   the cause of his coming.
I shall give this brave man   boons for boldness.
Bring him in quickly.   The band of my kinsmen
345 is gathered together.   Welcome our guest
to the dwelling of Danes."
                              Then Wulfgar went
through the hall's entry   with word from within:
"I am ordered to answer   that the lord of East-Danes
honors your father   and offers you welcome,
350 sailors who sought us   over the sea-waves,
bravely bent   on embarking hither.
Now you may march   in your mail and masks
to behold Hrothgar.   Here you must leave
war-shields and spears   sharpened for strife.
355 Your weapons can wait   for words to be spoken."

The mighty one rose   with many a man
marshaled about him,   though some were bidden
to stay with the weapons   and stand on watch.
Under Heorot's roof   the rest hastened
360 when Beowulf brought them   boldly before
the hearth of Hrothgar.   Helmed and hardy,
the war-chief shone   as he stood in skillfully
smithied chain-mail   and spoke to his host:

"Hail to you, Hrothgar!   I am Hygelac's
365 kinsman and comrade,   esteemed by the king
for deeds I have done   in the years of youth.
I heard in my homeland   how Grendel grieves you.
Seafarers say   that your splendid hall
stands idle and useless   after the sun
370 sinks each evening   from Heaven's height.
The most honored among us,   earls and elders,
have urged me to seek you,   certain my strength

---

9. Hrothgar is, in fact, king of all the Danes: North, South, East, and West. The different terms merely conform to the Anglo-Saxon alliterative pattern established in each line.

would serve in your struggle.   They have seen me return
bloody from binding   brutish giants,

375 a family of five   destroyed in our strife;
by night in the sea   I have slain monsters.
Hardship I had,   but our harms were avenged,
our enemies mastered.   Now I shall match
my grip against Grendel's   and get you an end

380 to this feud with the fiend.   Therefore one favor
I ask from you, Hrothgar,   sovereign of Spear-Danes,
shelter of shield-bearers,   friend to your folk:
that I and my officers,   we and no others,
be offered the honor   of purging your hall.

385 I have also heard   that the rash thing reckons
the thrust of a weapon   no threat to his thews,[1]
so I shall grab   and grapple with Grendel.
Let my lord Hygelac   hear and be glad
I foreswore   my sword and strong shield

390 when I fought for life   with that fearsome foe.
Whomever death takes,   his doom is doubtless
decreed by the Lord.   If I let the creature
best me when battle   begins in this building,
he will freely feast   as he often has fed

395 on men of much mettle.   My corpse will require
no covering cloth.   He will carry away
a crushed carcass   clotted with gore,
the fiend's fodder   gleefully eaten,
smearing his lonesome   lair on the moor.

400 No need to worry   who buries my body
if battle takes me.   Send back to my sovereign
this best of shirts   which has shielded my breast,
this choice chain-mail,   Hrethel's heirloom
and Weland's work.[2]   Fate goes as it will."

405 Helm of the Scyldings,   Hrothgar answered:
"It is fair that you seek   to defend us, my friend,
in return for the favor   offered your father
when a killing fanned   the fiercest of feuds
after he felled   the Wylfing, Heatholaf.

410 Wary of war,   the Weder-Geats wanted
Ecgtheow elsewhere,   so over the sea-swells
he sought the South-Danes,   strong Scyldings.
I had lately become   king of my kinsmen,
a youth ruling   this jewel of a realm,

415 this store-house of heroes,   with Heorogar gone,
my brother and better,   born of Healfdene.
I calmed your father's   quarrel with wergeld
sent over sea   straight to the Wylfings,
an ancient heirloom;   and Ecgtheow's oath

1. Well-developed sinew or muscle.

420 I took in return.
                   "It pains me to tell
what grief Grendel   has given me since,
what harm in Heorot,   hatred and shame
at his sudden onset.   My circle is shrunken;
my guardsmen are gone,   gathered by fate
425 into Grendel's grip.   How simply the Sovereign
of Heaven could hinder   deeds of this hell-fiend!
Beer-swollen boasters,   brave in their ale-cups,
often have sworn   to stay with their swords
drawn in the dark,   to strike down the demon.
430 Then in the morning   the mead-hall was drenched,
blood on the bench-boards,   blood on the floor,
the highest of houses   a horror at dawn.
Fewer were left   to keep faith with their lord
since those dear retainers   were taken by death.
435 But sit now to sup   and afterward speak
of soldierly pride,   if the spirit prompts you."

A bench was then cleared   there in the beer-hall
so all of the Geats   could sit together,
sturdy soldiers,   proud and stout-hearted.
440 A dutiful Dane   brought them bright ale-cups
and poured sweet mead   while the scop was singing
high-voiced in Heorot.   That host of warriors,
Weders and Scyldings,   shared in the wassails.

But envious Unferth,[3]   Ecglaf's son,
445 spat out his spite   from the seat he took
at his sovereign's feet.   The seafarer's quest
grieved him greatly,   for he would not grant
any man ever,   in all middle-earth,
more fame under heaven   than he himself had.

450 "Are you that Beowulf   Breca bested
when both of you bet   on swimming the straits,
daring the deep   in a dire struggle,
risking your lives   after rash boasting?
Though friend or foe,   no man could deflect
455 your foolhardy foray.   Arms flailing,
you each embraced   the billowing stream,
spanned the sea-lane   with swift-dipping hands
and wended over   the warring ocean.
Winter-like waves   were roiling the waters
460 as the two of you toiled   in the tumult of combers.
For seven nights   you strove to outswim him,
but he was the stronger   and saw at sunrise
the sea had swept him   to Heathoraem[4] shores.

---

3. Hrothgar's spokesman or court jester; his rude behavior toward Beowulf is consistent with other figures in epics and
romances who taunt the hero before he undertakes his exploits. "Unferth" may mean "strife."

4. Coastal tribe of central Sweden; see the Norwegian border.

Breca went back   to his own homeland,
465   his burg on the bluff,   stronghold of Brondings,
a fair realm and wealthy.   The wager was won;
Beanstan's son   had brought off his boast.
However you fared   in onslaughts elsewhere,
I doubt you will live   the length of a night
470   if you dare to linger   so near Grendel."

Then Beowulf spoke,   son of Ecgtheow:
"Listen, Unferth,   my fuddled friend
brimful of beer,   you blabber too much
about Breca's venture.   I tell you the truth:
475   my force in the flood   is more than a match
for any man   who wrestles the waves.
Boys that we were,   brash in our youth
and reckless of risk,   both of us boasted
that each one could swim   the open ocean.
480   So we set forth,   stroking together
sturdily seaward   with swords drawn
hard in our hands   to ward off whale-fish.
No swifter was he   in those heaving seas;
each of us kept   close to the other,
485   floating together   those first five nights.
Then the storm-surges   swept us apart:
winter-cold weather   and warring winds
drove from the north   in deepening darkness.
Rough waves rose   and sea-beasts raged,
490   but my breast was bound   in a woven mail-shirt.
Hard and hand-linked,   hemmed with gold,
it kept those creatures   from causing me harm.
I was drawn to the depths,   held fast by the foe,
grim in his grasp;   yet granted a stab,
495   I stuck in my sword-point,   struck down the horror.
The mighty sea-monster   met death by my hand.

"Often afterward   snatchers of swimmers
snapped at my heels.   With my strong sword
I served them fitly.   I would fatten no foes,
500   feed no man-banes   munching their morsels
when setting to feast   on the floor of the sea.
Instead at sunrise   the sword-stricken
washed up in windrows   to lie lifelessly,
lodged by the tide-line,   and nevermore trouble
505   sailors crossing   the steep-cliffed straits.
As God's beacon   brightened the East,
I spied a cape   across calming seas,
a windward wall.   So I was spared,
for fate often favors   an unmarked man
510   if he keeps his courage.   My sword was the slayer
of nine monsters.   I've not heard of many

who fended off   a more fearsome assault
while hurled by the waves   under heaven's vault.
Yet I broke the beasts' grip   and got off alive,
weary of warfare.   Swiftly surging
after the storm,   the sea-current swept me
to Finland's coast.
                                "Such close combat
or stark sword-strokes   you have not seen,
you or Breca.   No tale has told
how either of you two   ever attempted
so bold a deed   done with bright sword,
though I would not claim   a brother's bane
if the killing of kin   were all I'd accomplished.
For that you are certain   to suffer in Hell,
doomed with the damned   despite your swift wit.
I say straight out,   son of Ecglaf,
that ghastly Grendel,   however gruesome,
would never have done   such dreadful deeds,
harming your lord   here in his hall,
if your spirit were stern,   your will, warlike,
as you have affirmed.   The foe has found
that he need not reckon   with wrathful swords
or look with alarm   on the likes of you,
Scylding victor.   He takes his tribute,
sparing no man,   snatching and supping
whenever he wishes   with wicked delight,
expecting no strife   with spear-bearing Danes.
But soon, very soon,   I shall show him the strength
and boldness of Geats   giving him battle.
When morning comes   to light up the land,
you may go again   and gladly get mead
as the bright sun   beams in the South
and starts a new day   for the sons of men."

Gray-haired Hrothgar,   giver of hoard-wealth,
was happy to hear   Beowulf bolster
hope for his folk   with forthright avowal.
About the Bright-Danes'   battle-leader
rang warriors' laughter   and winsome words.
The queen, Wealtheow,[5]   by custom courteous,
greeted the party   aglitter with gold
and bore the full cup   first to her lord,
the keeper of East-Danes,   dear to his people,
bidding him drink   and be glad of his beer.
That soldierly sovereign   quaffed and supped
while his Helming princess   passed through the hall
offering everyone,   young man and old,

515

520

525

530

535

540

545

550

555

5. "Weal theow" means "foreign slave," and she may be British or Celtic in origin. Even after her marriage to Hrothgar, she continues to maintain her identity as the "lady of the Helmings," an epithet recalling her father Helm.

the dole he was due.   Adorned with rings,
she bore the burnished   mead-bowl to Beowulf,
last of them all,   and honored the Geat
560 with gracious words,   firm in her wisdom
and grateful to God   for granting her wish.
Here was the prayed-for   prince who would help
to end the ill deeds.   He emptied the cup
Wealtheow offered;   then the willing warrior,
565 Ecgtheow's son,   spoke as one ready
for strife and slaughter:
                              "When I set my ship
to sail on the sea   and steered her hence
with my squadron of swords,   I swore to fulfill
the will of the Scyldings   or die in the deed,
570 fall with the slain,   held fast by the foe,
my last day lived out   here in your hall."

The wife was well-pleased   with Beowulf's words,
this oath from the Geat;   and glinting with gold
the queen, Wealtheow,   went to her king.
575 Boasts were bandied   once more in the beer-hall,
the hearty speech   of a hopeful household,
forceful fighters.   But soon the sovereign,
son of Healfdene,   hankered for sleep.
He knew his enemy   brooded on battle
580 all day from dawn   until deepening dusk.
Covered by darkness,   the creature would come,
a shade under shadows.   The company stood.
One man to another,   Hrothgar hailed
brave Beowulf,   wishing him well
585 and granting him leave   to guard the wine-hall.

"So long as my hand   has hefted a shield,
I never have yielded   the Danes' mansion
to any man else,   whatever his mettle.
Now you shall hold   this highest of houses.
590 Be mindful of fame;   make your might known;
but beware of the brute.   You will want no boon
if you tackle this task   and live to request it."

Hrothgar and his princes   departed the hall;
the warder of Danes   went to his woman,
595 couched with his queen.   The King of Glory
had granted a guard   against Grendel's wrath,
as all had now learned.   One man had offered
to take on this task   and watch for the terror.
The leader of Geats   would gladly trust
600 the force of God's favor.   He flung off his mail-shirt,
then handed his helmet   and inlaid sword
to the steward assigned   safe-keeping of iron

and gilded war-gear.   Again the bold
Beowulf boasted   while bound for his bed:

605 "I am no weaker   in works of war,
no less a grappler   than Grendel himself.
Soon I shall sink him   into his death-sleep,
not with my sword   but solely by strength.
He is unschooled in skills   to strike against me,
610 to shatter my shield,   though feared for his fierceness.
So I shall bear   no blade in the night
if he sees fit   to fight without weapons.
May God in His wisdom   grant whom He wills
blessing in battle."
                                The brave soldier
615 stretched out for sleep,   and a bolster pillowed
his proud cheekbone.   About him were sprawled
the strong sea-warriors,   each one wondering
whether he ever   would walk once again
his beloved land,   or find his own folk
620 from childhood's time   in an untroubled town.
All had been told   how often before
dreadful death   had swept up the Danes
who lay in this hall.   But the Lord lent them
aid in their anguish,   weaving their war-luck,
625 for one man alone   had the might and main
to fight off the fiend,   crush him in combat,
proving who ruled   the races of men,
then and forever: God, the Almighty.⁶

Cunningly creeping,   a spectral stalker
630 slunk through the gloom.   The bowmen were sleeping
who ought to have held   the high-horned house,
all except one,   for the Lord's will
now became known: no more would the murderer
drag under darkness   whomever he wished.
635 Anger was wakeful,   watching the enemy;
hot-hearted Beowulf   was bent upon battle.

Then from the moor   under misty hillsides,
Grendel came gliding   girt with God's anger.
The man-scather sought   someone to snatch
640 from the high hall.   He crept under clouds
until he caught sight   of the king's court
whose gilded gables   he knew at a glance.
He often had haunted   Hrothgar's house;
but he never found,   before or after,
645 hardier hall-thanes   or harder luck.

---

6. This interpolation of Christian belief into what is essentially a pagan tradition has been taken as evidence of a conscious rewriting of much earlier material. The narrative assures its reader that Christian beliefs were still valid, regardless of what the characters in the story may have believed.

The joyless giant   drew near the door,
which swiftly swung back   at the touch of his hand
though bound and fastened   with forge-bent bars.
The building's mouth   had been broken open,
650   and Grendel entered   with ill intent.
Swollen with fury,   he stalked over flagstones
and looked round the manse   where many men lay.
An unlovely light   most like a flame
flashed from his eyes,   flared through the hall
655   at young soldiers dozing   shoulder to shoulder,
comradely kindred.   The cruel creature laughed
in his murderous mind,   thinking how many
now living would die   before the day dawned,
how glutted with gore   he would guzzle his fill.
660   It was not his fate   to finish the feast
he foresaw that night.
                                    Soon the Stalwart,
Hygelac's kinsman,   beheld how the horror,
not one to be idle,   went about evil.
For his first feat   he suddenly seized
665   a sleeping soldier,   slashed at the flesh,
bit through bones   and lapped up the blood
that gushed from veins   as he gorged on gobbets.
Swiftly he swallowed   those lifeless limbs,
hands and feet whole;   then he headed forward
670   with open palm   to plunder the prone.
One man angled   up on his elbow:
the fiend soon found   he was facing a foe
whose hand-grip was harder   than any other
he ever had met   in all Middle-Earth.
675   Cravenly cringing,   coward at heart,
he longed for a swift   escape to his lair,
his bevy of devils.   He never had known
from his earliest days   such awful anguish.

The captain, recalling   his speech to the king,
680   straightaway stood   and hardened his hold.
Fingers fractured.   The fiend spun round;
the soldier stepped closer.   Grendel sought
somehow to slip   that grasp and escape,
flee to the fens;   but his fingers were caught
685   in too fierce a grip.   His foray had failed;
the harm-wreaker rued   his raid on Heorot.
From the hall of the Danes   a hellish din
beset every soldier   outside the stronghold,
louder than laughter   of ale-sodden earls.
690   A wonder it was   the wine-hall withstood
this forceful affray   without falling to earth.
That beautiful building   was firmly bonded

by iron bands   forged with forethought
inside and out.   As some have told it,
695 the struggle swept on   and slammed to the floor
many mead-benches   massive with gold.
No Scylding elders   ever imagined
that any would harm   their elk-horned hall,
raze what they wrought,   unless flames arose
700 to enfold and consume it.   Frightful new sounds
burst from the building,   unnerved the North-Danes,
each one and all   who heard those outcries
outside the walls.   Wailing in anguish,
the hellish horror,   hateful to God,
705 sang his dispair,   seized by the grip
of a man more mighty   than any then living.

That shielder of men   meant by no means
to let the death-dealer   leave with his life,
a life worthless   to anyone elsewhere.
710 Then the young soldiers   swung their old swords
again and again   to save their guardian,
their kingly comrade,   however they could.
Engaging with Grendel   and hoping to hew him
from every side,   they scarcely suspected
715 that blades wielded   by worthy warriors
never would cut   to the criminal's quick.
The spell was spun   so strongly about him
that the finest iron   of any on earth,
the sharpest sword-edge   left him unscathed.
720 Still he was soon   to be stripped of his life
and sent on a sore   sojourn to Hell.
The strength of his sinews   would serve him no more;
no more would he menace   mankind with his crimes,
his grudge against God,   for the high-hearted kinsman
725 of King Hygelac   had hold of his hand.
Each found the other   loathsome in life;
but the murderous man-bane   got a great wound
as tendons were torn,   shoulder shorn open,
and bone-locks broken.   Beowulf gained
730 glory in war;   and Grendel went off
bloody and bent   to the boggy hills,
sorrowfully seeking   his dreary dwelling.
Surely he sensed   his life-span was spent,
his days upon days;   but the Danes were grateful:
735 their wish was fulfilled   after fearsome warfare.

Wise and strong-willed,   the one from afar
had cleansed Heorot,   hall of Hrothgar.
Great among Geats,   he was glad of his night-work
ending the evil,   his fame-winning feat,
740 fulfilling his oath   to aid the East Danes,

easing their anguish,   healing the horror
they suffered so long,   no small distress.
As token of triumph,   the troop-leader hung
the shorn-off shoulder   and arm by its hand:
745   the grip of Grendel   swung from the gable!

Many a warrior   met in the morning
around Hrothgar's hall,   so I have heard.
Folk-leaders fared   from near and far
over wide lands   to look on the wonder,
750   the track of the terror,   glad he had taken
leave of his life   when they looked on footprints
wending away   to the mere of monsters.
Weary and weak,   defeated in war,
he dripped his blood-trail   down to dark water,
755   tinting the terrible   tide where he sank,
spilling his lifeblood   to swirl in the surge.
There the doomed one   dropped into death
where he long had lurked   in his joyless lair,
and Hell received   his heathen soul.

760   Many went hence: young men and old
mounted white mares   and rode to the mere,
a joyous journey   on brave battle-steeds.
There Beowulf's   prowess was praised
and approved by all.   Everyone said
765   that over the Earth   and under bright sky,
from north to south   between sea and sea,
no other man   was more worthy of wearing
corselet or crown,   though no one denied
the grace of Hrothgar: that was a good king.

770   Sometimes they galloped   great-hearted bays;
races were run   where roads were smooth
on open upland.   Meanwhile a man
skilled as a singer,   versed in old stories,
wove a new lay   of truly-linked words.
775   So the scop started   his song of Beowulf's
wisdom and strength,   setting his spell
with subtle staves.   Of Sigemund[7] also
he said what he knew: many marvels,
deeds of daring   and distant journeys,
780   the wars of Waels' son,   his wildness, his sins,
unsung among men   save by Fitela,
Sigemund's nephew,   who knew his secrets
and aided his uncle   in every conflict
as comrade-at-need.   A whole clan of ogres

7. The story of Sigemund is also told in the Old Norse *Volsunga Saga* and with major variations in the Middle High German *Niebelungenlied.* The scop's comparison of Sigemund with Beowulf is ironic in that the order and the outcome of Beowulf's later encounter with a dragon will be reversed.

785　was slain by the Waelsing　wielding his sword.
　　　No small esteem　sprang up for Sigemund
　　　after his death-day.　Dauntless in war,
　　　he struck down a serpent　under gray stone
　　　where it held its hoard.　He fared alone
790　on this fearsome foray,　not with Fitela;
　　　but fate allowed him　to lunge with his blade,
　　　spitting the scaly　worm to the wall.
　　　His pluck repaid,　Sigemund was pleased
　　　to take his pick　of the piled-up treasure
795　and load bright arms　in his longboat's breast
　　　while the molten worm　melted away.

　　　Thus that wayfarer　famed far and wide
　　　among nations of men,　that mighty war-maker,
　　　shelter of shield-bearers,　outshone another:
800　unhappy Heremod,[8]　king of the Danes,
　　　whose strength, spirit,　and courage were spent.
　　　He fell among foes,　was taken by traitors
　　　and swiftly dispatched.　So his sorrows
　　　ended at last.　Too long had lords
805　and commoners suffered,　scourged by their king,
　　　who ought to have honored　his father's office,
　　　defending his homeland,　his hoard and stronghold.
　　　Evil had entered him.　Dearer to Danes
　　　and all humankind　was Hygelac's kinsman.

810　Still running heats,　the horses hurtled
　　　on sandy lanes.　The light of morning
　　　had swung to the south,　and many men sped,
　　　keen to behold　the hall of the king,
　　　the strange sights inside.　Hrothgar himself,
815　keeper of treasures　and leader of troops,
　　　came from the queen's　quarters to march
　　　with measured tread　the track to his mead-hall;
　　　the queen and her maidens　also came forth.
　　　He stopped on the stairs　and gazed at the gable,
820　glinting with gold　behind Grendel's hand.

　　　"My thanks for this sight　go straight to Heaven!
　　　Grendel has given me　grief and grievance;
　　　but God often works　wonders on wonders.
　　　Not long ago　I had no hope at all
825　of living to see　relief from my sorrows
　　　while slaughter stained　the highest of houses,
　　　wide-spilling woes　the wisest advisors
　　　despaired of stanching.　None of them knew
　　　how to fend off our foes:　the ghosts and ghasts

---

8. Heremod, an earlier Danish king, was the stock illustration of the unjust and unwise ruler. After bringing bloodshed upon his own house, Heremod took refuge among the Jutes, who eventually put him to death.

830 afflicting our folk   here in our fastness.
Now, praise Heaven,   a prince has proven
this deed could be done   that daunted us all.
Indeed the mother   who bore this young man
among mankind   may certainly say,
835 if she still is living,   that the Lord of Old
blessed her child-bearing.   Henceforth, Beowulf,
best of the brave,   I shall hold you in heart
as close as a son.   Keep our new kinship,
and I shall award you   whatever you wish
840 that is mine to command.   Many a time
I have lavished wealth   on lesser warriors,
slighter in strife.   You have earned your esteem.
May the All-Wielder   reward you always,
just as He gives you   these goods today."

845 Beowulf spoke,   son of Ecgtheow:
"We gladly engaged   in this work of war
and freely faced   the unknowable foe,
but I greatly regret   that you were not granted
the sight of him broken,   slathered with blood.
850 I sought to grip him   swiftly and strongly,
wrestle him down   to writhe on his death-bed
as life left him,   unless he broke loose.
It was not my fate   to fasten the man-bane
firmly enough.   The fiend was so fierce
855 he secured his escape   by leaving this limb
to ransom his life,   though little the wretch
has gained for his hurt,   held in the grip
of a dire wound,   awaiting death
as a savage man,   besmirched by his sins,
860 might wait to learn   what the Lord wills."

Unferth was silent.   He spoke no more boasts
about works of war   when warriors gazed
at the hand hanging   from Heorot's roof,
the fiend's fingers   jutting in front,
865 each nail intact,   those terrible talons
like spikes of steel.   Everyone said
that the strongest sword   from smithies of old,
the hardest iron   edge ever forged,
would never have harmed   that monstrous mauler,
870 those bloody claws   crooked for combat.

2. Grendel's Mother

Inside Heorot   many hands hastened
at Hrothgar's command: men and women
washed out the wine-hall,   unfurled on the walls
gold-woven hangings   to gladden their guests,

875   each of whom gazed   wide-eyed in wonder.
        Though bound with iron,   the bright building
        was badly battered,   its hinges broken.
        Only the roof   had escaped unscathed
        before the fell creature   cringed and fled,
880   stained by his sin   and despairing of life.
        Flee it who will,   a well-earned fate
        is not often altered,   for every earth-dweller
        and soul-bearing son   must seek out a spot
        to lay down his body,   lie on his death-bed,
885   sleep after feasting.   So came the season
        for Healfdene's son   to stride through his hall:
        the king himself   would sup with his kin.
        I have never heard   in any nation
        of such a great host   so graciously gathered,
890   arrayed on benches   around their ruler,
        glad of his fame   and glad for the feast.
        Many a mead-cup   those masterful kinsmen
        Hrothgar and Hrothulf   raised in the hall.
        All were then friends   who filled Heorot,
895   treason and treachery   not yet contrived.[1]

        Crowning his conquest,   the King of the Danes
        bestowed on the soldier   a battle-standard
        embroidered with gold,   a helmet, mail-shirt,
        and unblemished blade   borne out while ranks
900   of warriors watched.   Then Beowulf drank
        a flagon before them: he would feel no shame
        facing bold spearmen   with boons such as these.
        Not many men   on mead benches
        have given another   four golden gifts
905   in friendlier fashion.   The head-guard was flanged
        with windings of wire.   Facing forward,
        it warded off harm   when the wearer in war
        was obliged to bear shield   against enemy blades
        that were hammer-hardened   and honed by files.
910   The sovereign ordered   eight swift steeds
        brought to the court   on braided bridles.
        One bore a saddle   studded with gems
        and glinting gold-work: there the great king,
        son of Healfdene,   would sit during sword-strife,
915   never faltering,   fierce at the front,
        working his will   while the wounded fell.
        Then Hrothgar awarded   horses and weapons
        both to Beowulf,   bade that he keep them
        and wield them well.   So from his hoard

---

1. Possibly an allusion to the later usurpation of the Danish throne by Hrothgar's nephew Hrothulf.

920	he paid the hero a princely reward
	of heirlooms and arms for braving the battle;
	no man could fairly or truthfully fault them.
	That lord also lavished gifts on the Geats
	whom Beowulf brought over broad seas,
925	and wergeld he gave for the one Grendel
	had wickedly killed, though the creature would surely
	have murdered more had God in his wisdom,
	man in his strength failed to forestall it.
	So the Almighty has always moved men;
930	yet man must consistently strive to discern
	good from evil, evil from good
	while drunk with days he dwells in this world.
	Music and story now sounded together
	as Hrothgar's scop sang for the hall-fest
935	a tale often told when harp was held:[2]
	how Finn's followers, faithless Jutes,
	fell to fighting friends in his fortress;
	how Hnaef the Half-Dane, hero of Scyldings,
	was fated to fall in Frisian warfare;
940	how by shield-swagger harmless Hildeburh,
	faithful to Finn though daughter of Danes,
	lost her beloved brother and son
	who were both born to be struck by spears.
	Not without cause did Hoc's daughter
945	bewail the Lord's will when morning awoke:
	she who had known nothing but happiness
	beheld under heaven the horror of kin-strife.
	War had taken its toll of attackers;
	few men remained for Finn to muster,
950	too few to force the fight against Hengest,
	a dutiful thane who had rallied the Danes.
	As tokens of truce Finn offered these terms:
	a haven wholly emptied of foes,
	hall and high seat, with an equal share
955	in gifts given his own gathered kin.
	Each time he treated his sons to treasures
	plated with gold, a portion would go
	to sweeten Hengest's stay in his hall.
	The two sides swore a strict treaty;
960	and Finn freely affirmed to Hengest

2. The following episode is one of the most obscure in *Beowulf*. It seems that Hnaef and Hildeburh are both children of an earlier Danish king named Hoc and that Hildeburh has been sent to marry Finn, the son of Folcwalda and king of the Jutes and Frisians, in order to conclude a marriage alliance and thus settle a prior blood feud between the two tribes. Upon going to visit his sister and her husband, Hnaef is treacherously ambushed and killed by Finn's men; Hildeburh's son by Finn is also killed. In her role as peace-weaver, Hildeburh is torn by conflicting allegiances, foreshadowing the fate of Hrothgar's own daughter Freawaru in her marriage to Ingeld.

that all would honor   this oath to the Danes,
as his council decreed,   and further declared
no Frisian would ever,   by word or work,
challenge the peace   or mention with malice
965   the plight of survivors   deprived of their prince
and wintered-in   at the slayer's stronghold.
Should any Frisian   enter in anger,
the sword's edge   would settle the quarrel.

That oath offered,   the hoard was opened
970   for gold to array   the greatest of War-Danes.
Iron-hard guardians   gilded with gold,
bloody mail-shirts   and boar-tusked helms
were heaped on his bier,   awaiting the balefire.
Many a warrior,   weakened by wounds,
975   had faltered and fallen   with foes he had slain.
Hildeburh ordered   her own dear son
be placed on the pyre,   the prince and his uncle
shoulder to shoulder.   Their bodies were burned
while the stricken lady   sang out her sorrow.
980   Streamers of smoke   burst from the bier
as corpses kindled   with cruelest of flames.
Faces withered,   wounded flesh yawned,
and blood boiled out   as the blaze swallowed
with hateful hunger   those whom warfare
985   had borne away,   the best of both houses.
Their glory was gone.
                    The Frisians were fewer
heading for home;   their high stronghold
was empty of allies.   For Hengest also
that winter was woeful,   walled up in Frisia,
990   brooding on bloodshed   and longing to leave,
though knowing his vessel   never could breast
the wind-darkened swells   of a wide ocean
seething with storms,   or break the ice-bindings
that barred his bow   from the bitter waters.
995   Constrained to wait   for kindlier weather,
he watched until spring,   season of sunlight,
dawned on men's dwellings   as ever it did
and still does today.   Winter withdrew
and Earth blossomed.
                    Though the exile was eager
1000   to end his visit,   he ached for vengeance
before sailing home.   Loathe to foreswear
the way of this world,   he schemed to assail
the sons of slayers.   So Hengest heeded
Hunlaf's son,   who laid on his lap
1005   the sword War-Flame,   feared by all foes,
asking its edge   be offered the Jutes.

67

His heart was hot;   he could hold back no more;
gladly he answered   Guthlaf and Oslaf,
who wrathfully spoke   of the wrong they suffered,
1010   the shame of Scyldings   sharing their plight.
Then fierce-hearted Finn   fell in his turn,
stricken by swords   in his own stronghold.
The building was bloody   with bodies of foemen:
the king lay slain,   likewise his kin;
1015   and the queen was captured.   Scyldings carried
off in their ship   all of the chattels
found in Finn's fortress,   gemstones and jewels.
The lady was borne   to the land of her birth.

So that story   was sung to its end,
1020   then mirth mounted   once more in Heorot.
Revelry rang   as wine-bearers brought
finely-wrought flagons   filled to the brim.
Wearing her circlet,   Wealtheow walked
where uncle and nephew,   Hrothgar and Hrothulf,
1025   were sitting in peace,   two soldiers together,
each still believing   the other was loyal.
Likewise the officer,   Unferth, was honored
to sit at the feet   of the Scylding sovereign.
Everyone thought him   honest and trustworthy,
1030   blameless and brave,   though his blade had unjustly
stricken a kinsman.
                    So the queen spoke:
"Receive this cup,   sovereign of Scyldings,
giver of gold;   drink and be glad;
greet the Geats mildly   as well a man might,
1035   mindful of gifts   graciously given
from near and far,   now in your keeping.
They say you would name   that knight as a son
for purging the ring-hall.   Employ as you please
wealth and rewards,   but bequeath to your kin
1040   rule of this realm   when the Ruler of All
holds that you must.   I know that Hrothulf
will honor our trust   and treat these youths well
if you have to leave   this life before him.
I am counting on him   to recall our kindness
1045   when he was a child   and repay our children
for presents we gave   and pleasures we granted."

She turned to the bench   where her sons were seated,
Hrethric and Hrothmund.   Between the two brothers
Beowulf sat;   and the cup-bearer brought him
1050   words of welcome,   willingly gave him
as tokens of favor   two braided arm-bands,
jerkin, corselet,   and jeweled collar

grander than any   other on Earth.[3]
I have heard under heaven   of no higher treasure
1055 hoarded by heroes   since Hama stole off
to his fair fortress   with Freya's necklace,
shining with stones   set by the Fire-Dwarves.
So Hama earned   Eormanric's anger,
and fame for himself.   Foolhardy Hygelac,
1060 grandson of Swerting   and sovereign of Geats,
would wear it one day   on his final foray.
He fell in the fray   defending his treasure,
the spoils he bore   with his battle-standard.
Recklessly raiding   the realm of Frisia,
1065 the prince in his pride   had prompted misfortune
by crossing the sea   while clad in that collar.
He fell under shield,   fell to the Franks,
weaker warriors   stripping the slain
of armor and spoil   after the slaughter.
1070 Hygelac held   the graveyard of Geats.

The hall approved   the princely prize
bestowed by the queen,   and Wealtheow spoke
for the host to hear: "Keep this collar,
beloved Beowulf.   Bear this armor,
1075 wealth of our realm.   May it ward you well.
Swear that your strength   and kindly counsel
will aid these youngsters,   and I shall reward you.
Now your renown   will range near and far;
your fame will wax wide,   as wide as the water
1080 hemming our hills,   homes of the wind.
Be blessed, Beowulf,   with abundant treasures
as long as you live;   and be mild to my sons,
a model admired.   Here men are courtly,
honest and true,   each to the other,
1085 all to their ruler;   and after the revels,
bolstered with beer,   they do as I bid."

The lady left him   and sat on her seat.
The feast went on;   fine wine was flowing.
Men could not know   what fate would befall them,
1090 what evil of old   was decreed to come
for the earls that evening.   As always, Hrothgar
headed for home,   where the ruler rested.
A great many others   remained in the hall,
bearing bright benches   and rolling out beds
1095 while one drunkard,   doomed and death-ripened,

---

3. The narrative jumps ahead beyond Beowulf's return home to the Geats. His uncle, Hygelac, the king, will not only receive the collar from Beowulf but will die with it in battle among the Frisians. The collar thus connects different events at different times.

sprawled into sleep.   They set at their heads
round war-shields,   well-adorned wood.
Above them on boards,   their battle-helms rested,
ringed mail-shirts   and mighty spear-shafts
1100   waiting for strife.   Such was their wont
at home or afield,   wherever they fared,
in case their king   should call them to arms.
Those were stern people.
                                    They sank into slumber,
but one paid sorely   for sleep that evening,
1105   as often had happened   when grim Grendel
held the gold-hall,   wreaking his wrongs
straight to the end: death after sins.
It would soon be perceived   plainly by all
that one ill-wisher   still was alive,
1110   maddened by grief: Grendel's mother,
a fearsome female   bitterly brooding
alone in her lair   deep in dread waters
and cold currents   since Cain had killed
the only brother   born of his father.
1115   Marked by murder,   he fled from mankind
and went to the wastes.   Doomed evil-doers
issued from him.   Grendel was one,
but the hateful Hell-walker   found a warrior
wakefully watching   for combat in Heorot.
1120   The monster met there   a man who remembered
strength would serve him,   the great gift of God,
faith in the All-Wielder's   favor and aid.
By that he mastered   the ghastly ghoul;
routed, wretched,   the hell-fiend fled,
1125   forlornly drew near   his dreary death-place.
Enraged and ravenous,   Grendel's mother
swiftly set out   on a sorrowful journey
to settle the score   for her son's demise.

She slipped into Heorot,   hall of the Ring-Danes,
1130   where sleeping soldiers   soon would endure
an awful reversal.   Her onslaught was less
by as much as a woman's   mettle in war
is less than a man's   wielding his weapon:
the banded blade   hammered to hardness,
1135   a blood-stained sword   whose bitter stroke
slashes a boar-helm   borne into battle.
In the hall, sword-edge   sprang from scabbard;
broadshield was swung   swiftly off bench,
held firmly in hand.   None thought of helmet
1140   or sturdy mail-shirt   when terror assailed him.

Out she hastened,   out and away,
keen to keep living   when caught in the act.

She fastened on one,   then fled to her fen.
He was Hrothgar's   highest counselor,
1145 boon companion   and brave shield-bearer
slain in his bed.   Beowulf slept
elsewhere that evening,   for after the feast
the Geat had been given   a different dwelling.
A din of dismay   mounted in Heorot:
1150 the gory hand   was gone from the gable.
Dread had retaken   the Danes' dwelling.
That bargain was bad   for both barterers,
costing each one   a close comrade.

It was grim for the sovereign,   the grizzled soldier,
1155 to learn his old thane   was no longer living,
to know such a dear one   was suddenly dead.
Swiftly he sent   servants to fetch
battle-blessed Beowulf   early from bed,
together with all   the great-hearted Geats.
1160 He marched in their midst,   went where the wise one
was wondering whether   the All-Wielder
ever would alter   this spell of ill-fortune.
That much-honored man   marched up the floor,
and timbers dinned   with the tread of his troop.
1165 He spoke soberly   after the summons,
asking how soundly   the sovereign had slept.

Hrothgar answered,   head of his house:
"Ask not about ease!   Anguish has wakened
again for the Danes.   Aeschere is dead.
1170 He was Yrmenlaf's   elder brother,
my rune-reader   and keeper of counsel,
my shoulder's shielder,   warder in war
when swordsmen struck   at boar-headed helms.
Whatever an honored   earl ought to be,
1175 such was Aeschere.   A sleepless evil
has slipped into Heorot,   seized and strangled.
No one knows where   she will wander now,
glad of the gory   trophy she takes,
her fine fodder.   So she requites
1180 her kinsman's killer   for yesterday's deed,
when you grabbed Grendel   hard in your hand-grip.
He plagued and plundered   my people too long.
His life forfeit,   he fell in the fray;
but now a second   mighty man-scather
1185 comes to carry   the feud further,
as many a thane   must mournfully think,
seeing his sovereign   stricken with grief
at the slaying of one   who served so well.

"I have heard spokesmen   speak in my hall,
1190 country-folk saying   they sometimes spotted

a pair of prodigies   prowling the moors,
evil outcasts,   walkers of wastelands.
One, they descried,   had the semblance of woman;
the other, ill-shapen,   an aspect of man
1195   trudging his track,   ever an exile,
though superhuman   in stature and strength.
In bygone days   the border-dwellers
called him *Grendel*.   What creature begot him,
what nameless spirit,   no one could say.
1200   The two of them trekked   untraveled country:
wolf-haunted heights   and windy headlands,
the frightening fen-path   where falling torrents
dive into darkness,   stream beneath stone
amid folded mountains.   That mere[4] is not far,
1205   as miles are measured.   About it there broods
a forest of fir trees   frosted with mist.
Hedges of wood-roots   hem in the water
where each evening   fire-glow flickers
forth on the flood,   a sinister sight.
1210   That pool is unplumbed   by wits of the wise;
but the heath-striding hart   hunted by hounds,
the strong-antlered stag   seeking a thicket,
running for cover,   would rather be killed
at bay on the bank   before hiding its head
1215   under that welter.   It is no peaceful place
where water-struck waves   whipped into clouds,
surge and storm,   swept by the winds,
so the heights are hidden   and heaven weeps.
Now you alone   can relieve our anguish:
1220   look, if you will,   at the lay of the land;
and seek, if you dare,   that dreadful dale
where the she-demon dwells.   Finish this feud,
and I shall reward you   with age-old wealth,
twisted-gold treasures,   if you return."

1225   Beowulf spoke,   son of Ecgtheow:
"Grieve not, good man.   It is better to go
and avenge your friend   than mourn overmuch.
We all must abide   an end on this earth,
but a warrior's works   may win him renown
1230   as long as he lives   and after life leaves him.
Rise now, ruler;   let us ride together
and seek out the signs   of Grendel's mother.
I swear to you this: she shall not escape
in chasm or cave,   in cliff-climbing thicket
1235   or bog's bottom,   wherever she bides.
Suffer your sorrow   this one day only;
I wish you to wait,   wait and be patient."

4. A small lake.

The elder leapt up   and offered his thanks
to God Almighty,   Master of all,
1240 for such hopeful speech.   Then Hrothgar's horse,
a steed with mane braided,   was brought on its bridle.
The sage sovereign   set out in splendor
with shield-bearing soldiers   striding beside him.
Tracks on the trail   were easy to trace:
1245 they went from woodland   out to the open,
heading through heather   and murky moors
where the best of thanes   was borne off unbreathing.
He would live no longer   in Hrothgar's house.
Crossing the moorland,   the king mounted
1250 a stony path   up steepening slopes.
With a squad of scouts   in single file,
he rode through regions   none of them knew,
mountains and hollows   that hid many monsters.
The sovereign himself,   son of great forebears,
1255 suddenly spotted   a forest of fir-trees
rooted on rock,   their trunks tipping
over a tarn   of turbulent eddies.
Danes were downcast,   and Geats, grim;
every soldier   was stricken at heart
1260 to behold on that height   Aeschere's head.

As they looked on the lake,   blood still lingered,
welled to the surface.   A war-horn sounded
its bold battle-cry,   and the band halted.
Strange sea-dragons   swam in the depths;
1265 sinuous serpents   slid to and fro.
At the base of the bluff   water-beasts lay,
much like monsters   that rise in the morning
when seafarers sail   on strenuous journeys.
Hearing the horn's   high-pitched challenge,
1270 they puffed up with rage   and plunged in the pool.
One Geatish lad   lifted his bow
and loosing an arrow,   ended the life
of a wondrous wave-piercer.   War-shaft jutting
hard in its heart,   the swimmer slowed
1275 as death seized it.   With startling speed
the waters were torn   by terrible tuskers.
They heaved the hideous   hulk to the shore
with spear-hooked heads   as warriors watched.

Undaunted, Beowulf   donned battle armor.
1280 His woven war-corselet,   wide and ornate,
would safeguard his heart   as he searched underwater.
It knew how to armor   the breast of its bearer
if an angry grappler   grasped him in battle.
The bright war-helm   would hold his head
1285 when he sought the seafloor   in swirling flood.

A weapon-smith   had skillfully worked
its gilding of gold   in bygone days
and royally ringed it.   He added afterward
figures of boars   so blades of foemen
1290   would fail to bite.   One further aid
Beowulf borrowed: Unferth offered
the hilt of Hrunting,   his princely sword,
a poisoned war-fang   with iron-edged blade,
blood-hardened   in battles of old.
1295   It never had failed   in any man's grasp
if he dared to fare   on a dreadful foray
to fields of foes.   This was not the first time
it was forced to perform   a desperate deed.

Though strong and sly,   the son of Ecglaf
1300   had somehow forgotten   the slander he spoke,
bleary with beer.   He loaned his blade
to a better bearer,   a doer of deeds
that he would not dare.   His head never dipped
under wild waves,   and his fame waned
1305   when bravery failed him   as battle beckoned.
Not so, the other,   armed and eager.

Beowulf spoke,   son of Ecgtheow:
"Remember, wise master,   mover of men
and giver of gold,   since now I begin
1310   this foray full-willing,   how once before
you pledged to fill   the place of a father
if I should be killed   acquitting your cause.
Guard these young aides,   my partners in arms,
if death takes me.   The treasures you dealt,
1315   Hrothgar, my lord,   I leave to Hygelac.
Let the king of Geats   gaze on the gold
and see that I found   a fair bestower,
a generous host   to help while I could.
Let Unferth have back   his heirloom, Hrunting,
1320   this wonderful weapon,   wavy-skinned sword
renowned among men.   Now I shall conquer
or die in the deed."
                         So saying, he dived,
high-hearted and hasty,   awaiting no answer.
The waters swallowed   that stout soldier.
1325   He swam a half-day   before seeing sea-floor.
Straightaway someone   spied him as well:
she that had hidden   a hundred half-years
in the void's vastness.   Grim and greedy,
she glimpsed a creature   come from above
1330   and crept up to catch him,   clutch him, crush him.
Quickly she learned   his life was secure;
he was hale and whole,   held in the ring-mail.

Linked and locked,   his life-shielding shirt
was wrapped around him,   and wrathful fingers
1335   failed to rip open   the armor he wore.
The wolf of the waters   dragged him away
to her den in the deep,   where weapons of war,
though bravely wielded,   were worthless against her.
Many a mere-beast   banded about him,
1340   brandishing tusks   to tear at his shirt.

The soldier now saw   a high-roofed hall:
unharmed, he beheld   the foe's fastness
beyond the reach   of the roiling flood.
Fire-light flared;   a blaze shone brightly.
1345   The lordly one looked   on the hellish hag,
the mighty mere-wife.   He swung his sword
for a swift stroke,   not staying his hand;
and the whorled blade   whistled its war-song.
But the battle-flame   failed to bite her;
1350   its edge was unable   to end her life,
though Hrunting had often   hacked through helmets
and slashed mail-shirts   in hand-to-hand strife.
For the first time   the famous blade faltered.

Resolve unshaken,   courage rekindled,
1355   Hygelac's kinsman   was keen for conquest.
In a fit of fury,   he flung down the sword.
Steely and strong,   the ring-banded blade
rang on the stones.   He would trust in the strength
of his mighty hand-grip.   Thus should a man,
1360   unmindful of life,   win lasting renown.
Grabbing the tresses   of Grendel's mother,
the Geats' battle-chief,   bursting with wrath,
wrestled her down: no deed to regret
but a favor repaid   as fast as she fell.
1365   With her grim grasp   she grappled him still.
Weary, the warrior   stumbled and slipped;
the strongest foot-soldier   fell to the foe.
Astraddle the hall-guest,   she drew her dagger,
broad and bright-bladed,   bent on avenging
1370   her only offspring.   His mail-shirt shielded
shoulder and breast.   Barring the entry
of edge or point,   the woven war-shirt
saved him from harm.   Ecgtheow's son,
the leader of Geats,   would have lost his life
1375   under Earth's arch   but for his armor
and Heaven's favor   furnishing help.
The Ruler of All   readily aided
the righteous man   when he rose once more.

He beheld in a hoard   of ancient arms
1380   a battle-blessed sword   with strong-edged blade,

a marvelous weapon   men might admire
though over-heavy   for any to heft
when finely forged   by giants of old.
The Scyldings' shielder   took hold of the hilt
1385 and swung up the sword,   though despairing of life.
He struck savagely,   hit her hard neck
and broke the bone-rings,   cleaving clean through
her fated flesh.   She fell to the floor;
the sword sweated;   the soldier rejoiced.

1390 The blaze brightened,   shining through shadows
as clearly as Heaven's   candle on high.
Grim and angry,   Hygelac's guardsman
glanced round the room   and went toward the wall
with his weapon raised,   holding it hard
1395 by the inlaid hilt.   Its edge was ideal
for quickly requiting   the killings of Grendel.
Too many times   he had warred on the West-Danes.
He had slain Hrothgar's   hearth-mates in sleep,
eagerly eaten   fifteen of those folk
1400 and as many more borne   for his monstrous booty.
He paid their price   to the fierce prince,
who looked on the ground   where Grendel lay limp,
wound-weary,   defeated in war.
The lifeless one lurched   at the stroke of the sword
1405 that cleaved his corpse   and cut off his head.

At once the wise men   waiting with Hrothgar
and watching the waters   saw the waves seethe
with streaks of gore.   Gray-haired and glum,
age around honor,   they offered their counsel,
1410 convinced that no victor   would ever emerge
and seek out the sovereign.   All were certain
the mere-wolf had mauled him.   It was mid-afternoon,
and the proud Danes   departed the dale;
generous Hrothgar   headed for home.
1415 The Geats lingered   and looked on the lake
with sorrowful souls,   wistfully wishing
they still might see   their beloved leader.

The sword shrank   from battle-shed blood;
its blade began melting,   a marvel to watch,
1420 that war-icicle   waning away
like a rope of water   unwound by the Ruler
when Father releases   fetters of frost,
the true Sovereign   of seasons and times.
The Weders' warlord   took only two treasures
1425 from all he beheld: the head and the hilt,
studded with gems.   The sword had melted.
Its banded blade   was burnt by the blood,
so hot was the horror,   so acid the evil

that ended thereon.   Soon he was swimming:
1430   the strife-survivor   drove up from the deep
when his foe had fallen.   The foaming waves,
the wide waters   were everywhere cleansed;
that alien evil   had ended her life-days,
left the loaned world.
                       Landward he swam;
1435   the strong-minded savior   of sea-faring men
was glad of his burden,   the booty he brought.
Grateful to God,   the band of brave thanes
hastened gladly   to greet their chieftain,
astonished to see him   whole and unharmed.
1440   His helm and chain-mail   were swiftly unstrapped.
Calm under clouds,   the lake lay quietly,
stained by the slain.   They found the foot-path
and marched manfully,   making their way
back through the barrens.   Proud as princes,
1445   they hauled the head   far from the highland,
an effort for each   of the four who ferried it
slung from spear-shafts.   They bore their booty
straight to the gold-hall.   Battle-hardened,
all fourteen strode   from the field outside,
1450   a bold band of Geats   gathered about
their leader and lord,   the war-worthy man,
peerless in prowess   and daring in deeds.
He hailed Hrothgar   as Grendel's head
was dragged by the hair,   drawn through the hall
1455   where earls were drinking.   All were awe-stricken:
women and warriors   watched in wonder.

Beowulf spoke,   son of Ecgtheow:
"Hail, Hrothgar,   Healfdene's son.
Look on this token   we took from the lake,
1460   this glorious booty   we bring you gladly.
The struggle was stark;   the danger, dreadful.
My foe would have won   our war underwater
had the Lord not looked   after my life.
Hrunting failed me,   though finely fashioned;
1465   but God vouchsafed me   a glimpse of a great-sword,
ancient and huge,   hung from the wall.
All-Father often   fosters the friendless.
Wielding this weapon,   I struck down and slew
the cavern's keeper   as soon as I could.
1470   My banded war-blade   was burned away
when blood burst forth   in the heat of battle.
I bore the hilt here,   wrested from raiders.
Thus I avenged   the deaths among Danes
as it was fitting,   and this I assure you:
1475   henceforth in Heorot   heroes shall sleep

untroubled by terror.   Your warrior troop,
all of your thanes,   young men and old,
need fear no further   evil befalling,
not from that quarter,   king of the Scyldings."

1480   He gave the gold hilt   to the good old man;
the hoary war-chief   held in his hand
an ancient artifact   forged by giants.
At the devils' downfall,   this wondrous work
went to the Danes.   The dark-hearted demon,
1485   hater of humans,   Heaven's enemy,
committer of murders,   and likewise his mother,
departed this Earth.   Their power passed
to the wisest world-king   who ever awarded
treasure in Denmark   between the two seas.

1490   Hrothgar spoke   as he studied the hilt,
that aged heirloom   inscribed long ago
with a story of strife: how the Flood swallowed
the race of giants   with onrushing ocean.
Defiant kindred,   they fared cruelly,
1495   condemned for their deeds   to death by water.
Such were the staves   graven in gold-plate,
runes rightly set,   saying for whom
the serpent-ribbed sword   and raddled hilt[5]
were once fashioned   of finest iron.
1500   When the wise one spoke,   all were silent.

"Truth may be told   by the homeland's holder
and keeper of kinfolk,   who rightly recalls
the past for his people: this prince was born
bravest of fighters.   My friend, Beowulf,
1505   your fame shall flourish   in far countries,
everywhere honored.   Your strength is sustained
by patience and judgement.   Just as I promised,
our friendship is firmed,   a lasting alliance.
So you shall be   a boon to your brethren,
1510   unlike Heremod   who ought to have helped
Ecgwela's sons,   the Honor-Scyldings.
He grew up to grief   and grim slaughter,
doling out death   to the Danish nation.
Hot-tempered at table,   he cut down comrades,
1515   slew his own soldiers   and spurned humankind,
alone and unloved,   an infamous prince,
though mighty God   had given him greatness
and raised him in rank   over all other men.
Hidden wrath   took root in his heart,

---

5. On the sword hilt is the story of the flood, written in runes (letters of the early Germanic alphabet), and a decorative
pattern of twisted serpent shapes.

1520   bloodthirsty thoughts.   He would give no gifts
        to honor others.   Loveless, he lived,
        a lasting affliction   endured by the Danes
        in sorrow and strife.   Consider him well,
        his life and lesson.
                       "Wise with winters,
1525   I tell you this tale   as I mull and marvel
        how the Almighty   metes to mankind
        the blessings of reason,   rule and realm.
        He arranges it all.   For a time He allows
        the mind of a man   to linger in love
1530   with earthly honors.   He offers him homeland
        to hold and enjoy,   a fort full of fighters,
        men to command   and might in the world,
        wide kingdoms   won to his will.
        In his folly, the fool   imagines no ending.
1535   He dwells in delight   without thought of his lot.
        Illness, old age,   anguish or envy:
        none of these gnaw   by night at his mind.
        Nowhere are swords   brandished in anger;
        for him the whole world   wends as he wishes.
1540   He knows nothing worse   till his portion of pride
        waxes within him.   His soul is asleep;
        his gate, unguarded.   He slumbers too soundly,
        sunk in small cares.   The slayer creeps close
        and shoots a shaft   from the baneful bow.
1545   The bitter arrow   bites through his armor,
        piercing the heart   he neglected to guard
        from crooked counsel   and evil impulse.
        Too little seems all   he has long possessed.
        Suspicious and stingy,   withholding his hoard
1550   of gold-plated gifts,   he forgets or ignores
        what fate awaits him,   for the world's Wielder
        surely has granted   his share of glory.
        But the end-rune   is already written:
        the loaned life-home   collapses in ruin;
1555   some other usurps   and openly offers
        the hoarded wealth,   heedless of worry.

        "Beloved Beowulf,   best of defenders,
        guard against anger   and gain for yourself
        perpetual profit.   Put aside pride,
1560   worthiest warrior.   Now for awhile
        your force flowers,   yet soon it shall fail.
        Sickness or age   will strip you of strength,
        or the fangs of flame,   or flood-surges,
        the sword's bite   or the spear's flight,
1565   or fearful frailty   as bright eyes fade,
        dimming to darkness.   Afterward death

will sweep you away,   strongest of war-chiefs.

"I ruled the Ring-Danes   a hundred half-years,
stern under clouds   with sword and spear
1570   that I wielded in war   against many nations
across Middle-Earth,   until none remained
beneath spacious skies   to reckon as rivals.
Recompense happened   here in my homeland,
grief after gladness   when Grendel came,
1575   when the ancient enemy   cunningly entered.
Thereafter I suffered   constant sorrows
and cruelest cares.   But God has given me
long enough life   to look at this head
with my own eyes,   as enmity ends
1580   spattered with gore.   Sit and be glad,
war-worthy one: the feast is forthcoming,
and many gifts   will be granted tomorrow."

Gladly the Geat   sought out his seat
as the old man asked.   Hall-guests were given
1585   a second feast   as fine as the first.
The helm of Heaven   darkened with dusk,
and the elders arose.   The oldest of Scyldings
was ready to rest   his hoary-haired head
at peace on his pillow.   Peerless with shield,
1590   the leader of Geats   was equally eager
to lie down at last.   A thane was appointed
to serve as his esquire.   Such was the courtesy
shown in those days   to weary wayfarers,
soldiers sojourning   over the ocean.

1595   Beneath golden gables   the great-hearted guest
dozed until dawn   in the high-roofed hall,
when the black raven   blithely foretold
joy under Heaven.   Daybreak hastened,
sun after shadow.   The soldiers were ardent,
1600   the earls eager   to hurry homeward;
the stern minded man   would make for his ship,
fare back to his folk.   But first he bade
that Hrunting be sent   to the son of Ecglaf,
a treasure returned   with thanks for the loan
1605   of precious iron.   He ordered the owner
be told he considered   the sword a fine friend,
blameless in battle.   That man was gallant!
Keen for the crossing,   his weapons secure,
the warrior went   to the worthy Dane;
1610   the thane sought the throne   where a sovereign sat,
that steadfast hero,   Hrothgar the Great.

Beowulf spoke,   son of Ecgtheow:
"Now we must say   as far-sailing seamen,

we wish to make way   homeward to Hygelac.

1615 Here we were well   and warmly received.
If anything further   would earn your favor,
some deed of war   that remains to be done
for the master of men,   I shall always be ready.
Should word ever wend   over wide ocean
1620 that nearby nations   menace your marches,
as those who detest you   sometimes have tried,
I shall summon a thousand   thanes to your aid.
I know Hygelac,   though newly-anointed
the nation's shepherd,   will surely consent
1625 to honor my offer   in word and action.
If you ever need men,   I shall muster at once
a thicket of spears   and support you in strength.
Should Hrethric, your son,   sail overseas,
he shall find friends   in the fort of the Geats.
1630 It is well for the worthy   to fare in far countries."

Hrothgar offered   these answering words:
"Heaven's Sovereign   has set in your heart
this vow you have voiced.   I never have known
someone so young   to speak more wisely.
1635 You are peerless in strength,   princely in spirit,
straightforward in speech.   If a spear fells
Hrethel's son,   if a hostile sword-stroke
kills him in combat   or after, with illness,
slays your leader   while you still live,
1640 the Sea-Geats surely   could name no better
to serve as their king   and keeper of treasure,
should you wish to wield   rule in your realm.
I sensed your spirit   the instant I saw you,
precious Beowulf,   bringer of peace
1645 for both our peoples: War-Danes and Weders,
so often sundered   by strife in the past.
While I wield the rule   of this wide realm,
men will exchange   many more greetings
and riches will ride   in ring-bowed ships
1650 bearing their gifts   where the gannets bathe.
I know your countrymen   keep to old ways,
fast in friendship,   and war as well."

Then the hall's holder,   Healfdene's son,
gave his protector   twelve more treasures,
1655 bidding he bear   these tokens safely
home to his kin,   and quickly return.
That hoary-haired king   held and kissed him,
clasping his neck.   The noble Scylding
was too well aware   with the wisdom of age
1660 that he never might meet   the young man again
coming to council.   So close had they grown,

so strong in esteem,   he could scarcely endure
the surfeit of sorrow   that surged in his heart;
the flame of affection   burned in his blood.
1665 But Beowulf walked   away with his wealth;
proud of his prizes,   he trod on the turf.
Standing at anchor,   his sea-courser
chafed for its captain.   All the way home
Hrothgar's gifts   were often honored.
1670 That was a king   accorded respect
until age unmanned him,   like many another.

High-hearted,   the troop of young soldiers
strode to the sea,   wrapped in their ring-mesh,
linked and locked shirts.   The land-watcher spied
1675 the fighters faring,   just as before.
He called no taunts   from the top of the cliff
but galloped to greet them   and tell them the Geats
would always be welcome,   armored warriors
borne on their ship.   The broad-beamed boat
1680 lay by the beach,   laden with chain-mail,
chargers and treasures   behind its tall prow.
The mast soared high   over Hrothgar's hoard.

The boat-guard was given   a gold-bound sword;
thereafter that man   had honor enhanced,
1685 bearing an heirloom   to Heorot's mead-bench.
They boarded their vessel,   breasted the deep,
left Denmark behind.   A halyard hoisted
the sea-wind's shroud;   the sail was sheeted,
bound to the mast,   and the beams moaned
1690 as a fair wind wafted   the wave-rider forward.
Foamy-throated,   the longboat bounded,
swept on the swells   of the swift sea-stream
until welcoming capes   were sighted ahead,
the cliffs of Geat-land.   The keel grounded
1695 as wind-lift thrust it   straight onto sand.

The harbor-guard hastened   hence from his post.
He had looked long   on an empty ocean
and waited to meet   the much-missed men.
He moored the broad-beamed   bow to the beach
1700 with woven lines   lest the backwash of waves
bear off the boat.   Then Beowulf ordered
treasures unloaded,   the lordly trappings,
gold that was going   to Hygelac's hall,
close to the cliff-edge,   where the ring-giver kept
1705 his comrades about him.
                           That building was bold
at the hill's crown;   and queenly Hygd,
Haereth's daughter,   dwelt there as well.
Wise and refined,   though her winters were few,

	she housed in the stronghold. Open-handed,
1710	she granted generous gifts to the Geats,
	most unlike Modthryth,[6] a maiden so fierce
	that none but her father dared venture near.
	The brave man who gazed at Modthryth by day
	might reckon a death-rope already twisted,
1715	might count himself quickly captured and killed,
	the stroke of a sword prescribed for his trespass.
	Such is no style for a queen to proclaim:
	though peerless, a woman ought to weave peace,
	not snatch away life for illusory slights.

1720   Modthryth's temper   was tamed by marriage.
Ale-drinkers say   her ill-deeds ended
once she was given   in garlands of gold
to Hemming's kinsman.   She came to his hall
over pale seas,   accepted that prince,
1725   a fine young heir,   at her father's behest.
Thenceforth on the throne,   she was famed for fairness,
making the most   of her lot in life,
sustained by loving   her lordly sovereign.
That king, Offa,   was called by all men
1730   the ablest of any   ruling a realm
between two seas,   so I am told.
Gifted in war,   a wise gift-giver
everywhere honored,   the spear-bold soldier
held his homeland   and also fathered
1735   help for the heroes   of Hemming's kindred:
war-worthy Eomer,   grandson of Garmund.

Brave Beowulf   marched with his band,
strode up the sands   of the broad beach
while the sun in the south   beamed like a beacon.
1740   The earls went eagerly   up to the keep
where the strong sovereign,   Ongentheow's slayer,
the young war-king   doled out gold rings.
Beowulf's coming   was quickly proclaimed.
Hygelac heard   that his shoulder-shielder
1745   had entered the hall,   whole and unharmed
by bouts of battle.   The ruler made room
for the foot-guests crossing   the floor before him.

Saluting his lord   with a loyal speech
earnestly worded,   the winner in war
1750   sat facing the king,   kinsman with kinsman.
A mead-vessel moved   from table to table
as Haereth's daughter,   heedful of heroes,
bore the wine-beaker   from hand to hand.
Keen to elicit   his comrade's account

---

68

6. "Modthryth" may mean "arrogant in temper"; it may be a reference to an arrogant woman rather than a proper name.

in the high-roofed hall,   Hygelac graciously
asked how the Sea-Geats   fared on their foray:

"Say what befell   from your sudden resolve
to seek out strife   over salt waters,
to struggle in Heorot.   Have you helped Hrothgar
1760 ward off the well-known   cares of his kingdom?
You have cost me disquiet,   angst and anguish.
Doubting the outcome,   dearest of men,
for anyone meeting   that murderous demon,
I sought to dissuade you   from starting the venture.
1765 The South-Danes themselves   should have settled their feud
with ghastly Grendel.   Now I thank God
that I see you again,   safe and sound."

Beowulf spoke,   son of Ecgtheow:
"For a great many men   our meeting's issue
1770 is hardly hidden,   my lord Hygelac.
What a fine fracas   passed in that place
when both of us battled   where Grendel had brought
sore sorrow   on scores of War-Scyldings!
I avenged every one,   so that none of his kin
1775 anywhere need   exult at our night-bout,
however long   the loathsome race lives,
covered with crime.   When Hrothgar came
and heard what had happened   there in the ring-hall,
he sat me at once   with his own two sons.

1780 "The whole of his host   gathered in gladness;
all my life long   I never have known
such joy in a hall   beneath heaven's vault.
The acclaimed queen,   her kindred's peace-pledge,
would sometimes circle   the seated youths,
1785 lavishing rings   on delighted young lords.
Hrothgar's daughter   handed the elders
ale-cups aplenty,   pouring for each
old trooper in turn.   I heard the hall-sitters
call her Freawaru   after she proffered
1790 the studded flagon.   To Froda's fair son
that maiden is sworn.   This match seems meet
to the lord of Scyldings,   who looks to settle
his Heatho-Bard feud.   Yet the best of brides
seldom has stilled   the spears of slaughter
1795 so swiftly after   a sovereign was stricken.

"Ingeld and all   his earls will be rankled,
watching that woman   walk in their hall
with high-born Danes   doing her bidding.
Her escorts will wear   ancient heirlooms:
1800 Heatho-Bard swords   with braided steel blades,
weapons once wielded   and lost in war

along with the lives   of friends in the fray.
Eyeing the ring-hilts,   an old ash-warrior
will brood in his beer   and bitterly pine
1805   for the stark reminders   of men slain in strife.
He will grimly begin   to goad a young soldier,
testing and tempting   a troubled heart,
his whispered words   waking war-evil:

"'My friend, have you spotted   the battle-sword
1810   that your father bore   on his final foray?
Wearing his war-mask,   Withergyld fell
when foemen seized   the field of slaughter.
His priceless blade   became battle-plunder.
Today a son   of the Scylding who slew him
1815   struts on our floor,   flaunting his trophy,
an heirloom that you   should rightfully own.'

"He will prick and pique   with pointed words
time after time   till the challenge is taken,
the maiden's attendant   is murdered in turn,
1820   blade-bitten   to sleep in his blood,
forfeit his life   for his father's feat.
Another will run,   knowing the road.
So on both sides   oaths will be broken;
and afterward Ingeld's   anger will grow
1825   hotter, unchecked,   as he chills toward his wife.
Hence I would hold   the Heatho-Bards likely
to prove unpeaceable   partners for Danes."

"Now I shall speak   of my strife with Grendel,
further acquainting   the kingdom's keeper
1830   with all that befell   when our fight began.
Heaven's gem   had gone overhead;
in darkness the dire   demon stalked us
while we stood guard   unharmed in Heorot.
Hondscioh was doomed   to die with the onslaught,
1835   first to succumb,   though clad for combat
when grabbed by Grendel,   who gobbled him whole.
That beloved young thane   was eaten alive.
Not one to leave   the hall empty-handed,
the bloody-toothed terror   intended to try
1840   his might upon me.   A curious creel
hung from his hand,   cunningly clasped
and strangely sewn   with devilish skill
from skin of a dragon.   The demon would stuff me,
sinless, inside   like so many others;
1845   but rising in wrath,   I stood upright.
It is too long a tale,   how the people's plaguer
paid for his crimes   with proper requital;
but the feat reflected   finely, my lord,

on the land you lead.   Though the foe fled

1850 to live awhile longer,   he left behind him
as sign of the strife   a hand in Heorot.
Humbled, he fell   to the floor of the mere.

"The warder of Scyldings   rewarded my warfare
with much treasure   when morning arrived,

1855 and we sat for a feast   with songs and sagas.
He told many tales   he learned in his lifetime.
Sometimes a soldier   struck the glad harp,
the sounding wood;   sometimes strange stories
were spoken like spells,   tragic and true,

1860 rightly related.   The large-hearted lord
sometimes would start   to speak of his youth,
his might in war.   His memories welled;
ancient in winters,   he weighed them all.

"So we delighted   the livelong day

1865 until darkness drew   once more upon men.
Then Grendel's mother,   mourning her son,
swiftly set out   in search of revenge
against warlike Geats.   The grisly woman
wantonly slew   a Scylding warrior:

1870 aged Aeschere,   the king's counselor,
relinquished his life.   Nor in the morning
might death-weary Danes   bear off his body
to burn on a bier,   for the creature clutching him
fled to her fastness   under a waterfall.

1875 This was the sorest   of sorrows that Hrothgar
suffered as king.   Distraught, he beseeched me
to do in your name   a notable deed.
If I dived in the deep,   heedless of danger,
to war underwater,   he would reward me.

1880 "Under I went,   as now is well-known;
and I found the hideous   haunter of fens.
For a time we two   contested our hand-strength;
then I struck off her head   with a huge sword
that her battle-hall held,   and her hot blood

1885 boiled in the lake.   Leaving that place
was no easy feat,   but fate let me live.
Again I was granted   gifts that the guardian,
Healfdene's son,   had sworn to bestow.
The king of that people   kept his promise,

1890 allotting me all   he had earlier offered:
meed for my might,   with more treasures,
my choice from the hoard   of Healfdene's son.
These, my lord,   I deliver to you,
as proof of fealty.   My future depends

1895 wholly on you.   I have in this world
few close kin   but my king, Hygelac."

He bade the boar-banner   now be brought in,
the high helmet,   hard mail-shirt,
and splendid sword,   describing them thus:

1900
"When Hrothgar gave me   this hoarded gear,
the sage sovereign   entreated I tell
the tale of his gift: this treasure was held
by Heorogar, king,   who long was the lord
of Scylding people.   It should have passed

1905
to armor the breast   of bold Heoroweard,
the father's favorite,   faithful and brave;
but he willed it elsewhere,   so use it well."

I have heard how horses   followed that hoard,
four dappled mounts,   matching and fleet.

1910
He gave up his gifts,   gold and horses.
Kinsmen should always   act with honor,
not spin one another   in snares of spite
or secretly scheme   to kill close comrades.
Always the nephew   had aided his uncle;

1915
each held the other's   welfare at heart.
He gave to Queen Hygd   the golden collar,
wondrously wrought,   Wealtheow's token,
and also three steeds,   sleek and bright-saddled.
Thereafter her breast   was graced by the gift.

1920
So Ecgtheow's son   won his repute
as a man of mettle,   acting with honor,
yet mild-hearted   toward hearth-companions,
harming no one   when muddled with mead.
Bold in battle,   he guarded the guerdon

1925
that God had granted,   the greatest strength
of all humankind,   though once he was thought
weak and unworthy,   a sluggardly sloucher,
mocked for meekness   by men on the mead-bench,
and given no gifts   by the lord of the Geats.

1930
Every trouble   untwined in time
for the glory-blessed man.
                    A blade was brought
at the king's request,   Hrethel's heirloom
glinting with gold.   No greater treasure,
no nobler sword   was held in his hoard.

1935
He lay that brand   on Beowulf's lap
and also bestowed   a spacious estate,
hall and high seat.   When land and lordship
were left to them both,   by birthright and law,
he who ranked higher   ruled the wide realm.

3. The Dragon

1940
It happened long after,   with Hygelac dead,
that war-swords slew   Heardred, his son,

when Battle-Scylfings   broke his shield-wall
and hurtled headlong   at Hereric's nephew.
So Beowulf came   to rule the broad realm.

1945   For fifty winters   he fostered it well;
then the old king,   keeper of kinfolk,
heard of a dragon   drawn from the darkness.
He had long lain   in his lofty fastness,
the steep stone-barrow,   guarding his gold;

1950   but a path pierced it,   known to no person
save him who found it   and followed it forward.
That stranger seized   a singular treasure.
He bore it in hand   from the heathen hoard:
a finely-worked flagon   he filched from the lair

1955   where the dragon dozed.   Enraged at the robber,
the sneaking thief   who struck while he slept,
the guardian woke   glowing with wrath,
as his nearest neighbors   were soon to discern.
It was not by choice   that the wretch raided

1960   the wondrous worm-hoard.   The one who offended
was stricken himself,   sorely mistreated,
the son of a warrior   sold as a slave.
Escaped and seeking   a safe refuge,
he guiltily groped   his way below ground.

1965   There the intruder,   trembling with terror,
sensed an ancient   evil asleep.
His fate was to find   as fear unmanned him
his fingers feeling   a filigreed cup.
Many such goblets   had gone to the earth-house,

1970   legacies left   by a lordly people.
In an earlier age   someone unknown
had cleverly covered   those costly treasures.
That thane held the hoard   for the lifetime allowed him,
but gold could not gladden   a man in mourning.

1975   Newly-built   near the breaking waves,
a barrow stood   at the base of a bluff,
its entrance sculpted   by secret arts.
Earthward the warrior   bore the hoard-worthy
portion of plate,   the golden craftwork.

1980   The ringkeeper spoke   these words as he went:
"Hold now, Earth,   what men may not,
the hoard of the heroes,   earth-gotten wealth
when it first was won.   War-death has felled them,
an evil befalling   each of my people.

1985   The household is mirthless   when men are lifeless.
I have none to wear sword,   none to bear wine
or polish the precious   vessels and plates.
Gone are the brethren   who braved many battles.
From the hard helmet   the hand-wrought gilding

1990   drops in the dust.   Asleep are the smiths
who knew how to burnish   the war-chief's mask
or mend the mail-shirts   mangled in battle.
Shields and mail-shirts   molder with warriors
and follow no foes   to faraway fields.
1995   No harp rejoices   to herald the heroes,
no hand-fed hawk   swoops through the hall,
no stallion stamps   in the stronghold's courtyard.
Death has undone   many kindreds of men."

Stricken in spirit,   he spoke of his sorrow
2000   as last of his line,   drearily drifting
through day and dark   until death's flood-tide
stilled his heart.   The old night-scather
was happy to glimpse   the unguarded hoard.
Balefully burning,   he seeks out barrows.
2005   Naked and hateful   in a raiment of flame,
the dragon dreaded   by outland dwellers
must gather and guard   the heathen gold,
no better for wealth   but wise with his winters.

For three hundred winters   the waster of nations
2010   held that mighty   hoard in his earth-hall
till one man wronged him,   arousing his wrath.
The wretched robber   ransomed his life
with the prize he pilfered,   the plated flagon.
Beholding that marvel   men of old made,
2015   his fief-lord forgave   the skulker's offense.
One treasure taken   had tainted the rest.
Waking in wrath,   the worm reared up
and slid over stones.   Stark-hearted,
he spotted the footprints   where someone had stepped,
2020   stealthily creeping   close to his head.
The fortunate man   slips swiftly and safely
through the worst dangers   if the World's Warder
grants him that grace.
               Eager and angry,
the hoard-guard hunted   the thief who had haunted
2025   his hall while he slept.   He circled the stone-house,
but out in that wasteland   the one man he wanted
was not to be found.   How fearsome he felt,
how fit for battle!   Back in his barrow
he tracked the intruder   who dared to tamper
2030   with glorious gold.   Fierce and fretful,
the dragon waited   for dusk and darkness.
The rage-swollen holder   of headland and hoard
was plotting reprisal: flames for his flagon.
Then day withdrew,   and the dragon, delighted,
2035   would linger no longer   but flare up and fly.
His onset was awful   for all on the land,
and a cruel ending   soon came for their king.

When the ghastly specter   scattered his sparks
and set their buildings   brightly burning,

2040   flowing with flames   as householders fled,
he meant to leave   not one man alive.
That wreaker of havoc   hated and harried
the Geatish folk   fleeing his flames.
Far and wide   his warfare was watched

2045   until night waned   and the worm went winging
back to the hall   where his hoard lay hidden,
sure of his stronghold,   his walls and his war,
sure of himself,   deceived by his pride.

Then terrible tidings   were taken to Beowulf:
2050   how swiftly his own   stronghold was stricken,
that best of buildings   bursting with flames
and his throne melting.   The hero was heart-sore;
the wise man wondered   what wrong he had wrought
and how he trangressed   against old law,

2055   the Lord Everlasting,   Ruler of All.
His grief was great,   and grim thoughts
boiled in his breast   as never before.
The fiery foe   had flown to his coastlands,
had sacked and seared   his keep by the sea.

2060   For that the war-king   required requital.
He ordered a broad-shield   fashioned of iron,
better for breasting   baleful blazes
than the linden-wood   that warded his warriors.
Little was left   of the time lent him

2065   for life in the world;   and the worm as well,
who had haughtily held   his hoard for so long.
Scorning to follow   the far-flying foe
with his whole host,   the ring-giver reckoned
the wrath of a dragon   unworthy of dread.

2070   Fearless and forceful,   he often had faced
the straits of struggle   blessed with success.
Beowulf braved   many a battle
after ridding Hrothgar's   hall of its horrors
and grappling with Grendel's   gruesome kin.

2075   Not least of his clashes   had come when the king
Hygelac fell   while fighting the Frisians
in hand-to-hand combat.   His friend and fief-lord,
the son of Hrethel,   was slain in the onslaught,
stricken to death   by a blood-drinking blade.

2080   Beowulf battled   back to the beach
where he proved his strength   with skillful swimming,
for he took to the tide   bearing the trophies
of thirty warriors   won on the field.

None of the Hetware   needed to boast
2085   how they fared on foot,   flaunting their shields
against that fierce fighter,   for few remained
after the battle   to bear the tale home.

Over wide waters   the lone swimmer went,
the son of Ecgtheow   swept on the sea-waves
2090   back to his homeland,   forlorn with his loss,
and hence to Hygd   who offered her hoard:
rings and a realm,   a throne for the thane.
With Hygelac dead   she doubted her son
could guard the Geats   from foreigners' forays.
2095   Refusing her boon,   Beowulf bade
the leaderless lords   to hail the lad
as their rightful ruler.   He chose not to reign
by thwarting his cousin   but to counsel the king
and guide with good will   until Heardred grew older.

2100   It was Heardred who held   the Weder-Geats' hall
when outcast Scylfings   came seeking its safety:
Eanmund and Eadgils,   nephews of Onela.
That strong sea-king   and spender of treasures
sailed from Sweden   pursuing the rebels
2105   who challenged his right   to rule their realm.
For lending them haven,   Hygelac's son
suffered the sword-stroke   that spilled out his life.
The Swede headed home   when Heardred lay dead,
leaving Beowulf   lordship of Geats.
2110   That was a good king,   keeping the gift-seat;
yet Heardred's death   dwelled in his thoughts.
A long time later   he offered his aid
to end the exile   of destitute Eadgils.
He summoned an army,   and Ohthere's son,
2115   cold in his cares,   went over wide waters
with weapons and warriors   to kill off a king.

Such were the struggles   and tests of strength
the son of Ecgtheow   saw and survived.
His pluck was proven   in perilous onslaughts
2120   till that fateful day   when he fought the dragon.
As leader of twelve   trailing that terror,
the greatest of Geats   glowered with rage
when he looked on the lair   where the worm lurked.
By now he had found   how the feud flared,
2125   this fell affliction   befalling his kingdom,
for the kingly cup   had come to his hand
from the hand of him   who raided the hoard.
That sorry slave   had started the strife,
and against his will   he went with the warriors,
2130   a thirteenth man   bringing the band
to the barrow's brink   which he alone knew.

Hard by the surge   of the seething sea
gaped a cavern   glutted with golden
medallions and chains.   The murderous man-bane,
2135   hidden within,   hungered for warfare.
No taker would touch   his treasures cheaply:
the hoard's holder   would drive a hard bargain.

The proud war-king   paused on the sea-point
to lighten the hearts   of his hearth-companions,
2140   though his heart was heavy   and hankered for death.
It was nearing him now.   That taker of treasure
would sunder the soul   from his old bones and flesh.
So Beowulf spoke,   the son of Ecgtheow,
recalling the life   he was loathe to lose:

2145   "From boyhood I bore   battles and bloodshed,
struggles and strife: I still see them all.
I was given at seven   to house with King Hrethel,
my mother's father   and friend of our folk.
He kept me fairly   with feasts and fine gifts.
2150   I fared no worse   than one of his sons:
Herebeald, Hathcyn,   or princely Hygelac
who was later my lord.   The eldest, Herebeald,
unwittingly went   to a wrongful death
when Hathcyn's horn-bow   hurled an arrow.
2155   Missing the mark,   it murdered the kinsman;
a brother was shot   by the blood-stained shaft.
This blow to the heart   was brutal and baffling.
A prince had fallen.   The felon went free.[1]

"So it is sore   for an old man to suffer
2160   his son swinging   young on the gallows,
gladdening ravens.   He groans in his grief
and loudly laments   the lad he has lost.
No help is at hand   from hard-won wisdom
or the march of years.   Each morning reminds him
2165   his heir is elsewhere,   and he has no heart
to wait for a second   son in his stronghold
when death has finished   the deeds of the first.
He ceaselessly sees   his son's dwelling,
the desolate wine-hall,   the windswept grave-sward
2170   where swift riders   and swordsmen slumber.
No harp-string sounds,   no song in the courtyard.
He goes to his bed   sighing with sorrow,
one soul for another.   His home is hollow;
his field, fallow.
                    "So Hrethel suffered,
2175   hopeless and heart-sore   with Herebeald gone.

---

1. Even in cases of involuntary manslaughter, punishment was required to avenge the dead. In this instance, it seems that a ritual, sacrificial hanging was performed to spare Hathcyn for murdering his brother Herebeald.

He would do no deed   to wound the death-dealer
or harrow his household   with hatred and anger;
but bitter bloodshed   had stolen his bliss,
and he quit his life   for the light of the Lord.
2180 Like a luckier man,   he could leave his land
in the hands of a son,   though he loved him no longer.

"Then strife and struggle   of Geats and Swedes
crossed the wide water.   Warfare wounded
both sides in battle   when Hrethel lay buried.
2185 Ongentheow's sons,   fierce and unfriendly,
suddenly struck   at Hreosna-Beorh
and bloodied the bluff   with baneful slaughter.
Our foes in this feud   soon felt the wrath
of my kinsman the king   claiming our due,
2190 though the counterblow   cost his own life.
Hathcyn was killed,   his kingship cut short.
The slayer himself   was slain in the morning.
I have heard how Eofor   struck the old Scyfing.
Sword-ashen,   Ongentheow sank
2195 with his helm split: heedful of harm,
to kinsman and king,   the hand would not halt
the death-blow it dealt.
                                   "My own sword-arm
repaid my prince   for the gifts he granted.
He gave me a fiefdom,   the land I have loved.
2200 He never had need   to seek among Spear-Danes,
Gifthas or Swedes   and get with his gifts
a worse warrior.   I wielded my sword
at the head of our host;   so shall I hold
this blade that I bear   boldly in battle
2205 as long as life lasts.   It has worn well
since the day when Daeghrefn   died by my hand,
the Frankish foe   who fought for the Frisians,
bearing their banner.   He broke in my grip,
never to barter   the necklace he robbed
2210 from Hygelac's corpse.   I crushed that killer;
his bones snapped,   and his life-blood spilled.
I slew him by strength,   not by the sword.
Now I shall bear   his brand into battle:
hand and hard sword   will fight for the hoard."

2215 Now Beowulf spoke   his last battle-boast:
"In boyhood I braved   bitter clashes;
still in old age   I would seek out strife
and gain glory   guarding my people
if the man-bane comes   from his cave to meet me."

2220 Then he turned to his troop   for the final time,
bidding farewell   to bold helmet-bearers,
fast in friendship: "I would wear no sword,

no weapon at all   to ward off the worm
if I knew how to fight   this fiendish foe

2225   as I grappled with Grendel   one bygone night.
But here I shall find   fierce battle-fire
and breath envenomed;   therefore I bear
this mail-coat and shield.   I shall not shy
from standing my ground   when I greet the guardian,

2230   follow what will   at the foot of his wall.
I shall face the fiend   with a firm heart.
Let the Ruler of men   reckon my fate:
words are worthless   against the war-flyer.
Bide by the barrow,   safe in your byrnies,

2235   and watch, my warriors,   which of us two
will better bear   the brunt of our clash.
This war is not yours;   it is meted to me,
matching my strength,   man against monster.
I shall do this deed   undaunted by death

2240   and get you gold   or else get my ending,
borne off in battle,   the bane of your lord."

The hero arose,   helmed and hardy,
a war-king clad   in shield and corselet.
He strode strongly   under the stone-cliff:

2245   no faint-hearted man,   to face it unflinching!
Stalwart soldier   of so many marches,
unshaken when shields   were crushed in the clash,
he saw between stiles   an archway where steam
burst like a boiling   tide from the barrow,

2250   woeful for one   close to the worm-hoard.
He would not linger long   unburned by the lurker
or safely slip   through the searing lair.
Then a battle-cry broke   from Beowulf's breast
as his rightful wrath   was roused for the reckoning.

2255   His challenge sounded   under stark stone
where the hateful hoard-guard   heard in his hollow
the clear-voiced call   of a man coming.

No quarter was claimed;   no quarter given.
First the beast's breath   blew hot from the barrow

2260   as battle-bellows   boomed underground.
The stone-house stormer   swung up his shield
at the ghastly guardian.   Then the dragon's grim heart
kindled for conflict.   Uncoiling, he came
seeking the swordsman   who'd already drawn

2265   the keen-edged blade   bequeathed him for combat.
Each foe confronted   the other with fear.
His will unbroken,   the warlord waited
behind his tall shield,   helm and armor.
With fitful twistings   the fire-drake hastened

2270   fatefully forward.   His defense held high,

Beowulf felt   the blaze blister through
hotter and sooner   than he had foreseen.
So for the first time   fortune was failing
the mighty man   in the midst of a struggle.
2275 Wielding his sword,   he struck at the worm
and his fabled blade   bit to the bone
through blazoned hide: bit and bounced back,
no match for the foe   in this moment of need.

The peerless prince   was hard-pressed in response,
2280 for his bootless blow   had maddened the monster
and fatal flames   shot further than ever,
lighting the land.   The blade he bared
failed in the fray,   though forged from iron.
No easy end   for the son of Ecgtheow:
2285 against his will   he would leave this world
to dwell elsewhere,   as every man must
when his days are done.   Swiftly the death-dealer
moved to meet him.   From the murderous breast
bellows of breath   belched fresh flames.
2290 Enfolded in fire,   he who formerly
ruled a whole realm   had no one to help him
hold off the heat,   for his hand-picked band
of princelings had fled,   fearing to face
the foe with their lord.   Loving honor
2295 less than their lives,   they hid in the holt.
But one among them   grieved for the Geats
and balked at the thought   of quitting a kinsman.

This one was Wiglaf,   son of Weohstan,
kinsman of Aelfhere,   earl among Scylfings.
2300 Seeing his liege-lord   suffering sorely
with war-mask scorched   by the searing onslaught,
the thankful thane   thought of the boons
his sovereign bestowed: the splendid homestead
and folk-rights his father   formerly held.
2305 No shirker could stop him   from seizing his shield
of yellow linden   and lifting the blade
Weohstan won   when he slew Eanmund,
son of Ohthere.   Spoils of that struggle,
sword and scabbard,   smithwork of giants,
2310 a byrnie of ring-mail   and bright burnished helm
were granted as gifts,   a thane's war-garb,
for Onela never   acknowledged his nephews
but struck against both   of his brother's sons.
When Eadgils avenged   Eanmund's death,
2315 Weohstan fled.   Woeful and friendless,
he saved that gear   for seasons of strife,
foreseeing his son   someday might crave
sword and corselet.   He came to his kinsman,

the prince of the Geats,   and passed on his heirlooms,
2320   hoping Wiglaf   would wear them with honor.
Old then, and wise,   he went from the world.

This war was the first   young Wiglaf would fight
helping the king.   His heart would not quail
nor weapon fail   as the foe would find
2325   going against him;   but he made his grim mood
known to the men: "I remember the time
when taking our mead   in the mighty hall,
all of us offered   oaths to our liege-lord.
We promised to pay   for princely trappings
2330   by staunchly wielding   sword-blades in war
if need should arise.   Now we are needed
by him who chose,   from the whole of his host,
twelve for this trial,   trusting our claims
as warriors worthy   of wearing our blades,
2335   bearing keen spears.   Our king has come here
bent on battling   the man-bane alone,
because among warriors   one keeper of kinfolk
has done, undaunted,   the most deeds of daring.
But this day our lord   needs dauntless defenders
2340   so long as the frightful   fires keep flaring.
God knows I would gladly   give my own body
for flames to enfold   with the gold-giver.
Shameful, to shoulder   our shields homeward!
First we must fell   this fearsome foe
2345   and protect the life   of our people's lord.
It is wrong that one man   be wrathfully racked
for his former feats   and fall in this fight,
guarding the Geats.   We shall share our war-gear:
shield and battle-shirt,   helm and hard sword."

2350   So speaking, he stormed   through the reek of smoke,
with helmet on head,   to help his lord.
"Beloved Beowulf,   bear up your blade.
You pledged in your youth,   powerful prince,
never to let   your luster lessen
2355   while life was left you.   Now summon your strength.
Stand steadfast.   I shall stand with you."

After these words   the worm was enraged.
For a second time   the spiteful specter
flew at his foe,   and he wreathed in flames
2360   the hated human   he hungered to harm.
His dreadful fire-wind   drove in a wave,
charring young Wiglaf's   shield to the boss,
nor might a mail-shirt   bar that breath
from burning the brave   spear-bearer's breast.
2365   Wiglaf took cover   close to his kinsman,
shielded by iron   when linden was cinder.

Then the war-king,   recalling past conquests,
struck with full strength   straight at the head.
His battle-sword, Naegling,   stuck there and split,
2370 shattered in combat,   so sharp was the shock
to Beowulf's great   gray-banded blade.
He never was granted   the gift of a sword
as hard and strong   as the hand that held it.
I have heard that he broke   blood-hardened brands,
2375 so the weapon-bearer   was none the better.

The fearful fire-drake,   scather of strongholds,
flung himself forward   a final time,
wild with wounds   yet wily and sly.
In the heat of the fray,   he hurtled headlong
2380 to fasten his fangs   in the foe's throat.
Beowulf's life-blood   came bursting forth
on those terrible tusks.   Just then, I am told,
the second warrior   sprang from his side,
a man born for battle   proving his mettle,
2385 keen to strengthen   his kinsman in combat.
He took no heed   of the hideous head
scorching his hand   as he hit lower down.
The sword sank in,   patterned and plated;
the flames of the foe   faltered, faded.
2390 Quick-witted still,   the king unsheathed
the keen killing-blade   he kept in his corselet.
Then the Geats' guardian   gutted the dragon,
felling that fiend   with the help of his friend,
two kinsmen together   besting the terror.
2395 So should a thane   succor his sovereign.

That deed was the king's   crowning conquest;
Beowulf's work   in the world was done.
He soon felt his wound   swelling and stinging
where fell fangs   had fastened upon him,
2400 and evil venom   enveloped his heart.
Wisely he sought   a seat by the stone-wall,
and his gaze dwelled   on the dark doorway
delved in the dolmen,   the straight stiles
and sturdy archway   sculpted by giants.
2405 With wonderful kindness   Wiglaf washed
the clotting blood   from his king and kinsman;
his hands loosened   the lord's high helm.
Though banefully bitten,   Beowulf spoke,
for he knew his lifetime   would last no longer.
2410 The count of his days   had come to a close.
His joys were done.   Death drew near him.
"Now I would wish   to will my son
these weapons of war,   had I been awarded
an heir of my own,   holder of heirlooms.

2415   I fathered the Weders   for fifty winters.
          No warlike lord   of neighboring lands
          dared to assail us   or daunt us with dread.
          A watchful warden,   I waited on fate
          while keeping our people   clear of quarrels.
2420   I swore many oaths;   not one was wrongful.
          So I rejoice,   though sick with my death-wound,
          that God may not blame me   for baseless bloodshed
          or killing of kin   when breath quits my body.
          Hurry below   and look on the hoard,
2425   beloved Wiglaf.   The worm lies sleeping
          under gray stone,   sorely stricken
          and stripped of his gold.   Go swiftly and seize it.
          Get me giltwork   and glittering gems:
          I would set my sight   on that store of wealth.
2430   Loath would I be   to leave for less
          the life and lordship   I held for so long."

          I have heard how swiftly   the son of Weohstan
          hastened to heed   his wounded and weakening
          war-lord's behest.   In his woven mail-shirt,
2435   his bright byrnie,   he entered the barrow;
          and passing its threshold,   proud and princely,
          he glimpsed all the gold   piled on the ground,
          the walled-in wealth   won by the worm,
          that fierce night-flyer.   Flagons were standing,
2440   embossed wine-beakers   lying unburnished,
          their inlays loosened.   There were lofty helmets
          and twisted arm-rings   rotting and rusting.
          Gold below ground   may betray into grief
          any who hold it: heed me who will!

2445   Wiglaf saw also   a gold-woven standard,
          a wonder of handiwork,   skillfully filigreed,
          high above ground.   It gave off a glow
          that let him behold   the whole of the hoard.
          I am told he took   from that trove of giants
2450   goblets and platters   pressed to his breastplate,
          and the golden banner   glinting brightly.
          He spotted no sign   of the stricken dragon.
          The iron-edged brand   old Beowulf bore
          had mortally wounded   the warder of wealth
2455   and fiery foe   whose flames in the night
          welled so fiercely   before he was felled.

          Bent with his burden,   the messenger hastened
          back to his master,   burning to know
          whether the brave   but wound-weakened
2460   lord of the Weders   was lost to the living.
          Setting his spoils   by the storied prince
          whose lifeblood blackened   the ground with gore,

Wiglaf wakened   the war-lord with water,
and these words thrust   like spears through his breast
as the ancient one grimly   gazed on the gold:

"I offer my thanks   to the Almighty Master,
the King of Glory,   for granting my kindred
these precious things   I look upon last.
Losing my life,   I have bought this boon
to lighten my leave-day.   Look to our people,
for you shall be leader;   I lead no longer.
Gather my guard   and raise me a grave-mound
housing my ashes   at Hronesnaesse,
reminding my kin   to recall their king
after his pyre   has flared on the point.
Seafarers passing   shall say when they see it
'Beowulf's Barrow'   as bright longboats
drive over darkness,   daring the flood."

So the stern prince   bestowed on his sword-thane
and keen spear-wielder   the kingly collar,
his gold-plated helm   and hammered armor.
He told him to bear them   bravely in battle:
"Farewell, Wiglaf,   last Waegmunding.
I follow our fathers,   foredestined to die,
swept off by fate,   though strong and steadfast."
These heartfelt words   were the warrior's last
before his body   burned in the bale-fire
and his soul sought   the doom of the truthful.

Smitten with sorrow,   the young man saw
the old lord he loved   lying in pain
as life left him.   Slain and slayer
died there together: the dread earth-dragon,
deprived of his life,   no longer would lurk
coiled on the hoard.   Hard-hammered swords
had felled the far-flyer   in front of his lair.
No more would he sport   on the midnight sky,
proud of his wealth,   his power and pomp.
He sprawled on stone   where the war-chief slew him.
Though deeds of daring   were done in that land,
I have heard of no man   whose might would suffice
to face the fire-drake's   fuming breath
or help him escape   if he handled the hoard
once he had woken   its warder from sleep.
Beowulf paid   for that lode with his life;
his loan of days   was lost to the dragon.
Before long the laggards   limped from the woods,
ten cowards together,   the troth-breakers
who had failed to bare   their blades in battle
at the moment their master   needed them most.

2510   In shame they shouldered   their shields and spears.
    Armored for war,   they went to Wiglaf
    who sorrowfully sat   at their sovereign's shoulder.
    Laving his leader,   the foot-soldier failed
    to waken the fallen   fighter one whit,
2515   nor could he will   his lord back to life.
    The World's Warden   decided what deeds
    men might achieve   in those days and these.

    A hard answer   was easily offered
    by young Wiglaf,   Weohstan's son.
2520   With little love   he looked on the shirkers:
    "I tell you in truth,   takers of treasure,
    bench-sitting boasters   brave in the hall:
    Beowulf gave you   the gear that you wear,
    the most finely fashioned   found near or far
2525   for a prince to proffer   his thankless thanes;
    but he wasted his wealth   on a worthless troop
    who cast off their king   at the coming of war.
    Our lord had no need   to laud his liege-men;
    yet God, giver   of glory and vengeance,
2530   granted him strength   to stand with his sword.
    I could do little   to lengthen his life
    facing that foe,   but I fought nonetheless:
    beyond my power   I propped up my prince.
    The fire-drake faltered   after I struck him,
2535   and his fuming jaws   flamed less fiercely,
    but too few friends   flew to our king
    when evil beset him.   Now sword-bestowing
    and gold-getting   shall cease for the Geats.
    You shall have no joy   in the homeland you love.
2540   Your farms shall be forfeit,   and each man fare
    alone and landless   when foreign lords
    learn of your flight,   your failure of faith.
    Better to die   than dwell in disgrace."

    Then Wiglaf bade   that the battle-tidings
2545   be sent to the camp   over the sea-cliff
    where warriors waited   with shields unslung,
    sadly sitting   from dawn until noon
    to learn if their lord   and beloved leader
    had seen his last sunrise   or soon would return.
2550   The herald would leave them   little to doubt;
    he sped up the headland   and spoke to them all:

    "Now the wish-granter,   warlord of Weders,
    lies on his death-bed.   The leader of Geats
    stays in the slaughter-place,   slain by the worm
2555   sprawled at his side.   Dagger-stricken,
    the slayer was felled,   though a sword had failed
    to wound the serpent.   Weohstan's son,

Wiglaf is waiting   by Beowulf's body;
a living warrior   watches the lifeless,
2560   sad-heartedly   sitting to guard
the loved and the loathed.   Look now for war
as Franks and Frisians   learn how the king
has fallen in combat.   Few foreigners love us,
for Hygelac angered   the harsh Hugas
2565   when his fleet forayed   to far-off Frisia.
Fierce Hetware   met him with forces
bigger than his.   They broke him in battle;
that mail-clad chieftain   fell with his men.
Hygelac took   no trophies to thanes;
2570   no king of the Meroving   wishes us well.

    "I also foresee   strife with the Swedes,
feud without end,   for all know Ongentheow
slew Hrethel's son   when Hathcyn first forayed
near Ravenswood   with hot-headed Geats
2575   and raided the realm   of Scylf-land's ruler.
That fearsome old foe,   father of Ohthere,
quickly struck back.   He cut down our king
to rescue the queen   Hathcyn had captured.
Her captors had shorn   the crone of her gold,
2580   dishonored the aged   mother of Onela.
Ongentheow followed   hard on their heels.
Wounded, weary   and fiercely-harried,
those left unslain   by Swedish swords
limped off leaderless,   hid in the holt.
2585   A huge army   beleaguered them there.
All night long   Ongentheow taunted
the wretched raiders.   At daybreak, he swore,
he would slice them to slivers.   Some would swing
slung on his gallows,   sport for the ravens.
2590   But gladness came   again to grim Geats
hearing Hygelac's   horns in the morning,
the trumpet calls   of the troop that tracked them.
Hathcyn's brother,   bold with his band,
had rallied for battle.
                        "A bloody swath
2595   Scylfings and Geats   left on the landscape,
everywhere smeared   with gore from the stricken.
So the two folks   stirred further feuds.
Wise in warfare,   old Ongentheow
grimly stood off,   seeking the safety
2600   of higher ground.   He had heard of Hygelac's
strength in struggles,   his pride and prowess.
Mistrusting his force   to fend off the foray,
he feared for his family   and fell back to guard
the hoard hidden   behind his earthworks.
2605   Then Hrethel's people   pressed the pursuit:

the standards of Hygelac   stormed the stronghold.
There the Swede   was snared between swords.
Eofor humbled   that hoary-haired leader,
though Wulf struck first,   fierce with his weapon,
2610   and a cut vein colored   the king's white head.
Undaunted, Ongentheow   warded him off;
Wulf was wounded   the worse in return:
Ongentheow's blow   broke open his helm,
hurled him headlong,   helpless and bleeding
2615   though not destined   to die on that day.
Then Eofor faced   the folk-lord alone.
Sternly he stood   when his brother slumped:
Hygelac's soldier   with sword in his hand
and helmet on head,   hoarded smithwork
2620   shaped by old crafts,   shattered the shield-wall.
The king crumpled,   struck to the quick.

"Now the Geats gathered   after the slaughter.
Some bound the wound   of Eofor's brother
and bundled him off   the field of battle.
2625   Meanwhile one warrior   plundered the other:
Eofor stripped   the hard-hilted sword,
helm and corselet   from Ongentheow's corpse.
He handed that heap   of armor to Hygelac.
Pleased with his prizes,   the king pledged in turn
2630   to reward war-strokes   as lord of the Weders.
He gave great riches   to Wulf and Eofor.
Once they were home,   he honored each one
with a hundred thousand   in land and linked rings.
No man in middle-earth   ever begrudged them
2635   favor and fortune   bestowed for their feat.
Yet a further honor   was offered Eofor:
the king's only daughter   adorned his house,
awarded in wedlock   to Wonred's son.

"Full of this feud,   this festering hatred,
2640   the Swedes, I am certain,   will swiftly beset us,
as soon as they learn   our lord lies lifeless
who held his hoard,   his hall and his realm
against all foes   when heroes had fallen,
who fostered his folk   with fair kingship.
2645   Now must we hasten,   behold our sovereign,
and bear him for burial.   The brave one shall not
be beggared of booty   to melt on his bier.
Let funeral flames   greedily fasten
on gold beyond measure,   grimly gotten,
2650   lucre our leader   bought with his life.
No thane shall take   tokens to treasure
nor maiden be made   fairer with finery
strung at her throat.   Stripped of their wealth,
they shall wander woefully   all their lives long,

2655 lordless and landless now that their king
 has laid aside laughter, sport and song.
 Their hands shall heft many a spear-haft,
 cold in the morning. No call of the harp
 shall waken warriors after their battles;
2660 but the black raven shall boast to the eagle,
 crowing how finely he fed on the fated
 when, with the wolf, he went rending the slain."

 Thus the terrible tidings were told,
 and the teller had not mistaken the truth.
2665 The warriors all rose and woefully went
 to look on the wonder with welling tears.
 They found on the sand under Earnanaess
 their lifeless lord laid there to rest,
 beloved giver of gifts and gold rings,
2670 the war-king come at the close of his days
 to a marvelous death. At first the monster
 commanded their gaze: grim on the ground
 across from the king, the creature had crumpled,
 scaly and scorched, a fearsome fire-drake
2675 fifty feet long. He would fly no more,
 free in the darkness, nor drop to his den
 at the break of dawn. Death held the dragon;
 he never would coil in his cavern again.
 Beyond the serpent stood flagons and jars,
2680 plated flatware and priceless swords
 rotting in ruin, etched out with rust.
 These riches had rested in Earth's embrace
 for a thousand winters, the heritage held
 by warders of old, spell-enwoven
2685 and toilfully tombed that none might touch them,
 unless God Himself, granter of grace,
 true Lord of glory, allotted release
 to one of His choosing and opened the hoard.

 It little profited him who had wrongfully
2690 hidden the hand-wrought wealth within walls.
 His payment was scant for slaying the one
 with courage to claim it: the kill was quickly
 and harshly requited. So the kingly
 may come to strange ends when their strength is spent
2695 and time meted out. They may not remain
 as men among kin, mirthful with mead.
 Beowulf goaded the gold's guardian,
 raised up the wrath, not reckoning whether
 his death-day had dawned, not knowing the doom
2700 solemnly sworn by princes who placed
 their hoard in that hollow: the thief who held it
 would fall before idols, forge himself hell-bonds,
 waste in torment for touching the treasure.

He failed to consider   more fully and sooner
2705   who rightfully owned   such awesome riches.

So spoke Wiglaf,   son of Weohstan:
"By the whim of one man,   many warriors
sometimes may suffer,   as here has happened.
No means were at hand   to move my master;
2710   no counsel could sway   the kingdom's keeper
never to trouble   the treasure's taker,
but leave him lying   where long he had hidden,
walled with his wealth   until the world's ending.
He kept to his course,   uncovered the hoard.
2715   Fate was too strongly   forcing him hither.
I have entered that hall,   beheld everything
golden within,   though none too glad
for the opening offered   under its archway.
In haste I heaved   much from the hoard;
2720   a mighty burden   I bore from the barrow
straight to my sovereign.   He still was alive.
His wits were clear;   his words came quickly.
In anguish, the Ancient   asked that I say
he bade you to build   a barrow for him
2725   befitting the deeds   of a fallen friend.
You shall heap it high   over his ashes,
since he was the world's   worthiest warrior,
famed far and wide   for the wealth of his fortress.

"Now let us hurry   hence to the hoard.
2730   For a second time   I shall see that splendor
under the cliff-wall,   those wonders of craftwork.
Come, I shall take you   close to the trove,
where you may behold   heaps of broad gold.
Then let a bier   be readied to bear
2735   our beloved lord   to his long dwelling
under the watch   of the World's Warden."

Then Weohstan's heir   ordered the earls,
heads of houses   and fief holders,
to fetch firewood   fit for the folk-leader's
2740   funeral pyre.   "Flames shall now flare,
feed on the flesh   and fade into darkness,
an ending for him   who often endured
the iron showers   shot over shield-walls
when string-driven storms   of arrows arose
2745   with feathered fins   to steer them in flight
and barbed arrowheads   eager to bite."

Wisely Wiglaf,   son of Weohstan,
summoned the seven   most steadfast thanes.
They went in together,   eight earls entering
2750   under the evil   arch of the earth-house
with one man bearing   a blazing torch.

No lot was cast   to learn which liege-man
would plunder the loot   lying unguarded,
as each searcher   could see for himself;
2755   yet none was unhappy   to hurry that hoard
out into daylight.   They heaved the dragon
over the sea-cliff   where surges seized him:
the treasure's keeper   was caught by the tide.
Then they filled a wain   with filigreed gold
2760   and untold treasures;   and they carried the king,
their hoary-haired warlord,   to Hronesnaess.

There the king's kinsmen   piled him a pyre,
wide and well-made   just as he willed it.
They hung it with helmets,   shields and mail-shirts,
2765   then laid in its midst   their beloved lord,
renowned among men.   Lamenting their loss,
his warriors woke   the most woeful fire
to flare on the bluff.   Fierce was the burning,
woven with weeping,   and wood-smoke rose
2770   black over the blaze,   blown with a roar.
The fire-wind faltered   and flames dwindled,
hot at their heart   the broken bone-house.
Sunken in spirit   at Beowulf's slaying,
the Geats gathered   grieving together.
2775   Her hair wound up,   a woebegone woman
sang and resang   her dirge of dread,
foretelling a future   fraught with warfare,
kinfolk sundered,   slaughter and slavery
even as Heaven   swallowed the smoke.

2780   High on the headland   they heaped his grave-mound
which seafaring sailors   would spy from afar.
Ten days they toiled   on the scorched hilltop,
the cleverest men   skillfully crafting
a long-home built   for the bold in battle.
2785   They walled with timbers   the trove they had taken,
sealing in stone   the circlets and gems,
wealth of the worm-hoard   gotten with grief,
gold from the ground   gone back to Earth
as worthless to men   as when it was won.
2790   Then sorrowing swordsmen   circled the barrow,
twelve of his earls   telling their tales,
the sons of nobles   sadly saluting
deeds of the dead.   So dutiful thanes
in liege to their lord   mourn him with lays
2795   praising his peerless   prowess in battle
as it is fitting   when life leaves the flesh.
Heavy-hearted   his hearth-companions
grieved for Beowulf,   great among kings,
mild in his mien,   most gentle of men,
2800   kindest to kinfolk   and keenest for fame.

Iberia, the Meeting of Three Worlds

There are two common names for the period of eight hundred years during which Islamic forces controlled some portion of the Iberian Peninsula: the *Convivencia,* or coexistence, and the *Reconquista,* or reconquest. As these very different terms suggest, medieval Spain can be seen as an extraordinary confluence of the three dominant cultures of the modern West (Arabic, Christian, and Jewish) or as an embattled cohabitation. In either case, there is no denying the unique and multifaceted art and literature that emerged from it. Southern Spain was the portal through which the rich and ancient erudition of North Africa, the Middle East, and Greece made its way back into Europe after the fall of the Roman Empire.

Muslim armies first arrived in the Iberian peninsula in 711, sweeping northward into France, where they were eventually turned back by Charles Martel at Poitiers. The first dynasty of emirs in al-Andalus (Arabic for "the land of the Vandals," earlier rulers of the region) was the Umayyads, who controlled the entire peninsula outside of the northern quarter—the Christian kingdoms of Asturias, León, Navarre, Aragon, and Catalonia. Most of the cities of al-Andalus remained relatively independent. The great political and cultural centers were Córdoba, Granada, and, later, Seville; here were built the magnificent mosques and palaces still visible today, and here poets were drawn from all over the declining eastern empire. The long-established and highly regular forms of classical, courtly Arabic poetry were renewed through contact with the indigenous forms of Spain.

Poetry was the most prestigious literary mode and the chief cultural institution of the Arabic-speaking world, practiced by rulers, courtiers, philosophers, and religious leaders as well as professional poets. The incorporation of Greek philosophy from the tenth century on provided a common language and set of problems to Muslims, Christians, and Jews alike. The so-called "courtier rabbis" were especially important to this cultural mélange, benefiting from the Arab principle of toleration for those they called the *dhimmi,* or "people of the book." Wealthy and powerful, fluent in Arabic, pious and learned in Jewish tradition, the community of the Sephardim (as the Jews of Iberia called themselves) saw to the everyday workings of the kingdoms of al-Andalus. They also created an unprecedented corpus of secular Hebrew poetry out of Arabic forms, as if the poetic clash of sensuality, nature, and physical love with divinity were a way of mitigating the contradiction between their public and private lives.

Exile was a great theme, not only for the Hebrew poets adapting a classical Jewish motif to Arabic poetic forms, but to the Arab mystics describing their separation from paradise in the material world. Celebrations of wine, love, and song went hand in hand with an underlying conviction of the transience of physical experience. Even under the fairly stable government of the tenth and eleventh centuries, warfare was constant. Two movements during the eleventh century had far-reaching consequences. In 1035, the Almoravids, a strictly orthodox sect, arose in North Africa; at the same time, the Christian rulers of Castile and León began the centuries-long push southward that became known as the *Reconquista*. Invited into al-Andalus to counter the Castilian forces, Almoravid rule initiated a decline in Jewish participation in society. A pogrom in Granada in 1066 resulted in the massacre of 3,000 Jews. When Almoravid power dissipated in the mid-twelfth century, their role was taken over by the Almohads, a new reform movement that preached austere simplicity, rejected the doctrine of *dhimmi,* and caused a further exodus from al-Andalus of Jews and Mozarabs (Christians who had adopted Arabic language and culture without converting to Islam).

Medieval Iberia was a society both enraptured and disturbed by anything hybrid. Jews and Christians held high posts in al-Andalus; their poets and philosophers later found refuge and patronage in the courts of northern Spain, collaborating, for example, in

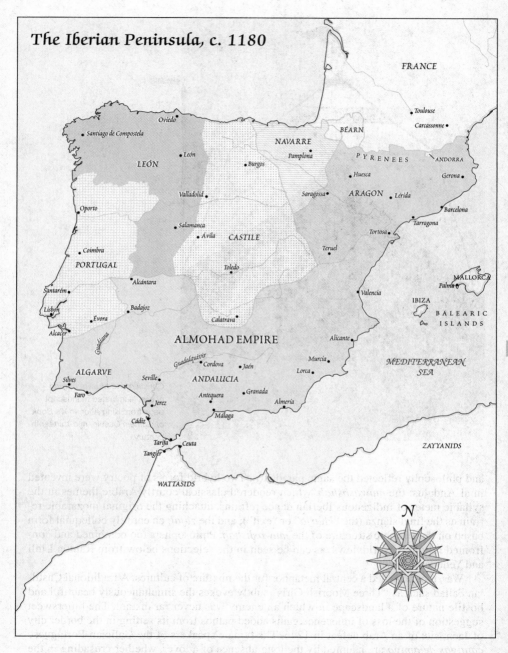

The Iberian Peninsula, c. 1180

the creation by Alfonso X of the thirteenth-century *cantigas de Santa Maria*, a huge collection of over 400 songs celebrating the Virgin Mary. Miniatures in the opulent manuscript depict Arab, Jewish, and Christian performers side by side, singing, dancing, and playing a wide variety of musical instruments. A Castilian general such as Rodrigo Díaz battled other Christians as well as Muslims, and, although a loyal vassal to King Alfonso VI, maintained close friendships and ties of allegiance to Muslim rulers. Poetry

Christian and Muslim playing chess, illuminated manuscript page from King Alfonso X's *Book of Games*, Castile, mid-thirteenth century.

and philosophy reflected the same paradoxes. Two hybrid forms of poetry were invented in al-Andalus: the *muwashshah*, which rendered classical courtly Arabic themes in the syllabic meter of indigenous Iberian dance refrains, attaching the original mozarabic refrain as the final stanza (the "*kharja*" or "exit"); and the *zajal,* an entirely colloquial form based on the strophic structure of the *muwashshah.* Philosophers too combined and confronted religious worldviews, as can be seen in the selections below from Ramón Llull and Yehuda ha-Levi.

War, too, provided a central metaphor for the mixture of cultures. A traditional Castilian ballad such as "Three Moorish Girls" subtly evokes the simultaneously beautiful and hostile nature of a landscape in which an enemy was never far distant. The bittersweet suggestion of the loss of innocence gains added pathos from its setting in the border city of Jaén, site of an Arab defeat in 1246. The female speakers of the Galician-Portuguese *cantigas de amigo* are haunted by the long absence of a lover, whether crusading in the distant East or the nearby South. Slogans of religious fervor often go hand in hand with episodes of intimate cooperation. But when Ferdinand and Isabella married to unite conclusively the kingdoms of Castile and Aragon, a sea change was imminent. The last Arab stronghold, Granada, surrendered in 1492, the same year in which the Jews were expelled from Spain, and in which Columbus reached the Americas. The "people of the book" would come together again in other countries under conditions of war, but never again would that hostile proximity also result in a cultural flowering of such local beauty and far-reaching influence.

PRONUNCIATIONS:
Al-Andalus: ahl-AHN-dah-loos
Averroës: ah-ve-RRO-es
Cordoba: KOR-do-bah
Dom Dinis: dohm DEE-nees
Ibn Al-'Arabi: ib'n ahl-ah-RAH-bee
Solomon Ibn Gabirol: SOHL-oh-mon ib'n GAH-bee-roll
Ibn Hazm: ib'n HAZ'm
Kharjas: KHAR-zhas
Ramon Llull: rah-MON LULL
Yehuda ha-Levi: ya-WHO-dah ha-LAY-vee

CASTILIAN BALLADS AND TRADITIONAL SONGS ■ (c. 11th–14th centuries)

During the late fifteenth century, as the final battles of the *Reconquista* were being decided, Ferdinand and Isabella began forging a national identity for Spain exclusive of Jews and Muslims. One aspect of this process was to collect the oral tradition of Castilian song into written form, a process initiated by Dom Dinis in the late thirteenth century. The result was a series of *Cancioneros,* or songbooks, and *Romanceros,* or books of ballads, including the *Cancionero de Palacio* (1438), *Cancionero de la Colombina* (1493), the *Cancionero musical del palacio* (1500), the *Cancionero general* (1511), the *Cancionero de romances* (1550), and the *Romancero general* (1600). The songs dated from the previous several centuries; many are probably of far earlier origin. In addition to universal motifs of love and celebration, these collections document the complex relationship of Castile over the past centuries with its southern neighbors in al-Andalus.

Ballad of Juliana[1]

> "Get on, you hounds, get on,
>   And may the furies take you.
> Thursday you kill the boar
>   And eat the meat on Friday.[2]

5
> "Today makes seven years
>   I've wandered in these hills.
> Now both my feet are bare,
>   Blood spurts from my toenails.

> "Now I drink fresh gore,
10
>   The meat I eat is raw,
> And sadly seek Juliana,
>   Who was the emperor's daughter.

---

1. From the *Cancionero de romances.* Translated by Edwin Honig.

2. It was long the custom in the Catholic church to abstain from eating meat on Fridays in memory of the crucifixion of Jesus on that day.

"Early St. John's morning,[3]
    While she gathered flowers,
15   The Moors took her away
    From her father's bowers."

Juliana hears this said
    Wrapt in the Moor's embrace;
Twin tears her two eyes shed
20   Fall on that Moor's face.

Abenámar[1]

"Abenámar, Abenámar
Moor of Moor's delight
The hour of your birth
Comets filled the night.[2]
5 The sea was calm as glass
The moon was waxing full
A Moor with stars like yours
Must never break the spell."
"I tell the truth, my lord,
10 Though it be death to tell."
"I thank you, Abenámar,
Your birth bespeaks you well.
What castles are those shining
High on yonder hill?"
15 "The Alhambra there, my lord,
The mosque tower further still,
And there, the Alixares,
Built so wondrous well.[3]
A Moor was paid to build them
20 A hundred crowns a day
And lost, for each day idle,
As much as he was paid.
When all was built and ready
The architect was slain
25 So he could build no others
For Andalusia's reign.
There lies Crimson Towers
A castle of renown
And there, the Generalife,

---

3. June 24, the midsummer festival of St. John's Day, marked the end of the festival season and the beginning of the work of harvesting. Its rituals included gathering grass for auguring and flowers for girls to wear in wreaths, dancing around a bonfire, eating, drinking, and of course lovemaking.

1. Translated by William M. Davis. Abenámar refers to Yusuf IV, or Ibn al-Ahmar, who gained the throne of Granada with the help of Juan II of Castilia in 1431. The poem relates their meeting against the spectacular backdrop of the city, which has the last word in the ballad.

2. Comets were traditionally taken as omens, either for good or for ill.

3. Perched on a hilltop in the Sierra Nevada, the Alhambra was a vast fortified town complex centered around the palace itself. The Alixares was a further palace with gardens.

Of matchless garden fame,"[4]
Then spoke King don Juan,
Mark what he will say:
"With your consent, Granada,
I'd marry you today;
With Córdoba for dowry,
Sevilla for display."[5]
"I am a wife, King John,
No widow, but a wife,
The Moor who is my husband
Loves me more than life."

Those mountains, mother[1]

Those mountains, mother
are steep to climb,
where streams rush down
to fields of thyme.[2]
Those mountains, mother
have flowers above:
up where they are,
I have my love.

I will not pick verbena[1]

I will not pick verbena
on the morrow of St. John,[2]
for my lover has gone.

I will not pick sunflowers,
honeysuckle or carnations.
Only sorrows will I pluck
and cruel frustrations,
for my lover has gone.

Three Moorish Girls[1]

I am in love with three Moorish lasses in Jaén,[2]
Axa, Fátima and Marién.

4. The Torres Bermejas, or Crimson Towers, are a group of fortified towers near the entrance to the Alhambra. The Generalife ("Garden of the Builder") is an extensive series of gardens and pavilions leading eastward from the Alhambra to the summer palace.

5. The other two major cities of al-Andalus. Córdoba had fallen to Ferdinand III of Castilia in 1236, and Seville to the same ruler 12 years later. Granada was the last stronghold to fall, holding out until 1492.

1. Translated by James Duffy. From Diego Pisador, *Libro de Música de Vihuela* (1552), a collection of settings of traditional songs for the *vihuela,* a guitar-shaped instrument whose strings were plucked like a lute.

2. Literally, *toronjil,* lemon balm, a fragrant and medicinal herb of the mint family.

1. Translated by James Duffy. Verbena is a flower and a medicinal herb.

2. The midsummer festival of St. John's Day came on June 24; it was the traditional end of the season of festivals.

1. From the *Cancionero del Palacio.* Translated by Angela Buxton.

2. Lying north of Granada in Andalusia, Jaén was for a long time the frontier between Christians and Moors in medieval Spain, and the region was the scene of many battles before it was captured by Ferdinand III in 1246.

Three pretty Moorish lasses
went to pick olives,
5 and they found them already picked in Jaén.[3]
Axa, Fátima and Marién.

And they found them picked,
and they came back dismayed,
and their colour was gone in Jaén.
10 Axa, Fátima and Marién.

Three such lively Moorish lasses
went to pick apples
and they found them already picked in Jaén.
Axa, Fátima and Marién.

MOZARABIC *KHARJAS* ▓ (10th–early 11th century)

The *kharja* epitomizes the melting pot that was medieval Iberia. Written in Mozarabic, a Romance vernacular that was the common spoken language of al-Andalus, these brief verses originated in the refrains of popular dance. Hispano-Arabic (and, later, Hebrew) poets adapted these refrains as the final stanza (*kharja* means "exit") of a poetic form they invented in the tenth century, called the *muwashshah*. The body of the poem is a courtly love song with traditional Arabic images but a syllabic meter based on the melody of the concluding vernacular stanza. The *kharja* responds to the refined and idealized male voice of the poem's body with the frank, colloquial voice of a flesh-and-blood woman. Sixty-one *kharjas* survive, representing the earliest known body of Romance lyric.

As if you were a stranger[1]

Como si filyol' alyenu,   As if you were a stranger,
non mas adormis a meu senu.   you no longer fall asleep on my breast.

Ah tell me, little sisters[2]

Garid vos, ay yermanellas,   Ah tell me, little sisters,
com contenir a meu male!   how to hold my pain!
Sin al-habib non vivireyu—   I'll not live without my beloved—
advolarey demandare.   I shall fly to seek him again.

My lord Ibrahim[3]

Meu sidi Ibrahim,   My lord Ibrahim,
ya tu omne dolǧe,   oh my sweet love,
vent' a mib   come to me
de nohte!   at night!

3. The ambiguity over whether it is the girls or the olives that were "plucked" is heightened by the fact that *morilla* (Moorish girl) can also mean a small berry, or *mora*.

1. Translated by Peter Dronke. From two *muwashshahat*: Yehuda ha-Levi, "Panegyric [poem of praise] for Abu l-Hasan ben Qamniel" and an anonymous love poem.

2. Translated by Peter Dronke. From the *muwashshah* by Yehuda ha-Levi, "Panegyric for Ishaq ibn Qrispin."

3. Translated by Peter Dronke. From a *muwashshah* by Muhammad ibn Ubada, a Silk Merchant of Málaga.

5　In non, si non queris,　　　　　　If not, if you don't want to,
　　yireym' a tib.　　　　　　　　　　I shall come to you.
　　Gar me a ob　　　　　　　　　　Tell me where
　　legarte!　　　　　　　　　　　　to see you!

I'll give you such love![4]

Tan t'amaray, illa con al-šarti　　　　I'll give you such love!—but only if
　　　　　　　　　　　　　　　　　　you'll bend

an taḡma' halhali ma' qurti!　　　　my anklets right over to my earrings!

Take me out of this plight[5]

Alsa-me de min hali—　　　　　　Take me out of this plight—
mon hali qad bare!　　　　　　　　my state is desperate!
Que faray, ya 'ummi?—　　　　　　Mother, what shall I do?—
Faneq bad lebare!　　　　　　　　The falcon is about to snatch![6]

Mother, I shall not sleep[7]

Non dormireyo, mamma,　　　　　Mother, I shall not sleep
a rayo de manyana:　　　　　　　When morning rises
í Bon Abū-l-Qāsim,　　　　　　　But dream of Abū-l-Qāsim,
la fage de matrama!　　　　　　　His features dawning.

71

IBN AL-'ARABI ■ (1165–1240)

Raised in Seville, the capital of the Almohad state, Ibn al-'Arabi converted to Sufism while still a teenager, following a warning vision. He traveled across Iberia seeking wisdom and guidance, including several meetings with the philosopher Ibn Rushd, then journeyed to North Africa and eastward on a pilgrimage to Mecca. He spent the last years of his life in Damascus. He produced numerous, often controversial esoteric works throughout his life; his poetry transposes those concerns through the lyric themes of nature, nostalgia, and love. Steeped in esoteric lore, a poem such as "Gentle now, doves" strives to render that lore immediately present through the experience of verse.

Gentle now, doves[1]

Gentle now, doves of the thornberry
and moringa thicket,[2]
don't add to my heartache
your sighs.

---

4. Translated by Peter Dronke. From an anonymous *muwashshah*.
5. Translated by Peter Dronke. From a *muwashshah* by Muhammad ibn Ubada.
6. The comparison of a lover to a falcon was a common image in love lyrics.
7. Translated by William M. Davis. From a *muwashshah* by Ibn Harun al-Asbahi of Lérida (12th century).
1. Translated by Michael Sells.
2. The thornberry or arak tree grows in Arabia, parts of Africa, and eastern India; its roots and twigs are used as tooth-

5   Gentle now,
or your sad cooing
will reveal the love I hide,
the sorrow I hide away.

I echo back, in the evening,
10   in the morning, echo,
the longing of a love-sick lover,
the moaning of the lost.

In a grove of Gháda[3]
spirits wrestled,
15   bending the limbs down over me,
passing me away.

They brought yearning,
breaking of the heart,
and other new twists of pain,
20   putting me through it.

Who is there for me in Jám',
and the Stoning-Ground at Mína,[4]
who for me at Tamarisk Grove,
or at the way-station of Na'mán?

25   Hour by hour
they circle my heart
in rapture, in love-ache,
and touch my pillars with a kiss.

As the best of creation
30   circled the Ká'ba,[5]
which reason with its proofs
called unworthy,

He kissed the stones there—
and he was entrusted with the word!
35   And what is the house of stone
compared to a man or a woman?

They swore, and how often!
they'd never change—piling up vows.
She who dyes herself red with henna
40   is faithless.

A white-blazed gazelle[6]
is an amazing sight,

---

3. The tamarisk is an evergreen-like shrub or small tree that grows in sandy terrain. Its leaves have been used in medicine; ghada wood produces a dense charcoal.

4. These are stations on the pilgrimage to Mecca. Pilgrims camp in Jam' or al-Muzdalifa on the ninth night; on the tenth, they travel to Mina, where they cast stones at a pillar representing the temptation of Shaitan, or Satan.

5. A small shrine near the center of the Great Mosque in Mecca, the Ká'ba is the most holy structure in Islam, held to be the center of the world, the direction in which Muslims perform their prayers. "The best of creation" is the Prophet Muhammad.

6. The gazelle is a conventional metaphor in Arabic love poetry for the beloved. As with Ibn al-'Arabi's other natural images, it also possesses a mystical meaning.

red-dye signaling,
eyelids hinting,

45   Pasture between breastbones
and innards.
Marvel,
a garden among the flames!

My heart can take on
50   any form:
a meadow for gazelles,
a cloister for monks,

For the idols, sacred ground,
Ká'ba for the circling pilgrim,
55   the tables of the Toráh,
the scrolls of the Qur'án.

I profess the religion of love;
wherever its caravan turns along the way,
that is the belief,
60   the faith I keep.

Like Bishr,
Hind and her sister,
love-mad Qays and his lost Láyla,
Máyya and her lover Ghaylán.[7]

SOLOMON IBN GABIROL ▓ (c. 1021–c. 1057)

Born in Málaga in southern Spain, Ibn Gabirol was orphaned at an early age. Physically weak, temperamental and ill-at-ease with the courtier life, he spent his formative years in Saragossa, an important center of Jewish culture, where he immersed himself in a career of letters. He wrote some twenty volumes on philosophy and religion, most of which haven't survived. His influential secular treatise, *The Source of Life,* was translated from the Arabic into Latin in the twelfth century. Only during the nineteenth century was it discovered that its author, Avicebron, was identical with the Andalusian Jew celebrated for his hymns and for his lyric poetry. Poems such as "She looked at me and her eyelids burned" demonstrate Ibn Gabirol's skill in forging philosophical and religious preoccupations into powerfully unified visual images.

She looked at me and her eyelids burned[1]

She looked at me and her eyelids burned,
While her goblet brimmed with tears;
The words overflowed her mouth, like strings of pearls,
And the smile on her lips defied compare with gold.

---

7. Names of celebrated Arab poets and lovers of previous centuries.
1. Translated by William M. Davis.

5　But the rebuke she sent my soul
Wounded me like the words of the creditor to the poor debtor.
Meanwhile, the cup passed from hand to hand like the sun amid the heavens,
And day receded, fleeting, like waves along the shore,
But my blood, receding at unison of day,
10　Tinged my cheeks bright red: she will not return.

Behold the sun at evening[1]

Behold the sun at evening, red
　As if she wore vermillion robes.
Slipping the wraps from north and south
　She covers in purple the western side.
5　The earth—she leaves it cold and bare
　To huddle in shadows all night long.
At once the sky is dark; you'd think
　Sackcloth it wore for Yequtiel.[2]

The mind is flawed, the way to wisdom blocked[1]

The mind is flawed, the way to wisdom blocked;
　The body alone is seen, the soul is hid,
And those who seek the world find only ill;
　A man can get no pleasure here on earth.[2]
5　The servant rises up and kills his lord,
　And serving girls attack their mistresses.
Sons are raising hands against their parents,
　Daughters too oppose their parents' will.
My friend, from what I've seen of life I'd say
10　The best that one can hope is to go mad.
However long you live you suffer toil,
　And in the end you suffer rot and worms.
Then finally the clay goes back to clay;
　At last the soul ascends to join the Soul.[3]

Winter wrote with the ink of its rains and showers[1]

Winter wrote with the ink of its rains and showers,
　The pen of its flashing lightning, and the hand of its clouds
A letter upon the garden in blue and purple,
　Of which no craftsman with all his skill could make the like,

1. Translated by Raymond P. Scheindlin.
2. This elegy was written on the occasion of the death of his patron, Yequtiel Ibn Hassan, in 1039. Sackcloth was a coarse fabric traditionally worn in mourning.
1. Translated by Raymond P. Scheindlin.
2. In the philosophical tradition of Neoplatonism, the soul is regarded as imprisoned in the body, its spiritual nature blocked by bodily needs and desire.
3. The soul is released by death to return to the great World Soul from which it had been torn to descend to its body on earth.
1. Translated by Raymond P. Scheindlin. Garden poetry was an important genre for both Arab and Jewish poets in Andalusia.

5
Therefore, when the earth longed to see the sky,
      She embroidered on the twigs of her flowerbeds something like the stars.

YEHUDA HA-LEVI ▪ (before 1075–1141)

Yehuda (or Judah) ha-Levi is the legendary figurehead of Sephardic Jewry, his life an emblem of the height and decline of its "Golden Age" in al-Andalus. A successful court physician, ha-Levi traveled throughout al-Andalus, frequently crossing into the Christian north, on whose border he had been born. Revered for his poetic gifts during his lifetime (over 800 of his poems survive), he became disenchanted with his success and the gilded life he led. In 1140 he left his home, setting sail for Jerusalem by way of Egypt, where he was seduced by the good life once again, tarrying as a court poet in Cairo and Alexandria for almost a year. He appears never to have reached the Promised Land, but in popular legend his pilgrimage led directly from Spain to the Western Wall of Jerusalem, where he died a violent death just before arriving. Only a few years after Yehuda ha-Levi's departure, Jewish power was fully dispersed by the Almohad dynasty; for the courtier rabbis, the Golden Age was over.

Poems like "My heart is in the East," "Your breeze, Western shore," and "From time's beginning" illustrate the ambivalence of Yehuda ha-Levi's attitude toward al-Andalus, his home from birth but also a place of exile where he was a man of influence yet also subject to Almoravid rule. He skillfully renewed the Arabic theme of the poet's longing for his lost homeland by merging individual longing with the national theme of the Exile of Israel. In addition to such poems of exile, he composed in a wide variety of forms from panegyric to religious meditations; included below are three poems of love and wine, another traditional genre.

Cups without wine are lowly[1]

Cups without wine are lowly
As a pot thrown on the ground
But, full of juice, they shine
Like the body with a soul.

Ofra does her laundry with my tears[1]

Ofra does her laundry with my tears
      And spreads it out before her beauty's rays.
With my two eyes she needs no flowing well;
      Nor sun needs she: Her face provides the blaze.

Once when I fondled him upon my thighs[1]

Once when I fondled him upon my thighs
      He caught his own reflection in my eyes
And kissed my eyes, deceitful imp; I knew
      It was his image he kissed, and not my eyes!

---

1. Translated by William M. Davis.
1. Translated by Raymond P. Scheindlin. *Ofra* in Hebrew means a female fawn and is often a term for the poet's beloved.
1. Adapted by Yehuda ha-Levi from an Arabic original by al-Mutanabbi; English translation by Raymond P. Scheindlin. Homosexuality was common in al-Andalus, and the male beloved was a stock figure in the Arabic love poetry adapted by the Jewish poets.

From time's beginning, You were love's abode[1]

From time's beginning, You were love's abode:
  My love encamped wherever it was You tented.
The taunts of foes for Your name's sake are sweet,
  So let them torture one whom You tormented.

5 I love my foes; for they learned wrath from You,
  For they pursue a body You have slain.
The day You hated me I loathed myself,
  For I will honor none whom You disdain.

Until Your anger pass, and You restore
10 This people whom You rescued once before.

Your breeze, Western shore, is perfumed[1]

Your breeze, Western shore, is perfumed.
The scent of nard° is in its wings, and the apple.   *an aromatic plant*
Your origin is in the merchants' treasuries,
Surely not from the store-house of the wind.[2]
5 You flutter the wings of the bird, giving him freedom;
You are like flowing myrrh[3] straight from the phial.
How much do people long for you, since, with your help,
They are carried by wooden beams on the backs of the waves.
Do not let your hand slacken its hold on the ship,
10 Whether the day is encamped, or blows fresh at the dawn.
Smooth out the deep, split the heart of the seas,
Come to the holy mountains. There you can rest.
Rebuke the East wind which enrages the sea,
Turning the waves into a boiling cauldron.
15 What shall a man do, chained to his Rock,
At one time confined, at another set free.
The essence of my request is in the hand of the Highest,
Who formed the mountains, who created the wind.

My heart is in the East[1]

My heart is in the East, and I in the depths of the West.
My food has no taste. How can it be sweet?
How can I fulfil my pledges and my vows,
When Zion is in the power of Edom, and I in the fetters of Arabia?[2]

---

1. Translated by Raymond P. Scheindlin. Yehuda ha-Levi adapts the Arabic situation of the lover who embraces abasement and rejection by her beloved, using it for Israel's attitude in exile from God.

1. Translated by David Goldstein.

2. Alluding to Psalm 135:7: "He bringeth forth the wind out of his treasuries."

3. Myrrh is a gum resin used for perfume. Like nard, it appears frequently in the Bible.

1. Translated by David Goldstein.

2. The poet asks how he can he travel to the Holy Land ("Zion") when he is a tolerated minority in Arab Iberia, and Palestine has been conquered by the Christians in the First Crusade. (After the conquest of Jerusalem in 1099, the Crusaders had slaughtered not only Muslims but Jews within the city.) The Edomites were enemies of the ancient Israelites; "Edom" became a code word for Rome when Israel was part of the Roman empire, and here means the Christian occupiers of Palestine.

5   It will be nothing to me to leave all the goodness of Spain.
       So rich will it be to see the dust of the ruined sanctuary.[3]

RAMÓN LLULL ■ (1232–1315)

A prolific polymath mystic, Ramón Llull wrote over 250 works, in Catalan and in Arabic, on nearly every subject there was. Born on the island of Majorca, during his youth he was a courtier and seneschal, or steward, before a mystical vision led him to retreat for nine years of hermitlike study in order to persuade the Jews and Muslims of the error of their faiths. Immersed in all three cultures of Iberia, his esoteric Christianity is well evident in the 366 allusive and lyrical aphorisms that make up the *Book of the Lover and the Beloved* (*Llibre d'amic et amat*), which forms chapter 99 of *Blanquerna* (1283), the first prose novel written in a romance language.

from Blanquerna: The Book of the Lover and the Beloved[1]

14. The Lover sought for one who should tell his Beloved how great trials he was enduring for love of Him, and how he was like to die. And he found his Beloved, who was reading in a book wherein were written all the griefs which love made him to suffer for his Beloved, and the joy which he had of his love.

16. "Say, thou bird that singest! Hast thou placed thyself in the care of my Beloved, that He may guard thee from indifference,[2] and increase in thee thy love?" The bird replied: "And who makes me to sing but the Lord of love, Who holds indifference to be sin?"

18. There was a contention between the eyes and the memory of the Lover, for the eyes said that it was better to behold the Beloved than to remember Him. But Memory said that remembrance brings tears to the eyes, and makes the heart to burn with love.

54. As one that was a fool went the Lover through a city, singing of his Beloved; and men asked him if he had lost his wits. "My Beloved," he answered, "has taken my will, and I myself have yielded up to Him my understanding; so that there is left in me naught but memory, wherewith I remember my Beloved."

69. The Lover extended and prolonged his thoughts of the greatness and everlastingness of his Beloved, and he found in Him neither beginning, nor mean,[3] nor end. And the Beloved said: "What measurest thou, O Fool?" The Lover answered: "I measure the lesser with the greater, defect with fulness, and beginning with infinity

---

3. The sanctuary, the Temple of Jerusalem, was destroyed by the Romans in 70 C.E. as a consequence of the Jewish rebellion of 66. The ruins that remain are part of the Western Wall, also known as the Wailing Wall.

1. Translated by E. Allison Peers. In the context of the novel, *The Book of the Lover and the Beloved* is written by the protagonist Blanquerna as an allegory of the faithful Christian and God, his Beloved, echoing the characters in the biblical Song of Songs (page 84). Like other mystical writings using the language of love, the numbered aphoristic sentences are equally applicable to the amorous situations they use to evoke a mystical state.

2. The translator uses "indifference" to translate the frequently occurring Catalan word *desamor*, which literally means "unlove," or "absence of love."

3. Middle

and eternity, to the end that humility, patience, charity and hope may be planted the more firmly in my remembrance."

70. The paths of love are both long and short. For love is clear, bright and pure, subtle yet simple, strong, diligent, brilliant, and abounding both in fresh thoughts and in old memories.

89. Love went apart with the Lover, and they had great joy of the Beloved; and the Beloved revealed himself to them. The Lover wept, and afterwards was in rapture, and Love swooned thereat.[4] But the Beloved brought life to His Lover by bringing to his memory His virtues.

98. The Beloved left the Lover, and the Lover sought Him in his thoughts, and enquired for Him of men in the language of love.

118. The Lover and the Beloved strove, and their love made peace between them. Which of them, think you, bore the stronger love toward the other?

130. With the pen of love, with the water of his tears, and on a paper of suffering, the Lover wrote letters to his Beloved. And in these he told how devotion tarried, how love was dying, and how sin and error were increasing the number of His enemies.

131. The Lover and the Beloved were bound in love with the bonds of memory, understanding, and will, that they might never be parted; and the cord wherewith these two loves were bound was woven of thoughts and griefs, sighs and tears.

132. The Lover lay in the bed of love: his sheets were of joys, his coverlet was of griefs, his pillow of tears. And none knew if the fabric of the pillow was that of the sheets or of the coverlet.

133. The Beloved clothed His Lover in vest, coat and mantle,[5] and gave him a helmet of love. His body He clothed with thoughts, his feet with tribulations, and his head with a garland of tears.

182. The Lover made complaint of his Beloved, because He caused Love so grievously to torment him. And the Beloved made reply by increasing his trials and perils, thoughts and tears.

194. One day the Lover ceased to remember his Beloved, and on the next day he remembered that he had forgotten Him. On the day when it came to the Lover that he had forgotten his Beloved, he was in sorrow and pain, and yet in glory and bliss—the one for his forgetfulness, and the other for his remembrance.

217. The Beloved chastened the heart of His Lover with rods of love, to make him love the tree whence He plucks the rods wherewith He chastens His lovers. And this is that tree whereon He suffered grief and dishonour and death, that He might bring back to love of Him those lovers whom He had lost.[6]

---

4. Because of that.
5. Sleeveless cloak.
6. This aphorism makes the Christian allegory more explicit than many of the others, with its recasting of the Passion of Christ in terms of the Lover and the Beloved.

An accomplished poet and patron of the arts, Dom Dinis opened his court to displaced poets from abroad: Provençal troubadours fleeing the Albigensian crusade in southwest France, Jews and Muslims fleeing the unrest in the southern half of the Iberian Peninsula. The coastal town of Santiago de Compostela was an important destination for medieval pilgrims and the performers who accompanied them. The Portuguese court was nourished by these influences, and Dom Dinis put this rich blend of talent to work copying and compiling luxurious illuminated manuscripts of songs.

Over a hundred texts of Dom Dinis's own songs have come down to us, along with the musical notation of seven compositions—all that we have, with seven of Martin Codax's, to indicate how the songs of the Galician-Portuguese tradition were actually performed. Most Occitanian and Northern French songs, with their more elusive melodies and extended, highly expressive lyrics, were rendered by voice alone, or with the spare accompaniment of the medieval fiddle. The Galician-Portuguese songs, although influenced by the French lyrics, also derived from a strong local tradition of refrain-based folk song. With catchier melodies and highly repetitive lyrics, these songs lent themselves to the greater instrumentation and dance beat of a small orchestra, which included the harp and the *pandeiro,* a square-frame drum, as well as the symphonie, a stringed instrument resembling a hurdy-gurdy.

Dom Dinis's version of the *canso* or love song is generally short with a refrain; he composed seventy-three of them. He also excelled in the *cantiga de amigo,* brief lyrics of love and longing written in the voice of a woman, usually waiting for or going to meet her lover. Nowhere else in medieval Europe were more women's songs composed, often superior in quality to the otherwise more common *cantiga de amor,* written in the voice of the male lover.

Provençals right well may versify[1]

> Provençals right well may versify
> And say they do with love
> But those with verse in flowertime
> And never else, I'd vow,
> 5   Their heart is not in torment
> As mine is for my lady.
>
> Although they're bound to versify
> And praise as best they can,
> Nonetheless, I'd vow
> 10   That those with verse in spring
> And never else, will bring
> No grief as deep as mine.
>
> For those who versify with joy
> About the verdant° time,   *greening*
> 15   The flowers do their bidding,
> In spring, but soon decline,
> Nor is their life perdition
> Nor death in life, like mine.

---

1. Translated by William M. Davis. The verb *trobar* ("versify," literally "to find") is a key word in the vocabulary of Occitan poetry referred to here by Dom Dinis, for it is also the source of the names, *troubadours* and *trobairitz.*

Of what are you dying, daughter[1]

Of what are you dying, daughter, of body so fair?
Mother, I'm dying for the love my friend bestowed.
It's dawn, and quickly he goes.

Of what are you dying, daughter, of body so lithe?
5   Mother, I'm dying for the love my lover bestowed.
It's dawn, and quickly he goes.

Mother, I'm dying for the love my friend bestowed
whenever I look at this sash I tie for his love.
It's dawn, and quickly he goes.

10   Mother, I'm dying for the love my lover bestowed
whenever I look at this sash that I wear for his love.
It's dawn, and quickly he goes.

Whenever I look at this sash that I tie for his love
and remember, pretty me, how he spoke with me.
15   It's dawn, and quickly he goes.

Whenever I look at this sash that I wear for his love
and remember, pretty me, how both of us spoke.
It's dawn, and quickly he goes.

O blossoms of the verdant pine

O blossoms of the verdant pine,
if you have news of my friend?
   O God, where is he?

O blossoms of the verdant bough,
5   if you have news of my beloved?
   O God, where is he?

If you have news of my friend,
who lied about what he promised to me?
   O God, where is he?

10   If you have news of my beloved,
who lied about what he swore to me?
   O God, where is he?

You ask me about that friend of yours,
and I tell you that he is well and alive.
15   O God, where is he?

You ask me about that friend of yours,
and I tell you that he is alive and well.
   O God, where is he?

1. This and the following poems are translated by Barbara Hughes Fowler.

And I tell you that he is well and alive,
and will be with you before very long.
>O God, where is he?

And I tell you that he is alive and well
and will be with you now very soon.
>O God, where is he?

The lovely girl arose at earliest dawn

The lovely girl
arose at earliest dawn,
and goes to wash her camisoles at the river swirl.
She goes to wash them at earliest dawn.

5   The elegant girl
arose at earliest dawn,
and goes to wash her petticoats at the river swirl.
>She goes to wash them at earliest dawn.

She goes to wash her camisoles.
10   She rose at earliest dawn.
The wind is scattering them at the river swirl.
She goes to wash them at earliest dawn.

She goes to wash her petticoats.
She rose at earliest dawn.
15   The wind has born them off at the river swirl.
She goes to wash them at earliest dawn.

The wind is scattering them.
She rose at earliest dawn.
At dawn she was enraged at the river swirl.
20   She goes to wash them at earliest dawn.

MARTIN CODAX ■ (fl. mid-13th century)

In 1914, a parchment leaf was found inside the binding of a book in Madrid. It contained the words and music to seven *cantigas de amigo,* or "songs for a friend," composed by Martin Codax in Galician-Portuguese at the court of Ferdinand III of Castile in the mid-thirteenth century. We know nothing about him except the name, but the poems provide rare firsthand evidence of how lyric was performed on the Iberian Peninsula. The high degree of parallelism from stanza to stanza in both words and melody mirrors the dominant image of the sea in the delicate form known as the *marinha,* or sea-song. End-rhyme intensifies the parallelism; in "O waves that I've come to see," for example, rhymes of words ending in *-er* and *-ar* play off each other like the waves of the sea that is serving the speaker as her mirror and confidante. The musical settings stretch out the key words, particularly *amigo* (friend, lover), stressing the mood they create, before finishing on the plaintive and brief monosyllables, *sin min,* "without me."

Ah God, if only my love could know[1]

Ah God, if only my love could know
how much I am alone in Vigo,[2]
   and go about in love.

Ah God, if he knew, my dearest one,
5   how I am in Vigo, all alone!
   and go about in love.

How in Vigo, alone, I stay—
and near me not a single spy,
   and go about in love.

10   How in Vigo I stay alone,
with no spies around me, none,
   and go about in love.

And I have no spies with me,
only my eyes, that weep with me,
15   and go about in love.

And near me now I have no spies
—only my pair of weeping eyes—
   and go about in love.

My beautiful sister, come hurry with me[1]

My beautiful sister, come hurry with me
to the church of Vigo beside the turbulent sea,
   and we shall marvel at the waves.

My beautiful sister, come hurry, please,
5   to the church of Vigo beside the tumultuous sea,
   and we shall marvel at the waves.

To the church of Vigo beside the turbulent sea,
and there will come here, mother, my friend,
   and we shall marvel at the waves.

10   To the church of Vigo beside the tumultuous sea,
and there will come here, my mother, my love,
   and we shall marvel at the waves.

1. Translated by Peter Dronke.
2. The area around Vigo, in Galicia on the northwest coast of the Iberian Peninsula south of Santiago de Compostela, has been inhabited since prehistory. During the middle ages, it was a port town dependent on the Cistercian monastery of Melón.
1. Translated by Barbara Hughes Fowler.

O waves that I've come to see[1]

> O waves that I've come to see,
> if you know, tell to me
> why my love lingers
> without me.
>
> 5   O waves that I've come to view,
> if you know, reveal to me
> why my love lingers
> without me.

[END OF IBERIA, THE MEETING OF THREE WORLDS]

MARIE DE FRANCE ▪ (mid-12th–early 13th century)

What we know for certain about the author of the *Lais* is neither more nor less than the name she gives herself: *Sui Marie e sui de France* ("I am Marie and am from France"). She wrote in the French dialect called Anglo-Norman, probably for the French-speaking Norman audience in England around the court of Henry II and Eleanor of Aquitaine. It has been conjectured from her familiarity with court life that she may have been an illegitimate half-sister to Henry; she was in all likelihood of noble blood. The *Lais* are her best and best-known work; a collection of animal fables and a translation of a Latin otherworld journey, *St. Patrick's Purgatory,* have also been attributed to her. The *Lais* is a group of short narratives in verse, tales of courtly love and adventure based on the oral traditions of Brittany. The Norman conquest of 1066 had opened up a vogue for the *matière de Bretagne,* the Celtic legends that included those of King Arthur and the lovers Tristan and Yseult.

Marie was writing at a time of enormous change in French society and culture. The tradition of tracing familial descent through the maternal side of the family had recently been supplanted by paternal ancestry. The orally based couplets of the traditional *chanson de geste,* or epic, had given way to the more musical and psychologically flexible eight-syllable couplets of the romance. As Marie translated her Celtic sources into French verse, she changed their focus as well, creating a series of ethical tests for her characters, male and female, in which she could explore the conflicts between social constraints and individual desire, and between real life and the world of fantasy. While rooted in the world of legend, the *Lais* are also concerned with the complex politics of the feudal court. The knight Lanval, for example, suffers first from his lack of status at Arthur's court, and then, like the later Gawain in *Sir Gawain and the Green Knight,* from his lack of poise in fending off the unwanted advances of a powerful ruler, Queen Guinevere.

Legendary motifs are strongly in evidence. The plot of *Bisclavret,* for example, turns on the protagonist's monthly transformation into a wolf. In other tales, we find self-guiding boats, magical women, a man who can transform himself into a bird, a woman who can appear invisibly to her lover, and a potion bestowing superhuman strength. Marie wields these motifs strategically to demarcate places where the cold reality of the feudal structure is incompatible with the more fanciful demands of the individual. In the conventional tale of chivalry, the knight would ride out, seeking to test himself through adventures. But in Marie's world, adventure tends to seek out the knights and ladies, and their response to

1. Translated by Barbara Hughes Fowler.

an unforeseen event or encounter will determine their failure or success in the world. In *Bisclavret,* the wife, the werewolf, and the king are presented in turn with crucial ethical decisions that have no obvious cultural precedent. The scenario of the brief tale *Chevrefoil,* based on the famous legend of Tristan and Yseult, is more limited. Here Marie ignores the best-known parts—the love potion accidentally drunk by Tristan and the bride he is bringing to King Mark or the efforts of the king and his courtiers to catch the adulterous couple in the act. Instead, Marie selects a little-known episode following the knight's banishment. The adventure that befalls the lovers is a chance meeting; their proper response to this opportunity determines the possibility of a brief, perfect moment of union.

Marie's characters do not reveal themselves through their thoughts, as modern protagonists tend to do. They discover themselves, and we are asked to analyze them, through their actions, and through comparison from one *lai* to the next. The *Lais* are structured like a series of permutations of a fixed set of variables in a laboratory experiment. We find the positive counterpart of Bisclavret's wife in *Eliduc,* for example, and his tragic counterpart in the bird-man of *Yonec.* It is evident that the *Lais* had a didactic component along with their role as court entertainment. The feudal system was based on the exchange of loyalty for land and protection, guided by a complex code of behavior, and resulting in a constantly shifting set of allegiances. The role of women in this society was especially contradictory. An apparently powerful queen and patron such as Eleanor of Aquitaine could just as easily be locked in a tower for fifteen years, as she was by Henry II between 1174 and 1189. Rulers such as Eleanor and Marie, countess of Champagne, could patronize the arts, and women such as Marie could be prominent poets and authors while possessing little or no actual power, being regarded primarily as items of barter, providers of land and heirs. These women were celebrated as goddesses of love while deprived of any agency to act on that love. Marie's female characters both embody this double bind and find ways of negotiating what modicum of freedom and happiness might be possible within it.

PRONUNCIATIONS:
Bisclavret: bees-KLAH-vray
Chevrefoil: CHEV-r'foy

from Lais

Prologue[1]

> Whoever has received knowledge
> and eloquence in speech from God
> should not be silent or secretive
> but demonstrate it willingly.
5   When a great good is widely heard of,
> then, and only then, does it bloom,
> and when that good is praised by many,
> it has spread its blossoms.
> The custom among the ancients—
10   as Priscian testifies—
> was to speak quite obscurely
> in the books they wrote,

---

1. Translated by Joan M. Ferrante and Robert W. Hanning. Like many medieval prologues, this one takes a series of commonplaces and gives them a particular spin. The first theme derives from Jesus's parable of the talents (Matthew 25.14–32). Marie justifies her writing the *lais* as the laudable exercise of a God-given talent.

so that those who were to come after
and study them
15   might gloss° the letter   *explain*
and supply its significance from their own wisdom.[2]
Philosophers knew this,
they understood among themselves
that the more time they spent,
20   the more subtle their minds would become
and the better they would know how to keep themselves
from whatever was to be avoided.
He who would guard himself from vice
should study and understand
25   and begin a weighty work
by which he might keep vice at a distance,
and free himself from great sorrow.[3]
That's why I began to think
about composing some good stories
30   and translating from Latin to Romance;
but that was not to bring me fame:
too many others have done it.
Then I thought of the *lais* I'd heard.
I did not doubt, indeed I knew well,
35   that those who first began them
and sent them forth
composed them in order to preserve
adventures they had heard.[4]
I have heard many told;
40   and I don't want to neglect or forget them.
To put them into word and rhyme
I've often stayed awake.

In your honor, noble King,[5]
who are so brave and courteous,
45   repository of all joys
in whose heart all goodness takes root,
I undertook to assemble these *lais*
to compose and recount them in rhyme.
In my heart I thought and determined,
50   sire, that I would present them to you.
If it pleases you to receive them,
you will give me great joy;
I shall be happy forever.

2. Priscian (fl. c. 500 C.E.) wrote what became the standard textbook of Latin grammar in the Middle Ages, the *Institutiones grammaticae* ("Grammatical Foundations"). "Glossing" a text meant not only explaining its grammatical constructions, but also revealing allegorical meaning hidden beneath the "letter" or literal meaning of the words.

3. Here, studying and glossing provide an occupation that both removes temptation toward more vicious activities and distracts the mind from sorrow. This could either mean the tribulations of Fortune (in a philosophical context) or the sufferings of love (in a courtly context, as below).

4. Rather than the classical themes she has been enumerating, Marie proposes the novelty of the *lais*, oral folktales rather than written manuscripts.

5. It was customary for the prologue to conclude with a dedication to the poet's patron, here most likely Henry II.

Do not think me presumptuous
55   if I dare present them to you.
Now hear how they begin.

Bisclavret (The Werewolf)

Since I am undertaking to compose *lais*,
I don't want to forget Bisclavret;
In Breton, the *lai*'s name is *Bisclavret*—
the Normans call it *The Werewolf*.[1]
5   In the old days, people used to say—
and it often actually happened—
that some men turned into werewolves
and lived in the woods.
A werewolf is a savage beast;
10   while his fury is on him
he eats men, does much harm,
goes deep in the forest to live.
But that's enough of this for now:
I want to tell you about the Bisclavret.

15   In Brittany there lived a nobleman
whom I've heard marvelously praised;
a fine, handsome knight
who behaved nobly.
He was close to his lord,
20   and loved by all his neighbors.
He had an estimable wife,
one of lovely appearance;
he loved her and she him,
but one thing was very vexing to her:
25   during the week he would be missing
for three whole days, and she didn't know
what happened to him or where he went.
Nor did any of his men know anything about it.
One day he returned home
30   happy and delighted;
she asked him about it.
"My lord," she said, "and dear love,
I'd very much like to ask you one thing—
if I dared;
35   but I'm so afraid of your anger
that nothing frightens me more."
When he heard that, he embraced her,
drew her to him and kissed her.
"My lady," he said, "go ahead and ask!
40   There's nothing you could want to know,

---

1. "*Garwaf*." As in the Prologue, Marie emphasizes the task of translation, explaining the meaning of key words in both languages.

that, if I knew the answer, I wouldn't tell you."
"By God," she replied, "now I'm cured!
My lord, on the days when you go away from me
I'm in such a state—
45   so sad at heart,
so afraid I'll lose you—
that if I don't get quick relief
I could die of this very soon.
Please, tell me where you go,
50   where you have been staying.
I think you must have a lover,
and if that's so, you're doing wrong."
"My dear," he said, "have mercy on me, for God's sake!
Harm will come to me if I tell you about this,
55   because I'd lose your love
and even my very self."
When the lady heard this
she didn't take it lightly;
she kept asking him,
60   coaxed and flattered him so much,
that he finally told her what happened to him—
he hid nothing from her.
"My dear, I become a werewolf:
I go off into the great forest,
65   in the thickest part of the woods,
and I live on the prey I hunt down."
When he had told her everything,
she asked further
whether he undressed or kept his clothes on.°   *as a werewolf*
70   "Wife," he replied, "I go stark naked."
"Tell me, then, for God's sake, where your clothes are."
"That I won't tell you;
for if I were to lose them,
and then be discovered,
75   I'd stay a werewolf forever.
I'd be helpless
until I got them back.
That's why I don't want their hiding place to be known."
"My lord," the lady answered,
80   "I love you more than all the world;
you mustn't hide anything from me
or fear me in any way:
that doesn't seem like love to me.
What wrong have I done? For what sin of mine
85   do you mistrust me about anything?
Do the right thing and tell me!"
She harassed and bedeviled him so,
that he had no choice but to tell her.
"Lady," he said, "near the woods,

90	beside the road that I use to get there,
	there's an old chapel
	that has often done me good service;
	under a bush there is a big stone,
	hollowed out inside;
95	I hide my clothes right there
	until I'm ready to come home."
	The lady heard this wonder
	and turned scarlet from fear;
	she was terrified of the whole adventure.
100	Over and over she considered
	how she might get rid of him;
	she never wanted to sleep with him again.
	There was a knight of that region
	who had loved her for a long time,
105	who begged for her love,
	and dedicated himself to serving her.
	She'd never loved him at all,
	nor pledged her love to him,
	but now she sent a messenger for him,
110	and told him her intention.
	"My dear," she said, "cheer up!
	I shall now grant you without delay
	what you have suffered for;
	you'll meet with no more refusals—
115	I offer you my love and my body;
	make me your mistress!"
	He thanked her graciously
	and accepted her promise,
	and she bound him to her by an oath.
120	Then she told him
	how her husband went away and what happened to him;
	she also taught him the precise path
	her husband took into the forest,
	and then she sent the knight to get her husband's clothes.
125	So Bisclavret was betrayed,
	ruined by his own wife.
	Since people knew he was often away from home
	they all thought
	this time he'd gone away forever.
130	They searched for him and made inquiries
	but could never find him,
	so they had to let matters stand.
	The wife later married the other knight,
	who had loved her for so long.
135	A whole year passed
	until one day the king went hunting;
	he headed right for the forest
	where Bisclavret was.

When the hounds were unleashed,
140 they ran across Bisclavret;
the hunters and the dogs
chased him all day,
until they were just about to take him
and tear him apart,
145 at which point he saw the king
and ran to him, pleading for mercy.
He took hold of the king's stirrup,
kissed his leg and his foot.
The king saw this and was terrified;
150 he called his companions.
"My lords," he said, "come quickly!
Look at this marvel—
this beast is humbling itself to me.
It has the mind of a man, and it's begging me for mercy!
155 Chase the dogs away,
and make sure no one strikes it.
This beast is rational—he has a mind.
Hurry up: let's get out of here.
I'll extend my peace to the creature;
160 indeed, I'll hunt no more today!"
Thereupon the king turned away.
Bisclavret followed him;
he stayed close to the king, and wouldn't go away;
he'd no intention of leaving him.
165 The king led him to his castle;
he was delighted with this turn of events,
for he'd never seen anything like it.
He considered the beast a great wonder
and held him very dear.
170 He commanded all his followers,
for the sake of their love for him, to guard Bisclavret well,
and under no circumstances to do him harm;
none of them should strike him;
rather, he should be well fed and watered.
175 They willingly guarded the creature;
every day he went to sleep
among the knights, near the king.
Everyone was fond of him;
he was so noble and well behaved
180 that he never wished to do anything wrong.
Regardless of where the king might go,
Bisclavret never wanted to be separated from him;
he always accompanied the king.
The king became very much aware that the creature loved him.
185 Now listen to what happened next.
The king held a court;
to help him celebrate his feast

and to serve him as handsomely as possible,
he summoned all the barons

190   who held fiefs from him.[2]
Among the knights who went,
and all dressed up in his best attire,
was the one who had married Bisclavret's wife.
He neither knew nor suspected

195   that he would find Bisclavret so close by.
As soon as he came to the palace
Bisclavret saw him,
ran toward him at full speed,
sank his teeth into him, and started to drag him down.

200   He would have done him great damage
if the king hadn't called him off,
and threatened him with a stick.
Twice that day he tried to bite the knight.
Everyone was extremely surprised,

205   since the beast had never acted that way
toward any other man he had seen.
All over the palace people said
that he wouldn't act that way without a reason:
that somehow or other, the knight had mistreated Bisclavret,

210   and now he wanted his revenge.
And so the matter rested
until the feast was over
and until the barons took their leave of the king
and started home.

215   The very first to leave,
to the best of my knowledge,
was the knight whom Bisclavret had attacked.
It's no wonder the creature hated him.
Not long afterward,

220   as the story leads me to believe,
the king, who was so wise and noble,
went back to the forest
where he had found Bisclavret,
and the creature went with him.

225   That night, when he finished hunting,
he sought lodging out in the countryside.
The wife of Bisclavret heard about it,
dressed herself elegantly,
and went the next day to speak with the king,

230   bringing rich presents for him.
When Bisclavret saw her coming,
no one could hold him back;
he ran toward her in a rage.

2. Who were bound to him in oaths of fealty.

Now listen to how well he avenged himself!
235 He tore the nose off her face.
What worse thing could he have done to her?
Now men closed in on him from all sides;
they were about to tear him apart,
when a wise man said to the king,
240 "My lord, listen to me!
This beast has stayed with you,
and there's not one of us
who hasn't watched him closely,
hasn't traveled with him often.
245 He's never touched anyone,
or shown any wickedness,
except to this woman.
By the faith that I owe you,
he has some grudge against her,
250 and against her husband as well.
This is the wife of the knight
whom you used to like so much,
and who's been missing for so long—
we don't know what became of him.
255 Why not put this woman to torture
and see if she'll tell you
why the beast hates her?[3]
Make her tell what she knows!
We've seen many strange things
260 happen in Brittany!"
The king took his advice;
he detained the knight.
At the same time he took the wife
and subjected her to torture;
265 out of fear and pain
she told all about her husband:
how she had betrayed him
and taken away his clothes;
the story he had told her
270 about what happened to him and where he went;
and how after she had taken his clothes
he'd never been seen in his land again.
She was quite certain
that this beast was Bisclavret.
275 The king demanded the clothes;
whether she wanted to or not
she sent home for them,
and had them brought to Bisclavret.
When they were put down in front of him

---

3. Torture was a common means of interrogation, especially for gaining confessions. The king's advisor takes the beast's attack as evidence of the lady's guilt.

280   he didn't even seem to notice them;
the king's wise man—
the one who had advised him earlier—
said to him, "My lord, you're not doing it right.
This beast wouldn't, under any circumstances,
285   in order to get rid of his animal form,
put on his clothes in front of you;
you don't understand what this means:
he's just too ashamed to do it here.
Have him led to your chambers
290   and bring the clothes with him;
then we'll leave him alone for a while.
If he turns into a man, we'll know about it."
The king himself led the way
and closed all the doors on him.
295   After a while he went back,
taking two barons with him;
all three entered the king's chamber.
On the king's royal bed
they found the knight asleep.
300   The king ran to embrace him.
He hugged and kissed him again and again.
As soon as he had the chance,
the king gave him back all his lands;
he gave him more than I can tell.
305   He banished the wife,
chased her out of the country.
She went into exile with the knight
with whom she had betrayed her lord.
She had several children
310   who were widely known
for their appearance:
several women of the family
were actually born without noses,
and lived out their lives noseless.[4]

315   The adventure that you have heard
really happened, no doubt about it.
The *lai* of Bisclavret was made
so it would be remembered forever.

Chevrefoil (The Honeysuckle)

I should like very much
to tell you the truth
about the *lai* men call *Chevrefoil*—
why it was composed and where it came from.

---

4. The *lai* includes a folktale-style explanation of the origin of a physical defect in the family. It also suggests that punishment for misbehavior will be passed through the generations.

5 Many have told and recited it to me
 and I have found it in writing,
 about Tristan and the queen
 and their love that was so true,
 that brought them much suffering
10 and caused them to die the same day.[1]
 King Mark was annoyed,
 angry at his nephew Tristan;
 he exiled Tristan from his land
 because of the queen whom he loved.[2]
15 Tristan returned to his own country,
 South Wales, where he was born,
 he stayed a whole year;
 he couldn't come back.
 Afterward he began to expose himself
20 to death and destruction.
 Don't be surprised at this:
 for one who loves very faithfully
 is sad and troubled
 when he cannot satisfy his desires.
25 Tristan was sad and worried,
 so he set out from his land.
 He traveled straight to Cornwall,
 where the queen lived,
 and entered the forest all alone—
30 he didn't want anyone to see him;
 he came out only in the evening
 when it was time to find shelter.
 He took lodging that night,
 with peasants, poor people.
35 He asked them for news
 of the king—what he was doing.
 They told him they had heard
 that the barons had been summoned by ban.
 They were to come to Tintagel
40 where the king wanted to hold his court;[3]
 at Pentecost they would all be there,[4]
 there'd be much joy and pleasure,
 and the queen would be there too.

1. The tragic love affair of Tristan and Yseult was based on a Celtic legend. There were various written sources Marie could have known, including the Anglo-Norman version of Thomas (c. 1170), composed at the court of Henry II, which was also Gottfried von Strassburg's source. The episode she recounts, however, doesn't exist in other versions, although she assumes her audience was familiar with them, not even naming Yseult ("the queen").

2. Mark, king of Cornwall, had sent Tristan to Ireland to win Yseult as his queen. A love potion caused the pair to fall in love, and when Mark discovered their affair, he banished his nephew.

3. The Norman castle of Tintagel, on the northwestern coast of Cornwall, was built on the site of a Celtic monastery held to be the birthplace of King Arthur.

4. Pentecost, or Whitsunday, commemorates the descent of the Holy Spirit upon the disciples, seven Sundays after the resurrection of Christ. It was a major spring festival in the Christian year, and, along with Christmas and Easter, a traditional time for a king to hold full court.

Tristan heard and was very happy;
45   she would not be able to go there
            without his seeing her pass.
            The day the king set out,
            Tristan also came to the woods
            by the road he knew
50   their assembly must take.
            He cut a hazel tree in half,
            then he squared it.
            When he had prepared the wood,
            he wrote his name on it with his knife.
55   If the queen noticed it—
            and she should be on the watch for it,
            for it had happened before
            and she had noticed it then—
            she'd know when she saw it,
60   that the piece of wood had come from her love.
            This was the message of the writing
            that he had sent to her:
            he had been there a long time,
            had waited and remained
65   to find out and to discover
            how he could see her,
            for he could not live without her.
            With the two of them it was just
            as it is with the honeysuckle
70   that attaches itself to the hazel tree:
            when it has wound and attached
            and worked itself around the trunk,
            the two can survive together;
            but if someone tries to separate them,
75   the hazel dies quickly
            and the honeysuckle with it.
            "Sweet love, so it is with us:
            You cannot live without me, nor I without you."
            The queen rode along;
80   she looked at the hillside
            and saw the piece of wood; she knew what it was,
            she recognized all the letters.
            The knights who were accompanying her,
            who were riding with her,
85   she ordered to stop:
            she wanted to dismount and rest.
            They obeyed her command.
            She went far away from her people
            and called her girl
90   Brenguein,[5] who was loyal to her.

---

5. Yseult's companion and waiting-woman; Brenguein plays an important role in the Tristan romances.

She went a short distance from the road;
and in the woods she found him
whom she loved more than any living thing.
They took great joy in each other.
95   He spoke to her as much as he desired,
she told him whatever she liked.
Then she assured him
that he would be reconciled with the king—
for it weighed on him
100   that he had sent Tristan away;
he'd done it because of the accusation.[6]
Then she departed, she left her love,
but when it came to the separation,
they began to weep.
105   Tristan went to Wales,
to wait until his uncle sent for him.
For the joy that he'd felt
from his love when he saw her,
by means of the stick he inscribed
110   as the queen had instructed,
and in order to remember the words,
Tristan, who played the harp well,
composed a new *lai* about it.
I shall name it briefly:
115   in English they call it *Goat's Leaf*
the French call it *Chevrefoil*.[7]
I have given you the truth
about the *lai* that I have told here.

DANTE ALIGHIERI ■ (1265–1321)

In the traces of autobiography he wove throughout his writings, Dante made it clear that there were two defining tragedies in his life: the death of his beloved Beatrice in 1290 and his exile from Florence in 1302, condemned to death should he ever return. Much else must have occurred in his life of which we know next to nothing—around 1285, he was married to one Gemma Donati, who bore him four children; he wrote his epic poem the *Commedia* during his peripatetic years of exile, finishing it right around the time of his death in Ravenna in 1321—but in the world of his poetry he chose to epitomize his life by an episode of unrequited love and a moment of high political drama.

Dante's Florence was an independent republic, and its status as a banking center had made it one of the most important cities in late medieval Europe. It was also, like much of Italy, torn by civil strife. In 1260, two coalitions of noble families had fought for control of the city: the victorious Ghibellines, allied with the Hohenstaufen ruler Manfred, and the defeated Guelfs, allied with the papacy and a group of north-central Italian cities. The Guelfs regained control of Florence seven years later, banishing the Ghibellines and confiscating their property. In 1295, Dante enrolled in one of the professional guilds that constituted the power base of the *popolo*, a

---

6. Like most courtly lovers, Tristan and Yseult were harassed by ill-wishing courtiers or *losengiers,* who try to trap them. King Mark, meanwhile, would prefer to believe that the affair does not exist.

7. As in *Bisclavret,* Marie emphasizes her title word (and the meaning embodied in it) through a focus on its translation.

popular party which sought to contain the feuding of the aristocratic families, now focused on the drive by Pope Boniface VIII to bring northern Italy under papal control. In 1300, Dante was appointed to a two-month term as one of the city's seven priors (chief magistrates). As the city was rocked with violence, the priors exiled leading members of the new clashing factions of Black and White Guelfs, including Dante's good friend, the poet Guido Cavalcanti, who would die later that year. While an emissary in Rome two years later, Dante was sentenced to death in absentia, probably as revenge for his part in the earlier decision. He spent the last two decades of his life in miserable exile, wandering from city to city and patron to patron, all over Italy and possibly as far as Paris.

Dante's earliest writings include *Il Fiore* (*The Flower*), a sonnet sequence adapted from *The Romance of the Rose*, and other writings related to the Northern Italian lyric movement of the *dolce stil novo,* or "sweet new style," as he would call it in the *Commedia*. The new Italian lyric was predominantly metaphysical, using Provençal forms and imagery to explore questions of philosophy, theology, and knowledge. Love was seldom sexual and seldom even social; the poet need barely have spoken to an idealized beloved like Dante's Beatrice or Cavalcanti's Giovanna. According to his poetic autobiography, *La vita nuova* (*The New Life,* 1292–1294), Dante first encountered the Florentine girl, Beatrice Portinari, when she was eight and he was nine years old; she died sixteen years later without Dante having ever exchanged more than a few words with her. While he suffers from her presence (and her absence) just as a courtly lover would have done, he also comes to regard his beloved as nothing less than a manifestation of Christ, descended to earth to inspire him with love in order to lead him to a deeper understanding and a better life.

Much of Dante's writing was concerned with the meaning of what he had already written. *La Vita nuova* placed a series of his most celebrated early lyrics in the context of his obsession with Beatrice, explaining in retrospect how each poem had come to be written and how each reflected a different stage in his love from afar and a different aspect of his divine beloved. In *Il Convivio* (*The Banquet*), written in exile between about 1304 and 1307 and left unfinished, Dante reinterpreted several long love lyrics, this time as allegories about Lady Philosophy. During the same period he wrote but didn't finish *De vulgari eloquentia* (*On the Vulgar Tongue*) in which he surveyed the lyric tradition as a defense for composing intellectually ambitious verse in an Italian vernacular rather than in Latin. Somewhere around 1310, he wrote *De Monarchia* (*On Monarchy*), a treatise on political philosophy arguing that an emperor was necessary to provide political stability to the world. The *Commedia* or *Comedy,* widely known as *The Divine Comedy,* incorporates all of Dante's earlier themes; it documents the difficulty of fulfilling his youthful ambitions, and the many ways in which the poet may or may not actually be worthy of doing so.

The Divine Comedy[1] The structure of the *Commedia* is dazzlingly simple and impossibly intricate, an attempt to mirror the essential mystery of the Trinity. Everything is divided into threes and ones, their ideal permutations of nine and ten, and the perfect number seven. The single poem is composed of three parts, or canticles, *Inferno, Purgatorio,* and *Paradiso,* each describing one of the three distinct realms of the afterlife that compose the single universe comprehended by the divine plan. Each canticle is made up of thirty-three cantos, for a total of ninety-nine, except that *Inferno* has one extra to make a perfect hundred. Usually the first canto is considered as a prelude to the rest; this is one example of the ways in which Dante introduced dissymmetry to prevent the overall order of his poem from becoming monotonous. Cantos, for example, range in length from 115 to 160 lines. The meter Dante invented for the *Commedia,* which he called *terza rima* (third rhyme), embodies the poem's tension between order and disorder, stability and change. The

1. Translated by Allen Mandelbaum.

eleven-syllable lines are divided into *terzinas,* or triplets, the first and third lines rhyming with each other, the second line introducing the main rhyme for the next *terzina*. So, for example, the first nine lines of the *Commedia:*

> Nel mezzo del cammin di nostra vita
> mi ritrovai per una selva oscura,
> ché la diritta via era smarrita.
> Ahi quanto a dir qual era è cosa dura
> esta selva selvaggia e aspra e forte
> che nel pensier rinova la paura!
> Tant' è amara che poco è più morte:
> ma per trattar del ben ch'i'vi trovai,
> dirò de l'altre cose ch'i' v'ho scorte.

(Ed. Petrocchi)

> When I had journeyed half of our life's way,
> I found myself within a shadowed forest,
> for I had lost the path that does not stray.
> Ah, it is hard to speak of what it was,
> that savage forest, dense and difficult,
> which even in recall renews my fear:
> so bitter—death is hardly more severe!
> But to retell the good discovered there,
> I'll also tell the other things I saw.

Each *terzina* is a self-contained argument, but the overlapping rhymes link one unit to the next, providing both closure and continuity. For example in line 3, *smarrita* ("lost") brings the opening image to a frightening close, but then the next rhymes of *dura* ("hard") and *paura* ("fear") recall and expand the previous description of the *selva oscura* ("dark forest"), while the new rhyme word *forte* ("difficult") looks forward to the next *terzina,* which rounds out the opening argument of all nine verses: he will tell us of the bad so that we will understand the good that came after.

The vision the poet recounts encompasses God's plan for the world, from its creation through to the Last Judgment. From the divine perspective, time doesn't exist, for in Dante's theology, God existed before time began and will still exist after time ceases. Everything that happens in the world, every thought and action, is known by God beforehand. From the human perspective, however, seeing only at best the deeds of the past, the lessons of history, and the memories of a life, this eternal scheme can hardly be comprehended, much less put into words. The formal structure of the poem is the most fundamental of the many ways in which Dante tries to impart this dual perspective to his readers. The transience, variety, and fascination of human life alternate with the eternity, unity, and fixity of the afterlife. Rather than simply relate what he saw in his vision and explain what it meant, the all-knowing poet slowly reveals it through a first-person persona (referred to in the notes to the poem as "the pilgrim") who is as unfamiliar as we are with what he is seeing. For the medieval Christian, the world and everything in it was a book created by God to be read and interpreted, and this is how Dante conceived the afterlife, as an enormously complex rebus, a puzzle to be deciphered. Each soul the pilgrim encounters presents a mystery; it is often unclear in terms of strict Catholic doctrine why a certain soul has been damned to hell or another saved in purgatory. Even though the poet claims to have been there and to have understood what everything in this plan means, he wants us instead to be confused, intrigued, and even outraged by what we see. The reader is to be converted, taught the way to salvation, but as an active participant.

There are three guides who lead the pilgrim on this journey: the classical Roman poet Virgil (70–19 B.C.E.), who takes him through Hell and Purgatory; Beatrice, who takes him through Paradise; and Saint Bernard of Clairvaux, who prepares him for the final momentary union with the godhead. In addition to their historical character, each of these figures can be understood as a personification in an allegory about the conversion of a human soul: Virgil as the role of Reason in comprehending the rational cost of sin, either damnation or expiation; Beatrice as the role of Love and Faith in moving beyond the physical bounds of sin into the heavens; Bernard as the role of mystic vision and theology in achieving a final, perfect fusion with God. Each can be understood also as a personification of letters and study: Virgil as the preparatory ground of the classics; Beatrice as the inspirational role of love poetry; Bernard as the conclusive grasp of theology and mysticism. Further, they personify key influences in Dante's own life, the depth and emotional commitment of his attachment especially to the poetry and legend of Virgil and to the person and memory of Beatrice. For the *Commedia* is also a deeply felt spiritual autobiography, moving from suicidal despair to hope and the fulfillment of the pilgrim's innermost wishes.

The landscape of this autobiography is an idiosyncratic version of medieval geography and myth. Dante places Hell within the earth, an inverted cone created when Satan fell from heaven through the southern hemisphere directly opposite the future site of Jerusalem. As Satan was lodged in the center of the earth, land fleeing his presence piled up in both directions. The land escaping to the north created the inhabited world and hollowed out the cone of Hell beneath it. To the south, a passage was created leading to the surface of the southern hemisphere, where the mountain of Purgatory arose, its seven terraces analogous to the nine circles of hell. At the top of the mountain of Purgatory sits the earthly paradise, where Adam and Eve first dwelt in Eden before they were banished to the world below. Paradise is located in the fiery Empyrean, beyond the planets and stars above. Dante tells us that the three realms are peopled by innumerable souls, but singles out various individuals as emblematic of each sin or quality. His selection is eclectic: men and women out of classical myth and Roman history, biblical figures, Florentines, other Italians, and Europeans, friends and enemies, poets and politicians, characters from medieval legend, and popes who hadn't even died yet in 1300 when the journey is supposed to occur. Dante chooses to persuade us of the extraordinary bliss of heaven and the intolerable torment of hell by painting them in the vivid colors we know so well from the world in which we live. He invests every one of these characters, every word they say and everything the pilgrim does with enormous significance, a significance that he makes us urgently need to know.

Inferno Hell serves double duty in the *Commedia*: it describes the consequences of a sinful life and it teaches the reader how to read the poem. Although from early on critics began mapping its nine circles (plus the vestibule, or ante-hell) and arguing about who did or didn't deserve to be where, Dante actually reveals the structure of Hell gradually, sometimes only partially, and often in ways a medieval reader would never have expected. This begins with Virgil, the most complex character in the poem. He was renowned for his virtue and considered a prophet of Christianity, and there was no pressing reason to condemn him to Hell at all. As with many of the souls encountered, however, Virgil's fate serves to define his place (Limbo) as a series of debates and dilemmas rather than a simple equation. In God's eyes, sin may be a simple and well-ordered business, but from the human perspective, it is not so easy to judge. Sin can be seductive, like Francesca da Rimini in the circle of the Lustful; it can inspire pity and fear, like Ugolino at the very bottom of Hell. Seldom, however, is it exactly what it seems, for Dante expects his readers to move back and forth through the poem, to compare what he says about a shade to what was known or written about him or her: he challenges his readers to be like himself, so immersed in the classics, the Bible, myth, history and thirteenth-century art and politics that they become emotional, life-and-death concerns. The portraits are striking in their own right, but the more we know about their models the more profound and far-reaching are the moral and ethical dilemmas they embody.

We unravel the meaning of each circle of Hell through the souls we are told it contains, by the dramatic encounters the two pilgrims have with certain of these souls, by the particular guardian (usually a mythological monster) assigned to each, by the particular landscape, by the style of the language, which ranges from the sublimity of epic to the simplicity of lyric to the earthiness of the folk tale, and by the nature of the torment. One soul terms Hell's torments the *contrapasso,* or counter-punishment. The principle of *contrapasso* is poetic justice: each soul receives what he or she most desired or did on earth, but in a perverse and unwanted form— the flatterers drown in excrement; the sowers of discord are split asunder. There is a tension throughout *Inferno* between the moral lessons we are to learn from the damned characters, and the fascination many of them exert on us, both positive and negative, in their quality as stubbornly alive and suffering individuals.

Many of the damned serve to demonstrate that there is a danger in knowing Hell too well. The underworld offers great temptation for rage and revenge, and it contains much of apparent pleasure and beauty as well: the worthies of Limbo, Francesca's love, Dante's mentor Brunetto Latini, the doting father of his friend and fellow poet Cavalcanti. This will also be a dilemma in *Purgatorio,* where the souls, although saved, must suffer much in weaning themselves from their ties to the world they loved, but in the *Inferno* the dilemma takes a starker form. The stakes are very high, not just for individuals but for society, and Dante is also careful to indicate which parts of Hell cause particular trouble, either to him or to his society: sins of desire, which are so close to the love and longing that can lead one to God; the complex and subdivided sins of fraud in the eighth circle, which attack the very bonds of sociability on which community relies. Dante doesn't want us to submit meekly to the journey through Hell; he expects us to go through it kicking and screaming, arguing and cursing, although he also expects that in the end he will win us over, as in the end he has won over himself.

PRONUNCIATIONS:

Beatrice: BAY-ah-TREE-che
Commedia: koh-ME-dee-ah
Contrapasso: kohn-trah-PAH-soh
Francesca: frahn-CHES-kah
Inferno: een-FAYR-noh
Guido Cavalcanti: GWEE-doh kah-vahl-KAHN-tee

La Vita Nuova: lah VEE-tah noo-OH-vah
Paradiso: pah-rah-DEE-soh
Purgatorio: poor-gah-TOR-ee-oh
terra rima: TAYR-tazh REE-mah
Ugolino: oo-goh-LEE-noh

Canto 1

The voyager-narrator astray by night in a dark forest. Morning and the sunlit hill. Three beasts that impede his ascent. The encounter with Virgil, who offers his guidance and an alternative path through two of the three realms the voyager must visit.

When I had journeyed half of our life's way,[2]
I found myself within a shadowed forest,

2. Canto 21.112–14 establishes the date of the journey as Easter weekend of 1300, the entry into the dark wood on the night of Maundy Thursday, the day before Good Friday. Born in 1265, Dante would have been 35, precisely midway in the biblical life span of 70 years. The adjective "our" expands the individual journey to one that involves the reader in an allegory of every person's life.

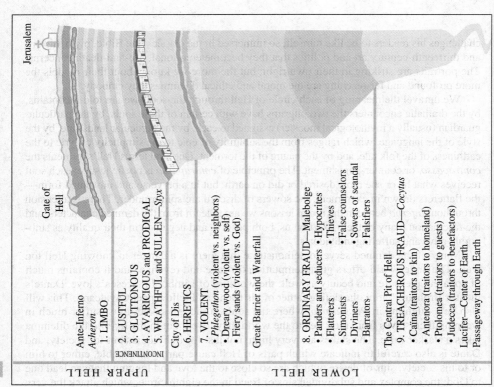

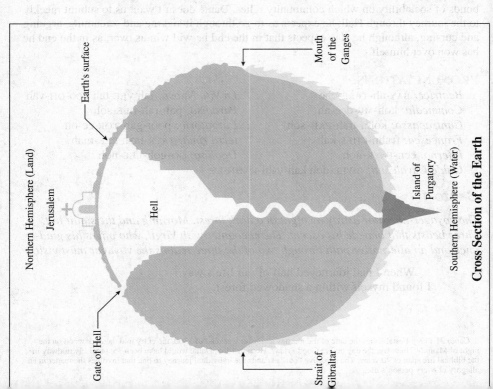

Cross Section of the Earth

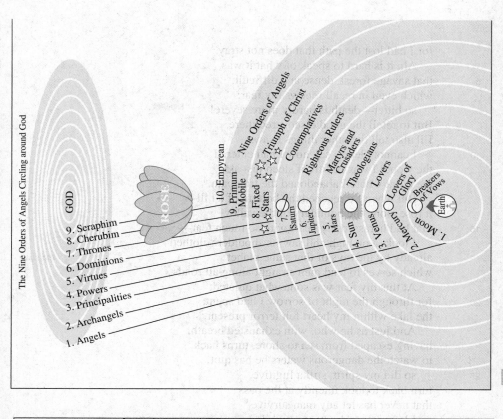

The Nine Orders of Angels Circling around God

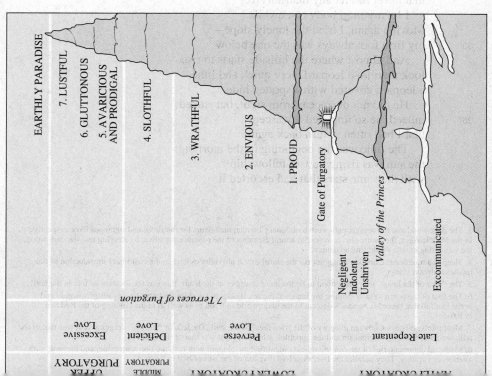

for I had lost the path that does not stray.[3]
  Ah, it is hard to speak of what it was,
that savage forest, dense and difficult,
which even in recall renews my fear:

  so bitter—death is hardly more severe!
But to retell the good discovered there,
I'll also tell the other things I saw.

  I cannot clearly say how I had entered
the wood; I was so full of sleep just at
the point where I abandoned the true path.[4]

  But when I'd reached the bottom of a hill—
it rose along the boundary of the valley
that had harassed my heart with so much fear—

  I looked on high and saw its shoulders clothed
already by the rays of that same planet°   *the sun*
which serves to lead men straight along all roads.

  At this my fear was somewhat quieted;
for through the night of sorrow I had spent,
the lake within my heart felt terror present.[5]

  And just as he who, with exhausted breath,
having escaped from sea to shore, turns back
to watch the dangerous waters he has quit,

  so did my spirit, still a fugitive,
turn back to look intently at the pass
that never has let any man survive.[6]

  I let my tired body rest awhile.
Moving again, I tried the lonely slope—
my firm foot always was the one below.[7]

  And almost where the hillside starts to rise—
look there!—a leopard, very quick and lithe,
a leopard covered with a spotted hide.[8]

  He did not disappear from sight, but stayed;
indeed, he so impeded my ascent
that I had often to turn back again.

  The time was the beginning of the morning;
the sun was rising now in fellowship
with the same stars that had escorted it

---

3. The dark wood and the straight path were traditional Christian metaphors for the sinful and righteous lives, respectively. In the Middle Ages, they were also common structural elements of the romance narrative: by straying into the dark wood, the wandering knight would find adventure.

4. Sleep is a traditional Christian metaphor for the sinful life; it also alludes here to the customary introduction of the medieval dream vision.

5. The "lake of the heart" was understood to be the inner chamber of the heart; this was the location of fear in the body.

6. The first of the poem's many similes: the image of the sea alludes to the shipwreck that begins Virgil's *Aeneid* and to the landfall that precedes Aeneas's descent to the underworld in Book 6, as well as to the crossing of the Red Sea in Exodus.

7. Most likely, this is a Christian allegory of the "two feet" of the soul. The left, or "firmer," dragging foot was that of the will, weighed down by original sin and the appetites, while the right was that of the intellect.

8. Medieval commentaries of the *Inferno* quickly identified the leopard with lust, the lion with pride, and the wolf with avarice, or cupidity. They parallel the later threefold division of the sins of hell in Canto 11.

40   when Divine Love first moved those things of beauty;[9]
      so that the hour and the gentle season
      gave me good cause for hopefulness on seeing

      that beast before me with his speckled skin;
      but hope was hardly able to prevent
45   the fear I felt when I beheld a lion.

      His head held high and ravenous with hunger—
      even the air around him seemed to shudder—
      this lion seemed to make his way against me.

      And then a she-wolf showed herself; she seemed
50   to carry every craving in her leanness;
      she had already brought despair to many.

      The very sight of her so weighted me
      with fearfulness that I abandoned hope
      of ever climbing up that mountain slope.

55   Even as he who glories while he gains
      will, when the time has come to tally loss,
      lament with every thought and turn despondent,

      so was I when I faced that restless beast,
      which, even as she stalked me, step by step
60   had thrust me back to where the sun is speechless.

      While I retreated down to lower ground,
      before my eyes there suddenly appeared
      one who seemed faint because of the long silence.

      When I saw him in that vast wilderness,
65   "Have pity on me," were the words I cried,
      "whatever you may be—a shade, a man."

      He answered me: "Not man; I once was man.
      Both of my parents came from Lombardy,
      and both claimed Mantua as native city.

70   And I was born, though late, *sub Julio,*
      and lived in Rome under the good Augustus—
      the season of the false and lying gods.

      I was a poet, and I sang the righteous
      son of Anchises who had come from Troy
75   when flames destroyed the pride of Ilium.[1]

      But why do you return to wretchedness?
      Why not climb up the mountain of delight,
      the origin and cause of every joy?"

      "And are you then that Virgil, you the fountain
80   that freely pours so rich a stream of speech?"
      I answered him with shame upon my brow.
      "O light and honor of all other poets,

---

9. The world was believed to have been created in spring, when the sun was in the constellation of Ares; Dante's journey takes place in the same season and under the same stars.

1. Virgil (70–19 B.C.E.) was born during the lifetime of Julius Caesar, who was assassinated in 44, too soon to have known the poet's writing. Virgil's patron was Caesar's adopted son, the emperor Augustus. Virgil identifies himself with his final work, the mythical epic of Aeneas, the "righteous son of Anchises," who journeyed from the destruction of Troy ("Ilium") to Italy to found the city of Rome.

may my long study and the intense love
that made me search your volume serve me now.

85   You are my master and my author, you—
the only one from whom my writing drew
the noble style for which I have been honored.

You see the beast that made me turn aside;
help me, o famous sage, to stand against her,
90   for she has made my blood and pulses shudder."

"It is another path that you must take,"
he answered when he saw my tearfulness,
"if you would leave this savage wilderness;

the beast that is the cause of your outcry
95   allows no man to pass along her track,
but blocks him even to the point of death;

her nature is so squalid, so malicious
that she can never sate her greedy will;
when she has fed, she's hungrier than ever.

100   She mates with many living souls and shall
yet mate with many more, until the Greyhound
arrives, inflicting painful death on her.

That Hound will never feed on land or pewter,
but find his fare in wisdom, love, and virtue;
105   his place of birth shall be between two felts.[2]

He will restore low-lying Italy
for which the maid Camilla died of wounds,
and Nisus, Turnus, and Euryalus.[3]

And he will hunt that beast through every city
110   until he thrusts her back again to Hell,
from which she was first sent above by envy.[4]

Therefore, I think and judge it best for you
to follow me, and I shall guide you, taking
you from this place through an eternal place,

115   where you shall hear the howls of desperation
and see the ancient spirits in their pain,
as each of them laments his second death;[5]

and you shall see those souls who are content
within the fire,° for they hope to reach—   ° of Purgatory
120   whenever that may be—the blessed people.

If you would then ascend as high as these,

---

2. Virgil explains the she-wolf's sway by means of the first of the poem's many prophecies. The poetical aptness of a Greyhound (*veltro*) to hunt down and kill the she-wolf is clear; possible identities are many and not mutually exclusive. There is some reference to the redemptive powers of Christ, but also to the desired coming of a secular leader who would be above corruption, seeking neither land nor money ("pewter"), and who would reestablish temporal authority in Christendom: perhaps Dante's benefactor Can Grande della Scala of Verona, whose domain was roughly limited by the two "felts" (*Feltros*) of Feltre and Montefeltro, perhaps a Holy Roman Emperor, elected by the casting of ballots in the felt-lined urns used at the time.

3. Virgil refers to Italy in terms of his own epic of the founding of the classical Roman empire, alluding to four characters who died in the civil war for the possession of Italy related in the second half of the *Aeneid*.

4. "But by the envy of the devil, death entered the world" (Wisdom 2:24).

5. Either the condemnation of the soul to hell after death, or the final condemnation to hell and reunion with the body that will occur during the Last Judgment.

a soul more worthy than I am will guide you;
I'll leave you in her care when I depart,
　　because that Emperor who reigns above,
125　since I have been rebellious to His law,
will not allow me entry to His city.
　　He governs everywhere, but rules from there;
there is His city, His high capital:
O happy those He chooses to be there!"
130　　　And I replied: "O poet—by that God
whom you had never come to know—I beg you,
that I may flee this evil and worse evils,
　　to lead me to the place of which you spoke,
that I may see the gateway of Saint Peter[6]
135　and those whom you describe as sorrowful."
　　　Then he set out, and I moved on behind him.

Canto 2

The following evening. Invocation to the Muses. The narrator's questioning of his worthiness to visit the deathless world. Virgil's comforting explanation that he has been sent to help Dante by three Ladies of Heaven. The voyager heartened. Their setting out.

　　　The day was now departing; the dark air
released the living beings of the earth
from work and weariness; and I myself
　　alone prepared to undergo the battle
5　both of the journeying and of the pity,
which memory, mistaking not, shall show.
　　　O Muses, o high genius, help me now;
O memory that set down what I saw,
here shall your excellence reveal itself![1]
10　　　I started: "Poet, you who are my guide,
see if the force in me is strong enough
before you let me face that rugged pass.
　　　You say that he who fathered Sylvius,
while he was still corruptible, had journeyed
15　into the deathless world with his live body.[2]
　　　For, if the Enemy of every evil
was courteous to him, considering
all he would cause and who and what he was,
　　that does not seem incomprehensible,
20　since in the empyrean heaven he was chosen
to father honored Rome and her empire;
　　　and if the truth be told, Rome and her realm

6. Either the gate of Purgatory or the entry to Paradise.

1. Echoes of the *Aeneid* continue: the invocation of the classical muses was a staple of the epic style. Dante adds the stress on the poet's memory of what he has seen.

2. In lines 13–27, Dante retells the story of *Aeneid* 6 in a Christian context. While still alive, Aeneas (father of Sylvius, ancestor of the founder of Rome) descended to the underworld, which included both a place of punishment and a paradise, in order to meet his father and learn the fate of his descendants.

were destined to become the sacred place,
the seat of the successor° of great Peter.   *the Pope*

25   And through the journey you ascribe to him,
he came to learn of things that were to bring
his victory and, too, the papal mantle.[3]

Later the Chosen Vessel travelled there,
to bring us back assurance of that faith

30   with which the way to our salvation starts.[4]

But why should I go there? Who sanctions it?
For I am not Aeneas, am not Paul;
nor I nor others think myself so worthy.

Therefore, if I consent to start this journey,

35   I fear my venture may be wild and empty.
You're wise; you know far more than what I say."

And just as he who unwills what he wills
and shifts what he intends to seek new ends
so that he's drawn from what he had begun,

40   so was I in the midst of that dark land,
because, with all my thinking, I annulled
the task I had so quickly undertaken.

"If I have understood what you have said,"
replied the shade of that great-hearted one,

45   "your soul has been assailed by cowardice,
which often weighs so heavily on a man—
distracting him from honorable trials—
as phantoms frighten beasts when shadows fall.

That you may be delivered from this fear,

50   I'll tell you why I came and what I heard
when I first felt compassion for your pain.[5]

I was among those souls who are suspended;°   *in Limbo*
a lady called to me, so blessed, so lovely
that I implored to serve at her command.

55   Her eyes surpassed the splendor of the star's;
and she began to speak to me—so gently
and softly—with angelic voice. She said:

'O spirit of the courteous Mantuan,
whose fame is still a presence in the world

60   and shall endure as long as the world lasts,

my friend, who has not been the friend of fortune,
is hindered in his path along that lonely
hillside; he has been turned aside by terror.

From all that I have heard of him in Heaven,

---

3. Aeneas's father gave him advice on the upcoming war and showed his son a procession of souls of future Romans that forecast the empire of Augustus; in Dante's version it also forecasts papal Rome.

4. The apostle Paul ("the Chosen Vessel") described in his second Epistle to the Corinthians (12.2–4) how he was "caught up into Paradise"; the apocryphal *Vision of St. Paul* narrates a descent into hell as well.

5. Virgil explains how he came to appear before Dante and provides a "divine" authorization for the journey (and the poem) that follows. The language of the account is less that of the high style of the *Aeneid* than of the lyric of courtly love.

65	he is, I fear, already so astray
	that I have come to help him much too late.
	Go now; with your persuasive word, with
	all that is required to see that he escapes,
	bring help to him, that I may be consoled.
70	For I am Beatrice who send you on;
	I come from where I most long to return;
	Love prompted me, that Love which makes me speak.
	When once again I stand before my Lord,
	then I shall often let Him hear your praises.'
75	Now Beatrice was silent. I began:
	'O Lady of virtue, the sole reason why
	the human race surpasses all that lies
	beneath the heaven with the smallest spheres,
	so welcome is your wish, that even if
80	it were already done, it would seem tardy;
	all you need do is let me know your will.
	But tell me why you have not been more prudent—
	descending to this center, moving from
	that spacious place where you long to return?'
85	'Because you want to fathom things so deeply,
	I now shall tell you promptly,' she replied,
	'why I am not afraid to enter here.
	One ought to be afraid of nothing other
	than things possessed of power to do us harm,
90	but things innocuous need not be feared.
	God, in His graciousness, has made me so
	that this, your misery, cannot touch me;
	I can withstand the fires flaming here.[6]
	In Heaven there's a gentle lady—one
95	who weeps for the distress toward which I send you,
	so that stern judgment up above is shattered.
	And it was she who called upon Lucia,[7]
	requesting of her: "Now your faithful one
	has need of you, and I commend him to you."
100	Lucia, enemy of every cruelty,
	arose and made her way to where I was,
	sitting beside the venerable Rachel.[8]
	She said: "You, Beatrice, true praise of God,
	why have you not helped him who loves you so
105	that—for your sake—he's left the vulgar crowd?
	Do you not hear the anguish in his cry?
	Do you not see the death he wars against
	upon that river ruthless as the sea?"
	No one within this world has ever been

6. Neither the fires of hell nor the damned have the power physically to harm any of the blessed, nor do their sufferings deserve any compassion—a cornerstone of Catholic doctrine that Dante sorely tests in the *Inferno*.

7. St. Lucy of Syracuse, a late-3rd-century virgin martyr who is patron saint of sight, and a symbol of illuminating grace.

8. Beatrice has her seat in heaven next to Rachel, younger sister of Leah in Genesis, and beloved of Jacob.

110   so quick to seek his good or flee his harm
        as I—when she had finished speaking thus—
            to come below, down from my blessed station;
        I trusted in your honest utterance,
        which honors you and those who've listened to you.'
115   When she had finished with her words to me,
        she turned aside her gleaming, tearful eyes,
        which only made me hurry all the more.
            And, just as she had wished, I came to you:
        I snatched you from the path of the fierce beast
120   that barred the shortest way up the fair mountain.
            What is it then? Why, why do you resist?
        Why does your heart host so much cowardice?
        Where are your daring and your openness
            as long as there are three such blessed women
125   concerned for you within the court of Heaven
        and my words promise you so great a good?"
            As little flowers, which the chill of night
        has bent and huddled, when the white sun strikes,
        grow straight and open fully on their stems,
130   so did I, too, with my exhausted force;
        and such warm daring rushed into my heart
        that I—as one who has been freed—began:
            "O she, compassionate, who has helped me!
        And you who, courteous, obeyed so quickly
135   the true words that she had addressed to you!
            You, with your words, have so disposed my heart
        to longing for this journey—I return
        to what I was at first prepared to do.
            Now go; a single will fills both of us:
140   you are my guide, my governor, my master."
        These were my words to him; when he advanced,
            I entered on the steep and savage path.

Canto 3

The inscription above the Gate of Hell. The Ante-Inferno, where the shades of those who lived without praise and without blame now intermingle with the neutral angels. He who made the great refusal. The River Acheron. Charon. Dante's loss of his senses as the earth trembles.

THROUGH ME THE WAY INTO THE SUFFERING CITY,
THROUGH ME THE WAY TO THE ETERNAL PAIN,
THROUGH ME THE WAY THAT RUNS AMONG THE LOST.
JUSTICE URGED ON MY HIGH ARTIFICER;
5   MY MAKER WAS DIVINE AUTHORITY,
THE HIGHEST WISDOM, AND THE PRIMAL LOVE.
BEFORE ME NOTHING BUT ETERNAL THINGS
WERE MADE, AND I ENDURE ETERNALLY.

ABANDON EVERY HOPE, WHO ENTER HERE.[1]

10   These words—their aspect was obscure—I read
inscribed above a gateway, and I said:
"Master, their meaning is difficult for me."
    And he to me, as one who comprehends:
"Here one must leave behind all hesitation;
15   here every cowardice must meet its death.
    For we have reached the place of which I spoke,
where you will see the miserable people,
those who have lost the good of the intellect."[2]
    And when, with gladness in his face, he placed
20   his hand upon my own, to comfort me,
he drew me in among the hidden things.
    Here sighs and lamentations and loud cries
were echoing across the starless air,
so that, as soon as I set out, I wept.
25   Strange utterances, horrible pronouncements,
accents of anger, words of suffering,
and voices shrill and faint, and beating hands—
    all went to make a tumult that will whirl
forever through that turbid, timeless air,
30   like sand that eddies when a whirlwind swirls.
    And I—my head oppressed by horror—said:
"Master, what is it that I hear? Who are
those people so defeated by their pain?"
    And he to me: "This miserable way
35   is taken by the sorry souls of those
who lived without disgrace and without praise.
    They now commingle with the coward angels,
the company of those who were not rebels
nor faithful to their God, but stood apart.
40   The heavens, that their beauty not be lessened,
have cast them out, nor will deep Hell receive them—
even the wicked cannot glory in them."[3]
    And I: "What is it, master, that oppresses
these souls, compelling them to wail so loud?"
45   He answered: "I shall tell you in few words.
    Those who are here can place no hope in death,
and their blind life is so abject that they
are envious of every other fate.
    The world will let no fame of theirs endure;

---

1. The famous inscription on the Gate of Hell announces several key laws of the realm: it is the negative counterpart to the city of God, but also created by divine order, subject to the Lord's authority, and ruled by justice and love. Evil is not independent from, but somehow part of the divine scheme since it was first created by Satan's rebellion at the beginning of time.

2. The rules may be clear, but their meaning is not. Virgil gives a first definition of the state of damnation: those ruled by their appetites rather than their reason. Truth, following Aristotle, is the good of the intellect; for Dante the highest good is God.

3. Dante invented a category of souls who belong neither in Heaven nor in Hell properly speaking: the "lukewarm," grouped with the neutral angels, those who neither rebelled with Satan nor sided with God.

50 both justice and compassion must disdain them;
    let us not talk of them, but look and pass."[4]
        And I, looking more closely, saw a banner
    that, as it wheeled about, raced on—so quick
    that any respite seemed unsuited to it.
55   Behind that banner trailed so long a file
    of people—I should never have believed
    that death could have unmade so many souls.
        After I had identified a few,
    I saw and recognized the shade of him
60 who made, through cowardice, the great refusal.[5]
        At once I understood with certainty:
    this company contained the cowardly,
    hateful to God and to His enemies.
        These wretched ones, who never were alive,
65 went naked and were stung again, again
    by horseflies and by wasps that circled them.
        The insects streaked their faces with their blood,
    which, mingled with their tears, fell at their feet,
    where it was gathered up by sickening worms.
70   And then, looking beyond them, I could see
    a crowd along the bank of a great river;
    at which I said: "Allow me now to know
        who are these people—master—and what law
    has made them seem so eager for the crossing,
75 as I can see despite the feeble light."
        And he to me: "When we have stopped along
    the melancholy shore of Acheron,°   *a river of Hell*
    then all these matters will be plain to you."
        At that, with eyes ashamed, downcast, and fearing
80 that what I said had given him offense,
    I did not speak until we reached the river.
        And here, advancing toward us, in a boat,
    an aged man—his hair was white with years[6]—
    was shouting: "Woe to you, corrupted souls!
85   Forget your hope of ever seeing Heaven:
    I come to lead you to the other shore,
    to the eternal dark, to fire and frost.
        And you approaching there, you living soul,
    keep well away from these—they are the dead."
90 But when he saw I made no move to go,
        he said: "Another way and other harbors—

---

4. Here the poetically apt punishment consists of the complete lack of fame for those who made no choices in life, and of goading insects and speeding banners, since they would not be goaded and chose no banners.

5. The one soul singled out among the lukewarm, fittingly, is not named. Early commentators mostly agreed he was Pope Celestine V, who abdicated ("the great refusal") only five months after his election as pope in 1294, allowing the election of Boniface VIII, pope from 1294 to 1303, one of the arch-villains of the *Commedia*.

6. The first figure out of pagan mythology encountered in Hell, the ferryman Charon was the son of Erebus and Night.

not here—will bring you passage to your shore:
a lighter craft will have to carry you."

My guide then: "Charon, don't torment yourself:
95 our passage has been willed above, where One[7]
can do what He has willed; and ask no more."

Now silence fell upon the wooly cheeks
of Charon, pilot of the livid marsh,
whose eyes were ringed about with wheels of flame.

100 But all those spirits, naked and exhausted,
had lost their color, and they gnashed their teeth
as soon as they heard Charon's cruel words;

they execrated God and their own parents
and humankind, and then the place and time
105 of their conception's seed and of their birth.

Then they forgathered, huddled in one throng,
weeping aloud along that wretched shore
which waits for all who have no fear of God.

The demon Charon, with his eyes like embers,
110 by signaling to them, has all embark;
his oar strikes anyone who stretches out.

As, in the autumn, leaves detach themselves,
first one and then the other, till the bough
sees all its fallen garments on the ground,[8]

115 similarly, the evil seed of Adam
descended from the shoreline one by one,
when signaled, as a falcon—called—will come.[9]

So do they move across the darkened waters;
even before they reach the farther shore,
120 new ranks already gather on this bank.

"My son," the gracious master said to me,
"those who have died beneath the wrath of God,
all these assemble here from every country;

and they are eager for the river crossing
125 because celestial justice spurs them on,
so that their fear is turned into desire.

No good soul ever takes its passage here;
therefore, if Charon has complained of you,
by now you can be sure what his words mean."

130 And after this was said, the darkened plain
quaked so tremendously—the memory
of terror then, bathes me in sweat again.

A whirlwind burst out of the tear-drenched earth,
a wind that crackled with a bloodred light,
135 a light that overcame all of my senses;
and like a man whom sleep has seized, I fell.

---

7. God, Christ, and the Holy Spirit are never named in Hell directly.
8. The simile of autumn leaves to describe dead souls reworks that of *Aeneid* 6.309–12.
9. A simile from medieval falconry: the moment when the falcon is lured down by the hunter.

Canto 4

Dante's awakening to the First Circle, or Limbo, inhabited by those who were worthy but lived before Christianity and/or without baptism. The welcoming of Virgil and Dante by Homer, Horace, Ovid, Lucan. The catalogue of other great-hearted spirits in the noble castle of Limbo.

    The heavy sleep within my head was smashed
by an enormous thunderclap, so that
I started up as one whom force awakens;

    I stood erect and turned my rested eyes
5   from side to side, and I stared steadily
to learn what place it was surrounding me.

    In truth I found myself upon the brink
of an abyss, the melancholy valley
containing thundering, unending wailings.

10   That valley, dark and deep and filled with mist,
is such that, though I gazed into its pit,
I was unable to discern a thing.[1]

    "Let us descend into the blind world now,"[2]
the poet, who was deathly pale, began;
15   "I shall go first and you will follow me."

    But I, who'd seen the change in his complexion,
said: "How shall I go on if you are frightened,
you who have always helped dispel my doubts?"

    And he to me: "The anguish of the people
20   whose place is here below, has touched my face
with the compassion you mistake for fear.

    Let us go on, the way that waits is long."
So he set out, and so he had me enter
on that first circle girdling the abyss.[3]

25   Here, for as much as hearing could discover,
there was no outcry louder than the sighs
that caused the everlasting air to tremble.

    The sighs arose from sorrow without torments,
out of the crowds—the many multitudes—
30   of infants and of women and of men.

    The kindly master said: "Do you not ask
who are these spirits whom you see before you?
I'd have you know, before you go ahead,

    they did not sin; and yet, though they have merits,
35   that's not enough, because they lacked baptism,
the portal of the faith that you embrace.

    And if they lived before Christianity,

---

1. The first glimpse of the geography of Hell proper. The pit was a standard component of medieval hells; the conelike valley the pilgrim will encounter was not.

2. Blind because bereft of sun and stars, and blind because bereft of spiritual clarity.

3. The first circle of Hell is Limbo, according to doctrine the place of children who died before baptism and of righteous Old Testament figures who lived before the coming of Christ. Dante took the liberty of adding a new category: the virtuous pagans, whose number includes Virgil.

they did not worship God in fitting ways;
and of such spirits I myself am one.

40   For these defects, and for no other evil,
we now are lost and punished just with this:
we have no hope and yet we live in longing."

    Great sorrow seized my heart on hearing him,
for I had seen some estimable men
45 among the souls suspended in that limbo.

    "Tell me, my master, tell me, lord," I then
began because I wanted to be certain
of that belief which vanquishes all errors,

    "did any ever go—by his own merit
50 or others'—from this place toward blessedness?"
And he, who understood my covert speech,[4]

    replied: "I was new-entered on this state
when I beheld a Great Lord enter here;
the crown he wore, a sign of victory.[5]

55   He carried off the shade of our first father,°   *Adam*
of his son Abel, and the shade of Noah,
of Moses, the obedient legislator,

    of father Abraham, David the king,
of Israel,° his father, and his sons,   *Jacob*
60 and Rachel, she for whom he worked so long,

    and many others—and He made them blessed;
and I should have you know that, before them,
there were no human souls that had been saved."

    We did not stay our steps although he spoke;
65 we still continued onward through the wood—
the wood, I say, where many spirits thronged.

    Our path had not gone far beyond the point
where I had slept, when I beheld a fire
win out against a hemisphere of shadows.

70   We still were at a little distance from it,
but not so far I could not see in part
that honorable men possessed that place.

    "O you who honor art and science both,
who are these souls whose dignity has kept
75 their way of being, separate from the rest?"

    And he to me: "The honor of their name,
which echoes up above within your life,
gains Heaven's grace, and that advances them."

    Meanwhile there was a voice that I could hear:
80 "Pay honor to the estimable poet;
his shadow, which had left us, now returns."

    After that voice was done, when there was silence,

---

4. The pilgrim wants to ask whether Virgil, his guide, can be saved. He doesn't receive the answer he desires.

5. The apocryphal Gospel of Nicodemus tells that between his crucifixion on Good Friday and his resurrection on Easter Sunday, Christ descended into Limbo and took its Old Testament figures with him up to Heaven. The Harrowing of Hell was proclaimed as dogma during the 13th century. Virgil died in 19 B.C.E.; hence he was newly arrived when Christ descended in 33 C.E.

I saw four giant shades approaching us;
in aspect, they were neither sad nor joyous.

85   My kindly master then began by saying:
"Look well at him who holds that sword in hand,
who moves before the other three as lord.

That shade is Homer, the consummate poet;
the other one is Horace, satirist;
90   the third is Ovid, and the last is Lucan.[6]

Because each of these spirits shares with me
the name called out before by the lone voice,
they welcome me—and, doing that, do well."

And so I saw that splendid school assembled,
95   led by the lord of song incomparable,°   *Homer*
who like an eagle soars above the rest.

Soon after they had talked a while together,
they turned to me, saluting cordially;
and having witnessed this, my master smiled;

100   and even greater honor then was mine,
for they invited me to join their ranks—
I was the sixth among such intellects.

So did we move along and toward the light,
talking of things about which silence here
105   is just as seemly as our speech was there.

We reached the base of an exalted castle,
encircled seven times by towering walls,
defended all around by a fair stream.[7]

We forded this as if upon hard ground;
110   I entered seven portals with these sages;
we reached a meadow of green flowering plants.

The people here had eyes both grave and slow;
their features carried great authority;
they spoke infrequently, with gentle voices.

115   We drew aside to one part of the meadow,
an open place both high and filled with light,
and we could see all those who were assembled.[8]

Facing me there, on the enameled green,
great-hearted souls were shown to me and I
120   still glory in my having witnessed them.

I saw Electra with her many comrades,
among whom I knew Hector and Aeneas,

---

6. Dante produces a pantheon of classical poets. Homer was known only by reputation in Dante's time. Virgil's friend and contemporary, Horace (65–8 B.C.E), is remembered here for his *Satires* and *Epistles*. Ovid (43 B.C.E–17 C.E.) and Lucan (39–65 C.E.) are the two classical poets Dante cites most frequently after Virgil, from Ovid primarily his epic compilation of myth, the *Metamorphoses,* and from Lucan his violent epic on the civil war between Caesar and Pompey, *De bello civili,* or *Pharsalia.*

7. The castle's form is allegorically related to the seven liberal arts and the tradition of the House of Fame, suitable for a group distinguished by their achievements in the arts, in heroism and in proper living but not in the faith required by Christian doctrine.

8. The description of the meadow enclosed by the castle walls is reminiscent of the Elysian Fields of Virgil's underworld, as well as of the *locus amoenus,* or "pleasing place" of courtly romances such as *The Romance of the Rose.* The list of "great-hearted souls" he meets blends mythical and historical, classical and medieval personages.

and Caesar, in his armor, falcon-eyed.[9]
I saw Camilla and Penthesilea
125 and, on the other side, saw King Latinus,
who sat beside Lavinia, his daughter.[1]
I saw that Brutus who drove Tarquin out,
Lucretia, Julia, Marcia, and Cornelia,
and, solitary, set apart, Saladin.[2]
130 When I had raised my eyes a little higher,
I saw the master of the men who know,
seated in philosophic family.[3]
There all look up to him, all do him honor:
there I beheld both Socrates and Plato,
135 closest to him, in front of all the rest;
Democritus, who ascribes the world to chance,
Diogenes, Empedocles, and Zeno,
and Thales, Anaxagoras, Heraclitus;
I saw the good collector of medicinals,
140 I mean Dioscorides; and I saw Orpheus,
and Tully, Linus, moral Seneca;[4]
and Euclid the geometer, and Ptolemy,
Hippocrates and Galen, Avicenna,
Averroës, of the great Commentary.[5]
145 I cannot here describe them all in full;
my ample theme impels me onward so:
what's told is often less than the event.
The company of six divides in two;
my knowing guide leads me another way,
150 beyond the quiet, into trembling air.
And I have reached a part where no thing gleams.

Canto 5

*The Second Circle, where the Lustful are forever buffeted by violent storm. Minos.
The catalogue of carnal sinners. Francesca da Rimini and her brother-in-law, Paolo
Malatesta. Francesca's tale of their love and death, at which Dante faints.*

9. The origins and apogee of Rome: Electra was mother of Dardanus, founder of Troy. Hector was the leader of the Trojan forces, the survivors of which Aeneas led to Italy. Caesar founded the imperial line of Rome.

1. Camilla and Penthesilea were female warriors. Latinus was king of Latium; the betrothal of his daughter Lavinia to Aeneas caused Turnus to begin the civil war.

2. Lucius Junius Brutus drove out Tarquin, the last of the legendary Roman kings, in 510 B.C.E. to become one of the first two consuls of the Roman republic. Four female exemplars of Roman virtue are then listed, followed by the Sultan of Egypt from 1171 to 1193, Saladin, who crushingly defeated the Crusaders, but whose magnanimity and generosity were a medieval commonplace.

3. The list of philosophers begins with Aristotle, so influential in Dante's time he need not be named, followed by Socrates, Plato, and seven other celebrated ancient Greek philosophers.

4. Dioscorides was a Greek physician of the 1st century C.E.; Linus and Orpheus were mythical Greek poets; Tully is the Roman orator and philosopher Marcus Tullius Cicero (106–43 B.C.E.), Seneca the moral philosopher and writer of tragedies who committed suicide at the command of Nero in 65 C.E.

5. The mathematician Euclid lived c. 300 B.C.E.; the geocentric theory of his fellow Alexandrian, the astronomer and geographer Ptolemy, who was active in the 2nd century C.E., was the basis of medieval astronomy. Hippocrates and Galen were Greek physicians. Avicenna (980–1037) and Averroës (1126–1198) were Muslim philosophers, both authors of influential commentaries on Aristotle.

So I descended from the first enclosure
down to the second circle, that which girdles
less space but grief more great,[1] that goads to weeping.

There dreadful Minos stands, gnashing his teeth:

5   examining the sins of those who enter,
he judges and assigns as his tail twines.[2]

I mean that when the spirit born to evil
appears before him, it confesses all;
and he, the connoisseur of sin, can tell

10   the depth in Hell appropriate to it;
as many times as Minos wraps his tail
around himself, that marks the sinner's level.

Always there is a crowd that stands before him:
each soul in turn advances toward that judgment;

15   they speak and hear, then they are cast below.

Arresting his extraordinary task,
Minos, as soon as he had seen me, said:
"O you who reach this house of suffering,
be careful how you enter, whom you trust;

20   the gate is wide, but do not be deceived!"
To which my guide replied: "But why protest?

Do not attempt to block his fated path:
our passage has been willed above, where One
can do what He has willed; and ask no more."

25   Now notes of desperation have begun
to overtake my hearing; now I come
where mighty lamentation beats against me.

I reached a place where every light is muted,
which bellows like the sea beneath a tempest,

30   when it is battered by opposing winds.

The hellish hurricane, which never rests,
drives on the spirits with its violence:
wheeling and pounding, it harasses them.

When they come up against the ruined slope,

35   then there are cries and wailing and lament,
and there they curse the force of the divine.

I learned that those who undergo this torment
are damned because they sinned within the flesh,
subjecting reason to the rule of lust.

40   And as, in the cold season, starlings' wings
bear them along in broad and crowded ranks,
so does that blast bear on the guilty spirits:
now here, now there, now down, now up, it drives them.

There is no hope that ever comforts them—

---

1. Although separated from the rest of Hell by the guardian and judge Minos, Limbo is called the first circle. The second circle, where the Lustful are punished, "girdles less space" because the cone shape of Hell narrows as it descends.

2. Minos was legendary king of Crete, and with his brother Rhadamanthus judge in Virgil's underworld. The tail, however, is a Dantesque touch that makes Minos more monster and less king, imitating the spiraling structure of Hell.

45   no hope for rest and none for lesser pain.

        And just as cranes in flight will chant their lays,
    arraying their long file across the air,
    so did the shades I saw approaching, borne

        by that assailing wind, lament and moan;
50   so that I asked him: "Master, who are those
    who suffer punishment in this dark air?"

        "The first of those about whose history
    you want to know," my master then told me,
    "once ruled as empress over many nations.

55   Her vice of lust became so customary
    that she made license licit in her laws
    to free her from the scandal she had caused.

        She is Semíramis, of whom we read
    that she was Ninus' wife and his successor:
60   she held the land the Sultan now commands.[3]

        That other spirit killed herself for love,
    and she betrayed the ashes of Sychaeus;[4]
    the wanton Cleopatra follows next.[5]

        See Helen, for whose sake so many years
65   of evil had to pass; see great Achilles,
    who finally met love—in his last battle.[6]

        See Paris, Tristan..."—and he pointed out
    and named to me more than a thousand shades
    departed from our life because of love.

70   No sooner had I heard my teacher name
    the ancient ladies and the knights, than pity
    seized me, and I was like a man astray.

        My first words: "Poet, I should willingly
    speak with those two who go together there
75   and seem so lightly carried by the wind."[7]

        And he to me: "You'll see when they draw closer
    to us, and then you may appeal to them

3. In Dante's time, Egypt was under the rule of the Sultan. There is some confusion here because Egypt was fairly distant from the Mesopotamian kingdom of Assyria, supposedly founded by Ninus and the lustful Semiramis.

4. Curiously, Virgil does not name Dido, whose story he had related in one of the most celebrated parts of the *Aeneid*. Sychaeus was Dido's husband, murdered by her brother Pygmalion, king of Tyre. Dido fled to North Africa, where she founded the city of Carthage, and, according to *Aeneid* 4, was seduced and abandoned by Aeneas, after which she killed herself in despair.

5. Cleopatra was the queen of Egypt of legendary beauty who was the lover first of Julius Caesar and then of Marc Antony, with whom she was defeated at the battle of Actium in 29 B.C.E. by Augustus. Rather than be taken as a prisoner to Rome, she killed herself with an asp.

6. The list switches from women to men with two legendary figures of the Trojan War: Helen, wife of Menelaus, king of Sparta, whose abduction by Paris was the origin of the war, and Achilles, the greatest of the Greek heroes. Homer had him killed under the walls of Troy by Paris; according to medieval legend, Paris lured him to his death at the temple of Apollo by promises that he would be given Priam's daughter Polyxena if he changed sides. Tristan was a celebrated figure of medieval romance, lover of Iseult, who was wife of King Mark of Cornwall, his uncle.

7. The first conversation recorded with a condemned soul is also the first appearance of two of Dante's contemporaries, the lovers Francesca da Rimini and Paolo Malatesta. Daughter of Guido da Polenta, lord of Ravenna, and aunt of Guido Novello, Dante's host at Ravenna at the end of his life, Francesca was married for political reasons to Paolo's older brother Gianciotto some time after 1275. Around 1285, at which time Francesca had a nine-year old daughter and Paolo was around 40 years old, Gianciotto apparently found the lovers out and killed them both. The language of the dialogue is suffused with the language of the *dolce stil novo*, the "sweet new style" of love lyric that first brought fame to Dante.

by that love which impels them. They will come."

No sooner had the wind bent them toward us
80 than I urged on my voice: "O battered souls,
if One does not forbid it, speak with us."

Even as doves when summoned by desire,
borne forward by their will, move through the air
with wings uplifted, still, to their sweet nest,

85 those spirits left the ranks where Dido suffers,
approaching us through the malignant air;
so powerful had been my loving cry.

"O living being, gracious and benign,
who through the darkened air have come to visit
90 our souls that stained the world with blood, if He

who rules the universe were friend to us,
then we should pray to Him to give you peace,
for you have pitied our atrocious state.

Whatever pleases you to hear and speak
95 will please us, too, to hear and speak with you,
now while the wind is silent, in this place.

The land where I was born lies on that shore
to which the Po together with the waters
that follow it descends to final rest.[8]

100 Love, that can quickly seize the gentle heart,
took hold of him because of the fair body
taken from me—how that was done still wounds me.

Love, that releases no beloved from loving,
took hold of me so strongly through his beauty
105 that, as you see, it has not left me yet.

Love led the two of us unto one death.
Caïna waits for him who took our life."[9]
These words were borne across from them to us.

When I had listened to those injured souls,
110 I bent my head and held it low until
the poet asked of me: "What are you thinking?"

When I replied, my words began: "Alas,
how many gentle thoughts, how deep a longing,
had led them to the agonizing pass!"

115 Then I addressed my speech again to them,
and I began: "Francesca, your afflictions
move me to tears of sorrow and of pity.

But tell me, in the time of gentle sighs,
with what and in what way did Love allow you
120 to recognize your still uncertain longings?"

And she to me: "There is no greater sorrow

---

8. Ravenna is on the Adriatic coast of northern Italy, between the Po River and the Rubicon.

9. Francesca's speech combines echoes of a famous *canzone* by Dante's friend Guido Guinizelli and its definitions of courtly love with harsh concluding phrases on her own fate. Caïna is the first of the four divisions of the ninth circle of Hell, named after Cain, who killed his brother Abel. This place where those who betray their kin are punished "waits for" Francesca's husband because he was still alive in 1300.

than thinking back upon a happy time
in misery—and this your teacher knows.

125　　Yet if you long so much to understand
the first root of our love, then I shall tell
my tale to you as one who weeps and speaks.

One day, to pass the time away, we read
of Lancelot—how love had overcome him.
We were alone, and we suspected nothing.

130　　And time and time again that reading led
our eyes to meet, and made our faces pale,
and yet one point alone defeated us.

When we had read how the desired smile
was kissed by one who was so true a lover,

135　　this one, who never shall be parted from me,
while all his body trembled, kissed my mouth.
A Gallehault indeed, that book and he
who wrote it, too; that day we read no more."[1]

And while one spirit said these words to me,

140　　the other wept, so that—because of pity—
I fainted, as if I had met my death.
And then I fell as a dead body falls.

Canto 6

76

*Dante's awakening to the Third Circle, where the Gluttonous, supine, are flailed by
cold and filthy rain and tormented by Cerberus. Ciacco and his prophecy concerning
Florence. The state of the damned after the Resurrection.*

Upon my mind's reviving—it had closed
on hearing the lament of those two kindred,
since sorrow had confounded me completely—

I see new sufferings, new sufferers

5　　surrounding me on every side, wherever
I move or turn about or set my eyes.

I am in the third circle, filled with cold,
unending, heavy, and accursèd rain;
its measure and its kind are never changed.

10　　Gross hailstones, water gray with filth, and snow
come streaking down across the shadowed air;
the earth, as it receives that shower, stinks.

Over the souls of those submerged beneath
that mess, is an outlandish, vicious beast,

15　　his three throats barking, doglike: Cerberus.[1]

---

1. The story of Lancelot, "flower of the knighthood of the world," and the love for Queen Guinevere, wife of his lord, King Arthur, that caused him to fail in his quest for the Holy Grail, was one of the most popular medieval romances. In the Old French romance, *Lancelot du lac,* it was Lancelot's friend Gallehault who arranged an interview between the pair and induced them to kiss. The book, as well as its author, are accused of being the "go-between" that led to the death and damnation of Francesca and her silent lover.

1. The mythical three-headed guardian of the underworld, described in *Aeneid* 6.417–23. Dante makes him paradoxically more human and more bestial. The guardian(s) of each circle generally relate to that circle's sin; here, the monster's gluttony is stressed by having his gullets silenced by lumps of earth rather than the honey cakes of the *Aeneid.*

His eyes are bloodred; greasy, black, his beard;
his belly bulges, and his hands are claws;
his talons tear and flay and rend the shades.

That downpour makes the sinners howl like dogs;
20   they use one of their sides to screen the other—
those miserable wretches turn and turn.

When Cerberus, the great worm, noticed us,
he opened wide his mouths, showed us his fangs;
there was no part of him that did not twitch.

25   My guide opened his hands to their full span,
plucked up some earth, and with his fists filled full
he hurled it straight into those famished jaws.

Just as a dog that barks with greedy hunger
will then fall quiet when he gnaws his food,
30   intent and straining hard to cram it in,

so were the filthy faces of the demon
Cerberus transformed—after he'd stunned
the spirits so, they wished that they were deaf.

We walked across the shades on whom there thuds
35   that heavy rain, and set our soles upon
their empty images that seem like persons.

And all those spirits lay upon the ground,
except for one who sat erect as soon
as he caught sight of us in front of him.

40   "O you who are conducted through this Hell,"
he said to me, "recall me, if you can;
for you, before I was unmade, were made."

And I to him: "It is perhaps your anguish
that snatches you out of my memory,
45   so that it seems that I have never seen you.

But tell me who you are, you who are set
in such a dismal place, such punishment—
if other pains are more, none's more disgusting."

And he to me: "Your city—one so full
50   of envy that its sack has always spilled—
that city held me in the sunlit life.[2]

The name you citizens gave me was Ciacco;
and for the damning sin of gluttony,
as you can see, I languish in the rain.

55   And I, a wretched soul, am not alone,
for all of these have this same penalty
for this same sin." And he said nothing more.

I answered him: "Ciacco, your suffering
so weights on me that I am forced to weep;
60   but tell me, if you know, what end awaits
      the citizens of that divided city;

2. Dante's native city of Florence, which figures prominently in the poem, appears for the first time, and in characteristically negative fashion.

is any just man there? Tell me the reason
why it has been assailed by so much schism."[3]
    And he to me: "After long controversy,
65   they'll come to blood; the party of the woods
will chase the other out with much offense.
    But then, within three suns, they too must fall;
at which the other party will prevail,
using the power of one who tacks his sails.°   *Pope Boniface*
70   This party will hold high its head for long
and heap great weights upon its enemies,
however much they weep indignantly.
    Two men are just, but no one listens to them.
Three sparks that set on fire every heart
75   are envy, pride, and avariciousness."
    With this, his words, inciting tears, were done;
and I to him: "I would learn more from you;
I ask you for a gift of further speech:
    Tegghiaio, Farinata, men so worthy,
80   Arrigo, Mosca, Jacopo Rusticucci,
and all the rest whose minds bent toward the good,
    do tell me where they are and let me meet them;
for my great longing drives me on to learn
if Heaven sweetens or Hell poisons them."[4]
85   And he: "They are among the blackest souls;
a different sin has dragged them to the bottom;
if you descend so low, there you can see them.
    But when you have returned to the sweet world,
I pray, recall me to men's memory:
90   I say no more to you, answer no more."
    Then his straight gaze grew twisted and awry;
he looked at me awhile, then bent his head;
he fell as low as all his blind companions.
    And my guide said to me: "He'll rise no more
95   until the blast of the angelic trumpet
upon the coming of the hostile Judge:°   *Christ*
    each one shall see his sorry tomb again
and once again take on his flesh and form,
and hear what shall resound eternally."
100   So did we pass across that squalid mixture
of shadows and of rain, our steps slowed down,
talking awhile about the life to come.
    At which I said: "And after the great sentence—
o master—will these torments grow, or else
105   be less, or will they be just as intense?"
    And he to me: "Remember now your science,

---

3. The first explicit discussion of contemporary political events. In spring of 1300, trouble was brewing between the two Guelf factions, the Whites, led by the Cerchi family, and the Blacks, led by the Donatis.

4. The pilgrim asks about some famous political figures who lived in Florence before the division between Blacks and Whites. All except Arrigo are found deeper in Hell.

which says that when a thing has more perfection,
so much the greater is its pain or pleasure.

    Though these accursed sinners never shall
110   attain the true perfection, yet they can
expect to be more perfect then than now."[5]

    We took the circling way traced by that road;
we said much more than I can here recount;
we reached the point that marks the downward slope.

115   Here we found Plutus, the great enemy.[6]

Canto 7

The demon Plutus. The Fourth Circle, where the Avaricious and the Prodigal, in opposite directions, roll weights in semicircles. Fortune and her ways. Descent into the Fifth Circle: the Wrathful and the Sullen, the former besmirched by the muddy Styx, the latter immersed in it.

    "Pape Satàn, pape Satàn aleppe!"[1]
so Plutus, with his grating voice, began.
The gentle sage, aware of everything,
    said reassuringly, "Don't let your fear
5   defeat you; for whatever power he has,
he cannot stop our climbing down this crag."

    Then he turned back to Plutus' swollen face
and said to him: "Be quiet, cursed wolf![2]
Let your vindictiveness feed on yourself.
10   His is no random journey to the deep:
it has been willed on high, where Michael
took revenge upon the arrogant rebellion."[3]

    As sails inflated by the wind collapse,
entangled in a heap, when the mast cracks,
15   so that ferocious beast fell to the ground.

    Thus we made our way down to the fourth ditch,
to take in more of that despondent shore
where all the universe's ill is stored.

    Justice of God! Who has amassed as many
20   strange tortures and travails as I have seen?
Why do we let our guilt consume us so?

    Even as waves that break above Charybdis,[4]
each shattering the other when they meet,

---

5. "Science" is Aristotelian philosophy as interpreted in Scholasticism. Aquinas held that the soul attains natural perfection only when unified with the body. For the dead, this perfection will be achieved only after the Last Judgment, when their souls be reunited with their bodies. The pains of the damned will be then be increased ("more perfect") just as will the pleasure of the blessed.

6. Pluto was mythological god of the underworld; Plutus was the Roman god of wealth. Dante appears to make no distinction between the two, making out of them a minor demon, guardian of the Fourth Circle.

1. A hodgepodge of Latin, Greek, and Hebrew appealing to Plutus's superior: "Oh Satan, oh Satan, the most powerful one!"

2. Recalling the cupidity of the she-wolf of Canto 1.

3. Alluding to the Archangel Michael's role as leader of the angels in the battle in heaven that resulted in the casting out of Satan and the rebel angels.

4. A famous whirlpool between the island of Sicily and the Italian coast, described in *Aeneid* 3.420–23.

so must the spirits here dance their round dance.

25   Here, more than elsewhere, I saw multitudes
to every side of me; their howls were loud
while, wheeling weights, they used their chests to push.

    They struck against each other; at that point,
each turned around and, wheeling back those weights,
30 cried out: "Why do you hoard?" "Why do you squander?"[5]

    So did they move around the sorry circle
from left and right to the opposing point;
again, again they cried their chant of scorn;

    and so, when each of them had changed positions,
35 he circled halfway back to his next joust.
And I, who felt my heart almost pierced through,

    requested: "Master, show me now what shades
are these and tell me if they all were clerics—
those tonsured ones who circle on our left."[6]

40   And he to me: "All these, to left and right
were so squint-eyed of mind in the first life—
no spending that they did was done with measure.

    Their voices bark this out with clarity
when they have reached the two points of the circle
45 where their opposing guilts divide their ranks.

    These to the left—their heads bereft of hair—
were clergymen, and popes and cardinals,
within whom avarice works its excess."

    And I to him: "Master, among this kind
50 I certainly might hope to recognize
some who have been bespattered by these crimes."

    And he to me: "That thought of yours is empty:
the undiscerning life that made them filthy
now renders them unrecognizable.

55   For all eternity they'll come to blows:
these here will rise up from their sepulchers
with fists clenched tight; and these, with hair cropped close.

    Ill giving and ill keeping have robbed both
of the fair world° and set them to this fracas—   *Heaven*
60 what that is like, my words need not embellish.

    Now you can see, my son, how brief's the sport
of all those goods that are in Fortune's care,
for which the tribe of men contend and brawl;

    for all the gold that is or ever was
65 beneath the moon could never offer rest
to even one of these exhausted spirits."

    "Master," I asked of him, "now tell me too:
this Fortune whom you've touched upon just now—

---

5. Here one sin is punished by confrontation with its opposite. In Dante's scheme, the excesses of avarice ("hoarding") and prodigality ("squandering") are equally to be avoided.

6. The tonsure is the shaven crown of the head signifying membership in a monastic or clerical order; the avarice of the clergy was proverbial.

what's she, who clutches so all the world's goods?"[7]

And he to me: "O unenlightened creatures,
how deep—the ignorance that hampers you!
I want you to digest my word on this.

Who made the heavens and who gave them guides
was He whose wisdom transcends everything;
that every part may shine unto the other,

He had the light apportioned equally;
similarly, for wordly splendors, He
ordained a general minister and guide

to shift, from time to time, those empty goods
from nation unto nation, clan to clan,
in ways that human reason can't prevent;

just so, one people rules, one languishes,
obeying the decision she has given,
which, like a serpent in the grass, is hidden.

Your knowledge cannot stand against her force;
for she foresees and judges and maintains
her kingdom as the other gods do theirs.

The changes that she brings are without respite:
it is necessity that makes her swift;
and for this reason, men change state so often.

She is the one so frequently maligned
even by those who should give praise to her—
they blame her wrongfully with words of scorn.

But she is blessed and does not hear these things;
for with the other primal beings, happy,
she turns her sphere and glories in her bliss.[8]

But now let us descend to greater sorrow,
for every star that rose when I first moved
is setting now;[9] we cannot stay too long."

We crossed the circle to the other shore;
we reached a foaming watercourse that spills
into a trench formed by its overflow.

That stream was even darker than deep purple;
and we, together with those shadowed waves,
moved downward and along a strange pathway.

When it has reached the foot of those malign
gray slopes, that melancholy stream descends,
forming a swamp that bears the name of Styx.

And I, who was intent on watching it,

70
75
80
85
90
95
100
105

7. Fortune was often pictured blindfolded, turning a wheel at random to distribute her goods. In Virgil's explanation, aimed at reconciling the principles of chance and inequality with those of divine justice and providence, Fortune is one of the Intelligences in the heavenly sphere, in charge of administering the riches of the world.

8. The Intelligences preside over the revolving heavens and turn the heaven assigned to them, as Fortune turns her sphere. They were commonly referred to as gods and goddesses.

9. The starry heavens make a complete circuit every 24 hours. The stars that were rising when Virgil first set out from Limbo around noon on Good Friday are now setting 12 hours later, after midnight of Holy Saturday.

110   could make out muddied people in that slime,
     all naked and their faces furious.

       These struck each other not with hands alone,
     but with their heads and chests and with their feet,
     and tore each other piecemeal with their teeth.

115   The kindly master told me: "Son, now see
     the souls of those whom anger has defeated;
     and I should also have you know for certain

       that underneath the water there are souls
     who sigh and make this plain of water bubble,
120   as your eye, looking anywhere, can tell.

       Wedged in the slime, they say: 'We had been sullen
     in the sweet air that's gladdened by the sun;
     we bore the mist of sluggishness in us:

       now we are bitter in the blackened mud.'
125   This hymn they have to gurgle in their gullets,
     because they cannot speak it in full words."

       And so, between the dry shore and the swamp,
     we circled much of that disgusting pond,
     our eyes upon the swallowers of slime.
130   We came at last upon a tower's base.

Canto 8

Still the Fifth Circle: the Wrathful and the Sullen. The tall tower. Phlegyas and the crossing of the Styx. Filippo Argenti and Dante's fury. Approach to Dis, the lower part of Hell: its moat, its walls, its gate. The demons, fallen angels, and their obstruction of the poets' entry into Dis.

       I say, continuing, that long before
     we two had reached the foot of that tall tower,
     our eyes had risen upward, toward its summit,

       because of two small flames that flickered there,
5   while still another flame returned their signal,
     so far off it was scarcely visible.

       And I turned toward the sea of all good sense;
     I said: "What does this mean? And what reply
     comes from that other fire? Who kindled it?"

10   And he to me: "Above the filthy waters
     you can already see what waits for us,
     if it's not hid by vapors from the marsh."

       Bowstring has not thrust from itself an arrow
     that ever rushed as swiftly through the air
15   as did the little bark that at that moment

       I saw as it skimmed toward us on the water,
     a solitary boatman at its helm.
     I heard him howl: "Now you are caught, foul soul!"

       "O Phlegyas, Phlegyas, such a shout is useless
20   this time," my master said; "we're yours no longer

than it will take to cross the muddy sluice."[1]
    And just as one who hears some great deception
was done to him, and then resents it, so
was Phlegyas when he had to store his anger.

25   My guide preceded me into the boat.
Once he was in, he had me follow him;
there seemed to be no weight until I boarded.[2]
    No sooner were my guide and I embarked
than off that ancient prow went, cutting water
30   more deeply than it does when bearing others.
    And while we steered across the stagnant channel,
before me stood a sinner thick with mud,
saying: "Who are you, come before your time?"
    And I to him: "I've come, but I don't stay;
35   but who are you, who have become so ugly?"
He answered: "You can see—I'm one who weeps."
    And I to him: "In weeping and in grieving,
accursèd spirit, may you long remain;
though you're disguised by filth, I know your name."[3]
40   Then he stretched both his hands out toward the boat,
at which my master quickly shoved him back,
saying: "Be off there with the other dogs!"
    That done, he threw his arms around my neck
and kissed my face and said: "Indignant soul,
45   blessèd is she who bore you in her womb!
    When in the world, he was presumptuous;
there is no good to gild his memory,
and so his shade down here is hot with fury.
    How many up above now count themselves
50   great kings, who'll wallow here like pigs in slime,
leaving behind foul memories of their crimes!"
    And I: "O master, I am very eager
to see that spirit soused within this broth
before we've made our way across the lake."
55   And he to me: "Before the other shore
comes into view, you shall be satisfied;
to gratify so fine a wish is right."
    Soon after I had heard these words, I saw
the muddy sinners so dismember him
60   that even now I praise and thank God for it.
    They all were shouting: "At Filippo Argenti!"
At this, the Florentine, gone wild with spleen,°   *ill temper*

---

1. In ancient myth, Phlegyas was son of Chryse and the war-god Mars, king of the Lapithae, and father of Ixion and Coronis. When Coronis was violated by Apollo, Phlegyas in fury set fire to the god's temple at Delphi. For this sacrilege, according to Virgil in *Aeneid* 6.821–23, he was punished eternally in Tartarus. Dante makes him an infernal boatman in the circle suited to his actions.

2. Reminiscent of Aeneas's crossing of the Styx in *Aeneid* 6.544–46, as Dante too has a real body.

3. Filippo Argenti (identified in line 61 of the canto) was so called because he had his horse shod in silver (*argento*). He was a member of the Adimari clan of Florence, Black Guelfs, and his brother obtained Dante's property from the Commune of Florence when the poet was exiled.

began to turn his teeth against himself.

    We left him there; I tell no more of him.

65 But in my ears so loud a wailing pounded
that I lean forward, all intent to see.

    The kindly master said: "My son, the city
that bears the name of Dis is drawing near,
70 with its grave citizens, its great battalions."[4]

    I said: "I can already see distinctly—
master—the mosques that gleam within the valley,
as crimson as if they had just been drawn

    out of the fire." He told me: "The eternal
flame burning there appears to make them red,
75 as you can see, within this lower Hell."

    So we arrived inside the deep-cut trenches
that are the moats of this despondent land:
the ramparts seemed to me to be of iron.

    But not before we'd ranged in a wide circuit
80 did we approach a place where that shrill pilot
shouted: "Get out; the entrance way is here."

    About the gates I saw more than a thousand—
who once had rained from Heaven[5]—and they cried
in anger: "Who is this who, without death,
85 can journey through the kingdom of the dead?"
And my wise master made a sign that said
he wanted to speak secretly to them.

    Then they suppressed—somewhat—their great disdain
and said: "You come alone; let him be gone—
90 for he was reckless, entering this realm.

    Let him return alone on his mad road—
or try to, if he can, since you, his guide
across so dark a land, you are to stay."

    Consider, reader, my dismay before
95 the sound of those abominable words:
returning here seemed so impossible.

    "O my dear guide, who more than seven times
has given back to me my confidence
and snatched me from deep danger that had menaced,
100 do not desert me when I'm so undone;
and if they will not let us pass beyond,
let us retrace our steps together, quickly."

    These were my words; the lord who'd led me there
replied: "Forget your fear, no one can hinder
105 our passage; One so great has granted it.

---

4. Dis was the god of the underworld in the religion of ancient Rome, and by extension the name for the underworld itself. Dante will use the term to refer to Satan; here he means lower Hell, which he depicts as a Muslim city.

5. The rebel angels fallen from Heaven with Lucifer; likened here to Muslim infidels, and for whom the verbal talisman no longer appears to guarantee safe passage. The change in organization and custom introduces the social nature and greater complexity of lower Hell.

But you wait here for me, and feed and comfort
your tired spirit with good hope, for I
will not abandon you in this low world."

So he goes on his way; that gentle father
110   has left me there to wait and hesitate,
for *yes* and *no* contend within my head.

I could not hear what he was telling them;
but he had not been long with them when each
ran back into the city, scrambling fast.

115   And these, our adversaries, slammed the gates
in my lord's face; and he remained outside,
then, with slow steps, turned back again to me.

His eyes turned to the ground, his brows deprived
of every confidence, he said with sighs:
120   "See who has kept me from the house of sorrow!"[6]

To me he added: "You—though I am vexed—
must not be daunted; I shall win this contest,
whoever tries—within—to block our way.

This insolence of theirs is nothing new;
125   they used it once before and at a gate
less secret—it is still without its bolts[7]—

the place where you made out the fatal text;
and now, already well within that gate,°   *the gate of Hell*
across the circles—and alone—descends
130   the one who will unlock this realm for us."

Canto 9

The gate of Dis. Dante's fear. The three Furies, invoking Medusa. Virgil's warning
to Dante lest he look at Gorgon, Medusa's head. A heavenly messenger. The flight
of the demons. Entry into Dis, where Virgil and Dante reach the Sixth Circle and its
Arch-Heretics, entombed in red-hot sepulchers.

The color cowardice displayed in me
when I saw that my guide was driven back,
made him more quickly mask his own new pallor.

He stood alert, like an attentive listener,
5   because his eye could hardly journey far
across the black air and the heavy fog.

"We have to win this battle," he began,
"if not . . . But one so great had offered help.
How slow that someone's coming seems to me!"

10   But I saw well enough how he had covered
his first words with the words that followed after—
so different from what he had said before;

---

6. This first of several times when Virgil will be thwarted or deceived in Hell (always by devils) begins a careful development of his strengths and limitations as guide to the afterlife.

7. According to Christian legend, when Christ entered Limbo to harrow Hell, the rebel angels attempted to block his passage. As the Matins of the Office of Holy Saturday have it: "Today our Savior shattered the gates and likewise the bolts of death."

nevertheless, his speech made me afraid,
because I drew out from his broken phrase
15 a meaning worse—perhaps—than he'd intended.

"Does anyone from the first circle, one
whose only punishment is crippled hope,
ever descend so deep in this sad hollow?"[1]

That was my question. And he answered so:
20 "It is quite rare for one of us to go
along the way that I have taken now.

But I, in truth, have been here once before:
that savage witch Erichtho, she who called
the shades back to their bodies, summoned me.

25 My flesh had not been long stripped off when she
had me descend through all the rings of Hell,
to draw a spirit back from Judas' circle.[2]

That is the deepest and the darkest place,
the farthest from the heaven that girds all:
30 so rest assured, I know the pathway well.

This swamp that breeds and breathes the giant stench
surrounds the city of the sorrowing,°   Dis
which now we cannot enter without anger."

And he said more, but I cannot remember
35 because my eyes had wholly taken me
to that high tower with the glowing summit

where, at one single point, there suddenly
stood three infernal Furies flecked with blood,
who had the limbs of women and their ways

40 but wore, as girdles, snakes of deepest green;
small serpents and horned vipers formed their hairs,
and these were used to bind their bestial temples.[3]

And he, who knew these handmaids well—they served
the Queen of never-ending lamentation[4]—
45 said: "Look at the ferocious Erinyes!

That is Megaera on the left, and she
who weeps upon the right, that is Allecto;
Tisiphone's between them." He was done.

Each Fury tore her breast with taloned nails;
50 each, with her palms, beat on herself and wailed
so loud that I, in fear, drew near the poet.

"Just let Medusa come; then we shall turn
him into stone," they all cried, looking down;

1. Here the pilgrim probes his guide's knowledge of lower Hell, a realm that, unlike the upper circles, has no direct parallels to the underworld described in the *Aeneid*.

2. Medieval legend had made Virgil a magician, but there is no known source for the strange tale he produces here to establish his expertise. Erichtho was a legendary sorceress who, in an especially gruesome episode in Lucan's *Pharsalia* (6.507–830), is employed to summon the spirit of a dead soldier to learn the outcome of the impending battle of Pharsalia. "Judas' circle" is the lowest part of the last circle of Hell.

3. The Furies (Greek: Erinyes) were daughters of Night, forces of vengeance feared by gods and men. They were depicted in Virgil's *Aeneid* and elsewhere as monstrous women, with snakes for hair.

4. Proserpina, queen of the underworld in classical myth.

"we should have punished Theseus' assault."[5]

55   "Turn round and keep your eyes shut fast, for should
the Gorgon show herself and you behold her,
never again would you return above,"

    my master said; and he himself turned me
around and, not content with just my hands,
60 used his as well to cover up my eyes.

    O you possessed of sturdy intellects,
observe the teaching that is hidden here
beneath the veil of verses so obscure.[6]

    And now, across the turbid waves, there passed
65 a reboantic° fracas—horrid sound,   *reverberating*
enough to make both of the shorelines quake:

    a sound not other than a wind's when, wild
because it must contend with warmer currents,
it strikes against the forest without let,

70   shattering, beating down, bearing off branches,
as it moves proudly, clouds of dust before it,
and puts to flight both animals and shepherds.

    He freed my eyes and said: "Now let your optic
nerve turn directly toward that ancient foam,
75 there where the mist is thickest and most acrid."

    As frogs confronted by their enemy,
the snake, will scatter underwater till
each hunches in a heap along the bottom,

    so did the thousand ruined souls I saw
80 take flight before a figure crossing Styx
who walked as if on land and with dry soles.[7]

    He thrust away the thick air from his face,
waving his left hand frequently before him;
that seemed the only task that wearied him.

85   I knew well he was Heaven's messenger,
and I turned toward my master; and he made
a sign that I be still and bow before him.

    How full of high disdain he seemed to me!
He came up to the gate, and with a wand,
90 he opened it, for there was no resistance.

    "O you cast out of Heaven, hated crowd,"
were his first words upon that horrid threshold,
"why do you harbor this presumptuousness?

    Why are you so reluctant to endure
95 that Will whose aim can never be cut short,
and which so often added to your hurts?

    What good is it to thrust against the fates?

5. In mythology, the serpent-haired Gorgon Medusa was so fearful that all who looked upon her head were turned to stone. The legendary Greek hero Theseus descended to Hades to abduct Proserpina.

6. A standard medieval formula for introducing a self-contained allegory, the meaning of which the reader must extract from beneath the "veil" of its surface story.

7. The reminiscence of Jesus walking on water at the Sea of Galilee (Matthew 14.21–33) adds to the effect of a repetition of the Harrowing of Hell.

Your Cerberus, if you remember well,
for that, had both his throat and chin stripped clean."[8]

100   At that he turned and took the filthy road,
and did not speak to us, but had the look
of one who is obsessed by other cares

    than those that press and gnaw at those before him;
and we moved forward, on into the city,
105 in safety, having heard his holy words.

    We made our way inside without a struggle;
and I, who wanted so much to observe
the state of things that such a fortress guarded,

    as soon as I had entered, looked about.
110 I saw, on every side, a spreading plain
of lamentation and atrocious pain.

    Just as at Arles, where Rhone becomes a marsh,
just as at Pola, near Quarnero's gulf,
that closes Italy and bathes its borders,[9]

115   the sepulchers make all the plain uneven,
so they did here on every side, except
that here the sepulchers were much more harsh;

    for flames were scattered through the tombs, and these
had kindled all of them to glowing heat;
120 no artisan could ask for hotter iron.

    The lid of every tomb was lifted up,
and from each tomb such sorry cries arose
as could come only from the sad and hurt.

    And I: "Master, who can these people be
125 who, buried in great chests of stone like these,
must speak by way of sighs in agony?"

    And he to me: "Here are arch-heretics
and those who followed them, from every sect;
those tombs are much more crowded than you think.

130   Here, like has been ensepulchered with like;
some monuments are heated more, some less."
And then he turned around and to his right;[1]
    we passed between the torments and high walls.

Canto 10

Still the Sixth Circle: the Heretics. The tombs of the Epicureans. Farinata degli Uberti. Cavalcante dei Cavalcanti. Farinata's prediction of Dante's difficulty in returning to Florence from exile. The inability of the damned to see the present, although they can foresee the future.

---

8. The legendary hero Hercules was often regarded as foreshadowing Christ, especially in his Twelve Labors, of which the fetching of Cerberus from the underworld was the final and most difficult.

9. The Provençal town of Arles and the northeastern Italian town of Pola were sites of Roman necropolises.

1. The poets bear left at every opportunity except here and in Canto 17.31; then always to the right on the Mountain of Purgatory. The exception here is perhaps related to the exceptional status of the sin of heresy.

Now, by a narrow path that ran between
those torments and the ramparts of the city,
my master moves ahead, I following.

"O highest virtue, you who lead me through
these circles of transgression, at your will,
do speak to me, and satisfy my longings.

Can those who lie within the sepulchers
be seen? The lids—in fact—have all been lifted;
no guardian is watching over them."

And he to me: "They'll all be shuttered up
when they return here from Jehosaphat
together with the flesh they left above.[1]

Within this region is the cemetery
of Epicurus and his followers,
all those who say the soul dies with the body.[2]

And so the question you have asked of me
will soon find satisfaction while we're here,
as will the longing you have hid from me."

And I: "Good guide, the only reason I
have hid my heart was that I might speak briefly,
and you, long since, encouraged me in this."

"O Tuscan, you who pass alive across
the fiery city with such seemly words,
be kind enough to stay your journey here.

Your accent makes it clear that you belong
among the natives of the noble city
I may have dealt with too vindictively."[3]

This sound had burst so unexpectedly
out of one sepulcher that, trembling, I
then drew a little closer to my guide.

But he told me: "Turn round! What are you doing?
That's Farinata who has risen there—
you will see all of him from the waist up."

My eyes already were intent on his;
and up he rose—his forehead and his chest—
as if he had tremendous scorn for Hell.

My guide—his hands encouraging and quick—
thrust me between the sepulchers toward him,
saying: "Your words must be appropriate."

When I'd drawn closer to his sepulcher,
he glanced at me, and as if in disdain,
he asked of me: "Who were your ancestors?"[4]

---

1. The Valley of Jehosaphat, source of the stream running between Jerusalem and the Mount of Olives, was expected to be the site of the Last Judgment.

2. The Greek philosopher Epicurus (341–270 B.C.E.) taught that the soul died with the body; consequently, the greatest good to be sought was pleasure, defined as the absence of pain through the cultivation of virtue. This denial of the immortality of the soul was quite current in Florence, especially with the Ghibellines.

3. The soul has identified Dante because of the Italian dialect he is speaking, from Tuscany, the region of Florence.

4. Farinata, a leader of the Florentine Ghibellines, had died just before Dante was born, so he asks about members of previous generations he would have known, and whether they were known to his illustrious family, the Uberti.

Because I wanted so to be compliant,
I hid no thing from him: I told him all.
45 At this he lifted up his brows a bit,
    then said: "They were ferocious enemies
of mine and of my parents and my party,
so that I had to scatter them twice over."[5]
    "If they were driven out," I answered him,
50 "they still returned, both times, from every quarter;
but yours were never quick to learn that art."[6]
    At this there rose another shade alongside,
uncovered to my sight down to his chin;
I think that he had risen on his knees.[7]
55   He looked around me, just as if he longed
to see if I had come with someone else;
but then, his expectation spent, he said
    in tears: "If it is your high intellect
that lets you journey here, through this blind prison,
60 where is my son? Why is he not with you?"
    I answered: "My own powers have not brought me;
he who awaits me there, leads me through here
perhaps to one your Guido did disdain."[8]
    His words, the nature of his punishment—
65 these had already let me read his name;
therefore, my answer was so fully made.
    Then suddenly erect, he cried: "What's that:
He '*did* disdain'? He is not still alive?
The sweet light does not strike against his eyes?"[9]
70   And when he noticed how I hesitated
a moment in my answer, he fell back—
supine—and did not show himself again.
    But that great-hearted one, the other shade
at whose request I'd stayed, did not change aspect
75 or turn aside his head or lean or bend;
    and taking up his words where he'd left off,
"If they were slow," he said, "to learn that art,
that is more torment to me than this bed.
    And yet the Lady who is ruler here
80 will not have her face kindled fifty times[1]

---

5. Farinata played a prominent role in the expulsion of the Guelfs from Florence in 1248 and in their crushing defeat at Montaperti in 1260, after which he successfully argued for renewed expulsions rather than the destruction of his native city.

6. The Guelfs returned in 1251 after the defeat of the Ghibellines in battle, and again in 1266 after another military victory. By contrast, the Ghibellines never returned to Florence as a party, and their most powerful families, including the Uberti, were excluded from the city by the terms of the peace of 1280.

7. The speaker is Cavalcante de' Cavalcanti, a notorious Epicurean and father of the famous poet and close friend of Dante, Guido Cavalcanti. An ardent Guelf, Guido was married to Farinata's daughter Beatrice to guarantee peace between the feuding factions. When the priors of Florence (including Dante) put an end to the hostilities in June 1300, the leading Blacks and leading Whites (including Guido) were banished. Guido died of malaria in August of the same year; hence Dante was indirectly responsible for his friend's death.

8. Guido too was a notorious Epicurean, celebrating "high intellect" as the greatest virtue in his poetry.

9. Guido is not yet dead, but his father misunderstands the meaning of Dante's words.

1. Proserpina is identified with Hecate, goddess of the moon, whose face is fully lit once a month.

before you learn how heavy is that art.[2]

And so may you return to the sweet world,
tell me: why are those citizens so cruel
against my kin in all of their decrees?"[3]

85 To which I said: "The carnage, the great bloodshed
that stained the waters of the Arbia red
have led us to such prayers in our temple."[4]

He sighed and shook his head, then said: "In that,
I did not act alone, but certainly
90 I'd not have joined the others without cause.

But where I was alone was *there* where all
the rest would have annihilated Florence,
had I not interceded forcefully."[5]

"Ah, as I hope your seed may yet find peace,"
95 I asked, "so may you help me to undo
the knot that here has snarled my course of thought.

It seems, if I hear right, that you can see
beforehand that which time is carrying,
but you're denied the sight of present things."

100 "We see, even as men who are farsighted,
those things," he said, "that are remote from us;
the Highest Lord allots us that much light.

But when events draw near or are, our minds
are useless; were we not informed by others,
105 we should know nothing of your human state.

So you can understand how our awareness
will die completely at the moment when
the portal of the future has been shut."[6]

Then, as if penitent for my omission,
110 I said: "Will you now tell that fallen man
his son is still among the living ones;

and if, a while ago, I held my tongue
before his question, let him know it was
because I had in mind the doubt you've answered."

115 And now my master was recalling me;
so that, more hurriedly, I asked the spirit
to name the others who were there with him.

He said: "More than a thousand lie with me:
the second Frederick is but one among them,

2. Farinata foretells Dante's own exile from Florence in 1302, and the difficulty he will have in learning the "art" of returning.

3. The Uberti had been banished from Florence in 1280 and never allowed to return. In 1283, Farinata and his wife had been posthumously excommunicated, their bones exhumed and scattered, and the goods of their heirs confiscated.

4. The hill of Montaperti was on the bank of a small stream near Siena called the Arbia.

5. Farinata recalls his lone opposition to the total destruction of Florence at the council that followed the battle of Montaperti.

6. Because time itself will end after the Last Judgment, they will have no more future to see.

120   as is the Cardinal;[7] I name no others."

      With that, he hid himself; and pondering
the speech that seemed to me so menacing,
I turned my steps to meet the ancient poet.

      He moved ahead, and as we made our way,
125   he said to me: "Why are you so dismayed?"
I satisfied him, answering him fully.

      And then that sage exhorted me: "Remember
the words that have been spoken here against you.
Now pay attention," and he raised his finger;
130   "when you shall stand before the gentle splendor
of one whose gracious eyes see everything,
then you shall learn—from her—your lifetime's journey."[8]

      Following that, his steps turned to the left,
leaving the wall and moving toward the middle
135   along a path that strikes into a valley
      whose stench, as it rose up, disgusted us.

Canto 11

*Still the Sixth Circle. Pope Anastasius' tomb. Virgil on the parts of Dis they now will visit,
where the modes of malice are punished: violence in the Seventh Circle's Three Rings;
"ordinary" fraud in the Eighth Circle; and treacherous fraud in the Ninth Circle. Hell's
previous circles, Two through Five, as circles of incontinence. Usury condemned.*

      Along the upper rim of a high bank
formed by a ring of massive broken boulders,
we came above a crowd more cruelly pent.°   *confined*
      And here, because of the outrageous stench
5   thrown up in excess by that deep abyss,
we drew back till we were behind the lid
of a great tomb, on which I made out this,
inscribed: "I hold Pope Anastasius,
enticed to leave the true path by Photinus."[1]
10   "It would be better to delay descent
so that our senses may grow somewhat used
to this foul stench; and then we can ignore it."
      So said my master, and I answered him:
"Do find some compensation, lest this time
15   be lost." And he: "You see, I've thought of that."
      "My son, within this ring of broken rocks,"

---

7. The Emperor Frederick II (1194–1250), known to his contemporaries as *Stupor Mundi*, "the wonder of the world," was King of Sicily and Naples, and head of the Holy Roman Empire from 1215 until his death. His contemporaries deemed him to be an Epicurean, believing neither in life after death nor in paradise. The Ghibelline Ottaviano degli Ubaldini was made Bishop of Bologna in 1240 and cardinal in 1244. His brother appears in *Purgatorio* and his uncle, Archbishop Ruggieri, in *Inferno* 33,14.

8. Beatrice, who sees all things in the perspective of God, will explain those mysteries which Virgil cannot, as he sees only by the natural light of human reason.

1. Anastasius II was pope from 496 to 498. Tradition appears to have confused him with Anastasius I, Byzantine emperor from 491 to 518, an adherent to the heresy of Photinus, which denied the divine origin of Christ.

he then began, "there are three smaller circles;[2]
like those that you are leaving, they range down.

　　Those circles are all full of cursed spirits;
so that your seeing of them may suffice,
learn now the how and why of their confinement.

　　Of every malice that earns hate in Heaven,
injustice is the end; and each such end
by force or fraud brings harm to other men.[3]

　　However, fraud is man's peculiar vice;
God finds it more displeasing—and therefore,
the fraudulent are lower, suffering more.

　　The violent take all of the first circle;
but since one uses force against three persons,
that circle's built of three divided rings.[4]

　　To God and to one's self and to one's neighbor—
I mean, to them or what is theirs—one can
do violence, as you shall now hear clearly.

　　Violent death and painful wounds may be
inflicted on one's neighbor; his possessions
may suffer ruin, fire, and extortion;

　　thus, murderers and those who strike in malice,
as well as plunderers and robbers—these,
in separated ranks, the first ring racks.

　　A man can set violent hands against
himself or his belongings; so within
the second ring repents, though uselessly,

　　whoever would deny himself your world,
gambling away, wasting his patrimony,
and weeping where he should instead be happy.

　　One can be violent against the Godhead,
one's heart denying and blaspheming Him
and scorning nature and the good in her;[5]

　　so, with its sign, the smallest ring has sealed
both Sodom and Cahors and all of those
who speak in passionate contempt of God.[6]

　　Now fraud, that eats away at every conscience,
is practiced by a man against another
who trusts in him, or one who has no trust.[7]

20

25

30

35

40

45

50

---

2. The seventh, eighth and ninth, "smaller" because further down in the cone.

3. "Malice" is the blanket term for all the sins of lower Hell, either by force (seventh circle) or by fraud (eighth and ninth), and distinguishes them from those of upper Hell.

4. "First circle" here means the first of lower Hell, the seventh, subdivided into three rings in order of gravity: the violence against one's neighbor, against self, and against God.

5. Any sin against Nature is considered an injury to God's order of Nature.

6. The Old Testament city of Sodom was identified with the act of sodomy, which in theological discussion was generally called simply "the vice against nature." Cahors is a town in southern France famous as a center of usury, the lending of money with a rate of interest. The third form of violence against God is blasphemy.

7. Fraud is the most complex and dangerous of sins because it is "man's peculiar vice." Dante divides it between simple fraud and treachery, where a bond of trust is broken.

55   This latter way seems only to cut off
   the bond of love that nature forges;[8] thus,
   nestled within the second circle[9] are:
    hypocrisy and flattery, sorcerers,
   and falsifiers, simony, and theft,
60   and barrators and panders and like trash.

    But in the former way of fraud, not only
   the love that nature forges is forgotten,
   but added love that builds a special trust;
    thus, in the tightest circle, where there is
65   the universe's center, seat of Dis,°   *Satan*
   all traitors are consumed eternally."

    "Master, your reasoning is clear indeed,"
   I said; "it has made plain for me the nature
   of this pit and the population in it.

70   But tell me: those the dense marsh holds, or those
   driven before the wind, or those on whom
   rain falls, or those who clash with such harsh tongues,
    why are they not all punished in the city
   of flaming red if God is angry with them?
75   And if He's not, why then are they tormented?"[1]

    And then to me, "Why does your reason wander
   so far from its accustomed course?" he said.
   "Or of what other things are you now thinking?

    Have you forgotten, then, the words with which
80   your *Ethics* treats of those three dispositions
   that strike at Heaven's will: incontinence
    and malice and mad bestiality?[2]

   And how the fault that is the least condemned
   and least offends God is incontinence?

85   If you consider carefully this judgment
   and call to mind the souls of upper Hell,
   who bear their penalties outside this city,
    you'll see why they have been set off from these
   unrighteous ones, and why, when heaven's vengeance
90   hammers at them, it carries lesser anger."

    "O sun that heals all sight that is perplexed,
   when I ask you, your answer so contents
   that doubting pleases me as much as knowing.

---

8. In Dante's ethics, humankind is created by love and love is the basis of the natural social bond; hence any act of fraud is a conscious severing of that bond just as the sins of upper Hell pervert (by excess or insufficiency) the innate desire for God's creation.

9. The eighth circle, which contains ten subdivisions in all, is the second circle of lower Hell.

1. The pilgrim's question raises a key tension in the depiction of Hell: do all souls suffer equally because all are damned, or do some suffer more than others? Are all sins equally evil, or are some worse than others?

2. In his *Nicomachean Ethics*, known to Dante through the commentaries and translations of Averroës, Aquinas, and others, Aristotle drew a distinction between three types of immoral practice. Incontinence signifies excess in any passion which, in moderation, is lawful, including all the vices punished in the second through fifth circles. "Mad bestiality" here means violence, and "malice," fraud. Aristotle's classification does not include heresy, and Virgil never mentions the sixth circle in this discussion; nor does he mention the lukewarm souls of Ante-Inferno or the souls of Limbo, whose sins were of omission rather than commission.

Go back a little to that point," I said,
95   "where you told me that usury offends
divine goodness; unravel now that knot."

"Philosophy, for one who understands,
points out, and not in just one place," he said,
100   "how nature follows—as she takes her course—
the Divine Intellect and Divine Art;
and if you read your *Physics* carefully,[3]
not many pages from the start, you'll see
that when it can, your art would follow nature,
just as a pupil imitates his master;
105   so that your art is almost God's grandchild.[4]
From these two, art and nature, it is fitting,
if you recall how *Genesis* begins,
for men to make their way, to gain their living;
and since the usurer prefers another
110   pathway, he scorns both nature in herself
and art, her follower; his hope is elsewhere.[5]
But follow me, for it is time to move;
the Fishes glitter now on the horizon
and all the Wain is spread out over Caurus;[6]
115   only beyond, can one climb down the cliff."

Canto 12

The Seventh Circle, First Ring: the Violent against their Neighbors. The Minotaur.
The Centaurs, led by Chiron, who assigns Nessus to guide Dante and Virgil across
the boiling river of blood (Phlegethon). In that river, Tyrants and Murderers,
immersed, watched over by the Centaurs.

The place that we had reached for our descent
along the bank was alpine; what reclined
upon that bank would, too, repel all eyes.
Just like the toppled mass of rock that struck—
5   because of earthquake or eroded props—
the Adige on its flank, this side of Trent,
where from the mountain top from which it thrust
down to the plain, the rock is shattered so
that it permits a path for those above:[1]
10   such was the passage down to that ravine.
And at the edge above the cracked abyss,

3. The *Physics* of Aristotle.

4. Nature, daughter of God, follows his eternal ideas and his art in her own operation; human art and industry, daughter of Nature, ought to follow her and her art in the same way.

5. God's command to Adam and Eve when he expelled them from Eden was that they should gain their living by the sweat of their brows (Genesis 3.19). Because the usurer gains his living from money rather than either from Nature or from her follower, art, he despises her twice over.

6. The position of the constellations indicates the time: two hours before sunrise, or 4 A.M.

1. The comparison is to the Slavini di Marco, a "toppled mass of rock" resulting from an enormous landslide between Trent and Verona on the Adige River in northeast Italy.

there lay outstretched the infamy of Crete,[2]
    conceived within the counterfeited cow;
and, catching sight of us, he bit himself

15 like one whom fury devastates within.
    Turning to him, my sage cried out: "Perhaps
you think this is the Duke of Athens here,
who, in the world above, brought you your death.
    Be off, you beast; this man who comes has not

20 been tutored by your sister; all he wants
in coming here is to observe your torments."
    Just as the bull that breaks loose from its halter
the moment it receives the fatal stroke,
and cannot run but plunges back and forth,

25   so did I see the Minotaur respond;
and my alert guide cried: "Run toward the pass;
it's better to descend while he's berserk."
    And so we made our way across that heap
of stones, which often moved beneath my feet

30 because my weight was somewhat strange for them.
    While climbing down, I thought. He said: "You wonder,
perhaps, about that fallen mass, watched over
by the inhuman rage I have just quenched.
    Now I would have you know: the other time

35 that I descended into lower Hell,
this mass of boulders had not yet collapsed;[3]
    but if I reason rightly, it was just
before the coming of the One who took
from Dis the highest circle's splendid spoils

40   that, on all sides, the steep and filthy valley
had trembled so, I thought the universe
felt love (by which, as some believe, the world
    has often been converted into chaos);
and at that moment, here as well as elsewhere,

45 these ancient boulders toppled, in this way.[4]
    But fix your eyes below, upon the valley,
for now we near the stream of blood, where those
who injure others violently, boil."
    O blind cupidity and insane anger,

50 which goad us on so much in our short life,
then steep us in such grief eternally!
    I saw a broad ditch bent into an arc

---

2. The Minotaur, half-man, half-bull, the result of a union between a bull and queen Pasiphaë of Crete, who hid within
an artificial cow to mate with the bull. King Minos of Crete extracted an annual tribute of seven Greek youths and seven
maidens to be thrown to the Minotaur in its labyrinth. Theseus, Duke of Athens, traveled to Crete as one of the sacrificial
youths and killed the Minotaur.

3. Virgil refers to the errand on which Erichtho sent him (Canto 9.22–27), which took place before the crucifixion of
Christ and the Harrowing of Hell, mentioned next.

4. According to a theory of the ancient philosopher Empedocles, the alternate supremacy of principles of hate, which
keeps things separate, and love, which unites all things, causes periodic destruction and construction in the scheme of
the universe; both are required for equilibrium. This is how Virgil understands the earthquake that marked Christ's death
(Matthew 27.51), the supreme sacrifice expressing God's love for his creation.

so that it could embrace all of that plain,
precisely as my guide had said before;

55 between it and the base of the embankment
raced files of Centaurs who were armed with arrows,[5]
as, in the world above, they used to hunt.

On seeing us descend, they all reined in;
and, after they had chosen bows and shafts,

60 three of their number moved out from their ranks;

and still far off, one cried: "What punishment
do you approach as you descend the slope?
But speak from there; if not, I draw my bow."

My master told him: "We shall make reply

65 only to Chiron,[6] when we reach his side;
your hasty will has never served you well."

Then he nudged me and said: "That one is Nessus,
who died because of lovely Deianira
and of himself wrought vengeance for himself.[7]

70 And in the middle, gazing at his chest,
is mighty Chiron, tutor of Achilles;
the third is Pholus, he who was so frenzied.[8]

And many thousands wheel around the moat,
their arrows aimed at any soul that thrusts

75 above the blood more than its guilt allots."

By now we had drawn near those agile beasts;
Chiron drew out an arrow; with the notch,
he parted his beard back upon his jaws.

When he'd uncovered his enormous mouth,

80 he said to his companions: "Have you noticed
how he who walks behind moves what he touches?

Dead souls are not accustomed to do that."
And my good guide—now near the Centaur's chest,
the place where his two natures met—replied:

85 "He is indeed alive, and so alone
it falls to me to show him the dark valley.
Necessity has brought him here, not pleasure.

For she° who gave me this new task was one   *Beatrice*
who had just come from singing halleluiah:

90 he is no robber; I am not a thief.

But by the Power that permits my steps
to journey on so wild a path, give us
one of your band, to serve as our companion;

and let him show us where to ford the ditch,

95 and let him bear this man upon his back,

5. In mythology, centaurs are half-man, half-horse, excellent archers, and notorious for their gluttony and violence.

6. An exceptional centaur, Chiron was traditionally depicted as an educator, scientist, and musician who tutored Achilles, Hercules, and other Greek heroes.

7. Dying of a poisoned arrow shot by Hercules after he tried to rape the hero's wife Deianira, Nessus gave Deianira a robe dipped in his blood which he claimed would preserve her husband's love. When she gave Hercules the robe, he was maddened by the poison in the blood, and burned himself to death to end the agony (Ovid, *Metamorphoses*, 9.127–69).

8. Pholus was killed during the Centaurs' battle with the Lapiths at the wedding of Pirithoüs.

for he's no spirit who can fly through air."

Then Chiron wheeled about and right and said
to Nessus: "Then, return and be their guide;
if other troops disturb you, fend them off."

100   Now, with our faithful escort, we advanced
along the bloodred, boiling ditch's banks,
beside the piercing cries of those who boiled.

I saw some who were sunk up to their brows,
and that huge Centaur said: "These are the tyrants
105 who plunged their hands in blood and plundering.

Here they lament their ruthless crimes; here are
both Alexander and the fierce Dionysius,
who brought such years of grief to Sicily.[9]

That brow with hair so black is Ezzelino;
110 that other there, the blonde one, is Obizzo
of Este, he who was indeed undone,

within the world above, by his fierce son."[1]
Then I turned to the poet, and he said:
"Now let him be your first guide, me your second."

115   A little farther on, the Centaur stopped
above a group that seemed to rise above
the boiling blood as far up as their throats.

He pointed out one shade, alone, apart,
and said: "Within God's bosom, he impaled
120 the heart that still drips blood upon the Thames."[2]

Then I caught sight of some who kept their heads
and even their full chests above the tide;
among them—many whom I recognized.

And so the blood grew always shallower
125 until it only scorched the feet; and here
we found a place where we could ford the ditch.

"Just as you see that, on this side, the brook
continually thins," the Centaur said,

"so I should have you know the rivulet,
130 along the other side, will slowly deepen
its bed, until it reaches once again

the depth where tyranny must make lament.
And there divine justice torments Attila
he who was such a scourge upon the earth,

9. "Alexander" may be either Alexander the Great of Macedonia (356–323 B.C.E.) or Alexander of Pherae, a tyrant of Thessaly of the same period, famed for his cruelty. Dionysius the elder was tyrant of Syracuse in Sicily during the early 4th century B.C.E.

1. Ezzelino III da Romano (1194–1259) was son-in-law of Emperor Frederick II, head of the Ghibellines in Upper Italy, and so infamous for his cruelty that the Pope proclaimed a crusade against him. Obizzo II d'Este (1247–1293) was an ardent Guelf and supporter of Charles of Anjou who fought against Manfred, natural son of Frederick. He was said to have been smothered by his son, Azzo VIII.

2. Guy, son of Simon de Montfort, killed his first cousin Prince Henry of Cornwall in March 1271 during the assembly of the cardinals to elect a pope, supposedly at the very moment of the elevation of the Host when Henry was on his knees. According to some accounts, Henry's heart was enclosed in a statue on London Bridge over the river Thames, still dripping blood because not yet avenged.

135   and Pyrrhus, Sextus;[3] to eternity
        it milks the tears that boiling brook unlocks
    from Rinier of Corneto, Rinier Pazzo,
    those two who waged such war upon the highroads."[4]
        Then he turned round and crossed the ford again.

Canto 13

*The Seventh Circle, Second Ring: the Violent against Themselves (Suicides) or
against their Possessions (Squanderers). The dreary wood, with the Suicides transformed into strange trees, and the Squanderers, hounded and rent by bitches. Pier
della Vigna. Lano and Jacopo da Santo Andrea. The anonymous Florentine suicide.*

        Nessus had not yet reached the other bank
    when we began to make our way across
    a wood on which no path had left its mark.
        No green leaves in that forest, only black;
5   no branches straight and smooth, but knotted, gnarled;
    no fruits were there, but briers bearing poison.
        Even those savage beasts that roam between
    Cécina and Corneto,[1] beasts that hate
    tilled lands, do not have holts° so harsh and dense.   *woods*
10   This is the nesting place of the foul Harpies,
    who chased the Trojans from the Strophades
    with sad foretelling of their future trials.[2]
        Their wings are wide, their necks and faces human;
    their feet are taloned, their great bellies feathered;
15   they utter their laments on the strange trees.
        And my kind master then instructed me:
    "Before you enter farther know that now
    you are within the second ring and shall
    be here until you reach the horrid sand;
20   therefore look carefully; you'll see such things
    as would deprive my speech of all belief."[3]
        From every side I heard the sound of cries,
    but I could not see any source for them,
    so that, in my bewilderment, I stopped.
25   I think that he was thinking that I thought
    so many voices moaned among those trunks
    from people who had been concealed from us.

3. Known as "the Scourge of God," Attila was King of the Huns (433–453). Pyrrhus is either the son of Achilles whose
savage murder of Priam and other Trojans was recorded in *Aeneid* 2 or a king of Epirus who made war on Rome in the
third century B.C.E. Sextus was the son of Pompey and a notorious pirate in Lucan's *Pharsalia*.

4. Two famous highwaymen of Dante's day.

1. The river Cecina and the town of Corneto mark the boundaries of the Maremma, a famously dense Tuscan wood.

2. Mythical monsters in the shapes of birds with clawed hands and women's faces, the Harpies, among other deeds,
fouled the Trojans' feast and drove Aeneas and his companions from the Strophades, islands in the Ionian Sea,
prophesying that they would face starvation and misfortune before reaching Italy (*Aeneid* 3.209–57).

3. This episode closely follows another adventure in *Aeneid* 3. Landed in Thrace, Aeneas tries to tear off a green branch
for an altar only to find black blood dripping from it. The tree entombs Polydorus, a son of Priam sent to purchase aid in
the Trojan War from the King of Thrace, who murdered him instead, stealing the gold proffered as payment.

Therefore my master said: "If you would tear
a little twig from any of these plants,
the thoughts you have will also be cut off."

30

Then I stretched out my hand a little way
and from a great thornbush snapped off a branch,
at which its trunk cried out: "Why do you tear me?"

And then, when it had grown more dark with blood,

35

it asked again: "Why do you break me off?
Are you without all sentiment of pity?

We once were men and now are arid stumps:
your hand might well have shown us greater mercy
had we been nothing more than souls of serpents."

40

As from a sapling log that catches fire
along one of its ends, while at the other
it drips and hisses with escaping vapor,

so from that broken stump issued together
both words and blood; at which I let the branch

45

fall, and I stood like one who is afraid.

My sage said: "Wounded soul, if, earlier,
he had been able to believe what he
had only glimpsed within my poetry,

then he would not have set his hand against you;

50

but its incredibility made me
urge him to do a deed that grieves me deeply.

But tell him who you were, so that he may,
to make amends, refresh your fame within
the world above, where he can still return."

55

To which the trunk: "Your sweet speech draws me so
that I cannot be still; and may it not
oppress you, if I linger now in talk.[4]

I am the one who guarded both the keys
of Frederick's heart and turned them, locking and

60

unlocking them with such dexterity
that none but I could share his confidence;
and I was faithful to my splendid office,
so faithful that I lost both sleep and strength.

The whore who never turned her harlot's eyes

65

away from Caesar's dwelling, she who is
the death of all and vice of every court,

inflamed the minds of everyone against me;
and those inflamed, then so inflamed Augustus
that my delighted honors turned to sadness.[5]

70

My mind, because of its disdainful temper,

4. The speaker, Pier della Vigna (c. 1190–1249), was minister and councilor to Emperor Frederick II. Accused (prob-ably falsely) of plotting with the pope to poison Frederick, he was arrested, thrown into prison, and blinded. He soon committed suicide, it is said by dashing his head against a wall. Pier was also a poet and accomplished letter-writer, as is reflected in the ornamented and mannered style of his speech.

5. The "whore" is envy, which was a sin of the eyes; "Caesar's dwelling" is the imperial court, and "Augustus" is the emperor, after the Roman emperor, Caesar Augustus.

believing it could flee disdain through death,
made me unjust against my own just self.

I swear to you by the peculiar roots
of this thornbush, I never broke my faith
with him who was so worthy—with my lord.

If one of you returns into the world,
then let him help my memory, which still
lies prone beneath the battering of envy."

The poet waited briefly, then he said
to me: "Since he is silent, do not lose
this chance, but speak and ask what you would know."

And I: "Do you continue; ask of him
whatever you believe I should request;
I cannot, so much pity takes my heart."

Then he began again: "Imprisoned spirit,
so may this man do freely what you ask,
may it please you to tell us something more

of how the soul is bound into these knots;
and tell us, if you can, if any one
can ever find his freedom from these limbs."

At this the trunk breathed violently, then
that wind became this voice: "You shall be answered
promptly. When the savage spirit quits

the body from which it has torn itself,
then Minos sends it to the seventh maw.
It falls into the wood, and there's no place

to which it is allotted, but wherever
fortune has flung that soul, that is the space
where, even as a grain of spelt, it sprouts.⁶

It rises as a sapling, a wild plant;
and then the Harpies, feeding on its leaves,
cause pain and for that pain provide a vent.

Like other souls, we shall seek out the flesh
that we have left, but none of us shall wear it;
it is not right for any man to have

what he himself has cast aside. We'll drag
our bodies here; they'll hang in this sad wood,
each on the stump of its vindictive shade."⁷

And we were still intent upon the trunk—
believing it had wanted to say more—
when we were overtaken by a roar,

just as the hunter is aware of chase
and boar as they draw near his post—he hears
the beasts and then the branches as they crack.

And there upon the left were two who, scratched

75

80

85

90

95

100

105

110

115

---

6. Like other wheats and grains, spelt grows readily and in thick clumps out of a single shoot.

7. Souls are to be rejoined with their bodies after the Last Judgment. Because the shade was unjust ("vindictive") to its own body through suicide, it will not be fully reunited with it.

and naked, fled so violently that
they tore away each forest bough they passed.
    The one in front: "Now come, death, quickly come!"
The other shade, who thought himself too slow,
120   was shouting after him: "Lano, your legs
      were not so nimble at the jousts of Toppo!"[8]
And then, perhaps because he'd lost his breath,
he fell into one tangle with a bush.
    Behind these two, black bitches filled the wood,
125   and they were just as eager and as swift
    as greyhounds that have been let off their leash.
    They set their teeth in him where he had crouched;
and, piece by piece, those dogs dismembered him
and carried off his miserable limbs.
130   Then he who was my escort took my hand;
he led me to the lacerated thorn
that wept in vain where it was bleeding, broken.
    "O Jacopo," it said, "da Santo Andrea,
what have you gained by using me as screen?
135   Am I to blame for your indecent life?"
    When my good master stood beside that bush,
he said: "Who were you, who through many wounds
must breathe with blood your melancholy words?"[9]
    And he to us: "O spirits who have come
140   to witness the outrageous laceration
that leaves so many of my branches torn,
    collect them at the foot of this sad thorn.
My home was in the city whose first patron
gave way to John the Baptist; for this reason,
145   he'll always use his art to make it sorrow;[1]
and if—along the crossing of the Arno—
some effigy of Mars had not remained,
    those citizens who afterward rebuilt
their city on the ashes that Attila
150   had left to them, would have travailed in vain.[2]
    I made—of my own house—my gallows place."

Canto 14

*The Seventh Circle, Third Ring: the Violent against God. The First Zone: Blas-
phemers, supine on fiery sands. Capaneus. Virgil on the Old Man of Crete, whose*

8. Lano of Siena and Jacopo da Santo Andrea of Padua, two notorious squanderers of 13th-century Italy.

9. Generally known as "the anonymous Florentine," this soul appears to represent the general self-destructiveness of his city itself rather than a particular inhabitant.

1. In pagan times, the citizens of Florence had chosen Mars as their special patron; when they switched to Christianity, they incurred the war-god's wrath when they converted his temple to a church dedicated to St. John.

2. According to legend, the statue of Mars was removed to a tower near the river Arno, and it fell into the river when the city was destroyed by Attila in 450 (confused here with the Ostrogoth king Totila, who had besieged the city in 542). It was said that the retrieval of the statue had permitted the Florentines to rebuild their city (in fact, it was neither destroyed nor rebuilt).

streaming tears form the rivers of Hell: Acheron, Phlegethon, Styx, and Cocytus. The sight of Lethe postponed.

<blockquote>

Love of our native city overcame me;
I gathered up the scattered boughs and gave
them back to him whose voice was spent already.

From there we reached the boundary that divides
the second from the third ring—and the sight
of a dread work that justice had devised.

To make these strange things clear, I must explain
that we had come upon an open plain
that banishes all green things from its bed.

The wood of sorrow is a garland round it,
just as that wood is ringed by a sad channel;
here, at the very edge, we stayed our steps.

The ground was made of sand, dry and compact,
a sand not different in kind from that
on which the feet of Cato had once tramped.[1]

O vengeance of the Lord, how you should be
dreaded by everyone who now can read
whatever was made manifest to me!

I saw so many flocks of naked souls,
all weeping miserably, and it seemed
that they were ruled by different decrees.

Some lay upon the ground, flat on their backs;
some huddled in a crouch, and there they sat;
and others moved about incessantly.

The largest group was those who walked about,
the smallest, those supine° in punishment;   lying down
but these had looser tongues to tell their torment.

Above that plain of sand, distended flakes
of fire showered down;[2] their fall was slow—
as snow descends on alps when no wind blows.

Just like the flames that Alexander saw
in India's hot zones, when fires fell,
intact and to the ground, on his battalions,

for which—wisely—he had his soldiers tramp
the soil to see that every fire was spent
before new flames were added to the old;[3]

so did the never-ending heat descend;
with this, the sand was kindled just as tinder
on meeting flint will flame—doubling the pain.

The dance of wretched hands was never done;

</blockquote>

Line numbers: 5, 10, 15, 20, 25, 30, 35, 40

---

1. Cato of Utica (95–46 B.C.E.), who led the Pompeian forces through the Libyan Desert in 47 B.C.E. (Lucan, *Pharsalia* 9); Dante placed him at the base of the Mountain of Purgatory (*Purgatorio* 1).

2. The rain of fire derives from the fire that fell upon Sodom and Gomorrah (Genesis 19.24) and also from Ezekiel 38.22.

3. The incident comes from an apocryphal letter from Alexander of Macedon to Aristotle; Dante condenses an incident of trampling on heavily falling snow with a rain of fire from the sky.

now here, now there, they tried to beat aside
the fresh flames as they fell. And I began
    to speak: "My master, you who can defeat
all things except for those tenacious demons
45   who tried to block us at the entryway,
    who is that giant there, who does not seem
to heed the singeing—he who lies and scorns
and scowls, he whom the rains can't seem to soften?"[4]
    And he himself, on noticing that I
50   was querying my guide about him, cried:
"That which I was in life, I am in death.
    Though Jove wear out the smith from whom he took,
in wrath, the keen-edged thunderbolt with which
on my last day I was to be transfixed;
55   or if he tire the others, one by one,
in Mongibello, at the sooty forge,
while bellowing: 'O help, good Vulcan, help!'[5]—
    just as he did when there was war at Phlegra[6]—
and casts his shafts at me with all his force,
60   not even then would he have happy vengeance."
    Then did my guide speak with such vehemence
as I had never heard him use before:
"O Capaneus, for your arrogance
    that is not quenched, you're punished all the more:
65   no torture other than your own madness
could offer pain enough to match your wrath."
    But then, with gentler face he turned to me
and said: "That man was one of seven kings
besieging Thebes; he held—and still, it seems,
70   holds—God in great disdain, disprizing° Him;   *scorning*
but as I told him now, his maledictions
sit well as ornaments upon his chest.
    Now follow me and—take care—do not set
your feet upon the sand that's burning hot,
75   but always keep them back, close to the forest."
    In silence we had reached a place where flowed
a slender watercourse out of the wood—
a stream whose redness makes me shudder still.
    As from the Bulicame pours a brook
80   whose waters then are shared by prostitutes,[7]
so did this stream run down across the sand.
    Its bed and both its banks were made of stone,
together with the slopes along its shores,

4. Capaneus was one of the legendary Seven against Thebes, kings who besieged the city; defying Jove as he scaled the walls, Capaneus was struck down by a thunderbolt.

5. Vulcan, god of fire and of the forge, with his assistants, the Cyclopes, made Jove's thunderbolts. His furnace was thought to be at Mt. Etna in Sicily, called Mongibello in Italian.

6. When the rebellious Giants stormed Olympus, Jove defeated them at the battle of Phlegra (literally "the place of burning") with the help of Hercules.

7. The Bulicame was a famous sulphurous hot spring near Viterbo, north of Rome. Its waters were piped into the houses of prostitutes there.

so that I saw our passageway lay there.

85   "Among all other things that I have shown you
since we first made our way across the gate
whose threshold is forbidden to no one,

    no thing has yet been witnessed by your eyes
as notable as this red rivulet,
90 which quenches every flame that burns above it."

    These words were spoken by my guide; at this,
I begged him to bestow the food for which
he had already given me the craving.[8]

    "A devastated land lies in midsea,
95 a land that is called Crete," he answered me.
"Under its king the world once lived chastely.

    Within that land there was a mountain blessed
with leaves and waters, and they called it Ida;
but it is withered now like some old thing.

100   It once was chosen as a trusted cradle
by Rhea for her son; to hide him better,
when he cried out, she had her servants clamor.[9]

    Within the mountain is a huge Old Man,
who stands erect—his back turned toward Damietta°—   *in Egypt*
105 and looks at Rome as if it were his mirror.

    The Old Man's head is fashioned of fine gold,
the purest silver forms his arms and chest,
but he is made of brass down to the cleft;

    below that point he is of choicest iron
110 except for his right foot, made of baked clay;
and he rests more on this than on the left.[1]

    Each part of him, except the gold, is cracked;
and down that fissure there are tears that drip;
when gathered, they pierce through that cavern's floor

115   and, crossing rocks into this valley, form
the Acheron and Styx and Phlegethon;
and then they make their way down this tight channel,

    and at the point past which there's no descent,
they form Cocytus; since you are to see
120 what that pool is, I'll not describe it here."

    And I asked him: "But if the rivulet
must follow such a course down from our world,
why can we see it only at this boundary?"

    And he to me: "You know this place is round;

8. The tale of the Old Man of Crete, used to explain the origin of the waterways of Hell, is a synthesis of Ovid's myth of the four ages—a golden age under Saturn, mythical king of Crete, when "the world once lived chastely," followed in declining order by silver, bronze and iron (*Metamorphoses* 1.89–150), and the prophet Daniel's account of a composite statue in the dream of Nebuchadnezzar (Daniel 2.31–35).

9. Rhea, or Cybele, was mother by Saturn of Jove. In order to avert a prophecy that he would be dethroned by one of his children, Saturn had devoured them one by one as they were born. Only Jove was saved when Rhea retired to Mt. Ida to give birth and substituted a stone for the child. To hide the infant's cries, she had her priests clash their weapons and chant.

1. Nebuchadnezzar's dream imagined a similar statue, broken to pieces by "a stone cut out of a mountain without hands." Dante adds the detail, reminiscent of the pilgrim's aborted climb in Canto 1.30, of the unevenly weighted feet, and the gloss of the statue as an allegory of the four ages.

125   and though the way that you have come is long,
    and always toward the left and toward the bottom,
      you still have not completed all the circle:
    so that, if something new appears to us,
    it need not bring such wonder to your face."[2]

130   And I again: "Master, where's Phlegethon
    and where is Lethe?[3] You omit the second
    and say this rain of tears has formed the first."

      "I'm pleased indeed," he said, "with all your questions;
    yet one of them might well have found its answer
135   already—when you saw the red stream boiling.

      You shall see Lethe, but past this abyss,
    there where the spirits go to cleanse themselves
    when their repented guilt is set aside."

      Then he declared: "The time has come to quit
140   this wood; see that you follow close behind me;
    these margins form a path that does not scorch,
      and over them, all flaming vapor is quenched."

Canto 15

*Still the Seventh Circle, Third Ring: the Violent against God. Second Zone: the Sod-
omites, endlessly crossing the fiery sands beneath the rain of fire. Brunetto Latini,
whom Dante treats as mentor. Priscian, Francesco d'Accorso, and Andrea dei Mozzi,
Bishop of Florence.*

      Now one of the hard borders bears us forward;
    the river mist forms shadows overhead
    and shields the shores and water from the fire.

      Just as between Wissant and Bruges, the Flemings,
5   in terror of the tide that floods toward them,
    have built a wall of dykes to daunt the sea;

      and as the Paduans, along the Brenta,
    build bulwarks to defend their towns and castles
    before the dog days fall on Carentana;[1]

10   just so were these embankments, even though
    they were not built so high and not so broad,
    whoever was the artisan who made them.

      By now we were so distant from the wood
    that I should not have made out where it was—
15   not even if I'd turned around to look—
      when we came on a company of spirits

---

2. There has been much discussion as to whether Virgil's explanation is consistent with geographical descriptions elsewhere in the canticle, but it is clear enough here: each river is basically level, circling a particular region of Hell, and linked to the others by a descending rivulet such as the one encountered here that leads from Phlegethon down to Cocytus. Because their descent has nearly always been in a leftward direction, the travelers haven't always crossed such connecting streams.

3. Well versed in his classical mythology, the pilgrim is puzzled over the absence of Lethe, the river of forgetting of which the souls in the Elysian Fields drink before returning to the world above (*Aeneid* 6).

1. Wissant and Bruges are given as the eastern and western boundaries of the Flemish seaboard, lined with great dykes to hold back the North Sea. The melt-off from the Carnic Alps ("Carentana") would swell the northern Italian river Brenta as it flowed down into the city of Padua.

who made their way along the bank; and each
stared steadily at us, as in the dusk,
 beneath the new moon, men look at each other.
20   They knit their brows and squinted at us—just
as an old tailor at his needle's eye.
   And when that family looked harder, I
was recognized by one, who took me by
the hem and cried out: "This is marvelous!"
25   That spirit having stretched his arm toward me,
I fixed my eyes upon his baked, brown features,
 so that the scorching of his face could not
  prevent my mind from recognizing him;
and lowering my face to meet his face,
30 I answered him: "Are you here, Ser Brunetto?"[2]
   And he: "My son, do not mind if Brunetto
Latini lingers for a while with you
and lets the file he's with pass on ahead."
   I said: "With all my strength I pray you, stay;
35 and if you'd have me rest awhile with you,
I shall, if that please him with whom I go."
   "O son," he said, "whoever of this flock
stops but a moment, stays a hundred years
and cannot shield himself when fire strikes.
40   Therefore move on; below—but close—I'll follow;
and then I shall rejoin my company,
who go lamenting their eternal sorrows."
   I did not dare to leave my path for his
own level; but I walked with head bent low
45 as does a man who goes in reverence.
   And he began: "What destiny or chance
has led you here below before your last
day came, and who is he who shows the way?"
   "There, in the sunlit life above," I answered,
50 "before my years were full, I went astray
within a valley. Only yesterday
 at dawn I turned my back upon it—but
when I was newly lost, he here appeared,
to guide me home again along this path."
55   And he to me: "If you pursue your star,
you cannot fail to reach a splendid harbor,
if in fair life, I judged you properly;
 and if I had not died too soon for this,
on seeing Heaven was so kind to you,

---

2. "Master" Brunetto, a term of respect. Brunetto Latini (c. 1220–1294) was a celebrated writer and Guelph political
figure who was active in Florentine affairs. Author of such works as a French prose encyclopedia and the Italian didactic
poem the *Tesoretto,* he was not actually Dante's teacher, but an important influence. He had no reputation as a sodomite,
and there has been much debate over whether Dante also intended the sin to be understood, as it often was in the Middle
Ages, in terms of a "sterile" or nonproductive use of language and learning.

60   I should have helped sustain you in your work.
       But that malicious, that ungrateful people
come down, in ancient times, from Fiesole—
still keeping something of the rock and mountain[3]—
       for your good deeds, will be your enemy:

65   and there is cause—among the sour sorbs,
the sweet fig is not meant to bear its fruit.[4]
       The world has long since called them blind, a people
presumptuous, avaricious, envious;
       be sure to cleanse yourself of their foul ways.

70   Your fortune holds in store such honor for you,
one party and the other will be hungry
for you—but keep the grass far from the goat.
       For let the beasts of Fiesole find forage
among themselves, and leave the plant alone—

75   if still, among their dung, it rises up—
       in which there lives again the sacred seed
of those few Romans who remained in Florence
when such a nest of wickedness was built."
       "If my desire were answered totally,"

80   I said to Ser Brunetto, "you'd still be
among, not banished from, humanity.
       Within my memory is fixed—and now
moves me—your dear, your kind paternal
image when, in the world above, from time to time

85   you taught me how man makes himself eternal;[5]
and while I live, my gratitude for that
must always be apparent in my words.
       What you have told me of my course, I write;
I keep it with another text, for comment

90   by one who'll understand, if I may reach her.
       One thing alone I'd have you plainly see:
so long as I am not rebuked by conscience,
I stand prepared for Fortune, come what may.
       My ears find no new pledge in that prediction;

95   therefore, let Fortune turn her wheel as she
may please, and let the peasant turn his mattock."°   *hoe*
       At this, my master turned his head around
and toward the right, and looked at me and said:
"He who takes note of this has listened well."

100   But nonetheless, my talk with Ser Brunetto
continues, and I ask of him who are

3. The tradition was that Florence was founded following Caesar's successful siege of the ancient town of Fiesole, on a hill four miles to the northeast, partly by Romans and partly by families from the destroyed town.

4. The sorb is related to the apple and the pear; the metaphor parallels the contrast between Fiesolan and Roman Florentines, with Dante as the fig and his tormenters as the "sour sorbs."

5. Brunetto wrote in the *Tresor* that "Glory gives the wise man a second life; that is to say, after his death the reputation which remains of his good works makes it seem as if he were still alive" (2.120.1).

his comrades of repute and excellence.

And he to me: "To know of some is good;
but for the rest, silence is to be praised;
105   the time we have is short for so much talk.

In brief, know that my company has clerics
and men of letters and of fame—and all
were stained by one same sin upon the earth.

That sorry crowd holds Priscian and Francesco
110   d'Accorso;[6] and among them you can see,
if you have any longing for such scurf,

the one the Servant of His Servants sent
from the Arno to the Bacchiglione's banks,
and there he left his tendons strained by sin.[7]

115   I would say more; but both my walk and words
must not be longer, for—beyond—I see
new smoke emerging from the sandy bed.

Now people come with whom I must not be.
Let my *Tesoro*, in which I still live,
120   be precious to you; and I ask no more."

And then he turned and seemed like one of those
who race across the fields to win the green
cloth at Verona; of those runners, he
appeared to be the winner, not the loser.[8]

Canto 16

Still the Seventh Circle, Third Ring, Second Zone: other Sodomites. Three Floren-
tines, Guido Guerra, Tegghiaio Aldobrandi, Jacopo Rusticucci. The decadence of
Florence. Phlegethon, cascading into the next zone. The cord of Dante, used by Virgil
to summon a monstrous figure from the waters.

No sooner had I reached the place where one
could hear a murmur, like a beehive's hum,
of waters as they fell to the next circle,

when, setting out together, three shades ran,
5   leaving another company that passed
beneath the rain of bitter punishment.

They came toward us, and each of them cried out:
"Stop, you who by your clothing seem to be
someone who comes from our indecent country!"[1]

---

6. Priscian (fl. c. 500 C.E.) was a celebrated Latin grammarian whose works were widely used in medieval schools. Francesco d'Accorso (1225–1293) was a renowned lawyer and professor of law at Bologna and Oxford.

7. Andrea de' Mozzi was bishop of Florence (on the Arno) until transferred by Pope Boniface VIII in 1295 to Vicenza (on the Bacchiglione) due to his unseemly living. He died there several months later, leaving a body, according to Brunetto, with muscles "strained" by sodomy. Boniface VIII is referred to, with irony, by the pope's name in official acts, "Servant of Servants."

8. This foot race was instituted in 1207 and run annually on the first Sunday in Lent outside Verona. According to Boccaccio, the runners were naked and the prize was a piece of green cloth.

1. According to the Florentine chronicler Villani, the dress of his people "was the most beautiful, the most noble, and the most decorous of that of any nation; it was in the manner of the togaed Roman."

10   Ah me, what wounds I saw upon their limbs,
  wounds new and old, wounds that the flames seared in!
  It pains me still as I remember it.

   When they cried out, my master paid attention;
  he turned his face toward me and then he said:
15 "Now wait: to these one must show courtesy.

   And were it not the nature of this place
  for shafts of fire to fall, I'd say that haste
  was seemlier for you than for those three."

   As soon as we stood still, they started up
20 their ancient wail again; and when they reached us,
  they formed a wheel, all three of them together.

   As champions, naked, oiled, will always do,
  each studying the grip that serves him best
  before the blows and wounds begin to fall,

25   while wheeling so, each one made sure his face
  was turned to me, so that their necks opposed
  their feet in one uninterrupted flow.[2]

   And, "If the squalor of this shifting sand,
  together with our baked and barren features,
30 makes us and our requests contemptible,"

   one said, "then may our fame incline your mind
  to tell us who you are, whose living feet
  can make their way through Hell with such assurance.

   He in whose steps you see me tread, although
35 he now must wheel about both peeled and naked,
  was higher in degree than you believe:

   he was a grandson of the good Gualdrada,
  and Guido Guerra was his name; in life
  his sword and his good sense accomplished much.

40   The other who, behind me, tramples sand—
  Tegghiaio Aldobrandi, one whose voice
  should have been heeded in the world above.

   And I, who share this punishment with them,
  was Jacopo Rusticucci; certainly,
45 more than all else, my savage wife destroyed me."[3]

   If I'd had shield and shelter from the fire,
  I should have thrown myself down there among them—
  I think my master would have sanctioned that;

   but since that would have left me burned and baked,
50 my fear won out against the good intention
  that made me so impatient to embrace them.

   Then I began: "Your present state had fixed
  not scorn but sorrow in me—and so deeply
  that it will only disappear slowly—

---

2. The theme of athletics introduced at the end of the previous canto continues here, referring either to ancient wrestlers, to the medieval trial by combat to settle judicial disputes, or to both.

3. Guido and Tegghiaio were prominent Guelfs of the mid 13th century; Rusticucci a less distinguished neighbor of Tegghiaio and also a Guelf. Dante had asked for news of the latter two in Canto 6. Jacopo blames his wife for his fate.

55   as soon as my lord spoke to me with words
that made me understand what kind of men
were coming toward us, men of worth like yours.

      For I am of your city; and with fondness,
I've always told and heard the others tell
60 of both your actions and your honored names.

      I leave the gall and go for the sweet apples
that I was promised by my truthful guide;
but first I must descend into the center."

      "So may your soul long lead your limbs and may
65 your fame shine after you," he answered then,
"tell us if courtesy and valor still

      abide within our city as they did
when we were there, or have they disappeared
completely;[4] for Guiglielmo Borsiere,

70   who only recently has come to share
our torments, and goes there with our companions,
has caused us much affliction with his words."[5]

      "Newcomers to the city and quick gains
have brought excess and arrogance to you,
75 o Florence, and you weep for it already!"

      So I cried out with face upraised; the three
looked at each other when they heard my answer
as men will stare when they have heard the truth.

      "If you can always offer a reply
80 so readily to others," said all three,
"then happy you who speak, at will, so clearly.

      So, if you can escape these lands of darkness
and see the lovely stars on your return,
when you repeat with pleasure, 'I was there,'

85   be sure that you remember us to men."
At this they broke their wheel; and as they fled,
their swift legs seemed to be no less than wings.

      The time it took for them to disappear—
more brief than time it takes to say "amen";
90 and so, my master thought it right to leave.

      I followed him. We'd only walked a little
when roaring water grew so near to us
we hardly could have heard each other speak.

      And even as the river that is first
95 to take its own course eastward from Mount Viso,
along the left flank of the Apennines

      (which up above is called the Acquacheta,
before it spills into its valley bed

---

4. True to the deference with which Dante treats them here, these Florentines are genuinely concerned with the fate of their city which, as in Canto 10, is too close for them to foresee.

5. Guiglielmo Borsiere was a pursemaker known for his courteous manners and bearing; he is the subject of a tale in Boccaccio's *Decameron* (1.8).

and flows without that name beyond Forlì),

100   reverberates above San Benedetto
dell'Alpe as it cascades in one leap,
where there is space enough to house a thousand;[6]

      so did we hear that blackened water roar
as it plunged down a steep and craggy bank,
105   enough to deafen us in a few hours.

      Around my waist I had a cord as girdle,
and with it once I thought I should be able
to catch the leopard with the painted hide.[7]

      And after I had loosened it completely,
110   just as my guide commanded me to do,
I handed it to him, knotted and coiled.

      At this, he wheeled around upon his right
and cast it, at some distance from the edge,
straight down into the depth of the ravine.

115   "And surely something strange must here reply,"
I said within myself, "to this strange sign—
the sign my master follows with his eye."

      Ah, how much care men ought to exercise
with those whose penetrating intellect
120   can see our thoughts—not just our outer act!

      He said to me: "Now there will soon emerge
what I await and what your thought has conjured:
it soon must be discovered to your sight."

      Faced with that truth which seems a lie, a man
125   should always close his lips as long as he can—
to tell it shames him, even though he's blameless;

      but here I can't be still; and by the lines
of this my Comedy, reader, I swear[8]—
and may my verse find favor for long years—
130   that through the dense and darkened air I saw

a figure swimming, rising up, enough
to bring amazement to the firmest heart,

      like one returning from the waves where he
went down to loose an anchor snagged upon
135   a reef or something else hid in the sea,

      who stretches upward and draws in his feet.

Canto 17

The monster Geryon. The Seventh Circle, Third Ring, Third Zone: the Violent against Nature and Art (Usurers), each seated beneath the rain of fire with a purse—bearing his family's heraldic emblem—around his neck. Descent to the Eighth Circle on the back of Geryon.

"Behold the beast who bears the pointed tail,
who crosses mountains, shatters weapons, walls!
Behold the one whose stench fills all the world!"
So did my guide begin to speak to me,
and then he signaled him to come ashore
close to the end of those stone passageways.
And he came on, that filthy effigy
of fraud, and landed with his head and torso
but did not draw his tail onto the bank.[1]
The face he wore was that of a just man,
so gracious was his features' outer semblance;
and all his trunk, the body of a serpent;
he had two paws, with hair up to the armpits;
his back and chest as well as both his flanks
had been adorned with twining knots and circlets.
No Turks or Tartars ever fashioned fabrics
more colorful in background and relief,
nor had Arachne ever loomed such webs.[2]
As boats will sometimes lie along the shore,
with part of them on land and part in water,
and just as there, among the guzzling Germans,
the beaver sets himself when he means war,[3]
so did that squalid beast lie on the margin
of stone that serves as border for the sand.
And all his tail was quivering in the void
while twisting upward its envenomed fork,
which had a tip just like a scorpion's.
My guide said: "Now we'd better bend our path
a little, till we reach as far as that
malicious beast which crouches over there."
Thus we descended on the right hand side[4]
and moved ten paces on the stony brink
in order to avoid the sand and fire.
When we had reached the sprawling beast, I saw—
a little farther on, upon the sand—
some sinners sitting near the fissured rock.
And here my master said to me: "So that

5

10

15

20

25

30

35

---

1. In classical mythology, Geryon was a giant possessing three bodies and three heads, slain by Hercules when the hero took his prized cattle as one of the Twelve Labors. Dante's description gives Geryon a threefold nature—man, beast and serpent—deriving some of the imagery from biblical sources.

2. Tartar and Turkish cloths were highly valued in the Middle Ages for their richness and intricacy of design; from a dogmatic Christian perspective, their infidel makers were also treacherous. In Greek mythology, the mortal Arachne challenged Minerva to a weaving contest; angry at the result, the goddess transformed her into a spider (Ovid, *Metamorphoses* 6.5–145).

3. According to popular belief, the beaver (common in Germany) caught fish by squirting oily drops while agitating the water with its tail; deceived by the drops, the fish came close enough to be grabbed.

4. The second of the two right-hand turns in Hell (the first was at 9.132); this one suggests the impossibility of approaching fraud in a straightforward manner.

you may experience this ring in full,
go now, and see the state in which they are.

40   But keep your conversation with them brief;
till you return, I'll parley with this beast,
to see if he can lend us his strong shoulders."

        So I went on alone[5] and even farther
along the seventh circle's outer margin,
45   to where the melancholy people sat.

        Despondency was bursting from their eyes;
this side, then that, their hands kept fending off,
at times the flames, at times the burning soil:

        not otherwise do dogs in summer—now
50   with muzzle, now with paw—when they are bitten
by fleas or gnats or by the sharp gadfly.

        When I had set my eyes upon the faces
of some on whom that painful fire falls,
I recognized no one; but I did notice

55   that from the neck of each a purse was hung
that had a special color and an emblem,
and their eyes seemed to feast upon these pouches.[6]

        Looking about—when I had come among them—
I saw a yellow purse with azure on it
60   that had the face and manner of a lion.

        Then, as I let my eyes move farther on,
I saw another purse that was bloodred,
and it displayed a goose more white than butter.

        And one who had an azure, pregnant sow
65   inscribed as emblem on his white pouch, said
to me: "What are you doing in this pit?

        Now you be off; and since you're still alive,
remember that my neighbor Vitaliano
shall yet sit here, upon my left hand side.

70   Among these Florentines, I'm Paduan;
I often hear them thunder in my ears,
shouting, 'Now let the sovereign cavalier,

        the one who'll bring the purse with three goats, come!'"
At this he slewed his mouth, and then he stuck
75   his tongue out, like an ox that licks its nose.

        And I, afraid that any longer stay
might anger him who'd warned me to be brief,
made my way back from those exhausted souls.

        I found my guide, who had already climbed
80   upon the back of that brute animal,
and he told me: "Be strong and daring now,

        for our descent is by this kind of stairs:

---

5. The first and only time in the *Inferno* in which the pilgrim moves alone, without Virgil.
6. The emblems on the moneylenders' pouches belong to distinguished Florentine and Paduan families well-known for their usury.

you mount in front; I want to be between,
so that the tail can't do you any harm."

85 As one who feels the quartan fever near
and shivers, with his nails already blue,[7]
the sight of shade enough to make him shudder,

so I became when I had heard these words;
90 but then I felt the threat of shame, which makes
a servant—in his kind lord's presence—brave.

I settled down on those enormous shoulders;
I wished to say (and yet my voice did not
come as I thought): "See that you hold me tight."

95 But he who—other times, in other dangers—
sustained me, just as soon as I had mounted,
clasped me within his arms and propped me up,

and said: "Now, Geryon, move on; take care to
keep your circles wide, your landing slow;
remember the new weight you're carrying."

100 Just like a boat that, starting from its moorings,
moves backward, backward, so that beast took off;
and when he felt himself completely clear,

he turned his tail to where his chest had been
and, having stretched it, moved it like an eel,
105 and with his paws he gathered in the air.

I do not think that there was greater fear
in Phaëthon when he let his reins go free—
for which the sky, as one still sees, was scorched—

nor in poor Icarus when he could feel
110 his sides unwinged because the wax was melting,
his father shouting to him, "That way's wrong!"[8]

than was in me when, on all sides, I saw
that I was in the air, and everything
had faded from my sight—except the beast.

115 Slowly, slowly, swimming, he moves on;
he wheels and he descends, but I feel only
the wind upon my face and the wind rising.

Already, on our right, I heard the torrent
resounding, there beneath us, horribly,
120 so that I stretched my neck and looked below.

Then I was more afraid of falling off,
for I saw fires and I heard laments,
at which I tremble, crouching, and hold fast.

And now I saw what I had missed before:

---

7. The quartan fever takes its name from the four-day cycle of shivering fits that accompanies it.

8. Phaëthon was son of Apollo and a mortal woman. Phaëthon persuaded his father to allow him to drive the chariot of the sun for a day, but he couldn't control the horses, and they ran so near to the earth that Jupiter killed Phaëthon with a thunderbolt to save the earth from burning (Ovid, *Metamorphoses* 2.1–138). In another myth, Icarus escaped with his father Daedalus from Crete with wings the inventor had fashioned together with wax. Ignoring his father's warning, Icarus flew too close to the sun, the wax melted, and he plummeted to his death in the sea (*Metamorphoses* 8.203–35; see pages 455–56.)

125   his wheeling and descent—because great torments
       were drawing closer to us on all sides.

         Just as a falcon long upon the wing—
       who, seeing neither lure nor bird, compels
       the falconer to cry, "Ah me, you fall!"—

130   descends, exhausted, in a hundred circles,
       where he had once been swift, and sets himself,
       embittered and enraged, far from his master;[9]

         such, at the bottom of the jagged rock,
       was Geryon, when he had set us down.

135   And once our weight was lifted from his back,
       he vanished like an arrow from a bow.

Canto 18

The Eighth Circle, called Malebolge ("Evil-Pouches"), with its Ten Pouches,
where "ordinary" fraud is punished. The First Pouch, with Panders and Seducers
scourged by horned demons. Venèdico Caccianemico. Jason. The Second Pouch, with
Flatterers immersed in excrement. Alessio Interminei. Thais.

         There is a place in Hell called Malebolge,
       made all of stone the color of crude iron,
       as is the wall that makes its way around it.

         Right in the middle of this evil field
5   is an abyss, a broad and yawning pit,
       whose structure I shall tell in its due place.

         The belt, then, that extends between the pit
       and that hard, steep wall's base is circular;
       its bottom has been split into ten valleys.

10   Just as, where moat on moat surrounds a castle
       in order to keep guard upon the walls,
       the ground they occupy will form a pattern,

         so did the valleys here form a design;
       and as such fortresses have bridges running
15   right from their thresholds toward the outer bank,

         so here, across the banks and ditches, ridges
       ran from the base of that rock wall until
       the pit that cuts them short and joins them all.

         This was the place in which we found ourselves
20   when Geryon had put us down; the poet
       held to the left, and I walked at his back.

         Upon the right I saw new misery,
       I saw new tortures and new torturers,
       filling the first of Malebolge's moats.

25   Along its bottom, naked sinners moved,
       to our side of the middle, facing us;

---

9. Trained not to descend until either it sights its prey or is called back by its master whirling a lure, the falcon will
remain aloft until compelled by exhaustion to come down.

beyond that, they moved with us, but more quickly—
    as, in the year of Jubilee, the Romans,
confronted by great crowds, contrived a plan

30   that let the people pass across the bridge,
    for to one side went all who had their eyes
upon the Castle, heading toward St. Peter's,

and to the other, those who faced the Mount.[1]
    Both left and right, along the somber rock,

35   I saw horned demons with enormous whips,
who lashed those spirits cruelly from behind.[2]

    Ah, how their first strokes made those sinners lift
their heels! Indeed no sinner waited for
a second stroke to fall—or for a third.

40   And as I moved ahead, my eyes met those
of someone else, and suddenly I said:
"I was not spared the sight of him before."

    And so I stayed my steps, to study him;
my gentle guide had stopped together with me

45   and gave me leave to take a few steps back.
    That scourged soul thought that he could hide himself
by lowering his face;[3] it helped him little,

for I said: "You, who cast your eyes upon
the ground, if these your features are not false,

50   must be Venèdico Caccianemico;[4]
but what brings you to sauces so piquant?"

    And he to me: "I speak unwillingly;
but your plain speech, that brings the memory
of the old world to me, is what compels me;

55   For it was I who led Ghisolabella
to do as the Marquis would have her do—
however they retell that filthy tale.

    I'm not the only Bolognese who weeps here;
indeed, this place is so crammed full of us

60   that not so many tongues have learned to say
    sipa between the Sàvena and Reno;[5]
if you want faith and testament of that,
just call to mind our avaricious hearts."

    And as he spoke, a demon cudgeled him

65   with his horsewhip and cried: "Be off, you pimp,
there are no women here for you to trick."

---

1. A rarity in medieval times: separate lanes for traffic in each direction. The first Jubilee or Holy Year was proclaimed by Pope Boniface VIII in 1300, granting indulgence (reduction of penance) for all those who visited the basilicas of St. Peter and San Paolo fuori le Mura; hundreds of thousands of pilgrims came.

2. The reader finally encounters the horned demons familiar from medieval iconography and earlier otherworld visions; in Dante's scheme, they are specific to the realm of fraud.

3. A change in behavior: the souls this deep in Hell prefer anonymity rather than the fame and salvaged reputation of those higher up.

4. Son of the head of the Guelf party of Bologna. He is said to have been bribed by his ally Obizzo II to gain him entry to his sister Ghisolobella's bedchamber.

5. *Sipa* is the word for "yes" in the old dialect spoken between the Sàvena and Reno streams that form the western and eastern bounds of the territory of Bologna. Dante singles out Bologna for its panders, or pimps.

I joined my escort once again; and then
with but few steps, we came upon a place
where, from the bank, a rocky ridge ran out.

70 We climbed quite easily along that height;
and turning right upon its jagged back,
we took our leave of those eternal circlings.

When we had reached the point where that ridge opens
below to leave a passage for the lashed,

75 my guide said: "Stay, and make sure that the sight
of still more ill-born spirits strikes your eyes,
for you have not yet seen their faces, since
they have been moving in our own direction."

From the old bridge we looked down at the ranks

80 of those approaching from the other side;
they too were driven onward by the lash.

And my good master, though I had not asked,
urged me: "Look at that mighty one who comes
and does not seem to shed a tear of pain:

85 how he still keeps the image of a king!
That shade is Jason, who with heart and head
deprived the men of Colchis of their ram.[6]

He made a landfall on the isle of Lemnos
after its women, bold and pitiless,

90 had given all their island males to death.

With polished words and love signs he took in
Hypsipyle, the girl whose own deception
had earlier deceived the other women.[7]

And he abandoned her, alone and pregnant;

95 such guilt condemns him to such punishment;
and for Medea, too, revenge is taken.

With him go those who cheated so: this is
enough for you to know of that first valley
and of the souls it clamps within its jaws."

100 We were already where the narrow path
reaches and intersects the second bank
and serves as shoulder for another bridge.

We heard the people whine in the next pouch
and heard them as they snorted with their snouts;

105 we heard them use their palms to beat themselves.

And exhalations, rising from below,
stuck to the banks, encrusting them with mold,
and so waged war against both eyes and nose.

The bottom is so deep, we found no spot

6. Jason was leader of the Argonauts on the expedition to Colchis to obtain the golden fleece. Along the way, they landed at Lemnos, where Jason seduced and then abandoned Hypsipyle, daughter of the king, leaving her with twin sons. After Medea, daughter of the king of the Colchians, had helped him to secure the fleece, Jason took her with him as his wife, but later left her for Creusa, daughter of Creon, king of Corinth. In revenge, she killed the two children she had borne him (Ovid, *Metamorphoses* 7.1–397). See also Euripides's version (page 281).

7. When the women of Lemnos had killed all the other men on the island, Hypsipyle had managed secretly to save her father's life (Statius, *Thebaid* 5.403–85).

110   to see it from, except by climbing up
    the arch until the bridge's highest point.

      This was the place we reached; the ditch beneath
    held people plunged in excrement that seemed
    as if it had been poured from human privies.°   *toilets*

115   And while my eyes searched that abysmal sight,
    I saw one with a head so smeared with shit,
    one could not see if he were lay or cleric.[8]

      He howled: "Why do you stare more greedily
    at me than at the others who are filthy?"

120   And I: "Because, if I remember right,
    I have seen you before, with your hair dry;
    and so I eye you more than all: you are
    Alessio Interminei of Lucca."[9]

      Then he continued, pounding on his pate:

125   "I am plunged here because of flatteries—
    of which my tongue had such sufficiency."

      At which my guide advised me: "See you thrust
    your head a little farther to the front,
    so that your eyes can clearly glimpse the face

130   of that besmirched, bedraggled harridan°   *shrew*
    who scratches at herself with shit-filled nails,
    and now she crouches, now she stands upright.

      That is Thaïs, the harlot who returned
    her lover's question, 'Are you very grateful

135   to me?' by saying, 'Yes, enormously.'[1]
      And now our sight has had its fill of this."

Canto 19

*The Eighth Circle, Third Pouch, where the Simonists are set, heads down, into
holes in the rock, with their protruding feet tormented by flames. Pope Nicholas III.
Dante's invective against simoniacal popes.*

      O Simon Magus! O his sad disciples!
    Rapacious ones, who take the things of God,
    that ought to be the brides of Righteousness,
      and make them fornicate for gold and silver!

5   The time has come to let the trumpet sound
    for you; your place is here in this third pouch.[1]
      We had already reached the tomb beyond

---

8. That is, he couldn't tell if the head was tonsured. Like their hypocrisy (see the sixth pouch), the flattery of clerics was proverbial.

9. Member of a prominent Guelf family of the Tuscan town of Lucca.

1. Thaïs is a courtesan in *Eunuchus,* a play by the ancient Roman playwright Terence. In fact, the flatterer in the scene referred to is the go-between, a soldier named Gnatho.

1. In the Bible, Simon Magus was a converted sorcerer who attempted to buy the power of conferring the Holy Ghost. He was rebuked by the apostle Peter for presuming that the gift of God might be purchased (Acts 8:9–24). From his name is derived the word "simony," which refers to the buying or selling of spiritual goods and offices. The metaphor of lines 3–4 relates this pouch with the previous one by depicting simonists as pimps of the Church, the Bride of Christ. Town criers would sound a trumpet to announce the public reading of judicial sentences; the word also alludes to the sounding of the angel's trumpet on Judgment Day.

and climbed onto the ridge, where its high point
hangs just above the middle of the ditch.

10   O Highest Wisdom, how much art you show
in heaven, earth, and this sad world below,
how just your power is when it allots![2]

    Along the sides and down along the bottom,
I saw that livid rock was perforated:
15   the openings were all one width and round.

    They did not seem to me less broad or more
than those that in my handsome San Giovanni
were made to serve as basins for baptizing;

    and one of these, not many years ago,
20   I broke for someone who was drowning in it:
and let this be my seal to set men straight.[3]

    Out from the mouth of each hole there emerged
a sinner's feet and so much of his legs
up to the thigh; the rest remained within.

25   Both soles of every sinner were on fire;
their joints were writhing with such violence,
they would have severed withes° and ropes of grass.   *thin branches*

    As flame on oily things will only stir
along the outer surface, so there, too,
30   that fire made its way from heels to toes.

    "Master," I said, "who is that shade who suffers
and quivers more than all his other comrades,
that sinner who is licked by redder flames?"

    And he to me: "If you would have me lead
35   you down along the steepest of the banks,
from him you'll learn about his self and sins."

    And I: "What pleases you will please me too:
you are my lord; you know I do not swerve
from what you will; you know what is unspoken."

40   At this we came upon the fourth embankment;
we turned and, keeping to the left, descended
into the narrow, perforated bottom.

    My good lord did not let me leave his side
until he'd brought me to the hole that held
45   that sinner who lamented with his legs.

    "Whoever you may be, dejected soul,
whose head is downward, planted like a pole,"
my words began, "do speak if you are able."

    I stood as does the friar who confesses
50   the foul assassin who, fixed fast, head down,

---

81

2. The apostrophe to the Lord praises the "art" which he has devoted to the design of hell as much as to that of heaven and earth.

3. Like most Florentine children of the time, Dante was baptized in the famous Baptistery of Florence, San Giovanni. It is possible Dante mentioned his motive in breaking the font to defend himself against accusations of sacrilege; it is certainly noteworthy that he placed it in a canto devoted to the misuse of sacred vessels and offices.

calls back the friar, and so delays his death;[4]

and he cried out: "Are you already standing,
already standing there, o Boniface?
The book has lied to me by several years.

55 Are you so quickly sated with the riches
for which you did not fear to take by guile
the Lovely Lady, then to violate her?"[5]

And I became like those who stand as if
they have been mocked, who cannot understand
60 what has been said to them and can't respond.

But Virgil said: "Tell this to him at once:
'I am not he—not whom you think I am.'"
And I replied as I was told to do.

At this the spirit twisted both his feet,
65 and sighing and with a despairing voice,
he said: "What is it, then, you want of me?

If you have crossed the bank and climbed so far
to find out who I am, then know that I
was one of those who wore the mighty mantle,

70 and surely was a son of the she-bear,
so eager to advance the cubs that I
pursed wealth above while here I purse myself.[6]

Below my head there is the place of those
who took the way of simony before me;
75 and they are stuffed within the clefts of stone.

I, too, shall yield my place and fall below
when he arrives, the one for whom I had
mistaken you when I was quick to question.

But I have baked my feet a longer time,
80 have stood like this, upon my head, than he
is to stand planted here with scarlet feet:

for after him, one uglier in deeds
will come, a lawless shepherd from the west,
worthy to cover him and cover me.[7]

85 He'll be a second Jason, of whom we read
in *Maccabees;* and just as Jason's king
was soft to him, so shall the king of France

---

4. In the punishment known as "the planting of grapevines," assassins were stuck head downward in a hole that was then filled with dirt, choking them to death.

5. The speaker, Pope Nicholas III, believes he is addressing Boniface VIII, who he knows will die in Rome in 1303, three years after the date of the present encounter, enabling Dante to place a soul in its "proper" place by anticipation. Boniface was surrounded by many accusations of nepotism and simony; as for the charge that he took "by guile the Lovely Lady," that he was elected pope by fraud: he was said to have offered his services to Charles of Anjou in his war in Sicily in return for support of his candidacy.

6. The Roman family of Giovanni Orsini, Pope Nicholas III, were commonly referred to as *filii orsae,* cubs of the she-bear, known as a rapacious beast especially fierce in protecting her young. Giovanni was elected pope ("the mighty mantle") in 1277 and died three years later, but his brief tenure was marked by nepotism and intrigue. Line 72 neatly expresses the *contrapasso:* the font in which he is placed is his purse in which he keeps the rewards he sought above.

7. Nicholas has to wait 23 years for Boniface to take the topmost place in the hole, but Boniface will need wait less than 11 for the next simonist pope to replace him: Clement V, who died in 1314 near Avignon. Born in Gascony ("from the west") and elected pope in 1304, Clement saw the Papal See removed from Rome to Avignon in southern France, where it remained for nearly 70 years in what is referred to as the "Babylonian Captivity."

be soft to this one."[8] And I do not know
if I was too rash here—I answered so:

90 "Then tell me now, how much gold did our Lord
ask that Saint Peter give to him before
he placed the keys within his care? Surely
the only thing he said was: 'Follow me.'[9]

And Peter and the others never asked
95 for gold or silver when they chose Matthias
to take the place of the transgressing soul.[1]

Stay as you are, for you are rightly punished;
and guard with care the money got by evil
that made you so audacious against Charles.[2]

100 And were it not that I am still prevented
by reverence for those exalted keys
that you had held within the happy life,

I'd utter words much heavier than these,
because your avarice afflicts the world:
105 it tramples on the good, lifts up the wicked.

You, shepherds, the Evangelist had noticed
when he saw her who sits upon the waters
and realized she fornicates with kings,

she who was born with seven heads and had
110 the power and support of the ten horns,
as long as virtue was her husband's pleasure.[3]

You've made yourselves a god of gold and silver;
how are you different from idolaters,
save that they worship one and you a hundred?

115 Ah, Constantine, what wickedness was born—
and not from your conversion—from the dower
that you bestowed upon the first rich father!"[4]

And while I sang such notes to him—whether
it was his indignation or his conscience
120 that bit him—he kicked hard with both his soles.

8. While still Archbishop of Bordeaux, Clement had negotiated his election as pope with the powerful King Philip the Fair of France, just as Jason had first been appointed High Priest of the Jews by bribing King Antiochus of Syria, endeavoring afterward to reintroduce Greek customs and pagan worship in place of the Jewish religion (2 Maccabees 4:13–16).

9. The apostle Peter was considered to have been the first pope: "And I say to thee, thou art Peter, and upon this rock I will build my Church.... And I will give thee the keys of the kingdom of heaven." (Matthew 16.18–19). "Follow me" were the words with which Jesus first called the brothers Simon (Peter) and Andrew to be his disciples (Matthew 4.18–19).

1. After Judas Iscariot had betrayed Jesus, Matthias was chosen by lot to fill his vacant place among the 12 apostles.

2. It was commonly believed that Nicholas had intrigued against Charles of Anjou when Charles had refused to marry Nicholas's niece.

3. In the Book of Revelation, attributed to the Evangelist, St. John, the whore "who sits upon the waters" (17.1–3) was most likely pagan Rome, while Dante interprets her as the Church corrupted by secular interests. The seven heads symbolize the seven sacraments; the ten horns the Ten Commandments.

4. Due to a skillful forgery known as "The Donation of Constantine," probably composed in the papal court during the 8th century, it was believed that the Emperor Constantine had given to the Church his temporal power in the west when he moved the imperial capital eastward to Constantinople in the 5th century. For Dante, this fraud marked the beginning of the ecclesiastical corruption denounced in this canto. "The first rich father" is Pope Sylvester I, to whom the Donation was said to have been made in exchange for curing Constantine of leprosy.

I do indeed believe it pleased my guide:
he listened always with such satisfied
expression to the sound of those true words.

125   And then he gathered me in both his arms
and, when he had me fast against his chest,
where he climbed down before, climbed upward now;

    nor did he tire of clasping me until
he brought me to the summit of the arch
that crosses from the fourth to the fifth rampart.

130   And here he gently set his burden down—
gently because the ridge was rough and steep,
and would have been a rugged pass for goats.

    From there another valley lay before me.

Canto 20

The Eighth Circle, Fourth Pouch, where Diviners, Astrologers, Magicians, all have
their heads turned backward. Amphiaraus. Tiresias. Aruns. Manto. Virgil on the
origin of Mantua, his native city. Eurypylus. Michael Scot and other moderns adept
at fraud.

    I must make verses of new punishment
and offer matter now for Canto Twenty
of this first canticle—of the submerged.

    I was already well prepared to stare
5   below, into the depth that was disclosed,
where tears of anguished sorrow bathed the ground;

    and in the valley's circle I saw souls
advancing, mute and weeping, at the pace
that, in our world, holy processions take.

10   As I inclined my head still more, I saw
that each, amazingly, appeared contorted
between the chin and where the chest begins;

    they had their faces twisted toward their haunches
and found it necessary to walk backward,
15   because they could not see ahead of them.[1]

    Perhaps the force of palsy[2] has so fully
distorted some, but that I've yet to see,
and I do not believe that that can be.

    May God so let you, reader, gather fruit
20   from what you read; and now think for yourself
how I could ever keep my own face dry

    when I beheld our image so nearby
and so awry that tears, down from the eyes,
bathed the buttocks, running down the cleft.

25   Of course I wept, leaning against a rock

---

1. In this *bolgia*, diviners and soothsayers are punished for their attempt to see the future by being condemned to see only backward.
2. A condition marked by the paralysis or uncontrollable tremor of a body or a body part.

along that rugged ridge, so that my guide
told me: "Are you as foolish as the rest?

Here pity only lives when it is dead:
for who can be more impious than he

30 who links God's judgment to passivity?

Lift, lift your head and see the one for whom
the earth was opened while the Thebans watched,
so that they all cried: 'Amphiaraus,
where are you rushing? Have you quit the fight?'

35 Nor did he interrupt his downward plunge
to Minos, who lays hands on every sinner.[3]

See how he's made a chest out of his shoulders;
and since he wanted so to see ahead,
he looks behind and walks a backward path.

40 And see Tiresias, who changed his mien
when from a man he turned into a woman,
so totally transforming all his limbs

that then he had to strike once more upon
the two entwining serpents with his wand

45 before he had his manly plumes again.[4]

And Aruns is the one who backs against
the belly of Tiresias—Aruns who,
in Luni's hills, tilled by the Carrarese,

who live below, had as his home, a cave

50 among white marbles, from which he could gaze
at stars and sea with unimpeded view.[5]

And she who covers up her breasts—which you
can't see—with her disheveled locks, who keeps
all of her hairy parts to the far side,

55 was Manto,[6] who had searched through many lands,
then settled in the place where I was born;
on this, I'd have you hear me now a while.

When Manto's father took his leave of life,
and Bacchus' city found itself enslaved,[7]

60 she wandered through the world for many years.

High up, in lovely Italy, beneath
the Alps that shut in Germany above

---

3. Amphiaraus was a great prophet and hero of Argos and another of the Seven against Thebes consigned to Hell. Foreseeing that he would die there, he had attempted to hide, but his hiding-place was revealed by his wife after she was
bribed with a necklace. He and his chariot were swallowed up by the earth as he was fleeing his pursuers at Thebes.

4. The famed soothsayer of Thebes, Tiresias, had been changed into a woman when he separated with his staff two cou-
pling serpents. Seven years later, he found the same serpents, struck them again, and was changed back to a man. Called
upon to mediate a dispute between Jupiter and Juno, he declared that women experience greater pleasure in lovemaking.
As a result, Juno in anger struck him blind, and Jupiter gave him the gift of prophecy. (Ovid, *Metamorphoses* 3.322–31).

5. Aruns was an Etruscan seer who according to Lucan foretold the civil war that ended in Caesar's triumph and
Pompey's death (*Pharsalia* 1.585–638). "Luni's hills" are near Carrara in northern Tuscany, famous for its white marble.

6. A prophetess of Thebes, daughter of Tiresias who, by some accounts, settled in Italy where the town of Mantua,
Virgil's birthplace, was named after her.

7. Thebes was consecrated to the god Bacchus and tradition made it his birthplace. After the war of the Seven against
Thebes, the city came under the tyranny of Creon.

Tirolo, lies a lake known as Benaco.[8]

65 A thousand springs and more, I think, must flow
out of the waters of that lake to bathe
Pennino, Garda, Val Camonica.

And at its middle is a place where three—
the bishops of Verona, Brescia, Trento[9]—
may bless if they should chance to come that way.

70 Peschiera, strong and handsome fortress, built
to face the Brescians and the Bergamasques
stands where the circling shore is at its lowest.[1]

There, all the waters that cannot be held
within the bosom of Benaco fall,

75 to form a river running through green meadows.

No sooner has that stream begun to flow
than it is called the Mincio, not Benaco—
until Govèrnolo, where it joins the Po.

It's not flowed far before it finds flat land;

80 and there it stretches out to form a fen
that in the summer can at times be fetid.

And when she passed that way, the savage virgin
saw land along the middle of the swamp,
untilled and stripped of its inhabitants.

85 And there, to flee all human intercourse,
she halted with her slaves to ply her arts;
and there she lived, there left her empty body.

And afterward, the people of those parts
collected at that place, because the marsh—

90 surrounding it on all sides—made it strong.

They built a city over her dead bones;
and after her who first had picked that spot,
they called it Mantua—they cast no lots.[2]

There once were far more people in its walls,

95 before the foolishness of Casalodi
was tricked by the deceit of Pinamonte.[3]

Therefore, I charge you, if you ever hear
a different tale of my town's origin,
do not let any falsehood gull° the truth."[4]   *dupe*

100 And I: "O master, that which you have spoken
convinces me and so compels my trust
that others' words would only be spent coals.

---

8. To recount the situation of Mantua, Virgil begins with a long account of the waters that flow from Lake Garda down into the river Po.

9. That is, an island where the boundaries and jurisdictions of these three dioceses meet.

1. Peschiera was a town and fortress at the southeast shore of the lake, about 20 miles southeast of Brescia and 50 miles from Bergamo.

2. An ancient custom was to choose the name of a town by casting lots.

3. The Brescian counts of Casalodi took control of Mantua in 1272. Pinamonte, a native Mantuan, treacherously advised Alberto to appease the populace by expelling many nobles from the city, including his own supporters. With Alberto defenseless, Pinamonte was able to seize power himself.

4. According to the *Aeneid* (10.198–200), Mantua was founded by her son, Ocnus.

But tell me if among the passing souls
you see some spirits worthy of our notice,
105   because my mind is bent on that alone."
Then he to me: "That shade who spreads his beard
down from his cheeks across his swarthy shoulders—
when Greece had been so emptied of its males
that hardly any cradle held a son,
110   he was an augur; and at Aulis, he
and Calchas set the time to cut the cables.
His name's Eurypylus; a certain passage
of my high tragedy has sung it so;
you know that well enough, who know the whole.[5]
115   That other there, his flanks extremely spare,
was Michael Scot,[6] a man who certainly
knew how the game of magic fraud was played.
See there Guido Bonatti; see Asdente,
who now would wish he had attended to
120   his cord and leather, but repents too late.[7]
See those sad women who had left their needle,
shuttle, and spindle to become diviners;
they cast their spells with herbs and effigies.
But let us go; Cain with his thorns already
125   is at the border of both hemispheres
and there, below Seville, touches the sea.[8]
Last night the moon was at its full; you should
be well aware of this, for there were times
when it did you no harm in the deep wood."
130   These were his words to me; meanwhile we journeyed.

Canto 21

The Eighth Circle, Fifth Pouch, with Barrators plunged into boiling pitch and guarded by demons armed with prongs. A newly arrived magistrate from Lucca. Ten demons assigned by Malacoda ("Evil-Tail"), the chief of the Malebranche ("Evil-Claws"), to escort Dante and Virgil. The remarkable signal for their march.

We came along from one bridge to another,
talking of things my Comedy is not
concerned to sing. We held fast to the summit,
then stayed our steps to spy the other cleft
5   of Malebolge and other vain laments.

5. On the advice of the prophet Calchas, the Greeks sacrificed Agamemnon's daughter Iphigenia to appease the goddess Diana. When they were preparing to return home from Troy, Eurypylus was sent to consult the oracle of Apollo, which advised that their return must also be purchased in blood. *Aeneid* (2.114–24, "my high tragedy") mentions both incidents, but attributes only the second of them to Eurypylus.

6. A famous scientist, philosopher, astrologer, and necromancer from Scotland who served for many years at the court of Frederick II at Palermo in Sicily.

7. Guido Bonatti of Forlì served as astrologer at the court of Guido da Montefeltro (see Canto 27); Asdente ("toothless") was a 13th-century shoemaker of Parma famed as a prophet and soothsayer.

8. Custom held that God had placed Cain in the moon following his murder of Abel; "thorns" refers to the moon spots. For the ideal observer in Jerusalem, the moon is setting in the west ("below Seville"); the time is 6 A.M.

I saw that it was wonderfully dark.[1]
  As in the arsenal of the Venetians,[2]
all winter long a stew of sticky pitch
boils up to patch their sick and tattered ships

10 that cannot sail (instead of voyaging,
some build new keels, some tow and tar the ribs
of hulls worn out by too much journeying;
  some hammer at the prow, some at the stern,
and some make oars, and some braid ropes and cords;

15 one mends the jib, another, the mainsail);
  so, not by fire but by the art of God,
below there boiled a thick and tarry mass
that covered all the banks with clamminess.
  I saw it, but I could not see within it;

20 no thing was visible but boiling bubbles,
the swelling of the pitch; and then it settled.
  And while I watched below attentively,
my guide called out to me: "Take care! Take care!"[3]
And then, from where I stood, he drew me near.

25 I turned around as one who is impatient
to see what he should shun but is dashed down
beneath the terror he has undergone,
  who does not stop his flight and yet would look.
And then in back of us I saw a black

30 demon as he came racing up the crags.
  Ah, he was surely barbarous to see!
And how relentless seemed to me his acts!
His wings were open and his feet were lithe;
  across his shoulder, which was sharp and high,

35 he had slung a sinner, upward from the thighs;
in front, the demon gripped him by the ankles.
  Then from our bridge, he called: "O Malebranche,
I've got an elder of Saint Zita for you!
Shove this one under—I'll go back for more—

40 his city is well furnished with such stores;
there, everyone's a grafter but Bonturo;
and there—for cash—they'll change a *no* to *yes*."[4]
  He threw the sinner down, then wheeled along
the stony cliff: no mastiff's ever been

45 unleashed with so much haste to chase a thief.
  The sinner plunged, then surfaced, black with pitch;
but now the demons, from beneath the bridge,

---

1. Even darker than the other, unlit pouches, because black with boiling pitch.
2. One of the most important shipyards in Europe, and the reason for the Venetian Republic's enduring power at sea.
3. One motivation for the guide's urgency may be that barratry (the buying and selling of public office, the secular equivalent of simony) would be the charge made against Dante when he was sentenced to exile in 1302.
4. St. Zita (1218–c. 1278) was the patron saint of Lucca; the elders were ten citizens holding executive power along with

shouted: "The Sacred Face has no place here;[5]
here we swim differently than in the Serchio;[6]

50 if you don't want to feel our grappling hooks,
don't try to lift yourself above that ditch."

They pricked him with a hundred prongs and more,
then taunted: "Here one dances under cover,
so try to grab your secret graft below."

55 The demons did the same as any cook
who has his urchins force the meat with hooks
deep down into the pot, that it not float.

Then my good master said to me: "Don't let
those demons see that you are here; take care

60 to crouch behind the cover of a crag.

No matter what offense they offer me,
don't be afraid; I know how these things go—
I've had to face such fracases before."[7]

When this was said, he moved beyond the bridgehead.

65 And on the sixth embankment, he had need
to show his imperturbability.

With the same frenzy, with the brouhaha
of dogs, when they beset a poor wretch who
then stops dead in his tracks as if to beg,

70 so, from beneath the bridge, the demons rushed
against my guide with all their prongs, but he
called out: "Can't you forget your savagery!

Before you try to maul me, just let one
of all your troop step forward. Hear me out,

75 and then decide if I am to be hooked."

At this they howled, "Let Malacoda go!"
And one of them moved up—the others stayed—
and as he came, he asked: "How can he win?"

"O Malacoda, do you think I've come,"

80 my master answered him, "already armed—
as you can see—against your obstacles,

without the will of God[8] and helpful fate?
Let us move on; it is the will of Heaven
for me to show this wild way to another."

85 At this the pride of Malacoda fell;
his prong dropped to his feet. He told his fellows:
"Since that's the way things stand, let us not wound him."

My guide then spoke to me: "O you, who crouch,
bent low among the bridge's splintered rocks,

90 you can feel safe—and now return to me."

At this I moved and quickly came to him.
The devils had edged forward, all of them;

---

5. The Sacred Face of Lucca was a venerated ancient Byzantine crucifix carved in dark wood. The demon's vulgar pleas-antry compares it to the pitch-covered rear end of the naked shade.

6. A Tuscan river near Lucca.

7. Probably referring to the episode with the rebel angels; the pattern in fact is that the demons generally *do* give Virgil more trouble than the classical monsters.

I feared that they might fail to keep their word:
just so, I saw the infantry when they
marched out, under safe conduct, from Caprona;[9]
they trembled when they passed their enemies.

My body huddled closer to my guide;
I did not let the demons out of sight;
the looks they cast at us were less than kind.

They bent their hooks and shouted to each other:
"And shall I give it to him on the rump?"
And all of them replied, "Yes, let him have it!"

But Malacoda, still in conversation
with my good guide, turned quickly to his squadron
and said: "Be still, Scarmiglione, still!"

To us he said: "There is no use in going
much farther on this ridge, because the sixth
bridge—at the bottom there—is smashed to bits.

Yet if you two still want to go ahead,
move up and walk along this rocky edge;
nearby, another ridge will form a path.[1]

Five hours from this hour yesterday,
one thousand and two hundred sixty-six
years passed since that roadway was shattered here.[2]

I'm sending ten of mine out there to see
if any sinner lifts his head for air;
go with my men—there is no malice in them."

"Step forward, Alichino and Calcabrina,"
he then began to say, "and you, Cagnazzo;
and Barbariccia, who can lead the ten.

Let Libicocco go, and Draghignazzo
and tusky Ciriatto and Graffiacane
and Farfarello and mad Rubicante.[3]

Search all around the clammy stew of pitch;
keep these two safe and sound till the next ridge
that rises without break across the dens."

"Ah me! What is this, master, that I see?"
I said. "Can't we do without company?
If you know how to go, I want no escort.

If you are just as keen as usual,

95

100

105

110

115

120

125

130

20

---

9. A castle in the territory of Pisa, on a hill near the river Arno. Following the death of Ugolino, leader of the Pisan Guelfs (see 33.4–75), his party was expelled from the city, and the castle was taken in 1289 by the Tuscan Guelfs, led by the Lucchese and Florentines, probably including Dante himself.

1. As it turns out, Malacoda is truthful about the nearer bridge, but deliberately deceitful about the farther.

2. The internal dating of the poem hinges on this information from the mouth of a devil. The bridges of Hell crumbled at the moment of Christ's death on the cross. In Dante's reckoning, Christ died at the age of 34, counted from the day of the Incarnation. Matthew gave the time of death as the sixth hour, or noon; Malacoda refers to a moment five hours earlier and one day following this event, that is, 7 A.M. on Holy Saturday, which fell on April 9 in the year 1300. Through other internal signals in the poem, this places the night in the dark wood on Thursday, April 7, the encounter with the three beasts and Virgil during the next day, and the entry through the Gate of Hell at sunset of Good Friday. It is now just past daybreak in the world above; they have consumed the night in their descent thus far.

3. Some of the devils' names have been coined by Dante: Malacoda ("evil-tail"), Malebranche ("evil-claws"), Cagnazzo ("big dog"). Several were also family names in Lucca.

can't you see how those demons grind their teeth?
Their brows are menacing, they promise trouble."
And he to me: "I do not want you frightened:
just let them gnash away as they may wish;
135   they do it for the wretches boiled in pitch."
They turned around along the left hand bank:
but first each pressed his tongue between his teeth
as signal for their leader, Barbariccia.
And he had made a trumpet of his ass.

Canto 22

Still the Eighth Circle, Fifth Pouch: the Barrators. The Barrator from Navarre. Fra Gomita and Michele Zanche, two Sardinians. The astuteness of the Navarrese that leads two demons to fall into the pitch.

Before this I've seen horsemen start to march
and open the assault and muster ranks[1]
and seen them, too, at times beat their retreat;
   and on your land, o Aretines, I've seen
5   rangers and raiding parties galloping,
the clash of tournaments, the rush of jousts,
   now done with trumpets, now with bells, and now
with drums, and now with signs from castle walls,
with native things and with imported ware;[2]
10   but never yet have I seen horsemen or
seen infantry or ship that sails by signal
of land or star move to so strange a bugle!
   We made our way together with ten demons:
ah, what ferocious company! And yet
15   "in church with saints, with rotters in the tavern."[3]
But I was all intent upon the pitch,
to seek out every feature of the pouch
and of the people who were burning in it.
   Just as the dolphins do, when with arched back,
20   they signal to the seamen to prepare
for tempest, that their vessel may be spared,[4]
   so here from time to time, to ease his torment,
some sinner showed his back above the surface,
then hid more quickly than a lightning flash.
25   And just as on the margin of a ditch,
frogs crouch, their snouts alone above the water,

---

1. The tone of the several cantos of the adventure with the devils of the fifth *bolgia* is closer to the popular style of the Italian *novella*, or short tale, than it is to the high, tragic style of many of the preceding cantos.

2. The Aretines are the people of the Tuscan commune of Arezzo. Dante is likely to have seen their cavalry in 1289 when the Florentine Guelfs defeated the Aretine Ghibellines at the Battle of Campaldino, and also later at Caprona.

3. A popular proverb that also suggests a reason for the shift in literary style.

4. It was believed that dolphins on the surface of the sea near a ship were the sign of an imminent storm.

so as to hide their feet and their plump flesh,

  so here on every side these sinners crouched;
but faster than a flash, when Barbariccia
30 drew near, they plunged beneath the boiling pitch.

  I saw—my heart still shudders in recall—
one who delayed, just as at times a frog
is left behind while others dive below;

  and Graffiacane, who was closest to him,
35 then hooked him by his pitch entangled locks
and hauled him up; he seemed to me an otter.

  By now I knew the names of all those demons—
I'd paid attention when the fiends were chosen;
I'd watched as they stepped forward one by one.

40 "O Rubicante, see you set your talons
right into him, so you can flay° his flesh!"   *tear off*
So did those cursed ones cry out together.

  And I: "My master, if you can, find out
what is the name of that unfortunate
45 who's fallen victim to his enemies."

  My guide, who then drew near that sinner's side,
asked him to tell his birthplace. He replied:
"My homeland was the kingdom of Navarre.

  My mother, who had had me by a wastrel,
50 destroyer of himself and his possessions,
had placed me in the service of a lord.

  Then I was in the household of the worthy
King Thibault;[5] there I started taking graft;
with this heat I pay reckoning for that."

55 And Ciriatto, from whose mouth there bulged
to right and left two tusks like a wild hog's,
then let him feel how one of them could mangle.

  The mouse had fallen in with evil cats;
but Barbariccia clasped him in his arms
60 and said: "Stand off there, while I fork him fast."

  And turning toward my master then, he said:
"Ask on, if you would learn some more from him
before one of the others does him in."

  At which my guide: "Now tell: among the sinners
65 who hide beneath the pitch, are any others
Italian?" And he: "I have just left

  one who was nearby there; and would I were
still covered by the pitch as he is hidden,
for then I'd have no fear of hook or talon."

70 And Libicocco said, "We've been too patient!"
and, with his grapple, grabbed him by the arm
and, ripping, carried off a hunk of flesh.

  But Draghignazzo also looked as if

5. King of Navarre in northern Spain and southwestern France.

75   to grab his legs; at which, their captain wheeled
      and threatened all of them with raging looks.
          When they'd grown somewhat less tumultuous,
      without delay my guide asked of that one
      who had his eyes still fixed upon his wound:
          "Who was the one you left to come ashore—
80   unluckily—as you just said before?"
      He answered: "Fra Gomita of Gallura,
          who was a vessel fit for every fraud;
      he had his master's enemies in hand,
      but handled them in ways that pleased them all.
85   He took their gold and smoothly let them off,
      as he himself says; and in other matters,
      he was a sovereign, not a petty, swindler.
          His comrade there is Don Michele Zanche
      of Logodoro; and their tongues are never
90   too tired to talk of their Sardinia.[6]
          Ah me, see that one there who grinds his teeth!
      If I were not afraid, I'd speak some more,
      but he is getting set to scratch my scurf."
          And their great marshal, facing Farfarello—
95   who was so hot to strike he rolled his eyes,
      said: "Get away from there, you filthy bird!"
          "If you perhaps would like to see or hear,"
      that sinner, terrified, began again,
      "Lombards or Tuscans, I can fetch you some;
100   but let the Malebranche stand aside
      so that my comrades need not fear their vengeance.
      Remaining in this very spot, I shall,
          although alone, make seven more appear
      when I have whistled, as has been our custom
105   when one of us has managed to get out."
          At that, Cagnazzo lifted up his snout
      and shook his head, and said: "Just listen to
      that trick by which he thinks he can dive back!"
          To this, he who was rich in artifice
110   replied: "Then I must have too many tricks,
      if I bring greater torment to my friends."[7]
          This was too much for Alichino and,
      despite the others, he cried out: "If you
      dive back, I shall not gallop after you
115   but beat my wings above the pitch; we'll leave
      this height; with the embankment as a screen,
      we'll see if you—alone—can handle us."

---

6. Two shades of Sardinia, at the time controlled by Pisa (Gallura and Logodoro were two of the four judicial divisions of the island). Fra Gomita was a friar who was hanged for abusing his position of deputy to the judge of Gallura. Little is known for certain about Michele Zanche except that he was father-in-law of his murderer Branca Doria (33.137).

7. Ciampolo thus continues his fraudulent ways in Hell.

O you who read, hear now of this new sport:
each turned his eyes upon the other shore,
120   he first who'd been most hesitant before.

The Navarrese, in nick of time, had planted
his feet upon the ground; then in an instant
he jumped and freed himself from their commander.

At this each demon felt the prick of guilt,
125   and most, he who had led his band to blunder;
so he took off and shouted: "You are caught!"

But this could help him little; wings were not
more fast than fear; the sinner plunged right under;
the other, flying up, lifted his chest:

130   not otherwise the wild duck when it plunges
precipitously, when the falcon nears
and then—exhausted, thwarted—flies back up.

But Calcabrina, raging at the trick,
flew after Alichino; he was keen
135   to see the sinner free and have a brawl;

and once the Navarrese had disappeared,
he turned his talons on his fellow demon
and tangled with him just above the ditch.

But Alichino clawed him well—he was
140   indeed a full-grown kestrel;° and both fell   *falcon*
into the middle of the boiling pond.

The heat was quick to disentangle them,
but still there was no way they could get out;
their wings were stuck, enmeshed in glue-like pitch.

145   And Barbariccia, grieving with the rest,
sent four to fly out toward the other shore
with all their forks, and speedily enough

on this side and on that they took their posts;
and toward those two—stuck fast, already cooked
150   beneath that crust—they stretched their grappling hooks.
We left them still contending with that mess.

Canto 23

*Still the Eighth Circle, Fifth Pouch: the Barrators. Pursuit by the demons, with Virgil
snatching up Dante and sliding down to the Sixth Pouch, where the Hypocrites file
along slowly, clothed in caps of lead. Two Jovial Friars of Bologna, Catalano and
Loderingo. Caiaphas. Virgil's distress at Malacoda's deceitfulness.*

Silent, alone, no one escorting us,
we made our way—one went before, one after—
as Friars Minor when they walk together.[1]

The present fracas made me think of Aesop—
5   that fable where he tells about the mouse

---

1. Franciscan monks called themselves Friars Minor because of their devotion to poverty and humility. It was their custom
to travel in bands of two, with the senior walking ahead of the other.

and frog; for "near" and "nigh" are not more close
   than are that fable and this incident,
if you compare with care how each begins
and then compare the endings that they share.[2]

10   And even as one thought springs from another,
so out of that was still another born,
which made the fear I felt before redouble.

       I thought: "Because of us, they have been mocked,
and this inflicted so much hurt and scorn
15   that I am sure they feel deep indignation.

       If anger's to be added to their malice,
they'll hunt us down with more ferocity
than any hound whose teeth have trapped a hare."

       I could already feel my hair curl up
20   from fear, and I looked back attentively,
while saying: "Master, if you don't conceal

       yourself and me at once—they terrify me,
those Malebranche; they are after us;
I so imagine them, I hear them now."

25   And he to me: "Were I a leaded mirror,[3]
I could not gather in your outer image
more quickly than I have received your inner.

       For even now your thoughts have joined my own;
in both our acts and aspects we are kin—
30   with both our minds I've come to one decision.

       If that right bank is not extremely steep,
we can descend into the other moat
and so escape from the imagined chase."

       He'd hardly finished telling me his plan
35   when I saw them approach with outstretched wings,
not too far off, and keen on taking us.

       My guide snatched me up instantly, just as
the mother who is wakened by a roar
and catches sight of blazing flames beside her,

40   will lift her son and run without a stop—
she cares more for the child than for herself—
not pausing even to throw on a shift;

       and down the hard embankment's edge—his back
lay flat along the sloping rock that closes
45   one side of the adjacent moat—he slid.

       No water ever ran so fast along
a sluice to turn the wheels of a land mill,

---

2. A large collection of animal fables was attributed to Aesop, a Greek author said to have lived in the early 6th century B.C.E. In this popular fable, a frog agrees to carry a mouse across a river. Halfway across, it dives down in an attempt to kill the mouse, but while the two are fighting, a hawk swoops down and captures either the frog (in the version of Marie de France), or both the mouse and the frog. The fable may apply to the end of the previous canto, with Calcabrina as frog and Alichino as mouse; it also foreshadows the discovery at the end of this canto that Malacoda as frog has lied to Virgil and Dante as mouse about the existence of a bridge.

3. Lead was the customary backing for mirrors of the time.

not even when its flow approached the paddles,[4]

as did my master race down that embankment
50   while bearing me with him upon his chest,
just like a son, and not like a companion.

His feet had scarcely reached the bed that lies
along the deep below, than those ten demons
were on the edge above us; but there was
55   nothing to fear; for that High Providence
that willed them ministers of the fifth ditch,
denies to all of them the power to leave it.

Below that point we found a painted people,
who moved about with lagging steps, in circles,
60   weeping, with features tired and defeated.

And they were dressed in cloaks with cowls so low
they fell before their eyes, of that same cut
that's used to make the clothes for Cluny's monks.[5]

Outside, these cloaks were gilded and they dazzled;
65   but inside they were all of lead, so heavy
that Frederick's capes were straw compared to them.[6]

A tiring mantle for eternity!
We turned again, as always, to the left,
along with them, intent on their sad weeping;
70   but with their weights that weary people paced
so slowly that we found ourselves among
new company each time we took a step.[7]

At which I told my guide: "Please try to find
someone whose name or deed I recognize;
75   and while we walk, be watchful with your eyes."

And one who'd taken in my Tuscan speech
cried out behind us: "Stay your steps, o you
who hurry so along this darkened air!

Perhaps you'll have from me that which you seek."
80   At which my guide turned to me, saying: "Wait,
and then continue, following his pace."

I stopped, and I saw two whose faces showed
their minds were keen to be with me; but both
their load and the tight path forced them to slow.

85   When they came up, they looked askance at me
a long while, and they uttered not a word
until they turned to one another, saying:

"The throbbing of his throat makes this one seem
alive; and if they're dead, what privilege

---

4. The mill is situated near a body of water, its paddles turned by water passed through canals or sluices.

5. Cluny was a famous Benedictine abbey in Burgundy. In a letter to his nephew, who had left the Cistercian order to join the Cluniacs, Bernard of Clairvaux noted with some sarcasm the luxury of their robes, "made of the finest and most expensive fabrics, with long sleeves and a full hood."

6. Emperor Frederick II was accustomed to punish criminals by fitting them with a leaden cape and then placing them into a cauldron. As the cauldron was heated, the lead would melt, removing the skin piece by piece.

7. This is one of the few parts of Hell in which the pilgrim directly imitates the movements of the damned.

82

90   lets them appear without the heavy mantle?"
        Then they addressed me: "Tuscan, you who come
to this assembly of sad hypocrites,
do not disdain to tell us who you are."
        I answered: "Where the lovely Arno flows,
95   there I was born and raised, in the great city;
I'm with the body I have always had.
        But who are you, upon whose cheeks I see
such tears distilled by grief? And let me know
what punishment it is that glitters so."
100   And one of them replied: "The yellow cloaks
are of a lead so thick, their heaviness
makes us, the balances beneath them, creak.[8]
        We both were Jovial Friars, and Bolognese;
my name was Catalano, Loderingo
105   was his, and we were chosen by your city
        together, for the post that's usually
one man's, to keep the peace; and what we were
is still to be observed around Gardingo."[9]
        I then began, "O Friars, your misdeeds..."
110   but said no more, because my eyes had caught
one crucified by three stakes on the ground.
        When he saw me, that sinner writhed all over,
and he breathed hard into his beard with sighs;
observing that, Fra Catalano said
115   to me: "That one impaled there, whom you see,
counseled the Pharisees that it was prudent
to let one man—and not one nation—suffer.[1]
        Naked, he has been stretched across the path,
as you can see, and he must feel the weight
120   of anyone who passes over him.
        Like torment, in this ditch, afflicts both his
father-in-law and others in that council,
which for the Jews has seeded so much evil."[2]
        Then I saw Virgil stand amazed above
125   that one who lay stretched out upon a cross
so squalidly in his eternal exile.[3]

---

8. Like the words of the hypocrite, the cloaks glitter on the outside but in reality are lead.

9. "Jovial Friars" were members of the Knights of the Blessed Virgin Mary, an order founded in Bologna in 1261 with the object of making peace between the warring factions in Italy's cities. The nickname was given them in reaction to the laxity of their rules. The Guelf Catalano di Guido di Ostia was associated with the Ghibelline Loderingo degli Andalò in founding the order; they were appointed by Pope Clement IV to serve jointly as chief magistrates of Florence, owing allegiance to the pope rather than to their political parties. Their appointment resulted in an uprising of Guelfs and expulsion of Ghibelline nobles along with destruction of their houses, including those of the Uberti, a leading family (Farinata's, see Canto 10), in the neighborhood of Gardingo near the Palazzo Vecchio.

1. Caiaphas was the high priest under Pontius Pilate who counseled the Pharisees that "one man," Jesus, should die (John 18.13).

2. Caiaphas was supported at the council of the Pharisees by his father-in-law Annas. "Seeded" refers to the Christian belief that the blood of Christ was the "seed" that led to the destruction of Jerusalem and the dispersal of the Jews.

3. All sinners are "exiled" from heaven, but the gibe carries extra weight in the context of the fate of the Jews. Virgil's "amazement" may partly result from the fact that these shades would not have been there on his last passage through Malebolge (9.16–30).

And he addressed the friar in this way:
"If it does not displease you—if you may—
tell us if there's some passage on the right
130   that would allow the two of us to leave
without our having to compel black angels
to travel to this deep, to get us out."
He answered: "Closer than you hope, you'll find
a rocky ridge that stretches from the great
135   round wall and crosses all the savage valleys,
    except that here it's broken—not a bridge.
But where its ruins slope along the bank
and heap up at the bottom, you can climb."
My leader stood a while with his head bent,
140   then said: "He who hooks sinners over there
gave us a false account of this affair."
At which the Friar: "In Bologna, I
once heard about the devil's many vices—
they said he was a liar and father of lies."[4]
145   And then my guide moved on with giant strides,
somewhat disturbed, with anger in his eyes;
at this I left those overburdened spirits,
    while following the prints of his dear feet.

Canto 24

Still the Eighth Circle, Sixth Pouch: the Hypocrites. Hard passage to the Seventh Pouch: the Thieves. Bitten by a serpent, a thieving sinner who turns to ashes and is then restored: Vanni Fucci. His prediction of the defeat of the Whites—Dante's party—at Pistoia.

In that part of the young year when the sun
begins to warm its locks beneath Aquarius
and nights grow shorter, equaling the days,
    when hoarfrost mimes the image of his white
5   sister upon the ground—but not for long,
because the pen he uses is not sharp—
    the farmer who is short of fodder rises
and looks and sees the fields all white, at which
he slaps his thigh, turns back into the house,
10   and here and there complains like some poor wretch
who doesn't know what can be done, and then
goes out again and gathers up new hope
    on seeing that the world has changed its face
in so few hours, and he takes his staff
15   and hurries out his flock of sheep to pasture.[1]

---

4. The hypocrite maliciously points out Virgil's ignorance of the ways of the devil that led to his deception by Malacoda (21.111), referring to his own experience as well as to the words of the Gospel (John 8.44).

1. The sun is in the sign of Aquarius between late January and late February. The "white sister" of hoarfrost is snow; both "write" upon the ground, but frost less deeply. The farmer mistakes one for the other, but only for the time it takes the rising sun to melt the frost.

So did my master fill me with dismay
when I saw how his brow was deeply troubled,
yet then the plaster soothed the sore as quickly:

for soon as we were on the broken bridge,
20 my guide turned back to me with that sweet manner
I first had seen along the mountain's base.[2]

And he examined carefully the ruin;
then having picked the way we would ascend,
he opened up his arms and thrust me forward.

25 And just as he who ponders as he labors,
who's always ready for the step ahead,
so, as he lifted me up toward the summit

of one great crag, he'd see another spur,
saying: "That is the one you will grip next,
30 but try it first to see if it is firm."

That was no path for those with cloaks of lead,[3]
for he and I—he, light; I, with support—
could hardly make it up from spur to spur.

And were it not that, down from this enclosure,
35 the slope was shorter than the bank before,
I cannot speak for him, but I should surely

have been defeated. But since Malebolge
runs right into the mouth of its last well,
the placement of each valley means it must

40 have one bank high and have the other short;
and so we reached, at length, the jutting where
the last stone of the ruined bridge breaks off.

The breath within my lungs was so exhausted
from climbing, I could not go on; in fact,
45 as soon as I had reached that stone, I sat.

"Now you must cast aside your laziness,"
my master said, "for he who rests on down
or under covers cannot come to fame;

and he who spends his life without renown
50 leaves such a vestige of himself on earth
as smoke bequeaths to air or foam to water.

Therefore, get up; defeat your breathlessness
with spirit that can win all battles if
the body's heaviness does not deter it.

55 A longer ladder still is to be climbed;
it's not enough to have left them behind;
if you have understood, now profit from it."[4]

Then I arose and showed myself far better
equipped with breath than I had been before:

2. When Virgil first appeared to Dante in Canto 1.

3. The hypocrites require no other guardian than the robes they wear.

4. Virgil's words liken the "heaviness" of Dante's body to the cloaks of the hypocrites, and also remind him that both fame and salvation will require a much longer climb later on: the one that leads them out of hell in Canto 34, or that of the Mountain of Purgatory in the next canticle.

60　　"Go on, for I am strong and confident."
　　　　We took our upward way upon the ridge,
with crags more jagged, narrow, difficult,
and much more steep than we had crossed before.

　　　　I spoke as we went on, not to seem weak;
65　at this, a voice came from the ditch beyond—
a voice that was not suited to form words.

　　　　I know not what he said, although I was
already at the summit of the bridge
that crosses there; and yet he seemed to move.

70　　　　I had bent downward, but my living eyes
could not see to the bottom through that dark;
at which I said: "O master, can we reach

　　　the other belt? Let us descend the wall,
for as I hear and cannot understand,
75　so I see down but can distinguish nothing."

　　　　"The only answer that I give to you
is doing it," he said. "A just request
is to be met in silence, by the act."

　　　　We then climbed down the bridge, just at the end
80　where it runs right into the eighth embankment,
and now the moat was plain enough to me;

　　　and there within I saw a dreadful swarm
of serpents so extravagant in form—
remembering them still drains my blood from me.[5]

85　　　　Let Libya boast no more about her sands;
for if she breeds chelydri, jaculi,
cenchres with amphisbaena, pareae,

　　　she never showed—with all of Ethiopia
or all the land that borders the Red Sea[6]—
90　so many, such malignant, pestilences.

　　　　Among this cruel and depressing swarm,
ran people who were naked, terrified,
with no hope of a hole or heliotrope.[7]

　　　　Their hands were tied behind by serpents; these
95　had thrust their head and tail right through the loins,
and then were knotted on the other side.

　　　　And—there!—a serpent sprang with force at one
who stood upon our shore, transfixing him
just where the neck and shoulders form a knot.

100　No *o* or *i* has ever been transcribed
so quickly as that soul caught fire and burned
and, as he fell, completely turned to ashes;

　　　and when he lay, undone, upon the ground,
the dust of him collected by itself

5. The fanciful list of serpents comes from Cato's crossing of the Libyan Desert in Lucan's *Pharsalia* 9.711–21.
6. Even if the Libyan Desert is expanded to include Africa south of Egypt as far as Zanzibar and east to the Red Sea.
7. The heliotrope was a stone supposedly found in northern Africa that rendered the wearer invisible.

and instantly returned to what it was:
                just so, it is asserted by great sages,
            that, when it reaches its five-hundredth year,
            the phoenix dies and then is born again;[8]
110   lifelong it never feeds on grass or grain,
            only on drops of incense and amomum;
            its final winding sheets are nard and myrrh.[9]
                And just as he who falls, and knows not how—
            by demon's force that drags him to the ground
            or by some other hindrance that binds man—
115   who, when he rises, stares about him, all
            bewildered by the heavy anguish he
            has suffered, sighing as he looks around;
                so did this sinner stare when he arose.
            Oh, how severe it is, the power of God
120   that, as its vengeance, showers down such blows!
                My guide then asked that sinner who he was;
            to this he answered: "Not long since, I rained
            from Tuscany into this savage maw.
                Mule that I was, the bestial life pleased me
125   and not the human; I am Vanni Fucci,
            beast; and the den that suited me—Pistoia."[1]
                And I to Virgil: "Tell him not to slip
            away, and ask what sin has thrust him here;
            I knew him as a man of blood and anger."
130   The sinner heard and did not try to feign
            but turned his mind and face, intent, toward me;
            and coloring with miserable shame,
                he said: "I suffer more because you've caught me
            in this, the misery you see, than I
135   suffered when taken from the other life.
                I can't refuse to answer what you ask:
            I am set down so far because I robbed
            the sacristy of its fair ornaments,
                and someone else was falsely blamed for that.[2]
140   But lest this sight give you too much delight,
            if you can ever leave these lands of darkness,
                open your ears to my announcement, hear:
            Pistoia first will strip herself of Blacks,
            then Florence will renew her men and manners.
145   From Val di Magra, Mars will draw a vapor
            which turbid clouds will try to wrap; the clash

---

8. The mythical Arabian phoenix was a bird that burned itself every 500 years on a pyre of incense, rising from the ashes in the form of a small worm that developed into a full-grown bird by the third day (Ovid, *Metamorphoses* 15.392–402).

9. Amomum and incense, nard and myrrh are fragrant plant extracts and tree resins; the former provide its food, the latter form the phoenix's "winding sheet," the cloth in which its corpse is wrapped.

1. The "mule" or illegitimate son of a noble family of Pistoia, northwest of Florence, Vanni Fucci was an ardent Black Guelf. Dante may have known him from the war against Pisa (1289–1293).

2. There are various reports concerning the robbery of the treasury of San Jacopo in the church of San Zeno at Pistoia; an innocent man was nearly executed for the crime.

between them will be fierce, impetuous,
        a tempest, fought upon Campo Piceno,
    until that vapor, vigorous, shall crack
150   the mist, and every White be struck by it.[3]
        And I have told you this to make you grieve."

Canto 25

Still the Eighth Circle, Seventh Pouch: the Thieves. Vanni Fucci and his obscene figs against God. The Centaur Cacus. Five Florentine Thieves, three of them humans and two of them serpents. The astounding metamorphoses undergone by four of them.

    When he had finished with his words, the thief
    raised high his fists with both figs cocked and cried:
    "Take that, o God; I square them off for you!"[1]
        From that time on, those serpents were my friends,
5   for one of them coiled then around his neck,
    as if to say, "I'll have you speak no more";
        another wound about his arms and bound him
    again and wrapped itself in front so firmly,
    he could not even make them budge an inch.
10   Pistoia, ah, Pistoia, must you last:
    why not decree your self-incineration,
    since you surpass your seed in wickedness?[2]
        Throughout the shadowed circles of deep Hell,
    I saw no soul against God so rebel,
15 not even he who fell from Theban walls.[3]
        He fled and could not say another word;
    and then I saw a Centaur full of anger,
    shouting: "Where is he, where's that bitter one?"
        I do not think Maremma has the number
20 of snakes that Centaur carried on his haunch
    until the part that takes our human form.[4]
        Upon his shoulders and behind his nape
    there lay a dragon with its wings outstretched;
    it sets ablaze all those it intercepts.
25   My master said: "That Centaur there is Cacus,
    who often made a lake of blood within
    a grotto underneath Mount Aventine.
        He does not ride the same road as his brothers
    because he stole—and most deceitfully—

---

3. The Blacks of Pistoia were expelled and their houses burned in 1301, but with the help of the ostensible peacemaker, Charles of Valois, they and the Blacks of Florence were able to expel the Florentine Whites, including Dante, in 1302 (lines 143–44). The "vapor" drawn by the war-god from Val di Magra is the Guelf leader Moroello Malaspina. The defeat of the Whites ("the mist" of line 150) may refer to events of 1302 or to the capture of the city in 1306.

1. The "fig" is an obscene gesture produced by thrusting out the fist while holding the thumb between the forefinger and middle finger.

2. According to legend, Pistoia was founded by survivors of the forces of Catiline, the conspirator against the Roman republic defeated nearby in 62 B.C.E.

3. The blasphemer Capaneus in Canto 14.46–72.

4. The beast-filled Tuscan wood of Maremma was referred to already in Canto 13.7–9 to describe the wood of suicides and squanderers; here, serpents are added to its contents.

30	from the great herd nearby; his crooked deeds
	⠀⠀ended beneath the club of Hercules,
	who may have given him a hundred blows—
	but he was not alive to feel the tenth."[5]
	⠀⠀While he was talking so, Cacus ran by
35	and, just beneath our ledge, three souls arrived;
	but neither I nor my guide noticed them
	⠀⠀until they had cried out: "And who are you?"
	At this the words we shared were interrupted,
	and we attended only to those spirits.
40	⠀⠀I did not recognize them, but it happened,
	as chance will usually bring about,
	that one of them called out the other's name,[6]
	⠀⠀exclaiming: "Where was Cianfa left behind?"
	At this, so that my guide might be alert,
45	I raised my finger up from chin to nose.
	⠀⠀If, reader, you are slow now to believe
	what I shall tell, that is no cause for wonder,
	for I who saw it hardly can accept it.
	⠀⠀As I kept my eyes fixed upon those sinners,
50	a serpent with six feet springs out against
	one of the three, and clutches him completely.
	⠀⠀It gripped his belly with its middle feet,
	and with its forefeet grappled his two arms;
	and then it sank its teeth in both his cheeks;
55	⠀⠀it stretched its rear feet out along his thighs
	and ran its tail along between the two,
	then straightened it again behind his loins.
	⠀⠀No ivy ever gripped a tree so fast
	as when that horrifying monster clasped
60	and intertwined the other's limbs with its.
	⠀⠀Then just as if their substance were warm wax,
	they stuck together and they mixed their colors,
	so neither seemed what he had been before;
	⠀⠀just as, when paper's kindled, where it still
65	has not caught flame in full, its color's dark
	though not yet black, while white is dying off.
	⠀⠀The other two souls stared, and each one cried:
	"Ah me, Agnello, how you change! Just see,
	you are already neither two nor one!"[7]

5. Cacus was the fire-breathing, half-human son of Vulcan and Medusa who stole cattle from Hercules. In order to conceal their tracks, Cacus dragged the cattle backward into his cave, but their bellowing alerted Hercules, who slew the thief (*Aeneid* 8.193–267). Dante makes Cacus a Centaur, and displaces the fire-breathing to a dragon familiar on its shoulder.

6. There are five souls involved in the complex action of this canto; all were thieves of noble Florentine families: Cianfa Donati, lost when he became a serpent (50) and eventually fusing (70–78) with Agnello de' Brunelleschi; Francesco Guercio ("squinting") de' Cavalcanti, the "blazing little serpent" (82) that steals the substance of "Buoso" (85), probably Buoso di Forese Donati, nephew of the Buoso Donati mentioned as a victim of counterfeiting in Canto 30.41–44, in the transformation that concludes at line 141; and Puccio Sciancato, "the only soul who'd not been changed" (149).

7. Agnello was reputed to have used disguises to facilitate his thieving. The transformation that follows closely resembles the merging of Salmacis and Hermaphroditus in *Metamorphoses* 4.373–79.

70   Then two heads were already joined in one,
when in one face where two had been dissolved,
two intermingled shapes appeared to us.

    Two arms came into being from four lengths;
the thighs and legs, the belly and the chest
75   became such limbs as never had been seen.

    And every former shape was canceled there:
that perverse image seemed to share in both—
and none; and so, and slowly, it moved on.

    Just as the lizard, when it darts from hedge
80   to hedge, beneath the dog days' giant lash,
seems, if it cross one's path, a lightning flash,

    so seemed a blazing little serpent moving
against the bellies of the other two,
as black and livid as a peppercorn.

85   Attacking one of them, it pierced right through
the part where we first take our nourishment;°   *the navel*
and then it fell before him at full length.

    The one it had transfixed stared but said nothing;
in fact he only stood his ground and yawned
90   as one whom sleep or fever has undone.

    The serpent stared at him, he at the serpent;
one through his wound, the other through his mouth
were smoking violently; their smoke met.

    Let Lucan now be silent, where he sings
95   of sad Sabellus and Nasidius,
and wait to hear what flies off from my bow.

    Let Ovid now be silent, where he tells
of Cadmus, Arethusa; if his verse
has made of one a serpent, one a fountain,[8]

100   I do not envy him; he never did
transmute two natures, face to face, so that
both forms were ready to exchange their matter.

    These were the ways they answered to each other:
the serpent split its tail into a fork;
105   the wounded sinner drew his steps together.

    The legs and then the thighs along with them
so fastened to each other that the juncture
soon left no sign that was discernible.

    Meanwhile the cleft tail took upon itself
110   the form the other gradually lost;
its skin grew soft, the other's skin grew hard.

    I saw the arms that drew in at his armpits
and also saw the monster's two short feet

8. Dante invokes (and outdoes) his two primary sources in this canto: the horrific deaths by snakebite of two Roman soldiers in the Libyan Desert in Lucan's *Pharsalia* 9 and the transformations of Ovid's *Metamorphoses,* in this case those of
Thebes's founder Cadmus into a serpent (4.576–89) and of the nymph Arethusa into a fountain (5.572–641).

grow long for just as much as those were shortened.
115   The serpent's hind feet, twisted up together,
became the member that man hides; just as
the wretch put out two hind paws from his member.
    And while the smoke veils each with a new color,
and now breeds hair upon the skin of one,
120   just as it strips the hair from off the other,
    the one rose up, the other fell; and yet
they never turned aside their impious eyelamps,
beneath which each of them transformed his snout:
    he who stood up drew his back toward the temples,
125   and from the excess matter growing there
came ears upon the cheeks that had been bare;
    whatever had not been pulled back but kept,
superfluous, then made his face a nose
and thickened out his lips appropriately.
130   He who was lying down thrust out his snout;
and even as the snail hauls in its horns,
he drew his ears straight back into his head;
    his tongue, which had before been whole and fit
for speech, now cleaves; the other's tongue, which had
135   been forked, now closes up; and the smoke stops.
    The soul that had become an animal,
now hissing, hurried off along the valley;
the other one, behind him, speaks and spits.
    And then he turned aside his new-made shoulders
140   and told the third soul: "I'd have Buoso run
on all fours down this road, as I have done."
    And so I saw the seventh ballast change
and rechange;[9] may the strangeness plead for me
if there's been some confusion in my pen.
145   And though my eyes were somewhat blurred, my mind
bewildered, those three sinners did not flee
so secretly that I could not perceive
    Puccio Sciancato clearly, he who was
the only soul who'd not been changed among
150   the three companions we had met at first;
    the other one made you, Gaville, grieve.[1]

Canto 26

Still the Eighth Circle, Seventh Pouch: the Thieves. Dante's invective against Florence. View of the Eighth Pouch, where Fraudulent Counselors are clothed in the

9. That is, the souls of the seventh *bolgia*, likened to the hold of a ship.
1. Murdered by the inhabitants of the village of Gaville, Francesco de' Cavalcanti was swiftly and savagely avenged by his family.

flames that burn them. Ulysses and Diomedes in one shared flame. Ulysses' tale of his final voyage.

Be joyous, Florence, you are great indeed,
for over sea and land you beat your wings;
through every part of Hell your name extends!

Among the thieves I found five citizens
5 of yours—and such, that shame has taken me;
with them, you can ascend to no high honor.

But if the dreams dreamt close to dawn are true,
then little time will pass before you feel
what Prato and the others crave for you.[1]

10 Were that already come, it would not be
too soon—and let it come, since it must be!
As I grow older, it will be more heavy.[2]

We left that deep and, by protruding stones
that served as stairs for our descent before,
15 my guide climbed up again and drew me forward;

and as we took our solitary path
among the ridge's jagged spurs and rocks,
our feet could not make way without our hands.

It grieved me then and now grieves me again
20 when I direct my mind to what I saw;
and more than usual, I curb my talent,

that it not run where virtue does not guide;
so that, if my kind star or something better
has given me that gift, I not abuse it.

25 As many as the fireflies the peasant
(while resting on a hillside in the season°   *summer*
when he who lights the world least hides his face),

just when the fly gives way to the mosquito,
sees glimmering below, down in the valley,
30 there where perhaps he gathers grapes and tills—

so many were the flames that glittered in
the eighth abyss; I made this out as soon
as I had come to where one sees the bottom.

Even as he who was avenged by bears
35 saw, as it left, Elijah's chariot—
its horses rearing, rising right to heaven—

when he could not keep track of it except
by watching one lone flame in its ascent,
just like a little cloud that climbs on high:[3]

40 so, through the gullet of that ditch, each flame

---

1. Ancient lore distinguished many sorts of dreams; only those dreamt near dawn were held to be prophetic, "true." Prato is a Tuscan town between Florence and Pistoia that envied Florentine power; the enigmatic prediction may refer to Cardinal Niccolò da Prato, who placed the city under interdiction after his peacemission failed in 1304.
2. The longer he must wait for a retribution to his city that will be just but bittersweet.
3. After the prophet Elisha was mocked by a group of boys, two bears came from the woods and killed 42 of them; he had already witnessed the ascent of his teacher, the prophet Elijah, to heaven in a fiery chariot (2 Kings 2.23–24).

must make its way; no flame displays its prey,
though every flame has carried off a sinner.

I stood upon the bridge and leaned straight out
to see; and if I had not gripped a rock,
I should have fallen off—without a push.

My guide, who noted how intent I was,
told me: "Within those fires there are souls;
each one is swathed in that which scorches him."

"My master," I replied, "on hearing you,
I am more sure; but I'd already thought
that it was so, and I had meant to ask:

Who is within the flame that comes so twinned
above that it would seem to rise out of
the pyre Eteocles shared with his brother?"[4]

He answered me: "Within that flame, Ulysses
and Diomedes suffer; they, who went
as one to rage, now share one punishment.[5]

And there, together in their flame, they grieve
over the horse's fraud that caused a breach—
the gate that let Rome's noble seed escape.

There they regret the guile that makes the dead
Deïdamia still lament Achilles;
and there, for the Palladium, they pay."

"If they can speak within those sparks," I said,
"I pray you and repray and, master, may
my prayer be worth a thousand pleas, do not

forbid my waiting here until the flame
with horns approaches us; for you can see
how, out of my desire, I bend toward it."

And he to me: "What you have asked is worthy
of every praise; therefore, I favor it.
I only ask you this: refrain from talking.

Let me address them—I have understood
what you desire of them. Since they were Greek,
perhaps they'd be disdainful of your speech."[6]

And when my guide adjudged the flame had reached

4. Eteocles and Polynices were twin sons of Oedipus, King of Thebes, and Jocasta. After they forced their father (and brother) to abdicate, he cursed them with enmity. They fought over the kingship, killed each other in single combat, and were burned on a single funeral pyre. So enduring was their hatred that the rising flames divided in two (Statius, *Thebaid* 429ff. and Lucan, *Pharsalia* 1.549–52).

5. Ulysses and Diomedes were Greek heroes of the Trojan War who often acted in tandem. One of their exploits was to steal the Palladium, a wooden image of Pallas Athena said to preserve the walls of Troy. In pretended remorse, they built an enormous, hollow wooden horse in which they and other Greeks hid, and which then led the deceived Trojans to breach their walls in order to bear it within the city (*Aeneid* 2.18–370). Rome's "noble seed" is Aeneas and his followers, who fled the city's destruction for Italy. Deïdamia was the mother of Pyrrhus; she died of grief after the boy's father, Achilles, sailed to Troy. In *Purgatorio* 22.114, she is said to be among the souls in Limbo.

6. Unlike Dante, Virgil had been fluent in Greek; moreover, his epic, like Homer's, was written in the high, tragic style characteristic of the speech in this encounter. Dante also chooses to stress the greatness and antiquity of the shade being interviewed.

a point where time and place were opportune,
this was the form I heard his words assume:
  "You two who move as one within the flame,
80 if I deserved of you while I still lived,
if I deserved of you much or a little
    when in the world I wrote my noble lines,
do not move on; let one of you retell
where, having gone astray, he found his death."
85   The greater horn within that ancient flame
began to sway and tremble, murmuring
just like a fire that struggles in the wind;
    and then he waved his flame-tip back and forth
as if it were a tongue that tried to speak,
90 and flung toward us a voice that answered:[7] "When
    I sailed away from Circe, who'd beguiled me
to stay more than a year there, near Gaeta—
before Aeneas gave that place a name[8]—
    neither my fondness for my son nor pity
95 for my old father nor the love I owed
Penelope, which would have gladdened her,
    was able to defeat in me the longing
I had to gain experience of the world
and of the vices and the worth of men.
100   Therefore, I set out on the open sea
with but one ship and that small company
of those who never had deserted me.
    I saw as far as Spain, far as Morocco,
along both shores; I saw Sardinia
105 and saw the other islands that sea bathes.
    And I and my companions were already
old and slow, when we approached the narrows
where Hercules set up his boundary stones
    that men might heed and never reach beyond:
110 upon my right, I had gone past Seville,
and on the left, already passed Ceüta.[9]
    'Brothers,' I said, 'o you, who having crossed
a hundred thousand dangers, reach the west,
to this brief waking-time that still is left
115   unto your senses, you must not deny
experience of that which lies beyond
the sun, and of the world that is unpeopled.

---

7. There is no known source for this account by Ulysses (the "greater" flame) of his death; it contradicts the prophecy of Tiresias in *Odyssey* 11.134–37 of a peaceful death at sea.

8. Circe was an enchantress who transformed Ulysses' men into swine. After forcing her to change them back, Ulysses tarried with Circe for a year before continuing his voyage to his home and family in Ithaca.

9. Ulysses and his men are at the western edge of the known world; on the African and European shores of the Mediterranean, the Pillars of Hercules were twin promontories formed when the hero split a mountain in two across the Mediterranean, usually identified with the modern promontories of Gibraltar in Spain and Jebel Musa in Morocco. It was thought impossible to sail beyond this boundary and return alive.

Consider well the seed that gave you birth:
you were not made to live your lives as brutes,
120   but to be followers of worth and knowledge.'

I spurred my comrades with this brief address
to meet the journey with such eagerness
that I could hardly, then, have held them back;

and having turned our stern toward morning,° we   *the east*
125   made wings out of our oars in a wild flight
and always gained upon our left-hand side.

At night I now could see the other pole
and all its stars; the star of ours had fallen
and never rose above the plain of the ocean.[1]

130   Five times the light beneath the moon had been
rekindled, and, as many times, was spent,[2]
since that hard passage faced our first attempt,

when there before us rose a mountain, dark
because of distance, and it seemed to me
135   the highest mountain I had ever seen.[3]

And we were glad, but this soon turned to sorrow,
for out of that new land a whirlwind rose
and hammered at our ship, against her bow.

Three times it turned her round with all the waters;
140   and at the fourth, it lifted up the stern
so that our prow plunged deep, as pleased an Other,°   *God*
until the sea again closed—over us.''

Canto 27

*Still the Eighth Circle, Eighth Pouch: the Fraudulent Counselors. Guido da
Montefeltro, for whom Dante provides a panorama of the state of political affairs in
Romagna. Guido's tale of the anticipatory—but unavailing—absolution given him by
Boniface VIII. The quarrel of a demon and St Francis over Guido's soul.*

The flame already was erect and silent—
it had no more to say. Now it had left
us with the permission of the gentle poet,

when, just behind it, came another flame
5   that drew our eyes to watch its tip because
of the perplexing sound that it sent forth.

Even as the Sicilian bull (that first
had bellowed with the cry—and this was just—
of him who shaped it with his instruments)

10   would always bellow with its victim's voice,
so that, although that bull was only brass,

---

1. The "other pole" is Antartica; they have crossed the equator and no longer see the stars of "our" pole, the northern hemisphere.

2. Five months had passed.

3. This is probably the Mountain of Purgatory; it also resonates with the pilgrim's unsuccessful attempt in Canto 1.

it seemed as if it were pierced through by pain;[1]

so were the helpless words that, from the first,
had found no path or exit from the flame,
15   transformed into the language of the fire.

But after they had found their way up toward
the tip, and given it that movement which
the tongue had given them along their passage,

we heard: "O you to whom I turn my voice,
20   who only now were talking Lombard, saying,
'Now you may leave—I'll not provoke more speech,'[2]

though I have come perhaps a little late,
may it not trouble you to stop and speak
with me; see how I stay—and I am burning![3]

25   If you have fallen into this blind world
but recently, out of the sweet Italian
country from which I carry all my guilt,

do tell me if the Romagnoles have peace
or war; I was from there—the hills between
30   Urbino and the ridge where Tiber springs."

I still was bent, attentive, over him,
when my guide nudged me lightly at the side
and said: "You speak; he is Italian."[4]

And I, who had my answer set already,
35   without delay began to speak to him:
"O soul that is concealed below in flame,

Romagna is not now and never was
quite free of war inside its tyrants' hearts;
but when I left her, none had broken out.

40   Ravenna stands as it has stood for years;
the eagle of Polenta shelters it
and also covers Cervia with his wings.[5]

The city that already stood long trial
and made a bloody heap out of the French,
45   now finds itself again beneath green paws.[6]

Both mastiffs of Verruchio, old and new,
who dealt so badly with Montagna, use

---

1. The Athenian artisan Perillus fabricated a bronze bull in which the victims of Phalaris, the 6th-century tyrant of Agrigentum in Sicily, could be roasted alive, their shrieks emerging as if the bellowing of a bull. Perillus was chosen to be first to test his apparatus.

2. "Lombardy" in the Middle Ages referred to northern Italy, including Virgil's birthplace of Mantua where, in Dante's belief, a version of the Lombard dialect was already spoken in antiquity. Given the focus on "high" language in the previous canto, it is a calculated shock to suggest to us in retrospect that Virgil was speaking to Ulysses in Italian (line 3).

3. The shade is Guido da Montefeltro (c.1220–1298), nicknamed the "Fox," who commanded a force of Ghibellines from Romagnola (the region north of Tuscany) and exiles from Bologna and Florence. In his *Convivio*, Dante had referred to the late-life conversion of Guido as exemplary and praised the leader as "our most noble Latin" (4.28.8).

4. By contrast to the previous canto (73–75), where Virgil addressed the Greek shades.

5. The Adriatic cities of Ravenna and Cervia were ruled from 1275 by the Guelf Polenta family, whose coat of arms displayed an eagle. The head of the family from 1275 until his death in 1310 was Guido da Polenta the elder, father of Francesca da Rimini (5.73–142).

6. Under the leadership of Guido da Montefeltro, Forlì, a central city of Romagna, successfully withstood a year-long siege by French and Guelf troops sent by Pope Martin IV; in 1282 they decimated the attacking force. The following year, the city came to terms with the pope and drove out Guido. The "green paws" belong to the coat of arms of the Ordelaffi family, new tyrants of Forlì as of 1300.

their teeth to bore where they have always gnawed.[7]
    The cities on Lamone and Santerno

50 are led by the young lion of the white lair;
from summer unto winter, he shifts factions.[8]
    That city with its side bathed by the Savio,
just as it lies between the plain and mountain,
lives somewhere between tyranny and freedom.[9]

55   And now, I pray you, tell me who you are:
do not be harder than I've been with you,
that in the world your name may still endure."[1]
    After the flame, in customary fashion,
had roared awhile, it moved its pointed tip

60 this side and that and then set free this breath:
    "If I thought my reply were meant for one
who ever could return into the world,
this flame would stir no more; and yet, since none—
if what I hear is true—ever returned

65 alive from this abyss, then without fear
of facing infamy, I answer you.
    I was a man of arms, then wore the cord,°   *of a monk*
believing that, so girt, I made amends;
and surely what I thought would have been true

70 had not the Highest Priest—may he be damned!—
made me fall back into my former sins;
and how and why, I'd have you hear from me.[2]
    While I still had the form of bones and flesh
my mother gave to me, my deeds were not

75 those of the lion but those of the fox.[3]
    The wiles and secret ways—I knew them all
and so employed their arts that my renown
had reached the very boundaries of earth.
    But when I saw myself come to that part

80 of life when it is fitting for all men
to lower sails and gather in their ropes,
    what once had been my joy was now dejection;
repenting and confessing, I became
a friar; and—poor me—it would have helped.

85   The prince of the new Pharisees,° who then   *Pope Boniface*
was waging war so near the Lateran—

---

7. Malatesta, lord of Rimini, had four sons, including Gianciotto, husband of Francesca da Rimini, her lover Paolo, and Malatestino da Verruchio, the "young mastiff." Both lords were harsh tyrants, killing the head of the Rimini Ghibellines, Montagna de' Parcitati, in 1295.

8. Maghinardo Pagani da Susinana, whose coat of arms displayed a lion on a white ground, ruled the cities of Faenza, on the Lamone, and Imola, on the Santerno River. Ghibelline by birth, he was also loyal to the Florentine Guelfs.

9. Cesena was on the Savio River, midway between Forlì and Rimini. It was a free municipality during this period, but dominated by Guido's powerful cousin, Galasso da Montefeltro.

1. Guido has been under the misconception that Dante was a shade; Dante doesn't yet know to whom he has been speaking.

2. After leading the Ghibellines, Guido made peace with Boniface VIII and joined the Franciscan order late in life. He died in 1298 at the age of 75. The incident that Dante has him recount here may have been invented.

3. A common distinction between force ("the lion") and guile ("the fox").

and not against the Jews or Saracens,° Arabs

for every enemy of his was Christian,

and none of them had gone to conquer Acre

90   or been a trader in the Sultan's lands—

took no care for the highest office or

the holy orders that were his, or for

my cord, which used to make its wearers leaner.[4]

But just as Constantine, on Mount Soracte,

95   to cure his leprosy, sought out Sylvester,[5]

so this one sought me out as his instructor,

to ease the fever of his arrogance.

He asked me to give counsel. I was silent—

his words had seemed to me delirious.

100   And then he said: 'Your heart must not mistrust:

I now absolve you in advance—teach me

to batter Penestrino to the ground.[6]

You surely know that I possess the power

to lock and unlock Heaven; for the keys

105   my predecessor did not prize are two.'[7]

Then his grave arguments compelled me so,

my silence seemed a worse offense than speech,

and I said: 'Since you cleanse me of the sin

that I must now fall into, Father, know:

110   long promises and very brief fulfillments

will bring a victory to your high throne.'[8]

Then Francis came, as soon as I was dead,

for me; but one of the black cherubim

told him: 'Don't bear him off; do not cheat me.[9]

115   He must come down among my menials;

the counsel that he gave was fraudulent;

since then, I've kept close track, to snatch his scalp;

one can't absolve a man who's not repented,

and no one can repent and will at once;

120   the law of contradiction won't allow it.'

O miserable me, for how I started

when he took hold of me and said: 'Perhaps

you did not think that I was a logician!'

He carried me to Minos; and that monster

---

4. Rather than waging a holy war—Acre was the principal port of the crusaders in Palestine—Boniface was engaged in a local feud (the Lateran Palace was the papal residence) with the Colonna family.

5. According to legend, the Emperor Constantine was afflicted by leprosy due to his persecution of the Christians. Led by a dream, he sought out Pope Sylvester I on Mt. Soracte north of Rome, who baptized and then cured him.

6. The castle at Penestrino southeast of Rome was the stronghold of the Colonna, who surrendered after Boniface had promised complete amnesty (the "long promises" of line 110). He immediately had the castle leveled.

7. The "keys of the kingdom of heaven" (Matthew 16.19) were the symbol of the pope's ultimate power over condemnation and absolution; according to Boniface, his predecessor, Celestine V, who abdicated, "did not prize" them.

8. The pope's promise to Guido to absolve him in advance of whatever evil he may counsel is an extreme version of the abuse of granting indulgences, or reduced penance, for sins not yet committed.

9. Coming for the soul of one of his order, St. Francis takes the place of the customary angel who struggles against the devil ("black cherubim") for possession of a soul.

125 twisted his tail eight times around his hide
  and then, when he had bit it in great anger,
   announced: 'This one is for the thieving fire';
  for which—and where, you see—I now am lost,
  and in this garb I move in bitterness."

130   And when, with this, his words were at an end,
  the flame departed, sorrowing and writhing
  and tossing its sharp horn. We moved beyond;
   I went together with my guide, along
  the ridge until the other arch that bridges
135 the ditch where payment is imposed on those
   who, since they brought such discord, bear such loads.

Canto 28

The Eighth Circle, Ninth Pouch, where the Sowers of Scandal and Schism, perpetually circling, are wounded and—after each healing—wounded again by a demon with a sword. Mohammed and Ali. Warning to Fra Dolcino. Curio. Mosca. Bertran de Born.

   Who, even with untrammeled° words and many   *unrestrained*
  attempts at telling, ever could recount
  in full the blood and wounds that I now saw?
   Each tongue that tried would certainly fall short
5 because the shallowness of both our speech
  and intellect cannot contain so much.
   Were you to reassemble all the men
  who once, within Apulia's fateful land,°   *southern Italy*
  had mourned their blood, shed at the Trojans' hands,[1]
10 as well as those who fell in the long war
  where massive mounds of rings were battle spoils—
  even as Livy writes, who does not err[2]—
   and those who felt the thrust of painful blows
  when they fought hard against Robert Guiscard;[3]
15 with all the rest whose bones are still piled up
   at Ceperano—each Apulian was
  a traitor there—and, too, at Tagliacozzo,
  where old Alardo conquered without weapons;[4]
   and then, were one to show his limb pierced through
20 and one his limb hacked off, that would not match
  the hideousness of the ninth abyss.
   No barrel, even though it's lost a hoop
  or end-piece, ever gapes as one whom I
  saw ripped right from his chin to where we fart:

1. The early Romans, descendants of Aeneas and his men, and their wars with the Tarentines (280–274 B.C.E.) and the Samnites (434–290 B.C.E.).

2. Livy (59 B.C.E.–17 C.E.) was the great historian of ancient Rome; his monumental *History* includes an account of the Second Punic War (219–202 B.C.E.), during which Hannibal brought to Carthage a heap of gold rings taken off of the fingers of slain Romans (33.12.1–2).

3. A Norman adventurer (1015–1085) who fought the Greeks and Saracens in Sicily and southern Italy.

4. Sites of bloody battles in the 1260s marked by treachery.

25 his bowels hung between his legs, one saw
his vitals and the miserable sack
that makes of what we swallow excrement.

    While I was all intent on watching him,
he looked at me, and with his hands he spread
30 his chest and said: "See how I split myself!

    See now how maimed Mohammed is![5] And he
who walks and weeps before me is Ali,[6]
whose face is opened wide from chin to forelock.

    And all the others here whom you can see
35 were, when alive, the sowers of dissension
and scandal, and for this they now are split.

    Behind us here, a devil decks us out
so cruelly, re-placing every one
of this throng underneath the sword edge when
40 we've made our way around the road of pain,
because our wounds have closed again before
we have returned to meet his blade once more.

    But who are you who dawdle on this ridge,
perhaps to slow your going to the verdict
45 that was pronounced on your self-accusations?"

    "Death has not reached him yet," my master answered,
"nor is it guilt that summons him to torment;
but that he may gain full experience,

    I, who am dead, must guide him here below,
50 to circle after circle, throughout Hell:
this is as true as that I speak to you."

    More than a hundred, when they heard him, stopped
within the ditch and turned to look at me,
forgetful of their torture, wondering.

55   "Then you, who will perhaps soon see the sun,
tell Fra Dolcino to provide himself
with food, if he has no desire to join me

    here quickly, lest when snow besieges him,
it bring the Novarese the victory
60 that otherwise they would not find too easy."[7]

    When he had raised his heel, as if to go,
Mohammed said these words to me, and then
he set it on the ground and off he went.

    Another sinner, with his throat slit through
65 and with his nose hacked off up to his eyebrows,
and no more than a single ear remaining,

---

5. The Prophet Mohammed (570–632) was considered in medieval Europe as an apostate Christian; from the same point of view, Islam was a decisive division of religious unity.

6. Mohammed's son-in-law. He was assassinated after only five years as caliph, in 661, leading to the division of Islam into two sects, the Sunnites and the Shiites or Fatimites.

7. In 1300 Fra Dolcino had become head of the reformist sect of the Apostolic Brothers; when the sect was pronounced as heretical in 1305 by Clement V because it believed in holding goods and women in common, thousands of its members fled to the hills between Novara and Vercelli in northwest Italy. Forced by starvation to surrender, many were burned alive, including Fra Dolcino and his companion, Margaret of Trent.

had—with the others—stayed his steps in wonder;
he was the first, before the rest, to open
his windpipe—on the outside, all bloodred—

70   and said: "O you whom guilt does not condemn,
and whom, unless too close resemblance cheats me,
I've seen above upon Italian soil,
        remember Pier da Medicina[8] if
you ever see again the gentle plain

75   that from Vercelli slopes to Marcabò.
        And let the two best men of Fano know—
I mean both Messer Guido and Angiolello—
that, if the foresight we have here's not vain,
        they will be cast out of their ship and drowned,

80   weighed down with stones, near La Cattolica,
because of a foul tyrant's treachery.[9]
        Between the isles of Cyprus and Majorca,[1]
Neptune has never seen so cruel a crime
committed by the pirates or the Argives.°   Greeks

85   That traitor who sees only with one eye
and rules the land which one who's here with me
would wish his sight had never seen, will call
        Guido and Angiolello to a parley,
and then will so arrange it that they'll need

90   no vow or prayer to Focara's wind!"[2]
        And I to him: "If you would have me carry
some news of you above, then tell and show me
who so detests the sight of Rimini."
        And then he set his hand upon the jaw

95   of a companion, opening his mouth
and shouting: "This is he, and he speaks not.
        A man cast out, he quenched the doubt in Caesar,
insisting that the one who is prepared
can only suffer harm if he delays."[3]

100   Oh, how dismayed and pained he seemed to me,
his tongue slit in his gullet: Curio,
who once was so audacious in his talk!
        And one who walked with both his hands hacked off,
while lifting up his stumps through the dark air,

105   so that his face was hideous with blood,

---

8. Early commentators described Pier da Medicina as a sower of discord in Romagna.

9. In c. 1312 Guido del Cassero and Angliolello di Carignano were thrown overboard by henchmen of Malatestino, lord of Rimini (the "young mastiff" of 27.46, and the "foul tyrant" and "one-eyed traitor" here), as they were on their way at his invitation to a meeting at the small coastal town of La Cattolica. Presumably, Malatestino planned to seize power in their town.

1. The two ends of the Mediterranean.

2. Focara was a proverbially windy and dangerous headland on the Adriatic between Fano and La Cattolica. Guido and Angiolello no longer need to worry about praying for safe passage.

3. While tribune in Rome in 50 B.C.E., Gaius Curio the younger was bought by Julius Caesar away from the Pompeian party. He fled the city after civil war broke out. Dante follows Lucan (*Pharsalia* 1.279–81) by making Curio responsible for Caesar's decision to cross the Rubicon, the stream separating Italy from Cisalpine Gaul; Roman law forbade a general from leading his army beyond the province he controlled.

cried out: "You will remember Mosca, too,
who said—alas—'What's done is at an end,'
which was the seed of evil for the Tuscans."[4]

110   I added: "—and brought death to your own kinsmen";
then having heard me speak, grief heaped on grief,
he went his way as one gone mad with sadness.

But I stayed there to watch that company
and saw a thing that I should be afraid
to tell with no more proof than my own self—

115   except that I am reassured by conscience,
that good companion, heartening a man
beneath the breastplate of its purity.

I surely saw, and it still seems I see,
a trunk without a head that walked just like

120   the others in that melancholy herd;

it carried by the hair its severed head,
which swayed within its hand just like a lantern;
and that head looked at us and said: "Ah me!"

Out of itself it made itself a lamp,

125   and they were two in one and one in two;
how that can be, He knows who so decrees.

When it was just below the bridge, it lifted
its arm together with its head, so that
its words might be more near us, words that said:

130   "Now you can see atrocious punishment,
you who, still breathing, go to view the dead:
see if there's any pain as great as this.

And so that you may carry news of me,
know that I am Bertran de Born, the one

135   who gave bad counsel to the fledgling king.[5]

I made the son and father enemies:
Achitophel with his malicious urgings
did not do worse with Absalom and David.[6]

Because I severed those so joined, I carry—

140   alas—my brain dissevered from its source,
which is within my trunk. And thus, in me
one sees the law of counter-penalty."

Canto 29

Still the Eighth Circle, Ninth Pouch: the Sowers of Scandal and Schism. Geri del Bello, an unavenged ancestor of Dante. The Tenth Pouch: the Falsifiers. The First Group, Falsifiers of Metals (Alchemists), plagued by scabs, lying on the earth, scratching furiously. Griffolino. Capocchio.

---

4. The feuding between the Guelfs and Ghibellines of Florence was viciously renewed in 1215 by the ardent Ghibelline Mosca de' Lamberti.

5. Bertran de Born (c. 1140–c. 1215) was Lord of Hautefort, a soldier and a famous troubadour who specialized in political songs. He was said to have urged Prince Henry of England to rebel against his father, Henry II.

6. Achitophel hanged himself after unsuccessfully encouraging David's son Absalom to rebel against his father (2 Samuel 15–17.23).

So many souls and such outlandish wounds
had made my eyes inebriate—they longed
to stay and weep. But Virgil said to me:

"Why are you staring so insistently?
Why does your vision linger there below
among the lost and mutilated shadows?

You did not do so at the other moats.
If you would count them all, consider: twenty-
two miles make up the circuit of the valley.[1]

The moon already is beneath our feet;
the time alloted to us now is short,[2]
and there is more to see than you see here."

"Had you," I answered him without a pause,
"been able to consider why I looked,
you might have granted me a longer stay."

Meanwhile my guide had moved ahead; I went
behind him, answering as I walked on,
and adding: "In that hollow upon which

just now, I kept my eyes intent, I think
a spirit born of my own blood laments
the guilt which, down below, costs one so much."[3]

At this my master said: "Don't let your thoughts
about him interrupt you from here on:
attend to other things, let him stay there;

for I saw him below the little bridge,
his finger pointing at you, threatening,
and heard him called by name—Geri del Bello.

But at that moment you were occupied
with him who once was lord of Hautefort;°   ° *Bertran de Born*
you did not notice Geri—he moved off."

"My guide, it was his death by violence,
for which he still is not avenged,"[4] I said,
"by anyone who shares his shame, that made

him so disdainful now; and—I suppose—
for this he left without a word to me,
and this has made me pity him the more."

And so we talked until we found the first
point of the ridge that, if there were more light,
would show the other valley to the bottom.

When we had climbed above the final cloister
of Malebolge, so that its lay brothers[5]
were able to appear before our eyes,

5

10

15

20

25

30

35

40

84

---

1. It is unclear why Dante chose this moment to provide the first exact measurement of any part of Hell.

2. If the moon is below them, the sun must be at its zenith above them, in Jerusalem: it is around 2 P.M. Only four hours remain of the 24 allotted to the journey through Hell.

3. This is Geri del Bello degli Alighieri, first cousin to Dante's father. A troublemaker, Geri was murdered by a member of the Sacchetti family; this was avenged by the Alighieri in 1310, and the families apparently continued feuding until 1342.

4. Family feuding and private vendettas were sanctioned by law in Dante's time; hence, Geri still had just cause for complaint against his family in 1300.

5. The cutting metaphor equates the shades of the tenth *bolgia* to working members of a religious house, the "final cloister" of the eighth circle.

I felt the force of strange laments, like arrows
whose shafts are barbed with pity; and at this,
45   I had to place my hands across my ears.
       Just like the sufferings that all the sick
of Val di Chiana's hospitals, Maremma's,
Sardinia's,° from July until September   *malarial regions*
       would muster if assembled in one ditch—
50   so was it here, and such a stench rose up
as usually comes from festering limbs.
       And keeping always to the left, we climbed
down to the final bank of the long ridge,
and then my sight could see more vividly
55   into the bottom, where unerring Justice,
the minister of the High Lord, punishes
the falsifiers she had registered.
       I do not think that there was greater grief
in seeing all Aegina's people sick[6]
60   (then, when the air was so infected that
       all animals, down to the little worm,
collapsed; and afterward, as poets hold
to be the certain truth, those ancient peoples
       received their health again through seed of ants)
65   than I felt when I saw, in that dark valley,
the spirits languishing in scattered heaps.
       Some lay upon their bellies, some upon
the shoulders of another spirit, some
crawled on all fours along that squalid road.
70   We journeyed step by step without a word,
watching and listening to those sick souls,
who had not strength enough to lift themselves.
       I saw two sitting propped against each other—
as pan is propped on pan to heat them up—
75   and each, from head to foot, spotted with scabs;
       and I have never seen a stableboy
whose master waits for him, or one who stays
awake reluctantly, so ply a horse
       with currycomb, as they assailed themselves
80   with clawing nails—their itching had such force
and fury, and there was no other help.
       And so their nails kept scraping off the scabs,
just as a knife scrapes off the scales of carp
or of another fish with scales more large.
85   "O you who use your nails to strip yourself,"
my guide began to say to one of them,
"and sometimes have to turn them into pincers,

---

6. When Jupiter carried off the nymph Aegina to the island of Oenone, their son Aeacus aroused Juno's jealousy by renaming the island after his mother. After Juno sent a devastating pestilence as punishment, Jupiter restored the island by changing its ants into men, called "Myrmidons" after the Greek word for *ant* (*Metamorphoses* 7.523–657).

tell us if there are some Italians
among the sinners in this moat—so may

90   your nails hold out, eternal, at their work."

"We two whom you see so disfigured here,
we are Italians," one said, in tears.
"But who are you who have inquired of us?"

My guide replied: "From circle down to circle,
95   together with this living man, I am
one who descends; I mean to show him Hell."

At this their mutual support broke off;
and, quivering, each spirit turned toward me
with others who, by chance, had heard his words.

100   Then my good master drew more close to me,
saying: "Now tell them what it is you want."
And I began to speak, just as he wished:

"So that your memory may never fade
within the first world from the minds of men,
105   but still live on—and under many suns—

do tell me who you are and from what city,
and do not let your vile and filthy torment
make you afraid to let me know your names."

One answered me: "My city was Arezzo
110   and Albero of Siena had me burned;
but what I died for does not bring me here.[7]

It's true that I had told him—jestingly—
'I'd know enough to fly through air'; and he,
with curiosity, but little sense,

115   wished me to show that art to him and, just
because I had not made him Daedalus,
had one who held him as a son burn me.

But Minos, who cannot mistake, condemned
my spirit to the final pouch of ten
120   for alchemy I practiced in the world."

And then I asked the poet: "Was there ever
so vain a people as the Sienese?
Even the French can't match such vanity."[8]

At this, the other leper, who had heard me,
125   replied to what I'd said: "Except for Stricca,
for he knew how to spend most frugally;

and Niccolò, the first to make men see
that cloves can serve as luxury (such seed,
in gardens where it suits, can take fast root);

130   and, too, Caccia d'Asciano's company,
with whom he squandered vineyards and tilled fields,

7. Griffolino was an alchemist of Arezzo who promised he could teach Albero of Siena flying, the art of Daedalus
(see 17.109–11). Angry at having been fleeced, Albero denounced Griffolino as a magician, and had him burned at
the stake.

8. The vanity of the French was proverbial; the young Sienese noblemen listed below all belonged to a group called the
"Spendthrift Club" and revelled in squandering their estates.

while Abbagliato showed such subtlety.
But if you want to know who joins you so
against the Sienese, look hard at me—
135   that way, my face can also answer rightly—
and see that I'm the shade of that Capocchio
whose alchemy could counterfeit fine metals.
And you, if I correctly take your measure,
recall how apt I was at aping nature."9

Canto 30

Still the Eighth Circle, Tenth Pouch: the Falsifiers. Gianni Schicchi and Myrrha in
the Second Group, Counterfeiters of Others' Persons. Master Adam in the Third
Group, Counterfeiters of Coins. Potiphar's wife and Sinon the Greek in the Fourth
Group, Falsifiers of Words, Liars. The quarrel between Adam and Sinon.

When Juno was incensed with Semele
and, thus, against the Theban family
had shown her fury time and time again,
then Athamas was driven so insane
5   that, seeing both his wife and their two sons,
as she bore one upon each arm, he cried:
"Let's spread the nets, to take the lioness
together with her cubs along the pass";
and he stretched out his talons, pitiless,
10   and snatched the son who bore the name Learchus,
whirled him around and dashed him on a rock;
she, with her other burden, drowned herself.1
And after fortune turned against the pride
of Troy, which had dared all, so that the king
15   together with his kingdom, was destroyed,
then Hecuba was wretched, sad, a captive;
and after she had seen Polyxena
dead and, in misery, had recognized
her Polydorus lying on the shore,2
20   she barked, out of her senses, like a dog—
her agony had so deformed her mind.
But neither fury—Theban, Trojan—ever
was seen to be so cruel against another,
in rending beasts and even human limbs,
25   as were two shades I saw, both pale and naked,
who, biting, ran berserk in just the way
a hog does when it's let loose from its sty.

---

9. Capocchio was burned alive in 1293 in Siena as an alchemist; apparently, he was acquainted with the young Dante.
Because it attempts to create gold out of baser metals, alchemy imitates or "apes" the work of nature.

1. The Theban princess Semele was loved by Jupiter and she bore him the god Bacchus. As part of her vengeance, Jupiter's wife Juno caused Semele's brother-in-law, the king of Thebes, to believe his wife and two sons were a lioness and cubs; after he killed one son, his wife drowned herself with the other (*Metamorphoses* 4.512–30).

2. Priam's queen, Hecuba, went mad after the fall of Troy following the killing of her daughter and son. According to Ovid, on seeing her son's unburied body Hecuba howled like a dog and jumped into the sea (*Metamorphoses* 13.404–575).

85

The one came at Capocchio and sank

his tusks into his neck so that, by dragging,

30   he made the hard ground scrape against his belly.

And he who stayed behind, the Aretine,

trembled and said: "That phantom's Gianni Schicchi,

and he goes raging, rending others so."[3]

And, "Oh," I said to him, "so may the other

35   not sink its teeth in you, please tell me who

it is before it hurries off from here."

And he to me: "That is the ancient soul

of the indecent Myrrha, she who loved

her father past the limits of just love.[4]

40   She came to sin with him by falsely taking

another's shape upon herself, just as

the other phantom who goes there had done,

that he might gain the lady of the herd,

when he disguised himself as Buoso Donati,

45   making a will as if most properly."

And when the pair of raging ones had passed,

those two on whom my eyes were fixed, I turned

around to see the rest of the ill-born.

I saw one who'd be fashioned like a lute

50   if he had only had his groin cut off

from that part of his body where it forks.

The heavy dropsy, which so disproportions

the limbs with unassimilated humors

that there's no match between the face and belly,

55   had made him part his lips like a consumptive,

who will, because of thirst, let one lip drop

down to his chin and lift the other up.[5]

"O you exempt from every punishment

in this grim world, and I do not know why,"

60   he said to us, "look now and pay attention

to this, the misery of Master Adam:

alive, I had enough of all I wanted;

alas, I now long for one drop of water.[6]

The rivulets that fall into the Arno

65   down from the green hills of the Casentino

with channels cool and moist, are constantly

before me; I am racked by memory—

---

3. The "Aretine" is Griffolino from the previous canto. Gianni Chichi (d. 1280) was a Florentine of the Cavalcanti family well known for his skill at mimicry. In one reported incident, he impersonated Buoso Donati at the request of Simone Donati, in order to dictate a new will in Simone's favor that included Buoso's mule, the best in Tuscany.

4. Myrrha conceived a passion for her father Cinyras, king of Cyprus. With the aid of her nurse, she entered her father's bedchamber in disguise and slept with him.

5. Dropsy, or edema, is an abnormal accumulation of watery fluid ("humors") in the body. A "consumptive" here is someone suffering from hectic fever, a wasting disease characterized by hot, dry skin and flushed cheeks.

6. Master Adam counterfeited the gold florin of Florence. Like the florin, his coins bore the seal of John the Baptist, but they were of 21 rather than 24 carats. In 1281 he suffered the penalty of counterfeiters: burned at the stake.

the image of their flow parches me more
than the disease that robs my face of flesh.

70   The rigid Justice that would torment me
uses, as most appropriate, the place
where I had sinned, to draw swift sighs from me.

There is Romena, there I counterfeited
the currency that bears the Baptist's seal;
75   for this I left my body, burned, above.

But could I see the miserable souls
of Guido, Alessandro, or their brother,
I'd not give up the sight for Fonte Branda.[7]

And one of them is in this moat already,
80   if what the angry shades report is true.
What use is that to me whose limbs are tied?

Were I so light that, in a hundred years,
I could advance an inch, I should already
be well upon the road to search for him

85   among the mutilated ones, although
this circuit measures some eleven miles
and is at least a half a mile across.

Because of them I'm in this family;
it was those three who had incited me
90   to coin the florins with three carats' dross."

And I to him: "Who are those two poor sinners
who give off smoke like wet hands in the winter
and lie so close to you upon the right?"

"I found them here," he answered, "when I rained
95   down to this rocky slope; they've not stirred since
and will not move, I think, eternally.

One is the lying woman who blamed Joseph;
the other, lying Sinon, Greek from Troy:[8]
because of raging fever they reek so."

100   And one of them, who seemed to take offense,
perhaps at being named so squalidly,
struck with his fist at Adam's rigid belly.

It sounded as if it had been a drum;
and Master Adam struck him in the face,
105   using his arm, which did not seem less hard,

saying to him: "Although I cannot move
my limbs because they are too heavy, I
still have an arm that's free to serve that need."

And he replied: "But when you went to burning,
110   your arm was not as quick as it was now;

7. Adam names three of the Conti Guidi family, who instigated his counterfeiting, including Guido II da Romena, who
died before 1300. The Fonte Branda is perhaps a now almost dry fountain near the castle of Romena.

8. After Joseph rejected the advances of Potiphar's wife, she accused him of attempting to seduce her (Genesis 39.6–20).
Sinon was a treacherous Greek who allowed himself to be captured by the Trojans, persuading them to take within their
walls the wooden horse the Greeks had left (and hidden inside) (*Aeneid* 2.18–370).

though when you coined, it was as quick and more."

     To which the dropsied one: "Here you speak true;
but you were not so true a witness there,
when you were asked to tell the truth at Troy."

115   "If I spoke false, you falsified the coin,"
said Sinon; "I am here for just one crime—
but you've committed more than any demon."

     "Do not forget the horse, you perjurer,"
replied the one who had the bloated belly,
120 "may you be plagued because the whole world knows it."

     The Greek: "And you be plagued by thirst that cracks
your tongue, and putrid water that has made
your belly such a hedge before your eyes."

     And then the coiner: "So, as usual,
125 your mouth, because of racking fever, gapes;
for if I thirst and if my humor bloats me,

     you have both dryness and a head that aches;
few words would be sufficient invitation
to have you lick the mirror of Narcissus."⁹

130   I was intent on listening to them
when this was what my master said: "If you
insist on looking more, I'll quarrel with you!"

     And when I heard him speak so angrily,
I turned around to him with shame so great
135 that it still stirs within my memory.

     Even as one who dreams that he is harmed
and, dreaming, wishes he were dreaming, thus
desiring that which is, as if it were not,

     so I became within my speechlessness:
140 I wanted to excuse myself and did
excuse myself, although I knew it not.

     "Less shame would wash away a greater fault
than was your fault," my master said to me;
"therefore release yourself from all remorse

145   and see that I am always at your side,
should it so happen—once again—that fortune
brings you where men would quarrel in this fashion:

     to want to hear such bickering is base."

Canto 31

Passage to the Ninth Circle. The central pit or well of Hell, where Cocytus, the last river of Hell, freezes. The Giants: Nimrod, Ephialtes, Briareus, Antaeus. Antaeus's compliance with Virgil's request to lower the two poets into the pit.

---

9. When the nymph Echo's love for the youth Narcissus was unrequited, she pined away until all that was left was her voice. In punishment, he was made to fall in love with his own reflection in a fountain, pining away as well, until he was transformed into a flower (*Metamorphoses* 3.351–510). To "lick" his mirror thus means to drink.

The very tongue that first had wounded me,
sending the color up in both my cheeks,
was then to cure me with its medicine—

as did Achilles' and his father's lance,
even as I have heard, when it dispensed
a sad stroke first and then a healing one.[1]

We turned our backs upon that dismal valley
by climbing up the bank that girdles it;
we made our way across without a word.

Here it was less than night and less than day,
so that my sight could only move ahead
slightly, but then I heard a bugle blast

so strong, it would have made a thunder clap
seem faint; at this, my eyes—which doubled back
upon their path—turned fully toward one place.

Not even Roland's horn, which followed on
the sad defeat when Charlemagne had lost
his holy army, was as dread as this.[2]

I'd only turned my head there briefly when
I seemed to make out many high towers; then
I asked him: "Master, tell me, what's this city?"

And he to me: "It is because you try
to penetrate from far into these shadows
that you have formed such faulty images.

When you have reached that place, you shall see clearly
how much the distance has deceived your sense;
and, therefore, let this spur you on your way."

Then lovingly he took me by the hand
and said: "Before we have moved farther on,
so that the fact may seem less strange to you,

I'd have you know they are not towers, but giants,
and from the navel downward, all of them
are in the central pit, at the embankment."

Just as, whenever mists begin to thin,
when, gradually, vision finds the form
that in the vapor-thickened air was hidden,

so I pierced through the dense and darkened fog;
as I drew always nearer to the shore,
my error fled from me, my terror grew;

for as, on its round wall, Montereggioni°   *a hill fortress*
is crowned with towers, so there towered here,
above the bank that runs around the pit,

---

1. Achilles's father Peleus gave him a spear that by its mere touch could cure any wound it had caused (*Metamorphoses* 13.171–2). Medieval poets often used the image to describe the lady's love, which could be healed only by opening a new wound in her lover.

2. A first image of the ninth circle's sin of treachery. In the medieval epic, *The Song of Roland,* after the hero Roland, leader of Charlemagne's rear-guard, has had his forces betrayed to and annihilated by the Saracens at Roncesvalles, he sounds his famous horn so loudly that the emperor returns to avenge his death.

with half their bulk, the terrifying giants,
whom Jove still menaces from Heaven when
45   he sends his bolts of thunder down upon them.

And I could now make out the face of one,
his shoulders and his chest, much of his belly,
and both his arms that hung along his sides.

Surely when she gave up the art of making
50   such creatures, Nature acted well indeed,
depriving Mars of instruments like these.[3]

And if she still produces elephants
and whales, whoever sees with subtlety
holds her—for this—to be more just and prudent;

55   for where the mind's acutest reasoning
is joined to evil will and evil power,
there human beings can't defend themselves.[4]

His face appeared to me as broad and long
as Rome can claim for its St. Peter's pine cone;[5]
60   his other bones shared in that same proportion;

so that the bank, which served him as an apron
down from his middle, showed so much of him
above, that three Frieslanders would in vain

have boasted of their reaching to his hair;
65   for downward from the place where one would buckle
a mantle, I saw thirty spans of him.[6]

"Raphèl maì amècche zabì almi,"
began to bellow that brute mouth, for which
no sweeter psalms would be appropriate.[7]

70   And my guide turned to him: "O stupid soul,
keep to your horn and use that as an outlet
when rage or other passion touches you![8]

Look at your neck, and you will find the strap
that holds it fast; and see, bewildered spirit,
75   how it lies straight across your massive chest."

And then to me: "He is his own accuser;
for this is Nimrod, through whose wicked thought
one single language cannot serve the world.

Leave him alone—let's not waste time in talk;
80   for every language is to him the same
as his to others—no one knows his tongue."

So, turning to the left, we journeyed on

---

3. Dante equates the Giants of Greek myth with those of the Bible, "expert in war" (Baruch 3.26–28).

4. According to Aquinas, "An evil man can do ten thousand times more harm than a beast by his reason which he can use to devise very diverse evils."

5. This bronze pine cone, over twelve feet high, was said to have stood near the Campus Martius in Rome; it was moved to the old basilica of St. Peter's.

6. The inhabitants of Friesland on the North Sea were known for their great height; the giant's top half is about thirty-five feet.

7. The giant is Nimrod, biblical ruler of Babylon, under whose direction the Tower of Babel was attempted (Genesis 10–11). His incomprehensible words, which no commentator has deciphered, are an apt retribution for his role in causing the confusion of the world's tongues.

8. The hunter's horn derives from the biblical description of Nimrod as a "mighty hunter before the Lord" (Genesis 10.9).

and, at the distance of a bow-shot, found
another giant, far more huge and fierce.

85　　　Who was the master who had tied him so,
I cannot say, but his left arm was bent
behind him and his right was bent in front,

　　　both pinioned by a chain that held him tight
down from the neck; and round the part of him
90　that was exposed, it had been wound five times.

　　　"This giant in his arrogance had tested
his force against the force of highest Jove,"
my guide said, "so he merits this reward.

　　　His name is Ephialtes;[9] and he showed
95　tremendous power when the giants frightened
the gods; the arms he moved now move no more."

　　　And I to him: "If it is possible,
I'd like my eyes to have experience
of the enormous one, Briareus."

100　　At which he answered: "You shall see Antaeus[1]
nearby. He is unfettered and can speak;
he'll take us to the bottom of all evil.

　　　The one you wish to see lies far beyond
and is bound up and just as huge as this one,
105　and even more ferocious in his gaze."

　　　No earthquake ever was so violent
when called to shake a tower so robust,
as Ephialtes quick to shake himself.

　　　Then I was more afraid of death than ever;
110　that fear would have been quite enough to kill me,
had I not seen how he was held by chains.

　　　And we continued on until we reached
Antaeus, who, not reckoning his head,
stood out above the rock wall full five ells.° 　　*fifteen feet*

115　　"O you, who lived within the famous valley
(where Scipio became the heir of glory
when Hannibal retreated with his men),[2]

　　　who took a thousand lions as your prey—
and had you been together with your brothers
120　in their high war, it seems some still believe

　　　the sons of earth would have become the victors—
do set us down below, where cold shuts in
Cocytus,[3] and do not disdain that task.

9. Son of Neptune; with his brother Otus, he stormed Olympus itself. Virgil placed them both in Tartarus (*Aeneid* 6.771–74).

1. The hundred-handed and fifty-headed giant Briareus joined the attack of his race against the gods; Jupiter slew him with a thunderbolt and buried him under Mt. Etna. Unlike the enchained giants here, Antaeus was born after the war against the gods. Son of Neptune and Earth, he was invincible while in contact with his mother. He lived in Libya and was said to feed on wild lions. Hercules slew him when he managed to lift Antaeus off the ground and crush him (*Pharsalia* 4.585–660).

2. The valley of the Bagradas River in north-central Tunisia was site of Scipio's decisive victory over Hannibal's forces in 202 B.C.E. during the Second Punic War between Rome and Carthage.

3. The frozen lake that covers the ninth circle at the bottom of Hell.

Don't send us on to Tityus or Typhon;[4]
125 this man can give you what is longed for here;
therefore bend down and do not curl your lip.

He still can bring you fame within the world,
for he's alive and still expects long life,
unless grace summon him before his time."

130 So said my master; and in haste Antaeus
stretched out his hands, whose massive grip had once
been felt by Hercules, and grasped my guide.

And Virgil, when he felt himself caught up,
called out to me: "Come here, so I can hold you,"
135 then made one bundle of himself and me.

Just as the Garisenda seems when seen
beneath the leaning side, when clouds run past
and it hangs down as if about to crash,[5]

so did Antaeus seem to me as I
140 watched him bend over me—a moment when
I'd have preferred to take some other road.

But gently—on the deep that swallows up
both Lucifer and Judas—he placed us;
nor did he, so bent over, stay there long,

145 but, like a mast above a ship, he rose.

Canto 32

The Ninth Circle, First Ring, called Caïna, where Traitors to their Kin are immersed in the ice, heads bent down. Camiscione dei Pazzi. The Second Ring, called Antenora: the Traitors to their Homeland or Party. Bocca degli Abati's provocation of Dante. Two traitors, one gnawing at the other's head.

Had I the crude and scrannel° rhymes to suit   *harsh*
the melancholy hole upon which all
the other circling crags converge and rest,

the juice of my conception would be pressed
5 more fully; but because I feel their lack,
I bring myself to speak, yet speak in fear;

for it is not a task to take in jest,
to show the base of all the universe—
nor for a tongue that cries out, "mama," "papa."

10 But may those ladies now sustain my verse
who helped Amphion when he walled up Thebes,
so that my tale not differ from the fact.[1]

O rabble, miscreated past all others,
there in the place of which it's hard to speak,

4. Two more giants: Tityus was thrown into Tartarus by Apollo and Diana for his attempted rape of their mother Latona; Typhon, incited by his mother, Earth, to attack the Olympian gods, was defeated by Jupiter.

5. One of the leaning towers of Bologna, Garisenda was built in 1110; a cloud passing opposite the direction of the slant gives the illusion of the tower falling out of the sky.

1. The Muses ("ladies") inspired the singer Amphion to charm the stones of Mt. Cithaeron with his lyre into arranging themselves as walls around Thebes (Horace, *Ars Poetica* 394–96; *Thebaid* 10.873–77). The invocation of the Muses marks a new beginning of the poem, and a mixed style of language and diction.

15   better if here you had been goats or sheep!
        When we were down below in the dark well,
        beneath the giant's feet and lower yet,
        with my eyes still upon the steep embankment,
        I heard this said to me: "Watch how you pass;
20   walk so that you not trample with your soles
        the heads of your exhausted, wretched brothers."
        At this I turned and saw in front of me,
        beneath my feet, a lake that, frozen fast,
        had lost the look of water and seemed glass.
25   The Danube where it flows in Austria,
        the Don beneath its frozen sky,° have never   *in Russia*
        made for their course so thick a veil in winter
        as there was here; for had Mount Tambernic
        or Pietrapana's mountain° crashed upon it,   *Italian alps*
30   not even at the edge would it have creaked.
        And as the croaking frog sits with its muzzle
        above the water, in the season when
        the peasant woman often dreams of gleaning,
        so, livid in the ice, up to the place
35   where shame can show itself, were those sad shades,
        whose teeth were chattering with notes like storks'.
        Each kept his face bent downward steadily;
        their mouths bore witness to the cold they felt,
        just as their eyes proclaimed their sorry hearts.
40   When I had looked around a while, my eyes
        turned toward my feet and saw two locked so close,
        the hair upon their heads had intermingled.
        "Do tell me, you whose chests are pressed so tight,"
        I said, "who are you?" They bent back their necks,
45   and when they'd lifted up their faces toward me,
        their eyes, which wept upon the ground before,
        shed tears down on their lips until the cold
        held fast the tears and locked their lids still more.
        No clamp has ever fastened plank to plank
50   so tightly; and because of this, they butted
        each other like two rams, such was their fury.
        And one from whom the cold had taken both
        his ears, who kept his face bent low, then said:
        "Why do you keep on staring so at us?
55   If you would like to know who these two are:
        that valley where Bisenzio descends,
        belonged to them and to their father Alberto.²
        They came out of one body; and you can
        search all Caïna,³ you will never find

---

2. The Conti Alberti had two castles in this region west of Florence. The Guelf Alessandro and the Ghibelline Napoleone were sons of Alberto degli Alberti; they killed each other quarreling over the inheritance of the Castle of Mangano.

3. Caïna, the first of the four subdivisions of Cocytus, is named after Cain, the first man to betray and kill a kinsman, his brother Abel (Genesis 4).

60 a shade more fit to sit within this ice—
  not him who, at one blow, had chest and shadow
shattered by Arthur's hand;[4] and not Focaccia;
and not this sinner here who so impedes
  my vision with his head, I can't see past him;
65 his name was Sassol Mascheroni; if
you're Tuscan, now you know who he has been.[5]
  And lest you keep me talking any longer,
know that I was Camiscion de' Pazzi;
I'm waiting for Carlino to absolve me."[6]

70 And after that I saw a thousand faces
made doglike by the cold; for which I shudder—
and always will—when I face frozen fords.[7]

  And while we were advancing toward the center
to which all weight is drawn—I, shivering
75 in that eternally cold shadow—I

  know not if it was will or destiny
or chance, but as I walked among the heads,
I struck my foot hard in the face of one.

  Weeping, he chided then: "Why trample me?
80 If you've not come to add to the revenge
of Montaperti, why do you molest me?"[8]

  And I: "My master, now wait here for me,
that I may clear up just one doubt about him;
then you can make me hurry as you will."

85 My guide stood fast, and I went on to ask
of him who still was cursing bitterly:
"Who are you that rebukes another so?"

  "And who are you who go through Antenora,
striking the cheeks of others," he replied,
90 "too roughly—even if you were alive?"

  "I am alive, and can be precious to you
if you want fame," was my reply, "for I
can set your name among my other notes."

  And he to me: "I want the contrary;
95 so go away and do not harass me—
your flattery is useless in this valley."

  At that I grabbed him by the scruff and said:
"You'll have to name yourself to me or else
you won't have even one hair left up here."

85

---

4. Modred, the traitorous nephew of King Arthur, slew his uncle; when Arthur pierced Mordred with a spear in return, a ray of sunlight passed through the wound.

5. Foccaccia was the nickname of the White Guelf Vanni de' Cancellieri of Pistoia, guilty of murdering a cousin in 1293. Sassol Mascheroni was a Florentine who murdered a kinsman for the sake of his inheritance.

6. The Ghibelline Camiscion de' Pazzi of the Val d'Arno treacherously killed his kinsman Ubertino. In 1302, his kinsman Carlino would betray the Florentine Whites and Ghibellines in the Castle of Piantravigne to the Blacks. As a traitor against his party, Carlino will "absolve" Camiscion by going to the next, worse ring of Cocytus, where those who betrayed party, country, or city are punished.

7. A subtle transition to the second ring, where the souls hold their heads erect rather than being able to shelter their eyes from the cold. The ring is named Antenora after the Trojan warrior Antenor, who was believed to have betrayed his city to the Greeks.

8. Bocca degli Abati, a Florentine Guelf who betrayed his party at the battle of Montaperti in 1260 when he cut off the hand of the Florentine standard-bearer at the crucial moment of the charge of Manfred's German cavalry.

100   And he to me: "Though you should strip me bald,
I shall not tell you who I am or show it,
not if you pound my head a thousand times."

His hairs were wound around my hand already,
and I had plucked from him more than one tuft
105   while he was barking and his eyes stared down,
      when someone else cried out: "What is it, Bocca?
Isn't the music of your jaws enough
for you without your bark? What devil's at you?"

    "And now," I said, "you traitor bent on evil,
110   I do not need your talk, for I shall carry
true news of you, and that will bring you shame."

    "Be off," he answered; "tell them what you like,
but don't be silent, if you make it back,
about the one whose tongue was now so quick.

115   Here he laments the silver of the Frenchmen;
'I saw,' you then can say, 'him of Duera,
down there, where all the sinners are kept cool.'[9]

    And if you're asked who else was there in ice,
one of the Beccheria is beside you—
120   he had his gullet sliced right through by Florence.

    Gianni de' Soldanieri, I believe,
lies there with Ganelon and Tebaldello,
he who unlocked Faenza while it slept."[1]

    We had already taken leave of him,
125   when I saw two shades frozen in one hole,
so that one's head served as the other's cap;

    and just as he who's hungry chews his bread,
one sinner dug his teeth into the other
right at the place where brain is joined to nape:

130   no differently had Tydeus gnawed the temples
of Menalippus, out of indignation,[2]
than this one chewed the skull and other parts.

    "O you who show, with such a bestial sign,
your hatred for the one on whom you feed,
135   tell me the cause," I said; "we can agree

    that if your quarrel with him is justified,
then knowing who you are and what's his sin,
I shall repay you yet on earth above,
    if that with which I speak does not dry up."

---

9. In 1265, the Ghibelline leader of Cremona, Buoso da Duera, betrayed Manfred, King of Naples, when he was bribed to allow the French troops to pass through Lombardy unmolested.

1. Tesauro de' Beccheria of Pavia, Abbot of Vallombrosa, was seized and beheaded in 1258 by the Florentine Guelfs on the charge of intriguing with the Ghibellines. Gianni de' Soldanieri was a Florentine Ghibelline who opposed his own party when the populace rose up against it following the defeat and death of Manfred at Benevento in 1266. Tebaldello opened the gates of his city to Guelf enemies in order to avenge a private grudge. As recorded in *The Song of Roland*, Ganelon betrayed the rearguard of Charlemagne at Roncesvalles; his name became synonymous with treachery.

2. King Tydeus was one of the Seven against Thebes. When mortally wounded by Menalippus, whom he slayed in return, the enraged Tydeus gnawed through his enemy's skull and ate part of his brain (*Thebaid* 8.739–62).

Canto 33

Still the Ninth Circle, Second Ring. Ugolino's tale of his and his sons' death in a Pisan prison. Dante's invective against Pisa. The Third Ring, Ptolomea, where Traitors against their Guests jut out from ice, their eyes sealed by frozen tears. Fra Alberigo and Branca Doria, still alive on earth but already in Hell.

That sinner raised his mouth from his fierce meal,
then used the head that he had ripped apart
in back: he wiped his lips upon its hair.

Then he began: "You want me to renew
5   despairing pain that presses at my heart
even as I think back, before I speak.

But if my words are seed from which the fruit
is infamy for this betrayer whom
I gnaw, you'll see me speak and weep at once.[1]

10   I don't know who you are or in what way
you've come down here; and yet you surely seem—
from what I hear—to be a Florentine.

You are to know I was Count Ugolino,
and this one here, Archbishop Ruggieri;
15   and now I'll tell you why I am his neighbor.[2]

There is no need to tell you that, because
of his malicious tricks, I first was taken
and then was killed—since I had trusted him;

however, that which you cannot have heard—
20   that is, the cruel death devised for me—
you now shall hear and know if he has wronged me.

A narrow window in the Eagles' Tower,
which now, through me, is called the Hunger Tower,
a cage in which still others will be locked,[3]

25   had, through its opening, already showed me
several moons, when I dreamed that bad dream
which rent the curtain of the future for me.[4]

This man appeared to me as lord and master;
he hunted down the wolf and its young whelps
30   upon the mountain that prevents the Pisans

---

1. Several phrases in this speech of Ugolino recall those of Francesca in Canto 5.

2. Count Ugolino della Gherardesca was banished from the traditionally Ghibelline city of Pisa for conspiring with the Guelf leader Giovanni Visconti in 1275, but returned to wealth and position the following year. Following a defeat by Genoa (which he was suspected of abetting) Ugolino was made magistrate of Pisa in 1284. He ceded three castles to Florence and Lucca to assuage the Guelf threat, which his enemies regarded as a betrayal. The following year, Ugolino feuded with his Guelf grandson, Nino Visconti, son of Giovanni, with whom he was sharing the magistracy. The Ghibelline Ruggieri degli Ubaldini was archbishop of Pisa, and magistrate in place of Ugolino in 1288. Ugolino apparently intrigued with Ruggiero against Nino but was betrayed by the archbishop and his Ghibelline allies, who invited the count back into the city only to lock him up with two of his sons (Gaddo and Uguiccone) and two grandsons (Anselm and a different Nino, nicknamed "Brigata") in the Tower of Gualandi, where they eventually were starved to death. Pisa was now controlled by the Ghibellines, with Guido da Montefeltro (see Canto 27) soon to be made their magistrate.

3. The Tower of Gualandi served as a prison until 1318. According to early commentators, moulting eagles were kept in its Mew, or tower, which became known after Ugolino's death as the Torre della Fame ("Tower of Hunger").

4. In the dream, Ruggieri ("lord and master") hunts down Ugolino and his children on Mt. San Giuliano, between Pisa and Lucca (where the count had political connections). The dogs likely represent the populace roused against Ugolino by Ruggieri; the Gualandi, Sismondi and Lanfranchi were prominent Ghibelline families of Pisa who joined the archbishop.

from seeing Lucca; and with lean and keen
and practiced hounds, he'd sent up front, before him,
Gualandi and Sismondi and Lanfranchi.

35 But after a brief course, it seemed to me
that both the father and the sons were weary;
I seemed to see their flanks torn by sharp fangs.

When I awoke at daybreak, I could hear
my sons, who were together with me there,
weeping within their sleep, asking for bread.

40 You would be cruel indeed if, thinking what
my heart foresaw, you don't already grieve;
and if you don't weep now, when would you weep?

They were awake by now; the hour drew near
at which our food was usually brought,
45 and each, because of what he'd dreamed, was anxious;

below, I heard them nailing up the door
of that appalling tower; without a word,
I looked into the faces of my sons.

I did not weep; within, I turned to stone.
50 They wept; and my poor little Anselm said:
'Father, you look so... What is wrong with you?'

At that I shed no tears and—all day long
and through the night that followed—did not answer
until another sun had touched the world.

55 As soon as a thin ray had made its way
into that sorry prison, and I saw,
reflected in four faces, my own gaze,

out of my grief, I bit at both my hands;
and they, who thought I'd done that out of hunger,
60 immediately rose and told me: 'Father,

it would be far less painful for us if
you ate of us; for you clothed us in this
sad flesh—it is for you to strip it off.'

Then I grew calm, to keep them from more sadness;
65 through that day and the next, we all were silent;
O hard earth, why did you not open up?

But after we had reached the fourth day, Gaddo,
throwing himself, outstretched, down at my feet,
implored me: 'Father, why do you not help me?'

70 And there he died; and just as you see me,
I saw the other three fall one by one
between the fifth day and the sixth; at which,

now blind, I started groping over each;
and after they were dead, I called them for
75 two days; then fasting had more force than grief."[5]

When he had spoken this, with eyes awry,

---

5. This line suggests that Ugolino resorted to cannibalism. Given the allusions to Christ on the cross in line 69 (Matthew 27.46), there is probably a religious overtone as well: Ugolino does not provide his children with spiritual any more than

again he gripped the sad skull in his teeth,
which, like a dog's, were strong down to the bone.

80   Ah, Pisa, you the scandal of the peoples
of that fair land where *si* is heard,° because   *Italy*
your neighbors are so slow to punish you,

    may, then, Caprara and Gorgona° move   *Mediterranean islands*
and build a hedge across the Arno's mouth,
so that it may drown every soul in you!

85   For if Count Ugolino was reputed
to have betrayed your fortresses, there was
no need to have his sons endure such torment.

    O Thebes renewed,[6] their years were innocent
and young—Brigata, Uguiccione, and
90 the other two my song has named above!

    We passed beyond, where frozen water wraps—
a rugged covering—still other sinners,
who were not bent, but flat upon their backs.

    Their very weeping there won't let them weep,
95 and grief that finds a barrier in their eyes
turns inward to increase their agony;

    because their first tears freeze into a cluster,
and, like a crystal visor, fill up all
the hollow that is underneath the eyebrow.

100   And though, because of cold, my every sense
had left its dwelling in my face, just as
a callus has no feeling, nonetheless,

    I seemed to feel some wind now, and I said:
"My master, who has set this gust in motion?
105 For isn't every vapor quenched down here?"[7]

    And he to me: "You soon shall be where your
own eye will answer that, when you shall see
the reason why this wind blasts from above."

    And one of those sad sinners in the cold
110 crust, cried to us: "O souls who are so cruel
that this last place has been assigned to you,

    take off the hard veils from my face so that
I can release the suffering that fills
my heart before lament freezes again."

115   To which I answered: "If you'd have me help you,
then tell me who you are; if I don't free you,
may I go to the bottom of the ice."[8]

    He answered then: "I am Fra Alberigo,
the one who tended fruits in a bad garden,
120 and here my figs have been repaid with dates."[9]

---

6. The ancient city of Thebes was notorious for crime and bloodshed.

7. The cause of wind was thought to be the heat of the sun.

8. A deceptive promise, since he is in fact headed to the "bottom of the ice."

9. Like Catalano and Loderingo (23.103–9), Alberigo was a member of the order of the Jovial Friars; like Tebaldello (32.122), he belonged to the Guelf Manfredi family of Faenza. Alberigo had two of his relatives killed at a banquet at his house in supposed reconciliation. The signal to the assassins was his order at the end of dinner to bring the fruit. He

"But then," I said, "are you already dead?"
And he to me: "I have no knowledge of
my body's fate within the world above.

For Ptolomea has this privilege:
125   quite frequently the soul falls here before
it has been thrust away by Atropos.[1]

And that you may with much more willingness
scrape these glazed tears from off my face, know this:
as soon as any soul becomes a traitor,

130   as I was, then a demon takes its body
away—and keeps that body in his power
until its years have run their course completely.

The soul falls headlong, down into this cistern;
and up above, perhaps, there still appears
135   the body of the shade that winters here

behind me; you must know him, if you've just
come down; he is Ser Branca Doria;[2]
for many years he has been thus pent up."

I said to him: "I think that you deceive me,
140   for Branca Doria is not yet dead;
he eats and drinks and sleeps and puts on clothes."

"There in the Malebranche's ditch above,
where sticky pitch boils up, Michele Zanche
had still not come," he said to me, "when this one—

145   together with a kinsman, who had done
the treachery together with him—left
a devil in his stead inside his body.

But now reach out your hand; open my eyes."
And yet I did not open them for him;
150   and it was courtesy to show him rudeness.

Ah, Genoese, a people strange to every
constraint of custom, full of all corruption,
why have you not been driven from the world?

For with the foulest spirit of Romagna,
I found one of you such that, for his acts,[3]
in soul he bathes already in Cocytus
    and up above appears alive, in body.

Canto 34

The Ninth Circle, Fourth Ring, called Judecca, where Traitors against their Bene-
factors are fully covered by ice. Dis, or Lucifer, emperor of that kingdom, his three

1. Ptolomea, where betrayers of guests and friends are punished, may be named for the Egyptian king Ptolemy XII (51–47 B.C.E.), murderer of Pompey (*Pharsalia* 8.536–712), or for a governor of Jericho who murdered his father-in-law, the high priest Simon the Maccabee, and two of his sons at a banquet in their honor in 134 B.C.E. (1 Maccabees 16.11–17). Ptolomea is apparently unique among the parts of Hell in that souls can be condemned to it before they are actually dead. (Atropos was the one of the three Fates responsible for cutting the thread of an individual's life.) The idea is perhaps the most extreme of the many heterodoxies included by Dante in his conception of the afterlife.
2. A Ghibelline of a famous Genoese family who murdered his father-in-law Michel Zanche at a banquet with the aid of another relation.
3. The "foulest spirit of Romagna" is Alberigo; the "Genoese" is Branca Doria.

mouths rending Judas, Brutus, and Cassius. Descent of Virgil and Dante down Lucifer's body to the other, southern hemisphere. Their vision of the stars.

"Vexilla regis prodeunt inferni[1]
toward us; and therefore keep your eyes ahead,"
my master said, "to see if you can spy him."
   Just as, when night falls on our hemisphere
5   or when a heavy fog is blowing thick,
a windmill seems to wheel when seen far off,
   so then I seemed to see that sort of structure.
And next, because the wind was strong, I shrank
behind my guide; there was no other shelter.
10   And now—with fear I set it down in meter—
I was where all the shades were fully covered
but visible as wisps of straw in glass.
   There some lie flat and others stand erect,
one on his head, and one upon his soles;
15   and some bend face to feet, just like a bow.
   But after we had made our way ahead,
my master felt he now should have me see
that creature who was once a handsome presence;[2]
   he stepped aside and made me stop, and said:
20   "Look! Here is Dis, and this the place where you
will have to arm yourself with fortitude."
   O reader, do not ask of me how I
grew faint and frozen then—I cannot write it:
all words would fall far short of what it was.
25   I did not die, and I was not alive;
think for yourself, if you have any wit,
what I became, deprived of life and death.
   The emperor of the despondent kingdom
so towered from the ice, up from midchest,
30   that I match better with a giant's breadth
   than giants match the measure of his arms;
now you can gauge the size of all of him
if it is in proportion to such parts.
   If he was once as handsome as he now
35   is ugly and, despite that, raised his brows
against his Maker, one can understand how
   every sorrow has its source in him!
I marveled when I saw that, on his head,
he had three faces: one—in front—bloodred;
40   and then another two that, just above
the midpoint of each shoulder, joined the first;
and at the crown, all three were reattached;
   the right looked somewhat yellow, somewhat white;

86.

1. "The banners of the king of Hell draw closer": modified from a Holy Week hymn, with Hell in place of Heaven, as Lucifer is the negative mirror image of Christ.

2. Lucifer, the "light-bearing" seraph, or angel, was most beautiful of them all before he fell, becoming Satan. Dante identifies him with Dis, the Roman god of the underworld.

the left in its appearance was like those°   *black Ethiopians*
45   who come from where the Nile, descending, flows.

       Beneath each face of his, two wings spread out,
as broad as suited so immense a bird:
I've never seen a ship with sails so wide.

       They had no feathers, but were fashioned like
50   a bat's; and he was agitating them,
so that three winds made their way out from him—
    and all Cocytus froze before those winds.
He wept out of six eyes; and down three chins,
tears gushed together with a bloody froth.[3]

55   Within each mouth—he used it like a grinder—
with gnashing teeth he tore to bits a sinner,
so that he brought much pain to three at once.

       The forward sinner found that biting nothing
when matched against the clawing, for at times
60   his back was stripped completely of its hide.

       "That soul up there who has to suffer most,"
my master said: "Judas Iscariot—
his head inside, he jerks his legs without.

       Of those two others, with their heads beneath,
65   the one who hangs from that black snout is Brutus—
see how he writhes and does not say a word!

       That other, who seems so robust, is Cassius[4]
But night is come again, and it is time
for us to leave; we have seen everything."[5]

70   Just as he asked, I clasped him round the neck;
and he watched for the chance of time and place,
and when the wings were open wide enough,

       he took fast hold upon the shaggy flanks
and then descended, down from tuft to tuft,
75   between the tangled hair and icy crusts.

       When we had reached the point at which the thigh
revolves, just at the swelling of the hip,
my guide, with heavy strain and rugged work,

       reversed his head to where his legs had been
80   and grappled on the hair, as one who climbs—
I thought that we were going back to Hell.

       "Hold tight," my master said—he panted like
a man exhausted— "it is by such stairs

---

3. The *contrapasso* of Dis reproduces his rebellion: he is depicted as a false, three-faced Trinity, winged like an angel (the seraph also had six wings), and lord of the realm, but a lord as hideous as he once was beautiful, whose only power is the mechanical beating of wings that freezes Cocytus and confines him in the ice of his own making, and the grinding of teeth that punishes the three traitors in his jaws.

4. The three arch-traitors are Judas Iscariot, who sold Christ (after whom this region of Judecca is named; he is gnawed head-first), and two conspirators against Julius Caesar, Marcus Junius Brutus and Gaius Cassius Longus (gnawed feet-first) both of whom killed themselves after their defeat at Philippi in 42 B.C.E., two years following Caesar's murder.

5. It is now 6 P.M. on Holy Saturday, 24 hours after the pair entered the Gate of Hell on Good Friday. The anticlimactic nature of Satan and the bottom of Hell shows evil as an empty negation or perversion of good desires and intentions rather than a powerful and independent force of its own.

that we must take our leave of so much evil."[6]

85   Then he slipped through a crevice in a rock
and placed me on the edge of it, to sit;
that done, he climbed toward me with steady steps.

      I raised my eyes, believing I should see
the half of Lucifer that I had left;

90   instead I saw him with his legs turned up;
and if I then became perplexed, do let
the ignorant be judges—those who can
not understand what point I had just crossed.

      "Get up," my master said, "be on your feet:

95   the way is long, the path is difficult;
the sun's already back to middle tierce."[7]

      It was no palace hall, the place in which
we found ourselves, but with its rough-hewn floor
and scanty light, a dungeon built by nature.

100   "Before I free myself from this abyss,
master," I said when I had stood up straight,
"tell me enough to see I don't mistake:

      Where is the ice? And how is he so placed
head downward? Tell me, too, how has the sun

105   in so few hours gone from night to morning?"

      And he to me: "You still believe you are
north of the center, where I grasped the hair
of the damned worm who pierces through the world.

      And you were there as long as I descended;

110   but when I turned, that's when you passed the point
to which, from every part, all weights are drawn.

      And now you stand beneath the hemisphere
opposing that which cloaks the great dry lands
and underneath whose zenith died the Man

115   whose birth and life were sinless in this world.[8]
Your feet are placed upon a little sphere
that forms the other face of the Judecca.

      Here it is morning when it's evening there;
and he whose hair has served us as a ladder

120   is still fixed, even as he was before.

      This was the side on which he fell from Heaven;
for fear of him, the land that once loomed here
made of the sea a veil and rose into

      our hemisphere; and that land which appears

125   upon this side—perhaps to flee from him—

6. Just as Hell can only be avoided by comprehending every last part of it, so the only way out of it is through its very heart, the body of Satan. Because the waist of his body is placed at the very center of the earth (and of the universe in Ptolemy's conception), the climb takes the pair from the northern into the southern hemisphere (held to be all water), causing the inversion of direction that so confuses the pilgrim.

7. The reference to the sun—all such references within Hell were given with respect to the moon and stars—tells us that in the southern hemisphere it is now 7:30 A.M. The climb through the southern half of the earth will take 21 or 22 hours, about the same amount of time as the descent through Hell.

8. Jerusalem was regarded as the center of the northern hemisphere of land; it was often represented on maps with the image of Christ hanging on the cross.

left here this hollow space and hurried upward."[9]

  There is a place below, the limit of
that cave, its farthest point from Beelzebub,°   *Satan*
a place one cannot see: it is discovered
130 by ear—there is a sounding stream that flows
along the hollow of a rock eroded
by winding waters, and the slope is easy.
  My guide and I came on that hidden road
to make our way back into the bright world;
135 and with no care for any rest, we climbed—
  he first, I following—until I saw,
through a round opening, some of those things
of beauty Heaven bears. It was from there
  that we emerged, to see—once more—the stars.

GEOFFREY CHAUCER ■ (c. 1340–1400)

Like so much else in the world of fourteenth-century England, Chaucer's family name was derived from the French: a maker of *chausses,* shoes or hose. His family had nothing to do with footwear, but Chaucer made his name as a poet with a translation from the French of *Le Roman de la rose,* and he established himself as a valuable servant to three successive English kings partly due to linguistic skills that enabled him to conduct royal business during journeys to France, Spain, and Italy. But what made Chaucer the first great authority of English literature was the way he transformed Continental themes, words, and literary genres into something indelibly and recognizably English. As Dante in his *Commedia* quite consciously created the first epic poem in vernacular Italian rather than Latin, so Chaucer set out in *The Canterbury Tales* to forge a work of poetry for an entire people, in a language—the London dialect that would become modern English—potentially accessible to all citizens, from the highest to the lowest.

  Chaucer's ancestors were prosperous vintners and property owners in Ipswich who by the late thirteenth century had moved seventy miles south to settle in London. Chaucer's father served in the household of King Edward III; Geoffrey began his career in 1357 similarly situated, working for the wife of Edward's son, Prince Henry. About ten years later, he made an advantageous marriage to the daughter of a knight of Hainault, and was soon made an *esquier* (esquire), or retainer in the royal household. He traveled frequently around England and abroad in the king's service, not only to nearby France, but to Florence in 1373, where he may have met Boccaccio (page 936), and Petrarch (page 962), and certainly learned of their poetry as well as of Dante's. Chaucer was evidently a skilled courtier; he survived countless power struggles, continued receiving posts and assignments after the accession of Richard II in 1377, and had his annuities confirmed when Henry IV supplanted Richard in 1399.

---

9. In Dante's invention, Lucifer's fall from Heaven provides a geological as well as a theological origin of Hell and Purgatory: when he fell into the southern hemisphere, directly opposite Jerusalem, the land that once filled it fled from him northward. Once he became fixed in the center of the earth, the land around him fled southward, raising the Mountain of Purgatory and hollowing out the cone of Hell.

Unlike the public lives of many medieval writers, Chaucer's lifetime of service was extremely well-documented, but of the nearly 500 items that mention his name only a few allude to his personal affairs and none at all to his poetry. Conversely, Chaucer's poetry rarely mentions the great events of his day, from the Black Death of his childhood to the grand dynastic struggles that must have deeply affected his life. His earlier writings show him immersed in the medieval occupations of translation and popularization. The translation of the foremost authority of medieval romance, *The Romance of the Rose*, was begun before 1372 and that of Boethius's *The Consolation of Philosophy* in the 1380s. *The Book of the Duchess*, which mimics the French genre of the *dits amoureux*, was written to commemorate the death of Blanche, Duchess of Lancaster, in 1369. Like *The Book of the Duchess, The House of Fame* (1378–1380) and *The Parliament of Fowls* (1380–1382) were first-person dream visions dealing with issues of fame, poetry, and love. Here, Chaucer developed a self-deprecating persona that nonetheless voices an ambition to equal Dante, the French romances, and the classical poets, as in this deflation of the grand opening of Virgil's *Aeneid*, "I wol now synge, yif I kan, / The armes and also the man." Up to the middle of the eighteenth century, the most frequently cited of Chaucer's works was a long verse romance, *Troilus and Cressida* (1382–1386), based on a romance by Boccaccio set during the Trojan War, and often considered the first psychological novel due to the depth of its depiction of character.

To write in English was not the obvious choice for a prodigiously learned and ambitious fourteenth-century *esquier,* although its use had increased as the century went on, culminating in Henry V's declared preference for it as the language of literature at his court. French had long been the language of statecraft and civil record-keeping, and of literature in many circles, especially the court. Latin was the language of ecclesiastical and theological discourse, including philosophy, and still an important literary language, especially in Italy. The London dialect adapted by Chaucer would have been primarily a practical language, with limited capacities for meter, rhyme, and vocabulary in comparison to Chaucer's French, Italian, and Latin sources. His genius was to expand the capacities of English without losing its flavor of reality as an everyday language. As with Dante, Chaucer's choice of a local vernacular incorporated the thematic contrast between decorum and plainness, spirit and matter, into the very language of the verse.

This effect is strongest in *The Canterbury Tales,* parts of which date from as early as the 1370s, but most of which was written in the late 1380s and early 1390s. Chaucer presents the stories told by a diverse collection of twenty-nine pilgrims (more or less) as they make their way from London to the shrine of Saint Thomas à Becket in Canterbury. The pilgrimage was an essential feature of medieval life, whether a brief journey within Kent or a more extended voyage to Santiago de Compostela in Spain or to the Holy Land—and the Wife of Bath has done them all. Undertaken to seek miraculous aid, to visit a famous biblical site, to renounce the world, or to expiate a sin, pilgrimage could also be imposed as penance on criminals, used as a front by charlatans, or undertaken by clergy who had fallen out with parish authorities. The pilgrimage brought together all the estates of society, although rarely involving the extreme social variety of Chaucer's pilgrims, from the devout knight, prioress, and merchant to a range of fairly secular-minded characters to the scurvy Miller and Reeve. Chaucer's pilgrimage is a literary conceit, but a conceit based on a wide and familiar practice.

Chaucer devotes far less time to the motivations behind the characters' decision to take a pilgrimage than he does to the interactions between them and to the many different stories he can tell through their varied persons. In the "General Prologue," he gives a thumbnail sketch of every character except his own stand-in, a self-effacing poet who tells two failed stories; these sketches are noteworthy for their memorable and idiosyncratic detail and for their stylistic range. The procession of characters is based on the estates satire, a comic catalogue of the different estates, or classes of society. Each character represents a type, defined primarily by his or her profession; however, each type is engraved in our memory through tellingly individual touches. We are told of the Miller, for example, that he possesses the strength needed to exercise his profession, but the demonstration of this strength takes a comically unlikely form: he breaks down doors with his head ("Ther was no dore that he nolde heve of harre, / Or breke it rennyng with his head").

In a similar fashion, each tale reflects the milieu of its teller and evokes a literary genre he or she would be familiar with—the Knight tells of chivalry, the Monk of the perils of trusting to Fortune, the Miller and the Reeve bawdy tales (*fabliaux*) about artisans. Yet each tale is constructed with consummate artistry to match the condition of each teller, a feat beyond the capacity of most if not all of Chaucer's characters. In "The Miller's Tale," for example, Chaucer invests the *fabliau* with a doubled and converging seduction plot and a thematic backdrop of mystery plays and courtly love conventions, remaining faithful to the parody and scatological humor of the genre while expanding its scope and heightening its comedy.

The proliferation of narrators and narrative styles often makes it difficult to know how we are meant to evaluate a particular character. Alisoun, the garrulous Wife of Bath, for instance, sums up and embodies centuries of the misogynist clichés and biblical commonplaces of the clerkly tradition and the *querelle des femmes* ("quarrel about women") but she does so with such energy and she travesties her sources with such gusto that the reader is more likely to side with her than against her. In the Prologue to her tale, she recounts the story of her life and five husbands—a prologue that overshadows and doubles the length of her Tale proper, the collection's only version of an Arthurian romance. Even here, digression and anachronism take pride of place over fidelity to her source. The knight's quest for the answer to the question "What thing is it that wommen moost desiren" extends her Prologue's debate over the battle of the sexes, marriage, and desire into the fantasy world of legend: a paradoxically fitting genre for one of Chaucer's most down-to-earth characters.

Unlike Dante, Chaucer left his *magnum opus* unfinished, in ten more or less ordered groupings. There is no numerical perfection, as in the even hundred cantos of the *Commedia* or the ten tellers, ten days and hundred stories of Boccaccio's *Decameron* (see page 936). Still, the interaction among characters, the sequencing of certain tales, and the repeated themes and motifs create a complex network of comparison. Although he was no stranger to the structures of symmetry so dear to much of medieval poetry, Chaucer prefers here to develop his tales through interruption and disorder, as in the Miller's drunken insistence on telling his tale out of order so that he can "quite," or pay back, the Reeve's insult. Rather than ordering spiritual and secular, courtly and *fabliau,* proper and obscene, Chaucer imagines the multifaceted teeming medieval world all thrown together, with characters looking the other way or staring each other down, reveling in the bickering and bantering in enforced coexistence encapsulated by the pilgrimage setting.

from The Canterbury Tales[1]
The General Prologue

When April with his showers sweet with fruit
The drought of March has pierced unto the root
And bathed each vein with liquor that has power
To generate therein and sire the flower;
5   When Zephyr° also has, with his sweet breath,   *the West Wind*
Quickened again, in every holt° and heath,   *woods*
The tender shoots and buds, and the young sun
Into the Ram one half his course has run,[2]

1. Translated by J. U. Nicolson.
2. The Ram is the zodiacal sign Aries, which lasts from mid-March to mid-April.

And many little birds make melody
10 That sleep through all the night with open eye
(So Nature[3] pricks them on to ramp and rage)—
Then do folk long to go on pilgrimage,
And palmers to go seeking out strange strands,
To distant shrines well known in sundry lands.[4]
15 And specially from every shire's° end   county's
Of England they to Canterbury wend,°   make their way
The holy blessed martyr there to seek
Who helped them when they lay so ill and weak.[5]
        Befell that, in that season, on a day
20 In Southwark, at the Tabard,[6] as I lay
Ready to start upon my pilgrimage
To Canterbury, full of devout homage,
There came at nightfall to that hostelry
Some nine and twenty in a company
25 Of sundry persons who had chanced to fall
In fellowship, and pilgrims were they all
That toward Canterbury town would ride.
The rooms and stables spacious were and wide,
And well we there were eased, and of the best.
30 And briefly, when the sun had gone to rest,
So had I spoken with them, every one,
That I was of their fellowship anon,°   soon
And made agreement that we'd early rise
To take the road, as you I will apprise.
35   But none the less, whilst I have time and space,
Before yet farther in this tale I pace,
It seems to me accordant with reason
To inform you of the state of every one
Of all of these, as it appeared to me,
40 And who they were, and what was their degree,
And even how arrayed° there at the inn;   dressed
And with a knight thus will I first begin.

        A knight there was, and he a worthy man,
Who, from the moment that he first began
45 To ride about the world, loved chivalry,
Truth, honour, freedom and courtesy.
Full worthy was he in his liege-lord's° war,   his feudal lord's
And therein had he ridden (none more far)
As well in Christendom as heathenesse,°   pagan lands
50 And honoured everywhere for worthiness.

3. Nature as a creative force was frequently personified as a goddess in the Middle Ages.

4. Pilgrims returning from the Holy Land would carry a palm frond as sign of their achievement; a palmer also designated an itinerant monk.

5. The cathedral town of Canterbury, the ecclesiastical center of England, is about 35 miles southeast of London. It contained the shrine of Archbishop Thomas à Becket, who was murdered by Henry II in 1170 and canonized by the pope three years later. For many centuries it was a primary pilgrimage destination in England.

6. The Canterbury road began in the rather disreputable borough of Southwark, just across London Bridge from London. There was in fact an inn called the Tabard in Southwark at the time.

At Alexandria, he, when it was won;[7]
Full oft the table's roster he'd begun
Above all nations' knights in Prussia.[8]
In Latvia raided he, and Russia,
55   No christened man so oft of his degree.
In far Granada at the siege was he
Of Algeciras,[9] and in Belmarie.°   *Morocco*
At Ayas was he and at Satalye°   *in Turkey*
When they were won; and on the Middle Sea°   *Mediterranean*
60   At many a noble meeting chanced to be.
Of mortal battles he had fought fifteen,
And he'd fought for our faith at Tramissene°   *in Algeria*
Three times in lists, and each time slain his foe.[1]
This self-same worthy knight had been also
65   At one time with the lord of Palatye°   *in Turkey*
Against another heathen in Turkey;
And always won he sovereign fame for prize.
Though so illustrious, he was very wise
And bore himself as meekly as a maid.
70   He never yet had any vileness said,
In all his life, to whatsoever wight.°   *person*
He was a truly perfect, gentle knight.
But now, to tell you all of his array,
His steeds were good, but yet he was not gay.°   *richly dressed*
75   Of simple fustian° wore he a jupon°   *coarse cloth / tunic*
Sadly discoloured by his habergeon;°   *breast plate*
For he had lately come from his voyage
And now was going on this pilgrimage.

      With him there was his son, a youthful squire,
80   A lover and a lusty bachelor,[2]
With locks well curled, as if they'd laid in press.
Some twenty years of age he was, I guess.
In stature he was of an average length,
Wondrously active, aye, and great of strength.
85   He'd ridden sometime with the cavalry
In Flanders, in Artois, and Picardy,[3]
And borne him well within that little space
In hope to win thereby his lady's grace.
Prinked out° he was, as if he were a mead,°   *dressed up / meadow*

---

7. The Egyptian city of Alexandria was conquered by Peter I of Cyprus in 1365 and left behind after a week of slaughter and plundering.

8. The Baltic region of Prussia was a stronghold of the Teutonic Knights, a religious order formed in the 12th century for the purpose of crusading. The Knight has been granted the place of honor among them.

9. A port city in the Andalusian kingdom of Granada near Gibraltar. It was conquered by the Christian forces of the Castilian ruler Alphonso IX in 1344.

1. One-on-one battles between opposing champions were common features of medieval warfare.

2. Squires were bachelors, or knights of the lowest orders, and would often serve as attendants or followers of bannerets, more senior knights who had the right to lead under their own banner.

3. Artois and Picardy are regions of northern France near Belgium, parts of which were controlled by the Counts of Flanders. The reference is probably to the disastrous "crusade" led by the bishop of Norwich against Flanders.

90 All full of fresh-cut flowers white and red.
    Singing he was, or fluting, all the day;
    He was as fresh as is the month of May.
    Short was his gown,° with sleeves both long and wide.   *outer robe*
    Well could he sit on horse, and fairly ride.
95 He could make songs and words thereto indite,°   *compose*
    Joust, and dance too, as well as sketch and write.
    So hot he loved that, while night told her tale,
    He slept no more than does a nightingale.
    Courteous he, and humble, willing and able,
100 And carved before his father at the table.[4]

        A yeoman had he, nor more servants, no,
    At that time, for he chose to travel so;[5]
    And he was clad in coat and hood of green.
    A sheaf of peacock arrows bright and keen
105 Under his belt he bore right carefully
    (Well could he keep his tackle yeomanly:
    His arrows had no draggled° feathers low),   *trailing*
    And in his hand he bore a mighty bow.
    A cropped head had he and a sun-browned face.
110 Of woodcraft knew he all the useful ways.
    Upon his arm he bore a bracer gay,°   *bright arm guard*
    And at one side a sword and buckler,° yea,   *small shield*
    And at the other side a dagger bright,
    Well sheathed and sharp as spear point in the light;
115 On breast a Christopher of silver sheen.[6]
    He bore a horn in baldric° all of green;   *shoulder strap*
    A forester he truly was, I guess.[7]

        There was also a nun, a prioress,[8]
    Who, in her smiling, modest was and coy;°   *quiet*
120 Her greatest oath was but "By Saint Eloy!"
    And she was known as Madam Eglantine.°   *briar rose*
    Full well she sang the services divine,
    Intoning through her nose, becomingly;
    And fair she spoke her French, and fluently,
125 After the school of Stratford-at-the-Bow,
    For French of Paris was not hers to know.[9]
    At table she had been well taught withal,°   *as well*
    And never from her lips let morsels fall,
    Nor dipped her fingers deep in sauce, but ate

4. One of the squire's customary tasks was to carve the meat for their knights.

5. In addition to his son, the Squire, the Knight is accompanied by a Yeoman, a free servant next in rank below a squire in the feudal order.

6. St. Christopher was the patron saint of travelers; his medallion gave protection on the road.

7. The Yeoman is a gamekeeper, charged with guarding his lord's game from poachers and with conducting the elaborate ceremonies of the hunt.

8. The superior of a religious house or order. The description includes many attributes of the courtly lady of the time, although her own position, and her lack of connection with the court, complicate the portrait.

9. Rather than Parisian French, the Prioress speaks the Anglo-Norman dialect she learned at school in Stratford-at-the-Bow, a village outside London.

130	With so much care the food upon her plate
	That never driblet fell upon her breast.
	In courtesy she had delight and zest.
	Her upper lip was always wiped so clean
	That in her cup was no iota seen
135	Of grease, when she had drunk her draught of wine.
	Becomingly she reached for meat to dine.
	And certainly delighting in good sport,° *diversions*
	She was right pleasant, amiable—in short.
	She was at pains to counterfeit the look
140	Of courtliness,° and stately manners took, *court manners*
	And would be held worthy of reverence.
	But, to say something of her moral sense,
	She was so charitable and piteous
	That she would weep if she but saw a mouse
145	Caught in a trap, though it were dead or bled.
	She had some little dogs, too, that she fed
	On roasted flesh, or milk and fine white bread.
	But sore she'd weep if one of them were dead,
	Or if men smote it with a rod to smart:
150	For pity ruled her, and her tender heart.
	Right decorous her pleated wimple° was; *nun's headdress*
	Her nose was fine; her eyes were blue as glass;
	Her mouth was small and therewith soft and red;
	But certainly she had a fair forehead;
155	It was almost a full span° broad, I own, *up to nine inches*
	For, truth to tell, she was not undergrown.
	Neat was her cloak, as I was well aware.
	Of coral small about her arm she'd bear
	A string of beads and gauded all with green;
160	And therefrom hung a brooch of golden sheen
	Whereon there was first written a crowned "A,"
	And under, *Amor vincit omnia*.[1]
	Another little nun with her had she,
	Who was her chaplain; and of priests she'd three.[2]
165	A monk there was, one made for mastery,° *very handsome*
	An outrider, who loved his venery;° *hunting*
	A manly man, to be an abbot able.[3]
	Full many a blooded° horse had he in stable: *of good breed*
	And when he rode men might his bridle hear
170	A-jingling in the whistling wind as clear,
	Aye, and as loud as does the chapel bell

---

1. "Love conquers all," a phrase from Virgil's tenth Eclogue. Nuns were generally forbidden to wear brooches.

2. A chaplain was a clergyman or nun who conducted services in a private chapel. Like the Knight's Squire, the Nun serves as attendant and secretary to her superior, the Prioress; like the Yeoman, the Priests (or Priest—there is some dispute over whether Chaucer in the end intended one or three) serve as subordinate attendants.

3. An outrider was a monk whose duties led him outside the confines of his abbey, something that would certainly aid this monk in indulging worldly tastes such as hunting. An abbot is the head of a community of monks.

Where this brave monk was master of the cell.[4]
The rule of Maurus or Saint Benedict,
By reason it was old and somewhat strict,[5]
175 This said monk let such old things slowly pace
And followed new-world manners in their place.
He cared not for that text a clean-plucked hen°   *at all*
Which holds that hunters are not holy men;
Nor that a monk, when he is cloisterless,
180 Is like unto a fish that's waterless;
That is to say, a monk out of his cloister.
But this same text he held not worth an oyster;
And I said his opinion was right good.
What? Should he study as a madman would
185 Upon a book in cloister cell? Or yet
Go labour with his hands and swink° and sweat,   *toil*
As Austin bids? How shall the world be served?[6]
Let Austin have his toil to him reserved.
Therefore he was a rider day and night;
190 Greyhounds he had, as swift as bird in flight.
Since riding and the hunting of the hare
Were all his love, for no cost would he spare.
I saw his sleeves were purfled° at the hand   *fringed*
With fur of grey, the finest in the land;
195 Also, to fasten hood beneath his chin,
He had of good wrought gold a curious pin:
A love-knot in the larger end there was.
His head was bald and shone like any glass,
And smooth as one anointed was his face.
200 Fat was this lord, he stood in goodly case.
His bulging eyes he rolled about, and hot
They gleamed and red, like fire beneath a pot;
His boots were soft; his horse of great estate.
Now certainly he was a fine prelate:°   *church dignitary*
205 He was not pale as some poor wasted ghost.
A fat swan loved he best of any roast.
His palfrey° was as brown as is a berry.   *saddle-horse*

    A friar there was, a wanton and a merry,
A limiter, a very festive man.[7]
210 In all the Orders Four is none that can
Equal his gossip and his fair language.

---

4. A small monastery or nunnery, usually dependent on a larger one.

5. The ascetic Rule of St. Benedict, brought to France by his disciple, St. Maurus.

6. St. Augustine ("Austin") was reputed author of an early monastic rule and a staunch believer in the need to withdraw one's desires from the things of this world. The ironic question asks who would do the work of the secular world, especially its heavy clerical duties, if not the clergy.

7. A friar was a member of one of the four begging orders instituted in the 13th century. Because they were supposed to own nothing of their own, they were legally permitted to beg within certain limits (hence the word "limiter"). As with the Monk before him, the portrait of the Friar partakes in a tradition of satirical depictions of the clergy.

He had arranged full many a marriage
Of women young, and this at his own cost.
Unto his order he was a noble post.°   *pillar*

215   Well liked by all and intimate was he
With franklins everywhere in his country,[8]
And with the worthy women of the town:
For at confessing he'd more power in gown
(As he himself said) than a good curate,

220   For of his order he was licentiate.°   *licensed confessor*
He heard confession gently, it was said,
Gently absolved too, leaving naught of dread.
He was an easy man to give penance
When knowing he should gain a good pittance;

225   For to a begging friar, money given
Is sign that any man has been well shriven.°   *confessed*
For if one gave (he dared to boast of this),
He took the man's repentance not amiss,
For many a man there is so hard of heart

230   He cannot weep however pains may smart.
Therefore, instead of weeping and of prayer,
Men should give silver to poor friars all bare.
His tippet° was stuck always full of knives   *scarf*
And pins, to give to young and pleasing wives.

235   And certainly he kept a merry note:
Well could he sing and play upon the rote.°   *fiddle*
At balladry he bore the prize away.
His throat was white as lily of the May;
Yet strong he was as ever champion.

240   In towns he knew the taverns, every one,
And every good host and each barmaid too—
Better than begging lepers, these he knew.
For unto no such solid man as he
Accorded it, as far as he could see,

245   To have sick lepers for acquaintances.
There is no honest advantageousness
In dealing with such poverty-stricken curs;
It's with the rich and with big victuallers.°   *food sellers*
And so, wherever profit might arise,

250   Courteous he was and humble in men's eyes.
There was no other man so virtuous.
He was the finest beggar of his house;
A certain district being farmed to him,
None of his brethren dared approach its rim;

255   For though a widow had no shoes to show,
So pleasant was his *In principio*,[9]
He always got a farthing ere he went.

---

8. A franklin was a landowner of free but not noble birth, and of ranking just below the gentry.
9. "In the beginning," the first words of Genesis and of the Gospel According to John in Latin.

He lived by pickings, it is evident.
And he could romp as well as any whelp.°   *pup*

260 On love days[1] could he be of mickle° help.   *great*
For there he was not like a cloisterer,°   *monk*
With threadbare cope° as is the poor scholar,   *cloak*
But he was like a lord or like a pope.
Of double worsted° was his semi-cope,°   *wool / short cloak*

265 That rounded like a bell, as you may guess.
He lisped a little, out of wantonness,
To make his English soft upon his tongue;
And in his harping, after he had sung,
His two eyes twinkled in his head as bright

270 As do the stars within the frosty night.
This worthy limiter was named Hubert.

    There was a merchant with forked beard, and girt
In motley° gown, and high on horse he sat,   *multicolored*
Upon his head a Flemish beaver hat;

275 His boots were fastened rather elegantly.[2]
His spoke his notions out right pompously,
Stressing the times when he had won, not lost.
He would the sea were held at any cost
Across from Middleburgh to Orwell town.[3]

280 At money-changing he could make a crown.
This worthy man kept all his wits well set;
There was no one could say he was in debt,
So well he governed all his trade affairs
With bargains and with borrowings and with shares.

285 Indeed, he was a worthy man withal,
But, sooth° to say, his name I can't recall.   *truth*

    A clerk from Oxford was with us also,
Who'd turned to getting knowledge, long ago.[4]
As meagre was his horse as is a rake,

290 Nor he himself too fat, I'll undertake,
But he looked hollow and went soberly.
Right threadbare was his overcoat; for he
Had got him yet no churchly benefice,°   *employment*
Nor was so worldly as to gain office.[5]

295 For he would rather have at his bed's head
Some twenty books, all bound in black and red,
Of Aristotle and his philosophy

---

1. Days appointed for settling disputes out of court.

2. In keeping with his position ("Merchant" primarily referred to an import-export dealer in such goods as wool, cloth, and furs), the Merchant is dressed very richly.

3. Middleburg was a Dutch port across the Channel from Orwell in England. The Merchant is concerned with piracy en route between the two towns.

4. A clerk was any man ordained to the ministry or the service of the Church; because few except the clergy could read and write, the term was also applied to anyone who could do so, especially one who worked as a scribe, secretary, or keeper of accounts. Education at Oxford or Cambridge was generally intended for those entering the clergy.

5. Employment in secular capacity as a private or government secretary or official.

Than rich robes, fiddle, or gay psaltery.° *harp*
Yet, and for all he was philosopher,
300 He had but little gold within his coffer;[6]
But all that he might borrow from a friend
On books and learning he would swiftly spend,
And then he'd pray right busily for the souls
Of those who gave him wherewithal for schools.
305 Of study took he utmost care and heed.
Not one word spoke he more than was his need;
And that was said in fullest reverence
And short and quick and full of high good sense.
Pregnant of moral virtue was his speech;
310 And gladly would he learn and gladly teach.

    A sergeant of the law,[7] wary and wise,
Who'd often gone to Paul's walk to advise,[8]
There was also, compact° of excellence. *full*
Discreet he was, and of great reverence;
315 At least he seemed so, his words were so wise.
Often he sat as justice in assize,
By patent or commission from the crown;[9]
Because of learning and his high renown,
He took large fees and many robes could own.
320 So great a purchaser° was never known. *land-buyer*
All was fee simple° to him, in effect, *owned outright*
Wherefore his claims could never be suspect.
Nowhere a man so busy of his class,
And yet he seemed much busier than he was.
325 All cases and all judgments could he cite
That from King William's time were apposite.[1]
And he could draw a contract so explicit
Not any man could fault therefrom elicit;
And every statute he'd verbatim quote.
330 He rode but badly° in a medley° coat, *simply / mixed-colored*
Belted in a silken sash, with little bars,
But of his dress no more particulars.

    There was a franklin° in his company; *large landholder*
White was his beard as is the white daisy.
335 Of sanguine° temperament by every sign, *optimistic*
He loved right well his morning sop° in wine. *bread*
Delightful living was the goal he'd won,
For he was Epicurus'° very son, *Greek philosopher*

---

6. Philosophers were commonly assumed also to be adepts in alchemy and other occult matters; the "philosopher's stone" could transmute base metals into gold.

7. Member of a high order of lawyers, equal to knights in prestige.

8. The porch of St. Paul's Cathedral in London, where clients would come to consult with lawyers.

9. Assizes were sessions held in county courts that heard all manner of civil cases; only sergeants of law could preside over them, appointed by the king.

1. This Man of Law supposedly knows all the reports of property transactions dating back to the reign of William the Conqueror (1066–1087).

340 That held opinion that a full delight
Was true felicity, perfect and right.
A householder, and that a great, was he;
Saint Julian[2] he was in his own country.
His bread and ale were always right well done;
A man with better cellars there was none.
345 Baked meat was never wanting in his house,
Of fish and flesh, and that so plenteous
It seemed to snow therein both food and drink
Of every dainty that a man could think.
According to the season of the year
350 He changed his diet and his means of cheer.   *pen*
Full many a fattened partridge did he mew,°
And many a bream and pike in fish-pond too.
Woe to his cook, except° the sauces were   *unless*
Poignant and sharp, and ready all his gear.
355 His table, waiting in his hall alway,
Stood ready covered through the livelong day.
At county sessions was he lord and sire,
And often acted as a knight of shire.°   *member of Parliament*
A dagger and a trinket-bag of silk
360 Hung from his girdle, white as morning milk.
He had been sheriff and been auditor;
And nowhere was a worthier vavasor.[3]

    A haberdasher and a carpenter,
An arras°-maker, dyer, and weaver   *tapestry*
365 Were with us, clothed in similar livery.°   *uniform*
All of one sober, great fraternity.°   *trade guild*
Their gear was new and well adorned it was;
Their weapons were not cheaply trimmed with brass,
But all with silver; chastely° made and well   *purely*
370 Their girdles° and their pouches too, I tell.   *belts*
Each man of them appeared a proper burgess°   *townsman*
To sit in guildhall on a high dais.[4]
And each of them, for wisdom he could span,
Was fitted to have been an alderman;
375 For chattels° they'd enough, and, too, of rent;   *possessions*
To which their goodwives gave a free assent,
Or else for certain they had been to blame.
It's good to hear "Madam" before one's name,
And go to church when all the world may see,
380 Having one's mantle borne right royally.[5]

    A cook they had with them, just for the nonce,°   *occasion*
To boil the chickens with the marrow-bones,

---

2. Patron saint of hospitality.

3. A feudal tenant ranking in nobility below a baron.

4. The guildhall was the meeting-place of a guild, often equivalent to the town hall. On its dais, or high platform, would sit the highest ranking officials.

5. An alderman's wife was given the title "Madam," allowing her to be treated as if she were nobility.

And flavour tartly and with galingale.°   *aromatic spices*
Well could he tell a draught of London ale.
385   And he could roast and seethe° and broil and fry,   *simmer*
And make a good thick soup, and bake a pie.
But very ill it was, it seemed to me,
That on his shin a deadly sore had he;
For sweet blanc-mange,° he made it with the best.   *stew*

390   There was a sailor, living far out west;
For aught I know, he was of Dartmouth town.[6]
He sadly rode a hackney,° in a gown,   *nag*
Of thick rough cloth falling to the knee.
A dagger hanging on a cord had he
395   About his neck, and under arm, and down.
The summer's heat had burned his visage brown;
And certainly he was a good fellow.
Full many a draught of wine he'd drawn, I trow,°   *believe*
Of Bordeaux vintage, while the trader slept.
400   Nice conscience was a thing he never kept.
If that he fought and got the upper hand,
By water he sent them home to every land.
But as for craft, to reckon well his tides,
His currents and the dangerous watersides
405   His harbours, and his moon, his pilotage,
There was none such from Hull to far Carthage.
Hardy, and wise in all things undertaken,
By many a tempest had his beard been shaken.
He knew well all the havens, as they were,
410   From Gottland to the Cape of Finisterre,
And every creek in Brittany and Spain;[7]
His vessel had been christened *Madeleine*.

     With us there was a doctor of physic;
In all this world was none like him to pick
415   For talk of medicine and surgery;
For he was grounded in astronomy.[8]
He often kept a patient from the pall
By horoscopes and magic natural.
Well could he tell the fortune ascendent
420   Within the houses for his sick patient.
He knew the cause of every malady,
Were it of hot or cold, of moist or dry,
And where engendered, and of what humour;[9]
He was a very good practitioner.

---

6. A port town on the English Channel.

7. Ports near and far: Hull in northeastern England, Carthage (formerly) in North Africa, Gottland in Scandinavia, Finisterre in Spain.

8. Stars and planets were held to have an important influence on the body.

9. According to classical and medieval medicine, illness was caused by an imbalance in the four elements that composed the body (air, water, fire, earth), as they were manifested in the four humors or fluids: blood (hot and moist), phlegm (cold and moist), yellow bile (hot and dry), and black bile (cold and dry).

425	The cause being known, down to the deepest root,
	Anon he gave to the sick man his boot.° *remedy*
	Ready he was, with his apothecaries,° *druggists*
	To send him drugs and all electuaries;° *medicines*
	By mutual aid much gold they'd always won—
430	Their friendship was a thing not new begun.
	Well read was he in Esculapius,
	And Deiscorides, and in Rufus,
	Hippocrates, and Hali, and Galen,
	Serapion, Rhazes, and Avicen,
435	Averrhoës, Gilbert, and Constantine,
	Bernard, and Gatisden, and John Damascene.[1]
	In diet he was measured as could be,
	Including naught of superfluity,
	But nourishing and easy. It's no libel
440	To say he read but little in the Bible.
	In blue and scarlet he went clad, withal,
	Lined with a taffeta° and with sendal; *rich silks*
	And yet he was right chary of expense;
	He kept the gold he gained from pestilence.
445	For gold in physic is a fine cordial,
	And therefore loved he gold exceeding all.
	There was a housewife come from Bath, or near,[2]
	Who—sad to say—was deaf in either ear.
	At making cloth she had so great a bent
450	She bettered those of Ypres and even of Ghent.[3]
	In all the parish there was no good wife
	Should offering make before her, on my life;[4]
	And if one did, indeed, so wroth was she
	It put her out of all her charity.
455	Her kerchiefs were of finest weave and ground;° *texture*
	I dare swear that they weighed a full ten pound
	Which, of a Sunday, she wore on her head.
	Her hose were of the choicest scarlet red,
	Close gartered, and her shoes were soft and new.
460	Bold was her face, and fair, and red of hue.
	She'd been respectable throughout her life,
	With five churched husbands bringing joy and strife,
	Not counting other company in youth;
	But thereof there's no need to speak, in truth.
465	Three times she'd journeyed to Jerusalem;
	And many a foreign stream she'd had to stem;
	At Rome she'd been, and she'd been in Boulogne,
	In Spain at Santiago, and at Cologne.° *pilgrimage sites*

88

1. Famous classical and medieval authorities on medicine from around the Mediterranean.
2. Named after its ancient Roman baths, Bath was a city in western England and the center of cloth manufacturing.
3. Trading and manufacturing centers of Flanders, famous for their cloth.
4. Offerings were given to the priest at the church altar in order of rank.

She could tell much of wandering by the way:

470 Gap-toothed was she, it is no lie to say.
Upon an ambler° easily she sat,   *easy-riding horse*
Well wimpled, aye, and over all a hat
As broad as is a buckler or a targe;°   *light shield*
A rug was tucked around her buttocks large,

475 And on her feet a pair of sharpened spurs.
In company well could she laugh her slurs.°   *faults*
The remedies of love she knew, perchance,
For of that art she'd learned the old, old dance.

There was a good man of religion, too,

480 A country parson, poor, I warrant you;
But rich he was in holy thought and work.
He was a learned man also, a clerk,
Who Christ's own gospel truly sought to preach;
Devoutly his parishioners would he teach.

485 Benign he was and wondrous diligent.
Patient in adverse times and well content,
As he was ofttimes proven; always blithe,
He was right loath to curse to get a tithe,[5]
But rather would he give, in case of doubt,

490 Unto those poor parishioners about,
Part of his income, even of his goods.
Enough° with little, coloured° all his moods.   *satisfied / harmonized*
Wide was his parish, houses far asunder,
But never did he fail, for rain or thunder,

495 In sickness, or in sin, or any state,
To visit to the farthest, small and great,
Going afoot, and in his hand a stave.
This fine example to his flock he gave,
That first he wrought° and afterwards he taught;   *worked*

500 Out of the gospel then that text he caught.
And this figure he added thereunto—
That, if gold rust, what shall poor iron do?
For if the priest be foul, in whom we trust,
What wonder if a layman yield to lust?

505 And shame it is, if priest take thought for keep,° *is involved*
A shitty shepherd, shepherding clean sheep.
Well ought a priest example good to give,
By his own cleanness, how his flock should live.
He never let his benefice for hire,

510 Leaving his flock to flounder in the mire,
And ran to London, up to old Saint Paul's
To get himself a chantry there for souls.[6]

---

5. Parishioners paid the Church a tithe, or a tenth part of their income.
6. A parish priest was usually granted his church and its lands for life. Some would rent out their post and get well-paid positions with minimal duties, such as saying masses for the dead in London chantries.

Nor in some brotherhood° did he withhold;° *guild / was he hired*
But dwelt at home and kept so well the fold
515 That never wolf could make his plans miscarry;
He was a shepherd and not mercenary.
And holy though he was, and virtuous,
To sinners he was not impiteous,
Nor haughty in his speech, nor too divine,
520 But in all teaching prudent and benign.
To lead folk into Heaven but by stress
Of good example was his busyness.
But if some sinful one proved obstinate,
Be who it might, of high or low estate,
525 Him he reproved, and sharply, as I know.
There is nowhere a better priest, I trow.
He had no thirst for pomp or reverence,
Nor made himself a special, spiced° conscience, *dainty*
But Christ's own lore, and His apostles' twelve
530 He taught, but first he followed it himselve.

With him there was a plowman, was his brother,
That many a load of dung, and many another
Had scattered, for a good true toiler, he,
Living in peace and perfect charity.
535 He loved God most, and that with his whole heart
At all times, though he played or plied his art,
And next, his neighbour, even as himself.
He'd thresh and dig, with never thought of pelf,° *money*
For Christ's own sake, for every poor wight,° *person*
540 All without pay, if it lay in his might.
He paid his taxes, fully, fairly, well,
Both by his own toil and by stuff he'd sell.
In a tabard° he rode upon a mare. *smock*
There were also a reeve and miller there;
545 A summoner, manciple and pardoner,
And these, beside myself, made all there were.

The miller was a stout churl,° be it known, *country man*
Hardy and big of brawn and big of bone;
Which was well proved, for when he went on lam° *fought*
550 At wrestling, never failed he of the ram.° *prize*
He was a chunky fellow, broad of build;
He'd heave a door from hinges if he willed,
Or break it through, by running, with his head.
His beard, as any sow or fox, was red,
555 And broad it was as if it were a spade.
Upon the coping° of his nose he had *bridge*
A wart, and thereon stood a tuft of hairs,
Red as the bristles in an old sow's ears;
His nostrils they were black and very wide.
560 A sword and buckler bore he by his side.

His mouth was like a furnace door for size.
He was a jester and could poetize,
But mostly all of sin and ribaldries.
He could steal corn and full thrice charge his fees;
565 And yet he had a thumb of gold, begad.
A white coat and blue hood he wore, this lad.
A bagpipe he could blow well, be it known,
And with that same he brought us out of town.

There was a manciple from an inn of court,
570 To whom all buyers might quite well resort
To learn the art of buying food and drink;[7]
For whether he paid cash or not, I think
That he so knew the markets, when to buy,
He never found himself left high and dry.
575 Now is it not of God a full fair grace
That such a vulgar man has wit to pace°   *outdo*
The wisdom of a crowd of learned men?
Of masters had he more than three times ten,
Who were in law expert and curious;
580 Whereof there were a dozen in that house
Fit to be stewards of both rent and land
Of any lord in England who would stand
Upon his own and live in manner good,
In honour, debtless (save his head were wood),
585 Or live as frugally as he might desire;
These men were able to have helped a shire
In any case that ever might befall;
And yet this manciple outguessed them all.

The reeve he was a slender, choleric man,
590 Who shaved his beard as close as razor can.[8]
His hair was cut round even with his ears;
His top was tonsured like a pulpiteer's.°   *preacher's*
Long were his legs, and they were very lean,
And like a staff, with no calf to be seen.
595 Well could he manage granary and bin;
No auditor could ever on him win.
He could foretell, by drought and by the rain,
The yielding of his seed and of his grain.
His lord's sheep and his oxen and his dairy,
600 His swine and horses, all his stores, his poultry,
Were wholly in this steward's managing;
And, by agreement, he'd made reckoning°   *settled accounts*
Since his young lord of age was twenty years;
Yet no man ever found him in arrears.°   *behind in payments*

---

7. A manciple was a servant or officer charged with provisioning a college, an inn of court, or a monastery. The inns of court controlled training in the legal profession.

8. The overseer or steward of an estate. Chaucer's Reeve suffers from an excess of the humor of yellow bile, hot and dry, making him choleric, or quick to anger.

605 There was no agent, hind,° or herd° who'd cheat   *servant / herdsman*
But he knew well his cunning and deceit;
They were afraid of him as of the death.
His cottage was a good one, on a heath;
By green trees shaded with this dwelling-place.
610 Much better than his lord could he purchase.
Right rich he was in his own private right,
Seeing he'd pleased his lord, by day or night,
By giving him, or lending, of his goods,
And so got thanked—but yet got coats and hoods.
615 In youth he'd learned a good trade, and had been
A carpenter, as fine as could be seen.
This steward sat a horse that well could trot,
And was all dapple-grey, and was named Scot.
A long surcoat° of blue did he parade,   *overcoat*
620 And at his side he bore a rusty blade.
Of Norfolk° was this reeve of whom I tell,   *in north England*
From near a town that men call Badeswell.
Bundled he was like friar from chin to croup,°   *rump*
And ever he rode hindmost of our troop.

625   A summoner was with us in that place,[9]
Who had a fiery-red, cherubic face,
For eczema he had; his eyes were narrow
As hot he was, and lecherous, as a sparrow;
With black and scabby brows and scanty beard;
630 He had a face that little children feared.
There was no mercury, sulphur, or litharge,
No borax, ceruse, tartar,[1] could discharge,
Nor ointment that could cleanse enough, or bite,
To free him of his boils and pimples white,
635 Nor of the bosses° resting on his cheeks.   *lumps*
Well loved he garlic, onions, aye and leeks,
And drinking of strong wine as red as blood.
Then would he talk and shout as madman would.
And when a deal of wine he'd poured within,
640 Then would he utter no word save Latin.
Some phrases had he learned, say two or three,
Which he had garnered out of some decree;
No wonder, for he'd heard it all the day;
And all you know right well that even a jay
645 Can call out "Wat" as well as can the pope.
But when, for aught else, into him you'd grope,
'Twas found he'd spent his whole philosophy;
Just "*Questio quid juris*" would he cry.[2]

---

9. A summoner was a petty court officer who summoned for court appearances and kept track of them.
1. These primarily mineral compounds were different remedies recommended by medieval medicine for the treatment of the Summoner's skin disorder.
2. "The question is, what point of law (applies)?"

He was a noble rascal, and a kind;
650   A better comrade 'twould be hard to find.
Why, he would suffer, for a quart of wine,
Some good fellow to have his concubine
A twelve-month, and excuse him to the full
(Between ourselves, though, he could pluck a gull).
655   And if he chanced upon a good fellow,
He would instruct him never to have awe,
In such a case, of the archdeacon's curse,°   excommunication
Except a man's soul lie within his purse;
For in his purse the man should punished be.
660   "The purse is the archdeacon's Hell," said he.
But well I know he lied in what he said,
A curse ought every guilty man to dread
(For curse can kill, as absolution save),
And 'ware° significavit³ to the grave.   beware
665   In his own power had he, and at ease,
The boys and girls of all the diocese,
And knew their secrets, and by counsel led.
A garland° had he set upon his head,   wreath
Large as a tavern's wine-bush on a stake;°   sign
670   A buckler had he made of bread they bake.

     With him there rode a gentle pardoner
Of Rouncival, his friend and his compeer;°   companion
Straight from the court of Rome had journeyed he.⁴
Loudly he sang "Come hither, love, to me,"
675   The summoner joining with a burden° round;   bass line
Was never horn of° half so great a sound.   made with
This pardoner had hair as yellow as wax,
But lank it hung as does a strike of flax;
In wisps hung down such locks as he'd on head,
680   And with them he his shoulders overspread;
But thin they dropped, and stringy, one by one.
But as to hood, for sport of it, he'd none,
Though it was packed in wallet° all the while.   bag
It seemed to him he went in latest style,
685   Dishevelled, save for cap, his head all bare.
As shiny eyes he had as has a hare.
He had a fine veronica sewed to cap.⁵
His wallet lay before him in his lap,
Stuffed full of pardons brought from Rome all hot.
690   A voice he had that bleated like a goat.

---

3. An ecclesiastical writ for the arrest of an excommunicated person.

4. A pardoner was licensed by the Church (and the Pope, at the "court of Rome") to sell indulgences, or papal pardons for sin. This Pardoner is connected to St. Mary Rouncesval in Charing Cross, London.

5. According to legend, St. Veronica had wiped Christ's face with her kerchief on his way to be crucified. The cloth retained an impression of the face, and was kept as a sacred relic in Rome. Reproductions would be carried by pilgrims as tokens of their pilgrimage.

No beard had he, nor ever should he have,
For smooth his face as he'd just had a shave;
I think he was a gelding° or a mare.°   *eunuch / homosexual*
But in his craft, from Berwick unto Ware,°   *in all of England*

695   Was no such pardoner in any place.
For in his bag he had a pillowcase
The which, he said, was Our True Lady's veil:
He said he had a piece of the very sail
That good Saint Peter had, what time he went

700   Upon the sea, till Jesus changed his bent.[6]
He had a latten° cross set full of stones   *brass*
And in a bottle had he some pig's bones.
But with these relics, when he came upon
Some simple parson, then this paragon

705   In that one day more money stood to gain
Than the poor dupe in two months could attain.
And thus, with flattery and suchlike japes,°   *tricks*
He made the parson and the rest his apes.
But yet, to tell the whole truth at the last,

710   He was, in church, a fine ecclesiast.
Well could he read a lesson or a story,
But best of all he sang an offertory;
For well he knew that when that song was sung,
Then might he preach, and all with polished tongue,

715   To win some silver, as he right well could;
Therefore he sang so merrily and so loud.

     Now have I told you briefly, in a clause,°   *short space*
The state, the array, the number, and the cause
Of the assembling of this company

720   In Southwark, at this noble hostelry
Known as the Tabard Inn, hard by the Bell.°   *another tavern*
But now the time is come wherein to tell
How all we bore ourselves that very night
When at the hostelry we did alight.

725   And afterward the story I engage
To tell you of our common pilgrimage.
But first, I pray you, of your courtesy,
You'll not ascribe it to vulgarity
Though I speak plainly of this matter here,

730   Retailing you their words and means of cheer;
Nor though I use their very terms, nor lie.
For this thing do you know as well as I:
When one repeats a tale told by a man,
He must report, as nearly as he can,

735   Every least word, if he remember it,

---

6. The Pardoner's fake relics include Mary's veil and part of the sail used by Peter as a fisherman before he was called by Jesus to be a disciple.

However rude it be, or how unfit;
Or else he may be telling what's untrue,
Embellishing and fictionizing too.
He may not spare, although it were his brother;
740   He must as well say one word as another.
Christ spoke right broadly out, in holy writ,
And, you know well, there's nothing low in it.
And Plato says, to those able to read:
"The word should be the cousin to the deed."[7]
745   Also, I pray that you'll forgive it me
If I have not set folk, in their degree
Here in this tale, by rank as they should stand
My wits are not the best, you'll understand.[8]

      Great cheer our host gave to us, every one,
750   And to the supper set us all anon;
And served us then with victuals of the best.
Strong was the wine and pleasant to each guest.
A seemly man our good host was, withal,
Fit to have been a marshal in some hall;[9]
755   He was a large man, with protruding eyes,
As fine a burgher as in Cheapside lies;[1]
Bold in his speech, and wise, and right well taught,
And as to manhood, lacking there in naught.
Also, he was a very merry man,
760   And after meat, at playing he began,
Speaking of mirth among some other things,
When all of us had paid our reckonings;
And saying thus: "Now masters, verily
You are all welcome here, and heartily:
765   For by my truth, and telling you no lie,
I have not seen, this year, a company
Here in this inn, fitter for sport than now.
Fain° would I make you happy, knew I how.   gladly
And of a game have I this moment thought
770   To give you joy, and it shall cost you naught.
      "You go to Canterbury; may God speed
And the blest martyr soon requite your meed.°   reward you
And well I know, as you go on your way,
You'll tell good tales and shape yourselves to play;
775   For truly there's no mirth nor comfort, none,
Riding the roads as dumb as is a stone;
And therefore will I furnish you a sport,
As I just said, to give you some comfort.

---

7. The saying is taken from Plato's *Timaeus,* but probably cited as a commonplace from a later source. According to the narrator, both Plato and Jesus, in the sayings attributed to him in the Gospels, held a principle of realism: things should be called by their true names, and words should be reported as they were said.

8. Rather than organized according to the social standing ("degree") of their tellers, the tales are given in the order in which they were supposedly told. The pretense of modesty was a standard theme of medieval rhetoric.

9. Master of ceremonies and arrangements at a banquet.

1. A major market area in London.

And if you like it, all, by one assent,

780　And will be ruled by me, of my judgment,
And will so do as I'll proceed to say,
Tomorrow, when you ride upon your way,
Then, by my father's spirit, who is dead,
If you're not gay, I'll give you up my head.

785　Hold up your hands, nor more about it speak."
　　　Our full assenting was not far to seek;
We thought there was no reason to think twice,
And granted him his way without advice,
And bade him tell his verdict just and wise,

790　　　"Masters," quoth he, "here now is my advice;
But take it not, I pray you, in disdain;
This is the point, to put it short and plain,
That each of you, beguiling the long day,
Shall tell two stories as you wend your way

795　To Canterbury town; and each of you
On coming home, shall tell another two,
All of adventures he has known befall.
And he who plays his part the best of all,
That is to say, who tells upon the road

800　Tales of best sense, in most amusing mode,
Shall have a supper at the others' cost
Here in this room and sitting by this post,
When we come back again from Canterbury.
And now, the more to warrant you'll be merry

805　I will myself, and gladly, with you ride
At my own cost, and I will be your guide.
But whosoever shall my rule gainsay°　　　　　　　　　*deny*
Shall pay for all that's bought along the way.
And if you are agreed that it be so,

810　Tell me at once, or if not, tell me no,
And I will act accordingly. No more."
　　　This thing was granted, and our oaths we swore,
With right glad hearts, and prayed of him, also,
That he would take the office, nor forgo

815　The place of governor of all of us,
Judging our tales; and by his wisdom thus
Arrange that supper at a certain price,
We to be ruled, each one, by his advice
In things both great and small; by one assent,

820　We stood committed to his government.
And thereupon, the wine was fetched anon;
We drank, and then to rest went every one,
And that without a longer tarrying.°　　　　　　　　　*delay*
　　　Next morning, when the day began to spring,

825　Up rose our host, and acting as our cock,
He gathered us together in a flock,
And forth we rode, a jog-trot° being the pace,　　　　*slow, steady pace*

Until we reached Saint Thomas' watering-place.[2]
And there our host pulled horse up to a walk,
830 And said: "Now, masters, listen while I talk.
You know what you agreed at set of sun.
If even-song and morning-song are one,[3]
Let's here decide who first shall tell a tale.
And as I hope to drink more wine and ale,
835 Whoso proves rebel to my government
Shall pay for all that by the way is spent.
Come now, draw cuts, before we farther win,
And he that draws the shortest shall begin.
Sir knight," said he, "my master and my lord,
840 You shall draw first as you have pledged your word.
Come near," quoth he, "my lady prioress:
And you sir, clerk, put by your bashfulness,
Nor ponder more; out hands, now, every man!"
          At once to draw a cut each one began,
845 And, to make short the matter, as it was,
Whether by chance or whatsoever cause,
The truth is, that the cut fell to the knight,
At which right happy then was every wight.
Thus that his story first of all he'd tell,
850 According to the compact, it befell,
As you have heard. Why argue to and fro?
And when this good man saw that it was so,
Being a wise man and obedient
To plighted° word, given by free assent,   *pledged*
855 He said: "Since I must then begin the game,
Why, welcome be the cut, and in God's name!
Now let us ride, and hearken what I say."
And at that word we rode forth on our way;
And he began to speak, with right good cheer,
860 His tale anon, as it is written here.

                              ***

The Wife of Bath's Prologue

"Experience, though no authority
Were in this world, were° good enough for me,   *would be*
To speak of woe that is in all marriage;
For, masters, since I was twelve years of age,
5 Thanks be to God Who is for aye° alive,   *ever*
Of husbands at church door have I had five;
For men so many times have wedded me;
And all were worthy men in their degree.°   *rank*
But someone told me not so long ago

2. A brook located a couple of miles from London.

10   That since Our Lord, save once, would never go
To wedding (that at Cana in Galilee),[1]
Thus, by this same example, showed He me
I never should have married more than once.
Lo and behold! What sharp words, for the nonce,
15   Beside a well Lord Jesus, God and man,
Spoke in reproving the Samaritan:
'For thou hast had five husbands,' thus said He,
'And he whom thou hast now to be with thee
Is not thine husband.'[2] Thus He said that day,
20   But what He meant thereby I cannot say;
And I would ask now why that same fifth man
Was not husband to the Samaritan?
How many might she have, then, in marriage?
For I have never heard, in all my age,
25   Clear exposition of this number shown,
Though men may guess and argue up and down.[3]
But well I know and say, and do not lie,
God bade us to increase and multiply;
That worthy text can I well understand.
30   And well I know He said, too, my husband
Should father leave, and mother, and cleave to me;[4]
But no specific number mentioned He,
Whether of bigamy or octogamy;°   *eight marriages*
Why should men speak of it reproachfully?
35   "Lo, there's the wise old king Dan Solomon;
I understand he had more wives than one;[5]
And now would God it were permitted me
To be refreshed one half as oft as he!
Which gift of God he had for all his wives!
40   No man has such that in this world now lives.
God knows, this noble king, it strikes my wit,
The first night he had many a merry fit
With each of them, so much he was alive!
Praise be to God that I have wedded five!
45   Welcome the sixth whenever come he shall.
Forsooth,° I'll not keep chaste for good and all;   *truly*
When my good husband from the world is gone,
Some Christian man shall marry me anon;
Of whom I did pick out and choose the best
50   Both for their nether° purse and for their chest.   *lower*
Different schools make divers perfect clerks,
Different methods learned in sundry works

1. Site of Jesus's first miracle (John 2.1–10). This was a standard passage for arguments in favor of monogamy, dating back to St. Jerome, from whose treatise *Adversus Jovinianum* (393) the bulk of the scriptural argument that follows was drawn.

2. John 4.5–30.

3. The Wife of Bath avoids the plain sense of the passage by claiming it must have some obscure mystical meaning.

4. Following standard practice in biblical interpretation, she counters one biblical precept with several others that seem to give the opposite instructions: God's instruction to Adam and Eve to "increase and multiply" (Genesis 1.28) and Jesus's words in Matthew 19.5–6 (in fact arguing against divorce), citing Adam and Eve.

5. King Solomon had a thousand wives and concubines (1 Kings 11.3).

	Make the good workman perfect, certainly.	
	Of full five husbands tutoring am I.	
55	For then, the apostle° says that I am free	Paul
	To wed, in God's name, where it pleases me.	
	He says that to be wedded is no sin;	
	Better to marry than to burn within.[6]	
	What care I though folk speak reproachfully	
60	Of wicked Lamech and his bigamy?	
	I know well Abraham was holy man,	
	And Jacob, too, as far as know I can;	
	And each of them had spouses more than two;	
	And many another holy man also.[7]	
65	Or can you say that you have ever heard	
	That God has ever by His express word	
	Marriage forbidden? Pray you, now, tell me;	
	Or where commanded He virginity?	
	I read as well as you no doubt have read	
70	The apostle when he speaks of maidenhead;	
	He said, commandment of the Lord he'd none.	
	Men may advise a woman to be one,	
	But such advice is not commandment, no;	
	He left the thing to our own judgment so.[8]	
75	For had Lord God commanded maidenhood,	
	He'd have condemned all marriage as not good;	
	And certainly, if there were no seed sown,	
	Virginity—where then should it be grown?[9]	
	Paul dared not to forbid us, at the least,	
80	A thing whereof his Master'd no behest.°	injunction
	The dart° is set up for virginity;	prize
	Catch it who can; who runs best let us see.	
	"But this word is not meant for every wight,	
	But where God wills to give it, of His might.	
85	I know well that the apostle was a maid;°	virgin
	Nevertheless, and though he wrote and said	
	He would that everyone were such as he,	
	All is not counsel to virginity;	
	And so to be a wife he gave me leave	
90	Out of permission; there's no shame should grieve	
	In marrying me, if that my mate should die,	
	Without exception,° too, of bigamy.	objection
	And though 'twere good no woman's flesh to touch,	
	He meant, in his own bed or on his couch;	
95	For peril 'tis fire and tow to assemble;	

---

6. Quoting 1 Corinthians 7.9 and 7.28.

7. Lamech was a descendant of the accursed Cain who was considered to have been the first bigamist (Genesis 4.19–24). By contrast, Abraham and Jacob were biblical patriarchs who also had several wives.

8. According to Paul, "if a virgin marry, she hath not sinned," since there was no commandment against marriage (1 Corinthians 7.25 and 28), but he did advise even those who had wives to remain celibate (7.29).

You know what this example may resemble.[1]
This is the sum: he held virginity
Nearer perfection than marriage for° frailty.   *out of*
And frailty's all, I say, save° he and she   *unless*
100   Would lead their lives throughout in chastity.
    "I grant this well, I have no great envy
Though maidenhood's preferred to bigamy;
Let those who will be clean, body and ghost,°   *soul*
Of my condition I will make no boast.
105   For well you know, a lord in his household,
He has not every vessel all of gold;
Some are of wood and serve well all their days.
God calls folk unto Him in sundry° ways,   *diverse*
And each one has from God a proper gift,
110   Some this, some that, as pleases Him to shift.
    "Virginity is great perfection known,
And continence e'en° with devotion shown.   *equally*
But Christ, Who of perfection is the well,
Bade not each separate man he should go sell
115   All that he had and give it to the poor
And follow Him in such wise going before.[2]
He spoke to those that would live perfectly;
And, masters, by your leave, such am not I.
I will devote the flower of all my age
120   To all the acts and harvests of marriage.
    "Tell me also, to what purpose or end
The genitals were made, that I defend,
And for what benefit was man first wrought?[3]
Trust you right well, they were not made for naught° *nothing*
125   Explain who will and argue up and down
That they were made for passing out, as known,
Of urine, and our two belongings small
Were just to tell a female from a male,
And for no other cause—ah, say you no?
130   Experience knows well it is not so;
And, so the clerics be not with me wroth,°   *angry*
I say now that they have been made for both,
That is to say, for duty and for ease
In getting,° when we do not God displease.   *procreation*
135   Why should men otherwise in their books set
That man shall pay unto his wife his debt?°   *marital duty*
Now wherewith should he ever make payment,
Except he used his blessed instrument?
Then on a creature were devised these things
140   For urination and engenderings.

---

1. 1 Corinthians 7.1: "It is good for a man not to touch a woman"; Alisoun adds a proverb ("example") that fire and tow (flax or hemp) placed too closely together will burn.

2. Matthew 19.21: "If thou wilt be perfect, go and sell what thou hast, and give to the poor, and thou shalt have treasure in heaven: and come and follow me."

3. Here, as most of her other arguments in favor of sexual activity, the Wife of Bath closely echoes Jean de Meun's con-

"But I say not that every one is bound,
Who's fitted out and furnished as I've found,
To go and use it to beget an heir;
Then men would have for chastity no care.
145 Christ was a maid, and yet shaped like a man,
And many a saint, since this old world began,
Yet has lived ever in perfect chastity.
I bear no malice to virginity;
Let such be bread of purest white wheat-seed,
150 And let us wives be called but barley bread;
And yet with barley bread (if Mark you scan)
Jesus Our Lord refreshed full many a man.[4]
In such condition as God places us
I'll persevere, I'm not fastidious.
155 In wifehood I will use my instrument
As freely as my Maker has it sent.
If I be niggardly,° God give me sorrow!   *stingy*
My husband he shall have it, eve and morrow,
When he's pleased to come forth and pay his debt.
160 I'll not delay, a husband I will get
Who shall be both my debtor and my thrall°   *slave*
And have his tribulations therewithal
Upon his flesh, the while I am his wife.
I have the power during all my life
165 Over his own good body, and not he.
For thus the apostle told it unto me;
And bade our husbands that they love us well.[5]
And all this pleases me wherof I tell."
        Up rose the pardoner, and that anon.
170 "Now dame," said he, "by God and by Saint John,
You are a noble preacher in this case!
I was about to wed a wife, alas!
Why should I buy this on° my flesh so dear?   *with*
No, I would rather wed no wife this year."
175   "But wait," said she, "my tale is not begun;
Nay, you shall drink from out another tun°   *barrel*
Before I cease, and savour worse than ale.
And when I shall have told you all my tale
Of tribulation that is in marriage,
180 Whereof I've been an expert all my age,
That is to say, myself have been the whip,
Then may you choose whether you will so sip
Out of that very tun which I shall broach.
Beware of it ere you too near approach;
185 For I shall give examples more than ten.

4. Jesus made enough food to feed five thousand out of five barley loaves and two small fishes. Bread made from barley was considered very low fare.

5. This is not exactly what Paul intended by his metaphors of debt and subordination (1 Corinthians 7.3–5), which advised husband and wife rather to be sparing in their possession of each other.

Whoso will not be warned by other men
By him shall other men corrected be.
The self-same words has written Ptolemy;
Read in his *Almagest* and find it there."[6]

190   "Lady, I pray you, if your will it were,"
Spoke up this pardoner, "as you began,
Tell forth your tale, nor spare° for any man,   refrain
And teach us younger men of your technique."
      "Gladly," said she, "since it may please, not pique.°   offend
195 But yet I pray of all this company
That if I speak from my own phantasy,°   fancy
They will not take amiss the things I say;
For my intention's only but to play.
      "Now, sirs, now will I tell you forth my tale.
200 And as I may drink ever wine and ale,
I will tell truth of husbands that I've had,
For three of them were good and two were bad.
The three were good men and were rich and old.
Not easily could they the promise hold
205 Whereby they had been bound to cherish me.
You know well what I mean by that, pardie!°   indeed
So help me God, I laugh now when I think
How pitifully by night I made them swink;°   toil
And by my faith I set by it no store.°   pay it no heed
210 They'd given me their gold, and treasure more;
I needed not do longer diligence
To win their love, or show them reverence.
They all loved me so well, by God above,
I never did set value on their love!
215 A woman wise will strive continually
To get herself loved, when she's not, you see.
But since I had them wholly in my hand,
And since to me they'd given all their land,
Why should I take heed, then, that I should please,
220 Save it were for my profit or my ease?
I set them so to work, that, by my fay,°   faith
Full many a night they sighed out 'Welaway!'°   woe is me
The bacon was not brought them home, I trow,°   trust
That some men have in Essex at Dunmowe.[7]
225 I governed them so well, by my own law,
That each of them was happy as a daw,°   crow
And fain to bring me fine things from the fair.
And they were right glad when I spoke them fair;°   kindly
For God knows that I nagged them mercilessly.
230   "Now hearken how I bore me properly,

6. The *Almagest*, written around 150 C.E. by the Greek astronomer and mathematician Ptolemy.

7. It was long the custom in this town to award a side of bacon to any married couple who managed not to quarrel for at least a year.

All you wise wives that well can understand.
　　"Thus shall you speak and wrongfully demand;
For half so brazenfacedly can no man
Swear to his lying as a woman can.
235 I say not this to wives who may be wise,
Except when they themselves do misadvise.
A wise wife, if she knows what's for her good,
Will swear the crow is mad, and in this mood
Call up for witness to it her own maid;[8]
240 But hear me now, for this is what I said.[9]
　　"'Sir Dotard,° is it thus you stand today?   *old imbecile*
Why is my neighbour's wife so fine and gay?
She's honoured over all where'er she goes;
I sit at home, I have no decent clo'es.
245 What do you do there at my neighbour's house?
Is she so fair? Are you so amorous?
Why whisper to our maid? *Benedicite!*°   *bless us*
Sir Lecher old, let your seductions be!
And if I have a gossip or a friend,
250 Innocently, you blame me like a fiend
If I but walk, for company, to his house!
You come home here as drunken as a mouse,
And preach there on your bench, a curse on you!
You tell me it's a great misfortune, too,
255 To wed a girl who costs more than she's worth;
And if she's rich and of a higher birth,
You say it's torment to abide her folly
And put up with her pride and melancholy.
And if she be right fair, you utter knave,
260 You say that every lecher will her have;
She may no while in chastity abide
That is assailed by all and on each side.
　　"'You say, some men desire us for our gold,
Some for our shape and some for fairness told;
265 And some, that she can either sing or dance,
And some, for courtesy and dalliance;
Some for her hands and for her arms so small;
Thus all goes to the devil in your tale.
You say men cannot keep a castle wall
270 That's long assailed on all sides, and by all.[1]
　　"'And if that she be foul, you say that she
Hankers for every man that she may see;
For like a spaniel will she leap on him

8. In a common fable, a talking crow informs a husband of his wife's infidelity; her maid backs up her lies.

9. Alisoun's exhaustive response is composed of passages from several well-worn misogynist treatises, including Theophrastus, Jerome, Matheolus, Jean de Meun, and Eustache Deschamps.

1. In *The Romance of the Rose,* from which these and the following lines are adapted, the Rose is imprisoned in a castle which the Lover is determined to take by any means.

	Until she finds a man to be victim;
275	And not a grey goose swims there in the lake
	But finds a gander willing her to take.
	You say, it is a hard thing to enfold
	Her whom no man will in his own arms hold.
	This say you, worthless, when you go to bed;
280	And that no wise man needs thus to be wed,
	No, nor a man that hearkens unto Heaven.
	With furious thunder-claps and fiery levin° *lightning*
	May your thin, withered, wrinkled neck be broke;
	"'You say that dripping eaves, and also smoke,
285	And wives contentious, will make men to flee
	But of their houses; ah, *benedicite!*
	What ails such an old fellow so to chide?
	"'You say that all we wives our vices hide
	Till we are married, then we show them well;
290	That is a scoundrel's proverb, let me tell!
	"'You say that oxen, asses, horses, hounds
	Are tried out variously, and on good grounds;
	Basins and bowls, before men will them buy,
	And spoons and stools and all such goods you try,
295	And so with pots and clothes and all array;
	But of their wives men get no trial, you say,
	Till they are married, base old dotard you!
	And then we show what evil we can do.
	"'You say also that it displeases me
300	Unless you praise and flatter my beauty,
	And save° you gaze always upon my face *unless*
	And call me "lovely lady" every place;
	And save you make a feast upon that day
	When I was born, and give me garments gay;
305	And save due honour to my nurse is paid
	As well as to my faithful chambermaid,
	And to my father's folk and his allies—
	Thus you go on, old barrel full of lies!
	"'And yet of our apprentice, young Jenkin,
310	For his crisp hair, showing like gold so fine,
	Because he squires me walking up and down,
	A false suspicion in your mind is sown;
	I'd give him naught, though you were dead tomorrow.
	"'But tell me this, why do you hide, with sorrow,
315	The keys to your strong box away from me?
	It is my gold as well as yours, pardie.
	Why would you make an idiot of your dame?
	Now by Saint James,² but you shall miss your aim,
	You shall not be, although like mad you scold,
320	Master of both my body and my gold;

89

2. Alisoun has made a pilgrimage to the shrine of St. James at Compostela.

One you'll forgo in spite of both your eyes;
Why need you seek me out or set on spies?
I think you'd like to lock me in your chest!
You should say: "Dear wife, go where you like best,
325   Amuse yourself, I will believe no tales;
You're my wife Alis true, and truth prevails."
We love no man that guards us or gives charge
Of where we go, for we will be at large.

    "'Of all men the most blessed may he be,
330   That wise astrologer, Dan Ptolemy,
Who says this proverb in his Almagest;
"Of all men he's in wisdom the highest
That nothing cares who has the world in hand."
And by this proverb shall you understand:
335   Since you've enough, why do you reck° or care   *worry*
How merrily all other folks may fare?
For certainly, old dotard, by your leave,
You shall have cunt all right enough at eve.
He is too much a niggard who's so tight
340   That from his lantern he'll give none a light.
For he'll have never the less light, by gad;
Since you've enough, you need not be so sad.

    "'You say, also, that if we make us gay
With clothing, all in costliest array,
345   That it's a danger to our chastity;
And you must back the saying up, pardie!
Repeating these words in the apostle's° name: *Paul's*
"In habits meet for chastity, not shame,
Your women shall be garmented," said he,
350   "And not with broidered hair, or jewellery,
Or pearls, or gold, or costly gowns and chic";
After your text and after your rubric°   *heading*
I will not follow more than would a gnat.
You said this, too, that I was like a cat;
355   For if one care to singe a cat's furred skin,
Then would the cat remain the house within;
And if the cat's coat be all sleek and gay,
She will not keep in house a half a day,
But out she'll go, ere° dawn of any day,   *before*
360   To show her skin and caterwaul° and play.   *howl like a cat*
This is to say, if I'm a little gay,
To show my rags I'll gad about all day.

    "'Sir Ancient Fool, what ails you with your spies?
Though you pray Argus, with his hundred eyes,
365   To be my body-guard and do his best,[3]

---

3. Argus was a hundred-eyed watchman in Greek and Roman myth who never closed all of his eyes at once. He was set by the jealous goddess Juno to guard the mortal woman Io and to prevent her husband Jupiter from sleeping with her. He did not succeed.

Faith, he sha'n't hold me, save I am modest;
I could delude him easily—trust me!
　　　"'You said, also, that there are three things—three—
The which things are a trouble on this earth,
370　And that no man may ever endure the fourth:
O dear Sir Rogue, may Christ cut short your life!
Yet do you preach and say a hateful wife
Is to be reckoned one of these mischances.
Are there no other kinds of resemblances
375　That you may liken thus your parables to,
But must a hapless wife be made to do?
　　　"'You liken woman's love to very Hell,
To desert land where waters do not well.
You liken it, also, unto wildfire;
380　The more it burns, the more it has desire
To consume everything that burned may be.
You say that just as worms destroy a tree,
Just so a wife destroys her own husband;
Men know this who are bound in marriage band.'
385　　　"Masters, like this, as you must understand,
Did I my old men charge and censure, and
Claim that they said these things in drunkenness;
And all was false, but yet I took witness
Of Jenkin and of my dear niece also.
390　O Lord, the pain I gave them and the woe,
All guiltless, too, by God's grief exquisite!
For like a stallion could I neigh and bite.
I could complain, though mine was all the guilt,
Or else, full many a time, I'd lost the tilt.°　　　　　　　joust
395　Whoso comes first to mill first gets meal ground;
I whimpered first and so did them confound.
They were right glad to hasten to excuse
Things they had never done, save in my ruse,
　　　"With wenches would I charge him, by this hand,
400　When, for some illness, he could hardly stand.
Yet tickled this the heart of him, for he
Deemed it was love produced such jealousy.
I swore that all my walking out at night
Was but to spy on girls he kept outright;
405　And under cover of that I had much mirth.
For all such wit is given us at birth;
Deceit, weeping, and spinning, does God give
To women, naturally, the while they live.
And thus of one thing I speak boastfully,
410　I got the best of each one, finally,
By trick, or force, or by some kind of thing,
As by continual growls or murmuring;
Especially in bed had they mischance,
There would I chide and give them no pleasance;

415 I would no longer in the bed abide
     If I but felt his arm across my side,
     Till he had paid his ransom unto me;
     Then would I let him do his nicety.
     And therefore to all men this tale I tell,
420 Let gain who may, for everything's to sell.
     With empty hand men may no falcons lure;
     For profit would I all his lust endure,
     And make for him a well-feigned appetite;
     Yet I in bacon never had delight;
425 And that is why I used so much to chide.
     For if the pope were seated there beside
     I'd not have spared them, no, at their own board.°   *table*
     For by my truth, I paid them, word for word.
     So help me the True God Omnipotent,
430 Though I right now should make my testament,
     I owe them not a word that was not quit.°   *repaid*
     I brought it so about, and by my wit,
     That they must give it up, as for the best,
     Or otherwise we'd never have had rest.
435 For though he glared and scowled like lion mad,
     Yet failed he of the end he wished he had.
          "Then would I say: 'Good dearie, see you keep
     In mind how meek is Wilkin, our old sheep;
     Come near, my spouse, come let me kiss your cheek!
440 You should be always patient, aye, and meek,
     And have a sweetly scrupulous tenderness,
     Since you so preach of old Job's patience, yes.
     Suffer always, since you so well can preach;
     And, save you do, be sure that we will teach
445 That it is well to leave a wife in peace.
     One of us two must bow,° to be at ease;   *submit*
     And since a man's more reasonable, they say,
     Than woman is, you must have patience aye,
     What ails you that you grumble thus and groan?
450 Is it because you'd have my cunt alone?
     Why take it all, lo, have it every bit;
     Peter!° Beshrew° you but you're fond of it!   *By St. Peter / curse*
     For if I would go peddle my *belle chose,*°   *beautiful thing*
     I could walk out as fresh as is a rose;
455 But I will keep it for your own sweet tooth.
     You are to blame, by God I tell the truth.'
          "Such were the words I had at my command.
     Now will I tell you of my fourth husband.
          "My fourth husband, he was a reveller,
460 That is to say, he kept a paramour;
     And young and full of passion then was I,
     Stubborn and strong and jolly as a pie.°   *magpie*
     Well could I dance to tune of harp, nor fail

To sing as well as any nightingale

465   When I had drunk a good draught of sweet wine.

Metellius, the foul churl and the swine,

Did with a staff deprive his wife of life

Because she drank wine;[4] had I been his wife

He never should have frightened me from drink;

470   For after wine, of Venus must I think:

For just as surely as cold produces hail,

A liquorish° mouth must have a lickerish° tail.   *greedy / lecherous*

In women wine's no bar of impotence,

This know all lechers by experience.

475   "But Lord Christ! When I do remember me

Upon my youth and on my jollity,

It tickles me about my heart's deep root.

To this day does my heart sing in salute

That I have had my world in my own time

480   But age, alas! that poisons every prime.

Has taken away my beauty and my pith;°   *vigor*

Let go, farewell, the devil go therewith!

The flour is gone, there is no more to tell,

The bran, as best I may, must I now sell;

485   But yet to be right merry I'll try, and

Now will I tell you of my fourth husband.

        "I say that in my heart I'd great despite

When he of any other had delight.

But he was quit, by God and by Saint Joce![5]

490   I made, of the same wood, a staff most gross;°   *paid him back in kind*

Not with my body and in manner foul,

But certainly I showed so gay a soul

That in his own thick grease I made him fry

For anger and for utter jealousy.

495   By God, on earth I was his purgatory,

For which I hope his soul lives now in glory.

For God knows, many a time he sat and sung

When the shoe bitterly his foot had wrung

There was no one, save God and he, that knew

500   How, in so many ways, I'd twist the screw.

He died when I came from Jerusalem,

And lies entombed beneath the great rood-beam,°   *crossbeam*

Although his tomb is not so glorious

As was the sepulchre of Darius,

505   The which Apelles wrought full cleverly;[6]

'Twas waste to bury him expensively.

Let him fare well. God give his soul good rest,

---

90

4. Alisoun refers to an ancient Roman incident of a man who beat his wife to death with a staff for drinking wine.

5. St. Jodocus, or Josse, was a Breton king who abdicated after a pilgrimage to Rome and became a hermit.

6. The Persian ruler Darius III was an opponent of Alexander the Great in the 4th century B.C.E. The story of his tomb comes from a medieval romance about Alexander.

He now is in the grave and in his chest.°   *coffin*

    "And now of my fifth husband will I tell.

510   God grant his soul may never get to Hell

And yet he was to me most brutal, too;

My ribs yet feel as they were black and blue,

And ever shall, until my dying day.

But in our bed he was so fresh and gay,

515   And therewithal he could so well impose,

What time he wanted use of my *belle chose*,

That though he'd beaten me on every bone,

He could re-win my love, and that full soon.

I guess I loved him best of all, for he

520   Gave of his love most sparingly to me.

We women have, if I am not to lie,

In this love matter, a quaint fantasy;

Look out a thing we may not lightly have,

And after that we'll cry all day and crave.

525   Forbid a thing, and that thing covet we;

Press hard upon us, then we turn and flee.

Sparingly offer we our goods, when fair;

Great crowds at market make for dearer ware,

And what's too common brings but little price;

530   All this knows every woman who is wise.

    "My fifth husband, may God his spirit bless!

Whom I took all for love, and not riches,

Had been sometime a student at Oxford,

And had left school and had come home to board

535   With my best gossip,° dwelling in our town,   *friend*

God save her soul! Her name was Alison.

She knew my heart and all my privity°   *secrets*

Better than did our parish priest, s'help me!

To her confided I my secrets all.

540   For had my husband pissed against a wall,

Or done a thing that might have cost his life,

To her and to another worthy wife,

And to my niece whom I loved always well,

I would have told it—every bit I'd tell,

545   And did so, many and many a time, God wot,°   *knows*

Which made his face full often red and hot

For utter shame; he blamed himself that he

Had told me of so deep a privity.

    "So it befell that on a time, in Lent[7]

550   (For oftentimes I to my gossip went,

Since I loved always to be glad and gay

And to walk out, in March, April, and May,

---

7. The springtime period of Lent was supposed to be a time of fasting and penitence leading up to Holy Week and Easter.

From house to house, to hear the latest malice),
Jenkin the clerk, and my gossip Dame Alis,
555 And I myself into the meadows went.
My husband was in London all that Lent;
I had the greater leisure, then, to play,
And to observe, and to be seen, I say,
By pleasant folk; what knew I where my face
560 Was destined to be loved, or in what place?
Therefore I made my visits round about
To vigils and processions of devout,
To preaching too, and shrines of pilgrimage,
To miracle plays, and always to each marriage,
565 And wore my scarlet skirt before all wights.
These worms and all these moths and all these mites,
I say it at my peril, never ate;
And know you why? I wore it early and late.° *all the time*
"Now will I tell you what befell to me.
570 I say that in the meadows walked we three
Till, truly, we had come to such dalliance,
This clerk and I, that, of my vigilance,° *in my foresight*
I spoke to him and told him how that he,
Were I a widow, might well marry me.
575 For certainly I say it not to brag,
But I was never quite without a bag
Full of the needs of marriage that I seek.
I hold a mouse's heart not worth a leek
That has but one hole into which to run,
580 And if it fail of that, then all is done.
"I made him think he had enchanted me;
My mother taught me all that subtlety.
And then I said I'd dreamed of him all night,
He would have slain me as I lay upright,
585 And all my bed was full of very blood;
But yet I hoped that he would do me good,
For blood betokens gold, as I was taught.
And all was false, I dreamed of him just—naught,
Save as I acted on my mother's lore,
590 As well in this thing as in many more.
"But now, let's see, what was I going to say?
Aha, by God, I know! It goes this way.
"When my fourth husband lay upon his bier,
I wept enough and made but sorry cheer,
595 As wives must always, for it's custom's grace,
And with my kerchief covered up my face;
But since I was provided with a mate,
I really wept but little. I may state.
"To church my man was borne upon the morrow
600 By neighbours, who for him made signs of sorrow;
And Jenkin, our good clerk, was one of them.

So help me God, when rang the requiem
After the bier, I thought he had a pair
Of legs and feet so clean-cut and so fair
605 That all my heart I gave to him to hold.
He was, I think, but twenty winters old,
And I was forty, if I tell the truth;
But then I always had a young colt's tooth.°   *youthful tastes*
Gap-toothed I was, and that became me well;
610 I had the print of holy Venus' seal.°   *a birthmark*
So help me God, I was a healthy one,
And fair and rich and young and full of fun;
And truly, as my husbands all told me,
I had the silkiest *quoniam*° that could be.   *you-know-what*
615 For truly, I am all Venusian
In feeling, and my brain is Martian.[8]
Venus gave me my lust, my lickerishness,
And Mars gave me my sturdy hardiness.
Taurus was my ascendant, with Mars therein.[9]
620 Alas, alas, that ever love was sin!
I followed always my own inclination
By vitue of my natal constellation;[1]
Which wrought me so I never could withdraw
My Venus-chamber from a good fellow.
625 Yet have I Mars's mark° upon my face,   *birthmark*
And also in another private place.
For God so truly my salvation be
As I have never loved for policy,
But ever followed my own appetite,
630 Though he were short or tall, or black or white;
I took no heed, so that° he cared for me,   *as long as*
How poor he was nor even of what degree.°   *estate*
    "What should I say now, save, at the month's end,
This jolly, gentle, Jenkin clerk, my friend,
635 Had wedded me full ceremoniously,
And to him gave I all the land and fee°   *goods*
That ever had been given me before;
But later I repented me full sore.
He never suffered me to have my way.
640 By God, he smote me on the ear, one day,
Because I tore out of his book a leaf,°   *folio page*
So that from this my ear is grown quite deaf.
Stubborn I was as is a lioness,
And with my tongue a very jay, I guess,

---

8. Her feelings are dominated by the planet Venus and ruled by love; her brain is dominated by the planet Mars and ruled by conflict.

9. Alisoun was born under Taurus, the second sign of the zodiac, ruled by Venus. Mars was also passing through Taurus at that time; hence the double influence.

1. By contrast, the proper approach for a medieval Christian would be to accept the influence of the stars and use his or her will to overcome their sinful aspects.

645	And walk I would, as I had done before,
	From house to house, though I should not, he swore.
	For which he often times would sit and preach
	And read old Roman tales to me and teach
	How one Sulpicius Gallus left his wife
650	And her forsook for term of all his life
	Because he saw her with bared head, I say,
	Looking out from his door, upon a day.[2]
	"Another Roman told he of by name
	Who, since his wife was at a summer-game
655	Without his knowing, he forsook her eke,[3]
	And then would he within his Bible seek
	That proverb of the old Ecclesiast[4]
	Where he commands so freely and so fast
	That man forbid his wife to gad about;
660	Then would he thus repeat, with never doubt:

'Whoso would build his whole house out of sallows,°   *willow branches*
And spur his blind horse to run over fallows,°   *ploughed land*
And let his wife alone go seeking hallows,°   *shrines*
Is worthy to be hanged upon the gallows.'

665	But all for naught, I didn't care a haw°	*at all*
	For all his proverbs, nor for his old saw,°	*saying*
	Nor yet would I by him corrected be.
	I hate one that my vices tells to me,
	And so do more of us—God knows!—than I.
670	This made him mad with me, and furiously,
	That I'd not yield to him in any case.
	"Now will I tell you truth, by Saint Thomas,
	Of why I tore from out his book a leaf,
	For which he struck me so it made me deaf.
675	"He had a book that gladly, night and day,
	For his amusement he would read alway.
	He called it 'Theophrastus' and 'Valerius,'[5]
	At which book would he laugh, uproarious.
	And, too, there sometime was a clerk at Rome,
680	A cardinal, that men called Saint Jerome,
	Who made a book against Jovinian;
	In which book, too, there was Tertullian,
	Chrysippus, Trotula, and Heloïse
	Who was abbess near Paris' diocese;
685	And too, the *Proverbs* of King Solomon,
	And Ovid's *Art,* and books full many a one,

---

2. The *Memorable Deeds and Sayings* of Valerius Maximus (1st century C.E.) recorded this "harsh" but "logical" choice of the consul Gaius Suspicius Gallus.

3. Valerius Maximus also recorded this anecdote about the consul Publius Sempronius Sophus divorcing his wife.

4. The author of the biblical book, Ecclesiasticus, a collection of maxims.

5. Authors of two famous Latin tracts against marriage.

And all of these were bound in one volume.[6]
And every night and day 'twas his custom,
When he had leisure and took some vacation
690 From all his other worldly occupation,
To read, within this book, of wicked wives.
He knew of them more legends and more lives
Than are of good wives written in the Bible.
For trust me, it's impossible, no libel,
695 That any cleric shall speak well of wives,
Unless it be of saints and holy lives,
But naught for other women will they do.
Who painted first the lion, tell me who?[7]
By God, if women had but written stories,
700 As have these clerks within their oratories,°   *chapels*
They would have written of men more wickedness
Than all the race of Adam could redress.
The children of Mercury and of Venus
Are in their lives antagonistic thus;
705 For Mercury loves wisdom and science,
And Venus loves but pleasure and expense.
Because they different dispositions own,
Each falls when other's in ascendant shown.
And God knows Mercury is desolate
710 In Pisces, wherein Venus rules in state;
And Venus falls when Mercury is raised;
Therefore no woman by a clerk is praised.[8]
A clerk, when he is old and can naught do
Of Venus' labours worth his worn-out shoe,
715 Then sits he down and writes, in his dotage,
That women cannot keep vow of marriage!
    "But now to tell you, as I started to,
Why I was beaten for a book, *pardieu.*°   *by God*
Upon a night Jenkin, who was our sire,
720 Read in his book, as he sat by the fire,
Of Mother Eve who, by her wickedness,
First brought mankind to all his wretchedness,
For which Lord Jesus Christ Himself was slain,
Who, with His heart's blood, saved us thus again.
725 Lo here, expressly of woman, may you find
That woman was the ruin of mankind.

---

6. Jenkins's volume contains key sources in clerkly misogyny, from the church fathers Jerome and Tertullian, the Bible, and the Roman poet Ovid, author of *The Art of Love*. Unusually, his collection includes the writings of two women: Trotula, a medieval physician who wrote several works on gynecology; and Heloïse, who argued against marriage with her lover Abelard, before becoming an abbess.

7. The Wife of Bath refers to a fable first told by Aesop, and more recently by Marie de France, that recounts the response of a lion when confronted with the image of a peasant killing a lion.

8. Another astrological explanation: the planet Mercury was associated with the learning proper to the clerk, Venus with the qualities they attributed to women. In terms of the zodiac, when one is ascendant, as Venus in Pisces, the other is descendant—hence, for Alisoun, the conflict between clerks and women.

     "Then read he out how Samson lost his hairs,
     Sleeping, his leman° cut them with her shears;   *lover*
     And through this treason lost he either eye.[9]

730   "Then read he out, if I am not to lie,
     Of Hercules, and Deianira's desire
     That caused him to go set himself on fire.[1]

      "Nothing escaped him of the pain and woe
     That Socrates had with his spouses two;

735   How Xantippe threw piss upon his head;
     This hapless man sat still, as he were dead;
     He wiped his head, no more durst he complain
     Than 'Ere the thunder ceases comes the rain.'[2]

      "Then of Pasiphaë, the queen of Crete,
740   For cursedness he thought the story sweet;
     Fie! Say no more—it is an awful thing—
     Of her so horrible lust and love-liking.

      "Of Clytemnestra, for her lechery,
     Who caused her husband's death by treachery,
745   He read all this with greatest zest, I vow.

      "He told me, too, just when it was and how
     Amphiaraus at Thebes lost his life;
     My husband had a legend of his wife
     Eriphyle who, for a brooch of gold,
750   In secrecy to hostile Greeks had told
     Whereat her husband had his hiding place,
     For which he found at Thebes but sorry grace.[3]

      "Of Livia and Lucia told he me,
     For both of them their husbands killed, you see,
755   The one for love, the other killed for hate;
     Livia her husband, on an evening late,
     Made drink some poison, for she was his foe.
     Lucia, lecherous, loved her husband so
     That, to the end he'd always of her think,
760   She gave him such a philtre, for love-drink,
     That he was dead or ever it was morrow;
     And husbands thus, by same means, came to sorrow.[4]

      "Then did he tell how one Latumius
     Complained unto his comrade Arrius
765   That in his garden grew a baleful tree
     Whereon, he said, his wives, and they were three,
     Had hanged themselves for wretchedness and woe.

---

9. The story of Delilah's betrayal of Samson to the Philistines, by cutting off the hair that gave him his great strength, was originally told in the biblical book of Judges. Like the other passages cited here, it had become proverbial.

1. In fact, Deianira's role in the death of her husband, the hero Hercules, was accidental.

2. Jerome is the source for this version of the philosopher Socrates and his proverbially shrewish wife.

3. Episodes from Greek legend: Pasiphaë's passion for a bull, the adulterous Clytemnestra's murder of her husband Agamemnon on his return from Troy, and Eriphyle's betrayal of her husband's hiding place, sending him to a death in Thebes he had already foreseen.

4. Two episodes from Roman history: Livia was said to have murdered her husband with the help of her lover; Lucia (or Lucilla) was said to have killed her husband, the poet Lucretius, accidentally with a love potion.

'O brother,' Arrius said, 'and did they so?
Give me a graft of that same blessed tree
770   And in my garden planted it shall be!'
    "Of wives of later date he also read,
How some had slain their husbands in their bed
And let their lovers shag them all the night
While corpses lay upon the floor upright.
775   And some had driven nails into the brain
While husbands slept and in such wise were slain.
And some had given them poison in their drink.
He told more evil than the mind can think.
And therewithal he knew of more proverbs
780   Than in this world there grows of grass or herbs.
'Better,' he said, 'your habitation be
With lion wild or dragon foul,' said he,
'Than with a woman who will nag and chide.'
'Better,' he said, 'on the housetop abide
785   Than with a brawling wife down in the house;
Such are so wicked and contrarious
They hate the thing their husband loves, for aye.'
He said, 'a woman throws her shame away
When she throws off her smock,' and further, too:
790   'A woman fair, save she be chaste also,
Is like a ring of gold in a sow's nose.'
Who would imagine or who would suppose
What grief and pain were in this heart of mine?
    "And when I saw he'd never cease, in fine,
795   His reading in this cursed book at night,
Three leaves of it I snatched and tore outright
Out of his book, as he read on; and eke
I with my fist so took him on the cheek
That in our fire he reeled and fell right down.
800   Then he got up as does a wild lion,
And with his fist he struck me on the head,
And on the floor I lay as I were dead.
And when he saw how limp and still I lay,
He was afraid and would have run away,
805   Until at last out of my swoon I made:
'Oh, have you slain me, you false thief?' I said,
'And for my land have you thus murdered me?
Kiss me before I die, and let me be.'
    "He came to me and near me he knelt down,
810   And said: 'O my dear sister Alison,
So help me God, I'll never strike you more;
What I have done, you are to blame therefor.
But all the same forgiveness now I seek!'
And thereupon I hit him on the cheek,
815   And said: 'Thief, so much vengeance do I wreak!
Now will I die, I can no longer speak!'

But at the last, and with much care and woe,
We made it up between ourselves. And so
He put the bridle reins within my hand
820　To have the governing of house and land;
And of his tongue and of his hand, also;
And made him burn his book, right then, oho!
And when I had thus gathered unto me
Masterfully, the entire sovereignty,
825　And he had said: 'My own true wedded wife,
Do as you please the term of all your life,
Guard your own honour and keep fair my state'—
After that day we never had debate.
God help me now, I was to him as kind
830　As any wife from Denmark unto Ind,°　　　　　　*India*
And also true, and so was he to me.
I pray to God, Who sits in majesty,
To bless his soul, out of His mercy dear!
Now will I tell my tale, if you will hear."

835　The friar laughed when he had heard all this.
"Now dame," said he, "so have I joy or bliss
This is a long preamble to a tale!"
　　　And when the summoner heard this friar's hail,
"Lo," said the summoner, "by God's arms two!
840　A friar will always interfere, mark you.
Behold, good men, a housefly and a friar
Will fall in every dish and matters higher.[5]
Why speak of preambling, you in your gown?
What! Amble, trot, hold peace, or go sit down;
845　You hinder our diversion thus to inquire."
　　　"Aye, say you so, sir summoner?" said the friar,
"Now by my faith I will, before I go,
Tell of a summoner such a tale, or so,
That all the folk shall laugh who're in this place."
850　　"Otherwise, friar, I beshrew° your face,"　　　　　*curse*
Replied this summoner, "and beshrew me
If I do not tell tales here, two or three,
Of friars ere I come to Sittingbourne,[6]
That certainly will give you cause to mourn,
855　For well I know your patience will be gone."
　　　Our host cried out, "Now peace, and that anon!"
And said he: "Let the woman tell her tale.
You act like people who are drunk with ale.
Do, lady, tell your tale, and that is best."
860　　"All ready, sir," said she, "as you request,

---

5. That is, will eat anything and meddle in any business. There was a longstanding dislike between clergy possessing land and goods and mendicants, who did not.

6. On the pilgrimage route, about 40 miles from London and 16 from Canterbury.

If I have license of° this worthy friar."   *permission from*
    "Yes, dame," said he, "to hear you's my desire."

The Wife of Bath's Tale

Now in the olden days of King Arthur,
Of whom the Britons speak with great honour,
All this wide land was land of faëry
The elf-queen, with her jolly company,
5   Danced often times on many a green mead;°   *meadow*
This was the old opinion, as I read.[1]
I speak of many hundred years ago;
But now no man can see the elves, you know.
For now the so-great charity and prayers
10   Of limiters and other holy friars
That do infest each land and every stream
As thick as motes° are in a bright sunbeam,   *dust particles*
Blessing halls, chambers, kitchens, ladies' bowers,°   *chambers*
Cities and towns and castles and high towers,
15   Manors and barns and stables, aye and dairies—
This causes it that there are now no fairies.[2]
For where was wont to walk full many an elf,
Right there walks now the limiter himself
In noons and afternoons and in mornings,
20   Saying his matins and such holy things,
As he goes round his district in his gown.[3]
Women may now go safely up and down,
In every copse° or under every tree;   *thicket*
There is no other incubus than he,[4]
25   And would do them nothing but dishonour.
      And so befell it that this King Arthur
Had at his court a lusty bachelor°   *young knight*
Who, on a day, came riding from river;
And happened that, alone as she was born,
30   He saw a maiden walking through the corn,
From whom, in spite of all she did and said,
Straightway by force he took her maidenhead;
For which violation was there such clamour,
And such appealing unto King Arthur,
35   That soon condemned was this knight to be dead
By course of law, and should have lost his head,

1. Although its specific source is unknown, "The Wife of Bath's Tale" is drawn from the "Matter of Britain," a collection of tales and romances about the deeds of the legendary King Arthur and his court. See also the *lais* of Marie de France (page 731).

2. In her offhand way, Alisoun allows Chaucer to draw out an important theme of the Matter of Britain: the tension between the ancient pre-Christian Celtic religion, including its fairies, elves, and magic, and the Christian belief system that was replacing it.

3. A friar limiter (allowed to beg within certain limits), like the one who has just finished interrupting her tale.

4. An incubus was an evil spirit who descended on people in their sleep; with women especially it sought sexual activity. Their existence was recognized by both church and state during the Middle Ages.

Peradventure,° such being the statute then;   *as it chanced*
But that the other ladies and the queen
So long prayed of the king to show him grace,
40   He granted life, at last, in the law's place,
And gave him to the queen, as she should will,
Whether she'd save him, or his blood should spill.
    The queen she thanked the king with all her might,
And after this, thus spoke she to the knight,
45   When she'd an opportunity, one day:
"You stand yet," said she, "in such poor a way
That for your life you've no security.
I'll grant you life if you can tell to me
What thing it is that women most desire.
50   Be wise, and keep your neck from iron dire!°   *dreadful iron*
And if you cannot tell it me anon,
Then will I give you license to be gone
A twelvemonth° and a day, to search and learn   *year*
Sufficient answer in this grave concern.
55   And your knight's word I'll have, ere forth you pace,
To yield your body to me in this place."
    Grieved was this knight, and sorrowfully he sighed;
But there! he could not do as pleased his pride.
And at the last he chose that he would wend,°   *depart*
60   And come again upon the twelvemonth's end,
With such an answer as God might purvey;°   *provide*
And so he took his leave and went his way.
    He sought out every house and every place
Wherein he hoped to find that he had grace
65   To learn what women love the most of all;
But nowhere ever did it him befall
To find, upon the question stated here,
Two persons who agreed with statement clear.
    Some said that women all loved best riches,
70   Some said, fair fame, and some said, prettiness;
Some, rich array, some said 'twas lust abed
And often to be widowed and re-wed.
    Some said that our poor hearts are aye most eased
When we have been most flattered and thus pleased
75   And he went near the truth, I will not lie;
A man may win us best with flattery;
And with attentions and with busyness
We're often limed,° the greater and the less.   *ensnared*
    And some say, too, that we do love the best
80   To be quite free to do our own behest,
And that no man reprove us for our vice,
But saying we are wise, take our advice.
For truly there is no one of us all,
If anyone shall rub us on a gall,°   *sore spot*
85   That will not kick because he tells the truth.
Try, and he'll find who does so, I say sooth.°

No matter how much vice we have within,
We would be held for wise and clean of sin.
   And some folk say that great delight have we
90   To be held constant, also trustworthy,
And on one purpose steadfastly to dwell,
And not betray a thing that men may tell.
But that tale is not worth a rake's handle;
By God, we women can no thing conceal,
95   As witness Midas. Would you hear the tale?[5]
   Ovid, among some other matters small,
Said Midas had beneath his long curled hair,
Two ass's ears that grew in secret there
The which defect he hid, as best he might,
100   Full cunningly from every person's sight,
And, save his wife, no one knew of it, no.
He loved her most, and trusted her also;
And he prayed of her that to no creature
She'd tell of his disfigurement impure.
105   She swore him: Nay, for all this world to win
She would do no such villainy or sin
And cause her husband have so foul a name;
Nor would she tell it for her own deep shame.
Nevertheless, she thought she would have died
110   Because so long the secret must she hide;
It seemed to swell so big about her heart
That some word from her mouth must surely start;
And since she dared to tell it to no man,
Down to a marsh, that lay hard by, she ran;
115   Till she came there her heart was all afire,
And as a bittern booms in the quagmire,
She laid her mouth low to the water down:
"Betray me not, you sounding water blown,"
Said she, "I tell it to none else but you:
120   Long ears like asses' has my husband two!
Now is my heart at ease, since that is out;
I could no longer keep it, there's no doubt."
Here may you see, though for a while we bide,
Yet out it must; no secret can we hide.
125   The rest of all this tale, if you would hear,
Read Ovid: in his book does it appear.
   This knight my tale is chiefly told about
When what he went for he could not find out,
That is, the thing that women love the best,
130   Most saddened was the spirit in his breast;
But home he goes, he could no more delay.
The day was come when home he turned his way;

---

5. Ovid recounts the tale in Book 11 of the *Metamorphoses,* although the Wife of Bath has replaced the original version's barber with a wife.

And on his way it chanced that he should ride
In all his care, beneath a forest's side,
135 And there he saw, a-dancing him before,
Full four and twenty ladies, maybe more;
Toward which dance eagerly did he turn
In hope that there some wisdom he should learn.
But truly, ere he came upon them there,
140 The dancers vanished all, he knew not where.[6]
No creature saw he that gave sign of life,
Save, on the greensward sitting, an old wife;
A fouler person could no man devise.
Before the knight this old wife did arise,
145 And said: "Sir knight, hence lies no travelled way.
Tell me what thing you seek, and by your fay.
Perchance you'll find it may the better be;
These ancient folk know many things," said she.
    "Dear mother," said this knight assuredly,
150 "I am but dead, save I can tell, truly,
What thing it is that women most desire;
Could you inform me, I'd pay well your hire."
    "Plight me your troth° here, hand in hand," said she,   *promise me*
"That you will do, whatever it may be,
155 The thing I ask if it lie in your might;
And I'll give you your answer ere the night."
    "Have here my word," said he. "That thing I grant."
    "Then," said the crone, "of this I make my vaunt°   *boast*
Your life is safe; and I will stand thereby,
160 Upon my life, the queen will say as I.
Let's see which is the proudest of them all
That wears upon her hair kerchief or caul,°   *ornamented hairnet*
Shall dare say no to that which I shall teach;
Let us go now and without longer speech."
165   Then whispered she a sentence in his ear,
And bade him to be glad and have no fear.
    When they were come unto the court, this knight
Said he had kept his promise as was right,
And ready was his answer, as he said.
170 Full many a noble wife, and many a maid,
And many a widow, since they are so wise,
The queen herself sitting as high justice,
Assembled were, his answer there to hear;
And then the knight was bidden to appear.[7]
175   Command was given for silence in the hall,

---

6. The *locus amoenus,* or pleasing place, reached after a long wandering journey, was a central locale in medieval romance. See, for example, the *lais* of Marie de France (page 731).

7. The setting and the type of question recall the "courts of love" of Eleanor of Aquitaine and her daughter Marie, who had been primarily responsible for reviving the *matière de Bretagne* and who were patrons to many of the most important poets and writers of the time, including Marie de France, Andreas Capellanus, and Chrétien de Troyes.

And that the knight should tell before them all
What thing all worldly women love the best.
This knight did not stand dumb, as does a beast,
But to this question presently answered
180 With manly voice, so that the whole court heard:
"My liege lady, generally," said he,
"Woman desire to have the sovereignty
As well upon their husband as their love,
And to have mastery their man above;°   *over their man*
185 This thing you most desire, though me you kill
Do as you please, I am here at your will."
      In all the court there was no wife or maid
Or widow that denied the thing he said,
But all held, he was worthy to have life.
190   And with that word up started the old wife
Whom he had seen a-sitting on the green.
"Mercy," cried she, "my sovereign lady queen!
Before the court's dismissed, give me my right.
'Twas I who taught the answer to this knight;
195 For which he did plight troth to me, out there,
That the first thing I should of him require
He would do that, if it lay in his might.
Before the court, now, pray I you sir knight,"
Said she, "that you will take me for your wife;
200 For well you know that I have saved your life.
If this be false, say nay, upon your fay!"
      This knight replied: "Alas and welaway!
That I so promised I will not protest.
But for God's love pray make a new request,
205 Take all my wealth and let my body go."
      "Nay then," said she, "beshrew us if I do!
For though I may be foul and old and poor,
I will not, for all metal and all ore
That from the earth is dug or lies above,
210 Be aught except your wife and your true love."
      "My love?" cried he, "nay, rather my damnation!
Alas! that any of my race and station
Should ever so dishonoured foully be!"
      But all for naught; the end was this, that he
215 Was so constrained he needs must go and wed,
And take his ancient wife and go to bed.
      Now, peradventure, would some men say here,
That, of my negligence, I take no care
To tell you of the joy and all the array
220 That at the wedding feast were seen that day.
Make a brief answer to this thing I shall;
I say, there was no joy or feast at all;
There was but heaviness and grievous sorrow;
For privately he wedded on the morrow,°   *the next day*

225   And all day, then, he hid him like an owl;[8]
         So sad he was, his old wife looked so foul.
            Great was the woe the knight had in his thought
         When he, with her, to marriage bed was brought;
         He rolled about and turned him to and fro.
230   His old wife lay there, always smiling so
         And said: "O my dear husband, *ben'cite!*
         Fares every knight with wife as you with me?
         Is this the custom in King Arthur's house?
         Are knights of his all so fastidious?
235   I am your own true love and, more, your wife;
         And I am she who saved your very life;
         And truly, since I've never done you wrong,
         Why do you treat me so, this first night long?
         You act as does a man who's lost his wit;
240   What is my fault? For God's love tell me it,
         And it shall be amended, if I may."
            "Amended!" cried this knight, "Alas, nay, nay!
         It will not be amended ever, no!
         Your are so loathsome, and so old also,
245   And therewith of so low a race were born,
         It's little wonder that I toss and turn.
         Would God my heart would break within my breast!"
            "Is this," asked she, "the cause of your unrest?"
            "Yes, truly," said he, "and no wonder 'tis."
250   "Now, sir," said she, "I could amend all this,
         If I but would, and that within days three,
         If you would bear yourself well towards me.
            "But since you speak of such gentility
         As is descended from old wealth, till ye
255   Claim that for that you should be gentlemen,
         I hold such arrogance not worth a hen.
         Find him who is most virtuous alway,
         Alone or publicly, and most tries aye
         To do whatever noble deeds he can,
260   And take him for the greatest gentleman.
         Christ wills we claim from Him gentility,
         Not from ancestors of landocracy.°   *landed gentry*
         For though they give us all their heritage,
         For which we claim to be of high lineage,
265   Yet can they not bequeath, in anything,
         To any of us, their virtuous living,
         That made men say they had gentility,
         And bade us follow them in like degree.
            "Well does that poet wise of great Florence,

---

8. Owls emerge only at night.

270 Called Dante, speak his mind in this sentence;
    Somewhat like this may it translated be:
    'Rarely unto the branches of the tree
    Doth human worth mount up: and so ordains
    He Who bestows it; to Him it pertains.'[9]
275 For of our fathers may we nothing claim
    But temporal things, that man may hurt and maim.
        "And everyone knows this as well as I,
    If nobleness were implanted naturally
    Within a certain lineage, down the line,
280 In private and in public, I opine,
    The ways of gentleness they'd alway show
    And never fall to vice and conduct low.
        "Take fire and carry it in the darkest house
    Between here and the Mount of Caucasus,°   *east of the Black Sea*
285 And let men shut the doors and from them turn;
    Yet will the fire as fairly blaze and burn
    As twenty thousand men did it behold;
    Its nature and its office it will hold,
    On peril of my life, until it die.
290   "From this you see that true gentility
    Is not allied to wealth a man may own,
    Since folk do not their deeds, as may be shown,
    As does the fire, according to its kind.
    For God knows that men may full often find
295 A lord's son doing shame and villainy;
    And he that prizes his gentility
    In being born of some old noble house,
    With ancestors both noble and virtuous,
    But will himself do naught of noble deeds
300 Nor follow him to whose name he succeeds,
    He is not gentle,° be he duke or earl;   *noble*
    For acting churlish makes a man a churl.
    Gentility is not just the renown
    Of ancestors who have some greatness shown,
305 In which you have no portion of your own.
    Your own gentility comes from God alone;
    Thence comes our true nobility by grace,
    It was not willed us with our rank and place
        "Think how noble, as says Valerius,
310 Was that same Tullius Hostilius,
    Who out of poverty rose to high estate.[1]
    Seneca and Boethius inculcate,°   *urge*
    Expressly (and no doubt it thus proceeds),

9. The passage is translated from *Purgatorio* 7.121–23, where Dante bemoaned the inability of good character to be transmitted as reliably as a good name. For Dante this demonstrated the difference between fallibly human conceptions of fate and inscrutably divine conceptions of justice.

1. The *Memorable Deeds and Sayings* of Valerius Maximus record the legendary life of the herdsman Tullius Hostilius, who rose to become the third king of Rome.

That he is noble who does noble deeds;[2]
315 And therefore, husband dear, I thus conclude:
Although my ancestors mayhap° were rude,°   *perhaps / uncultured*
Yet may the High Lord, and so hope I,
Grant me the grace to live right virtuously.
Then I'll be gentle when I do begin
320 To live in virtue and to do no sin.

    "And when you me reproach for poverty,
The High God, in Whom we believe, say I,
In voluntary poverty lived His life.
And surely every man, or maid, or wife
325 May understand that Jesus, Heaven's King,
Would not have chosen vileness of living.
Glad poverty's an honest thing, that's plain,
Which Seneca and other clerks maintain.
Whoso will be content with poverty,
330 I hold him rich, though not a shirt has he.
And he that covets much is a poor wight,
For he would gain what's all beyond his might
But he that has not, nor desires to have,
Is rich, although you hold him but a knave.

335   "True poverty, it sings right naturally;
Juvenal gaily says of poverty:[3]
'The poor man, when he walks along the way,
Before the robbers he may sing and play.'
Poverty's odious good, and, as I guess,
340 It is a stimulant to busyness;
A great improver, too, of sapience
In him that takes it all with due patience.
Poverty's this, though it seem misery—
Its quality may none dispute, say I.
345 Poverty often, when a man is low,
Makes him his God and even himself to know.
And poverty's an eye-glass, seems to me,
Through which a man his loyal friends may see.
Since you've received no injury from me,
350 Then why reproach me for my poverty.

    "Now, sir, with age you have upbraided me;
And truly, sir, though no authority
Were in a book, you gentles° of honour   *gentle folk*
Say that men should the aged show favour,
355 And call him father, of your gentleness;
And authors could I find for this, I guess.

    "Now since you say that I am foul and old,
Then fear you not to be made a cuckold;
For dirt and age, as° prosperous I may be,   *however*

2. Referring to the *Moral Epistles* of Seneca the Younger (d. 65 C.E.) and to the *Consolation of Philosophy* of the Roman philosopher Boethius, which Chaucer had translated during the 1380s.
3. The Roman satirist Juvenal, in his tenth Satire.

360 Are mighty wardens over chastity.
Nevertheless, since I know your delight,
I'll satisfy your worldly appetite.
    "Choose, now," said she, "one of these two things, aye,
To have me foul and old until I die,
365 And be to you a true and humble wife,
And never anger you in all my life;
Or else to have me young and very fair
And take your chance with those who will repair
Unto your house, and all because of me,
370 Or in some other place, as well may be.
Now choose which you like better and reply."
    This knight considered, and did sorely sigh,
But at the last replied as you shall hear:
"My lady and my love, and wife so dear,
375 I put myself in your wise governing;
Do you choose which may be the more pleasing,
And bring most honour to you, and me also.
I care not which it be of these things two;
For if you like it, that suffices me."
380   "Then have I got of you the mastery,
Since I may choose and govern, in earnest?"
    "Yes, truly, wife," said he, "I hold that best."
    "Kiss me," said she, "we'll be no longer wroth,
For by my truth, to you I will be both;
385 That is to say, I'll be both good and fair.
I pray God I go mad, and so declare,
If I be not to you as good and true
As ever wife was since the world was new.
And, save I be, at dawn, as fairly seen
390 As any lady, empress, or great queen
That is between the east and the far west,
Do with my life and death as you like best.
Throw back the curtain and see how it is."
    And when the knight saw verily all this,
395 That she so very fair was, and young too,
For joy he clasped her in his strong arms two,
His heart bathed in a bath of utter bliss;
A thousand times, all in a row, he'd kiss.
And she obeyed his wish in everything
400 That might give pleasure to his love-liking.
    And thus they lived unto their lives' fair end,
In perfect joy; and Jesus to us send
Meek husbands, and young ones, and fresh in bed,
And good luck to outlive them that we wed.
405 And I pray Jesus to cut short the lives
Of those who'll not be governed by their wives;
And old and querulous niggards with their pence,
And send them soon a mortal pestilence!

The Early Modern Period

Don Cristobal Colon, Admiral of Ships Bound for the Indies. In Honorius Philoponus, *Nova typis transacta navigatio* (1621). In this image from a book by a German monk on missionary voyages, Columbus is poised at Europe's shore, the vast sea stretching away toward the Indies he can see in his mind's eye. The portrait combines eras as well as regions: Columbus is shown with a modern compass and ship, but he seems to bear the globe on his shoulder like the classical giant Atlas, while his feet rest on an ancient Christian symbol, the Anchor of Faith. While one hand gestures toward his charts, the other hand raises up toward God. The globe shows the major islands Columbus "discovered," Cuba and Hispaniola or "Spagnolla," but much more space is given to the lands Columbus himself never believed were there: not India at all but entirely separate continents. Brazil, Peru, Mexico, and North America beckon Honorius's reader to go beyond Columbus to new explorations, conquests and conversions in the still unmapped regions approaching the "Circumference of the Center of Gravity."

IN MANY REGIONS OF THE WORLD, THE CENTURIES BETWEEN about 1400 and 1650 mark a time of transition from ancient, largely separate traditions to the rapidly evolving and interconnected world of modernity; the term "early modern" is increasingly used to describe this transitional era. The literatures of the early modern period reflect three great global movements: of worldwide exploration and conquest; of rational and scientific inquiry; and of the growing literary use of vernacular or common speech. These three developments are closely related. The world opened out dramatically after 1492, as the Eastern and Western hemispheres came into direct contact, and even before then contacts were intensifying as China's Ming dynasty extended its sway across the Indian Ocean, the expanding Ottoman Empire linked vast territories from Mesopotamia to eastern Europe, and European navigators explored the coasts of Africa and India. Greatly increased contact between widely separated cultures stimulated reflection on religious doctrines, political structures, and cultural practices of all sorts. And as old traditions came newly into question, the ancient languages that had conveyed them, such as Latin and Sanskrit, began to be supplemented and even replaced by modern vernaculars, as writers sought modes of expression that would reflect the changing reality around them.

The Early Modern World

The early modern world was marked politically by two opposing forces: expansive imperial outreach by several major powers, and national consolidation and resistance to outside rule. At times, these forces could actually work together, as when the Castilian monarchs Ferdinand and Isabella conquered the Muslim kingdom of Grenada in southern Spain in 1492; beginning in that very year, the unified nation became a major launching-point for American exploration and imperial conquest. Yet unified nations could also gain new independence from outside control: the Protestant countries of Germany and Scandinavia broke free of papal authority and the related political sway of the Holy Roman Empire, and France, though remaining largely Catholic, asserted an increasingly unified cultural identity and political independence.

An important aspect of political and cultural self-definition became the establishment of national languages and literatures. Local languages achieved new status in many parts of the world. Korea had long been in China's shadow both politically and culturally, but a new dynasty was established in 1392 by a general named Yi Songgye. The Chosŏn dynasty lasted until 1910 and cultivated specifically Korean arts and culture. Like Japanese, Korean had always been written using Chinese characters, but the mid-1400s saw the establishment of a Korean alphabet. French, German, English, and other national languages were increasingly used in place of Latin for serious literary work, and Italy itself was an early leader in "the vernacular revolution" as writers such as Dante and Boccaccio began to use Italian as well as Latin.

Exploration and Conquest

Long-distance exploration began in earnest in the late 1400s, with Portuguese navigators exploring the coast of Africa in the 1480s and Vasco da Gama reaching as far as India in the 1490s. Columbus's epochal voyage of 1492 was followed by a flood

The World in 1500

Legend:
- Incan Empire
- Holy Roman Empire
- Muscovy
- Ottoman Empire
- Timurids
- Ming Empire

PACIFIC OCEAN

NEW ZEALAND
Moas

Paleosiberians
Samoyeds
Ugrians
Turkic peoples
Tungus
Buryats
KHANATE OF THE OIRATS
GOBI
MING EMPIRE
Beijing
Nanjing
KOREA
JAPAN
PHILIPPINE ISLANDS
SULTANATE OF TERNATE
NEW GUINEA
Yumun
MAJAPAHIT
Australian Aborigines

TIBET
SHAN STATES
ANNAM
LAOS
CAMBODIA
CHAMPA
SIAM
BRUNEI
PEGU
GUJARATIS
SULTANATE OF MALACCA
Malacca
ACEH
MALAI STATES
CEYLON
MADAGASCAR
Malays

CHAGATAI KHANATE
SHAYBANIDS
KHANATE OF SIBIR
KHANATE OF ASTRAKHAN
KHANATE OF KAZAN
KHANATE OF RYAZAN
THE GOLDEN HORDE
MUSCOVY
Moscow
Pskov
LITHUANIA
SWEDEN
NORWAY
Copenhagen
POLAND
BOHEMIA
HUNGARY
GEORGIAN STATES
SAFAVIDS
GILHAN
AK KOYUNLU
OTTOMAN EMPIRE
Constantinople

TIMURIDS
KASHMIR
MULTAN
SIND
LODI SULTANATE OF DELHI
SMALL STATES
GUJARAT
RAJPUTS
AHMADNAGAR
BIJAPUR
VIJAYANAGAR

ARABIAN PENINSULA
Beduins
HADRAMAUT
OMAN
YEMEN
ADAL
ETHIOPIA
FUNJ
MAKURIA
MAMLUKS
Cairo
SWAHILI CITY STATES
Kilwa

INTERLACUSTRINE STATES
Bantus
MARAVI
MITABA
TORWA
BENGUELA
NDONGO
KALAHARI DESERT
Khoisan peoples

SAHARA
Beduins
Tuaregs
HAUSA STATES
KANEM-BORNU
TUNJUR
KONGO
NGOTO
KAKONGO
BENIN
AKAN STATES
SONGHAY
MALI
TAKRUR
WATTASIDS
ZAYYANIDS
HAFSIDS
Ceuta

HOLY ROMAN EMPIRE
SCOTLAND
IRELAND
ENGLAND
London
Paris
FRANCE
NAVARRE
PORTUGAL
SPAIN
Madrid
Lisbon

ATLANTIC OCEAN
INDIAN OCEAN
PACIFIC OCEAN

Inuit
NORTHWEST COAST CULTURES
ROCKY MOUNTAINS
GREAT PLAINS
PLAINS VILLAGES
PUEBLOS
Forest hunters and gatherers
Plains hunters and gatherers
MISSISSIPPIAN CULTURES
Woodland Culture
AZTEC EMPIRE
Tenochtitlan
Maya peoples
WEST INDIES
Lucayans
HISPANIOLA
Carib
Arawaks

Sumo
Misquito
CHICHA
ORINOQUENOI
Carib
ARUAKI
TAPAJO
ONIGLATAL
ARUAK
MANOA
AMAZON
Machu Picchu
ANDES
INCA EMPIRE
Cuzco
PATAGONIA
Nomadic hunters
Tupi
Ge
Guarani
Tupinguim
Nomadic hunters

N

of explorations westward and then the conquest of the Aztec and Incan empires in the early 1500s; Dutch, British, and French colonies followed Spanish settlements in North America in the early 1600s. New worlds are constantly being discovered in early modern literature. In 1516, Sir Thomas More claimed that one of Amerigo Vespucci's sailors had gone on from Brazil to find the ideal island republic of *Utopia*. At the close of the early modern period, Milton's Satan voyages from Hell to the "boundless Continent" of Earth, where he hopes to increase his "Honor and Empire... / By conquering this new World" (*Paradise Lost* 4.390–91). The rapid expansion of European exploration and settlement involved discoveries in both directions. In one Aztec poem from around 1550, the poet describes traveling to Rome to meet Pope Clement VII:

> The pope is on God's mat and seat and speaks for him.
> Who is this reclining on a golden chair? Look! It's the pope.
> He has his turquoise blowgun and he's shooting in the world.
> It seems it's true, he has his cross and golden staff,
> and these are shining in the world.

Several major empires were extending their reach in other parts of the world as well. In West Africa, the Songhai empire expanded during the 1500s from its base in Mali. In China, the Ming dynasty, founded in 1368, ruled until 1644 at the close of the early modern period. Where previous dynasties had largely looked inward, or at most had been active in East Asia, Ming China extended its influence over an unprecedented region. The emperor Cheng Tsu (r. 1402–1424) sent a fleet of warships commanded by the enterprising eunuch admiral Cheng Ho to establish trading bases and exact tribute not only from Japan and Korea but from southern India and even the east coast of Africa. In the 1500s, the Mughal Empire encompassed almost all of northern India and what is now Pakistan, while in the fifteenth through sixteenth centuries the Ottoman Empire expanded from Turkey to control Greece, the Balkans, Hungary, the Crimea, Mesopotamia, Syria, Palestine, Egypt, and the north coast of Africa all the way to Morocco at the western end of the Mediterranean. The Ottoman ruler Suleiman I, who reigned for almost half a century beginning in 1520, became known in Europe as "Suleiman the Magnificent" for the splendor of his court and his many victories.

Scientific Conquest and Inquiry

The increasing interest in scientific inquiry and technological innovation also aided imperial outreach: modern armies and navies could now overwhelm much larger forces not equipped with rifles, cannon, and warships. The practitioners of science or "natural philosophy" could even think of themselves as conquering warriors. As the physician and alchemist Paracelsus explained in his *Great Surgery Book* in 1536, "Every experiment is like a weapon which must be used in a particular way—a spear to thrust, a club to strike. Experimenting requires a man who knows when to thrust and when to strike, each according to need and fashion." In these same years, the Polish astronomer Nicolas Copernicus was making the observations that would lead to his revolutionary assertion that the earth and other planets revolve around the sun, not the sun around the earth—a disorienting change of perspective that questioned both classical authority and church doctrine. All phenomena and all traditions became subjects for probing, skeptical inquiry. In the 1570s Michel de Montaigne founded a new kind of writing, the essay or *essai*—French for "trial, experiment"—to convey his speculations on past and present events and on his own character. As he wrote in an inscription for his library, "I do not understand; I pause, I examine."

In Mughal India, the undogmatic ruler Akbar the Great (r. 1556–1605) organized discussions among a series of religious leaders—Zoroastrians, Christians, and Hindus as well as Muslims. Though Akbar never abandoned Islam, the religion of his birth, he came to regard Muhammad as not necessarily the last or the greatest of prophets, and he proclaimed tolerance for all religions in his realm. He reformed the judicial system in a similar spirit of inquiry, decreeing that judges "should not be satisfied with witnesses or oaths, but proceed by manifold inquiries, by the study of physiognomy, and the exercise of foresight." In Ming China, new emphasis was given to individual merit as demonstrated on civil service examinations. While established, wealthy families continued to have advantages in preparing their sons for these elaborate examinations, increasing numbers of people without marked wealth or connections were able to come into the government.

The importance given to the examination stimulated the establishment of Chinese schools, both by the government and by private scholars; like the many new universities of Europe, these schools became centers of debate and of probing scholarship. The fifteenth and sixteenth centuries saw an outpouring of Chinese scholarship that assembled and assessed the classic works of the past. The most ambitious imperial anthology ran to no fewer than eleven thousand volumes. Textual scholars sought to establish correct texts, and one sixteenth-century scholar was so bold as to question the authenticity of portions of the classic *Book of Songs*, a text that had been a founding document for earlier Confucian orthodoxy (see page 370).

The Ming scholars' interest in restoring and critically assessing their literary heritage went along with a heightened individualism and a new attention to colloquial prose fiction. A similar confluence can be seen in Europe as well, in the intensive reengagement with ancient texts and artworks that became known as "the Renaissance." European writers and other artists engaged with new intensity with classic forms, creating modern epics, plays, poems, and fictions out of the materials of Greek and Latin tradition.

The Rise of Print Culture

A crucial development in the early modern period was the invention of printing, which enabled texts to be widely circulated in multiple copies and made ownership affordable to people not possessing extensive private means. The world's first movable type was developed in China by a printer named Pi Sheng in around 1000, using pottery rather than metal type, though the complexity of the thousands of Chinese characters meant that texts could still more readily be written by hand. Increasingly sophisticated methods of woodblock printing allowed for the printing of more and more texts, often to the displeasure of government officials unable to control private mass-production of texts.

The Peking Mission. **The Jesuit mission to China in the late 16th century was strictly speaking a failure, insofar as very few Chinese were converted by the small band of Italians, Spaniards, and Germans who lived among them for several decades. But the mission was about more than conversion. The top panel depicts three priests, Matteo Ricci, Adam Schaal, and Ferdinand Verbiest, representative less of their religious beliefs than of the recent innovations in Western science: the compass, the astrolabe, the quadrant. At the same time, science could be the path that led to conversion; Ricci would collaborate with one bureaucrat, Li Zhizao, on several mathematical works before Li became a Christian. Two such converts are shown in the lower panel, turned to face the cross which, the illustration says, "the Christians have now accustomed the Chinese to let themselves be buried with."**

In Europe, the invention of movable metal type in the 1450s revolutionized the production and circulation of texts. Among other consequences, the spread of print culture gave impetus to the protestant Reformation beginning in the early 1500s, which stressed individual reading and understanding of Scripture. Such individual reading was newly possible with the spread of printed copies of the Bible, increasingly published in vernacular languages that people could read without needing the expense and leisure required to learn Latin. Not only men but also women—rarely given classical educations—could take an active role in the writing and reading of vernacular texts, and all sorts of literary production were stimulated by the new possibilities of print and the new availability of the vernacular languages as resources for serious writing. Writers around the world began to explore the brave new worlds open to them through vernacular languages and print culture.

Early Modern Europe

In 1632, the aging astronomer Galileo Galilei declared before the Roman Inquisition that he had entertained "the false opinion that the Sun is the center of the world and immovable, and that the earth is not the center of the same and that it moves." The early modern period saw the position of the earth radically reimagined by Galileo and his predecessor Copernicus; it also witnessed the renewed tenacity of the restraints on that imagination. In addition to the increased power of the papacy embodied in the Inquisition, the political map was redrawn. Spain and France had become absolutist states as former kingdoms and duchies were united under a single crown or, in the case of Spain, two crowns: the marriage of Ferdinand of Aragon and Isabella of Castile transformed the greater part of the Iberian peninsula into a powerful military presence. Likewise, England and Poland emerged in the fifteenth centuries as formidable monarchies. At the same time, in 1579 Europe experienced what one historian has called its "first modern war of national liberation" when the northern provinces of the Netherlands rose up against Spain. The English monarchy would soon face its own rebellion, culminating in the execution of Charles I in 1649. The economically thriving duchies of Germany, on the other hand, were the very heart of the Holy Roman Empire, revived in 1438 under the first representatives of what would be the long-lived Habsburg Dynasty. Even if Holy Roman Emperor Charles V called Luther a heretic at a crucial confrontation in 1520, the German princes, who would retain considerable autonomy, refused to go along with the accusation. As a result, much of what we now know as Germany embraced Luther's revolution, throwing off its shackles to the Catholic Church shortly after Charles V's proclamation. After a lifetime struggling against the German Protestants, Charles would abdicate his throne and retire to a monastery in Spain.

This redrawing of the earth's perimeters and its geopolitical makeup extended both westward and eastward. In the wake of the religious divisiveness brought about by the Protestants, Calvinists founded colonies off the coast of Brazil, Puritans defied the elements at Plymouth Rock, and Jesuits started schools in Ceylon (Sri Lanka) and China. These new wanderings were a concerted effort to win souls for Christ and to acquire gold, bread baskets, and new subjects for Europe's sovereign states. The Islamic presence in the Middle East and northwest Asia had grown steadily under the Sultan Osman, one of the early rulers of the Ottoman Empire. In 1453, Osman's armies captured the city of Constantinople, strategically situated on the edge of the Black Sea. Named for Constantine, the Roman emperor who had made Christianity the religion of his empire, Constantinople became Istanbul, and the great church of Santa Sophia became a mosque. The old spice route that had enabled enterprising merchants such as Marco Polo to pass through Turkey, Afghanistan, India, and even China was closed down, forcing other traders to find new routes to the Indies. Columbus's misguided pursuit of a new spice route to Asia led him instead to new worlds, while Vasco da Gama would reach the real India by ship in 1498. By 1521, Magellan would circumnavigate the globe.

The capture of Constantinople had other far-reaching effects. The Turks eventually advanced as far west as Vienna, and their threatening proximity polarized opposition to Islam, sparking talk of new Crusades. Isabella and Ferdinand overthrew the Arab kingdom of Granada in 1492, permanently banishing Muslims from

Europe in 1590

GOTLAND
Edinburgh
IRELAND
Dublin
York
ENGLAND
NORTH SEA
DENMARK-NORWAY
SWEDEN
Stockholm
RUSSIA
Riga
COURLAND
Copenhagen
BALTIC SEA
Königsberg
PRUSSIA
Hamburg
Warsaw
POLAND-LITHUANIA
London
Canterbury
NETHERLANDS
Utrecht
Münster
Brussels
Cologne
BRANDENBURG
Berlin
HOLY ROMAN EMPIRE
Wittenberg
Mühlberg
SAXONY
Schmalkalden
Prague
Cracow
ATLANTIC OCEAN
Crépy
Paris
Nemours
Orléans
Troyes
Worms
Speyer
Nuremberg
Augsburg
BAVARIA
AUSTRIAN HABSBURG POSSESSIONS
Vienna
HUNGARY
Buda
Debrecen
TRANSILVANIA
MOLDAVIA
Nantes
FRANCE
FRANCHE-COMTE
Basle
Zurich
SWISS CONFEDERATION
Geneva
Trent
Milan
Venice
Gyulafehervar
Cognac
Lyon
SAVOY
DUCHY OF MILAN
PARMA
Genoa
VENETIAN TERRITORIES
Belgrade
WALLACHIA
NAVARRE
Bordeaux
Bergerac
Toulouse
Avignon
MODENA
PAPAL STATES
URBINO
FLORENCE
Florence
PAPAL STATES
Rome
MONTENEGRO
OTTOMAN EMPIRE
BEARN
REPUBLIC OF GENOA
STATO DEI PRESIDI
REPUBLIC OF RAGUSA
Salonica
PORTUGAL
Madrid
SPAIN
Lisbon
Barcelona
Seville
BALEARIC ISLANDS
SARDINIA
NAPLES
Naples
MEDITERRANEAN SEA

N

| Spain | Denmark-Norway | Poland-Lithuania |
| French | Holy Roman Empire | Ottoman Empire |

a region that had once been the intellectual capital of southern Europe. Moreover, for a millennium Constantinople had served as the capital of the Byzantine Empire, home to a sophisticated civilization. As the Ottomans progressively conquered Athens, Damascus, Belgrade, and Rhodes, for the first time since antiquity, a large number of Greek-speaking scholars fled to western Europe, taking the quickest sea route to Venice. Among other things, their presence would enable the restoration of the Greek legacy of antiquity, dominated in the west for over a thousand years by Latinity. Plato, Homer, Sappho, the Greek tragedians, and eventually a freshly studied Aristotle became newly available to scholars and, eventually, the general reader.

Continuities and Changes

At the same time, the Renaissance was not the radical break with the past that it is commonly thought to be. There was much in Galileo's world that Dante would easily have recognized. One was the ubiquity of war and civic strife, though on a newly global scale. The so-called Hundred Years' War between England and France, which featured such "heroes" as Joan of Arc, finally ended in 1453, the year of the Turks' victory at Istanbul, but only after it had devastated much of western Europe. The victorious French didn't find respite for long: a series of battles throughout the early sixteenth century with the Holy Roman Empire decimated their army, thanks largely to the Empire's savvy deployment of Spanish musketeers, marking the end of an era of knightly combat. The so-called Wars of Italy made the vulnerable peninsula a veritable battleground for over sixty years, culminating with the absorption of Milan and Naples into the Spanish empire by 1559. A few years later, an angry mob tossed two of Emperor Ferdinand II's ministers from a window in Prague Castle; this "defenestration of Prague" set in motion the events that would ultimately lead to the Thirty Years' War (1618–1648), which engulfed most of central Europe.

Secondly, plague remained a constant blight on the landscape. The most severe epidemic ever to strike Europe was the Black Death of 1348–1350, apparently starting when a Genoese vessel fresh from a diseased Orient pulled into Messina; Giovanni Boccaccio grimly recorded its devastating effects on Florence in the opening pages of his *Decameron*. Little had changed by the time of Galileo's recantation; the astronomer narrowly missed dying himself in the virulent plague that swept across southern Europe in 1627 and 1628. Largely because of the recurrence of disease, Europe's major cities, with few exceptions, would never attain during the Renaissance the populations they had in Dante's lifetime. The closest that early modern Florence ever got to its pre-1348 population of 100,000 was 75,000.

Finally, Dante probably would not have been surprised by the steady decline of the aristocracy and the rise of the merchant class, although he wouldn't have been particularly pleased. Energetic merchants and prosperous guild members challenged the ways in which a man's worth was valued: did it depend on bloodline and clerical privilege, or could honest labor and thrifty behavior play a major part? The Medici, who would rule Florence for centuries, began as merchants and became prominent bankers; the merchant-banker Jakob Fugger of Augsburg, in southern Germany, came from a family of weavers, and at his death had emperors in his debt. Even as social relationships continued to be reconfigured throughout the Renaissance, however, the commercial growth and economic expansion that Dante's era had enjoyed came to an end with the Black Death of 1348. Depression and inflation characterized Europe until the sixteenth century, when the influx of gold and silver troves found in the New World—as well as in the mines of central Europe financed by Jakob Fugger and his contemporaries—helped the sagging economy. As business recovered, the Holy

Roman Empire did as well, invigorated by dynastic marriages that brought Spain within its orb; at the same time, the papacy, now firmly reestablished in Rome, sought to extend its political and temporal authority into a central Italy that had long avoided the sway of the "eternal city" to its south.

In the mid-fifteenth century when Nicholas V launched a major urban renovation, Rome was no more than a swamp dotted with half-buried ruins; two hundred years later it would witness the triumphant construction of Saint Peter's. François I, inspired by trips to Italy, would refashion Paris in the 1530s and 1540s, a project continued by Catherine de' Medici and lavishly extended by Louis XIV. Lisbon flourished under the Henrys, Madrid under the Phillips, and the attractions of Elizabeth's and James's courts brought the European Renaissance fully to London. The presence of wealthy sovereigns busy setting up court was not only good for business. It was also good for culture, and the arts thrived in capital cities that sought to outdo each other in power and prestige.

At the same time, the new-world discoveries had made those countries bordering the Atlantic Ocean the maritime powers of the epoch, outpacing the cities that dotted the Mediterranean. Venice alone retained its importance as a major port city, and that largely because of the unique circumstances that enabled the republic to retain its independence from territorial rulers. England, the Netherlands, and Spain were the beneficiaries of a somewhat belated Renaissance. The *siglo de oro* or "golden century" celebrated by Spain was the century in which Shakespeare, Donne, Milton, Cervantes, Lope de Vega, Calderón, Tirso de Molina, Vermeer, Rembrandt, and many more artists and writers flourished.

Looking Backward and Looking Forward

The backward glance to antiquity provoked the "rebirth" implicit in the term "renaissance." At the heart of this rebirth was the movement known as humanism: a manner of seeing the world which, as its name implies, placed man rather than God at the center. Initially, humanism can be said to have started out quietly enough. Petrarch desperately wanted to hear Virgil's genuine voice, to discover his true intentions rather than the ones visited upon him by Christian allegorists. The recovery of ancient thought and practice would not be limited, however, to pagan authors. In particular, humanists in northern Europe, buoyed by the creation of new centers of learning to accommodate their focus on letters—between 1472 and 1516, universities were founded at Munich, Uppsala, Copenhagen, and Wittenberg, and five new colleges instituted at Oxford and Cambridge—turned their attention to Scripture as well as writings of the early church.

Milton's great epic, *Paradise Lost*, also indulges in a profound backward look to the origins of creation itself. Written in the wake of the failed Puritan republic in which Milton had played a central role, *Paradise Lost* is opposed to idealizations of any kind. Yet it seeks a new type of unity in the simple fact of all men's and women's distance from God. There is a looming sense in *Paradise Lost* as to the finality of that loss, long before Milton's time, while the last words of the poem are a move forward—albeit a hesitant, somewhat reluctant one—as Adam and Eve, exiled from Eden, go out into the great world:

> Some natural tears they dropped, but wiped them soon;
> The world was all before them, where to choose
> Their place of rest, and providence their guide:
> They hand in hand with wandering steps and slow,
> Through Eden took their solitary way.

Product of the classical traditions that had inspired Petrarch, as well as of the vernacular poetry that had earned England a Renaissance all its own, *Paradise Lost* was begun a decade after Galileo's death. As if in anticipation of the encyclopedias that would become a distinctive mark of the eighteenth century, Milton's poem is, like them, a thoughtful compilation of the best the ancients and the moderns had to offer.

Authors and Authorships

The technological, educational, and social advances of the fifteenth and sixteenth centuries facilitated the emergence of a new phenomenon that could encompass a wide range of individuals, men as well as women: that of published authorship. Limited literacy in Latin had confined the technical act of writing mostly to clerics. Even highly cultured medieval monarchs such as Alfonso X of Castile were said to have relied exclusively on scribes. The need for a class of highly cultured individuals at Europe's courts and capitals would continue, however, even when the various European vernaculars began to rival Latin. The young Machiavelli and Petrarch worked as secretaries, respectively, for the city of Florence and for a French pope; Milton's skill in languages led to his appointment as Secretary for the Foreign Tongues by Oliver Cromwell's Council of State. Many of these sophisticated centers were governed by newly made men (or women) whose claims to power were shaky: the Medici, Cromwell himself, and Elizabeth Tudor, who kept her chief rival to the English throne, her cousin Mary Stuart, in the Tower for many years until having her beheaded on the eve of the Spanish Armada. They were eager for works acknowledging their legitimacy, and writers were quick to take up the challenge to provide stately poems to honor patrons or would-be patrons.

But if patronage provided one major catalyst for writing, there were others as well. The popular theaters in Spain and England gave Lope de Vega and Shakespeare possibilities for careers as both actors and playwrights, while later in the seventeenth century, Aphra Behn made respectable earnings from her plays and her poetry. Other attempts to live off one's writing were not as successful: Cervantes failed dismally to support himself. For a growing number of people, writing was simply one aspect of their daily activities. Many of them were women: Marguerite de Navarre, Sor Juana Inéz de la Cruz, and Vittoria Colonna were able to compose their own poetry and religious works in rooms of their own, thanks to associations with royalty, the relatively quiet rhythms of convent life, or a wealthy widowhood.

The fictional characters created by these authors are increasingly articulate about the limitations of human inquiry, and their probing the limits of their own minds may signal early modernity's most dramatic innovation with respect to its medieval legacy. Characters come increasingly to obey the laws of psychological realism, and their authors do as well, even if from behind cleverly constructed personae. Petrarch, Montaigne, and Cervantes speak to us with a new directness and openness. These voices are stylized, of course, but the stylization consists largely in the conviction that exposing one's most intimate life in its domestic and spiritual details is warranted by the occasion itself.

Part of this new accessibility has much to do with improved record-keeping on the part of cities, states, and religious organizations. The need to record, to scrutinize, in order to find out "truths" amidst contingencies links Calvin's Geneva, the Inquisitorial trials of Galileo and his contemporaries, and the arrival of Matteo Ricci, a Jesuit missionary, in the court of the emperor of China. Part of it also has to do with the fragmentation not only of a world, but of the literary genres that marked that world. Epic and tragedy, two classical imports much revised in the course of the early modern period, would find their share of practitioners. Other literary forms, some of them also salvaged from classical antiquity, were less monolithic and therefore perhaps less formidable. Those on the peripheries of elite culture found it easier to take up these lesser genres: the letter, the lyric, the essay, the autobiography, the short story and eventually the novel, in many ways a hodgepodge of all of the above. For most women, and for many men, entrance onto the literary scene began as simply the raising of a personal voice in reflection, in challenge, or in jest.

There was a volatile relationship between their words and the societies in which these authors lived. Not only was Galileo the victim of a judicial process, but all of Erasmus's works were placed on the Roman Index of Prohibited Books, along with writings by Rabelais, Boccaccio, and Petrarch. Catholicism was not alone in persecuting potential heretics and subversives, however; Thomas More was decapitated for refusing to take the oath of allegiance to King Henry VIII after Henry repudiated the pope, and Martin Luther sanctioned the massacre of German peasants who had risen in rebellion. As a result, authors often attempted to couch their radical arguments within deliberately distancing and sometimes disorienting frames. Erasmus's *Praise of Folly* is one example, Boccaccio's *Decameron* another. Others were

Aztec screenfold book c. 1500.

careful to display a heightened sense of self-consciousness about the finally fictive status of their works. More's "Utopia" means "nowhere," while Shakespeare's Prospero reveals to Miranda and to us that the storm he had created is only the result of a sleight-of-hand, and Vermeer's paintings, with their mirrors and drawing easels, constantly remind us of their own construction. The gleaning and publication of a supposedly self-evident truth, as Galileo learned, could be fraught with difficulties. And as in Galileo's case, such difficulties emerged from the perceived conflicts between profoundly held religious beliefs and the awareness of a new worldliness that militated against those very beliefs.

It is thus not surprising that the culture of early modern Europe is marked throughout by reflections on its vulnerabilities. In many ways, this is a culture that emerges to protect a singular voice that at first boldly, and then perhaps more hesitatingly, called attention to the origins of art not in God or universals handed down for centuries, but in the thoughtful and creative self.

Mesoamerica: Before Columbus and After Cortés

The traditional Amerindian cultures are often called "pre-Columbian," literally referring to the era before Columbus's voyage of 1492, and more generally including the period before a given culture's first substantial European contact. At the time of the Conquest, some twenty million people lived in Mesoamerica. Cities had begun to form in the first millennium B.C.E., dominated by pyramid temples. The Maya were the major presence in their region until the Aztecs migrated into central Mexico from the arid north in the thirteenth century; they were forced to settle in undesirable marshlands around the large lake in the Valley of Mexico. They gradually expanded a pair of islands into their double capital city, Tenochtitlán-Tlatelolco. The Aztecs came to control much of central and southern Mexico, and Tenochtitlán became the greatest city ever seen in the hemisphere, with many as 350,000 inhabitants, magnificent pyramids and palaces, and separate districts for the production of jewelry, textiles, pottery, and weapons.

The major Mesoamerican cities became both religious and political centers, with temple and court establishments centered on magnificent temple pyramids and lavish palaces, filled with frescoes and elaborate furnishings, and surrounded by pleasure gardens. There was much literary activity, more in oral than written form, as hieroglyphics were used as prompts to memory rather than to compose freestanding texts. Mythological and historical tales were told and retold, most memorably recorded in the Mayan *Popol Vuh* or Council Book, and hymns and songs were sung to the accompaniment of flutes, drums, and rattles. Though the region's cultures were not at all advanced technologically—most tools were of stone or wood; goods had to be carried by people, as the Mesoamericans did not use beasts of burden or even the wheel—the Mayan and Aztec artisans developed remarkably delicate artworks.

As the Aztecs built their empire, the difficulties of transportation and supply made it hard to carry on sustained warfare at any distance from home; instead, they extended their sway by complex negotiations and through the selective, exemplary violence of human sacrifice. Beginning in the late 1420s and under the emperor's chief advisor Tlacaelel, human sacrifice became widespread, with thousands of foreign captives being sacrificed on major festivals, in a theater of terror to which neighboring rulers were pointedly invited. By the early 1500s, the Aztecs' enemies and even most of their allies were bitterly resentful of the Aztecs' sacrifices, heavy taxation, and conscription of youths to serve as warriors and build temples and palaces. They were more than ready for things to change.

Cortés arrived in Mexico in 1519 and by August of 1521, aided by the Aztecs' enemies—and their restless allies—he had succeeded in overthrowing the Aztecs and destroying Tenochtitlán. Cortés's lieutenant, Pedro de Alvarado, conquered the highland Mayan center of Guatemala in 1523, and in 1532 another Spaniard, Francisco Pizarro, took a small force to Peru, home of the other greatest New World Empire, that of the Incas. Professing friendship for the Incan emperor Atahualpa, Pizarro seized him, extracted ransom, and executed him. With the region's great empires defeated, the New World was open to piecemeal conquest and settlement by Europe, with Portuguese settlers gaining control over Brazil, the Spanish dominating the rest of South and Central America, and Spanish, French, and English colonizers vying for control over North America. The colonial period lasted in the region until Mexico and Guatemala achieved independence from Spain in 1821. At that time, Mexico's territory included Texas, California, and much of the American southwest; in a series of conflicts with the growing United States, the present borders were eventually established in 1848.

Over the centuries, a rich and varied culture has evolved in Mexico and Central America among the increasingly mixed populations of the descendants of the Spanish settlers and the native Amerindians. A major element in this evolution has been a powerful literary heritage, from the rhetorically charged writings of the conquistadors and the haunting poetry of their adversaries, to the elevated lyrics of the great Sor Juana Inés de la Cruz in the seventeenth century, to such contemporary writers as Octavio Paz, Carlos Fuentes, and the Guatemalan Miguel Ángel Asturias, winner of the 1967 Nobel Prize for Literature, who translated the *Popol Vuh* into Spanish and incorporated many of its themes into his novels. Today, hundreds of thousands of people in Mexico and Central America still speak native languages as their first or even sole language, and poetry is still being composed in Mayan and in Nahuatl, as members of the indigenous cultures seek to assess and adapt their heritage in the contemporary world.

YEAR	THE WORLD	LITERATURE
1300		1300s Aztecs begin producing painted screenfold books
1310		
1320	1325 Founding of Aztec capital, Tenochtitlán	1321 Dante dies
1330	1337–1453 Hundred Years' War between England and France	
1340	1348–1350 Black Death in Europe	
1350		1353–1354 Petrarch writing *Canzoniere* and Boccaccio, *Decameron*
1360	1363 Timur (Tamerlane) begins conquests in central Asia, Persia, Russia, and India 1368 Chinese overthrow Mongols; Ming dynasty replaces Yuan dynasty	Early 1360s St. Catherine, *Letters*
1370	1378 Pope Gregory XI leaves Avignon for Rome; beginning of Great Schism	
1380		
1390		
1400		1404 Christine de Pizan, *Book of the City of Ladies*
1410		
1420	1428–1440 Reign of Aztec emperor Itzcoatl; Aztecs become dominant regional power 1429 Joan of Arc leads siege at Orleans; burned at stake (1431)	
1430	1434 Cosimo de' Medici becomes ruler of Florence	1430s–1519 Elaboration of court poetry in service of the Aztec empire 1430s Leon Battista Alberti, *On Painting*
1440	1440 Portuguese begin slave trade in Africa 1444 Mehmed II becomes sultan of Ottoman Empire	
1450	1450 Lorenzo Valla proves *Donation of Constantine* a forgery 1453 Gutenberg prints first Bible using movable metal type; Turks seize Constantinople; end of Byzantine Empire	1450s François Villon, poetic works

933

continued

YEAR	THE WORLD	LITERATURE
1460		
1470	1474 Isabella becomes Queen of Castile	1470s Lucrezia Tornabuoni
	1478 Spanish Inquisition begins	de' Medici, *Sacred Stories*
1480	1488 Bartolomeu Dias explores Cape of Good Hope	
1490	1492 Jews expelled from Spain; Columbus explores West Indies	1493 Columbus writes first letters to Queen Isabella detailing his discoveries
		1494 Aldus Manutius establishes an important printing press in Venice
	1497 Leonardo da Vinci, *Last Supper*	
	1498 Vasco da Gama reaches India; Savonarola burned at stake in Florence	
	1499–1501 Amerigo Vespucci explores coast of Brazil	
1500	1500 Michelangelo, *David*	1509 Erasmus, *The Praise of Folly*
	1502–1520 Reign of Moctezuma II in Mexico	
1510	1511 Cuba becomes Spanish colony	
	1514 Copernicus publishes work on heliocentric theory	1513 Niccolò Machiavelli, *The Prince*
	1517 Luther writes 95 theses contesting Church's practice of granting indulgences	1516 Thomas More, *Utopia*
	1519–1522 Magellan circumnavigates globe	1519–1521 Cortés writes five long letters to Charles V on his exploits
	1519 Hernán Cortés invades Aztec empire, places Moctezuma under house arrest	
1520	1521 Three–month siege of Tenochtitlán ends in fall of Aztec empire. Cortés gains control over central and southern Mexico	
	1523 Pedro de Alvarado conquers Guatemala. Pope Clement VII sends a dozen missionaries to organize the conversion of the Mexican population	1522 Martin Luther translates New Testament
		1524 Aztec-Spanish dialogues on the merits of traditional religion versus Christianity
	1525–1526 Peasants' rebellion in Germany; Thomas Muntzer executed	1524–1525 Erasmus and Luther debate free will
	1527 Sack of Rome by Holy Roman Emperor Charles V	1527 Baldassare Castiglione, *The Courtier*
	1529 Turks invade Austria; Bernardino de Sahagún arrives in Mexico	
1530	1532 Francisco Pizarro conquers Incan empire in Peru	1530s Lyrics of Michelangelo and Vittoria Colonna
	1533 Jean Calvin goes to Geneva	1532 François Rabelais, *Pantagruel*
	1534 Henry VIII excommunicated	1534 Rabelais, *Gargantua*
	1535 Thomas More beheaded	
	1539 First printing press in New World (Mexico)	
1540	1540 Jesuits approved by Pope as official order; Treaties signed between Turkey and Venice	1540s Clement Marot translates the Psalms; Marguerite de Navarre, *Heptameron*
		1540–1560s Wu Cheng'en, *Journey to the West*

YEAR	THE WORLD	LITERATURE
	1545–1562 Council of Trent reforms Catholic practices in response to Protestant challenges	1547–1580s Bernardino de Sahagún collects materials from native informants for his *General History of the Affairs of New Spain* and poetry collections
1550		
	1555 Calvinist mission to Brazil 1557 Erasmus's works put on Index of Prohibited Books 1559 Elizabeth I becomes Queen of England	1555 Louise Labé, *Works*
1560		
	1562–1598 French Wars of Religion 1568–1648 War in Netherlands, ending with independence from Spain	1560s Bartolomé de las Casas, *Apolgetic History* 1564–1565 Bernal Díaz del Castillo, *True History of the Conquest of New Spain*
1570		
	1572 Battle of Lepanto, Spanish Catholic naval forces defeat Ottomans; St. Bartholomew's Day massacre 1578 King Sebastiaõ and Portuguese troops killed in northern Africa	1570s Luis Vaz de Camões, *The Lusiads*; Jean de Léry, *History of a Voyage to Brazil* 1577 Teresa of Avila, *Interior Castle*
1580		
	1582 Gregorian Calendar implemented 1580 Union of Portugal and Spain 1585 First English settlement in North America 1588 Spanish Armada defeated by England	1580s Jan Kochanowski, *Laments*; Michel de Montaigne, *Essays*
1590		
	1598 Restoration of shogunate in Japan	
1600		
	1609 Spain approaching bankruptcy; Moors expelled	1605 Miguel de Cervantes, *Don Quixote*, Book 1
1610		
	1618–1648 Thirty Years' War	1611 William Shakespeare, *The Tempest* 1614 Lope de Vega, *Fuenteovejuna* 1615 Cervantes, *Don Quixote*, Book 2
1620	1620 Plymouth Colony founded in Massachusetts 1621 Philip IV becomes King of Spain 1628 Recurrence of plague in Europe	1624 John Donne, *Devotions upon Emergent Occasions* 1629 Hernando Ruiz de Alarcón, *Treatise on the Superstitions of the Natives of This New Spain*
1630		
	1633 Galileo recants before the Inquisition	
1640		
	1640 Portuguese war of independence begins 1642–1649 English Civil War 1649 Charles I beheaded	1641 René Descartes, *Meditations*
1650		
		1650 Anne Bradstreet, *The Tenth Muse Lately Sprung Up in America*
1660		
	1660 Restoration and return of Charles II to England	1667 John Milton, *Paradise Lost* 1667–1670 Sor Juana Inés de la Cruz writes first purely Mexican ~~poems in Spanish~~

"These stories were told neither in a church, of whose affairs one must speak with a chaste mind and a pure tongue…nor in the schools of philosophers…[but] in a garden, in a place designed for pleasure, among people who, though young in years, were nonetheless fully mature and not to be led astray by stories." Thus does Giovanni Boccaccio defend his *Decameron* from its imagined detractors in the epilogue to his masterpiece. As its title indicates, the *Decameron* is the (fictional) record of ten days: days spent telling one hundred tales during one of the worst plagues ever to strike Europe. Centuries later, some readers were still blushing at the raciness of some of the stories told by ten young men and women who have fled plague-infested Florence; the tale of naive but insatiable Alibech, who exhausts an amorous hermit, was translated into English only in the late nineteenth century. Boccaccio himself had second thoughts in the wake of the visit of a monk to Florence a decade after the *Decameron* was finished, when Boccaccio had taken religious orders. Admonished to change his sinful ways, Boccaccio was moved by the conversation to wish to destroy his earlier "evil" writings. Only a timely letter from his good friend Francis Petrarch prevented the author from burning a work that has been hailed as the first European example of an immensely popular genre, the *novella* or short story.

Florence was a fertile place for the birth of such a collection. The same town that had exiled Dante in 1302 had become, by midcentury, a bustling commercial center, run by the city's merchant class rather than by its aristocrats. The stability of its banks and the success of its merchants, Boccaccio's father among them, produced the vibrant, wealthy city in which Boccaccio was born. This thriving city is not the plague-ridden town we see in the macabre preface, although it and other Tuscan cities like it reappear in all their local color in many tales told in the gardens to which Boccaccio's young conversationalists flee. The true birthplaces of the Renaissance in Italy, these towns were the first to witness the transition from a recognizably medieval era dominated by feudal relationships to a new age of which Boccaccio—occasionally thought of as "still" medieval—is representative in many ways. But if bustling Italian towns and their bourgeois inhabitants dominate many of the stories, they aren't the only hubs of activity. Boccaccio's eclectic storytellers take us from Babylon to the tangled pine forest outside Ravenna to the court of the king of Spain.

Boccaccio went to a wide range of sources for his tales, including Ovid's *Metamorphoses,* clerical manuals, French *lais,* and Arabic tales. Like Shakespeare, he was an avid borrower who transformed what he borrowed. The *Decameron* also reflects the courtly world which Boccaccio had known firsthand when he lived in Naples in the 1320s and 1330s. Here he spent some distasteful years first studying banking and law, then found Naples much more to his liking when he turned to poetry and joined the flourishing intellectual community of King Robert of Anjou. Boccaccio wrote his first works in Robert's court: his *Filostrato,* which would become the basis for Chaucer's *Troilus and Criseyde;* his epic *Filocolo,* about the misfortunes of the Muslim Biancifiore; and *Thesiad of the Marriage of Emilia.* All works in the vernacular, they look back to classical epic and culture while incorporating the meters and themes of medieval romance and contemporary Italian poetry. But this productive period in King Robert's court ended abruptly in 1341, when the Florentine bank for which Boccaccio's father worked met with disaster. Father and son regretfully returned to Florence where, in time, the young Boccaccio's house in Certaldo just south of the city would become the center of Florence's fledgling humanist movement.

The episode of the near book-burning might suggest that the *Decameron* represents the culmination of Boccaccio's youthful period, which includes one of the first psychological novels of European literature (*The Elegy of Madonna Fiammetta*) and the first modern pastoral (*Nymphs of Fiesole*). Such works, several of which feature men and women gathered in gardens to tell tales, were indeed good preparation for a collection of stories of knights, ladies, and magnanimous kings. At the same time, the *Decameron* is like nothing Boccaccio had written before, and like nothing Europe had seen before. Its encyclopedic scale looks ahead to Boccaccio's later Latin compendia, including his (unfinished) *Genealogy of the Pagan Gods* and *Lives of Famous Men,* begun under Petrarch's tutelage and carried out in the midst of Boccaccio's commitment to unraveling the obscurities of ancient texts (to the extent that he could boast of being one of the first Italians to have learned ancient Greek). Boccaccio's solicitude for women is visible in the *Decameron*'s preface when he suggests that his tales are for female readers who are forced to "spend most of their time cooped up within the narrow confines of their rooms." His attention to women is also evident in his collection of biographies of notable classical women, *De mulieribus claris,* dedicated, not incidentally, to a Florentine woman, Andrea Acciaiuoli. Finally, the Latinate style of Boccaccio's Italian is a testimony to his lifelong engagement with classical literature, while the fact that the *Decameron* is written in the vernacular may suggest the admiration Boccaccio had for his fellow Florentine Dante (whose daughter he visited in a nunnery to present her with ten gold florins from the Commune of Florence as partial restitution for her father's losses). He had to discontinue a series of public lectures on the *Inferno* because of illness in 1374, and shortly thereafter died.

Yet while the *Decameron* may adhere, like the *Divine Comedy,* to a careful structure, the sensibility of Boccaccio's work is markedly different from Dante's. Death in the *Decameron*'s introduction is portrayed as final, with no suggestion of a Dantesque afterlife, either infernal or redemptive. Rarely have the ravages of disease been so relentlessly described, and with them, the almost complete destruction of community and the bonds that hold it together. In this sense, the ten conversationalists' escape to the countryside is at once a strategy for survival (reminiscent of Scheherazade's witty tale-telling escapades in *The Thousand and One Nights*) and an attempt to restore what has been lost. But the world outside Florence cannot sustain them forever. The order created at the villa is only a tentative one. The songs they sing at the end of each day, the delicate feasts they enjoy, the beautiful Valley of the Ladies eloquently described on the seventh day, all point toward a kind of preciousness and fleeting beauty of their lives which are too fragile to last, but healing and of great comfort while they do.

The actual stories, on the other hand, largely reflect a different reality, far more durable and rugged. Only a very few transpire in places as pristine as the gardens in Fiesole, and the vast majority of them deal with the messy contingencies of everyday life: marriage to a husband who is impotent, or tyrannical, or adulterous; the lechery and greed of friars; the stupidity of one's neighbors and colleagues; the stinginess of a king. Yet for most of these problems the tales' protagonists find solutions. Many succeed through savvy and wit, as when Nathan the Wise confounds a Sultan who seeks to confound him. Some, particularly in the last day's stories, succeed through greatness of heart, as in the problematic tale of the patient wife Griselda. In some cases, though—particularly the tragedies of Day Four—there are no solutions to be found. Yet by taking into account the tragic along with the ribald, Chaucer's "gode Boccace" demonstrates how attentive he was to the vicissitudes of life and the narratives into which they can be placed, winning for the *Decameron* enthusiastic readers and imitators from every culture and every rung of the social ladder.

PRONUNCIATIONS:

Giovanni Boccaccio: jo-VAN-ni bo-KATCH-oh
Dioneo: dee-oh-NAY-oh

from Decameron[1]

from First Day

[Introduction]

Here begins the First Day of the Decameron, *wherein first of all the author explains the circumstances in which certain persons, who presently make their appearance, were induced to meet for the purpose of conversing together, after which, under the rule of* Pampinea, *each of them speaks on the subject they find most congenial.*

Whenever, fairest ladies,[2] I pause to consider how compassionate you all are by nature, I invariably become aware that the present work will seem to you to possess an irksome and ponderous opening. For it carries at its head the painful memory of the deadly havoc wrought by the recent plague,[3] which brought so much heartache and misery to those who witnessed, or had experience of it. But I do not want you to be deterred, for this reason, from reading any further, on the assumption that you are to be subjected, as you read, to an endless torrent of tears and sobbing. You will be affected no differently by this grim beginning than walkers confronted by a steep and rugged hill, beyond which there lies a beautiful and delectable plain. The degree of pleasure they derive from the latter will correspond directly to the difficulty of the climb and the descent. And just as the end of mirth is heaviness, so sorrows are dispersed by the advent of joy.

This brief unpleasantness (I call it brief, inasmuch as it is contained within few words) is quickly followed by the sweetness and the pleasure which I have already promised you, and which, unless you were told in advance, you would not perhaps be expecting to find after such a beginning as this. Believe me, if I could decently have taken you whither I desire by some other route, rather than along a path so difficult as this, I would gladly have done so. But since it is impossible without this memoir to show the origin of the events you will read about later, I really have no alternative but to address myself to its composition.

I say, then, that the sum of thirteen hundred and forty-eight years had elapsed since the fruitful Incarnation of the Son of God, when the noble city of Florence, which for its great beauty excels all others in Italy, was visited by the deadly pestilence. Some say that it descended upon the human race through the influence of the heavenly bodies, others that it was a punishment signifying God's righteous anger at our iniquitous way of life. But whatever its cause, it had originated some years earlier in the East, where it had claimed countless lives before it unhappily spread westward, growing in strength as it swept relentlessly on from one place to the next.

In the face of its onrush, all the wisdom and ingenuity of man were unavailing. Large quantities of refuse were cleared out of the city by officials specially appointed for the purpose, all sick persons were forbidden entry, and numerous instructions were issued for safeguarding the people's health, but all to no avail. Nor were the countless petitions humbly directed to God by the pious, whether by means of formal processions or in any other guise, any less ineffectual. For in the early spring of the

---

1. Translated from the Italian by G. H. McWilliam.

2. In his introduction to the *Decameron,* Boccaccio directly addresses women as his primary audience: "So in order that I may to some extent repair the omissions of Fortune, which (as we may see in the case of the more delicate sex) was always more sparing of support wherever natural strength was more deficient, I intend to provide succour and diversion for the ladies, but only for those who are in love."

year we have mentioned, the plague began, in a terrifying and extraordinary manner, to make its disastrous effects apparent. It did not take the form it had assumed in the East, where if anyone bled from the nose it was an obvious portent of certain death. On the contrary, its earliest symptom, in men and women alike, was the appearance of certain swellings in the groin or the armpit, some of which were egg-shaped whilst others were roughly the size of the common apple. Sometimes the swellings were large, sometimes not so large, and they were referred to by the populace as *gavòccioli.*[4] From the two areas already mentioned, this deadly *gavòcciolo* would begin to spread, and within a short time it would appear at random all over the body. Later on, the symptoms of the disease changed, and many people began to find dark blotches and bruises on their arms, thighs, and other parts of the body, sometimes large and few in number, at other times tiny and closely spaced. These, to anyone unfortunate enough to contract them, were just as infallible a sign that he would die as the *gavòcciolo* had been earlier, and as indeed it still was.

Against these maladies, it seemed that all the advice of physicians and all the power of medicine were profitless and unavailing. Perhaps the nature of the illness was such that it allowed no remedy: or perhaps those people who were treating the illness (whose numbers had increased enormously because the ranks of the qualified were invaded by people, both men and women, who had never received any training in medicine), being ignorant of its causes, were not prescribing the appropriate cure. At all events, few of those who caught it ever recovered, and in most cases death occurred within three days from the appearance of the symptoms we have described, some people dying more rapidly than others, the majority without any fever or other complications.

But what made this pestilence even more severe was that whenever those suffering from it mixed with people who were still unaffected, it would rush upon these with the speed of a fire racing through dry or oily substances that happened to be placed within its reach. Nor was this the full extent of its evil, for not only did it infect healthy persons who conversed or had any dealings with the sick, making them ill or visiting an equally horrible death upon them, but it also seemed to transfer the sickness to anyone touching the clothes or other objects which had been handled or used by its victims.

It is a remarkable story that I have to relate. And were it not for the fact that I am one of many people who saw it with their own eyes, I would scarcely dare to believe it, let alone commit it to paper, even though I had heard it from a person whose word I could trust. The plague I have been describing was of so contagious a nature that very often it visibly did more than simply pass from one person to another. In other words, whenever an animal other than a human being touched anything belonging to a person who had been stricken or exterminated by the disease, it not only caught the sickness, but died from it almost at once. To all of this, as I have just said, my own eyes bore witness on more than one occasion. One day, for instance, the rags of a pauper who had died from the disease were thrown into the street, where they attracted the attention of two pigs. In their wonted fashion, the pigs first of all gave the rags a thorough mauling with their snouts after which they took them between their teeth and shook them against their cheeks. And within a short time they began to writhe as though they had been poisoned, then they both dropped dead to the ground, spreadeagled upon the rags that had brought about their undoing. ✳ ✳ ✳

---

4. Little goiters in local dialect.

In the face of so much affliction and misery, all respect for the laws of God and man had virtually broken down and been extinguished in our city. For like everybody else, those ministers and executors of the laws who were not either dead or ill were left with so few subordinates that they were unable to discharge any of their duties. Hence everyone was free to behave as he pleased. * * *

Some people, pursuing what was possibly the safer alternative, callously maintained that there was no better or more efficacious remedy against a plague than to run away from it. Swayed by this argument, and sparing no thought for anyone but themselves, large numbers of men and women abandoned their city, their homes, their relatives, their estates and their belongings, and headed for the countryside, either in Florentine territory or, better still, abroad. It was as though they imagined that the wrath of God would not unleash this plague against men for their iniquities irrespective of where they happened to be, but would only be aroused against those who found themselves within the city walls; or possibly they assumed that the whole of the population would be exterminated and that the city's last hour had come.

Of the people who held these various opinions, not all of them died. Nor, however, did they all survive. On the contrary, many of each different persuasion fell ill here, there, and everywhere, and having themselves, when they were fit and well, set an example to those who were as yet unaffected, they languished away with virtually no one to nurse them. It was not merely a question of one citizen avoiding another, and of people almost invariably neglecting their neighbours and rarely or never visiting their relatives, addressing them only from a distance; this scourge had implanted so great a terror in the hearts of men and women that brothers abandoned brothers, uncles their nephews, sisters their brothers, and in many cases wives deserted their husbands. But even worse, and almost incredible, was the fact that fathers and mothers refused to nurse and assist their own children, as though they did not belong to them. * * *

Whenever people died, their neighbours nearly always followed a single, set routine, prompted as much by their fear of being contaminated by the decaying corpse as by any charitable feelings they may have entertained towards the deceased. Either on their own, or with the assistance of bearers whenever these were to be had, they extracted the bodies of the dead from their houses and left them lying outside their front doors, where anyone going about the streets, especially in the early morning, could have observed countless numbers of them. Funeral biers would then be sent for, upon which the dead were taken away, though there were some who, for lack of biers, were carried off on plain boards. It was by no means rare for more than one of these biers to be seen with two or three bodies upon it at a time; on the contrary, many were seen to contain a husband and wife, two or three brothers and sisters, a father and son, or some other pair of close relatives. And times without number it happened that two priests would be on their way to bury someone, holding a cross before them, only to find that bearers carrying three or four additional biers would fall in behind them; so that whereas the priests had thought they had only one burial to attend to, they in fact had six or seven, and sometimes more. Even in these circumstances, however, there were no tears or candles or mourners to honour the dead; in fact, no more respect was accorded to dead people than would nowadays be shown towards dead goats. For it was quite apparent that the one thing which, in normal times, no wise man had ever learned to accept with patient resignation (even though it struck so seldom and unobtrusively), had now been brought home to the feeble-minded as well, but the scale of the calamity caused them to regard it with indifference.

Such was the multitude of corpses (of which further consignments were arriving every day and almost by the hour at each of the churches), that there was not sufficient consecrated ground for them to be buried in, especially if each was to have its own plot in accordance with long-established custom. So when all the graves were full, huge trenches were excavated in the churchyards, into which new arrivals were placed in their hundreds, stowed tier upon tier like ships' cargo, each layer of corpses being covered over with a thin layer of soil till the trench was filled to the top. * * *

What more remains to be said, except that the cruelty of heaven (and possibly, in some measure, also that of man) was so immense and so devastating that between March and July of the year in question, what with the fury of the pestilence and the fact that so many of the sick were inadequately cared for or abandoned in their hour of need because the healthy were too terrified to approach them, it is reliably thought that over a hundred thousand human lives were extinguished within the walls of the city of Florence? Yet before this lethal catastrophe fell upon the city, it is doubtful whether anyone would have guessed it contained so many inhabitants.[5]

Ah, how great a number of splendid palaces, fine houses, and noble dwellings, once filled with retainers, with lords and with ladies, were bereft of all who had lived there, down to the tiniest child! How numerous were the famous families, the vast estates, the notable fortunes, that were seen to be left without a rightful successor! How many gallant gentlemen, fair ladies, and sprightly youths, who would have been judged hale and hearty by Galen, Hippocrates and Aesculapius[6] (to say nothing of others), having breakfasted in the morning with their kinsfolk, acquaintances and friends, supped that same evening with their ancestors in the next world!

The more I reflect upon all this misery, the deeper my sense of personal sorrow; hence I shall refrain from describing those aspects which can suitably be omitted, and proceed to inform you that these were the conditions prevailing in our city, which was by now almost emptied of its inhabitants, when one Tuesday morning (or so I was told by a person whose word can be trusted) seven young ladies were to be found in the venerable church of Santa Maria Novella, which was otherwise almost deserted.[7] They had been attending divine service, and were dressed in mournful attire appropriate to the times. Each was a friend, a neighbour, or a relative of the other six, none was older than twenty-seven or younger than eighteen, and all were intelligent, gently bred, fair to look upon, graceful in bearing, and charmingly unaffected. I could tell you their actual names, but refrain from doing so for a good reason, namely that I would not want any of them to feel embarrassed, at any time in the future, on account of the ensuing stories, all of which they either listened to or narrated themselves. For nowadays, laws relating to pleasure are somewhat restrictive, whereas at that time, for the reasons indicated above, they were exceptionally lax, not only for ladies of their own age but also for much older women. Besides, I have no wish to supply envious tongues, ever ready to censure a laudable way of life, with a chance to besmirch the good name of these worthy ladies with their lewd and filthy gossip. And therefore, so that we may perceive distinctly what each of them had to say, I propose to refer to them by names which are either wholly or partially appropriate to the qualities of

---

5. The number is probably excessive. Before the plague, Florence is estimated as having had 100,000 citizens, making it one of the largest cities in Italy. As many as half of them died between 1348–1349.

6. Hippocrates and Galen were ancient Greek physicians; Aesculapius was the Roman god of medicine.

7. The church was built by the Dominicans during the 13th century on what were then the outskirts of Florence.

each. The first of them, who was also the eldest, we shall call Pampinea, the second Fiammetta, Filomena the third, and the fourth Emilia; then we shall name the fifth Lauretta, and the sixth Neifile, whilst to the last, not without reason, we shall give the name of Elissa.[8]

Without prior agreement but simply by chance, these seven ladies found themselves sitting, more or less in a circle, in one part of the church, reciting their paternosters.[9] Eventually, they left off and heaved a great many sighs, after which they began to talk among themselves on various different aspects of the times through which they were passing. But after a little while, they all fell silent except for Pampinea, who said:

"Dear ladies, you will often have heard it affirmed, as I have, that no man does injury to another in exercising his lawful rights. Every person born into this world has a natural right to sustain, preserve, and defend his own life to the best of his ability—a right so freely acknowledged that men have sometimes killed others in self-defence, and no blame whatever has attached to their actions. Now, if this is permitted by the laws, upon whose prompt application all mortal creatures depend for their well-being, how can it possibly be wrong, seeing that it harms no one, for us or anyone else to do all in our power to preserve our lives? If I pause to consider what we have been doing this morning, and what we have done on several mornings in the past, if I reflect on the nature and subject of our conversation, I realize, just as you also must realize, that each of us is apprehensive on her own account. This does not surprise me in the least, but what does greatly surprise me (seeing that each of us has the natural feelings of a woman) is that we do nothing to requite ourselves against the thing of which we are all so justly afraid.

"Here we linger for no other purpose, or so it seems to me, than to count the number of corpses being taken to burial, or to hear whether the friars of the church, very few of whom are left, chant their offices at the appropriate hours, or to exhibit the quality and quantity of our sorrows, by means of the clothes we are wearing, to all those whom we meet in this place. And if we go outside, we shall see the dead and the sick being carried hither and thither, or we shall see people, once condemned to exile by the courts for their misdeeds, careering wildly about the streets in open defiance of the law, well knowing that those appointed to enforce it are either dead or dying; or else we shall find ourselves at the mercy of the scum of our city who, having scented our blood, call themselves sextons and go prancing and bustling all over the place, singing bawdy songs that add insult to our injuries. Moreover, all we ever hear is 'So-and-so's dead' and 'So-and-so's dying'; and if there were anyone left to mourn, the whole place would be filled with sounds of wailing and weeping.

"And if we return to our homes, what happens? I know not whether your own experience is similar to mine, but my house was once full of servants, and now that there is no one left apart from my maid and myself, I am filled with foreboding and feel as if every hair of my head is standing on end. Wherever I go in the house, wherever I pause to rest, I seem to be haunted by the shades of the departed, whose faces no longer appear as I remember them but with strange and horribly twisted expressions that frighten me out of my senses.

"Accordingly, whether I am here in church or out in the streets or sitting at home, I always feel ill at ease, the more so because it seems to me that no one possessing

---

8. The names carry varying mythological weight. Filomena means "nightingale," Laureta is associated with the laurel, and Elissa was another name for Dido, queen of Carthage in Virgil's *Aeneid.*

9. Our fathers, customary prayers.

private means and a place to retreat to is left here apart from ourselves. But even if such people are still to be found, they draw no distinction, as I have frequently heard and seen for myself, between what is honest and what is dishonest; and provided only that they are prompted by their appetites, they will do whatever affords them the greatest pleasure, whether by day or by night, alone or in company. It is not only of lay people that I speak, but also of those enclosed in monasteries, who, having convinced themselves that such behaviour is suitable for them and is only unbecoming in others, have broken the rules of obedience and given themselves over to carnal pleasures, thereby thinking to escape, and have turned lascivious and dissolute.

"If this be so (and we plainly perceive that it is), what are we doing here? What are we waiting for? What are we dreaming about? Why do we lag so far behind all the rest of the citizens in providing for our safety? Do we rate ourselves lower than all other women? Or do we suppose that our own lives, unlike those of others, are bound to our bodies by such strong chains that we may ignore all those things which have the power to harm them? In that case we are deluded and mistaken. We have only to recall the names and the condition of the young men and women who have fallen victim to this cruel pestilence, in order to realize clearly the foolishness of such notions.

"And so, lest by pretending to be above such things or by becoming complacent we should succumb to that which we might possibly avoid if we so desired, I would think it an excellent idea (though I do not know whether you would agree with me) for us all to get away from this city, just as many others have done before us, and as indeed they are doing still. We could go and stay together on one of our various country estates, shunning at all costs the lewd practices of our fellow citizens and feasting and merrymaking as best we may without in any way overstepping the bounds of what is reasonable.

"There we shall hear the birds singing, we shall see fresh green hills and plains, fields of corn undulating like the sea, and trees of at least a thousand different species; and we shall have a clearer view of the heavens, which, troubled though they are, do not however deny us their eternal beauties, so much more fair to look upon than the desolate walls of our city. Moreover the country air is much more refreshing, the necessities of life in such a time as this are more abundant, and there are fewer obstacles to contend with. For although the farmworkers are dying there in the same way as the townspeople here in Florence, the spectacle is less harrowing inasmuch as the houses and people are more widely scattered. Besides, unless I am mistaken we shall not be abandoning anyone by going away from here; on the contrary, we may fairly claim that we are the ones who have been abandoned, for our kinsfolk are either dead or fled, and have left us to fend for ourselves in the midst of all this affliction, as though disowning us completely.

"Hence no one can reproach us for taking the course I have advocated, whereas if we do nothing we shall inevitably be confronted with distress and mourning, and possibly forfeit our lives into the bargain. Let us therefore do as I suggest, taking our maidservants with us and seeing to the dispatch of all the things we shall need. We can move from place to place, spending one day here and another there, pursuing whatever pleasures and entertainments the present times will afford. In this way of life we shall continue until such time as we discover (provided we are spared from early death) the end decreed by Heaven for these terrible events. You must remember, after all, that it is no more unseemly for us to go away and thus preserve our own honour than it is for most other women to remain here and forfeit theirs."

* * *

[The Women, Along with Three Young Men Arrive in Fiesole.][1]

Scarcely had they travelled two miles from Florence before they reached the place at which they had agreed to stay.

The spot in question was some distance away from any road, on a small hill that was agreeable to behold for its abundance of shrubs and trees, all bedecked in green leaves. Perched on its summit was a palace, built round a fine, spacious courtyard, and containing loggias, halls, and sleeping apartments, which were not only excellently proportioned but richly embellished with paintings depicting scenes of gaiety. Delectable gardens and meadows lay all around, and there were wells of cool, refreshing water. The cellars were stocked with precious wines, more suited to the palates of connoisseurs than to sedate and respectable ladies. And on their arrival the company discovered, to their no small pleasure, that the place had been cleaned from top to bottom, the beds in the rooms were made up, the whole house was adorned with seasonable flowers of every description, and the floors had been carpeted with rushes.

Soon after reaching the palace, they all sat down, and Dioneo, a youth of matchless charm and readiness of wit, said:

"It is not our foresight, ladies, but rather your own good sense, that has led us to this spot. I know not what you intend to do with your troubles; my own I left inside the city gates when I departed thence a short while ago in your company. Hence you may either prepare to join with me in as much laughter, song and merriment as your sense of decorum will allow, or else you may give me leave to go back for my troubles and live in the afflicted city."

Pampinea, as though she too had driven away all her troubles, answered him in the same carefree vein.

"There is much sense in what you say, Dioneo," she replied. "A merry life should be our aim, since it was for no other reason that we were prompted to run away from the sorrows of the city. However, nothing will last for very long unless it possesses a definite form. And since it was I who led the discussions from which this fair company has come into being, I have given some thought to the continuance of our happiness, and consider it necessary for us to choose a leader, drawn from our own ranks, whom we would honour and obey as our superior, and whose sole concern will be that of devising the means whereby we may pass our time agreeably. But so that none of us will complain that he or she has had no opportunity to experience the burden of responsibility and the pleasure of command associated with sovereign power, I propose that the burden and the honour should be assigned to each of us in turn for a single day. It will be for all of us to decide who is to be our first ruler, after which it will be up to each ruler, when the hour of vespers approaches, to elect his or her successor from among the ladies and gentlemen present. The person chosen to govern will be at liberty to make whatever arrangements he likes for the period covered by his rule, and to prescribe the place and the manner in which we are to live."[2]

* * *

1. In the intervening pages, the seven women have met up with three men, who have joined them in the church: Pamphilo, Filostrato, and Dioneo (who is described as "more attractive and wittier than either of the other young men"). They agree that they can live virtuously together, and they leave the plague-ridden city together for Fiesole, a hill-town northeast of Florence.

2. Pampinea is elected queen for the first day, and following a siesta, suggests to her companions that they proceed to spend "this hotter part of the day" in telling stories, "an activity that may afford some amusement to the narrator and to the company at large. By the time each one of you has narrated a little tale of his own or her own, the sun will be setting, the heat will have abated and we shall be able to go and amuse ourselves wherever you choose." The company agrees to her suggestion, and she decrees that on the first day, "each of us should be free to speak upon whatever topic he prefers."

Third Story: [The Three Rings]

Melchizedek the Jew, with a story about three rings, avoids a most dangerous trap laid for him by Saladin.

Neifile's story was well received by all the company, and when she fell silent, Filomena began at the queen's behest to address them as follows:

The story told by Neifile reminds me of the parlous state in which a Jew once found himself. Now that we have heard such fine things said concerning God and the truth of our religion,[1] it will not seem inappropriate to descend at this juncture to the deeds and adventures of men. So I shall tell you a story which, when you have heard it, will possibly make you more cautious in answering questions addressed to you. It is a fact, my sweet companions, that just as folly often destroys men's happiness and casts them into deepest misery, so prudence extricates the wise from dreadful perils and guides them firmly to safety. So clearly may we perceive that folly leads men from contentment to misery, that we shall not even bother for the present to consider the matter further, since countless examples spring readily to mind. But that prudence may bring its reward, I shall, as I have promised, prove to you briefly by means of the following little tale:

Saladin, whose worth was so great that it raised him from humble beginnings to the sultanate of Egypt and brought him many victories over Saracen and Christian kings,[2] had expended the whole of his treasure in various wars and extraordinary acts of munificence, when a certain situation arose for which he required a vast sum of money. Not being able to see any way of obtaining what he needed at such short notice, he happened to recall a rich Jew, Melchizedek by name, who ran a money-lending business in Alexandria,[3] and would certainly, he thought, have enough for his purposes, if only he could be persuaded to part with it. But this Melchizedek was such a miserly fellow that he would never hand it over of his own free will, and the Sultan was not prepared to take it away from him by force. However, as his need became more pressing, having racked his brains to discover some way of compelling the Jew to assist him, he resolved to use force in the guise of reason. So he sent for the Jew, gave him a cordial reception, invited him to sit down beside him, and said:

"O man of excellent worth, many men have told me of your great wisdom and your superior knowledge of the ways of God. Hence I would be glad if you would tell me which of the three laws, whether the Jewish, the Saracen, or the Christian, you deem to be truly authentic."

The Jew, who was indeed a wise man, realized all too well that Saladin was aiming to trip him up with the intention of picking a quarrel with him, and that if he were to praise any of the three more than the others, the Sultan would achieve his object. He therefore had need of a reply that would save him from falling into the trap, and having sharpened his wits, in no time at all he was ready with his answer.

"My lord," he said, "your question is a very good one, and in order to explain my views on the subject, I must ask you to listen to the following little story:

---

1. The second story of the first day was about a Jew called Abraham who travels from Paris to Rome to see for himself how depraved the church hierarchy is. Yet he decides to convert to Christianity, seeing how the religion has "grown in popularity and become more splendid and illustrious" despite the church's corruption: "I can only conclude that, being a more holy and genuine religion than any of the others, it deservedly has the Holy Ghost as its foundation and support."

2. Salah-ed-din was sultan of Syria and Egypt in the 12th century. Under his rule the Muslims regained the city of Jerusalem from the Christians in 1187.

3. In Egypt.

"Unless I am mistaken, I recall having frequently heard that there was once a great and wealthy man who, apart from the other fine jewels contained in his treasury, possessed a most precious and beautiful ring. Because of its value and beauty, he wanted to do it the honour of leaving it in perpetuity to his descendants, and so he announced that he would bequeath the ring to one of his sons, and that whichever of them should be found to have it in his keeping, this man was to be looked upon as his heir, and the others were to honour and respect him as the head of the family.

"The man to whom he left the ring, having made a similar provision regarding his own descendants, followed the example set by his predecessor. To cut a long story short, the ring was handed down through many generations till it finally came to rest in the hands of a man who had three most splendid and virtuous sons who were very obedient to their father, and he loved all three of them equally. Each of the three young men, being aware of the tradition concerning the ring, was eager to take precedence over the others, and they all did their utmost to persuade the father, who was now an old man, to leave them the ring when he died.

"The good man, who loved all three and was unable to decide which of them should inherit the ring, resolved, having promised it to each, to try and please them all. So he secretly commissioned a master-craftsman to make two more rings, which were so like the first that even the man who had made them could barely distinguish them from the original. And when he was dying, he took each of his sons aside in turn, and gave one ring to each.

"After their father's death, they all desired to succeed to his title and estate, and each man denied the claims of the others, producing his ring to prove his case. But finding that the rings were so alike that it was impossible to tell them apart, the question of which of the sons was the true and rightful heir remained in abeyance, and has never been settled.

"And I say to you, my lord, that the same applies to the three laws which God the Father granted to His three peoples, and which formed the subject of your inquiry. Each of them considers itself the legitimate heir to His estate, each believes it possesses His one true law and observes His commandments. But as with the rings, the question as to which of them is right remains in abeyance."

Saladin perceived that the fellow had ingeniously side-stepped the trap he had set before him, and he therefore decided to make a clean breast of his needs, and see if the Jew would come to his assistance. This he did, freely admitting what he had intended to do, but for the fact that the Jew had answered him so discreetly.

Melchizedek gladly provided the Sultan with the money he required. The Sultan later paid him back in full, in addition to which he showered magnificent gifts upon him, made him his lifelong friend, and maintained him at his court in a state of importance and honour.

from Third Day[1]

Tenth Story: [Locking the Devil Up in Hell]

Alibech becomes a recluse, and after being taught by the monk, Rustico, to put the devil back in Hell, she is eventually taken away to become the wife of Neerbal.

---

1. The theme for the third day, under the rule of Neifile, is about people who achieved something they desired, or recovered something they lost. Dioneo, who by prior agreement always tells the final tale of each day, is also exempt from the rules regarding the theme.

Dioneo had been following the queen's story closely, and on perceiving that it was finished, knowing that he was the only speaker left, he smiled and began without waiting to be bidden:

Gracious ladies, you have possibly never heard how the devil is put back into Hell, and hence, without unduly straying from the theme of your discussions for today, I should like to tell you about it. By learning how it is done, there may yet be time perhaps for you to save our souls from perdition, and you will also discover that, even though Love is more inclined to take up his abode in a gay palace and a dainty bedchamber than in a wretched hovel, there is no denying that he sometimes makes his powers felt among pathless woods, on rugged mountains, and in desert caves; nor is this surprising, since all living things are subject to his sway.

Now, to come to the point, there once lived in the town of Gafsa, in Barbary,[2] a very rich man who had numerous children, among them a lovely and graceful young daughter called Alibech. She was not herself a Christian, but there were many Christians in the town, and one day, having on occasion heard them extol the Christian faith and the service of God, she asked one of them for his opinion on the best and easiest way for a person to "serve God," as they put it. He answered her by saying that the ones who served God best were those who put the greatest distance between themselves and earthly goods, as happened in the case of people who had gone to live in the remoter parts of the Sahara.[3]

She said no more about it to anyone, but next morning, being a very simple-natured creature of fourteen or thereabouts, Alibech set out all alone, in secret, and made her way towards the desert, prompted by nothing more logical than a strong adolescent impulse. A few days later, exhausted from fatigue and hunger, she arrived in the heart of the wilderness, where, catching sight of a small hut in the distance, she stumbled towards it, and in the doorway she found a holy man, who was astonished to see her in those parts and asked her what she was doing there. She told him that she had been inspired by God, and that she was trying, not only to serve Him, but also to find someone who could teach her how she should go about it.

On observing how young and exceedingly pretty she was, the good man was afraid to take her under his wing lest the devil should catch him unawares. So he praised her for her good intentions, and having given her a quantity of herb-roots, wild apples and dates to eat, and some water to drink, he said to her:

"My daughter, not very far from here there is a holy man who is much more capable than I of teaching you what you want to know. Go along to him." And he sent her upon her way.

When she came to this second man, she was told precisely the same thing, and so she went on until she arrived at the cell of a young hermit, a very devout and kindly fellow called Rustico, to whom she put the same inquiry as she had addressed to the others. Being anxious to prove to himself that he possessed a will of iron, he did not, like the others, send her away or direct her elsewhere, but kept her with him in his cell, in a corner of which, when night descended, he prepared a makeshift bed out of palm-leaves, upon which he invited her to lie down and rest.

Once he had taken this step, very little time elapsed before temptation went to war against his willpower, and after the first few assaults, finding himself outmanoeuvred on all fronts, he laid down his arms and surrendered. Casting aside pious thoughts, prayers, and penitential exercises, he began to concentrate his mental faculties upon the youth and beauty of the girl, and to devise suitable ways and means for approaching her in such a fashion that she should not think it lewd of him to make the sort of proposal he had in mind. By putting certain questions to her, he soon discovered that she had never been intimate with the opposite sex and was every bit as innocent as she seemed; and he therefore thought of a possible way to persuade her, with the pretext of serving God, to gratify his desires. He began by delivering a long speech in which he showed her how powerful an enemy the devil was to the Lord God, and followed this up by impressing upon her that of all the ways of serving God, the one that He most appreciated consisted in putting the devil back in Hell, to which the Almighty had consigned him in the first place.

The girl asked him how this was done, and Rustico replied:

"You will soon find out, but just do whatever you see me doing for the present." And so saying, he began to divest himself of the few clothes he was wearing, leaving himself completely naked. The girl followed his example, and he sank to his knees as though he were about to pray, getting her to kneel directly opposite.

In this posture, the girl's beauty was displayed to Rustico in all its glory, and his longings blazed more fiercely than ever, bringing about the resurrection of the flesh.[4] Alibech stared at this in amazement, and said:

"Rustico, what is that thing I see sticking out in front of you, which I do not possess?"

"Oh, my daughter," said Rustico, "this is the devil I was telling you about. Do you see what he's doing? He's hurting me so much that I can hardly endure it."

"Oh, praise be to God," said the girl, "I can see that I am better off than you are, for I have no such devil to contend with."

"You're right there," said Rustico. "But you have something else instead, that I haven't."

"Oh?" said Alibech. "And what's that?"

"You have Hell," said Rustico. "And I honestly believe that God has sent you here for the salvation of my soul, because if this devil continues to plague the life out of me, and if you are prepared to take sufficient pity upon me to let me put him back into Hell, you will be giving me marvellous relief, as well as rendering incalculable service and pleasure to God, which is what you say you came here for to begin with."

"Oh, Father," replied the girl in all innocence, "if I really do have a Hell, let's do as you suggest just as soon as you are ready."

"God bless you, my daughter," said Rustico. "Let us go and put him back and then perhaps he'll leave me alone."

At which point he conveyed the girl to one of their beds, where he instructed her in the art of incarcerating that accursed fiend.

Never having put a single devil into Hell before, the girl found the first experience a little painful, and she said to Rustico:

"This devil must certainly be a bad lot, Father, and a true enemy of God, for as well as plaguing mankind, he even hurts Hell when he's driven back inside it."

---

4. A punning allusion to the Last Judgment.

"Daughter," said Rustico, "it will not always be like that." And in order to ensure that it wouldn't, before moving from the bed they put him back half a dozen times, curbing his arrogance to such good effect that he was positively glad to keep still for the rest of the day.

During the next few days, however, the devil's pride frequently reared its head again, and the girl, ever ready to obey the call to duty and bring him under control, happened to develop a taste for the sport, and began saying to Rustico:

"I can certainly see what those worthy men in Gafsa meant when they said that serving God was so agreeable. I don't honestly recall ever having done anything that gave me so much pleasure and satisfaction as I get from putting the devil back in Hell. To my way of thinking, anyone who devotes his energies to anything but the service of God is a complete blockhead."

She thus developed the habit of going to Rustico at frequent intervals, and saying to him:

"Father, I came here to serve God, not to idle away my time. Let's go and put the devil back in Hell."

And sometimes, in the middle of their labours, she would say:

"What puzzles me, Rustico, is that the devil should ever want to escape from Hell. Because if he liked being there as much as Hell enjoys receiving him and keeping him inside, he would never go away at all."

By inviting Rustico to play the game too often, continually urging him on in the service of God, the girl took so much stuffing out of him that he eventually began to turn cold where another man would have been bathed in sweat. So he told her that the devil should only be punished and put back in Hell when he reared his head with pride, adding that by the grace of Heaven, they had tamed him so effectively that he was pleading with God to be left in peace. In this way, he managed to keep the girl quiet for a while, but one day, having begun to notice that Rustico was no longer asking for the devil to be put back in Hell, she said:

"Look here, Rustico. Even though your devil has been punished and pesters you no longer, my Hell simply refuses to leave me alone. Now that I have helped you with my Hell to subdue the pride of your devil, the least you can do is to get your devil to help me tame the fury of my Hell."

Rustico, who was living on a diet of herb-roots and water, was quite incapable of supplying her requirements, and told her that the taming of her Hell would require an awful lot of devils, but promised to do what he could. Sometimes, therefore, he responded to the call, but this happened so infrequently that it was rather like chucking a bean into the mouth of a lion, with the result that the girl, who felt that she was not serving God as diligently as she would have liked, was found complaining more often than not.

But at the height of this dispute between Alibech's Hell and Rustico's devil, brought about by a surplus of desire on the one hand and a shortage of power on the other, a fire broke out in Gafsa, and Alibech's father was burnt to death in his own house along with all his children and every other member of his household, so that Alibech inherited the whole of his property. Because of this a young man called Neerbal who had spent the whole of his substance in sumptuous living, having heard that she was still alive, set out to look for her, and before the authorities were able to appropriate her late father's fortune on the grounds that there was no heir, he succeeded in tracing her whereabouts. To the great relief of Rustico, but against her own wishes, he took her back to Gafsa and married her, thus inheriting a half-share in her father's enormous fortune.

Before Neerbal had actually slept with her, she was questioned by the women of Gafsa about how she had served God in the desert, and she replied that she had served Him by putting the devil back in Hell, and that Neerbal had committed a terrible sin by stopping her from performing so worthy a service.

"How do you put the devil back in Hell?" asked the women.

Partly in words and partly through gestures, the girl showed them how it was done, whereupon the women laughed so much that they are laughing yet; and they said:

"Don't let it worry you, my dear. People do the job every bit as well here in Gafsa, and Neerbal will give you plenty of help in serving the Lord."

The story was repeated throughout the town, being passed from one woman to the next, and they coined a proverbial saying there to the effect that the most agreeable way of serving God was to put the devil back in Hell. The dictum later crossed the sea to Italy, where it survives to this day.

And so, young ladies, if you stand in need of God's grace, see that you learn to put the devil back in Hell, for it is greatly to His liking and pleasurable to the parties concerned, and a great deal of good can arise and flow in the process.

* * *

So aptly and cleverly worded did Dioneo's tale appear to the virtuous ladies, that they shook with mirth a thousand times or more. And when he had brought it to a close, the queen, acknowledging the end of her sovereignty, removed the laurel from her head and placed it very gracefully on Filostrato's, saying:

"Now we shall discover whether the wolf can fare any better at leading the sheep than the sheep have fared in leading the wolves."[5]

On hearing this, Filostrato laughed and said: "Had you listened to me, the wolves would have taught the sheep by now to put the devil back in Hell, no less skilfully than Rustico taught Alibech. But you have not exactly been behaving like sheep, and therefore you must not describe us as wolves. However, you have placed the kingdom in my hands, and I shall govern it as well as I am able." * * *

Seventh Day[1]

Fourth Story: [The Woman Who Locked Her Husband Out]

[Thus Lauretta began her tale:]

O Love, how manifold and mighty are your powers! How wise your counsels, how keen your insights! What philosopher, what artist could ever have conjured up all the arguments, all the subterfuges, all the explanations that you offer spontaneously to those who nail their colours to your mast? Every other doctrine is assuredly behind-hand in comparison with yours, as may clearly be seen from the cases already brought to our notice. And to these, fond ladies, I shall now add yet another, by telling you of the expedient adopted by a woman of no great intelligence, who to my way of think-ing could only have been motivated by Love.

---

5. Filostrato will be the first man to lead the day's tale-telling.

1. Tales of the seventh day, over which Dioneo rules, are to be about "tricks which, either in the cause of love or for mo-tives of self-preservation, women have played upon their husbands, irrespective of whether or not they were found out."

In the city of Arezzo,[2] then, there once lived a man of means, Tofano[3] by name, who, having taken to wife a woman of very great beauty, called Monna Ghita, promptly grew jealous of her without any reason. On perceiving how jealous he was, the lady took offence and repeatedly asked him to explain the reason, but since he could only reply in vague and illogical terms, she resolved to make him suffer in good earnest from the ill which hitherto he had feared without cause.

Having observed that a certain young man, a very agreeable sort of fellow to her way of thinking, was casting amorous glances in her direction, she secretly began to cultivate his acquaintance. And when she and the young man had carried the affair to the point where it only remained to translate words into deeds, she once again took the initiative and devised a way of doing it. She had already discovered that one of her husband's bad habits was a fondness for drink, and so she began not only to commend him for it, but to encourage him deliberately whenever she had the chance. With a little practice, she quickly acquired the knack of persuading him to drink himself into a stupor, almost as often as she chose, and once she saw that he was blind drunk, she put him to bed and forgathered with her lover. This soon became a regular habit of theirs, and they met together in perfect safety. Indeed, the lady came to rely so completely on the fellow's talent for drinking himself unconscious that she made bold, not only to admit her lover to the premises, but on occasion to go and spend a goodly part of the night with him at his own house, which was no great distance away.

The amorous lady had been doing this for quite some time when her unfortunate husband happened to notice that although she encouraged him to drink, she herself never drank at all, which made him suspect (as was indeed the case) that his wife was making him drunk so that she could do as she pleased when he was asleep. In order to prove whether this was so, he returned home one evening, having refrained from drinking for the whole day, and pretended to be as drunk as a lord, scarcely able to speak or stand on his feet. Being taken in by all this, and concluding that he would sleep like a log without imbibing any more liquor, his wife quickly put him to bed, then left the house and made her way, as on previous occasions, to the house of her lover, where she stayed for half the night.

Hearing no sound from his wife, Tofano got up, went and bolted the door from the inside, and stationed himself at the window so that he would see her coming back and let her know that he had tumbled to her mischief; and there he remained until she returned. Great indeed was the woman's distress when she came home to find that she was locked out, and she began to apply all her strength in an effort to force the door open.

Tofano put up with this for a while, then he said:

"You're wasting your energies, woman. You can't possibly get in. Go back to wherever it is that you've been until this hour of the night, and rest assured that you won't return to this house till I've made an example of you in front of your kinsfolk and neighbours."

Then his wife began to plead with him for the love of God to let her in, saying that she had not been doing anything wrong, as he supposed, but simply keeping vigil with a neighbour of hers, who could neither sleep the whole night because it was too long, nor keep vigil in the house by herself.

Her pleas were totally unavailing, for the silly ass was clearly determined that all the Aretines should learn about his dishonour, of which none of them had so far heard anything. And when she saw that it was no use pleading with him, the woman resorted to threats, and said:

"If you don't let me in, I shall make you the sorriest man on earth."

To which Tofano replied:

"And how are you going to do that?"

The lady had all her wits about her, for Love was her counsellor, and she replied:

"Rather than face the dishonour which in spite of my innocence you threaten me with, I shall hurl myself into this well, and when they find me dead inside it, they will all think that it was you who threw me into it when you were drunk; and so either you will have to run away, lose everything you possess, and live in exile, or you will have your head chopped off for murdering your wife, which in effect is what you will have done."

But having made up his stupid mind, Tofano was not affected in the slightest by these words, and so his wife said:

"Now look here, I won't let you torment me any longer; may God forgive you, I'll leave my distaff here, and you can put it back where it belongs."

The night was so dark that you could scarcely see your hand in front of your face, and having uttered these words, the woman groped her way towards the well, picked up an enormous stone that was lying beside it, and with a cry of "God forgive me!" she dropped it into the depths. The stone struck the water with a tremendous thump, and when Tofano heard this he was firmly convinced that she had thrown herself in. So he seized the pail and its rope, rushed head-long from the house, and ran to the well to assist her. His wife was lying in wait near the front door, and as soon as she saw him running to the well, she stepped inside the house, bolted the door, and went to the window, where she stood and shouted:

"You should water down your wine when you're drinking it, and not in the middle of the night."

When he heard her voice, Tofano saw that he had been outwitted and made his way back to the house. And on finding that he couldn't open the door, he ordered her to let him in.

Whereas previously she had addressed him in little more than a whisper, his wife now began to shout almost at the top of her voice, saying:

"By the cross of God, you loathsome sot, you're not going to come in here to-night. I will not tolerate this conduct of yours any longer. It's time I showed people the sort of man you are and the hours you keep."

Being very angry, Tofano too began to shout, pouring out a stream of abuse, so that the neighbours, men and women alike, hearing all this racket, got up out of bed and appeared at their windows, demanding to know what was going on.

The woman's eyes filled with tears, and she said: "It's this villain of a man, who returns home drunk of an evening, or else he falls asleep in some tavern or other and then comes back at this hour. I've put up with it for God knows how long and remonstrated with him until I was blue in the face. But I can't put up with it any longer, and so I've decided to take him down a peg or two by locking him out, to see whether he will mend his ways."

Tofano on the other hand, like the fool that he was, explained precisely what had happened, and came out with a whole lot of threats and abuse, whereupon his wife spoke up again, saying to the neighbours:

"You see the sort of man he is! What would you say if I were in the street and he was in the house, instead of the other way round? In God's faith I've no doubt you would believe what he was saying. So you can see what a crafty fellow he is. He accuses me of doing the very thing that he appears to have done himself. He thought he could frighten me by dropping something or other down the well; but I wish to God that he really had thrown himself in, and drowned himself at the same time, so that all the wine he's been drinking would have been well and truly diluted."

The neighbours, men and women alike, all began to scold Tofano, putting the blame on him alone and reviling him for slandering his poor wife; and in brief, they created such an uproar that it eventually reached the ears of the woman's kinsfolk.

Her kinsfolk hurried to the scene, and having listened to the accounts of several of the neighbours, they took hold of Tofano and hammered him till he was black and blue. They then went into the house, collected all the woman's belongings, and took her back with them, threatening Tofano with worse to follow.

Seeing what a sorry plight he had landed himself in on account of his jealousy, Tofano, since he was really very fond of his wife, persuaded certain friends of his to intercede on his behalf with the lady's kinsfolk, with whom he succeeded in making his peace and arranging for her to come back to him. And not only did he promise her that he would never be jealous again, but he gave her permission to amuse herself to her heart's content, provided she was sensible enough not to let him catch her out. So, like the stupid peasant, he first was mad and then was pleasant. Long live love, therefore, and a plague on all skinflints!

Tenth Day[1]

Tenth Story: [The Patient Griselda]

The Marquis of Saluzzo, obliged by the entreaties of his subjects to take a wife, follows his personal whims and marries the daughter of a peasant. She bears him two children, and he gives her the impression that he has put them to death. Later on, pretending that she has incurred his displeasure and that he has remarried, he arranges for his own daughter to return home and passes her off as his bride, having meanwhile turned his wife out of doors in no more than the shift she is wearing. But on finding that she endures it all with patience, he cherishes her all the more deeply, brings her back to his house, shows her their children, who have now grown up, and honours her as the Marchioness, causing others to honour her likewise.

Sweet and gentle ladies, [said Dioneo] this day has been devoted, so far as I can see, to the doings of kings and sultans and people of that sort; and therefore, so as not to place too great a distance between us, I want to tell you of a marquis, whose actions, even though things turned out well for him in the end, were remarkable not so much for their munificence as for their senseless brutality.[2] Nor do I advise anyone to follow his example, for it was a great pity that the fellow should have drawn any profit from his conduct.

1. For the final day, over which Panfilo presides, "the discussion turns upon those who have performed liberal or munificent deeds, whether in the cause of love or otherwise." As always, Dioneo goes last and is exempt from the thematic rule.

2. In Italian, "matta bestialitade" (mad bestiality), a phrase which echoes Dante's description of one of the "three dispositions / that strike at Heaven's will: incontinence / and malice and mad bestiality" (*Inferno* XI: 81–2); the phrase covers those found in the Seventh Circle, the violent against their neighbours, themselves, nature, and God.

A very long time ago, there succeeded to the marquisate of Saluzzo[3] a young man called Gualtieri, who, having neither wife nor children, spent the whole of his time hunting and hawking, and never even thought about marrying or raising a family, which says a great deal for his intelligence. His followers, however, disapproved of this, and repeatedly begged him to marry so that he should not be left without an heir nor they without a lord. Moreover, they offered to find him a wife whose parentage would be such as to strengthen their expectations and who would make him exceedingly happy.

So Gualtieri answered them as follows:

"My friends, you are pressing me to do something that I had always set my mind firmly against, seeing how difficult it is to find a person who will easily adapt to one's own way of living, how many thousands there are who will do precisely the opposite, and what a miserable life is in store for the man who stumbles upon a woman ill-suited to his own temperament. Moreover it is foolish of you to believe that you can judge the character of daughters from the ways of their fathers and mothers, hence claiming to provide me with a wife who will please me. For I cannot see how you are to know the fathers, or to discover the secrets of the mothers; and even if this were possible, daughters are very often different from either of their parents. Since, however, you are so determined to bind me in chains of this sort, I am ready to do as you ask; but so that I have only myself to blame if it should turn out badly, I must insist on marrying a wife of my own choosing. And I hereby declare that no matter who she may be, if you fail to honour her as your lady you will learn to your great cost how serious a matter it is for you to have urged me to marry against my will."

To this the gentlemen replied that if only he would bring himself to take a wife, they would be satisfied.

Now, for some little time, Gualtieri had been casting an appreciative eye on the manners of a poor girl from a neighbouring village, and thinking her very beautiful, he considered that a life with her would have much to commend it. So without looking further afield, he resolved to marry the girl; and having summoned her father, who was very poor indeed, he arranged with him that he should take her as his wife.

This done, Gualtieri brought together all his friends from the various parts of his domain, and said to them:

"My friends, since you still persist in wanting me to take a wife, I am prepared to do it, not because I have any desire to marry, but rather in order to gratify your wishes. You will recall the promise you gave me, that no matter whom I should choose, you would rest content and honour her as your lady. The time has now come when I want you to keep that promise, and for me to honour the promise I gave to you. I have found a girl after my own heart, in this very district, and a few days hence I intend to marry her and convey her to my house. See to it, therefore, that the wedding-feast lacks nothing in splendour, and consider how you may honourably receive her, so that all of us may call ourselves contented—I with you for keeping your promise, and you with me for keeping mine."

As of one voice, the good folk joyously gave him their blessing, and said that whoever she happened to be, they would accept her as their lady and honour her as such in all respects. Then they all prepared to celebrate the wedding in a suitably grand and sumptuous manner, and Gualtieri did the same. A rich and splendid nuptial feast was

3. Saluzzo is in northwestern Italy, in the region of Piedmont.

arranged, to which he invited many of his friends, his kinsfolk, great nobles and other people of the locality; moreover he caused a quantity of fine, rich robes to be tailored to fit a girl whose figure appeared to match that of the young woman he intended to marry; and lastly he laid in a number of rings and ornamental belts, along with a precious and beautiful crown, and everything else that a bride could possibly need.

Early on the morning of the day he had fixed for the nuptials, Gualtieri, his preparations now complete, mounted his horse together with all the people who had come to do him honour, and said:

"Gentlemen, it is time for us to go and fetch the bride."

He then set forth with the whole of the company in train, and eventually they came to the village and made their way to the house of the girl's father, where they met her as she was returning with water from the fountain, making great haste so that she could go with other women to see Gualtieri's bride arriving. As soon as Gualtieri caught sight of her, he called to her by her name, which was Griselda, and asked her where her father was, to which she blushingly replied:

"My lord, he is at home."

So Gualtieri dismounted, and having ordered everyone to wait for him outside, he went alone into the humble dwelling, where he found the girl's father, whose name was Giannùcole,[4] and said to him:

"I have come to marry Griselda, but first I want to ask her certain questions in your presence." He then asked her whether, if he were to marry her, she would always try to please him and never be upset by anything he said or did, whether she would obey him, and many other questions of this sort, to all of which she answered that she would.

Whereupon Gualtieri, having taken her by the hand, led her out of the house, and in the presence of his whole company and of all the other people there he caused her to be stripped naked. Then he called for the clothes and shoes which he had had specially made, and quickly got her to put them on, after which he caused a crown to be placed upon the dishevelled hair of her head. And just as everyone was wondering what this might signify, he said:

"Gentlemen, this is the woman I intend to marry, provided she will have me as her husband." Then, turning to Griselda, who was so embarrassed that she hardly knew where to look, he said: "Griselda, will you have me as your wedded husband?"

To which she replied:

"I will, my lord."

"And I will have you as my wedded wife," said Gualtieri, and he married her then and there before all the people present. He then helped her mount a palfrey, and led her back, honourably attended, to his house, where the nuptials were as splendid and as sumptuous, and the rejoicing as unrestrained, as if he had married the King of France's daughter.

Along with her new clothes, the young bride appeared to take on a new lease of life, and she seemed a different woman entirely. She was endowed, as we have said, with a fine figure and beautiful features, and lovely as she already was, she now acquired so confident, graceful and decorous a manner that she could have been taken for the daughter, not of the shepherd Giannùcole, but of some great nobleman, and consequently everyone who had known her before her marriage was filled with astonishment. But apart from this, she was so obedient to her husband, and so compliant to his wishes, that he thought himself the happiest and most contented man on earth. At the same time she was so gracious and benign towards her husband's subjects, that each and every one of them was glad to honour her, and accorded her his unselfish devotion, praying for her happiness, prosperity, and greater glory. And whereas they had been wont to say that Gualtieri had shown some lack of discretion in taking this woman as his wife, they now regarded him as the wisest and most discerning man on earth. For no one apart from Gualtieri could ever have perceived the noble qualities that lay concealed beneath her ragged and rustic attire.

In short, she comported herself in such a manner that she quickly earned widespread acclaim for her virtuous deeds and excellent character not only in her husband's domain but also in the world at large; and those who had formerly censured Gualtieri for choosing to marry her were now compelled to reverse their opinion.

Not long after she had gone to live with Gualtieri she conceived a child, and in the fullness of time, to her husband's enormous joy, she bore him a daughter. But shortly thereafter Gualtieri was seized with the strange desire to test Griselda's patience, by subjecting her to constant provocation and making her life unbearable.

At first he lashed her with his tongue, feigning to be angry and claiming that his subjects were thoroughly disgruntled with her on account of her lowly condition, especially now that they saw her bearing children; and he said they were greatly distressed about this infant daughter of theirs, of whom they did nothing but grumble.

The lady betrayed no sign of bitterness on hearing these words, and without changing her expression she said to him:

"My lord, deal with me as you think best for your own good name and peace of mind, for I shall rest content whatever you decide, knowing myself to be their inferior and that I was unworthy of the honour which you so generously bestowed upon me."

This reply was much to Gualtieri's liking, for it showed him that she had not been puffed with pride by any honour that he or others had paid her.

A little while later, having told his wife in general terms that his subjects could not abide the daughter she had borne him, he gave certain instructions to one of his attendants, whom he sent to Griselda. The man looked very sorrowful, and said:

"My lady, if I do not wish to die, I must do as my lord commands me. He has ordered me to take this daughter of yours, and to..." And his voice trailed off into silence.

On hearing these words and perceiving the man's expression, Griselda, recalling what she had been told, concluded that he had been instructed to murder her child. So she quickly picked it up from its cradle, kissed it, gave it her blessing, and albeit she felt that her heart was about to break, placed the child in the arms of the servant without any trace of emotion, saying:

"There: do exactly as your lord, who is my lord too, has instructed you. But do not leave her to be devoured by the beasts and the birds, unless that is what he has ordered you to do."

The servant took away the little girl and reported Griselda's words to Gualtieri, who, marvelling at her constancy, sent him with the child to a kinswoman of his in Bologna, requesting her to rear and educate her carefully, but without ever making it known whose daughter she was.

Then it came about that his wife once more became pregnant, and in due course she gave birth to a son, which pleased Gualtieri enormously. But not being content with the mischief he had done already, he abused her more viciously than ever, and one day he glowered at her angrily and said:

"Woman, from the day you produced this infant son, the people have made my life a complete misery, so bitterly do they resent the thought of a grandson of Giannùcole succeeding me as their lord. So unless I want to be deposed, I'm afraid I shall be forced to do as I did before, and eventually to leave you and marry someone else."

His wife listened patiently, and all she replied was:

"My lord, look to your own comfort, see that you fulfil your wishes, and spare no thought for me, since nothing brings me pleasure unless it pleases you also."

Before many days had elapsed, Gualtieri sent for his son in the same way that he had sent for his daughter, and having likewise pretended to have had the child put to death, he sent him, like the little girl, to Bologna. To all of this his wife reacted no differently, either in her speech or in her looks, than she had on the previous occasion, much to the astonishment of Gualtieri, who told himself that no other woman could have remained so impassive. But for the fact that he had observed her doting upon the children for as long as he allowed her to do so, he would have assumed that she was glad to be rid of them, whereas he knew that she was too judicious to behave in any other way.

His subjects, thinking he had caused the children to be murdered, roundly condemned him and judged him a cruel tyrant, whilst his wife became the object of their deepest compassion. But to the women who offered her their sympathy in the loss of her children, all she ever said was that the decision of their father was good enough for her.

Many years after the birth of his daughter, Gualtieri decided that the time had come to put Griselda's patience to the final test. So he told a number of his men that in no circumstances could he put up with Griselda as his wife any longer, having now come to realize that his marriage was an aberration of his youth. He would therefore do everything in his power to obtain a dispensation from the Pope, enabling him to divorce Griselda and marry someone else. For this he was chided severely by many worthy men, but his only reply was that it had to be done.

On learning of her husband's intentions, from which it appeared she would have to return to her father's house, in order perhaps to look after the sheep as she had in the past, meanwhile seeing the man she adored being cherished by some other woman, Griselda was secretly filled with despair. But she prepared herself to endure this final blow as stoically as she had borne Fortune's earlier assaults.

Shortly thereafter, Gualtieri arranged for some counterfeit letters of his to arrive from Rome, and led his subjects to believe that in these, the Pope had granted him permission to abandon Griselda and remarry.

He accordingly sent for Griselda, and before a large number of people he said to her:

"Woman, I have had a dispensation from the Pope, allowing me to leave you and take another wife. Since my ancestors were great noblemen and rulers of these lands, whereas yours have always been peasants, I intend that you shall no longer be my wife, but return to Giannùcole's house with the dowry you brought me, after which I shall bring another lady here. I have already chosen her and she is far better suited to a man of my condition."

On hearing these words, the lady, with an effort beyond the power of any normal woman's nature, suppressed her tears and replied:

"My lord, I have always known that my lowly condition was totally at odds with your nobility, and that it is to God and to yourself that I owe whatever standing

I possess. Nor have I ever regarded this as a gift that I might keep and cherish as my own, but rather as something I have borrowed; and now that you want me to return it, I must give it back to you with good grace. Here is the ring with which you married me: take it. As to your ordering me to take away the dowry that I brought, you will require no accountant, nor will I need a purse or a pack-horse, for this to be done. For it has not escaped my memory that you took me naked as on the day I was born. If you think it proper that the body in which I have borne your children should be seen by all the people, I shall go away naked. But in return for my virginity, which I brought to you and cannot retrieve, I trust you will at least allow me, in addition to my dowry, to take one shift away with me."

Gualtieri wanted above all else to burst into tears, but maintaining a stern expression he said:

"Very well, you may take a shift."

All the people present implored Gualtieri to let her have a dress, so that she who had been his wife for thirteen years and more would not have to suffer the indignity of leaving his house in a shift, like a pauper; but their pleas were unavailing. And so Griselda, wearing a shift, barefoot, and with nothing to cover her head, having bidden them farewell, set forth from Gualtieri's house and returned to her father amid the weeping and the wailing of all who set eyes upon her.

Giannùcole, who had never thought it possible that Gualtieri would keep his daughter as his wife, and was daily expecting this to happen, had preserved the clothes she discarded on the morning Gualtieri had married her. So he brought them to her, and Griselda, having put them on, applied herself as before to the menial chores in her father's house, bravely enduring the cruel assault of hostile Fortune.

No sooner did Gualtieri drive Griselda away, than he gave his subjects to understand that he was betrothed to a daughter of one of the Counts of Panago.[5] And having ordered that grandiose preparations were to be made for the nuptials, he sent for Griselda and said to her:

"I am about to fetch home this new bride of mine, and from the moment she sets foot inside the house, I intend to accord her an honourable welcome. As you know, I have no women here who can set the rooms in order for me, or attend to many of the things that a festive occasion of this sort requires. No one knows better than you how to handle these household affairs, so I want you to make all the necessary arrangements. Invite all the ladies you need, and receive them as though you were mistress of the house. And when the nuptials are over, you can go back home to your father."

Since Griselda was unable to lay aside her love for Gualtieri as readily as she had dispensed with her good fortune, his words pierced her heart like so many knives. But she replied.

"My lord, I am ready to do as you ask."

And so, in her coarse, thick, woollen garments, Griselda returned to the house she had quitted shortly before in her shift, and started to sweep and tidy the various chambers. On her instructions, the beds were draped with hangings, the benches in the halls were suitably adorned, the kitchen was made ready; and she set her hand, as though she were a petty serving wench, to every conceivable household task, never stopping to draw breath until she had everything prepared and arranged as befitted the occasion.

5. Panago, or Panico, is in the province of Emilio-Romagna, near Bologna.

Having done all this, she caused invitations to be sent, in Gualtieri's name, to all the ladies living in those parts, and began to await the event. And when at last the nuptial day arrived, heedless of her beggarly attire, she bade a cheerful welcome to each of the lady guests, displaying all the warmth and courtesy of a lady of the manor.

Gualtieri's children having meanwhile been carefully reared by his kinswoman in Bologna, who had married into the family of the Counts of Panago, the girl was now twelve years old, the loveliest creature ever seen, whilst the boy had reached the age of six. Gualtieri had sent word to his kinswoman's husband, asking him to do him the kindness of bringing this daughter of his to Saluzzo along with her little brother, to see that she was nobly and honourably escorted, and to tell everyone he met that he was taking her to marry Gualtieri, without revealing who she really was to a living soul.

In accordance with the Marquis's request, the gentleman set forth with the girl and her brother and a noble company, and a few days later, shortly before the hour of breakfast, he arrived at Saluzzo, where he found that all the folk thereabouts, and numerous others from neighbouring parts, were waiting for Gualtieri's latest bride.

After being welcomed by the ladies, she made her way to the hall where the tables were set, and Griselda, just as we have described her, went cordially up to meet her, saying:

"My lady, you are welcome."

The ladies, who in vain had implored Gualtieri to see that Griselda remained in another room, or to lend her one of the dresses that had once been hers, so that she would not cut such a sorry figure in front of his guests, took their seats at table and addressed themselves to the meal. All eyes were fixed upon the girl, and everyone said that Gualtieri had made a good exchange. But Griselda praised her as warmly as anyone present, speaking no less admiringly of her little brother.

Gualtieri felt that he had now seen all he wished to see of the patience of his lady, for he perceived that no event, however singular, produced the slightest change in her demeanour, and he was certain that this was not because of her obtuseness, as he knew her to be very intelligent. He therefore considered that the time had come for him to free her from the rancour that he judged her to be hiding beneath her tranquil outward expression. And having summoned her to his table, before all the people present he smiled at her and said:

"What do you think of our new bride?"

"My lord," replied Griselda, "I think very well of her. And if, as I believe, her wisdom matches her beauty, I have no doubt whatever that your life with her will bring you greater happiness than any gentleman on earth has ever known. But with all my heart I beg you not to inflict those same wounds upon her that you imposed upon her predecessor, for I doubt whether she could withstand them, not only because she is younger, but also because she has had a refined upbringing, whereas the other had to face continual hardship from her infancy."

On observing that Griselda was firmly convinced that the young lady was to be his wife, and that even so she allowed no hint of resentment to escape her lips, Gualtieri got her to sit down beside him, and said:

"Griselda, the time has come for you to reap the reward of your unfailing patience, and for those who considered me a cruel and bestial tyrant, to know that whatever I have done was done of set purpose, for I wished to show you how to be a wife, to teach these people how to choose and keep a wife, and to guarantee my own peace and quiet for as long as we were living beneath the same roof. When I came to take a wife, I was greatly afraid that this peace would be denied me, and in order to prove otherwise I tormented and provoked you in the ways you have seen. But as I have never known you to oppose my wishes, I now intend, being persuaded that you can offer me all the happiness I desired, to restore to you in a single instant that which I took from you little by little, and delectably assuage the pains I have inflicted upon you. Receive with gladsome heart, then, this girl whom you believe to be my bride, and also her brother. These are our children, whom you and many others have long supposed that I caused to be cruelly murdered; and I am your husband, who loves you above all else, for I think I can boast that there is no other man on earth whose contentment in his wife exceeds my own."

Having spoken these words, he embraced and kissed Griselda, who by now was weeping with joy; then they both got up from table and made their way to the place where their daughter sat listening in utter amazement to these tidings. And after they had fondly embraced the girl and her brother, the mystery was unravelled to her, as well as to many of the others who were present.

The ladies rose from table in transports of joy, and escorted Griselda to a chamber, where, with greater assurance of her future happiness, they divested her of her tattered garments and clothed her anew in one of her stately robes. And as their lady and their mistress, a rôle which even in her rags had seemed to be hers, they led her back to the hall, where she and Gualtieri rejoiced with the children in a manner marvellous to behold.

Everyone being delighted with the turn that events had taken, the feasting and the merrymaking were redoubled, and continued unabated for the next few days. Gualtieri was acknowledged to be very wise, though the trials to which he had subjected his lady were regarded as harsh and intolerable, whilst Griselda was accounted the wisest of all.

The Count of Panago returned a few days later to Bologna, and Gualtieri, having removed Giannùcole from his drudgery, set him up in a style befitting his father-in-law, so that he lived in great comfort and honour for the rest of his days. As for Gualtieri himself, having married off his daughter to a gentleman of renown, he lived long and contentedly with Griselda, never failing to honour her to the best of his ability.

What more needs to be said, except that celestial spirits may sometimes descend even into the houses of the poor, whilst there are those in royal palaces who would be better employed as swineherds than as rulers of men? Who else but Griselda could have endured so cheerfully the cruel and unheard of trials that Gualtieri imposed upon her without shedding a tear? For perhaps it would have served him right if he had chanced upon a wife, who, being driven from the house in her shift, had found some other man to shake her skin-coat for her,[6] earning herself a fine new dress in the process.

* * *

Dioneo's story had ended, and the ladies, some taking one side and some another, some finding fault with one of its details and some commending another, had talked about it at length, when the king,[7] having raised his eyes to observe that the sun had already sunk low in the evening sky, began, without getting up, to address them as follows:

"Graceful ladies, the wisdom of mortals consists, as I think you know, not only in remembering the past and apprehending the present, but in being able, through a

6. Dioneo often uses erotic metaphors of this kind.
7. Panfilo.

knowledge of each, to anticipate the future, which grave men regard as the acme of human intelligence.

"Tomorrow, as you know, a fortnight will have elapsed since the day we departed from Florence to provide for our relaxation, preserve our health and our lives, and escape from the sadness, the suffering and the anguish continuously to be found in our city since this plague first descended upon it. These aims we have achieved, in my judgement, without any loss of decorum. For as far as I have been able to observe, albeit the tales related here have been amusing, perhaps of a sort to stimulate carnal desire, and we have continually partaken of excellent food and drink, played music, and sung many songs, all of which things may encourage unseemly behaviour among those who are feeble of mind, neither in word nor in deed nor in any other respect have I known either you or ourselves to be worthy of censure. On the contrary, from what I have seen and heard, it seems to me that our proceedings have been marked by a constant sense of propriety, an unfailing spirit of harmony, and a continual feeling of brotherly and sisterly amity. All of which pleases me greatly, as it surely redounds to our communal honour and credit.

"Accordingly, lest aught conducive to tedium should arise from a custom too long established, and lest, by protracting our stay, we should cause evil tongues to start wagging, I now think it proper, since we have all in turn had our share of the honour still invested in me, that with your consent we should return from whence we came. If, moreover, you consider the matter carefully, our company being known to various others hereabouts, our numbers could increase in such a way as to destroy all our pleasure. And so, if my advice should command your approval, I shall retain the crown that was given me until our departure, which I propose should take effect tomorrow morning. But if you decide otherwise, I already have someone in mind upon whom to bestow the crown for the next day to follow."

The ladies and the young men, having debated the matter at considerable length, considered the king's advice, in the end, to be sensible and just, and decided to do as he had said. He therefore sent for the steward and conferred with him with regard to the following morning's arrangements, and having dismissed the company till supper-time, he rose to his feet.

The ladies and the other young men followed suit, and turned their attention to various pastimes as usual. When it was time for supper, they disposed of the meal with infinite relish, after which they turned to singing and music and dancing. * * *

Next morning they arose at the crack of dawn, by which time all their baggage had been sent on ahead by the steward, and with their wise king leading the way they returned to Florence. Having taken their leave of the seven young ladies in Santa Maria Novella, whence they had all set out together, the three young men went off in search of other diversions; and in due course the ladies returned to their homes.[8]

---

8. Thus ends the narrative part of the *Decameron*. Boccaccio follows with a brief epilogue, in which he anticipates the criticism that he has taken too many liberties with his stories. He defends himself by pointing out that the stories are told in a garden, not in a church; that only corrupt minds will find things to corrupt in his stories; and that after all, he "could only transcribe the stories as they were actually told, . . . But even if one could assume that I was the inventor as well as the scribe of these stories (which was not the case), I still insist that I would not feel ashamed if some fell short of perfection, for there is no craftsman other than God whose work is whole and faultless in every respect." He closes by reminding his reader that everything in the world is subject to constant change, including his own tongue. He then thanks God, and asks the "sweet ladies" whom he addressed in his introduction to remember him "if perchance these stories should bring you any profit."

Francis Petrarch is one of the crucial figures who launched the modern era, an era that embodied the very contradictions that characterized Petrarch himself. For most of his life, he fervently upheld the superiority of Latin, but he spent forty years working on his collection of lyric poetry in Italian. He cultivated the persona of the independent scholar, but attached himself to powerful, at times repugnant patrons—such as the Visconti—who could fund his personal library, which became the largest manuscript collection in Europe. He took his own religious profession lightly, but lambasted popes for not returning to Rome and advocated a Crusade. While the image that has come down to us of Petrarch is of a modernist—perhaps our first—he looks backward as much as forward. To a modern eye his least satisfying works are his attempts to write in the ancient genres of the epic and the eclogue, as well as his allegorical poems in Italian. But his look back across the long Middle Ages to what was for him the Golden Age of Rome also revealed to him the great ancients—Cicero, Virgil, Augustine—as familiar figures rather than unapproachable icons, writers from whom he might learn what it is to be human and whose words he might plunder. As he wrote in one of his letters: "the skillful juxtaposition of others' words and concepts often makes them ours." In juxtaposing "others' words" in order to articulate what, indeed, was "his," Petrarch launched the cult of the personality, and few personalities are as complex or as fascinating as that of Petrarch.

Born in 1304 to a father who, like Dante, had been exiled from Florence for his political sympathies, Petrarch spent his earliest years in Italy, near Arezzo. When he was only eight, his father took his family to Avignon in southern France where he would continue his profession as notary for the French Pope, Clement V. Although Petrarch was sent to Bologna to pursue legal studies, it quickly became clear that the law was not his passion. He returned to Avignon in 1326 after his father's death and began pursuing what *was* his passion: the study of classical antiquity through the collecting and transcribing of ancient manuscripts. With its enormous library and its large number of scholars connected to the papal court, Avignon offered the young Franciscus Petracchi—he would change his name only later to the more Latin-sounding Petrarca—the opportunity to begin honing his scholarly skills. The late 1320s saw his pioneering edition of the Roman historian Livy, the first venture to organize the scattered manuscripts of the *History of Rome* into a coherent whole. He also mingled with like-minded men who would become his companions and in some cases, his patrons for life, including the monk Dionigi da Borgo San Sepolcro, who gave Petrarch the small copy of Augustine's *Confessions* that he carried with him until his death. Southern France also offered him the restful climes of Vaucluse, a village on the Sorgue River where he bought a house and escaped from Avignon to write his first literary works in the 1330s and early 1340s: his (incomplete) epic, *Africa,* based on the heroic events of the Roman general Scipio Africanus; his collection of lives of famous men, *De viris illustribus;* and the first of his poems in Italian about a woman whom he had supposedly first glimpsed in a church in Avignon on April 6, 1327: the unattainable "Laura," whose identity remains unknown. Having decided to embrace the life of a man of the church—a decision which didn't prevent him from fathering two children—Petrarch was awarded with a canonry in the nearby cathedral of Lombez, an appointment that carried few responsibilities but sufficient income to pursue his writing.

One significant measure of Petrarch's widespread fame by the time he was thirty-six was an invitation, in 1340, to be crowned poet laureate by the University of Paris—an invitation that was matched, supposedly only hours later, by the Roman Senate. Petrarch accepted the honor from Rome and was crowned on the Capitoline Hill the following year. The next decade would see the writing of the *Secretum,* a dialogue between Petrarch and Augustine, who upbraids him for his passion for Laura, and the undertaking of a carefully organized collection of letters to both living and dead figures, inspired by Petrarch's discovery in Verona of Cicero's epistles. But the 1340s saw a number of changes in Petrarch's life that would considerably influence his future writing. He enthusiastically supported a short-lived attempt of the nobleman Cola di Rienzo to unite Italy's reigning principates, but the venture ended in disaster and eventually Cola's death at the stake as a heretic. Petrarch's brother Gherardo decided in 1343 to become a monk, depriving Petrarch of one of his most constant companions; his letter on Mount Ventoux, probably composed after Gherardo's withdrawal from the world, looks back to the happier days of the 1320s when the two were virtually inseparable. And the Black Death recorded so gruesomely by Boccaccio in the opening pages of his *Decameron* took as its victims a number of Petrarch's close friends, among them his most steadfast patron, Giacomo Colonna, and his beloved "Laura." Such devastation inspired the *Triumph of Death,* an allegorical pageant that unfolds before a stunned and saddened Petrarch, and the one hundred final poems of the *Canzoniere* that mourn the loss of the poet's lady.

Canzoniere Petrarch spent many years writing, revising, and ordering and reordering the 366-poem sequence known as the *Canzoniere* or *Rime sparse* ("Scattered rhymes"). The chronology he carefully constructs from these "fragments" allows us to participate in the unfolding not simply of an unrequited passion, but of a life. That this life speaks to us with such directness, despite the formality of the metrical and verse constraints within which Petrarch worked, is one of the paradoxes of the sequence, and one that poets after him struggled to repeat with varying degrees of success.

While Petrarch wrote in a variety of metrical forms, including the flexible *canzone* and the sestina, the one that he employed most is the sonnet, perfecting the form to the extent that fourteen-line poems with a clear break between their eighth and ninth lines are simply referred to as "Petrarchan sonnets." For the most part, the four stanzas that comprise the sonnet are syntactically compact units: the octet is broken into two stanzas of four lines each, with an *abba* rhyme scheme; the sestet is composed of two stanzas of three lines each, with a *cdc* rhyme. Such compactness allows for suggestive but brief sketches of Laura's beauty and the speaker's unrequited love; the discreteness of the stanza (a word that means "room") dictates that connections among them depend more on comparison and allusion than syntactical complexity. At the same time, the continuity of rhyme and Petrarch's frequent use of assonance and alliteration—plays with language and sound that the Italian language encourages, with its fluidity and inherent musicality—create a subtle, often sensuous impression of unity.

Italian though the *Canzoniere* may be, it represents in many ways a continued dialogue with classical culture. Mythological allusions abound, particularly to myths retold by Ovid. The Virgilian legacy is also strongly marked, as in the echo of Aeneas's frustrated glimpse of Venus (90) and the extended meditation on the poignant nightingale simile from the tale of Orpheus in Virgil's fourth *Georgic* (311, 353, 365). Such classical references aren't included simply for the sake of displaying intellectual wares. They help to situate Petrarch's often unanchored persona and give form to the elusive Laura: from the transformed laurel tree, to the threatening Diana who forbids Actaeon's speech, to the graceful Aurora who, in death, leaves an aging Petrarch behind on earth.

Yet Petrarch models his sequence equally on modern innovations. The sonnet, for one thing, derived from the formal experimentations of both the French Provençal school and the late thirteenth-century practitioners of the *dolce stil nuovo* ("sweet new style") to which Petrarch pays homage in his seventieth poem. Petrarch quotes lines from Arnaut Daniel, Guido Cavalcanti, and the great Dante himself, only to move beyond them in a final stanza where he tellingly quotes—who else?—himself. The idea of a poetry "book" looks back to the Roman poets Catullus and Propertius (whose manuscripts Petrarch had discovered and transcribed) but Petrarch gives his sequence a Christian focus, starting with his confessional lament and closing with a recantation addressed not to Laura but to the "Virgin mother," Mary.

Petrarch uses devotional imagery to describe Laura, first glimpsed in a church on Good Friday. Yet there is something potentially idolatrous about this earthly passion. Petrarch's supposed inability to choose between Christian salvation and his idolatrous love is poignantly foreshadowed in the *Canzoniere,* especially in those sonnets where he mourns the fact that life is swiftly overtaking him and that he has nothing to show for his gray locks but a handful of poems. Unlike the supremely divine Beatrice of Dante's own poetry book, the *Vita nuova,* Laura finally cannot function as the medium for the poet's salvation.

Often castigated for his preciousness, as well as for a misogynistic treatment of Laura, Petrarch reveals himself as fully aware of the choices he has made and their implications. The real Laura, the Petrarchan narrator knows all too well, is nowhere to be found in his poems. One of the many conflicts of the *Canzoniere,* in fact, is the tension between the poet's fiction and the world beyond it. From time to time, Petrarch directly addresses political events as well as the patrons who generously supported him. Though his lyrics are primarily about his interior life, Petrarch also speaks to the contexts that privilege such a life.

Canzoniere

During the Life of My Lady Laura[1]

1

O you[2] who hear within these scattered verses
the sound of sighs with which I fed my heart
in my first errant youthful days when I
in part was not the man I am today;

5　for all the ways in which I weep and speak
between vain hopes, between vain suffering,
in anyone who knows love through its trials,
in them, may I find pity and forgiveness.

But now I see how I've become the talk
10　so long a time of people all around
(it often makes me feel so full of shame),

and from my vanities there comes shame's fruit,
and my repentance, and the clear awareness
that worldly joy is just a fleeting dream.

3

It was the day the sun's ray had turned pale
with pity for the suffering of his Maker
when I was caught (and I put up no fight),[3]
my lady, for your lovely eyes had bound me.

5　It seemed no time to be on guard against
Love's blows; therefore, I went my way

---

1. Translated from the Italian by Mark Musa.

2. Petrarch uses *Voi* to address his reader, which can be read as the plural form of "you" or as the formal address to a single reader, as contrasted with the more informal *tu.*

3. The day Petrarch was "taken" by his Lady is Good Friday, or 6 April 1327.

secure and fearless—so, all my misfortunes
began in midst of universal woe.

Love found me all disarmed and saw the way
10   was clear to reach my heart down through the eyes,
which have become the halls and doors of tears.

It seems to me it did him little honor
to wound me with his arrow in my state
and to you, armed, not show his bow at all.

16

The old man takes his leave, white-haired and pale,
of the sweet place where he filled out his age
and leaves his little family, bewildered
to see its own dear father disappear;

5   from there, dragging along his ancient limbs
throughout the very last days of his life,
helping himself with good will all he can,
broken by years, and wearied by the road,

he comes to Rome, pursuing his desire,
10   to look upon the likeness of the One
that he still hopes to see up there in Heaven.[4]

Just so, alas, sometimes I go, my lady,
searching, as much as possible, in others
for your true, your desirable form.

35

Alone and deep in thought I measure out
the most deserted fields, with slow, late steps,
with eyes intent to flee whatever sign
of human footprint left within the sand.

5   I find no other shield for my protection
against the knowing glances of mankind,
for in my bearing all bereft of joy
one sees from outside how I burn within.

So now, I think, only the plains and mountains,
10   the rivers and the forests know the kind
of life I lead, the one concealed from all.

And still, I never seem to find a path
too harsh, too wild for Love to always join
me and to speak to me, and I to him!

---

4. The allusion is to the veil with which Veronica is said to have wiped Christ's face while he was carrying the cross; Christ's image was preserved on the cloth, which was kept in St. Peter's and attracted large numbers of pilgrims to see it. Petrarch is drawing on a simile from Dante's *Paradiso*, Canto 31, in which a pilgrim from Croatia who comes to see the "Veronica" is compared to Dante himself.

52

Diana never pleased her lover more,
when just by chance all of her naked body
he saw bathing within the chilly waters,[5]

than did the simple mountain shepherdess
5   please me, the while she bathed the pretty veil
that holds her lovely blonde hair in the breeze.[6]

So that even now in hot sunlight she makes me
tremble all over with the chill of love.

90

She'd let her gold hair flow free in the breeze
that whirled it into thousands of sweet knots,
and lovely light would burn beyond all measure
in those fair eyes whose light is dimmer now.

5   Her face would turn the color pity wears,
a pity true or false I did not know,
and I with all Love's tinder in my breast—
it's no surprise I quickly caught on fire.

The way she walked was not the way of mortals
10 but of angelic forms, and when she spoke
more than an earthly voice it was that sang:[7]

a godly spirit and a living sun
was what I saw, and if she is not now,
my wound still bleeds, although the bow's unbent.

126

Clear, cool, sweet, running waters
where she, for me the only
woman, would rest her lovely body;
kind branch on which it pleased her
5   (I sigh to think of it)
to make a column for her lovely side;
and grass and flowers which her gown,
richly flowing, covered
with its angelic folds;
10 sacred air serene
where Love with those fair eyes opened my heart:
listen all of you together
to these my mournful, my last words.[8]

5. The goddess of chastity who lives among her nymphs in the woods, Diana was surprised by the hunter Actaeon while she was bathing. For his transgression, she turned him into a stag; and he was torn apart by his own dogs. Throughout the *Canzoniere,* Petrarch often refers to himself through a series of metamorphosed figures.

6. "From the breeze" is *a l'aura* in Italian—one of Petrarch's many wordplays on Laura's name.

7. In the forests of Carthage in *Aeneid* 1 the goddess Venus appears to Aeneas disguised as a young maiden, speaking to him with a more than human voice.

8. This depiction of the *locus amoenus* or beautiful place is drawn from Vaucluse, on the south bank of the Sorgue River, where Petrarch bought a house in the mid 1330s, finding there the serenity and peace he couldn't have in Avignon. The "clear, cool, sweet waters" are those of the Sorgue.

15   If it, indeed, must be my fate,
     and Heaven works its ways,
     that Love close up these eyes while they still weep,
     let grace see my poor body
     be buried there among you
20   and let my soul return to its home naked;
     then death would be less harsh
     if I could bear this hope
     unto that fearful crossing,
     because the weary soul
     could never in a more secluded port,
25   in a more tranquil grave,
     flee from my poor belabored flesh and bones.

     And there will come a time, perhaps,
     that to the well-known place
     the lovely animal returns,[9] and tamed,
30   and there where she first saw me
     that day which now is blessed,
     she turns her eyes with hope and happiness
     in search of me, and—ah, the pity—
     to see me there as dust
35   among the stones, Love will
     inspire her and she will sigh
     so sweetly she will win for me some mercy
     and force open the heavens
     drying her eyes there with her lovely veil.

40   Falling from gracious boughs,
     I sweetly call to mind,
     were flowers in a rain upon her bosom,
     and she was sitting there
     humble in such glory
45   now covered in a shower of love's blooms:
     a flower falling on her lap,
     some fell on her blond curls,
     like pearls set into gold
     they seemed to me that day;
50   some fell to rest on ground, some on the water,
     and some in lovelike wandering
     were circling down and saying, "Here Love reigns."

     How often I would say
     at that time, full of awe:
55   "For certain she was born up there in Heaven!"[1]
     And her divine behavior,
     her face and words and her sweet smile

9. Laura herself.
1. The imagery in the preceding stanza recalls Dante's description of the Garden of Eden, from *Purgatory* 30, and Laura is here modeled on Dante's Beatrice who appears "within a cloud of flowers."

so filled me with forgetfulness
and so divided me
60   from the true image
that I would sigh and say:
"Just how and when did I come here?"
thinking I was in Heaven, not where I was;
and since then I have loved
65   this bank of grass and find peace nowhere else.

If you had all the beauty you desired,
you could with boldness leave
the wood and make your way among mankind.[2]

195

From day to day my face and hair are changing,
but I still bite the sweetly baited hook
and hold tight to the green and enlimed branches
of the tree that has no care of cold or heat.[3]

5   The sea will lose its water, sky its stars
before I fear no longer and desire
her lovely shade, and I not love and hate
the deep and loving wound I hide so badly.

I do not hope to ever rest my labors
10   until I am deboned, defleshed, demuscled,
or till my enemy shows me her pity.

All things that cannot be will be before
another or she or Death will heal the wound
that Love with her fair eyes made in my heart.

After the Death of My Lady Laura
267[4]

O God! that lovely face, that gentle look,
O God! that charming way of hers, so proud!
O God! those words that any wild, harsh heart
could tame and cowards turn to courageous men!

5   And, O God, that sweet smile whence came the arrow
of death, the only good I hope for now!
Royal soul, the worthiest of all to rule,
if only you had not joined us so late:

it is for you I burn, in you I breathe
10   for I am yours alone; deprived of you,
I suffer less for all my other pains;

2. The last stanza, referred to as the *congedo* or leave-taking, is addressed to the poem itself.
3. The tree is the evergreen laurel, another play on Laura's name.
4. With this poem, the poet is confronted with Laura's death by plague, which occurred on 6 April 1348. In the manuscript, there is a space between poems 266 and 267.

with hope you filled me once and with desire
the time I left that highest charm alive,
but all those words were scattered in the wind.

277

If Love does not give me some new advice,
I shall be forced to change my life with death,
such fear and grief afflict my saddened soul
because desire lives and hope is dead,

5   and so bewildered, unconsoled my life
is totally, that night and day it weeps,
weary without a helm in stormy seas
and on a dubious course with no true guide.

An imaginary guide is driving it,
10   the true one's underground—no, she's in Heaven
whence she shines even brighter through my heart,

not through my eyes, because a veil of sorrow
forbids them to behold the longed-for light
and turns my hair to grey before its time.

291

When I see coming down the sky Aurora
with roses on her brow and gold in hair,
Love seizes me and losing all my color
I sigh as I say, "Laura is there now.⁵

5   "O glad Tithonus,⁶ you know when it's time
to hold your precious treasure once again;
but I, what can I do with my sweet laurel?
To see her once again I have to die.

"Your partings aren't so difficult to take—
10   at least at nighttime she returns to you,
and she does not despise your head of white;

"my nights she saddens and my days she darkens,
the one who carried off my thoughts with her
and left me of herself only her name."

311

That nightingale so tenderly lamenting
perhaps his children or his cherished mate,
in sweetness fills the sky and countryside
with many notes of grief skillfully played,

5   and all night long he stays with me it seems,
reminding me of my harsh destiny;

5. "Ivi è Laura ora," playing on "Dawn" (l'Aurora).
6. A mortal who fell in love with Dawn; at her request, the gods granted him eternal life, but since she hadn't asked that

I have no one to blame except myself
for thinking Death could not rule such a goddess.[7]

How easy to deceive one who is sure!
Those two lights, lovely, brighter than the sun,
whoever thought would turn the earth so dark?

And now I know what this fierce fate of mine
would have me learn as I live on in tears:
that nothing here can please and also last.

353[8]

O lovely little bird singing away
in tones of grief for all the time gone by,
you see the night and winter at your side,
the day and all those happy months behind;

aware as you are of your grievous troubles
could you be so of my plight as your own,
you would fly straight to the bosom of this wretch
to share with him some of his painful grief.

I cannot say our portions would be equal,
since she you weep for may still have her life
with which Heaven and Death for me are stingy;

but the forbidding season and the hour,
the memory of sweet years and bitter ones,
invites me to discuss with you my pity.

365

I go my way lamenting those past times
I spent in loving something which was mortal
instead of soaring high, since I had wings
that might have taken me to higher levels.

You who see all my shameful, wicked errors,
King of all Heaven, invisible, immortal,
help this frail soul of mine for she has strayed,
and all her emptiness fill up with grace,

so that, having once lived in storms, at war,
I may now die in peace, in port; and if my stay
was vain, at least let my departure count.

Over the little life that still remains to me,
and at my death, deign that your hand be present:
You know You are the only hope I have.

10

5

10

5

10

7. The first half of the poem is drawn from Virgil's extended nightingale simile in the fourth *Georgic*.

8. Originally, Petrarch had made this sonnet the next to last poem (365) in the collection; it shows his ongoing fascination with the weeping bird as an analogy for himself as singer.

Michel de Montaigne introduces his longest essay, "Apology for Raymond Sebond," with a vivid portrait of the household in which he grew up. "Inflamed with that new ardor with which King Francis I embraced letters, [my father] sought with great diligence and expense the acquaintance of learned men, receiving them at his house like holy persons having some particular inspiration of divine wisdom." According to the essayist, his father, Eyquem de Montaigne, a prosperous merchant who had received little formal education, treated scholars with "reverence and religion" only because he was wholly unqualified to judge them. "Myself," Montaigne continues, "I like them well enough, but I do not worship them."

This attack on his father's naive enthusiasm for "learned men" may also seem to be an indictment of the time and considerable expense Eyquem spent on his son's education. Brought up with a German tutor who taught him Latin as his mother tongue, the future author of some of the finest and most spirited works in the French language—the incomparable *Essays*—was sent to the prestigious Collège de Guienne in Bordeaux, trained in law, and went on to become a magistrate in the Parliament of Bordeaux. But at the age of thirty-seven, Montaigne abruptly chose to retire from Parliament and retreat to the family home that had become his (and from which he took his last name). Here he had the beams in his library carved with his favorite quotations from classical authors, and in a medallion he had made for himself in 1576, he inscribed the question, *Que sçay-je?*—"what do I know?" The answer, one pondered throughout a lifetime in his *Essays,* was *Rien* (or "nothing")—nothing, that is, save himself. "I would rather be an authority on myself than on Cicero," he remarks in his final essay, "Of Experience," and it is clear from the sum total of the *Essays* that any claim to be an authority on Cicero would be instantly suspect.

And yet to a certain extent, such a query represents the very fruit of Renaissance learning. Two hundred years earlier, Petrarch had posed the same question, framed as an attack on the pedantic nature of scholastic learning that had dominated the medieval universities: "What good is it to know the nature of the beasts and the birds, the fish and the snakes, if we ignore and don't bother to learn the nature of man: why we are born, from whence we come, where are we going?" Montaigne's compatriot Rabelais had challenged the dry university education that produced unthinking parrots; far better the humanist training that addressed the whole man. Moreover, like Erasmus, Montaigne turned for his most valued model to the one ancient figure who didn't presume on his own considerable knowledge, who believed that there is nothing "so ridiculous as that this miserable and puny creature, who is not even master of himself...should call himself master and emperor of the universe": the Greek philosopher Socrates. Or as Montaigne describes him: "Socrates was a man, and wanted neither to be nor to seem anything else" ("On some verses of Virgil"). But unlike Rabelais or Erasmus—or even Socrates, for that matter—Montaigne deploys in his 107 essays an intensely personal voice that became more frankly autobiographical as the years went on. Thanks to the meticulous care that Montaigne devoted to his writings, we are able to see how his thinking developed over a period of twenty years.

The *Essays* began as a "commonplace book," a collection of pithy quotations with selective commentary on topics as diverse as "smells," "sleep," "war horses," and "liars." Perhaps, as Montaigne suggests in one of his shortest essays, "Of Idleness," he began writing in order to harness the "idle thoughts" that plagued him in the years immediately after his retirement. But his book eventually grew to voluminous size, as Montaigne created a new and flexible narrative form which he christened with the French word *essais*—trials or attempts, on which he puns in "Of repentance": "If my mind could gain a firm footing, I would not make essays, I would make decisions; but it is always in apprenticeship and on trial." And these "trials" increasingly revolved around none other than Montaigne himself, revealed in all his foibles. His memory is so poor that he has often picked up a book believing it to be the first time, only to find his extensive notes scribbled in the margins; he has only modest strengths (there are few friends more loyal than he), and he has suffered from a variety of physical ailments, ranging from a concussion he suffered when he fell from his horse, to the maladies which increase as he ages, such as the painful bouts with kidney stones that sent him to Italy and Germany in 1580 in search of spas that could grant him relief. (His lively *Travel Journal* is the product of his trip, which was interrupted when he was summoned to return to Bordeaux to preside for two terms as mayor.) Although there is plenty of engagement with Virgil, Lucretius, Sextus Empiricus, and countless other classical writers (occasionally quoted inaccurately, thereby verifying what Montaigne says about his poor memory), Montaigne uses these borrowings to take us from the potentially abstract realms of philosophy and Roman history to the most immediate of concerns: his health, his love affairs, his inability to stay at the table after he has finished eating a meal, and his—and our—impending death.

Some have criticized Montaigne for this egoistic turn inward, reflective, perhaps, of the new bourgeois consciousness that privileged the private space over the public and civic space. The seventeenth-century philosopher and mathematician Blaise Pascal, who was greatly influenced by the *Essays,* was nonetheless one of many who chastised his predecessor for his obsessive self-preoccupation and his vacillation over the burning issues of his day. Yet Montaigne, writing at the height of France's religious wars, had seen enough blood and incivility to know that fanatical partisanship on disputed questions was not the answer to the ills plaguing post-Reformation Europe. The fact that he was called in to negotiate between the Catholic Henri de Guise and the Protestant Henry of Navarre suggests that others prized his ability to refrain from too quickly taking sides and to weigh all possible options before coming—if coming—to decisions. It also suggests that Montaigne deliberately underplayed the important political role he did have, both before and after his "retirement." In the same way, the ventures into the New World didn't prove to Montaigne the superiority of European culture. They demonstrated something quite to the contrary: the barbaric nature of European practices, as Montaigne wittily suggests in his classic essay "Of Cannibals." At the same time, he knew that he couldn't simply deny the culture that had created him. As he mentions in his preface to the *Essays,* since he had not been born "among those nations which are said to live still in the sweet freedom of nature's first laws," he was unable to portray himself "entire and wholly naked." Stepping outside oneself to become another was an impossibility, in the same way that placing oneself at the universe's center was the highest folly.

This brings us to what may be called the paradox of Montaigne's massive project: why did he write, and, more significantly, publish his *Essays*? They began, Montaigne suggests, not merely as a cure for idleness but as consolation for a friendship that had ended tragically in 1563 when Montaigne's "soulmate" from school, Étienne de la Boétie, died of the plague. It is telling in this light that Marie de Gornay, a young woman whom Montaigne befriended and made his adoptive daughter and literary executrix, lovingly attended to the *Essays* after Montaigne's death in 1592, transcribing his marginalia and overseeing the publication of the posthumous version in 1595. Particularly in his later essays, Montaigne tries to create a familiar, even intimate, relationship with his readers, anxious to convey simply himself, rather than to pass on profound wisdom; "it should not be held against me if I publish what I write," he says in "Of practice." "What is useful to me may also by accident be useful to another. Moreover, I am not spoiling anything, I am using only what is mine." The "accident" of the essays' utility thereby becomes a convenient aftermath of what Montaigne imagines to be the essays' real purpose, the portrayal of himself in all his dimensions. Another accidental aftermath might also have been this: to find a true friend who might understand him, and, perhaps, be understood in turn. Mademoiselle de Gornay is said to have claimed that she knew Montaigne long before she met him. No doubt many since then have also felt well-acquainted with the man who seemed to have taken the sincerest pleasure in being among the first to expose himself, almost if not completely naked, to generations of avid readers.

The *Essays* went through numerous publications, beginning in 1580 with a publication of the first two (of three) books, in Bordeaux, where Montaigne would soon be mayor.

Several editions with numerous additions and modifications followed. The 1588 edition, published in Paris, was the first to contain the third book of essays. Between 1588 and 1592, the year of his death, Montaigne continued to reflect on and augment his literary creation; the posthumous 1595 edition incorporates the many changes he made in the margins to his 1588 text. While the various strata of the essays will not generally be noted below, it is important to recognize that the essays changed significantly over time.

PRONUNCIATION:
   *Michel de Montaigne: mee-*SHELL *duh mon-*TEN

from Essays[1]

Of Idleness

Just as we see that fallow land, if rich and fertile, teems with a hundred thousand kinds of wild and useless weeds, and that to set it to work we must subject it and sow it with certain seeds for our service; and as we see that women, all alone, produce mere shapeless masses and lumps of flesh, but that to create a good and natural offspring they must be made fertile with a different kind of seed; so it is with minds. Unless you keep them busy with some definite subject that will bridle and control them, they throw themselves in disorder hither and yon in the vague field of imagination.

> Thus, in a brazen urn, the water's light
> Trembling reflects the sun's and moon's bright rays,
> And, darting here and there in aimless flight,
> Rises aloft, and on the ceiling plays.
> > VIRGIL[2]

And there is no mad or idle fancy that they do not bring forth in this agitation:

> Like a sick man's dreams,
> They form vain visions.
> > HORACE

The soul that has no fixed goal loses itself; for as they say, to be everywhere is to be nowhere:

> He who dwells everywhere, Maximus, nowhere dwells.
> > MARTIAL

Lately when I retired to my home, determined so far as possible to bother about nothing except spending the little life I have left in rest and seclusion, it seemed to me I could do my mind no greater favor than to let it entertain itself in full idleness and stay and settle in itself, which I hoped it might do more easily now, having become weightier and riper with time. But I find—

> Ever idle hours breed wandering thoughts
> > LUCAN

---

1. Translated by Donald Frame. Book 1, Chapter 8, of the *Essays*.
2. The citation is from Virgil's *Aeneid*, Book 8. Like the passage from Martial, it was added by Montaigne to his revised edition of the *Essays* published in 1588. Montaigne constantly weaves quotations from classical writers into his prose, often to express his meaning succinctly, and to give a general resonance to his own experience. The most notable of these references will be footnoted.

—that, on the contrary, like a runaway horse, it gives itself a hundred times more trouble than it took for others, and gives birth to so many chimeras and fantastic monsters, one after another, without order or purpose, that in order to contemplate their ineptitude and strangeness at my pleasure, I have begun to put them in writing, hoping in time to make my mind ashamed of itself.

Of the Power of the Imagination[1]

A strong imagination creates the event, say the scholars. I am one of those who are very much influenced by the imagination. Everyone feels its impact, but some are overthrown by it.[2] Its impression on me is piercing. And my art is to escape it, not to resist it. I would live solely in the presence of gay, healthy people. The sight of other people's anguish causes very real anguish to me, and my feelings have often usurped the feelings of others. A continual cougher irritates my lungs and throat. I visit less willingly the sick toward whom duty directs me than those toward whom I am less attentive and concerned. I catch the disease that I study, and lodge it in me. I do not find it strange that imagination brings fevers and death to those who give it a free hand and encourage it.

Simon Thomas was a great doctor in his time. I remember that one day, when he met me at the house of a rich old consumptive with whom he was discussing ways to cure his illness, he told him that one of these would be to give me occasion to enjoy his company; and that by fixing his eyes on the freshness of my face and his thoughts on the blitheness and overflowing vigor of my youth, and filling all his senses with my flourishing condition, he might improve his constitution. But he forgot to say that mine might get worse at the same time.

Gallus Vibius strained his mind so hard to understand the essence and impulses of insanity that he dragged his judgment off its seat and never could get it back again; and he could boast of having become mad through wisdom.[3] There are some who through fear anticipate the hand of the executioner. And one man who was being unbound to have his pardon read him dropped stone dead on the scaffold, struck down by his mere imagination. We drip with sweat, we tremble, we turn pale and turn red at the blows of our imagination; reclining in our feather beds we feel our bodies agitated by their impact, sometimes to the point of expiring. And boiling youth, fast asleep, grows so hot in the harness that in dreams it satisfies its amorous desires:

> So that as though it were an actual affair,
> They pour out mighty streams, and stain the clothes they wear.
> LUCRETIUS

And although it is nothing new to see horns grow overnight on someone who did not have them when he went to bed, nevertheless what happened to Cippus, king of Italy, is memorable; having been in the daytime a very excited spectator at a bullfight and having all night in his dreams had horns on his head, he grew actual horns on his forehead by the power of his imagination. Passion gave the son of Croesus the voice that nature had refused him. And Antiochus took fever from the beauty of Stratonice too vividly imprinted in his soul. Pliny says he saw Lucius Cossitius changed from a woman into a

---

1. Book 1, Chapter 21.

2. The remainder of this paragraph and the next are from post-1588 publications of the *Essays*, and reflects the increasingly intimate reflections of the late editions.

3. Cited in the Roman philosopher Seneca's *Controversies;* Gallus was a declaimer who apparently went mad.

man on his wedding day. Pontanus and others report similar metamorphoses as having happened in Italy in these later ages. And through his and his mother's vehement desire,

> Iphis the man fulfilled vows made when he was a girl.[4]
>
> OVID

Passing through Vitry-le-François, I might have seen a man whom the bishop of Soissons had named Germain at confirmation, but whom all the inhabitants of that place had seen and known as a girl named Marie until the age of twenty-two. He was now heavily bearded, and old, and not married. Straining himself in some way in jumping, he says, his masculine organs came forth; and among the girls there a song is still current by which they warn each other not to take big strides for fear of becoming boys, like Marie Germain. It is not so great a marvel that this sort of accident is frequently met with. For if the imagination has power in such things, it is so continually and vigorously fixed on this subject that in order not to have to relapse so often into the same thought and sharpness of desire, it is better off if once and for all it incorporates this masculine member in girls.

Some attribute to the power of imagination the scars of King Dagobert and of Saint Francis.[5] It is said that thereby bodies are sometimes removed from their places. And Celsus tells of a priest who used to fly with his soul into such ecstasy that his body would remain a long time without breath and without sensation. Saint Augustine names another who whenever he heard lamentable and plaintive cries would suddenly go into a trance and get so carried away that it was no use to shake him and shout at him, to pinch him and burn him, until he had come to; then he would say that he had heard voices, but as if coming from afar, and he would notice his burns and bruises. And that this was no feigned resistance to his senses was shown by the fact that while in this state he had neither pulse nor breath.

It is probable that the principal credit of miracles, visions, enchantments, and such extraordinary occurrences comes from the power of imagination, acting principally upon the minds of the common people, which are softer. Their belief has been so strongly seized that they think they see what they do not see.

I am still of this opinion, that those comical inhibitions by which our society is so fettered that people talk of nothing else are for the most part the effects of apprehension and fear. For I know by experience that one man, whom I can answer for as for myself, on whom there could fall no suspicion whatever of impotence and just as little of being enchanted, having heard a friend of his tell the story of an extraordinary impotence into which he had fallen at the moment when he needed it least, and finding himself in a similar situation, was all at once so struck in his imagination by the horror of this story that he incurred the same fate. And from then on he was subject to relapse, for the ugly memory of his mishap checked him and tyrannized him. He found some remedy for this fancy by another fancy: which was that by admitting this weakness and speaking about it in advance, he relieved the tension of his soul, for when the trouble had been presented as one to be expected, his sense of responsibility diminished and weighed upon him less. When he had a chance of his own choosing, with his mind

97

4. After noting a number of supposedly historical metamorphoses—the account of Cippus, for example, is taken from Pliny's *Natural History*, the story of Croesus, who spoke in a man's voice for the first time only when he saw his father on his deathbed, is from Herodotus—Montaigne turns to Ovid's *Metamorphoses* for the story of Iphis. A girl raised as a boy, she falls in love with the bride she is given to marry, and the goddess Isis transforms her into a young man.

5. Dagobert had been covered by scars provoked by his fear of gangrene. St. Francis of Assisi was said to bear the stigmata, the wounds made on Christ's body by the nails of the cross.

unembroiled and relaxed and his body in good shape, to have his bodily powers first tested, then seized and taken by surprise, with the other party's full knowledge of his problem, he was completely cured in this respect. A man is never after incapable, unless from genuine impotence, with a woman with whom he has once been capable.

This mishap is to be feared only in enterprises where our soul is immoderately tense with desire and respect, and especially if the opportunity is unexpected and pressing; there is no way of recovering from this trouble. I know one man who found it helpful to bring to it a body that had already begun to be sated elsewhere, so as to lull his frenzied ardor, and who with age finds himself less impotent through being less potent. And I know another who was helped when a friend assured him that he was supplied with a counterbattery of enchantments that were certain to save him. I had better tell how this happened.

A count, a member of a very distinguished family, with whom I was quite intimate,[6] upon getting married to a beautiful lady who had been courted by a man who was present at the wedding feast, had his friends very worried and especially an old lady, a relative of his, who was presiding at the wedding and holding it at her house. She was fearful of these sorceries, and gave me to understand this. I asked her to rely on me. I had by chance in my coffers a certain little flat piece of gold on which were engraved some celestial figures, to protect against sunstroke and take away a headache by placing it precisely on the suture of the skull; and, to keep it there, it was sewed to a ribbon intended to be tied under the chin: a kindred fancy to the one we are speaking of. Jacques Peletier had given me this singular present. I thought of making some use of it, and said to the count that he might incur the same fate as others, there being men present who would like to bring this about; but that he should boldly go to bed and I would do him a friendly turn and would not, if he needed it, spare a miracle which was in my power, provided that he promised me on his honor to keep it most faithfully secret; he was only to make a given signal to me, when they came to bring him the midnight meal, if things had gone badly with him. He had had his soul and his ears so battered that he did find himself fettered by the trouble of his imagination, and gave me his signal. I told him then that he should get up on the pretext of chasing us out, and playfully take the bathrobe that I had on (we were very close in height) and put it on him until he had carried out my prescription, which was this: when we had left, he should withdraw to pass water, say certain prayers three times and go through certain motions; each of these three times he should tie the ribbon I was putting in his hand around him and very carefully lay the medal that was attached to it on his kidneys, with the figure in such and such a position; this done, having tied this ribbon firmly so that it could neither come untied nor slip from its place, he should return to his business with complete assurance and not forget to spread my robe over his bed so that it should cover them both. These monkey tricks are the main part of the business, our mind being unable to get free of the idea that such strange means must come from some abstruse science. Their inanity gives them weight and reverence. All in all, it is certain that the characters on my medal proved themselves more venereal than solar, more useful for action than for prevention. It was a sudden and curious whim that led me to do such a thing, which was alien to my nature. I am an enemy of subtle and dissimulated acts and hate trickery in myself, not only for sport but also for someone's profit. If the action is not vicious, the road to it is.

Amasis, king of Egypt, married Laodice, a very beautiful Greek girl; and he, who showed himself a gay companion everywhere else, fell short when it came to enjoying

6. Montaigne is probably referring to the count of Gurson, Louis de Foix, who married his relative, Diane de Foix de Candale, in 1579. Montaigne was very close to the family, and dedicated one of his best-known essays, "Of the Education of Children" (1.26), to Diane de Foix.

her, and threatened to kill her, thinking it was some sort of sorcery. As is usual in matters of fancy, she referred him to religion; and having made his vows and promises to Venus, he found himself divinely restored from the first night after his oblations and sacrifices.[7]

Now women are wrong to greet us with those threatening, quarrelsome, and coy countenances, which put out our fires even as they light them. The daughter-in-law of Pythagoras used to say that the woman who goes to bed with a man should put off her modesty with her skirt and put it on again with her petticoat. The soul of the assailant, when troubled with many various alarms, is easily discouraged; and when imagination has once made a man suffer this shame—and it does so only at the first encounters, inasmuch as these are more boiling and violent, and also because in this first intimacy a man is much more afraid of failing—having begun badly, he gets from this accident a feverishness and vexation which lasts into subsequent occasions.

Married people, whose time is all their own, should neither press their undertaking nor even attempt it if they are not ready; it is better to fail unbecomingly to handsel the nuptial couch, which is full of agitation and feverishness, and wait for some other more private and less tense opportunity, than to fall into perpetual misery for having been stunned and made desperate by a first refusal. Before taking possession, the patient should try himself out and offer himself, lightly, by sallies at different times, without priding himself and obstinately insisting on convincing himself definitively. Those who know that their members are naturally obedient, let them take care only to counteract the tricks of their fancies.

People are right to notice the unruly liberty of this member, obtruding so importunately when we have no use for it, and failing so importunately when we have the most use for it, and struggling for mastery so imperiously with our will, refusing with so much pride and obstinacy our solicitations, both mental and manual.

If, however, in the matter of his rebellion being blamed and used as proof to condemn him, he had paid me to plead his cause, I should perhaps place our other members, his fellows, under suspicion of having framed this trumped-up charge out of sheer envy of the importance and pleasure of the use of him, and of having armed everyone against him by a conspiracy, malignantly charging him alone with their common fault.[8] For I ask you to think whether there is a single one of the parts of our body that does not often refuse its function to our will and exercise it against our will. They each have passions of their own which rouse them and put them to sleep without our leave. How many times do the forced movements of our face bear witness to the thoughts that we were holding secret, and betray us to those present. The same cause that animates this member also animates, without our knowledge, the heart, the lungs, and the pulse; the sight of a pleasing object spreading in us imperceptibly the flame of a feverish emotion. Are there only these muscles and these veins that stand up and lie down without the consent, not only of our will, but even of our thoughts? We do not command our hair to stand on end or our skin to shiver with desire or fear. The hand often moves itself to where we do not send it. The tongue is paralyzed, and the voice congealed, at their own time. Even when, having nothing to put in to fry, we should

---

7. The story is told in Herodotus's *History*, Book 2, Chapter 181. The vow to Aphrodite (Venus) was made, however, by poor Laodice herself, who promised to present a statue to Aphrodite's temple in Cyrene should her husband have intercourse with her. Montaigne not infrequently misremembers or misquotes his sources.

8. Although Montaigne is unique in coming to the defense of the penis, the "trial" of body parts has a long history in ancient literature. The fable of the belly and the limbs has its origin in Livy's Roman history, Book 2, in which Menenius Agrippa tells a Roman mob of the importance of the stomach in the commonwealth and is able to prevent them from violence. Shakespeare's *Coriolanus* opens with this scene as Menenius tells the "mutinous Citizens" of "a time when all the body's members / Rebell'd against the belly" (1.1.97–98).

like to forbid it, the appetite for eating and drinking does not fail to stir the parts that are subject to it, no more nor less than that other appetite; and it likewise abandons us inopportunely when it sees fit. The organs that serve to discharge the stomach have their own dilatations and compressions, beyond and against our plans, just like those that are destined to discharge the kidneys. To vindicate the omnipotence of our will, Saint Augustine alleges that he knew a man who commanded his behind to produce as many farts as he wanted, and his commentator Vives goes him one better with another example of his own time, of farts arranged to suit the tone of verses pronounced to their accompaniment; but all this does not really argue any pure obedience in this organ; for is there any that is ordinarily more indiscreet or tumultuous? Besides, I know one so turbulent and unruly, that for forty years it has kept its master farting with a constant and unremitting wind and compulsion, and is thus taking him to his death.[9]

But as for our will, on behalf of whose rights we set forth this complaint, how much more plausibly may we charge it with rebellion and sedition for its disorderliness and disobedience! Does it always will what we would will it to will? Doesn't it often will what we forbid it to will, and that to our evident disadvantage? Is it any more amenable than our other parts to the decisions of our reason?

To conclude, I would say this in defense of the honorable member whom I represent: May it please the court to take into consideration that in this matter, although my client's case is inseparably and indistinguishably linked with that of an accessory, nevertheless he alone has been brought to trial; and that the arguments and charges against him are such as cannot—in view of the status of the parties—be in any manner pertinent or relevant to the aforesaid accessory. Whereby is revealed his accusers' manifest animosity and disrespect for law. However that may be, Nature will meanwhile go her way, protesting that the lawyers and judges quarrel and pass sentence in vain. Indeed, she would have done no more than is right if she had endowed with some particular privilege this member, author of the sole immortal work of mortals. Wherefore to Socrates generation is a divine act; and love, a desire for immortality and itself an immortal daemon.

Perhaps it is by this effect of the imagination that one man here gets rid of the scrofula which his companion carries back to Spain.[1] This effect is the reason why, in such matters, it is customary to demand that the mind be prepared. Why do the doctors work on the credulity of their patient beforehand with so many false promises of a cure, if not so that the effect of the imagination may make up for the imposture of their decoction? They know that one of the masters of the trade left them this in writing, that there have been men for whom the mere sight of medicine did the job.

And this whole caprice has just come to hand apropos of the story that an apothecary, a servant of my late father, used to tell me, a simple man and Swiss, of a nation little addicted to vanity and lying. He had long known a merchant at Toulouse, sickly and subject to the stone, who often needed enemas, and ordered various kinds from his doctors according to the circumstances of his illness. Once they were brought to him, nothing was omitted of the accustomed formalities; often he tested them by hand to make sure they were not too hot. There he was, lying on his stomach, and all the motions were gone through—except that no injection was made. After this ceremony, the apothecary having retired and the patient being accommodated as if he had really taken the enema, he

---

9. Augustine's *City of God* 14.24 refers to such a man in the context of a chapter entitled "That if men had remained innocent and obedient in Paradise, the generative organs should have been in subjection to the will as the other members are." Juan Luis Vives, a Spanish humanist, wrote commentaries and treatises on education. The "turbulent and unruly" organ is probably Montaigne's.

1. The king of France had the reputation of having the "royal touch" that cured scrofula, a disease of the lymph glands in the neck.

felt the same effect from it as those who do take them. And if the doctor did not find its operation sufficient, he would give him two or three more, of the same sort. My witness swears that when to save the expense (for he paid for them as if he had taken them) this sick man's wife sometimes tried to have just warm water used, the effect revealed the fraud; and having found that kind useless, they were obliged to return to the first method.

A woman, thinking she had swallowed a pin with her bread, was screaming in agony as though she had an unbearable pain in her throat, where she thought she felt it stuck; but because externally there was neither swelling nor alteration, a smart man, judging that it was only a fancy and notion derived from some bit of bread that had scratched her as it went down, made her vomit, and, on the sly, tossed a crooked pin into what she threw up. The woman, thinking she had thrown it up, felt herself suddenly relieved of her pain. I know that one gentleman, having entertained a goodly company at his house, three or four days later boasted, as a sort of joke (for there was nothing in it), that he had made them eat cat in a pie; at which one lady in the party was so horrified that she fell into a violent stomach disorder and fever, and it was impossible to save her. Even animals are subject like ourselves to the power of imagination. Witness dogs, who let themselves die out of grief for the loss of their masters. We also see them yap and twitch in their dreams, and horses whinny and writhe.

But all this may be attributed to the narrow seam between the soul and body, through which the experience of the one is communicated to the other. Sometimes, however, one's imagination acts not only against one's own body, but against someone else's. And just as a body passes on its sickness to its neighbor, as is seen in the plague, the pox, and soreness of the eyes, which are transmitted from one body to the other—

> By looking at sore eyes, eyes become sore;
> From body into body ills pass o'er
>
> OVID

—likewise the imagination, when vehemently stirred, launches darts that can injure an external object. The ancients maintained that certain women of Scythia, when animated and enraged against anyone, would kill him with their mere glance. Tortoises and ostriches hatch their eggs just by looking at them, a sign that their sight has some ejaculative virtue. And as for sorcerers, they are said to have baleful and harmful eyes:

> Some evil eye bewitched my tender lambs.
>
> VIRGIL

To me, magicians are poor authorities. Nevertheless, we know by experience that women transmit marks of their fancies to the bodies of the children they carry in their womb; witness the one who gave birth to the Moor. And there was presented to Charles, king of Bohemia and Emperor, a girl from near Pisa, all hairy and bristly, who her mother said had been thus conceived because of a picture of Saint John the Baptist hanging by her bed.[2]

With animals it is the same: witness Jacob's sheep,[3] and the partridges and hares that the snow turns white in the mountains. Recently at my house a cat was seen watching a bird on a treetop, and, after they had locked gazes for some time, the bird

---

2. There are many accounts in ancient and medieval literature of an infant who bears no resemblance to its parents but to an image or painting on which a mother had been looking while she was pregnant or when she conceived. Some of these involve a black child born to white parents.

3. In Genesis 30, Jacob has goats mate in front of boughs from which he has peeled back the bark. The lambs are born with patterns on their wool resembling those on the branches, either speckled or spotted.

let itself fall as if dead between the cat's paws, either intoxicated by its own imagination or drawn by some attracting power of the cat. Those who like falconry have heard the story of the falconer who, setting his gaze obstinately upon a kite in the air, wagered that by the sole power of his gaze he would bring it down, and did. At least, so they say—for I refer the stories that I borrow to the conscience of those from whom I take them.[4] The reflections are my own, and depend on the proofs of reason, not of experience; everyone can add his own examples to them; and he who has none, let him not fail to believe that there are plenty, in view of the number and variety of occurrences. If I do not apply them well, let another apply them for me.

So in the study that I am making of our behavior and motives, fabulous testimonies, provided they are possible, serve like true ones. Whether they have happened or no, in Paris or Rome, to John or Peter, they exemplify, at all events, some human potentiality, and thus their telling imparts useful information to me. I see it and profit from it just as well in shadow as in substance. And of the different readings that histories often give, I take for my use the one that is most rare and memorable. There are authors whose end is to tell what has happened. Mine, if I could attain it, would be to talk about what can happen. The schools are justly permitted to suppose similitudes when they have none at hand. I do not do so, however, and in that respect I surpass all historical fidelity, being scrupulous to the point of superstition. In the examples that I bring in here of what I have heard, done, or said, I have forbidden myself to dare to alter even the slightest and most inconsequential circumstances. My conscience does not falsify one iota; my knowledge, I don't know.

In this connection, I sometimes fall to thinking whether it befits a theologian, a philosopher, and such people of exquisite and exact conscience and prudence, to write history. How can they stake their fidelity on the fidelity of an ordinary person? How be responsible for the thoughts of persons unknown and give their conjectures as coin of the realm? Of complicated actions that happen in their presence they would refuse to give testimony if placed under oath by a judge; and they know no man so intimately that they would undertake to answer fully for his intentions. I consider it less hazardous to write of things past than present, inasmuch as the writer has only to give an account of a borrowed truth.

Some urge me to write the events of my time, believing that I see them with a view less distorted by passion than another man's, and from closer, because of the access that fortune has given me to the heads of different parties.[5] What they forget is that even for all the glory of Sallust, I would not take the trouble, being a sworn enemy of obligation, assiduity, perseverance; and that there is nothing so contrary to my style as an extended narration. I cut myself off so often for lack of breath; I have neither composition nor development that is worth anything; I am more ignorant than a child of the phrases and terms that serve for the commonest things. And so I have chosen to say what I know how to say, accommodating the matter to my power. If I took a subject that would lead me along, I might not be able to measure up to it; and with my freedom being so very free, I might publish judgments which, even according to my own opinion and to reason, would be illegitimate and punishable. Plutarch might well say to us, concerning his accomplishments in this line, that the credit belongs to others if his examples are wholly and everywhere true; but that their being

---

4. The original essay, first published in 1580, ended here; Montaigne added the remainder of the essay after 1588.
5. One of the rare references Montaigne makes to his public activities as mayor and diplomat.

useful to posterity, and presented with a luster which lights our way to virtue, that is his work.[6] There is no danger—as there is in a medicinal drug—in an old story being this way or that.

Of Cannibals[1]

When King Pyrrhus passed over into Italy, after he had reconnoitered the formation of the army that the Romans were sending to meet him, he said: "I do not know what barbarians these are" (for so the Greeks called all foreign nations), "but the formation of this army that I see is not at all barbarous." The Greeks said as much of the army that Flamininus brought into their country, and so did Philip, seeing from a knoll the order and distribution of the Roman camp, in his kingdom, under Publius Sulpicius Galba.[2] Thus we should beware of clinging to vulgar opinions, and judge things by reason's way, not by popular say.

I had with me for a long time a man who had lived for ten or twelve years in that other world which has been discovered in our century, in the place where Villegaignon landed, and which he called Antarctic France.[3] This discovery of a boundless country seems worthy of consideration. I don't know if I can guarantee that some other such discovery will not be made in the future, so many personages greater than ourselves having been mistaken about this one. I am afraid we have eyes bigger than our stomachs, and more curiosity than capacity. We embrace everything, but we clasp only wind.

Plato brings in Solon, telling how he had learned from the priests of the city of Saïs in Egypt that in days of old, before the Flood, there was a great island named Atlantis, right at the mouth of the Strait of Gibraltar, which contained more land than Africa and Asia put together, and that the kings of that country, who not only possessed that island but had stretched out so far on the mainland that they held the breadth of Africa as far as Egypt, and the length of Europe as far as Tuscany, undertook to step over into Asia and subjugate all the nations that border on the Mediterranean, as far as the Black Sea; and for this purpose crossed the Spains, Gaul, Italy, as far as Greece, where the Athenians checked them; but that some time after, both the Athenians and themselves and their island were swallowed up by the Flood.[4]

It is quite likely that that extreme devastation of waters made amazing changes in the habitations of the earth, as people maintain that the sea cut off Sicily from Italy—

> 'Tis said an earthquake once asunder tore
> These lands with dreadful havoc, which before
> Formed but one land, one coast
>
> VIRGIL

98

---

6. The great Greek biographer Plutarch (1st century C.E.), cited often by Montaigne, wrote 50 *Lives* of prominent Greek and Roman figures such as Julius Caesar, Cicero, and Pericles.

1. Book 1, Chapter 31.

2. Plutarch recounts the first two stories, of Pyrrhus's and the Greeks' comments on the Romans. The account of Philip, King of Macedon—another Greek unimpressed by a Roman army—is found in Livy.

3. Brazil, where Nicolas Durand de Villegaignon led an expedition in 1555–1556, with the hope of gaining some military clout. Among those who traveled with him were a group of Calvinist sympathizers, including the Calvinist Jean de Léry as well as a Franciscan friar named André Thevet. Both Thevet and Léry published extensive writings of their travels, from which Montaigne borrowed freely.

4. The legendary lost island of Atlantis is mentioned by Plato in the *Timaeus*.

—Cyprus from Syria, the island of Euboea from the mainland of Boeotia; and elsewhere joined lands that were divided, filling the channels between them with sand and mud:

> A sterile marsh, long fit for rowing, now
> Feeds neighbor towns, and feels the heavy plow.
>
> HORACE

But there is no great likelihood that that island was the new world which we have just discovered; for it almost touched Spain, and it would be an incredible result of a flood to have forced it away as far as it is, more than twelve hundred leagues; besides, the travels of the moderns have already almost revealed that it is not an island, but a mainland connected with the East Indies on one side, and elsewhere with the lands under the two poles; or, if it is separated from them, it is by so narrow a strait and interval that it does not deserve to be called an island on that account.

It seems that there are movements, some natural, others feverish, in these great bodies, just as in our own. When I consider the inroads that my river, the Dordogne, is making in my lifetime into the right bank in its descent, and that in twenty years it has gained so much ground and stolen away the foundations of several buildings, I clearly see that this is an extraordinary disturbance; for if it had always gone at this rate, or was to do so in the future, the face of the world would be turned topsy-turvy. But rivers are subject to changes: now they overflow in one direction, now in another, now they keep to their course. I am not speaking of the sudden inundations whose causes are manifest. In Médoc, along the seashore, my brother, the sieur d'Arsac,[5] can see an estate of his buried under the sands that the sea spews forth; the tops of some buildings are still visible; his farms and domains have changed into very thin pasturage. The inhabitants say that for some time the sea has been pushing toward them so hard that they have lost four leagues of land. These sands are its harbingers; and we see great dunes of moving sand that march half a league ahead of it and keep conquering land.

The other testimony of antiquity with which some would connect this discovery is in Aristotle, at least if that little book *Of Unheard-of Wonders* is by him. He there relates that certain Carthaginians, after setting out upon the Atlantic Ocean from the Strait of Gibraltar and sailing a long time, at last discovered a great fertile island, all clothed in woods and watered by great deep rivers, far remote from any mainland; and that they, and others since, attracted by the goodness and fertility of the soil, went there with their wives and children, and began to settle there. The lords of Carthage, seeing that their country was gradually becoming depopulated, expressly forbade anyone to go there any more, on pain of death, and drove out these new inhabitants, fearing, it is said, that in course of time they might come to multiply so greatly as to supplant their former masters and ruin their state. This story of Aristotle does not fit our new lands any better than the other.

This man I had was a simple, crude fellow—a character fit to bear true witness; for clever people observe more things and more curiously, but they interpret them; and to lend weight and conviction to their interpretation, they cannot help altering history a little. They never show you things as they are, but bend and disguise them according to the way they have seen them; and to give credence to their judgment and

---

5. Montaigne had five brothers; the "sieur of Arsac" was younger than he.

attract you to it, they are prone to add something to their matter, to stretch it out and amplify it. We need a man either very honest, or so simple that he has not the stuff to build up false inventions and give them plausibility; and wedded to no theory. Such was my man; and besides this, he at various times brought sailors and merchants, whom he had known on that trip, to see me. So I content myself with his information, without inquiring what the cosmographers say about it.

We ought to have topographers who would give us an exact account of the places where they have been. But because they have over us the advantage of having seen Palestine, they want to enjoy the privilege of telling us news about all the rest of the world. I would like everyone to write what he knows, and as much as he knows, not only in this, but in all other subjects; for a man may have some special knowledge and experience of the nature of a river or a fountain, who in other matters knows only what everybody knows. However, to circulate this little scrap of knowledge, he will undertake to write the whole of physics. From this vice spring many great abuses.

Now, to return to my subject, I think there is nothing barbarous and savage in that nation, from what I have been told, except that each man calls barbarism whatever is not his own practice; for indeed it seems we have no other test of truth and reason than the example and pattern of the opinions and customs of the country we live in. *There* is always the perfect religion, the perfect government, the perfect and accomplished manners in all things. Those people are wild, just as we call wild the fruits that Nature has produced by herself and in her normal course; whereas really it is those that we have changed artificially and led astray from the common order, that we should rather call wild. The former retain alive and vigorous their genuine, their most useful and natural, virtues and properties, which we have debased in the latter in adapting them to gratify our corrupted taste. And yet for all that, the savor and delicacy of some uncultivated fruits of those countries is quite as excellent, even to our taste, as that of our own. It is not reasonable that art should win the place of honor over our great and powerful mother Nature. We have so overloaded the beauty and richness of her works by our inventions that we have quite smothered her. Yet wherever her purity shines forth, she wonderfully puts to shame our vain and frivolous attempts:

> Ivy comes readier without our care;
> In lonely caves the arbutus grows more fair;
> No art with artless bird song can compare.
> PROPERTIUS

All our efforts cannot even succeed in reproducing the nest of the tiniest little bird, its contexture, its beauty and convenience; or even the web of the puny spider. All things, says Plato, are produced by nature, by fortune, or by art; the greatest and most beautiful by one or the other of the first two, the least and most imperfect by the last.

These nations, then, seem to me barbarous in this sense, that they have been fashioned very little by the human mind, and are still very close to their original naturalness. The laws of nature still rule them, very little corrupted by ours; and they are in such a state of purity that I am sometimes vexed that they were unknown earlier, in the days when there were men able to judge them better than we. I am sorry that Lycurgus and Plato did not know of them;[6] for it seems to me that what we actually

---

6. Lycurgus was a legendary Spartan legislator who radically reformed his city's laws. Among Plato's many treatises was the *Republic,* where he talks about the ideal society.

see in these nations surpasses not only all the pictures in which poets have idealized the golden age and all their inventions in imagining a happy state of man, but also the conceptions and the very desire of philosophy. They could not imagine a naturalness so pure and simple as we see by experience; nor could they believe that our society could be maintained with so little artifice and human solder. This is a nation, I should say to Plato, in which there is no sort of traffic, no knowledge of letters, no science of numbers, no name for a magistrate or for political superiority, no custom of servitude, no riches or poverty, no contracts, no successions, no partitions, no occupations but leisure ones, no care for any but common kinship, no clothes, no agriculture, no metal, no use of wine or wheat. The very words that signify lying, treachery, dissimulation, avarice, envy, belittling, pardon—unheard of.[7] How far from this perfection would he find the republic that he imagined: *Men fresh sprung from the gods* [Seneca].

> These manners nature first ordained.
> VIRGIL

For the rest, they live in a country with a very pleasant and temperate climate, so that according to my witnesses it is rare to see a sick man there; and they have assured me that they never saw one palsied, bleary-eyed, toothless, or bent with age. They are settled along the sea and shut in on the land side by great high mountains, with a stretch about a hundred leagues wide in between. They have a great abundance of fish and flesh which bear no resemblance to ours, and they eat them with no other artifice than cooking. The first man who rode a horse there, though he had had dealings with them on several other trips, so horrified them in this posture that they shot him dead with arrows before they could recognize him.

Their buildings are very long, with a capacity of two or three hundred souls; they are covered with the bark of great trees, the strips reaching to the ground at one end and supporting and leaning on one another at the top, in the manner of some of our barns, whose covering hangs down to the ground and acts as a side. They have wood so hard that they cut with it and make of it their swords and grills to cook their food. Their beds are of a cotton weave, hung from the roof like those in our ships, each man having his own; for the wives sleep apart from their husbands.

They get up with the sun, and eat immediately upon rising, to last them through the day; for they take no other meal than that one. Like some other Eastern peoples, of whom Suidas[8] tells us, who drank apart from meals, they do not drink then; but they drink several times a day, and to capacity. Their drink is made of some root, and is of the color of our claret wines. They drink it only lukewarm. This beverage keeps only two or three days; it has a slightly sharp taste, is not at all heady, is good for the stomach, and has a laxative effect upon those who are not used to it; it is a very pleasant drink for anyone who is accustomed to it. In place of bread they use a certain white substance like preserved coriander. I have tried it; it tastes sweet and a little flat.

The whole day is spent in dancing. The younger men go to hunt animals with bows. Some of the women busy themselves meanwhile with warming their drink, which is their chief duty. Some one of the old men, in the morning before they begin

---

7. Gonzalo's irritating speech to Sebastian in *The Tempest* (see page 1090) borrows from these two lines as translated by Montaigne's earliest English translator, John Florio.

8. The Suidas was the name given to a great Greek encyclopedia, compiled around the 10th century C.E.

to eat, preaches to the whole barnful in common, walking from one end to the other, and repeating one single sentence several times until he has completed the circuit (for the buildings are fully a hundred paces long). He recommends to them only two things: valor against the enemy and love for their wives. And they never fail to point out this obligation, as their refrain, that it is their wives who keep their drink warm and seasoned.

There may be seen in several places, including my own house, specimens of their beds, of their ropes, of their wooden swords and the bracelets with which they cover their wrists in combats, and of the big canes, open at one end, by whose sound they keep time in their dances. They are close shaven all over, and shave themselves much more cleanly than we, with nothing but a wooden or stone razor. They believe that souls are immortal, and that those who have deserved well of the gods are lodged in that part of heaven where the sun rises, and the damned in the west.

They have some sort of priests and prophets, but they rarely appear before the people, having their home in the mountains. On their arrival there is a great feast and solemn assembly of several villages—each barn, as I have described it, makes up a village, and they are about one French league from each other. The prophet speaks to them in public, exhorting them to virtue and their duty; but their whole ethical science contains only these two articles: resoluteness in war and affection for their wives. He prophesies to them things to come and the results they are to expect from their undertakings, and urges them to war or holds them back from it; but this is on the condition that when he fails to prophesy correctly, and if things turn out otherwise than he has predicted, he is cut into a thousand pieces if they catch him, and condemned as a false prophet. For this reason, the prophet who has once been mistaken is never seen again.

Divination is a gift of God; that is why its abuse should be punished as imposture. Among the Scythians, when the soothsayers failed to hit the mark, they were laid, chained hand and foot, on carts full of heather and drawn by oxen, on which they were burned.[9] Those who handle matters subject to the control of human capacity are excusable if they do the best they can. But these others, who come and trick us with assurances of an extraordinary faculty that is beyond our ken, should they not be punished for not making good their promise, and for the temerity of their imposture?

They have their wars with the nations beyond the mountains, further inland, to which they go quite naked, with no other arms than bows or wooden swords ending in a sharp point, in the manner of the tongues of our boar spears. It is astonishing what firmness they show in their combats, which never end but in slaughter and bloodshed; for as to routs and terror, they know nothing of either.

Each man brings back as his trophy the head of the enemy he has killed, and sets it up at the entrance to his dwelling. After they have treated their prisoners well for a long time with all the hospitality they can think of, each man who has a prisoner calls a great assembly of his acquaintances. He ties a rope to one of the prisoner's arms, by the end of which he holds him, a few steps away, for fear of being hurt, and gives his dearest friend the other arm to hold in the same way; and these two, in the presence of the whole assembly, kill him with their swords. This done, they roast him and eat him in common and send some pieces to their absent friends. This is not, as people think, for nourishment, as of old the Scythians used to do; it is to betoken an extreme revenge. And the proof of this came when they saw the Portuguese, who had joined

9. The story is from Herodotus; the term "Scythians" was used to describe the peoples from the north, who supposedly practiced a number of barbaric customs such as scalping and flaying their enemy.

forces with their adversaries, inflict a different kind of death on them when they took them prisoner, which was to bury them up to the waist, shoot the rest of their body full of arrows, and afterward hang them.[1] They thought that these people from the other world, being men who had sown the knowledge of many vices among their neighbors and were much greater masters than themselves in every sort of wickedness, did not adopt this sort of vengeance without some reason, and that it must be more painful than their own; so they began to give up their old method and to follow this one.

I am not sorry that we notice the barbarous horror of such acts, but I am heartily sorry that, judging their faults rightly, we should be so blind to our own. I think there is more barbarity in eating a man alive than in eating him dead; and in tearing by tortures and the rack a body still full of feeling, in roasting a man bit by bit, in having him bitten and mangled by dogs and swine (as we have not only read but seen within fresh memory, not among ancient enemies, but among neighbors and fellow citizens, and what is worse, on the pretext of piety and religion),[2] than in roasting and eating him after he is dead. Indeed, Chrysippus and Zeno, heads of the Stoic sect, thought there was nothing wrong in using our carcasses for any purpose in case of need, and getting nourishment from them; just as our ancestors, when besieged by Caesar in the city of Alésia, resolved to relieve their famine by eating old men, women, and other people useless for fighting.[3]

> The Gascons once, 'tis said, their life renewed
> By eating of such food.
>
> JUVENAL

And physicians do not fear to use human flesh in all sorts of ways for our health, applying it either inwardly or outwardly. But there never was any opinion so disordered as to excuse treachery, disloyalty, tyranny, and cruelty, which are our ordinary vices.

So we may well call these people barbarians, in respect to the rules of reason, but not in respect to ourselves, who surpass them in every kind of barbarity.

Their warfare is wholly noble and generous, and as excusable and beautiful as this human disease can be; its only basis among them is their rivalry in valor. They are not fighting for the conquest of new lands, for they still enjoy that natural abundance that provides them without toil and trouble with all necessary things in such profusion that they have no wish to enlarge their boundaries. They are still in that happy state of desiring only as much as their natural needs demand; anything beyond that is super-fluous to them.[4]

They generally call those of the same age, brothers; those who are younger, children; and the old men are fathers to all the others. These leave to their heirs in common the full possession of their property, without division or any other title at all than just the one that Nature gives to her creatures in bringing them into the world.

If their neighbors cross the mountains to attack them and win a victory, the gain of the victor is glory, and the advantage of having proved the master in valor and virtue; for apart from this they have no use for the goods of the vanquished, and they

---

1. The Portuguese had settled in Brazil long before the French.

2. A reference to the wars of religion that had divided France since the early 1570s.

3. "Our ancestors" are the Galls, referred to by Caesar himself in his *Gallic Wars*. The quote by Juvenal that follows also refers to the Gascons or Galls.

4. Much of this description of the native Brazilians (the Tupinamba Indians) is drawn from Jean de Léry's account.

return to their own country, where they lack neither anything necessary nor that great thing, the knowledge of how to enjoy their condition happily and be content with it. These men of ours do the same in their turn. They demand of their prisoners no other ransom than that they confess and acknowledge their defeat. But there is not one in a whole century who does not choose to die rather than to relax a single bit, by word or look, from the grandeur of an invincible courage; not one who would not rather be killed and eaten than so much as ask not to be. They treat them very freely, so that life may be all the dearer to them, and usually entertain them with threats of their coming death, of the torments they will have to suffer, the preparations that are being made for that purpose, the cutting up of their limbs, and the feast that will be made at their expense. All this is done for the sole purpose of extorting from their lips some weak or base word, or making them want to flee, so as to gain the advantage of having terrified them and broken down their firmness. For indeed, if you take it the right way, it is in this point alone that true victory lies:

> It is no victory
> Unless the vanquished foe admits your mastery.
> CLAUDIAN

The Hungarians, very bellicose fighters, did not in olden times pursue their advantage beyond putting the enemy at their mercy. For having wrung a confession from him to this effect, they let him go unharmed and unransomed, except, at most, for exacting his promise never again to take up arms against them.

We win enough advantages over our enemies that are borrowed advantages, not really our own. It is the quality of a porter, not of valor, to have sturdier arms and legs; agility is a dead and corporeal quality; it is a stroke of luck to make our enemy stumble, or dazzle his eyes by the sunlight; it is a trick of art and technique, which may be found in a worthless coward, to be an able fencer. The worth and value of a man is in his heart and his will; there lies his real honor. Valor is the strength, not of legs and arms, but of heart and soul; it consists not in the worth of our horse or our weapons, but in our own. He who falls obstinate in his courage, *if he has fallen, he fights on his knees* [Seneca]. He who relaxes none of his assurance, no matter how great the danger of imminent death; who, giving up his soul, still looks firmly and scornfully at his enemy—he is beaten not by us, but by fortune; he is killed, not conquered.

The most valiant are sometimes the most unfortunate. Thus there are triumphant defeats that rival victories. Nor did those four sister victories, the fairest that the sun ever set eyes on—Salamis, Plataea, Mycale, and Sicily—ever dare match all their combined glory against the glory of the annihilation of King Leonidas and his men at the pass of Thermopylae.[5]

Who ever hastened with more glorious and ambitious desire to win a battle than Captain Ischolas to lose one? Who ever secured his safety more ingeniously and painstakingly than he did his destruction? He was charged to defend a certain pass in the Peloponnesus against the Arcadians. Finding himself wholly incapable of doing this, in view of the nature of the place and the inequality of the forces, he made up his mind that all who confronted the enemy would necessarily have to remain on the field. On the other hand, deeming it unworthy both of his own virtue and magnanimity and

5. The first three victories were triumphs by the Greeks over the Persians in 479–480 B.C.E.; simultaneously the Greeks halted Carthaginian expansion in Sicily with a stunning victory at Himera. With a slender army, Leonidas held back the Persians for several days at the pass of Thermopylae, inflicting heavy casualities; when a native showed the Persians a mountain path that would enable them to attack the Greeks from the rear, Leonidas was killed and his army defeated.

of the Lacedaemonian name to fail in his charge, he took a middle course between these two extremes, in this way. The youngest and fittest of his band he preserved for the defense and service of their country, and sent them home; and with those whose loss was less important, he determined to hold this pass, and by their death to make the enemy buy their entry as dearly as he could. And so it turned out. For he was presently surrounded on all sides by the Arcadians, and after slaughtering a large number of them, he and his men were all put to the sword. Is there a trophy dedicated to victors that would not be more due to these vanquished? The role of true victory is in fighting, not in coming off safely; and the honor of valor consists in combating, not in beating.

To return to our story. These prisoners are so far from giving in, in spite of all that is done to them, that on the contrary, during the two or three months that they are kept, they wear a gay expression; they urge their captors to hurry and put them to the test; they defy them, insult them, reproach them with their cowardice and the number of battles they have lost to the prisoners' own people.

I have a song composed by a prisoner which contains this challenge, that they should all come boldly and gather to dine off him, for they will be eating at the same time their own fathers and grandfathers, who have served to feed and nourish his body. "These muscles," he says, "this flesh and these veins are your own, poor fools that you are. You do not recognize that the substance of your ancestors' limbs is still contained in them. Savor them well; you will find in them the taste of your own flesh." An idea that certainly does not smack of barbarity. Those that paint these people dying, and who show the execution, portray the prisoner spitting in the face of his slayers and scowling at them. Indeed, to the last gasp they never stop braving and defying their enemies by word and look. Truly here are real savages by our standards; for either they must be thoroughly so, or we must be; there is an amazing distance between their character and ours.

The men there have several wives, and the higher their reputation for valor the more wives they have. It is a remarkably beautiful thing about their marriages that the same jealousy our wives have to keep us from the affection and kindness of other women, theirs have to win this for them. Being more concerned for their husbands' honor than for anything else, they strive and scheme to have as many companions as they can, since that is a sign of their husbands' valor.

Our wives will cry "Miracle!" but it is no miracle. It is a properly matrimonial virtue, but one of the highest order. In the Bible, Leah, Rachel, Sarah, and Jacob's wives gave their beautiful handmaids to their husbands; and Livia seconded the appetites of Augustus, to her own disadvantage; and Stratonice, the wife of King Deiotarus, not only lent her husband for his use a very beautiful young chambermaid in her service, but carefully brought up her children, and backed them up to succeed to their father's estates.[6]

And lest it be thought that all this is done through a simple and servile bondage to usage and through the pressure of the authority of their ancient customs, without reasoning or judgment, and because their minds are so stupid that they cannot take any other course, I must cite some examples of their capacity. Besides the warlike song I have just quoted, I have another, a love song, which begins in this vein: "Adder, stay; stay, adder, that from the pattern of your coloring my sister may draw the fashion and the workmanship of a rich girdle that I may give to my love; so may your beauty and

---

6. Leah and Rachel are Jacob's wives; Sarah is the wife of Abraham, who sent her Egyptian maid Hagar to her husband that he might have an heir. Livia bore Augustus no children; King Deiotarus and Stratonice, allies of Rome during the first century B.C.E., are written of in Plutarch's *Bravery of Women*.

your pattern be forever preferred to all other serpents." This first couplet is the refrain of the song. Now I am familiar enough with poetry to be a judge of this: not only is there nothing barbarous in this fancy, but it is altogether Anacreontic.[7] Their language, moreover, is a soft language, with an agreeable sound, somewhat like Greek in its endings.

Three of these men, ignorant of the price they will pay some day, in loss of repose and happiness, for gaining knowledge of the corruptions of this side of the ocean; ignorant also of the fact that of this intercourse will come their ruin (which I suppose is already well advanced: poor wretches, to let themselves be tricked by the desire for new things, and to have left the serenity of their own sky to come and see ours!)— three of these men were at Rouen, at the time the late King Charles IX was there.[8] The king talked to them for a long time; they were shown our ways, our splendor, the aspect of a fine city. After that, someone asked their opinion, and wanted to know what they had found most amazing. They mentioned three things, of which I have forgotten the third, and I am very sorry for it; but I still remember two of them. They said that in the first place they thought it very strange that so many grown men, bearded, strong, and armed, who were around the king (it is likely that they were talking about the Swiss of his guard) should submit to obey a child, and that one of them was not chosen to command instead. Second (they have a way in their language of speaking of men as halves of one another), they had noticed that there were among us men full and gorged with all sorts of good things, and that their other halves were beggars at their doors, emaciated with hunger and poverty; and they thought it strange that these needy halves could endure such an injustice, and did not take the others by the throat, or set fire to their houses.

I had a very long talk with one of them; but I had an interpreter who followed my meaning so badly, and who was so hindered by his stupidity in taking in my ideas, that I could get hardly any satisfaction from the man. When I asked him what profit he gained from his superior position among his people (for he was a captain, and our sailors called him king), he told me that it was to march foremost in war. How many men followed him? He pointed to a piece of ground, to signify as many as such a space could hold; it might have been four or five thousand men. Did all his authority expire with the war? He said that this much remained, that when he visited the villages dependent on him, they made paths for him through the underbrush by which he might pass quite comfortably.

All this is not too bad—but what's the use? They don't wear breeches.

Of Repentance[1]

Others form man; I tell of him, and portray a particular one, very ill-formed, whom I should really make very different from what he is if I had to fashion him over again. But now it is done.

Now the lines of my painting do not go astray, though they change and vary. The world is but a perennial movement. All things in it are in constant motion—the earth, the rocks of the Caucasus, the pyramids of Egypt—both with the common motion and with their own. Stability itself is nothing but a more languid motion.

7. Anacreon was a 6th century B.C.E. Greek lyric poet.

8. The occasion dates to 1562. Charles IX, who succeeded to the throne in 1560, would have been only 12 at the time, which explains the men's comment that they thought it odd "that so many grown men...should submit to obey a child."

1. Book 3, Chapter 2.

I cannot keep my subject still. It goes along befuddled and staggering, with a natural drunkenness. I take it in this condition, just as it is at the moment I give my attention to it. I do not portray being: I portray passing. Not the passing from one age to another, or, as the people say, from seven years to seven years, but from day to day, from minute to minute. My history needs to be adapted to the moment. I may presently change, not only by chance, but also by intention. This is a record of various and changeable occurrences, and of irresolute and, when it so befalls, contradictory ideas: whether I am different myself, or whether I take hold of my subjects in different circumstances and aspects. So, all in all, I may indeed contradict myself now and then; but truth, as Demades said, I do not contradict. If my mind could gain a firm footing, I would not make essays,[2] I would make decisions; but it is always in apprenticeship and on trial.

I set forth a humble and inglorious life; that does not matter. You can tie up all moral philosophy with a common and private life just as well as with a life of richer stuff. Each man bears the entire form of man's estate.

Authors communicate with the people by some special extrinsic mark; I am the first to do so by my entire being, as Michel de Montaigne, not as a grammarian or a poet or a jurist. If the world complains that I speak too much of myself, I complain that it does not even think of itself.[3]

But is it reasonable that I, so fond of privacy in actual life, should aspire to publicity in the knowledge of me? Is it reasonable too that I should set forth to the world, where fashioning and art have so much credit and authority, some crude and simple products of nature, and of a very feeble nature at that? Is it not making a wall without stone, or something like that, to construct books without knowledge and without art? Musical fancies are guided by art, mine by chance.

At least I have one thing according to the rules: that no man ever treated a subject he knew and understood better than I do the subject I have undertaken; and that in this I am the most learned man alive. Secondly, that no man ever penetrated more deeply into his material, or plucked its limbs and consequences cleaner, or reached more accurately and fully the goal he had set for his work. To accomplish it, I need only bring it to fidelity; and that is in it, as sincere and pure as can be found. I speak the truth, not my fill of it, but as much as I dare speak; and I dare to do so a little more as I grow old, for it seems that custom allows old age more freedom to prate and more indiscretion in talking about oneself. It cannot happen here as I see it happening often, that the craftsman and his work contradict each other: "Has a man whose conversation is so good written such a stupid book?" or "Have such learned writings come from a man whose conversation is so feeble?"

If a man is commonplace in conversation and rare in writing, that means that his capacity is in the place from which he borrows it, and not in himself. A learned man is not learned in all matters; but the capable man is capable in all matters, even in ignorance.

In this case we go hand in hand and at the same pace, my book and I. In other cases one may commend or blame the work apart from the workman; not so here; he who touches the one, touches the other. He who judges it without knowing it will injure himself more than me; he who has known it will completely satisfy me. Happy beyond my deserts if I have just this share of public approval, that I make men of understanding feel that I was capable of profiting by knowledge, if I had had any, and that I deserved better assistance from my memory.

---

2. Montaigne plays here in the French with the meanings of the word *essayer*, "to try," "to prove."
3. This bold claim is a late one, added after the 1588 publication of the essays.

Let me here excuse what I often say, that I rarely repent and that my conscience is content with itself—not as the conscience of an angel or a horse, but as the conscience of a man; always adding this refrain, not perfunctorily but in sincere and complete submission: that I speak as an ignorant inquirer, referring the decision purely and simply to the common and authorized beliefs. I do not teach, I tell.

There is no vice truly a vice which is not offensive, and which a sound judgment does not condemn; for its ugliness and painfulness is so apparent that perhaps the people are right who say it is chiefly produced by stupidity and ignorance. So hard it is to imagine anyone knowing it without hating it.

Malice sucks up the greater part of its own venom, and poisons itself with it. Vice leaves repentance in the soul, like an ulcer in the flesh, which is always scratching itself and drawing blood. For reason effaces other griefs and sorrows; but it engenders that of repentance, which is all the more grievous because it springs from within, as the cold and heat of fevers is sharper than that which comes from outside. I consider as vices (but each one according to its measure) not only those that reason and nature condemn, but also those that man's opinion has created, even false and erroneous opinion, if it is authorized by laws and customs.

There is likewise no good deed that does not rejoice a wellborn nature. Indeed there is a sort of gratification in doing good which makes us rejoice in ourselves, and a generous pride that accompanies a good conscience. A boldly vicious soul may perhaps arm itself with security, but with this complacency and satisfaction it cannot provide itself. It is no slight pleasure to feel oneself preserved from the contagion of so depraved an age, and to say to oneself: "If anyone should see right into my soul, still he would not find me guilty either of anyone's affliction or ruin, or of vengeance or envy, or of public offense against the laws, or of innovation and disturbance, or of failing in my word; and in spite of what the license of the times allows and teaches each man, still I have not put my hand either upon the property or into the purse of any Frenchman, and have lived only on my own, both in war and in peace; nor have I used any man's work without paying his wages." These testimonies of conscience give us pleasure; and this natural rejoicing is a great boon to us, and the only payment that never fails us.

To found the reward for virtuous actions on the approval of others is to choose too uncertain and shaky a foundation. Especially in an age as corrupt and ignorant as this, the good opinion of the people is a dishonor. Whom can you trust to see what is praiseworthy? God keep me from being a worthy man according to the descriptions I see people every day giving of themselves in their own honor. *What were vices now are moral acts* [Seneca].

Certain of my friends have sometimes undertaken to call me on the carpet and lecture me unreservedly, either of their own accord or at my invitation, as a service which, to a well-formed soul, surpasses all the services of friendship, not only in usefulness, but also in pleasantness. I have always welcomed it with the wide-open arms of courtesy and gratitude. But to speak of it now in all conscience, I have often found in their reproach or praise such false measure that I would hardly have erred to err rather than to do good in their fashion.

Those of us especially who live a private life that is on display only to ourselves must have a pattern established within us by which to test our actions, and, according to this pattern, now pat ourselves on the back, now punish ourselves. I have my own laws and court to judge me, and I address myself to them more than anywhere else. To be sure, I restrain my actions according to others, but I extend them only according to myself. There is no one but yourself who knows whether you are cowardly and cruel, or loyal and devout. Others do not see you, they guess at you by uncertain conjectures; they see not so much your nature as your art. Therefore do not cling to their judgment; cling to your own. *You must use your own judgment.... With regard to virtues and vices, your own conscience has great weight: take that away, and everything falls* [Cicero].

But the saying that repentance follows close upon sin does not seem to consider the sin that is in robes of state, that dwells in us as in its own home. We can disown and retract the vices that take us by surprise, and toward which we are swept by passion; but those which by long habit are rooted and anchored in a strong and vigorous will cannot be denied. Repentance is nothing but a disavowal of our will and an opposition to our fancies, which leads us about in all directions. It makes this man disown his past virtue and his continence:

> Why had I not in youth the mind I have today?
> Or why, with old desires, have red cheeks flown away?
>   HORACE

It is a rare life that remains well ordered even in private. Any man can play his part in the side show and represent a worthy man on the boards; but to be disciplined within, in his own bosom, where all is permissible, where all is concealed—that's the point. The next step to that is to be so in our own house, in our ordinary actions, for which we need render account to no one, where nothing is studied or artificial. And therefore Bias, depicting an excellent state of family life, says it is one in which the master is the same within, by his own volition, as he is outside for fear of the law and of what people will say. And it was a worthy remark of Julius Drusus to the workmen who offered, for three thousand crowns, to arrange his house so that his neighbors would no longer be able to look into it as they could before. "I will give you six thousand," he said; "make it so that everyone can see in from all sides." The practice of Agesilaus is noted with honor, of taking lodging in the churches when traveling, so that the people and the gods themselves might see into his private actions.[4] Men have seemed miraculous to the world, in whom their wives and valets have never seen anything even worth noticing. Few men have been admired by their own households.

No man has been a prophet, not merely in his own house, but in his own country,[5] says the experience of history. Likewise in things of no importance. And in this humble example you may see an image of greater ones. In my region of Gascony they think it a joke to see me in print. The farther from my lair the knowledge of me spreads, the more I am valued. I buy printers in Guienne,[6] elsewhere they buy me. On this phenomenon those people base their hopes who hide themselves while alive and present, to gain favor when dead and gone. I would rather have less of it. And I cast myself on the world only for the share of favor I get now. When I leave it, I shall hold it quits.

The people escort this man back to his door, with awe, from a public function. He drops his part with his gown; the higher he has hoisted himself, the lower he falls back; inside, in his home, everything is tumultuous and vile. Even if there is order there, it takes a keen and select judgment to perceive it in these humble private actions. Besides, order is a dull and somber virtue. To win through a breach, to conduct an embassy, to govern

---

4. The three references to Bias, Julius Drusus, and Agesilaus are all drawn from various works of Plutarch.

5. Jesus remarks that "No man is accepted as a prophet in his own country" when the people of Nazareth resist his teachings (Luke 4.24).

6. A city near Montaigne's home, in southwest France.

a people, these are dazzling actions. To scold, to laugh, to sell, to pay, to love, to hate, and to deal pleasantly and justly with our household and ourselves, not to let ourselves go, not to be false to ourselves, that is a rarer matter, more difficult and less noticeable.

Therefore retired lives, whatever people may say, accomplish duties as harsh and strenuous as other lives, or more so. And private persons, says Aristotle, render higher and more difficult service to virtue than those who are in authority. We prepare ourselves for eminent occasions more for glory than for conscience. The shortest way to attain glory would be to do for conscience what we do for glory. And Alexander's virtue seems to me to represent much less vigor in his theater than does that of Socrates in his lowly and obscure activity. I can easily imagine Socrates in Alexander's place; Alexander in that of Socrates, I cannot.[7] If you ask the former what he knows how to do, he will answer, "Subdue the world"; if you ask the latter, he will say, "Lead the life of man in conformity with its natural condition"; a knowledge much more general, more weighty, and more legitimate.

The value of the soul consists not in flying high, but in an orderly pace. Its greatness is exercised not in greatness, but in mediocrity. As those who judge and touch us inwardly make little account of the brilliance of our public acts, and see that these are only thin streams and jets of water spurting from a bottom otherwise muddy and thick; so likewise those who judge us by this brave outward appearance draw similar conclusions about our inner constitution, and cannot associate common faculties, just like their own, with these other faculties that astonish them and are so far beyond their scope. So we give demons wild shapes. And who does not give Tamerlane raised eyebrows, open nostrils, a dreadful face, and immense size, like the size of the imaginary picture of him we have formed from the renown of his name?[8] If I had been able to see Erasmus in other days, it would have been hard for me not to take for adages and apophthegms everything he said to his valet and his hostess.[9] We imagine much more appropriately an artisan on the toilet seat or on his wife than a great president, venerable by his demeanor and his ability. It seems to us that they do not stoop from their lofty thrones even to live.

As vicious souls are often incited to do good by some extraneous impulse, so are virtuous souls to do evil. Thus we must judge them by their settled state, when they are at home, if ever they are; or at least when they are closest to repose and their natural position.

Natural inclinations gain assistance and strength from education; but they are scarcely to be changed and overcome. A thousand natures, in my time, have escaped toward virtue or toward vice through the lines of a contrary training:

> As when wild beasts grow tame, shut in a cage,
> Forget the woods, and lose their look of rage,
> And learn to suffer man; but if they taste
> Hot blood, their rage and fury is replaced,
> Their reminiscent jaws distend, they burn,
> And for their trembling keeper's blood they yearn.
>   LUCAN

7. Montaigne alludes to Alexander the Great (356–323 B.C.E.), student of Aristotle and master of the Hellenic empire that would be extended under his sway into Syria, Egypt, and India.

8. Tamerlane, or Tamburlaine, was Timur Khan, who conquered the Mongols early in his military career and went to advance as far west as Turkey and Arabia. He died in 1405.

9. The industrious Dutch scholar and humanist Desiderius Erasmus spent his lifetime compiling the *Adagia*, a collection of adages or proverbs. ("Apophthegms" are witty sayings.)

We do not root out these original qualities, we cover them up, we conceal them. Latin is like a native tongue to me; I understand it better than French; but for forty years I have not used it at all for speaking or writing.[1] Yet in sudden and extreme emotions, into which I have fallen two or three times in my life—one of them when I saw my father, in perfect health, fall back into my arms in a faint—I have always poured out my first words from the depths of my entrails in Latin; Nature surging forth and expressing herself by force, in the face of long habit. And this experience is told of many others.

Those who in my time have tried[2] to correct the world's morals by new ideas, reform the superficial vices; the essential ones they leave as they were, if they do not increase them; and increase is to be feared. People are likely to rest from all other well-doing on the strength of these external, arbitrary reforms, which cost us less and bring greater acclaim; and thereby they satisfy at little expense the other natural, consubstantial, and internal vices.

Just consider the evidence of this in our own experience. There is no one who, if he listens to himself, does not discover in himself a pattern all his own, a ruling pattern, which struggles against education and against the tempest of the passions that oppose it. For my part, I do not feel much sudden agitation; I am nearly always in place, like heavy and inert bodies. If I am not at home, I am always very near it. My excesses do not carry me very far away. There is nothing extreme or strange about them. And besides I have periods of vigorous and healthy reaction.

The real condemnation, which applies to the common run of men of today, is that even their retirement is full of corruption and filth; their idea of reformation, blurred; their penitence, diseased and guilty, almost as much as their sin. Some, either from being glued to vice by a natural attachment, or from long habit, no longer recognize its ugliness. On others (in whose regiment I belong) vice weighs heavily, but they counterbalance it with pleasure or some other consideration, and endure it and lend themselves to it for a certain price; viciously, however, and basely. Yet it might be possible to imagine a disproportion so extreme that the pleasure might justly excuse the sin, as we say utility does; not only if the pleasure was incidental and not a part of the sin, as in theft, but if it was in the very exercise of the sin, as in intercourse with women, where the impulse is violent, and, they say, sometimes invincible.

The other day when I was at Armagnac, on the estate of a kinsman of mine, I saw a country fellow whom everyone nicknames the Thief. He gave this account of his life: that born a beggar, and finding that by earning his bread by the toil of his hands he would never protect himself enough against want, he had decided to become a thief; and he had spent all his youth at this trade in security, by virtue of his bodily strength. For he reaped his harvest and vintage from other people's lands, but so far away and in such great loads that it was inconceivable that one man could have carried off so much on his shoulders in one night. And he was careful besides to equalize and spread out the damage he did, so that the loss was less insupportable for each individual. He is now, in his old age, rich for a man in his station, thanks to this traffic, which he openly confesses. And to make his peace with God for his acquisitions, he says that he spends his days compensating, by good deeds, the successors of the

---

1. Montaigne says in *Essays* I.26 that his father hired a tutor when he was born to teach him Latin as his first language: "I was over six before I understood any more French or Perigordian than Arabic."
2. Once again, Montaigne plays with the verb "essayer" as he talks about those who have tried ("ceux qui ont essaié") to change the world's morals.

people he robbed; and that if he does not finish this task (for he cannot do it all at once), he will charge his heirs with it, according to the knowledge, which he alone has, of the amount of wrong he did to each. Judging by this description, whether it is true or false, this man regards theft as a dishonorable action and hates it, but hates it less than poverty; he indeed repents of it in itself, but in so far as it was thus counterbalanced and compensated, he does not repent of it. This is not that habit that incorporates us with vice and brings even our understanding into conformity with it; nor is it that impetuous wind that comes in gusts to confuse and blind our soul, and hurls us for the moment headlong, judgment and all, into the power of vice.

I customarily do wholeheartedly whatever I do, and go my way all in one piece. I scarcely make a motion that is hidden and out of sight of my reason, and that is not guided by the consent of nearly all parts of me, without division, without internal sedition. My judgment takes all the blame or all the praise for it; and the blame it once takes, it always keeps, for virtually since its birth it has been one; the same inclination, the same road, the same strength. And in the matter of general opinions, in childhood I established myself in the position where I was to remain.

There are some impetuous, prompt, and sudden sins: let us leave them aside. But as for these other sins so many times repeated, planned, and premeditated, constitutional sins, or even professional or vocational sins, I cannot imagine that they can be implanted so long in one and the same heart, without the reason and conscience of their possessor constantly willing and intending it to be so. And the repentance which he claims comes to him at a certain prescribed moment is a little hard for me to imagine and conceive.

I do not follow the belief of the sect of Pythagoras, that men take on a new soul when they approach the images of the gods to receive their oracles.[3] Unless he meant just this, that the soul must indeed be foreign, new, and loaned for the occasion, since their own showed so little sign of any purification and cleanness worthy of this office.

They do just the opposite of the Stoic precepts, which indeed order us to correct the imperfections and vices that we recognize in us, but forbid us to be repentant and glum about them. These men make us believe that they feel great regret and remorse within; but of amendment and correction, or interruption, they show us no sign. Yet it is no cure if the disease is not thrown off. If repentance were weighing in the scale of the balance, it would outweigh the sin. I know of no quality so easy to counterfeit as piety, if conduct and life are not made to conform with it. Its essence is abstruse and occult; its semblance, easy and showy.

As for me, I may desire in a general way to be different; I may condemn and dislike my nature as a whole, and implore God to reform me completely and to pardon my natural weakness. But this I ought not to call repentance, it seems to me, any more than my displeasure at being neither an angel nor Cato.[4] My actions are in order and conformity with what I am and with my condition. I can do no better. And repentance does not properly apply to the things that are not in our power; rather does regret. I imagine numberless natures loftier and better regulated than mine, but for all that, I do not amend my faculties; just as neither my arm nor my mind becomes more vigorous by imagining another that is so. If imagining and desiring a nobler conduct

3. Seneca discusses this particular doctrine in his letters.

4. Marcus Cato (to whom Montaigne probably refers) was known as the "conscience of Rome" in his staunch opposition to Caesar and empire. Dante makes him guardian to the mountain of Purgatory.

than ours produced repentance of our own, we should have to repent of our most innocent actions, inasmuch as we rightly judge that in a more excellent nature they would have been performed with greater perfection and dignity, and we should wish to do likewise.

When I consider the behavior of my youth in comparison with that of my old age, I find that I have generally conducted myself in orderly fashion, according to my lights; that is all my resistance can accomplish. I do not flatter myself; in similar circumstances I should always be the same. It is not a spot, it is rather a tincture with which I am stained all over. I know no superficial, halfway, and perfunctory repentance. It must affect me in every part before I will call it so, and must grip me by the vitals and afflict them as deeply and as completely as God sees into me.

In business matters, several good opportunities have escaped me for want of successful management. However, my counsels have been good, according to the circumstances they were faced with; their way is always to take the easiest and surest course. I find that in my past deliberations, according to my rule, I have proceeded wisely, considering the state of the matter proposed to me, and I should do the same a thousand years from now in similar situations. I am not considering what it is at this moment, but what it was when I was deliberating about it.

The soundness of any plan depends on the time; circumstances and things roll about and change incessantly. I have fallen into some serious and important mistakes in my life, not for lack of good counsel but for lack of good luck. There are secret parts in the matters we handle which cannot be guessed, especially in human nature— mute factors that do not show, factors sometimes unknown to their possessor himself, which are brought forth and aroused by unexpected occasions. If my prudence has been unable to see into them and predict them, I bear it no ill will; its responsibility is restricted within its limitations. It is the outcome that beats me; and if it favors the course I have refused, there is no help for it; I do not blame myself; I accuse my luck, not my work. That is not to be called repentance.

Phocion had given the Athenians some advice that was not followed. When however the affair came out prosperously against his opinion, someone said to him: "Well, Phocion, are you glad that the thing is going so well?" "Indeed I am glad," he said, "that it has turned out this way, but I do not repent of having advised that way."[5]

When my friends apply to me for advice, I give it freely and clearly, and without hesitating as nearly everyone else does because, the affair being hazardous, it may come out contrary to my expectations, wherefore they may have cause to reproach me for my advice; that does not worry me. For they will be wrong, and I should not have refused them this service.

I have scarcely any occasion to blame my mistakes or mishaps on anyone but myself. For in practice I rarely ask other people's advice, unless as a compliment and out of politeness, except when I need scientific information or knowledge of the facts. But in things where I have only my judgment to employ, other people's reasons can serve to support me, but seldom to change my course. I listen to them all favorably and decently; but so far as I can remember, I have never up to this moment followed any but my own. If you ask me, they are nothing but flies and atoms that distract my will. I set little value on my own opinions, but I set just as little on those of others. Fortune pays me properly. If I do not take advice, I give still less. Mine is seldom asked, but it is followed even less; and I know of no public or private enterprise that my advice restored to its feet and

5. Recounted in Plutarch; Phocion, a soldier, advised the Athenians against a war that they ended up winning.

to the right path. Even the people whom fortune has made somewhat dependent on it have let themselves be managed more readily by anyone else's brains. Being a man who is quite as jealous of the rights of my repose as of the rights of my authority, I prefer it so; by leaving me alone, they treat me according to my professed principle, which is to be wholly contained and established within myself. To me it is a pleasure not to be concerned in other people's affairs and to be free of responsibility for them.

In all affairs, when they are past, however they have turned out, I have little regret. For this idea takes away the pain: that they were bound to happen thus, and now they are in the great stream of the universe and in the chain of Stoical causes. Your fancy, by wish or imagination, cannot change a single point without overturning the whole order of things, and the past and the future.

For the rest, I hate that accidental repentance that age brings. The man who said of old that he was obliged to the years for having rid him of sensuality had a different viewpoint from mine;[6] I shall never be grateful to impotence for any good it may do me. *Nor will Providence ever be so hostile to her own work that debility should be ranked among the best things* [Quintilian]. Our appetites are few in old age; a profound satiety seizes us after the act. In that I see nothing of conscience; sourness and weakness imprint on us a sluggish and rheumatic virtue. We must not let ourselves be so carried away by natural changes as to let our judgment degenerate. Youth and pleasure in other days did not make me fail to recognize the face of vice in voluptuousness; nor does the distaste that the years bring me make me fail to recognize the face of voluptuousness in vice. Now that I am no longer in that state, I judge it as though I were in it.

I who shake up my reason sharply and attentively, find that it is the very same I had in my more licentious years, except perhaps in so far as it has grown weaker and worse as it has grown old. And I find that even if it refuses, out of consideration for the interests of my bodily health, to put me in the furnace of this pleasure, it would not refuse to do so, any more than formerly, for my spiritual health. I do not consider it any more valiant for seeing it *hors de combat.* My temptations are so broken and mortified that they are not worth its opposition. By merely stretching out my hands to them, I exorcise them. If my reason were confronted with my former lust, I fear that it would have less strength to resist than it used to have. I do not see that of itself it judges anything differently than it did then, nor that it has gained any new light. Wherefore, if there is any convalescence, it is a deformed convalescence.

Miserable sort of remedy, to owe our health to disease! It is not for our misfortune to do us this service, it is for the good fortune of our judgment. You cannot make me do anything by ills and afflictions except curse them. They are for people who are only awakened by whipping. My reason runs a much freer course in prosperity. It is much more distracted and busy digesting pains than pleasures. I see much more clearly in fair weather. Health admonishes me more cheerfully and so more usefully than sickness. I advanced as far as I could toward reform and a regulated life when I had health to enjoy. I should be ashamed and resentful if the misery and misfortune of my decrepitude were to be thought better than my good, healthy, lively, vigorous years, and if people were to esteem me not for what I have been, but for ceasing to be that.

99

6. The "man" is Sophocles, reported by Cicero in his *On Aging.*

In my opinion it is living happily, not, as Antisthenes said, dying happily, that constitutes human felicity.[7] I have made no effort to attach, monstrously, the tail of a philosopher to the head and body of a dissipated man; or that this sickly remainder of my life should disavow and belie its fairest, longest, and most complete part. I want to present and show myself uniformly throughout. If I had to live over again, I would live as I have lived. I have neither tears for the past nor fears for the future. And unless I am fooling myself, it has gone about the same way within me as without. It is one of the chief obligations I have to my fortune that my bodily state has run its course with each thing in due season. I have seen the grass, the flower, and the fruit; now I see the dryness—happily, since it is naturally. I bear the ills I have much more easily because they are properly timed, and also because they make me remember more pleasantly the long felicity of my past life.

Likewise my wisdom may well have been of the same proportions in one age as in the other; but it was much more potent and graceful when green, gay, and natural, than it is now, being broken down, peevish, and labored. Therefore I renounce these casual and painful reformations.

God must touch our hearts. Our conscience must reform by itself through the strengthening of our reason, not through the weakening of our appetites. Sensual pleasure is neither pale nor colorless in itself for being seen through dim and bleary eyes. We should love temperance for itself and out of reverence toward God, who has commanded it, and also chastity; what catarrh lends us, and what I owe to the favor of my colic, is neither chastity nor temperance. We cannot boast of despising and fighting sensual pleasure, if we do not see or know it, and its charms, its powers, and its most alluring beauty.

I know them both; I have a right to speak; but it seems to me that in old age our souls are subject to more troublesome ailments and imperfections than in our youth. I used to say so when I was young; then they taunted me with my beardless chin. I still say so now that my gray hair gives me authority to speak. We call "wisdom" the difficulty of our humors, our distaste for present things. But in truth we do not so much abandon our vices as change them, and, in my opinion, for the worse. Besides a silly and decrepit pride, a tedious prattle, prickly and unsociable humors, superstition, and a ridiculous concern for riches when we have lost the use of them, I find there more envy, injustice, and malice. Old age puts more wrinkles in our minds than on our faces; and we never, or rarely, see a soul that in growing old does not come to smell sour and musty. Man grows and dwindles in his entirety.

Seeing the wisdom of Socrates and several circumstances of his condemnation, I should venture to believe that he lent himself to it to some extent, purposely, by prevarication, being seventy, and having so soon to suffer an increasing torpor of the rich activity of his mind, and the dimming of its accustomed brightness.[8]

What metamorphoses I see old age producing every day in many of my acquaintances! It is a powerful malady, and it creeps up on us naturally and imperceptibly. We need a great provision of study, and great precaution, to avoid the imperfections it loads upon us, or at least to slow up their progress. I feel that, notwithstanding all my retrenchments, it gains on me foot by foot. I stand fast as well as I can. But I do not know where it will lead even me in the end. In any event, I am glad to have people know whence I shall have fallen.

7. The fourth-century Athenian Antisthenes was a Cynic, who saw freedom from the passions as the only key to happiness.

8. Socrates was sentenced to death in 399 B.C.E. on the charge of having corrupted the youth of Athens. As recounted by Plato in the *Apology,* he responded ambiguously to the charges against him rather than pleading for his life as expected.

"There's one thing I can say to you in passing, that there's nothing so pleasant in the world for an honest man as to be squire to a knight errant, that seeks adventures." So says Sancho Panza to his wife at the end of the first part of the book that bears the knight errant's name. Indeed, this most beloved of novels is a novel of and about the road. Neither epic nor chivalric poem, neither pastoral romance nor picaresque, *Don Quixote* maintains a guarded and ironic distance from all these readily identifiable genres, even as its prologue beckons its *desoccupado lector* or idle reader to travel with Alonso Quixano, alias Don Quixote, and his endlessly talkative squire.

In *Don Quixote,* these are travels in the world of early seventeenth-century Spain: a world from which Jews and then Moors had been banished, where the forces of the Inquisition were ubiquitous and the importance of *limpieza de sangre*—purity of blood—was paramount. This was a world in which Miguel de Cervantes, like his knight errant, may not have been always at home. Son of an impoverished doctor, he departed for Italy following a fight when he was twenty-one to serve in the household of a cardinal in Rome. Ten years after his return, he petitioned to work in colonial Latin America (he was told in no uncertain terms to look for something in Spain). Beginning in the early 1580s, Cervantes tried to make a go of the profession of writing, succeeding only with the publication of *Don Quixote* when he was fifty-eight, considerably older than the *hidalgo* who made his fortune. Yet Cervantes and his creation are no direct mirrors for one another. Don Quixote never leaves Spain and can only dream of meaningful military action. Cervantes joined the Spanish army shortly after arriving in Italy, fighting in 1571 in the major battle of Lepanto that annihilated the Turkish fleet and restored Catholic Europe's faith in its military superiority over the Muslims. Five years later, the boat he was taking back to Spain was captured by pirates, and he was sold to a Greek in Algiers, where he remained for several years. Such episodes lie behind "The Captive's Tale" from the first part of the novel, while Cervantes's later experience in Spanish jails no doubt informs the lively chapter on the galley slaves. Nor was Cervantes a gentleman—a member of the lesser nobility that with the accession of Philip III to the throne found itself with less and less to do. One of the most powerful monarchies in Europe, even after the British defeated its naval Armada, the Spanish crown, whimsical enough to move its quarters from Madrid to Valladolid and back again in the space of five years, was also one of the most centralized.

Along with his family and innumerable courtiers, Cervantes moved back and forth with Phillip as well, no doubt hoping to win courtly approval for a government position—he had tried his hand at tax collecting for a number of years—or an occasional commission for a patriotic work, such as his play *The Seige of Numantia*. But it was only with the publication of *Don Quixote* in 1605 that Cervantes came to the attention of his fellow Spaniards and probably his king. The success of Part I was so great (as Cervantes has one fictional enthusiast put it, "Children finger it; young people read it; grown men know it by heart, and old men praise it") that pirated editions of the work began to appear almost immediately, and one Alonso Fernández de Avellaneda was motivated in 1613 to write a sequel. An ailing Cervantes completed a second part that attacks Avellaneda in its preface and has Sancho and Don Quixote laughing at the "inaccurate" sequel. But the jabs at Avellaneda are merely one aspect of the work's self-consciousness regarding its place in a world of "idle readers." In Part 2, published in 1615, just a year before the author's death, Cervantes acknowledges that his character has acquired a history and reputation all his own, and Don Quixote is constantly running into people who have already read about him and who expect him to live up to his reputation. Initially a product of the many books of chivalry he had wasted his patrimony on, Don Quixote becomes, in Part 2, the product of another book: his own. Throughout Part 2, he is forced to confront his own fictionality in a world of "real" people.

Like Jorge Luis Borges and other modernist writers he inspired, Cervantes is fascinated with the madness that ensues when the real and the fictive are confused. *Don Quixote* offers a genealogy of the knight's madness, and in a certain sense provides a requiem to a Renaissance man who thrived on folly. On the one hand, Don Quixote comes from a long line of mad heroes, from Chrètien de Troye's Ivain to the "mad Roland" (*Orlando furioso*) of Ludovico Ariosto's sixteenth-century poem, who goes beserk when he discovers that his beloved Angelica yielded her virginity to a Moorish footsoldier—a drama that Don Quixote sadly realizes he cannot imitate: "For I dare swear that my Dulcinea del Toboso has never seen a real Moor in his real Moorish dress in all her life." But on the other hand, the romances of chivalry, and the chivalric code behind them, had long had a tenuous relationship to reality; as the historian Gerhart Ladner has noted, the knight's only choices are to transcend the world or be destroyed by it. The knight in shining armor from Arthurian legend would find his life's work in pledging eternal fealty to a woman he would never possess and performing great deeds in her name—a model of ideal behavior that few could or would ever want to attain, an idealism marked both by profound Christian faith and by a fiercely sublimated eroticism. While manuals of chivalric behavior were legion after Ramon Lull's best-selling *Book of the Order of Chivalry,* by the seventeenth century, there was little inclination to find in the vestiges of medieval chivalry anything other than entertainment.

For a time, the missionary zeal inspired by the discovery of the Americas, especially among followers of the Spanish Jesuit Loyola, and the new wars with the Turks which Cervantes experienced firsthand had renewed the fervor for the chivalric glories of the past. But this fervor had diminished by the time Cervantes sat down to write his novel. In large part, it is the absence of a community that takes chivalry seriously that renders Cervantes's hero so marginal (a marginality exacerbated, as Borges has wryly remarked, by the name of Don Quixote's village: "Don Quixote de la Mancha, that now has the sound of nobility in Spanish, was intended to sound then as Don Quixote of Kansas City.") At every turn, the knight encounters greed, self-interest, and cold-blooded calculation that are the antitheses of a knight errantry meant "to redress wrongs, aid widows and protect maidens." In his first adventure, in an inn he imagines to be a castle, he finds not a castellan and ladies-in-waiting but a greedy owner, prostitutes, and a laborer who showers Don Quixote with stones. When Don Quixote later seeks solace among goatherds, he launches into a long speech about the pastoral origins of a golden age when men were considerate of their fellow human beings, a speech the goatherds listen to "in fascination and bewilderment." But the knight and his squire will end their sojourn in the supposedly idyllic countryside when they are beaten and bruised by a band of angry rustics defending their mares from the amorous advances of Don Quixote's horse, Rocinante. Shortly thereafter Don Quixote will wade into a flock of sheep and do battle with them thinking they are two powerful armies, and his "tilting at windmills" mistaken for giants has become proverbial for foolish enthusiasm.

Cervantes nonetheless complicates this repeated juxtaposition of Don Quixote's version of events and the way they "really" are, particularly in regard to the characters with whom the knight has most sustained contact. On occasion, Don Quixote's madness brings out the good in others, as he evokes their sympathy and enables them to express a compassion to which they are unaccustomed. The innkeeper doesn't demand payment from the injured knight, and the laborer who takes Don Quixote back to La Mancha after his first round of adventures "waits till it was rather darker [to ride into the village], so that no one should see the battered gentleman on so shameful a mount." Far more than sympathy is exacted from Sancho Panza, who initially rides off with Don Quixote for purely mercenary motives—he wants to govern the island promised him as reward for his patient services—but who becomes seduced by the profound pleasures of the life of knight-errantry: it is clearly a life more exciting, more meaningful, than his sedentary life in the village. Between him and Don Quixote grows a bond fashioned from sharing intimate moments, ranging from their lengthy discourses in the lonely Sierra Morena, to their vomiting over one another after the episode of the sheep.

At the same time, Sancho Panza becomes adept at learning Don Quixote's language and at exploiting it, as when he claims that a peasant girl he met on the road was an enchanted Dulcinea. Yet there are far more subtle ways in which Don Quixote's companions are influenced by his vision of the world—a world where "every man is the child of his works" and one has faith in things not seen. While Don Quixote's madness is surely ridiculous, and his naive belief in the old chivalric stories is condemned, the reader is often led to the same query posed by two gentlemen with whom Don Quixote dines late in Part 2: "One moment they thought him a man of sense, and the next he slipped into craziness; nor could they decide what degree to assign him between wisdom and folly."

Where Cervantes himself stands in relationship to his hero is a puzzle. This is in part because of the playful distance he placed between himself and Don Quixote's story. The story after Chapter 10 comes to us from a Moorish enchanter named Cide Hamete Benengeli and is translated by a Moor the author meets in the marketplace. But since "men of that [Arabic] nation [are] ready liars," neither the history itself nor the translation can be trusted. Moreover, as Cervantes matures as a writer, Don Quixote tends to slip from our sight. He is very much the focus of Part 1, save for the story of "The Captive's Tale." But in Part 2, other characters take center stage for extended periods of time, as the university student Sansón Carrasco and a seemingly sadistic duke and duchess increasingly manipulate the book's events. Perhaps the novel must inevitably prepare for the moment when the world which Don Quixote had made so colorful must go on without him: Alonxo Quixano may be unable to survive the destruction of his fantasy, but others must continue in its absence.

Cervantes himself, though, did not live long after the publication of Part 2. A flurry of literary activity in his last few years had led him to write his *Exemplary Novels* (1613), a collection

100

Gustave Doré, engraving for Cervantes's *Don Quixote.* Doré was a prominent sculptor and painter in mid-nineteenth-century France, but he is best remembered for his illustrations for literary masterpieces such as Rabelais's works, *Paradise Lost* and Dante's *Inferno* (with many a gruesome punishment vividly displayed for the reader's entertainment). *Don Quixote* attracted Doré's attention as well, and in 1862—two years before publishing an illustrated Bible—the artist gave the world arresting images such as this one, showing Don Quixote's collision with a windmill, while a frantic Sancho Panza yells from afar.

of short stories that subverts the genre of the picaresque, and he then wrote an ambitious romance, *Persiles and Sigismunda,* published posthumously. But Cide Hamete's observation at the close of his manuscript, "For me alone Don Quixote was born and I for him," may be true for Cervantes himself. Perhaps the great irony of this work by one of the master ironists of all time is that Don Quixote is a victim of the fictions he has read; yet it is he who, along with his faithful servant, is the most compelling and immediate of the novel's characters. He is the one most likely to pull us as readers—and perhaps Cervantes as author—into the dangerous new world of the novel, as refracted through the endearingly mad habitations of his mind.

PRONUNCIATIONS:

Cide Hamete Benengeli: SEE-day ha-MEE-tay ben-en-HEL-lee
Don Jerónimo: DON hay-RO-nee-mo
Don Quixote: DON kee-HO-tay
Dulcinea: dole-see-NAY-ah
Gines de Pasamonte: he-NACE day pahs-ah-MON-tay
Rocinante: ro-see-NAN-tay
Roque Guinart: RO-kay gee-NAR
Quejana: kay-HAN-na
Quesada: kay-SAH-da

Don Quixote[1]

Part 1

Chapter 1

Concerning the famous hidalgo[2] Don Quixote de la Mancha's position, character and way of life

In a village in La Mancha, the name of which I cannot quite recall,[3] there lived not long ago one of those country gentlemen or hidalgos who keep a lance in a rack, an ancient leather shield, a scrawny hack and a greyhound for coursing. A midday stew with rather more shin of beef than leg of lamb, the leftovers for supper most nights, lardy eggs on Saturdays, lentil broth on Fridays and an occasional pigeon as a Sunday treat ate up three-quarters of his income. The rest went on a cape of black broadcloth, with breeches of velvet and slippers to match for holy days, and on weekdays he walked proudly in the finest homespun. He maintained a housekeeper the wrong side of forty, a niece the right side of twenty and a jack of all trades who was as good at saddling the nag as at plying the pruning shears. Our hidalgo himself was nearly fifty; he had a robust constitution, dried-up flesh and a withered face, and he was an early riser and a keen huntsman. His surname's said to have been Quixada, or Quesada (as if he were a jawbone, or a cheesecake):[4] concerning this detail there's some discrepancy among the authors who have written on the subject, although a credible conjecture does suggest he might have been a plaintive Quexana. But this doesn't matter much, as far as our story's concerned, provided that the narrator doesn't stray one inch from the truth.

1. Translated by John Rutherford.
2. *Hidalgo* literally means a person "of some distinction," a member of the lowest rung of the nobility who would have been exempt from taxation. Don Quixote is neither a *don* nor a knight or *caballero*, who would have had jurisdiction over land.
3. La Mancha is an arid region of Castile in south-central Spain, not far from the major cities of Toledo and Madrid.
4. A *quixote* is a piece of armor, a far cry from the comic images suggested by the variants of his name (a *quijado* is a

Now you must understand that during his idle moments (which accounted for most of the year) this hidalgo took to reading books of chivalry with such relish and enthusiasm that he almost forgot about his hunting and even running his property, and his foolish curiosity reached such extremes that he sold acres of arable land to buy these books of chivalry, and took home as many of them as he could find; he liked none of them so much as those by the famous Feliciano de Silva,[5] because the brilliance of the prose and all that intricate language seemed a treasure to him, never more so than when he was reading those amorous compliments and challenges delivered by letter, in which he often found: "The reason for the unreason to which my reason is subjected, so weakens my reason that I have reason to complain of your beauty." And also when he read: "...the lofty heavens which with their stars divinely fortify you in your divinity, and make you meritorious of the merits merited by your greatness." Such subtleties used to drive the poor gentleman to distraction, and he would rack his brains trying to understand it all and unravel its meaning, something that Aristotle himself wouldn't have been capable of doing even if he'd come back to life for this purpose alone. He wasn't very happy about the wounds that Sir Belianis kept on inflicting and receiving, because he imagined that, however skilful the doctors who treated him, his face and body must have been covered with gashes and scars. But, in spite of all that, he commended the author for ending his book with that promise of endless adventure, and often felt the urge to take up his quill and bring the story to a proper conclusion, as is promised there; and no doubt he'd have done so, and with success too, if other more important and insistent preoccupations hadn't prevented him. He had frequent arguments with the village priest (a learned man—a Sigüenza graduate no less) about which had been the better knight errant, Palmerin of England or Amadis of Gaul;[6] but Master Nicolás, the village barber, argued that neither of them could hold a candle to the Knight of Phoebus, and that if anyone at all could be compared to him it was Don Galaor, Amadis of Gaul's brother, because there was no emergency he couldn't cope with: he wasn't one of your pernickety knights, nor was he such a blubberer as his brother, and he was every bit his equal as far as courage was concerned.

In short, our hidalgo was soon so absorbed in these books that his nights were spent reading from dusk till dawn, and his days from dawn till dusk, until the lack of sleep and the excess of reading withered his brain, and he went mad. Everything he read in his books took possession of his imagination: enchantments, fights, battles, challenges, wounds, sweet nothings, love affairs, storms and impossible absurdities. The idea that this whole fabric of famous fabrications was real so established itself in his mind that no history in the world was truer for him. He would declare that El Cid, Ruy Díaz, had been an excellent knight, but that he couldn't be compared to the Knight of the Burning Sword,[7] who with just one back-stroke had split two fierce and enormous giants clean down the middle. He felt happier about Bernardo del Carpio, because he'd slain Roland the Enchanted at Roncesvalles, by the same method used by Hercules when he suffocated Antaeus, the son of Earth—with a bear-hug.[8] He was full of praise for the giant Morgante[9] because, despite belonging to a proud and

5. A 16th-century writer of the chivalric romances that had been vastly popular in Spain.

6. A third-rate university was to be found at Sigüenza, a town northwest of Madrid. Palmerin of England was the protagonist of a Portuguese chivalric romance, Amadis of Gaul that of Spain's most famous romance, *Amadís de Gaula*, written by Garci Rodríguez de Montalvo in 1508. Montalvo combined battle scenes with those of courtly love, and ended his work with the rather unusual flourish of a marriage.

7. The Cid was the hero of *The Poem of the Cid,* the first epic poem written in Spain; he was noted for his deeds against the Moors. The Knight of the Burning Sword is a character in one of Feliciano de Silva's romances, *The Ninth Book of Amadis of Gaul* (1530).

8. The Castilian warrior Bernardo del Carpio appears in mid-16th-century Spanish works as the defeater of Roland, Charlemagne's most powerful knight. He quickly attained the status of Spain's national hero. Antaeus derived his strength from his contact with "mother" Earth; Hercules lifted him up until he became weak, then killed him.

insolent breed, he alone was affable and well-mannered. But his greatest favourite was Reynald of Montalban, most of all when he saw him sallying forth from his castle and plundering all those he met, and when in foreign parts he stole that image of Muhammad made of solid gold, as his history records.[1] He'd have given his house-keeper, and even his niece into the bargain, to trample the traitor Ganelon in the dust.[2]

And so, by now quite insane, he conceived the strangest notion that ever took shape in a madman's head, considering it desirable and necessary, both for the increase of his honour and for the common good, to become a knight errant, and to travel about the world with his armour and his arms and his horse in search of adventures, and to prac-tise all those activities that he knew from his books were practised by knights errant, redressing all kinds of grievances, and exposing himself to perils and dangers that he would overcome and thus gain eternal fame and renown. The poor man could already see himself being crowned Emperor of Trebizond,[3] at the very least, through the might of his arm; and so, possessed by these delightful thoughts and carried away by the strange pleasure that he derived from them, he hastened to put into practice what he so desired.

His first step was to clean a suit of armour that had belonged to his forefathers and that, covered in rust and mould, had been standing forgotten in a corner for centuries. He scoured and mended it as best he could; yet he realized that it had one important defect, which was that the headpiece was not a complete helmet but just a simple steel cap; he was ingenious enough, however, to overcome this problem, constructing out of cardboard something resembling a visor and face-guard which, once inserted into the steel cap, gave it the appearance of a full helmet. It's true that, to test its strength and find out whether it could safely be exposed to attack, he drew his sword and dealt it two blows, with the first of which he destroyed in a second what it had taken him a week to create. He couldn't help being concerned about the ease with which he'd shattered it, and to guard against this danger he reconstructed it, fixing some iron bars on the inside, which reassured him about its strength; and, preferring not to carry out any further tests, he deemed and pronounced it a most excellent visored helmet.

Then he went to visit his nag, and although it had more corns than a barleyfield and more wrong with it than Gonella's horse, which *tantum pellis et ossa fuit*, it seemed to him that neither Alexander's Bucephalus nor the Cid's Babieca was its equal.[4] He spent four days considering what name to give the nag; for (he told himself) it wasn't fitting that the horse of such a famous knight errant, and such a fine horse in its own right, too, shouldn't have some name of eminence; and so he tried to find one that would express both what it had been before it became a knight's horse and what it was now, for it was appropriate that, since its master had changed his rank, it too should change its name, and acquire a famous and much-trumpeted one, as suited the new order and new way of life he professed. And so, after a long succession of names that he invented, eliminated and struck out, added, deleted and remade in his mind and in his imagination, he finally decided to call it *Rocinante*, that is, *Hackafore*, a name which, in his opinion, was lofty and sonorous and expressed what the creature had been when it was a humble hack, before it became what it was now—the first and foremost of all the hacks in the world.

1. Reynald (Rinaldo) appears in the two major chivalric romances of the Italian Renaissance, Boiardo's *Orlando Innam-orato* (Orlando [Roland] in love) and Ludovico Ariosto's *Orlando furioso* (Mad Orlando).

2. In the original *Song of Roland,* the jealous Ganelon betrays Charlemagne and Roland to the Moors and causes the army's defeat at Roncesvalles.

3. A region of the Byzantine empire; the name was used broadly for Asiatic Turkey.

4. Pietro Gonella was a famous jester in Ferrara. The Latin phrase means "all skin and bone." The wild horse Bucephalus was tamed by the young Alexander, who then rode him during his conquests of India and the East, while Babieca was the Cid's famous steed.

Having given his horse a name, and one so much to his liking, he decided to give himself a name as well, and this problem kept him busy for another eight days, at the end of which he decided to call himself *Don Quixote,* that is, *Sir Thighpiece,* from which, as has already been observed, the authors of this most true history concluded that his surname must have been Quixada, and not Quesada as others had affirmed. Yet remembering that brave Amadis hadn't been content to call himself Amadis alone, but had added the name of his kingdom and homeland, to make it famous, and had styled himself Amadis of Gaul, so Don Quixote, as a worthy knight, decided to add his own country to his name and call himself *Don Quixote de la Mancha,* by doing which, in his opinion, he declared in a most vivid manner both his lineage and his homeland, and honoured the latter by taking it as his surname.

Having, then, cleaned his armour, turned his steel cap into a visored helmet, baptized his nag and confirmed himself, he realized that the only remaining task was to find a lady of whom he could be enamoured; for a knight errant without a lady-love is a tree without leaves or fruit, a body without a soul. He said to himself:

"If, for my wicked sins or my good fortune, I encounter some giant, as knights errant usually do, and I dash him down in single combat, or cleave him asunder, or, in short, defeat and vanquish him, will it not be proper to have someone to whom I can send him as a tribute, so that he can come before my sweet lady and fall to his knees and say in humble tones of submission: 'I, my lady, am the giant Caraculiambro, the Lord of the Isle of Malindrania,[5] vanquished in single combat by the never sufficiently praised knight Don Quixote de la Mancha, who has commanded me to present myself before Your Highness so that Your Highness may dispose of me as you will'"?

Oh my, how our worthy knight rejoiced once he'd spoken these words—even more, once he'd found someone he could call his lady! The fact was—or so it is generally believed—that in a nearby village there lived a good-looking peasant girl, with whom he'd once been in love (although it appears that she was never aware of this love, about which he never told her). She was called Aldonza Lorenzo, and this was the woman upon whom it seemed appropriate to confer the title of the lady of his thoughts; and seeking a name with some affinity with his own, which would also suggest the name of a princess and a fine lady, he decided to call her *Dulcinea del Toboso,* because she was a native of El Toboso: a name that, in his opinion, was musical and magical and meaningful, like all the other names he'd bestowed upon himself and his possessions.

Chapter 2

Concerning the ingenious Don Quixote's first sally

Once he'd made these preparations he decided not to wait any longer before putting his plans into action, encouraged by the need that he believed his delay was creating in the world: so great was his determination to redress grievances, right wrongs, correct injustices, rectify abuses and fulfil obligations. And so, without telling anyone about his plans or being seen by anyone, one morning, before dawn because it was going to be one of those sweltering July days, he donned his armour, mounted Rocinante, with his ill-devised visor in place, took up his leather shield, seized his

---

5. An imaginary island; the giant's name translates roughly as "face of an ass."

lance and rode out into the fields through the side-door in a yard wall, in raptures of joy on seeing how easy it had been to embark upon his noble enterprise. But no sooner was he outside the door than he was assailed by a terrible thought, which almost made him abandon his undertaking: he remembered that he hadn't been knighted and by the laws of chivalry shouldn't and indeed couldn't take up arms against any knight; and that even if he had been knighted, he would, as a novice, have been obliged to bear white arms, that is to say a shield without any insignia on it, until he'd won them by his own prowess. These thoughts made him waver in his plans; but, since his madness prevailed over all other considerations, he decided to have himself knighted by the first person he chanced upon, in imitation of many others who'd done the same, as he'd read in the books that had reduced him to this state. As for the white arms, he resolved to give his lance and his armour such a scouring, as soon as an opportunity arose, as to make them cleaner and whiter than ermine; and thus he calmed down and continued on his chosen way, which in reality was none other than the way his horse chose to follow, for he believed that in this consisted the essence of adventure.

As our fledgling adventurer rode along, he said to himself:

"Who can doubt but that in future times, when the true history of my famous deeds sees the light, the sage who chronicles them will, when he recounts this my first sally, so early in the morning, write in this manner: 'Scarce had ruddy Apollo spread over the face of the wide and spacious earth the golden tresses of his beauteous hair, and scarce had the speckled little birds with their harmonious tongues hailed in musical and mellifluous melody the approach of rosy Aurora who, rising from her jealous husband's soft couch, disclosed herself to mortals in the portals and balconies of La Mancha's horizon, when the famous knight Don Quixote de la Mancha, quitting the slothful feathers of his bed, mounted his famous steed Rocinante and began to ride over the ancient and far-famed Plain of Montiel'"?[1]

And it was true that this was where he was riding. And he added:

"Happy will be the age, the century will be happy, which brings to light my famous exploits, worthy to be engraved on sheets of bronze, carved on slabs of marble and painted on boards of wood as a monument for all posterity. O sage enchanter, whomsoever you may be, to whom it falls to be the chronicler of this singular history, I beg you not to overlook my good Rocinante, my eternal companion in all my travels and wanderings."

Then he turned and said, as if he really were in love:

"O Princess Dulcinea, mistress of this hapless heart! Great injury have you done me in reproaching and dismissing me, with the cruel command not to appear in the presence of your wondrous beauty. Vouchsafe, my lady, to be mindful of this your subject heart, which suffers such sorrow for love of you."

He strung these absurdities together with many others, all in the style of those that he'd learned from his books. This made his progress so slow, and the sun was rising so fast and becoming so hot, that his brains would have melted, if he'd had any.

He rode on almost throughout that day and nothing happened worth mentioning, which reduced him to despair because he was longing for an early encounter with someone on whom he could test the worth of his mighty arm. Some authors say that the first adventure that befell him was that of the Pass of Lápice, others claim that it was that of the windmills, but what I've been able to discover about this matter,

1. Site of a major battle in 1369.

and indeed what I've found recorded in the annals of La Mancha, is that he rode on throughout that day, and that at nightfall both he and his nag were exhausted and half dead from starvation; and that, looking all around to see if he could spot some castle or shepherds' hut where they might retire and find some remedy for their great hunger and dire want, he caught sight of an inn not far from the road along which he was travelling, which was as if he had seen a star leading him not just to the portals but to the very palace of his redemption. He quickened his pace, and he reached the inn as night was falling.

Sitting by the inn door there happened to be two young women, of the sort known as ladies of easy virtue, on their way to Seville with some muleteers who'd chanced to break their journey that night at the inn. And since whatever our adventurer thought, saw or imagined seemed to him to be as it was in the books he'd read, as soon as he saw the inn he took it for a castle with its four towers and their spires of shining silver, complete with its drawbridge and its deep moat and all the other accessories that such castles commonly boast. He approached the inn that he took for a castle, and at a short distance from it he drew rein, waiting for some dwarf to appear upon the battlements and announce with a trumpet-blast the arrival of a knight. But finding that there was some delay, and that Rocinante was impatient to get to the stable, he rode on towards the inn door and saw the two dissolute wenches sitting there, and thought that they were two beautiful maidens or fine ladies taking their ease at the castle gate. At this point a swineherd who was gathering together some pigs (begging nobody's pardon, because that's what they're called) from a stubble field happened to sound his horn to round them up, and Don Quixote thought that his wish had been fulfilled and that a dwarf was announcing his arrival; so it was with unusual satisfaction that he reached the inn and the ladies, who, on observing the approach of a man dressed like that in armour and clutching a lance and a leather shield, started to run in terror back into the inn. But Don Quixote, conjecturing their fear from their flight, and raising his cardboard visor to reveal his dry and dusty face, addressed them with courteous demeanour and tranquil voice:

"Flee not, nor fear the least affront; for in the order of knighthood which I profess it neither belongs nor behoves to offer any such, much less to high-born maidens, as your presence testifies you to be."

The girls had been peering at him and trying to make out his face, hidden behind the ill-made visor; but when they heard themselves called maidens, a term so much at odds with their profession, they couldn't contain their laughter, which was so hearty that Don Quixote flared up and exclaimed:

"Moderation befits the fair; furthermore, laughter which springs from a petty cause is a great folly; but I say this unto you not to grieve you nor yet to sour your disposition; for mine is none other than to serve you."

This language, which the ladies didn't understand, together with the sorry figure cut by the knight, only redoubled their laughter and his wrath, and things would have come to a pretty pass if it hadn't been for the appearance at that moment of the innkeeper, a man who, being very fat, was very peaceable, and who on seeing such an ungainly figure, with such ill-matched equipment as the long stirrups, the lance, the leather shield and the infantryman's body-armour, was more than willing to join the maidens in their merry-making. But he was also intimidated by all these paraphernalia and, deciding to address the knight in a civil manner, he said:

"If, sir caballero, you're looking for somewhere to stay the night, you'll find plenty of everything you need here—all except a bed that is, we haven't got any of those."

Don Quixote, observing the humility of the governor of the castle, for they were what he took the innkeeper and the inn to be, replied:

> "For me, sir castellano,[2] anything will suffice, because
> My arms are my bed-hangings,
> And my rest's the bloody fray."[3]

The host thought that Don Quixote had called him castellano because he'd taken him for one of the Castilian conmen, whereas in reality he was an Andalusian, a prime picaroon from the Playa district of Sanlúcar, no less a thief than Cacus,[4] and no less an evildoer than any experienced page-boy, and he replied:

"In that case,

> Your bed must be the hard, hard rock,
> And your sleep to watch till day

—and that being so, you go ahead and dismount in the certainty of finding in this humble abode plenty of opportunities not to sleep for a whole year, let alone one night."

And with these words he went and held Don Quixote's stirrup, and the knight dismounted with the greatest difficulty, not having broken his fast all day long.

He then instructed the innkeeper to take great care of his horse, for a finer steed had never eaten barley. The innkeeper looked at the animal, which didn't seem half as good as Don Quixote had claimed, and, after housing it in the stable, went back to receive orders from his guest, whom the maidens, now reconciled, were helping out of his armour. Although they'd taken off his breast and back plates, they couldn't fathom how to disengage his gorget or remove his imitation visor, tied on with green ribbons that would have to be cut, since it was impossible to undo the knots; but he would by no means consent to this, and kept his helmet on all night, making the funniest and strangest figure imaginable. As these trollops unarmed him, he, thinking they were illustrious ladies of the castle, wittily declaimed:

> "And never sure was any knight
> So served by damsel or by dame
> As Quixote was, one happy night
> When from his village first he came:
> Maids waited on that man of might,
> Princesses on his steed, whose name...

is Rocinante, good ladies, and mine is Don Quixote de la Mancha; for although I had intended not to discover myself until the deeds done for your benefit and service should have made me known, yet the necessity to accommodate this ancient ballad of Sir Lancelot[5] to our present purpose has been the occasion of your knowing my name ere it were meet; but a time will come when you will command and I shall obey, and when the might of this arm will manifest the desire I have to serve you."

The girls, who weren't used to such rhetorical flourishes, didn't answer, but just asked if he'd like a bite to eat.

"I would fain eat anything," replied Don Quixote, "for, by my troth, much good would it do me."

2. Governor or constable of a castle.
3. The lines are from a well-known Spanish ballad.
4. The Playa district was an area of thieves and swindlers, while in Roman legend the brigand Cacus is said to have stolen the cattle of Hercules.
5. One of King Arthur's knights; Don Quixote has just altered the words to a popular ballad about him.

It happened to be a Friday, so there was no food in the inn except a few helpings of what is known in Castile as *abadejo,* in Andalusia as *bacallao* and in other parts of Spain as *curadillo*—in other words the humble salt cod; but in these parts it was strangely called *truchuela.* They asked him if he'd like some of this troutling, because that was all the fish there was.

"If you have a goodly number of troutlings," replied Don Quixote, "they will serve me as well as a trout, because it makes no difference to me whether I am given eight separate reals or a single piece of eight. What is more, it might even be that these troutlings are like veal, which is better than beef, or like kid, which is better than goat. But whatever this fish is, let it be served; for the travails and the burden of arms cannot be borne on an empty stomach."

A table was set at the door of the inn, where it was cooler, and the innkeeper brought a dish of inadequately soaked and worse cooked salt cod, and a loaf of bread as black and mouldy as the hidalgo's armour; and it was a source of great mirth to watch him eat because, since he was wearing his helmet and holding up the visor, he couldn't put any food into his mouth with his own hands, and somebody else had to do so for him, a task performed by one of the ladies. But when they tried to give him some drink, they found this an impossible task, and he wouldn't have drunk a drop if the innkeeper hadn't bored a hole through a length of cane and put one end into his mouth and poured the wine into the other; and Don Quixote suffered it all with great patience, so as not to allow his helmet-ribbons to be cut. In the midst of these activities a sow-gelder happened to arrive at the inn, and as he did so he sounded his pan-pipes four or five times, which convinced Don Quixote that he was indeed in some famous castle, and that he was being served to the accompaniment of music, and that the salt cod was trout, the bread baked from the whitest wheat-flour, the prostitutes fine ladies and the innkeeper the lord of the castle; and it all confirmed that his decision to sally forth had been a wise one. Yet what most bothered him was that he hadn't yet been knighted, because he knew that he couldn't lawfully embark on any adventure without first having been admitted to the order of chivalry.

Chapter 3

Which relates the amusing way in which Don Quixote had himself knighted

And so, troubled by this thought, Don Quixote made short work of his meagre lodging-house supper, and then called for the innkeeper and, shutting himself up with him in the stable, fell upon his knees before him and said:

"I shall ne'er, O valorous knight, arise from where I kneel, until your courtesy vouchsafes me a boon which I desire to beg of you and which will redound to your own praise and to the benefit of humankind."

The innkeeper, seeing his guest at his feet and hearing such pleadings, gazed down at him in perplexity, not knowing what to do or say, and kept telling him to stand up; but he kept refusing, and the innkeeper had to promise to grant his request.

"No less did I expect from your munificence, sir," replied Don Quixote. "Know therefore that the boon which I have begged and which your liberality has vouchsafed me is that tomorrow you shall knight me; and tonight, in the chapel of this your castle, I will keep the vigil of arms; and tomorrow, as I have said, what I so desire shall be accomplished, so that I can legitimately roam through the four corners of the world in quest of adventures for the relief of the needy, as is the duty of chivalry and of knights errant such as I, whose desire towards such exploits is inclined."

The innkeeper, who, as I've said, was something of a wag, and had already suspected that his guest wasn't in his right mind, found his suspicion confirmed when he heard these words and, to have something to laugh at that night, decided to humour him; so he said that he was quite right to pursue these objectives, and that such desires were natural and fitting in such a knight as he seemed to be and as his gallant presence testified; and that he himself in his younger days had followed the same honourable profession, roaming through different parts of the world in search of adventure, without omitting to visit such districts as Percheles and Islas de Riarán in Malaga, Compás in Seville, Azoguejo in Segovia, Olivera in Valencia, Rondilla in Granada, Playa in Sanlúcar, Potro in Cordova and Ventillas in Toledo,[1] and many other places where he'd exercised the dexterity of his hands and the nimbleness of his heels, doing many injuries, wooing many widows, ruining a few maidens and swindling a few orphans, and, in short, making himself known in most of the law courts and tribunals in Spain; and that he'd finally retired to his castle, where he lived on his own means and on those of others, accommodating all knights errant, whatever their status or position, solely because of the great affection he felt for them and so that they could share their wealth with him, to repay him for his kindness.

He also told Don Quixote that in his castle there wasn't any chapel where he could keep the vigil of arms, because it had been demolished to build a new one, but he knew that in case of need vigil might be kept anywhere, and Don Quixote could do so that night in a courtyard within the castle; and in the morning, God willing, the proper ceremonies would be performed to make him into a knight, so very thoroughly that no knight in the whole wide world could be more of a knight than he.

He asked Don Quixote if he had any money on him; Don Quixote replied that he did not have so much as a single real,[2] because he had never read in histories of knights errant that any of them had ever carried money. To this the innkeeper retorted that he was deluding himself—even if it wasn't written in the histories, because their authors had considered that there wasn't any need to record something as obviously necessary as money or clean shirts, that wasn't any reason to believe that they'd travelled without supplies of both; so he could take it as true and proven that all knights errant, of which so many books are full to overflowing, kept their purses well lined in readiness for any eventuality, and that they also carried shirts and small chests full of ointments for curing the wounds they received; because there wasn't always someone available to treat them in every field or desert where they engaged in combat and were injured, unless they had some wise enchanter for a friend, and he came to their aid, summoning through the air, on some cloud, a damsel or a dwarf with a flask of water of such magical properties that, on tasting just one drop, they were instantly cured of their wounds and injuries, as if they'd never been hurt. But, just in case this didn't happen, the knights of old had considered it wise to see that their squires were provided with money and other necessities such as lint and ointments to dress their wounds; and if any such knight happened not to have a squire (a most unusual occurrence), he himself would carry all these supplies in small saddle-bags that were scarcely visible, on the crupper of his steed, as if they were something else of much

1. All notorious lowlife districts in some of Spain's major cities.
2. A coin worth about five cents.

greater importance because, except in such circumstances, carrying saddle-bags was rather frowned upon among knights errant; and the innkeeper therefore advised Don Quixote—although he could, if he wished, command him as the godson that he was about to become—never again to travel without money and all the other supplies just mentioned, and he'd discover when he least expected it how useful they could be.

Don Quixote promised to do exactly as he'd been told, and then he was given orders to keep the vigil of arms in a large yard on one side of the inn; and he gathered his armour together and placed it on a water-trough next to a well, and, taking up his leather shield and seizing his lance, he began with stately bearing to pace back and forth in front of the trough; and as his pacing began, night was beginning to fall.

The innkeeper told everyone in the hostelry about his guest's insanity, his vigil and the knighting that he awaited. They wondered at such a strange kind of madness and went to watch him from a distance, and saw that, with a composed air, he sometimes paced to and fro and, at other times, leaning on his lance, gazed at his armour without looking away for some while. Night fell, but the moon was so bright that it competed with the source of its brightness, and every action of the novice knight could be clearly observed by all. And now one of the muleteers staying at the inn decided to water his animals, and to do so he had to remove from the trough the armour placed there by Don Quixote, who, on seeing him approach, cried out:

"O rash knight, whomsoever you may be, coming to lay hands on the armour of the most valiant knight errant who ever girded sword! Take care what you do, and touch it not, unless you wish to pay with your life for your temerity."

The muleteer wouldn't toe the line (it would have been better for the rest of his anatomy if he had); instead, grasping the armour by its straps, he hurled it to one side. When Don Quixote saw this, he raised his eyes to heaven and, fixing his thoughts, as it seemed, on his lady Dulcinea, he said:

"Assist me, dear lady, in this first affront suffered by this breast that is enthralled to you; let not your favour and your succour abandon me in this first moment of peril."

And with these and other similar words he dropped his leather shield, raised his lance with both hands, and dealt the muleteer so powerful a blow to the head that he fell on the ground in such a sorry state that had it been followed by another blow he wouldn't have needed a doctor to treat him. Then Don Quixote replaced his armour and continued pacing to and fro with the same composure as before. After a while another muleteer, not knowing what had happened (because the first one still lay stunned), also came to water his animals and, as he went to remove the armour from the trough, Don Quixote, without uttering a word or asking anybody for her favour, again dropped his leather shield and raised his lance, and didn't break it over the second muleteer's head but rather broke the head, into more than three pieces, because he criss-crossed it with two blows. All the people in the hostelry came running at the noise, the innkeeper among them. When Don Quixote saw them, he took up his leather shield and, with one hand on his sword, declared:

"O beauteous lady, strength and vigour of my enfeebled heart! Now is the time for you to turn the eyes of your greatness towards this your hapless knight, on the brink of so mighty an adventure."

With this he felt so inspirited that if all the muleteers in the world had attacked him he wouldn't have retreated one inch. The wounded men's companions, seeing them in such a state, began to rain stones on Don Quixote, who fended them off with his leather shield as best he could, unwilling to move away from the water-trough and leave his armour unprotected. The innkeeper was yelling at them to let him be—he'd already told them he was a madman, and as such would go scot-free even if he killed the lot of them. Don Quixote was shouting too, even louder, calling them perfidious traitors and the lord of the castle a poltroon and a base-born knight, who allowed knights errant to be treated in such a way and who, if he had been admitted to the order of chivalry, would have been made to regret his treachery:

"But to you, vile and base rabble, I pay no heed; stone me, come, draw near, assail me as best you can, for you will soon see how you are made to pay for your folly and your insolence."

He spoke with such vehemence and spirit that he struck fear into his assailants; and this, together with the innkeeper's arguments, persuaded them to stop, and he allowed them to remove the wounded, and continued keeping the vigil of arms, with the same composure as before.

The innkeeper wasn't amused by his guest's capers, and decided to put an end to them by giving him his wretched order of chivalry before any further calamities occurred. And so he approached him and apologized for the insolent behaviour of that rabble, about which he'd known nothing; but they had been properly punished for their impudence. He said that, as he'd mentioned before, there wasn't any chapel in the castle, and in any case there wasn't any need of one for what was left to be done; because the essence of being knighted lay in the cuff on the neck and the touch on the shoulder, according to his information about the ceremonial of the order, and all of that could be done in the middle of a field if necessary, and his guest had already fulfilled the bit about keeping the vigil of arms, because two hours of it were quite enough, and he'd been at it for over four. Don Quixote believed every word; he was there ready to obey him, and could he please expedite the process as much as possible, for if he were to be attacked again, after having been knighted, he did not intend to leave a single soul alive in the castle except those whom its lord commanded be spared and whom, out of respect for him, he would not harm.

The castellan, thus forewarned and now even more concerned, hurried away to fetch a ledger in which he kept the muleteers' accounts for straw and barley and, accompanied by a lad carrying a candle-end and by the two maidens, he came back to Don Quixote and ordered him to kneel; and, after reading for a while from his ledger, as if reciting some devout prayer, he raised his hand and cuffed him on the neck and then, with Don Quixote's own sword, gave him a handsome thwack on the shoulder, all the while muttering as if praying. And then he commanded one of the maidens to gird on the novice knight's sword, a task performed with much grace and discretion, with which she needed to be well provided so as not to burst out laughing at each stage of the ceremony; but the exploits that they'd watched him perform kept their laughter in check. As the good lady girded on his sword, she said:

"May God make you a most fortunate knight and give you good fortune in your battles."

Don Quixote asked what was her name, so that he should thenceforth know to whom he was indebted for the favour received, because he intended to bestow upon her a share of the honour he was to win by the might of his arm. She humbly replied that her name was La Tolosa, and that she was the daughter of a cobbler from Toledo who lived near the Sancho Bienaya market stalls, and that wherever she was she'd serve him and regard him as her lord. Don Quixote replied that, for his sake and as a favour to him, she should thenceforth take the title of a lady, and call herself Doña Tolosa. She promised to do so, and the other maiden buckled on his spurs; there ensued almost exactly the same dialogue as with the lady of the sword. He asked what was her name, she said it was La Molinera, because she was the daughter of an honourable miller from Antoquera, and Don Quixote also asked her to take a title, and call herself Doña Molinera, and offered her further services and favours.

Now that these unprecedented ceremonies had been performed, at top speed, Don Quixote couldn't wait to be on horseback sallying forth in search of adventures, and he saddled and mounted Rocinante and, having embraced his host, made such extraordinary statements as he thanked him for the favour of dubbing him knight that it would be impossible to do them justice in writing. The innkeeper, concerned only to be rid of his guest, replied to his rhetoric in no less high-flown although somewhat briefer terms, and was so delighted to see the back of the man that he didn't demand any payment for his stay at the inn.

Chapter 4

About what happened to our knight when he left the inn

It must have been about daybreak when Don Quixote left the inn, so happy, so gallant, so delighted at being a properly dubbed knight that the very girths of his horse were bursting with his joy. But remembering his host's advice about the essential supplies that he should take with him, and in particular money and shirts, he decided to return home and equip himself with them and with a squire, resolving to take into his service a neighbour, a poor farmer who had a large family but was well suited to the squirely office. With this in mind he turned Rocinante towards his home village, and the nag, half sensing its old haunts, began to trot with such zest that its hooves seemed not to touch the ground.

He hadn't gone far when he thought he could hear, coming from a dense wood on his right, faint sounds as of someone moaning, and he said:

"I thank heaven for the favour it now grants me, providing me with such an early opportunity to fulfil the duties of my profession and gather the fruit of my honourable intentions. These cries come, no doubt, from some man or woman in distress, who stands in need of my protection and assistance."

He turned right and rode over to where he thought the sounds were coming from. A few steps into the wood he saw a mare tied by the reins to an evergreen oak, and tied to another a lad of about fifteen, naked from the waist up, and this was the one who was crying out, not without reason, because a burly farmer was flogging him with a leather belt, accompanying each blow with a word of reproof and advice:

"Keep your mouth shut and your eyes open."

And the lad replied:

"I won't do it again, sir, by Christ who died on the Cross I swear I won't, I promise that from now on I'll take more care of the flock."

When Don Quixote saw what was happening, he fired up and said:

"Discourteous knight: it ill becomes you to assault one who cannot defend himself; mount your steed and take up your lance," (for the man also had a lance leaning up against the oak to which his mare was tethered) "and I shall force you to recognize that your actions are those of a coward."

The farmer, seeing such a figure bearing down on him, encased in armour and brandishing a lance under his nose, gave himself up for dead and meekly replied:

"This lad I'm punishing, sir knight, is one of my servants, and his job is to look after a flock of sheep for me, but he's so careless that every day one of them goes missing; and although what I'm punishing is his carelessness, or his wickedness, he says I'm doing it because I'm a skinflint, so as not to pay him his wages—but I swear by God and by my eternal soul that he's lying."

"You dare to use that word in my presence, you villainous wretch?"[1] said Don Quixote. "I swear by the sun that shines down on us that I am minded to run you through with this lance. Pay him immediately, and do not answer back; otherwise, by God who rules us, I shall exterminate and annihilate you this very instant. Untie him."

The farmer bowed his head and, without uttering a word, untied his servant, whom Don Quixote asked how much his master owed him. The reply was nine months at seven reals a month. Don Quixote worked it out and found that it came to seventy-three reals, which he told the farmer to hand over there and then, if he didn't want to die. The fearful countryman swore by the tight corner he was in and by the oath he'd already sworn (he hadn't sworn any oath at all), that it wasn't as much as all that, because an allowance and deduction had to be made for three pairs of shoes he'd given the lad, and one real paid for two blood-lettings when he'd been ill.

"That is all very well," replied Don Quixote, "but the shoes and the blood-lettings will be set against the flogging you have given him without due cause: for if he has done some damage to the hide of the shoes that you bought him, you have damaged his own hide, and if the barber bled him when he was ill, you have done the same to him in good health; so that on this account he owes you nothing."

"The problem is, sir knight, I haven't got any money on me; if Andrés would like to come home with me, I'll pay him every single real I owe him."

"Me, go with him, ever again?" said the lad. "No fear! No sir, I wouldn't even dream of it—so that as soon as we're alone again he can flay me like St Bartholomew?"[2]

"He shall do no such thing," replied Don Quixote. "My command will be sufficient to ensure his obedience; and provided that he gives me his oath by the laws of the order of chivalry into which he has been admitted, I shall allow him to go free, and personally guarantee the payment."

"Think what you're saying, sir," said the lad. "My master here isn't a knight at all, and he's never been admitted into any order of chivalry—he's just Juan Haldudo, the rich farmer from Quintanar."

"That is of little consequence," replied Don Quixote, "there is no reason why someone with a plebeian name should not be a knight, for every man is the child of his own deeds."

"That's as may be," said Andrés, "but this master of mine, what deeds is he the child of, seeing as how he refuses to pay me any wages for my sweat and toil?"

"I'm not refusing you anything at all, my dear Andrés," replied the farmer. "Please do be so kind as to come with me—I swear by all the orders of chivalry in the world to pay you, as I said, every single real I owe you, and with brass knobs on too."

"You may dispense with the brass knobs," said Don Quixote. "Pay him in silver reals, and that will satisfy me; and take good care to do exactly as you have sworn to do, for otherwise, by that same oath, I swear that I will come back to punish you, and that I will find you, even if you hide yourself away like a lizard. And if you wish to know who is issuing these commands, so as to be the more obliged to obey them,

---

1. The word in question is "lying"; Don Quixote takes the farmer's words as a personal assault, since he has chosen to defend the young boy.
2. A martyr who was flayed alive.

know that I am the valiant Don Quixote de la Mancha, the righter of wrongs and injustices; and God be with you, and do not forget for one moment what you have promised and sworn, under pain of the penalties prescribed."

And as he said this he spurred Rocinante, and before very long he had got under way. The farmer followed him with his gaze, and as soon as he was certain that he'd ridden out of the wood and was out of sight, he turned to his servant Andrés and said:

"Come here, my son, I want to pay you what I owe you, just as that righter of wrongs has ordered."

"I swear you will, too," said Andrés, "and you'll do well to obey that good knight's commands, God bless him, because he's such a brave man and such a good judge, by all that's holy, that if you don't pay me he'll come back and do what he said he'd do."

"And I swear I will, too," said the farmer, "but, since I'm so very fond of you, I think I'll increase the debt first, just so as to increase the repayment."

And seizing him by the arm, he tied him back to the evergreen oak and flogged him half dead.

"And now, Señor Andrés," said the farmer, "you can call upon your righter of wrongs. As you'll see, he isn't going to right this particular wrong in a hurry. But I don't think I've done with the wronging quite yet, because I'm feeling the urge to skin you alive, just as you feared I would."

But at length he untied him and told him he could go off in search of his judge so that this gentleman could carry out the sentence he'd pronounced. Andrés crept sullenly away, swearing that he was going in search of the brave Don Quixote de la Mancha to tell him exactly what had happened, and that the farmer would pay for it sevenfold. But, for all that, Andrés departed in tears and his master was left laughing.

This was how the valiant Don Quixote redressed that wrong; and delighted with what had happened, and considering that he had made a most happy and glorious beginning to his knight-errantry, he rode towards his village full of satisfaction, and murmuring:

"Well may you call yourself fortunate above all women who dwell on this earth, O Dulcinea del Toboso, fairest of the fair, for it has befallen your lot to hold subjected and enslaved to your every wish and desire a knight as valiant and far-famed as is and shall be Don Quixote de la Mancha, who (as all the world knows) was but yesterday admitted to the order of chivalry and today has righted the greatest injury and wrong ever devised by unreason and perpetrated by cruelty: today he has wrested the scourge from the hand of that pitiless enemy who was so unjustly flogging that delicate child."

As he was saying this he came to a crossroads, and this brought to his mind those other crossroads where knights errant would pause to consider which way to go; and, to imitate them, he remained motionless for a while; but after careful thought he let go of the reins, surrendering his will to that of his nag, which followed its original inclination—to head for its stable. After a couple of miles, Don Quixote spotted a throng of people who, as it afterwards transpired, were merchants from Toledo on their way to Murcia to buy silk.[3] There were six of them, each beneath his sunshade, accompanied by four servants on horseback and three footmen. As soon as Don Quixote saw them, he imagined that here was the opportunity for a new adventure; and, wishing to imitate in every way he believed he could the passages of arms he'd

3. Murcia is on the southwest coast of Spain.

read about in his books, he decided that one he had in mind was perfect for this situation. And so, with a gallant bearing and a resolute air, he steadied himself in his stirrups, clutched his lance, lifted his leather shield to his chest and, taking up his position in the middle of the highway, awaited the arrival of these knights errant, for this was what he judged them to be; and when they came within sight and earshot, Don Quixote raised his voice and, striking a haughty posture, declared:

"You will none of you advance one step further unless all of you confess that in all the world there is no maiden more beauteous than the Empress of La Mancha, the peerless Dulcinea del Toboso."

The merchants halted when they heard these words and saw the strange figure uttering them, and from the figure and the words they realized that the man was mad; but they had a mind to stay and see what would be the outcome of the required confession and one of them, waggish and sharp-witted, said:

"Sir knight, we don't know who this worthy lady is; do let us see her, because if she's as beautiful as you claim she is, we'll most freely and willingly confess that what you say is true."

"If I were to let you see her," retorted Don Quixote, "what merit would there be in confessing so manifest a truth? The whole point is that, without seeing her, you must believe, confess, affirm, swear and uphold it; if not, monstrous and arrogant wretches, you shall face me in battle forthwith. For whether you present yourselves one by one, as the order of chivalry requires, or all together, as is the custom and wicked practice of those of your ilk, here I stand and wait for you, confident in the justice of my cause."

"Sir knight," replied the merchant, "I beg you, in the name of all us princes gathered here, that—so as not to burden our consciences by confessing something never seen or heard by any of us, particularly since it is so detrimental to the Empresses and Queens of La Alcarria and Extremadura[4]—you be pleased to show us a portrait of that lady, even if no bigger than a grain of wheat; because the skein can be judged by the thread, as they say, and this will leave us satisfied and reassured, and leave you pleased and contented; indeed I believe we are already so far inclined in her favour that, even if her portrait shows that one of her eyes has gone skew-whiff and that sulphur and cinnabar ooze out of the other one, we will, just to please you, say in her favour whatever you want us to say."

"It does not ooze, you infamous knaves," replied Don Quixote, burning with anger. "It does not ooze, I repeat, with what you say, but with ambergris and civet kept in finest cotton; and she is not skew-whiff or hunch-backed, but straighter than a Guadarrama spindle.[5] And you shall pay for the great blasphemy you have uttered against such beauty as that of my lady!"

And so saying he charged with lowered lance at the blasphemer in such fury that, if good fortune hadn't made Rocinante trip and fall on the way, things would have gone badly for the reckless merchant. But Rocinante did fall, and his master rolled over the ground for some distance, and he tried to get up, but he couldn't, so encumbered was he by his lance, his leather shield, his spurs and his helmet, together with the burden of all the rest of his ancient armour. And as he struggled in vain to rise he cried:

4. La Alcarria, known for its production of honey, and Extremadura, on the border of Portugal, are relatively underdeveloped regions in Spain; the designation is thus vaguely insulting.
5. Guadarrama is a mountainous area outside of Madrid well-known for its cloth production.

"Flee not, you paltry cowards; you wretches, bide your time. 'Tis my horse's fault and not my own that I am lying here."

One of the footmen—not, it seems, a very well-intentioned one—on hearing all this bluster from the poor fallen fellow, couldn't resist giving him an answer on his ribs. And coming up to him he grabbed his lance and, breaking it into pieces, took one of them and began to give our Don Quixote such a pounding that, in spite of all his armour, he ended up as well threshed as the finest chaff. The muleteer's masters were shouting to him not to hit so hard, and to stop, but the lad was by now so caught up in his game that he wouldn't leave it until he'd played all the cards of his fury, and, picking up the other pieces of the lance, he shattered them, too, on the poor fallen man who, in the face of the storm of blows raining down, never stopped shouting as he threatened heaven and earth and those brigands, as he imagined them to be.

The lad grew tired, and the merchants continued their journey, supplied with enough to talk about throughout it on the subject of the poor pounded knight. Once he found himself alone, he again tried to get up; but if he hadn't been able to do so when fit and well, how was he going to manage it now that he was pummelled to pieces? Even so he considered himself lucky, in the belief that this was a fitting misfortune for knights errant, and he blamed his horse for it all; and it was impossible to get up, so very bruised and battered was his body.

Chapter 5

In which the story of our knight's misfortune is continued

Finding, then, that he couldn't move, it occurred to him to resort to his usual remedy, which was to think about some passage from his books; and his madness brought to his memory the episode from the story of Baldwin and the Marquis of Mantua in which Carloto leaves Baldwin wounded in the forest, a tale known to every little boy, not unfamiliar to youths, celebrated and even believed by old men, yet with no more truth in it than the miracles of Muhammad.[1] It was perfect for the predicament in which he found himself; and so, with many manifestations of extreme suffering, he began to writhe about on the ground and to say in the faintest of voices what the wounded knight of the forest is said to have said:

> Where are you, mistress of my heart?
> Are you not pained by my distress?
> Maybe you know not of my plight,
> Maybe you're false and pitiless.

And on he went reciting the ballad right up to the lines that go:

> O noble Marquis, gentle sire,
> My uncle and my lord by blood...

Fortune decreed that at this point a farmer from his own village, one of his neighbours, happened to be returning home after taking a hundredweight of wheat to the mill. Seeing a man lying there the farmer came up and asked him who he was and what was the matter with him, moaning away like that. No doubt Don Quixote

1. Don Quixote is thinking of a ballad about the son of Charlemagne (Carloto), who wounds the nephew of the Marquis of Mantua; the Marquis in turn will seek perpetual revenge. The anti-Islamic sentiment is not unusual in the period.

thought that this was the Marquis of Mantua, his uncle, and so his only response was to continue reciting his ballad, informing the man of his misfortune and of the love that the Emperor's son felt for his wife, exactly as the ballad relates.

The farmer was astonished to hear all this nonsense; and, removing the man's visor, which had been battered to pieces, he wiped his face, which was covered in dust. And once he'd done wiping he recognized him and said:

"Señor Quixana," (for this must have been his name when he was sane and hadn't yet turned from a placid hidalgo into a knight errant) "who's done this to you?"

But he continued to reply with his ballad to everything he was asked. Sizing up the situation, the farmer took his back and breast plates off as best he could, to see if he was wounded, but couldn't see any blood or signs of any hurt. He managed to lift him up, and with great difficulty hoisted him on to the donkey, since this seemed the more tranquil animal. He picked up the armour and arms, including the fragments of the lance, and tied them on to Rocinante, which he took by the reins, and taking his donkey by the halter he set off in the direction of his village, deep in thought as he heard the nonsense being spoken by Don Quixote, who was no less pensive and so badly bruised that he couldn't keep his seat on the donkey, and every so often breathed sighs loud enough to reach heaven; so that the farmer again felt he should ask what was wrong, and it must have been the devil himself who made Don Quixote recall tales to fit the events, because at that moment, forgetting all about Baldwin, he remembered Abindarráez the Moor being captured and taken as a prisoner to his castle by the Governor of Antequera, Rodrigo de Narváez. So that when the farmer asked him again how he felt and what was the matter with him, he replied with the very same words and arguments used by the captive Moor to reply to Rodrigo de Narváez, as he'd read the story in Jorge de Montemayor's *Diana*,[2] making such appropriate use of it that the farmer wished himself to the devil for having to listen to such a pack of absurdities. He realized his neighbour was mad, and hurried on to the village so as not to have to put up with Don Quixote's interminable harangue more than necessary. It concluded like this:

"You must know, Señor Don Rodrigo de Narváez, that this fair Jarifa I have mentioned is now the beauteous Dulcinea del Toboso, for whom I have performed, do perform and shall perform the most famous deeds of chivalry that have been witnessed, are witnessed and shall be witnessed in this world."

The farmer replied:

"Look here sir, as I'm a sinner I'm not Don Rodrigo de Narváez, nor the Marquis of Mantua, but Pedro Alonso, your neighbour; and you aren't Baldwin, nor Abindarráez, but the honourable hidalgo Señor Quixana."

"I know who I am," retorted Don Quixote, "and I know that I can be not only all those whom I have mentioned, but every one of the Twelve Peers of France, and every one of the Nine Worthies as well, because all the deeds performed by them both singly and together will be exceeded by mine."[3]

2. A popular pastoral romance; begun by Gil Polo, its second part was written by Jorge de Montemayor in the mid-16th century. The episode about Abindarráez, the captive Moor, is from the novel.

3. The 12 peers were the warriors of Charlemagne's court in late 8th-century France. The nine worthies consisted of three groups of Christians, Jews, and Gentiles; Charlemagne, David, and Alexander are among them. Along with the Knights of the Round Table, a band of worthies assembled by the legendary King Arthur of England, these three groups of warriors provide constant (even interchangeable) points of comparison for the deluded Quixote.

With these exchanges and other similar ones they approached the village at night-fall, but the farmer waited until it was darker so that nobody could see the battered hidalgo so wretchedly mounted. When he thought the time had come he entered the village and went straight to Don Quixote's house, which was in an uproar: the priest and the barber, great friends of Don Quixote's, were there, and his housekeeper was shouting:

"And what's your opinion, Father Pero Pérez sir," (for this was the priest's name) "about my master's misfortune? Three days it's been now without a trace of him, his nag, his leather shield, his lance or his armour. A fine pickle I'm in! It's my belief, as sure as I was born to die, that his brain's been turned by those damned chivalry books of his he reads all the time—I remember often hearing him say to himself that he wanted to be a knight errant and go off in search of adventures. The devil take all those books, and Barabbas[4] take them too, for scrambling the finest mind in all La Mancha!"

The niece said much the same and even more:

"And let me tell you this, Master Nicolás," (for this was the barber's name). "My uncle would often be reading those evil books of misadventure for two whole days and nights on end, and then he'd throw his book down, grab his sword and slash the walls of his room, and once he was exhausted he'd say that he'd killed four giants as big as four towers, and that the sweat pouring from him was blood from the wounds received in battle, and then he'd drink a pitcher of cold water and feel calm and well again, claiming that the water was a most precious draught brought by the famous sage Squiffy, a great enchanter and friend of his.[5] But I'm the one to blame for it all, not telling you gentlemen about my uncle's madness so you could have done something about it and burned those unchristian books of his before it came to all this; he's got lots and lots of them, and they do deserve to be put to the flames, like heretics."

"I agree with that," said the priest, "and I swear that before another day has passed they'll be put on public trial and condemned to the flames so that they can't make anyone reading them do what my friend must have done."

All this was overheard by Don Quixote and the farmer, who could no longer have any doubts about his neighbour's illness, and so he began to shout:

"Open up to Sir Baldwin and the Marquis of Mantua, who's sore wounded here, and to the Moor Abindarráez, brought captive by the valiant Rodrigo de Narváez, the Governor of Antequera."

These shouts brought all four running into the porch, and as the men recognized their friend, and the women their master and uncle, who hadn't dismounted from the donkey because he couldn't, they ran to embrace him. He said:

"Stop, all of you, for I am sore wounded through the fault of my steed. Carry me to my bed and, if you are able, summon the wise Urganda[6] to heed and tend my wounds."

"Just look at him, in the name of the devil!" cried the housekeeper. "Didn't I know in the marrow of my bones what was wrong with the master? Up you go, sir, up you go to bed, we'll cure you well enough without any need for that there Ugandan woman. Damn those chivalry books, damn the lot of them, getting you into such a state!"

4. The thief whom Pilate released to the Jews when they requested that he be freed rather than Jesus.
5. An enchanter (Alquife) from *Amadis of Gaul*.
6. Alquife's wife.

They took him to his bed and, examining him for wounds, couldn't find any; he told them that it had been a general, overall battering sustained when he and his steed Rocinante suffered a terrible fall as he was doing battle with ten giants, the most lawless and reckless giants to be found almost anywhere on the face of the earth.

"I see, I see!" said the priest. "So there are giants in the game as well, are there? I swear by this Holy Cross that I'll burn them tomorrow, before the day is over."

They asked Don Quixote a thousand questions, and his only reply was to request food and to be allowed to sleep, for this was his greatest need. And then the priest asked the farmer to tell him exactly how he'd found Don Quixote. The farmer told him the whole story, including the nonsense that on being discovered and transported the knight had uttered, which made the priest even more anxious to do what the very next day he did do: call on his friend the barber Master Nicolás, with whom he walked to Don Quixote's house.

from *Chapter 6*

About the amusing and exhaustive scrutiny that the priest and the barber made in the library of our ingenious hidalgo

Who was still asleep. The priest asked the niece for the keys of the room where the books, the authors of the mischief, were kept, and she was happy to hand them over. They went in, the housekeeper too, and found more than a hundred large volumes, finely bound, and some small ones; and as soon as the housekeeper saw them, she ran out of the room and back again clutching a bowl of holy water and some hyssop, and said:

"Here you are, reverend father, you take this and sprinkle the room with it, just in case there's one of those hordes of enchanters from those books in here, and he puts a spell on us as a punishment for the torments they'll undergo once we've wiped them off the face of the earth."

The priest laughed at the housekeeper's simple-mindedness, and told the barber to hand him the books one by one so that he could see what was in them, since he might find some that didn't deserve to be committed to the flames.[1]

"No," said the niece, "there's no reason to let any of them off, they're all to blame. Better throw the whole lot of them out of the windows into the courtyard, and make a pile of them, and set fire to them, or take them to the backyard and make the bonfire there, where the smoke won't be such a nuisance."

The housekeeper said much the same, so anxious were both women to see those innocents massacred, but the priest wouldn't agree without at least reading the titles. The first one that Master Nicolás put into his hands was *The Four Books of Amadis of Gaul,* and the priest said:

"This is a strange coincidence: I've heard that this was the very first chivalry romance to be printed in Spain, and that all the others have their origin and beginning in it; so it seems to me that, as the prophet of such a pernicious sect, it should be condemned to the flames without delay."

---

1. The auto-de-fé which the priest is orchestrating—a public exhibition of those convicted of heresy—would have been a familiar sight in the days of the Inquisition; at times such an exhibition culminated in the death by fire of the heretic. There were calls to burn chivalric books as well in the mid-16th century when the fashion of chivalric romances was at its height.

"No, no," said the barber. "I've also heard that it's the very best of all the books of this kind that have ever been written; and so, being unique in its artistry, it ought to be pardoned."

"You're right," said the priest, "so its life is spared for the time being. Let's see that one next to it."

"This," said the barber, "is *The Exploits of Esplandian,* Amadis of Gaul's legitimate son."[2]

"Well, to be sure," said the priest, "the excellence of the father isn't going to be of any avail to the son. Here you are, ma'am, open that window and throw it into the yard, the first faggot on the bonfire we're going to make."

The housekeeper was delighted to do so, and the good Esplandian flew out into the courtyard, where he patiently awaited the flames with which he was threatened.

"Let's see the next one," said the priest.

"This," said the barber, "is *Amadis of Greece,* and all the books on this side, I think, are members of that same family."[3]

"Then out into the yard with the lot of them," said the priest. "Just to be able to burn Queen Pintiquiniestra, and the shepherd Darinel, and his eclogues, and his author's devilish, contorted language, I'll burn the father that begot me, too, if I catch him going about as a knight errant."

"I agree," said the barber.

"So do I," added the niece.

"That being so," said the housekeeper, "let's have them here, and out into the courtyard they all go."

They gave them to her, and since there were so many of them she spared herself the stairs again and flung them out of the window....

And not wanting to weary himself any more reading chivalry romances, the priest ordered the housekeeper to take all the big books and throw them out into the yard. His command didn't fall on deaf ears, because she'd rather have been burning those books than weaving the finest and largest piece of fabric in the world, and, seizing about eight of them, she heaved them out of the window. But because she took up so many of them together, one fell at the barber's feet and, curious to know what it was, he saw: *History of the Famous Knight Tirante the White.*[4]

"Good heavens!" cried the priest. "Fancy Tirante the White being here! Give it to me, my friend: I reckon I've found in this book a treasure of delight and a mine of entertainment. In it you'll discover Don Quirieleisón de Montalbán, a most courageous knight, and his brother Tomás de Montalbán, and the knight Fonseca, together with the fight that the brave Tirante had with the mastiff, and the witticisms of the maiden Placerdemivida, and the amours and the trickery of the widow Reposada, and the lady empress in love with her squire Hipólito. Let me tell you this, my friend; as far as its style is concerned this is the best book in the world. In it knights eat and sleep and die in their beds and make wills before they die, and other such things that are usually omitted from books of this sort. But in spite of all this I do have to say that the man who wrote it deserved to be sent to the galleys for life, for not knowing what he was doing when he was writing such nonsense. Take it home and read it, and you'll see that what I say is true."

"That I'll do," replied the barber, "but what about these other little books here?"

---

2. Written by the author of *Amadis of Gaul* and published two years later.
3. The Amadis story provoked a number of imitations.
4. A late 15th-century Catalan chivalric romance.

"They can't be books of chivalry," said the priest, "but books of poetry."

And, opening one of them he saw that it was Jorge de Montemayor's *Diana* and, convinced that they were all of the same sort, he said:

"These don't deserve to be burned with the others, because they aren't and never will be as damaging as those books of chivalry have been—these are books for the intellect, and do nobody any harm."

"Oh sir," cried the niece, "please have them burned like the rest, because it could well happen that once my uncle gets over his chivalry illness he starts reading all these other books and takes it into his head to become a shepherd and wander about the forests and meadows singing and playing music and, what would be even worse than that, turn into a poet, which they say is a catching and incurable disease."

"The girl's right," said the priest, "and it'll be a good idea to remove this dangerous stumbling-block from our friend's way."

* * *

Chapter 7

About our worthy knight Don Quixote de la Mancha's second sally

And now Don Quixote began to bellow:

"Come, come, you valiant knights; 'tis now you must display the worth of your mighty arms, for the courtiers are getting the better of the tourney."

They ran to see what the commotion was all about, and this put a stop to the scrutiny of the remaining books; as a result it's believed that *Carolea* and *The Lion of Spain,* together with *The Exploits of the Emperor* by Luis de Avila,[1] went to the flames without any trial at all, because they must have been among the remainder; and perhaps if the priest had examined them they wouldn't have received such a severe sentence.

By the time they reached Don Quixote's room he was out of bed, shouting and raving, laying about him with his sword in all directions with slashes and backstrokes, as wide awake as if he'd never slept. They wrestled him back to bed, and once he'd calmed down a little, he turned to the priest and said:

"Indeed, my Lord Archbishop Turpin, it is a disgrace for us, who call ourselves the Twelve Peers, so meekly to allow those knights courtiers to carry off the victory in this tournament, after we knights adventurers had won all the honours on the previous three days."[2]

"Hush, my friend," said the priest, "God will grant a change of fortune so that what is lost today is won tomorrow, and for the moment you should look to your health—you seem to be overtired, if not sore wounded."

"Wounded I am not," said Don Quixote, "but weak and exhausted I am indeed, for the bastard Roland has been pounding me with the trunk of an evergreen oak, and all out of envy, because he can see that I am the only man who opposes his bravado. But my name would not be Reynald of Montalbán if, as soon as I rise from this bed, I did not make him pay for it, in spite of all his magic spells.[3] For the present,

---

1. *La Carolea* and *The Lion of Spain* were heroic poems about Charles V (1500–1558), who was both Holy Roman Emperor and king of Spain; *The Exploits of the Emperor* chronicled Charles V's deeds in prose.

2. Turpin was archbishop at Charlemagne's court and the fabled author of the *Song of Roland*.

3. Reynald (Rinaldo) was Roland's cousin; Roland (Orlando) is conceived as virtually invulnerable to injury in the Italian romance tradition.

however, bring me victuals, for they, I know, will be more to my purpose, and leave it to me to seek my revenge."

And that's what they did: they gave him some food, and he fell asleep again, and they fell to marvelling at his madness.

That night the housekeeper burned to ashes all the books in the courtyard and the house, and some must have perished that deserved to be treasured in perpetual archives; but fate, and the scrutineer's laziness, wouldn't permit it, and in them was fulfilled the proverb which says that the just sometimes pay for sinners.

One of the remedies that the priest and the barber had prescribed at that time for their friend's malady was to have his library walled up and sealed off, so that he couldn't find his books when he got up—maybe if the cause was removed the effect might cease—and to tell him that an enchanter had carried them off, with the library and all; and this was done without delay. Two days later Don Quixote did get up, and his first action was to go and look at his books; and, since he couldn't find the room in which he'd left them, he wandered all over the house searching for it. He kept going up to the place where the door used to be, and feeling for it with his hands, and running his eyes backwards and forwards over the walls without uttering a word; and after some time doing this he asked his housekeeper where his library was. Well trained in her answer, she said:

"And what library do you think you're looking for? There's no library and no books left in this house, because the devil himself took them away."

"No it wasn't the devil," replied the niece, "it was an enchanter who came one night on a cloud, after you'd gone away, and he climbed off a serpent he was riding and he went into the library and I don't know what he got up to in there, because a bit later he flew away over the roof and left the house full of smoke; and when we made up our minds to go and see what he'd done, we couldn't find any books or any library. All we remember is that as that wicked old man flew away he shouted that because of a secret grudge he bore the owner of the books and the library, he'd done the house the damage that we were about to discover. He also said that he was called the sage Munaton."

"Frestón is what he must have said," said Don Quixote.

"I don't know," said the housekeeper, "whether he was called Frestón or Piston or whatever, all I know is his name ended in ton."[4]

"That is indeed his name," said Don Quixote, "and he is a wise enchanter, a great enemy of mine, who bears me much malice, because he knows by his arts and his learning that the time will come when I shall engage in single combat a knight who is a favourite of his, and defeat him, without his being able to do anything to prevent it, and for this reason he tries to make as much mischief for me as he can; but I can promise him that he is powerless to gainsay or avert what heaven has decreed."

"Who can doubt that?" said the niece. "But uncle, why do you have to go and get involved in these arguments? Wouldn't it be better to stay quietly at home instead of looking for better bread than what's made from wheat, and forgetting that many a man's gone out shearing and come back shorn?"

"My dear niece!" replied Don Quixote. "How wrong you are! Before anyone shears me I will pluck the beards off the chins of all those who even contemplate touching a single hair of mine!"

---

4. Probably Frestón, an enchanter in the chivalric romance *Don Belianís de Grecia*.

Neither woman answered him back, because they could see that he was growing heated.

And yet he did stay quietly at home for a whole fortnight without showing any signs of wanting to re-enact his former follies, and during this time he talked all kinds of amusing bunkum with his friends the priest and the barber, as he declared that what the world most needed was knights errant and a rebirth of knight-errantry. Sometimes the priest contradicted him and sometimes he gave in to him, because if he didn't make use of this tactic it would be impossible to restore his sanity.

During this fortnight Don Quixote set to work on a farmer who was a neighbour of his, an honourable man (if a poor man can be called honourable) but a little short of salt in the brain-pan. To be brief, Don Quixote told him, reasoned with him and promised him so much that the poor villager decided to go away with him and serve him as squire. Don Quixote told the man, among other things, that he ought to be delighted to go, because at some time or other he could well have an adventure in which he won an island in the twinkling of an eye and installed his squire as governor. These and other similar promises persuaded Sancho Panza, for this was the farmer's name, to leave his wife and children and go into service as his neighbour's squire.

Don Quixote immediately set about raising money, and by selling one possession, pawning another, and always making a bad bargain, he scraped together a reasonable sum. He also found himself a little round infantryman's shield, borrowed from a friend, and, patching up his shattered helmet as best he could, he told his squire Sancho the day and time he intended to set out, so that he too could obtain whatever he considered most necessary. Don Quixote was particularly insistent on saddle-bags, and Sancho said that indeed he would bring some, and he'd bring a very fine donkey of his too, because he wasn't all that much given to going very far on foot. At this Don Quixote hesitated, racking his brains to try and remember if any knight errant had ever been escorted by a donkey-mounted squire, but none came to mind; yet for all that he decided that Sancho should ride his donkey, proposing to provide him with a more honourable mount at the earliest opportunity, by unhorsing the first discourteous knight he came across. Don Quixote stocked up with shirts and everything else he could, following the advice that the innkeeper had given him; and once all these preparations had been made, without Panza saying goodbye to his wife and children, or Don Quixote to his housekeeper and niece, they left the village unseen one night, and by daybreak they'd ridden so far they felt certain no one would be able to find them however hard he looked.

Sancho Panza rode his ass like a patriarch, complete with saddle-bags and leather bottle, longing to be the governor of the island his master had promised him. Don Quixote happened to take the same road he'd followed on his first sally, across the plain of Montiel, with less discomfort than before, because it was early morning and the sun, being low, didn't bother them. Sancho Panza said to his master:

"You'll be sure, won't you, sir knight, not to forget what you promised me about the island. I'll be up to governing it all right, however big it is."

To which Don Quixote replied:

"I would have you know, my good friend Sancho Panza, that it was a custom much in use among the knights errant of old to make their squires the governors of the islands or kingdoms that they conquered, and I have determined that such an ancient usage shall not lapse through my fault. Quite on the contrary, I intend to improve upon it: for those knights would sometimes—more often than not, perhaps—wait until their squires were old men and, once they were tired of serving and of suffering bad days and worse nights, give them some title, such as count or at the most marquis of some valley or paltry province; but if your life and mine are spared, it could well be that within six days I shall conquer a kingdom with others annexed, any one of which would be perfect for you to be crowned king of it. And you must not think that there would be anything extraordinary about that: incidents and accidents befall us knights in such unprecedented and unimagined ways that I might easily be able to give you even more than I have promised."

"And so," said Sancho Panza, "if by one of those miracles you've just said I became king, then Juana Gutiérrez, my old woman, would be queen no less, and the kids would be princes and princesses."

"Who can doubt it?" replied Don Quixote.

"I can," retorted Sancho Panza. "To my mind, even if God rained kingdoms down on this earth none of them would sit well on my Mari Gutiérrez's head. Look here, sir, she wouldn't be worth two brass farthings as a queen—countess would suit her better, and even that'd be hard going for her."

"Commend the matter to God, Sancho," replied Don Quixote, "and he will give her what is best for her; but you must not be so daunted that you agree to content yourself with anything less than being a provincial governor."

"I shan't do that, sir," replied Sancho, "not with such a fine master as you, who'll be able to give me everything that's good for me and I can cope with."

Chapter 8

About the brave Don Quixote's success in the dreadful and unimaginable adventure of the windmills, together with other events worthy of happy memory

As he was saying this, they caught sight of thirty or forty windmills standing on the plain, and as soon as Don Quixote saw them he said to his squire:

"Fortune is directing our affairs even better than we could have wished: for you can see over there, good friend Sancho Panza, a place where stand thirty or more monstrous giants with whom I intend to fight a battle and whose lives I intend to take; and with the booty we shall begin to prosper. For this is a just war, and it is a great service to God to wipe such a wicked breed from the face of the earth."

"What giants?" said Sancho Panza.

"Those giants that you can see over there," replied his master, "with long arms: there are giants with arms almost six miles long."

"Look you here," Sancho retorted, "those over there aren't giants, they're windmills, and what look to you like arms are sails—when the wind turns them they make the millstones go round."

"It is perfectly clear," replied Don Quixote, "that you are but a raw novice in this matter of adventures. They are giants; and if you are frightened, you can take yourself away and say your prayers while I engage them in fierce and arduous combat."

And so saying he set spurs to his steed Rocinante, not paying any attention to his squire Sancho Panza, who was shouting that what he was charging were definitely windmills not giants. But Don Quixote was so convinced that they were giants that he neither heard his squire Sancho's shouts nor saw what stood in front of him, even though he was by now upon them; instead he cried:

"Flee not, O vile and cowardly creatures, for it is but one solitary knight who attacks you."

A gust of wind arose, the great sails began to move, and Don Quixote yelled:

"Though you flourish more arms than the giant Briareus,[1] I will make you pay for it."

So saying, and commending himself with all his heart to his lady Dulcinea, begging her to succour him in his plight, well protected by his little round infantryman's shield, and with his lance couched, he advanced at Rocinante's top speed and charged at the windmill nearest him. As he thrust his lance into its sail the wind turned it with such violence that it smashed the lance into pieces and dragged the horse and his rider with it, and Don Quixote went rolling over the plain in a very sore predicament. Sancho Panza rushed to help his master at his donkey's fastest trot and found that he couldn't stir, such was the toss that Rocinante had given him.

"For God's sake!" said Sancho. "Didn't I tell you to be careful what you were doing, didn't I tell you they were only windmills? And only someone with windmills on the brain could have failed to see that!"

"Not at all, friend Sancho," replied Don Quixote. "Affairs of war, even more than others, are subject to continual change. All the more so as I believe, indeed I am certain, that the same sage Frestón who stole my library and my books has just turned these giants into windmills, to deprive me of the glory of my victory, such is the enmity he feels for me; but in the end his evil arts will avail him little against the might of my sword."

"God's will be done," replied Sancho Panza.

He helped his master to his feet, and his master remounted Rocinante, whose shoulder was half dislocated. And talking about this adventure they followed the road towards the Pass of Lápice, because Don Quixote said they couldn't fail to encounter plentiful and varied adventures there, as it was a much frequented spot. But he was dejected by the destruction of his lance, and he told his squire so, and added:

"I remember reading that a Spanish knight called Diego Pérez de Vargas, having broken his sword in battle, tore a weighty bough or trunk from an evergreen oak, and did such deeds with it that day, and thrashed so many Moors, that he was nicknamed Machuca, that is to say, the thrasher; and from that day onwards his surname and that of his descendants was changed to Vargas y Machuca.[2] I have told you this because from the first oak tree that comes before me I intend to tear off another such trunk, as good as the one I have in mind, and with it I intend to do such deeds as to make you consider yourself most fortunate to be deemed worthy to behold them, and to witness that which can hardly be believed."

"God's will be done," said Sancho. "I believe every word you say. But do sit up straighter, you're riding all lopsided, it must be that hammering you got when you fell off your horse."

"That is indeed the case," replied Don Quixote, "and if I do not utter any complaint about the pain it is because knights errant are not permitted to complain about wounds, even if their entrails are spilling out of them."

"If that's so there's nothing more for me to say," replied Sancho, "but God knows I'd like you to complain if anything hurts. As for me, I can tell you I'm going to moan like anything about the slightest little pain, unless that stuff about not complaining goes for knight errants' squires as well."

---

1. One of the mythological Titans, Briareus had 100 arms.
2. "Machuca" was the subject of ballads; he was instrumental at the 13th-century battle of Jerez.

Don Quixote couldn't help laughing at his squire's simple-mindedness, and declared that he could moan as and when he pleased, whether he felt any pain or not, for he had not yet read anything to the contrary in the order of chivalry. Sancho pointed out that it was time to eat. His master replied that he didn't need any food yet, but that Sancho could eat whenever he liked. So Sancho settled himself down as best he could on his donkey and, taking out of his saddle-bags what he'd put into them, he jogged along and munched away behind his master, and every so often he'd take a swig from his leather bottle with such relish that the most self-indulgent innkeeper in Malaga[3] would have envied him. And as Sancho trotted on, drinking his fill, he didn't remember any of the promises his master had made him, and reckoned that going in search of adventures, however dangerous they might be, was more like good fun than hard work.

To cut a long story short, they spent that night under some trees, and from one of them Don Quixote tore a dead branch that might almost serve as a lance, and fastened on to it the iron head that he'd taken off the broken one. He didn't sleep in all the night, thinking about his lady Dulcinea, to conform with what he'd read in his books, where knights errant spent many sleepless nights in glades and deserts, engrossed in the recollection of their ladies. Not so Sancho Panza who, with his stomach full, and not of chicory water either, slept right through until morning; and, if his master hadn't called him, neither the rays of the sun, falling full on his face, nor the songs of the birds that, in great throngs and with expansive joy, greeted the coming of the new day, would have been capable of awaking him. He got up, had his breakfast swig and found his leather bottle rather slimmer than the evening before; and his heart sank, because it didn't look as if this lack was going to be remedied as soon as he'd have liked. Don Quixote refused breakfast because, as we know, he had decided to subsist on savoury recollections. They continued along the road to the Pass of Lápice, and at about three o'clock in the afternoon they sighted it.

"Over there, brother Sancho Panza," said Don Quixote when he saw it, "we can dip our arms right up to our elbows in what people call adventures. But take note that, even if you see me in the greatest peril imaginable, you must not seize your sword to defend me, unless you should see that those who attack me are rabble and common people, in which case you can most certainly come to my aid; but should they be knights and gentlemen, it is on no account licit or permitted by the laws of chivalry for you to assist me, until you yourself be knighted."

"You can be sure, sir," replied Sancho, "of being fully obeyed there, specially since I'm a peaceful man by nature and don't like getting involved in rows and brawls. Though I do have to say that when it comes to defending myself I'm not going to take much notice of those there laws of yours, because divine and human justice both let anyone defend himself against attack."

"I do not disagree in the slightest," replied Don Quixote, "but as regards assisting me against knights, you must keep your natural impetuosity under control."

"I'll do that all right," replied Sancho. "I'll keep that particular promise as strictly as the Sabbath."

As they talked away like this, two friars of the order of St Benedict appeared on the road, each seated upon a dromedary: their mules were no less tall than that. They came complete with their riding masks and their sunshades. Behind them was a coach

---

3. A port-town on the southern coast of Spain.

with four or five horsemen escorting it, and two footmen walking. In the coach, as was later discovered, there was a Basque lady on her way to Seville to join her husband, who was going to America to take up an important post. The friars weren't travelling with her, they just happened to be on the same road; but as soon as Don Quixote caught sight of them he said to his squire:

"Either I am much mistaken or this will be the most famous adventure ever witnessed; for those black figures over there must be and no doubt are enchanters abducting a princess in that coach, and I must redress this wrong to the utmost of my power."

"This'll be worse than the windmills," said Sancho. "Look here, sir, those there are Benedictine friars, and the coach must just be taking some travellers on their way. Look, look, do take care what you're doing, this could be one of the devil's own tricks."

"I have already told you, Sancho," replied Don Quixote, "that you know next to nothing on the subject of adventures. What I say is true, as you will soon see."

So saying, he rode forward and planted himself in the middle of the road down which the friars were plodding and, when he thought they were near enough to hear him, he cried:

"Diabolical and monstrous wretches, release this very moment the noble princesses whom you are abducting in that coach, or prepare to be killed this instant as a just punishment for your wicked works."

The friars reined in their mules and sat there in astonishment at the figure cut by Don Quixote and at the words he'd spoken, to which they replied:

"Sir knight, we aren't diabolical or monstrous at all, we're just two Benedictine friars going about our business, and we haven't the faintest idea whether there are any abducted princesses in this coach."

"Soft words will not work with me, for I know you only too well, perfidious knaves!" said Don Quixote.

And without awaiting any more replies he spurred Rocinante and charged with levelled lance at the friar in front with such determination and fury that, if the friar hadn't thrown himself from his mule, the knight would have brought him to the ground sore vexed and indeed sore wounded, if not stone dead. The other friar, seeing how his companion was being treated, dug his heels into his castle of a mule and made off across the plain faster than the wind.

Sancho Panza, seeing the friar sprawling on the ground, slipped off his donkey, ran over to him and began to strip him of his habits. And now two of the friars' servants came up and asked what he thought he was doing stripping their master like that. Sancho replied that the clothes were rightly his, the spoils of the battle his master Don Quixote had won. The servant-lads, who lacked a sense of humour and knew nothing about spoils and battles, seeing that Don Quixote had gone off to talk to the ladies in the coach, fell upon Sancho, knocked him to the ground, gave his beard a thorough plucking and his body a merciless kicking, and left him lying there breathless and senseless. Without pausing for an instant the friar remounted, terrified and trembling and drained of all colour, and spurred his mule in the direction of his companion, who was waiting a good distance away to see what would be the outcome of this nightmare; and not wanting to stop for the conclusion of the incident they continued on their way, making more signs of the cross than if they had the very devil at their backs.

Don Quixote, as has been said, was talking to the lady in the coach, and saying:

"You may now, in your ineffable loveliness, my lady, dispose of your person as best pleases you, for the pride of your ravishers lies on the ground, o'erthrown by this mighty arm of mine; and that you may not pine to know the name of your deliverer, be informed that I am Don Quixote de la Mancha, knight adventurer and errant, and captive to the peerless and beauteous Doña Dulcinea del Toboso; and in requital of the benefit you have received from me, all I desire is that you turn back to El Toboso and on my behalf present yourself before that lady and inform her of what I have accomplished for your deliverance."

Everything that Don Quixote said was overheard by one of the squires escorting the coach, a Basque; who, seeing that the man didn't want to let the coach continue on its way, but was saying that it must turn back at once to El Toboso, rode up to Don Quixote and, seizing him by the lance, said in bad Castilian and worse Basque:[4]

"Go on way, knight, and go with devil. By God made me, if not leaving coach, you as killed by Basque as stand there."

Don Quixote understood him perfectly, and with great composure he replied:

"If you were a knight and a gentleman, which you are not, I should already have punished your folly and audacity, you wretched creature."

To which the Basque replied:

"Me not gentleman? I swear God you lie as me Christian. If leaving lance and taking sword, soon see you monkey making! Basque on land, gentleman on sea, gentleman for devil, and see lie if other saying."

"'Now you shall see,' quoth Agrages,"[5] quoted Don Quixote.

And throwing his lance to the ground, he drew his sword, took up his little round shield and set upon the Basque, intending to kill him. The Basque, seeing the knight advance, would have preferred to dismount from his mule, which was a hired one and therefore a bad one and not to be trusted, but all he had time to do was to draw his sword; and it was lucky for him that he happened to be next to the coach, from which he was able to snatch a cushion to serve as a shield; and then the two men went for each other as if they were mortal enemies. The rest of the party would have made peace between them but they couldn't, because the Basque was saying in his topsy-turvy tongue that if they didn't let him finish his battle he'd kill his mistress and anyone else who got in his way. The lady in the coach, astonished and terrified at this sight, made the coachman drive a safe distance off, and then settled down to watch the desperate struggle, in the course of which the Basque dealt Don Quixote such a mighty blow on the shoulder, over the top of his shield, that if he hadn't been wearing armour he'd have been split down the middle. When Don Quixote felt the impact of the terrible stroke he cried:

"O lady of my soul, Dulcinea, flower of all beauty, succour this your knight who, through his desire to satisfy your great goodness, finds himself in this dire peril!"

Uttering these words, gripping his sword, raising his shield and launching himself at the Basque was the work of a moment, as Don Quixote resolved to venture everything on the fortune of a single blow. The Basque, seeing Don Quixote advance, could see from his spirited bearing what a brave man he was, and decided to follow his example; so he stood his ground, well protected by his cushion but unable to turn the mule one way or the other because by now, exhausted and unaccustomed to such pranks, it couldn't budge a single step.

4. The Basque region is in northern Spain. Basques were renowned for their fighting abilities, and their traditional limberness also made them good dancers. Their language is unrelated to Spanish. Castilian is another word for what has become the Spanish language.

5. A warrior from the *Amadis de Gaul* who typically says this phrase at the start of a fight.

So Don Quixote was advancing, as described, on the well-shielded Basque, with his sword aloft, determined to split him in half, and the Basque was awaiting him with his sword also aloft, and upholstered in his protective cushion, and all the bystanders were terrified and wondering what was going to be the outcome of the prodigious blows with which the two men were threatening each other; and the lady in the coach and her maids were making a thousand vows and offerings to all the images and holy places in Spain for God to deliver their squire and themselves from this great peril. But the trouble is that at this very point the author of this history leaves the battle unfinished, excusing himself on the ground that he hasn't found anything more written about these exploits of Don Quixote than what he has narrated. It is true, though, that the second author of this work refused to believe that such a fascinating history had been abandoned to the laws of oblivion, or that the chroniclers of La Mancha had been so lacking in curiosity that they hadn't kept papers relating to this famous knight in their archives or their desks; and so, with this in mind, he didn't despair of finding the end of this delectable history, which indeed, with heaven's help, he did find in the way that will be narrated in the second part.

Second Part of the Ingenious Hidalgo DON QUIXOTE de la Mancha

Chapter 9

In which the stupendous battle between the gallant Basque and the valiant man from La Mancha is brought to a conclusion

In the first part of this history we left the valiant Basque and the famous Don Quixote with naked swords aloft, about to deliver two such devastating downstrokes that if their aim was true they would at the very least split each other from top to bottom and cut each other open like pomegranates; and at this critical point the delightful history stopped short and was left truncated, without any indication from its author about where the missing section might be found.

This worried me, because the pleasure afforded by the little I had read turned to displeasure as I considered what an uphill task awaited me if I wanted to find the great bulk of material that, as I imagined, was missing from this delectable tale. It seemed impossible and contrary to all good practice that such an excellent knight shouldn't have had some sage who'd have made it his job to record his unprecedented deeds, something never lacked by any of those knights errant

> Who go, as people say,
> Adventuring their way,[1]

because every one of them had one or two sages, made to measure for him, who not only recorded his exploits but also depicted his least thoughts and most trivial actions, however hidden from the public gaze they were; and such an excellent knight couldn't have been so unfortunate as to be totally lacking in what Platir and the like had more than enough of.[2] So I couldn't bring myself to believe that such a superb history had been left maimed and mutilated, and I laid the blame on malicious time,

---

1. Likely to be a refrain from a contemporary ballad, one repeated several times in the novel.

2. A knight whose deeds were supposedly recorded.

the devourer and demolisher of all things, which had either hidden or destroyed what was missing.

It also struck me that, since modern books like *The Undeceptions of Jealousy* and *The Nymphs and Shepherds of Henares* had been found in his library, his history must also be a recent one, and that, even if it hadn't been put into writing, it must live on in the memory of the people of his village and others near by. All these thoughts left me feeling puzzled and eager for exact and authentic knowledge of the complete life and works of our famous Spaniard Don Quixote de la Mancha, the light and mirror of the chivalry of that land, and the first man in our times, in these calamitous times of ours, to devote himself to the toils and exercise of knight-errantry, and to the redressing of wrongs, the succouring of widows and the protecting of maidens, those maidens who used to ride about, up hill and down dale, with their whips and their palfreys, carrying their maidenhead with them; for unless raped by some blackguard, or by some peasant with his hatchet and his iron skullcap, or by some monstrous giant, there were maidens in those times gone by who, at the age of eighty and not having slept a single night under a roof, went to their graves with their maidenheads as intact as the mothers who'd borne them. I say, then, that for these and many other reasons our gallant Don Quixote is worthy of continuous and memorable praise—which shouldn't be denied me, either, for all the hard work and diligence I devoted to searching out the conclusion to this agreeable history; although I'm well aware that if heaven, chance and fortune hadn't helped me, the world would have been left without the pleasurable entertainment that an attentive reader of this work can enjoy for nearly two hours. And this is how I found the missing part:

One day when I was in the main shopping street in Toledo, a lad appeared, on his way to sell some old notebooks and loose sheets of paper to a silk merchant; and since I'll read anything, even scraps of paper lying in the gutter, this leaning of mine led me to pick up one of the notebooks that the lad had for sale, and I saw it was written in characters that I recognized as Arabic. Although I knew that much, I couldn't read them, and so I looked around to see if there was some Spanish-speaking Moor in the street, and it wasn't very hard to find one, because even if I'd been looking for a translator from another better and older language,[3] I should have found him, too. In short, chance provided me with a man who, when I told him what I wanted and put the book in his hands, opened it in the middle and after reading a little began to laugh. I asked him why, and he replied that he was laughing at something written in the margin of the book by way of annotation. I told him to tell me what it was and, still laughing, he replied:

"As I said, this is written here in the margin: 'This woman Dulcinea del Toboso, so often mentioned in this book, is said to have been a dabber hand at salting pork than any other woman in La Mancha.'"

When I heard "Dulcinea del Toboso" I was dumbfounded, because it immediately suggested that the notebooks contained the history of Don Quixote. So I told him to read me the title-page that very instant and he did so, making an extempore translation from the Arabic, and it said: *History of Don Quixote de la Mancha, written by Cide Hamete Benengeli, an Arab historian.*[4] I had to draw on all the discretion

---

3. Hebrew. Despite the supposed banishing of both Moors and Jews from Spain in the late 15th and early 16th centuries, quite a few remained; many had become converts or *conversos*.

4. "Cide" (as in El Cid) means "Lord" in Arabic, and "Hamete" means "He who praises." "Benengeli," on the other hand, derives from the Spanish word for eggplant.

I possess not to reveal how happy I felt when I heard the title of the book; and, getting in ahead of the silk merchant, I bought all the papers and notebooks from the lad for half a real; and if the lad himself had had any discretion and had noticed how much I wanted them, he could well have expected and indeed exacted more than six reals. Then I went off with the Moor to the cathedral cloister and asked him to translate the notebooks, or at least all those that had to do with Don Quixote, into Castilian, without adding or omitting a single word, and I offered to pay him whatever he asked. He was satisfied with fifty pounds of raisins and two bushels of wheat, and promised to make a good, faithful translation, and to be quick about it, too. But to ensure the smooth working of our agreement, and not to let such a find out of my sight, I brought the Moor home with me, and in little more than a month and a half he translated the whole text just as it is set down here.

In the first notebook there was a realistic picture of Don Quixote's battle with the Basque, with both of them in the positions described in the history, their swords aloft, one protected by his little round infantry man's shield and the other by his cushion, and the Basque's mule so lifelike that you could tell from a mile off that it was a hired one. At the Basque's feet were written the words *Don Sancho de Azpetia,* which must have been his name; and at Rocinante's feet were these other words: *Don Quixote.* Rocinante was depicted in such wonderful detail—as long as a wet week and as lean as a lath, with a jutting spine and far gone in consumption—that it was easy to see how appropriately he had been named Rocinante. Next to him stood Sancho Panza, holding his ass by the halter, and at his feet were the words *Sancho Zancas;* and he must, to judge from the picture, have had a short body, a plump paunch and long shanks, these last two features being expressed in the words Panza and Zancas[5] respectively, because he's given both these surnames at different points in this history. Other details could be observed, but none of them is important, or relevant to the truthful narration of this history—and no history is bad so long as it is truthful.

If there is any objection to be made about the truthfulness of this history, it can only be that its author was an Arab, and it's a well-known feature of Arabs that they're all liars; but since they're such enemies of ours, it's to be supposed that he fell short of the truth rather than exaggerating it. And this is, indeed, what I suspect he did, because where he could and should have launched into the praises of such an excellent knight, he seems to have been careful to pass them over in silence, which is something he shouldn't have done or even thought of doing, because historians should and must be precise, truthful and unprejudiced, without allowing self-interest or fear, hostility or affection, to turn them away from the path of truth, whose mother is history: the imitator of time, the storehouse of actions and the witness to the past, an example and a lesson to the present and a warning to the future. In this history I know that everything anyone could want to find in the most delectable history is to be found; and if anything worthwhile is missing from it, it's my belief that it's the dog of an author who wrote it that's to blame, rather than any defect in the subject. At all events the second part began like this, according to the translation:

The keen-edged swords of the two valiant and enraged combatants, thus raised aloft, seemed to be threatening the very heavens, earth and watery abysses, such was the determination displayed by both men. The first to deliver his blow was the wrathful Basque, and he did so with such force and fury that, if his sword had not twisted in the

5. "Panza" means belly or paunch; "zancas" means legs.

course of its descent, that stroke alone would have been enough to put an end to the fearful fight and to all our knight's adventures; but fortune, which had better things in store for him, turned his opponent's blade aside so that, although it struck his left shoulder, all the damage it did was to disarm him on that side, carrying with it a large part of his helmet together with half his ear, all of which tumbled to the ground in hideous ruin, leaving him in a sorry state indeed.

By God, who could describe the rage that took possession of the heart of the man of La Mancha on seeing himself treated in this way? All that can be said is that it was so great that he rose at last in his stirrups and, gripping his sword with both hands, brought it down with such fury full on the Basque's cushion and head that his admirable protection was of no avail and, as if a mountain had fallen on top of him, blood began to trickle from his nose, and from his mouth, and from his ears, and he started to slide off his mule, from which he would no doubt have fallen had he not clung to its neck; but even so he lost his stirrups and dropped his reins, and the animal, terrified by the awful blow, began to gallop this way and that, and soon bucked its rider off.

Don Quixote was calmly watching this scene, and when he saw the Basque fall he jumped from his horse, ran up to him and, putting the tip of his sword between his eyes, told him to surrender or he would cut off his head. The Basque was so stunned that he could not reply, and his fate would have been sealed, so blind with rage was Don Quixote, if the ladies in the coach, who had been watching the fight in consternation, had not hastened to where he stood and pleaded with him to do them the great kindness and favour of sparing their squire's life. To which Don Quixote, haughty and grave, replied:

"To be sure, fair ladies, I am well content to do as you request; but I insist on one condition to which you must agree, which is that this knight promise me to repair to the village of El Toboso and present himself on my behalf before the peerless Doña Dulcinea, that she may dispose of him according to her pleasure."

The fearful, disconsolate ladies, without stopping to think about what Don Quixote was demanding or even asking who Dulcinea was, promised that the squire would do whatever was required of him.

"Since you have given me your word, I shall do him no further harm, even though he richly merits it."

Chapter 10

About what happened next between Don Quixote and the Basque, and the peril with which he was threatened by a mob of men from Yanguas

By this time Sancho Panza had struggled to his feet, somewhat mauled by the friars' servants, and had stood watching Don Quixote's battle, as in his heart he prayed to God to be so kind as to give his master the victory and let him win some island of which he could make his squire the governor, as promised. So once Sancho saw that the fight was over and that his master was about to remount Rocinante, he went over to hold his stirrup and, before he started climbing, knelt down before him and, grasping his hand, kissed it and said:

"Don Quixote sir, please make me the governor of the island you've just won in this dreadful battle. However big it is, I'm sure I'll be strong enough to govern it as well as anyone who ever governed islands anywhere in the world."

To which Don Quixote replied:

"I would have you know, brother Sancho, that this adventure and others like it are not island adventures but roadside adventures, in which there is nothing to be won but a broken head and a missing ear. Be patient, for there will be adventures that will enable me to make you not only a governor but something greater still."

Sancho thanked him profusely and, again kissing his hand, and the skirts of his armour too, helped him on to Rocinante, and himself mounted his donkey and set out after his master, who, without a word of farewell to the ladies in the coach, rode off at a brisk pace into a nearby wood. Sancho followed as fast as his donkey could trot, but Rocinante's speed was such that Sancho fell further and further behind and had to call out to his master to wait for him. Don Quixote did so, reining Rocinante in until his weary squire caught up with him, and said:

"What I'm thinking, sir, is that it'd be a good idea to go and take refuge in some church somewhere, because that man you fought is in a really bad way, and it wouldn't surprise me if we were reported to the Holy Brotherhood and they came to arrest us.[1] And by God, if they do that, we'll sweat blood before we get out of prison."

"Not at all, Sancho," said Don Quixote. "Where have you ever seen or read of a knight errant standing trial, whatever outrages he is accused of?"

"I don't know anything about getting out of rages, I've never been in one in my life—all I do know is that people who go fighting in the fields are dealt with by the Holy Brotherhood, and I'm not going to poke my nose into that other thing you said."

"Do not worry, my friend," replied Don Quixote, "for I shall rescue you from the Chaldeans themselves if need be,[2] let alone the Holy Brotherhood. But tell me, pray: have you ever seen a knight more valiant than I on all the face of the earth? Have you ever read in histories of any knight who is or has been more spirited in the attack, more persevering in the pursuit, more dexterous in the wounding or more skilful in the unhorsing?"

"To tell you the honest truth," replied Sancho, "I haven't ever read a history, because I can't read or write, but what I will dare bet is that in all the days of my born life I've never served a braver master than you—and I pray God these braveries of yours aren't paid for where I just said. And what I pray you to do is to see to that ear of yours, you're losing a lot of blood from it. Here in my saddle-bags I've got some lint and white ointment."

"All this would have been quite unnecessary," replied Don Quixote, "if I had remembered to make a flask of the Balsam of Fierabras: for but one drop of it would have saved us both time and medicine."[3]

"What flask and what balsam is that?" said Sancho Panza.

"It is," said Don Quixote, "a balsam the recipe for which I carry in my memory, and if provided with it one need not fear death or contemplate dying from any kind of wound. And so, once I make some and give it to you, all you have to do when you see that in some battle I have been cut in two (as often happens) is to take the part of my body that has fallen to the ground and, before the blood congeals, neatly and carefully place it on top of the part remaining in the saddle, being quite sure to make it fit exactly. Then you will have me drink just two mouthfuls of the balsam, and I shall be as sound as a bell."

---

1. Created during Ferdinand's and Isabella's reign, the Holy Brotherhood dealt largely with rural criminals and highway robbers.

2. The Chaldeans were a group of tribes who became dominant in Babylonia and were regarded as enemies of the Israelites.

3. The balsam in which Christ's body was embalmed, supposedly possessed of miraculous powers of healing. Fierabras is a giant who steals the balsam from the Christians in the legends surrounding the history of Charlemagne; Charlemagne himself eventually retrieves it.

"If that's so," said Sancho, "I here and now renounce being governor of the island you've promised me, and all I want in payment for my many good services is for you to let me have the recipe for that wonderful potion—to my mind it'll fetch more than two reals an ounce anywhere, so it's all I need to live an honourable and easy life. But first I'd better know if it costs a lot to make."

"For less than three reals you can make twelve pints of it," replied Don Quixote.

"Strike me blind!" replied Sancho. "What are you waiting for, why not make some here and now and show me how?"

"Enough of that, my friend," replied Don Quixote. "I intend in due course to show you even greater secrets and do you even greater favours. But now let us see to this ear of mine, for it is hurting more than I should like."

Sancho took lint and ointment out of his saddle-bags. But when Don Quixote saw his broken helmet he was on the point of going berserk, and, placing his hand on his sword and raising his eyes to heaven, he said:

"I swear by the Creator of all things, and by the four evangelists and all their holy writings, that I will lead the life led by the great Marquis of Mantua when he swore to avenge his nephew Baldwin's death, and until then 'ne'er at table to eat bread nor with his wife to lie,' and other such things that, although I cannot remember them now, can be taken as spoken, until I have exacted full vengeance on the perpetrator of this outrage."

When Sancho heard this he said:

"I'd just like to point out, Don Quixote sir, that if that knight has done as he was told and has gone to present himself before my lady Dulcinea del Toboso, then he's done his duty and doesn't deserve another punishment unless he commits another crime."

"You have spoken well and to the purpose," replied Don Quixote, "and so I hereby annul my oath as regards exacting fresh vengeance on him; but I swear anew and confirm that I will lead the life I have just described until I wrest from some knight another helmet at least as fine as this. And do not imagine, Sancho, that I am doing this without a solid basis, for I have a clear model to follow: exactly the same thing happened, down to the very last detail, with Mambrino's helmet, which cost Sacripante so dear."[4]

"You just send all those oaths of yours to the devil, sir," retorted Sancho, "they're bad for your health and worse for your conscience. Or else tell me this—supposing days and days go by and we don't come across anyone in a helmet, what then? Have we got to honour the oath, regardless of all the inconvenience and discomfort, always sleeping in our clothes, never under a roof, and those hundreds of other penances in the mad old Marquis of Mantua's vow, that you're so set on reviving? Just think about it, sir—it isn't men in armour you'll find on these here roads but carters and muleteers, who not only don't wear helmets but have probably never even heard of them."

"You are mistaken about that," said Don Quixote, "because before we have been riding along these highways and byways for two hours we shall see more men in arms than fell upon Albracca to carry off the fair Angelica."[5]

4. Rinaldo, elsewhere cited as Reynaldo of Montelban, steals the enchanted helmet of the Moorish king Sacripante in Book 1 of Boiardo's *Orlando Innamorato*.
5. Daughter of a Moorish king who dwells in the castle of Albracca; in Boiardo's poem, the castle is beseiged by Agricane and his men.

"All right, then, so be it," said Sancho, "and please God we come well out of all this and the time soon arrives to conquer this island that's going to cost me so dear—and then I can die happy."

"I have already told you, Sancho, not to worry about all that; for if finding an island presents any problems, there is always the kingdom of Denmark or the kingdom of Soliadisa,[6] which would fit you like a glove, and still more so being as it is on terra firma, which should make you even happier. But let us leave these matters until it is time to deal with them; and now see if you have anything to eat in your saddle-bags, so that we can go without delay in search of some castle where we can stay for the night and make the balsam about which I have told you; for I swear to God that my ear is very painful."

"There's an onion here, and a bit of cheese, and a few scraps of bread," said Sancho, "but that isn't food for a valiant knight like you."

"How mistaken you are!" replied Don Quixote. "I would have you know, Sancho, that it is an honour for knights errant not to eat for a whole month, and if they do eat, it must be what they find readiest to hand, and you would know this well enough if you had read as many histories as I have; for in all those very very many that I have read, I have not found any mention of knights errant eating, except when it happened that some sumptuous banquet was held for them, but otherwise they used to live on next to nothing. And although it is evident that they could not have gone without eating and satisfying all the other needs of nature, because, after all, they were men like us, it is also evident that since they spent most of their time wandering in woods and wildernesses, without cooks, their everyday food must have been country fare, like that which you are offering me now. And so, friend Sancho, do not be afflicted by what pleases me; do not seek to build the world anew, or to turn knight-errantry on its head."

"I'm sorry I'm sure," said Sancho. "Not knowing how to read or write, as I said before, I haven't been able to find out about all these rules of knighthood. From now on I'll put all sorts of nuts and raisins into the saddle-bags for you, being as you are a knight, and for me, not being one, I'll put in feathered provisions of greater substance."

"I am not saying, Sancho," replied Don Quixote, "that it is obligatory for knights errant not to eat anything other than those nuts to which you refer; but that they must have been their usual sustenance, together with certain herbs, known to them and to me, which they found in the fields."

"It's a good idea," said Sancho, "to know about those there herbs. I fancy we're going to need that knowledge one fine day."

Then he took out what he'd said he'd brought, and the two men ate together in peace and good fellowship. But anxious to find somewhere to stay that night they didn't linger over their dry and frugal meal. They remounted and hurried on, to try and reach a village before nightfall, but both the day and their hopes of doing so came to an end as they were passing some goatherds' huts, and they decided to spend the night there. Sancho's sorrow at not reaching a village was matched by his master's delight at sleeping in the open air, because he considered that each time he did so he performed an act of possession that provided fresh proof of his chivalry.

---

6. Perhaps Cervantes (or Quixote) is confusing names here; Soliadisa is a princess, not a kingdom, in a 16th-century romance.

from *Chapter 18*

Which relates the conversation that Sancho Panza had with his master Don Quixote, and other adventures worth relating

* * * As Don Quixote and his squire discussed these matters, Don Quixote saw that a huge, dense cloud of dust was approaching them along the road, and he turned to Sancho and said:

"This is the day, O Sancho, when will be seen the good that fortune has in store for me; this is the day, I say, when the might of my arm will be displayed as never before, and when I shall do deeds that will remain written in the book of fame for the ages to come. Do you see that cloud of dust rising up over there, Sancho? Well, it is being raised by a vast army from countless different nations, marching towards us."

"In that case there must be two armies," said Sancho, "because opposite it, back there behind us, there's another dust cloud just like it."

Don Quixote turned round and saw that Sancho was right; and then he was beside himself with joy, because he knew that these were two armies marching to clash in the middle of that broad plain. Every minute of every hour his imagination was filled with those battles, enchantments, adventures, extravagances, loves and challenges that books of chivalry recount, and everything he said, thought or did was channelled into such affairs. And the dust clouds were being raised by two great droves of sheep approaching from opposite directions along the same road, but the dust prevented the sheep from being seen until they came close. And Don Quixote was so insistent they were armies that Sancho believed him, and said:

"So what are we going to do now, sir?"

"What are we going to do?" said Don Quixote. "Favour and assist the needy and helpless. And you should know, Sancho, that this army approaching from in front of us is led and directed by the great Emperor Alifanfarón, lord of the great island of Taprobana;[1] the other army coming up behind me belongs to his enemy, the King of the Garamantes, known as Pentapolín of the Uprolled Sleeve, because he always goes into battle with his right arm bare."[2]

"But why do these two lords hate each other so much?" asked Sancho.

"They hate each other," replied Don Quixote, "because this Alifanfarón is a wild pagan, and he is in love with Pentapolín's daughter, who is a very beauteous and, moreover, charming lady, and a Christian, and her father will not give her in marriage to the pagan king unless this man first abjures the religion of his false prophet Muhammad and is converted to Christianity."

"My eye!" said Sancho. "Pentapolín's doing just the right thing, and I'm going to help him in every way I can."

"Then you will be doing your duty, Sancho," said Don Quixote, "because to take part in battles of this kind it is not necessary to be knighted."

"I'm very well aware of that," replied Sancho, "but where are we going to put this ass of mine so that we can be sure of finding it again once the fighting's over? Because I don't expect going into battle on something like this is what people usually do."

"That is true," said Don Quixote. "What you can do with the ass is to leave it free to have its own adventures, whether it goes missing or not, because we shall possess

---

1. Taprobana is Sri Lanka, the emperor a fantasy of Don Quixote's.
2. The Garamantes were a fierce people from Africa; Pentapolín is another invention of Don Quixote.

so many horses when we emerge victorious that even Rocinante will be in danger of being replaced by another. But now pay attention to me and keep your eyes open, for I am going to inform you about the most important knights in these two armies. And so that you can see and observe them better, let us withdraw to that hill over there, from where both armies must be visible."

This they did, and from the hill they would indeed have had a clear view of the two flocks that were armies for Don Quixote, if the clouds of dust they were raising hadn't interfered with the view. Yet seeing in his imagination what he didn't see and didn't exist, he began to proclaim:

"That knight you can see over there in yellow armour, with a crowned lion lying submissive at a damsel's feet on his shield, is the valiant Laurcalco, Lord of the Silver Bridge; the other one, with golden flowers on his armour, and on his shield three silver crowns on a blue field, is the much-feared Micocolembo, the Grand Duke of Quirocia; that other one on his right, with gigantic limbs, is the fearless Brandabarbarán de Boliche, Lord of the Three Arabias, wearing that serpent's skin for armour and, instead of a shield, bearing a door which is reputed to be one of the doors of the temple pulled down by Samson when in dying he avenged himself on his enemies.[3] But look in the other direction and you will see at the front of the other army the ever victorious, never vanquished Timonel de Carcajona, the Prince of Nueva Vizcaya, with his armour quartered blue, green, white and yellow, and on his shield he has a golden cat on a tawny field with the word *Miau,* which is the beginning of his lady's name, for it is said that she is the peerless Miulina, the daughter of Duke Alfeñiquén of the Algarve; that other knight who burdens the back of that powerful steed, with armour as white as snow and white arms—that is to say a shield without any device on it—is a novice knight from France, called Pierres Papin, Lord of the Baronies of Utrique; that other one, striking his iron spurs into the flanks of that dazzling, fleet zebra, and with armour of blue vair,[4] is the powerful Duke of Nerbia, Espartafilardo of the Wood, who bears on his shield the device of an asparagus plant, with a motto in Castilian that says: 'Divine my fortune.'"

And he went on naming imaginary knights from one army and the other and, swept along by the fancies of his unique madness, he improvised armour, colours, devices and mottoes for all of them; and without a pause he continued:

"This other army, facing us, is formed of people of many races: here are those who have drunk the sweet waters of famous Xanthus; mountaineers who tread the Massilian fields; those who sift fine gold dust in Arabia Felix; those who enjoy the famous, cool banks of clear Thermodon; those who bleed golden Pactolus along many different channels; and the Numidians, breakers of promises; the Persians, bowmen of great renown; the Parthians and the Medes, who fight as they flee; the Arabs, who move their dwellings; the Scythians, as cruel as they are pale; the Ethiopians, with pierced lips, and other infinite peoples, whose faces I see and recognize, even though I do not remember their names. In this other squadron come those who drink the crystalline waters of olive-bearing Betis; those who wash their faces in the liquor of the ever rich and golden Tagus; those who enjoy the beneficent waters of the divine Genil; those who tread the lush pastures of the Tartesian fields; those who take delight in the Elysian meadows of Jerez; men of La Mancha, rich and crowned with yellow ears of corn; men

---

3. Once again, for most of this paragraph Don Quixote is indulging in his own fictions. Samson was the Hebrew warrior who was blinded by Delilah and pulled down a temple on top of himself and his enemies, the Philistines.

4. Weasel fur.

clad in iron, ancient relics of Gothic blood; those who bathe in the Pisuerga, renowned for the gentleness of its current; those who graze their flocks and herds on the broad meadows of winding Guadiana, famous for its secret course; those who shiver in the cold of the bosky Pyrenees and among the white snowflakes of the lofty Apennines: in short, all those whom Europe contains and encloses within its boundaries."[5]

Great God, how many provinces he mentioned, how many races he named, giving to each one of them, with wonderful readiness, its own attributes, steeped as he was in everything he'd read in his lying books! Sancho Panza was hanging on his every word, and didn't utter a single one himself, and every so often he'd turn his head to try to spot the knights and giants his master was naming; and since he couldn't see any of them, he said:

"Look sir, the devil can take any of those men or giants or knights you say there are hereabouts—at least I can't see them, perhaps it's all a magic spell, like those ghosts last night."

"How can you say that?" retorted Don Quixote. "Do you not hear the neighing of the horses, the sounding of the bugles, the beating of the drums?"

"All I can hear," replied Sancho, "is lots of sheep bleating."

And he was right, because the two flocks were coming close.

"It is your fear, Sancho," said Don Quixote, "that is preventing you from seeing or hearing properly; because one of the effects of fear is to muddle the senses and make things seem to be what they are not; and if you are so frightened, stand aside and leave me alone, for I am sufficient by myself to give the victory to whichever army I decide to support."

As he said this he put spurs to Rocinante and, with his lance at the ready, he sped down the hill like a thunderbolt. Sancho shouted after him:

"Come back, come back, Don Quixote sir, I swear to God they're sheep you're charging! Come back! By the bones of my poor old father! What madness is this? Look, there aren't any giants or knights, or cats, or armour, or shields quartered or left in one piece, or blue vairs, or the devil. What are you doing? Lord have mercy on us sinners!"

But nothing would make Don Quixote turn back. Instead he galloped on, crying:

"Come, you knights, fighting beneath the banners of the valiant Emperor Pentapolín of the Uprolled Sleeve, follow me, and you shall see with what ease I give him his revenge over his enemy Alifanfarón of Taprobana!"

With this he rode into the army of sheep and began to spear them with as much fury and determination as if he really were attacking mortal enemies. The shepherds and farmers accompanying the flock were screaming at him to stop, but, seeing that this didn't have any effect, they drew their slings from their belts and started to salute him about the ears with stones the size of fists. Don Quixote didn't take any notice of the stones; instead he galloped this way and that, crying:

"Where are you, proud Alifanfarón? Come here: a lone knight am I, who wishes, in single combat, to try your strength and take your life, as punishment for the distress you have caused the valiant Pentapolín the Garamante."

As he said this a large smooth pebble came and struck him in the side and buried two of his ribs in his body. This left him in such a state that he felt certain he was

---

5. In this paragraph, Don Quixote mentions real places and warlike peoples. In the "first squadron" are found the Trojans, who lived near the river Xanthus, and numerous other races from countries in Africa and Asia, including Turkey (site of the Thermodon River) and Lydia (site of the Pactolus). The "other squadron" includes peoples from Spain and Italy; all the rivers he lists here run through the Iberian peninsula, including the "winding Guadiana," which flows through La Mancha and frequently makes its "secret course" underground. The Pyrenees are the mountains on the border between Spain and France; the Apennines are mountains running down the center of Italy.

either dead or sore wounded and, remembering his remedy, he took out the oil-bottle, put it to his mouth and began to pour the liquor into his stomach;[6] but before he could swallow what he considered to be a sufficient amount, another of those sugared almonds came and hit his hand and his bottle with such force that it smashed the bottle, taking out three or four teeth as well, and crushing two fingers.

Such was the first blow, and such was the second, that the poor knight couldn't stop himself from sliding off his horse. The shepherds came up to look at him, and thought they'd killed him, so they made haste to round up their flock, pick up the dead sheep, of which there were more than a few, and make themselves scarce, without looking any further into the matter.

All this time Sancho had been on the hill, watching his master's follies, tearing his beard and cursing the moment when fortune had brought them together. When he saw that Don Quixote was lying on the ground and that the shepherds had gone away, he ventured down the hill and approached him, and found him in a terrible state, although still conscious. And Sancho said:

"Didn't I tell you, Don Quixote sir, to turn back, because what you were attacking wasn't armies, it was flocks of sheep?"

"This just shows how my enemy, that scoundrel of an enchanter, can transform things and make them disappear. I would have you know, Sancho, that it is very easy for such people to make us look like whatever they want, and this villain who is persecuting me, envious of the glory he saw I was about to conquer in this battle, turned the armies of enemy forces into flocks of sheep. If you do not believe me, Sancho, I beg you to do something that will correct your mistake and make you see that I am telling you the truth: mount your ass and stalk them, and you will soon see how, once they have gone a little way, they turn back into what they were at first and, ceasing to be sheep, become real men again, just as I described them to you. But do not go yet, because I have need of your assistance: come here and see how many of my teeth are missing, for it seems to me that there is not one left in my mouth."

Sancho came so close that his eyes were nearly inside his master's mouth; and by now the balsam had done its work in Don Quixote's stomach, and, just as Sancho was peering in, he discharged all its contents with the violence of a shotgun and they exploded in the face of the compassionate squire.

"Holy Mother of God!" cried Sancho. "What's up now? The man's dying, he must be—he's spewing blood!"

But when he examined the evidence more closely he could tell from the colour, taste and smell that it wasn't blood but the balsam he'd seen him drinking from the oil-bottle, and this disgusting discovery so turned his stomach that he vomited his guts all over his master, and both of them were left in the same fine mess. Sancho staggered over to his ass to look in the saddle-bags for something with which to clean himself and see to his master's wounds, and when he couldn't find them he almost went insane. He cursed himself again, and decided in his heart to leave his master and go back home, even if that did mean forfeiting what he was owed for services rendered and his hopes of governing the promised island.

Don Quixote now struggled to his feet, with his left hand clapped to his mouth to stop his remaining teeth from falling out, took hold with the other hand of the reins

---

6. This is the holy balsam of Fierebras that cures all ills, which Don Quixote managed to concoct in Chapter 17 after he and Sancho Panza were badly beaten at an inn Don Quixote took for a castle. Don Quixote drinks the potion as a cure, and undergoes such "seizures and spasms" that not only he but everyone else in the inn "thought that his end had come."

of the faithful Rocinante, who was so loyal and good-natured that he hadn't budged from his master's side, and went over to his squire, who was leaning over his ass with his hand on his cheek, in the posture of a man overwhelmed by thought. And when Don Quixote saw all these signs of deep distress, he said:

"Allow me to remind you, Sancho, that no man is worth more than any other, unless he achieves more than the other. All these storms falling upon us are signs that the weather will soon clear and that things will go well for us; for neither good nor bad can last for ever, and from this we can deduce that since this bad spell has lasted for a long time, a good one cannot be far away. So you must not be distressed about the misfortunes that I undergo, for you have no part in them."

"No part in them?" retorted Sancho. "The bloke who got blanket-tossed yesterday— was he by any chance any other than my own father's son? And the saddle-bags I've lost today, with all my valuables in them—do they belong to any other than the same?"[7]

"You have lost your saddle-bags, Sancho?" said Don Quixote.

"Yes I have," replied Sancho.

"So we have nothing to eat today," replied Don Quixote.

"We wouldn't have," replied Sancho, "if it wasn't for those herbs you say you know all about growing in the fields, the ones that unfortunate knight errants like you go and pick to make up for lack of food in fixes like this."

"For all that," replied Don Quixote, "I would sooner have a two-pound loaf of white bread or indeed an eight-pound loaf of bran bread and a couple of dozen salted pilchards, than all the herbs described by Dioscorides, even in Dr. Laguna's magnificent edition.[8] But anyway, climb on to your donkey, good Sancho, and follow me, because God, who is the provider of all things, will not fail us, especially since we are engaged in his service; because he does not fail the gnats in the air, or the worms in the earth, or the tadpoles in the water. And he is so merciful that he makes his sun rise on the evil and on the good, and sends his rain on the just and on the unjust."

"You'd have done better as a preacher," said Sancho, "than as a knight errant."

"Knights errant have always known and still must know about everything, Sancho," said Don Quixote, "for there were knights errant in centuries past who would stop to preach a sermon or deliver a speech in the middle of a fair just as if they were graduates of the University of Paris; from which we can infer that the sword has never blunted the pen, nor the pen the sword."[9]

"All right, I'll take your word for it," replied Sancho, "and now let's get going and find somewhere to stay the night, and God grant it's a place where there aren't any blankets, or blanket-tossers, or ghosts, or enchanted Moors—because if there are any of those, I'll send this adventuring lark to the devil, lock, stock and barrel."

"You must pray to God for that, my son," said Don Quixote. "And now guide us where you will, for on this occasion I wish to leave the choice of a lodging to you. But first lend me your hand and feel with your finger how many teeth are missing on this upper right side, because that is where I feel the pain."

Sancho put his fingers in and, as he felt around, he asked:

"How many back teeth did you use to have on this side?"

"Four," replied Don Quixote, "apart from the wisdom tooth, all of them whole and sound."

"Are you quite sure of what you're saying, sir?" said Sancho.

"Yes, four, if not five," replied Don Quixote, "because I have never had any teeth extracted, nor have any fallen out or been destroyed by decay or infection."

"Well, down here below," said Sancho, "you've only got two and a half now, and up above not even half a tooth, it's as smooth as the palm of my hand."

"Oh, unhappy me!" said Don Quixote as he heard the sad news his squire was giving him. "I would rather have lost an arm, so long as it was not my sword arm. For I would have you know, Sancho, that a mouth without teeth is like a mill without a millstone, and that a tooth is much more worthy of esteem than a diamond. But those of us who profess the order of chivalry in all its severity are subject to this. Mount your donkey, my friend, and lead the way, and I shall follow at whatever pace you prefer."

Sancho did so, heading towards where he thought they might find a place to stay without leaving the highway, which was uninterrupted in that part.

As they plodded along, because the pain in Don Quixote's jaws didn't give him any respite or any inclination to ride faster, Sancho tried to amuse him and cheer him up by chatting to him, and said, among other things, what is recorded in the next chapter.

Chapter 22

About how Don Quixote freed many wretches who, much against their will, were being taken where they would have preferred not to go

Cide Hamete Benengeli, the Arab author from La Mancha, relates in this most grave, grandiloquent, meticulous, delightful and imaginative history that after the conversation between the famous Don Quixote de la Mancha and his squire Sancho Panza recorded at the end of the twenty-first chapter, Don Quixote raised his eyes and saw that some twelve men on foot, strung by the neck, like beads, on a great iron chain, and with shackles on their hands, were plodding towards them along the road. Two men on horseback and two others on foot were escorting them. The mounted men were carrying firelocks and the others swords and spears, and as soon as Sancho Panza saw them he said:

"Here comes a chain-gang of convicts, on their forced march to the King's galleys."

"What do you mean, forced march?" demanded Don Quixote. "Is it possible that the King uses force on anyone?"

"I don't mean that," replied Sancho, "just that they've been sentenced to serve the King in his galleys for their crimes, and they've got a long walk to get there."

"In short," replied Don Quixote, "whatever the details may be, these people, wherever they are going, are being forced to march there, and are not doing it of their own free will."

"That's right," said Sancho.

"In that case," said his master, "this situation is calling out for the exercise of my profession: the redressing of outrages and the succour and relief of the wretched."

"Look, sir," said Sancho. "Justice, and that means the King himself, isn't doing these people any outrages, only punishing them for their crimes."

At this point the chain-gang came up, and Don Quixote, in courteous language, asked the guards to be so kind as to inform him of the reason or reasons why they were bearing those people off in that way. One of the guards on horseback replied that they were all convicts, detained at His Majesty's pleasure and on their way to the galleys, and that there was nothing else to be said and nothing else that he had any business to know.

"All the same," said Don Quixote, "I should like to hear from each one of them individually the cause of his misfortune."

He added other such polite expressions to persuade them to tell him what he wanted to know that the other guard on horseback said:

"We do have here the documents and certificates with the sentences that each of these wretches has been given, but this is no time to stop to take them out and read them; so you'd better come and ask the men yourself, and they'll tell you if they want to—and they will want to, because these are fellows who really enjoy getting up to their evil tricks and bragging about them afterwards."

With this permission, which Don Quixote would have taken for himself if it hadn't been given him, he approached the chain-gang and asked the first convict what sins had put him in that plight. The convict replied that he was there for being in love.

"For no more than that?" replied Don Quixote. "If they send men to the galleys for being in love, I could have been rowing in them for a long time by now."

"It isn't love of the sort you think," said the convict. "Mine was for a washing-basket that was chock-a-block with linen, and I loved it so much, and I hugged it so tight, that if the law hadn't taken it off me by force I still wouldn't have let go of it of my own freewill to this day. I was caught red-handed, there wasn't any need for torture, the trial's over and done with, they gave me a hundred of the best plus three in the tubs and that's that."

"What are tubs?" asked Don Quixote.

"Tubs is galleys," replied the convict.

He was a young man of maybe twenty-four, and he said he was a native of Piedrahita. Don Quixote put the same question to the second convict, who was so overcome by melancholy that he didn't offer a word in reply, but the first one answered for him and said:

"This one, sir, is here for being a canary-bird, that is to say for being a singer and musician."

"What?" said Don Quixote. "Do men go to the galleys for being singers and musicians, too?"

"Yes, sir," replied the convict, "because there's nothing worse than singing in your throes."

"On the contrary," said Don Quixote, "I have often heard it said that one can sing away sorrows and cast away care."

"Here it's the opposite," said the convict. "Sing just that once and you'll weep for the rest of your life."

"I fail to understand," said Don Quixote.

But one of the guards explained:

"Sir knight, among these ungodly people singing in your throes means confessing under torture. This sinner was tortured and he confessed to his crime—he's a prigger of prancers, in other words a horse-thief—and because he confessed he was sentenced to six years in the galleys and two hundred strokes of the lash, and these he's already been given; and he's always sad and lost in his thoughts, because the other criminals back there in prison and here in the chain-gang despise and mock and maltreat him and make his life impossible for confessing and not having the guts to keep saying no. They say, you see, that "nay" has no more letters in it than "aye," and that a delinquent's a lucky man if his life or death depends on his own tongue and not on witnesses or evidence, and it's my belief they aren't far wrong."

"That is my understanding, too," replied Don Quixote.

He moved on to the third convict and put the same question to him; the reply was ready and assured:

"I'm off to our old friends the tubs for five years, for the lack of ten ducats."

"I will most gladly give you twenty," said Don Quixote, "to relieve you of such distress."

"That looks to me," replied the convict, "like having money in the middle of the ocean when you're starving and there isn't anywhere to buy what you need. I'm saying this because if I'd had those twenty ducats you're offering me when I needed them, I'd have used them to grease the clerk's pen and liven up my lawyer's wits, and now I'd be in the middle of Zocodover Square in Toledo instead of in the middle of this road, like a greyhound on a leash. But God is good, and you've just got to be patient."

Don Quixote went on to the fourth convict, a man with a venerable face and a white beard reaching below his chest who, when asked why he was there, began to weep and didn't reply; but the fifth convict acted as interpreter and said:

"This honourable man is going to the galleys for four years, having been paraded in state through the customary streets, all dressed up and on a fine horse."

"That means, I think," said Sancho, "that he was exposed to public shame."[1]

"That's right," said the convict, "and the crime he was given this punishment for was stockbroking, or to be more exact bodybroking. What I mean to say is that this gentleman's here for being a pimp, and also for having a touch of the sorcerer about him."

"If it were not for the touch of the sorcerer," said Don Quixote, "for being a pimp alone he does not deserve to go to row in the galleys, but rather to be the admiral in charge of them. Because the pimp's trade is no ordinary trade; it must be carried out by intelligent people and it is absolutely essential to any well-ordered society, and only the well-born should exercise it; and there should be an official inspector of pimps, as there is of other trades, and a maximum permitted number of them established and published, as is the case with stockbrokers, and this would be the way to forestall many evils that arise from the fact that this trade is in the hands of untrained and unqualified people such as little strumpets, page-boys and other scoundrels of no age or experience who, when at a critical moment some decisive action is called for, make a mess of the whole thing because they cannot tell their right hands from their left. I should like to go on to give the reasons why it would be advisable to make a careful selection of those who do such a necessary job in society, but this is not the place: one day I shall present my ideas to the proper authorities. All I shall say now is that the distress caused me by the sight of these white hairs and this venerable face in such a plight through his being a pimp is dissipated by the addition of his being a sorcerer. I know, of course, that there are no spells in the world that can control a person's will, as some simple people believe; for our free will is sovereign, and there is no herb or enchantment that can control it. What some silly little strumpets and deceitful rogues do is to make certain poisonous mixtures that they use to turn men mad, claiming that they have the power to make them fall in love, whereas it is, as I have just said, impossible to coerce the will."

"Right you are," said the old man, "and honestly, sir, I wasn't guilty of being a sorcerer, though I couldn't deny the charge of being a pimp. But I never thought I was doing any harm, all I wanted was for everyone to be happy and live in peace and

1. A common form of punishment in early modern Europe; he would have been flogged and then paraded through the city's main streets with a placard denouncing his crimes.

quiet, without any quarrels or sadness—but these good intentions weren't any use to prevent me from being sent where I don't expect to come back from, what with my advanced age and my bladder trouble, that doesn't give me a moment's peace."

And here he started weeping again, and Sancho felt so sorry for him that he took a real from inside his shirt and handed it over. Don Quixote moved on to the next man and asked what was his crime, and he replied with no less brio than the last, indeed with rather more of it:

"I'm here because I fooled around too much with two girl-cousins of mine, and with two girl-cousins of somebody else's; and, in short, I fooled around so much with the lot of them that as a result the family tree's become so complicated that I don't know who the devil would be able to work it out. It was all proved against me, there weren't any strings for me to pull, I hadn't got any money, I was within an inch of having my neck stretched, I was sentenced to the galleys for six years and I accepted my fate: it's the punishment for my crime, I'm still young, long live life, while there's life there's hope. If, sir knight, you've got anything on you that you could spare for us poor wretches, God will repay you for it in heaven, and here on earth we'll take care to pray to God that your life and your health may be as long and as good as you obviously deserve."

He was wearing a student's gown, and one of the guards said that he was a great talker and a first-rate latiner.

Behind all of these was a man of thirty, very good-looking except that he squinted a little. He was shackled in a different way from the others: he had a chain on his ankle so long that he'd wound it all round his body, and two neck-irons, one linking him to the other convicts and the other, one of the sort called a keep-friend or friend's foot, from which descended two bars to his waist, where his wrists were manacled to them with great padlocks, so that he could neither raise his hands to his mouth nor lower his head to his hands. Don Quixote asked why this man was wearing so many more fetters than the others. The guard replied that it was because he'd committed more crimes than all the others put together, and that he was so reckless and such a villain that, even though he was shackled up like that, they didn't feel at all safe with him, and feared he was going to escape.

"What crimes can he have committed, though," asked Don Quixote, "if he was not given a worse punishment than the galleys?"

"He's going for ten years," replied the guard, "which is civil death, more or less. All you need to know is that this man is the famous Ginés de Pasamonte, also known as Ginesillo de Parapilla."[2]

"Look you here, sergeant," said the convict, "just watch your step, and don't be in such a hurry to fix names and nicknames on to people. I'm called Ginés, not Ginesillo, and my family name is Pasamonte, not the Parapilla you said, and I'd advise you lot to stop poking your noses into other people's business."

"Less impudence, you double-dyed villain," replied the sergeant, "unless you want me to shut your mouth for you."

"It isn't hard to spot," replied the convict, "that at the moment I'm reduced to what God has seen fit to send me; but one day somebody's going to find out whether I'm called Ginesillo de Parapilla or not."

---

2. Ginesillo is the diminutive for Ginés, and implies a lack of respect.

"Isn't that what people call you, then, you liar?" said the guard.

"Yes, that's what they call me," replied Ginés, "but I'll stop them calling me that, or else I'll pull out every single hair from my I know what. If you've got something to give us, sir knight, let's have it, and then you can clear off, because you're beginning to get on my nerves with all your prying into other people's lives—and if you want to know about mine, let me tell you I'm Ginés de Pasamonte, and my life has been written by these very fingers here."

"Now he's telling the truth," said the sergeant. "He's written his own life-history himself and a good one it is, too, and he pawned the book in prison for two hundred reals."

"And I mean to redeem it," said Ginés. "And I would, even if I'd pawned it for two hundred ducats."

"Is it as good as all that?" said Don Quixote.

"It's so good," replied Ginés, "that I wouldn't give a fig for *Lazarillo de Tormes* and all the others of that kind that have been or ever will be written.[3] What I can tell you is that it deals with facts, and that they're such fine and funny facts no lies could ever match them."

"And what is the title of your book?" asked Don Quixote.

"The Life of Ginés de Pasamonte," replied the man of that name.

"And have you finished it?" asked Don Quixote.

"How can I have finished it," he replied, "if my life hasn't finished yet? What's written so far is from my birth to when I was sentenced to the galleys this last time."

"Have you been to the galleys before, then?" asked Don Quixote.

"I have, serving God and the King for four years, so I know what biscuits taste like and I know what the lash tastes like," replied Ginés. "And I'm not too worried about going back, because it'll give me a chance to finish my book—there are lots of things left for me to say, and in Spanish galleys there's more than enough peace and quiet, not that I need much of that for what I've got left to write, because I know it all by heart."

"You seem to be an able fellow," said Don Quixote.

"And an unfortunate one, too," replied Ginés, "because misfortunes always pursue men of genius."

"They pursue villains," said the sergeant.

"I've already told you, sergeant," replied Pasamonte, "to watch your step—you weren't given that staff to ill-treat us poor wretches, but to guide and take us to where His Majesty commands. Otherwise—by the blood of...!—all sorts of things might come out in the wash one day, like those stains that were made at the inn, for example. So everyone keep his mouth shut, and live a good life, and speak even better words, and let's get moving, because this little joke has been going on for far too long."

The sergeant raised his staff to hit Pasamonte in reply to his threats, but Don Quixote thrust himself between them and begged the sergeant not to maltreat the fellow, for it was only to be expected that one whose hands were so tightly bound would loosen his tongue a little. And turning to the chain-gang he said:

"From everything that you have told me, dearly beloved brethren, I have gathered that, although it is for your crimes you have been sentenced, the punishments you are to suffer give you little pleasure, and that you are on your way to receive them with

---

3. *The Life of Lazarillo of Tormes* was a popular novel in mid–16th-century Spain about a young boy forced to make his way in the world. The anonymous novel, written as an autobiography, launched the genre of the "picaresque," or works about down-and-out rogues (*picaro* means rascal). Ginés is obviously capitalizing on the public's thirst for such works.

reluctance and against your will; and it could be that one man's lack of courage under torture, another's lack of money, another's lack of strings to pull and, to be brief, the judge's perverse decisions, were the causes of your downfall and of his failure to recognize the right that was on your side. All of which is now so powerfully present in my mind that it is persuading, telling and even obliging me to demonstrate on you the purpose for which heaven sent me into this world and made me profess in it the order of chivalry that I do profess, and the vow that I made to favour the needy and those oppressed by the powerful. But because I know that one essential part of prudence is never to do by force what can be achieved by consent, I hereby request these guards and this sergeant to be so kind as to release you and allow you to go in peace, for there will be no lack of other men to serve the King in happier circumstances, and it does seem excessively harsh to make slaves of those whom God and nature made free. What is more, guards," added Don Quixote, "these poor men have done nothing to you. Let each answer for his sins in the other world; there is a God in heaven who does not neglect to punish the wicked and reward the virtuous, and it is not right for honourable men to be the executioners of others, if they have no personal concern in the matter. I am making my request in this mild and measured manner so that, if you accede to it, I shall have reason for thanking you; but if you do not accede voluntarily, this lance and this sword and the might of my arm will force you to comply."

"That's a good one that is!" said the sergeant. "That's a fine joke he's come out with at long last! He wants us to hand the King's prisoners over to him, as if we had the authority to let them go or he had the authority to tell us to! You'd better clear off and make tracks, sir, and straighten that chamber-pot you've got on your head, and don't go around trying to put the cat among the pigeons."

"You are the cat, and the rat, and the villain, too!" retorted Don Quixote. He matched his deeds to his words and his attack was such a sudden one that he tumbled the man to the ground with a pike-wound before he had a chance to defend himself; and it was fortunate for Don Quixote that this was the guard with the firelock. The other guards were amazed and disconcerted by this unexpected development, but they rallied, and those on horseback seized their swords, and those on foot their spears, and they all fell upon Don Quixote, who was calmly awaiting them; yet he'd have fared badly if the convicts, seeing their chance to be free, hadn't succeeded by breaking the chain on which they were threaded. The hurly-burly was such that the guards, trying both to control the convicts, who were unshackling themselves, and to attack Don Quixote, who was attacking them, chased around in circles and achieved nothing.

Sancho, for his part, helped with the freeing of Ginés de Pasamonte, who was the first to spring into action as he launched himself at the fallen sergeant, snatched up his sword and his firelock and, pointing this at one man and then at another, without firing it, made all the guards disappear as they fled both from the gun and from the stones being hurled at them by the escaped convicts.

This incident saddened Sancho, because he supposed that the fleeing men would go and inform the Holy Brotherhood, who would sound the alarm and come out in pursuit of the wrongdoers; and Sancho said so to his master, and begged him to agree to a quick getaway to hide in the forests in the nearby sierra.

"That is a good idea," said Don Quixote, "but there is something I must do first."

And he called out to the convicts, who were creating a furor as they stripped the sergeant naked; they gathered around to see what he wanted, and he said:

"It is a mark of well-born people to be grateful for benefits received, and one of the sins most offensive to God is ingratitude. I am saying this because you have seen, gentlemen, manifest before your eyes, the benefit that you have received from me; in payment of which it is my wish and desire that you should set out without delay, bearing that chain that I have taken from your necks, for the city of El Toboso, and present yourselves before the lady Dulcinea del Toboso, and tell her that her knight, the Knight of the Sorry Face,[4] presents his compliments, and relate to her, stage by stage, every detail of this famous adventure up to and including my restoration of the liberty that you so desired; and once you have done this you can go wherever you like, and may good fortune attend you."

Ginés de Pasamonte replied on behalf of them all, and said:

"This that you order us to do, dear lord and liberator, is utterly and totally out of the question, because we can't travel together—we've got to split up and go alone, each along his own road, and try to find a way into the very bowels of the earth so as not to be caught by the Holy Brotherhood, who'll be coming out after us, for certain. What you can do and what it'd be right for you to do is to replace that toll or tax payable to the lady Dulcinea del Toboso by a certain number of Ave Marias and Credos, which we'll say for your kindness, and this is something that can be done by night and by day, running away and resting, in peace and in war; but to think that we're going back to the flesh-pots of Egypt,[5] in other words picking up our chain again and setting off for El Toboso, is like thinking it's night-time already when it isn't yet ten in the morning—it's like trying to get figs from thistles."

"By my faith," cried Don Quixote, by now in a fury, "you little bastard, Don Ginesillo de Paropillo or whatever you're called—now you shall go there alone, with your tail between your legs and the whole chain on your back!"

Pasamonte wasn't a long-suffering sort, and from Don Quixote's absurd desire to set them free he'd realized that the man wasn't very sane, so when he found himself thus addressed, he tipped his companions the wink and they edged away and began to rain so many stones on Don Quixote that, however he ducked and dodged behind his little round shield, he couldn't fend them off; and poor Rocinante paid no more attention to the spurs than if he'd been made of bronze. Sancho sheltered behind his ass from the hailstorm falling on them both. Don Quixote couldn't prevent countless stones from hitting his body with enough force to knock him to the ground, and as soon as he did fall the student leapt on him, snatched the basin from his head and smashed it three or four times on his back and as many more times on the earth, pounding it almost to pieces. Then they stripped him of a surcoat he was wearing over his armour and would have stripped him of his stockings, too, if his leg armour hadn't made this impossible. They took Sancho's topcoat and left him in his shirtsleeves, and they shared the rest of the spoils of battle, and each went his own way, more concerned to escape from the dreaded Holy Brotherhood than to burden himself with the chain and go to present himself before the lady Dulcinea del Toboso.

The ass and Rocinante, Sancho and Don Quixote were left alone: the ass hanging its head, lost in its thoughts, flapping its ears every so often in the belief that the storm of stones wasn't yet over, because it was still raging inside its skull; Rocinante

---

4. In Chapter 19, Sancho hits upon a fitting epithet for Don Quixote: *Caballero de la Triste Figura*, or Knight of the Sad or Sorry Face. Don Quixote immediately takes a liking to the name, declaring that "the sage whose task it is to write the history of my exploits must have thought it right for me to take some appellation, as all previous knights have done": he therefore magically must have placed the epithet in Sancho's mind.

5. Back to the lap of luxury; the phrase is from Exodus 16.

stretched out by his master's side, because he'd also been brought down by a stone; Sancho in his shirtsleeves and fearful of the Holy Brotherhood; and Don Quixote sulking at being left in such a sorry state by men for whom he had done so much.

*　*　*

from *Chapter 25*

Concerning the strange things that happened to the brave knight of La Mancha in the Sierra Morena, and his imitation of the penance of Beltenebros[1]

*　*　* "What I say, Sancho," replied Don Quixote, "is that you must do as you please, for your idea does not seem a bad one; and I also say that you shall depart three days from now, because I want you to spend this time witnessing what I do and say for her sake, so that you can tell her about it."

"And what else have I got to see," asked Sancho, "apart from what I've seen already?"

"You are well informed about these matters, I must say!" Don Quixote retorted. "Now I must tear my garments, scatter my armour and dash my head against these rocks, and perform other similar actions that will amaze you."

"For God's sake," said Sancho Panza, "do be careful how you go around dashing your head, because you could pick on such a rock and hit it in such a place that you put paid to the whole penance business with the very first knock you gave it. And if you really think head-dashing's essential and this job can't be done without it, to my mind you ought to be content, since it's all make-believe, a fake and a sham, to dash your head against the water, or something soft like cotton, and leave the rest to me—I'll tell my lady you were knocking it against a jutting crag, harder than diamonds."

"I am grateful to you for meaning well, friend Sancho," replied Don Quixote, "but I would have you know that I am doing all these things not in jest but very much in earnest; for to behave otherwise would be to contravene the commands of chivalry, which instruct one never to tell a lie, on pain of being punished as a recidivist;[2] and to do one thing instead of another is the same as lying. So my blows on the head must be real, firm and effective, with no element of the sophistical or the fantastic about them. And you will have to leave me some lint to cure my wounds, for fate has left us without our balsam."

"Losing the ass was worse," replied Sancho, "because the lint and all was lost with it. And I'd ask you very kindly not to bring that damned potion up again—just hearing it mentioned turns not only my stomach but my very soul inside-out. And I'd also ask you, as regards those three days you allocated for watching the crazy things you're going to do, to make believe they're over and done with, because I'll be happy to take them for granted as if seen and approved, and I'll tell my lady wonders. So you write your letter and then send me packing, because I'm longing to come back and get you out of this purgatory where I'm leaving you."

"Purgatory you call it, Sancho?" said Don Quixote. "You would do better to call it hell, or worse, if there is anything worse."

1. Don Quixote and Sancho have reached the desolate region of the Sierra Morena, where Don Quixote prepares to perform penance in imitation of Amadis de Gaul, who took the name "Beltenebros," or "beautiful shadows." Sancho is preparing to depart to report to Dulcinea what he has seen of his master's penitence.
2. A backslider or repeat offender.

10

"In hell," replied Sancho, "*nulla est retentio,* so I've heard say."[3]

"I do not understand what you mean by *retentio,*" said Don Quixote.

"*Retentio* means," replied Sancho, "that people in hell never get out, and can't get out. It'll be the reverse with you, though, so long as I get my heels working, if I'm wearing spurs to make Rocinante move, that is—and you just wait till I reach El Toboso, and come before my lady Dulcinea, and then I'll tell her such stories about the acts of madness and stupidity, which comes to the same thing, that you've done and are doing as will make her as sweet as a nut, even if she's as hard as a cork-oak when I start work on her. And I'll come back through the air like a sorcerer with her honeyed answer, and I'll rescue you from this purgatory that seems like hell but isn't, because there's a hope of getting out of it, which people in hell haven't got, as I've just said, and I don't suppose you'll want to disagree with that."

"True," said the Knight of the Sorry Face, "but how are we going to manage to write that letter?"

"And that donkey-warrant," added Sancho.

"It will all be included," said Don Quixote, "and, since we have no paper, it would be appropriate to write it, as the ancients did, on leaves from the trees, or on tablets of wax; yet it would be as difficult to find these now as paper itself. But I have just thought of a good place, indeed an excellent one, to write it: the notebook that used to belong to Cardenio,[4] and you must take care to have it copied in a clear hand on to a sheet of paper in the first village with a schoolmaster, or else any sexton will copy it for you; but do not ask a clerk to copy it, because they use a corrupt and degenerate hand that Satan himself would not be able to read."

"And what's to be done about your signature?" asked Sancho.

"The letters of Amadis are never signed," replied Don Quixote.

"That's as may be," replied Sancho, "but the warrant must be signed, and if it's copied out they'll say the signature's a fake and I'll be left without my donkeys."

"The warrant will be signed in the notebook, and when my niece sees it she will not raise any objections about complying with it. And as regards the love-letter, you will have it signed: 'Yours until death, The Knight of the Sorry Face.' It will matter little that it is signed in another hand, because as far as I remember Dulcinea cannot read or write, and she has never seen a letter written by me, because the love between us has always been platonic, never going beyond a modest glance. And even this has been so occasional that I can truly swear that, in the twelve years I have loved her more than the light of these eyes that the earth will one day devour, I have not seen her as many as four times; and it is possible that on those four occasions she has not even once noticed that I was looking at her, such is the reserve and seclusion in which her father Lorenzo Corchuelo and her mother Aldonza Nogales have brought her up."

"Oho!" said Sancho. "So Lorenzo Corchuelo's daughter is the lady Dulcinea del Toboso, also known as Aldonza Lorenzo, is she?"

"She is," said Don Quixote, "and she it is who deserves to be the mistress of the entire universe."

"I know her well," said Sancho, "and let me tell you she pitches a bar as far as the strongest lad in all the village. Good God, she's a lusty lass all right, hale and hearty, strong as an ox, and any knight errant who has her as his lady now or in the future can

---

3. While Sancho's explanation is a canny one, his Latin is mangled; he should have said "in hell, *nulla est redemptio*" (nothing is redeemed) rather than "nothing is retained." The line is from the service for the dead.

4. Sancho and Don Quixote were first alerted to Cardenio's whereabouts when they discovered a satchel with his notebooks in Chapter 23.

count on her to pull him out of the mire! The little baggage, what muscles she's got on her, and what a voice! Let me tell you she climbed up one day to the top of the church belfry to call to some lads of hers who were in a fallow field of her father's, and even though they were a good couple of miles off they could hear her just as if they'd been standing at the foot of the tower. And the best thing about her is she isn't at all priggish, she's a real courtly lass, enjoys a joke with everyone and turns everything into a good laugh. And now I can say, Sir Knight of the Sorry Face, that not only is it very right and proper for you to get up to your mad tricks for her sake—you've got every reason to give way to despair and hang yourself, too, and nobody who knows about it will say you weren't justified, even if it does send you to the devil. And I wish I was on my way already, just to take a look at her, because I haven't seen her for days, and she must be changed by now, because women's faces get spoiled by always being out in the fields, in the sun and the wind. And I must be honest with you, Don Quixote sir—until now I've been completely mistaken, because I really and truly believed that the lady Dulcinea must be some princess you were in love with, or at least someone who deserved all those fine gifts you've sent her, that Basque and those convicts, and lots of others that there must have been, too, considering how many victories you must have won before I became your squire. But all things considered, what will the lady Aldonza Lorenzo I mean the lady Dulcinea del Toboso care whether the knights you defeat and send to her get down on their bended knees before her? Because when they turn up she might be combing flax or threshing wheat in the yard, and then they'd be all embarrassed and she'd burst out laughing and turn up her nose at the gift."

"I have often told you before now, Sancho," said Don Quixote, "that you are a chatterbox and that, although you are a dim-witted fellow, you often try to be too clever by half; but, so that you can see how stupid you are and how intelligent I am, I want you to listen to a little story. There was once a widow who was beautiful, young, unattached, rich and, above all, carefree, and who fell in love with a certain lay brother, a well-fleshed, corpulent young man; his superior found out, and said to the good widow one day, by way of friarly reprehension:

"'I am surprised, madam, and not without good reason, that a woman of your quality, as beautiful and as wealthy as you are, should have fallen in love with such a low, vulgar and ignorant fellow, when in this house there are so many bachelors, masters and doctors of divinity among whom you could have chosen as among pears at a fruit-stall, saying: "I'll have this one; no, not that."'

"But she replied to him with wit and dash:

"'You are much mistaken, sir, and very old-fashioned in your ideas, if you think I have made a bad choice, however stupid he may seem to you; because for what I want of him he knows as much philosophy as Aristotle, and more.'"

"And so, Sancho, for what I want of Dulcinea del Toboso, she is as good as the most exalted princess in the world. Yes indeed, for not all poets who praise ladies under a name that they choose for them really have any such mistresses at all. Do you really believe that the Amaryllises, Phyllises, Sylvias, Dianas, Galateas, Alidas and others that fill books, ballads, barbers' shops and theatre stages were real ladies of flesh and blood, and the mistresses of those that praise and have praised them?[5] No, of course not, the poets themselves invent most of them, to have something to write

---

5. All names of female characters from the many pastoral romances written in the second half of the 16th century. Cervantes's own pastoral romance was called *La Galatea*.

their poetry about, and to make people think that they are in love and that they have it in them to be lovers. And so it is enough for me to be convinced that the good Aldonza Lorenzo is beautiful and virtuous, and the question of lineage is not very important, because nobody is going to be enquiring into it to see whether she is entitled to robes of nobility, and for me she is the greatest princess in the world. For I would have you know, Sancho, if you do not know it already, that there are just two qualities that inspire love more than any others, and these are great beauty and good repute, and these two qualities are to be found in abundance in Dulcinea, because no woman can equal her in beauty, and few can approach her in good repute. And to put it in a nutshell, I imagine that everything I say is precisely as I say it is, and I depict her in my imagination as I wish her to be, both in beauty and in rank, and Helen cannot rival her, nor can Lucretia or any other of the famous women of past ages, whether Greek, Barbarian or Roman, equal her.[6] And people can say what they like, because if I am reproached by the ignorant for this, I shall not be punished by even the most severe judges."

"And I say you're right as right can be," replied Sancho, "and I'm an ass—but I don't know why I'm talking about asses, because you don't mention ropes in the house of the man that hanged himself. Let's have the letter, though, and then I'll be off."

Don Quixote took out the notebook and, drawing a little aside, he began with great deliberation to write the letter; and as he finished he called Sancho and said that he was going to read it aloud, so that Sancho could learn it by heart, in case he lost it on the way, because with his bad luck anything could happen. To which Sancho replied:

"You just write it down two or three times in the book and then let me have it, and I'll take good care of it—it's madness to think I'm going to learn it by heart, because my memory's so bad I often forget my own name. But read it to me all the same, I'll enjoy listening to it, because it must be a beauty."

"Listen, then; it goes like this," said Don Quixote.

Letter from Don Quixote to Dulcinea del Toboso

Sovereign and noble lady,

One sore-wounded by the dart of absence and lacerated to the very fabric of his heart, O sweetest Dulcinea del Toboso, wishes you the good health that he does not enjoy. If your beauteousness scorns me, if your worth does not favour me, if your disdain is my humiliation, I shall ill be able, albeit I am well furnished with longanimity,[7] to suffer a grief that is not merely intense but protracted. My good squire Sancho will render you a full account, O lovely ingrate, O beloved enemy of mine, of the state to which I am reduced for your sake. If it be your wish to succour me, I am yours, and if not, do what you will, for by ending my life I shall satisfy your cruelty and my desire.

Yours until death,
THE KNIGHT OF THE SORRY FACE

"By my dear father's bones!" cried Sancho. "That's the very finest thing I ever did hear! Damn it all, how well you say everything you want to say, and how well

---

6. Lucretia was the chaste wife of the Roman Collatinus; when raped by Sextus Tarquinius, son of the despot Tarquinius Superbus, she killed herself, after calling on her family to bring down Rome's king. They did so, founding the Roman republic.

7. Long-suffering or forbearance.

it all suits the signature 'The Knight of the Sorry Face'! To be sure you're the very devil, there isn't anything you don't know!"

"Everything is needed," replied Don Quixote, "in the profession that I follow."

"Come on, then," said Sancho, "turn over the page and write the warrant for the three donkeys, and sign it clear as clear, so they know your signature as soon as they see it."

"Very well," said Don Quixote.

And once he'd written it he read it out:

On receipt of this my first donkey-warrant, please order that three of the five that I left at home in your charge be given to my squire Sancho Panza. Which three donkeys I hereby order to be delivered to him and duly paid for, in return for the like number received from him here; and this bill, together with his receipt, will be sufficient for this transaction. Given in the heart of the Sierra Morena on the twenty-second of August of the current year.

"That's good," said Sancho. "Now sign it."

"There is no need for me to sign it," said Don Quixote. "All I have to do is to append my flourish, which counts as a signature, and that is sufficient for three asses, and even for three hundred."

"I'll believe you," replied Sancho. "Now let me go and saddle Rocinante, and you get ready to give me your blessing, because I'm leaving straight away, without waiting to see any of these antics you're going to get up to, though I'll tell her I saw you do so many of them that she'll be more than satisfied."

"At least, Sancho, I want you, because it is essential—what I mean to say is that I want you to see me naked, performing a dozen or two dozen mad deeds, which will only take me half an hour, so that having seen them with your own eyes you can safely swear to any others that you may care to add; and I can assure you that you will not tell her of as many as I intend to perform."

"For the love of God, sir, don't make me see you naked, I'll feel so sorry for you I shan't be able to help crying. And my head's in such a state after crying so much last night for my dun that I'm in no condition for any more tears, so if you want me to see some of your antics, do them with your clothes on—quick antics, just the most relevant ones. What's more, there isn't any need for all this as far as I'm concerned, and, as I said, it would mean I'd come back all the sooner with the news that you want and deserve to hear. If not, the lady Dulcinea had better look out, because if she doesn't reply as she ought to, I take my solemn oath that I'll kick and punch the right answer out of her guts. Because who can put up with a famous knight errant like you going mad, without any reason at all, for a . . .? And the lady had better not make me say it, or else by God I'll upset the apple cart, and hang the consequences! And I can! She doesn't know what I'm like! If she did, she'd stand in fear of me, she would!"

"And so, Sancho," said Don Quixote, "it seems that you are no saner than I am."

"No, I'm not as mad as you," said Sancho, "but I am angrier. Leaving all that aside, though, what are you going to eat while I'm away? Are you going to waylay goatherds and steal your food, like Cardenio?"

"You must not worry about that," replied Don Quixote, "for even if I had any food, all I should eat would be whatever herbs and other fruit of the land this meadow and these trees provide; for the beauty of my plan lies precisely in not eating and in other equivalent mortifications. And so goodbye."

"But do you know what I'm scared of? Not finding the way back here where I'm leaving you, because it's so secluded."

"You take good note of the landmarks, and I shall try not to move far off," said Don Quixote, "and I shall even take the precaution of climbing the highest of these crags here to see if I can spot you when you return. In addition, your surest way of not getting lost and missing me will be to cut some of this broom growing so abundantly hereabouts, and to drop a branch every so often until you reach the plain, and they will serve as guide-marks on your return, like the thread in Perseus's labyrinth."[8]

"That's what I'll do," replied Sancho Panza.

He cut some broom, asked his master for his blessing and, not without many tears on both sides, said goodbye. And climbing on to Rocinante, whom Don Quixote warmly entrusted to Sancho's safe-keeping, with the instruction to take as good care of him as of his own person, he headed off towards the plain, scattering broom-branches every so often, as his master had advised. And so he rode away, even though Don Quixote was still insisting that he should watch a couple of his wild deeds, at least. But Sancho hadn't gone a hundred steps when he turned and came back and said:

"I think you were right, sir, and to be able to swear with a clear conscience that I've seen you doing mad deeds, I'd better see one of them at least, although I must say I've seen a big enough one already—you staying here."

"Did I not tell you so?" said Don Quixote. "Just wait a minute, Sancho, I shall perform them in the saying of a creed."

And pulling down his breeches as fast as ever he could, he stood there in his shirt and then did two leaps in the air followed by two somersaults, revealing things that made Sancho turn Rocinante so as not to have to see them again; and he felt fully satisfied that he could swear his master was mad. And we shall allow him to go his way until his return, which was speedy.

* * *

from *Chapter 52*

About Don Quixote's fight with the goatherd, and the singular adventure of the penitents, which he brought to a happy conclusion by the sweat of his brow[1]

* * * The goatherd[2] looked at Don Quixote, and finding him such a sorry sight he asked the barber—who was sitting next to him—in some bewilderment:

"Who is this man, sir, that cuts such a figure and speaks in such a way?"

"Who should he be," answered the barber, "but the famous Don Quixote de la Mancha, the redresser of injuries, the righter of wrongs, the protector of damsels, the terror of giants and the victor in battles?"

8. A reference to the labyrinth in which the Minotaur was housed, and which Theseus (not Perseus) successfully navigated by means of a thread.

1. In the intervening chapters, Don Quixote leaves the Sierra Morena, hears a variety of tales from Cardenio and others, and suffers the effects of an enchantment orchestrated by the barber and the priest, who are trying to bring him back to La Mancha. Don Quixote is bound hand and foot while sleeping in an inn and placed as a captive in an ox-cart, with which the disguised barber and priest will take him home. A canon from Toledo, along with his servants and several "peace-officers" or members of the Holy Brotherhood, have joined the company as well.

2. The goatherd is a young man named Eugenio, who has just finished telling a story about his love for a woman who eloped with a trickster and has been put by her father in a convent. The current discussion is taking place in an inn, after Don Quixote is let temporarily out of his cage and promises not to run away: "I do indeed give my word," he says, "and in any case, a person who is enchanted, as I am, is not at liberty to dispose of his person as he wishes, because the man who enchanted him can prevent him from moving for three centuries on end, and if he flees he will bring him back in the twinkling of an eye."

"That sounds to me," replied the goatherd, "like what you read in books about knights errant, who used to do all those things you said this man does, but it's my opinion that either you're joking or some of the rooms in this character's upper storey are empty."

"You are a villainous wretch," Don Quixote burst out, "and you are the one who is empty and a fool, and I am fuller than the whore of a bitch who bore you ever was."

And with these words he snatched up a loaf and hurled it at the goatherd's face with such furious force that he flattened his nose; and the goatherd, who couldn't take a jest and found himself being assaulted in earnest, disregarded the carpet and the tablecloths and all the people who were eating, and leapt upon Don Quixote, seized him by the throat with both hands and wouldn't have hesitated to throttle him if Sancho Panza hadn't rushed over, grabbed the goatherd by the shoulders and flung him down on the table, breaking plates, smashing cups and overturning and scattering everything else. As soon as Don Quixote found himself free he jumped on top of the goatherd, who, bloody-faced and pounded by Sancho's feet, was crawling over the tablecloths in search of a knife with which to take some gory revenge, but the canon and the priest were making sure this couldn't happen; and then the barber intervened to enable the goatherd to climb on top of Don Quixote, at whom he flailed away until as much blood was pouring from the poor knight's face as from his own. The canon and the priest were laughing fit to burst, the peace-officers were jumping with joy, everyone was cheering the two men on as dogs are cheered on when they're fighting; only Sancho Panza was in despair, because he couldn't wriggle free of the grasp of one of the canon's servants who was preventing him from going to help his master.

In short, just when everyone was enjoying this festival of fun, except the two battered, scratching warriors, they heard a trumpet call, so mournful that it made them all turn towards where it seemed to be coming from; but the man who was most affected by the sound was Don Quixote who, although he was under the goatherd, much against his will and most severely mauled, said to him:

"Brother devil, for that is what you must be, since you have found the resolve and the strength to overpower me: I request that we agree on a truce for just one hour, because the sorrowful sound of that trumpet which we can hear appears to be summoning me to a new adventure."

The goatherd, who by now was tired of thumping and being thumped, climbed off without more ado, and Don Quixote stood up and looked with the others in the direction of the sounds, and as he did so a horde of men dressed as penitents in white suddenly came into sight as they descended one of the sides of the valley. What had happened was that the clouds had withheld their moisture from the earth that year, and processions, public prayers and acts of penitence were being organized in all the villages in the area to entreat God to open the hands of his mercy and send down some rain; and to this end the people from a nearby village were coming in a procession to a holy chapel on one side of the valley.[3] Don Quixote, seeing the processionists' strange dress, and not pausing to remember that he must have seen such penitents many times before, imagined that this was the subject for an adventure, and that it was his task alone, as a knight errant, to undertake it; and he was further confirmed in this belief when he saw a holy image swathed in mourning that they were carrying, and

3. Such processions to pray for changes in weather were fairly common, particularly in rural areas. The participants would generally pray and sing while flogging themselves in penitence for sins of the community, and would often carry with them large statues or images of Mary and the saints.

thought it was some eminent lady whom those arrant and insolent knaves were bearing off against her will; and no sooner had this idea found its way into his head than he charged over to where Rocinante was grazing, unhooked both the horse's bit and his own shield from the pommel, put the bit in its place in the twinkling of an eye, told Sancho to give him his sword, mounted Rocinante, took up his shield and cried to all present:

"And now, O doughty company, you shall perceive how important it is that knights who profess the order of knight-errantry should exist in the world; now, I say, you shall perceive, in the freeing of that good lady who is being carried away captive, whether or not knights errant are worthy of esteem."

And as he said this he put thighs to Rocinante, because he wasn't wearing any spurs, and at a canter, because we don't read anywhere in this true history that Rocinante ever ventured on a full gallop, he advanced on the penitents, despite all the efforts of the priest and the canon and the barber to stop him; but it was impossible, and Sancho couldn't do anything to dissuade him, either, by yelling:

"What are you going to do now, Don Quixote sir? What demons have you got inside your breast egging you on against our holy Catholic faith? I'll be damned—look, look, that's a penitents' procession, and that lady they're carrying on the platform is the blessed image of the immaculate Virgin. Be careful, sir, what you're doing—this time I'm really sure it isn't what you think it is."

But Sancho laboured in vain, because his master was so set on confronting the men in white and freeing the lady in black that he didn't hear a word; and even if he had heard one he wouldn't have turned back, not if it had been the King himself ordering him. So on he cantered towards the procession and then he halted Rocinante, who was by now ready to take a rest, and he cried in a hoarse and agitated voice:

"O you who hide your faces, perchance because you are evil: pay attention and listen to what I have to say to you."

The first to stop were the men carrying the image, and one of the four priests chanting the litanies took one look at Don Quixote's strange figure, Rocinante's thinness and other ludicrous aspects of the knight's appearance, and replied with the words:

"If you want to say something to us, my good man, say it quickly, because our brethren here are tearing their flesh to shreds, and we cannot and must not stop to listen to anything unless it's brief enough to be said in a couple of words."

"I shall say it all in one word," replied Don Quixote, "and it is this: you must at this very instant set free that beautiful lady, whose tears and sorrowful face are clear proof that you are bearing her off against her will and that you have done her some very great mischief; and I, who came into this world to redress such injuries, will not permit you to take one step forward unless you give her the liberty that she desires and deserves."

These words made all those who heard them realize that Don Quixote must be some madman, and they burst into hearty laughter, which was like pouring gunpowder on to the fire of Don Quixote's wrath: without another word he drew his sword and charged at the platform. One of the men carrying it left his companions holding it up, came out to meet Don Quixote brandishing the forked prop on which he helped to support it whenever they paused for a rest, used this prop to ward off a mighty sword-stroke that the knight aimed at him and that cut it in two and then, with the part left in his hand, delivered such a blow to the shoulder of his enemy's sword arm, which the shield couldn't protect against brute strength, that poor Don Quixote tumbled to the ground in dire straits. Sancho Panza, who came puffing after his master, saw him fall and cried out to his demolisher not to hit him again, he was only a poor enchanted knight who'd never done anyone any harm in all the days of his born life. But what stopped the peasant wasn't Sancho's shouts but seeing that Don Quixote wasn't stirring, not so much as a hand or a foot; and so, in the belief that he'd killed him, he hoisted his tunic up to his waist and ran away across the fields like a deer.

And now Don Quixote's companions arrived on the scene, as did the other processionists, who saw their opponents come running up with the peace-officers clutching their crossbows, feared the worst and swarmed around the holy image with their hoods raised from their faces, brandishing their scourges while the priests wielded their great processional candle-sticks, awaiting the assault in the determination to defend themselves and even attack their assailants if they could; but fortune treated them better than they'd thought it would, because all Sancho did was to throw himself upon his master's body and pour over him the most piteous and laughable lament ever heard, in the belief that he was dead. Our priest was recognized by one of the priests in the procession, and this calmed the fears that had developed in both squadrons. The first priest gave the second one a brief account of Don Quixote, and then he went with the throng of penitents to see whether the poor knight was dead, and they all heard Sancho Panza saying, with tears in his eyes:

"O flower of chivalry, whose well-spent life just one thump with a cudgel has done for! O pride of your family, honour and glory of all La Mancha and all the world—now that you've gone from it, it'll fill up with evil-doers who won't be frightened of being punished for their wicked ways! O you who were more open-handed than all the Alexanders, because for only eight months' service you said you'd give me the best island that ever had the sea all round it! O you who were humble to the haughty and haughty to the humble, tackler of dangers, taker of insults, in love without a cause, imitator of the good, scourge of the wicked, enemy of villains—in a word, knight errant, and that says it all!"

Sancho's cries and groans revived Don Quixote, and what he first said was:

"He who lives absent from you, sweetest Dulcinea, is subject to even greater calamities than this. Help me, dear Sancho, to climb on to the enchanted cart: I am no longer in any fit state to burden Rocinante's saddle, for this shoulder of mine has been smashed to smithereens."

"I'll do that with a will, sir," replied Sancho, "and let's go back to our village with these gentlemen, who only want what's best for you, and there we'll work out a way to make another sally that'll bring us more profit and renown."

"You are speaking sound sense," replied Don Quixote, "and it will be wise indeed to wait for the presently prevailing malign influence of the stars to dissipate."

The canon and the priest and the barber told him that he would be quite right to do as he'd said; and so, having been most wonderfully entertained by Sancho Panza's absurdities, they put Don Quixote back on the cart. The religious procession formed up again, and went on its way. The goatherd said goodbye to everyone. The peace-officers refused to go any further, and the priest paid them what he owed them. The canon asked the priest to let him know what happened to Don Quixote, whether he recovered from his madness or continued in the same state, and then begged their leave to continue his journey.

And so the party split up and each followed his own road, leaving the priest and the barber, Don Quixote and Panza and the good Rocinante, as patient as his master in the face of everything he'd undergone. The carter yoked his oxen, put Don Quixote on top of a truss of hay, followed with his usual sedateness the route indicated by the priest; and six days later they reached their village, which they entered at noon, and as it happened to be a Sunday everybody was in the square, through the middle of which the cart trundled on its way. Everyone went over to see what was in the cart, and when they recognized their neighbour they were astonished, and a lad ran to tell the house-keeper and the niece that their master and uncle had come back, thin and pale, and lying on top of a pile of hay in an ox-cart. It was pitiful to hear the cries these two good ladies let loose, the slaps they gave themselves, the curses they again directed at those damned books of chivalry; all of which they renewed when they saw Don Quixote coming in through the door.

At the news of Don Quixote's arrival Sancho Panza's wife hurried to his house, because she had discovered that her husband had gone away with him as his squire, and when she saw Sancho the first thing she asked was whether the ass was well. Sancho replied that the ass was better than its master was.[4]

"Thanks be to God for his great goodness to me," she replied. "And now tell me, husband, what have you got out of all this squiring of yours? How many fine skirts have you brought back for me? How many pairs of shoes for your children?"

"I haven't brought any of all that, wife," said Sancho. "But I've got other stuff that's much more special and important."

"I'm very pleased to hear it, too," his wife replied. "Now show me this stuff that's so much more important and special, husband—I'd love to see it to cheer up this heart of mine that's been so sad and out of sorts all these ages that you've been away."

"I'll let you see it when we get home," said Panza, "and meantime you can count yourself lucky, because if it's God's will for us to go off again in search of adventures you'll soon see me made an earl or the governor of an island, and not any old island either but the very best island there is."

"May heaven grant it, husband, we need it badly enough. But tell me, what's all this about islands? I don't understand you."

"Honey wasn't made for the mouths of asses," Sancho retorted. "You'll see in due course, wife, and you'll get a surprise, I can tell you, when you hear all your vassals calling you your ladyship."

"What's this you're saying, Sancho, about ladyships, islands and vassals?" replied Juana Panza, for this was the name of Sancho's wife, not that they were blood relations but because it's the custom in La Mancha for women to take their husbands' surnames.

"Don't you be in such a hurry, Juana, to know about all these things; I'm tell-ing you the truth, and that's enough for you, so shut up. All I will say, since I'm on the subject, is that there's nothing better in life than being an honest man who's the squire of a knight errant who goes in search of adventures. It is true that most of the adventures you find don't turn out as well as what you'd like them to, because out of a hundred you come across ninety-nine usually go skew-whiff. I know that from experience, because I've ended up blanket-tossed in some and beaten black and blue in others. But in spite of all that, it's great to be waiting to see what's going to happen next as you ride across mountains, explore forests, climb crags, visit castles and put up at inns as and when you like, and not the devil a farthing to pay."

While Sancho Panza and his wife Juana Panza chatted away like this, Don Quix-ote's housekeeper and niece welcomed their master, undressed him and laid him on

---

4. The ass mysteriously returns to Sancho after its theft by Ginés de Pasamonte, an oversight that Cervantes will make fun of in Part 2.

his ancient bed. He was peering at them through unfocused eyes, and couldn't fathom where on earth he was. The priest told the niece to make sure to pamper her uncle and have him watched so that he didn't escape again, and described what they'd had to do to bring him back home. And then the two women again raised the roof with their outcry; again they renewed their cursing of the books of chivalry; again they implored heaven to cast the authors of all those lies and absurdities into the depths of the bottomless pit. All this left them bewildered and fearful that as soon as their master and uncle felt a little better they'd lose him again; and that was indeed what happened.

But although the author of this history has searched with the most meticulous care for an account of the deeds performed by Don Quixote during his third sally, he hasn't been able to find any information about them, not at least in writings by reputable authors; tradition alone has preserved, in the memory of La Mancha, the belief that the third time Don Quixote left home he went to Saragossa, where he took part in some famous jousts and underwent experiences worthy of his courage and intelligence. But the author could not discover any information about how Don Quixote met his end, nor would he ever have even known about it if good fortune had not sent him an aged doctor who had in his possession a lead casket which, he said, had been found among the foundations of an old, ruined chapel that was being rebuilt. In this casket there were some parchments with texts written in Roman letters but in Castilian verse, describing many of his exploits and giving accounts of Dulcinea del Toboso's beauty, Rocinante's looks, Sancho Panza's loyalty and Don Quixote's grave, in various epitaphs and eulogies about his life and works. And those that could be read and understood have been set down here by the trustworthy author of this original and matchless history, who only asks from his readers, in recompense for the immense trouble that he has taken to scrutinize and explore all the archives in La Mancha so as to be able to bring it to the light of day, that they give it the same credit that people of good sense give to books of chivalry, so highly prized by all; and this will make him feel well rewarded and satisfied, and encourage him to search out other histories, perhaps less authentic than this one but no less ingenious or entertaining.

105

[*Several verses by local wits praising Don Quixote and Sancho follow, ending with the following poems.*]

Hobgoblin, a member of the Argamasilla Academy,[5] on the grave of Don Quixote

EPITAPH

Here lies a knight, a man of pluck,
Rich in thumpings, poor in luck,
Who, perched on Rocinante's back,
Rode up this path and down that track.
And Sancho Panza is the dolt
Who lies beside him in this vault;
The loyallest man in our empire
Who ever earned the name of squire.

---

5. Argamasilla is a village in La Mancha; this may be the "forgotten" town from which Don Quixote hails. Academies were men's clubs that convened on civic and festive occasions, and churned out mediocre verses to honor important events; the academy mentioned here is completely imaginary, as the silly names of its members attest.

Ding-dong, a member of the Argamasilla Academy, on the grave of
Dulcinea del Toboso

EPITAPH

> Fair Dulcinea here is laid
> And though she was a meaty maid
> Death turned her into dust and clay
> In his horrendous, dreadful way.
> Of a true breed she surely came,
> She was the great Don Quixote's flame,
> She wore with style a lady's gown:
> The glory of Toboso town.

These were the verses that were legible; since the others were worm-eaten, they
were handed to an academician for him to decipher. It is reported that he has done so,
after long vigils and much toil, and that he intends to publish them, as we await Don
Quixote's third sally.

Forse altri canterà con miglior plectio.[6]

Part 2[1]

Chapter 3

About the ridiculous discussion between Don Quixote, Sancho Panza and Sansón Carrasco, BA

Don Quixote remained deep in thought as he awaited the young graduate Carrasco, from
whom he was expecting to hear news about himself published in a book, as Sancho had
said; and he couldn't persuade himself that such a history existed—the blood of the enemies that he had killed was not yet dry on the blade of his sword, and people were already
claiming that his noble deeds of chivalry had appeared in print! Despite this, though, it did
occur to him that some sage, friendly or hostile, must have published his deeds by way of
enchantment: if friendly, to exalt them and place them above the most renowned exploits
ever performed by any knight errant; if hostile, to dismiss them and present them as being
meaner than the wretchedest deeds that the basest squire had ever been described as doing,
but then again (he said to himself), squires' exploits had never been recorded; and if it was
true that this history did exist, the fact that it concerned a knight errant was a guarantee
that it would be grandiloquent, lofty, illustrious, magnificent and true.

This thought offered him some consolation, but then he lost heart again when he
remembered that the name Cide suggested that the author was a Moor, and not a word
of truth was to be expected from any of those, since the whole lot of them are deceiv-
ers, liars and story-tellers. He was afraid that the author might have handled his love

---

6. "Perhaps others will sing with better lyre than I." From *Orlando furioso* (canto 30, stanza 16).

1. Part 2 of *Don Quixote* was published in 1615, ten years after Part 1. After an introductory chapter, Chapter 2 has
Don Quixote eager to discover what others are saying about him, and he urges Sancho to sally forth to find one Sansón
Carrasco. Carrasco has just returned from his studies at Salamanca University and has told Sancho that his story has been
put into a book called *The Ingenious Hidalgo Don Quixote de la Mancha*. As Sancho reports to Don Quixote, "he says
I'm named in it with my very own name of Sancho Panza, and the lady Dulcinea del Toboso too, and things are even
mentioned when you and I were alone when we did them"—prompting Don Quixote to declare "that the author of our
history must be some wise enchanter."

affair in an indelicate manner that would cause detraction and damage to the chastity of his lady Dulcinea del Toboso; he hoped that he had portrayed his faithfulness and the unswerving correctness of his behaviour towards her, snubbing queens, empresses and damsels of all ranks, and holding in leash the powerful urges of his natural passions; and in this state, engrossed in these and many other thoughts careering about his brain, he was found by Sancho and Carrasco, whom Don Quixote greeted with gracious courtesy.

Despite his name[2] the new graduate wasn't a big man, although he was a great leg-puller; his complexion was dull but his wits were sharp; he'd have been about twenty-four, with a moon face, a snub nose and a large mouth, all signs that he had a waggish disposition and loved joking and jesting, as he showed when he saw Don Quixote by throwing himself on to his knees before him and saying:

"Pray give me your hands, Don Quixote de la Mancha; I swear by this habit of St Peter that I'm wearing, even though I've only taken minor orders,[3] that you are one of the most famous knights errant that have ever existed or indeed ever will exist in the whole wide world. A blessing on Cide Hamete Benengeli for having written the history of your great deeds, and a double blessing on the diligent man who took care to have it translated from Arabic into our Castilian vernacular, for the amusement and entertainment of all."

Don Quixote brought him to his feet and said:

"It is true, then, is it, that a history of me exists, and that it was a Moor and a sage who wrote it?"

"It's so true, sir," said Sansón, "that I'm to understand that more than twelve thousand copies of the history are in print at this moment; and if you don't believe me, just ask Portugal, Barcelona and Valencia, where they were printed; and there's a report that it's being printed now in Antwerp, and all the signs are that there's no language in the world into which it won't be translated."[4]

"One of the things," Don Quixote put in, "that must give the greatest happiness to a virtuous and eminent man is to find himself with a good name on everybody's lips, and in print, while he is still alive. I said "with a good name" because, if the opposite were the case, no death could equal it."

"As far as good names and good reputations are concerned," the young graduate said, "you have gained the palm from all other knights errant, because the Moor in his language, and the Christian in his, took good care to depict most vividly for us your gallantry, your courage in confronting perils, your patience in adversity, your long-suffering in misfortune and when wounded, and your chastity and continence in that most platonic love-affair between you and my lady Doña Dulcinea del Toboso."

"I've never heard anyone," Sancho butted in, "calling my lady Dulcinea Doña, but just the lady Dulcinea del Toboso—so the history's wrong about that, for starters."

"That isn't an important objection," Carrasco replied.

"Certainly not," said Don Quixote, "but tell me, sir, which of my deeds are most highly praised in the history?"

"About that," the young graduate replied, "opinions differ, as tastes do: some prefer the adventure of the windmills, which you thought were Briareuses and giants;

---

2. Sansón is Spanish for Samson, the Hebrew warrior who possessed great strength as long as he didn't cut his hair.

3. Carrasco would have been wearing a habit of someone who was a minor cleric.

4. By 1615, *Don Quixote* had already been translated into English as well as French; numerous editions in Spanish had been published in Valencia, Barcelona, Lisbon, and Madrid as well as Brussels and Milan.

others, the adventure of the fulling-mill; others, the description of the two armies that turned out to be two flocks of sheep; one man praises the adventure of the corpse being taken to Segovia to be buried; another says that the best one of them all is the freeing of the convicts; yet another that none of them equals the adventure of the two Benedictine giants and the fight with the brave Basque."

"Could you please tell me, sir," Sancho put in, "whether they've included the adventure of the men from Yanguas, when good old Rocinante had the bright idea of reaching for the stars?"

"The sage didn't leave anything out," replied Sansón. "He includes and describes it all, even the capers cut by Sancho in the blanket."

"I didn't cut any capers in the blanket," Sancho retorted. "I cut them in the air, and more of them than I'd have chosen to."

"I suppose," added Don Quixote, "that every history that has ever been written has its ups and its downs, especially those that deal with chivalric exploits, for they cannot recount successful adventures alone."

"For all that," the young graduate replied, "some of those who've read the history say that they'd have been happier if its authors had overlooked some of the countless beatings that Don Quixote received in various confrontations."

"That's where the truth of the history comes in," said Sancho.

"But they could, in all fairness, have kept quiet about them," said Don Quixote, "because there is no need to narrate actions that do not alter or undermine the truth of the history, if they are going to result in the discrediting of the hero. I am sure that Aeneas was not as pious as Virgil depicts him, nor was Ulysses as prudent as Homer says."

"That's true," Sansón replied, "but it's one thing to write as a poet and quite another to write as a historian: the poet can narrate or sing events not as they were but as they should have been, and the historian must record them not as they should have been but as they were, without adding anything to the truth or taking anything away from it."

"Well if this Moorish bloke's after telling the truth," said Sancho, "I bet the thumpings they handed out to me will be in there among the ones my master got, because they never took the measure of his shoulders without taking it of my whole body. But that's no surprise, because as my master says, all the limbs have got to share the headache."

"You are a sly dog, Sancho," replied Don Quixote. "I must say your memory works well enough when you want it to."

"Even if I did want to forget the thrashings I've been given," said Sancho, "the bruises wouldn't let me, still fresh here on my ribs."

"Keep quiet, Sancho," said Don Quixote, "and stop interrupting our friend from the university, whom I entreat to continue telling me what is said about me in this history."

"And about me, too," said Sancho. "They say I'm one of the main caricatures in it, too."

"*Characters,* not *caricatures,* friend Sancho," said Sansón.

"Oh no, not another blunders-expert!" said Sancho. "If you two start up on that again, we'll all be here till the ends of our lives."

"May God give me a bad life, Sancho," replied the young graduate, "if you aren't the second most important character in the history, and there are those who'd rather hear you talk than the finest of the others, even though there are also people who say you were too gullible in believing you could ever become governor of that island offered you by Don Quixote here."

"All is not yet lost," said Don Quixote, "and as Sancho matures he will, with the experience that only the passing years can bring, become more suited and better qualified for the post of governor than he is at present."

"For God's sake, sir," said Sancho, "the island I can't govern at my age. I shan't be able to govern when I'm as old as Moses. The problem is that this island of yours is biding its time God only knows where, not that I haven't got the gumption to govern it."

"Entrust the matter to God's good care, Sancho," said Don Quixote, "for everything will turn out well, better perhaps than you think: not a leaf stirs on a tree unless God wishes it to."

"That's true enough," said Sansón, "and, if it is God's will, there shall be a thousand islands for Sancho to govern, let alone one."

"I've seen governors about the place," said Sancho, "that to my mind can't hold a candle to me, yet, for all that, they get called my lord and they eat off plates of silver."

"Those aren't governors of islands," replied Sansón, "but of other less demanding things; because those who govern islands must at the very least have some knowledge of syntax."

"I could cope with the sin," said Sancho, "but I'll pass on the tax—it's something I haven't ever come to grips with. But to leave me being governor in God's hands, and may he send me where I can be of most service to him—what I say, Sansón Carrasco sir, is that I'm very very glad that the author of this here history has talked about me in such a way that what he says doesn't give offence, because I swear to you as a loyal squire that if he'd said anything that wasn't fit to be said about a pure-bred Christian, which is what I am, the deafest of the deaf would have heard what I'd have had to say to him."

"That would have been a miracle," Sansón replied.

"Miracle or no miracle," said Sancho, "everyone should watch out how he talks or writes about the next man and not just shove down the first thing that comes into his brain-box."

"One of the faults that have been found in this history," said the young graduate, "is that the author included a tale called *Inappropriate Curiosity;* not that it's a bad one or badly told, but it's out of place and has nothing to do with the history of the great Don Quixote."[5]

"I bet," replied Sancho, "that the bastard's gone and made a right old hotchpotch."

"I do now have to say," said Don Quixote, "that the author of my history is no sage but some ignorant prattler, who started writing it in a haphazard and unplanned way and let it turn out however it would, like Orbaneja, the famous artist of Úbeda,[6] who, when asked what he was painting, replied: 'Whatever emerges.' On one occasion he was painting a cockerel so badly and so unlike a real cockerel that he had to write in capital letters by its side: 'This is a cockerel.' My history must be like that, needing a commentary to make it intelligible."

"No, no," replied Sansón, "it's so very intelligible that it doesn't pose any difficulties at all: children leaf through it, adolescents read it, grown men understand it and old men praise it, and, in short, it's so well-thumbed and well-perused and well-known by all kinds of people that as soon as they see a skinny nag pass by they say: 'Look, there goes Rocinante.' And the people who have most taken to it are the page-boys. There's not a lord's antechamber without its *Quixote:* if one person puts

---

106

5. In Chapters 33–35, the priest read aloud to the company a tale that the innkeeper found among some other papers; it concerns the exploits of two Florentine gentlemen who are best friends.

6. An unknown Spanish painter.

it aside, another picks it up; some ask to be lent it, others run up and snatch it away. All in all, this history provides the most delightful and least harmful entertainment ever, because nowhere in it can one find the slightest suspicion of language that isn't wholesome or thoughts that aren't Catholic."

"To write in any other way," said Don Quixote, "would be to write not truths but falsehoods, and historians who have recourse to falsehoods should be burnt, like counterfeiters; and I do not know what could have made the author turn to stories about other people when there was so much to write about me: I suppose he was relying on the saying, 'It's all fish that comes to the net.' Yet the truth of the matter is that just by recording my thoughts, my sighs, my tears, my worthy designs and my missions he could have written a volume bigger than all the works of El Tostado[7] put together, or at any rate as big. Be that as it may, my understanding of the matter, my dear sir, is that to write histories and other books one needs a fine mind and a mature understanding. To tell jokes and write wittily is the work of geniuses; the most intelligent character in a play is the fool, because the actor playing the part of a simpleton must not be one. History is, as it were, sacred, because it must be truthful, and where there is truth there is God, because he is truth; and yet, in spite of all this, there are those who toss off books as if they were pancakes."

"There's no book so bad," said the young graduate, "that there isn't something good in it."

"About that there is no doubt," Don Quixote replied, "but it often happens that men who have deservedly achieved and won fame by their writings lose it completely or find it diminished in part as soon as they publish them."

"The reason for that," said Sansón, "is that printed works are read at leisure and their defects are easily spotted, and the more famous the author the more closely they're scrutinized. Men renowned for their genius—great poets, illustrious historians—are usually envied by those whose pleasure and pastime is to pass judgement on what others have written, without ever having published anything themselves."

"That is not surprising," said Don Quixote, "because there are many theologians who cannot preach, yet are experts at identifying the faults and the excesses of those who can."

"It is exactly as you say, Don Quixote," said Carrasco, "but I do wish that such critics were more forgiving and less censorious, and did not pay such attention to the spots on the brilliant sun of the work they grumble at; for if *aliquando bonus dormitat Homerus*,[8] they should also remember how very long Homer stayed awake to give us the light of his work with the least possible shadow; and it could even be that what they think are faults are in reality beauty spots, which often increase the loveliness of a face; so, you see, anyone publishing a book exposes himself to enormous risk, because it's absolutely impossible to write one in such a way that it satisfies and pleases all those who read it."

"The book that has been written about me," said Don Quixote, "will not have pleased many people."

"Quite the contrary: since *stultorum infinitus est numerus*,[9] innumerable are those who have relished this history. Some have found fault with the author's memory and accused him of deception because he forgets to tell us who was the thief that stole

Sancho's dun[1]—the incident isn't narrated and we just have to infer that somebody has stolen it, and a little later we find Sancho riding the very same donkey without having recovered it. They also say that the author forgot to state what Sancho did with the hundred escudos he found in the travelling bag in the Sierra Morena, which are never mentioned again; and there are many people who would like to know what happened to them, or what he spent them on, which is one of the essential points omitted from the book."

Sancho replied:

"Right now, Señor Carrasco, I'm in no state to go into any accounts or explanations, because I've just gone all a-flutter in my tummy, and if I don't get a couple of swigs of the old stuff inside me to put it right I'll soon be nothing but skin and bone. I'll have to go home for it, and the wife's waiting for me—as soon as I've done eating I'll come back and answer all the questions you and anyone else want to put to me, both about the loss of the ass and about the spending of the hundred escudos."

And without awaiting a reply or saying another word he went home. Don Quixote insisted that the graduate must share his humble board. The graduate accepted the invitation and stayed for the meal, a couple of squabs were added to the pot, the conversation at table was about deeds of chivalry, Carrasco played along with his host, the banquet came to an end, they had their afternoon nap, Sancho returned and the previous conversation was resumed.

Chapter 4

In which Sancho Panza provides the answers to the young graduate Sansón Carrasco's doubts and questions; together with other events worth knowing and telling

Sancho Panza returned to Don Quixote's house and to the previous conversation, and he said:

"To what Señor Sansón said about people wanting to know who stole my donkey, and how and when, it is my reply that on the very same night when we went to hide from the Holy Brotherhood in the Sierra Morena, after the adventure or misadventure of the convicts, and the other one of the dead body being taken to Segovia, me and my master rode into a clump of trees where my master leaned on his lance and I sat on my dun, both of us dead beat after the fights we'd had, and we dozed off just as if we were lying on half-a-dozen feather mattresses, and in particular I fell so very fast asleep that whoever it was managed to come and prop up the pack-saddle, with me sitting there and all, on top of four poles one in each corner, and get the dun out from underneath without me noticing a thing."

That is easy enough to do, and no new occurrence: it is what happened to Sacripante when he was at the siege of Albracca and that famous thief Brunello removed his horse from between his legs using the same trick.[1]

"Dawn broke," Sancho resumed, "and as soon as I gave myself a good shake the poles caved in and I came down with an almighty thump, and I looked around for my donkey and I couldn't find it, and the tears filled my eyes and I made such a lament that if the author of our history hasn't put it in he can take it from me he hasn't put anything worthwhile in. A few days later, I can't rightly remember how many, I was

---

1. Cervantes actually corrected this oversight in Book 1, reporting on Ginés's theft.
1. In *Orlando furioso,* Brunello is notorious for his thievery; he steals Sacripante's horse in Canto 27.

walking along with Princess Micomicona when I spotted my donkey, and on top of it wearing gipsy clothes was that character Ginés de Pasamonte, that crook, that great villain me and my master set free from the chain."[2]

"That isn't the mistake," Sansón replied. "The mistake is that before the ass has reappeared the author says Sancho's riding it!"

"I don't know what to say to that," said Sancho, "but maybe the historian got it wrong, or it might have been a slip of the printer's."

"I'm sure you're right," said Sansón, "but what happened to the hundred escudos? Did they disappear into thin air?"

Sancho replied:

"I laid them out on the well-being of my person and of my wife and children, and those escudos are the only reason why my wife's putting up with me going off along all those highways and byways serving my master Don Quixote, because if after all that time I'd come back home penniless and donkeyless I'd have been in for it—and if there's anything else you want to know about me here I am, and I'll answer to the King himself in person, and there's no cause for anybody to be poking their noses into whether I brought money back with me or not and whether I spent it or not. Because if the thumpings I was given on my travels had to be paid for in hard cash, even if they were only priced at four maravedís apiece another hundred escudos wouldn't be enough to pay for the half of them, and people can put their hands on their hearts and say what they'd have done, and stop making out that what's white's black and what's black's white—each of us is how God made him and many are much worse."

"I'll take care," said Carrasco, "to warn the author of the history that if he prints it again he mustn't forget what the worthy Sancho has just said—for this will carry it to even greater heights."

"Are there any other features of this book that need correcting, my dear young graduate?" Don Quixote asked.

"Yes, there must be," he replied, "but none of them can be as important as those that I have mentioned."

"And does the author," Don Quixote asked, "by any chance promise a second part?"

"Yes, he does," Sansón replied, "but he says he hasn't found it and doesn't know who's got it, so we can't tell whether it'll come out or not—and both because of this and because some people are saying, 'Second parts are never any good,' and others are saying, 'What's already been written about Don Quixote is quite enough,' there are doubts about the appearance of this second part; although other people who are jovial rather than saturnine say, 'Let's have more quixotry—let Don Quixote charge and Sancho Panza talk, and that'll keep us happy, whatever he writes.'"

"And what is the author's position?"

"He says," Sansón replied, "that as soon as he does find the history, for which he's searching with the utmost diligence, he's going to have it printed immediately, more for the profit he can make out of it than to win anybody's praise."

At which Sancho remarked:

"So the author's hoping to make some money out of it, is he? That'd be a miracle, because it'll be hurry, hurry, hurry, like a tailor on the day before a fiesta, and rushed jobs are never as well done as they ought to be. That Moorish bloke, or whatever he

2. In Chapter 44 of Book 1. Princess Micomicona is really the young Dorotea, an accomplice in the priest's and barber's elaborate plans to lure Don Quixote out of the Sierra Morena. She pretends to be a princess who needs her kingdom restored to her by none other than Don Quixote himself.

is, had better take care to be on his mettle—me and my master are going to hand him such a supply of raw materials in the shape of adventures and all kinds of other doings that he'll be able to write not just one second part but a hundred of them. I suppose that character thinks we're resting on our laurels here—well, if he holds up our feet to be shod he'll soon see if there's anything wrong with our hooves. All I can say is that if my master took my advice we'd be out in the fields by now, redressing grievances and righting wrongs as all the best knight errants do."

Sancho had hardly finished speaking when they heard Rocinante neighing, which Don Quixote took as a most happy omen, so he decided to make another sally in three or four days' time. He informed the young graduate of his decision, and asked his advice about where to start the campaign; and the reply was that they should travel to the kingdom of Aragon and the city of Saragossa, where solemn jousts were soon to be held to celebrate St George's day[3]—and these would give Don Quixote the chance to outshine all the knights in Aragon, which would be the same as outshining all the knights in the world. Sansón commended Don Quixote's decision as a most honourable and courageous one, and warned him to be more cautious when he confronted dangers, because his life was not his own: it belonged to all those who needed his aid and protection in their misfortunes. * * *

Chapter 10

Which describes Sancho's cunning enchantment of the lady Dulcinea, and other events as ridiculous as they are true

As the author of this great history reaches the events that he narrates in this chapter, he says that he'd have preferred to pass over them in silence, fearing he wouldn't be believed, because here Don Quixote's mad deeds approached the limits of the imaginable, and indeed went a couple of bowshots beyond them. But in the end, and in spite of these fears and misgivings, he described those deeds exactly as they happened, without adding or subtracting one atom of truth or concerning himself with any accusations that might be made that he was lying; and he was right to do so, because the truth might be stretched thin but it never breaks, and it always surfaces above lies, as oil floats on water.

And so, continuing his history, he says that as soon as Don Quixote had hidden in the glade, wood or oak-grove close to El Toboso, he ordered Sancho to return to the city and not to appear in his presence again without having spoken on his behalf to his lady and besought her to be so gracious as to grant her hapless knight an audience and deign to bestow her blessing on him, so that he could hope for the greatest success in all his undertakings and difficult enterprises, thanks to her. Sancho agreed to do exactly as he was told, and to bring back as good a reply as he had brought back the first time.[1]

"On your way, then, my friend," replied Don Quixote, "and do not be plunged into confusion when you find yourself in the presence of the light of the sun of beauty that you are now going to seek. Happy are you above all the squires in the world! Stay alert, and make sure that you do not fail to observe the way in which she receives you: whether her colour changes as you deliver my message; whether

3. April 23, feast day of the proverbial slayer of dragons.
1. This was in Part 1 when Don Quixote was in the Sierra Morena; Sancho returns to Don Quixote in Chapter 27 with instructions by the priest and barber to tell him that Dulcinea had replied by word of mouth, commanding Don Quixote to come and see her at once.

she seems disturbed or disquieted on hearing my name; whether her cushion seems not to be able to hold her, if perchance you find her seated upon the rich dais proper to her dignity—and if she is standing, watch her to see whether she shifts her weight from one foot to the other; whether she repeats her answer maybe two or three times; whether she changes it from a kind one to a harsh one, or from a cruel one to a loving one; whether she raises her hand to her hair to pat it into place, even though it is not untidy; and in short, my son, watch her every action, her every movement, because if you tell me about them I shall deduce how she feels in the most secret places of her heart about my love for her; for I would have you know, Sancho, if you do not know it already, that the external actions and movements made by lovers while the conversation concerns their love are messengers between them giving totally reliable accounts of what is happening in their souls. So off you go, my friend, and may better fortune than mine guide you and send you a happier outcome than that which I, here in this my bleak solitude, fear and expect.''

"Yes, I'm going, and I'll soon be back," said Sancho. "And do try and stop that poor little heart of yours from shrinking so, it must be about the size of a hazel nut by now, and remember what they say, a good heart conquers ill fortune, and where there isn't any bacon there aren't any hooks to hang it from and, as they also say, the hare leaps up where you least expect it to. I'm only mentioning all this because if we didn't find my lady's palace or castle last night, now it's daytime I do intend to find it, when I'm least expecting to, and once I've found it, you just leave her to me."

"This I will say, Sancho," said Don Quixote. "I do hope that God gives me even better fortune in my aspirations than you have in choosing proverbs appropriate to our discussions."

After this, Sancho turned away and gave his dun the stick, and Don Quixote was left sitting on his nag, resting in his stirrups and leaning on his lance, overwhelmed by sorrowful and confused musings, where we shall leave him and go off with Sancho Panza, who was no less pensive and bewildered than his master; so much so, that he was hardly out of the wood when, looking back and seeing that Don Quixote was no longer in sight, he climbed off his donkey, sat down at the foot of a tree, and began to talk to himself and to say:

"Pray be so good as to tell us, brother Sancho, where it is that you're going. To look for some donkey that you've lost? No, most certainly not. So what are you look-ing for? Oh, I'm just going to look for some princess, that's all, the sun of beauty and the whole of heaven in one person. And where do you expect to find all that, Sancho? Where? In the great city of El Toboso. Very well, and on whose behalf are you going to look for her? On behalf of the famous knight Don Quixote de la Mancha, who rights wrongs and gives food to the thirsty and drink to the hungry. That is all most com-mendable. And do you know where she lives, Sancho? My master says she must live in a royal palace or a splendid castle. And have you ever seen her by any chance? Neither me nor my master have ever clapped eyes on the woman. And do you think it would be right and proper for the men of El Toboso, if they found out that you're here intend-ing to spirit away their princesses and raise a rumpus among their ladies, to come and give you such a going-over that they didn't leave a bone unbroken in your body? Yes, they'd be in the right, unless they bore in mind that I'm just an errand-boy, and

> You're but a messenger, my friend,
> You don't deserve the blame.[2]

2. From a ballad about the hero Bernardo del Carpio, the Castilian who defeats Roland.

No, you can't rely on that, Sancho, because the people of La Mancha are as hot-tempered as they're honourable, and they won't let anyone play around with them. God Almighty, if they suspect what you're up to, I can promise you a bad time of it! No, you can get lost, Old Nick, you're not catching me in a hurry! Oh yes, I'm going to go stirring up a hornet's nest for the sake of somebody else's pleasure, I am! What's more, looking for Dulcinea in El Toboso would be like looking for a student in Salamanca or a girl called María in Madrid. Yes, yes, it was the devil, the devil and nobody else that got me into this mess!'"

The result of Sancho's soliloquy was that he talked to himself again, and said:

"On the other hand, there's a remedy for all things but death, under whose yoke we must all pass, like it or not, at the end of our lives. I've seen a thousand signs that this master of mine is a raving lunatic, and I'm not much better myself, because I'm even stupider than he is, following him and serving him as I do, if there's any truth in the proverb that says a man is known by the company he keeps, and that other one about birds of a feather flocking together. So him being as he is mad, and with a madness that usually makes him take one thing for another and think that white is black and black is white, as anyone could see when he said that those windmills were giants, and those friars' mules were dromedaries, and those flocks of sheep were enemy armies, and all sorts of other stuff like that, it won't be all that difficult to make him believe that some peasant girl, the very first one I come across, is lady Dulcinea—and if he doesn't believe it I'll swear she is, and if he swears she isn't I'll swear she is again, and if he insists I'll insist even more, and so I'll make sure I always have the last word, come what may. Maybe by insisting like this I'll make him stop sending me off on all these errands, seeing what a mess I make of them—or on the other hand maybe he'll think, as I expect he will, that one of those evil enchanters that he says hate him so much has changed her looks to spite him and do him harm."

These thoughts calmed Sancho's breast, and he counted the business as good as settled; and he waited where he was until the afternoon, to leave enough time for Don Quixote to believe that he'd gone to El Toboso and come back; and events fell out so well for him that when he got up to climb on his dun he saw three peasant girls coming towards him from El Toboso on three jackasses, or she-asses, because the author isn't explicit on this point, though it's more likely that they were she-asses, this being what peasant girls usually ride on; but since it doesn't matter much one way or the other, there's no need to stop to elucidate the matter. So, to cut a long story short, as soon as Sancho saw the peasant girls he rode back to his master Don Quixote as fast as he could go, and found him sighing and breathing a thousand amorous laments. When Don Quixote saw Sancho he said:

"What news, Sancho my friend? Can I mark this day with a white stone or with a black stone?"[3]

"It'll be best," Sancho replied, "for you to mark it in bright red paint, like new professors' names on college walls, so that everyone who sees it sees it clearly."

"That means," said Don Quixote, "that you bring good news."

"Such good news," Sancho replied, "that all you've got to do to find the lady Dulcinea del Toboso is to clap spurs to Rocinante and ride out of the wood—she's on her way with two of her maids to see you."

---

3. From the Roman practice of using white stones to mark lucky days, black stones unlucky ones.

"Good God! What are you saying, friend Sancho?" said Don Quixote. "You had better not be deceiving me, or attempting to beguile my real grief with false joy."

"What would I gain from deceiving you?" Sancho replied, "specially now I'm so close to showing you the truth of what I'm saying. Just get your spurs into action, sir, and come with me, and you'll see the princess, our mistress, on her way here, dressed and bedecked just like what she is. She and her maids are all one blaze of flaming gold, all spindlefuls of pearls, they're all diamonds, all rubies, all brocade more than ten levels deep, with their hair flowing over their shoulders like sunbeams playing with the wind, and what's more each of them's riding her piebald poultry, a sight for sore eyes."

"I think you mean *palfrey*, Sancho."

"There isn't that much of a difference," Sancho replied, "between poultry and palfrey, but whatever they're riding they're looking as spruce and ladylike as you could ever wish, specially my lady Princess Dulcinea—she fair takes your breath away, she does."

"Let us go, Sancho my son," Don Quixote said, "and as a reward for this news, as splendid as it is unexpected, I hereby promise you the best spoils I win in the first adventure that I undertake, and if this does not satisfy you I promise you all the foals born this year to my three mares: as you know, they are awaiting the happy event on the village green."

"I'll take the foals," replied Sancho, "because it isn't too clear that the spoils of the first adventure are going to be that brilliant."

As he said this, they emerged from the wood and saw the three peasant girls not far away. Don Quixote surveyed the road to El Toboso, and since all he could see was these three peasants he became alarmed and asked Sancho if the ladies had been outside the city when he'd left them.

"What do you mean, outside the city?" Sancho replied. "Do you keep your eyes in the back of your head or something, to stop you from seeing that they're these ladies here, shining like the very sun at noon?"

"All I can see, Sancho," said Don Quixote, "is three peasant girls on three donkeys."

"God save my soul from damnation!" Sancho replied. "Is it possible for three palfreys or whatever they're called, as white as the driven snow, to seem to you like donkeys? Good Lord, I'd pull out every single hair on my chin if that was true!"

"Well, I am telling you, friend Sancho," said Don Quixote, "that it is as true that they are asses, or maybe she-asses, as it is that I am Don Quixote and you are Sancho Panza; or at least this is how it seems to me."

"Hush, sir," said Sancho, "you mustn't talk like that—open those eyes of yours and come and do homage to the lady of your life, now she's so close at hand."

And as he said this he rode forward to greet the three peasant girls, and, dismounting from his dun, he seized one of their asses by the halter, fell to his knees and said:

"O queen and princess and duchess of beauty, may your highness and your mightiness be pleased to receive into your grace and goodwill this your hapless knight, standing over there like a marble statue, all flustered and flummoxed at finding himself in your magnificent presence. I am his squire Sancho Panza, and he is the harassed knight Don Quixote de la Mancha, also known as the Knight of the Sorry Face."

Don Quixote had by now knelt at Sancho's side and was staring with clouded vision and bulging eyes at the woman whom Sancho called queen and lady; and since all he could see there was a peasant girl, and not a very pretty one at that, because she was moon-faced and flat-nosed, he was dumbstruck and didn't dare open his mouth. The peasant girls were equally astonished, at the sight of such an ill-assorted pair kneeling in front of one of them and impeding her progress. But she broke the silence and spoke with neither goodwill nor grace:

"Get out of the bloody way and let us through, we're in a hurry!"

To which Sancho replied:

"O princess and universal lady of El Toboso! How is it that your magnanimous heart is not melted by the sight of the column and foundation of knight-errantry kneeling here in your sublimated presence?"

When one of the other girls heard this, she said:

"Come to cast pearls before swine, have we? Look at these fine gents trying to make fun of us village girls, as if we didn't know how to take the piss as well! You two go on your way, and let us go on ours, if you want to stay in one piece."

"Arise, Sancho," Don Quixote put in. "I can see that fortune, not content with my sufferings, has blocked all the roads along which some happiness might have come to this wretched soul contained within my flesh. And you, O perfection of all the excellence that the heart can desire, acme of human courtesy, the sole remedy of this afflicted heart that adores you: even though the malicious enchanter is hounding me, and has placed clouds and cataracts over my eyes, and for them alone and not for other eyes has altered and transformed your face of peerless beauty into that of some poor peasant wench, I beg you—so long as he has not also changed my face into that of some monster, to make me abominable in your sight—not to refuse to look on me with gentleness and love, seeing in my position of submission and prostration before your disguised beauty the self-humiliation of my soul's adoration."

"Hark at old grandad!" the village girl replied. "Don't I just love oily eyewash like that! Come on, shift over and let us through, thank you very much."

Sancho shifted over and let her through, delighted to have extricated himself from that particular muddle. As soon as the peasant girl who'd played the part of Dulcinea found herself free she prodded her poultry with a nail on a stick that she was carrying and it broke into a canter across the field. And feeling the nail, which annoyed it more than usual, it started to prance and buck, and dumped Lady Dulcinea among the daisies; Don Quixote rushed to pick her up and Sancho hurried to put the pack-saddle, which had slipped round under the ass's belly, back into place. Once Sancho had done this, Don Quixote went to lift his enchanted lady in his arms and place her on the ass; but the lady saved him the trouble by jumping to her feet, taking a couple of strides backwards, bounding up to the ass, bringing both hands down on to its rump and vaulting, as swift as a falcon, on to the pack-saddle, where she sat astride as if she were a man; and then Sancho said:

"By holy St Roch,[4] our lady and mistress is nimbler than a hobby-hawk, and she could teach the best rider from Cordova or Mexico how to jump on to a horse Arab-style! Over the crupper she went in one leap, and without any spurs she's making her palfrey gallop like a zebra. And her maids aren't being outdone, they're going like the wind, too."

4. Saint Roch (or Roque), 14th-century figure from Montpellier who healed plague victims and who is invoked against disease.

And Sancho was right, because once Dulcinea was mounted the other two girls spurred after her, not turning their heads back for more than a mile. Don Quixote pursued them with his gaze, and when they were out of sight he turned to Sancho and said:

"Sancho, what is your opinion about this grudge that the enchanters bear me? You can see how far their malice and hatred extend, for they have deprived me of the joy that I could have experienced on beholding my lady in her true being. I was indeed born to be a mirror of misfortune, the eternal target for the arrows of adversity. And you should also note, Sancho, that those traitors were not content just to transform my Dulcinea, but had to transform her into a figure as wretched and ugly as that peasant wench, and at the same time they took away from her what is so characteristic of fine ladies; the sweet smell that they derive from living among ambergris and flowers. Because I would have you know, Sancho, that when I went to replace Dulcinea on her palfrey (as you call it, although I thought it was a donkey), I was half suffocated by a blast of raw garlic that poisoned my very soul."

"Oh you miserable wretches!" Sancho burst out. "Oh you fateful and spiteful enchanters, I'd like to see you all hanging by your gills like pilchards on a string! Aren't you clever, aren't you powerful and aren't you bloody well active! You ought to have been happy, you villains, with turning those eyes of pearl of my lady's into oak-apples, and her tresses of purest gold into hairs from the tail of a sorrel ox, and, all in all, every one of her features from good to bad, without messing about with her smell, too—from her smell we'd at least have been able to work out what was hidden under that ugly outside although, to tell you the truth, I never did see her ugliness but only her beauty, which was boosted no end by a mole she had on the right side of her lip, a bit like a moustache, with seven or eight blond hairs like threads of gold growing out of it, more than a handsbreadth long."

"According to the rules of correspondence between facial moles and bodily moles," said Don Quixote, "Dulcinea must have another mole on the thick of the thigh on the same side as the one on her face; but hairs of the length that you have indicated are very long indeed for moles."

"Well, I can tell you," Sancho replied, "they were there all right, just as if she'd been born with them."

"I believe you, my friend," replied Don Quixote, "because nature has given Dulcinea nothing that is not complete and perfect; and so, if she had a hundred moles like the one you have described, on her they would not be moles but moons—resplendent moons and shining stars. But tell me, Sancho, the object that seemed to me like a pack-saddle, which you straightened for her—was it an ordinary saddle or a lady's saddle with arms?"

"It was nothing less than a great tall Arab-style saddle," Sancho replied, "with a saddle-cloth so precious it's worth half a kingdom."

"And to think that I could not see any of that, Sancho!" said Don Quixote. "I say it again, and I shall say it a thousand times: I am the most unfortunate of men."

The sly rogue Sancho had his work cut out to hide his laughter as he listened to the nonsense being blurted by his master, whom he had deceived with such finesse. In the end, after the two had talked for a good while longer, they remounted and followed the road that led towards Saragossa, where they planned to arrive in time for the solemn festivities held each year in that famous city. But before they arrived certain things happened to them, so many, so important and so strange, that they deserve to be written and read about, as will be seen in what follows.

* * *

Chapter 72

Concerning the arrival of Don Quixote and Sancho at their village[1]

Don Quixote and Sancho spent all that day at the village inn, waiting for nightfall: one of them to bring his exercise in flagellation to a conclusion in the open air, and the other to witness its completion and with it the accomplishment of his desires. Meanwhile a traveller arrived on horseback with three or four servants, one of whom said to the man who seemed to be their master:

"You can rest here, Don Álvaro Tarfe sir, while the sun is high—the inn seems clean and cool."

When Don Quixote heard this he said to Sancho:

"Look, Sancho, when I thumbed through that book containing the second part of my history, I think I came across the name Don Álvaro Tarfe."

"You could be right," Sancho replied. "Let's wait for him to dismount and then we'll ask him."

The gentleman dismounted, and the innkeeper's wife gave him a ground-floor room opposite Don Quixote's, decorated with painted cloths of the same sort. The recent arrival went to change into more comfortable clothes and, strolling out into the cool, spacious porch, where Don Quixote was pacing up and down, he asked:

"And where might you be bound for, my dear sir?"

And Don Quixote replied:

"To a village near here, where I live. And where are you going?"

"I am on my way to Granada, sir," the gentleman replied, "my home town."

"And a very fine town it is, too!" Don Quixote replied. "But please be so kind as to tell me your name; because I think it is going to be of more interest to me to know it than I can well explain."

"My name is Don Álvaro Tarfe," the guest said.

To which Don Quixote replied:

"I do believe you must be the very same Don Álvaro Tarfe who appears in the second part of the *History of Don Quixote de la Mancha,* recently printed and published by a novice author."

"Indeed I am," the gentleman replied, "and that man Don Quixote, the protagonist of the history, was a very close friend of mine, and I was the one who took him away from home, or at least I persuaded him to travel to Saragossa to take part in jousts held there, where I was going; and the truth of the matter is that I did him many favours and prevented the executioner from tickling his ribs for his recklessness."

"And please tell me, Señor Don Álvaro, am I at all like that Don Quixote to whom you refer?"

"No, certainly not," the guest replied, "not in the slightest."

"And did that Don Quixote," said our one, "have with him a squire called Sancho Panza?"

---

1. In Barcelona, Don Quixote experiences humiliating defeat at the hands of a mysterious challenger, the Knight of the White Moon, who is really the graduate Sansón Carrasco in disguise. Carrasco exacts from him the promise that for one year hence, he will remain in his village. The dejected Quixote starts toward La Mancha, and in Chapter 71 Sancho approaches the end of his "penance," administering in the dark such a severe flogging to a nearby tree that Don Quixote, unaware of the trick, fears for his squire's life.

"Yes, he did," Don Álvaro replied, "and although he had the reputation of being a comical fellow, not one of his attempts to be funny that I heard ever succeeded."

"I can believe that all right," Sancho butted in, "because not everybody's good at being funny, and that Sancho you're talking about, my good sir, must be some great scoundrel, as much a crook as he's unfunny; I'm the real Sancho Panza, and I'm so funny it's as if fun had rained down on me from heaven, and if you don't believe me just give me a try, and follow me around for a year or so, and you'll see how the fun gushes out of me at every turn, so much of it and such high quality that even though most of the time I don't know what I'm saying I make everyone listening to me laugh. And the real Don Quixote de la Mancha, the famous one, the brave and wise one, the lover, the righter of wrongs, the guardian of minors and orphans, the protector of widows and the slaughterer of maidens, the one whose only lady is the peerless Dulcinea del Toboso, is this gentleman here present, who's my master. All other Don Quixotes and all other Sancho Panzas besides us two are so much jiggery-pokery, figures from dreamland."

"And I believe you too, by God!" Don Álvaro Tarfe replied. "Because you've said more funny things, my friend, in the half-a-dozen words you've just spoken than the other Sancho Panza managed in all the words I heard from him. He was better at gorging himself than at talking, and was more foolish than funny, and I consider it a certain fact that the enchanters who pursue Don Quixote the Good have been chasing after me with Don Quixote the Bad. But I don't know what to say—I'd go as far as to swear that I left him in the Toledo madhouse awaiting treatment, and now another Don Quixote pops up here, quite different from mine."

"I do not know," said Don Quixote, "whether I am good, but I do know that I am not the bad Quixote, as proof of which I should like you to know, Don Álvaro Tarfe sir, that I have never in my life set foot in Saragossa; on the contrary, having been told that the fantasy Don Quixote had taken part in the jousts in that city, I refused to go there, to prove to all the world that he is a fraud; and so I went straight on to Barcelona, the storehouse of courtesy, the refuge of strangers, the hospital of the poor, the homeland of the brave, the avenger of the affronted and the appreciative returner of firm friendship, unique in its setting and its beauty. And although what happened to me there was not very pleasant, indeed was most disagreeable, I can bear it all without heaviness of heart, just for the sake of having seen Barcelona. In short, Don Álvaro Tarfe sir, I am the Don Quixote de la Mancha of whom fame speaks—not that wretch who sought to usurp my name and exalt himself with my thoughts. I entreat you, sir, as you are a gentleman, to be so kind as to make a formal declaration before the mayor of this village to the effect that you have never in all the days of your life seen me until now, and that I am not the Don Quixote who appears in the second part, nor is this squire of mine Sancho Panza the man whom you knew."

"I shall be delighted to do so," Don Álvaro replied, "even though it amazes me to see two Don Quixotes and two Sancho Panzas at the same time, as identical in name as they are antithetical in action; and I repeat and confirm that I have not seen what I have seen and that what has happened to me has not happened."

"I'm sure," said Sancho, "that you must be under a spell too, like my lady Dulcinea, and would to God I could get rid of it for you by giving myself another three thousand odd lashes like the ones I'm giving myself for her—and I'd do it without expecting anything for it, either."

"I don't understand this talk of lashes," said Don Álvaro.

And Sancho replied that it was a long story, but he'd tell it if they happened to be going the same way. By now it was time for lunch; Don Quixote and Don Álvaro ate together. The village mayor happened to walk into the inn with a notary, and to the said mayor Don Quixote presented a petition to the effect that it was his wish and right that Don Álvaro Tarfe, the gentleman who was there present, should depose before His Worship that the said deponent did not know Don Quixote de la Mancha, who was also there present, and that the said Don Quixote was not the man who appeared in print in a history entitled *The Second Part of Don Quixote de la Mancha* written by one Avellaneda, from Tordesillas. And the mayor took all the appropriate steps: the deposition was drawn up with all the legal requisites, as is proper in such cases, which delighted Don Quixote and Sancho, as if such a deposition were vital to their welfare, and as if their deeds and their words didn't clearly show the difference between the two Don Quixotes and between the two Sanchos. Many courtesies and offers were exchanged between Don Álvaro and Don Quixote, in the course of which the great man of La Mancha displayed such good sense that he disabused Don Álvaro of his error; and Don Álvaro reached the conclusion that he must indeed have been enchanted, since he'd seen with his own eyes two such contrasting Don Quixotes.

Evening came, they left the village and after a couple of miles the road forked, one way leading to Don Quixote's village and the other to where Don Álvaro was going. In this short interval Don Quixote told him about his calamitous defeat, and about Dulcinea's enchantment and disenchantment, all of which filled Don Álvaro with fresh amazement; and then he embraced Don Quixote and Sancho and went on his way, as did Don Quixote, who spent that night among some more trees, to give Sancho the opportunity to complete his penance, which he did as he had on the previous night, at the expense of the bark of the beeches rather than the skin of his back, of which he took such good care that the lashes wouldn't have brushed a fly off it if there had been one there. The deluded Don Quixote didn't fail to count a single stroke, and found that together with the previous night's score the total was three thousand and twenty-nine. It seems that the sun rose early to witness the sacrifice, and by its light the pair continued on their way, discussing Don Álvaro's delusion and what a good idea it had been to have him make his deposition before the proper authorities in such a correct and formal manner. That day and that night they pressed on, and nothing worth mentioning happened to them, except that during the night Sancho completed his task, to Don Quixote's unutterable joy, and he waited eagerly for daylight, to see if he could find his lady Dulcinea along the way, disenchanted; and as he rode there was not a woman whom he did not approach to examine her and discover whether she was Dulcinea del Toboso, because he was absolutely certain that Merlin's promises could not be false. Full of these thoughts and expectations they climbed a hill, from the top of which they could see their village, and Sancho fell to his knees, exclaiming:

"Open your eyes, my longed-for village, and see your son Sancho Panza returning, not very rich but very well lashed. Open your arms, too, to welcome your son Don Quixote, who has been conquered by another's arm but comes here as the conqueror of himself; and that, he's told me, is the best conquering you can wish for. I've got some money with me, because if I've been given a good lashing I've had a ride on a good horse, as the thief said to the executioner."

"Stop all that nonsense," said Don Quixote, "and let's put our best feet forward as we make our entry into the village, where we'll give free play to our imaginations and settle our plans for the pastoral life that we're going to lead."

And with this they went down the hill towards their village.

Chapter 73

About the omens that Don Quixote encountered as he entered his village, together with other events that adorn and authenticate this great history

As they approached it, according to Cide Hamete Benengeli, Don Quixote saw two boys squabbling on the threshing floor, and one said to the other:

"Don't keep on, Periquillo—that's something that's never ever going to happen."

Don Quixote overheard him, and said to Sancho:

"Didn't you hear, friend Sancho, what that boy said—'that's something that's never ever going to happen'?"

"And who cares," said Sancho, "what the boy said?"

"Who cares?" replied Don Quixote. "Can't you see that if you apply these words to my hopes, they mean that I'll never see Dulcinea again?"

Sancho was about to reply when he was stopped by the sight of a hare dashing across the fields, chased by many greyhounds and huntsmen, and in its terror it sought shelter and squatted between the dun's feet. Sancho picked it up and presented it to Don Quixote, who was saying:

"*Malum signum! Malum signum!*[1] Hare flees, greyhounds chase: Dulcinea appears not!"

"You're a strange one," said Sancho. "Let's suppose that this here hare is Dulcinea del Toboso and those there greyhounds chasing it are the knavish enchanters that turned her into a peasant girl—she runs away, I grab her and put her into your charge, and now she's in your arms and you're caring for her, so how can that be a bad sign, and what bad omen can you see in that?"

The two squabbling boys came to look at the hare, and Sancho asked one of them why they'd been quarrelling. The answer came from the one who'd said "that's something that's never ever going to happen"—he had taken a cricket cage from the other boy and was never ever going to give it back to him. Sancho took four quarter-reals out of his waist-pouch and gave them to the boy for the cage, which he placed in Don Quixote's hands, saying:

"Here you are, sir—your omens foiled and come to nought, and I might be a fool but to my mind they haven't got any more to do with our affairs than last year's clouds. And if I'm not much mistaken, I've heard the village priest saying that sensible Christian persons shouldn't pay any attention to such nonsense, and you yourself told me the same thing a few days back, and showed me that all Christians who heeded omens were idiots. But there's no need for me to keep on about it—let's go into the village."

The huntsmen came up and asked for their hare, and Don Quixote gave it back to them; the pair continued, and in a meadow on the outskirts of the village they found

---

1. "A bad sign, a bad sign!", often uttered by doctors. Hares were bad omens.

the priest and the graduate Carrasco at their devotions. It should be mentioned that Sancho Panza had draped over his dun and the bundle of armour, as a kind of sumpter-cloth, the buckram robe with flames painted all over it that he'd been made to wear in the Duke's castle on the night Altisidora came back to life.[2] And he'd also put the inquisitional cardboard cone on the donkey's head, the most original transformation and adornment ever effected on any ass in the world.[3] The pair were immediately recognized by the priest and the graduate, who ran over to them with open arms. Don Quixote dismounted and embraced them warmly, while the village boys—boys' lynx eyes see everything—spotted the donkey's headgear and came to stare at it, calling to each other:

"Come over here, lads, if you want to see an ass looking as spruce as a sparrow and an old hack as skinny as a skeleton—and then you can have a good giggle at the dun and Rocinante, too."

Finally, surrounded by boys and accompanied by the priest and the graduate, they entered the village and went to Don Quixote's house, and at the door they found the housekeeper and the niece, who'd already been told of his arrival. So too had Teresa Panza, Sancho's wife, who, dishevelled and half naked, clutching her daughter Sanchica by the hand, hurried out to meet her husband; and when she saw that he wasn't as smart as she thought a governor ought to be, she said:

"Why are you looking like that, husband? I'd say you've come here on foot and it hasn't done your feet much good either—you look more unruly, than a ruler."

"Shut up, Teresa," Sancho replied. "Often where there are hooks there isn't any bacon to hang on them, so let's go home, and then you'll hear marvels. I've brought some money back with me, and that's what counts, and I've earned it with my own wiles, without doing any harm to anybody."

"So long as you've brought some money back, good husband," Teresa said, "you can have earned it this way or that for all I care—however you've earned it you won't have started up any new customs in the world."

Sanchica hugged her father and asked him if he'd brought anything for her, she'd been longing to see him like rain in a drought; and with her hanging on to one side of his belt and pulling his dun along behind her, and his wife holding his hand, they made for their house, leaving Don Quixote in his, in the care of his niece and his housekeeper, and in the company of the priest and the graduate.

Without a moment's delay, Don Quixote took the graduate and the priest aside and gave them a brief account of his defeat and of the promise that he'd made not to leave the village for a year,[4] which he intended to keep to the letter, without breaking it in the slightest detail, as became a true knight errant, bound by all the discipline and order of knight-errantry—and he added that his intention was to become a shepherd for the year, and amuse himself in the solitude of the fields, where he could give free rein to his thoughts of love as he practised that virtuous pastoral way of life, and that he entreated them, if they didn't have too much to do and weren't prevented by more important matters, to consent to be his companions; he'd buy sheep enough to qualify

2. Reference to a recent episode (Chapter 69) in which, as part of yet another plan engineered by the Duke and Duchess, Altisidora had feigned to be in love with Don Quixote. In fact, the episode prompts Cide Hamete himself to say in Chapter 70 that he "considers that the perpetrators of the hoax were as mad as the victims, and that the Duke and Duchess, going to such lengths to make fun of two fools, were within a hairsbreadth of looking like fools themselves."

3. Those denounced by the Inquisition and forced to repent publicly had to wear tall white cones on their heads, along with a sign stating their sin.

4. The promise exacted of Don Quixote by the supposed Knight of the White Moon, Carrasco himself.

them as shepherds, and he could tell them that the most essential part of the business was already settled, because he'd provided them with names that would fit like gloves. The priest told him to say what they were. Don Quixote replied that he himself was going to be called the shepherd Quixotiz, the graduate the shepherd Carrascón, the priest the shepherd Curambro and Sancho Panza the shepherd Panzino.[5]

They were both astonished at Don Quixote's latest delusion; but to prevent him from wandering away from the village again on his chivalric exploits, and in the hope that during the year he might be cured, they consented to his new project, acclaimed his folly as sound sense and agreed to join him in his new way of life.

"And what's more," said Sansón Carrasco, "as everybody knows, I'm a famous poet and at every turn I'll write pastoral verse or courtly verse or whatever verse best suits my purpose, to keep us amused in the Godforsaken places where we're going a-wandering; and what's most essential, gentlemen, is for each of us to choose the name of the shepherdess he's going to honour in his verses, and for us not to leave a single tree, however hard the wood, where her name isn't carved, as is the habit and custom among shepherds in love."

"That is most fitting," Don Quixote replied, "even though I have no need to search for the name of a fictitious shepherdess, because I already have the peerless Dulcinea del Toboso, the glory of these riverbanks, the ornament of these meadows, the mainstay of beauty, the cream of all the graces, and, in short, one worthy to receive all praise, however hyperbolical it might appear to be."

"Quite right too," said the priest, "but the rest of us will look for nice obliging shepherdesses who'll be just what the doctor ordered."

To which Sansón Carrasco added:

"And if they haven't got appropriate names, we'll give them the names of the shepherdesses that come printed in all those books—the world's full of them: Phyllises, Amaryllises, Dianas, Fléridas, Galateas, Belisardas; and since they're sold in the market squares, we've got every right to buy them and keep them for ourselves. If my lady or, more accurately, my shepherdess happens to be called Ana, I'll sing her praises under the name of Anarda; if she's Francisca, I'll call her Francenia; if she's Lucía, Lucinda; and so on and so forth. And if Sancho Panza is going to join the club, he can sing his wife's praises with the name Teresaina."

Don Quixote laughed at the invention of the name, and the priest lauded his virtuous and honourable decision, and again offered to accompany them for as long as he could spare from his unavoidable duties. With this they took their leave and advised and begged him to take care of his health, and to indulge in everything that was good for him. As fate would have it, his niece and housekeeper overheard the conversation between the three men, and as soon as Don Quixote was alone they walked in, and the niece said:

"What's all this, uncle? Just when we were thinking you'd come back home to stay, and to live a quiet and honourable life here, you want to go off into yet more labyrinths, turning yourself into a

> Little Shepherd, coming, coming,
> Little Shepherd, going, going?[6]

---

5. All diminutives, reflective of shepherds' lowly status.
6. From a Christmas carol.

Well, the plain fact is the straw's a bit old for making whistles."

To which the housekeeper added:

"And are you going to be able to put up with the heat of the summer afternoons, the damp of the winter nights, the howling of the wolves, out there in the country? Of course not—that's a job for strong men, brought up and hardened to it pretty well since they were babes in arms. And of the two evils it's better to be a knight errant than a shepherd. Look, sir, take my advice, which I'm not giving you on a belly full of bread and wine but on an empty stomach and fifty years of experience—stay at home, look after your property, go often to confession, give alms to the poor, and on my conscience be it if I'm wrong."

"Hush, my daughters," Don Quixote replied, "I know what's good for me. Take me to my bed now, because I don't feel very well, and rest assured that, whether an actual knight errant or a would-be shepherd, I shall never fail to provide for your needs, as you will see for yourselves."

And his good daughters (as the housekeeper and the niece surely were) took him to his bed, where they gave him some food and lavished all possible attentions on him.

Chapter 74

Concerning how Don Quixote fell ill, the will that he made, and his death

Since what is human is not eternal, but is in continuous decline from its beginnings to its conclusion, this being particularly true of men's lives, and since Don Quixote's life had not been granted any special privilege by heaven to halt the course of its decline, it reached its end when he was least expecting it to; because, either out of the depression brought on by his defeat or by divine ordination, he was seized by a fever that kept him in bed for six days, during which time he was often visited by his friends the priest, the graduate and the barber, while his good squire Sancho Panza never left his bedside. In the belief that dejection at his defeat and the disappointment of his hopes for Dulcinea's deliverance and disenchantment had brought him to this state, they tried in every way they knew to raise his spirits; and the graduate told him to cheer up and get out of bed to make a start on the pastoral life, for which he'd already written an eclogue that would be bad news for all the eclogues Sannazaro had ever produced[1]—and with his own money he'd bought two splendid dogs to keep watch over the flock, one of them called Barcino and the other Butrón, which a herdsman from Quintanar had sold him. But none of this roused Don Quixote from his melancholy.

His friends called in the doctor, who felt his pulse and wasn't happy with what he found, and said that to be on the safe side he should look to the well-being of his soul, because the well-being of his body was in some danger. Don Quixote listened with great composure, but not so his housekeeper, his niece and his squire, who started to weep tender tears as if he were already lying dead before them. The doctor's opinion was that depression and despondency were killing him. Don Quixote asked to be left alone, because he needed a little sleep. They did as he asked, and he slept for more than six hours at a stretch, as the saying goes: indeed he slept for so long that the housekeeper and the niece thought that he was going to die in his sleep. But he did eventually awake, and he bellowed:

1. The Neapolitan Jacopo Sannazaro wrote *Arcadia*, the first pastoral romance; published in 1504, it juxtaposes verse eclogues with a prose sequence that tells the story of a desperate lover's attempts to escape his sorrow and live among the shepherds. It inspired more than a century's worth of pastoral literature.

"Blessed be Almighty God, who has done me such good! Indeed his mercy knows no bounds, and the sins of men do not lessen or obstruct it."

The niece paid careful attention to her uncle's words, and they seemed more rational than usual, during his recent illness at least, and she asked him:

"What are you saying, sir? Has something happened? What's this mercy you're on about, and these sins of men?"

"The mercy, niece," Don Quixote replied, "is that which God has this instant shown me, unobstructed, as I said, by my sins. My mind has been restored to me, and it is now clear and free, without those gloomy shadows of ignorance cast over me by my wretched, obsessive reading of those detestable books of chivalry. Now I can recognize their absurdity and their deceitfulness, and my only regret is that this discovery has come so late that it leaves me no time to make amends by reading other books that might be a light for my soul. It is my belief, niece, that I am at death's door; I should like to make myself ready to die in such a way as to indicate that my life has not been so very wicked as to leave me with a reputation as a madman; for even though this is exactly what I have been, I'd rather not confirm this truth in the way in which I die. Call my good friends, my dear: the priest, the graduate Sansón Carrasco, and Master Nicolás the barber, because I want to confess my sins and make my will."

But she was saved her trouble by the entrance of all three. As soon as Don Quixote saw them he said:

"You must congratulate me, my good sirs, because I am no longer Don Quixote de la Mancha but Alonso Quixano, for whom my way of life earned me the nickname of 'the Good.' I am now the enemy of Amadis of Gaul and the whole infinite horde of his descendants; now all those profane histories of knight-errantry are odious to me; now I acknowledge my folly and the peril in which I was placed by reading them; now, by God's mercy, having at long last learned my lesson, I abominate them all."

When the three heard all this they were certain that he was in the grips of some new madness. And Sansón said:

"Now that we've had news, Don Quixote sir, that the lady Dulcinea has been disenchanted, you come out with all that? Now that we're on the point of becoming shepherds, to spend all our time singing and living like lords, you want to turn yourself into a hermit? Stop it for goodness sake, and come to your senses, and forget all that idle nonsense."

"The nonsense in which I have been involved so far," Don Quixote replied, "has been real enough as regards the harm it has done me, but my death will, with heaven's help, turn it to my benefit. Gentlemen: I can feel that I am dying, and dying quickly; please leave jests aside and bring me a confessor to confess me and a notary to write down my will, because at times like this a man must not trifle with his soul. And so I implore you to send someone for the notary while the priest confesses me."

They looked at each other, amazed at Don Quixote's words, and although they didn't know what to think they ended up by believing him; and one of the signs that led them to conclude that he really was dying was the ease with which he had turned from a madman into a sane man; for to what he had already said he added some more that was so well expressed, so Christian and so coherent that it removed all doubt from their minds and convinced them that he was indeed sane.

The priest ordered everybody out of the room and was left alone with him, and confessed him.

The graduate went to fetch the notary and returned a little later with him and with Sancho Panza, who had been told by the graduate about the state his master was in and who, finding the housekeeper and the niece in tears, began to pucker his lips and shed some of his own. The confession ended and the priest emerged, saying:

"Alonso Quixano the Good really is dying, and he really is sane; we'd better go back in so that he can make his will."

This news was a terrible stimulus for the housekeeper's, the niece's and the good squire Sancho Panza's swollen eyes, so much so that it made the tears burst from them, and a thousand deep sighs burst from their breasts; because the truth is, as has been said before, that while Don Quixote was plain Alonso Quixano the Good—and while he was Don Quixote, too—he was always of gentle disposition and affable behaviour, and well loved not only by his own household but by everybody who knew him. The notary went in with the others and once he had drawn up the heading and Don Quixote had disposed of his soul with all the necessary Christian formalities, they reached the part concerning the disposal of property, and he said:

"Likewise it is my will that with respect to certain monies in the possession of Sancho Panza, whom in my madness I made my squire, inasmuch as between the two of us there has been a certain amount of haggling, of give and take, he should not be held accountable for them, nor should any claim be made against him but that, if anything remains after he has paid himself what I owe him, it should all be his, although there will be little enough of it, and much good may it do him; and if, just as when I was mad I helped to procure for him the governorship of an island, I could now that I am sane make him the ruler of a kingdom, I would do it, because the straightforwardness of his character and the fidelity of his conduct deserve it."

And turning his face towards Sancho, he said:

"Forgive me, my friend, for making you seem mad, like me, and for making you fall into my own error of believing that knights errant ever have existed or do exist."

"Oh no, don't die, master!" Sancho replied, crying. "Take my advice and live for a long long time, because the maddest thing a man can do in this life is to let himself die, just like that, without anybody killing him or any other hands except the hands of depression doing away with him. Come on, don't be lazy, get out of that bed of yours, and let's go off into the countryside dressed up as shepherds as we said we would—and perhaps behind some bush or other we'll find the lady Dulcinea, disenchanted and looking as pretty as a picture. If you're dying from sadness because you were defeated, you just blame me and say you were knocked down because I didn't girth Rocinante properly—and what's more you must have read in your books of chivalry that it's an everyday event for knights to knock each other down, and for the one who's defeated today to be the victor tomorrow."

"Very true," said Sansón, "and the worthy Sancho Panza has hit the nail right on the head."

"Not so fast, gentlemen," said Don Quixote: "you won't find this year's birds in last year's nests. I was mad, and now I am sane: I was Don Quixote de la Mancha and now, as I said, I am Alonso Quixano the Good. May my repentance and my sincerity restore me in your eyes to the esteem in which I used to be held, and let the notary continue taking down my will:

"Likewise I bequeath all my estate in its entirety to my niece Antonia Quixana, here present, once what is needed for my other bequests has been deducted from the most readily disposable part of it; and it is my will that the first of these shall be the payment of the wages that I owe my housekeeper for all the time that she has been serving me, and in addition twenty ducats for a dress. I appoint the priest and the graduate Sansón Carrasco, here present, to be my executors.

"Likewise it is my will that if my niece Antonia Quixana should wish to marry, it must be to a man about whom it has first been formally established that he does not so much as know what books of chivalry are; and if it is discovered that he does, and, despite that, my niece still insists on marrying him, and she does so, she is to forfeit everything that I have left her, and my executors can distribute it in pious works as they see fit.

"Likewise I request the aforementioned gentlemen, my executors, if they are fortunate enough to meet the author who is said to have written a history that is circulating under the title of *The Second Part of the Exploits of Don Quixote de la Mancha,* to beg him on my behalf, as earnestly as they can, to forgive me for unintentionally having provided him with the opportunity to write all the gross absurdities contained in that book; because I am leaving this life with scruples of conscience for having given him an excuse for writing them."

Here he ended his testament, and was overcome by a fainting fit that prostrated him on his bed. The company was thrown into alarm and hurried to help him, and during the three days that he lived after making his will he fainted frequently. The whole house was in turmoil; but still the niece ate, the housekeeper toasted and Sancho Panza enjoyed himself; because inheriting always does something to dispel or temper in the heir the thoughts of the grief that the dead man will, of course, leave behind him.

Eventually Don Quixote's last day on earth arrived, after he had received all the sacraments and had expressed, in many powerful words, his loathing of books of chivalry. The notary was present, and he said that he'd never read in any book of chivalry of any knight errant dying in his bed in such a calm and Christian manner as Don Quixote, who, amidst the tears and lamentations of everybody present, gave up the ghost; by which I mean to say he died.

At which the priest asked the notary to write out a certificate to the effect that Alonso Quixano the Good, commonly known as Don Quixote de la Mancha, had passed on from this life, and died from natural causes. And he said that he was requesting this certificate to deprive any author other than Cide Hamete Benengeli of the opportunity to bring him falsely back to life and write endless histories of his exploits.

This was the end of the Ingenious Hidalgo of La Mancha, the name of whose village Cide Hamete couldn't quite recall, so that all the towns and villages of La Mancha could fight among themselves for the right to adopt him and make him their own son, just as the seven cities of Greece contended for Homer.[2] The lamentations of Sancho, the niece and the housekeeper are omitted from this account, as are the fresh epitaphs that were placed upon his tomb, although Sansón Carrasco did have this one put there:

> This is a doughty knight's repose;
> So high his matchless courage rose
> That, as it's plain enough to see,
> He granted death no victory,
> Not even when in death's last throes.
> This world he didn't ever prize:
> He was a scarecrow in its eyes,
> And yet he was its bugbear, too.
> He had the luck, with much ado,
> To live a madman, yet die wise.

And the sage Cide Hamete said to his pen:

---

2. The birthplace of the poet called Homer is unknown.

"Here you shall rest, hanging from this rack on this length of brass wire, O quill of mine—whether well trimmed or not I do not know—and here you shall live on for many centuries, unless presumptuous and knavish historians take you down to profane you. But before they touch you, you can warn them and tell them as best you can:

> 'Hands off, hands off, you paltry knaves;
> My noble king, let none
> Attempt this enterprise: you know
> It's kept for me alone.'[3]

For me alone was Don Quixote born, and I for him; it was for him to act, for me to write; we two are as one, in spite of that false writer from Tordesillas who has had and may even again have the effrontery to write with a coarse and clumsy ostrich quill about my valiant knight's deeds, because this is not a burden for his shoulders or a subject for his torpid wit. And you can warn him, if you do happen to meet him, to leave Don Quixote's weary mouldering bones at rest in his tomb, and not to try to take him, in the face of all the prerogatives of death, to Old Castile,[4] making him rise from the grave where he really and truly does lie stretched out at full length, quite incapable of any third sally or fresh campaign; because to make fun of all those campaigns waged by so very many knights errant his two are quite sufficient, such has been the approval and delight of all those who have known of them, both in Spain and in foreign realms. And so you will have carried out your Christian mission, giving good advice to one who wishes you ill, and I shall feel proud and satisfied to have been the first author to enjoy the full fruit of his writings, as I desired, because my only desire has been to make men hate those false, absurd histories in books of chivalry, which thanks to the exploits of my real Don Quixote are even now tottering, and without any doubt will soon tumble to the ground. Farewell."

108

WILLIAM SHAKESPEARE ■ (1564–1616)

William Shakespeare (or Shaxspeare, or Shakyspere, or Shakspere, or Shackespeare— there are over two dozen different spellings of his name), the oldest of five siblings, enjoyed a relatively comfortable bourgeois childhood in Stratford-on-Avon. His mother, Mary Arden, was the daughter of an affluent farmer; his father was a wool-dealer and glover who went into local politics. Stratford-on-Avon was a booming country town on a river that brought in a great deal of traffic, and the town's general prosperity enabled it to hire first-class teachers for the grammar school, where its most famous citizen became well-read in classics, history, and rhetoric.

Little is known of the period between Shakespeare's departure from Stratford Grammar School in 1578 and his marriage in 1582 to Anne Hathaway—he may have apprenticed as a glover for his father—and there are again no records of him until 1587, when he shows up in London, acting and possibly already writing plays. His extraordinarily rapid rise to the top of the competitive theater industry is attested to by his success in purchasing a coat-of-arms in 1596 and, a year later, the biggest house in Stratford. In 1599, he was one of five actors in the Lord Chamberlain's Men to hold half the lease for the new Globe Theatre, built by the acting company after their lease at James Burbage's Theatre had expired. By then not only was he listed as "principal comedian" for the company, but he

---

3. Lines from a popular ballad about the siege of Granada, the last part of the Moorish kingdom to fall into Christian hands (in 1492).

4. A northern region of central Spain, formerly part of the Kingdom of Castile. This may be an ironic gesture on Cervantes's part; almost all of *Don Quixote* takes place in what was once Castile, and almost all of the characters except for the meddling Duke and Duchess are from Castile.

had already written and produced his great history plays and his comedies, one of them—*The Merry Wives of Windsor*, with the burly Falstaff as its protagonist and a town not unlike his native Stratford as its setting—at the specific request of his queen, Elizabeth I. It may have been Elizabeth's formidable presence that inspired Shakespeare to create for his other comedies some of the classiest heroines in dramatic literature, albeit ones played by boys; notably, the self-possessed Rosalynde, who commandeers the events that transpire in Arden in *As You Like It*, and Viola, in *Twelfth Night*, who wins for herself a duke.

The season of Shakespeare's great tragedies followed, and with it, a change of monarchs and a corresponding change in Shakespeare's status. King James I, formerly James VI of Scotland, ruled England after Elizabeth's death in 1603, and promptly elevated Shakespeare's troupe to the King's Men, authorizing the actors to wear livery and inviting them to play some thirteen times a year at court. *Julius Caesar* and *Hamlet* predate James's succession, while *Othello*, *Macbeth*, and *King Lear* were written shortly after James became king. They were followed by works that do not fit nicely into distinct categories. *Antony and Cleopatra*, with its flirtatious Egyptian queen, lacks the momentum and drive of the earlier tragedies, and *Measure for Measure* ends too uneasily to be confused with the earlier comedies. Shakespeare's increasing interest in experimenting with dramatic structure is evident in the final plays of his career: *Winter's Tale*, *Cymbeline*, *Pericles*, and *The Tempest*. With their exotic settings and fantastic plots, their mixture of deaths and comic rebirths, they represent yet again a sharp departure from what had come before, while returning to themes that had always sparked Shakespeare's interest—jealousy, the trials of kingship, the possibilities afforded by escape to a pastoral world. Shakespeare officially retired from the stage in 1613, the year the capacious Globe Theatre burned down while *Henry VIII*, which Shakespeare wrote in collaboration with John Fletcher, was being performed. In April of 1616 he died in Stratford, having bequeathed to the English-speaking world several long narrative poems, over a hundred and fifty sonnets, and thirty-seven plays.

During a period of enforced absence from the stage—a combination of recurrent plague and bans against actors for unruly behavior—William Shakespeare, fresh from his first tragedy (the bloody *Titus Andronicus*) and his comedy *The Taming of the Shrew*, turned to poetry. This at least is one theory for the genesis of Shakespeare's 154 sonnets. While they were remarked upon as early as 1598, they weren't published until 1609, toward the end of the playwright's career, and well after the vogue for sonnet-making in England had passed. But as many readers have realized, there is something timeless in these sonnets—and the theme of art's timelessness is one on which Shakespeare's complex, cunning narrator himself insists as he tells his beloved that in his "war with Time for love of you / As he takes from you, I ingraft you new." Like Petrarch, Shakespeare is forced to settle for fame rather than reciprocity in love. But he does so by staging a series of intricate, emotional dramas that broaden the sonnet sequence's domain while unsettling the Petrarchan exaltation of chastity and love.

The focus of attention for the first 126 sonnets is a young man, probably an aristocrat whose social station is higher than the narrator's. The relationship of the narrator to the young man is, however, far more complicated than that found in Michelangelo. The volume opens with the so-called "procreation poems," eighteen sonnets in which Shakespeare urges the young man to have a child so that the world will not lose him forever when he dies; the final sonnets in this sequence then suggest that only poetry can truly "give life to thee." Many of the subsequent poems to the young man are taken up with the "pow'rful rime" of both the poet and, increasingly, rival poets who threaten to write about the young man as well. But these poems also illustrate the torment of the jealous lover whose faith in his supposedly chaste young man, as in his literary medium, is considerably shaken. The poem in which the poet bids his lover "Farewell: thou art too dear for my possessing" represents one low point of the collection, while the arrival of the "dark lady" onto the sonnets' stage with sonnet 127 shatters once and for all the delicate equilibrium attained earlier. Sonnet 147 closes, "I have sworn thee fair, and thought thee bright, / Who art as black as hell, as dark as night"; once mistress only to the narrator, this unsettling female presence is now actively pursuing the young man as well.

The order of the sonnets in the 1609 volume is contested, since there is no evidence that Shakespeare ever authorized his poems' publication. Still, it is possible to argue that the sequence may initially develop a Petrarchan quest for poetic glory, only to undo that quest and all it stands for. On the other hand, the narrator's stance is so changeable, as he himself admits, and Shakespeare's understanding of the dynamics of Petrarchism so penetrating, that perhaps the sonnets are never serious about their mission of preserving the "timeless" reputation of their author or of the young man who occupies center stage.

from Sonnets[1]

1

From fairest creatures we desire increase,
That thereby beauty's rose might never die,
But as the riper should by time decease,
His tender heir might bear his memory;
5   But thou, contracted° to thine own bright eyes,   *betrothed*
Feed'st thy light's flame with self-substantial° fuel,   *of your own making*
Making a famine where abundance lies,
Thyself thy foe, to thy sweet self too cruel.
Thou that art now the world's fresh ornament
10   And only herald to the gaudy° spring,   *bright*
Within thine own bud buriest thy content
And, tender churl, mak'st waste in niggarding.°   *hoarding*
    Pity the world, or else this glutton be,
    To eat the world's due, by the grave and thee.[2]

3

Look in thy glass, and tell the face thou viewest
Now is the time that face should form another,
Whose fresh repair° if now thou not renewest,   *condition*
Thou dost beguile the world, unbless some mother.[3]
5   For where is she so fair whose uneared womb
Disdains the tillage of thy husbandry?[4]
Or who is he so fond° will be the tomb   *foolish*
Of his self-love, to stop posterity?
Thou art thy mother's glass, and she in thee
10   Calls back the lovely April of her prime;
So thou through windows of thine age shalt see,
Despite of wrinkles, this thy golden time.[5]

1. The 1609 edition of the *Sonnets,* published by Thomas Thorpe, was prefaced with this dedication, followed by Thorpe's initials: "To the Only Begetter of these ensuing sonnets Mr. W. H. All happiness and that eternity promised by our ever-living poet wisheth the well-wishing adventurer in setting forth."

2. The last line gives the cannibalistic image of the "tender churl" eating "the world's due," i.e., his offspring, by refusing to procreate.

3. Prevent a woman from enjoying the blessings of motherhood.

4. Cultivation, but with a play on "husband."

5. Just as he furnishes his mother a "glass" through which she might see her youth, so would his children afford him a "window" in his old age to his "golden time."

But if thou live rememb'red not to be,
Die single, and thine image dies with thee.

17

Who will believe my verse in time to come
If it were filled with your most high deserts?
Though yet, heaven knows, it is but as a tomb
Which hides your life and shows not half your parts.
5 If I could write the beauty of your eyes
And in fresh numbers number all your graces,
The age to come would say, "This poet lies
Such heavenly touches ne'er touched earthly faces."
So should my papers, yellowed with their age,
10 Be scorned, like old men of less truth than tongue,
And your true rights be termed a poet's rage
And stretchèd metre° of an antique song.   *exaggerations*
     But were some child of yours alive that time,
     You should live twice—in it and in my rime.[6]

55

Not marble nor the gilded monuments
Of princes shall outlive this pow'rful rime,
But you shall shine more bright in these contents
Than° unswept stone, besmeared with sluttish° time.   *than in / lazy*
5 When wasteful war shall statues overturn,
And broils° root out the work of masonry,   *tumults*
Nor° Mars his sword nor war's quick fire shall burn   *Neither*
The living record of your memory.
'Gainst death and all oblivious enmity°   *oblivion*
10 Shall you pace forth; your praise shall still find room
Even in the eyes of all posterity
That wear this world out to the ending doom.
     So, till the judgment° that° yourself arise,   *Judgment Day / when*
     You live in this, and dwell in lovers' eyes.

73

That time of year thou mayst in me behold
When yellow leaves, or none, or few, do hang
Upon those boughs which shake against the cold,
Bare ruined choirs where late the sweet birds sang.
5 In me thou seest the twilight of such day
As after sunset fadeth in the west,
Which by and by black night doth take away,
Death's second self that seals up all in rest.
In me thou seest the glowing of such fire
10 That° on the ashes of his youth doth lie,   *As*
As the death bed whereon it must expire,

6. This sonnet concludes the so-called "procreation sonnets" in which the narrator is encouraging the young man to

Consumed with that which it was nourished by.
    This thou perceiv'st, which makes thy love more strong,
    To love that well which thou must leave ere long.

87

Farewell: thou art too dear° for my possessing,   *costly*
And like enough thou know'st thy estimate.°   *value*
The charter of thy worth gives thee releasing;[7]
My bonds° in thee are all determinate.°   *claims / expired*
5 For how do I hold thee but by thy granting,
And for that riches where is my deserving?
The cause of this fair gift in me is wanting,
And so my patent° back again is swerving.   *deed or title*
Thyself thou gav'st, thy own worth then not knowing,
10 Or me, to whom thou gav'st it, else mistaking;
So thy great gift, upon misprision growing,°   *originating in error*
Comes home again, on better judgment making.
    Thus have I had thee as a dream doth flatter,
    In sleep a king, but waking no such matter.°   *substance*

116

Let me not to the marriage of true minds
Admit impediments;[8] love is not love
Which alters when it alteration finds
Or bends with the remover to remove.
5 O, no, it is an ever-fixèd mark°   *landmark*
That looks on tempests and is never shaken;
It is the star to every wand'ring bark,
Whose worth's unknown, although his height be taken.[9]
Love's not Time's fool, though rosy lips and cheeks
10 Within his bending sickle's compass° come;   *range*
Love alters not with his brief hours and weeks,
But bears it out even to the edge of doom.°   *the last day*
    If this be error, and upon° me proved,   *against*
    I never writ, nor no man ever loved.

126

O thou, my lovely boy, who in thy power
Dost hold Time's fickle glass,° his sickle hour;°   *mirror / hourglass*
Who hast by waning grown, and therein show'st
Thy lovers withering as thy sweet self grow'st;
5 If Nature, sovereign mistress over wrack,°   *ruin*
As thou goest onwards, still will pluck thee back,
She keeps thee to this purpose, that her skill
May Time disgrace and wretched minutes kill.

7. You are worth so much that you have the privilege of being able to "release" yourself from all obligations to me.

8. The marriage service directs the congregation, "If any of you know cause or just impediment why these persons should not be joined together...."

Yet fear her, O thou minion of her pleasure!

10 She may detain, but not still° keep, her treasure;   *always*

Her audit,° though delayed, answered must be,   *final reckoning*

And her quietus° is to render° thee.[1]   *settlement / surrender*

127

In the old age black was not counted fair,[2]

Or, if it were, it bore not beauty's name;

But now is black beauty's successive heir,

And beauty slandered with a bastard shame;[3]

5 For since each hand hath put on nature's power,

Fairing the foul with art's false borrowed face,

Sweet beauty hath no name, no holy bower,

But is profaned, if not lives in disgrace.

Therefore my mistress' brows are raven black,

10 Her eyes so suited,° and they mourners seem   *dressed in black*

At such° who, not born fair, no beauty lack,   *For*

Sland'ring creation with a false esteem:

　　Yet so they mourn, becoming° of their woe,   *gracing*

　　That every tongue says beauty should look so.

130

My mistress' eyes are nothing like the sun;

Coral is far more red than her lips' red;

If snow be white, why then her breasts are dun;°   *dark*

If hairs be wires, black wires grow on her head.

5 I have seen roses damasked,° red and white,   *mingled*

But no such roses see I in her cheeks;

And in some perfumes is there more delight

Than in the breath that from my mistress reeks.

I love to hear her speak; yet well I know

10 That music hath a far more pleasing sound:

I grant I never saw a goddess go;

My mistress, when she walks, treads on the ground.[4]

　　And yet, by heaven, I think my love as rare

　　As any she° belied with false compare.°   *any woman / comparison*

The Tempest　Like his contemporary Montaigne, whose remarkable essay "Of Cannibals" informs *The Tempest,* Shakespeare was an armchair traveler. And like Montaigne, he seldom took anything at face value. For his plays, he devoured novellas by Italians, chapbooks by Englishmen, snatches of songs by Spaniards, and tourist propaganda by the New Virginians, who in 1610 were boasting that "after some planting and husbanding the Americas could supply not only England's needs but those of other nations as well." Virginia, that is to say, could be

---

1. This is the only poem in the series that lacks the final two lines, perhaps suggesting the dramatic "rendering" of the young man. This is also the final sonnet addressed directly to the young man; with 127, the "dark lady" sonnets begin.

2. "Fair" as in both "beautiful" and "blonde."

3. "Fair" beauty is rendered illegitimate, as women turn increasingly to cosmetics.

4. Perhaps an allusion to *Aeneid* 1, in which Aeneas watches his mother Venus part from him: "her gown was long and to the ground; even her walk was sign enough she was a goddess"; the moment is later echoed in Petrarch and others.

Carthage to England's Rome: the breadbasket for a Europe that still perenially suffered from plague and bad harvests. First performed in 1611, *The Tempest* is a recasting and rigorous questioning of pamphlets such as these, as it explores the anxieties that accompanied England's belated foray into a New World already occupied by Spanish plantations to the south and French missionaries to the north, not to mention by the native peoples themselves. Shipwreck and drowning, drunken brawls, seditious murder, tense confrontations between natives and Europeans, tender romance, and all within three hours: *The Tempest* is one of only two of Shakespeare's plays that respect the unities of time and place. And all of it is orchestrated by an exiled duke named Prospero, whose exceptional skills at magic and theatrical arts have resulted in many an audience seeing him as a self-portrait of his notoriously elusive creator.

The Tempest opened the voluminous collection overseen and published by Shakespeare's fellow actors in 1623. The First Folio, as it has been traditionally called, groups Shakespeare's works by genre. The fact that *The Tempest* is followed by *Two Gentlemen of Verona* and *Merry Wives of Windsor* suggests that the actors perceived it as a comedy. And so, in many respects, it is. It celebrates the magician's powers and those of the theater in which Shakespeare spent his adult life. It effects reconciliations undreamed of and lures us and its characters into brave new worlds; written on the edge of the baroque, it remarks throughout on theater's capacity to use illusion for peaceful resolutions—the most resounding of which is the love affair between Prospero's daughter Miranda and the dashing Ferdinand. An island spirit named Ariel is Prospero's Puckish servant, who does his master's bidding by transforming himself into (mostly female) roles and controlling characters as though they were puppets, first befuddling them, then bringing them together on the stage for revelations of life and death. Yet Shakespeare is also conscious of art's limitations, especially when confronted by the messiness of politics and family affairs. *The Tempest* is relentlessly realistic with respect to the extent to which "human nature" resists even the most artful Machiavellian tactics. Indeed, Prospero, the play's reigning Machiavellian, while provoking sympathy for his plight at his brother Antonio's hands, was a bad ruler who ignored office of state to pursue his magical arts; and it is only on the island that Prospero finds a means of bringing statecraft and witchcraft together for manipulative, at times, sadistic effect. The doubleness of Prospero's achievement is highlighted at the play's end, when Prospero must address the gaping Europeans' wonder not over a beautiful Miranda but over his "deformed" slave: "the thing of darkness" that he acknowledges, in a perplexing moment, as his own. Indeed, Caliban, whose name may be an anagram for "cannibal," represents a terrain which Machiavelli, in his cynical portrait of the ideal Renaissance ruler of a century earlier, had barely imagined: colonial encounters abroad with defiant indigenous peoples. The tumultuous relationship between Prospero and Caliban would inspire the later meditations of Caribbean and Latin American writers, especially Aimé Césaire, whose own twentieth-century *Tempest* is a postcolonial classic.

Yet Caliban is no "cannibal," and some of his lines—as when he reminds Prospero that once he "lov'd thee, / And show'd thee all the qualities o'th'isle, / The fresh springs, brine-pits, barren place and fertile"—are some of the most poetic in the play. At the same time, he is versatile enough to speak in bantering prose with the "jester" Trinculo and with Stephano, a "drunken butler," who contemplate taking the island over as theirs. Shakespeare's own ability to move back and forth between stunning poetry and prosaic wit distinguishes almost his entire dramatic canon, as he draws for his characters on extremely diverse segments of society and convincingly creates a world through their language; Elizabethans said they would go to *hear,* not *see,* a play, and this emphasis on the ear suggests for us the power that the dramatic word could have. But Shakespeare also derives his fast-paced dialogues and moving verse from a wealth of literary and dramatic traditions, both ancient and contemporary. The vibrant practices of the Italian professional theater or the *commedia dell'arte*—literally, the actor's guild, although the expression has come to designate the improvised scenarios of masked actors such as the hunchbacked merchant, the bumbling doctor, the wily servant—have long been considered an influence particu-larly on *The Tempest,* with its slapstick scenes of low life. On the other hand, Rome's most accomplished poet, Virgil, furnished not only the source of the wondering lines spoken by Ferdinand when he imagines Miranda to be a goddess, but the chaotic storm with which both the *Aeneid* and *The Tempest* open. And Ovid's *Metamorphoses* gave Shakespeare the powerful verses recited by Prospero when he abjures his "rough magic" and promises to drown his book: they are the words of Medea, the vengeful sorceress of Greek and Roman myth. If Shakespeare on the one hand lends to his characters' language the cadences of ev-eryday life, on the other he infuses it with the resonant poetry of earlier literary geniuses, and thereby participates in the broader cultural project of the English Renaissance, making the legacy of Roman empire and the European Renaissance alike England's own.

And yet not entirely its own. The haunting poetry of the waif Ariel—"Full fathom five thy father lies, / Of his bones are coral made"—would have been sung to an uncompre-hending Ferdinand and audience alike, as though Shakespeare was making us and Fer-dinand experience the unsettling feeling of what it is like to be in a place where we have lost our normal bearings. But this may in fact be what all of Shakespeare's theater tries to accomplish. The geography of London was such that the public theaters were on the other side—the wrong side—of the Thames River from the city's official neighborhoods, and the entertainment district was in some sense discontinuous with the real London. Simi-larly, *The Tempest* takes place like so many of Shakespeare's plays not at "home" but somewhere else: in this case, on an unnamed island in the Mediterranean that vanishes off the surface of the map as soon as the play is done. In remarking again and again on the insubstantialities of a play that has given us a narrative about marriage between old world and new, between the seasoned colonist Ferdinand and the innocent Miranda, Shakespeare points to the strange insubstantialities of stories about love and conquest alike. At the same time, in calling attention to the extent to which the problematic figure of Prospero is behind those stories, Shakespeare takes care to insinuate that he, like his audience, bears responsibility for what can happen to narratives once they are set in motion.

PRONUNCIATIONS:
Prospero: PROS-pe-ro
Trinculo: TRIN-coo-lo

The Tempest

The Names of the Actors

ALONSO, *King of Naples*
SEBASTIAN, *his brother*
PROSPERO, *the right Duke of Milan*
ANTONIO, *his brother, the usurping Duke*
   of Milan
FERDINAND, *son to the King of Naples*
GONZALO, *an honest old councillor*
ADRIAN *and* ⎫
FRANCISCO, ⎬ *lords*
⎭
CALIBAN, *a savage and deformed slave*
TRINCULO, *a jester*

STEPHANO, *a drunken butler*
MASTER *of a ship*
BOATSWAIN
MARINERS
MIRANDA, *daughter to Prospero*
ARIEL, *an airy spirit*
IRIS ⎫
CERES ⎪
JUNO ⎬ *(presented by) spirits*
NYMPHS ⎪
REAPERS ⎭

[*Other Spirits attending on Prospero*]

Scene: An uninhabited island

Act 1

Scene 1

[*A tempestuous noise of thunder and lightning heard. Enter a Shipmaster and a Boatswain.*][1]

MASTER: Boatswain!

BOATSWAIN: Here, Master. What cheer?

MASTER: Good, speak to the mariners. Fall to 't yarely,[2] or we run ourselves aground. Bestir, bestir!

[*Exit.*]

[*Enter Mariners.*]

BOATSWAIN: Heigh, my hearts! Cheerly, cheerly, my hearts! Yare, yare! Take in the topsail. Tend[3] to the Master's whistle.—Blow[4] till thou burst thy wind, if room enough![5]

[*Enter Alonso, Sebastian, Antonio, Ferdinand, Gonzalo, and others.*]

ALONSO: Good Boatswain, have care. Where's the Master? Play[6] the men.

BOATSWAIN: I pray now, keep below.

ANTONIO: Where is the Master, Boatswain?

BOATSWAIN: Do you not hear him? You mar our labor. Keep your cabins! You do assist the storm.

GONZALO: Nay, good, be patient.

BOATSWAIN: When the sea is. Hence! What cares these roarers[7] for the name of king?
15 To cabin! Silence! Trouble us not.

GONZALO: Good, yet remember whom thou hast aboard.

BOATSWAIN: None that I more love than myself. You are a councillor; if you can command these elements to silence and work the peace of the present, we will not hand[8] a rope more. Use your authority. If you cannot, give thanks
20 you have lived so long and make yourself ready in your cabin for the mischance of the hour, if it so hap.—Cheerly, good hearts!—Out of our way, I say.

[*Exit.*]

GONZALO: I have great comfort from this fellow. Methinks he hath no drowning mark upon him; his complexion is perfect gallows.[9] Stand fast, good Fate, to
25 his hanging! Make the rope of his destiny our cable, for our own doth little advantage.[1] If he be not born to be hanged, our case is miserable.

[*Exeunt (courtiers).*]

[*Enter Boatswain.*]

---

1. Location: On board ship.
2. Quickly.
3. Attend.
4. Addressed to the wind.
5. As long as we have sea room enough.
6. Ply? Urge the men to exert themselves.
7. Waves or wind.
8. Handle.
9. Alludes to the proverb "He that's born to be hanged need fear no drowning."
1. Doesn't do much good.

BOATSWAIN: Down with the topmast! Yare! Lower, lower! Bring her to try wi' the
       main course.[2] [*A cry within.*] A plague upon this howling! They are louder
       than the weather or our office.[3]

[*Enter Sebastian, Antonio, and Gonzalo.*]

30   Yet again? What do you here? Shall we give o'er and drown? Have you a
       mind to sink?
SEBASTIAN: A pox o'your throat, you bawling, blasphemous, incharitable dog!
BOATSWAIN: Work you, then.
ANTONIO: Hang, cur! Hang, you whoreson, insolent noisemaker! We are less afraid
35   to be drowned than thou art.
GONZALO: I'll warrant him for drowning,[4] though the ship were no stronger than a
       nutshell and as leaky as an unstanched[5] wench.
BOATSWAIN: Lay her ahold,[6] ahold! Set her two courses.[7]
       Off to sea again! Lay her off!

[*Enter Mariners, wet.*]

MARINERS: All lost! To prayers, to prayers! All lost!

[*The Mariners run about in confusion, exiting at random.*]

BOATSWAIN: What, must our mouths be cold?[8]
GONZALO: The King and Prince at prayers! Let's assist them,
       For our case is as theirs.
SEBASTIAN: I am out of patience.
ANTONIO: We are merely° cheated of our lives by drunkards.   *utterly*
45   This wide-chapped° rascal! Would thou mightst lie drowning   *wide-jawed*
       The washing of ten tides![9]
GONZALO: He'll be hanged yet,
       Though every drop of water swear against it
       And gape at wid'st to glut° him.   *gobble*
       [*A confused noise within.*]   "Mercy on us!"—
       "We split, we split!"—"Farewell my wife and children!"—
50   "Farewell, brother!"—"We split, we split, we split!"

                                                     [*Exit Boatswain.*]

ANTONIO: Let's all sink wi' the King.
SEBASTIAN: Let's take leave of him.

                                                 [*Exit (with Antonio).*]

GONZALO: Now would I give a thousand furlongs of sea for an acre of barren ground:
       long heath, brown furze; anything. The wills above be done! But I would
55   fain die a dry death.

                                                              [*Exit.*]

2. Sail her close to the wind.
3. The noise we make at our work.
4. Guarantee against.
5. Loose (suggesting also "menstrual").
6. Close to the wind.
7. Sets of sails.
8. Must we drown in the cold sea; or, let us heat up our mouths with liquor

Scene 2[1]

[Enter Prospero (in his magic cloak) and Miranda.]

MIRANDA: If by your art, my dearest father, you have
                      Put the wild waters in this roar, allay them.
                      The sky, it seems, would pour down stinking pitch,
                      But that the sea, mounting to th' welkin's cheek,°   *the sky's face*
5   Dashes the fire out. O, I have suffered
                      With those that I saw suffer! A brave° vessel,   *splendid*
                      Who had, no doubt, some noble creature in her,
                      Dashed all to pieces. O, the cry did knock
                      Against my very heart! Poor souls, they perished.
10   Had I been any god of power, I would
                      Have sunk the sea within the earth or ere°   *before*
                      It should the good ship so have swallowed and
                      The freighting° souls within her.   *forming the cargo*
PROSPERO: Be collected.°   *composed*
                      No more amazement.° Tell your piteous° heart   *consternation / pitying*
15   There's no harm done.
MIRANDA: O, woe the day!
PROSPERO: No harm.
                      I have done nothing but in care of thee,
                      Of thee, my dear one, thee, my daughter, who
                      Art ignorant of what thou art, naught knowing
                      Of whence I am, nor that I am more better
20   Than Prospero, master of a full° poor cell,   *very*
                      And thy no greater father.
MIRANDA: More to know
                      Did never meddle° with my thoughts.   *mingle*
PROSPERO: 'Tis time
                      I should inform thee farther. Lend thy hand
                      And pluck my magic garment from me. So,

[laying down his magic cloak and staff]

25   Lie there, my art.—Wipe thou thine eyes. Have comfort.
                      The direful spectacle of the wreck,° which touched   *shipwreck*
                      The very virtue° of compassion in thee,   *essence*
                      I have with such provision° in mine art   *foresight*
                      So safely ordered that there is no soul—
30   No, not so much perdition° as an hair   *loss*
                      Betid° to any creature in the vessel   *happened*
                      Which thou heard'st cry, which thou saw'st sink. Sit down.
                      For thou must now know farther.
MIRANDA *[sitting]*:   You have often
                      Begun to tell me what I am, but stopped
35   And left me to a bootless inquisition,°   *fruitless inquiry*
                      Concluding, "Stay, not yet."
PROSPERO: The hour's now come;
                      The very minute bids thee ope thine ear.
                      Obey, and be attentive. Canst thou remember

A time before we came unto this cell?
40   I do not think thou canst, for then thou wast not
      Out° three years old.   *fully*

MIRANDA: Certainly, sir, I can.

PROSPERO: By what? By any other house or person?
      Of anything the image, tell me, that
      Hath kept with thy remembrance.

MIRANDA: 'Tis far off,
45   And rather like a dream than an assurance
      That my remembrance warrants.[2] Had I not
      Four or five women once that tended me?

PROSPERO: Thou hadst, and more, Miranda. But how is it
      That this lives in thy mind? What seest thou else
50   In the dark backward and abysm of time?[3]
      If thou rememberest aught ere thou cam'st here,
      How thou cam'st here thou mayst.

MIRANDA: But that I do not.

PROSPERO: Twelve year since, Miranda, twelve year since,
      Thy father was the Duke of Milan and
55   A prince of power.

MIRANDA: Sir, are not you my father?

PROSPERO: Thy mother was a piece° of virtue, and   *masterpiece*
      She said thou wast my daughter; and thy father
      Was Duke of Milan, and his only heir
      And princess no worse issued.°   *no less nobly born*

MIRANDA: O the heavens!
60   What foul play had we, that we came from thence?
      Or blessèd was 't we did?

PROSPERO: Both, both, my girl.
      By foul play, as thou sayst, were we heaved thence,
      But blessedly holp° hither.   *helped*

MIRANDA: O, my heart bleeds
      To think o' the teen° that I have turned you to,[4]   *trouble*
65   Which is from° my remembrance! Please you, farther.   *out of*

PROSPERO: My brother and thy uncle, called Antonio—
      I pray thee mark me—that a brother should
      Be so perfidious!—he whom next° thyself   *next to*
      Of all the world I loved, and to him put
70   The manage° of my state, as at that time   *management*
      Through all the seigniories[5] it was the first,
      And Prospero the prime duke, being so reputed
      In dignity, and for the liberal arts
      Without a parallel; those being all my study,
75   The government I cast upon my brother
      And to my state grew stranger,[6] being transported°   *carried away*
      And rapt in secret studies. Thy false uncle—
      Dost thou attend me?

---

2. A certainty that my memory guarantees.
3. Abyss of the past.
4. I've caused you to remember.
5. Cit<u>states of a ...</u>

MIRANDA: Sir, most heedfully.

PROSPERO: Being once perfected° how to grant suits,   *grown skillful*

80   How to deny them, who t' advance and who

       To trash for overtopping,[7] new created

       The creatures that were mine, I say, or° changed 'em,   *either*

       Or else new formed 'em; having both the key[8]

       Of officer and office, set all hearts i' the state

85   To what tune pleased his ear, that° now he was   *so that*

       The ivy which had hid my princely trunk

       And sucked my verdure out on 't. Thou attend'st not.

MIRANDA: O, good sir, I do.

PROSPERO: I pray thee, mark me.

       I, thus neglecting worldly ends, all dedicated

90   To closeness° and the bettering of my mind   *seclusion*

       With that which, but by being so retired,

       O'erprized° all popular rate°, in my false brother   *outvalued / estimation*

       Awaked an evil nature; and my trust,

       Like a good parent,[9] did beget of° him   *in*

95   A falsehood in its contrary as great

       As my trust was, which had indeed no limit,

       A confidence sans° bound. He being thus lorded°   *without / made a lord*

       Not only with what my revenue yielded

       But what my power might else exact, like one

100   Who, having into° truth by telling of it,   *unto*

       Made such a sinner of his memory

       To° credit his own lie,[1] he did believe   *as to*

       He was indeed the Duke, out° o' the substitution   *as a result*

       And executing th' outward face of royalty

105   With all prerogative. Hence his ambition growing—

       Dost thou hear?

MIRANDA: Your tale, sir, would cure deafness.

PROSPERO: To have no screen between this part he played

       And him he played it for, he needs will be°   *insisted on becoming*

       Absolute Milan.[2] Me, poor man, my library

110   Was dukedom large enough. Of temporal royalties

       He thinks me now incapable; confederates°—   *allies himself*

       So dry° he was for sway—wi' the King of Naples   *thirsty*

       To give him annual tribute, do him homage,

       Subject his coronet to his crown, and bend

115   The dukedom yet° unbowed—alas, poor Milan!—   *previously*

       To most ignoble stooping.

MIRANDA: O the heavens!

PROSPERO: Mark his condition° and th' event°, then tell me   *pact / outcome*

       If this might be a brother.

MIRANDA: I should sin

       To think but nobly of my grandmother.

---

7. To check for going too fast, like hounds.

8. Key for unlocking; tool for tuning stringed instruments.

9. Alludes to the proverb that good parents often bear bad children; see line 120.

120	Good wombs have borne bad sons.	

PROSPERO: Now the condition.

     This King of Naples, being an enemy

     To me inveterate, hearkens° my brother's suit,   *listens to*

     Which was that he, in lieu o' the premises[3]

     Of homage and I know not how much tribute,

125   Should presently° extirpate° me and mine   *immediately / remove*

     Out of the dukedom and confer fair Milan,

     With all the honors, on my brother. Whereon,

     A treacherous army levied, one midnight

     Fated° to th' purpose did Antonio open   *devoted*

130   The gates of Milan, and, i' the dead of darkness,

     The ministers° for the purpose hurried thence   *agents*

     Me and thy crying self.

MIRANDA: Alack, for pity!

     I, not remembering how I cried out then,

     Will cry it o'er again. It is a hint°   *occasion*

135   That wrings[4] mine eyes to 't.

PROSPERO: Hear a little further,

     And then I'll bring thee to the present business

     Which now's upon 's, without the which this story

     Were most impertinent.°   *irrelevant*

MIRANDA: Wherefore° did they not   *why*

     That hour destroy us?

PROSPERO: Well demanded,° wench.   *asked*

140   My tale provokes that question. Dear, they durst not,

     So dear the love my people bore me, nor set

     A mark so bloody on the business, but

     With colors fairer painted their foul ends.

     In few,° they hurried us aboard a bark,°   *few words / ship*

145   Bore us some leagues to sea, where they prepared

     A rotten carcass of a butt,° not rigged,   *tub*

     Nor tackle, sail, nor mast; the very rats

     Instinctively have quit it. There they hoist us,

     To cry to th' sea that roared to us, to sigh

150   To th' winds whose pity, sighing back again,

     Did us but loving wrong.

MIRANDA: Alack, what trouble

     Was I then to you!

PROSPERO: O, a cherubin

     Thou wast that did preserve me. Thou didst smile,

     Infusèd with a fortitude from heaven,

155   When I have decked° the sea with drops full salt,   *adorned*

     Under my burden groaned, which raised in me

     An undergoing stomach,° to bear up   *courage to endure*

     Against what should ensue.

MIRANDA: How came we ashore?

PROSPERO: By Providence divine.

---

3. In exchange for the guarantee.

160	Some food we had, and some fresh water, that	
A noble Neapolitan, Gonzalo,	
Out of his charity, who being then appointed	
Master of this design, did give us, with	
Rich garments, linens, stuffs,° and necessaries,	*supplies*
165	Which since have steaded much.° So, of his gentleness,	*been of much use*
Knowing I loved my books, he furnished me	
From mine own library with volumes that	
I prize above my dukedom.	

MIRANDA: Would I might
But ever see that man!

PROSPERO: Now I arise. [*He puts on his magic cloak.*]
170   Sit still, and hear the last of our sea sorrow.
Here in this island we arrived; and here

Have I, thy schoolmaster, made thee more profit°	*profit more*
Than other princes'° can, that have more time	*princesses*
For vainer hours and tutors not so careful.	

MIRANDA: Heavens thank you for 't! And now, I pray you, sir—
For still 'tis beating in my mind—your reason
For raising this sea storm?

PROSPERO: Know thus far forth:
By accident most strange, bountiful Fortune,
Now my dear lady, hath mine enemies
180   Brought to this shore; and by my prescience

I find my zenith° doth depend upon	*apex of fortune*
A most auspicious star, whose influence	
If now I court not, but omit,° my fortunes	*neglect*
Will ever after droop. Here cease more questions.	
185	Thou art inclined to sleep. 'Tis a good dullness,°	*drowsiness*
And give it way. I know thou canst not choose.	

[*Miranda sleeps.*]

Come away,° servant, come! I am ready now.	*come here*
Approach, my Ariel, come.	

[*Enter Ariel.*]

ARIEL: All hail, great master, grave sir, hail! I come
190   To answer thy best pleasure; be 't to fly,
To swim, to dive into the fire, to ride

On the curled clouds, to thy strong bidding task°	*make demands upon*
Ariel and all his quality.°	*cohorts or abilities*

PROSPERO: Hast thou, spirit,

Performed to point° the tempest that I bade thee?	*in detail*

ARIEL: To every article.

I boarded the King's ship. Now on the beak,°	*prow*
Now in the waist,° the deck,° in every cabin,	*midships / poop*

I flamed amazement.[5] Sometimes I'd divide
And burn in many places; on the topmast,

---

5. Struck terror by appearing as St. Elmo's fire, an electric discharge seen at the prominent parts of ships in stormy

200	The yards, and bowsprit would I flame distinctly,°	*in different places*
	Then meet and join. Jove's lightning, the precursors	
	O' the dreadful thunderclaps, more momentary	
	And sight-outrunning° were not. The fire and cracks	*swifter than sight*
	Of sulfurous roaring the most mighty Neptune	
205	Seem to besiege and make his bold waves tremble,	
	Yea, his dread trident shake.	

PROSPERO: My brave spirit!
   Who was so firm, so constant, that this coil°   *uproar*
   Would not infect his reason?

ARIEL: Not a soul
   But felt a fever of the mad and played
210   Some tricks of desperation. All but mariners
   Plunged in the foaming brine and quit the vessel,
   Then all afire with me. The King's son, Ferdinand,
   With hair up-staring°—then like reeds, not hair—   *standing on end*
   Was the first man that leapt; cried, "Hell is empty,
215   And all the devils are here!"

PROSPERO: Why, that's my spirit!
   But was not this nigh shore?

ARIEL: Close by, my master.

PROSPERO: But are they, Ariel, safe?

ARIEL: Not a hair perished.
   On their sustaining garments[6] not a blemish,
   But fresher than before; and, as thou bad'st me,
220   In troops I have dispersed them 'bout the isle.
   The King's son have I landed by himself,
   Whom I left cooling of the air with sighs
   In an odd angle° of the isle, and sitting,   *corner*
   His arms in this sad knot. [*He folds his arms.*]

PROSPERO: Of the King's ship,
225   The mariners, say how thou hast disposed,
   And all the rest o' the fleet.

ARIEL: Safely in harbor
   Is the King's ship; in the deep nook,° where once   *bay*
   Thou called'st me up at midnight to fetch dew[7]
   From the still-vexed° Bermudas,[8] there she's hid;   *ever stormy*
230   The mariners all under hatches stowed,
   Who, with a charm joined to their suffered° labor,   *undergone*
   I have left asleep. And for the rest o' the fleet,
   Which I dispersed, they all have met again
   And are upon the Mediterranean float°   *sea*
235   Bound sadly home for Naples,
   Supposing that they saw the King's ship wrecked

---

6. Garments that buoyed them up in the sea.

7. For magical purposes; see line 322.

8. Perhaps refers to the then-recent Bermuda shipwreck of 1609, when one of nine ships sailing from England to Virginia was driven onto the Bermuda coast in a severe storm. As in *The Tempest,* all on board survived, although the news took a while to reach those in England, who had presumed the crew lost.

And his great person perish.

PROSPERO: Ariel, thy charge
Exactly is performed. But there's more work.
What is the time o' the day?

ARIEL: Past the mid season.°   *noon*

PROSPERO: At least two glasses.° The time twixt six and now   *hourglasses*
Must by us both be spent most preciously.

ARIEL: Is there more toil? Since thou dost give me pains,°   *labors*
Let me remember° thee what thou hast promised,   *remind*
Which is not yet performed me.

PROSPERO: How now? Moody?
245   What is't thou canst demand?

ARIEL: My liberty.

PROSPERO: Before the time be out? No more!

ARIEL: I prithee,
Remember I have done thee worthy service,
Told thee no lies, made thee no mistakings, served
Without or grudge or grumblings. Thou did promise
250   To bate° me a full year.   *remit*

PROSPERO: Dost thou forget
From what a torment I did free thee?

ARIEL: No.

PROSPERO: Thou dost, and think'st it much to tread the ooze
Of the salt deep,
To run upon the sharp wind of the north,
255   To do me° business in the veins[9] o' the earth   *do for me*
When it is baked° with frost.   *hardened*

ARIEL: I do not, sir.

PROSPERO: Thou liest, malignant thing! Hast thou forgot
The foul witch Sycorax, who with age and envy°   *malice*
Was grown into a hoop?[1] Hast thou forgot her?

ARIEL: No, sir.

PROSPERO: Thou hast. Where was she born? Speak. Tell me.

ARIEL: Sir, in Argier.°   *Algiers*

PROSPERO: O, was she so? I must
Once in a month recount what thou hast been,
Which thou forget'st. This damned witch Sycorax,
265   For mischiefs manifold and sorceries terrible
To enter human hearing, from Argier,
Thou know'st, was banished. For one thing she did°   *becoming pregnant*
They would not take her life. Is not this true?

ARIEL: Ay, sir.

PROSPERO: This blue-eyed[2] hag was hither brought with child°   *pregnant*
And here was left by the sailors. Thou, my slave,
As thou report'st thyself, was then her servant;
And, for° thou wast a spirit too delicate   *because*

9. Of minerals, or underground streams.
1. So bent with age as to resemble a hoop.
2. With dark circles under her eyes, implying pregnancy.

275 To act her earthy and abhorred commands,
Refusing her grand hests,° she did confine thee, *orders*
By help of her more potent ministers
And in her most unmitigable rage,
Into a cloven pine, within which rift
280 Imprisoned thou didst painfully remain
A dozen years; within which space she died
And left thee there, where thou didst vent thy groans
As fast as mill wheels strike.[3] Then was this island—
Save° for the son that she did litter° here, *except / give birth to*
A freckled whelp,° hag-born—not honored with *animal offspring*
A human shape.

ARIEL: Yes, Caliban her son.

PROSPERO: Dull thing, I say so:[4] he, that Caliban
Whom now I keep in service. Thou best know'st
What torment I did find thee in. Thy groans
Did make wolves howl, and penetrate the breasts
290 Of ever-angry bears. It was a torment
To lay upon the damned, which Sycorax
Could not again undo. It was mine art,
When I arrived and heard thee, that made gape° *open wide*
The pine and let thee out.

ARIEL: I thank thee, master.

PROSPERO: If thou more murmur'st, I will rend an oak
And peg thee in his° knotty entrails till *its*
Thou hast howled away twelve winters.

ARIEL: Pardon, master.
I will be correspondent° to command *obedient*
And do my spriting[5] gently.° *graciously*

PROSPERO: Do so, and after two days
I will discharge thee.

ARIEL: That's my noble master!
What shall I do? Say what? What shall I do?

PROSPERO: Go make thyself like a nymph o' the sea. Be subject
To no sight but thine and mine, invisible
To every eyeball else. Go take this shape
305 And hither come in 't. Go, hence with diligence!

                                        [*Exit (Ariel).*]

Awake, dear heart, awake! Thou hast slept well.
Awake!

MIRANDA: The strangeness of your story put
Heaviness° in me. *drowsiness*

PROSPERO: Shake it off. Come on,
We'll visit Caliban, my slave, who never
Yields us kind answer.

---

3. As the blades of a mill wheel strike water.
4. Exactly, that's what I said, you dimwit.
5. Duties as a spirit.

MIRANDA: 'Tis a villain, sir,
        I do not love to look on.
PROSPERO: But, as 'tis,
        We cannot miss° him. He does make our fire,   do without
        Fetch in our wood, and serves in offices°   functions
        That profit us.—What ho! Slave! Caliban!
        Thou earth, thou! Speak.
CALIBAN [within]:   There's wood enough within.
PROSPERO: Come forth, I say! There's other business for thee.
        Come, thou tortoise! When?[6]

        [Enter Ariel like a water nymph.]

        Fine apparition! My quaint° Ariel,   ingenious
        Hark in thine ear. [He whispers.]
ARIEL: My lord, it shall be done.

                                                                        [Exit.]

PROSPERO: Thou poisonous slave, got° by the devil himself   begotten
        Upon thy wicked dam,° come forth!   mother

        [Enter Caliban.]

CALIBAN: As wicked dew as e'er my mother brushed
        With raven's feather from unwholesome fen°   marsh
        Drop on you both! A southwest° blow on ye   diseased wind
325   And blister you all o'er!
PROSPERO: For this, be sure, tonight thou shalt have cramps,
        Side-stitches that shall pen thy breath up. Urchins[7]
        Shall forth at vast° of night that they may work[8]   desolate time
        All exercise on thee. Thou shalt be pinched
330   As thick as honeycomb, each pinch more stinging
        Than bees that made 'em.
CALIBAN: I must eat my dinner.
        This island's mine, by Sycorax my mother,
        Which thou tak'st from me. When thou cam'st first,
        Thou strok'st me and made much of me, wouldst give me
335   Water with berries in 't, and teach me how
        To name the bigger light, and how the less,
        That burn by day and night. And then I loved thee
        And showed thee all the qualities° o' th' isle,   resources
        The fresh springs, brine pits, barren place and fertile.
340   Cursed be I that did so! All the charms°   spells
        Of Sycorax, toads, beetles, bats, light on you!
        For I am all the subjects that you have,
        Which first was mine own king; and here you, sty° me   put me in a sty
        In this hard rock, whiles you do keep from me
        The rest o' th' island.

6. Expression of impatience.
7. Hedgehogs (here, goblins in the shape of hedgehogs).
8. Malignant spirits were thought to prowl at night.

PROSPERO: Thou most lying slave,
         Whom stripes° may move, not kindness! I have used thee,   *lashes*
         Filth as thou art, with humane care, and lodged thee
         In mine own cell, till thou didst seek to violate
         The honor of my child.
CALIBAN: O ho, O ho! Would 't had been done!
         Thou didst prevent me; I had peopled else°   *otherwise populated*
         This isle with Calibans.
MIRANDA:[9]   Abhorrèd slave,
         Which any print° of goodness wilt not take,   *imprint*
         Being capable of all ill! I pitied thee,
355   Took pains to make thee speak, taught thee each hour
         One thing or other. When thou didst not, savage,
         Know thine own meaning, but wouldst gabble like
         A thing most brutish, I endowed thy purposes°   *meanings*
         With words that made them known. But thy vile race,°   *nature*
360   Though thou didst learn, had that in 't which good natures
         Could not abide to be with; therefore wast thou
         Deservedly confined into this rock,
         Who hadst deserved more than a prison.
CALIBAN: You taught me language, and my profit on 't
365   Is I know how to curse. The red° plague rid° you   *bubonic / destroy*
         For learning me your language!
PROSPERO: Hagseed, hence!
         Fetch us in fuel, and be quick, thou 'rt best,[1]
         To answer other business:[2] Shrugg'st thou, malice?
         If thou neglect'st or dost unwillingly
370   What I command, I'll rack thee with old[3] cramps,
         Fill all thy bones with aches,[4] make thee roar
         That beasts shall tremble at thy din.
CALIBAN: No, pray thee.
         [*Aside.*] I must obey. His art is of such power
         It would control my dam's god, Setebos,[5]
         And make a vassal of him.
PROSPERO: So, slave, hence!

                                        [*Exit Caliban.*]

[*Enter Ferdinand; and Ariel, invisible,[6] playing and singing. (Ferdinand does not see
Prospero and Miranda.)*]

                    [*Ariel's Song.*]

ARIEL: *Come unto these yellow sands,*
                    And then take hands;
                Curtsied when you have, and kissed

9. This speech is sometimes assigned by editors to Prospero.
1. You'd be well advised.
2. Perform other tasks.
3. Such as old people have.
4. Pronounced "aitches."
5. A god of the Patagonians, at the tip of South America, named in Richard Eden's *History of Travel,* 1577.
6. To the other characters.

> *The wild waves whist;*[7]
380 > *Foot it featly° here and there,*   *dance nimbly*
> *And, sweet sprites, bear*
> *The burden. Hark, hark!*
> [Burden,° dispersedly (within): *Bow-wow.*]   *Refrain*
> *The watchdogs bark.*
385 > [Burden, dispersedly within: *Bow-wow.*]
> *Hark, hark! I hear*
> *The strain of strutting chanticleer*
> *Cry Cock-a-diddle-dow.*

FERDINAND: Where should this music be? I' th' air or th' earth?
390 It sounds no more; and sure it waits upon
Some god o' th' island. Sitting on a bank,
Weeping again the King my father's wreck,
This music crept by me upon the waters,
Allaying both their fury and my passion°   *lamentation*
395 With its sweet air. Thence I have followed it,
Or it hath drawn me rather. But 'tis gone.
No, it begins again.

[*Ariel's Song.*]

ARIEL: *Full fathom five thy father lies.*
> *Of his bones are coral made.*
400 > *Those are pearls that were his eyes.*
> *Nothing of him that doth fade*
> *But doth suffer a sea change*
> *Into something rich and strange.*
> *Sea nymphs hourly ring his knell.*
> [Burden (within): *Ding dong.*]
405 > *Hark, now I hear them, ding dong bell.*

FERDINAND: The ditty does remember° my drowned father.   *allude to*
This is no mortal business, nor no sound
That the earth owes.° I hear it now above me.   *owns*
PROSPERO [*to Miranda*]: The fringèd curtains of thine eye advance°   *raise*
And say what thou seest yond.
MIRANDA: What is 't? A spirit?
Lord, how it looks about! Believe me, sir,
It carries a brave° form. But 'tis a spirit.   *excellent*
PROSPERO: No, wench, it eats and sleeps and hath such senses
As we have, such. This gallant which thou seest
415 Was in the wreck; and, but he's something stained°   *disfigured*
With grief, that's beauty's canker,° thou mightst call him   *cankerworm*
A goodly person. He hath lost his fellows
And strays about to find 'em.
MIRANDA: I might call him
A thing divine, for nothing natural

---

7. Kissed the waves into silence.

I ever saw so noble.

PROSPERO [*aside*]: It goes on, I see,
As my soul prompts° it.—Spirit, fine spirit, I'll free thee   *would like*
Within two days for this.

FERDINAND [*seeing Miranda*]: Most sure,° the goddess   *this is certainly*
On whom these airs° attend!—Vouchsafe° my prayer   *songs / grant*
May know if you remain° upon this island,   *dwell*
425 And that you will some good instruction give
How I may bear me° here. My prime request,   *conduct myself*
Which I do last pronounce, is—O you wonder![8]—
If you be maid[9] or no?

MIRANDA: No wonder, sir,
But certainly a maid.

FERDINAND: My language? Heavens!
430 I am the best° of them that speak this speech,   *in birth*
Were I but where 'tis spoken.

PROSPERO [*coming forward*]: How? The best?
What wert thou if the King of Naples heard thee?

FERDINAND: A single[1] thing, as I am now, that wonders
To hear thee speak of Naples.° He does hear me,   *King of Naples*
435 And that he does I weep. Myself am Naples,
Who with mine eyes, never since at ebb,° beheld   *dry*
The King my father wrecked.

MIRANDA: Alack, for mercy!

FERDINAND: Yes, faith, and all his lords, the Duke of Milan
And his brave son[2] being twain.

PROSPERO [*aside*]: The Duke of Milan
440 And his more braver° daughter could control° thee,   *splendid / refute*
If now 'twere fit to do 't. At the first sight
They have changed eyes.°—Delicate Ariel,   *exchanged love looks*
I'll set thee free for this. [*To Ferdinand.*] A word, good sir.
I fear you have done yourself some wrong.° A word!   *told a lie*

MIRANDA [*aside*]: Why speaks my father so ungently? This
Is the third man that e'er I saw, the first
That e'er I sighed for. Pity move my father
To be inclined my way!

FERDINAND: O, if a virgin,
And your affection not gone forth, I'll make you
The Queen of Naples.

PROSPERO: Soft, sir! One word more.
[*Aside.*] They are both in either's powers; but this swift business
I must uneasy° make, lest too light winning   *difficult*
Make the prize light. [*To Ferdinand.*] One word more: I charge thee
That thou attend° me. Thou dost here usurp   *listen to*
455 The name thou ow'st° not, and hast put thyself   *ownest*

---

8. Miranda's name means "to be wondered at."
9. As opposed to either a goddess or a married woman.
1. Solitary, being at once King of Naples and myself; feeble.
2. Antonio's son is not mentioned elsewhere.

Upon this island as a spy, to win it
From me, the lord on 't.

FERDINAND: No, as I am a man.

MIRANDA: There's nothing ill can dwell in such a temple.
    If the ill spirit have so fair a house,
    Good things will strive to dwell with 't.

PROSPERO: Follow me.—
    Speak not you for him; he's a traitor.—Come,
    I'll manacle thy neck and feet together.
    Seawater shalt thou drink; thy food shall be
    The fresh-brook mussels, withered roots, and husks
    Wherein the acorn cradled. Follow.

FERDINAND: No!
    I will resist such entertainment° till   *treatment*
    Mine enemy has more power.

[*He draws, and is charmed from moving.*]

MIRANDA: O dear father,
    Make not too rash° a trial° of him, for   *harsh / judgment*
    He's gentle,° and not fearful.[3]   *noble*

PROSPERO: What, I say,
470   My foot° my tutor?—Put thy sword up, traitor,   *subordinate*
    Who mak'st a show but dar'st not strike, thy conscience
    Is so possessed with guilt. Come, from thy ward,°   *defensive posture*
    For I can here disarm thee with this stick
    And make thy weapon drop. [*He brandishes his staff.*]

MIRANDA [*trying to hinder him*]:   Beseech you, father!

PROSPERO: Hence! Hang not on my garments.

MIRANDA: Sir, have pity!
    I'll be his surety.°   *guarantee*

PROSPERO: Silence! One word more
    Shall make me chide thee, if not hate thee. What,
    An advocate for an impostor? Hush!
    Thou think'st there is no more such shapes as he,
480   Having seen but him and Caliban. Foolish wench,
    To° the most of men this is a Caliban,   *compared to*
    And they to him are angels.

MIRANDA: My affections
    Are then most humble; I have no ambition
    To see a goodlier man.

PROSPERO [*to Ferdinand*]:   Come on, obey.
485   Thy nerves° are in their infancy again   *sinews*
    And have no vigor in them.

FERDINAND: So they are.
    My spirits,° as in a dream, are all bound up.   *vital powers*
    My father's loss, the weakness which I feel,
    The wreck of all my friends, nor this man's threats
490   To whom I am subdued, are but light° to me,   *unimportant*

3. Frightening; cowardly.

Might I but through my prison once a day
Behold this maid. All corners else° o' th' earth   *other regions*
Let liberty make use of; space enough
Have I in such a prison.

PROSPERO [*aside*]:   It works. [*To Ferdinand.*] Come on.—
495   Thou hast done well, fine Ariel! [*To Ferdinand.*] Follow me.
[*To Ariel.*] Hark what thou else shalt do me.°   *for me*

MIRANDA [*to Ferdinand*]:   Be of comfort.
My father's of a better nature, sir,
Than he appears by speech. This is unwonted°   *unusual*
Which now came from him.

PROSPERO [*to Ariel*]:   Thou shalt be as free
500   As mountain winds; but then° exactly do   *until then*
All points of my command.

ARIEL: To th' syllable.

PROSPERO [*to Ferdinand*]:   Come, follow. [*To Miranda.*] Speak not for him.

                                        [*Exeunt.*]

Act 2

Scene 1[1]

[*Enter Alonso, Sebastian, Antonio, Gonzalo, Adrian, Francisco, and others.*]

GONZALO [*to Alonso*]:   Beseech you, sir, be merry. You have cause,
So have we all, of joy, for our escape
Is much beyond our loss. Our hint° of woe   *occasion*
Is common; every day some sailor's wife,
5   The masters of some merchant, and the merchant,[2]
Have just our theme of woe. But for the miracle,
I mean our preservation, few in millions
Can speak like us. Then wisely, good sir, weigh
Our sorrow with our comfort.

ALONSO: Prithee, peace.

SEBASTIAN [*aside to Antonio*]:   He receives comfort like cold porridge.[3]

ANTONIO [*aside to Sebastian*]:   The visitor[4] will not give him o'er[5] so.

SEBASTIAN: Look, he's winding up the watch of his wit; by and by it will strike.

GONZALO [*to Alonso*]:   Sir—

SEBASTIAN [*aside to Antonio*]:   One. Tell.°   *keep count*

GONZALO: When every grief is entertained
That's offered, comes to th' entertainer—

SEBASTIAN: A dollar.[6]

GONZALO: Dolor comes to him, indeed. You have spoken truer than you purposed.

SEBASTIAN: You have taken it wiselier than I meant you should.

GONZALO [*to Alonso*]:   Therefore, my lord—

1. Location: Another part of the island.
2. Officers of some merchant vessel and the owner himself.
3. Broth, with a pun on *peace* (peas), often used in porridge.
4. One taking comfort to the sick, as Gonzalo is doing.
5. Let him alone.
6. Widely circulated coin. (Sebastian puns on *entertainer* in the sense of inn-keeper; to Gonzalo, *dollar* suggests "dolor," or grief.)

ANTONIO: Fie, what a spendthrift is he of his tongue!

ALONSO [*to Gonzalo*]: I prithee, spare.° *forbear*

GONZALO: Well, I have done. But yet—

SEBASTIAN [*aside to Antonio*]: He will be talking.

ANTONIO [*aside to Sebastian*]: Which, of he or Adrian, for a good wager, first begins to crow?[7]

SEBASTIAN: The old cock.° *Gonzalo*

ANTONIO: The cockerel.° *Adrian*

SEBASTIAN: Done. The wager?

ANTONIO: A laughter.[8]

SEBASTIAN: A match!° *agreed*

ADRIAN: Though this island seem to be desert°— *uninhabited*

ANTONIO: Ha, ha, ha!

SEBASTIAN: So, you're paid.

ADRIAN: Uninhabitable and almost inaccessible—

SEBASTIAN: Yet—

ADRIAN: Yet—

ANTONIO: He could not miss 't.

ADRIAN: It must needs be of subtle, tender, and delicate temperance.° *climate*

ANTONIO: Temperance° was a delicate wench.[9] *girl's name*

SEBASTIAN: Ay, and a subtle,° as he most learnedly delivered.[1] *sexually tricky*

ADRIAN: The air breathes upon us here most sweetly.

SEBASTIAN: As if it had lungs, and rotten ones.

ANTONIO: Or as 'twere perfumed by a fen.

GONZALO: Here is everything advantageous to life.

ANTONIO: True, save° means to live. *except*

SEBASTIAN: Of that there's none, or little.

GONZALO: How lush and lusty° the grass looks! How green! *healthy*

ANTONIO: The ground indeed is tawny.° *dull brown*

SEBASTIAN: With an eye° of green in 't. *spot*

ANTONIO: He misses not much.

SEBASTIAN: No. He doth but° mistake the truth totally. *merely*

GONZALO: But the rarity of it is—which is indeed almost beyond credit—

SEBASTIAN: As many vouched rarities[2] are.

GONZALO: That our garments, being, as they were, drenched in the sea, hold notwithstanding their freshness and glosses, being rather new-dyed than stained with salt water.

ANTONIO: If but one of his pockets[3] could speak, would it not say he lies?

SEBASTIAN: Ay, or very falsely pocket up[4] his report.

GONZALO: Methinks our garments are now as fresh as when we put them on first in Afric, at the marriage of the King's fair daughter Claribel to the King of Tunis.

SEBASTIAN: 'Twas a sweet marriage, and we prosper well in our return.

---

7. Speak.
8. Whoever laughs, wins.
9. Antonio is mocking Adrian's Puritan phrase, *tender, and delicate temperance,* by applying it to a young woman.
1. Puritan cant for "well-phrased." (Sebastian joins Antonio in baiting the Puritans.)
2. Wonders guaranteed to be true.
3. I.e., because they are muddy.
4. Suppress.

ADRIAN: Tunis was never graced before with such a paragon to[5] their queen.

GONZALO: Not since widow Dido's[6] time.

ANTONIO [*aside to Sebastian*]:   Widow? A pox o' that! How came that "widow" in? Widow Dido!

SEBASTIAN: What if he had said "widower Aeneas" too? Good Lord, how you take it!

ADRIAN [*to Gonzalo*]:   "Widow Dido" said you? You make me study of that. She was
70 of Carthage, not of Tunis.

GONZALO: This Tunis, sir, was Carthage.

ADRIAN: Carthage?

GONZALO: I assure you, Carthage.

ANTONIO: His word is more than the miraculous harp.[7]

SEBASTIAN: He hath raised the wall, and houses too.

ANTONIO: What impossible matter will he make easy next?

SEBASTIAN: I think he will carry this island home in his pocket and give it his son for an apple.

ANTONIO: And, sowing the kernels of it in the sea, bring forth more islands.

GONZALO: Ay.[8]

ANTONIO: Why, in good time.

GONZALO [*to Alonso*]:   Sir, we were talking that our garments seem now as fresh as when we were at Tunis at the marriage of your daughter, who is now queen.

ANTONIO: And the rarest that e'er came there.

SEBASTIAN: Bate,° I beseech you, widow Dido.   *except*

ANTONIO: O, widow Dido? Ay, widow Dido.

GONZALO: Is not, sir, my doublet as fresh as the first day I wore it? I mean, in a sort.[9]

ANTONIO: That "sort"[1] was well fished for.

GONZALO: When I wore it at your daughter's marriage.

ALONSO: You cram these words into mine ears against
     The stomach of my sense.[2] Would I had never
     Married° my daughter there! For, coming thence,   *married off*
     My son is lost and, in my rate,° she too,   *estimation*
     Who is so far from Italy removed
95 I ne'er again shall see her. O thou mine heir
     Of Naples and of Milan, what strange fish
     Hath made his meal on thee?

FRANCISCO: Sir, he may live.
     I saw him beat the surges° under him   *waves*
     And ride upon their backs. He trod the water,
100 Whose enmity he flung aside, and breasted
     The surge most swoll'n that met him. His bold head
     'Bove the contentious waves he kept, and oared
     Himself with his good arms in lusty stroke

5. For.

6. Queen of Carthage, deserted by Aeneas. (She was, in fact, a widow when Aeneas, a widower, met her, but Antonio may be amused at Gonzalo's prudish use of "widow" for a woman deserted by her lover.)

7. The harp of Amphion, which raised the walls of Thebes; Gonzalo has exceeded that deed by recreating ancient Carthage mistakenly on the site of modern-day Tunis.

8. This and Antonio's rejoinder have not been satisfactorily explained.

9. Comparatively.

1. Play on the idea of drawing lots, or else fishing for something to say.

2. My appetite to hear them.

To th' shore, that o'er his° wave-worn basis° bowed, *its / base*
105 As° stooping to relieve him. I not doubt *as if*
He came alive to land.

ALONSO:　　　　　　　　　No, no, he's gone.

SEBASTIAN [*to Alonso*]:　Sir, you may thank yourself for this great loss,
That° would not bless our Europe with your daughter, *you who*
But rather loose° her to an African, *release; lose*
110 Where she at least is banished from your eye,
Who hath cause to wet the grief on 't.

ALONSO:　　　　　　　　　Prithee, peace.

SEBASTIAN:　You were kneeled to and importuned otherwise
By all of us, and the fair soul herself
Weighed between loathness and obedience at
115 Which end o' the beam should bow.[3] We have lost your son,
I fear, forever. Milan and Naples have
More widows in them of this business' making
Than we bring men to comfort them.
The fault's your own.

ALONSO:　　　　　　　So is the dear'st° o' the loss. *heaviest*

GONZALO:　My lord Sebastian,
The truth you speak doth lack some gentleness
And time to speak it in. You rub the sore
When you should bring the plaster.° *bandage*

SEBASTIAN:　　　　　　　Very well.

ANTONIO:　And most chirurgeonly.° *like a surgeon*

GONZALO [*to Alonso*]:　It is foul weather in us all, good sir,
When you are cloudy.

SEBASTIAN [*to Antonio*]:　　　Fowl weather?

ANTONIO [*to Sebastian*]:　　　　　　Very foul.

GONZALO:　Had I plantation[4] of this isle, my lord—

ANTONIO [*to Sebastian*]:　He'd sow 't with nettle seed.

SEBASTIAN:　　　　　　　Or docks, or mallows.[5]

GONZALO:　And were the king on 't, what would I do?

SEBASTIAN:　Scape° being drunk for want° of wine. *escape / only for lack*

GONZALO:　I' the commonwealth I would by contraries[6]
Execute all things; for no kind of traffic° *trade*
Would I admit; no name of magistrate;
Letters° should not be known; riches, poverty, *learning*
135 And use of service,° none; contract, succession,° *servants / inheritance*
Bourn,° bound of land, tilth,° vineyard, none; *borders / tilled soil*
No use of metal, corn,° or wine, or oil; *grain*
No occupation; all men idle, all,
And women too, but innocent and pure;
No sovereignty—

SEBASTIAN:　　　　　　Yet he would be king on 't.

ANTONIO:　The latter end of his commonwealth forgets the beginning.

---

3. Which side of the moral scale was heavier.
4. Colonization; planting.
5. Antidotes to nettle stings.
6. In contrast to custom.

GONZALO: All things in common nature should produce
Without sweat or endeavor. Treason, felony,
Sword, pike,° knife, gun, or need of any engine°   lance / weapon
145 Would I not have; but nature should bring forth,
Of its own kind, all foison,° all abundance,   plenty
To feed my innocent people.
SEBASTIAN: No marrying 'mong his subjects?
ANTONIO: None, man, all idle—whores and knaves.
GONZALO: I would with such perfection govern, sir,
T' excel the Golden Age.[7]
SEBASTIAN: 'Save° His Majesty!   God save
ANTONIO: Long live Gonzalo!
GONZALO: And—do you mark me, sir?
ALONSO: Prithee, no more. Thou dost talk nothing to me.
GONZALO: I do well believe Your Highness, and did it to minister occasion[8] to these
155 gentlemen, who are of such sensible[9] and nimble lungs that they always use
to laugh at nothing.
ANTONIO: 'Twas you we laughed at.
GONZALO: Who in this kind of merry fooling am nothing to you; so you may con-
tinue, and laugh at nothing still.
ANTONIO: What a blow was there given!
SEBASTIAN: An[1] it had not fallen flat-long.[2]
GONZALO: You are gentlemen of brave mettle; you would lift the moon out of her
sphere if she would continue in it five weeks without changing.

[Enter Ariel (invisible) playing solemn music.]

SEBASTIAN: We would so, and then go a-batfowling.[3]
ANTONIO: Nay, good my lord, be not angry.
GONZALO: No, I warrant you, I will not adventure my discretion[4] so weakly. Will
you laugh me asleep? For I am very heavy.[5]
ANTONIO: Go sleep, and hear us.

[All sleep except Alonso, Sebastian, and Antonio.]

ALONSO: What, all so soon asleep? I wish mine eyes
Would, with themselves, shut up my thoughts. I find
They are inclined to do so.
SEBASTIAN: Please you, sir,
Do not omit° the heavy offer of it.   neglect
It seldom visits sorrow; when it doth,
It is a comforter.
ANTONIO: We two, my lord,
Will guard your person while you take your rest,
And watch your safety.

7. In Hesiod, an age of innocence and abundance.
8. Provide opportunity.
9. Sensitive.
1. If.
2. Fallen flat.
3. Hunting birds at night with sticks (bats); duping a fool (Gonzalo).
4. Risk my reputation for discretion.
5. Sleep.

ALONSO: Thank you. Wondrous heavy.

[Alonso sleeps. Exit Ariel.]

SEBASTIAN: What a strange drowsiness possesses them!

ANTONIO: It is the quality o' the climate.

SEBASTIAN: Why

180 Doth it not then our eyelids sink? I find not
Myself disposed to sleep.

ANTONIO: Nor I. My spirits are nimble.
They fell together all, as by consent;°   *agreement*
They dropped, as by a thunderstroke. What might,
Worthy Sebastian, O, what might—? No more.

185 And yet methinks I see it in thy face,
What thou shouldst be. Th' occasion speaks° thee, and   *summons*
My strong imagination sees a crown
Dropping upon thy head.

SEBASTIAN: What, art thou waking?

ANTONIO: Do you not hear me speak?

SEBASTIAN: I do, and surely

190 It is a sleepy language, and thou speak'st
Out of thy sleep. What is it thou didst say?
This is a strange repose, to be asleep
With eyes wide open—standing, speaking, moving—
And yet so fast asleep.

ANTONIO: Noble Sebastian,

195 Thou lett'st thy fortune sleep—die, rather; wink'st°   *shut your eyes*
Whiles thou art waking.

SEBASTIAN: Thou dost snore distinctly;°   *articulately*
There's meaning in thy snores.

ANTONIO: I am more serious than my custom. You
Must be so too if heed° me, which to do   *you heed*
Trebles thee o'er.[6]

SEBASTIAN: Well, I am standing water.

ANTONIO: I'll teach you how to flow.

SEBASTIAN: Do so. To ebb
Hereditary sloth[7] instructs me.

ANTONIO: O,
If you but knew how you the purpose cherish°   *enrich*
Whiles thus you mock it! How, in stripping it,

205 You more invest° it! Ebbing men, indeed,   *clothe*
Most often do so near the bottom run
By their own fear or sloth.

SEBASTIAN: Prithee, say on:
The setting° of thine eye and cheek proclaim   *expression*
A matter from thee, and a birth indeed

210 Which throes° thee much to yield.   *pains*

---

6. Will make you three times as powerful.

7. Natural laziness; the position of younger son.

ANTONIO: Thus, sir:

Although this lord of weak remembrance,° this   *memory*

Who shall be of as little memory°   *as little remembered*

When he is earthed,° hath here almost persuaded—   *buried*

For he's a spirit of persuasion, only

215   Professes° to persuade—the King his son's alive,   *functions*

'Tis as impossible that he's undrowned

As he that sleeps here swims.

SEBASTIAN: I have no hope

That he's undrowned.

ANTONIO: O, out of that "no hope"

What great hope have you! No hope that way is

220   Another way so high a hope that even

Ambition cannot pierce a wink° beyond,   *glimpse*

But doubt discovery there. Will you grant with me

That Ferdinand is drowned?

SEBASTIAN: He's gone.

ANTONIO: Then tell me,

Who's the next heir of Naples?

SEBASTIAN: Claribel.

ANTONIO: She that is Queen of Tunis; she that dwells

Ten leagues beyond man's life; she that from Naples

Can have no note,° unless the sun were post°—   *news / messenger*

The Man i' the Moon's too slow—till newborn chins

Be rough and razorable; she that from° whom   *leaving*

230   We all were sea-swallowed, though some cast⁸ again,

And by that destiny to perform an act

Whereof what's past is prologue, what to come

In yours and my discharge.°   *business*

SEBASTIAN: What stuff is this? How say you?

'Tis true my brother's daughter's Queen of Tunis,

235   So is she heir of Naples, twixt which regions

There is some space.

ANTONIO: A space whose every cubit°   *unit of length*

Seems to cry out, "How shall that Claribel

Measure us° back to Naples? Keep in Tunis,   *the cubits*

And let Sebastian wake." Say this were death

240   That now hath seized them, why, they were no worse

Than now they are. There be that can rule Naples

As well as he that sleeps, lords that can prate°   *prattle*

As amply and unnecessarily

As this Gonzalo. I myself could make

245   A chough° of as deep chat. O, that you bore   *jackdaw*

The mind that I do! What a sleep were this

For your advancement! Do you understand me?

SEBASTIAN: Methinks I do.

---

8. Thrown up; cast, as in a play.

ANTONIO: And how does your content° desire
    Tender° your own good fortune? regard

SEBASTIAN: I remember
250   You did supplant your brother Prospero.

ANTONIO: True.
    And look how well my garments sit upon me,
    Much feater° than before. My brother's servants more suitably
    Were then my fellows.° Now they are my men.° equals / servants

SEBASTIAN: But, for your conscience?

ANTONIO: Ay, sir, where lies that? If 'twere a kibe,° sore on the heel
    'Twould put me to° my slipper; but I feel not make me wear
    This deity in my bosom. Twenty consciences
    That stand twixt me and Milan, candied° be they sugared
    And melt ere they molest!° Here lies your brother, interfere
260   No better than the earth he lies upon,
    If he were that which now he's like—that's dead,
    Whom I, with this obedient steel, three inches of it,
    Can lay to bed forever; whiles you, doing thus,
    To the perpetual wink° for aye° might put sleep / ever
265   This ancient morsel, this Sir Prudence, who
    Should not° upbraid our course. For all the rest, would not be able to
    They'll take° suggestion as a cat laps milk; respond to
    They'll tell the clock° to any business that chime in
    We say befits the hour.

SEBASTIAN: Thy case, dear friend,
270   Shall be my precedent. As thou gott'st Milan,
    I'll come by Naples. Draw thy sword. One stroke
    Shall free thee from the tribute which thou payest,
    And I the king shall love thee.

ANTONIO: Draw together;
    And when I rear my hand, do you the like
    To fall it° on Gonzalo. [*They draw.*] let it fall

SEBASTIAN: O, but one word. [*They talk apart.*]

[*Enter Ariel (invisible), with music and song.*]

ARIEL [*to Gonzalo*]:   My master through his art foresees the danger
    That you, his friend, are in, and sends me forth—
    For else his project dies—to keep them living.

[*Sings in Gonzalo's ear.*]

            While you here do snoring lie,
280   *Open-eyed conspiracy*
                His time°doth take. opportunity
             If of life you keep a care,
             Shake off slumber, and beware.
                Awake, awake!

ANTONIO: Then let us both be sudden.° quick

GONZALO [*waking*]:   Now, good angels preserve the King!

[*The others wake.*]

ALONSO: Why, how now, ho, awake? Why are you drawn?
     Wherefore this ghastly looking?

GONZALO: What's the matter?

SEBASTIAN: Whiles we stood here securing° your repose,   *guarding*
290   Even now, we heard a hollow burst of bellowing
     Like bulls, or rather lions. Did 't not wake you?
     It struck mine ear most terribly.

ALONSO: I heard nothing.

ANTONIO: O, 'twas a din to fright a monster's ear,
     To make an earthquake! Sure it was the roar
     Of a whole herd of lions.

ALONSO: Heard you this, Gonzalo?

GONZALO: Upon mine honor, sir, I heard a humming,
     And that a strange one too, which did awake me.
     I shaked you, sir, and cried. As mine eyes opened,
     I saw their weapons drawn. There was a noise,
300   That's verily.° 'Tis best we stand upon our guard,   *true*
     Or that we quit this place. Let's draw our weapons.

ALONSO: Lead off this ground, and let's make further search
     For my poor son.

GONZALO: Heavens keep him from these beasts!
     For he is, sure, i' th' island.

ALONSO: Lead away.

ARIEL [*aside*]: Prospero my lord shall know what I have done.
     So, King, go safely on to seek thy son.

[*Exeunt (separately).*]

Scene 2[9]

[*Enter Caliban with a burden of wood. A noise of thunder heard.*]

CALIBAN: All the infections that the sun sucks up
     From bogs, fens, flats,° on Prosper fall, and make him   *swamps*
     By inchmeal° a disease! His spirits hear me,   *inch by inch*
     And yet I needs must° curse. But they'll nor° pinch,   *have to / neither*
5   Fright me with urchin shows,° pitch me i' the mire,   *hedgehog goblins*
     Nor lead me, like a firebrand,[1] in the dark
     Out of my way, unless he bid 'em. But
     For every trifle are they set upon me,
     Sometimes like apes, that mow° and chatter at me   *make faces*
10   And after bite me; then like hedgehogs, which
     Lie tumbling in my barefoot way and mount
     Their pricks at my footfall. Sometimes am I
     All wound with adders, who with cloven tongues
     Do hiss me into madness.

[*Enter Trinculo.*]

9. Location: another part of the island.
1. In the form of a will-'o-th'-wisp, a light that appears at night over marshy ground, often a metaphor for false hope.

Lo, now, lo!
Here comes a spirit of his, and to torment me
For bringing wood in slowly. I'll fall flat.
Perchance he will not mind° me. [*He lies down.*] notice

TRINCULO: Here's neither bush nor shrub to bear off[2] any weather at all. And another
20 storm brewing; I hear it sing i' the wind. Yond same black cloud, yond huge
one, looks like a foul bombard[3] that would shed his[4] liquor. If it should
thunder as it did before, I know not where to hide my head. Yond same
cloud cannot choose but fall by pailfuls. [*Seeing Caliban.*] What have we
here, a man or a fish? Dead or alive? A fish, he smells like a fish; a very
25 ancient and fishlike smell; a kind of not-of-the-newest poor-John.[5] A
strange fish! Were I in England now, as once I was, and had but this fish
painted,[6] not a holiday fool there but would give a piece of silver. There
would this monster make a man.[7] Any strange beast there makes a man.
When they will not give a doit[8] to relieve a lame beggar, they will lay out
30 ten to see a dead Indian. Legged like a man, and his fins like arms! Warm, o'
my troth! I do now let loose my opinion, hold it no longer: this is no fish, but
an islander, that hath lately suffered[9] by a thunderbolt. [*Thunder.*] Alas, the
storm is come again! My best way is to creep under his gaberdine.[1] There is
no other shelter hereabout. Misery acquaints a man with strange bedfel-
35 lows. I will here shroud[2] till the dregs of the storm be past. [*He creeps under
Caliban's garment.*]

[*Enter Stephano, singing, (a bottle in his hand).*]

STEPHANO: "I shall no more to sea, to sea,
        Here shall I die ashore—"
This is a very scurvy tune to sing at a man's funeral.
Well, here's my comfort. [*Drinks.*]

[*Sings.*]

40   "*The master, the swabber, the boatswain, and I,*
            The gunner and his mate,
        Loved Mall, Meg, and Marian, and Margery,
            But none of us cared for Kate.
            For she had a tongue with a tang,
45   *Would cry to a sailor, 'Go hang!'*
        She loved not the savor of tar nor of pitch,
        Yet a tailor might scratch her where'er she did itch.
            Then to sea, boys, and let her go hang!"

This is a scurvy tune too. But here's my comfort. [*Drinks.*]

2. Ward off.
3. Leather bottle.
4. Its.
5. Salted fish.
6. Painted on a sign outside a booth at a fair.
7. Make a man's fortune; be indistinguishible from an Englishman.
8. Small coin.
9. Died.
1. Cloak.
2. Take shelter.

CALIBAN: Do not torment me! O!

STEPHANO: What's the matter?[3] Have we devils here? Do you put tricks upon 's with savages and men of Ind,[4] ha? I have not scaped drowning to be afeard now of your four legs. For it hath been said, "As proper[5] a man as ever went on four[6] legs cannot make him give ground"; and it shall be said so again
55 while Stephano breathes at' nostrils.

CALIBAN: This spirit torments me! O!

STEPHANO: This is some monster of the isle with four legs, who hath got, as I take it, an ague. Where the devil should he learn[7] our language? I will give him some relief, if it be but for that.[8] If I can recover[9] him and keep him tame
60 and get to Naples with him, he's a present for any emperor that ever trod on neat's leather.[1]

CALIBAN: Do not torment me, prithee. I'll bring my wood home faster.

STEPHANO: He's in his fit now and does not talk after the wisest. He shall taste of my bottle. If he have never drunk wine afore, it will go near to remove his
65 fit. If I can recover him and keep him tame, I will not take too much[2] for him. He shall pay for him that hath him, and that soundly.

CALIBAN: Thou dost me yet but little hurt; thou wilt anon,[3] I know it by thy trembling. Now Prosper works upon thee.

STEPHANO: Come on your ways. Open your mouth. Here is that which will give
70 language to you, cat.[4] Open your mouth. This will shake your shaking, I can tell you, and that soundly. [*Giving Caliban a drink.*] You cannot tell who's your friend. Open your chaps[5] again.

TRINCULO: I should know that voice. It should be—but he is drowned, and these are devils. O, defend me!

STEPHANO: Four legs and two voices—a most delicate[6] monster! His forward voice now is to speak well of his friend; his backward voice is to utter foul speeches and to detract. If all the wine in my bottle will recover him, I will help[7] his ague. Come. [*Giving a drink.*] Amen! I will pour some in thy other mouth.

TRINCULO: Stephano!

STEPHANO: Doth thy other mouth call me?[8] Mercy, mercy! This is a devil, and no monster. I will leave him. I have no long spoon.[9]

TRINCULO: Stephano! If thou beest Stephano, touch me and speak to me, for I am Trinculo—be not afeard—thy good friend Trinculo.

3. What's going on here?
4. India.
5. Handsome.
6. The expression supplies *two* legs, but Stephano thinks he sees a creature with four.
7. Could he have learned.
8. His speaking our language.
9. Restore.
1. Cowhide.
2. No price will be too much.
3. Presently.
4. Allusion to the proverb "Liquor will make a cat talk."
5. Jaws.
6. Ingenious.
7. Cure.
8. Call my name (know who I am).
9. Allusion to the proverb "He who sups with the devil must have a long spoon."

6

STEPHANO: If thou beest Trinculo, come forth. I'll pull thee by the lesser legs. If
85   any be Trinculo's legs, these are they. [*Pulling him out.*] Thou art very Tr-
            inculo indeed! How cam'st thou to be the siege[1] of this mooncalf?[2] Can he
            vent[3] Trinculos?

TRINCULO: I took him to be killed with a thunderstroke. But art thou not drowned,
            Stephano? I hope now thou art not drowned. Is the storm overblown?[4]
90   I hid me under the dead mooncalf's gaberdine for fear of the storm. And
            art thou living, Stephano? O Stephano, two Neapolitans scaped! [*He capers
            with Stephano.*]

STEPHANO: Prithee, do not turn me about. My stomach is not constant.[5]

CALIBAN: These be fine things, an if[6] they be not spirits.
95   That's a brave[7] god, and bears celestial liquor.
            I will kneel to him.

STEPHANO: How didst thou scape? How cam'st thou hither? Swear by this bot-
            tle how thou cam'st hither. I escaped upon a butt of sack[8] which the sailors
            heaved o'erboard—by this bottle, which I made of the bark of a tree with
100   mine own hands since I was cast ashore.

CALIBAN [*kneeling*]:   I'll swear upon that bottle to be thy true subject, for the liquor
            is not earthly.

STEPHANO: Here. Swear then how thou escapedst.

TRINCULO: Swum ashore, man, like a duck. I can swim like a duck, I'll be sworn.

STEPHANO: Here, kiss the book.[9] Though thou canst swim like a duck, thou art
            made like a goose.[1] [*Giving him a drink.*]

TRINCULO: O Stephano, hast any more of this?

STEPHANO: The whole butt, man. My cellar is in a rock by the seaside, where my
            wine is hid.—How now, mooncalf? How does thine ague?

CALIBAN: Hast thou not dropped from heaven?

STEPHANO: Out o' the moon, I do assure thee. I was the Man i' the Moon when
            time was.[2]

CALIBAN: I have seen thee in her, and I do adore thee.
            My mistress showed me thee, and thy dog, and thy bush.[3]

STEPHANO: Come, swear to that. Kiss the book. I will furnish it anon with new
            contents. Swear. [*Giving him a drink.*]

TRINCULO: By this good light, this is a very shallow monster! I afeard of him? A
            very weak monster! The Man i' the Moon? A most poor credulous monster!
            Well drawn,[4] monster, in good sooth!

1. Excrement.
2. Monster.
3. Excrete.
4. Blown over.
5. Unsteady.
6. If.
7. Magnificent.
8. Barrel of Canary wine.
9. I.e., the bottle (ironic allusion to swearing on the Bible).
1. With a long neck.
2. Once upon a time.
3. The Man in the Moon was popularly imagined to have with him a dog and a thorn-bush.
4. Drawn from the bottle.

CALIBAN [to Stephano]:   I'll show thee every fertile inch o' th' island,
       And I will kiss thy foot. I prithee, be my god.
TRINCULO: By this light, a most perfidious and drunken monster! When 's god's
       asleep, he'll rob his bottle.
CALIBAN: I'll kiss thy foot. I'll swear myself thy subject.
STEPHANO: Come on then. Down, and swear.

       [Caliban kneels.]

TRINCULO: I shall laugh myself to death at this puppy-headed monster. A most
       scurvy monster! I could find in my heart to beat him—
STEPHANO: Come, kiss.
TRINCULO: But that the poor monster's in drink.[5] An abominable monster!
CALIBAN: I'll show thee the best springs. I'll pluck thee berries.
       I'll fish for thee and get thee wood enough.
       A plague upon the tyrant that I serve!
       I'll bear him no more sticks, but follow thee,
       Thou wondrous man.
TRINCULO: A most ridiculous monster, to make a wonder of a poor drunkard!
CALIBAN: I prithee, let me bring thee where crabs° grow,   crab apples
       And I with my long nails will dig thee pignuts,°   peanuts
       Show thee a jay's nest, and instruct thee how
       To snare the nimble marmoset.° I'll bring thee   small monkey
140   To clustering filberts, and sometimes I'll get thee
       Young scamels[6] from the rock. Wilt thou go with me?
STEPHANO: I prithee now, lead the way without any more talking.—Trinculo, the
       King and all our company else being drowned, we will inherit[7] here.—Here,
       bear my bottle.—Fellow Trinculo, we'll fill him by and by[8] again.
CALIBAN [sings drunkenly]:   Farewell, master, farewell, farewell!
TRINCULO: A howling monster; a drunken monster!

CALIBAN: No more dams I'll make for fish,
                                  Nor fetch in firing°   firewood
                                  At requiring,
150   Nor scrape trenchering,°nor wash dish.   wooden plates
                                  'Ban, 'Ban, Ca-Caliban
                                  Has a new master. Get a new man!°   servant

       Freedom, high-day![9] High-day, freedom! Freedom, high-day, freedom!
STEPHANO: O brave monster! Lead the way. [Exeunt.]

                                  Act 3

                                 Scene 1[1]

       [Enter Ferdinand, bearing a log.]

FERDINAND: There be some sports are painful,° and their labor   strenuous
       Delight in them sets off.° Some kinds of baseness   compensates

5. Drunk.
6. Unexplained, but either a shellfish or a rock-nesting bird.
7. Take possession.
8. Soon.
9. Holiday.
1. Location: Before Prospero's cell.

Are nobly undergone, and most poor matters°   *poorest affairs*
Point to rich ends. This my mean° task   *lowly*
5   Would be as heavy to me as odious, but°   *but that*
The mistress which I serve quickens° what's dead   *brings to life*
And makes my labors pleasures. O, she is
Ten times more gentle than her father's crabbed,
And he's composed of harshness. I must remove
10 Some thousands of these logs and pile them up,
Upon a sore injunction.° My sweet mistress   *severe command*
Weeps when she sees me work and says such baseness
Had never like executor. I forget;
But these sweet thoughts do even refresh my labors,
Most busy lest[2] when I do it.

[*Enter Miranda; and Prospero (at a distance, unseen).*]

MIRANDA: Alas now, pray you,
Work not so hard. I would the lightning had
Burnt up those logs that you are enjoined° to pile!   *commanded*
Pray, set it down and rest you. When this burns,
'Twill weep° for having wearied you. My father   *exude resin*
20 Is hard at study. Pray now, rest yourself.
He's safe for these three hours.

FERDINAND: O most dear mistress,
The sun will set before I shall discharge
What I must strive to do.

MIRANDA: If you'll sit down,
I'll bear your logs the while. Pray, give me that.
I'll carry it to the pile.

FERDINAND: No, precious creature,
I had rather crack my sinews, break my back,
Than you should such dishonor undergo
While I sit lazy by.

MIRANDA: It would become me
As well as it does you; and I should do it
30 With much more ease, for my good will is to it,
And yours it is against.

PROSPERO [*aside*]:   Poor worm, thou art infected!
This visitation[3] shows it.

MIRANDA: You look wearily.

FERDINAND: No, noble mistress, 'tis fresh morning with me
When you are by° at night. I do beseech you—   *nearby*
35 Chiefly that I might set it in my prayers—
What is your name?

MIRANDA: Miranda.—O my father,
I have broke your hest° to say so.   *command*

FERDINAND: Admired Miranda![4]

2. Busy, but with my mind on other things.
3. Visit; attack of plague (in the metaphor of *infected*).
4. Her name means "to be admired or wondered at."

Indeed the top of admiration, worth
What's dearest to the world! Full many a lady

40   I have eyed with best regard, and many a time
The harmony of their tongues hath into bondage
Brought my too diligent° ear. For several° virtues   *attentive / different*
Have I liked several women, never any
With so full soul° but some defect in her   *so wholeheartedly*

45   Did quarrel with the noblest grace she owed°   *owned*
And put it to the foil.⁵ But you, O you,
So perfect and so peerless, are created
Of every creature's best!

MIRANDA: I do not know
One of my sex; no woman's face remember,

50   Save, from my glass, mine own. Nor have I seen
More that I may call men than you, good friend,
And my dear father. How features are abroad°   *elsewhere*
I am skilless° of; but, by my modesty,°   *ignorant / virginity*
The jewel in my dower, I would not wish

55   Any companion in the world but you;
Nor can imagination form a shape,
Besides yourself, to like of.° But I prattle   *care for*
Something° too wildly, and my father's precepts   *somewhat*
I therein do forget.

FERDINAND: I am in my condition°   *rank*

60   A prince, Miranda; I do think, a king—
I would,° not so!—and would no more endure   *wish*
This wooden slavery than to suffer
The flesh-fly⁶ blow° my mouth. Hear my soul speak: *lay eggs*
The very instant that I saw you did

65   My heart fly to your service, there resides
To make me slave to it, and for your sake
Am I this patient log-man.

MIRANDA: Do you love me?

FERDINAND: O heaven, O earth, bear witness to this sound,
And crown what I profess with kind event°   *favorable outcome*

70   If I speak true! If hollowly,° invert°   *falsely / turn*
What best is boded° me to mischief!° I   *in store for / harm*
Beyond all limit of what else i' the world
Do love, prize, honor you.

MIRANDA [*weeping*]:   I am a fool
To weep at what I am glad of.

PROSPERO [*aside*]:   Fair encounter

75   Of two most rare affections! Heavens rain grace
On that which breeds between 'em!

FERDINAND: Wherefore weep you?

MIRANDA: At mine unworthiness, that dare not offer

---

5. Overthrow; contrast.

6. Insect that lays eggs in dead flesh.

What I desire to give, and much less take
What I shall die[7] to want.° But this is trifling,   *lack*
80 And all the more it seeks to hide itself
The bigger bulk it shows. Hence, bashful cunning,°   *coyness*
And prompt me, plain and holy innocence!
I am your wife, if you will marry me;
If not, I'll die your maid.[8] To be your fellow°   *equal*
85 You may deny me, but I'll be your servant
Whether you will° or no.   *desire it*

FERDINAND: My mistress, dearest,
And I thus humble ever.

MIRANDA: My husband, then?

FERDINAND: Ay, with a heart as willing
90 As bondage e'er of freedom.° Here's my hand.   *to win freedom*

MIRANDA [*clasping his hand*]:
And mine, with my heart in 't. And now farewell
Till half an hour hence.

FERDINAND: A thousand thousand!°   *farewells*

        [*Exeunt (Ferdinand and Miranda, separately).*]

PROSPERO: So glad of this as they I cannot be,
Who are surprised with all; but my rejoicing
95 At nothing can be more. I'll to my book,
For yet ere suppertime must I perform
Much business appertaining.°   *relevant*

        [*Exit.*]

Scene 2[9]

[*Enter Caliban, Stephano, and Trinculo.*]

STEPHANO: Tell not me. When the butt is out,[1] we will drink water, not a drop before. Therefore bear up and board 'em.[2] Servant monster, drink to me.

TRINCULO: Servant monster? The folly of this island! They say there's but five upon this isle. We are three of them; if th' other two be brained[3] like us, the state
5 totters.

STEPHANO: Drink, servant monster, when I bid thee. Thy eyes are almost set[4] in thy head. [*Giving a drink.*]

TRINCULO: Where should they be set[5] else? He were a brave[6] monster indeed if they were set in his tail.

7. Probably with unconscious sexual meaning.
8. Servant; virgin.
9. Location: Another part of the island.
1. Empty.
2. Drink up (using the language of a nautical assault).
3. Have brains.
4. Sunk, like the sun.
5. Placed.
6. Fine.

STEPHANO: My man-monster hath drowned his tongue in sack. For my part, the sea cannot drown me. I swam, ere I could recover[7] the shore, five and thirty leagues off and on. By this light, thou shalt be my lieutenant, monster, or my standard.[8]

TRINCULO: Your lieutenant, if you list;[9] he's no standard.[1]

STEPHANO: We'll not run,[2] Monsieur Monster.

TRINCULO: Nor go[3] neither, but you'll lie[4] like dogs and yet say nothing neither.

STEPHANO: Mooncalf, speak once in thy life, if thou beest a good mooncalf.

CALIBAN: How does thy honor? Let me lick thy shoe.
I'll not serve him. He is not valiant.

TRINCULO: Thou liest, most ignorant monster, I am in case[5] to jostle a constable. Why, thou debauched fish, thou, was there ever man a coward that hath drunk so much sack[6] as I today? Wilt thou tell a monstrous lie, being but half a fish and half a monster?

CALIBAN: Lo, how he mocks me! Wilt thou let him, my lord?

TRINCULO: "Lord," quoth he? That a monster should be such a natural![7]

CALIBAN: Lo, lo, again! Bite him to death, I prithee.

STEPHANO: Trinculo, keep a good tongue in your head. If you prove a mutineer—the next tree![8] The poor monster's my subject, and he shall not suffer indignity.

CALIBAN: I thank my noble lord. Wilt thou be pleased
To hearken once again to the suit I made to thee?

STEPHANO: Marry, will I. Kneel and repeat it. I will stand, and so shall Trinculo.

[*Caliban kneels.*]

[*Enter Ariel, invisible.*]

CALIBAN: As I told thee before, I am subject to a tyrant,
A sorcerer, that by his cunning hath
35　　Cheated me of the island.

ARIEL [*mimicking Trinculo*]: Thou liest.

CALIBAN: Thou liest, thou jesting monkey, thou!
I would my valiant master would destroy thee.
I do not lie.

STEPHANO: Trinculo, if you trouble him any more in 's tale, by this hand, I will supplant[9] some of your teeth.

TRINCULO: Why, I said nothing.

STEPHANO: Mum, then, and no more.—Proceed.

CALIBAN: I say by sorcery he got this isle;

7. Reach.
8. Standard-bearer.
9. Prefer.
1. Not able to stand up.
2. Retreat; urinate.
3. Walk.
4. Tell lies; lie down; excrete.
5. Fit condition.
6. Spanish white wine.
7. Fool; as opposed to "unnatural."
8. I.e., you'll hang.
9. Remove.

45	From me he got it. If thy greatness will	
	Revenge it on him—for I know thou dar'st,	
	But this thing° dare not—	*Trinculo*
STEPHANO:	That's most certain.	
CALIBAN:	Thou shalt be lord of it, and I'll serve thee.	
STEPHANO:	How now shall this be compassed? Canst thou bring me to the party?[1]	
CALIBAN:	Yea, yea, my lord. I'll yield him thee asleep,	
	Where thou mayst knock a nail into his head.	
ARIEL:	Thou liest; thou canst not.	
CALIBAN:	What a pied ninny's° this! Thou scurvy patch!°—	*motley fool / clown*
55	I do beseech thy greatness, give him blows	
	And take his bottle from him. When that's gone	
	He shall drink naught but brine, for I'll not show him	
	Where the quick freshes° are.	*freshwater springs*
STEPHANO:	Trinculo, run into no further danger. Interrupt the monster one word	
60	further and, by this hand, I'll turn my mercy out o' doors and make a stock-fish[2] of thee.	
TRINCULO:	Why, what did I? I did nothing. I'll go farther off.	
STEPHANO:	Didst thou not say he lied?	
ARIEL:	Thou liest.	
STEPHANO:	Do I so? Take thou that. [*He beats Trinculo.*] As you like this, give me the lie[3] another time.	
TRINCULO:	I did not give the lie. Out o' your wits and hearing too? A pox o' your bottle! This can sack and drinking do. A murrain[4] on your monster, and the devil take your fingers!	
CALIBAN:	Ha, ha, ha!	
STEPHANO:	Now, forward with your tale. [*To Trinculo.*] Prithee, stand further off.	
CALIBAN:	Beat him enough. After a little time	
	I'll beat him too.	
STEPHANO:	Stand farther.—Come, proceed.	
CALIBAN:	Why, as I told thee, 'tis a custom with him	
	I' th' afternoon to sleep. There thou mayst brain him,	
	Having first seized his books; or with a log	
	Batter his skull, or paunch° him with a stake,	*stab in the belly*
	Or cut his weasand° with thy knife. Remember	*windpipe*
80	First to possess his books, for without them	
	He's but a sot,° as I am, nor hath not	*fool*
	One spirit to command. They all do hate him	
	As rootedly as I. Burn but his books.	
	He has brave utensils°—for so he calls them—	*furnishings*
85	Which, when he has a house, he'll deck withal.°	*furnish with them*
	And that most deeply to consider is	
	The beauty of his daughter. He himself	
	Calls her a nonpareil. I never saw a woman	
	But only Sycorax my dam and she;	

1. Person.
2. Dried cod, prepared by beating.
3. Call me a liar.
4. Cattle disease.

90 But she as far surpasseth Sycorax	
As great'st does least.	

STEPHANO: Is it so brave° a lass?   *splendid*

CALIBAN: Ay, lord. She will become° thy bed, I warrant,   *suit (sexually)*
         And bring thee forth brave brood.

STEPHANO: Monster, I will kill this man. His daughter and I will be king and
95   queen—save Our Graces!—and Trinculo and thyself shall be viceroys. Dost
     thou like the plot, Trinculo?

TRINCULO: Excellent.

STEPHANO: Give me thy hand. I am sorry I beat thee; but, while thou liv'st, keep a
     good tongue in thy head.

CALIBAN: Within this half hour will he be asleep.
         Wilt thou destroy him then?

STEPHANO: Ay, on mine honor.

ARIEL [*aside*]:   This will I tell my master.

CALIBAN: Thou mak'st me merry; I am full of pleasure.
         Let us be jocund. Will you troll the catch°   *sing the song*
105   You taught me but whilere?°   *just now*

STEPHANO: At thy request, monster, I will do reason, any reason.[5]—
         Come on, Trinculo, let us sing. [*Sings.*]

                "Flout° 'em and scout° 'em   *scoff at / deride*
                And scout 'em and flout 'em!
110   Thought is free."

CALIBAN: That's not the tune.

     [*Ariel plays the tune on a tabor° and pipe.*]   *small drum*

STEPHANO: What is this same?

TRINCULO: This is the tune of our catch, played by the picture of Nobody.[6]

STEPHANO: If thou beest a man, show thyself in thy likeness. If thou beest a devil,
115   take 't as thou list.[7]

TRINCULO: O, forgive me my sins!

STEPHANO: He that dies pays all debts. I defy thee. Mercy upon us!

CALIBAN: Art thou afeard?

STEPHANO: No, monster, not I.

CALIBAN: Be not afeard. The isle is full of noises,
         Sounds, and sweet airs, that give delight and hurt not.
         Sometimes a thousand twangling instruments
         Will hum about mine ears, and sometimes voices
         That, if I then had waked after long sleep,
125   Will make me sleep again; and then, in dreaming,
         The clouds methought would open and show riches
         Ready to drop upon me, that when I waked
         I cried to dream again.

STEPHANO: This will prove a brave kingdom to me, where I shall have my music
130   for nothing.

5. Anything reasonable.
6. Familiar image with head, arms, legs, but no trunk.
7. Suit yourself.

CALIBAN: When Prospero is destroyed.

STEPHANO: That shall be by and by.° I remember the story. *right away*

TRINCULO: The sound is going away. Let's follow it, and after do our work.

STEPHANO: Lead, monster; we'll follow. I would I could see this taborer! He lays
135   it on.[8]

TRINCULO: Wilt come? I'll follow, Stephano.

[Exeunt (following Ariel's music).]

Scene 3[9]

[Enter Alonso, Sebastian, Antonio, Gonzalo, Adrian, Francisco, etc.]

GONZALO: By'r lakin,[1] I can go no further, sir.
    My old bones aches. Here's a maze trod indeed
    Through forthrights° and meanders! By your patience, *straight paths*
    I needs must rest me.

ALONSO: Old lord, I cannot blame thee,
5   Who am myself attached° with weariness, *seized*
    To th' dulling of my spirits. Sit down and rest.
    Even here I will put off my hope, and keep it
    No longer for° my flatterer. He is drowned *as*
    Whom thus we stray to find, and the sea mocks
10   Our frustrate° search on land. Well, let him go. *frustrated*

[*Alonso and Gonzalo sit.*]

ANTONIO [*aside to Sebastian*]:   I am right glad that he's so out of hope.
    Do not, for° one repulse, forgo the purpose *because of*
    That you resolved t' effect.

SEBASTIAN [*to Antonio*]:   The next advantage
    Will we take throughly.° *thoroughly*

ANTONIO [*to Sebastian*]:   Let it be tonight,
15   For, now they are oppressed with travel, they
    Will not, nor cannot, use such vigilance
    As when they are fresh.

SEBASTIAN [*to Antonio*]:   I say tonight. No more.

[*Solemn and strange music; and Prospero on the top,[2] invisible.*]

ALONSO: What harmony is this? My good friends, hark!

GONZALO: Marvelous sweet music!

[*Enter several strange shapes, bringing in a banquet, and dance about it with gentle actions of salutations; and, inviting the King, etc., to eat, they depart.*]

ALONSO: Give us kind keepers,° heavens! What were these? *guardian angels*

SEBASTIAN: A living drollery.[3] Now I will believe
    That there are unicorns; that in Arabia

---

8. I.e., plays the drum vigorously.
9. Location: Another part of the island.
1. By our Ladykin (Virgin Mary).
2. An upper level of the theater.
3. Puppet show with live actors.

There is one tree, the phoenix' throne, one phoenix
At this hour reigning there.

ANTONIO: I'll believe both;
25   And what does else want credit,° come to me   *lack credibility*
And I'll be sworn 'tis true. Travelers ne'er did lie,
Though fools at home condemn 'em.

GONZALO: If in Naples
I should report this now, would they believe me
If I should say I saw such islanders?
30   For, certes,° these are people of the island,   *certainly*
Who, though they are of monstrous shape, yet note,
Their manners are more gentle, kind, than of
Our human generation you shall find
Many, nay, almost any.

PROSPERO [*aside*]:   Honest lord,
35   Thou hast said well, for some of you there present
Are worse than devils.

ALONSO: I cannot too much muse
Such shapes, such gesture, and such sound, expressing—
Although they want° the use of tongue—a kind   *lack*
Of excellent dumb discourse.

PROSPERO [*aside*]:   Praise in departing.[4]

FRANCISCO: They vanished strangely.

SEBASTIAN: No matter, since
They have left their viands° behind, for we have stomachs.°   *food / appetites*
Will't please you taste of what is here?

ALONSO: Not I.

GONZALO: Faith, sir, you need not fear. When we were boys,
Who would believe that there were mountaineers
45   Dewlapped[5] like bulls, whose throats had hanging at 'em
Wallets° of flesh? Or that there were such men   *wattles*
Whose heads stood in their breasts?[6] Which now we find
Each putter-out of five for one[7] will bring us
Good warrant of.

ALONSO: I will stand to° and feed,   *take the risk*
50   Although my last[8]—no matter, since I feel
The best is past. Brother, my lord the Duke,
Stand to, and do as we. [*They approach the table.*]

[*Thunder and lightning. Enter Ariel, like a harpy,[9] claps his wings upon the table,
and with a quaint[1] device the banquet[2] vanishes.*]

4. Save your praise for the end of the performance (proverbial).
5. With folds of flesh at the neck.
6. Like the Anthropophagi described in *Othello* 1.3.146.
7. Traveler whose insurance policy guarantees five to one repayment on his return.
8. Even if this were my last meal.
9. Monster with a woman's face and breasts and a vulture's body, supposed to bring divine vengeance.
1. Ingenious.
2. The food only.

ARIEL: You are three men of sin, whom Destiny—
          That hath to° instrument this lower world   *as its*
55   And what is in 't—the never-surfeited sea
          Hath caused to belch up you, and on this island
          Where man doth not inhabit, you 'mongst men
          Being most unfit to live. I have made you mad;
          And even with suchlike valor men hang and drown
          Their proper° selves.   *own*

[*Alonso, Sebastian, and Antonio draw their swords.*]

60   You fools! I and my fellows
          Are ministers of Fate. The elements
          Of whom° your swords are tempered° may as well   *which / composed*
          Wound the loud winds, or with bemocked-at° stabs   *scorned*
          Kill the still-closing° waters, as diminish   *ever-closing*
65   One dowl° that's in my plume. My fellow ministers   *feather*
          Are like° invulnerable. If you could hurt,   *likewise*
          Your swords are now too massy° for your strengths   *massive*
          And will not be uplifted. But remember—
          For that's my business to you—that you three
70   From Milan did supplant good Prospero;
          Exposed unto the sea, which hath requit° it,   *avenged*
          Him and his innocent child; for which foul deed
          The powers, delaying, not forgetting, have
          Incensed the seas and shores, yea, all the creatures,
75   Against your peace. Thee of thy son, Alonso,
          They have bereft; and do pronounce by me
          Ling'ring perdition,° worse than any death   *ruin*
          Can be at once, shall step by step attend
          You and your ways; whose wraths to guard you from—
80   Which here, in this most desolate isle, else° falls   *or else*
          Upon your heads—is nothing° but heart's sorrow   *there is no way*
          And a clear° life ensuing.   *innocent*

[*He vanishes in thunder; then, to soft music, enter the shapes again, and dance,
with mocks and mows,[3] and carrying out the table.*]

PROSPERO: Bravely the figure of this harpy hast thou
          Performed, my Ariel; a grace it had devouring.[4]
85   Of my instruction hast thou nothing bated°   *omitted*
          In what thou hadst to say. So,° with good life°   *similarly / acting*
          And observation strange,° my meaner ministers   *close attention*
          Their several kinds° have done. My high charms work,   *separate parts*
          And these mine enemies are all knit up
90   In their distractions.° They now are in my power;   *trances*
          And in these fits I leave them, while I visit
          Young Ferdinand, whom they suppose is drowned,
          And his and mine loved darling.

                                                          [*Exit above.*]

3. Grimaces and gestures.

4. Causing the banquet to disappear, with puns on "grace" as the blessing at meals and "devouring" as in "ravishing grace."

GONZALO: I' the name of something holy, sir, why stand you
            In this strange stare?
ALONSO: O, it is monstrous, monstrous!
            Methought the billows° spoke and told me of it;°   *waves / my sin*
            The winds did sing it to me, and the thunder,
            That deep and dreadful organ pipe, pronounced
            The name of Prosper; it did bass° my trespass.   *boom*
100   Therefore my son i' th' ooze is bedded; and
            I'll seek him deeper than e'er plummet sounded,°   *probed*
            And with him there lie mudded.

                                                                 [*Exit.*]

SEBASTIAN: But one fiend at a time,
            I'll fight their legions o'er.°   *one by one*
ANTONIO: I'll be thy second.

                                        [*Exeunt (Sebastian and Antonio).*]

GONZALO: All three of them are desperate. Their great guilt,
105   Like poison given to work a great time after,
            Now 'gins to bite the spirits. I do beseech you,
            That are of suppler joints, follow them swiftly
            And hinder them from what this ecstasy°   *madness*
            May now provoke them to.
ADRIAN: Follow, I pray you.

                                                           [*Exeunt omnes.*]

Act 4

Scene 1[1]

[*Enter Prospero, Ferdinand, and Miranda.*]

PROSPERO: If I have too austerely punished you,
            Your compensation makes amends, for I
            Have given you here a third[2] of mine own life,
            Or that for which I live; who once again
5   I tender° to thy hand. All thy vexations   *offer*
            Were but my trials of thy love, and thou
            Hast strangely° stood the test. Here, afore heaven,   *extraordinarily*
            I ratify this my rich gift. O Ferdinand,
            Do not smile at me that I boast her off;°   *boast of her*
10   For thou shalt find she will outstrip all praise
            And make it halt° behind her.   *limp*
FERDINAND: I do believe it
            Against an oracle.[3]

---

1. Location: Before Prospero's cell.
2. The other two thirds being his knowledge and his power?
3. Even if an oracle should deny it.

PROSPERO: Then, as my gift and thine own acquisition
             Worthily purchased, take my daughter. But
15   If thou dost break her virgin-knot before
             All sanctimonious° ceremonies may   *sacred*
             With full and holy rite be ministered,
             No sweet aspersion° shall the heavens let fall   *blessing*
             To make this contract grow; but barren hate,
20   Sour-eyed disdain, and discord shall bestrew
             The union of your bed with weeds⁴ so loathly
             That you shall hate it both. Therefore take heed,
             As Hymen's lamps shall light you.⁵
FERDINAND: As I hope
             For quiet days, fair issue,° and long life,   *offspring*
25   With such love as 'tis now, the murkiest den,
             The most opportune place, the strong'st suggestion°   *temptation*
             Our worser genius can,° shall never melt   *bad angel can make*
             Mine honor into lust, to take away
             The edge of that day's celebration
30   When I shall think or Phoebus' steeds are foundered⁶
             Or Night kept chained below.
PROSPERO: Fairly spoke.
             Sit then and talk with her. She is thine own.

             [Ferdinand and Miranda sit and talk together.]

             What, Ariel! My industrious servant, Ariel!

             [Enter Ariel.]

ARIEL: What would my potent master? Here I am.
PROSPERO: Thou and thy meaner fellows° your last service   *subordinates*
             Did worthily perform, and I must use you
             In such another trick. Go bring the rabble,
             O'er whom I give thee power, here to this place.
             Incite them to quick motion, for I must
40   Bestow upon the eyes of this young couple
             Some vanity° of mine art. It is my promise,   *show*
             And they expect it from me.
ARIEL: Presently?°   *now*
PROSPERO: Ay, with a twink.°   *now*
ARIEL: Before you can say "Come" and "Go,"
45   And breathe twice, and cry "So, so,"
             Each one, tripping on his toe,
             Will be here with mop and mow.°   *antics and gestures*
             Do you love me, master? No?
PROSPERO: Dearly, my delicate Ariel. Do not approach
50   Till thou dost hear me call.

---

4. As opposed to flowers.

5. Hymen was the Greek and Roman god of marriage, whose torches burned brightly for a happy marriage and smokily for a troubled one.

6. Either the sun-god's horses are lame.

ARIEL:	Well; I conceive.°	*understand*
		[*Exit.*]
PROSPERO:	Look thou be true;° do not give dalliance	*true to your word*
	Too much the rein. The strongest oaths are straw	
	To the fire i' the blood. Be more abstemious,	
	Or else good night your vow!	
FERDINAND:	I warrant you, sir,	
55	The white cold virgin snow upon my heart	
	Abates the ardor of my liver.[7]	
PROSPERO:	Well.	
	Now come, my Ariel! Bring a corollary,°	*surplus*
	Rather than want° a spirit. Appear, and pertly!°—	*lack / briskly*
	No tongue! All eyes! Be silent. [*Soft music.*]	

[*Enter Iris.*[8]]

IRIS:	Ceres,[9] most bounteous lady, thy rich leas°	*meadows*
	Of wheat, rye, barley, vetches,° oats, and peas;	*fodder*
	Thy turfy mountains, where live nibbling sheep,	
	And flat meads° thatched with stover,° them to keep;	*meadows / fodder*
65	Thy banks with pionèd and twillèd brims,[1]	
	Which spongy° April at thy hest° betrims	*wet / command*
	To make cold nymphs chaste crowns; and thy broom groves,°	*clumps of gorse*
	Whose shadow the dismissèd° bachelor loves,	*rejected*
	Being lass-lorn; thy poll-clipped° vineyard;	*pruned*
	And thy sea marge,° sterile and rocky hard,	*shore*
70	Where thou thyself dost air: the queen o' the sky,°	*Juno*
	Whose watery arch° and messenger am I,	*rainbow*
	Bids thee leave these, and with her sovereign grace,	

[*Juno descends (slowly in her car).*]

	Here on this grass plot, in this very place,	
	To come and sport. Her peacocks[2] fly amain.°	*at full speed*
75	Approach, rich Ceres, her to entertain.°	*receive*

[*Enter Ceres.*]

CERES:	Hail, many-colored messenger, that ne'er	
	Dost disobey the wife of Jupiter,	
	Who with thy saffron° wings upon my flowers	*yellow*
	Diffusest honeydrops, refreshing showers,	
80	And with each end of thy blue bow° dost crown	*rainbow*
	My bosky° acres and my unshrubbed down,	*wooded*
	Rich scarf to my proud earth. Why hath thy queen	
	Summoned me hither to this short-grassed green?	

7. Supposed seat of the passions.
8. Goddess of the rainbow and Juno's messenger.
9. Goddess of fertility.
1. Dug under by the current and protected by woven layers of branches.
2. Birds sacred to Juno, that drew her chariot.

IRIS:	A contract of true love to celebrate,	
85	And some donation freely to estate°	bestow
	On the blest lovers.	
CERES:	Tell me, heavenly bow,	
	If Venus or her son,[3] as thou dost know,	
	Do now attend the Queen? Since they did plot	
	The means that dusky Dis my daughter got,[4]	
90	Her and her blind boy's scandaled° company	disgraceful
	I have forsworn.	
IRIS:	Of her society	
	Be not afraid. I met her deity°	her Divine Majesty
	Cutting the clouds towards Paphos,[5] and her son	
	Dove-drawn with her. Here thought they to have done°	placed
95	Some wanton charm upon this man and maid,	
	Whose vows are that no bed-right shall be paid	
	Till Hymen's torch be lighted; but in vain.	
	Mars's hot minion° is returned again;	Venus
	Her waspish-headed° son has broke his arrows,	spiteful
100	Swears he will shoot no more, but play with sparrows[6]	
	And be a boy right out.°	outright

[*Juno alights.*]

CERES:	Highest Queen of state,	
	Great Juno, comes; I know her by her gait.	
JUNO:	How does my bounteous sister?° Go with me	fellow goddess
	To bless this twain, that they may prosperous be,	
105	And honored in their issue.°	offspring

[*They sing.*]

JUNO:	*Honor, riches, marriage blessing,*
	Long continuance, and increasing,
	Hourly joys be still° upon you! constantly
	Juno sings her blessings on you.

CERES:	*Earth's increase, foison° plenty,* abundance
	Barns and garners° never empty, granaries
	Vines with clustering bunches growing,
	Plants with goodly burden bowing;
	Spring come to you at the farthest
115	*In the very end of harvest![7]*
	Scarcity and want shall shun you;
	Ceres' blessing so is on you.

---

3. Cupid, often portrayed as blindfolded.
4. Pluto (Dis), god of the underworld, kidnapped Ceres's daughter Proserpina.
5. In Cyprus, center of Venus's cult.
6. Thought to be lustful, sparrows were sacred to Venus.
7. I.e., with no winter in between.

FERDINAND: This is a most majestic vision, and
              Harmonious charmingly. May I be bold
120   To think these spirits?
PROSPERO: Spirits, which by mine art
              I have from their confines called to enact
              My present fancies.
FERDINAND: Let me live here ever!
              So rare a wondered° father and a wife   *wonderful*
              Makes this place Paradise.

              [*Juno and Ceres whisper, and send Iris on employment.*]

PROSPERO: Sweet now, silence!
125   Juno and Ceres whisper seriously;
              There's something else to do. Hush and be mute,
              Or else our spell is marred.
IRIS [*calling offstage*]:
              You nymphs, called naiads, of the windring° brooks,   *winding*
              With your sedged° crowns and ever-harmless looks,   *made of reeds*
130   Leave your crisp° channels, and on this green land   *rippling*
              Answer your summons; Juno does command.
              Come, temperate° nymphs, and help to celebrate   *chaste*
              A contract of true love. Be not too late.

              [*Enter certain nymphs.*]

              You sunburned sicklemen, of August° weary,   *the harvest*
135   Come hither from the furrow and be merry.
              Make holiday; your rye-straw hats put on,
              And these fresh nymphs encounter every one
              In country footing.°   *dancing*

              [*Enter certain reapers, properly habited. They join with the nymphs in a graceful
              dance, towards the end whereof Prospero starts suddenly, and speaks; after which, to
              a strange, hollow, and confused noise, they heavily vanish.*]

PROSPERO [*aside*]:   I had forgot that foul conspiracy
140   Of the beast Caliban and his confederates
              Against my life. The minute of their plot
              Is almost come. [*To the Spirits.*] Well done! Avoid;° no more!   *be off*
FERDINAND [*to Miranda*]:   This is strange. Your father's in some passion
              That works° him strongly.   *affects*
MIRANDA: Never till this day
145   Saw I him touched with anger so distempered.
PROSPERO: You do look, my son, in a moved sort,°   *troubled state*
              As if you were dismayed. Be cheerful, sir.
              Our revels now are ended. These our actors,
              As I foretold you, were all spirits and
150   Are melted into air, into thin air;
              And, like the baseless° fabric of this vision,   *insubstantial*
              The cloud-capped towers, the gorgeous palaces,
              The solemn temples, the great globe itself,°   *(glances at theater)*

155 Yea, all which it inherit,° shall dissolve,   *occupy it*
And, like this insubstantial pageant faded,
Leave not a rack° behind. We are such stuff   *cloud*
As dreams are made on,° and our little life   *of*
Is rounded° with a sleep. Sir, I am vexed.   *surrounded*
Bear with my weakness. My old brain is troubled.
160 Be not disturbed with my infirmity.
If you be pleased, retire into my cell
And there repose. A turn or two I'll walk
To still my beating° mind.   *agitated*

FERDINAND, MIRANDA: We wish your peace.

            [Exeunt (Ferdinand and Miranda).]

PROSPERO: Come with a thought!° I thank thee, Ariel. Come.   *right now*

   [Enter Ariel.]

ARIEL: Thy thoughts I cleave to. What's thy pleasure?
PROSPERO: Spirit,
We must prepare to meet with Caliban.
ARIEL: Ay, my commander. When I presented° Ceres,   *played; introduced*
I thought to have told thee of it, but I feared
Lest I might anger thee.
PROSPERO: Say again, where didst thou leave these varlets?
ARIEL: I told you, sir, they were red-hot with drinking;
So full of valor that they smote the air
For breathing in their faces, beat the ground
For kissing of their feet; yet always bending
175 Towards their project. Then I beat my tabor,
At which, like unbacked° colts, they pricked their ears,   *unbroken*
Advanced° their eyelids, lifted up their noses   *raised*
As they smelt music. So I charmed their ears
That calflike they my lowing followed through
180 Toothed briers, sharp furzes, pricking gorse, and thorns,
Which entered their frail shins. At last I left them
I' the filthy-mantled° pool beyond your cell,   *scummed*
There dancing up to the chins, that the foul lake
O'erstunk their feet.
PROSPERO: This was well done, my bird.
185 Thy shape invisible retain thou still.
The trumpery° in my house, go bring it hither,   *cheap goods*
For stale° to catch these thieves.   *decoy*
ARIEL: I go, I go.

                    [Exit.]

PROSPERO: A devil, a born devil, on whose nature
Nurture can never stick; on whom my pains,
190 Humanely taken, all, all lost, quite lost!
And as with age his body uglier grows,

So his mind cankers.° I will plague them all,   *festers*
Even to roaring.

[*Enter Ariel, loaden with glistering apparel, etc.*]

Come, hang them on this line.°   *lime tree*

[(*Ariel hangs up the showy finery; Prospero and Ariel remain, invisible.*) *Enter
Caliban, Stephano, and Trinculo, all wet.*]

CALIBAN: Pray you, tread softly, that the blind mole may
195   Not hear a foot fall. We now are near his cell.
STEPHANO: Monster, your fairy, which you say is a harmless fairy, has done little
      better than played the jack[8] with us.
TRINCULO: Monster, I do smell all horse piss, at which my nose is in great indignation.
STEPHANO: So is mine. Do you hear, monster? If I should take a displeasure against
      you, look you—
TRINCULO: Thou wert but a lost monster.
CALIBAN: Good my lord, give me thy favor still.
      Be patient, for the prize I'll bring thee to
205   Shall hoodwink° this mischance. Therefore speak softly.   *cover over*
      All's hushed as midnight yet.
TRINCULO: Ay, but to lose our bottles in the pool—
STEPHANO: There is not only disgrace and dishonor in that, monster, but an
      infinite loss.
TRINCULO: That's more to me than my wetting. Yet this is your harmless fairy,
      monster!
STEPHANO: I will fetch off my bottle, though I be o'er ears[9] for my labor.
CALIBAN: Prithee, my king, be quiet. Seest thou here,
      This is the mouth o' the cell. No noise, and enter.
215   Do that good mischief which may make this island
      Thine own forever, and I thy Caliban
      For aye thy footlicker.
STEPHANO: Give me thy hand. I do begin to have bloody thoughts.
TRINCULO [*seeing the finery*]:   O King Stephano! O peer![1]
220   O worthy Stephano! Look what a wardrobe here is for thee!
CALIBAN: Let it alone, thou fool, it is but trash.
TRINCULO: O ho, monster! We know what belongs to a frippery.[2] O King Stephano!
      [*He puts on a gown.*]
STEPHANO: Put off that gown, Trinculo. By this hand, I'll have that gown.
TRINCULO: Thy Grace shall have it.
CALIBAN: The dropsy[3] drown this fool! What do you mean
      To dote thus on such luggage? Let 't alone
      And do the murder first. If he awake,
      From toe to crown he'll fill our skins with pinches,
230   Make us strange stuff.

8. Knave; jack o' lantern, will o' th' wisp.
9. Submerged or drowned.
1. Alludes to the ballad beginning "King Stephen was a worthy peer..."
2. Old-clothes shop.
3. Disease in which joints fill with fluid.

STEPHANO: Be you quiet, monster.—Mistress line, is not this my jerkin?[4] [*He takes it down.*] Now is the jerkin under the line.[5] Now, jerkin, you are like to lose your hair and prove a bald jerkin.

TRINCULO: Do, do! We steal by line and level,[6] an 't like[7] your Grace.

STEPHANO: I thank thee for that jest. Here's a garment for 't. [*He gives a garment.*] Wit shall not go unrewarded while I am king of this country. "Steal by line and level" is an excellent pass of pate.[8] There's another garment for 't.

TRINCULO: Monster, come, put some lime[9] upon your fingers, and away with the rest.

CALIBAN: I will have none on 't. We shall lose our time,
And all be turned to barnacles,[1] or to apes
With foreheads villainous low.

STEPHANO: Monster, lay to[2] your fingers. Help to bear this away where my hogs-head of wine is, or I'll turn you out of my kingdom. Go to, carry this.

TRINCULO: And this.

STEPHANO: Ay, and this.

[*They load Caliban with more and more garments.*]

[*A noise of hunters heard. Enter divers spirits, in shape of dogs and hounds, hunting them about, Prospero and Ariel setting them on.*]

PROSPERO: Hey, Mountain, hey!

ARIEL: Silver! There it goes, Silver!

PROSPERO: Fury, Fury! There, Tyrant, there! Hark! Hark! [*Caliban, Stephano, and Trinculo are driven out.*]
250 Go, charge my goblins that they grind their joints
With dry[3] convulsions, shorten up their sinews
With agèd cramps, and more pinch-spotted make them
Than pard or cat o'mountain.[4]

ARIEL: Hark, they roar!

PROSPERO: Let them be hunted soundly. At this hour
255 Lies at my mercy all mine enemies.
Shortly shall all my labors end, and thou
Shalt have the air at freedom. For a little
Follow, and do me service.

[*Exeunt.*]

ACT 5

Scene 1[1]

[*Enter Prospero in his magic robes, (with his staff,) and Ariel.*]

PROSPERO: Now does my project gather to a head.
My charms crack° not, my spirits obey, and Time   *fail*

---

4. Leather jacket.
5. Lime tree; pun on the equator, south of which sailors supposedly caught scurvy and lost their hair.
6. Methodically (pun on *line*).
7. If it please.
8. Witticism.
9. Bird-lime (sticky and good for stealing).
1. Geese.
2. Start using.
3. Aged.
4. Leopard or wildcat.
1. Location: Before Prospero's cell.

Goes upright with his carriage.[2] How's the day?
ARIEL: On the sixth hour, at which time, my lord,
5 You said our work should cease.
PROSPERO: I did say so,
When first I raised the tempest. Say, my spirit,
How fares the King and 's followers?
ARIEL: Confined together
In the same fashion as you gave in charge,
Just as you left them; all prisoners, sir,
10 In the line grove which weather-fends° your cell.   *protects from weather*
They cannot budge till your release.° The King,   *you release them*
His brother, and yours abide all three distracted,°   *mad*
And the remainder mourning over them,
Brim full of sorrow and dismay; but chiefly
15 Him that you termed, sir, the good old lord, Gonzalo.
His tears runs down his beard like winter's drops
From eaves of reeds.° Your charm so strongly works 'em   *thatched roof*
That if you now beheld them your affections°   *feelings*
Would become tender.
PROSPERO: Dost thou think so, spirit?
ARIEL: Mine would, sir, were I human.
PROSPERO: And mine shall.
Hast thou, which art but air, a touch,° a feeling   *a sense*
Of their afflictions, and shall not myself,
One of their kind, that relish° all° as sharply   *feel / quite*
Passion as they, be kindlier moved than thou art?
25 Though with their high wrongs I am struck to the quick,
Yet with my nobler reason 'gainst my fury
Do I take part. The rarer° action is   *nobler*
In virtue than in vengeance. They being penitent,
The sole drift of my purpose doth extend
30 Not a frown further. Go release them, Ariel.
My charms I'll break, their senses I'll restore,
And they shall be themselves.
ARIEL: I'll fetch them, sir.

                                             [Exit.]

[Prospero traces a charmed circle with his staff.]

PROSPERO:[3] Ye elves of hills, brooks, standing lakes, and groves,
And ye that on the sands with printless foot
35 Do chase the ebbing Neptune, and do fly him
When he comes back; you demi-puppets° that   *fairies*
By moonshine do the green sour ringlets° make,   *circles in grass*

---

2. Time's burden is light.

3. This famous passage, lines 33–50, is an embellished paraphrase of Golding's translation of Ovid's *Metamorphoses* 7.197–219.

Whereof the ewe not bites; and you whose pastime
Is to make midnight mushrooms, that rejoice
40 To hear the solemn curfew;° by whose aid,   *evening bell*
Weak masters° though ye be, I have bedimmed   *forces*
The noontide sun, called forth the mutinous winds,
And twixt the green sea and the azured vault°   *the sky*
Set roaring war; to the dread rattling thunder
45 Have I given fire, and rifted° Jove's stout oak[4]   *split*
With his own bolt; the strong-based promontory
Have I made shake, and by the spurs° plucked up   *roots*
The pine and cedar; graves at my command
Have waked their sleepers, oped, and let 'em forth
50 By my so potent art. But this rough magic
I here abjure, and when I have required°   *requested*
Some heavenly music—which even now I do—
To work mine end upon their senses that[5]
This airy charm° is for, I'll break my staff,   *music*
55 Bury it certain fathoms in the earth,
And deeper than did ever plummet sound
I'll drown my book. [*Solemn music.*]

[*Here enters Ariel before; then Alonso, with a frantic gesture, attended by Gonzalo; Sebastian and Antonio in like manner, attended by Adrian and Francisco. They all enter the circle which Prospero had made, and there stand charmed; which Prospero observing, speaks:*]

[*To Alonso.*] A solemn air,° and° the best comforter   *song / which is*
To an unsettled fancy, cure thy brains,
60 Now useless, boiled within thy skull! [*To Sebastian and Antonio.*] There stand,
For you are spell-stopped.—
Holy Gonzalo, honorable man,
Mine eyes, e'en sociable° to the show° of thine,   *sympathetic / sight*
Fall° fellowly drops. [*Aside.*] The charm dissolves apace, *let fall*
65 And as the morning steals upon the night,
Melting the darkness, so their rising senses
Begin to chase the ignorant fumes that mantle°   *envelop*
Their clearer reason.—O good Gonzalo,
My true preserver, and a loyal sir
70 To him thou follow'st! I will pay thy graces°   *favors*
Home° both in word and deed.—Most cruelly   *fully*
Didst thou, Alonso, use me and my daughter.
Thy brother was a furtherer° in the act.—   *accomplice*
Thou art pinched for 't now, Sebastian. [*To Antonio.*] Flesh and blood,
75 You, brother mine, that entertained ambition,
Expelled remorse° and nature,° whom, with Sebastian,   *pity / natural feeling*

4. Tree sacred to Jove.
5. The senses of those whom.

Whose inward pinches therefore are most strong,
Would here have killed your king, I do forgive thee,
Unnatural though thou art.—Their understanding
80 Begins to swell, and the approaching tide
Will shortly fill the reasonable shore°   *shore of the mind*
That now lies foul and muddy. Not one of them
That yet looks on me, or would know me.—Ariel,
Fetch me the hat and rapier in my cell.

[*Ariel goes to the cell and returns immediately.*]

85 I will discase° me and myself present   *disrobe*
As I was sometime Milan.[6] Quickly, spirit!
Thou shalt ere long be free.

[*Ariel sings and helps to attire him.*]

ARIEL: *Where the bee sucks, there suck I.*
                         In a cowslip's bell I lie;
90   *There I couch° when owls do cry.*   *lie*
                         On the bat's back I do fly
                         After° summer merrily.   *pursuing*
                         Merrily, merrily shall I live now
                         Under the blossom that hangs on the bough.

PROSPERO: Why, that's my dainty Ariel! I shall miss thee,
But yet thou shalt have freedom. So, so, so.
To the King's ship, invisible as thou art!
There shalt thou find the mariners asleep
Under the hatches. The Master and the Boatswain
100 Being awake, enforce them to this place,
And presently,° I prithee.   *right away*
ARIEL: I drink the air° before me and return   *consume space*
Or ere° your pulse twice beat.   *before*

                                                                          [*Exit.*]

GONZALO: All torment, trouble, wonder, and amazement
105 Inhabits here. Some heavenly power guide us
Out of this fearful° country!   *frightening*
PROSPERO: Behold, sir King,
The wrongèd Duke of Milan, Prospero.
For more assurance that a living prince
Does now speak to thee, I embrace thy body;
110 And to thee and thy company I bid
A hearty welcome. [*Embracing him.*]
ALONSO: Whe'er thou be'st he or no,
Or some enchanted trifle° to abuse° me,   *trick / deceive*
As late° I have been, I not know. Thy pulse   *lately*

---

6. As I looked when I was Duke of Milan.

Beats as of flesh and blood; and, since I saw thee,
115 Th' affliction of my mind amends, with which
I fear a madness held me. This must crave°— _require_
An if this be° at all—a most strange story. _is happening_
Thy dukedom I resign, and do entreat
Thou pardon me my wrongs. But how should Prospero
Be living, and be here?

PROSPERO [_to Gonzalo_]:   First, noble friend,
Let me embrace thine age,° whose honor cannot _yourself_
Be measured or confined. [_Embracing him._]

GONZALO: Whether this be
Or be not, I'll not swear.

PROSPERO: You do yet taste
Some subtleties° o' th' isle, that will not let you _illusions_
125 Believe things certain. Welcome, my friends all!

[_Aside to Sebastian and Antonio._]

But you, my brace° of lords, were I so minded, _pair_
I here could pluck° his Highness' frown upon you _pull down_
And justify° you traitors. At this time _prove_
I will tell no tales.

SEBASTIAN: The devil speaks in him.

PROSPERO: No.
130 [_To Antonio._] For you, most wicked sir, whom to call brother
Would even infect my mouth, I do forgive
Thy rankest fault—all of them; and require
My dukedom of thee, which perforce° I know _necessarily_
Thou must restore.

ALONSO: If thou be'st Prospero,
135 Give us particulars of thy preservation,
How thou hast met us here, whom three hours since
Were wrecked upon this shore; where I have lost—
How sharp the point of this remembrance is!—
My dear son Ferdinand.

PROSPERO: I am woe° for 't, sir. _sorry_

ALONSO: Irreparable is the loss, and patience
Says it is past her cure.

PROSPERO: I rather think
You have not sought her help, of whose soft grace
For the like loss I have her sovereign° aid _effective_
And rest myself content.

ALONSO: You the like loss?

PROSPERO: As great to me as late,° and supportable _recent_
To make the dear° loss, have I means much weaker _grievous_
Than you may call to comfort you; for I
Have lost my daughter.

ALONSO: A daughter?
O heavens, that they were living both in Naples,
150 The king and queen there! That° they were, I wish _so that_

Myself were mudded° in that oozy bed   *buried in mud*
    Where my son lies. When did you lose your daughter?
PROSPERO: In this last tempest. I perceive these lords
    At this encounter do so much admire°   *wonder*
155   That they devour their reason° and scarce think   *are open-mouthed*
    Their eyes do offices° of truth, their words   *perform services*
    Are natural breath. But, howsoever you have
    Been jostled from your senses, know for certain
    That I am Prospero and that very duke
160   Which was thrust forth of Milan, who most strangely
    Upon this shore, where you were wrecked, was landed
    To be the lord on 't. No more yet of this,
    For 'tis a chronicle of day by day,°   *many days' telling*
    Not a relation for a breakfast nor
165   Befitting this first meeting. Welcome, sir.
    This cell's my court. Here have I few attendants,
    And subjects none abroad.° Pray you, look in.   *elsewhere*
    My dukedom since you have given me again,
    I will requite° you with as good a thing,   *repay*
170   At least bring forth a wonder to content ye
    As much as me my dukedom.

[*Here Prospero discovers° Ferdinand and Miranda, playing at chess.*]   *discloses*

MIRANDA: Sweet lord, you play me false.
FERDINAND: No, my dearest love,
    I would not for the world.
MIRANDA: Yes, for a score of kingdoms you should wrangle,
    And I would call it fair play.[7]
ALONSO: If this prove
    A vision° of the island, one dear son   *illusion*
    Shall I twice lose.
SEBASTIAN: A most high miracle!
FERDINAND [*approaching his father*]:   Though the seas threaten, they are merciful;
    I have cursed them without cause. [*He kneels.*]
ALONSO: Now all the blessings
180   Of a glad father compass° thee about!   *encompass*
    Arise, and say how thou cam'st here.

[*Ferdinand rises.*]

MIRANDA: O, wonder!
    How many goodly creatures are there here!
    How beauteous mankind is! O brave° new world   *splendid*
    That has such people in 't!
PROSPERO: 'Tis new to thee.
ALONSO: What is this maid with whom thou wast at play?
    Your eld'st° acquaintance cannot be three hours.   *longest*
    Is she the goddess that hath severed us,

7. Miranda would still love Ferdinand, even if he did not play fair.

And brought us thus together?

FERDINAND: Sir, she is mortal;
    But by immortal Providence she's mine.
190   I chose her when I could not ask my father
    For his advice, nor thought I had one. She
    Is daughter to this famous Duke of Milan,
    Of whom so often I have heard renown,
    But never saw before; of whom I have
195   Received a second life; and second father
    This lady makes him to me.

ALONSO: I am hers.
    But O, how oddly will it sound that I
    Must ask my child forgiveness!

PROSPERO: There, sir, stop.
    Let us not burden our remembrances with
    A heaviness° that's gone.   *sadness*

GONZALO: I have inly° wept,   *inwardly*
    Or should have spoke ere this. Look down, you gods,
    And on this couple drop a blessèd crown!
    For it is you that have chalked forth the way
    Which brought us hither.

ALONSO: I say amen, Gonzalo!

GONZALO: Was Milan° thrust from Milan, that his issue   *the Duke of Milan*
    Should become kings of Naples? O, rejoice
    Beyond a common joy, and set it down
    With gold on lasting pillars: In one voyage
    Did Claribel her husband find at Tunis,
210   And Ferdinand, her brother, found a wife
    Where he himself was lost; Prospero his dukedom
    In a poor isle; and all of us ourselves°   *our senses*
    When no man was his own.°   *sane*

ALONSO [*to Ferdinand and Miranda*]: Give me your hands.
    Let grief and sorrow still° embrace his heart   *always*
    That doth not wish you joy!

GONZALO: Be it so! Amen!

[*Enter Ariel, with the Master and Boatswain amazedly following.*]

    O, look, sir, look, sir! Here is more of us.
    I prophesied, if a gallows were on land,
    This fellow could not drown.—Now, blasphemy,°   *blasphemer*
    That swear'st grace o'erboard, not an oath on shore?
220   Hast thou no mouth by land? What is the news?

BOATSWAIN: The best news is that we have safely found
    Our King and company; the next, our ship—
    Which, but three glasses° since, we gave out° split—   *hours / reported*
    Is tight and yare° and bravely rigged as when   *shipshape*
    We first put out to sea.

ARIEL [*aside to Prospero*]: Sir, all this service
    Have I done since I went.

PROSPERO [*aside to Ariel*]:   My tricksy° spirit!   *ingenious*

ALONSO: These are not natural events; they strengthen
　　　　From strange to stranger. Say, how came you hither?

BOATSWAIN: If I did think, sir, I were well awake,
230　　　　I'd strive to tell you. We were dead of sleep,
　　　　And—how we know not—all clapped under hatches,
　　　　Where but even now, with strange and several° noises   *various*
　　　　Of roaring, shrieking, howling, jingling chains,
　　　　And more diversity of sounds, all horrible,
235　　　　We were awaked; straightway at liberty;
　　　　Where we, in all her trim,° freshly beheld   *sail*
　　　　Our royal, good, and gallant ship, our Master
　　　　Cap'ring° to eye° her. On a trice, so please you,   *dancing / see*
　　　　Even in a dream, were we divided from them
　　　　And were brought moping° hither.   *in a daze*

ARIEL [*aside to Prospero*]:   Was't well done?

PROSPERO [*aside to Ariel*]:   Bravely, my diligence. Thou shalt be free.

ALONSO: This is as strange a maze as e'er men trod,
　　　　And there is in this business more than nature
　　　　Was ever conduct° of. Some oracle   *conductor*
　　　　Must rectify our knowledge.

PROSPERO: Sir, my liege,
　　　　Do not infest° your mind with beating on   *bother*
　　　　The strangeness of this business. At picked° leisure,   *chosen*
　　　　Which shall be shortly, single° I'll resolve° you,   *privately / explain*
　　　　Which to you shall seem probable, of every°   *every one of*
250　　　　These happened accidents;° till when, be cheerfull   *incidents*
　　　　And think of each thing well. [*Aside to Ariel.*] Come hither, spirit.
　　　　Set Caliban and his companions free.
　　　　Untie the spell. [*Exit Ariel.*] How fares my gracious sir?
　　　　There are yet missing of your company
255　　　　Some few odd lads that you remember not.

[*Enter Ariel, driving in Caliban, Stephano, and Trinculo, in their stolen apparel.*]

STEPHANO: Every man shift[8] for all the rest,[9] and let no man take care for himself;
　　　　for all is but fortune. Coragio,[1] bully monster,[2] coragio!

TRINCULO: If these be true spies[3] which I wear in my head, here's a goodly sight.

CALIBAN: O Setebos, these be brave° spirits indeed!   *handsome*
260　　　　How fine° my master is! I am afraid   *well-dressed*
　　　　He will chastise me.

SEBASTIAN: Ha, ha!
　　　　What things are these, my lord Antonio?

8. Provide.
9. Stephano drunkenly gets wrong the saying "Every man for himself."
1. Courage.
2. Gallant monster (ironical).
3. Sharp eyes.

Will money buy 'em?

ANTONIO: Very like. One of them
     Is a plain fish, and no doubt marketable.

PROSPERO: Mark but the badges of these men,° my lords,   servants
     Then say if they be true.° This misshapen knave,   honest
     His mother was a witch, and one so strong
     That could control the moon, make flows and ebbs,
     And deal in her° command without° her power.   the moon's / beyond
270 These three have robbed me, and this demidevil—
     For he's a bastard° one—had plotted with them   counterfeit
     To take my life. Two of these fellows you
     Must know and own.° This thing of darkness I   acknowledge
     Acknowledge mine.

CALIBAN: I shall be pinched to death.

ALONSO: Is not this Stephano, my drunken butler?

SEBASTIAN: He is drunk now. Where had he wine?

ALONSO: And Trinculo is reeling ripe.° Where should they   stumbling drunk
     Find this grand liquor that hath gilded[4] 'em?
     [To Trinculo.] How cam'st thou in this pickle?[5]

TRINCULO: I have been in such a pickle since I saw you last that, I fear me, will
     never out of my bones. I shall not fear flyblowing.[6]

SEBASTIAN: Why, how now, Stephano?

STEPHANO: O, touch me not! I am not Stephano, but a cramp.

PROSPERO: You'd be king o' the isle, sirrah?[7]

STEPHANO: I should have been a sore[8] one, then.

ALONSO [pointing to Caliban]:   This is a strange thing as e'er I looked on.

PROSPERO: He is as disproportioned in his manners
     As in his shape.—Go, sirrah, to my cell.
     Take with you your companions. As you look
290 To have my pardon, trim° it handsomely.   decorate

CALIBAN: Ay, that I will; and I'll be wise hereafter
     And seek for grace.° What a thrice-double ass   favor
     Was I to take this drunkard for a god
     And worship this dull fool!

PROSPERO: Go to. Away!

ALONSO: Hence, and bestow your luggage where you found it.

SEBASTIAN: Or stole it, rather.

                         [Exeunt Caliban, Stephano, and Trinculo.]

PROSPERO: Sir, I invite Your Highness and your train
     To my poor cell, where you shall take your rest

---

4. Intoxicated; covered with gold (suggesting horse urine).
5. Predicament; pickling brine (here, horse urine).
6. Being soiled by fly eggs (he is protected by being pickled).
7. Address to an inferior (here, a reprimand).
8. Tyrannical; sorry; aching.

	For this one night; which, part of it, I'll waste°	spend
300	With such discourse as, I not doubt, shall make it	
	Go quick away: the story of my life,	
	And the particular accidents° gone by	events
	Since I came to this isle. And in the morn	
	I'll bring you to your ship, and so to Naples,	
305	Where I have hope to see the nuptial	
	Of these our dear-belovèd solemnized;	
	And thence retire me to my Milan, where	
	Every third thought shall be my grave.	

ALONSO: I long

To hear the story of your life, which must

Take° the ear strangely.   *captivate*

PROSPERO: I'll deliver° all;   *tell*

And promise you calm seas, auspicious gales,

And sail so expeditious that shall catch

Your royal fleet far off. [*Aside to Ariel.*] My Ariel, chick,

That is thy charge. Then to the elements

315 Be free, and fare thou well!—Please you, draw near.

[*Exeunt omnes (except Prospero).*]

EPILOGUE

[*Spoken by Prospero.*]

	Now my charms are all o'erthrown,	
	And what strength I have's mine own,	
	Which is most faint. Now, 'tis true,	
	I must be here confined by you	
5	Or sent to Naples. Let me not,	
	Since I have my dukedom got	
	And pardoned the deceiver, dwell	
	In this bare island by your spell,°	silence
	But release me from my bands°	bonds
10	With the help of your good hands.°	applause
	Gentle breath of yours my sails	
	Must fill, or else my project fails,	
	Which was to please. Now I want°	lack
	Spirits to enforce,° art to enchant,	control
15	And my ending is despair,	
	Unless I be relieved by prayer,°	this very speech
	Which pierces so that it assaults°	gains the attention of
	Mercy itself, and frees° all faults.	earns pardon for
	As you from crimes° would pardoned be,	sins
20	Let your indulgence° set me free.	humoring; pardon

[*Exit.*]

The Conquest and Its Aftermath

When Hernán Cortés sailed from Cuba in 1519 to invade Mexico with his little army, he went in defiance of his superior Diego Velázquez, the governor of the recently established Spanish colony at Cuba. Velázquez was well aware of the precariousness of his foothold in the area and was not yet ready to attempt a major invasion on the mainland; at most, Cortés was authorized simply to establish an outlying base colony. Any sensible person, in fact, would never have thought of doing more with so small a force, but Cortés was convinced that God would enable him to succeed against all odds. To recruit men for his expedition, he had banners made that proclaimed, "Brothers and comrades, let us follow the sign of the Holy Cross in true faith, for under this sign we shall conquer." Having assembled his forces, he sailed first to the Yucatan coast, where his ships were attacked by hostile natives and he could only stay briefly on shore. There, however, he had the good fortune to come upon a sailor, Jerónimo de Aguilar, who had been shipwrecked on the coast several years before; he had settled in and learned the local Mayan language in the process.

Cortés could now communicate with the natives, and he soon had a second stroke of good fortune: he took on board a young Mexican noblewoman who was fluent in Mayan as well as in her native Nahuatl. Now Cortés could communicate with the Aztecs, through a double process of translation: Jerónimo de Aguilar could translate from Spanish into Mayan, and she could translate from Mayan into Nahuatl. Having her baptized as Doña Maria, Cortés made her his common-law wife, interpreter, and confidante; she became known to the Indians as "La Malinche."

Cortés next made a successful landing on the gulf coast of Mexico, at a swampy site he grandly dubbed La Villa Rica de la Vera Cruz, "The Rich Town of the True Cross." Though by all rights his mission should have ended there, he burned his boats so as to keep his troops from leaving. In letters to Charles V, Cortés claimed that his men had threatened to desert the new colony, but probably he was really preventing anyone from returning to Cuba to help his great rival, Diego Velázquez, establish authority on the mainland. The ships destroyed, Cortés and some four hundred men began the march into the interior. As they made their way toward the Aztec capital of Tenochtitlán, Cortés began to hear of the natives' widespread anger against their Aztec overlords. He also soon received ambassadors from the Aztec king, Moctezuma II, who was concerned to learn whether Cortés might possibly be the returning god Quetzalcoatl, as rumored, or whether he was an impostor.

Later accounts both by Spanish historians and by native chroniclers probed the enigma of Moctezuma's shifting responses to the news of Cortés's approach, which he alternately welcomed and rebuffed. Once Cortés reached the capital, he succeeded in placing Moctezuma under house arrest, a development that fatally damaged Moctezuma's prestige among his allies. Some sources describe the Aztec king as gullibly convinced that Cortés was indeed the returning Quetzalcoatl, yet a different picture emerges from close reading of accounts such as those given here by Bernal Díaz del Castillo. Even as he appears to welcome Cortés with open arms, Moctezuma tries a variety of strategies to put him off from approaching the capital. As the historian Davíd Carrasco has argued in a book called *Quetzalcoatl and the Irony of Empire,* the Aztec ruling house had shorn up its political power by claiming to be ruling on behalf of the absent divine Toltec king. Moctezuma could hardly refuse to welcome him outright, particularly after Cortés got wind of the old legend and began to intimate that he was indeed the returned monarch, or at least his ambassador (with the Spanish king Charles V in place of Quetzalcoatl). Further, even though it soon became clear that Cortés and his rough-and-ready troops were no divinities, it appears likely that Moctezuma hoped to use the newcomers to reinforce his fragile position at home among his restive allies. He was unaware that Cortés—who protested

Cortés accepting the Aztecs' surrender, from a native chronicle called the *Lienzo de Tlaxcala,* (1550). Wearing an improbable feathered headdress, Cortés is shown with La Malinche standing behind him as translator, as he accepts the surrender of the Aztec leader Cuauhtemoc. The Tlaxcalans, who had sided with the Spanish, are shown with a Spanish soldier in the lower right. The Nahuatl caption says *Yc poliuhque mexica,* "Here perished the Mexica."

friendship and admiration for him—was actively negotiating with his neighbors to destroy his empire.

After several months of a sort of standoff in Tenochtitlán, Cortés was forced to return to the coast to defeat a Spanish force sent from Cuba to bring him to heel. He left behind his hotheaded captain Pedro de Alvarado to keep watch over Moctezuma; while Cortés was away, however, Alvarado rightly or wrongly concluded that the natives were about to rise against him, and he engineered a massacre of many of the nobility in the midst of a religious festival. The enraged Aztecs retaliated in full force. During a bloody night known as the *noche triste* ("night of sorrows"), they succeeded in driving the Spaniards from the city. As they regrouped onshore, the would-be conquistadors could see captured comrades, high on the summit of Huitzilopochtli's temple, made to dance in the war god's honor before having their hearts cut out.

Undeterred by this disaster, Cortés soon returned to the Valley of Mexico with more men, and began campaigning among the Aztecs' neighbors to make a decisive strike against the capital. Aided by a combined force of 200,000 native warriors, Cortés mounted a long siege of Tenochtitlán, whose position out in Lake Texcoco, ordinarily very secure, became a trap once the inhabitants lost control of the causeways linking the city to the mainland. Starvation began to set in, and the situation became still more grave when plague broke out in the crowded city. By August of 1521, after weeks of street-to-street fighting, Cortés had destroyed the Aztecs' capital and was master of their empire. As an anonymous account from Tlatelolco recalled in 1528,

> Broken spears lie in the roads;
> we have torn our hair in our grief.
> The houses are roofless now,
> and their walls are red with blood.
>
> ......
>
> We have pounded our hands in despair
> against the adobe walls,
> for our inheritance, our city, is lost and dead.
> The shields of our warriors were its defense,
> but they could not save it.

In his *True History of the Conquest of New Spain,* Cortés's soldier Bernal Díaz del Castillo describes with real regret the destruction of the capital and the neighboring cities, cities so magnificent that when they first saw them, he and his comrades thought they must be dreaming. "Today," he wrote in 1564, "everything is torn down, lost, so there is nothing left." He was right that much had been destroyed: palaces and temples were pulled down, their stones used to build churches; "idolatrous" native books were burned en masse; over the course of the century as much as ninety percent of the native population perished from warfare, brutal mistreatment, and imported diseases like smallpox and plague. Yet more of the culture survived than either Bernal Díaz or the Tlatelolcan chronicler believed: religious and medical practices carried on out of Spanish view or recast into Spanish forms; historical traditions preserved in native languages with the convenient technology of the Roman alphabet; poems old and new, sung in memory of past greatness and in response to present struggles. Even amid the destruction of Tenochtitlán, one post-Conquest poem says, poetry sustained the Aztec nobles as the Spaniards tortured them in search of gold:

> Yet peacefully were Motelchiuh and Tlacotzin taken away.
> They fortified themselves with song in Acachinanco
> when they went to be delivered to the fire in Coyohuacan.

PRONUNCIATIONS:

Hernán Cortés: air-NAHN core-TEZ
Malinche: mah-LEAN-chay
Moctezuma: mock-tay-ZOO-mah
Tenochtitlán: tay-nokh-tea-TLAN
Tlatelolco: tlah-tell-OLE-co

BERNAL DÍAZ DEL CASTILLO ■ (1492–1584)

Born in the very year in which Christopher Columbus made his momentous first voyage across the Atlantic, Bernal Díaz grew up to become a soldier, adventurer, and the most vivid chronicler of the conquest of Mexico. Son of a magistrate in a provincial city in Spain, he received enough education to develop a fluent prose style and an enduring love of adventure stories and knightly romances, including the tales of Amadis of Gaul whose fictional exploits would later inspire Cervantes's hero Don Quixote. In his early twenties he sailed for the newly discovered New World, taking part in an unsuccessful quest for gold in Panama in 1514 and then attempting to establish himself in Cuba. There he signed on as a soldier serving Hernán Cortés, becoming part of the force with which Cortés invaded Mexico in 1519. After the two and a half years of struggle and hardship that culminated in the fall of Tenochtitlán, Bernal Díaz sought to achieve fame and fortune in Spain's new empire, but with only moderate success. The major political offices and land grants went to others with closer links to Cortés or with higher social standing and better connections at the royal court in Madrid.

Eventually, Bernal Díaz had to content himself with a modest position in Guatemala, where he served as a magistrate, carrying on his father's profession in a very different world. In the 1560s—irritated by an early history of the Conquest that gave credit largely to Cortés alone—Bernal Díaz decided to record his own reminiscences and set the record straight. His account didn't arouse the interest he had hoped; it remained unpublished until 1632, long after his death in Guatemala in 1584 at the age of ninety-two. As he wrote in a preface to his manuscript, "as luck would have it, I have gained nothing of value to leave to my children and descendants but this my true story, and they will presently find out what a wonderful story it is."

Writing with lively directness and with remarkably clear recall of events forty years before, Bernal Díaz didn't hesitate to reconstruct or even invent speeches, but comparison with other sources shows that he rarely seems to have misremembered events. He gives unforgettable portraits of Cortés and of Moctezuma ("Montezuma," as he calls him). He details Cortés's bold moves and shrewd negotiations while also criticizing his high-handedness and greed, and he gives us the fullest contemporary account of Doña Marina, also known as "La Malinche," the Aztec noblewoman who became Cortés's interpreter and wife. He records as well both Moctezuma's ambivalent, shifting responses and the heroic valor of the Aztec warriors in the face of the Spanish invasion. Altogether, *The True History of the Conquest of New Spain* is an unparalleled, soldier's-eye view of the Conquest, and a prime testimony to the wonder and mystery of the first European encounters with the great civilizations of Mesoamerica.

PRONUNCIATIONS:

Coyoacan: coy-oh-AH-cahn
Huexotzingo: way-shot-ZINC-go
Huichilobos: we-chill-LOW-bose
Iztapalapa: eats-tah-pah-LAH-pah
Malinche: mah-LEAN-chay
Montezuma: mon-tay-ZOU-mah
Narvaez: nar-VAH-yez
Texcoco: tesh-COH-coh
Tezcatepuca: tez-cat-eh-POU-cah
Tlaxcala: tlash-CAH-la

from The True History of the Conquest of New Spain[1]

[Preface]

I have observed that the most celebrated chroniclers, before they begin to write their histories, first set forth a Prologue and Preface with the argument expressed in lofty rhetoric in order to give lustre and repute to their statements, so that the studious readers who peruse them may partake of their melody and flavour. But I, being no Latin scholar, dare not venture on such a preamble or prologue, for in order properly to

1 Translated by Alfred Percival Maudslay.

extol the adventures which we met with and the heroic deeds we accomplished during the Conquest of New Spain and its provinces in the company of that valiant and doughty Captain, Don Hernando Cortés (who later on, on account of his heroic deeds, was made Marqués del Valle) there would be needed an eloquence and rhetoric far beyond my powers. That which I have myself seen and the fighting I have gone through, with the help of God, I will describe quite simply, as a fair eye witness without twisting events one way or another. I am now an old man, over eighty-four years of age, and I have lost my sight and hearing, and, as luck would have it, I have gained nothing of value to leave to my children and descendants but this my true story, and they will presently find out what a wonderful story it is.

[Cortés Prepares His Expedition]

As soon as Hernando Cortés had been appointed General he began to search for all sorts of arms, guns, powder and crossbows, and every kind of warlike stores which he could get together, and all sorts of articles to be used for barter, and other things necessary for the expedition.

Moreover he began to adorn himself and be more careful of his appearance than before, and he wore a plume of feathers with a medal, and a gold chain, and a velvet cloak trimmed with knots of gold, in fact he looked like a gallant and courageous Captain. However, he had no money to defray the expenses I have spoken about, for at that time he was very poor and much in debt, although he had a good *encomienda*[2] of Indians who were getting him a return from his gold mines, but he spent all of it on his person and on finery for his wife, whom he had recently married, and on entertaining some guests who had come to visit him. For he was affable in his manner and a good talker, and he had twice been chosen mayor of the town of Santiago Baracoa where he had settled, and in that country it is esteemed a great honour to be chosen as mayor.

When some merchant friends of his saw that he had obtained this command as Captain General, they lent him four thousand gold dollars in coin and gave him merchandise worth another four thousand dollars secured on his Indians and estates. Then he ordered two standards and banners to be made, worked in gold with the royal arms and a cross on each side with a legend which said, "Comrades, let us follow the sign of the holy Cross with true faith, and through it we shall conquer." And he ordered a proclamation to be made with the sound of drums and trumpets in the name of His Majesty and by Diego Velásquez in the King's name, and in his own as Captain General, to the effect that whatsoever person might wish to go in his company to the newly discovered lands to conquer them and to settle there, should receive his share of the gold, silver and riches which might be gained, and an *encomienda* of Indians after the country had been pacified, and that to do these things Diego Velásquez held authority from His Majesty. * * *

We continued to enlist soldiers and to buy horses, which at that time were both scarce and costly, and as Alonzo Hernándes Puertocarrero neither possessed a horse nor the wherewithal to buy one, Hernando Cortés bought him a gray mare, and paid for it with some of the golden knots off the velvet cloak which as I have said he had made at Santiago de Cuba.

[*Cortés's expedition sails along the Yucatan coast. They are driven off from some places, but find Jerónimo de Aguilar and take him on board as interpreter. They land further along the coast and fight a major battle, killing eight hundred natives. Their chiefs ("Caciques") then come to make peace.*]

---

2. A royal grant of peasants and land.

Early the next morning many Caciques and chiefs of Tabasco and the neighbouring towns arrived and paid great respect to us all, and they brought a present of gold, consisting of four diadems and some gold lizards, and two ornaments like little dogs, and earrings and five ducks, and two masks with Indian faces and two gold soles for sandals, and some other things of little value. I do not remember how much the things were worth; and they brought cloth, such as they make and wear, which was quilted stuff.

This present, however, was worth nothing in comparison with the twenty women that were given us, among them one very excellent woman called Doña Marina, for so she was named when she became a Christian. Cortés received this present with pleasure. * * * Cortés allotted one of the women to each of his captains and Doña Marina, as she was good looking and intelligent and without embarrassment, he gave to Alonzo Hernández Puertocarrero. When Puertocarrero went to Spain, Doña Marina lived with Cortés, and bore him a son named Don Martin Cortés. * * *

Before telling about the great Montezuma and his famous City of Mexico and the Mexicans, I wish to give some account of Doña Marina, who from her childhood had been the mistress and Cacica of towns and vassals. It happened in this way:

Her father and mother were chiefs and Caciques of a town called Paynala, which had other towns subject to it, and stood about eight leagues from the town of Coatzacoalcos.[3] Her father died while she was still a little child, and her mother married another Cacique, a young man, and bore him a son. It seems that the father and mother had a great affection for this son and it was agreed between them that he should succeed to their honours when their days were done. So that there should be no impediment to this, they gave the little girl, Doña Marina, to some Indians from Xicalango, and this they did by night so as to escape observation, and they then spread the report that she had died, and as it happened at this time that a child of one of their Indian slaves died they gave out that it was their daughter and the heiress who was dead.

The Indians of Xicalango gave the child to the people of Tabasco and the Tabasco people gave her to Cortés. I myself knew her mother, and the old woman's son and her halfbrother, when he was already grown up and ruled the town jointly with his mother, for the second husband of the old lady was dead. When they became Christians, the old lady was called Marta and the son Lázaro. I knew all this very well because in the year 1523 after the conquest of Mexico and the other provinces, when Cristóbal de Olid revolted in Honduras, and Cortés was on his way there, he passed through Coatzacoalcos and I and the greater number of the settlers of that town accompanied him on that expedition as I shall relate in the proper time and place. As Doña Marina proved herself such an excellent woman and good interpreter throughout the wars in New Spain, Tlaxcala, and Mexico (as I shall show later on) Cortés always took her with him, and during that expedition she was married to a gentleman named Juan Jaramillo at the town of Orizaba.

Doña Marina was a person of the greatest importance and was obeyed without question by the Indians throughout New Spain. * * * Doña Marina knew the language of Coatzacoalcos, which is that common to Mexico, and she knew the language of Tabasco, as did also Jerónimo de Aguilar, who spoke the language of Yucatan and Tabasco, which is one and the same. So that these two could understand one another clearly, and Aguilar translated into Castilian for Cortés.

3. A Nahuatl-speaking coastal city near the beginning of the Mayan-speaking Yucatan Peninsula.

This was the great beginning of our conquests and thus, thanks be to God, things prospered with us. I have made a point of explaining this matter, because without the help of Doña Marina we could not have understood the language of New Spain and Mexico.

* * *

During the morning, we arrived at a broad Causeway and continued our march towards Iztapalapa,[4] and when we saw so many cities and villages built in the water and other great towns on dry land and that straight and level Causeway going towards Mexico, we were amazed and said that it was like the enchantments they tell of in the legend of Amadis, on account of the great towers and cues and buildings rising from the water, and all built of masonry. And some of our soldiers even asked whether the things that we saw were not a dream. It is not to be wondered at that I here write it down in this manner, for there is so much to think over that I do not know how to describe it, seeing things as we did that had never been heard of or seen before, not even dreamed about.

Thus, we arrived near Iztapalapa, to behold the splendour of the other Caciques who came out to meet us, who were the Lord of the town named Cuitlahuac, and the Lord of Culuacan, both of them near relations of Montezuma. And then when we entered the city of Iztapalapa, the appearance of the palaces in which they lodged us! How spacious and well built they were, of beautiful stone work and cedar wood, and the wood of other sweet-scented trees, with great rooms and courts, wonderful to behold, covered with awnings of cotton cloth.

When we had looked well at all of this, we went to the orchard and garden, which was such a wonderful thing to see and walk in, that I was never tired of looking at the diversity of the trees, and noting the scent which each one had, and the paths full of roses and flowers, and the many fruit trees and native roses, and the pond of fresh water. There was another thing to observe, that great canoes were able to pass into the garden from the lake through an opening that had been made so that there was no need for their occupants to land. And all was cemented and very splendid with many kinds of stone monuments with pictures on them, which gave much to think about. Then the birds of many kinds and breeds which came into the pond. I say again that I stood looking at it and thought that never in the world would there be discovered other lands such as these, for at that time there was no Peru, nor any thought of it. Of all these wonders that I then beheld to-day all is overthrown and lost, nothing left standing.

Let us go on, and I will relate that the Caciques of that town and of Coyoacan brought us a present of gold, worth more than two thousand pesos.

Early next day we left Iztapalapa with a large escort of those great Caciques whom I have already mentioned. We proceeded along the Causeway which is here eight paces in width and runs so straight to the City of Mexico that it does not seem to me to turn either much or little, but, broad as it is, it was so crowded with people that there was hardly room for them all, some of them going to and others returning from Mexico, besides those who had come out to see us, so that we were hardly able to pass by the crowds of them that came; and the towers and cues[5] were full of people as

4. City on the southern shore of Lake Texcoco; endpoint of one of the three main causeways linking Tenochtitlán to the mainland.
5. Pyramids.

well as the canoes from all parts of the lake. It was not to be wondered at, for they had never before seen horses or men such as we are.

Gazing on such wonderful sights, we did not know what to say, or whether what appeared before us was real, for on one side, on the land, there were great cities, and in the lake ever so many more, and the lake itself was crowded with canoes, and in the Causeway were many bridges at intervals, and in front of us stood the great City of Mexico, and we—we did not even number four hundred soldiers! and we well remembered the words and warnings given us by the people of Huexotzingo and Tlaxcala, and the many other warnings that had been given that we should beware of entering Mexico, where they would kill us, as soon as they had us inside.

Let the curious readers consider whether there is not much to ponder over in this that I am writing. What men have there been in the world who have shown such daring? But let us get on, and march along the Causeway. When we arrived where another small causeway branches off (leading to Coyoacan, which is another city) where there were some buildings like towers, which are their oratories, many more chieftains and Caciques approached clad in very rich mantles, the brilliant liveries of one chieftain differing from those of another, and the causeways were crowded with them. The Great Montezuma had sent these great Caciques in advance to receive us, and when they came before Cortés they bade us welcome in their language, and as a sign of peace, they touched their hands against the ground, and kissed the ground with the hand.

There we halted for a good while, and Cacamatzin, the Lord of Texcoco, and the Lord of Iztapalapa and the Lord of Tacuba and the Lord of Coyoacan went on in advance to meet the Great Montezuma, who was approaching in a rich litter accompanied by other great Lords and Caciques, who owned vassals. When we arrived near to Mexico, where there were some other small towers, the Great Montezuma got down from his litter, and those great Caciques supported him with their arms beneath a marvellously rich canopy of green coloured feathers with much gold and silver embroidery and with pearls and chalchihuites suspended from a sort of bordering, which was wonderful to look at. The Great Montezuma was richly attired according to his usage, and he was shod with sandals, the soles were of gold and the upper part adorned with precious stones. The four Chieftains who supported his arms were also richly clothed according to their usage, in garments which were apparently held ready for them on the road to enable them to accompany their prince, for they did not appear in such attire when they came to receive us. Besides these four Chieftains, there were four other great Caciques who supported the canopy over their heads, and many other Lords who walked before the Great Montezuma, sweeping the ground where he would tread and spreading cloths on it, so that he should not tread on the earth. Not one of these Chieftains dared even to think of looking him in the face, but kept their eyes lowered with great reverence, except those four relations, his nephews, who supported him with their arms.

When Cortés was told that the Great Montezuma was approaching, and he saw him coming, he dismounted from his horse, and when he was near Montezuma, they simultaneously paid great reverence to one another. Montezuma bade him welcome and our Cortés replied through Doña Marina wishing him very good health. And it seems to me that Cortés, through Doña Marina, offered him his right hand, and Montezuma did not wish to take it, but he did give his hand to Cortés and then Cortés brought out a necklace which he had ready at hand, made of glass stones, which

I have already said are called Margaritas, which have within them many patterns of diverse colours, these were strung on a cord of gold and with musk so that it should have a sweet scent, and he placed it round the neck of the Great Montezuma and when he had so placed it he was going to embrace him, and those great Princes who accompanied Montezuma held back Cortés by the arm so that he should not embrace him, for they considered it an indignity.

Then Cortés through the mouth of Doña Marina told him that now his heart rejoiced at having seen such a great Prince, and that he took it as a great honour that he had come in person to meet him and had frequently shown him such favour.

Then Montezuma spoke other words of politeness to him, and told two of his nephews who supported his arms, the Lord of Texcoco and the Lord of Coyoacan, to go with us and show us to our quarters, and Montezuma with his other two relations, the Lord of Cuitlahuac and the Lord of Tacuba who accompanied him, returned to the city, and all those grand companies of Caciques and chieftains who had come with him returned in his train. As they turned back after their Prince we stood watching them and observed how they all marched with their eyes fixed on the ground without looking at him, keeping close to the wall, following him with great reverence. Thus space was made for us to enter the streets of Mexico, without being so much crowded. But who could now count the multitude of men and women and boys who were in the streets and on the azoteas,[6] and in canoes on the canals, who had come out to see us. It was indeed wonderful, and, now that I am writing about it, it all comes before my eyes as though it had happened but yesterday. Coming to think it over it seems to be a great mercy that our Lord Jesus Christ was pleased to give us grace and courage to dare to enter into such a city; and for the many times He has saved me from danger of death, as will be seen later on, I give Him sincere thanks, and in that He has preserved me to write about it, although I cannot do it as fully as is fitting or the subject needs. Let us make no words about it, for deeds are the best witnesses to what I say here and elsewhere.

* * *

[Hearing of a skirmish between native warriors and the men he had left behind at Vera Curz, Cortés decides to use the excuse to take Montezuma prisoner.]

When Cortés entered, after having made his usual salutations, he said to him through our interpreters: "Señor Montezuma, I am very much astonished that you, who are such a valiant Prince, after having declared that you are our friend, should order your Captains, whom you have stationed on the coast near to Tuxpan, to take arms against my Spaniards, and that they should dare to rob the towns which are in the keeping and under the protection of our King and master and to demand of them Indian men and women for sacrifice, and should kill a Spaniard, one of my brothers, and a horse." (He did not wish to speak of the Captain nor of the six soldiers who died as soon as they arrived at Villa Rica, for Montezuma did not know about it, nor did the Indian Captains who had attacked them.) Cortés went on to say: "Being such a friend of yours I ordered my Captains to do all that was possible to help and serve you, and you have done exactly the contrary to us. Also in the affair at Cholula your Captains and a large force of warriors had received your own commands to kill us. I forgave it at the time out of my great regard for you, but now again your vassals and Captains have become insolent, and hold secret consultations stating that you wish us to be killed. I do not wish to begin a war on this account nor to destroy this city, I am

6. Roof terraces.

willing to forgive it all, if silently and without raising any disturbance you will come with us to our quarters, where you will be as well served and attended to as though you were in your own house, but if you cry out or make any disturbance you will immediately be killed by these my Captains, whom I brought solely for this purpose."

When Montezuma heard this he was terrified and dumbfounded, and replied that he had never ordered his people to take arms against us, and that he would at once send to summon his Captains so that the truth should be known, and he would chastise them, and at that very moment he took from his arm and wrist the sign and seal of Huichilobos, which was only done when he gave an important and weighty command which was to be carried out at once. With regard to being taken prisoner and leaving his Palace against his will, he said that he was not the person to whom such an order could be given, and that he would not go. Cortés replied to him with very good arguments and Montezuma answered him with even better, showing that he ought not to leave his house. In this way more than half an hour was spent over talk, and when Juan Velásquez de Leon and the other Captains saw that they were wasting time over it and could not longer await the moment when they should remove him from his house and hold him a prisoner, they spoke to Cortés somewhat angrily and said: "What is the good of your making so many words, let us either take him prisoner, or stab him, tell him once more that if he cries out or makes an uproar we will kill him, for it is better at once to save our lives or to lose them," and as Juan Velásquez said this with a loud and rather terrifying voice, for such was his way of speaking, Montezuma, who saw that our Captains were angered, asked Doña Marina what they were saying in such loud tones.

As Doña Marina was very clever, she said: "Señor Montezuma, what I counsel you is to go at once to their quarters without any disturbance at all, for I know that they will pay you much honour as a great Prince such as you are, otherwise you will remain here a dead man, but in their quarters you will learn the truth." Then Montezuma said to Cortés: "Señor Malinche, if this is what you desire, I have a son and two legitimate daughters, take them as hostages, and do not put this affront on me, what will my chieftains say if they see me taken off as a prisoner?" Cortés replied to him that he must come with them himself and there was no alternative. At the end of much more discussion that took place, Montezuma said that he would go willingly, and then Cortés and our Captains bestowed many caresses on him and told him that they begged him not to be annoyed, and to tell his captains and the men of his guard that he was going of his own free will, because he had spoken to his Idol Huichilobos and the priests who attended him, and that it was beneficial for his health and the safety of his life that he should be with us. His rich litter, in which he was used to go out with all the Captains who accompanied him, was promptly brought, and he went to our quarters where we placed guards and watchmen over him.

All the attentions and amusements which it was possible for him to have, both Cortés and all of us did our best to afford him, and he was not put under any personal restraint, and soon all the principal Mexican Chieftains and his nephews came to talk with him, and to learn the reason of his seizure, and whether he wished them to attack us. Montezuma answered them that he was delighted to be here some days with us of his own free will and not by force, and that when he wished for anything he would tell them so, and that they must not excite themselves nor the City, nor were they to take it to heart, for what had happened about his being there was agreeable to his Huichilobos, and certain priests who knew had told him so, for they had spoken to the Idol about it. In this way which I have now related the capture of the Great Montezuma was effected.

There, where he remained, he had his service and his women and his baths in which he bathed himself, and twenty great chiefs always stayed in his company holding their ancient offices, as well as his councillors and captains, and he stayed there a prisoner without showing any anger at it, and Ambassadors from distant lands came there with their suites, and brought him his tribute, and he carried on his important business.

I will not say anything more at present about this imprisonment, and will relate how the messengers whom Montezuma sent with his sign and seal to summon the Captains who had killed our soldiers, brought them before him as prisoners and what he said to them I do not know, but he sent them on to Cortés, so that he might do justice to them, and their confession was taken when Montezuma was not present and they confessed that what I have already stated was true, that their Prince had ordered them to wage war and to extract tribute, and that if any Teules should appear in defence of the towns, they too should be attacked or killed. When Cortés heard this confession he sent to inform Montezuma how it implicated him in the affair, and Montezuma made all the excuses he could, and our captain sent him word that he believed the confession himself, but that although Montezuma deserved punishment in conformity with the ordinances of our King, to the effect that any person causing others, whether guilty or innocent, to be killed, shall die for it, yet he was so fond of him and wished him so well, that even if that crime lay at his door, he, Cortés, would pay the penalty with his own life sooner than allow Montezuma's to pass away. With all this that Cortés sent to tell him, Montezuma felt anxious, and without any further discussion Cortés sentenced those captains to death and to be burned in front of Montezuma's palace. This sentence was promptly carried out, and, so that there could be no obstruction while they were being burned, Cortés ordered shackles to be put on Montezuma himself, and when this was done Montezuma roared with rage, and if before this he was scared, he was then much more so.

After the burning was over our Cortés with five of our captains went to Montezuma's apartment and Cortés himself took off the fetters, and he spoke such loving words to him that his anger soon passed off, for our Cortés told him that he not only regarded him as a brother, but much more, and that, as he was already Lord and King of so many towns and provinces, if it were possible he would make him Lord of many more countries as time went on, such as he had not been able to subdue, and which did not now obey him, and he told him that if he now wished to go to his Palace, that he would give him leave to go. Cortés told him this through our interpreters and while Cortés was saying it the tears apparently sprang to Montezuma's eyes. He answered with great courtesy, that he thanked him for it (but he well knew that Cortés' speech was mere words), and that now at present it was better for him to stay there a prisoner, for there was danger, as his chieftains were numerous, and his nephews and relations came every day to him to say that it would be a good thing to attack us and free him from prison, that as soon as they saw him outside they might drive him to it. He did not wish to see revolutions in his city, but if he did not comply with their wishes possibly they would want to set up another Prince in his place. And so he was putting those thoughts out of their heads by saying that Huichilobos had sent him word that he should remain a prisoner.

[As Cortés solidified his position in Mexico, he sent letters and gold directly to the king in Spain, ignoring his superior, Diego Velázquez, governor of Cuba. Angered, Velázquez sent a force of four hundred men, commanded by his lieutenant Pánfilo de Narváez, to Vera Cruz to supplant Cortés. Cortés hurried to the coast with most *of his men, leaving Pedro de Alvarado and a small force to keep Montezuma under house arrest. Cortés defeated Narvaez, and enlisted most of Narvaez's men in his own service.]*

Let us return now to Narvaez and a black man whom he brought covered with smallpox, and a very black affair it was for New Spain, for it was owing to him that the whole country was stricken and filled with it, from which there was great mortality, for according to what the Indians said they had never had such a disease, and, as they did not understand it, they bathed very often, and on that account a great number of them died; so that dark as was the lot of Narvaez, still blacker was the death of so many persons who were not Christians.

Let me say how ill luck suddenly turns the wheel, and after great good fortune and pleasure follows sadness; it so happened that at this moment came the news that Mexico was in revolt, and that Pedro de Alvarado was besieged in his fortress and quarters, and that they had set fire to this same fortress in two places, and had killed seven of his soldiers and wounded many others, and he sent to demand assistance with great urgency and haste. This news was brought by two Tlaxcalans without any letter, but a letter soon arrived by two other Tlaxcalans sent by Pedro de Alvarado in which he told the same story. When we heard this bad news, God knows how greatly it depressed us.

By forced marches we began our journey to Mexico, Narvaez and Salvatierra remaining as prisoners in Villa Rica.

Just at this moment, as we were ready to start, there arrived four great chieftains sent to Cortés by the great Montezuma to complain to him of Pedro de Alvarado, and what they said, with tears streaming from their eyes, was that Pedro de Alvarado sallied out from his quarters with all the soldiers that Cortés had left with him, and, for no reason at all, fell on their chieftains and Caciques who were dancing and celebrating a feast in honour of their Idols Huichilobos and Tezcatepuca, Pedro de Alvarado having given them leave to do so. He killed and wounded many of them and in defending themselves they had killed six of his soldiers. Thus they made many complaints against Pedro de Alvarado, and Cortés, somewhat disgusted, replied to the messengers that he would go to Mexico and put it all to rights. So they went off with that reply to their great Montezuma, who it is said, resented it as a very bad one and was enraged at it.

[The Battle for the City]

Diego de Ordás set out in the way that he was ordered with his four hundred soldiers, but he had hardly reached the middle of the street along which he was to march, when so many squadrons of Mexican warriors fell on him and so many more were on the roofs of the houses, and they made such fierce attacks that on the first assault they killed eight soldiers and wounded all the rest, and Diego de Ordás himself was wounded in three places, and in this manner he could not advance one step further but had to return little by little to his quarters. During the retreat they killed another good soldier named Lyscano who, with a broadsword, had done the work of a very valiant man.

At that moment, while many squadrons came out against Ordás, many more approached our quarters and shot off so many javelins and stones from slings, and arrows, that they wounded on that occasion alone over forty-six of our men, and twelve of them died of their wounds; and such a number of warriors fell upon us that Diego de Ordás, who was coming in retreat, could not reach our quarters on account of the fierce assaults they made on him, some from the rear and others in front and others from the roofs.

Little availed our cannon, or our muskets, crossbows and lances, or the thrusts we gave them, or our good fighting, for although we killed and wounded many of them, yet they managed to reach us by pushing forward over the points of our swords and lances, and closing up their squadrons never desisted from their brave attack, nor could we push them away from us. * * *

We passed the night in dressing wounds and in mending the breaches in the walls that the enemy had made, and in getting ready for the next day. Then, as soon as it was dawn, our Captain decided that all of us and Narvaez' men should sally out to fight with them and that we should take the cannon and muskets and crossbows and endeavour to defeat them, or at least to make them feel our strength and valour better than the day before. I may state that when we came to this decision, the Mexicans were arranging the very same thing. We fought very well, but they were so strong, and had so many squadrons which relieved each other from time to time, that even if ten thousand Trojan Hectors and as many more Roldans[7] had been there, they would not have been able to break through them.

* * *

We made attacks on the Mexicans every day and succeeded in capturing many idol towers, houses, canals, and other openings and bridges which they had constructed from house to house, and we filled them all up with adobes and the timbers from the houses that we pulled down and destroyed and we kept guard over them, but notwithstanding all this trouble that we took, the enemy came back and deepened them and widened the openings and erected more barricades. * * *

I well understand that interested readers will be surfeited with seeing so many fights every day but one cannot do less, for during the ninety and three days that we besieged this strong and great City we had war and combats every day and every night as well. However, when it seemed to us that we were victorious, great disasters were really coming upon us, and we were in the greatest danger of perishing in all three camps, as will be seen later on. * * *

When we had retreated near to our quarters and had already crossed a great opening where there was much water the arrows, javelins and stones could no longer reach us. Sandoval, Francisco de Lugo and Andrés de Tápia were standing with Pedro de Alvarado each one relating what had happened to him and what Cortés had ordered, when again there was sounded the dismal drum of Huichilobos and many other shells and horns and things like trumpets and the sound of them all was terrifying, and we all looked towards the lofty Cue where they were being sounded, and saw that our comrades whom they had captured when they defeated Cortés were being carried by force up the steps, and they were taking them to be sacrificed. When they got them up to a small square in front of the oratory, where their accursed idols are kept, we saw them place plumes on the heads of many of them and with things like fans in their hands they forced them to dance before Huichilobos, and after they had danced they immediately placed them on their backs on some rather narrow stones which had been prepared as places for sacrifice, and with stone knives they sawed open their chests and drew out their palpitating hearts and offered them to the idols that were there, and they kicked the bodies down the steps, and Indian butchers who were waiting below cut off the arms and feet and flayed the skin off the faces, and prepared it afterwards like glove leather with the beards on, and kept those for the festivals when they celebrated drunken orgies, and the flesh they ate in *chilmole*.[8] In the same way they

---

7. Rolandor, a great hero of medieval romance.
8. Chili sauce.

sacrificed all the others and ate the legs and arms and offered the hearts and blood to their idols, as I have said, and the bodies, that is their entrails and feet, they threw to the tigers and lions which they kept in the house of the carnivores which I have spoken about in an earlier chapter.

When we saw those cruelties all of us in our camp said the one to the other: "Thank God that they are not carrying me off to-day to be sacrificed."

It should also be noted that we were not far away from them, yet we could render them no help, and could only pray God to guard us from such a death.

* * *

From all three camps we were now advancing into the City, Cortés on his side, Sandoval on his and Pedro de Alvarado on our side, and we reached the spot where the spring was, that I have already spoken about, where the Mexicans drank the brackish water, and we broke it up and destroyed it so that they might not make use of it. Some Mexicans were guarding it and we had a good skirmish with them. We could already move freely through all parts of the streets we had captured, for they were already levelled and free from water and openings and the horses could move very easily.

Thus the ten Companies of Pedro de Alvarado advanced fighting and reached Tlatelolco, and there were so many Mexicans guarding their Idols and lofty cues, and they had raised so many barricades that we were fully two hours before we were able to capture them and get inside. Now that the horses had space to gallop, although most of them were wounded, they helped us very much, and the horsemen speared many Mexicans.

[*Day after day, the Spanish penetrate further into the city, systematically levelling blocks of houses as they proceed. As they take the last districts of the city, the new ruler Cuauhtemoc ("Guatemoc") tries to flee by canoe. He is caught and brought to Cortés.*]

While they were bringing him, Cortés ordered a guest chamber to be prepared as well as could be done at the time, with mats and cloths and seats, and a good supply of the food which Cortés had reserved for himself. Sandoval and Holguin soon arrived with Guatemoc, and the two captains between them led him up to Cortés, and when he came in front of him he paid him great respect, and Cortés embraced Guatemoc with delight, and was very affectionate to him and his captains. Then Guatemoc said to Cortés: "Señor Malinche, I have surely done my duty in defence of my City, and I can do no more and I come by force and a prisoner into your presence and into your power. Take that dagger that you have in your belt and kill me at once with it," and when he said this he wept tears and sobbed and other great Lords whom he had brought with him also wept. Cortés answered him through Doña Marina and Aguilar very affectionately, that he esteemed him all the more for having been so brave as to defend the City, and he was deserving of no blame, on the contrary it was more in his favour than otherwise.

What he wished was that Guatemoc had made peace of his own free will before the city had been so far destroyed, and so many of his Mexicans had died, but now that both had happened there was no help for it and it could not be mended, let his spirit and the spirit of his Captains take rest, and he should rule in Mexico and over his provinces as he did before. Then Guatemoc and his Captains said that they accepted his favour, and Cortés asked after his wife and other great ladies, the wives of other Captains who, he had been told, had come with Guatemoc. Guatemoc himself answered and said that he had begged Gonzalo de Sandoval and García Holguin that they might remain in the canoes while he came to see what orders Malinche gave them. Cortés at once sent for them and ordered them all to be given of the best that at that time there was in the camp to eat, and as it was late and was beginning to rain, Cortés arranged for them to go to Coyoacan, and took Guatemoc and all his family and household and many chieftains with him, and he ordered Pedro de Alvarado, Gonzalo de Sandoval and the other captains each to go to his own quarters and camp, and we went to Tacuba, Sandoval to Tepeaquilla and Cortés to Coyoacan. Guatemoc and his captains were captured on the thirteenth day of August at the time of vespers on the day of Señor San Hipólito in the year one thousand five hundred and twenty-one, thanks to our Lord Jesus Christ and our Lady the Virgin Santa Maria, His Blessed Mother. Amen.

THE AZTEC-SPANISH DIALOGUES OF 1524

Following the military conquest of Mexico, it soon became clear that the spiritual conquest of the population was going to involve a much longer struggle. In 1524 the Pope authorized the Spanish emperor Charles V to send a select band of "twelve Apostles" to Mexico to oversee this process. Not long after their arrival, the twelve staged a public disputation with a group of Aztec priests and nobles; this extraordinary text is the result of those debates. Over several days, the Spanish friars and the Aztec spokesmen took turns in making the case for and against conversion. Hoping for a decisive and exemplary success, the friars arranged for extensive notes to be taken in Nahuatl, to provide a written record that could be used to persuade groups elsewhere. Forty years later, the tireless Bernardino de Sahagún organized the transcript and enlisted the aid of several of his native seminarians and four native elders "to transcribe it into suitably polished Nahuatl," as he wrote in a preface to the compilation. This revised manuscript was never published, perhaps because it proved to give such eloquent expression to the Aztec priests' reasons for remaining loyal to their gods even after their spectacular defeat by the Europeans. Preserved in secret archives at the Vatican and long forgotten, it was rediscovered and published only in 1924.

According to a Spanish summary that Sahagún wrote at the beginning of the manuscript, the dialogues did conclude with the conversion of the native speakers, but the second half of the manuscript has been lost. In the fourteen surviving chapters, the friars argue that the native gods are really devils who have rightly been overthrown by God, while the native elders defend their loyalty to the gods who have sustained their culture over many centuries. Jorge Klor de Alva's sensitive translation divides the elevated rhetoric of the speeches into units of sense, approximating the effect that oral delivery might have had, as the Aztec nobles attempt to negotiate a space for traditional beliefs and values in a radically changed world.

from The Aztec-Spanish Dialogues of 1524[1]

[The Friars' Opening Speech]

>Listen well, our beloved,
>you who caused yourselves to bear witness here,
>20   you who came out together here,
>you Mexicas, you Tenochcas, you lords, you speakers,
>please approach hither and consider well.
>If only it be able to settle where your heart makes a home,

---

1. Translated by Jorge Klor de Alva.

25   (when we set it forth, when we say it)
      the word of the message.

      Let us not disconcert you as to something,
      take care lest you see us as something superior,
      indeed, we are only your peers, we are only common people,
      we are men such as you are, we are surely not gods.
30   We are also inhabitants on the earth, we also drink, we also eat,
      we also die of cold, we are also overwhelmed by heat,
      we are also mortal, we are also destructible.
      Indeed, we are only messengers, we were only sent here,
      to the place of your homeland, to your water, to your mountain.
35   We came bearing it, his honorable breath, his honorable word,
      of this one who everywhere in the world, on the earth,
      is the great speaker of divine things,
      his name is Holy Father Pope.
                              * * *
      And it is not something else for which we came,
      for which we were sent hither;
125   only on account of spiritual compassion for you,
      for your salvation.
      Then, nothing earthly does he desire,
      the great speaker of divine things,
      hence, neither jade, nor gold,
130   nor quetzal plumes, nor anything precious.
      Now, only your completely total salvation he desires.
                              * * *
270   But, perhaps, you ask, now, perhaps, you say,
      this one, the divine word you mention with reverence,
      where did it come from? Where did it appear?
      Who gave it to you? Who showed it to you?
      Where did the great speaker of divine things acquire it?
275   Be so kind as to raise your ears, so you will be able to hear,
      from where came the divine word we come to give you,
      we come to make you comprehend.
      Understand and pursue earnestly the truth of it,
      that your heart may be properly filled.
280   Indeed, already it has been a long time,
      since He, the True God, Speaker,[2]
      Possessor of the Near, Possessor of the Surrounding,[3]
      He by Whom All Live, showed it to His most beloved,
      to His servants, these whose heart was very good, upright,
285   His great knowledge, His choices,
      their name is patriarchs, prophets.
      And, indeed, here on the earth a man He came to make Himself,
      He was able, as a man, to appeal to them,

---

2. *Tlatoani* in Nahuatl, the traditional term for "ruler."
3. Epithets of the god Tezcatlipoca, now transferred to the Christian God.

	the apostles, the evangelists.
290	And they are those to whom He gave
	His venerable breath, His venerable word, the divine word.
	And He commanded them so they will paint it,
	so that it will be preserved on the earth,
	so that the men on the earth will be instructed by the divine word.
295	And the Holy Father guards all the divine words they left,
	these formerly mentioned, His beloved of Our Lord, God.
	All is in the divine book, it lies blackened, it lies colored.
	All is there, everything is conserved,
	these which now are the very marvelous divine words.
300	And likewise, he made us bear it hither now, he, the Holy Father,
	so that we will give it to you, we will notify you of it.
	Indeed, this one, the divine word,
	does not resemble the speech of the common people on the earth.
	Indeed, very marvelous, true is His venerable breath, His venerable word,
305	the Creator of Men's and this one of the Savior of Men,
	the One Sole God, the Speaker,
	Possessor of the Near, Possessor of the Surrounding,
	On account of that it is properly named divine word;
	very truly the one followed.
310	Absolutely no one will be able to contradict it,
	even though he is a great knower of things on earth.

* * *

	There it is told, indeed, how on the earth,
580	there, is His precious dominion as a man, Our Lord Jesus Christ.
	He, the Only True God, Speaker,
	Creator of Men, and Savior of Men, Jesus Christ,
	here on the earth He founded His precious dominion,
	His honorable mat, His honorable seat, He set down,
585	and it is this whose name is dominion of heaven,
	moreover, its name is Holy Catholic Church.[4]
	Because of that, it is called the dominion of heaven,
	indeed, absolutely no one will enter heaven
	if he will not belong to it, the Holy Church.

* * *

	There where He resides, He by Whom All Live, Jesus Christ,
640	it is very necessary for you that you detest them,
	you despise them, you hate them, and you spit on them,
	these whom you have always regarded as gods.
	These gods which you esteemed, indeed, are truly not gods,
645	indeed, they only make a mockery of anyone.
	Furthermore, moreover, it is very necessary that you avoid them,
	that you abandon them, all these various transgressions,
	these injuries to the heart of the Possessor of the Near,
	Possessor of the Surrounding,
	He by Whom All Live, which you have continually caused.

---

4. *Sancta yglesia catholica* in the Nahuatl text.

[The Aztecs' Reply]

After it ended, it terminated,
this the venerable speech of the twelve Fathers,
at once one of those lords, speakers,
695 stood up, he greeted the divine guardians,
and a little bit, one lip, two lips,
by this he returned their venerable breath, their venerable words.
He said: Our lords, you have endured much,
indeed, when you came to approach us on this land,
700 indeed, when you came to govern it
from your honorable water, your honorable mountain.
From where? What kind of place is it, the place of our lords,
there, from where you came?
Indeed, from among the clouds, from among the mist, you have come out.
705 Indeed, before you, about you we carefully observe, admire,
the possessors of the water, the possessors of the mountain.
Here we acquire it, we seize it, the new word,
as if it were something celestial, that which you say.
And here it is shown to us, it is opened for us,
710 His precious coffer, His precious hamper,
that of the Man, Our Lord, Possessor of Heaven, Possessor of Earth.
And, thus, he sends you hither, the man, the great speaker,
from where his breath is made known,
from the place of our lords, the Holy Father, and the Emperor.
715 Indeed, here before us you place the turquoise, the bracelet,
here we marvel at it as if it were a round jade
able to shine without its shade, without its defect,
and as if it were a large precious quetzal plume, extremely green.
Indeed, they left, He destroyed them,
720 He burnt them, the Man, Our Lord,
the speakers, these who came to be,
these who came to live on the earth,
and who came to guard it, who came to govern it,
your honorable mat, your honorable seat,
725 for a brief day, for a moment,
here in Mexico, in Tenochtitlan,
and here in Aculhuacan, Tetzcoco, here in Tlacopan:
Motecuhzomatzin,[5]
Ahuitzotzin, Axayacatzin, Tizocicatzin, and Itzcoatzin,
the elder Motecuhzoma and Nezahualcoyotzin,
730 Nezahualpilli, Totoquihuaztli, and the elder Tezozomoctli.
If it had occurred during their time,
indeed, they would have returned
your precious breath, your precious word.
Likewise, they would have entreated you
735 by reason of your precious love for people,
which we admire here.

5. A list follows of ten earlier kings.

But, we, what now, immediately, will we say?
Supposing that we, we are those who shelter the people,
we are mothers to the people, we are fathers to the people,
740   perchance, then, are we, here before you, to destroy it, the ancient law;
the one which was greatly esteemed by our grandparents, our women;
the one which they would go speaking of favorably,
the one which they would go admiring, the lords, the speakers?

And these, oh our lords,
745   indeed, they are there, they still guide us,
these who carry us, these who govern us,
in relation to these being served,
indeed, these who are our gods, these who have their merit,
that of the tail, of the wing,
750   the ones who offer things, the ones who offer incense,
and those named the feathered serpents.
These are knowers of the word,
and their charge with which they trouble themselves,
by night, by day, is the act of burning *copal,*
755   the act of offering incense, thorns, *acxoyatl,*[6] the act of blood letting.
These see, these trouble themselves,
with the journey, the orderly course of the heavens,
according to how the night is divided.
And these continually look at it, these continually relate it,
760   these continually cause the book to cackle.
The black, the color, is in the paintings they continually carry.
Indeed, they are the ones who continually carry us,
they guide us, they cause the path to speak to us.
They are the ones who put it in order,
765   such as how a year falls,
such as how the count of the destinies-feasts follows its path,
and each one of the complete counts.
They trouble themselves with it,
they have their charge, their commission,
770   their duty which is the divine word.
And we are those, indeed, who but have as our sole task
(what is called) divine water, fire. And only we speak on it,
we trouble ourselves with the tribute, of the tail, the wing;
so that it seizes its headdress of heron feathers, its jacket of cords,
775   and its digging stick, its tumpline;[7]
that which is placed in front of the hearth;
in this way people are made "slaves."
Let us, for now, assemble them,
the ones who offer things, the feathered serpents.
780   Let us give them His precious breath, His precious word,
this one of the Man, Our Lord.
So that they, perhaps, will restore it, will return it,

---

6. Needles used for ritual bloodletting.
7. A band running across the forehead and back behind the shoulders to support a pack.

785

this which we have seized, this which we have grasped,
from your honorable breasts, your honorable heads,
we will elevate it, our lords.
If only you would calm your precious hearts, your precious flesh;
remain on your honorable mat, your honorable seat.

[The Aztecs' Second Speech][8]

915

And now, what, in what manner, what sort of thing will we say,
which we will raise to your honorable ears?

* * *

Have we, perhaps, been negligent in doing things?
Oh, where, by chance, are we truly to go?
Indeed, we are common people, we are destructible, we are mortal.

935

Oh, indeed, let us die, oh, indeed, let us perish,
since, indeed, the gods have been defeated!
If only it would settle itself,
your honorable heart, your honorable flesh (Oh, our lords).
Indeed, on account of this, we divide something very little,

940

now, on account of this, we open it very little,
his coffer, his hamper, this one of the man, our lord.

You tell them, indeed, that we do not know Him,
the Possessor of the Near, Possessor of the Surrounding,
the Possessor of Heaven, Possessor of Earth.

945

You tell them, indeed, that our gods are not real gods.
It is a new word, this one you tell them,
and because of it we are distressed,
because of it we are extremely frightened.
Indeed, these our makers,

950

these who came to be, these who came to live on the earth,
did not speak in this way.
Verily, they gave us their law.
They followed them as true, they served them,
they honored them, the gods.

955

They taught us all their forms of serving, their modes of honoring.
Thus, before them we eat earth, thus, we bleed ourselves,
thus, we discharge the debt ourselves, thus, we burn *copal*,
and, thus, we cause something to be killed.
They used to say that, verily, they, the gods, by whose grace one lives,

960

they merited us.
When? Where? While it was still night.
And they used to say, indeed, they give us our supper, our breakfast,
and all that is drinkable, edible,
this our meat, the corn, the bean,

965

the wild amaranth, the lime-leaved sage.
They are those from whom we request the water, the rain,
by which the things of the earth are made.

---

8. After hearing renewed Spanish arguments that their gods are really devils, the Aztecs take time to consult and then return to speak further.

Furthermore, they are rich themselves, they are happy themselves,
they are possessors of goods, they are owners of goods,
970 by which always, forever, it germinates there, it grows green in their house.
Where? What kind of place is it, the place of Tlaloc?[9]
Hunger never occurs there, nothing is diseased, nothing is poor.
And also, they give to the people prowess, courage, the chase, and the
    lip-grass,
the instrument by which something is bound, the loincloth, the mantle,
975 the flowers, the tobacco,
the jade, the quetzal plumes, the gold.

And when, where were these thus summoned,
when implored, when held as gods, when honored?
It is already a very long time.
980 When? At another time it was in Tula.
When? At another time it was in Huapalcalco.
When? At another time it was in Xochitlalpan.
When? At another time it was in Tamoanchan.
At another time it was in Yoallichan.
985 When? At another time it was in Teotihuacan.
Indeed, they, everywhere in the world,
they caused the people to construct with stones their mat, their seat.
They gave to the people the lordship, the dominion, the fame, the glory.

And, perchance, now, are we those who will destroy it, the ancient law?
990 The law of the Chichimecs? The law of the Toltecs?
The law of the Colhuaque? The law of the Tepanecs?
Already our heart is this way:
through him one is made to live,
through him one is given birth,
995 on account of him one is made to grow,
on account of him one is made to mature,
by means of this one, who is summoned,
by means of this one, who is implored.
Hear, our lords, beware of doing something to them,
1000 this your precious tail, your precious wing,
so much the more so that it will be abandoned,
so much the more so that it will be destroyed.
In this way also the old man,
in this way also the old woman had her growth, had her increase in age.
1005 Oh, that the gods be not angry with us.
Oh, that their anger, their wrath, not come.
And let us beware that on account of that
it not rise before us, on us, the tail, the wing.
Let us beware that on account of that we not stir it up,
1010 let us beware that on account of that we not provoke it,
by saying to it: no longer will it summon them,
no longer will it implore them.

9. The heavenly realm of Tlaloc, god of rain.

In the meantime, calmly, peacefully,
consider it, our lords, whatever is necessary.

1015 Indeed, our heart is not able to be full.
And, indeed, absolutely we do not yet agree to it ourselves,
we do not yet make it true for ourselves.
We ourselves will cause you injury to the heart.
Indeed, here they lie, the possessors of water, the possessors of mountains,

1020 the lords, the speakers, these who carry it, these who bear it, the world.
It is enough that we have already left it alone,
we have lost it, we have had it taken away,
we have had it prohibited, the mat, the seat.
Indeed, if we will only remain there,

1025 we will only cause them to be restricted.
Do it to us, whatever it is you will desire.
Indeed, we return it all by this, by this we respond to it,
your precious breath, your precious word, our lords.

[The Friars Reply]

Indeed, we will tell you everything,
we will cause you to hear it, if you desire it.

1115 And we will be able to cause you to have a full heart,
because we guard it, the divine book, the divine word,
there where it lies visible, it lies painted,
it lies arranged, all that which is His precious word,
this one of the Possessor of the Near, Possessor of the Surrounding.

* * *

You did not guard it, the divine book, the divine word.

1145 It never came to reach you,
His precious breath, His precious word,
this one of the Possessor of Heaven, the Possessor of Earth.
And, then, you are blind, you are deaf,
as if in darkness, in gloom, you live.

1150 On account of this your faults are, furthermore, not very great.
But now, if you do not desire to hear it,
the precious breath, the precious word of God
(this one He gives to you), you will be in much danger.
And God, Who has commenced your destruction,

1155 will conclude it, you will be completely lost.

Our beloved, so that you may hear it rightly, that which you desire,
likewise, so that your heart will be able to be full,
it is necessary that first we will cause you to hear,
we will manifest to you, of what precious sort is Our Lord God,

1160 He by Whom All Live, This One we came to show you.
And, indeed, already it is late, now, already, the time to eat is distant.
Tomorrow at dawn, when the sun comes out,
everybody will come hither,
here one will be assembled, something will be heard.

1165 For now all may depart, please go, eat something.
For now rest, let your heart be settled.

The court poets of the Aztecs and their allies created the most extensive and exquisite body of poetry ever known to have existed in Mesoamerica. Many of these lyrics are marked by a gentle melancholy and a delicate aestheticism, with poems often taking poetry itself as their subject. Poetry was commonly described metaphorically in Nahuatl as *in xochitl in cuicatl,* "flowers and birdsong," emblems of beauty in a transient world. The poets delighted in creating beautiful images and in elegant plays on words, and often intertwined friendship and poetry together as the greatest human values. As one poem puts it in the collection known as *Cantares Mexicanos:*

> We lift our songs, our flowers,
> these songs of the Only Spirit.
> Then friends embrace,
> the companions in each others' arms.
> So it has been said by Tochihuitzin,
> so it has been said by Coyolchiuqui:
> We come here only to sleep,
> we come here only to dream.

The same images and methods came to be used for very different purposes as the Aztec empire grew over the course of the century before the Spanish conquest. Court poets began to celebrate the beauties of conquest, and death in battle became an act of almost poetic virtue: "Jaguar flowers are opening," one poem declares; "knife-death flowers are becoming delicious upon the field." As another poem puts it, "We'll dare to go where fame, where glory, is gotten, where nobility is gotten, where flower death is won."

Aztec poetry underwent a further revolution with the coming of Cortés and the fall of the Aztec empire. Now the surviving poets had to consider the brevity of human life in a new way, involving not only individual mortality but the swift defeat of the greatest empire the region had ever known. Both the traditional themes and the unsettling colonial context are apparent in the poems as they have come down to us, chiefly in two manuscripts compiled between 1550 and 1585: the *Cantares Mexicanos* ("Songs of the Mexicans") and the *Romances de los Señores de la Nueva España* ("Ballads of the Lords of New Spain"). Written in the Roman alphabet but in the Aztecs' language, Nahuatl, these collections of close to two hundred poems record songs that likely come from a range of times. Some appear to be purely pre-Conquest poems, showing no trace of later events; others seem to be traditional poems revised in light of the Conquest; others (like the "Fish Song" and the "Water-Pouring Song" below) were clearly composed as direct responses to the Conquest itself.

The poems interweave the natural imagery of brightly colored tropical birds and flowers with a social landscape of great nobles, such as the Aztec king Moctezuma and the pre-Conquest ruler Nezahualcoyotl (1402–1472), king of the allied city of Texcoco. Often the poet sings in the name of these rulers or other nobles, and traditionally many poems were ascribed to Nezahualcoyotl himself, much as the Hebrew psalms were ascribed to King David. In post-Conquest times, the poems at times refer to still-living figures, at other times recall great heroes of the past, invoking their aid in the ongoing struggle for life and liberty. Even the most pressing historical events are seen through the prism of metaphor, as in the "Fish Song," whose speaker presents the Aztecs as fish, hoping the new bishop will stop eating them now that Lent is over and Easter has come. The long, haunting "Water-Pouring Song" shows the nobles pressed into service hauling water, and the poet turns their water jugs into images of Aztec culture and finally of the poem itself.

The "Water-Pouring Song" extends its range abroad, recounting a trip across the ocean by the Mexican leader Martin Ecatl in 1525 to meet Spain's emperor Charles V, and it includes a surreal encounter with Pope Clement VII, sitting on his mat with his turquoise blowgun. The post-Conquest poems often speak directly to the new God whom the Spaniards have brought, Dios (or Tios, or Tiox, as they call him) and his companions Jesus, Mary, and the Holy Spirit (*spilitu xanto* in the manuscript). Often God is addressed as Ipalnemoani, "Giver of Life," or as Tloque Nahuaque, "The Ever Present, Ever Near," traditional names for the great god Tezcatlipoca. Never named outright or seen directly, the old gods often seem still to be in the wings in these poems.

As it is set down in the manuscripts, Aztec poetry is written not in verse form but in paragraphs of varying lengths, sometimes prefaced with syllables that indicate rhythms to be used (*titico titico titico, toco toco toti*). A modern translator has a choice: to break these paragraphs into shorter lines corresponding to verses, usually guided by repetitions and variations in phrasing; or to retain the paragraphing of the manuscripts, presenting the poems as chants rather than as lyric utterances. The first selection here is set in verse form, which is how the poems have usually been published by Mexican scholars; the rest of the selections are given in paragraph form, in the eloquent contemporary translations of John Bierhorst.

The largest compilation of Aztec poetry, the *Cantares* manuscript, was apparently assembled by native informants under the direction of the Spanish friar Bernardino de Sahagún, compiler of the great historical and cultural survey called the *General History of the Affairs of New Spain*. Sahagún was evidently seeking to collect the poems to serve as a sort of sourcebook he could use in composing hymns and psalms in Nahuatl for his parishioners to use. Fascinated by the native cultures and deeply learned in Nahuatl, Sahagún had no interest in preserving the poems for their own sake; on the contrary, in his preface to his book of psalms he wrote that his parishioners' "persistence in singing their old songs arouses a good deal of suspicion as to the sincerity of their Christian Faith." It is a fitting poetic irony that these poems have been preserved for us today thanks to Sahagún's effort to study and then replace them so that "the praises of idols and idolatry be buried as they deserve."

PRONUNCIATIONS:

Dozens of names of people and places appear in the following poems; only a few of the most common are listed here. Generally Nahuatl names are pronounced as they are spelled, following Spanish usage at the time; *x* is pronounced *sh; h* is silent (*hua* has the sound *wa*); and *que* has the sound *kay*. Names are usually accented on the next to last syllable.

cuicatl: KWEE-cah'l
Cantares Mexicanos: cahn-TAR-race may-he-CAH-nohs
Huexotzinco: way-show-TZEEN-coh
Moctezuma: mock-tay-ZOOM-ah
Nahuatl: NAH-waht'l
Nezahualcoyotl: nets-ah-wahl-COY-yaht'l
Tezozomoc: tet-zoh-TZOH-mock
xochitl: SHOW-cheet'l
Sahagún: sah-ah-GOUN

Songs of the Aztec Nobility

Make your beginning, you who sing[1]

Xi huel om pehua
ti cuicanitl.
Ma oc xocon tzotzona
moxochihuehueuh.
5 Ma ic xi quimahuiltia
in tepilhuan
in cuauhtin in ocelo.
Cuel achic tiquitotlanehuia.

In zan iyollo ya quinequi
10 in ipal nemohuani
in cozcatli in quetzalli
in quipuztequiz oncan.
in quimmonequiz
quimontepehuatiuh
15 in cuauhtin in ocelo.
Cuel achic tiquitotlanehuia.

Quexquich cozcatli
quexquich quetzalli
tlatilo. Oo
20 ac a chalchiuhitli
ac a teocuitlatl.
In ma ye ica on xon ahuiyacan
ma ye ica on popolihui
a in totlaocol antepilhuan.

25 Auh in tocuic
auh in toxochiuh
ya in tonequimilol
xon ahuiyacan
ic malinticac
30 cuauhyotl ocelyotl
ica tiyazque
in canon ye yuhcan.

Zaniyo ye nican
titocnihua in tlalticpac.
35 Zan cuel achica tontiximati
zan titotlanehuico ye nican.
Ohua zan cuel achic
in inahuac in ipal nemoani
zan tocontlanehuico
40 ichimalxochiuh
a ixtlahuacateca.

Make your beginning,
you who sing.
May you beat again
your flowered drum,
may you give joy
to my lords,
the eagles, the jaguars.[2]
Briefly are we here together.

The one heart's desire
of the Giver of Life
is jewels, is quetzal plumes—
to tear them apart.
This is his desire:
to scatter apart
the eagles, the jaguars.
Briefly are we here together.

How many jewels,
how many quetzal plumes,
have been destroyed? Ah,
though it was jade,
though it was gold.
So may you now be happy:
for surely too will perish
our sorrow, my lords.

And these our songs,
these our flowers,
they are our shrouds.
So be happy:
woven into them
is the eagle, the jaguar;
we will go with them
there where it is all the same.

It is only here
we have friends, on earth.
Only briefly do we know one another,
only here are we together
Ah, only briefly here
do we share with the Giver of Life;
we are only given a loan
of his flowered shield—
soon it must be returned.

1. Translated by David Damrosch.
2. Orders of warriors.

In ma oc ompa papaqui in toyollo	So let us rejoice within our hearts,
yeehuaya in tlalticpac	all who are on earth;
zan cuel achica tontiximati	only briefly do we know one another,
zan titotlanehuico ye nican.	only here are we together.
Maca xi tlaocoyacan antepilhuan	So do not be saddened, my lords:
ayac ayac	no one, no one
mocauhtiaz in tlalticpac.	is left behind on earth.

from Water-Pouring Song[1]

1

There were plume willows at the turquoise-green waters in Chapolco. We Mexicans
had reached jade water's flowing-out place. Ah! And the waters are His, and He
drinks them, it's true. Drinks them, it's true. And ah, this Mexico arrives in that
Chapolco yonder. Aya!

It resembles that time of our utmost eagerness when we Mexicans set out from Acocolco[2] to reach this place that is here. And ah, the waters are His, and He drinks
them, it's true.

When the Captain arrived in Mexico and Moctezuma went out to meet him, then he
got down from his horse; and he adorned him with a gold necklace, spoke to him,
and embraced him. And the waters are His, and He drinks them, it's true.

And right away he says to him, "You've wearied yourself in reaching your city, this
Mexico. You've come to govern your mat and your seat. For but a moment and a
day I've tended things for you. Poor is your vassal." He speaks to him, embraces
him. And the waters are His, and He drinks them, it's true.

Now woe! He gives off smoke! This is how he enters, this conquistador, this Captain.
Now all the lords are yet alive: Commander Atlixcatzin and the troop chief Tepe-
huatzin. And as these princes come forth pouring water, Mexico is handed over.
Oh! the waters are His, and He drinks them, it's true.

"We who've come to Water's Midst to marvel are Tlaxcalans: Mexican princes are
pouring out their waters!" Lord Moctezuma's hauling vats of water. And the city
passes on, ensconced in water-whorl flowers. Thus Mexico is handed over. Oh!
the waters are His, and He drinks them, it's true.

Iye! The lady María[3] comes shouting. María comes saying, "O Mexicans, your water
jars go here! Let all the lords come carrying." And Acolhuacan's Quetzalacxoyatl
arrives. And Cuauhpopoca. Oh! the waters are His, and He drinks them, it's true.

O Life Giver, these urgently required ones have been broken, these, our water jars, and
we are Mexicans. A cry goes up. They're picking them off at Eagle Gate, where
recognition is achieved. Oh! the waters are His, and He drinks them, it's true.

They've been ruined with water hauling, and they're smoking—Nezahualquentzin
and the troop chief Tepehuatzin. It's because we Mexicans are hauling water.
And the waters are His, and He drinks them, it's true.

---

1. Translated by John Bierhorst.
2. As the Aztecs' ancestors migrated south into the Valley of Mexico, they lived for a time at Acocolco.
3. Cortés's interpreter and common-law wife Doña María or Malinche.

And so they're flowing. Indeed the ruler Moctezuma himself comes forth to pour
one out. As roseate-swan flowers, as flower shoots, as trogons, as pine flowers,
would he go off whirling his garlands: thus he glorifies Tenochcans. Oh! the waters are His, and He drinks them, it's true.

Oh never would our water pitchers be destroyed. These broad ones, these turquoise
gems, are strewn as gold. Ensconced in roseate-swan hand-flowers, he's moved
on to You. Shattered, he's moved on to Water's Midst, where waters and the
navel lie: and so he glorifies Tenochcans. Oh! the waters are His, and He drinks
them, it's true.

3

O nephews, hail! And hear a work assignment: we've come to do our water pouring.
Now who will go and fetch the jadestone jars that we must carry? And yonder
we're assembled, at Shore of the Bells, at the Place of Green Waters.

Oh none with us shall work for tribute. We're to pass away. Our guardian Don Diego
Tehuetzquiti is to lead us. And yonder we're assembled, at Shore of the Bells, at
the Place of Green Waters.

Our cups are born. It seems they're twirling—and as maize flowers—at the water's
edge. These jade-water drums! At Chapultepec's side! Let all our brothers pour.
Clean waters, then, will flow in beauty.

But I wonder, am I blessed? And so I grieve. O friends, where am I to go that I might
pour these? For my heart desires them. Let Yonder be the church![4]

I weep, I sorrow, and I sing: I've broken these, my turquoise gems, my pearls, these
water jars.

And merely in this manner let it be that I return them. Chirping for these flowers, let
me head for home. At Flower Waters let me weep, composing them: I've broken
these, my turquoise gems, my pearls, these water jars.

Indeed I seek those lords who drew the water. Nezahualtecolotl and Lord Coaihuitl.
In serenity I come to pour these waters at the emperor's. And may you all take
heart. Hey Don Pedrotli![5]

Nobility will flow in beauty here. Could our carried waters perish then? Take heart.
Hey Don Pedrotli!

4

God and Only Spirit, you and you alone lay down the mirror and the flame that stands
here in the world,[6]

Where there used to be the black and color of your creatures who were carried-water
masters, who were lords.

I pass, I pass away, I pass beyond, that I might reach the plume-shore turquoise lode.
There I'll fetch my limpid green one. Ah!

"O Ixtlilxochitl! O Mexicans!" So it is that they who were swallowed are painted as
shields—these hidden ones.

O charges of the flood-and-blaze! And so it is that they shall pour them. And it's
in this manner that Tenochcans are to labor. Oh it seems that they themselves
are done for, they, Cuauhtemoc, Coanacoch, ah! and Tetlepanquetzatzin: they've
heard the multitude.

---

4. *Iquelexia* in the manuscript, from the Spanish *iglesia*, "church."
5. Don Pedro Temilotzin, a leader of resistance after the Conquest.
6. God ("Tiox") has taken over the power of Tezcatlipoca, "Smoking Mirror."

So it is that they who were swallowed are painted as spears. Indeed, the lord Captain[7]
  has said it: "Paint them as turquoise pictures: the Mexicans' labor's in pictures!"
  And oh it would seem that this labor's been taken from everywhere into the city.
Now they who've wept in sadness are the lords and rulers. It's our destiny and circumstance: they've painted them as turquoise pictures!
We must go to hear them. Ho, Cuauhtemoc! Oquiztzin! Huanitl! He's handed down
  His judgment: our carried waters will never be destroyed. Take heart. And where
  in time are we to go? To the emperor![8]
Take heart, nephews. Cuauhtemoc! Let's go have these captured ones, our pitchers,
  be a raining mist of trogons. Off they go to fall as dew. Let our garlands flow
  profusely and as gold. Let us make our entry side by side with these, our carried
  waters. Off to the emperor!
Indeed I seek those lords who drew the water: Nezahualtecolotl and Lord Coaihuitl.
  In serenity I come to pour these waters at the emperor's. May you all take heart.
Thus nobility will flow in beauty. Could our babes then perish? May you all take
  heart.

5

I, Lord Xicotencatl, am the one who's saying, "Pass away, and not in vain! Fetch your
  shields, flowers, water jars. They're your pitchers—that is, your well-wrought
  blade-jar urns!" With these we'll carry water: we'll go get water there in
  Mexico—Chapolco! Yes, in Water's Midst.
"Pass away, and not in vain, O nephew." Brothers! Nephews! Princes of the flood!
I'm pouring water, Lord Cuauhtencoz. Let's all go and carry water. Yes, we'll get the
  water. Hey!
Now brother Motelchiuh must shout. O friends, it's said that we're to fetch him in the
  dawn, him, our carried water, this very limpid one, this limpid green one, gleaming like an emerald. And yonder we arrive. O cup!
Pass away, and not in vain! Must Nanahuatl have a craving? O brother, O Commander Cuitlachihuitl! Truly he's well wrought, like gold, this painted one, our
  water jar—and he's gone painting Lord Axayacatl. Scattered, we're to pass beyond. And yonder we arrive. O cup!
Jade water sprinkles. My adornments fall in a raining mist. My Tlaxcalan uncles have
  come to give me Huanitl, my flower-water charge. O Chichimecs, pass away,
  and not in vain.
Blaze flowers, shield flowers, are blossoming in quantity: these flower shoots are
  bursting: they're scattered plentifully, because it seems they've come to take
  them, these, these golden ones, as captives. And yes, in bearing off these precious
  water jars of mine, I fetch those painted green ones. O my great ones!
O Acolhuacan's Don Antonio! Let me take you away! Hail, nephew! O Tehuetzquiti!
  And they pass away reviving as reed flowers, as colored banners, pass away as
  captives. This is how I carry off these painted green ones, these precious water
  jars of mine. See me, O great ones!
And I who recall these painted ones, these precious water jars—am Fray Pedro! Before he went away, the bishop Don Fray Juan purified this city with a golden
  balm and sprinkled it with water.

7. Cortés, who had illustrated reports prepared to send home to Spain.
8. In 1525 Cortés brought a group of Aztec nobles to Spain; some went on to Rome, where they met Pope Clement VII.

Yes, it seems that our beloved father, the bishop, has gone away. And before he went, he purified this city with a golden balm and sprinkled it with water.

Let's be off to Plume-Shore Chapultepec! And these handflowers? They pass away as turquoise swans reviving, for they've been captured, they, our pitcher jades. Hail, brothers! But be cautious. Beware of being broken, for Our Lord would scold us.

So let them follow onward. Go carefully! And yonder we're assembled. To Mexico, where tunas[9] lie, they're off to be revived as turquoise swans.

Friends, willow men, behold the pope, who's representing God, who speaks for him. The pope is on God's mat and seat and speaks for him.

Who is this reclining on a golden chair? Look! It's the pope. He has his turquoise blowgun and he's shooting in the world.

It seems it's true: it seems he has his cross and golden staff, and these are shining in the world.

I grieve in Rome and see his flesh, and he's San Pedro, San Pablo![1]

It seems that from the four directions they've been captured: you've made them enter the golden refuge, and it's shining.

It seems the pope's home lies painted in golden butterflies. It's beaming.

6

Wind arises, roaring, hissing. The ocean seethes, and the boat goes creaking along.

We see great waves flowing over us, wonderful things of God. It's raining flowers, and the boat goes creaking along.

Friends, rejoice in these waters. You're splitting it open, O Don Martín! It's broken to pieces here on the ocean.

O Life Giver, you're alive in this place of fear. The waves are rolling over us. Let's go perish at the navel, at the roundel.

"No one in this boat is precious, friends. Can we return?" Let's go be counted at the navel, at the roundel!

Alas, I grieve. The emerald dew is on us. And where are we to go?

Life Giver causes grief. If only He were my friend, if only He were a kinsman. No one cares anymore about anyone here in the boat.

Inside this boat, this place of fear, jade waters are flowing over us, seething. Ah, these garlands roar, these fish are flying. See them!

Ah, and yonder stands the tree of sustenance, stands our palace. And these garlands roar, these fish are flying. See them!

9

We've been required right here, and this would seem to be the emperor's home. Would that His waters might make an appearance. They're being recited! Would God agree?

Let's call to the Only Spirit. It may be that in this manner we, the vassals, are allowed to spend a day near him and in his presence.

We, mere Mexicans, are off to marvel on the sea, the emperor commanding us: he's told us, "Go and see the holy father."

He's said: What do I need? Gold! Everybody bow down! Call out to God in excelsis![2]

9. Prickly pears, grown for their fruit.
1. The Pope was regarded as the successor of the apostles Peter and Paul.
2. In the highest (Latin).

And it's just for this that he sends us to Rome. He's told us, "Go and see the holy father."

Our hearts will be content, for he sends us on to Rome. He's told us, "Go and see the holy father."

It would seem that at the pope's, where the cavern house of colors stands, are golden words that give us life.

On account of trumpets there's a stirring. Aya! And they're honored where it stands: God's words, these trogons! They're ensconced in war capes. Ah, they give us life.

Bring them in, you princes. They're our comrades. Where? With God in Rome! Aya, there the pope is paying honor.

There in Rome she dwells, she the mother called Santa Cecelia! Aya, there the pope is paying honor.

Your flowers, it would seem, are budding, greening, in Willow Place, O Axayacatl. Indeed, you went away deserving. It's where the tunas lie!

White feather flowers are sifting down at Water Face. And it would seem that they're your flowers, Lord Axayacatl. Indeed, you went away deserving. It's where the tunas lie!

In the Place Unknown, where all are shorn, in heaven and as jades, perhaps, or turquoises, they're marshaled, they, the princes. They're with God.

Lord Oquiztzin flies along, perhaps, as a roseate swan. Perhaps Tlacotzin is an eagle plume. Yes, all are alive, and they're with God.

Take a look at the Only Spirit's flower field. There's a freshening in that place of heart pleasers: there's a plume dew raining all around.

Yonder dwells the turquoise swan-bird Don Martín. An egret bird is pleasured, and it's Coaihuitl. There's Don Juan!

Red feather trees are blossoming in God's home, and princes are inhaling them. Lord Anahuacatl and perhaps Commander Cuitlachihuitl are rejoicing in heaven.

They've been broken as plume jades or perhaps as turquoise gems: they're princes, and they're Mexicans, these Huexotzincans. Lord Anahuacatl and perhaps Commander Cuitlachihuitl are rejoicing in heaven.

Moctezuma, you creature of heaven, you sing in Mexico[1]

Moctezuma, you creature of heaven, you sing in Mexico, in Tenochtitlan.

Here where eagle multitudes were ruined, your bracelet house stands shining—there in the home of God our father.

There and in that place they come alive, ah! on the field! For a moment they come whirling, they the eagles, ah! the nobles Ixtlilcuechahuac and Matlaccuiatzin.

And in that place these nobles gain renown and honor: bells are scattered, dust and lords grow golden.

Onward, friends! We'll dare to go where fame, where glory's, gotten, where nobility is gotten, where flower death is won.

Your name and honor live, O princes. Prince Tlacahuepan! Ixtlilcuechahuac! You've gone and won war death.

Sky dawn is rising up. The multitude, the birds, are shrilling. Precious swans are being created. Turquoise troupials are being created.

Lucky you, arrayed in chalk and plumes. O flower-drunk Moctezuma! Precious swans are being created. Turquoise troupials are being created.

1. Translated by John Bierhorst.

Cortés's venture in Mexico was primarily military, but not exclusively so. Accompanying Cortés on his entrance into Mexico City in 1520 were several Franciscan friars, whose presence marked a secondary reason for Spanish intervention in the New World: the spreading of Catholicism. For those Indians who survived death by disease or guns, there was another kind of subjection: to the missions, comprised of colleges and "seminaries" where the native peoples were instructed through catechism, preaching, and perhaps surprisingly, theater, often presented on feast days such as Corpus Christi.

In the hands of Sor Juana, the Mexican nun who would write over 150 years after Cortés, such theater drew on not one but two vibrant traditions: that of seventeenth-century Spain, particularly the *auto sacramental* or religious drama, and the rituals of the indigenous Aztecs, marked by considerable pageantry and dance. Written in 1688, *The Divine Narcissus,* if it was performed at all, was shown only in Madrid, not Mexico. Part of the *loa* or prefatory act (excerpted below) explicitly debates its propriety for the Spanish stage, since it was written in the "backward" colonies. But the *loa* is also strikingly anticolonial. Like so many Mexican works, it commemorates the conquest of New World by Old (represented by the figures of Zeal and Religion). Yet the new-world characters of Occident and America are dignified in their resistance to these European figures revealed, by turns, as unnecessarily violent and hypocritical. Perhaps most intriguing is Sor Juana's grasp of Aztec customs and her occasional use of Nahuatl words in the play, as well as the final triumph of the *dios de las Semillas* whom America praises at the beginning of the *loa* as the Aztec fertility god. As much as he can be seen as a hybrid of Christ and an Aztec deity, his name—"the god of seeds"—persists at the end of the *loa,* despite the fact that the Europeans have obviously emerged victorious.

from The Loa for the Auto Sacramental of the Divine Narcissus[1]

An Allegory[2]

Speaking Characters

Occident   Religion
America   Musician
Zeal   Soldiers

Scene 1

[*Enter Occident, a gallant-looking Aztec, wearing a crown. By his side is America, an Aztec woman of poised self-possession. They are dressed in the* mantas *and* huipiles *worn for singing a* tocotín.[3] *They seat themselves on two chairs. On each side, Aztec men and women dance with feathers and rattles in their hands, as is customary for those doing this dance. While they dance, Music sings.*]

---

1. Translated by Patricia A. Peters and Renée Domeier, O.S.B. The *loa* was the often lengthy preamble to a play, in this case an *auto sacramental* or one-act sacramental or Eucharist play performed for a religious feast day.
2. *Por alegorías* suggests that the play should be read allegorically—that is, using the characters to represent something else.
3. *Manta* is the Spanish word for a blanket or poncho, while *huipile* is a blouse. A *tocotín* was a traditional Nahuatl ballad, of which Sor Juana wrote at least two.

MUSIC: O, Noble Mexicans,
            whose ancient ancestry
            comes forth from the clear light
            and brilliance of the Sun,[4]
5   since this, of all the year,
            is your most happy feast
            in which you venerate
            your greatest deity,
            come and adorn yourselves
10   with vestments of your rank;
            let your holy fervor be
            made one with jubilation;
            and celebrate in festive pomp
            the great God of the Seeds![5]
15   Since the abundance of
            our native fields and farms
            is owed to him alone
            who gives fertility,
            then offer him your thanks,
20   for it is right and just
            to give from what has grown,
            the first of the new fruits.
            From your own veins, draw out
            and give, without reserve,
25   the best blood, mixed with seed,
            so that his cult be served,
            and celebrate in festive pomp,
            the great God of the Seeds!

[*Occident and America sit, and Music ceases.*]

OCCIDENT: Of all the deities to whom
30   our rites demand I bend my knee—
           among two thousand gods or more
            who dwell within this royal city
            and who require the sacrifice
            of human victims still entreating
35   for life until their blood is drawn
            and gushes forth from hearts still beating
            and bowels still pulsing—I declare,
            among all these, (it bears repeating),
            whose ceremonies we observe,

---

4. The Mexicans believed that the Sun was their original "father": "The Sun cast down an arrow and made a hole, from which a man emerged...and following, a woman," a story Sor Juana could have read about in the writings of Franciscans such as Father Juan de Torquemada, published in Spain in the early 17th century.

5. There were several Aztec fertility gods, among them, Centéotl, god of corn; Xiuhteuctli, god of the grass; and Tláloc, god of water and the fecundity of the earth. However, in the context of the *loa*, it seems that Sor Juana is referring to Huitzilopochtli, who was the god of war and the most powerful deity of Tenochtitlán, the Aztecs' capital and what is now Mexico City. Identified with the sun, he was the one who demanded the blood sacrifices that will be referred to by Music.

40	the greatest is, surpassing all
	this pantheon's immensity
	the great God of the Seeds.

AMERICA: And you are right, since he alone
daily sustains our monarchy
45   because our lives depend on his
providing crops abundantly;
and since he gives us graciously
the gift from which all gifts proceed,
our fields rich with golden maize,
50   the source of life through daily bread,
we render him our highest praise.
Then how will it improve our lives
if rich America abounds
in gold from mines whose smoke deprives
55   the fields of their fertility
and with their clouds of filthy soot
will not allow the crops to grow
which blossom now so fruitfully
from seeded earth?[6] Moreover, his
60   protection of our people far
exceeds our daily food and drink,
the body's sustenance. Indeed,
he feeds us with his very flesh
(first purified of every stain).
65   We eat his body, drink his blood,
and by this sacred meal are freed
and cleansed from all that is profane,
and thus, he purifies our soul.[7]
And now, attentive to his rites,
70   together let us all proclaim:

THEY [OCCIDENT, AMERICA, DANCERS] AND MUSIC: We celebrate in festive pomp,
the great God of the Seeds!

Scene 2

[They exit dancing. Enter Christian Religion as a Spanish lady, Zeal as a Captain General in armor, and Spanish soldiers.][8]

RELIGION: How, being Zeal, can you suppress
the flames of righteous Christian wrath
75   when here before your very eyes
idolatry, so blind with pride,
adores, with superstitious rites
an idol, leaving your own bride,

---

6. An allusion to the extensive mining being practiced by the Spaniards throughout Mexico.

7. Sor Juana may be referring to the Aztec ritual of sacrifice in which those who had imbibed the "god" were slaughtered on the altar.

8. "Religion" represents the missionaries and the spiritual conquest of the Mexicans; "Zeal" the military wing of the conquest.

the holy faith of Christ disgraced?

ZEAL: Religion, trouble not your mind
or grieve my failure to attack,
complaining that my love is slack,
for now the sword I wear is bared,
its hilt in hand, clasped ready and

85   my arm raised high to take revenge.
Please stand aside and deign to wait
till I requite your grievances.

[*Enter Occident and America dancing, and accompanied by Music, who enters from the other side.*]

MUSIC: And celebrate in festive pomp,
the great God of the Seeds!

ZEAL: Here they come! I will confront them.

RELIGION: And I, in peace, will also go
(before your fury lays them low)
for justice must with mercy kiss;
I shall invite them to arise

95   from superstitious depths to faith.

ZEAL: Let us approach while they are still
absorbed in their lewd rituals.

MUSIC: And celebrate in festive pomp,
the great God of the Seeds!

[*Zeal and Religion cross the stage.*]

RELIGION: Great Occident, most powerful;
America, so beautiful
and rich; you live in poverty
amid the treasures of your land.
Abandon this irreverent cult

105   with which the demon has waylaid you.
Open your eyes! Follow the path
that leads straightforwardly to truth,
to which my love yearns to persuade you.

OCCIDENT: Who are these unknown people, so

110   intrusive in my sight, who dare
to stop us in our ecstasy?
Heaven forbid such infamy!

AMERICA: Who are these nations, never seen,
that wish, by force, to pit themselves

115   against my ancient power supreme?

OCCIDENT: Oh, you alien beauty fair;
oh, pilgrim woman from afar,
who comes to interrupt my prayer,
please speak and tell me who you are.

RELIGION: Christian Religion is my name,
and I intend that all this realm
will make obeisance unto me.

OCCIDENT: An impossible concession!
AMERICA: Yours is but a mad obsession!
OCCIDENT: You will meet with swift repression.
AMERICA: Pay no attention; she is mad!
           Let us go on with our procession.
MUSIC AND ALL [*Aztecs on stage*]:   And celebrate in festive pomp,
           the great God of the Seeds!
ZEAL: How is this, barbarous Occident?
           Can it be, sightless Idolatry,
           that you insult Religion,
           the spouse I cherish tenderly?
           Abomination fills your cup
135   and overruns the brim, but see
           that God will not permit you to
           continue drinking down delight,
           and I am sent to deal your doom.
OCCIDENT: And who are you who frightens all
140   who only look upon your face?
ZEAL: I am Zeal. Does that surprise you?
           Take heed! for when your excesses
           bring disgrace to fair Religion,
           then will Zeal arise to vengeance;
145   for insolence I will chastise you.
           I am the minister of God,
           Who growing weary with the sight
           of overreaching tyrannies
           so sinful that they reach the height
150   of error, practiced many years,
           has sent me forth to penalize you.
           And thus, these military hosts
           with flashing thunderbolts of steel,
           the ministers of His great wrath
155   are sent, His anger to reveal.
OCCIDENT: What god? What sin? What tyranny?
           What punishment do you foresee?
           Your reasons make no sense to me,
           nor can I make the slightest guess
160   who you might be with your insistence
           on tolerating no resistance,
           impeding us with rash persistence
           from lawful worship as we sing.
MUSIC: And celebrate with festive pomp,
165   the great God of the Seeds!
AMERICA: Madman, blind, and barbarous,
           with mystifying messages
           you try to mar our calm and peace,
           destroying the tranquility
170   that we enjoy. Your plots must cease,
           unless, of course, you wish to be

reduced to ashes, whose existence
even the winds will never sense.

[*to Occident*]

And you, my spouse, and your cohort,
175   close off your hearing and your sight
to all their words; refuse to heed
their fantasies of zealous might;
proceed to carry out your rite.
Do not concede to insolence
180   from foreigners intent to dull
our ritual's magnificence.

MUSIC: And celebrate with festive pomp,
the great God of the Seeds!

ZEAL: Since our initial offering
185   of peaceful terms, you held so cheap,
the dire alternative of war,
I guarantee you'll count more dear.
Take up your arms! To war! To war!

[*Drums and trumpets sound.*]

OCCIDENT: What miscarriages of justice
190   has heaven sent against me?
What are these weapons, blazing fire,
before my unbelieving eyes?
Get ready, guards! Aim well, my troops,
Your arrows at this enemy!

AMERICA: What lightening bolts does heaven send
to lay me low? What molten balls
of burning lead so fiercely rain?
What centaurs crush with monstrous force
and cause my people such great pain?

[*within*]

200   To arms! To arms! War! War!

[(*Drums and trumpets*) *sound.*]

Long life to Spain! Long live her king!

[*The battle begins. Indians enter through one door and flee through another with the Spanish pursuing at their heels. From back stage, Occident backs away from Religion and America retreats before Zeal's onslaught.*]

* * *

AMERICA: There is much more I want to see,
and my desire to know is now
by holy inspiration led.

OCCIDENT: And I desire more keenly still
to know about the life and death
400   of the God you say is in the bread.

RELIGION: Then come along with me, and I
shall make for you a metaphor,
a concept clothed in rhetoric
so colorful that what I show
405   to you, your eyes will clearly see;
for now I know that you require
objects of sight instead of words,
by which faith whispers in your ears
too deaf to hear; I understand,
410   for you necessity demands
that through the eyes, faith find her way
to her reception in your hearts.[1]

OCCIDENT: Exactly so. I do prefer
to see the things you would impart.

Scene 5

RELIGION: Then come.

ZEAL: Religion, answer me:
what metaphor will you employ
to represent these mysteries?

RELIGION: An *auto*[2] will make visible
through allegory images
420   of what America must learn
and Occident implores to know
about the questions that now burn
within him so.

ZEAL: What will you call
this play in allegory cast?

RELIGION: *Divine Narcissus,* let it be,
because if that unhappy maid
adored an idol which disguised
in such strange symbols the attempt
the demon made to counterfeit

---

9. In the ensuing scene, America and the Occident are defeated. Zeal is ready to annihilate them, but Religion protests that they be kept alive, insisting that they can be converted. Claiming that she will speak like St. Paul, Religion suggests to Occident and America that the many miracles they recount of fertility and growth are the work not of their "mendacious deities" but of "the One True God" who gave his life for theirs. Particularly striking are the numerous similarities Religion elucidates between the Aztecs' religion and Christianity.

1. Illustrations were often used by the missionaries to teach the indigenous Mexicans, as made clear in a work such as *Rhetorica Christiana* by the missionary Diego Valadés. Theater too, particularly the *autos sacramentales* of which Sor Juana's work is an example, was thought to be a highly effective teaching tool.

2. An *auto sacramental* or "Mystery Play."

430 the great and lofty mystery
    of the most Blessed Eucharist,[3]
    then there were also, I surmise,
    among more ancient pagans hints
    of such high marvels symbolized.

ZEAL: Where will your drama be performed?

RELIGION: In the crown city of Madrid,
    which is the center of the Faith,
    the seat of Catholic majesty,
    to whom the Indies owe their best
440 beneficence, the blessed gift
    of Holy Writ, the Gospel light
    illuminating all the West.[4]

ZEAL: That you should write in Mexico
    for royal patrons don't you see
445 to be an impropriety?[5]

RELIGION: Is it beyond imagination
    that something made in one location
    can in another be of use?
    Furthermore, my writing it
450 comes, not of whimsical caprice,
    but from my vowed obedience
    to do what seems beyond my reach.[6]
    Well, then, this work, however rough
    and little polished it might be,
455 results from my obedience,
    and not from any arrogance.

ZEAL: Then answer me, Religion, how
    (before you leave the matter now),
    will you respond when you are chid
460 for loading the whole Indies on
    a stage to transport to Madrid?

RELIGION: The purpose of my play can be
    none other than to glorify
    the Eucharistic Mystery;
465 and since the cast of characters
    are no more than abstractions which
    depict the theme with clarity,

3. Possibly an allusion to the one-act play that will follow the *loa*, for which Sor Juana drew on the myth of Narcissus. In her rendition, Narcissus is Christ, in love with the semblance of himself that is humanity, while the figure of Echo is the demonic fallen Angel who tries to tempt him from his love for *naturaleza Humana* or humankind. The work ends with Narcissus's death and resurrection and a hymn celebrating the Eucharist.

4. The performance history of *The Divine Narcissus* is unclear, although it was published in a separate edition in 1690. Madrid is called "center of the faith" because it was the religious and publishing center for the evangelization of the Indies.

5. Probably because the Mexicans were deemed inferior to the Spaniards.

6. Sor Juana was asked to write the *loa* by her close friend María Luisa Manrique de Lara y Gonzaga, the Condesa of Pardes. Sor Juana addresses her as "Phyllis" in several poems, and the countess in turn would take Sor Juana's poems to Spain and arrange for their first publication in 1689.

then surely no one should object
if they are taken to Madrid;
470 distance can never hinder thought
with persons of intelligence,
nor seas impede exchange of sense.
ZEAL: Then, prostrate at his royal feet,
beneath whose strength two worlds are joined
475 we beg for pardon of the King;
RELIGION: and from her eminence, the Queen;[7]
AMERICA: whose sovereign and anointed feet
the humble Indies bow to kiss;
ZEAL: and from the Royal High Council;
RELIGION: and from the ladies, who bring light
into their hemisphere;
AMERICA: and from
their poets, I most humbly beg
forgiveness for my crude attempt,
desiring with these awkward lines
485 to represent the Mystery.[8]
OCCIDENT: Let's go, for anxiously I long to see
exactly how this God of yours
will give Himself as food to me.

[*America, Occident, and Zeal sing:*]

The Indies know
490 and do concede
who is the true
God of the Seeds.
In loving tears
which joy prolongs
495 we gladly sing
our happy songs.
ALL: Blest be the day
when I could see
and worship the
500 great God of Seeds.

[*They all exit, dancing and singing.*]

[END OF THE CONQUEST AND ITS AFTERMATH]

---

7. Many *loas* close with such a request for pardon directed to the king, queen, the Royal Council, and the women and poets of the court.

8. Note America's use of the first person in speaking of the "crude attempt" of the *loa;* perhaps a personal allusion to Sor Juana, who is herself, of course, "American."

The Ancient World

The Ancient Near East • Bertil Albrektson, *History and the Gods,* 1967. • Cyril Aldred, *Akhenaten, Pharaoh of Egypt: A New Study,* 1968. • Robert Alter, *The Art of Biblical Narrative,* 1981. • Robert Alter, *The Art of Biblical Poetry,* 1985. • Robert Alter and Frank Kermode, eds., *The Literary Guide to the Bible,* 1987. • Jan Assmann, *The Mind of Egypt: History and Meaning in the Time of the Pharaohs,* 2002. • Jan Assmann, *The Search for God in Ancient Egypt,* 2001. • John Barton, *Reading the Old Testament: Method in Biblical Study,* 1984. • Jean Bottéro, *Mesopotamia: Writing, Reasoning and the Gods,* 1992. • Brevard Childs, *Introduction to the Old Testament as Scripture,* 1979. • Frank M. Cross, *Canaanite Myth and Hebrew Epic,* 1973. • Stephanie Dalley, *Myths from Mesopotamia,* 1989. • David Damrosch, *The Narrative Covenant: Transformations of Genre in the Growth of Biblical Literature,* 1987. • Michael Fishbane, *Biblical Interpretation in Ancient Israel,* 1985. • Benjamin Foster, *From Distant Days: Myths, Tales and Poetry of Ancient Mesopotamia,* 1995. • Henri Frankfort et al., *Before Philosophy,* 1954. • Northrop Frye, *The Great Code: The Bible and Literature,* 1982. • Norman Gottwald, *The Hebrew Bible: A Socio-Literary Introduction,* 1985. • James Kugel, *The Bible as It Was,* 1997. • James Kugel, *The Idea of Biblical Poetry,* 1981. • Amélie Kuhrt, *The Ancient Near East c. 3000–300 BC,* 1995. • Miriam Lichtheim, *Ancient Egyptian Literature,* 3 vols., 1975–1980. • Ilana Pardes, *The Biography of Ancient Israel: National Narratives in the Bible,* 2000. • J. N. Postgate, *Early Mesopotamia: Society and Economy at the Dawn of History,* 1992. • James B. Pritchard, *Ancient Near Eastern Texts Relating to the Old Testament,* 1976. • Paul Ricoeur, *The Symbolism of Evil,* 1969. • Herbert Schneidau, *Sacred Discontent: The Bible and Western Tradition,* 1976. • William K. Simpson, ed., *The Literature of Ancient Egypt,* 1973. • Daniel Snell, *Life in the Ancient Near East,* 1997. • Meir Sternberg, *The Poetics of Biblical Narrative,* 1985. • Joyce Tyldesley, *Daughters of Iris: Women of Ancient Egypt,* 1995. • John Van Seters, *In Search of History: Historiography in the Ancient World and the Origins of Biblical History,* 1983.

The Epic of Gilgamesh • David Damrosch, "Gilgamesh and Genesis," in *The Narrative Covenant,* 1987. • Andrew George, ed., *The Epic of Gilgamesh,* 1999. • Rivkah Harris, *Gender and Aging in Mesopotamia: The Gilgamesh Epic and Other Ancient Literature,* 2000. • Alexander Heidel, *The Gilgamesh Epic and Old Testament Parallels,* 1949. • Derrek Hines, *Gilgamesh,* 2002. • John Maier, ed., *Gilgamesh: A Reader,* 1997. • Benjamin Caleb Ray, "The Gilgamesh Epic: Myth and Meaning," in *Myth and Method,* eds. Laurie L. Patton and Wendy Doniger, 1996. • Jeffrey H. Tigay, *The Evolution of the Gilgamesh Epic,* 2002.

Genesis • Bernard W. Anderson, ed., *Creation in the Old Testament,* 1984. • Eugene Combs, *The Foundations of Political Order in Genesis and the Chondogya Upanishad,* 1987. • R. Gilboa, *Intercourses in the Book of Genesis: Mythic Motifs in Creator-Created Relationships,* 1998. • Dorothy Irvin, *Mytharion: The Comparison of Tales from the Old Testament and the Ancient Near East,* 1978. • Jon D. Levenson, *Creation and the Persistence of Evil: The Jewish Drama of Divine Omnipotence,* 1988. • Terry J. Prewitt, *The Elusive Covenant: A Structural-Semiotic Reading of Genesis,* 1990. • Ellen van Wolde, *Stories of the Beginning: Genesis 1–11 and Other Creation Stories,* 1997. • Claus Westermann, *Genesis: An Introduction,* 1992.

The Song of Songs • Blaise Arminjon, *Cantata of Love: A Verse-by-Verse Reading of the Song of Songs,* 1988. • Ariel Bloch and Chana Bloch, *The Song of Songs: A New Translation with an Introduction and Commentary,* 1994. • Athalva Brenner and Carole R. Fontaine, eds., *The Song of Songs: A Feminist Companion to the Bible,* 2000. • Marvin Pope, *The Song of Songs,* 1977. • Luis Stadelmann, *Love and Politics: A New Commentary on the Song of Songs,* 1992.

Classical Greece • John Boardman, Jasper Griffin, and Oswyn Murray, eds., *The Oxford History of the Classical World,* 1986. • Paul Cartledge, *The*

Greeks, 2002. • J. N. Davidson, *Courtesans and Fishcakes*, 1998. • Thomas R. Martin, *Ancient Greece*, 1996. • Robin Osborne, *Greece in the Making: 1200–479 BC*, 1996. • *Perseus* (database on ancient Greek civilization): www.perseus.tufts.edu • Jean-Pierre Vernant, ed., *The Greeks*, 1995.

Homer • George Dimock, *The Unity of the Odyssey,* 1989. • Nancy Felson-Rubin, *Regarding Penelope: From Character to Poetics,* 1994. • Ralph Hexter, *A Guide to the Odyssey,* 1993. • A. B. Lord, *The Singer of Tales,* 1960. • Gregory Nagy, *The Best of the Achaeans,* 1979. • Seth Schein, *The Mortal Hero: An Introduction to Homer's Iliad,* 1987. • Seth Schein, *Reading the Odyssey*, 1991. • W. G. Thalmann, *The Odyssey: An Epic of Return,* 1997.

Sappho • Page DuBois, *Sappho Is Burning,* 1995. • Denys Page, *Sappho and Alcaeus,* 1955. • E. M. Voigt, *Sappho et Alcaeus,* 1971. • *Sappho's Lyre: Archaic Lyric and Women Poets of Ancient Greece,* 1991. • *If Not, Winter: Fragments of Sappho,* trans. Anne Carson, 2002.

Sophocles • Harold Bloom, ed., *Sophocles's Oedipus Rex,* 1988. • Helene B. Foley, *Female Acts in Greek Tragedy,* 2001. • B. M. W. Knox, *Oedipus at Thebes,* 1957. • Charles Segal, *Oedipus Tyrannus: Tragic Heroism and the Limits of Knowledge,* 1993. • J.-P. Vernant and P. Vidal-Naquet, *Myth and Tragedy in Ancient Greece,* trans. J. Lloyd, 1988.

Euripides • Page duBois, *Centaurs and Amazons,* 1982. • E. Segal, ed., *Euripides: A Collection of Critical Essays,* 1968.

Plato • W. K. C. Guthrie, *A History of Greek Philosophy,* vol. 3, 1969. • A. Nightingale, *Genres in Dialogue,* 1995. • R. B. Rutherford, *The Art of Plato,* 1995.

Early South Asia • Edward C. Dimock et al., eds. *Literatures of India: An Introduction,* 1974. • Ainslie Embree, ed., *Sources of Indian Tradition,* 1988. • David Ludden, *India and South Asia: A Short History,* 2002. • Sheldon Pollock, ed., *Literary Cultures in History: Reconstructions from South Asia,* 2003. • Sheldon Pollock, "Introduction," and "Sanskrit Literature from the Inside Out," in *Literary Cultures in History,* ed. S. Pollock, 2003. • Joseph Schwartzberg, ed., *A Historical Atlas of South Asia,* 1992. • Romila Thapar, *Early India,* 2002. • Susie Tharu and K. Lalitha, eds., *Women Writing in India, 600 B.C. to the Present,* 1991–1993. • Herman Tieken, *Kavya in South India,* 2001.

***Ramayana* of Valmiki** • John Brockington, *The Sanskrit Epics,* 1998. • Robert Goldman et al., trans., *The Ramayana of Valmiki: An Epic of Ancient India,* 1984–. • Robert P. Goldman and Sally Sutherland, eds., *The Epic Tradition,* 2004. • Sheldon Pollock, "Ramayana and Political Imagination in India," *Journal of Asian Studies* 52.2 (1993), 261–97. • A. K. Ramanujan, "Three Hundred Ramayanas: Five Examples and Three Thoughts on Translation," in *Many Ramayanas,* ed. Paula Richman, 1994. • Paula Richman, ed. *Many Ramayanas: The Diversity of a Narrative Tradition in South Asia,* 1991. • Paula Richman, ed. *Questioning Ramayanas: A South Asian Tradition,* 2000.

China: The Classical Tradition • Cyril Birch, *Anthology of Chinese Literature,* vol. I, 1965. • Anne Birrell, *Chinese Mythology,* 1993. • Wing-tsit Chan, *A Sourcebook in Chinese Philosophy,* 1963. • Raymond Dawson, ed., *The Legacy of China,* 1964. • William Theodore de Bary, ed., *Sources of Chinese Tradition,* 1999. • Patricia B. Ebrey, ed., *Chinese Civilization and Society: A Sourcebook,* 1981. • C. P. Fitzgerald, *China: A Short Cultural History,* 1967. • Yu-lan Fung, *A History of Chinese Philosophy,* 1953. • Jacques Gernet, *A History of Chinese Civilization,* 1982. • James Legge, trans., *The Chinese Classics,* 1892. • Michael Loewe and Edward Shaughnessy, eds., *The Cambridge History of Ancient China,* 1999. • Frederick Mote, *Intellectual Foundations of China,* 1971. • William Nienhauser, ed., *The Indiana Companion to Traditional Chinese Literature,* 1986. • Stephen Owen, *An Anthology of Chinese Literature, Beginnings to 1911,* 1996. • Paul Ropp, ed., *The Heritage of China,* 1990. • Benjamin Schwartz, *The World of Thought in Ancient China,* 1985. • Burton Watson, *Early Chinese Literature,* 1962. • Arthur Waley, *Three Ways of Thought in Ancient China,* 1939. • Pauline Yu et al., eds., *Ways With Words: Writing About Reading Texts from Early China,* 2000.

The Book of Songs • Joseph R. Allen, ed., *The Book of Songs,* trans. Arthur Waley, 1996. • Marcel Granet, *Festivals and Songs of Ancient China,* 1932. • Bernhard Karlgren, trans., *The Book of Odes,* 1950. • William McNaughton, *The Book of Songs,* 1971. • Ezra Pound, trans., *The Confucian Odes,* 1954. • Haun Saussy, *The Problem of a Chinese Aesthetic,* 1993. • Steven Van Zoeren, *Poetry and Personality: Reading, Exegesis and Hermeneutics in Traditional China,* 1991. • Arthur Waley, trans., *The Book* of Songs, 1937. • C. H. Wang, *The Bell and the Drum*, 1974.

Confucius • Roger T. Ames and Henry Rosemont, trans., *The Analects of Confucius: A Philosophical Translation*, 1998. • Herrlee Creel, *Confucius: The Man and the Myth*, 1949. • Raymond Dawson, trans., *The Analects*, 1993. • Herbert Fingarette, *Confucius, the Secular as Sacred*, 1972. • David L. Hall and Roger T. Ames, *Thinking through Confucius*, 1987. • D. C. Lau, trans., *Confucius: The Analects*, 1979. • Simon Leys, trans., *The Analects of Confucius*, 1997. • Pertti Nikkilä, *Preference and Choice in the Confucian Analects*, 1997. • Yuri Pines, *Foundations of Confucian Thought*, 2002. • Edward L. Shaughnessy, *Before Confucius: Studies in the Creation of the Confucius Classics*, 1997. • Bryan W. Van Norden, ed., *Confucius and the Analects: New Essays*, 2002. • Arthur Waley, *The Analects of Confucius*, 1938.

Rome and the Roman Empire • Alessandro Barchiesi, *The Poet and the Prince: Ovid and Augustan Discourse*, 1997. • Anthony A. Barrett, *Livia: First Lady of Imperial Rome*, 2002. • Mary Beard, John North, and Simon Price, *Religions of Rome*, vol. 1: *A History*; vol. 2: *A Sourcebook*, 1998. • John Boardman, Jasper Griffin, and Oswyn Murray, *The Oxford History of the Roman World*, 2001. • Anthony J. Boyle, ed., *Roman Epic*, 1993. • Susan Braund, *Roman Verse Satire*, 1992. • Caesar, *The Conquest of Gaul*, trans. S. A. Handford, 1982. • Kitty Chisholm and John Ferguson, eds., *Rome, the Augustan Age: A Source Book*, 1981. • Peter Connolly and Hazel Dodge, *The Ancient City: Life in Classical Athens and Rome*, 1998. • Gian Biagio Conte, *Latin Literature: A History*, trans. Joseph B. Solodow, 1994. • Werner Eck, *The Age of Augustus*, trans. Deborah Lucas Schneider, 2003. • Catherine Edwards, *Writing Rome: Textual Approaches to the City*, 1996. • Elaine Fantham, Helene Peet Foley, Natalie Boymel Kampen, and H. A. Shapiro, *Women in the Classical World: Image and Text*, 1995. • Diane Favro, *The Urban Image of Imperial Rome*, 1998. • Dennis Feeney, *Literature and Religion at Rome: Cultures, Contexts, and Beliefs*, 1998. • M. I. Finley, *The Ancient Economy*, 1999. • Karl Galinsky, *Augustan Culture*, 1996. • Edward Gibbon, *The History of the Decline and Fall of the Roman Empire*, 1776–1788. • Emily Gowers, *The Loaded Table: Representations of Food in Roman Literature*, 1996. • Jasper Griffin, *Latin Poets and Roman Life*, 1985. • Thomas N. Habinek, *The Politics of Latin Literature*, 1998 • Thomas Habinek and Alessandro Schiesaro, eds., *The Roman Cultural Revolution*, 1997. • Judith P. Hallett and Marilyn B. Skinner, eds., *Roman Sexualities*, 1998. • Philip R. Hardie, *The Epic Successors of Virgil: A Study in the Dynamics of a Tradition*, 1993. • Fritz Heichelheim et al., *A History of the Roman People*, 2002. • Peter V. Jones and Keith C. Sidwell, *The World of Rome: An Introduction to Roman Culture*, 1997. • Josephus, *The Jewish War*, 1970. • Livy, *History of Rome*, 14 vols., Loeb Classical Library, 1964–1970. • Livy, *History of Rome from Its Foundation*, 4 vols., 1960–1982. • R. O. A. M. Lyne, *The Latin Love Poets: From Catullus to Horace*. Oxford: Clarendon, 1980. • Ramsay MacMullen, *Romanization in the Time of Augustus*, 2000. • Plutarch, *The Parallel Lives*, 11 vols., trans. Bernadotte Perrin, Loeb Classical Library, 1967. • David Quint, *Epic and Empire: Politics and Generic Form from Virgil to Milton*. Princeton: Princeton University Press, 1993. • Nancy H. Ramage and Andrew Ramage, *Roman Art: From Romulus to Constantine*, 1991. • Amy Richlin, *The Garden of Priapus: Sexuality and Aggression in Roman Humor*, 1992. • Howard H. Scullard, *From the Gracchi to Nero: A History of Rome 133 B.C. to A.D. 68*, 1990. • Ronald Syme, *The Roman Revolution*, 2002. • Robert Turcan, *The Gods of Ancient Rome: Religion in Everyday Life from Archaic to Imperial Times*, 2001. • Paul Veyne, *Roman Erotic Elegy: Love, Poetry and the West*, 1988. • Paul Veyne, ed., *A History of Private Life: I. From Pagan Rome to Byzantium*, 1987. • J. M. Wallace-Hadrill, *Augustan Rome*, 1993. • Peter White, *Promised Verse: Poets in the Society of Augustan Rome*, 1993. • Paul Zanker, *The Power of Images in the Age of Augustus*, 1988.

Virgil • Francis Cairns, *Virgil's Augustan Epic*, 1989. • Wendell Clausen, *Virgil's "Aeneid" and the Tradition of Hellenistic Poetry*, 1987. • Steele Commager, ed., *Virgil: A Collection of Critical Essays*, 1966. • Domenico Comparetti, *Vergil in the Middle Ages*, 1966. • K. W. Gransden, *Virgil's "Iliad": An Essay on Epic Narrative*, 1984. • Jasper Griffin, *Virgil*, 1986. • P. R. Hardie, *Virgil's "Aeneid": Cosmos and*

Imperium, 1986. • S. J. Harrison, *Oxford Readings in Vergil's "Aeneid,"* 1990. • W. R. Johnson, *Darkness Visible: A Study of Vergil's "Aeneid,"* 1976. • Charles Martindale, ed., *The Cambridge Companion to Virgil*, 1997. • Charles Martindale, ed., *Virgil and His Influence*, 1984. • Michael C. J. Putnam, *Virgil's "Aeneid": Interpretation and Influence*, 1995. • Kenneth Quinn, *Virgil's "Aeneid": A Critical Description*, 1968. • David Slavitt, *Virgil*, 1992. • Theodore Ziolkowski, *Virgil and the Moderns*, 1993.

Ovid • Karl Galinsky, *Ovid's Metamorphoses: An Introduction to the Basic Aspects*, 1975. • Philip Hardie, *Ovid's Poetics of Illusion*, 2002. • Philip Hardie, ed., *The Cambridge Companion to Ovid*, 2002. • P. E. Knox, *Ovid's Metamorphoses and the Traditions of Augustan Poetry*, 1986. • Sara Mack, *Ovid*, 1988. • Brooks Otis, *Ovid as an Epic Poet*, 1966. • Joseph B. Solodow, *The World of Ovid's Metamorphoses*, 1988. • Garth Tissol, *The Face of Nature: Wit, Narrative, and Cosmic Origins in Ovid's Metamorphoses*, 1997.

Catullus • William Fitzgerald, *Catullan Provocations. Lyric Poetry and the Drama of Position*, 1995. • Richard Jenkyns, *Three Classical Poets—Sappho, Catullus, and Juvenal*, 1982. • Charles Martin, *Catullus*, 1992. • Kenneth Quinn, *The Catullan Revolution*, 1959. • Arthur Leslie Wheeler, *Catullus and the Traditions of Ancient Poetry*, 1934. • T. P. Wiseman, *Catullus and His World: A Reappraisal*, 1985.

Horace • David Armstrong, *Horace*, 1989. • Steele Commager, *The Odes of Horace*, 1962. • Eduard Fraenkel, *Horace*, 1957. • Niall Rudd, ed., *Horace 2000: A Celebration. Essays for the Bimillennium*, 1993. • Niall Rudd, ed., *The Satires of Horace*, 1966. • David Alexander West, *Reading Horace*, 1967. • L. P. Wilkinson, *Horace and His Lyric Poetry*, 1951.

The Medieval Era

Medieval China • Cyril Birch, ed., *Studies in Chinese Literary Genres*, 1974. • Tse-tsung Chow, ed., *Wen-lin: Studies in Chinese Humanities*, 1968. • Christopher Leigh Connery, *The Empire of the Text: Writing and Authority in Early Imperial China*, 1998. • A. R. Davis, *The Penguin Book of Chinese Verse*, 1971. • Hans Frankel, *The Flowering Plum and the Palace Lady: Interpretations of Chinese Poetry*, 1976. • Donald Holzman, *Chinese Literature in Transition from Antiquity to the Middle Ages*, 1998. • Wu-chi Liu, *An Introduction to Chinese Literature*, 1966. • Wu-chi Liu and Irving Lo, eds., *Sunflower Splendor: Three Thousand Years of Chinese Poetry*, 1976. • Michael Loewe, *Everyday Life in Early Imperial China*, 1968. • Stephen Owen, *Traditional Chinese Poetry and Poetics: Omen of the World*, 1984. • Stephen Owen, *Remembrances: The Experience of the Past in Classical Chinese Literature*, 1986. • Scott Pearce, Audrey Spiro and Patricia Ebrey, eds., *Culture and Power in the Reconstitution of the Chinese Realm, 200–600*, 2001. • Burton Watson, *Chinese Lyricism*, 1970. • Burton Watson, *The Columbia Book of Chinese Poetry*, 1984. • Pauline Yu, *The Reading of Imagery in the Chinese Poetic Tradition*, 1987.

Poetry of the Tang Dynasty • Witter Bynner, *The Jade Mountain*, 1964. • François Cheng, *Chinese Poetic Writing*, 1982. • Arthur Cooper, *Li Po and Tu Fu*, 1973. • David Gordon, *Equinox: A Gathering of T'ang Poets*, 1975. • A. C. Graham, *Poems of the Late T'ang*, 1965. • Shuen-fu Lin and S. Owen, eds., *The Vitality of the Lyric Voice*, 1986. • James J. Y. Liu, *The Art of Chinese Poetry*, 1962. • Stephen Owen, *The Poetry of the Early T'ang*, 1977. • Stephen Owen, *The Great Age of Chinese Poetry: The High T'ang*, 1981. • Stephen Owen, *The End of the Chinese "Middle Ages": Essays in Mid-Tang Literary Culture*, 1996. • Vikram Seth, *Three Chinese Poets*, 1992. • Hugh Stimson, *Fifty-five T'ang Poems*, 1976. • Arthur Wright and Denis Twitchett, *Perspectives on the T'ang*, 1973. • David Young, trans., *Five T'ang Poets*, 1990.

Wang Wei • Tony Barnstone et al., *Laughing Lost in the Mountains—Selected Poems of Wang Wei*, 1989. • Yin-nan Chang and Lewis C. Walmsley, *Poems by Wang Wei*, 1958. • G. W. Robinson, *Poems of Wang Wei*, 1973. • Marsha L. Wagner, *Wang Wei*, 1981. • Lewis C. Walmsley and Dorothy B. Walmsley, *Wang Wei: The Painter-Poet*, 1968. • Eliot Weinberger and Octavio Paz, *Nineteen Ways of Looking at Wang Wei*, 1987. • Wai-lim Yip, *Hiding the Universe: Poems by Wang Wei*, 1972. • Pauline Yu, *The Poetry of Wang Wei: New Translations and Commentary*, 1980.

Li Bo • Rewi Alley, trans., *Li Pai: 200 Selected Poems*, 1980. • Shigeyoshi Obata, *The Works* of Li Po, 1922. • J. P. Seaton and James Cryer, trans., *Bright Moon, Perching Bird: Poems*, 1987. • Arthur Waley, *The Poetry and Career of Li Po*, 1950. • Siu-kit Wong, *The Genius of Li Po*, 1984.

Tu Fu • Rewi Alley, trans., *Tu Fu: Selected Poems*, 1962. • Eva Shan Chou, *Reconsidering Tu Fu: Literary Greatness and Cultural Context*, 1995. • A. R. Davis, *Tu Fu*, 1971. • Sam Hamill, trans., *Facing the Snow: Visions of Tu Fu*, 1988. • David Hawkes, *A Little Primer of Tu Fu*, 1967. • William Hung, *Tu Fu: China's Greatest Poet*, 1952. • David McCraw, *Du Fu's Laments from the South*, 1992.

Bo Juyi • Howard S. Levy, *Translations from Po Chü-i's Collected Works*, 1978. • Arthur Waley, *The Life and Times of Po Chü-i*, 1949.

Japan • Geoffrey Bownas and Anthony Thwaite, trans. and ed., *The Penguin Book of Japanese Verse*, 1964. • Robert Brower and Earl Miner, *Japanese Court Poetry*, 1961. • Steven D. Carter, trans. and ed., *Traditional Japanese Poetry: An Anthology*, 1991. • William T. de Bary, ed., *Sources of Japanese Tradition*, 1958. • John Whitney Hall, *Japan: From Prehistory to Modern Times*, 1970. • Haruo Shirane, *Early Modern Japanese Literature, An Anthology*, 2001. • Donald Keene, *Japanese Literature: An Introduction for Western Readers*, 1953. • Donald Keene, ed., *Anthology of Japanese Literature: From the Earliest Era to the Mid-Nineteenth Century*, 1955. • Donald Keene, *Seeds in the Heart: Japanese Literature from Earliest Times to the late 16th Century*, 1993. • Donald Keene, *World Within Walls: Japanese Literature of the Pre-Modern Era, 1600–1867*, 1976. • Jin'ichi Konishi, *A History of Japanese Literature*, vols. 1–3, 1984, 1986 and 1991. • Helen Craig McCullough, ed., *Classical Japanese Prose: An Anthology*, 1990. • Helen Craig McCullough, trans. and ed., *Genji and Heike: Selections from "The Tale of Genji" and "The Tale of the Heike,"* 1994. • Earl Miner, *An Introduction to Japanese Court Poetry*, 1968. • Earl Miner, Hiroko Odagiri, and Robert E. Morrell, *The Princeton Companion to Classical Japanese Literature*, 1985. • Ivan Morris, *The World of the Shining Prince: Court Life in Ancient Japan*, 1964. • Edward Putzar, *Japanese Literature: An Historical Outline*, 1973. • J. Thomas Rimer, *A Reader's Guide to Japanese Literature*, 1988. • George Sansom, *Japan: A Short Cultural History*, 1948. • Conrad Totman, *Japan before Perry: A Short History*, 1981. • Makoto Ueda, *Literary and Art Theories*

in Japan, 1967. • H. Paul Varley, *Japanese Culture*, 1984.

Murasaki Shikibu • Norma Field, *The Splendor of Longing in the Tale of Genji*, 1987. • Edward Kamens, ed., *Approaches to Teaching Murasaki Shikibu's The Tale of Genji*, 1993. • Ivan Morris, *The Tale of Genji Scroll*, 1971. • H. Richard Okada, *Figures of Resistance: Language, Poetry, and Narrating in The Tale of Genji and Other Mid-Heian Texts*, 1991. • Edward Seidensticker, trans., *The Tale of Genji*, 1981. • Haruo Shirane, *The Bridge of Dreams: A Poetics of "The Tale of Genji,"* 1987. • Amanda Mayer Stinchecum, "Who Tells the Tale? 'Ukifune': A Study in Narrative Voice." *Monumenta Nipponica* 35 (1980): 375–403. • Royall Tyler, trans., *The Tale of Genji*, 2001. • Arthur Waley, trans., *The Tale of Genji*, 1957.

Classical Arabic and Islamic Literatures • *The Encyclopaedia of Islam*, 1986. • *The Cambridge History of Iran*, 1968. • T. J. Andrae, *Muhammad: the Man and His Faith*, 1936. • J. Ashtiani et al., eds., *Abbasid Belles-Lettres*, 1988. • J. Bacharach, *A Middle Eastern Studies Handbook*, 1984. • A. F. Beeston et al., eds., *Arabic Literature to the End of the Ummayad Period*, 1983. • R. Blachère, *Histoire de la Littérature Arabe*, 3 vols., 1952–1966. • C. E. Bosworth, *The Islamic Dynasties*, 1967. • Peter Brown, *The World of Late Antiquity*, 1971. • A. J. Butler, *The Arab Conquest of Egypt*, 1902. • J. M. Cook, *The Persian Empire*, 1983. • D. Eikelman, *The Middle East: An Anthropological Approach*, 1981. • H. A. R. Gibb, *Arabic Literature*, 1963. • H. A. R. Gibb, *Islam*, 1969. • H. A. R. Gibb, *Muhammadansim*, 1949. • H. A. R. Gibb, *Studies on the Civilisation of Islam*, 1962. • G. E. von Grunebaum, *Medieval Islam: A Study in Cultural Orientation*, 1953. • Sabry Hafez, *The Genesis of Arabic Narrative Discourse*, 1993. • H. W. Hazard, *Atlas of the Islamic History*, 1957. • P. M. Holts et al., eds., *The Cambridge History of Islam*, 1970. • Albert Hourani, *A History of the Arab Peoples*, 1991. • Albert Hourani, *Syria and Lebanon*, 1946. • G. F. Hourani, *Arab Seafaring in the Indian Ocean in Ancient and Medieval Times*, 1951. • T. Khalidi, *Classical Arab Islam*, 1985. • S. Lane-Poole, *The Muhammadan Dynasties*, 1925. • I. M. Lapidus, *A History of Muslim Societies*, 1988. • Bernard Lewis, *Istanbul and the Civilisation of the Ottoman Empire*, 1963. • Bernard Lewis, ed. *The World of Islam*, 1976. • S. Moscati, *The Semites in Ancient History*, 1959. • J. D. Pearson et al., eds., *Index Islamicus*, 1958. • F. Rahman, *Islam*, 1979.

• R. Roolvink, *Historical Atlas of the Muslim Peoples,* 1957. • M. Ruthven, *Islam in the World,* 1984. • Jean Sargent, *Introduction to the History of the Muslim East,* 1965. • J. Sauvaget, *Introduction à l'histoire de l'orient musulman,* 1961. • I. Shahid, *Rome and the Arabs,* 1984. • L. Udovitch, ed., *The Islamic Middle East 700–1900: Studies in Economic and Social History,* 1981. • W. M. Watt, *Muhammad: Prophet and Statesman,* 1961. • W. M. Watt, *Muhammad at Mecca,* 1953. • W. M. Watt, *Muhammad at Medina,* 1956.

The Qur'an • A. J. Arberry, *The Qur'an Interpreted,* 1955. • H. Berkeland, *Old Muslim Opposition against Interpretation of the Qur'an,* 1955. • J. Bowker, *Jesus in the Qur'an,* 1965. • J. Burton, *The Collection of the Qur'an,* 1977. • K. Cragg, *The Event of the Qur'an,* 1971. • K. Cragg, *The Mind of the Qur'an,* 1973. • Ali Dashti, *Twenty-Three Years: A Study of the Prophetic Career of Muhammad,* 1985. • F. Gabrieli, *Muhammad and the Conquests of Islam,* 1968. • H. Gätje, *Qur'an and Its Exegeses,* 1976. • J. B. Glubb, *The Life and Times of Muhammad,* 1979. • M. H. Haykal, *The Life of Muhammad,* 1976. • R. G. Hovannisian, ed., *Islam's Understanding of Itself,* 1983. • T. Isutsu, *Ethico-Religious Concepts in the Qur'an,* 1966. • T. Isutsu, *God and Man in the Qur'an,* 1964. • J. Jansen, *The Interpretation of the Qur'an in Modern Egypt,* 1974. • A. Jeffery, *Reader on Islam,* 1962. • J. Jomier, *The Bible and the Qur'an,* 1964. • M. Lings, *Muhammad: His Life Based on the Earliest Sources,* 1983. • Henry Mercier and Lucien Tremlett, *The Qur'an,* 1973. • A. Abul Qaswm, *The Recitation and Interpretation of the Qur'an,* 1979. • D. Rahbar, *God of Justice: A Study in the Ethical Doctrine of the Qur'an,* 1960. • Fazlur Rahman, *Islam,* 1966. • M. Rodinson, *Mohammed,* 1971. • M. S. Seale, *Qur'an and Bible,* 1978. • S. H. Shamma, *The Ethical System underlying the Qur'an,* 1959. • W. Montgomery Watt, *Muhammad at Mecca,* 1953. • W. Montgomery Watt, *Muhammad at Medina,* 1966. • A. J. Wensinck, *Muhammad and the Jews of Mecca,* 1975.

The Thousand and One Nights • Daniel E. Beaumont, *Slave of Desire: Sex, Love, and Death in The 1001 Nights,* 2002. • Sir Richard F. Burton, trans., *The Arabian Nights: Tales from a Thousand and One Nights,* introduction by A. S. Byatt, 2001. • Peter L. Caracciolo, ed., *The "Arabian Nights" in English Literature,* 1988. • André Clot, *Harun al-Rashid and the World of the Thousand and One Nights,* 1989. • Ferial J. Ghazoul, *Nocturnal Poetics: The Arabian Nights in Comparative Perspective,* 1996. Husain Haddawy, trans., *The Arabian Nights,* 1990. • Husain Haddawy, trans., *The Arabian Nights II: Sinbad and Other Popular Stories,* 1995. • Robert Irwin, *The Arabian Nights: A Companion,* 1995. • Muhsin Mahdi, ed., *The Thousand and One Nights (Alf Layla wa-Layla) from the Earliest Known Sources,* 3 vols., 1984–1994. • Powys Mathers, trans., *The Book of the Thousand Nights and One Night,* 4 vols., from the French translation of J. C. Mardrus, 1964. • David Pinault, *Story-Telling Techniques in the Arabian Nights,* 1992. • Iqbal 'Ali Shah, *Alone in Arabian Nights,* 1933. • Douglas Brooke Wheelton Sladen, *Oriental Cairo: The City of the "Arabian Nights,"* 1987.

Medieval Europe • *The New Cambridge Medieval History,* 1995–2003. • Erich Auerbach, *Literary Language and Its Public in Late Latin Antiquity and in the Middle Ages,* trans. Ralph Manheim, 1993. • Erich Auerbach, *Mimesis: The Representation of Reallity in Western Litrature,* trans. Willard R. Trask, 1968. • W. R. J. Barron, ed., *The Arthur of the English: The Arthurian Legend in Medieval English Life and Literature,* 2001. • Marc Bloch, *Feudal Society,* trans. L. A. Manyon, 1964. • R. Howard Bloch, *Medieval Misogyny and the Invention of Western Romantic Love,* 1991. • Renate Blumenfeld-Kosinski, *Reading Myth: Classical Mythology and Its Interpretations in Medieval French Literature,* 1997. • John Boswell, *Christianity, Social Tolerance, and Homosexuality: Gay People in Western Europe from the Beginning of the Christian Era to the Fourteenth Century,* 1980. • Chirstopher Brooke, *Europe in the Central Middle Ages, 962–1154,* 2000. • Peter Brown, *The World of Late Antiquity A.D. 150–750,* 1989. • Peter Brown and Jacques Le Goff, eds., *The Rise of Western Christendom: Triumph and Diversity A.D. 200–1000,* 1997. • Carolyn Walker Bynum, *Holy Feast and Holy Fast: The Significance of Food to Medieval Women,* 1987. • Franco Cardini, *Europe and Islam,* trans. Caroline Besmish, 2001. • Mary Carruthers, *The Book of Memory: A Study of Memory in Medieval Culture,* 1990. • Roger Collins, *Early Medieval Europe, 300–1000,* 1999. • Ernst Robert Curtius, *European Literature and the Latin Middle Ages,* trans. Willard Trask, 1973. • Peter Dronke, *Medieval Latin and the Rise of the European Love Lyric,* 1968. • Peter Dronke, *The Medieval Lyric,* 1996. • Peter Dronke, *Women Writers of the Middle Ages: A Critical Study of Texts from Perpetua (203) to Marguerite Porete (1310),* 1984. • Georges

Duby, *France in the Middle Ages 987–1460: From Hugh Capet to Joan of Arc*, trans. Juliet Vale, 1991. • Georges Duby, ed., *Revelations of the Medieval World*. vol. 2 of *A History of Private Life*, 1987–1991. • Angus Fletcher, *Allegory, the Theory of a Symbolic Mode*, 1964. • Boris Ford, ed., *Medieval Literature: The European Inheritance*, 1983. • Barbara Harvey, ed., *The Twelfth and Thirteenth Centuries. 1066–c. 1280*, 2001. • George Holmes, ed., *The Oxford Illustrated History of Medieval Europe*, 1988. • Burce Holsinger, *Music, Body, and Desire in Medieval Culture: Hildegard of Bingen to Chaucer*, 2001. • Johan Huizinga, *The Autumn of the Middle Ages*, trans. Rodney J. Payton and Ulrich Mammitzsch, 1996. • W. T. H. Jackson, *The Hero and the King: An Epic Theme*, 1982. • Roberta L. Krueger, *The Campbridge Companion to Medieval Romance*, 2000. • Jacques Le Goff, *Intellectuals in the Middle Ages*, trans. Teresa Lavender Fagan, 1993. • Jacques Le Goff, *The Medieval Imagination*, trans. Arthur Goldhammer, 1988. • Bernard Lewis and Dominique Schnapper, eds., *Muslims in Europe*, 1994. • C. S. Lewis, *The Allegory of Love: A Study in Medieval Tradition*, 1958. • C. S. Lewis, *The Discarded Image: An Introduction to Medieval and Renaissance Literature*, 1994. • María Rose Menocal, *Shards of Love: Exile and the Origins of the Lyric*, 1994. • William Paden, ed., *Medieval Lyric: Genres in Historical Context*, 2002. • Lee Patterson, *Negotiating the Past: The Historical Understanding of Medieval Literature*, 1987. • James J. Paxson, *The Poetics of Personification*, 1994. • David L. Pike, *Passage through Hell: Modernist Descents, Medieval Underworlds*, 1997. • Michael A. Signer and John Van Engen, eds., *Jews and Christians in Twelfth-Century Europe*, 2001. • J. Riley Smith, ed., *The Oxford Illustrated History of the Crusades*, 1995. • Brian Stock, *The Implications of Literacy: Written Language and Models of Interpretation in the Eleventh and Twelfth Centuries*, 1983. • R. N. Swanson, *The Twelfth-Century Renaissance*, 1999. • Barbara Tuchman, *A Distant Mirror: The Calamitous Fourteenth Century*, 1978.

Beowulf • Adrien Bonjour, *The Digressions in Beowulf*, 1950. • R. W. Chambers and C. L. Wrenn, *Beowulf: An Introduction to the Study of the Poem*, 1959. • Craig R. Davis, *Beowulf and the Demise of Germanic Legend in England*, 1996. • Susan E. Deskis, *Beowulf and the Medieval Proverb Tradition*, 1996. • James W. Earl, *Thinking About Beowulf*, 1994. • John Miles Foley, *Traditional Oral Epic: The Odyssey, Beowulf, and the Serbo-Croatian Return Song*, 1990. • Ritchie Girvan and Rupert Bruce-Mitford, *Beowulf and the Seventh Century*, 1971. • John M. Hill, *The Anglo-Saxon Warrior Ethic*, 2000. • Edward B. Irving, *A Reading of Beowulf*, 1968. • J. D. A. Ogilvy, and Donald C. Baker, *Reading Beowulf: An Introduction to the Poem, Its Background, and Its Style*, 1983. • Gillian R. Overing, *Language, Sign, and Gender in Beowulf*, 1990. • Fred C. Robinson, *Beowulf and the Appositive Style*, 1985. • Kenneth Sisam, *The Structure of Beowulf*, 1965. • J. Michael Stitt, *Beowulf and the Bear's Son: Epic, Saga, and Fairytale in Northern Germanic Tradition*, 1992. • J. R. R. Tolkien, *Beowulf and the Critics*, ed. Michael D. C. Drout, 2002. • Dorothy Whitelock, *The Audience of Beowulf*, 1951.

Iberia, The Meeting of Three Worlds • Samuel Armistead, Mishael M. Caspi, et al., eds., *Jewish Culture and the Hispanic World*, 2001. • Eliahu Ashtor, *The Jews of Moslem Spain*, 1992. • Yitzhak Baer, *A History of the Jews in Christian Spain*, 1992. • Stacy N. Beckwith, *Charting Memory: Recalling Medieval Spain*, 1999. • Gilbert Chase, *The Music of Spain*, 1941. • Richard Fletcher, *Moorish Spain*, 1993. • Daniel Frank, ed., *The Jews of Medieval Islam: Community, Society, and Identity*, 1995. • Jane S. Gerber, *The Jews of Spain: A History of the Sephardic Experience*, 1994. • L. P. Harvey, *Islamic Spain 1250–1500*, 1992. • Salma Khadra Jayyusi, *The Legacy of Muslim Spain*, 2 vols. 1992. • John Esten Keller and Annette Grant Cash, *Daily Life Depicted in the Cantigas de Santa Maria*, 1998. • Hugh Kennedy, *Muslim Spain and Portugal: A Political History of Al-Andalus*, 1997. • Vivian B. Mann, Thomas F. Glick, and Jerrilynn D. Dodds, *Convivencia: Jews, Muslims, and Christians in Medieval Spain*, 1992. • Manuela Marin, Julio Samsó, and Maribel Fierro, *The Formation of Al-Andalus*, 2 vols., 1998. • María Rosa Menocal, *The Arabic Role in Medieval Literary History: A Forgotten Heritage*, 1987. • María Rosa Menocal, *Shards of Love: Exile and the Origins of the Lyric*, 1994. • María Rosa Menocal and Harold Bloom, *The Ornament of the World: How Muslims, Jews, and Christians Created a Culture of Tolerance in Medieval Spain*, 2002. • María Rosa Menocal, Raymond Scheindlin, and Michael Sells, eds., *The Literature of Al-Andalus*, 2000. • Louise Mirrer, *Women, Jews, and Muslims in the Texts of Reconquest Castile*, 1996. • A. R. Nykl, *Hispano-Arabic Poetry and Its Relation to the Old Provençal Troubadours*, 1946. • Bernard

F. Reilly, *The Medieval Spains*, 1993. • Julian Ribera, *Music in Ancient Arabia and Spain*, 1929. • Lucy A. Sponsler, *Women in the Medieval Spanish Epic and Lyric Traditions*, 1975. • David Wasserstein, *The Rise and Fall of the Party-Kings: Politics and Society in Islamic Spain 1002–1086*, 1985.

Castilian Ballads and Traditional Songs • Ingrid Bahler and Katherine Gyékényesi Gatto, *Of Kings and Poets: Cancionero Poetry of the Trastámara Courts*, 1992. • Robert Stevenson, *Spanish Music in the Age of Columbus*, 1960. • Ruth H. Webber, ed., *Hispanic Balladry Today*, 1989.

Mozarabic Kharjas • Samuel G. Armistead, "A Brief History of *Kharja* Studies." *Hispania* 70: 8–15, 1987 • Richard Hitchcock, *The Kharjas: A Critical Bibliography*, 1977. • Alan Jones, *Romance 'Kharjas' in Andalusian Arabic Muwassah Poetry: A Paleographical Analysis*, 1988. • Samuel Stern, *Hispano-Arabic Strophic Poetry: Studies*, 1974. • Otto Zwartjes, *Love Songs from al-Andalus: History, Structure, and Meaning of the Kharja*, 1997.

Ibn 'Arabi • A. E. Affifi, *The Mystical Philosophy of Muhyid din-Ibnul 'Arabi*, 1939. • Henri Corbin, *Creative Imagination in the Sufism of Ibn 'Arabi*, trans. Ralph Manheim, 1958. • Seyyed Hossain Nasr, *Three Muslim Sages*, 1969.

Yehudah ha-Levi and Solomon Ibn Gabirol • Ross Brann, *The Compunctious Poet: Cultural Ambiguity and Hebrew Poetry in Muslim Spain*, 1991. • David Hartman, *Israelis and the Jewish Tradition: An Ancient People Debating Its Future*, 2000. • Rudolf Kayser, *The Life and Time of Jehudah Halevi*, trans. Frank Gaynor, 1949. • Raphael Loewe, *Ibn Gabirol*, 1990. • Arie Schippers, *Spanish Hebrew Poetry and the Arabic Literary Tradition: Arabic Themes in Hebrew Andalusian Poetry*, 1994.

Ramon Llull • J. N. Hillgarth, *Raymond Llull and Llullism in Fourteenth-Century France*, 1971. • Mark D. Johnston, *The Evangelical Rhetoric of Ramon Llull: Lay Learning and Piety in the Christian West Around 1300*, 1996. • Mark D. Johnston, *The Spiritual Logic of Ramon Llull*, 1987. • E. Allison Peers, *Ramon Llull: A Biography*, 1969. • Frances A. Yates, *Llull and Bruno: Collected Essays*, vol. 1, 1982.

Dom Dinis and Martin Codax • Sheila R. Ackerlind, *King Dinis of Portugal and the Alfonsine Heritage*, 1990. • Frede Jensen, *The Earliest Portuguese Lyrics*, 1978.

Marie de France • R. Howard Bloch, *The Anonymous Marie de France*, 2003. • Margaret M. Boland, *Architectural Structure in the Lais of Marie de France*, 1995. • Glyn S. Burgess, *The Lais of Marie de France: Text and Context*, 1987. • Caroline Walker Bynum, *Metamorphosis and Identity*, 2001. • Paula Clifford, *Marie de France: Lais*, 1982. • Mortimer J. Donovan, *The Breton Lay: A Guide to Varieties*, 1969. • Chantal Maréchal, ed., *In Quest of Marie de France: A Twelfth-Century Poet*, 1992. • Emanuel J. Mickel, Jr., *Marie de France*, 1974.

Dante Alighieri • William Anderson, *Dante the Maker*, 1980. • Peter Armour, *Dante's Griffin and the History of the World*, 1989. • Peter Armour, *The Door of Purgatory: A Study of Multiple Symbolism in Dante's Purgatorio*, 1983. • Erich Auerbach, *Dante Poet of the Secular World*, 1961. • Erich Auerbach, "Figura," in *Scenes from the Drama of European Literature*, 1984. • Michele Barbi, *Life of Dante*, 1954. • Teodolinda Barolini, *Dante's Poets: Textuality and Truth in the Comedy*, 1983. • Teodolinda Barolini, *The Undivine Comedy: Detheologizing Dante*, 1992. • Steven Botterill, *Dante and the Mystical Tradition: Bernard of Clairvaux in the Commedia*, 1994. • Patrick Boyde, *Dante, Philomythes and Philosopher: Man in the Cosmos*, 1981. • Patrick Boyde, *Human Vices and Human Worth in Dante's Comedy*, 2000. • Anthony K. Cassell, *Inferno I*, 1989. • A. C. Charity, *Events and Their Afterlife: The Dialectics of Christian Typology in the Bible and Dante*, 1966. • Marc Cogan, *The Design in the Wax: The Structure of the Divine Comedy and Its Meaning*, 1999. • Alison Cornish, *Reading Dante's Stars*, 2000. • Charles Davis, *Dante and the Idea of Rome*, 1957. • Charles Davis, *Dante's Italy and Other Essays*, 1984. • Alessandro Passerin d'Entrèves, *Dante as a Political Thinker*, 1952. • Peter Dronke, *Dante and Medieval Latin Traditions*, 1986. • Robert M. Durling and Ronald L. Martínez, *Time and the Crystal: Studies in Dante's Rime Petrose*, 1990. • Francis Fergusson, *Dante*, 1966. • Frances Fergusson, *Dante's Drama of the Mind: A Modern Reading of Purgatorio*, 1953. • Joan M. Ferrante, *The Political Vision of the Divine Comedy*, 1984. • Kenelm Foster, *The Two Dantes and Other Studies*, 1977. • Wallace Fowlie, *A Reading of Dante's Inferno*, 1981. • William Franke, *Dante's Interpretive Journey*, 1996. • John Freccero, ed., *Dante: A Collection of Critical Essays*, 1965. • John Freccero, *Dante: The Poetics of*

Conversion, ed. Rachel Jacoff, 1986. • Eileen
Gardiner, trans., *Visions of Heaven and Hell
Before Dante*, 1989. • Etienne Gilson, *Dante
and Philosophy*, trans. David Moore, 1963. •
Cecil Grayson, ed., *The World of Dante*, 1980.
• Robert Pogue Harrison, *The Body of Beatrice*,
1988. • Robert Hollander, *Allegory in Dante's
Commedia*, 1969. • Robert Hollander, *Dante: A
Life in Works*, 2001. • George Holmes, *Dante*,
1980. • Rachel Jacoff, ed., *The Cambridge
Companion to Dante*, 1993. • Rachel Jacoff
and Jeffrey Schnapp, ed., *The Poetry of Allu-
sion: Virgil and Ovid in Dante's Commedia*,
1991. • Rachel Jacoff and William A. Stephany,
Inferno II, 1989. • Robin Kirkpatrick, *Dante's
Inferno: Difficulty and Dead Poetry*, 1987. •
John Kleiner, *Mismapping the Underworld:
Daring and Error in Dante's Comedy*, 1994. •
Richard Lansing, ed., *Dante: The Critical Com-
plex*, 8 vols., 2003. • Jacques Le Goff, *The Birth
of Purgatory*, 1984. • Ronald Macdonald, *The
Burial Places of Memory: Epic Underworlds in
Vergil, Dante and Milton*, 1987. • Allen Man-
delbaum, et al., eds., *Lectura Dantis: Inferno*,
1998. • Antonio C. Mastrobuono, *Dante's Jour-
ney of Sanctification*, 1990. • Jerome Mazzaro,
The Figure of Beatrice, 1981. • Joseph Anthony
Mazzeo, *Structure and Thought in the Parad-
iso*, 1958. • Giuseppe Mazzotta, ed., *Critical
Essays on Dante*, 1991. • Giuseppe Mazzotta,
*Dante, Poet of the Desert: History and Alle-
gory in the Divine Comedy*, 1979. • Giuseppe
Mazzotta, *Dante's Vision and the Circle of
Knowledge*, 1993. • María Rosa Menocal, *The
Arabic Role in Medieval Literary History*,
1987. • Edward G. Miller, *Sense Perception
in Dante's Commedia*, 1996. • Alison Morgan,
Dante and the Medieval Other World, 1990.
• Mary A. Orr, *Dante and the Early Astronomers*, 1961. • Shirley J. Paolini, *Confessions
of Sin and Love in the Middle Ages: Dante's
Commedia and St. Augustine's Confessions*,
1982. • Ricardo Quinones, *Dante Alighieri*,
1979. • Brenda Deen Schildgen, *Dante and the
Orient*, 2002. • Jeffrey Schnapp, *The Trans-
figuration of History at the Center of Dante's
Paradise*, 1986. • John A. Scott, *Dante's Political Purgatory*, 1996. • J. E. Shaw, *Essays on
the Vita Nuova*, 1929. • Maria Picchio Sim-
onelli, *Inferno III*, 1993. • Charles S. Singleton, *Dante's Commedia: Elements of Structure*,
1977. • Charles S. Singleton, *An Essay on the
Vita Nuova*, 1949. • Charles S. Singleton, *Journey to Beatrice*, 1958. • Madison U. Sowell,
ed., *Dante and Ovid: Essays in Intertextuality*,
1991. • Jeremy Tambling, ed., *Dante*, 1999. •

Miguel Tasín Palacios, *Islam and the Divine
Comedy*, 1968. • J. F. Took, *Dante, Lyric Poet
and Philosopher: An Introduction to the Minor
Works*, 1990. • Paget Toynbee, *Dante Alighieri,
His Life and Works*, 1965.

Geoffrey Chaucer • Malcolm Andrew, *Critical
Essays on Chaucer's Canterbury Tales*, 1991.
• Peter Beidler, ed., *The Wife of Bath*, 1996. •
C. David Benson, *Chaucer's Drama of Style:
Poetic Variety and Contrast in The Canter-
bury Tales*, 1986. • Piero Boitano, *Chaucer
and the Italian Trecento*, 1983. • Piero Boitano
and Jill Mann, eds., *The Cambridge Chaucer
Companion*, 1986. • Muriel Bowden, *A Com-
mentary on the General Prologue to "The
Canterbury Tales,"* 1967. • Susan Crane, *Gen-
der and Romance in Chaucer's "Canterbury
Tales,"* 1994. • W. A. Davenport, *Chaucer
and His English Contemporaries: Prologue
and Tale in "The Canterbury Tales,"* 1998.
• Alfred David, *The Strumpet Muse: Art and
Morals in Chaucer's Poetry*, 1976. • Carolyn
Dinshaw, *Chaucer's Sexual Poetics*, 1989. •
E. Talbot Donaldson, *Speaking of Chaucer*,
1970. • Sigmund Eisner, *A Tale of Wonder: A
Source Study of The Wife of Bath's Tale*, 1969. •
John M. Fyler, *Chaucer and Ovid*, 1979. • Jodi-
Anne George, ed., *Geoffrey Chaucer: The Gen-
eral Prologue to the "Canterbury Tales,"* 2000.
• Warren Ginsberg, *Chaucer's Italian Tradi-
tion*, 2002. • John C. Hirsch, *Chaucer and the
Canterbury Tales: A Short Introduction*, 2003.
• Donald R. Howard, *Chaucer: His Life, His
Works, His World*, 1987. • Donald R. Howard,
The Idea of the Canterbury Tales, 1976. • Peggy
Knapp, *Chaucer and the Social Contest*, 1990.
• Stephen Knight, *Geoffrey Chaucer*, 1986.
• V. A. Kolve, *Chaucer and the Imagery of Nar-
rative*, 1984. • H. Marshall Leicester Jr., *The Dis-
enchanted Self: Representing the Subject in the
Canterbury Tales*, 1990. • Kathryn L. Lynch, ed.,
Chaucer's Cultural Geography, 2002. • Jill
Mann, *Chaucer and Medieval Estates Sat-
ire: The Literature of Social Classes and the
General Prologue to the "Canterbury Tales,"*
1973. • Robert P. Miller, ed., *Chaucer: Sources
and Backgrounds*, 1977. • A. J. Minnis, *Chaucer and Pagan Antiquity*, 1982. • A. J. Minnis,
ed., *Chaucer's Boece and the Medieval Tradition of Boethius*, 1993. • Charles Muscatine,
Chaucer and the French Tradition, 1957. •
Richard Neuse, *Chaucer's Dante: Allegory
and Epic Theater in The Canterbury Tales*,
1991. • Paul A. Olson, *The Canterbury Tales
and the Good Society*, 1986. • Lee Patterson,

Chaucer and the Subject of History, 1991. • S. H. Rigby, *Chaucer in Context: Society, Allegory, and Gender,* 1996. • D. W. Robertson, *Chaucer's London,* 1968. • D. W. Robertson, *A Preface to Chaucer,* 1962. • Beryl Rowland, ed., *Companion to Chaucer Studies,* 1979. • Brenda Deen Schildgen, *Pagans, Tartars, Moslems, and Jews in Chaucer's "Canterbury Tales,"* 2001. • Paul Strohm, *Social Chaucer,* 1989. • David Wallace, *Chaucerian Polity: Absolutist Lineages and Associational Forms in England and Italy,* 1997. • Winthrop Wetherbee, *Geoffrey Chaucer: "The Canterbury Tales,"* 1989.

The Early Modern Period

Early Modern Europe • Erich Auerbach, *Mimesis: The Representation of Reality in Western Literature,* 1953. • Leonard Barkan, *Unearthing the Past: Archaeology and Aesthetics in the Making of Renaissance Culture,* 2000. • Hans Baron, *The Crisis of the Early Italian Renaissance,* 1966. • Harry Berger, Jr., *Second World and Green World: Studies in Renaissance Fiction-Making,* 1988. • John Bossy, *Christianity in the West, 1400–1700,* 1985. • Karl Brandi, *The Emperor Charles V,* 1980. • Fernand Braudel, *The Mediterranean and the Mediterranean World in the Age of Philip II,* 2 vols., 1972. • Jerry Brotton, *Trading Territories: Mapping the Early Modern World,* 1997. • Peter Burke, *Popular Culture in Early Modern Europe,* 1978. • Douglas Bush, *Classical Influences in Renaissance Literature,* 1952. • Stanley Chojnacki, *Women and Men in Renaissance Venice,* 2000. • Louise Clubb, *Italian Drama in Shakespeare's Time,* 1989. • Marcia L. Colish, *Medieval Foundations of the Western Intellectual Tradition,* 1998. • Natalie Davis, *Society and Culture in Early Modern France,* 1976. • Robert M. Durling, *The Figure of the Poet in Renaissance Epic,* 1965. • J. H. Elliott, *The Old World and the New, 1492–1650,* 1970. • Eugenio Garin, *Italian Humanism: Philosophy and Civic Life in the Renaissance,* 1965. • Deno Geanakoplos, *Greek Scholars in Venice,* 1962. • Richard Goldthwaite, *The Building of Renaissance Florence,* 1981. • Thomas Greene, *The Light in Troy: Imitation and Discovery in Renaissance Poetry,* 1982. • Thomas Greene, *The Descent from Heaven: A Study in Epic Continuity,* 1963. • Timothy Hampton, *Writing from History: The Rhetoric of Exemplarity in Renaissance Literature,* 1990. • Francis Haskell, *Patrons and Painters,* 1963. • Henry Kamen, *Philip of Spain,* 1997. • Dale Kent, *The Rise of the Medici,* 1978. • Nannerl O. Keohane, *Philosophy and the State in France,* 1980. • Christiane Klapisch-Zuber, *Women, Religion and Ritual in Early Modern Italy,* trans. Lydia G. Cochrane, 1985. • Jill Kraye, *The Cambridge Companion to Renaissance Humanism,* 1989. • Paul Oskar Kristeller, *Renaissance Thought and Its Sources,* 1979. • Frederic C. Lane, *Venice: A Maritime Republic,* 1973. • Frank Lestringant, *Mapping the Renaissance World: The Geographical Imagination in the Age of Discovery,* 1994. • Garrett Mattingly, *The Armada,* 1959. • Samuel Eliot Morison, *The European Discovery of America,* 1974. • Edward Muir, *Ritual in Early Modern Europe,* 1997. • David Norbrook, *Poetry and Politics in the English Renaissance,* 1984. • Erwin Panofsky, *Renaissance and Renascences in Western Art,* 1969. • Patricia Parker, *Inescapable Romance,* 1979. • Boies Penrose, *Travel and Discovery in the Renaissance, 1420–1620,* 1952. • Mary Elizabeth Perry, *Gender and Disorder in Early Modern Seville,* 1990. • J. G. A. Pocock, *The Machiavellian Moment,* 1975. • David Quint, *Epic and Empire,* 1993. • Albert Rabil Jr., ed., *Renaissance Humanism: Foundations, Forms, and Legacy,* 3 vols., 1988. • Edward Rosen, *Copernicus and the Scientific Revolution,* 1984. • David B. Ruderman, *Jewish Thought and Scientific Discovery in Early Modern Europe,* 1995. • Londa Schiebinger, *The Mind Has No Sex? Women in the Origins of Modern Science,* 1989. • Charles B. Schmitt, *Studies in Renaissance Philosophy and Science,* 1981. • Robert Schwoebel, *The Shadow of the Crescent: The Renaissance Image of the Turks, 1453–1517,* 1973. • Robert W. Scribner, *Popular Culture and Popular Movements in Reformation Germany,* 1987. • Nancy Siraisi, *Medieval and Early Renaissance Medicine,* 1990. • Dava Sobel, *Galileo's Daughter,* 2000. • Jonathan D. Spence, *The Memory Palace of Matteo Ricci,* 1985. • Dora Thornton, *The Scholar in his Study: Ownership and Experience in Renaissance Italy,* 1998. • Richard Trexler, *Public Life in Renaissance Florence,* 1980. • Charles Trinkaus, *In Our Image and Likeness,* 1970. • Jane Tylus, *Writing and Vulnerablity in the Late Renaissance,* 1993. • William Wallace, *Galileo and His Sources,* 1984. • Merry Wiesner-Hanks, *Women and Gender in Early Modern Europe,* 1993. • Edgar Wind, *Pagan Mysteries in the Renaissance,* 1968. • Frances

Yates, *The French Academies of the Sixteenth Century,* 1947.

Giovanni Boccaccio • Thomas Bergin, *Boccaccio,* 1982. • Vittore Branca, *Boccaccio: The Man and His Works,* 1976. • Pier Massimo Forni, *Adventures in Speech: Rhetoric and Narration in Boccaccio's Decameron,* 1996. • Victoria Kirkham, *The Sign of Reason in Boccaccio's Fiction,* 1993. • Millicent Marcus, *An Allegory of Form: Literary Self-Consciousness in the Decameron,* 1979. • Giuseppe Mazzotta, *The World at Play in Boccaccio's "Decameron,"* 1986. • Aldo Scaglione, *Nature and Love in the Middle Ages,* 1963. • Daniel Williman, ed., *The Black Death: The Impact of the Fourteenth-Century Plague,* 1982.

Francis Petrarch • Hans Baron, *From Petrarch to Leonardo Bruni,* 1968. • Thomas Bergin, *Petrarch,* 1970. • Morris Bishop, *Petrarch and His World,* 1963. • Robert M. Durling, "The Ascent of Mount Ventoux and the Crisis of Allegory," *Italian Quarterly* 18, 1974: 7–28. • John Freccero, "The Fig Tree and the Laurel," *Diacritics* 5, 1975: 34–40. • Giuseppe Mazzotta, *The Worlds of Petrarch,* 1993. • Sara Sturm-Maddox, *Petrarch's Laurels,* 1992. • Charles Trinkaus, *The Poet as Philosopher,* 1979. • Marguerite Waller, *Petrarch's Poetics and Literary History,* 1980. • E. H. Wilkins, *Life of Petrarch,* 1961. • E. H. Wilkins, *The Making of the "Canzoniere,"* 1951.

Michel de Montaigne • Harold Bloom, ed., *Montaigne's "Essays,"* 1987. • Donald Frame, *Montaigne: A Biography,* 1965. • Hugo Friedrich, *Montaigne,* 1968. • Fredi Chiappelli, ed., *First Images of America: The Impact of the New World on the Old,* 2 vols., 1976. • George Hoffmann, *Montaigne's Career,* 1998. • Glyn Norton, *Montaigne and the Introspective Mind,* 1975. • David Quint, *Montaigne and the Quality of Mercy,* 1998. • R. A. Sayce, *Essays of Montaigne,* 1972. • Jean Starobinski, *Montaigne in Motion,* 1985.

Miguel de Cervantes • Jean Canavaggio, *Cervantes,* 1990. • Anne J. Cruz, *Discourses of Poverty: Social Reform and the Picaresque Novel in Early Modern Spain,* 1999. • Ruth El Saffar, *Critical Essays on Cervantes,* 1986. • Alban Forcione, *Cervantes and the Humanist Vision,* 1982. • Maria Antonia Garcés, *Cervantes in Algiers: A Captive's Tale,* 2002. • Timothy Hampton, *Writing from History,* 1990. • Steven D. Hutchinson, *Cervantine Journeys,* 1992. • Carroll B. Johnson, *Don Quixote: The Quest for Modern Fiction,* 1990. • Carroll B. Johnson, *Cervantes and the Material World,* 2000. • Walter Kaiser, *Praisers of Folly,* 1963. • Georg Lukács, *Theory of the Novel,* 1971. • Melveena McKendrick, *Cervantes,* 1980. • Lowry Nelson Jr., *Cervantes: A Collection of Critical Essays,* 1969. • Edwin Williamson, *The Half-Way House of Fiction: Don Quixote and Arthurian Romance,* 1984.

William Shakespeare • Jean Wilson, *The Shakespeare Legacy,* 1995. • Leslie Fiedler, *The Stranger in Shakespeare,* 1972. • Charles Frey, *"The Tempest* and the New World," *Shakespeare Quarterly* 30, 1979. • Northrop Frye, *A Natural Perspective,* 1965. • Stephen Greenblatt, *Marvellous Possessions: The Wonder of the New World,* 1991. • Stephen Greenblatt, "Learning to Curse," in *First Images of America,* ed. Fredi Chiappelli, 1976. • Donna Hamilton, *Virgil and The Tempest: The Politics of Imitation,* 1990. • D. G. James, *The Dream of Prospero,* 1967. • Jeffrey Knapp, *An Empire Nowhere: England, America, and Literature from "Utopia" to "The Tempest,"* 1994. • James Schiffer, ed., *Shakespeare's Sonnets: Critical Essays,* 1999. • Murray M. Schwartz and Coppélia Kahn, eds., *Representing Shakespeare,* 1980. • Bruce Smith, *Homosexual Desire in Shakespeare's England,* 1991. • Stephen Orgel, "Prospero's Wife," in *Representing the English Renaissance,* ed. Stephen Greenblatt, 1988. • Alden T. and Virginia Vaughan, *Shakespeare's Caliban: A Cultural History,* 1991. • Helen Vendler, *The Art of Shakespeare's Sonnets,* 1997. • Stephen Greenblatt, *Renaissance Self-Fashioning,* 1980.

Mesoamerica: Before Columbus and After Cortés • Joan D. Barghusen, *The Aztecs,* 2000. • Robert Carmack, *The Legacy of Mesoamerica,* 1996. • Davíd Carrasco, *Quetzalcoatl and the Irony of Empire,* 1982. • Inga Clendinen, *Aztecs: An Interpretation,* 1991. • Michael D. Coe, *The Maya,* 1987. • Michael D. Coe, *The Maya Scribe and His World,* 1973. • David Damrosch, "The Pope's Blowgun," in *What Is World Literature?,* 2003. • Nancy M. Farriss, *Maya Society Under Colonial Rule: The Collective Enterprise of Survival,* 1984. • Enrique Florescano, *Memory, Myth, and Time in Mexico,* 1994. • Gary H. Gossen and Miguel León-Portilla, eds., *South and Meso-American Native Spirituality,* 1993. • Ross Hassig, *Time, History, and Belief in Aztec and Colonial Mexico,* 2001. • Alvin M. Josephy, ed., *America in 1492: The World of the Indian Peoples Before the Arrival* *of Columbus*, 1993. • Charles A. F. P. Maza, *Pre-Columbian Socio-Political Structure in the Valley of Mexico*, 1997. • Anthony Pagden, *European Encounters with the New World*, 1994. • Miguel León-Portilla, *The Aztec Image of Self and Society*, 1992. • Miguel León-Portilla, *The Broken Spears: The Aztec Account of the Conquest of Mexico*, 1992. • Miguel León-Portilla, ed., *Native Mesoamerican Spirituality*, 1980. • Bernardino de Sahagún, *The Florentine Codex: General History of the Things of New Spain*, Arthur J. O. Anderson and C. E. Dibble, eds., 1950–1982. • Mary Miller and Karl Taube, *The Gods and Symbols of Ancient Mexico and the Maya*, 1993.

The Conquest and Its Aftermath • Marvin Lunenfield, ed., *1492, Discovery, Invasion, Encounter: Sources and Interpretation*, 1991. • Stuart B. Schwartz, ed., *Victors and Vanquished: Spanish and Nahua Views of the Conquest of Mexico*, 2000. • Patricia Seed, *Ceremonies of Possession in Europe's Conquest of the New World, 1492–1640*, 1995. • Tzvetan Todorov, *The Conquest of America*, 1983. • David M. Traboulay, *Columbus and Las Casas: The Conquest and Christianization of America, 1492–1566*, 1994. • Michael Wood, *Conquistadors*, 2000.

Bernal Díaz del Castillo • Herbert Cerwin, *Bernal Díaz: Historian of the Conquest*, 1963. • Charles Gibson, *The Black Legend: Anti-Spanish Attitudes in the Old World and the New*, 1971. • Lewis Hanke, *All Mankind is One*, 1970.

• Bernal Díaz del Castillo, *The Discovery and Conquest of Mexico*, 1956.

Songs of the Aztec Nobility • John Bierhorst, ed., *Cantares Mexicanos, Songs of the Aztecs*, 1985. • David Damrosch, "The Aesthetics of Conquest: Aztec Poetry Before and After Cortés," *Representations* 33, 1991. • T. J. Knab, ed., *Scattering of Jades: Stories, Poems, and Prayers of the Aztecs*, 1994. • Miguel León-Portilla, *Fifteen Poets of the Aztec World*, 1992. • Irene Nicholson, *Firefly in the Night: A Study of Ancient Mexican Poetry and Symbolism*, 1959.

Sor Juana Inés de la Cruz • Electa Arenal and Stacey Schlau, eds., *Untold Sisters: Hispanic Nuns in their Own Works*, 1989. • Jean Franco, *Plotting Women: Gender and Representation in Mexico*, 1989. • James Henderson, *Ten Notable Women of Latin America*, 1978. • Juana Inéz de la Cruz, *A Woman of Genius: The Intellectual Autobiography of Sor Juana Inés de la Cruz*, 1982. • Pamela Kirk, *Sor Juana Inéz de la Cruz: Religion, Art, and Feminism*, 1998. • Irving Leonard, *Baroque Times in Old Mexico*, 1966. • Stephanie Merrim, ed., *Feminist Perspectives on Sor Juana Inéz de la Cruz*, 1999. • Stephanie Merrim, *Early Modern Women's Writing and Sor Juana Inéz de la Cruz*, 1999. • Octavio Paz, *Sor Juana, or, The Traps of Faith*, 1988. • Ruth S. El Saffar, *Rapture Encaged: The Suppression of the Feminine in Western Culture*, 1994. • George Tavard, *Juana Inés de la Cruz and the Theology of Beauty*, 1991.

Photo Credits

Page 282: Maenad cup: Staatliche Antikensammmlungen, Munich. Erich Lessing/Art Resource, New York.

Page 332: Contemporary Indian comic book *Ramayana: The Death of Ravana*: Amar Chitra/Katha, Bombay.

Page 486: Calligraphy of the name of the Prophet Muhammad: The Nasser D. Khalili Collection of Islamic Art (Cal 70) © Nour Foundation.

Page 477: *King Arthur and His Knights*: Musee de la Tapisserie, Bayeux, © Giraudon/Art Resource, New York.

Page 505: Liang Kai, *Li Bo Chanting a Poema*: Tokyo National Museum.

Page 714: *Christian and Muslim playing chess* from the *Book of Games*: Institut Amatller D'A Hispanic.

Page 919: *Don Cristobal Colon, Admiral of Ship Bound for the Indies*: Bibliotheque Nationale d France.

Page 924: *The Peking Mission*: Bodleian Library University of Oxford.

Page 930: Aztec screenfold book: Liverpool Cit Museum/Werner Forman/Art Resource, New York

Page 1001: Gustave Doré, engraving for cervantes' *Don Quixotea*: Public Domain.

Page 1146: *Cortes accepting the Aztecs' surrender* The Art Archive.

index

Abenámar, 716
Aeneid, 397
Ah God, if only my love could know, 730
Ah how quickly, Postumus, Postumus, 475
Ah! it's fearsome-oh! it's high!, 506
Ah tell me, little sisters, 718
Alone I sit amid the dark bamboo, 502
Analects, 380
A new home at the mouth of Meng Wall, 501
Apology, 315
A pot of wine among the flowers, 504
As if you were a stranger, 718
Autumn Meditations, 512
Aztec-Spanish Dialogues of 1524, 1159

Ballad of Juliana, 715
Ballad of the Army Carts, 511
Bamboo Lodge, 502
Beck, The, 375
Bed front bright moon radiance, 483
Before my bed the bright moon's gleam, 483
Behold the sun at evening, 722
Beowulf, 648
Bird Call Valley, 502
Birth to the People, 377
Bisclavret (The Werewolf), 734
Blanquerna: The Book of the Lover and the Beloved, 725
Blowing flutes cross to the distant shore, 514
Boccaccio, Giovanni, 936
    Decameron, First Day, 938
    Decameron, Seventh Day, 950
    Decameron, Tenth Day, 953
    Decameron, Third Day, 946
Bo Juyi, 514
    A Song of Unending Sorrow, 515
Book of Songs, The, 370

The Beck, 375
Birth to the People, 377
Cypress Boat (26), 372
Cypress Boat (45), 373
I Beg of You, Zhong Zi, 373
In the Wilds Is a Dead Doe, 372
In the wilds there is a dead deer, 372
Lies a dead deer on younder plain, 372
Locusts, 371
May Heaven Guard, 374
Oak Clumps, 376
The Ospreys Cry, 371
Plop Fall the Plums, 372
So They Appeared, 379
What Plant Is Not Faded?, 376
Bring in the Wine, 507
By Yangtse and Han, a stranger who thinks of home, 514

Canterbury Tales, The, 870
Canzoniere, 964
Carts rattle and squeak, 511
Castilian Ballads and Traditional Songs, 715
Catullus, 467
    3: Cry out lamenting, Venuses & Cupids, 468
    5: Lesbia, let us live only for loving, 468
    13: You will dine well with me, my dear Fabullus, 469
    51: To me that man seems like a god in heaven, 469
    76: If any pleasure can come to a man through recalling, 470
    85: I hate & love, 470
    107: If ever something which someone with no expectation, 470
Ceaseless flows that beck, 375
Cervantes Saavedra, Miguel de, 999
    Don Quixote, 1002
Chaucer, Geoffrey, 868

The Canterbury Tales, 870
    The General Prologue, 870
    The Wife of Bath's Prologue, 890
    The Wife of Bath's Tale, 910
Chevrefoil (The Honeysuckle), 740
China's Emperor, craving beauty that might shake an empire, 515
Codax, Martin, 729
    Ah God, if only my love could know, 730
    My beautiful sister, come hurry with me, 730
    O waves that I've come to see, 731
Come, goddess, 237
Confucius, 379
    Analects, 380
Cruz, Juana Inés de la, 1175
    The Loa for the Auto Sacramental of the Divine Narcissus, 1175
Cry out lamenting, Venuses & Cupids, 468
Cups without wine are lowly, 723
Cypress Boat
    26, 372
    45, 373

Dante Alighieri, 743
    The Divine Comedy: Inferno, 746
Decameron, 938
Deer Enclosure, 501
Díaz del Castillo, Bernal, 1147
    The True History of the Conquest of New Spain, 1148
Dinis (Dom), King of Portugal, 727
    The lovely girl arose at earliest dawn, 729
    O blossoms of the verdant pine, 728
    Provençals right well may versify, 727
    Of what are you dying, daughter, 728

Dismounting I give you wine to drink, 502
Divine Comedy, The Inferno, 746
Don Quixote, 1002
Doorman's feet, The, 240
Drinking Alone with the Moon, 504
Du Fu, 510
  Autumn Meditations, 512
  Ballad of the Army Carts, 511
  Moonlit Night, 511
  Spring Prospect, 512
  Traveling at Night, 512
  Yangtse and Han, 514

Empty mountain, no man is seen, 501
Epic of Gilgamesh, 29
Essays (Montaigne), 973
Euripides, 281
  The Medea, 284

"Fair, fair," cry the ospreys, 371
Farewell, 502
Farewell: thou art too dear for my possessing, 1087
Farewell to a Friend, 509
Farewell to Yuan the Second on His Mission to Anxi, 502
Fighting South of the Ramparts, 506
From fairest creatures we desire increase, 1085
From time's beginning, You were love's abode, 724

Gems of dew wilt and wound the maple trees in the wood, 512
Genesis 1–11, 75
Gentle now, doves, 719
"Get on, you hounds, get on," 715

He looks to me to be in heaven, 238
Homer, 95
  The Iliad, 98
  The Odyssey, 152
Honestly, I wish I were dead, 239
Horace, 471
  Ode 1.9: You see Soracte standing white and deep, 474
  Ode 2.14: Ah how quickly, Postumus, Postumus, 475
  Satire 1.5: Leaving the big city behind, 471

I am in love with three Moorish lasses in Jaén, 717
I Beg of You, Zhong Zi, 373
Ibn 'Arabi (Ibn al-'Arabi), 719
  Gentle now, doves, 719
Ibn Gabirol, Solomon, 721
  Behold the sun at evening, 722
  The mind is flawed, the way to wisdom blocked, 722
  She looked at me and her eyelids burned, 721
  Winter wrote with the ink of its rains and showers, 722
I do not know the Temple of Gathered Fragrance, 503
If any pleasure can come to a man through recalling, 470
If ever something which someone with no expectation, 470
I hate & love, 470
Iliad, The, 98
I'll give you such love!, 719
Inferno, 746
In Fuzhou, far away, my wife is watching, 511
In late years I care for tranquility alone—, 503
In middle years I am rather fond of the Dao, 503
In Response to Vice-Magistrate Zhang, 503
In the old age black was not counted fair, 1088
In the Quiet Night, 509
In the Wilds Is a Dead Doe, 371
In the wilds there is a dead deer, 371
In Wei City morning rain dampens the light dust, 502
I will not pick verbena, 717

Jewel Stairs' Grievance, The, 508

Lais, 732
Lake Yi, 502
Last year we were fighting at the source of the Sangkan, 506
Leaving the big city behind I found lodgins at Aricia, 471
Lesbia, let us live only for loving, 468
Let me not to the marriage of true minds, 1087
Li Bo, 503
  Bring in the Wine, 507

Drinking Alone with the Moon, 504
Farewell to a Friend, 509
Fighting South of the Ramparts, 506
In the Quiet Night, 509
The Jewel Stairs' Grievance, 508
Listening to a Monk from Shu Playing the Lute, 509
Question and Answer in the Mountains, 510
The River Merchant's Wife: a Letter, 508
The Road to Shu Is Hard, 506
Sitting Alone by Jingting Mountain, 509
Lies a dead deer on younder plain, 372
Like the sweet-apple, 240
Listening to a Monk from Shu Playing the Lute, 509
Listen well, our beloved, 1159
Llull, Ramón, 725
  Blanquerna: The Book of the Lover and the Beloved, 725
Locusts, 371
Look in thy glass, and tell the face thou viewest, 1085
Lovely girl arose at earliest dawn, The, 729
Love shakes my heart, 239

Make your beginning, you who sing, 1169
Man at leisure, cassia flowers fall, 502
Marie de France, 731
  Lais, 732
    Prologue, 732
    Bisclavret (The Werewolf), 734
    Chevrefoil (The Honeysuckle), 740
May Heaven Guard, 661
Medea, The, 284
Meng Wall Cove, 501
Metamorphoses, 444
Mind is flawed, the way to wisdom blocked, The, 722
Moctezuma, you creature of heaven, you sing in Mexico, 1174
Montaigne, Michel de, 971
  Essays: Of Cannibals, 981
  Essays: Of Idleness, 973

202

Essays: Of Repentance, 989
Essays: Of the Power of the Imagination, 973
Moonlit Night, 511
Mother, I shall not sleep, 719
Murasaki Shikibu, 517
  The Tale of Genji, 520
My beautiful sister, come hurry with me, 730
My heart is in the East, 724
My lord Ibrahim, 718
My mistress' eyes are nothing like the sun, 1088

Not marble nor the gilded monuments, 1086

Oak Clumps, 376
O blossoms of the verdant pine, 728
Odes, 474
  Ah how quickly, Postumus, Postumus, 475
  You see Soracte standing white and deep, 474
Odyssey, The, 152
Oedipus the King, 243
Of bodies changed to other forms I tell, 444
Of Cannibals, 981
Of Idleness, 973
Ofra does her laundry with my tears, 723
Of Repentance, 989
Of the Power of the Imagination, 973
Of what are you dying, daughter, 728
O God! that lovely face, that gentle look, 968
Once when I fondled him upon my thighs, 723
Ospreys Cry, The, 371
O thou, my lovely boy, who in thy power, 1087
Ovid, 442
  Metamorphoses, 444
O waves that I've come to see, 731
O you who hear within these scattered verses, 964

Petrarch, Francis, 962
  Canzoniere: After the Death of My Lady Laura, 968
  Canzoniere: During the Life of My Lady Laura, 964

Plato, 315
  Apology, 315
Plop Fall the Plums, 372
Poquelin, Jean-Baptiste. *See* **Molière**
Prologue (Lais), 732
Provençals right well may versify, 727

Question and Answer in the Mountains, 509
Quiet Night Thought, 483
Qur'an, 592

Ramayana of Valmiki, The, 331
Rich-throned immortal Aphrodite, 236
River Merchant's Wife: a Letter, The, 508
Road to Shu Is Hard, The, 506

Sappho, 236
  Come, goddess, 236
  The doorman's feet, 240
  He looks to me to be in heaven, 238
  Honestly, I wish I were dead, 239
  Like the sweet-apple, 240
  Love shakes my heart, 239
  Rich-throned immortal Aphrodite, 236
  . . . she worshipped you, 239
  Some think a fleet, 238
Satires
  Leaving the big city behind I found lodgings at Aricia, 471
Shakespeare, William, 1083
  The Sonnets, 1085
  The Tempest, 1090
She looked at me and her eyelids burned, 721
She who in the beginning gave birth to the people, 377
. . . she worshipped you, 239
Sing, goddess, the anger of Peleus' son Achilleus, 98
Sing to me of the man, Muse, the man of twists and turns, 152
Sitting Alone by Jingting Mountain, 509
Slender grass, a faint wind on the shore, 512
Some think a fleet, 238
Song of Songs, The, 84
Song of Unending Sorrow, A, 515

Songs of the Aztec Nobility
  Make your beginning, you who sing, 1169
  Moctezuma, you creature of heaven, you sing in Mexico, 1174
  Water-Pouring Song, 1170
Sonnets, The, 1085
Sophocles, 240
  Oedipus the King, 243
Sophora Path, 502
So They Appeared, 379
Spring Prospect, 512

Take me out of this plight, 719
Tale of Genji, The, 520
Tempest, The, 1090
That time of year thou mayst in me behold, 1086
The bypath is shaded by sophoras, 502
The country shattered, mountains and rivers remain, 512
The flocks of birds have flown high and away, 509
The floor before my bed is bright, 509
The jewelled steps are already quite white with dew, 508
The locusts' wings say "throng, throng", 371
The monk from Shu with his green lute-case walked, 509
There were plume willows at the turquoise-green waters in Chapolco, 1170
The waters of the Yellow River come down from the sky, 507
They ask me why I live in the green mountains, 510
Thick grow the oak clumps, 376
Those mountains, mother, 717
Thoughts on a Quiet Night, 483
Thousand and One Nights, The, 606
Three Moorish Girls, 717
To me that man seems like a god in heaven, 468
Traveling at Night, 512
True History of the Conquest of New Spain, The, 1148

Unsteady is that cypress boat, 373

Verdant mountains behind the northern ramparts, 509

Virgil, 393
Aeneid, 397
Visiting the Temple of Gathered
    Fragrance, 503

Wang River Collection, The, 501
    Bamboo Lodge, 502
    Deer Enclosure, 501
    Lake Yi, 502
    Meng Wall Cove, 501
    Sophora Path, 502
Wang Wei, 500
    Bird Call Valley, 502
    Farewell, 502
    Farewell to Yuan the
        Second on His Mission
        to Anxi, 502
    In Response to Vice-
        Magistrate Zhang, 503

Visiting the Temple of
    Gathered Fragrance, 503
The Wang River
    Collection, 501
    Zhongnan Retreat, 503
Water-Pouring Song, 1170
What Plant Is Not Faded?, 376
When April with his showers
    sweet with fruit, 870
While my hair was still cut
    straight across my
    forehead, 508
Who will believe my verse in
    time to come, 1086
Winter wrote with the ink of its
    rain and showers, 722

Yangtse and Han, 514
Yehuda ha-Levi, 723

Cups without wine are
    lowly, 723
My heart is in the East, 724
Ofra does her laundry with my
    tears, 723
Once when I fondled him upon
    my thighs, 723
From time's beginning, You
    were love's abode, 724
Your breeze, Western shore, is
    perfumed, 724
Your breeze, Western shore, is
    perfumed, 724
You see Soracte standing white
    and deep, 474
You will dine well with me, my
    dear Fabullus, 469

Zhongnan Retreat, 503